WEST'S LEGAL ENVIRONMENT OF BUSINESS

Text and Cases ◆ Sixth Edition

Ethical, Regulatory, International, and E-Commerce Issues

Frank B. Cross
Herbert D. Kelleher
Centennial Professor in Business Law
University of Texas at Austin

Roger LeRoy Miller
Institute for University Studies
Arlington, Texas

THOMSON
WEST

Australia · Canada · Mexico
Singapore · Spain
United Kingdom · United States

D0087028

THOMSON
WEST

West's Legal Environment of Business
TEXT AND CASES
Ethical, Regulatory, International, and E-Commerce Issues
SIXTH EDITION

Frank B. Cross and Roger LeRoy Miller

Vice President and Editorial Director:
Jack Calhoun

Publisher, Business Law and Accounting:
Rob Dewey

Acquisition Editor:
Steve Silverstein

Senior Developmental Editor:
Jan Lamar

Editorial Assistant:
Todd McKenzie

Executive Marketing Manager:
Lisa L. Lysne

Production Manager:
Bill Stryker

Technology Project Editor:
Christine A. Wittmer

Manufacturing Coordinator:
Charlene Taylor

Marketing Coordinator:
Jenny Stevens

Compositor:
Parkwood Composition Service

Printer:
RR Donnelley, Willard

Art Director:
Michelle Kunkler

Internal Designer:
Bill Stryker

Cover Designer:
Jennifer Lambert

Web Coordinator:
Scott Cook

STUDENT EDITIONS:
ISBN-13: 978-0-324-37613-5
ISBN-10: 0-324-37613-8 (Text Only)
ISBN-13: 978-0-324-30391-9
ISBN-10: 0-324-30391-2 (with Online Legal Research Guide)
ISBN-13: 978-0-324-37718-7
ISBN-10: 0-324-37718-5 (with *West's Legal Environment of Business* NOW: Online Assignments)

INSTRUCTOR'S EDITIONS:
ISBN-13: 978-0-324-37708-8
ISBN-10: 0-324-37708-8 (Text Only)
ISBN-13: 978-0-324-37709-5
ISBN-10: 0-324-37709-6 (with Online Legal Research Guide)
ISBN-13: 978-0-324-37716-3
ISBN-10: 0-324-37716-9 (with *West's Legal Environment of Business* NOW: Online Assignments)

INTERNATIONAL LOCATIONS

ASIA (including India)
Thomson Learning
5 Shenton Way
#01-01 UIC Building
Singapore 068808

AUSTRALIA/NEW ZEALAND
Thomson Learning Australia
102 Dodds Street
Southbank, Victoria 3006
Australia

LATIN AMERICA
Thomson Learning
Seneca, 53
Colonia Polanco
11560 Mexico
D.F.Mexico

CANADA
Thomson Nelson
1120 Birchmount Road
Toronto, Ontario
Canada M1K 5G4

UK/EUROPE/MIDDLE
EAST/AFRICA
Thomson Learning
High Holborn House
50-51 Bedford Road
London WC1R 4LR
United Kingdom

SPAIN (includes Portugal)
Thomson Paraninfo
Calle Magallanes, 25
28015 Madrid, Spain

... and all the study and review tools in the *Study Guide*

The student *Study Guide*, prepared by the text author Roger LeRoy Miller and William Eric Hollowell, is a valuable study and review tool. It contains the following helpful chapter-by-chapter features:

- A brief chapter introduction and chapter outline

- True-false, fill-in-the-blank, and multiple-choice questions as well as short essay problems to help you test yourself and prepare for exams

- Issue spotters

- A separate appendix at the end of the study guide containing answers to all questions and issue spotters

If your bookstore does not carry this study guide (ISBN 0-324-40205-8), you can order it directly online by visiting the "bookstore" at this text's Companion Web site http://wleb.westbuslaw.com

Study Guide

Sixth Edition

WEST'S LEGAL ENVIRONMENT OF BUSINESS

Text and Cases

Cross   Miller

Ethical, Regulatory, International, and E-Commerce Issues

Prepared by WILLIAM ERIC HOLLOWELL and ROGER LEROY MILLER

Contents in Brief

❖ Appendices

Contents

❖ | Appendices

CONCEPT SUMMARIES LIST

EXHIBITS LIST

EMERGING TRENDS

CONTEMPORARY LEGAL DEBATES

CHAPTER REVIEWING FEATURES

PREFACE: To the Student

Welcome to the world of the legal environment of business. You are about to embark on the study of one of the most important topics you should master in today's changing world. A solid understanding of the legal environment of business can, of course, help you if you are going into the world of business. If you decide on a career in accounting, economics, finance, political science, or history, understanding how the legal environment works is crucial. Moreover, in your role as a consumer, you will be faced with some legal issues throughout your lifetime—renting an apartment, buying a house, obtaining a mortgage, leasing a car, and so on. In your role as an employee (if you don't go into business for yourself), you will need to know what rights you have and what rights you don't have. Even when you contemplate marriage, you will be faced with legal issues.

What You Will Find in This Text

As you will see as you thumb through the pages in this text, we have tried to make your study of the legal environment of business as efficient and enjoyable as possible. To this end, you will find the following aids:

1. **Mastering Terminology**—through *key terms* that are boldfaced, listed at the end of each chapter, and explained fully in a *glossary* at the end of the book.
2. **Understanding Concepts**—through numerous *Concept Summaries* and *Exhibits.*
3. **Observing the Law in the Context of the Real World**—through a *Reviewing Feature* at the end of every chapter.

4. **Seeing How Legal Issues Can Arise**—through *Video Questions* based on Web-available short videos, many from actual Hollywood movies.
5. **Figuring Out How the Law Is Evolving**—through a feature called *Emerging Trends.*
6. **Determining the Current Controversies in Today's Law**—through a feature called *Contemporary Legal Debates.*

The above list, of course, is representative only. You will understand much more of what the law is about as you read through the *court cases* presented in this book, including *longer case excerpts,* which will give you a feel for how the courts really decide cases, in the courts' language.

Improving Your Ability to Perform Legal Reasoning and Analysis

While business law may seem to be a mass of facts, your goal in taking this course should also be an increased ability to figure out how legal situations will be resolved, by using legal reasoning and analysis. To this end, you will find the following key learning features to assist you in mastering legal reasoning and analysis:

- **Finding and Analyzing the Law**—In an appendix following Chapter 1, this section explains
  1. Legal citations
  2. Standard elements of a case
  3. The different types of opinions a court can issue
  4. How to read and understand cases

- *Briefing a Case*—You will see in Appendix A at the end of this text how to brief cases and analyze case problems. This explanation teaches you how to break down the elements of a case and will improve your ability to answer the *case problems* in each chapter.
- *Questions with Sample Answers*—At the end of each chapter, there are several hypothetical factual scenarios that present legal issues. One such question has a *sample answer* presented in Appendix I. This allows you to practice and to see if you are answering such hypothetical problems correctly.
- *Case Problems with Sample Answers*—Each chapter has a series of chapter-ending *case problems.* You can find an answer to one problem in each chapter on this book's companion student Web site at: **http://wleb.westbuslaw.com**. You can easily compare your answer to the court's opinion in each real case.
- *Impact of This Case on Today's Law*—Each landmark and classic case concludes with a short section that explains the relevance of older case law to the way courts reason today.
- *What If the Facts Were Different?*—This section, found at the end of selected cases, encourages you to think about how the outcome of a case might be different if the facts were altered.

The Companion Student Web Site

As already mentioned, the companion student Web site at **http://wleb.westbuslaw.com** provides you with short videos on various legal topics and with sample answers to one case problem per chapter. In addition, you will find the following:

- *Online quizzes* for every chapter.
- A *glossary* of terms (as well as a Spanish-English glossary).

- *Interactive exercises* that introduce you to how to research the law online.
- *Relevant Web sites* for additional research for *Emerging Trends* features as well as links to the URLs listed in the *Law on the Web* section at the end of each chapter.
- *Court case updates* for recent court decisions relating to topics covered in the text.

Interactive Assignments on the Web

Some of you may have instructors who provide assignments using our world-class interactive Web-based system, called *West's Legal Environment of Business NOW: Online Assignments.*

West's Legal Environment of Business NOW: Online Assignments allows you to improve your mastery of legal concepts and terminology, legal reasoning and analysis, and much more. Your instructor will give you further information if she or he decides to use this Web-based system.

Of course, whether or not you are using the NOW system, you will wish to consider purchasing the *Study Guide*, which can help you get a better grade in your course (see the inside front cover for details).

The law is all around you and will be for the rest of your life. We hope that you begin your first course in the legal environment of business with the same high degree of excitement that we, the authors, always have when we work on improving this text. *West's Legal Environment of Business* has withstood the test of time—several million students before you have already used and benefited by it.

F.B.C.

R.L.M.

Dedication

To Bill Hayes,

One of the world's
best architects.

Thanks,

R.L.M.

To my parents and sisters.
F.B.C.

UNIT ONE
The Foundations

CONTENTS

CHAPTER 1

Business and Its Legal Environment

One of the important functions of law in any society is to provide stability, predictability, and continuity so that people can be sure of how to order their affairs. If any society is to survive, its citizens must be able to determine what is legally right and legally wrong. They must know what sanctions will be imposed on them if they commit wrongful acts. If they suffer harm as a result of others' wrongful acts, they must know how they can seek redress. By setting forth the rights, obligations, and privileges of citizens, the law enables individuals to go about their business with confidence and a certain degree of predictability. The stability and predictability created by the law provide an essential framework for all civilized activities, including business activities.

What do we mean when we speak of "the law"? Although this term has had, and will continue to have, different definitions, they are all based on a general observation: at a minimum, **law** consists of *enforceable rules governing relationships among individuals and between individuals and their society.* These "enforceable rules" may consist of unwritten principles of behavior established by a nomadic tribe. They may be set forth in a law code, such as the Code of Hammurabi in ancient Babylon (c. 1780 B.C.E.) or the law code of one of today's European nations. They may consist of written laws and court decisions created by modern legislative and judicial bodies, as in the United States. Regardless of how such rules are created, they all have one thing in common: they establish rights, duties, and privileges that are consistent with the values and beliefs of their society or its ruling group.

Those who embark on a study of law will find that these broad statements leave unanswered some important questions concerning the nature of law. Part of the study of law, often referred to as **jurisprudence,** involves learning about different schools of jurisprudential thought and discovering how the approaches to law characteristic of each school can affect judicial decision making. We open this introductory chapter with an examination of that topic. We then look at an important question for any student reading this text: How does the legal environment affect business decision making? We next describe the basic sources of American law, the common law tradition, and some general classifications of law. We conclude the chapter with sections offering practical guidance on several topics, including how to find the sources of law discussed in this chapter (and referred to throughout the text) and how to read and understand court opinions.

SECTION 1 | Schools of Jurisprudential Thought

You may think that legal philosophy is far removed from the practical study of business law and the legal environment. In fact, it is not. As you will learn in the chapters of this text, how judges apply the law to specific disputes, including disputes relating to the business world, depends in part on their philosophical approaches to law.

Clearly, judges are not free to decide cases solely on the basis of their personal philosophical views or on their opinions about the issues before the court. A judge's function is not to *make* the laws—that is the function of the legislative branch of government—but to interpret and apply them. From a practical point of view, however, the courts play a significant role in defining what the law is. This is because laws enacted by legislative bodies tend to be expressed in general terms. Judges thus have some flexibility in interpreting and applying the law. It is because of this flexibility that different courts can, and often do, arrive at different conclusions in cases that involve nearly identical issues, facts, and applicable laws. This flexibility also means that each judge's unique personality, legal philosophy, set of values, and intellectual attributes necessarily frame the judicial decision-making process to some extent.

We look now at some of the significant schools of legal, or jurisprudential, thought that have evolved over time.

The Natural Law School

An age-old question about the nature of law has to do with the finality of a nation's laws, such as the laws of the United States at the present time. For example, what if a particular law is deemed to be a "bad" law by a substantial number of that nation's citizens? Must a citizen obey the law if it goes against his or her conscience to do so? Is there a higher or universal law to which individuals can appeal? One who adheres to the natural law tradition would answer these questions in the affirmative. **Natural law** denotes a system of moral and ethical principles that are inherent in human nature and that people can discover through the use of their natural intelligence, or reason.

The natural law tradition is one of the oldest and most significant schools of jurisprudence. It dates back to the days of the Greek philosopher Aristotle (384–322 B.C.E.), who distinguished between natural law and the laws governing a particular nation. According to Aristotle, natural law applies universally to all humankind.

The notion that people have "natural rights" stems from the natural law tradition. Those who claim that a specific foreign government is depriving certain citizens of their human rights implicitly are appealing to a higher law that has universal applicability. The question of the universality of basic human rights also comes into play in the context of international business operations. Should rights extended to workers in the United States, such as the right to be free of discrimination in the workplace, be extended to workers employed by a U.S. firm doing business in another country that does not provide for such rights? This question is rooted implicitly in a concept of universal rights that has its origins in the natural law tradition.

The Positivist School

In contrast, **positive law,** or national law (the written law of a given society at a particular point in time), applies only to the citizens of that nation or society. Those who adhere to the **positivist school** believe that there can be no higher law than a nation's positive law. According to the positivist school, there is no such thing as "natural rights." Rather, human rights exist solely because of laws. If the laws are not enforced, anarchy will result. Thus, whether a law is "bad" or "good" is irrelevant. The law is the law and must be obeyed until it is changed—in an orderly manner through a legitimate lawmaking process. A judge with positivist leanings probably would be more inclined to defer to an existing law than would a judge who adheres to the natural law tradition.

The Historical School

The **historical school** of legal thought emphasizes the evolutionary process of law by concentrating on the origin and history of the legal system. Thus, this school looks to the past to discover what the principles of contemporary law should be. The legal doctrines that have withstood the passage of time—those that have worked in the past—are deemed best suited for shaping present laws. Hence, law derives its legitimacy and authority from adhering to the standards that historical development has shown to be workable. Adherents of the historical school are more likely than those of other schools to strictly follow decisions made in past cases.

Legal Realism

In the 1920s and 1930s, a number of jurists and scholars, known as legal realists, rebelled against the historical approach to law. **Legal realism** is based on the idea that law is just one of many institutions in society and that it is shaped by social forces and needs. The law is a human enterprise, and judges should take social and economic realities into account when deciding cases. Legal realists also believe that the law can never be applied with total uniformity. Given that judges are human beings with unique personalities, value systems, and intellects, obviously different judges will bring different reasoning processes to the same case.

Legal realism strongly influenced the growth of what is sometimes called the **sociological school** of jurisprudence. This school views law as a tool for promoting justice in society. In the 1960s, for example, the justices of the United States Supreme Court played a leading role in the civil rights movement by upholding long-neglected laws calling for equal treatment for all Americans, including African Americans and other minorities. Generally, jurists who adhere to this philosophy of law are more likely to depart from past decisions than are those jurists who adhere to the other schools of legal thought.

CONCEPT SUMMARY 1.1 | Schools of Jurisprudential Thought

SCHOOL OF THOUGHT	DESCRIPTION
THE NATURAL LAW SCHOOL	One of the oldest and most significant schools of legal thought. Those who believe in natural law hold that there is a universal law applicable to all human beings. This law is discoverable through reason and is of a higher order than positive (national) law.
THE POSITIVIST SCHOOL	A school of legal thought centered on the assumption that there is no law higher than the laws created by the government. Laws must be obeyed, even if they are unjust, to prevent anarchy.
THE HISTORICAL SCHOOL	A school of legal thought that stresses the evolutionary nature of law and that looks to doctrines that have withstood the passage of time for guidance in shaping present laws.
LEGAL REALISM	A school of legal thought, popular during the 1920s and 1930s, that left a lasting imprint on American jurisprudence. Legal realists generally advocated a less abstract and more realistic and pragmatic approach to the law, an approach that would take into account customary practices and the circumstances in which transactions take place. Legal realism strongly influenced the growth of the *sociological school* of jurisprudence, which views law as a tool for promoting social justice.

SECTION 2 | Business Activities and the Legal Environment

As those entering the world of business will learn, laws and government regulations affect virtually all business activities—from hiring and firing decisions to workplace safety, to the manufacturing and marketing of products, to business financing, and so on. To make good business decisions, a basic knowledge of the laws and regulations governing these activities is beneficial—if not essential. Realize also that in today's world a knowledge of "black-letter" law is not enough. Businesspersons are also pressured to make ethical decisions. Thus, the study of business law necessarily involves an ethical dimension.

MANY DIFFERENT LAWS MAY AFFECT A SINGLE BUSINESS TRANSACTION

As you will note, each chapter in this text covers a specific area of the law and shows how the legal rules in that area affect business activities. Though compartmentalizing the law in this fashion promotes conceptual clarity, it does not indicate the extent to which a number of different laws may apply to just one transaction.

Consider an example. Suppose that you are the president of NetSys, Inc., a company that creates and maintains computer network systems for its clients, including business firms. NetSys also markets software for customers who require an internal computer network. One day, Hernandez, an operations officer for Southwest Distribution Corporation (SDC), contacts you by e-mail about a possible contract concerning SDC's computer network. In deciding whether to enter into a contract with SDC, you should consider, among other things, the legal requirements for an enforceable contract. Are there different requirements for a contract for services and a contract for products? What are your options if SDC **breaches** (breaks, or fails to perform) the contract? The answers to these questions are part of contract law and sales law.

Other questions might concern payment under the contract. How can you guarantee that NetSys will be paid? For example, if payment is made with a check that is returned for insufficient funds, what are your options? Answers to these questions can be found in the laws that relate to negotiable instruments (such as checks) and creditors' rights. Also, a dispute may occur over the rights to NetSys's software, or there may be a question of liability if the software is defective. There may be an issue as to whether you and Hernandez have the authority to make the deal in the first place. A disagreement may arise from circumstances such as an accountant's evaluation of the contract. Resolutions of these questions may be found in areas of the law that relate to intellectual property, e-commerce, torts, product liability, agency, business organizations, or professional liability.

Finally, if any dispute cannot be resolved amicably, then the laws and the rules concerning courts and court procedures spell out the steps of a lawsuit. Exhibit 1–1 illustrates the various areas of law that may influence business decision making.

ETHICS AND BUSINESS DECISION MAKING

Merely knowing the areas of law that may affect a business decision is not sufficient in today's business world. Businesspersons must also take ethics into account. As you will learn in Chapter 4, *ethics* is generally defined as the study of what constitutes right or wrong behavior. In today's business world, business decision makers must consider not just whether a decision is profitable and legal but also whether it is ethical.

Throughout this text, you will learn about the relationship between the law and ethics, as well as about some of the types of ethical questions that often arise in the business context. For example, the unit-ending *Focus on Ethics* features in this text are devoted solely to the exploration of ethical dimensions of selected topics treated within the unit. Additionally, Chapter 4 offers a detailed look at the importance of ethical

EXHIBIT 1–1 Areas of the Law That May Affect Business Decision Making

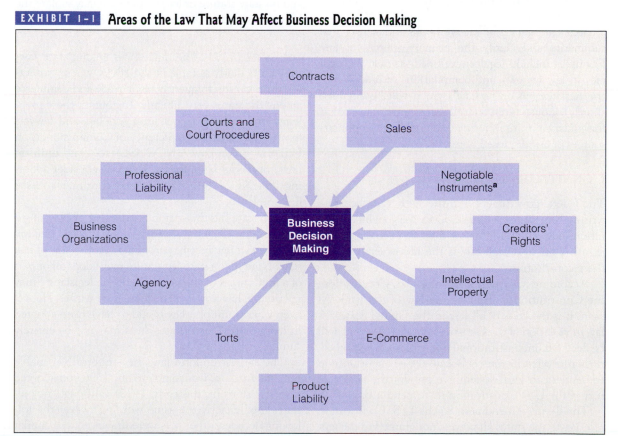

a. A *negotiable instrument*, such as a check or promissory note, can be defined as a signed writing that contains an unconditional promise or order to pay an exact sum of money, either when demanded or at a specified future date. Negotiable instruments, which are not covered in this text, function commercially as either a substitute for cash (such as when a person writes a check to purchase goods) or as a credit device (such as when a buyer gives a seller a promissory note promising to pay the purchase price at a later date).

considerations in business decision making. Finally, various other elements in this text, such as the ethical questions that conclude selected chapters, are designed to introduce you to ethical aspects of specific cases involving real-life situations.

SECTION 3 | Sources of American Law

There are numerous sources of American law. *Primary sources of law*, or sources that establish the law, include the following:

1. The U.S. Constitution and the constitutions of the various states.
2. Statutory law—including laws passed by Congress, state legislatures, or local governing bodies.
3. Regulations created by administrative agencies, such as the Food and Drug Administration.
4. Case law and common law doctrines.

We describe each of these important sources of law in the following pages.

Secondary sources of law are books and articles that summarize and clarify the primary sources of law. Examples include legal encyclopedias, treatises, articles in law reviews, and compilations of law, such as the *Restatements of the Law* (which will be discussed shortly). Courts often refer to secondary sources of law for guidance in interpreting and applying the primary sources of law discussed here.

CONSTITUTIONAL LAW

The federal government and the states have separate written constitutions that set forth the general organization, powers, and limits of their respective governments. **Constitutional law** is the law as expressed in these constitutions.

According to Article VI of the U.S. Constitution, the Constitution is the supreme law of the land. As such, it is the basis of all law in the United States. A law in violation of the Constitution, if challenged, will be declared unconstitutional and will not be enforced, no matter what its source. Because of its importance in the American legal system, we present the complete text of the U.S. Constitution in Appendix B.

The Tenth Amendment to the U.S. Constitution reserves to the states all powers not granted to the federal government. Each state in the union has its own constitution. Unless it conflicts with the U.S. Constitution or a federal law, a state constitution is supreme within the state's borders.

STATUTORY LAW

Laws enacted by legislative bodies at any level of government, such as the statutes passed by Congress or by state legislatures, make up the body of law generally referred to as **statutory law.** When a legislature passes a statute, that statute ultimately is included in the federal code of laws or the relevant state code of laws (these codes are discussed later in this chapter).

Statutory law also includes local **ordinances**—statutes (laws, rules, or orders) passed by municipal or county governing units to govern matters not covered by federal or state law. Ordinances commonly have to do with city or county land use (zoning ordinances), building and safety codes, and other matters affecting the local unit.

A federal statute, of course, applies to all states. A state statute, in contrast, applies only within the state's borders. State laws thus may vary from state to state. No federal statute may violate the U.S. Constitution, and no state statute or local ordinance may violate the U.S. Constitution or the relevant state constitution.

UNIFORM LAWS The differences among state laws were particularly notable in the 1800s, when conflicting state statutes frequently made trade and commerce among the states very difficult. To counter these problems, in 1892 a group of legal scholars and lawyers formed the National Conference of Commissioners on Uniform State Laws (NCCUSL) to draft **uniform laws,** or model laws, for the states to consider adopting. The NCCUSL still exists and continues to issue uniform laws.

Each state has the option of adopting or rejecting a uniform law. *Only if a state legislature adopts a uniform law does that law become part of the statutory law of that state.* Note that a state legislature may adopt all or part of a uniform law as it is written, or the legislature may rewrite the law however the legislature wishes. Hence, even when a uniform law is said to have been adopted in many states, those states' laws may not be entirely "uniform."

The earliest uniform law, the Uniform Negotiable Instruments Law, was completed by 1896 and adopted in every state by the early 1920s (although not all states used exactly the same wording). Over the following decades, other acts were drawn up in a similar manner. In all, over two hundred uniform acts have been issued by the NCCUSL since its inception. The most ambitious uniform act of all, however, was the Uniform Commercial Code.

THE UNIFORM COMMERCIAL CODE   The Uniform Commercial Code (UCC), which was created through the joint efforts of the NCCUSL and the American Law Institute,[1] was first issued in 1952. All fifty states,[2] the District of Columbia, and the Virgin Islands have adopted the UCC. It facilitates commerce among the states by providing a uniform, yet flexible, set of rules governing commercial transactions. The UCC assures businesspersons that their contracts, if validly entered into, normally will be enforced.

As you will read in later chapters, from time to time the NCCUSL revises the articles contained in the UCC and submits the revised versions to the states for adoption. During the 1990s, for example, four articles (Articles 3, 4, 5, and 9) were revised, and two new articles (Articles 2A and 4A) were added. In 2003, amendments to Articles 2 and 2A were approved. Because of its importance in the area of commercial law, we cite the UCC frequently in Chapter 11. We also present excerpts from the UCC in Appendix C.

ADMINISTRATIVE LAW

An important source of American law is **administrative law,** which consists of the rules, orders, and decisions of administrative agencies. An **administrative agency** is a federal, state, or local government agency established to perform a specific function. Administrative law and procedures, which will be examined in detail in Chapter 6, constitute a dominant element in the regulatory environment of business. Rules issued by various administrative agencies now affect virtually every aspect of a business's operations, including its capital structure and financing, its hiring and firing procedures, its relations with employees and unions, and the way it manufactures and markets its products.

FEDERAL AGENCIES   At the national level, numerous **executive agencies** exist within the cabinet departments of the executive branch. The Food and Drug Administration, for example, is an agency within the Department of Health and Human Services. Executive agencies are subject to the authority of the president, who has the power to appoint and remove officers of federal agencies. There are also major **independent regulatory agencies** at the federal level, such as the Federal Trade Commission, the Securities and Exchange Commission, and the Federal Communications Commission. The president's power is less pronounced in regard to independent agencies, whose officers serve for fixed terms and cannot be removed without just cause.

STATE AND LOCAL AGENCIES   There are administrative agencies at the state and local levels as well. Commonly, a state agency (such as a state pollution-control agency) is created as a parallel to a federal agency (such as the Environmental Protection Agency). Just as federal statutes take precedence over conflicting state statutes, so federal agency regulations take precedence over conflicting state regulations.

CASE LAW AND COMMON LAW DOCTRINES

The rules of law announced in court decisions constitute another basic source of American law. These rules of law include interpretations of constitutional provisions, of statutes enacted by legislatures, and of regulations created by administrative agencies. Today, this body of judge-made law is referred to as **case law,** or the *common law*. Because of the importance of the common law in our legal system, we look at the origins and characteristics of the common law tradition in some detail in the pages that follow.

SECTION 4 | The Common Law Tradition

Because of our colonial heritage, much of American law is based on the English legal system, which originated in medieval England and continued to evolve in the following centuries. A knowledge of this system is necessary to an understanding of the American legal system today.

EARLY ENGLISH COURTS

The origins of the English legal system—and thus the U.S. legal system as well—date back to 1066, when the Normans conquered England. William the Conqueror and his successors began the process of unifying the country under their rule. One of the means they used to do this was the establishment of the king's

---

1. This institute was formed in the 1920s and consists of practicing attorneys, legal scholars, and judges.
2. Louisiana has not adopted Articles 2 and 2A (covering contracts for the sale and lease of goods), however.

CONCEPT SUMMARY 1.2 | Sources of American Law

SOURCE	DESCRIPTION
CONSTITUTIONAL LAW	The law as expressed in the U.S. Constitution and the state constitutions. The U.S. Constitution is the supreme law of the land. State constitutions are supreme within state borders to the extent that they do not violate a clause of the U.S. Constitution or a federal law.
STATUTORY LAW	Laws (statutes and ordinances) created by federal, state, and local legislatures and governing bodies. None of these laws may violate the U.S. Constitution or the relevant state constitution. Uniform statutes, when adopted by a state, become statutory law in that state.
ADMINISTRATIVE LAW	The rules, orders, and decisions of federal, state, or local government administrative agencies.
CASE LAW AND COMMON LAW DOCTRINES	Judge-made law, including interpretations of constitutional provisions, of statutes enacted by legislatures, and of regulations created by administrative agencies.

courts, or *curiae regis.* Before the Norman Conquest, disputes had been settled according to the local legal customs and traditions in various regions of the country. The king's courts sought to establish a uniform set of customs for the country as a whole. What evolved in these courts was the beginning of the **common law**—a body of general rules that applied throughout the entire English realm. Eventually, the common law tradition became part of the heritage of all nations that were once British colonies, including the United States.

COURTS OF LAW AND REMEDIES AT LAW The early English king's courts could grant only very limited kinds of **remedies** (the legal means to enforce a right or redress a wrong). If one person wronged another in some way, the king's courts could award as compensation one or more of the following: (1) land, (2) items of value, or (3) money. The courts that awarded this compensation became known as **courts of law,** and the three remedies were called **remedies at law.** (Today, the remedy at law normally takes the form of money **damages**—money given to a party whose legal interests have been injured.) Even though the system introduced uniformity in the settling of disputes, when a complaining party wanted a remedy other than economic compensation, the courts of law could do nothing, so "no remedy, no right."

COURTS OF EQUITY AND REMEDIES IN EQUITY Equity is a branch of law, founded on what might be described as notions of justice and fair dealing, that

seeks to supply a remedy when no adequate remedy at law is available. When individuals could not obtain an adequate remedy in a court of law because of strict technicalities, they petitioned the king for relief. Most of these petitions were decided by an adviser to the king, called a **chancellor,** who was said to be the "keeper of the king's conscience." When the chancellor thought that the claims were fair, new and unique remedies were granted. Eventually, formal chancery courts, or **courts of equity,** were established.

The remedies granted by the equity courts became known as **remedies in equity,** or equitable remedies. These remedies include *specific performance* (ordering a party to perform an agreement as promised), an *injunction* (ordering a party to cease engaging in a specific activity or to undo some wrong or injury), and *rescission* (the cancellation of a contractual obligation). We discuss these and other equitable remedies in more detail at appropriate points in the chapters that follow.

As a general rule, today's courts, like the early English courts, will not grant equitable remedies unless the remedy at law—money damages—is inadequate. For example, suppose that you form a contract (a legally binding agreement—see Chapter 9) to purchase a parcel of land that you think will be just perfect for your future country home. Further suppose that the seller breaches this agreement. You could sue the seller for the return of any deposits or down payment you might have made on the land, but this is not the remedy you really seek. What you want is to have the court order the seller to go through with the contract. In other words, you want the court to grant the equitable remedy of specific performance because money damages are inadequate in this situation.

EQUITABLE MAXIMS In fashioning appropriate remedies, judges often were (and continue to be) guided by so-called **equitable maxims**—propositions or general statements of equitable rules. Exhibit 1–2 lists some important equitable maxims. The last maxim listed in that exhibit—"Equity aids the vigilant, not those who rest on their rights"—merits special attention. It has become known as the equitable doctrine of **laches** (a term derived from the Latin *laxus*, meaning "lax" or "negligent"), and it can be used as a defense. A **defense** is an argument raised by the **defendant** (the party being sued) indicating why the **plaintiff** (the suing party) should not obtain the remedy sought. (Note that in equity proceedings, the party bringing a lawsuit is called the **petitioner,** and the party being sued is referred to as the **respondent.**)

The doctrine of laches arose to encourage people to bring lawsuits while the evidence was fresh. What constitutes a reasonable time, of course, varies according to the circumstances of the case. Time periods for different types of cases are now usually fixed by **statutes of limitations.** After the time allowed under a statute of limitations has expired, no action can be brought, no matter how strong the case was originally.

EXHIBIT 1–2 Equitable Maxims

1. *Whoever seeks equity must do equity.* (Anyone who wishes to be treated fairly must treat others fairly.)

2. *Where there is equal equity, the law must prevail.* (The law will determine the outcome of a controversy in which the merits of both sides are equal.)

3. *One seeking the aid of an equity court must come to the court with clean hands.* (Plaintiffs must have acted fairly and honestly.)

4. *Equity will not suffer a wrong to be without a remedy.* (Equitable relief will be awarded when there is a right to relief and there is no adequate remedy at law.)

5. *Equity regards substance rather than form.* (Equity is more concerned with fairness and justice than with legal technicalities.)

6. *Equity aids the vigilant, not those who rest on their rights.* (Equity will not help those who neglect their rights for an unreasonable period of time.)

LEGAL AND EQUITABLE REMEDIES TODAY

The establishment of courts of equity in medieval England resulted in two distinct court systems: courts of law and courts of equity. The systems had different sets of judges and granted different types of remedies. Parties who sought legal remedies, or remedies at law, would bring their claims before courts of law. Parties seeking equitable relief, or remedies in equity, would bring their claims before courts of equity. During the nineteenth century, however, most states in the United States adopted rules of procedure that resulted in combined courts of law and equity—although some states, such as Arkansas, still retain the distinction. A party now may request both legal and equitable remedies in the same action, and the trial court judge may grant either or both forms of relief.

The distinction between legal and equitable remedies remains relevant to students of business law, however, because these remedies differ. To seek the proper remedy for a wrong, one must know what remedies are available. Additionally, certain vestiges of the procedures used when there were separate courts of law and equity still exist. For example, a party has the right to demand a jury trial in an action at law, but not in an action in equity. In the old courts of equity, the chancellor heard both sides of an issue and decided what should be done. Juries were considered inappropriate. In actions at law, however, juries participated in determining the outcome of cases, including the amount of damages to be awarded. Exhibit 1–3 on the next page summarizes the procedural differences between an action at law and an action in equity.

THE DOCTRINE OF STARE DECISIS

One of the unique features of the common law is that it is *judge-made* law. The body of principles and doctrines that forms the common law emerged over time as judges decided actual legal controversies.

CASE PRECEDENTS AND CASE REPORTERS When possible, judges attempted to be consistent and to base their decisions on the principles suggested by earlier cases. They sought to decide similar cases in a similar way and considered new cases with care because they knew that their decisions would make new law. Each interpretation became part of the law on the subject and served as a legal **precedent**—that is, a decision that furnished an example or authority for deciding

EXHIBIT 1-3 **Procedural Differences between an Action at Law and an Action in Equity**

PROCEDURE	ACTION AT LAW	ACTION IN EQUITY
Initiation of lawsuit	By filing a complaint	By filing a petition
Parties	Plaintiff and defendant	Petitioner and respondent
Decision	By jury or judge	By judge (no jury)
Result	Judgment	Decree
Remedy	Monetary damages	Injunction, specific performance, or rescission

subsequent cases involving similar legal principles or facts.

By the early fourteenth century, portions of the most important decisions of each year were being gathered together and recorded in *Year Books*, which became useful references for lawyers and judges. In the sixteenth century, the *Year Books* were discontinued, and other forms of case publication became available. Today, cases are published, or "reported," in volumes called **reporters,** or *reports*. We describe today's case reporting system in detail later in this chapter.

STARE DECISIS AND THE COMMON LAW The practice of deciding new cases with reference to former decisions, or precedents, became a cornerstone of the English and American judicial systems. The practice formed a doctrine known as **stare decisis**[3] (a Latin phrase meaning "to stand on decided cases"). Under this doctrine, judges are obligated to follow the precedents established within their jurisdictions. The term *jurisdiction* refers to an area in which a court or courts have the power to apply the law—see Chapter 2.

The doctrine of *stare decisis* helps the courts to be more efficient, because if other courts have carefully analyzed a similar case, their legal reasoning and opinions can serve as guides. *Stare decisis* also makes the law more stable and predictable. If the law on a given subject is well settled, someone bringing a case to court can usually rely on the court to make a decision based on what the law has been in the past.

A TYPICAL SCENARIO To illustrate how the doctrine of *stare decisis* works, consider an example. Suppose that the lower state courts in California have reached conflicting conclusions on whether drivers are liable for accidents they cause while merging into freeway traffic. Some courts have held drivers liable even though the

drivers looked and did not see any oncoming traffic and even though witnesses (passengers in their cars) testified to that effect. To settle the law on this issue, the California Supreme Court decides to review a case involving this fact pattern. The court rules that in such a situation, the driver who is merging into traffic is liable for any accidents caused by the driver's failure to yield to freeway traffic—even if the driver looked carefully and did not see an approaching vehicle.

The California Supreme Court's decision on this matter is a **binding authority**—a case precedent or statute that must be followed. (Nonbinding legal authorities on which judges may rely for guidance, such as precedents established in other jurisdictions, are referred to as *persuasive authorities*.) In other words, the California Supreme Court's decision will influence the outcome of all future cases on this issue brought before the California state courts. Similarly, a decision on a given question by the United States Supreme Court (the nation's highest court) is binding on all courts.

DEPARTURES FROM PRECEDENT Although courts are obligated to follow precedents, sometimes a court will depart from the rule of precedent if it decides that the precedent should no longer be followed. If a court decides that a ruling precedent is simply incorrect or that technological or social changes have rendered the precedent inapplicable, the court might rule contrary to the precedent. Cases that overturn precedent often receive a great deal of publicity.[4]

---

3. Pronounced *ster*-ay dih-*si*-ses.

4. For example, when the United States Supreme Court held in the 1950s that racial segregation in the public schools was unconstitutional, it expressly overturned a Supreme Court precedent upholding the constitutionality of "separate-but-equal" segregation. The Supreme Court's departure from precedent received a tremendous amount of publicity as people began to realize the ramifications of this change in the law. See *Brown v. Board of Education of Topeka*, 347 U.S. 483, 74 S.Ct. 686, 98 L.Ed. 873 (1954). (Legal citations are explained later in this chapter.)

Note that judges have some flexibility in applying precedents. For example, a trial court may avoid applying a Supreme Court precedent by arguing that the facts of the case before the court are distinguishable from the facts in the Supreme Court case and that, therefore, the Supreme Court's ruling on the issue does not apply to the case before the court.

WHEN THERE IS NO PRECEDENT Occasionally, the courts must decide cases for which no precedents exist, called *cases of first impression*. For example, as you will read throughout this text, disputes involving transactions conducted via the Internet have presented new problems for the courts. When existing laws governing free speech, pornography, fraud, jurisdiction, and other areas were drafted, cyberspace did not exist. Although new laws are being created to govern such disputes, in the meantime the courts have to decide, on a case-by-case basis, what rules should be applied.

Generally, in deciding cases of first impression, courts may consider a number of factors, including persuasive authorities (such as cases from other jurisdictions, if there are any), legal principles and policies underlying previous court decisions or existing statutes, fairness, social values and customs, **public policy** (governmental policy based on widely held societal values), and data and concepts drawn from the social sciences. Which of these sources is chosen or receives the greatest emphasis depends on the nature of the case being considered and the particular judge or judges hearing the case. In cases of first impression, as in all cases, judges must have legal reasons for ruling as they do on particular issues. When a court issues a written opinion on a case (we discuss court opinions later in this chapter), the opinion normally contains a carefully reasoned argument justifying the decision.

STARE DECISIS AND LEGAL REASONING

Legal reasoning is the reasoning process used by judges in deciding what law applies to a given dispute and then applying that law to the specific facts or circumstances of the case. Through the use of legal reasoning, judges harmonize their decisions with those that have been made before, as the doctrine of *stare decisis* requires.

Students of business law and the legal environment also engage in legal reasoning. For example, you may

be asked to provide answers for some of the case problems that appear at the end of every chapter in this text. Each problem describes the facts of a particular dispute and the legal question at issue. If you are assigned a case problem, you will be asked to determine how a court would answer that question, and why. In other words, you will need to give legal reasons for whatever conclusion you reach.[5] We look here at the basic steps involved in legal reasoning and then describe some forms of reasoning commonly used by the courts in making their decisions.

BASIC STEPS IN LEGAL REASONING At times, the legal arguments set forth in court opinions are relatively simple and brief. At other times, the arguments are complex and lengthy. Regardless of the length of a legal argument, however, the basic steps of the legal reasoning process remain the same. These steps, which you also can follow when analyzing cases and case problems, form what is commonly referred to as the *IRAC method* of legal reasoning. IRAC is an acronym formed from the first letters of the following words: Issue, Rule, Application, and Conclusion. To apply the IRAC method, you would ask the following questions:

1. *What are the key facts and issues?* For example, suppose that a plaintiff comes before the court claiming *assault* (a wrongful and intentional action in which one person makes another fearful of immediate physical harm—part of a class of actions called *torts*). The plaintiff claims that the defendant threatened her while she was sleeping. Although the plaintiff was unaware that she was being threatened, her roommate heard the defendant make the threat. The legal issue, or question, raised by these facts is whether the defendant's actions constitute the tort of assault, given that the plaintiff was not aware of those actions at the time they occurred.

2. *What rules of law apply to the case?* A rule of law may be a rule stated by the courts in previous decisions, a state or federal statute, or a state or federal administrative agency regulation. In our hypothetical case, the plaintiff **alleges** (claims) that the defendant committed a tort. Therefore, the applicable law is the common law of torts—specifically, tort law governing assault (see Chapter 12 for more detail on torts). Case precedents involving similar facts and issues thus

---

5. See Appendix A for further instructions on how to analyze case problems.

would be relevant. Often, more than one rule of law will be applicable to a case.

3. *How do the rules of law apply to the particular facts and circumstances of this case?* This step is often the most difficult one because each case presents a unique set of facts, circumstances, and parties. Although cases may be similar, no two cases are ever identical in all respects. Normally, judges (and lawyers and law students) try to find **cases on point**—previously decided cases that are as similar as possible to the one under consideration. (Because of the difficulty—and importance—of this step in the legal reasoning process, we discuss it in more detail in the next subsection.)

4. *What conclusion should be drawn?* This step normally presents few problems. Usually, the conclusion is evident if the previous three steps have been followed carefully.

FORMS OF LEGAL REASONING Judges use many types of reasoning when following the third step of the legal reasoning process—applying the law to the facts of a particular case. Three common forms of reasoning are deductive reasoning, linear reasoning, and reasoning by analogy.

—Deductive Reasoning. Deductive reasoning is sometimes called *syllogistic reasoning* because it employs a **syllogism**—a logical relationship involving a major premise, a minor premise, and a conclusion. For example, consider the hypothetical case presented earlier, in which the plaintiff alleged that the defendant committed assault by threatening her while she was sleeping. The judge might point out that "under the common law of torts, an individual must be *aware* of a threat of danger for the threat to constitute assault" (major premise); "the plaintiff in this case was unaware of the threat at the time it occurred" (minor premise); and "therefore, the circumstances do not amount to an assault" (conclusion).

—Linear Reasoning. A second important form of legal reasoning that is commonly employed might be thought of as "linear" reasoning because it proceeds from one point to another, with the final point being the conclusion. An analogy will help make this form of reasoning clear. Imagine a knotted rope, with each knot tying together separate pieces of rope to form a tight length. As a whole, the rope represents a linear progression of thought logically connecting various

points, with the last point, or knot, representing the conclusion. For example, suppose that a tenant in an apartment building sues the landlord for damages for an injury resulting from an allegedly inadequately lit stairway. The court may engage in a reasoning process involving the following "pieces of rope":

1. The landlord, who was on the premises the evening the injury occurred, testifies that none of the other nine tenants who used the stairway that night complained about the lights.

2. The fact that none of the tenants complained is the same as if they had said the lighting was sufficient.

3. That there were no complaints does not prove that the lighting was sufficient but does prove that the landlord had no reason to believe that it was not.

4. The landlord's belief was reasonable because no one complained.

5. Therefore, the landlord acted reasonably and was not negligent with respect to the lighting in the stairway.

On the basis of this reasoning, the court concludes that the tenant is not entitled to compensation on the basis of the stairway's allegedly insufficient lighting.

—Reasoning by Analogy. Another important type of reasoning that judges use in deciding cases is reasoning by *analogy*. To reason by **analogy** is to compare the facts in the case at hand to the facts in other cases and, to the extent that the patterns are similar, to apply the same rule of law to the present case. To the extent that the facts are unique, or "distinguishable," different rules may apply. For example, in case A, the court held that a driver who crossed a highway's center line was negligent. Case B involves a driver who crosses the line to avoid hitting a child. In determining whether case A's rule applies in case B, a judge would consider what the reasons were for the decision in A and whether B is sufficiently similar for those reasons to apply. If the judge holds that B's driver is not liable, that judge must indicate why case A's rule is not relevant to the facts presented in case B.

THERE IS NO ONE "RIGHT" ANSWER

Many persons believe that there is one "right" answer to every legal question. In most situations involving a legal controversy, however, there is no single correct result. Good arguments can often be made to support either side of a legal controversy. Quite often, a case does not present the situation of a "good" person suing a "bad" person. In many cases, both parties have acted in good faith in some measure or have acted in bad faith to some degree.

Additionally, as already mentioned, each judge has her or his own personal beliefs and philosophy, which shape, at least to some extent, the process of legal reasoning. This means that the outcome of a particular lawsuit before a court can never be predicted with absolute certainty. In fact, even though in some cases, the weight of the law would seem to favor one party's position, judges, through creative legal reasoning, have found ways to rule in favor of the other party in the interests of preventing injustice.

SECTION 5 | The Common Law Today

Today, the common law continues to be applied throughout the United States. Common law doctrines and principles govern all areas *not* covered by statutory or administrative law. In a dispute concerning a particular employment practice, for example, if a statute regulates that practice, the statute will apply rather than the common law doctrine that applied prior to the enactment of the statute.

THE CONTINUING IMPORTANCE OF THE COMMON LAW

Because the body of statutory law has expanded greatly since the beginning of this nation, thus narrowing the applicability of common law doctrines, it might seem that the common law has dwindled in importance. This is not true, however. For one thing, even in areas governed by statutory law, there is a significant interplay between statutory law and the common law. For example, many statutes essentially codify existing common law rules, and regulations issued by various administrative agencies usually are based, at least in part, on common law principles. Additionally, the courts, in interpreting statutory law, often rely on the common law as a guide to what the legislators intended.

Furthermore, how the courts interpret a particular statute determines how that statute will be applied. If you wanted to learn about the coverage and applicability of a particular statute, for example, you would necessarily have to locate the statute and study it. You would also need to see how the courts in your jurisdiction have interpreted and applied the statute. In other words, you would have to learn what precedents have been established in your jurisdiction with respect to

---

CONCEPT SUMMARY 1.3 | The Common Law Tradition

ASPECT	DESCRIPTION
ORIGINS OF THE COMMON LAW	The American legal system is based on the common law tradition, which originated in medieval England. Following the conquest of England in 1066 by William the Conqueror, king's courts were established throughout England, and the common law was developed in these courts.
LEGAL AND EQUITABLE REMEDIES	The distinction between remedies at law (money or items of value, such as land) and remedies in equity (including specific performance, injunction, and rescission of a contractual obligation) originated in the early English courts of law and courts of equity, respectively.
CASE PRECEDENTS AND THE DOCTRINE OF STARE DECISIS	In the king's courts, judges attempted to make their decisions consistent with previous decisions, called precedents. This practice gave rise to the doctrine of *stare decisis*. This doctrine, which became a cornerstone of the common law tradition, obligates judges to abide by precedents established in their jurisdictions.
STARE DECISIS AND LEGAL REASONING	Legal reasoning refers to the reasoning process used by judges in applying the law to the facts and issues of specific cases. Legal reasoning involves becoming familiar with the key facts of a case, identifying the relevant legal rules, linking those rules to the facts, and drawing a conclusion. In linking the legal rules to the facts of a case, judges may use deductive reasoning, linear reasoning, or reasoning by analogy.

that statute. Often, the applicability of a newly enacted statute does not become clear until a body of case law develops to clarify how, when, and to whom the statute applies.

RESTATEMENTS OF THE LAW

The American Law Institute (ALI) has drafted and published compilations of the common law called *Restatements of the Law*, which generally summarize the common law rules followed by most states. There are *Restatements of the Law* in the areas of contracts, torts, agency, trusts, property, restitution, security, judgments, and conflict of laws. The *Restatements*, like other secondary sources of law, do not in themselves have the force of law but are an important source of legal analysis and opinion on which judges often rely in making their decisions.

Many of the *Restatements* are now in their second or third editions. We refer to the *Restatements* frequently in subsequent chapters of this text, indicating in parentheses the edition to which we are referring. For example, we refer to the second edition of the *Restatement of the Law of Contracts* simply as the *Restatement (Second) of Contracts*.

SECTION 6 | Classifications of Law

Because the body of law is so large, one must break it down by some means of classification. A number of classification systems have been devised. For example, one classification system divides law into substantive law and procedural law. **Substantive law** consists of all laws that define, describe, regulate, and create legal rights and obligations. **Procedural law** consists of all laws that delineate the methods of enforcing the rights established by substantive law. Other classification systems divide law into federal law and state law, private law (dealing with relationships between private entities) and public law (addressing the relationship between persons and their governments), national law and international law, and so on. Here we look at still another classification system, which divides law into civil law and criminal law, as well as at what is meant by the term *cyberlaw*.

CIVIL LAW AND CRIMINAL LAW

Civil law spells out the rights and duties that exist between persons and between persons and their governments, and the relief available when a person's

rights are violated. Typically, in a civil case, a private party sues another private party (although the government can also sue a party for a civil law violation) to make that other party comply with a duty or pay for the damage caused by failure to comply with a duty. Much of the law that we discuss in this text is civil law. Contract law, for example, covered in Chapters 9 and 10, is civil law. The whole body of tort law (see Chapters 12 and 13) is civil law.

Criminal law, in contrast, is concerned with wrongs committed *against the public as a whole*. Criminal acts are defined and prohibited by local, state, or federal government statutes. Criminal defendants are thus prosecuted by public officials, such as a district attorney (D.A.), on behalf of the state, not by their victims or other private parties. (See Chapter 7 for a further discussion of the distinction between civil law and criminal law.)

CYBERLAW

Over the last ten years, the use of the Internet to conduct business transactions has led to new types of legal issues. In response, courts have had to adapt traditional laws to situations that are unique to our age. (For a discussion of one such situation, see this chapter's *Contemporary Legal Debates* feature on pages 16 and 17.) Additionally, legislatures have created laws to deal specifically with such issues. The growing body of law that deals specifically with issues raised by cyberspace transactions is often referred to as **cyberlaw.** Cyberlaw is not really a classification of law; rather, it is an informal term used to describe how traditional classifications of law, such as civil law and criminal law, are being applied to online activities.

Realize, too, that cyberlaw is not a new *type* of law. For the most part, it consists of traditional legal principles that have been modified and adapted to fit situations that are unique to the online world. Of course, in some areas new statutes have been enacted, at both the federal and state levels, to cover specific types of problems stemming from online communications.

Anyone preparing to enter today's business world will find it useful to know how old and new laws are being applied to activities conducted online, such as advertising, contracting, banking, filing documents with the courts or government agencies, employment relations, and a variety of other transactions. For that reason, many sections in this text are devoted to cyberlaw issues.

SECTION 7 | How to Find Primary Sources of Law

This text includes numerous citations to primary sources of law—federal and state statutes, the U.S. Constitution and state constitutions, regulations issued by administrative agencies, and court cases. (A **citation** is a reference to a publication in which a legal authority—such as a statute or a court decision or other source—can be found.) In this section, we explain how you can use citations to find primary sources of law.

FINDING STATUTORY AND ADMINISTRATIVE LAW

When Congress passes laws, they are collected in a publication titled *United States Statutes at Large*. When state legislatures pass laws, they are collected in similar state publications. Most frequently, however, laws are referred to in their codified form—that is, the form in which they appear in the federal and state codes. In these codes, laws are compiled by subject.

UNITED STATES CODE The *United States Code* (U.S.C.) arranges all existing federal laws of a public and permanent nature by subject. Each of the fifty subjects into which the U.S.C. arranges the laws is given a title and a title number. For example, laws relating to commerce and trade are collected in Title 15, "Commerce and Trade." Titles are subdivided by sections. A citation to the U.S.C. includes title and section numbers. Thus, a reference to "15 U.S.C. Section 1" means that the statute can be found in Section 1 of Title 15. ("Section" may also be designated by the symbol §, and "Sections," by §§.) Sometimes a citation includes the abbreviation *et seq.*, as in "15 U.S.C. Sections 1 *et seq.*" The term is an abbreviated form of *et sequitur*, which in Latin means "and the following"; when used in a citation, it refers to sections that concern the same subject as the numbered section and follow it in sequence.

Commercial publications of these laws and regulations are available and are widely used. For example, West Group publishes the *United States Code Annotated* (U.S.C.A.). The U.S.C.A. contains the complete text of laws included in the U.S.C., plus notes on court decisions that interpret and apply specific sections of the statutes, as well as the text of presidential proclamations and executive orders. The U.S.C.A. also includes research aids, such as cross-references to related statutes, historical notes, and library references. A citation to the U.S.C.A. is similar to a citation to the U.S.C.: "15 U.S.C.A. Section 1."

STATE CODES State codes follow the U.S.C. pattern of arranging law by subject. They may be called codes, revisions, compilations, consolidations, general statutes, or statutes, depending on the preferences of the states. In some codes, subjects are designated by number. In others, they are designated by name. For example, "13 Pennsylvania Consolidated Statutes Section 1101" means that the statute can be found in Title 13, Section 1101, of the Pennsylvania code. "California Commercial Code Section 1101" means that the statute can be found under the subject heading "Commercial Code" of the California code in Section 1101. Abbreviations may be used. For example, "13 Pennsylvania Consolidated Statutes Section 1101" may often be abbreviated "13 Pa. C.S. §1101," and "California Commercial Code Section 1101" may be abbreviated "Cal. Com. Code §1101."

ADMINISTRATIVE RULES Rules and regulations adopted by federal administrative agencies are initially published in the *Federal Register*, a daily publication of the U.S. government. Later, they are incorporated into the *Code of Federal Regulations* (C.F.R.). Like the U.S.C., the C.F.R. is divided into fifty titles. Rules within each title are assigned section numbers. A full citation to the C.F.R. includes title and section numbers. For example, a reference to "17 C.F.R. Section 230.504" means that the rule can be found in Section 230.504 of Title 17.

FINDING CASE LAW

Before discussing the case reporting system, we need to look briefly at the court system (which will be discussed in detail in Chapter 2). There are two types of courts in the United States, federal courts and state courts. Both the federal and state court systems consist of several levels, or tiers, of courts. *Trial courts,* in which evidence is presented and testimony given, are on the bottom tier (which also includes lower courts handling specialized issues). Decisions from a trial court can be appealed to a higher court, which commonly would be an intermediate *court of appeals,* or an *appellate court.* Decisions from these intermediate courts of appeals may be appealed to an even higher

International Jurisdiction and the Internet

As you will learn in Chapter 2, *jurisdiction* is an important legal concept that relates to the authority of a court to hear and decide a case. Within the United States, there is a federal court system, which has jurisdiction over specific types of cases. There are also fifty state court systems, each having jurisdiction over certain types of cases. In today's interconnected world, the issue of jurisdiction has become critical. Specifically, businesses using the Internet can reach individuals in any part of the world. Does that mean that every court everywhere has jurisdiction over, say, an Internet-based company in Chicago? This is one of today's legal debates.

THE MINIMUM-CONTACTS REQUIREMENT

Domestically, jurisdiction over individuals and businesses is based on the requirement of minimum contacts as outlined in *International Shoe Co. v. State of Washington.*[a] Essentially, this requirement means that a business must have a minimum level of contacts with residents of a particular state for that state's courts to exercise jurisdiction over the firm—see Chapter 2. In the context of the Internet, most courts have *not* viewed the mere existence of a *passive* Web site as sufficient minimum contacts to exercise jurisdiction over a person or entity located out of state. Rather, a site must offer some

degree of interactivity (such as allowing a person to order goods from the site) to meet the minimum-contacts requirement. Internationally, other countries' courts are applying the requirement of minimum contacts as developed by the U.S. courts. As a result, a business in the United States offering products for sale via its Web site must comply with the laws of any jurisdiction in which it targets customers for its products.

THE FRENCH CASE AGAINST YAHOO

To understand some of the problems created by Internet commerce, consider a French court's judgment against the U.S.-based Internet company Yahoo!, Inc. Yahoo operates an online auction site on which Nazi memorabilia have been offered for sale. In France, the display of any objects representing symbols of Nazi ideology subjects the person or entity displaying such objects to both criminal and civil liability. The International League against Racism and Anti-Semitism filed suit in Paris against Yahoo for displaying Nazi memorabilia and offering them for sale via its Web site. The French court in which the suit was filed asserted jurisdiction over the U.S.-based company on the ground that the materials on the company's U.S.-based servers could be viewed on a Web site accessible in France. The French court ordered Yahoo to eliminate all Internet access in France to the Nazi memorabilia offered for sale through its online auctions.

---

a. 326 U.S. 310, 66 S.Ct. 154, 90 L.Ed. 95 (1945).

---

court, such as a state supreme court or the United States Supreme Court.

STATE COURT DECISIONS Most state trial court decisions are not published. Except in New York and a few other states that publish selected opinions of their trial courts, decisions from state trial courts are merely filed in the office of the clerk of the court, where the decisions are available for public inspection. Written decisions of the appellate, or reviewing, courts, however, are published and distributed. As you will note, most of the state court cases presented in this book are from state appellate courts. The reported appellate decisions are published in volumes called *reports* or *reporters*, which are numbered consecutively. State appellate court decisions are found in the state reporters of that particular state. Official

reports are volumes that are published by the state, whereas unofficial reports are privately published.

—*Regional Reporters.* State court opinions appear in regional units of the National Reporter System, published by West Group. Most lawyers and libraries have the West reporters because they report cases more quickly, and are distributed more widely, than the state-published reporters. In fact, many states have eliminated their own reporters in favor of West's National Reporter System. The National Reporter System divides the states into the following geographic areas: *Atlantic* (A. or A.2d), *South Eastern* (S.E. or S.E.2d), *South Western* (S.W., S.W.2d, or S.W.3d), *North Western* (N.W. or N.W.2d), *North Eastern* (N.E. or N.E.2d), *Southern* (So. or So.2d), and *Pacific* (P., P.2d, or P.3d). (The *2d* and *3d* in the preceding abbre-

Yahoo took the case to a federal district court in the United States to resolve a much larger issue: Can a foreign court dictate what will or will not appear on a U.S. company's Web site? Or does such an order violate the U.S. constitutional right to free speech and expression under the First Amendment? The federal district court agreed with Yahoo's argument that the French court's order violated the First Amendment and was thus not enforceable in the United States.[b] In 2004, however, the U.S. Court of Appeals for the Ninth Circuit reversed the district court's decision on the ground that U.S. courts lacked personal jurisdiction over the French groups involved. According to the majority opinion, "If Yahoo violates the speech laws of another nation, it must wait for the foreign litigants to come to the United States to enforce the judgment before its First Amendment claim may be heard by a U.S. court."[c]

In the world of business, the *Yahoo* case represents the first time a U.S. court was asked to decide whether to honor a foreign judgment in the context of the Internet. The Ninth Circuit's ruling leaves open the possibility that Yahoo, and

anyone else who posts anything on the Internet, could be held answerable to the laws of any country in which the message might be received. Several other countries—including Belarus, Cuba, Iran, Iraq, North Korea, the People's Republic of China, Saudi Arabia, and Syria—have even stricter restrictions on free speech than France. What will happen if those countries start suing Internet companies for posting what they view as "politically undesirable" speech is still a matter of debate.

WHERE DO YOU STAND?

In general, no country wants to give up jurisdiction because domestic courts wish to protect their own citizens. Nonetheless, some contend that extending the jurisdiction of courts to include any company that uses the Internet—regardless of where that company is located—will have a "chilling" effect on the growth of Internet commerce, as well as on the dissemination of ideas. Others argue that national governments should have the right to enforce laws prohibiting certain forms of speech or certain types of product sales within their national borders in the interest of protecting the welfare of their citizenry. What is your position on this issue? In what situations, if any, should jurisdiction be extended internationally because the Internet was used?

---

b. *Yahoo!, Inc. v. La Ligue Contre le Racisme et l'Antisemitisme,* 169 F.Supp.2d 1181 (N.D.Cal. 2001).

c. *Yahoo!, Inc. v. La Ligue Contre le Racisme et l'Antisemitisme,* 379 F.3d 1120 (9th Cir. 2004).

---

viations refer to *Second Series* and *Third Series,* respectively.) The states included in each of these regional divisions are indicated in Exhibit 1–4 on the next page, which illustrates West's National Reporter System.

—**Case Citations.**   After an appellate decision has been published, it is normally referred to (cited) by the name of the case (sometimes called the *style* of the case); the volume, name, and page number of the state's official reporter (if different from West's National Reporter System); the volume, unit, and page number of the National Reporter; and the volume, name, and page number of any other selected reporter. (Citing a reporter by volume number, name, and page number, in that order, is common to all citations; often, as in this book, the year the decision was made will be included in parentheses, just after the citations to reporters.)

When more than one reporter is cited for the same case, each reference is called a *parallel citation.*[6]

For example, consider the following case citation: *Yale Diagnostic Radiology v. Estate of Harun Fountain,* 267 Conn. 351, 838 A.2d 179 (2004). We see that the opinion in this case may be found in Volume 267 of the official *Connecticut Reports,* on page 351. The parallel citation is to Volume 838 of the *Atlantic*

---

6. Note that Wisconsin has adopted a "public domain citation system" in which the format is somewhat different. For example, a Wisconsin Supreme Court decision might be designated "2003 WI 40," meaning that the case was decided in the year 2003 by the Wisconsin Supreme Court and was the fortieth decision issued by that court during that year. (Parallel citations to the *Wisconsin Reports* and *West's North Western Reporter* are still required when citing Wisconsin cases, but they must follow the public domain citation.)

EXHIBIT 1-4   National Reporter System—Regional/Federal

Regional Reporters	Coverage Beginning	Coverage
Atlantic Reporter (A. or A.2d)	1885	Connecticut, Delaware, Maine, Maryland, New Hampshire, New Jersey, Pennsylvania, Rhode Island, Vermont, and District of Columbia.
North Eastern Reporter (N.E. or N.E.2d)	1885	Illinois, Indiana, Massachusetts, New York, and Ohio.
North Western Reporter (N.W. or N.W.2d)	1879	Iowa, Michigan, Minnesota, Nebraska, North Dakota, South Dakota, and Wisconsin.
Pacific Reporter (P., P.2d, or P.3d)	1883	Alaska, Arizona, California, Colorado, Hawaii, Idaho, Kansas, Montana, Nevada, New Mexico, Oklahoma, Oregon, Utah, Washington, and Wyoming.
South Eastern Reporter (S.E. or S.E.2d)	1887	Georgia, North Carolina, South Carolina, Virginia, and West Virginia.
South Western Reporter (S.W., S.W.2d, or S.W.3d)	1886	Arkansas, Kentucky, Missouri, Tennessee, and Texas.
Southern Reporter (So. or So.2d)	1887	Alabama, Florida, Louisiana, and Mississippi.

Federal Reporters		
Federal Reporter (F., F.2d, or F.3d)	1880	U.S. Circuit Courts from 1880 to 1912; U.S. Commerce Court from 1911 to 1913; U.S. District Courts from 1880 to 1932; U.S. Court of Claims (now called U.S. Court of Federal Claims) from 1929 to 1932 and since 1960; U.S. Courts of Appeals since 1891; U.S. Court of Customs and Patent Appeals since 1929; and U.S. Emergency Court of Appeals since 1943.
Federal Supplement (F.Supp. or F.Supp.2d)	1932	U.S. Court of Claims from 1932 to 1960; U.S. District Courts since 1932; and U.S. Customs Court since 1956.
Federal Rules Decisions (F.R.D.)	1939	U.S. District Courts involving the Federal Rules of Civil Procedure since 1939 and Federal Rules of Criminal Procedure since 1946.
Supreme Court Reporter (S.Ct.)	1882	U.S. Supreme Court since the October term of 1882.
Bankruptcy Reporter (Bankr. or B.R.)	1980	Bankruptcy decisions of U.S. Bankruptcy Courts, U.S. District Courts, U.S. Courts of Appeals, and U.S. Supreme Court.
Military Justice Reporter (M.J.)	1978	U.S. Court of Military Appeals and Courts of Military Review for the Army, Navy, Air Force, and Coast Guard.

NATIONAL REPORTER SYSTEM MAP

Reporter, Second Series, page 179. In presenting appellate opinions in this text, in addition to the reporter, we give the name of the court hearing the case and the year of the court's decision. Sample citations to state court decisions are explained in Exhibit 1–5 starting on the next page.

FEDERAL COURT DECISIONS Federal district (trial) court decisions are published unofficially in West's *Federal Supplement* (F.Supp. or F.Supp.2d), and opinions from the circuit courts of appeals are reported unofficially in West's *Federal Reporter* (F., F.2d, or F.3d). Cases concerning federal bankruptcy law are published unofficially in West's *Bankruptcy Reporter* (Bankr. or B.R.).

The official edition of all decisions of the United States Supreme Court for which there are written opinions is the *United States Reports* (U.S.), which is published by the federal government. The series includes reports of Supreme Court cases dating from the August term of 1791, although many of the Supreme Court's decisions were not reported in the early volumes. Unofficial editions of Supreme Court cases include West's *Supreme Court Reporter* (S.Ct.), which includes cases dating from the Court's term in October 1882; and the *Lawyers' Edition of the Supreme Court Reports* (L.Ed. or L.Ed.2d), published by the Lawyers Cooperative Publishing Company (now a part of West Group). The latter contains many of the decisions not reported in the early volumes of the *United States Reports*. Sample citations for federal court decisions are also listed and explained in Exhibit 1–5.

UNPUBLISHED OPINIONS Many court opinions that are not yet published or that are not intended for publication can be accessed through Westlaw® (abbreviated in citations as "WL"), an online legal database maintained by West Group. When no citation to a published reporter is available for cases cited in this text, we give the WL citation (see Exhibit 1–5 for an example).

OLD CASE LAW On a few occasions, this text cites opinions from old, classic cases dating to the nineteenth century or earlier; some of these are from the English courts. The citations to these cases may not conform to the descriptions given above because the reporters in which they were published were often known by the names of the persons who compiled the reporters, and the reporters have since been replaced.

SECTION 8 | How to Read and Understand Case Law

The decisions made by the courts establish the boundaries of the law as it applies to virtually all business relationships. It thus is essential that businesspersons know how to read and understand case law. The cases that we present in this text have been condensed from the full text of the courts' opinions and are presented in a special format. In each case, we have summarized the background and facts, as well as the court's decision and remedy, in our own words and have included only selected portions of the court's opinion ("in the language of the court"). For those who wish to review court cases to perform research projects or to gain additional legal information, however, the following sections will provide useful insights into how to read and understand case law.

CASE TITLES

The title of a case, such as *Adams v. Jones*, indicates the names of the parties to the lawsuit. The *v.* in the case title stands for *versus*, which means "against." In the trial court, Adams was the plaintiff—the person who filed the suit. Jones was the defendant. If the case is appealed, however, the appellate court will sometimes place the name of the party appealing the decision first, so the case may be called *Jones v. Adams* if Jones is appealing. Because some appellate courts retain the trial court order of names, it is often impossible to distinguish the plaintiff from the defendant in the title of a reported appellate court decision. You must carefully read the facts of each case to identify the parties. Otherwise, the discussion by the appellate court may be difficult to understand.

TERMINOLOGY

The following terms, phrases, and abbreviations are frequently encountered in court opinions and legal publications. Because it is important to understand what is meant by these terms, phrases, and abbreviations, we define and discuss them here.

PARTIES TO LAWSUITS As mentioned previously, the party initiating a lawsuit is referred to as the *plaintiff* or *petitioner*, depending on the nature of the action, and the party against whom a lawsuit is brought is the *defendant* or *respondent*. Lawsuits frequently involve

EXHIBIT 1-5 **How to Read Citations**

State Courts

269 Neb. 82, 690 N.W.2d 778 (2005) [a]

> *N.W.* is the abbreviation for West's publication of state court decisions rendered in the *North Western Reporter* of the National Reporter System. *2d* indicates that this case was included in the *Second Series* of that reporter. The number 690 refers to the volume number of the reporter; the number 778 refers to the first page in that volume on which this case can be found.

> *Neb.* is an abbreviation for *Nebraska Reports,* Nebraska's official reports of the decisions of its highest court, the Nebraska Supreme Court.

125 Cal.App.4th 949, 23 Cal.Rptr.3d 233 (2005)

> *Cal.Rptr.* is the abbreviation for West's unofficial reports—titled *California Reporter*—of the decisions of the California Supreme Court and California appellate courts.

1 N.Y.3d 280, 803 N.E.2d 757, 771 N.Y.S.2d 484 (2003)

> *N.Y.S.* is the abbreviation for West's unofficial reports—titled *New York Supplement*—of the decisions of New York courts.

> *N.Y.* is the abbreviation for *New York Reports,* New York's official reports of the decisions of its court of appeals. The New York Court of Appeals is the state's highest court, analogous to other states' supreme courts. (In New York, a supreme court is a trial court.)

267 Ga.App. 832, 600 S.E.2d 800 (2004)

> *Ga.App.* is the abbreviation for *Georgia Appeals Reports,* Georgia's official reports of the decisions of its court of appeals.

Federal Courts

___ U.S. ___ , 125 S.Ct. 847, ___ L.Ed.2d ___ (2005)

> *L.Ed.* is an abbreviation for *Lawyers' Edition of the Supreme Court Reports,* an unofficial edition of decisions of the United States Supreme Court.

> *S.Ct.* is the abbreviation for West's unofficial reports—titled *Supreme Court Reporter*—of decisions of the United States Supreme Court.

> *U.S.* is the abbreviation for *United States Reports,* the official edition of the decisions of the United States Supreme Court.

a. The case names have been deleted from these citations to emphasize the publications. It should be kept in mind, however, that the name of a case is as important as the specific numbers of the volumes in which it is found. If a citation is incorrect, the correct citation may be found in a publication's index of case names. The date of a case is also important because in addition to providing a check on error in citations, the value of a recent case as an authority is likely to be greater than that of an earlier case.

EXHIBIT 1-5 **How to Read Citations (Continued)**

Federal Courts (continued)

394 F.3d 520 (7th Cir. 2005)

7th Cir. is an abbreviation denoting that this case was decided in the United States Court of Appeals for the Seventh Circuit.

340 F.Supp.2d 1051 (D.S.D. 2004)

D.S.D. is an abbreviation indicating that the United States District Court for the District of South Dakota decided this case.

English Courts

9 Exch. 341, 156 Eng.Rep. 145 (1854)

Eng.Rep. is an abbreviation for *English Reports, Full Reprint,* a series of reports containing selected decisions made in English courts between 1378 and 1865.

Exch. is an abbreviation for *English Exchequer Reports,* which includes the original reports of cases decided in England's Court of Exchequer.

Statutory and Other Citations

18 U.S.C. Section 1961(1)(A)

U.S.C. denotes *United States Code,* the codification of *United States Statutes at Large.* The number 18 refers to the statute's U.S.C. title number and 1961 to its section number within that title. The number 1 refers to a subsection within the section and the letter A to a subdivision within the subsection.

UCC 2–206(1)(b)

UCC is an abbreviation for *Uniform Commercial Code.* The first number 2 is a reference to an article of the UCC and 206 to a section within that article. The number 1 refers to a subsection within the section and the letter b to a subdivision within the subsection.

Restatement (Second) of Contracts, Section 162

Restatement (Second) of Contracts refers to the second edition of the American Law Institute's *Restatement of the Law of Contracts.* The number 162 refers to a specific section.

17 C.F.R. Section 230.505

C.F.R. is an abbreviation for *Code of Federal Regulations,* a compilation of federal administrative regulations. The number 17 designates the regulation's title number, and 230.505 designates a specific section within that title.

(Continued)

EXHIBIT 1-5 **How to Read Citations (Continued)**

Westlaw® Citations[b]

2005 WL 27554

WL is an abbreviation for Westlaw®. The number 2005 is the year of the document that can be found with this citation in the Westlaw® database. The number 27554 is a number assigned to a specific document. A higher number indicates that a document was added to the Westlaw® database later in the year.

Uniform Resource Locators (URLs)[c]

http://www.westlaw.com[d]

The suffix *com* is the top level domain (TLD) for this Web site. The TLD *com* is an abbreviation for "commercial," which normally means that a for-profit entity hosts (maintains or supports) this Web site.

westlaw is the host name—the part of the domain name selected by the organization that registered the name. In this case, West Group registered the name. This Internet site is the Westlaw database on the Web.

www is an abbreviation for "World Wide Web." The Web is a system of Internet servers that support documents formatted in *HTML* (hypertext markup language). HTML supports links to text, graphics, and audio and video files.

http://www.uscourts.gov

This is "The Federal Judiciary Home Page." The host is the Administrative Office of the U.S. Courts. The TLD *gov* is an abbreviation for "government." This Web site includes information and links from, and about, the federal courts.

http://www.law.cornell.edu/index.html

This part of a URL points to a Web page or file at a specific location within the host's domain. This page is a menu with links to documents within the domain and to other Internet resources.

This is the host name for a Web site that contains the Internet publications of the Legal Information Institute (LII), which is a part of Cornell Law School. The LII site includes a variety of legal materials and links to other legal resources on the Internet. The TLD *edu* is an abbreviation for "educational institution" (a school or a university).

http://www.ipl.org/ref

ref is an abbreviation for "Internet Public Library Reference Center," which is a map of the topics into which the links at this Web site have been categorized.

ipl is an abbreviation for "Internet Public Library," which is an online service that provides reference resources and links to other information services on the Web. The IPL is supported chiefly by the School of Information at the University of Michigan. The TLD *org* is an abbreviation for "organization" (normally nonprofit).

b. Many court decisions that are not yet published or that are not intended for publication can be accessed through Westlaw®, an online legal database.

c. URLs are frequently changed as sites are redesigned and may not be working for other reasons, such as when a Web site has been deleted. If you are unable to find sites in this text with the specified URLs, go to the text's Web site at **http://wleb. westbuslaw.com**, where you may find an updated URL for the site or a URL for a similar site.

d. The basic form for a URL is "service://hostname/path." The Internet service for all of the URLs in this text is *http* (hypertext transfer protocol). Most Web browsers will add this prefix automatically when a user enters a host name or a hostname/path.

more than one plaintiff and/or defendant. When a case is appealed from the original court or jurisdiction to another court or jurisdiction, the party appealing the case is called the **appellant.** The **appellee** is the party against whom the appeal is taken. (In some appellate courts, the party appealing a case is referred to as the *petitioner,* and the party against whom the suit is brought or appealed is called the *respondent.*)

JUDGES AND JUSTICES The terms *judge* and *justice* are usually synonymous and represent two designations given to judges in various courts. All members of the United States Supreme Court, for example, are referred to as *justices,* and *justice* is the formal title usually given to judges of appellate courts, although this is not always the case. In New York, a *justice* is a judge of the trial court (which is called the Supreme Court), and a member of the Court of Appeals (the state's highest court) is called a *judge.* The term *justice* is commonly abbreviated to J., and *justices,* to JJ. A Supreme Court case might refer to Justice Kennedy as Kennedy, J., or to Chief Justice John Roberts as Roberts, C.J.

DECISIONS AND OPINIONS Most decisions reached by reviewing, or appellate, courts are explained in written **opinions.** The opinion contains the court's reasons for its decision, the rules of law that apply, and the judgment.

—Unanimous, Concurring, and Dissenting Opinions. When all judges or justices unanimously agree on an opinion, the opinion is written for the entire court and can be deemed a *unanimous opinion.* When there is not a unanimous opinion, a *majority opinion* is written; the majority opinion outlines the view supported by the majority of the judges or justices deciding the case. If a judge agrees, or concurs, with the majority's decision, but for different reasons, that judge may write a *concurring opinion.* A *dissenting opinion* presents the views of one or more judges who disagree with the majority's decision. The dissenting opinion is important because it may form the basis of the arguments used years later in overruling the precedential majority opinion.

—Other Types of Opinions. Occasionally, a court issues a *per curiam* opinion. *Per curiam* is a Latin phrase meaning "of the court." In *per curiam* opinions, there is no indication of which judge or justice authored the opinion. This term may also be used for an announcement of a court's disposition of a case that is not accompanied by a written opinion. Some of the cases

presented in this text are *en banc* decisions. When an appellate court reviews a case *en banc,* which is a French term (derived from a Latin term) for "in the bench," generally all of the judges "sitting on the bench" of that court review the case.

A SAMPLE COURT CASE

To illustrate the elements in a court opinion, we present an annotated opinion in Exhibit 1–6 beginning on the next page. The opinion is from an actual case that the U.S. Court of Appeals for the Sixth Circuit decided in 2005.

BACKGROUND OF THE CASE A group of restaurant, bar, and bowling alley owners and an association of restaurant owners—collectively making up an organization called D.A.B.E., Inc.—filed a suit in a federal district court against the city of Toledo, Ohio. The plaintiffs alleged that a city ordinance establishing tight restrictions on smoking in public places constituted a "taking" of the plaintiffs' right to their property. They also argued that the ordinance conflicted with a state law on the same subject and that therefore the ordinance was void. The court issued a judgment in favor of the city. The plaintiffs appealed to the U.S. Court of Appeals for the Sixth Circuit.

EDITORIAL PRACTICE You will note that triple asterisks (* * *) and quadruple asterisks (* * * *) frequently appear in the opinion. The triple asterisks indicate that we have deleted a few words or sentences from the opinion for the sake of readability or brevity. Quadruple asterisks mean that an entire paragraph (or more) has been omitted. Additionally, when the opinion cites another case or legal source, the citation to the case or other source has been omitted to save space and to improve the flow of the text. These editorial practices are continued in the other court opinions presented in this book. In addition, whenever we present a court opinion that includes a term or phrase that may not be readily understandable, a bracketed definition or paraphrase has been added.

BRIEFING CASES Knowing how to read and understand court opinions and the legal reasoning used by the courts is an essential step in undertaking accurate legal research. Yet a further step is "briefing," or summarizing, the case. Legal researchers routinely brief cases by reducing the texts of the opinions to their essential elements. Generally, when you brief a case, you first summarize the background and facts of the case, as the authors have done for the cases presented within this text. You then indicate the issue (or issues) before the court. An important element in the case brief is, of course, the court's decision on the issue and the legal reasoning used by the court in reaching that decision. Detailed instructions on how to brief a case are given in Appendix A, which also includes a briefed version of the sample court case presented in Exhibit 1–6.

EXHIBIT 1–6 **A Sample Court Case**

This section contains the case citation— the name of the case, the name of the court that heard the case, the year of the court's decision, and reporters in which the court's opinion can be found.	**D.A.B.E., INC. v. CITY OF TOLEDO** United States Court of Appeals, Sixth Circuit, 2005. 393 F.3d 692.
This line gives the name of the judge who authored the opinion of the court.	BOYCE F. MARTIN, JR., Circuit Judge. * * * *
The court divides the opinion into three parts, headed by Roman numerals. The first part of the opinion summarizes the factual background of the case.	I. The City of Toledo has regulated smoking in public places
A law passed by a local government unit, such as a city or a county.	since 1987 * * *. In early 2003, the City Council * * * enacted a new Clean Indoor Air **Ordinance**, No. 509-03.
Present or current.	Ordinance No. 509-03 regulates the ability to smoke in public places, such as retail stores, theaters, courtrooms, libraries, muse- ums, health-care facilities, and—most relevant to the **instant** case—restaurants and bars. In enclosed public places, smoking is generally prohibited except in a "separate smoking lounge" that is designated for the exclusive purpose of smoking * * *. * * * * * * * Appellants * * * [challenge] the ordinance on two grounds: first, that it constitutes a * * * taking of their property in violation of the Fifth [Amendment to the U.S.
Prevented from taking effect.	Constitution] * * *; and second, that it is **preempted** by Section 3791.031 of the Ohio Revised Code, a state law that reg- ulates smoking in places of public assembly but that does not apply to restaurants, bowling alleys and bars. * * * *
The second major section of the opinion sets out and applies the law to the plaintiffs' arguments.	II. * * * *
The first part of this section addresses the claim that the ordinance is a taking of the plaintiffs' property.	A. * * * **Taking Claim** The * * * Fifth Amendment * * * provides that private property shall not "be taken for public use, without just compen-

EXHIBIT 1-6 **A Sample Court Case (Continued)**

Financially sustainable; capable of working, functioning, or developing adequately.	sation." * * * [A] statute regulating the uses that can be made of property effects a taking if it denies an owner **economically viable** use of his land. * * *
The words of a writing in their apparent or obvious meaning.	The evidence presented in this case fails to establish that, **on its face**, the Clean Indoor Air Ordinance denies appellants economically viable use of their respective properties. Appellants have submitted affidavits alleging that they have lost—or fear they will lose—customers as a result of the ordinance, because smoking is an activity in which many customers wish to engage while patronizing their establishments. * * *
	* * * First, there is nothing on the face of the Clean Indoor Air Ordinance that prevents the beneficial use of appellants' property. To the contrary, the ordinance has absolutely no effect on any aspect of appellants' businesses other than to restrict the areas in which appellants' patrons may smoke.
Absolutely, unqualifiedly.	Second, the ordinance does not **categorically** prohibit smoking inside appellants' establishments; it merely regulates the conditions under which smoking is permitted. We recognize that the construction of separate smoking lounges in most cases will require some financial investment, but an ordinance does not effect a taking merely because compliance with it requires the expenditure of money. Finally, for obvious reasons, the ordinance does not purport to regulate alternative uses of appellants' respective properties. Therefore, * * * it is clear that appellants have failed to establish that the Clean Indoor Air Ordinance, on its face, effects a * * * taking of their property.
The second part of this section addresses the assertion that the city ordinance is void because a state statute already covers the subject and thus takes precedence.	**B. Preemption Claim** Appellants' second argument is that the Clean Indoor Air Ordinance conflicts with—and, therefore, is preempted by—Section 3791.031(A) of the Ohio Revised Code. A state statute takes precedence over a local ordinance when * * * the ordinance is in conflict with the statute * * * . * * * [T]he test is whether the ordinance permits or licenses that which the statute forbids or prohibits, and vice versa. To the extent that the statute does not address or apply to an item or issue, however, an ordinance regulating the excluded item or issue does not conflict with the statute, even if it deals with the same general subject matter. * * *

(Continued)

EXHIBIT 1-6 **A Sample Court Case (Continued)**

In this case, Section 3791.031 of the Ohio Revised Code regulates indoor smoking throughout the State of Ohio within "places of public assembly." It explicitly provides, however, that "[r]estaurants, food service establishments, dining rooms, cafes, cafeterias, or other rooms used primarily for the service of food, as well as bowling alleys and places licensed by the division of liquor control to sell intoxicating beverages for consumption on the premises, are not places of public assembly." * * *

Appellants argue that because smoking is allowed in their establishments under state law but not under the ordinance, there is a conflict that renders the ordinance preempted by state law. The City argues, by contrast, that the statute "simply does not regulate the establishments" that are subject to the ordinance and, therefore, municipalities within the State of Ohio are free to regulate smoking within these establishments * * * .

* * * [B]y stating that certain types of establishments—such as restaurants, bars, bowling alleys, etc.—"are not places of public assembly," the legislature indicated not that these establishments were immune to smoking-related regulation, but that they simply did not fall within the * * * statute.

Our independent research reveals that other courts that have considered whether smoking-related ordinances are preempted by state law have reached similar conclusions. * * * The [statute] prohibits smoking in certain locations; it does not contain the slightest hint that the legislature intended to create a positive right to smoke in all public places where it did not expressly forbid smoking. Nothing in the [statute] is inconsistent with a local **jurisdiction's** decision to impose greater limits on public smoking. * * *

A government body with the authority to act within a certain geographic area.

* * * *

In the third major section of this opinion, the court states its decision and gives its order.

III.

For these reasons, the district court's judgment is AFFIRMED.

TERMS AND CONCEPTS TO REVIEW

administrative agency 7	cyberlaw 14	plaintiff 9
administrative law 7	damages 8	positive law 3
allege 11	defendant 9	positivist school 3
analogy 12	defense 9	precedent 9
appellant 23	equitable maxim 9	procedural law 14
appellee 23	executive agency 7	public policy 11
binding authority 10	historical school 3	remedy 8
breach 4	independent regulatory	remedy at law 8
case law 7	agency 7	remedy in equity 8
case on point 12	jurisprudence 2	reporter 10
chancellor 8	laches 9	respondent 9
citation 15	law 2	sociological school 4
civil law 14	legal realism 3	*stare decisis* 10
common law 8	legal reasoning 11	statute of limitations 9
constitutional law 6	natural law 3	statutory law 6
court of equity 8	opinion 23	substantive law 14
court of law 8	ordinance 6	syllogism 12
criminal law 14	petitioner 9	uniform law 6

QUESTIONS AND CASE PROBLEMS

1–1. How does statutory law come into existence? How does it differ from the common law? If statutory law conflicts with the common law, which law will govern?

1–2. QUESTION WITH SAMPLE ANSWER

After World War II, which ended in 1945, an international tribunal of judges convened at Nuremberg, Germany. The judges convicted several Nazis of "crimes against humanity." Assuming that the Nazi war criminals who were convicted had not disobeyed any law of their country and had merely been following their government's (Hitler's) orders, what law had they violated? Explain.

For a sample answer to this question, go to Appendix I at the end of this text.

1–3. Assume that you want to read the entire court opinion in the case of *Kelly v. Arriba Soft Corp.*, 280 F.3d 934 (9th Cir. 2002). The case considers whether a photographer's images could be legally displayed on another person's Web site without the photographer's permission. Explain specifically where you would find the court's opinion.

1–4. This chapter discussed a number of sources of American law. Which source of law takes priority in the following situations, and why?

(a) A federal statute conflicts with the U.S. Constitution.
(b) A federal statute conflicts with a state constitutional provision.
(c) A state statute conflicts with the common law of that state.
(d) A state constitutional amendment conflicts with the U.S. Constitution.

1–5. In the text of this chapter, we stated that the doctrine of *stare decisis* "became a cornerstone of the English and American judicial systems." What does *stare decisis* mean, and why has this doctrine been so fundamental to the development of our legal tradition?

1–6. What is the difference between a concurring opinion and a majority opinion? Between a concurring opinion and a dissenting opinion? Why do judges and justices write concurring and dissenting opinions, given that these opinions will not affect the outcome of the case at hand, which has already been decided by majority vote?

1-7. Courts can overturn precedents and thus change the common law. Should judges have the same authority to overrule statutory law? Explain.

1-8. "The judge's role is not to make the law but to uphold and apply the law." Do you agree or disagree with this statement? Discuss fully the reasons for your answer.

1-9. Assume that Arthur Rabe is suing Xavier Sanchez for breaching a contract in which Sanchez promised to sell Rabe a Van Gogh painting for $3 million.

(a) In this lawsuit, who is the plaintiff and who is the defendant?

(b) Suppose that Rabe wants Sanchez to perform the contract as promised. What remedy would Rabe seek from the court?

(c) Now suppose that Rabe wants to cancel the contract because Sanchez fraudulently misrepresented the painting as an original Van Gogh when in fact it is a copy. What remedy would Rabe seek?

(d) Will the remedy Rabe seeks in either situation be a remedy at law or a remedy in equity? What is the difference between legal and equitable remedies?

(e) Suppose that the trial court finds in Rabe's favor and grants one of these remedies. Sanchez then appeals the decision to a higher court. On appeal, which party will be the appellant (or petitioner), and which party will be the appellee (or respondent)?

LAW | on the Web

Today, business law and legal environment professors and students can go online to access information on virtually every topic covered in this text. A good point of departure for online legal research is the Web site for *West's Legal Environment of Business Law*, Sixth Edition, which can be found at http://wleb.westbuslaw.com. There you will find numerous materials relevant to this text and to business law generally, including links to various legal resources on the Web. Additionally, every chapter in this text ends with a *Law on the Web* feature that contains selected Web addresses.

You can access many of the sources of law discussed in Chapter 1 at the FindLaw Web site, which is probably the most comprehensive source of free legal information on the Internet. Go to

http://www.findlaw.com

The Legal Information Institute (LII) at Cornell Law School, which offers extensive information about U.S. law, is also a good starting point for legal research. The URL for this site is

http://www.law.cornell.edu

The Library of Congress offers extensive links to state and federal government resources at

http://www.loc.gov

The Virtual Law Library Index, created and maintained by the Indiana University School of Law, provides an index of legal sources categorized by subject at

http://www.law.indiana.edu/v-lib/index.html#libdoc

LEGAL RESEARCH EXERCISES ON THE WEB

Go to **http://wleb.westbuslaw.com**, the Web site that accompanies this text. Select "Chapter 1" and click on "Internet Exercises." There you will find the following Internet research exercises that you can perform to learn more about some important sources of law discussed in Chapter 1 and other useful legal sites on the Web.

Activity 1–1: **LEGAL PERSPECTIVE**
Internet Sources of Law

Activity 1–2: **MANAGEMENT PERSPECTIVE**
Online Assistance from Government Agencies

Activity 1–3: **SOCIAL PERSPECTIVE**
The Case of the Speluncean Explorers

CHAPTER 2
The Court System

Today in the United States there are fifty-two court systems—one for each of the fifty states, one for the District of Columbia, and a federal system. Keep in mind that the federal courts are not superior to the state courts; they are simply an independent system of courts, which derives its authority from Article III, Section 2, of the U.S. Constitution. By the power given to it under Article I of the U.S. Constitution, Congress has extended the federal court system beyond the boundaries of the United States to U.S. territories such as Guam, Puerto Rico, and the Virgin Islands.[1] As we shall see, the United States Supreme Court is the final controlling voice over all of these fifty-two systems, at least when questions of federal law are involved.

Every businessperson will likely face a lawsuit at some time in his or her career. It is thus important for anyone involved in business to have an understanding of the American court systems, as well as the various methods of dispute resolution that can be pursued outside the courts. In this chapter, after examining the judiciary's role in the American governmental system, we discuss some basic requirements that must be met before a party may bring a lawsuit before a particular court. We then look at the court systems of the United States in some detail and follow a hypothetical civil case through a court. We examine alternative methods of settling disputes in Chapter 3.

SECTION 1 | The Judiciary's Role in American Government

As you learned in Chapter 1, the body of American law includes the federal and state constitutions, statutes passed by legislative bodies, administrative law, and the case decisions and legal principles that form the common law. These laws would be meaningless, however, without the courts to interpret and apply them. This is the essential role of the judiciary—the courts—in the American governmental system: to interpret the laws and apply them to specific situations.

As the branch of government entrusted with interpreting the laws, the judiciary can decide, among other things, whether the laws or actions of the other two branches are constitutional. The process for making such a determination is known as **judicial review.** The power of judicial review enables the judicial branch to act as a check on the other two branches of government, in line with the system of checks and balances established by the U.S. Constitution.[2]

The power of judicial review is not mentioned in the Constitution (although many constitutional scholars conclude that the founders intended the judiciary to have this power). Rather, this power was explicitly established by the United States Supreme Court in 1803 by its decision in *Marbury v. Madison,*[3] in which the Supreme Court stated, "It is emphatically the province and duty of the Judicial Department to say what the law is. . . . If two laws conflict with each other, the courts must decide on the operation of each. . . . So if the law be in opposition to the Constitution . . . [t]he Court must determine which of these conflicting rules governs the case. This is the very essence of judicial duty." Since the *Marbury v. Madison* deci-

---

1. In Guam and the Virgin Islands, territorial courts serve as both federal courts and state courts; in Puerto Rico, they serve only as federal courts.

2. In a broad sense, judicial review occurs whenever a court "reviews" a case or legal proceeding—as when an appellate court reviews a lower court's decision. When referring to the judiciary's role in American government, however, the term *judicial review* is used to indicate the power of the judiciary to decide whether actions of the other two branches of government violate the Constitution.

3. 5 U.S. (1 Cranch) 137, 2 L.Ed. 60 (1803).

sion, the power of judicial review has remained unchallenged. Today, this power is exercised by both federal and state courts.

SECTION 2 | Basic Judicial Requirements

Before a lawsuit can be brought before a court, certain requirements must be met. These requirements relate to jurisdiction, venue, and standing to sue. We examine each of these important concepts here.

JURISDICTION

In Latin, *juris* means "law," and *diction* means "to speak." Thus, "the power to speak the law" is the literal meaning of the term **jurisdiction.** Before any court can hear a case, it must have two types of jurisdiction: jurisdiction over the person (defendant) or property involved and jurisdiction over the subject matter of the dispute.

JURISDICTION OVER PERSONS OR PROPERTY

Generally, a particular court can exercise *in personam* **jurisdiction** (personal jurisdiction) over any person or business that resides in a certain geographic area. A state trial court, for example, normally has jurisdictional authority over residents (including businesses) of a particular area of the state, such as a county or district. A state's highest court (often called the state supreme court)[4] has jurisdictional authority over all residents within the state.

A court can also exercise jurisdiction over property that is located within its boundaries. This kind of jurisdiction is known as *in rem* **jurisdiction,** or "jurisdiction over the thing." For example, suppose a dispute arises over the ownership of a boat in dry dock in Fort Lauderdale, Florida. The boat is owned by an Ohio resident, over whom a Florida court normally cannot exercise personal jurisdiction. The other party to the dispute is a resident of Nebraska. In this situation, a lawsuit concerning the boat could be brought in a Florida state court on the basis of the court's *in rem* jurisdiction.

—Long Arm Statutes. Under the authority of a state **long arm statute,** a court can exercise personal jurisdiction over certain out-of-state defendants based on activities that took place within the state. Before a court can exercise jurisdiction over an out-of-state defendant under a long arm statute, though, it must be demonstrated that the defendant had sufficient contacts, or *minimum contacts*, with the state to justify the jurisdiction.[5] Generally, this means that the defendant must have enough of a connection to the state for the judge to conclude that it is fair for the state to exercise power over the defendant. For example, if an out-of-state defendant caused an automobile accident or sold defective goods within the state, a court will usually find that minimum contacts exist to exercise jurisdiction over that defendant. Similarly, a state may exercise personal jurisdiction over a nonresident defendant who is sued for breaching a contract that was formed within the state.

—Corporate Contacts. In regard to corporations,[6] the minimum-contacts requirement is usually met if the corporation does business within the state, advertises or sells its products within the state, or places its goods into the "stream of commerce" with the intent that the goods be sold in the state. Suppose that a business incorporated under the laws of Maine and headquartered in that state has a branch office or manufacturing plant in Georgia. Does this facility constitute sufficient contacts with the state of Georgia to allow a Georgia court to exercise jurisdiction over the corporation? Yes, it does. If the Maine corporation advertises and sells its products in Georgia, or places goods within the stream of commerce with the expectation that the goods will be purchased by Georgia residents, those activities will likely suffice to meet the minimum-contacts requirement.

Some corporations, however, do not sell or advertise products or place any goods in the stream of commerce. Determining what constitutes minimum contacts in these situations can be more difficult, as the following case—involving an out-of-state creditor that refused to fix an alleged error in a resident's credit report—illustrates.

---

4. As will be discussed shortly, a state's highest court is often referred to as the state supreme court, but there are exceptions. For example, in New York the supreme court is a trial court.

5. The minimum-contacts standard was established in *International Shoe Co. v. State of Washington*, 326 U.S. 310, 66 S.Ct. 154, 90 L.Ed. 95 (1945).

6. In the eyes of the law, corporations are "legal persons"—entities that can sue and be sued. See Chapter 18.

| CASE 2.1 | Bickford v. Onslow Memorial Hospital Foundation, Inc. |

Supreme Judicial
Court of Maine, 2004.
2004 ME 111,
855 A.2d 1150.
*http://www.courts.state.
me.us/opinions/supreme* **a**

BACKGROUND AND FACTS *Roy Bickford was married in July 1997 and moved to Maine with his wife in June 1998. In September, his wife left him. She moved to North Carolina that December. The couple agreed that each would pay his or her own debts as of August 18, 1998. They divorced in 1999. Bickford's wife obtained medical care for her daughter at Onslow Memorial Hospital in North Carolina. Bickford was not legally related to his wife's daughter and never agreed to pay for the services. Without telling him, however, the hospital held him financially responsible and notified credit reporting agencies that he had been "placed in collection" for failing to pay. He asked the hospital to correct this statement, but it refused. Meanwhile, his bank would not qualify him for a mortgage because of the apparent outstanding debt. Bickford filed a suit in a Maine state court against Onslow Memorial Hospital Foundation, Inc., asserting various torts.* **b** *The defendant asked the court to dismiss the complaint on the ground that Maine did not have personal jurisdiction over the hospital. The hospital treats patients in North Carolina and does not own any property, have any contractual relationships, or solicit any business or funding in Maine or from Maine residents. The court dismissed the complaint. Bickford appealed to the Maine Supreme Judicial Court, the state's highest court.*

IN THE LANGUAGE OF THE COURT

SAUFLEY, C.J. [Chief Justice]

 * * * *

 * * * For Maine to exercise jurisdiction over a nonresident defendant, three conditions must exist * * * : (1) Maine must have a legitimate interest in the subject matter of this litigation; (2) the defendant, by its conduct, reasonably could have anticipated litigation in Maine; and (3) the exercise of jurisdiction by Maine's courts comports [is consistent] with traditional notions of fair play and substantial justice. * * * We address each condition in turn.

 * * * *

Maine has a legitimate interest in allowing its residents a forum [court] in which to seek redress when out-of-state creditors refuse to correct erroneous credit reports. Credit reports substantially influence the ability of individuals to obtain financing for purchases that are vital to their lives and livelihoods. If a creditor actively refuses to correct the false credit report of a Maine resident, Maine has a legitimate interest in protecting the resident, *whether or not the creditor is located outside of Maine's boundaries.* * * * [Emphasis added.]

 * * * *

In addressing [the] second [condition] Bickford relies on two United States Supreme Court cases in which the defendants were authors, editors, or publishers of periodicals that enjoyed circulation and readership in the states where suit was commenced. In each case, the Court emphasized that the effect of the allegedly [false] material was felt in the state where the suit was filed. Nonetheless, the commission outside the forum state of an act that has consequences in the forum state is *by itself* an insufficient contact where all the events necessary to give rise to a tort claim occurred outside the forum state. Rather, *the effect of the out-of-state conduct in Maine is merely a factor to be considered in light of the relevant facts that apply to the minimum contacts analysis.* [Emphasis added.]

We need not decide whether simply filing a report with a national credit agency that might share its information with lenders in Maine could establish a connection between the hospital and Maine that would justify Maine's exercise of control. In the present case, Bickford alleges that the hospital went beyond the mere act of reporting a credit incident. He alleges that the hospital realized the impact its report was having on a Maine resident after it engaged in an exchange with Bickford about the status of the credit report. Because the hospital was thereafter on notice that it was injuring a Maine resident by failing to take steps to eliminate the use of the allegedly [false] statement, it could reasonably have anticipated being required to respond to litigation in Maine courts. The hospital's conduct affected a Maine resident, and after Bickford contested the report, the hospital can be understood to have intentionally

---

a. In the "August 2004" section, click on the name of the case to access the opinion. The Judicial Branch of the State of Maine maintains this Web site.

b. A *tort* is wrongful conduct that causes injury to another. See Chapters 12 and 13.

CASE 2.1 | Continued

directed its conduct toward a Maine resident. We conclude that the hospital could reasonably anticipate being haled into court in Maine.

    *   *   *   *

We must next address the third [condition's] requirement that the exercise of jurisdiction comport with traditional notions of fair play and substantial justice. The determination of fairness for purposes of personal jurisdiction depends upon the facts of each case. In making this determination, we consider the number, nature, and purpose of the defendant's contacts with Maine, the connection between those contacts and the cause of action, the interest of Maine in the controversy, and the convenience to both parties.

Maine has a strong interest in protecting its residents from abuses in credit reporting, and the hospital's alleged contact with Maine forms the basis for Bickford's tort claims against the hospital. Although the hospital's contact with Maine has not been voluminous, its action as a creditor failing to correct an erroneous report has allegedly resulted in a substantial impact on a Maine resident. Although it is inconvenient for the hospital to defend a suit in Maine and potential witnesses are out-of-state, it would also be burdensome for Bickford, whose credit has allegedly been compromised, to prosecute an action in North Carolina. *   *   * [Thus] it [does not offend] traditional notions of fair play and substantial justice to hale the hospital into court in Maine.

DECISION AND REMEDY *Maine's Supreme Judicial Court vacated the lower court's dismissal of Bickford's complaint and remanded the case to the lower court for "further proceedings consistent with this opinion." Maine's exercise of personal jurisdiction over the hospital met the three required conditions: Maine had a legitimate interest in the subject of the suit, the defendant reasonably could have anticipated litigation in Maine, and Maine's exercise of jurisdiction was in line with "traditional notions of fair play and substantial justice."*

WHAT IF THE FACTS WERE DIFFERENT? *Suppose that the hospital had only reported the incident to a credit agency but had not been in contact with Bickford and thus had no notice of Bickford's claims. How might this have affected the court's ruling in this case?*

JURISDICTION OVER SUBJECT MATTER Subject-matter jurisdiction refers to the limitations on the types of cases a court can hear. Certain courts are empowered to hear certain kinds of disputes.

—General and Limited Jurisdiction. In both the federal and state court systems, there are courts of *general* (unlimited) *jurisdiction* and courts of *limited jurisdiction*. A court of general jurisdiction can decide cases involving a broad array of issues. An example of a court of general jurisdiction is a state trial court or a federal district court. An example of a state court of limited jurisdiction is a probate court. **Probate courts** are state courts that handle only matters relating to the transfer of a person's assets and obligations after that person's death, including issues relating to the custody and guardianship of children. An example of a federal court of limited subject-matter jurisdiction is a bankruptcy court. **Bankruptcy courts** handle only bankruptcy proceedings, which are governed by federal bankruptcy law (discussed in Chapter 15).

A court's jurisdiction over subject matter is usually defined in the statute or constitution creating the court. In both the federal and state court systems, a court's subject-matter jurisdiction can be limited not only by the subject of the lawsuit but also by the sum in controversy, whether the case is a felony (a more serious type of crime) or a misdemeanor (a less serious type of crime), or whether the proceeding is a trial or an appeal.

—Original and Appellate Jurisdiction. A court's subject-matter jurisdiction is also frequently limited to hearing cases at a particular stage of the dispute. Courts in which lawsuits begin, trials take place, and evidence is presented are referred to as courts of original jurisdiction. Courts having original jurisdiction are courts of the first instance, or trial courts. In the federal court system, the *district courts* are trial courts. In the various state court systems, the trial courts are known by different names, as will be discussed shortly.

Courts having appellate jurisdiction act as reviewing courts, or appellate courts. In general, cases can be brought before appellate courts only on appeal from an order or a judgment of a trial court or other lower court. In other words, the distinction between courts of original jurisdiction and courts of appellate jurisdiction normally lies in whether the case is being heard for the first time.

JURISDICTION OF THE FEDERAL COURTS   Because the federal government is a government of limited powers, the jurisdiction of the federal courts is limited. Federal courts have subject-matter jurisdiction in two situations.

—*Federal Questions.*   Article III of the U.S. Constitution establishes the boundaries of federal judicial power. Section 2 of Article III states that "[t]he judicial Power shall extend to all Cases, in Law and Equity, arising under this Constitution, the Laws of the United States, and Treaties made, or which shall be made, under their Authority." In effect, this clause means that whenever a plaintiff's cause of action is based, at least in part, on the U.S. Constitution, a treaty, or a federal law, a **federal question** arises. Any lawsuit involving a federal question comes under the judicial authority of the federal courts and can originate in a federal court. People who claim that their constitutional rights have been violated, for example, can begin their suits in a federal court. Note that in a case based on a federal question, a federal court will apply federal law.

—*Diversity of Citizenship.*   Federal district courts can also exercise original jurisdiction over cases involving **diversity of citizenship.** This term applies whenever a federal court has jurisdiction over a case that does not involve a question of federal law. The most common type of diversity jurisdiction has two requirements:[7] (1) the plaintiff and defendant must be residents of different states, and (2) the dollar amount in controversy must exceed $75,000. For purposes of diversity jurisdiction, a corporation is a citizen of both the state in which it is incorporated and the state in which its principal place of business is located. A case involving diversity of citizenship can be filed in the appropriate federal district court. If the case starts in a state court, it can sometimes be transferred, or "removed," to a federal court. A large percentage of the cases filed in federal courts each year are based on diversity of citizenship.

As noted, a federal court will apply federal law in cases involving federal questions. In a case based on diversity of citizenship, in contrast, a federal court will apply the relevant state law (which is often the law of the state in which the court sits).

EXCLUSIVE VERSUS CONCURRENT JURISDICTION
When both federal and state courts have the power to hear a case, as is true in suits involving diversity of citizenship, **concurrent jurisdiction** exists. When cases can be tried only in federal courts or only in state courts, **exclusive jurisdiction** exists. Federal courts have exclusive jurisdiction in cases involving federal crimes, bankruptcy, and most patent and copyright claims; in suits against the United States; and in some areas of admiralty law (law governing transportation on the seas and ocean waters). State courts also have exclusive jurisdiction over certain subjects—for example, divorce and adoption.

When concurrent jurisdiction exists, a party may choose to bring a suit in either a federal court or a state court. The party's lawyer will consider several factors in counseling the litigant as to which choice is preferable. The lawyer may prefer to litigate the case in a state court because she or he is more familiar with the state court's procedures, or perhaps the attorney believes that the state court's judge or jury would be more sympathetic to the client's case. Alternatively, the lawyer may advise the client to sue in federal court. Perhaps the state court's **docket** (the court's schedule listing the cases to be heard) is crowded, and the case could be brought to trial sooner in a federal court. Perhaps some feature of federal practice or procedure could offer an advantage in the client's case. Other important considerations include the law in the particular jurisdiction, how that law has been applied in the jurisdiction's courts, and what the results in similar cases have been in that jurisdiction.

JURISDICTION IN CYBERSPACE

The Internet's capacity to bypass political and geographic boundaries undercuts the traditional basis for a court to assert personal jurisdiction. This basis includes a party's contacts with a court's geographic jurisdiction. As already discussed, for a court to compel a defendant to come before it, there must be at least minimum contacts—the presence of a salesperson within the state, for example. Are there sufficient minimum contacts if the only connection to a jurisdiction is an ad on a Web site originating from a remote location?

7. Diversity jurisdiction also exists in cases between (1) a foreign country and citizens of a state or of different states and (2) citizens of a state and citizens or subjects of a foreign country. These bases for diversity jurisdiction are less commonly used.

THE "SLIDING-SCALE" STANDARD The courts are developing a standard—called a "sliding-scale" standard—for determining when the exercise of personal jurisdiction over an out-of-state defendant is proper. In developing this standard, the courts have identified three types of Internet business contacts: (1) substantial business conducted over the Internet (with contracts and sales, for example); (2) some interactivity through a Web site; and (3) passive advertising. Jurisdiction is proper for the first category, improper for the third, and may or may not be appropriate for the second.[8] An Internet communication is typically considered passive if people have to voluntarily access it to read the message and active if it is sent to specific individuals.

In certain situations, even a single contact can satisfy the minimum-contacts requirement. In one case, for example, a Texas resident, Connie Davis, sent an unsolicited e-mail message to numerous Mississippi residents advertising a pornographic Web site. Davis falsified the "from" header in the e-mail so that it looked as if Internet Doorway had sent the e-mail. Internet Doorway filed a lawsuit against Davis in Mississippi, claiming that its reputation and goodwill in the community had been harmed. The federal court in Mississippi held that Davis's single e-mail to Mississippi residents satisfied the minimum-contacts requirement for jurisdiction. The court concluded that Davis, by sending the e-mail solicitation, should reasonably have expected that she could be "haled into court in a distant jurisdiction to answer for the ramifications."[9]

In the following case, the court considered whether jurisdiction could be exercised over defendants whose only contacts with the jurisdiction were through their Web site.

---

8. For a leading case on this issue, see *Zippo Manufacturing Co. v. Zippo Dot Com, Inc.*, 952 F.Supp. 1119 (W.D.Pa. 1997).

9. *Internet Doorway, Inc. v. Parks*, 138 F.Supp.2d 773 (S.D.Miss. 2001).

CASE 2.2

United States
Court of Appeals,
Sixth Circuit, 2002.
289 F.3d 865.
http://pacer.ca6.uscourts.
gov/opinions/main.php [a]

Bird v. Parsons

HISTORICAL AND TECHNOLOGICAL SETTING *The creation of a Web site requires the reservation of a cyberlocation, called an Internet Protocol (IP) address, and a computer to host the contents of the site. To make using the Internet easier, a domain name is assigned to correspond to an IP address. A person who wants a specific domain name must apply for the name with a domain name registrar. To access a Web site, a user enters in a browser a domain name corresponding to an IP address and then is routed electronically to the computer that hosts the site at that address. Because not every person who establishes a site hosts it on his or her own Internet server, surrogate hosts license space on their servers to site owners.*

BACKGROUND AND FACTS *Darrell Bird, a citizen of Ohio, has operated Financia, Inc., a national computer software business, since 1983. Financia, Inc., owns the domain name financia.com. Dotster, Inc., a domain name registrar incorporated in Washington, operates its registry at http://www.dotster.com.[b] Dotster allows registrants who lack an Internet server to which a name can be assigned to park their names on Dotster's "Futurehome" page. Marshall Parsons registered the name efinancia.com on Dotster's site in 2000 and parked the name on the Futurehome page with the address http://www.efinancia.com. George DeCarlo and Steven Vincent, on behalf of Dotster, activated Parsons's site. The name efinancia.com was soon offered for sale at http://www.afternic.com, an auction site for the sale of domain names. Bird filed a suit against Dotster and others in a federal district court, alleging, in part, trademark infringement, copyright infringement, and cybersquatting.[c] Dotster, DeCarlo, and Vincent (the "Dotster defendants") asked the court to dismiss the complaint against them for, among other reasons, lack of personal jurisdiction. The court dismissed the suit. Alleging that Dotster sold 4,666 registrations to Ohio residents, Bird appealed to the U.S. Court of Appeals for the Sixth Circuit.*

---

a. This is a page within the Web site of the U.S. Court of Appeals for the Sixth Circuit. In the left-hand column, click on "Opinions Search." In the "Short Title contains" box, type "Parsons" and click on "Submit Query." In the "Opinion" box corresponding to the name of the case, click on the number to access the opinion.
b. Dotster's registration process is in conjunction with the Domain Registration of Internet Assigned Names and Numbers, which is maintained by Network Solutions, Inc. (owned by VeriSign), and regulated by the Internet Corporation for Assigned Names and Numbers (ICANN) (see Chapter 14). Dotster is an ICANN-accredited registrar.
c. *Cybersquatting* is registering another person's trademark as a domain name and offering it for sale. This is a violation of the Anticybersquatting Consumer Protection Act of 1999. Cybersquatting and trademark and copyright infringement will be discussed in more detail in Chapter 14.

CONTINUED ▶

CASE 2.2 | Continued

IN THE LANGUAGE OF THE COURT

RONALD LEE GILMAN, Circuit Judge.

* * * *

* * * [J]urisdiction over the Dotster defendants is permissible only if their contacts with Ohio satisfy [a] three-part test * * * :

> First, the defendant must purposefully avail himself of the privilege of acting in the forum state [the state in which the lawsuit is initiated] or causing a consequence in the forum state. Second, the cause of action must arise from the defendant's activities there. Finally, the acts of the defendant or consequences caused by the defendant must have a substantial enough connection with the forum state to make the exercise of jurisdiction over the defendant reasonable.

* * * We conclude that by maintaining a website on which Ohio residents can register domain names and by allegedly accepting the business of 4,666 Ohio residents, the Dotster defendants have satisfied the *purposeful-availment* [use] *requirement*. * * * [Emphasis added.]

The second requirement * * * involves an analysis of whether Bird's claims arise from the Dotster defendants' contacts with Ohio. * * *

The operative facts in the present case include Bird's allegation that the Dotster defendants committed copyright and trademark law violations by registering Parsons's domain name efinancia.com. Both the Dotster defendants' contacts with Ohio and Bird's claim of copyright and trademark violations stem from these defendants' operation of the Dotster website. As a result, the operative facts are at least marginally related to the alleged contacts between the Dotster defendants and Ohio. * * *

The final requirement * * * is that the exercise of jurisdiction be reasonable in light of the connection that allegedly exists between the Dotster defendants and Ohio. * * *

Although the Dotster defendants might face a burden in having to defend a lawsuit in Ohio, they cannot reasonably object to this burden given that Dotster has allegedly transacted business with 4,666 Ohio residents. Ohio has a legitimate interest in protecting the business interests of its citizens, *even though all of Bird's claims involve federal law*. Bird has an obvious interest in obtaining relief, and *Ohio might be the only forum where jurisdiction would exist over all of the defendants*. Although the state of Washington also has an interest in this dispute, because the claim involves its citizens, this interest does not override the other factors suggesting that personal jurisdiction in Ohio is reasonable. [Emphasis added.]

DECISION AND REMEDY *The U.S. Court of Appeals for the Sixth Circuit concluded that the lower court erred in granting the Dotster defendants' motion to dismiss for lack of personal jurisdiction. Bird had established that the court's exercise of jurisdiction over the Dotster defendants was proper.*

INTERNATIONAL JURISDICTIONAL ISSUES Because the Internet is international in scope, international jurisdictional issues have understandably come to the fore. We have already discussed some of these issues in the *Contemporary Legal Debates* feature in Chapter 1. The world's courts seem to be developing a standard that echoes the requirement of "minimum contacts" applied by the U.S. courts. Most courts are indicating that minimum contacts—doing business within the jurisdiction, for example—are enough to exercise jurisdiction over a defendant. The effect of this standard is that a business firm may have to comply with the laws in any jurisdiction in which it actively targets customers for its products.

VENUE

Jurisdiction has to do with whether a court has authority to hear a case involving specific persons, property, or subject matter. **Venue**[10] is concerned with the most appropriate location for a trial. For example, two state courts (or two federal courts) may have the authority

---

10. Pronounced *ven-yoo*.

CONCEPT SUMMARY 2.1 | Jurisdiction

TYPE OF JURISDICTION	DESCRIPTION
PERSONAL	Exists when a defendant is located within the territorial boundaries within which a court has the right and power to decide cases. Jurisdiction may be exercised over out-of-state defendants under state long arm statutes. Courts have jurisdiction over corporate defendants that do business within the state, as well as corporations that advertise, sell, or place goods into the stream of commerce in the state.
PROPERTY	Exists when the property that is subject to a lawsuit is located within the territorial boundaries within which a court has the right and power to decide cases.
SUBJECT MATTER	Limits the court's jurisdictional authority to particular types of cases. 1. *Limited jurisdiction*—Exists when a court is limited to a specific subject matter, such as probate or divorce. 2. *General jurisdiction*—Exists when a court can hear cases involving a broad array of issues.
ORIGINAL	Exists with courts that have the authority to hear a case for the first time (trial courts).
APPELLATE	Exists with courts of appeal and review; generally, appellate courts do not have original jurisdiction.
FEDERAL	1. *Federal questions*—When the plaintiff's cause of action is based at least in part on the U.S. Constitution, a treaty, or a federal law, a federal court can exercise jurisdiction. 2. *Diversity of citizenship*—A federal court can exercise jurisdiction in cases between citizens of different states when the amount in controversy exceeds $75,000, in cases between a foreign country and citizens of a state or of different states, and in cases between citizens of a state and citizens or subjects of a foreign country.
CONCURRENT	Exists when both federal and state courts have authority to hear the same case.
EXCLUSIVE	Exists when only state courts or only federal courts have authority to hear a case.
JURISDICTION IN CYBERSPACE	Because the Internet does not have physical boundaries, traditional jurisdictional concepts have been difficult to apply in cases involving activities conducted via the Web. Gradually, the courts are developing standards to use in determining when jurisdiction over a Web site owner or operator in another state is proper.

to exercise jurisdiction over a case, but it may be more appropriate or convenient to hear the case in one court than in the other.

Basically, the concept of venue reflects the policy that a court trying a suit should be in the geographic neighborhood (usually the county) where the incident leading to the lawsuit occurred or where the parties involved in the lawsuit reside. Venue in a civil case typically is where the defendant resides, whereas venue in a criminal case normally is where the crime occurred. Pretrial publicity or other factors, though, may require a change of venue to another community, especially in criminal cases in which the defendant's right to a fair and impartial jury has been impaired.

STANDING TO SUE

In order to bring a lawsuit before a court, a party must have **standing to sue,** or a sufficient "stake" in a matter to justify seeking relief through the court system. In other words, to have standing, a party must have a legally protected and tangible interest at stake in the litigation. The party bringing the lawsuit must have suffered a harm or been threatened with a harm by the action about which he or she has complained. At times, a person can have standing to sue on behalf of another person. For example, suppose that a child suffers serious injuries as a result of a defectively manufactured toy. Because the child is a minor, another person, such as a parent or legal guardian, can bring a lawsuit on the child's behalf.

Standing to sue also requires that the controversy at issue be a **justiciable**[11] **controversy**—a controversy that is real and substantial, as opposed to hypothetical or academic. For instance, in the above example, the child's parent could not sue the toy manufacturer merely on the ground that the toy was defective. The issue would become justiciable only if the child had actually been injured due to the defect in the toy as marketed. In other words, the parent normally could not ask the court to determine what damages might be obtained if the child had been injured, because this would be merely a hypothetical question.

SECTION 3 | The State and Federal Court Systems

As mentioned earlier in this chapter, each state has its own court system. Additionally, there is a system of federal courts. Although no two state court systems are exactly the same, the right-hand side of Exhibit 2–1 illustrates the basic organizational framework characteristic of the court systems in many states. The exhibit also shows how the federal court system is structured. We turn now to an examination of these court systems, beginning with the state courts.

STATE COURT SYSTEMS

Typically, a state court system includes several levels, or tiers, of courts. As indicated in Exhibit 2–1, state courts may include (1) local trial courts of limited jurisdiction, (2) state trial courts of general jurisdiction, (3) state courts of appeals (intermediate appellate courts), and (4) the state's highest court (often called the state supreme court). Judges in the state court system are usually elected by the voters for specified terms. In some states, however, judges are appointed by an elected official and then confirmed by a public vote.

Generally, any person who is a party to a lawsuit has the opportunity to plead the case before a trial court and then, if he or she loses, before at least one level of appellate court. Finally, if a federal statute or federal constitutional issue is involved in the decision of a state supreme court, that decision may be further appealed to the United States Supreme Court.

TRIAL COURTS Trial courts are exactly what their name implies—courts in which trials are held and testimony taken. State trial courts have either general or limited jurisdiction. Trial courts that have general jurisdiction as to subject matter may be called county, district, superior, or circuit courts.[12] State trial courts of general jurisdiction have jurisdiction over a wide

---

11. Pronounced jus-*tish*-a-bul.

12. The name in Ohio and Pennsylvania is Court of Common Pleas; the name in New York is Supreme Court, Trial Division.

EXHIBIT 2-1 **The State and Federal Court Systems**

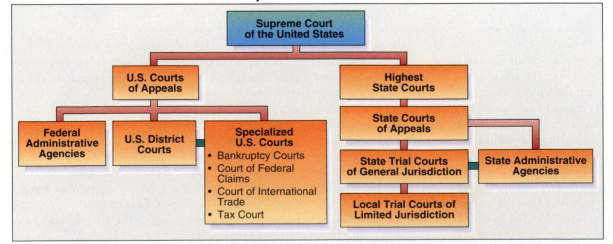

variety of subjects, including both civil disputes and criminal prosecutions. In some states, trial courts of general jurisdiction may hear appeals from courts of limited jurisdiction.

Courts of limited jurisdiction as to subject matter are often called special inferior trial courts or minor judiciary courts. **Small claims courts** are inferior trial courts that hear only civil cases involving claims of less than a certain amount, such as $5,000 (the amount varies from state to state). Suits brought in small claims courts are generally conducted informally, and lawyers are not required. In a small number of states, lawyers are not even allowed to represent people in small claims courts for most purposes. Decisions of small claims courts may sometimes be appealed to a state trial court of general jurisdiction.

Other courts of limited jurisdiction include domestic relations courts, which handle primarily divorce actions and child-custody disputes; local municipal courts, which mainly deal with traffic cases; and probate courts, as mentioned earlier.

APPELLATE, OR REVIEWING, COURTS Every state has at least one court of appeals (appellate court, or reviewing court), which may be an intermediate appellate court or the state's highest court. About three-fourths of the states have intermediate appellate courts. Generally, courts of appeals do not conduct new trials, in which evidence is submitted to the court and witnesses are examined. Rather, an appellate court panel of three or more judges reviews the record of the case on appeal, which includes a transcript of the trial proceedings, and then determines whether the trial court committed an error.

Usually, appellate courts focus on questions of law, not questions of fact. A **question of fact** deals with what really happened in regard to the dispute being tried—such as whether a party actually burned a flag. A **question of law** concerns the application or interpretation of the law—such as whether flag-burning is a form of speech protected by the First Amendment to the Constitution. Only a judge, not a jury, can rule on questions of law. Appellate courts normally defer to the trial court's findings on questions of fact because the trial court judge and jury were in a better position to evaluate testimony—by directly observing witnesses' gestures, demeanor, and other nonverbal behavior during the trial. At the appellate level, the judges review the written transcript of the trial, which does not include these nonverbal elements. Thus, an appellate court will tamper with a trial court's finding of fact only

when the finding is clearly erroneous (that is, when it is contrary to the evidence presented at trial) or when there is no evidence to support the finding.

HIGHEST STATE COURTS The highest appellate court in a state is usually called the supreme court but may be designated by some other name. For example, in both New York and Maryland, the highest state court is called the Court of Appeals. In Maine and Massachusetts, the highest court is labeled the Supreme Judicial Court. In West Virginia, the highest state court is the Supreme Court of Appeals.

The decisions of each state's highest court on all questions of state law are final. Only when issues of federal law are involved can the United States Supreme Court overrule a decision made by a state's highest court. For example, suppose that a city ordinance prohibits citizens from engaging in door-to-door advocacy without first registering with the mayor's office and receiving a permit. Further suppose that a religious group sues the city, arguing that the law violates the freedoms of speech and religion guaranteed by the First Amendment. If the state supreme court upholds the law, the group could appeal the decision to the United States Supreme Court—because a constitutional (federal) issue is involved.

THE FEDERAL COURT SYSTEM

The federal court system is basically a three-tiered model consisting of (1) U.S. district courts (trial courts of general jurisdiction) and various courts of limited jurisdiction, (2) U.S. courts of appeals (intermediate courts of appeals), and (3) the United States Supreme Court.

Unlike state court judges, who are usually elected, federal court judges—including the justices of the Supreme Court—are appointed by the president of the United States, subject to confirmation by the U.S. Senate. Article III of the Constitution states that federal judges "hold their offices during good Behaviour." In effect, this means that federal judges have lifetime appointments. Although they can be impeached (removed from office) for misconduct, this is rarely done. In the entire history of the United States, only seven federal judges have been removed from office through impeachment proceedings.

U.S. DISTRICT COURTS At the federal level, the equivalent of a state trial court of general jurisdiction is the district court. U.S. district courts have original jurisdiction in federal matters, and federal cases typically originate in district courts. There are other federal courts with original, but special (or limited), jurisdiction, such as the federal bankruptcy courts and others shown earlier in Exhibit 2–1 on page 38.

There is at least one federal district court in every state. The number of judicial districts can vary over time, primarily owing to population changes and corresponding changes in caseloads. At the present time, there are ninety-four federal judicial districts. Exhibit 2–2 shows the boundaries of the U.S. district courts, as well as the U.S. courts of appeals (discussed next).

U.S. COURTS OF APPEALS   In the federal court system, there are thirteen U.S. courts of appeals—referred to as U.S. circuit courts of appeals. Twelve of the federal courts of appeals (including the Court of Appeals for the D.C. Circuit) hear appeals from the federal district courts located within their respective judicial circuits, or geographic boundaries (shown in Exhibit 2–2).[13] The Court of Appeals for the Thirteenth Circuit, called the Federal Circuit, has national appellate jurisdiction over certain types of cases, such as those involving patent law and those in which the U.S. government is a defendant. The decisions of a circuit court of appeals are binding on all courts within the circuit court's jurisdiction and are final in most cases, but appeal to the United States Supreme Court is possible.

UNITED STATES SUPREME COURT   At the highest level in the three-tiered federal court system is the United States Supreme Court. According to the language of Article III of the U.S. Constitution, there is only one national Supreme Court. All other courts in the federal system are considered "inferior." Congress is empowered to create other inferior courts as it deems necessary. The inferior courts that Congress has created include the second tier in our model—the U.S. circuit courts of appeals—as well as the district courts and the various federal courts of limited, or specialized, jurisdiction.

The United States Supreme Court consists of nine justices. Although the Supreme Court has original, or trial, jurisdiction in rare instances (set forth in Article III, Sections 1 and 2), most of its work is as an appeals court. The Supreme Court can review any case decided

by any of the federal courts of appeals, and it also has appellate authority over cases involving federal questions that have been decided in the state courts. The Supreme Court is the final arbiter of the Constitution and federal law.

—Appeals to the Supreme Court.   To bring a case before the Supreme Court, a party requests the Court to issue a writ of *certiorari*.[14] A **writ of *certiorari*** is an order issued by the Supreme Court to a lower court requiring the latter to send it the record of the case for review. The Court will not issue a writ unless at least four of the nine justices approve of it. This is called the **rule of four.** Whether the Court will issue a writ of *certiorari* is entirely within its discretion, and most petitions for writs are denied. (Thousands of cases are filed with the Supreme Court each year, yet it hears, on average, less than one hundred of these cases.[15]) A denial is not a decision on the merits of a case, nor does it indicate agreement with the lower court's opinion. Also, denial of the writ has no value as a precedent. Denial simply means that the lower court's decision remains the law in that jurisdiction.

—Petitions Granted by the Court.   Typically, the Court grants petitions in cases that raise important constitutional questions or cases that conflict with other state or federal court decisions. Similarly, if federal appellate courts are rendering inconsistent opinions on an important issue, the Supreme Court may review the case and issue a decision to define the law on the matter. The justices, however, never explain their reasons for hearing certain cases and not others, so it is difficult to predict which type of case the Court might select.

SECTION 4 | Judicial Procedures: Following a Case through the Court

American and English courts follow the *adversarial system of justice.* Although clients are allowed to represent themselves in court (called *pro se* representation),[16] most parties to lawsuits hire attorneys to

---

13. Historically, judges were required to "ride the circuit" and hear appeals in different courts around the country, which is how the name *circuit court* came about.

14. Pronounced sur-shee-uh-*rah*-ree.
15. From the mid-1950s through the early 1990s, the Supreme Court reviewed more cases per year than it has since then. In the Court's 1982–1983 term, for example, the Court issued written opinions in 151 cases. In contrast, during the Court's 2004–2005 term, the Court issued written opinions in only 80 cases.
16. This right was definitively established in *Faretta v. California,* 422 U.S. 806, 95 S.Ct. 2525, 45 L.Ed.2d 562 (1975).

EXHIBIT 2–2 Geographic Boundaries of the U.S. District Courts and Courts of Appeals

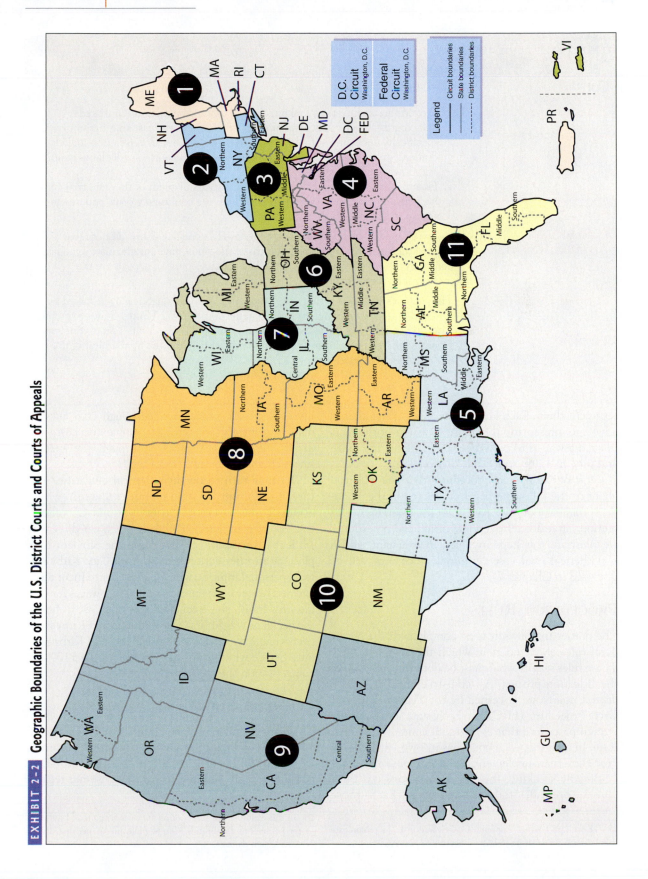

CONCEPT SUMMARY 2.2 | Types of Courts

COURT	DESCRIPTION
TRIAL COURTS	Trial courts are courts of original jurisdiction in which actions are initiated. 1. *State courts*—Courts of general jurisdiction can hear any case that has not been specifically designated for another court; courts of limited jurisdiction include domestic relations courts, probate courts, municipal courts, small claims courts, and others. 2. *Federal courts*—The federal district court is the equivalent of the state trial court. Federal courts of limited jurisdiction include the bankruptcy court and others shown in Exhibit 2–1 on page 38.
INTERMEDIATE APPELLATE COURTS	Courts of appeals are reviewing courts; generally, appellate courts do not have original jurisdiction. About three-fourths of the states have intermediate appellate courts; in the federal court system, the U.S. circuit courts of appeals are the intermediate appellate courts.
SUPREME COURT	The highest state court is that state's supreme court, although it may be called by some other name. Appeal from state supreme courts to the United States Supreme Court is possible only if a federal question is involved. The United States Supreme Court is the highest court in the federal court system and the final arbiter of the Constitution and federal law.

represent them. Each lawyer acts as his or her client's advocate, presenting the client's version of the facts in such a way as to convince the judge (or the judge and jury, in a jury trial) that this version is correct.

Most of the judicial procedures that you will read about in the following pages are rooted in the adversarial framework of the American legal system. In this section, after a brief overview of judicial procedures, we illustrate the steps involved in a lawsuit with a hypothetical civil case (criminal procedures will be discussed in Chapter 7).

PROCEDURAL RULES

The parties to a lawsuit must comply with the procedural rules of the court in which the lawsuit is filed. These rules specify what must be done at each stage of the litigation process. All civil trials held in federal district courts are governed by the **Federal Rules of Civil Procedure (FRCP)**.[17] Each state also has rules of civil procedure that apply to all courts within that state. In addition, each court has its own local rules of procedure that supplement the federal or state rules.

Broadly speaking, the litigation process has three phases: pretrial, trial, and posttrial. Each phase

involves specific procedures. Although civil lawsuits may vary greatly in terms of complexity, cost, and detail, they typically progress through the specific stages charted in Exhibit 2–3.

We now turn to our hypothetical civil case. The case arose from an automobile accident, which occurred when a car driven by Antonio Carvello, a resident of New Jersey, collided with a car driven by Jill Kirby, a resident of New York. The accident took place at an intersection in New York City. Kirby suffered personal injuries, which caused her to incur medical and hospital expenses as well as lost wages for four months. In all, she calculated that the cost to her of the accident was $100,000.[18] Carvello and Kirby have been unable to agree on a settlement, and Kirby now must decide whether to sue Carvello for the $100,000 compensation she feels she deserves.

CONSULTING WITH AN ATTORNEY

The first step taken by virtually anyone contemplating a lawsuit is to obtain the advice of a qualified attorney. In the hypothetical Kirby-Carvello case, Kirby may consult with an attorney, who will advise her regard-

---

17. The United States Supreme Court's authority to promulgate these rules is set forth in 28 U.S.C. Sections 2071–2077.

18. In this example, we are ignoring damages for pain and suffering or for permanent disabilities. Often, plaintiffs in personal-injury cases seek such damages.

EXHIBIT 2-3 **Stages in a Typical Lawsuit**

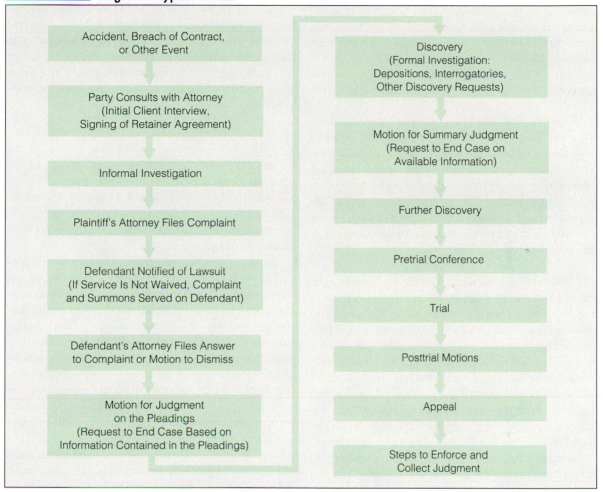

ing what she can expect to gain from a lawsuit, her probability of success if she sues, what procedures will be involved, and how long it may take to resolve the issue through the judicial process. Depending on the court hearing the case, the time costs of the litigation may be significant. Personal-injury cases may take two to three years to resolve, so this is an important factor for Kirby to consider.

LEGAL FEES Another crucial factor that Kirby must consider is, of course, the cost of the attorney's time—the legal fees that she will have to pay in an attempt to collect damages from the defendant, Carvello. Attorneys base their fees on such factors as the difficulty of a matter, the amount of time involved, the experience and skill of the attorney in the particular area of the law, and the cost of doing business. In the United States, legal fees range from $75 to $500 per

hour or even higher (the average fee per hour is between $150 and $275). In addition, the client is also responsible for paying various expenses relating to the case (called "out-of-pocket" costs), including court filing fees, travel expenses, and the cost of expert witnesses and investigators, for example.

—Types of Fee Arrangements. For a particular legal matter, an attorney may charge one type of fee or a combination of several types. *Fixed fees* may be charged for the performance of such services as drafting a simple will. *Hourly fees* may be computed for matters that will involve an indeterminate period of time. Any case brought to trial, for example, may involve an expenditure of time that cannot be precisely estimated in advance. *Contingency fees* are fixed as a percentage (usually between 25 and 40 percent) of a client's recovery in certain types of lawsuits,

such as a personal-injury lawsuit.[19] If the lawsuit is unsuccessful, the attorney receives no fee. If Kirby retains an attorney on a contingency-fee basis, she normally will not have to pay any fees unless she wins the case. (She will, however, have to pay the court fees and any other expenses incurred by the attorney on her behalf.)

—Courts Can Award Attorneys' Fees. Many state and federal statutes allow for an award of attorneys' fees in certain legal actions, such as probate matters (settling a person's estate after death). In these cases, a judge sets the amount of the fee, based on such factors as the results obtained by the attorney and the fee customarily charged for similar services. In some situations, a client may receive an award of attorneys' fees as part of her or his recovery.

SETTLEMENT CONSIDERATIONS Frequently, the extent to which an attorney will pursue a resolution of a legal problem is determined largely by the amount of time and funds the client wishes to invest in the process. If the client decides that he or she can afford a lengthy trial and one or more appeals, the attorney may pursue those actions. Often, however, once a client learns the costs involved in litigation he or she may decide to settle the claim for a lower amount by using one of the methods of alternative dispute resolution discussed in Chapter 3, such as negotiation or mediation.

Another important factor in deciding whether to pursue litigation is the defendant's ability to pay the damages sought. Even if Kirby is awarded damages, it may be difficult to enforce the court's judgment. (We will discuss the problems involved in enforcing a judgment later in this chapter.)

PRETRIAL PROCEDURES

The pretrial litigation process involves the filing of the *pleadings*, the gathering of evidence (called *discovery*), and possibly other procedures, such as a pretrial conference and jury selection.

THE PLEADINGS The *complaint* and *answer* (and other documents discussed below), taken together, are known as the **pleadings.** The pleadings formally notify each party of the claims of the other and specify the

issues (disputed questions) involved in the case. To an extent, the pleadings remove the element of surprise from a case. Because the attorneys learn from the pleadings what the other side will be claiming at trial, the lawyers can focus on preparing better arguments and gathering the most persuasive evidence to support their positions. The two basic pleadings are the complaint and answer.

—The Plaintiff's Complaint. Kirby's action against Carvello will commence when her lawyer files a **complaint**[20] with the clerk of the trial court in the appropriate geographic area—the proper venue. (Typically, the lawyer or her or his assistant delivers the complaint in person to the trial court clerk. Increasingly, however, courts are experimenting with electronic filing.)

In most states, the court would be one having general jurisdiction; in some, however, it might be a court having special jurisdiction with regard to subject matter. The complaint will contain (1) a statement alleging, or asserting, the facts necessary for the court to take jurisdiction; (2) a short statement of the facts necessary to show that the plaintiff is entitled to a remedy; and (3) a statement of the remedy the plaintiff is seeking. A typical complaint is shown in Exhibit 2–4.

The complaint will state that Kirby was driving her car through a green light at the specified intersection, exercising good driving habits and reasonable care, when Carvello negligently drove his vehicle through a red light and into the intersection from a cross street, striking Kirby's car and causing serious personal injury and property damage. The complaint will go on to state that Kirby is seeking $100,000 in damages. (Note that in some state civil actions, the amount of damages sought is not specified.)

—Service of Process. Before the court can exercise jurisdiction over the defendant (Carvello)—in effect, before the lawsuit can begin—the court must have proof that the defendant was notified of the lawsuit. The process of notifying the defendant of a lawsuit is called **service of process.** Service of process involves serving the defendant with a summons and a copy of the complaint—that is, delivering these items to the defendant. The **summons** notifies defendant Carvello that he must answer the complaint within a specified time period (twenty days in the federal courts) or suffer a default judgment against him. A **default judgment** in

---

19. Note that attorneys may charge a contingency fee in only certain types of cases and are typically prohibited from entering this type of fee arrangement in criminal cases, divorce cases, and cases involving distribution of assets after death.

---

20. Sometimes, the document filed with the court is called a *petition* or a *declaration* instead of a complaint.

EXHIBIT 2-4 **A Typical Complaint**

IN THE UNITED STATES DISTRICT COURT
FOR THE SOUTHERN DISTRICT OF NEW YORK

CIVIL NO. 7-1047

JILL KIRBY

Plaintiff,

v.   COMPLAINT

ANTONIO CARVELLO

Defendant.

The plaintiff brings this cause of action against the defendant, alleging as follows:

1. This action is between the plaintiff, who is a resident of the State of New York, and the defendant, who is a resident of the State of New Jersey. There is diversity of citizenship between the parties.
2. The amount in controversy, exclusive of interest and costs, exceeds the sum of $75,000.
3. On September 10th, 2006, the plaintiff, Jill Kirby, was exercising good driving habits and reasonable care in driving her car through the intersection of Boardwalk and Pennsylvania Avenue, New York City, New York, when the defendant, Antonio Carvello, negligently drove his vehicle through a red light at the intersection and collided with the plaintiff's vehicle.
4. As a result of the collision, the plaintiff suffered severe physical injury, which prevented her from working, and property damage to her car.

WHEREFORE, the plaintiff demands judgment against the defendant for the sum of $100,000 plus interest at the maximum legal rate and the costs of this action.

By _____*Joseph Roe*_____

Joseph Roe
Attorney for Plaintiff
100 Main Street
New York, New York

1/2/07

Kirby's favor would mean that she would be awarded the damages alleged in her complaint because Carvello failed to respond to the allegations. A typical summons is shown in Exhibit 2–5.

—*Method of Service.* How service of process occurs depends on the rules of the court or jurisdiction in which the lawsuit is brought. Under the Federal Rules of Civil Procedure (FRCP), service of process in federal court cases may be effected by anyone who is not a party to the lawsuit and who is at least eighteen years of age. In state courts, the process server is often a county sheriff or an employee of an independent company that provides process service in the local area. Usually, the server effects the service by handing the summons to the defendant personally or by leaving it at the defendant's residence or place of business. In some states, a summons can be served by mail if the defendant so agrees. When the defendant cannot be reached, special rules provide alternative means of service; for example, leaving the summons with a designated person, such as the state's secretary of state, or publishing a notice in the local newspaper.

—*Serving Corporate Defendants.* In cases involving corporate defendants, the summons and complaint may be served on an officer or on a *registered agent* (representative) of the corporation. The name of a corporation's registered agent can usually be obtained from the secretary of state's office in the state where the company incorporated its business (and, frequently, from the secretary of state's office in any state where the corporation does business).

—*Waiver of Formal Service of Process.* In many instances, the defendant is already aware that a lawsuit is being filed and is willing to waive (give up) her or his right to be served personally. The FRCP and many states' rules allow defendants to waive formal service of process, provided that certain procedures are followed. Kirby's attorney, for example, could mail to defendant Carvello a copy of the complaint, along with "Waiver of Service of Summons" forms for Carvello to sign. If Carvello signs and returns the forms within thirty days, formal service of process is waived. Moreover, under the FRCP, defendants who agree to waive formal service of process receive addi-

---

EXHIBIT 2-5 **A Typical Summons**

UNITED STATES DISTRICT COURT
FOR THE SOUTHERN DISTRICT OF NEW YORK

Jill Kirby)
                                      Plaintiff,)   **Civil Action, File Number 7-1047**
v.   )
Antonio Carvello)   *Summons*
                                      Defendant.)

To the above-named Defendant:

You are hereby summoned and required to serve upon Joseph Roe, plaintiff's attorney, whose address is 100 Main Street, New York, New York, an answer to the complaint which is herewith served upon you, within 20 days after service of this summons upon you, exclusive of the day of service. If you fail to do so, judgment by default will be taken against you for the relief demanded in the complaint.

Samuel Raeburn   February 10, 2007
CLERK   DATE

Mary Doakes
BY DEPUTY CLERK

tional time to respond to the complaint (sixty days, instead of twenty days). Some states provide similar incentives to encourage defendants to waive formal service of process and thereby reduce associated costs and foster cooperation between the parties.

—*The Defendant's Response.*   Typically, the defendant's response to the complaint takes the form of an **answer.** In an answer, the defendant either admits or denies each of the allegations in the plaintiff's complaint and may also set forth any defenses to those allegations. Under the federal rules, any allegations that are not denied by the defendant will be deemed by the court to have been admitted. If Carvello admits to all of Kirby's allegations in his answer, a judgment will be entered for Kirby. If Carvello denies Kirby's allegations, the matter will proceed further.

—*Affirmative Defenses.*   Carvello can also admit the truth of Kirby's complaint but raise new facts to show that he should not be held liable for Kirby's damages. This is called raising an **affirmative defense.** As will be discussed in subsequent chapters, defendants in both civil and criminal cases can raise affirmative defenses. For example, a defendant accused of physically harming another might claim that he or she acted in self-defense. A defendant charged with breach of contract might defend on the ground (legal basis) of mistake or the fact that the contract was oral when it was required by law to be in writing. In the Kirby-Carvello case, assume that Carvello has obtained evidence that Kirby was not exercising good driving habits at the time the accident occurred (she was looking at a child in the backseat of her car instead of watching the road). Carvello could assert Kirby's own negligence as a defense. In some states, a plaintiff's contributory negligence operates as a complete defense. In most states, however, the plaintiff's own negligence constitutes only a partial defense (see Chapter 13).

—*Counterclaims.*   Carvello could also deny Kirby's allegations and set forth his own claim that the accident occurred as a result of Kirby's negligence and that therefore Kirby owes Carvello for the damage to his car. This is appropriately called a **counterclaim.** If Carvello files a counterclaim, Kirby will have to submit an answer to the counterclaim.

DISMISSALS AND JUDGMENTS BEFORE TRIAL
Many actions for which pleadings have been filed never come to trial. The parties may, for example,

negotiate a settlement of the dispute at any stage of the litigation process. There are also numerous procedural avenues for disposing of a case without a trial. Many of them involve one or the other party's attempts to get the case dismissed through the use of various motions.

A **motion** is a procedural request submitted to the court by an attorney on behalf of her or his client. When one party files a motion with the court, that party must also send to, or serve on, the opposing party a *notice of motion.* The notice of motion informs the opposing party that the motion has been filed. **Pretrial motions** include the motion to dismiss, the motion for judgment on the pleadings, and the motion for summary judgment, as well as the other motions listed in Exhibit 2–6 on the next page.

—*Motion to Dismiss.*   Either party can file a **motion to dismiss** requesting the court to dismiss the case for the reasons provided in the motion. A defendant could file a motion to dismiss if the plaintiff's complaint fails to state a claim for which relief (a remedy) can be granted. Such a motion asserts that even if the facts alleged in the complaint are true, they do not give rise to any legal claim against the defendant. If, for example, the allegations in Kirby's complaint do not amount to negligence on Carvello's part, Carvello could move to dismiss the case for failure to state a claim. Defendant Carvello could also file a motion to dismiss if he believed that he had not been properly served, that the complaint had been filed in the wrong court (for example, that the court lacked personal or subject-matter jurisdiction or that the venue was improper), or for other specific reasons.

Often, instead of filing an answer with the court, a defendant files a motion to dismiss. If the court denies the motion, the defendant generally is given an extension of time to file an answer. If the defendant fails to file the appropriate pleading, a judgment will normally be entered for the plaintiff. If the court grants the motion to dismiss, the defendant is not required to answer the complaint, and the plaintiff generally is given time to file an amended complaint. If the plaintiff does not file this amended complaint, a judgment will be entered against the plaintiff, and the plaintiff will not be allowed to bring suit on the matter again. The court can also dismiss a case on its own motion.

—*Motion for Judgment on the Pleadings.*   After the pleadings are closed—after the complaint, answer, and any other pleadings have been filed—either of the

EXHIBIT 2-6 Pretrial Motions

MOTION TO DISMISS

A motion normally filed by the defendant in which the defendant asks the court to dismiss the case for a specified reason, such as improper service, lack of personal jurisdiction, or the plaintiff's failure to state a claim for which relief can be granted.

MOTION TO STRIKE

A motion filed by the defendant in which the defendant asks the court to strike (delete) from the complaint certain paragraphs contained in the complaint. Motions to strike help to clarify the underlying issues that form the basis for the complaint by removing paragraphs that are redundant or irrelevant to the action.

MOTION TO MAKE MORE DEFINITE AND CERTAIN

A motion filed by the defendant to compel the plaintiff to clarify the basis of the plaintiff's cause of action. The motion is filed when the defendant believes that the complaint is too vague or ambiguous for the defendant to respond to it in a meaningful way.

MOTION FOR JUDGMENT ON THE PLEADINGS

A motion that may be filed by either party in which the party asks the court to enter a judgment in his or her favor based on information contained in the pleadings. A judgment on the pleadings will only be made if there are no facts in dispute and the only question is how the law applies to a set of undisputed facts.

MOTION TO COMPEL DISCOVERY

A motion that may be filed by either party in which the party asks the court to compel the other party to comply with a discovery request. If a party refuses to allow the opponent to inspect and copy certain documents, for example, the party requesting the documents may make a motion to compel production of those documents.

MOTION FOR SUMMARY JUDGMENT

A motion that may be filed by either party in which the party asks the court to enter judgment in his or her favor without a trial. Unlike a motion for judgment on the pleadings, a motion for summary judgment can be supported by evidence outside the pleadings, such as witnesses' affidavits, answers to interrogatories, and other evidence obtained prior to or during discovery.

parties can file a **motion for judgment on the pleadings.** This motion may be filed when it appears from the pleadings that the plaintiff has failed to state a cause of action for which relief may be granted. The motion will only be granted when the pleadings indicate that no facts are in dispute and the only question is how the law applies to a set of agreed-on facts. For example, assume for a moment that in the Kirby-Carvello case, defendant Carvello admitted to all of Kirby's allegations in his answer and raised no affirmative defenses. In this situation, Kirby would file a motion for judgment on the pleadings in her favor.

The difference between this motion and a motion for summary judgment, discussed next, is that with a motion for a judgment on the pleadings, a court may consider only what is contained in the pleadings. In a motion for summary judgment, in contrast, the court may also consider sworn statements and other materials that would be admissible as evidence at trial.

—Motion for Summary Judgment. A **motion for summary judgment** is similar to a motion for judgment on the pleadings in that the party filing the motion is asking the court to grant a judgment in that

party's favor without a trial. As with a motion for judgment on the pleadings, a court will grant a motion for summary judgment only if it determines that no facts are in dispute and the only question is how the law applies to the facts. A motion for summary judgment can be made before or during a trial, but it will be granted only if, when the evidence is viewed in the light most favorable to the other party, there clearly are no factual disputes in contention.

To support a motion for summary judgment, one party can submit evidence obtained at any point prior to trial (including during the *discovery* stage of litigation—to be discussed next) that refutes the other party's factual claim. The evidence may consist of **affidavits** (sworn statements by parties or witnesses), as well as documents, such as a contract. Of course, the evidence must be *admissible* evidence—that is, evidence that the court would allow to be presented during the trial. If Carvello, for example, had an affidavit from a city official that the stoplight was not working when he drove through the intersection, he could submit that as evidence with a motion for summary judgment. As mentioned, the use of additional evidence is one feature that distinguishes the motion for summary judgment from the motion to dismiss and the motion for judgment on the pleadings.

DISCOVERY Before a trial begins, the parties can use a number of procedural devices to obtain information and gather evidence about the case. Kirby, for example, will want to know how fast Carvello was driving, whether he had been drinking or was under the influence of any medication, and whether he was wearing corrective lenses if he was required by law to do so while driving. The process of obtaining information from the opposing party or from witnesses prior to trial is known as **discovery.** Discovery includes gaining access to witnesses, documents, records, and other types of evidence.

The Federal Rules of Civil Procedure and similar state rules set forth the guidelines for discovery activity. The rules governing discovery are designed to make sure that a witness or a party is not unduly harassed, that privileged material is safeguarded, and that only information relevant to the case at hand—or likely to lead to the discovery of relevant information—is discoverable.

Discovery prevents surprises at trial by giving both parties access to evidence that might otherwise be hidden. This allows the litigants to learn as much as they can about what to expect at a trial before they reach the courtroom. Discovery also serves to narrow the issues so that trial time is spent on the main questions in the case.

—Depositions and Interrogatories. At a minimum, discovery involves the use of depositions, interrogatories, or both. A **deposition** is sworn testimony by a party to the lawsuit or by any witness, recorded by an authorized court official. The person deposed gives testimony and answers questions asked by the attorneys from both sides. The questions and answers are recorded, sworn to, and signed. These answers, of course, will help the attorneys prepare their cases. Depositions also give attorneys the opportunity to evaluate how their witnesses will conduct themselves at trial. In addition, depositions can be employed in court to impeach (challenge the credibility of) a party or a witness who changes testimony at the trial. A deposition can also be used as testimony if the witness is not available at trial.

Interrogatories are written questions for which written answers are prepared and then signed under oath. The main difference between interrogatories and written depositions is that interrogatories are directed to a party to the lawsuit (the plaintiff or the defendant), not to a witness, and the party can prepare answers with the aid of an attorney. Whereas depositions are useful for eliciting candid responses from a party and answers not prepared in advance, interrogatories are designed to obtain accurate information about specific topics, such as how many contracts were signed, and when. The scope of interrogatories is also broader because parties are obligated to answer questions, even if doing so means disclosing information from their records and files.

—Requests for Admissions. One party can serve the other party with a written request for an admission of the truth of matters relating to the trial. Any fact admitted under such a request is conclusively established as true for the trial. For example, Kirby can ask Carvello to admit that his driver's license was suspended at the time of the accident. A request for admission shortens the trial because the parties will not have to spend time proving facts on which they already agree.

—Requests for Documents, Objects, and Entry upon Land. A party can gain access to documents and other items not in her or his possession in order to inspect and examine them. Likewise, a party can gain "entry upon land" to inspect the premises. Carvello, for example, can gain permission to inspect and copy Kirby's car repair bills.

—Request for Examinations. When the physical or mental condition of one party is in question, the

Who Bears the Costs of Electronic Discovery?

Generally, the party responding to a discovery request must pay the expenses involved in obtaining the requested materials. A court can limit the scope of the request or shift some of the cost to the requesting party, however, if compliance would be too burdensome or the cost would be too great. One matter that has become the subject of much debate today is how these traditional rules governing discovery will apply to requests for electronic evidence.

WHY COURTS MIGHT SHIFT THE COSTS OF ELECTRONIC DISCOVERY

Electronic discovery (e-discovery) has dramatically increased the costs associated with complying with discovery requests. It is no longer simply a matter of photocopying paper documents. Now the responding party may need to hire computer forensics experts to make "image" copies of desktop, laptop, and server hard drives, as well as removable storage media (including CD-ROMs, DVDs, and Zip drives), back-up tapes, voice mail, cell phones, and any other device that digitally stores data.

In cases that involve multiple parties or large corporations with many offices and employees, the e-discovery process can easily run into hundreds of thousands of dollars, if not more. For example, in one case concert promoters alleged that thirty separate defendant companies had engaged in discriminatory practices. The federal district court hearing the case found that the complete restoration of the back-up tapes of just one of

those defendants would cost $9.75 million. Acquiring 200,000 e-mail messages from another defendant would cost between $43,000 and $84,000, with an additional $247,000 to have an attorney review the retrieved documents. Restoring the 523 back-up tapes of a third defendant would cost $395,000, and $120,000 for the attorney to review them. The judge hearing the case decided that both plaintiffs and defendants would share in these discovery costs.[a]

WHAT FACTORS DO COURTS CONSIDER IN DECIDING WHETHER TO SHIFT COSTS?

Increasingly, courts are shifting part of the costs of obtaining e-discovery to the party requesting it (which is usually the plaintiff). At what point, however, should this cost-shifting occur? In *Zubulake v. UBS Warburg LLC,*[b] the court set forth a three-step analysis for deciding disputes over discovery costs:

1. | If the data are kept in an accessible format, the usual rules of discovery apply: the responding party should pay the costs of producing responsive data. A court should consider cost-shifting *only* when electronic data are relatively inaccessible, such as in back-up tapes or deleted files.

2. | The court should determine what data may be found on the inaccessible media. Requiring the responding party to

a. *Rowe Entertainment, Inc. v. William Morris Agency,* 2002 WL 975713 (S.D.N.Y. 2002).
b. 2003 WL 21087884 (S.D.N.Y. 2003).

opposing party can ask the court to order a physical or mental examination by an independent examiner. If the court agrees to make the order, the opposing party can obtain the results of the examination. Note that the court will make such an order only when the need for the information outweighs the right to privacy of the person to be examined.

—*Electronic Discovery.* Any relevant material, including information stored electronically, can be the object of a discovery request. Electronic evidence, or **e-evidence,** consists of all computer-generated or electronically recorded information, such as e-mail, voice mail, spreadsheets, word processing documents, and other data. E-evidence can reveal significant facts that are not discoverable by other means. For example, whenever a person is working on a computer, informa-

tion is being recorded on the hard disk without ever being saved by the user. This information includes the file's location, path, creator, date created, date last accessed, concealed notes, earlier versions, passwords, and formatting. It reveals information about how, when, and by whom a document was created, accessed, modified, and transmitted. This information can only be obtained from the file in its electronic format—not from printed-out versions.

The federal rules and most state rules (as well as court decisions) now specifically allow individuals to obtain discovery of electronic "data compilations" (or e-evidence). Although traditional means, such as interrogatories and depositions, may still be employed to find out whether e-evidence exists, the parties must usually hire an expert to retrieve the evidence in its electronic format. Using special software, the expert

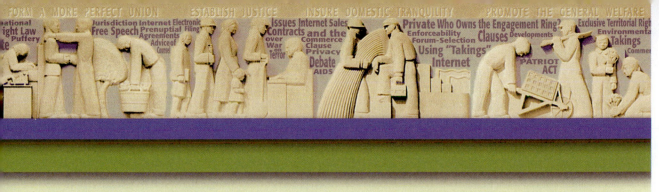

restore and produce responsive documents from a small sample of the requested medium is a sensible approach in most cases.

3. The court should consider a series of other factors, including, for example, the availability of the information from other sources, the total cost of production compared with the amount in controversy, and each party's ability to pay these costs.

Other courts, however, have declined to follow the *Zubulake* court's approach.[c]

PROPOSED CHANGES TO THE FEDERAL RULES OF CIVIL PROCEDURE

After five years of study, an advisory committee working for the federal judiciary has proposed changing the Federal Rules of Civil Procedure (FRCP) to better accommodate e-discovery. According to the committee, the enormous volume of electronic data, coupled with increasingly frequent requests for electronic evidence, or e-evidence, make this form of discovery more burdensome, costly, and time consuming than traditional discovery. The committee has therefore proposed that the parties only be required to provide electronic data that are "reasonably accessible." In addition, the committee recommends a "safe harbor" that would shield parties from

sanctions for failing to provide e-evidence as long as they have taken "reasonable steps to preserve the information" that they knew was discoverable.

Critics claim that the proposed new rules will allow more leeway to parties responding to e-discovery requests because they will be penalized only if they *willfully* fail to preserve e-evidence. (The current rules, in contrast, penalize even inadvertent destruction of evidence.) Many argue that the new rules simply are not necessary and that courts can do a better job of controlling the costs of e-discovery on a case-by-case basis.

WHERE DO YOU STAND?

As just discussed, the courts are still debating who should bear the costs of e-discovery. The federal judiciary has proposed changes to the FRCP that may decrease the burden on the responding party—the party that is asked to produce the e-evidence—by allowing it to produce only data that are "reasonably accessible." Should discovery of e-evidence be treated differently than other types of discovery just because it is more expensive? Should there be one rule establishing who pays the costs of e-discovery in all cases, or should the court determine who should bear the expense of providing e-evidence on a case-by-case basis? At what point, if ever, should the costs of producing e-discovery be shifted to the requesting party?

---

c. See, for example, *Toshiba America Electronic Components, Inc. v. Superior Court,* 124 Cal.App.4th 762, 21 Cal.Rptr.3d 532 (2004).

---

can reconstruct e-mail exchanges to establish who knew what and when they knew it. The expert can even recover files that the user thought had been deleted from the computer. Reviewing back-up copies of documents and e-mail provides useful—and often quite damaging—information about how a particular matter progressed over several weeks or months.

Electronic discovery has significant advantages, but it is also time consuming and expensive. Who should pay the costs associated with electronic discovery? For a discussion of this issue, see this chapter's *Contemporary Legal Debates* feature.

PRETRIAL CONFERENCE After discovery has taken place and before the trial begins, the attorneys may meet with the trial judge in a **pretrial conference.** The purpose of this conference is to clarify the issues that

remain in dispute after discovery has taken place and to explore the possibility of settling the conflict without a trial. If a settlement is not possible at this time, the parties and the judge discuss the manner in which the trial will be conducted. In particular, the parties may attempt to establish ground rules to restrict the number of expert witnesses or the admissibility of certain types of evidence, for example. Once the pretrial conference concludes, both parties must turn their attention to the trial itself and, if the trial is to be a jury trial, to the selection of jurors who will hear the case.

THE RIGHT TO A JURY TRIAL The Seventh Amendment to the U.S. Constitution guarantees the right to a jury trial for cases at law in federal courts when the amount in controversy exceeds $20. Most states have similar guarantees in their own constitutions, although many states set a higher minimum. For example, Iowa requires the dollar amount of damages to be at least $1,000 before there is a right to a jury trial. The right to a trial by jury need not be exercised, and many cases are tried without a jury. If there is no jury, the judge determines the truth of the facts alleged in the case. In most states and in federal courts, one of the parties must request a jury, or the judge presumes the parties waive this right.

JURY SELECTION   Prior to the commencement of any jury trial, a panel of jurors must be assembled. The clerk of the court will usually notify local residents by mail that they have been selected for jury duty. These prospective jurors are chosen in various ways, but often the court clerk selects names at random from lists of registered voters or lists of persons to whom the state has issued driver's licenses. These individuals then report to the courthouse on the date specified in the notice. There they are gathered into a single pool of jurors, and the process of selecting those jurors who will actually hear the case begins. Although some types of trials require twelve-person juries, most civil matters can be heard by six-person juries.

—Voir Dire.   The process by which the jury is selected is known as **voir dire**.[21] In most jurisdictions, *voir dire* consists of oral questions that attorneys for the plaintiff and the defendant ask a group of prospective jurors to determine whether a potential juror is biased or has any connection with a party to the action or with a prospective witness. Usually, jurors are questioned one at a time, although when large numbers of jurors are involved, the attorneys may direct their questions to groups of jurors instead to minimize the amount of time spent in jury selection. Sometimes, jurors are asked to fill out written questionnaires. Some trial attorneys use psychologists and other professionals to help them select jurors.

—*Challenges during* Voir Dire.   During *voir dire*, a party may challenge a certain number of prospective jurors *peremptorily*—that is, ask that these individuals not be sworn in as jurors without providing any reason for excluding them. The total number of peremptory challenges allowed each side is determined by statute or by the court. Furthermore, a party may challenge

any juror *for cause*—that is, provide a reason why an individual should not be sworn in as a juror. If the judge grants the challenge, the individual is asked to step down. A prospective juror, however, may not be excluded by the use of discriminatory challenges, such as those based on racial criteria[22] or gender.[23] Of course, *proving* that a particular challenge is discriminatory can be difficult because an attorney may give another reason for the challenge even though the underlying basis may be discriminatory.

After both sides have completed their challenges, those jurors who have been excused will be permitted to leave. The remaining jurors—those who have been found acceptable by the attorneys for both sides—will be seated in the jury box.

—*Alternate Jurors.*   Because unforeseeable circumstances or illness may necessitate that one or more of the sitting jurors be dismissed, the court, depending on the rules of the particular jurisdiction and the expected length of the trial, may choose to have up to three alternate jurors present throughout the trial. If a juror has to be excused in the middle of the trial, then an alternate may take his or her place without disrupting the proceedings. Once the jury members are seated, the judge will swear in the jury members, and the trial itself can begin.

THE TRIAL

Various rules and procedures govern the trial phase of the litigation process. There are rules governing what kind of evidence will or will not be admitted during the trial, as well as specific procedures that the participants in the lawsuit must follow.

RULES OF EVIDENCE   Whether evidence will be admitted in court is determined by the **rules of evidence**—a series of rules that have been created by the courts to ensure that any evidence presented during a trial is fair and reliable. The Federal Rules of Evidence govern the admissibility of evidence in federal courts.

---

21. Pronounced *vwahr deehr*. These old French verbs mean "to speak the truth." In legal language, the phrase refers to the process of questioning jurors to learn about their backgrounds, attitudes, and similar attributes.

22. *Batson v. Kentucky,* 476 U.S. 79, 106 S.Ct. 1712, 90 L.Ed.2d 69 (1986).

23. *J.E.B. v. Alabama ex rel. T.B.,* 511 U.S. 127, 114 S.Ct. 1419, 128 L.Ed.2d 89 (1994). (*Ex rel.* is an abbreviation of the Latin *ex relatione*. The phrase refers to an action brought on behalf of the state, by the attorney general, at the instigation of an individual who has a private interest in the matter.)

CONCEPT SUMMARY 2.3 | Pretrial Procedures

PROCEDURE	DESCRIPTION
PLEADINGS	1. *The plaintiff's complaint*—The plaintiff's statement of the cause of action and the parties involved, filed with the court by the plaintiff's attorney. After the filing, the defendant is notified of the suit through service of process. 2. *The defendant's response*—The defendant's response to the plaintiff's complaint may take the form of an answer, in which the defendant may admit to or deny the plaintiff's allegations. The defendant may raise an affirmative defense and/or assert a counterclaim.
PRETRIAL MOTIONS	1. *Motion to dismiss*—A motion requesting the judge to dismiss the case for reasons that are provided in the motion (such as failure to state a claim for which relief can be granted). 2. *Motion for judgment on the pleadings*—May be made by either party; will be granted only if no facts are in dispute and only questions of law are at issue. 3. *Motion for summary judgment*—May be made by either party; will be granted only if no facts are in dispute and only questions of law are at issue. Unlike the motion for judgment on the pleadings, the motion for summary judgment may be supported by evidence outside the pleadings, such as testimony and other evidence obtained during the discovery phase of litigation.
DISCOVERY	The process of gathering evidence concerning the case; involves (1) *depositions* (sworn testimony by either party or any witness); (2) *interrogatories* (in which parties to the action write answers to questions with the aid of their attorneys); and (3) requests for admissions, documents, examinations, or other information relating to the case.
PRETRIAL CONFERENCE	A pretrial hearing, at the request of either party or the court, to identify the matters in dispute after discovery has taken place and to explore the possibility of settling the dispute without a trial. If no settlement is possible, the parties plan the course of the trial.
JURY SELECTION	In a jury trial, the selection of members of the jury from a pool of prospective jurors. During a process known as *voir dire,* the attorneys for both sides may challenge prospective jurors either for cause or peremptorily (for no cause).

—Evidence Must Be Relevant to the Issues. Evidence will not be admitted in court unless it is relevant to the matter in question. **Relevant evidence** is evidence that tends to prove or disprove a fact in question or to establish the degree of probability of a fact or action. For example, evidence that a suspect's gun was in the home of another person when a victim was shot would be relevant—because it would tend to prove that the suspect did not shoot the victim.

Even relevant evidence may not be admitted in court if its reliability is questionable or if its probative (proving) value is substantially outweighed by other important considerations of the court. For example, a video or a photograph that shows in detail the severity of a victim's injuries would be relevant evidence, but the court might exclude this evidence on the ground that it would emotionally inflame the jurors.

—Hearsay Evidence Not Admissible. Generally, hearsay is not admissible as evidence. **Hearsay** is defined as any testimony given in court about a statement made by someone else who was not under oath at the time of the statement. Literally, it is what someone heard someone else say. For example, if a witness in the Kirby-Carvello case testified in court concerning what he or she heard another observer say about the accident, that testimony would be hearsay, or secondhand knowledge. Admitting hearsay into evidence carries many risks because, even though it may be relevant, there is no way to test its reliability.

OPENING STATEMENTS At the commencement of the trial, both attorneys are allowed to make **opening statements** concerning the facts that they expect to prove during the trial. The opening statement provides an opportunity for each lawyer to give a brief version of the facts and the supporting evidence that will be used during the trial.

EXAMINATION OF WITNESSES Because Kirby is the plaintiff, she has the burden of proving that her allegations are true.

—*Plaintiff Presents Evidence.* Kirby's attorney begins the presentation of Kirby's case by calling the first witness for the plaintiff and examining, or questioning, the witness. (For both attorneys, the types of questions and the manner of asking them are governed by the rules of evidence.) This questioning is called **direct examination.** After Kirby's attorney is finished, the witness is subject to **cross-examination** by Carvello's attorney. Then Kirby's attorney has another opportunity to question the witness in *redirect examination,* and Carvello's attorney may follow the redirect examination with a *recross-examination.* When both attorneys have finished with the first witness, Kirby's attorney calls the succeeding witnesses in the plaintiff's case, each of whom is subject to examination by the attorneys in the manner just described.

—*Potential Motion and Judgment.* At the conclusion of the plaintiff's case, the defendant's attorney has the opportunity to ask the judge to direct a verdict for the defendant on the ground that the plaintiff has presented no evidence to support the plaintiff's claim. This is called a **motion for a directed verdict** (federal courts use the term *judgment as a matter of law* instead of *directed verdict*). In considering the motion, the judge looks at the evidence in the light most favorable to the plaintiff and grants the motion only if there is insufficient evidence to raise an issue of fact. (Motions for directed verdicts at this stage of a trial are seldom granted.)

—*Defendant's Evidence.* The defendant's attorney then presents the evidence and witnesses for the defendant's case. Witnesses are called and examined by the defendant's attorney. The plaintiff's attorney has the right to cross-examine them, and there may be a redirect examination and possibly a recross-examination. At the end of the defendant's case, either attorney can move for a directed verdict, and the test again is whether the jury can, through any reasonable interpretation of the evidence, find for the party against whom the motion has been made. After the defendant's attorney has finished introducing evidence, the plaintiff's attorney can present a **rebuttal,** which includes additional evidence to refute the defendant's case. The defendant's attorney can, in turn, refute that evidence in a **rejoinder.**

CLOSING ARGUMENTS After both sides have rested their cases, each attorney presents a closing argument. In the **closing argument,** each attorney summarizes the facts and evidence presented during the trial, indicates why the facts and evidence support his or her client's claim, reveals the shortcomings of the points made by the opposing party during the trial, and generally urges a verdict in favor of the client. Each attorney's comments must be relevant to the issues in dispute.

JURY INSTRUCTIONS After the closing arguments, the judge instructs the jury (assuming it is a jury trial) in the law that applies to the case. The instructions to the jury are often called *charges*. A charge includes statements of the applicable laws, as well as a review of the facts as they were presented during the case. Because the jury's role is to serve as the fact finder, the factual account contained in the charge is not binding on the jurors. Indeed, they may completely disregard the facts as noted in the charge. They are not free to ignore the statements of law, however. The charge will help to channel the jurors' deliberations.

THE JURY'S VERDICT After receiving the instructions, the jury retires to the jury room to deliberate the case. In a civil case, the standard of proof is a *preponderance of the evidence*. In other words, the plaintiff (Kirby, in our hypothetical case) need not provide indisputable proof that she is entitled to a judgment. She need only show that her factual claim is more likely to be true than the defendant's. (As you will read in Chapter 7, in a criminal trial the prosecution has a higher standard of proof to meet—it must prove its case *beyond a reasonable doubt*.)

Note that some civil claims must be proved by "clear and convincing evidence," meaning that the evidence must show that the truth of the party's claim is highly probable. This standard applies in suits involving charges of fraud, suits to establish the terms of a lost will, some suits relating to oral contracts, and other suits in which the circumstances are thought to present a particular danger of deception.

CONCEPT SUMMARY 2.4 | Trial Procedures

PROCEDURE	DESCRIPTION
OPENING STATEMENTS	Each party's attorney is allowed to present an opening statement indicating what the attorney will attempt to prove during the course of the trial.
EXAMINATION OF WITNESSES	1. Plaintiff's introduction and direct examination of witnesses, cross-examination by defendant's attorney, possible redirect examination by plaintiff's attorney, and possible recross-examination by defendant's attorney. 2. At the close of the plaintiff's case, the defendant may make a motion for a directed verdict (or judgment as a matter of law), which, if granted by the court, will end the trial before the defendant presents witnesses. 3. Defendant's introduction and direct examination of witnesses, cross-examination by plaintiff's attorney, possible redirect examination by defendant's attorney, and possible recross-examination by plaintiff's attorney. 4. Possible rebuttal of defendant's argument by plaintiff's attorney, who presents more evidence. 5. Possible rejoinder by defendant's attorney to meet that evidence.
CLOSING ARGUMENTS	Each party's attorney argues in favor of a verdict for his or her client.
JURY INSTRUCTIONS	The judge instructs (or charges) the jury as to how the law applies to the issue.
JURY VERDICT	The jury renders its verdict, thus bringing the trial to an end.

Once the jury has reached a decision, it may issue a **verdict** in favor of one party; the verdict specifies the jury's factual findings and the amount of damages to be paid by the losing party. After the announcement of the verdict, which marks the end of the trial itself, the jurors will be dismissed.

POSTTRIAL MOTIONS

After the jury has rendered its verdict, either party may make a posttrial motion. The prevailing party usually files a motion for a judgment in accordance with the verdict. The nonprevailing party frequently files one of the motions discussed next.

MOTION FOR A NEW TRIAL   At the end of the trial, a motion can be made to set aside an adverse verdict and any judgment and to hold a new trial. The **motion for a new trial** will be granted only if the judge (1) is convinced, after looking at all the evidence, that the jury was in error but (2) does not feel it is appropriate to grant judgment for the other side. This will usually occur when the jury verdict is obviously the result of a misapplication of the law or a misunderstanding of the evidence presented at trial.

A new trial can also be granted on the grounds of newly discovered evidence, misconduct by the participants (such as the attorneys, the judge, or the jury) during the trial, or error by the judge. For example, in one personal-injury case, the plaintiff brought suit against Honda, a Japanese corporation. The plaintiff's attorney, during closing arguments, remarked that the case was about Honda's "corporate greed." When the jury returned a verdict in favor of the plaintiff, the court granted the defendant's motion for a new trial, based on the attorney's "improper and inflammatory" remarks to the jury.[24]

MOTION FOR JUDGMENT N.O.V.   If Kirby wins, and if Carvello's attorney has previously moved for a directed verdict, Carvello's attorney can now make a **motion for judgment n.o.v.**—from the Latin *non obstante veredicto*, meaning "notwithstanding the verdict." (Federal courts use the term *judgment as a matter of law* instead of judgment n.o.v.) The standards for granting a judgment n.o.v. often are the same as those for granting a motion to dismiss or a motion for a

---

24. *LeBlanc v. American Honda Motor Co.*, 141 N.H. 579, 688 A.2d 556 (1997).

directed verdict. Carvello can state that even if the evidence is viewed in the light most favorable to Kirby, a reasonable jury should not have found in Kirby's favor. If the judge finds this contention to be correct or decides that the law requires the opposite result, the motion will be granted. If the motion is denied, Carvello may then appeal the case. (Kirby may also appeal the case, even though she won at trial. She might appeal, for example, if she received a smaller monetary award than she had sought.)

The Appeal

Either party may appeal not only the jury's verdict but also any pretrial or posttrial motion. Many of the appellate court cases that appear in this text involve appeals of motions to dismiss, motions for summary judgment, or other motions that were denied by trial court judges. Note that few trial court decisions are reversed on appeal. In most appealed cases (approximately 90 percent), the trial court's decision is affirmed and thus becomes final.

FILING THE APPEAL If Carvello decides to appeal the verdict in Kirby's favor, then his attorney must file a *notice of appeal* with the clerk of the trial court within a prescribed period of time. Carvello then becomes the *appellant*. The clerk of the trial court sends to the reviewing court (usually an intermediate court of appeals) the *record on appeal*. The record contains all the pleadings, motions, and other documents filed with the court and a complete written transcript of the proceedings, including testimony, arguments, jury instructions, and judicial rulings.

Carvello's attorney will file an appellate **brief** with the reviewing court. The brief contains (1) a short statement of the facts; (2) a statement of the issues; (3) the rulings by the trial court that Carvello contends are erroneous and prejudicial (biased in favor of one of the parties); (4) the grounds for reversal of the judgment; (5) a statement of the applicable law; and (6) arguments on Carvello's behalf, citing applicable statutes and relevant cases as precedents. The attorney for the *appellee* (Kirby, in our hypothetical case) usually files an answering brief. Carvello's attorney can file a reply, although it is not required. The reviewing court then considers the case.

The expenses associated with an appeal can be considerable, and sometimes the party who wins the appeal is awarded some of the associated costs. In the following case, the appellants argued that they should be reimbursed for the $16,065 they spent to prepare and file their briefs electronically.

CASE 2.3 | **Phansalkar v. Andersen Weinroth & Co.**

United States
Court of Appeals,
Second Circuit, 2004.
356 F.3d 188.

PER CURIAM [By the whole court]:
* * * *
[Andersen Weinroth & Company (AW)] is a small * * * partnership that finds and creates investment opportunities for itself, its partners, and outside investors. * * *
* * * *
AW * * * paid [its] partners' * * * expenses, and provided them with opportunities to make certain investments * * * . These "Investment Opportunities" * * * were part of each partner's compensation * * * .
* * * *
[Rohit] Phansalkar joined AW in or about February 1998 as a nominal partner. * * * Throughout his tenure at AW, Phansalkar * * * was offered opportunities to invest in certain transactions.

Phansalkar remained at AW until June 2000, at which time he left to become the Chairman and [Chief Executive Officer] of Osicom Technologies, Inc. * * * AW * * * took the position that, after Phansalkar left AW, he was no longer entitled to the returns on certain Investment Opportunities that he had been given and had acted upon while at AW.
* * * *
* * * On October 16, 2000, Phansalkar filed this action against AW * * * . Phansalkar asserted claims for * * * breach of contract [among other things].
* * * *

CASE 2.3 | Continued

* * * The court calculated damages on Phansalkar's * * * claim in the amount of $4,417,655.40 plus * * * interest.[a]
* * * *

On September 16, 2003, this Court [the U.S. Court of Appeals for the Second Circuit] reversed a judgment of approximately $4.4 million entered by the U.S. District Court for the Southern District of New York in favor of Phansalkar. On September 29, 2003, the AW parties submitted an itemized bill of costs. As appellants who have won a reversal, they are clearly entitled to costs for the docketing [scheduling] of the appeal and for printing the "necessary" copies of the regular and special appendices of appellants' main brief and reply brief, an amount totaling $16,112. That entitlement is supported by Rule 39 [of the Federal Rules of Appellate Procedure and] by this Court's Local Instructions for Bill of Costs * * * . In addition, the AW parties seek $16,065 in costs associated with preparing and submitting companion appendices and briefs in hyperlinked CD-ROM format.

The AW parties and Phansalkar vigorously dispute whether an agreement was ever reached over how these CD-ROM costs would be allocated between them following this appeal. There is no dispute, however, that if such an agreement was reached, it was never committed to writing * * * . The issue raised by the parties, which this Court has not yet decided, is whether Rule 39 and the rules of this Court contemplate [an award] of the costs of preparing such electronic submissions.
* * * *

Under Rule 25(a)(2)(D) of the Federal Rules of Appellate Procedure,

[a] court of appeals may by local rule permit papers to be filed, signed, or verified by electronic means that are consistent with technical standards, if any, that the Judicial Conference of the United States establishes.

This Court was among the first [federal courts of appeals] to promulgate such a local rule, by * * * order on October 17, 1997. That order was supplemented on January 30, 1998, with * * * Order 98-2 * * * , which states that *the submission of electronic format briefs is "allowed and encouraged" as long as "[a]ll parties have consented * * * or a motion to file has been granted."* Several other [federal courts of appeals] have adopted local rules that permit or even require the filing of electronic briefs, usually on companion disks. The submission of an electronic version of a paper brief very likely entails small incremental costs. [Emphasis added.]

CD-ROM submissions that hyperlink briefs to relevant sections of the appellate record are more versatile, more useful, and considerably more expensive. Our January 30, 1998, order allows and encourages the use of such "interactive CD-ROM" formats. The [U.S. Court of Appeals for the] Federal Circuit also allows CD-ROM briefs to be filed with the prior consent of both the court and the opposing party. To date, only the [U.S. Court of Appeals for the] First Circuit appears to have adopted formally a local rule that applies to submission of hyperlinked CD-ROM briefs. *Such submissions can assist judicial review and are welcomed, but they are not necessarily [part of an award] as costs.* [Emphasis added.]

We have found no local rule or holding from another circuit that allocates CD-ROM costs. No guidance can be found in the relevant text of Rule 39, which authorizes [an award] of costs incurred to produce "necessary" copies of briefs, appendices, and portions of the record relevant to an appeal and a variety of other costs of appeal, such as filing fees. * * * [I]n the absence of a specific textual reference in Rule 39, *an expense can be an allowable cost of appeal when it is analogous to one of the costs specifically authorized by Rule 39(e).* Citing this test, and our administrative orders encouraging the use of CD-ROM's, the AW parties argue that CD-ROM expenses are allowable costs under Rule 39. [Emphasis added.]

However, * * * several other factors * * * are also important in determining if a cost is authorized by Rule 39: whether the party seeking disallowance has clearly consented to the expense; whether a court has previously approved the expense; and whether the alternative arrangement costs less than the expense specifically authorized by the Rule. None of

---

a. This statement of the facts is taken from the court's previous opinion in this case, which can be found at *Phansalkar v. Andersen Weinroth & Co.*, 344 F.3d 184 (2d Cir. 2003).

CONTINUED ▶

CASE 2.3 | Continued these factors assists the AW parties. In particular, it appears that a substantial portion of the costs were duplicative. Since the AW parties incurred costs both to produce hard copies of their appellate materials *and* to produce hyperlinked CD-ROM copies, Rule 25(a)(2)(D) suggests that the CD-ROM costs in this case were duplicative rather than an analog of hard copy production costs. [Awarding] the CD-ROM costs under such circumstances is inconsistent with our past applications of Rule 39.

Finally, it is decisive that there is no written stipulation or understanding between the parties concerning the allocation of the incremental costs of this useful technology.

*   *   *   *

For the reasons set forth above, the motion to disallow costs of $16,065 for CD-ROM preparation is hereby GRANTED.

QUESTIONS

1. Under the Federal Rules of Appellate Procedure, was it appropriate for the court to refuse the appellants' request for the cost of producing appellate documents in hyperlinked CD-ROM format? Why or why not?
2. Would the result in this case have been different if the court had required, rather than merely encouraged, the submission of electronic copies of the appeal documents? Explain.

APPELLATE REVIEW A court of appeals does not hear any evidence. Its decision concerning a case is based on the record on appeal and the briefs. The attorneys can present oral arguments, after which the case is taken under advisement. The court then issues a written opinion. In general, appellate courts do not reverse findings of fact unless the findings are unsupported or contradicted by the evidence.

An appellate court has the following options after reviewing a case:

1. The court can *affirm* the trial court's decision.
2. The court can *reverse* the trial court's judgment if it concludes that the trial court erred or that the jury did not receive proper instructions.
3. The appellate court can *remand* (send back) the case to the trial court for further proceedings consistent with its opinion on the matter.
4. The court might also affirm or reverse a decision *in part.* For example, the court might affirm the jury's finding that Carvello was negligent but remand the case for further proceedings on another issue (such as the extent of Kirby's damages).
5. An appellate court can also *modify* a lower court's decision. If the appellate court decides that the jury awarded an excessive amount in damages, for example, the court might reduce the award to a more appropriate, or fairer, amount.

HIGHER APPELLATE COURTS If the reviewing court is an intermediate appellate court, the court may allow the losing party to appeal the decision to the state's highest court, usually called its supreme court. Such a petition corresponds to a petition for a writ of *certiorari* in the United States Supreme Court. If the petition is granted, new briefs must be filed before the state supreme court, and the attorneys may be allowed or requested to present oral arguments. Like the intermediate appellate courts, the supreme court may reverse or affirm the appellate court's decision or remand the case.

At this point, the case has reached its end unless a federal question is at issue—a question concerning a constitutional right, for example, or a question as to how a federal statute should be interpreted. If a federal question is involved, the losing party (or the winning party, if that party is dissatisfied with the relief obtained) may appeal the decision to the United States Supreme Court by petitioning the Court for a writ of *certiorari.* As mentioned earlier, the Supreme Court may or may not grant the writ, depending on the significance of the issue in dispute.

ENFORCING THE JUDGMENT

The uncertainties of the litigation process are compounded by the lack of guarantees that any judgment will be enforceable. Even if the jury awards Kirby the full amount of damages requested ($100,000), for example, Carvello's auto insurance coverage might have lapsed, in which event the company would not pay any of the damages. Alternatively, Carvello's insurance policy might be limited to $50,000, meaning that Carvello personally would have to pay the remaining $50,000.

CONCEPT SUMMARY 2.5 | Posttrial Options

PROCEDURE	DESCRIPTION
POSTTRIAL MOTIONS	1. *Motion for a new trial*—If the judge is convinced that the jury was in error, the motion normally will be granted. 2. *Motion for judgment n.o.v. ("notwithstanding the verdict")*—The party making the motion must have filed a motion for a directed verdict at the close of all the evidence during the trial; the motion will be granted if the judge is convinced that the jury was in error.
APPEAL	Either party can appeal the trial court's judgment to an appropriate court of appeals. 1. *Filing the appeal*—The appealing party must file a notice of appeal with the clerk of the trial court, who forwards the record on appeal to the appellate court. Attorneys file appellate briefs. 2. *Appellate review*—The appellate court does not hear evidence but bases its opinion, which it issues in writing, on the record on appeal and the attorneys' briefs and oral arguments. The court may affirm or reverse all (or part) of the trial court's judgment and/or remand the case for further proceedings consistent with its opinion. Most decisions are affirmed on appeal. 3. In some cases, further review may be sought from a higher appellate court, such as a state supreme court. If a federal question is involved, the case may ultimately be appealed to the United States Supreme Court.

REQUESTING COURT ASSISTANCE IN COLLECTING THE JUDGMENT If the defendant does not have the funds available to pay the judgment, the plaintiff can go back to the court and request the court to issue a *writ of execution*—an order directing the sheriff to seize and sell the defendant's nonexempt assets (certain assets are exempted by law from creditors' actions). The proceeds of the sale would then be used to pay the damages owed, and any excess proceeds of the sale would be returned to the defendant. Alternatively, the nonexempt property itself could be transferred to the plaintiff in lieu of an outright payment. (Creditors' remedies, including those of judgment creditors, as well as exempt and nonexempt property, will be discussed in more detail in Chapter 15.)

AVAILABILITY OF ASSETS The problem of collecting a judgment is less pronounced, of course, when a party is seeking to satisfy a judgment against a defendant, such as a major corporation, that has substantial assets that can be easily located. Usually, one of the factors considered before a lawsuit is initiated is whether the defendant has sufficient assets to cover the amount of damages sought, should the plaintiff win the case. In addition, during the discovery process, attorneys should seek information to locate the defendant's assets that might potentially be used to satisfy a judgment.

REVIEWING THE COURT SYSTEM

Stan Garner resides in Illinois and promotes boxing matches for SuperSports, Inc., an Illinois corporation. Garner created the concept of "Ages" promotion—a three-fight series of boxing matches pitting an older fighter (George Foreman) against a younger fighter, such as John Ruiz or Riddick Bowe. The concept included titles for each of the three fights ("Challenge of the Ages," "Battle of the Ages," and "Fight of the Ages"), as well as promotional epithets to characterize the two fighters. Garner contacted George Foreman and his manager, who both reside in Texas,

(Continued)

REVIEWING THE COURT SYSTEM—Continued

to sell the idea, and they arranged a meeting at Caesar's Palace in Las Vegas, Nevada. At some point in the negotiations, Foreman's manager signed a nondisclosure agreement prohibiting him from disclosing Garner's promotional concepts unless the parties signed a contract. Nevertheless, after negotiations between Garner and Foreman fell through, Foreman used Garner's "Battle of the Ages" concept to promote a subsequent fight. Garner filed a suit against Foreman and his manager in a federal district court located in Illinois, alleging breach of contract. Using the information presented in the chapter, answer the following questions.

1. On what basis might the federal district court in Illinois exercise jurisdiction in this case?

2. Does the federal district court have original or appellate jurisdiction?

3. Suppose that Garner had filed his action in an Illinois state court. Could an Illinois state court exercise personal jurisdiction over Foreman or his manager? Why or why not?

4. Assume that Garner had filed his action in a Nevada state court. Would that court have personal jurisdiction over Foreman or his manager? Why or why not?

5. List and describe three procedural devices that Garner might use during the discovery process to gather evidence in support of his claims.

TERMS AND CONCEPTS TO REVIEW

QUESTIONS AND CASE PROBLEMS

2–1. Marya Callais, a citizen of Florida, was walking one day near a busy street in Tallahassee, Florida, when a large crate flew off a passing truck and hit her, causing numerous injuries. She incurred a great deal of pain and suffering, plus significant medical expenses, and she could not work for six months. She wants to sue the trucking firm for $300,000 in damages. The firm's headquarters are in Georgia, although the company does business in Florida. In what court might Callais bring suit—a Florida state court, a Georgia state court, or a federal court? What factors might influence her decision?

2–2. **QUESTION WITH SAMPLE ANSWER**
The defendant in a lawsuit is appealing the trial court's decision in favor of the plaintiff. On appeal, the defendant claims that the evidence presented at trial to support the plaintiff's claim was so scanty that no reasonable jury could have found for the plaintiff. Therefore, argues the defendant, the appellate court should reverse the trial court's decision. May an appellate court ever reverse a trial court's findings with respect to questions of fact? Discuss fully.

For a sample answer to this question, go to Appendix I at the end of this text.

2–3. Appellate courts normally see only written transcripts of trial proceedings when they are reviewing cases. Today, in some states, videotapes are being used as the official trial reports. If the use of videotapes as official reports continues, will this alter the appellate process? Should it? Discuss fully.

2–4. When and for what purpose is each of the following motions made? Which of them would be appropriate if a defendant claimed that the only issue between the parties was a question of law and that the law was favorable to the defendant's position?

(a) A motion for judgment on the pleadings.
(b) A motion for a directed verdict.
(c) A motion for summary judgment.
(d) A motion for judgment *n.o.v.*

2–5. **MOTION FOR JUDGMENT N.O.V.** Gerald Adams worked as a cook for Uno Restaurants, Inc., at Warwick Pizzeria Uno Restaurant & Bar in Warwick, Rhode Island. One night, shortly after Adams's shift began, he noticed that the kitchen floor was saturated with a foul-smelling liquid coming from the drains and backing up water onto the floor. He complained of illness and went home, where he contacted the state health department. A department representative visited the restaurant and closed it for the night, leaving instructions to sanitize the kitchen and clear the drains. Two days later, in the restaurant, David Badot, the manager, shouted at Adams in the presence of other employees.

When Adams shouted back, Badot fired Adams and had him arrested. Adams filed a suit in a Rhode Island state court against Uno, alleging that he had been unlawfully terminated for contacting the health department. A jury found in favor of Adams. Arguing that Adams had been fired for threatening Badot, Uno filed a motion for judgment as a matter of law (also known as a motion for judgment *n.o.v.*). What does a court weigh in considering whether to grant such a motion? Should the court grant the motion in this case? Why or why not? [*Adams v. Uno Restaurants, Inc.,* 794 A.2d 489 (R.I. 2002)]

2–6. E-JURISDICTION. American Business Financial Services, Inc. (ABFI), a Pennsylvania firm, sells and services loans to businesses and consumers. First Union National Bank, with its principal place of business in North Carolina, provides banking services. Alan Boyer, an employee of First Union, lives in North Carolina and has never been to Pennsylvania. In the course of his employment, Boyer learned that the bank was going to extend a $150 million line of credit to ABFI. Boyer then attempted to manipulate the stock price of ABFI for personal gain by sending disparaging e-mails to ABFI's independent auditors in Pennsylvania. Boyer also posted negative statements about ABFI and its management on a Yahoo bulletin board. ABFI filed a suit in a Pennsylvania state court against Boyer, First Union, and others, alleging wrongful interference with a contractual relationship, among other things. Boyer filed a motion to dismiss the complaint for lack of personal jurisdiction. Could the court exercise jurisdiction over Boyer? Explain. [*American Business Financial Services, Inc. v. First Union National Bank,* __ A.2d __ (Pa.Comm.Pl. 2002)]

2–7. **CASE PROBLEM WITH SAMPLE ANSWER**
To establish a Web site, a person must have an Internet service provider or hosting company, register a domain name, and acquire domain name servicing. Pfizer, Inc., Pfizer Ireland Pharmaceuticals, and Warner-Lambert Co. (collectively, Pfizer) filed a suit in a federal district court against Domains By Proxy, Inc., and other persons alleged to be behind two Web sites—genericlipitors.com and econopetcare.com. Among the defendants were an individual and a company that, according to Pfizer, were located in a foreign country. Without investigating other means of serving these two defendants, Pfizer asked the court for permission to accomplish service of process via e-mail. Under what circumstances is service via e-mail proper? Would it be appropriate in this case? Explain. [*Pfizer, Inc. v. Domains By Proxy,* __ F.Supp.2d __ (D.Conn. 2004)]

To view a sample answer for this case problem, go to this book's Web site at http://wleb.westbuslaw.com, select "Chapter 2," and click on "Case Problem with Sample Answer."

2–8. JURISDICTION. KaZaA BV was a company formed under the laws of the Netherlands. KaZaA distributed KaZaA Media Desktop (KMD) software, which enabled users to exchange, via a peer-to-peer transfer network, digital media, including movies and music. KaZaA also operated the KaZaA.com Web site, through which it distributed the KMD software to millions of California residents and other users. Metro-Goldwyn-Mayer Studios, Inc., and other parties in the entertainment industries based in California filed a suit in a federal district court against KaZaA and others, alleging copyright infringement. KaZaA filed a counterclaim, but while legal action was pending, the firm passed its assets and its Web site to Sharman Networks, Ltd., a company organized under the laws of Vanuatu (an island republic east of Australia) and doing business principally in Australia. Sharman explicitly disclaimed the assumption of any of KaZaA's liabilities. When the plaintiffs added Sharman as a defendant, Sharman filed a motion to dismiss on the ground that the court did not have jurisdiction. Would it be fair to subject Sharman to suit in this case? Explain. [*Metro-Goldwyn-Mayer Studios, Inc. v. Grokster, Ltd.*, 243 F.Supp.2d.1073 (C.D.Cal. 2003)]

2–9. STANDING TO SUE. Michael and Karla Covington live in Jefferson County, Idaho. When they bought their home, a gravel pit was across the street. In 1995, the county converted the pit to a landfill. Under the county's operation, the landfill accepted major appliances, household garbage, spilled grain, grass clippings, straw, manure, animal carcasses, containers with hazardous content warnings, leaking car batteries, and waste oil, among other things. The deposits were often left uncovered, attracting insects and other scavengers and contaminating the groundwater. Fires broke out, including at least one started by an intruder who entered the property through an unlocked gate. The Covingtons complained to the state, which inspected the landfill, but no changes were made to address their concerns. Finally, the Covingtons filed a suit in a federal district court against the county and the state, charging violations of federal environmental laws. Those laws were designed to minimize the risks of injuries from fires, scavengers, groundwater contamination, and other pollution dangers. Did the Covingtons have standing to sue? What principles apply? Explain. [*Covington v. Jefferson County*, 358 F.3d 626 (9th Cir. 2004)]

2–10. VIDEO QUESTION

Go to this text's Web site at **http://wleb.westbuslaw. com** and select "Chapter 2." Click on "Video Questions" and view the video titled *Jurisdiction in Cyberspace*. Then answer the following questions.

(a) What standard would a court apply to determine whether it has jurisdiction over the out-of-state computer firm in the video?

(b) What factors is a court likely to consider in assessing whether sufficient contacts existed when the only connection to the jurisdiction is through a Web site?

(c) How do you think the court would resolve the issue in this case?

LAW | on the Web

For updated links to resources available on the Web, as well as a variety of other materials, visit this text's Web site at **http://wleb.westbuslaw.com**.

For the decisions of the United States Supreme Court, as well as information about the Supreme Court, go to

http://supremecourtus.gov

Another Web site offering information about the United States Supreme Court, including information on the justices and links to opinions they have authored, can be accessed at

http://oyez.nwu.edu

The Web site for the federal courts offers information on the federal court system and links to all federal courts at

http://www.uscourts.gov

Procedural rules for several of the state courts are also online and can be accessed via the courts' Web pages. You can find links to the Web pages for state courts at the Web site of the National Center for State Courts. Go to

http://www.ncsc.dni.us/court/sites/courts.htm

LEGAL RESEARCH EXERCISES ON THE WEB

Go to http://wleb.westbuslaw.com, the Web site that accompanies this text. Select "Chapter 2" and click on "Internet Exercises." There you will find the following Internet research exercises that you can perform to learn more about topics covered in this chapter.

Activity 2–1:   **LEGAL PERSPECTIVE**
                Civil Procedure

Activity 2–2:   **TECHNOLOGICAL PERSPECTIVE**
                Virtual Courtrooms

Activity 2–3:   **HISTORICAL PERSPECTIVE**
                The Judiciary's Role in American Government

CHAPTER 3

Alternative and Online Dispute Resolution

Trials are costly and time consuming. It has been said that this is the result of "too many lawyers, too many lawsuits, and too many laws." In fact, since 1960, the number of lawyers has tripled, the number of lawsuits has tripled, and the number of laws has multiplied, while the numbers of judges and courts have not kept pace.

Although it is true that the number of lawsuits filed has grown rapidly, only 5 to 10 percent of lawsuits filed actually go to trial. Most cases are settled or dismissed long before the parties enter a courtroom. Moreover, the number of cases that are litigated does not appear to be growing any faster than the population. When compared with the large number of transactions that occur in our highly complex society, the rate of litigation appears low to some.

Nevertheless, in any individual case, it may be months before a hearing can even be scheduled. Depending on the complexity of the case, the extent of discovery proceedings required, and the delaying tactics of the opposing party, years may be spent in litigation. Even in the best of situations, the civil procedures discussed in Chapter 2 all require much time and money. As the cost and complexity of litigation have grown, businesspersons and other individuals have asked, "Is there a more appropriate way to resolve disputes?"

SECTION 1 | The Search for Alternatives to Litigation

A number of solutions have been proposed, and some have been implemented, to reduce the congestion in our court system and to reduce the litigation costs facing all members of society. The enforcement of arbitration clauses, the use of court-referred arbitration and mediation, and the emergence of an increasing number of private forums for dispute resolution have all helped to reduce the caseload of the courts.

Another solution to the problem involves putting caps on damage awards, particularly for pain and suffering. Without the probability of obtaining multimillion-dollar judgments for pain and suffering, some potential litigants will be deterred from undertaking lawsuits to obtain damages. Another avenue of attack is to penalize those who bring frivolous lawsuits. Rule 11 of the Federal Rules of Civil Procedure allows for disciplinary sanctions against lawyers and litigants who bring frivolous lawsuits in federal courts.

Many courts require *mediation* or *arbitration* before a case goes to trial. There are proposals to further reduce delay and expenses in federal civil cases, and proposals are being considered by the states as well. Some of the proposals can be viewed as case-management plans. One proposal, for example, would require each federal district court to implement procedures for placing cases on different tracks, with simple cases being handled more quickly than complex ones.

POLITICS AND LAW

Because reforms of any system affect individuals and groups differently, they seldom are accomplished easily and quickly. Reform of the court system is a prime example. At the federal level, members of Congress long have been concerned with bringing court costs and delay under control. These concerns gave rise to the enactment of legislation in the early 1990s that required the federal courts to develop a plan to cut costs and reduce delay within the federal judicial system.

NEW METHODS AND ARRANGEMENTS

The search for alternative means to resolve disputes has produced several distinct methods and arrangements. These range from neighbors sitting down over a cup of coffee to work out their differences to huge multinational corporations agreeing to resolve a dispute through a formal hearing before a panel of experts. All of these alternatives to traditional litigation make up what is broadly termed **alternative dispute resolution (ADR).**

ADR describes any procedure or device for resolving disputes outside the traditional judicial process. ADR is normally a less expensive and less time-consuming process than formal litigation. In some cases, it also has the advantage of being more private. Except in cases involving court-annexed arbitration (discussed later in this chapter), no public record of ADR proceedings is created; only the parties directly involved are privy to the information presented during the process. This is a particularly important consideration in many business disputes, because such cases may involve sensitive commercial information. As you will read later in this chapter, today ADR also includes online methods of resolving disputes.

SECTION 2 | Negotiation and Mediation

Alternative dispute resolution methods differ in the degree of formality involved and the extent to which third parties participate in the process. Generally, negotiation is the least formal method and involves no third parties. Mediation may be similarly informal but does involve the participation of a third party.

NEGOTIATION

In the process of **negotiation,** the parties come together informally, with or without attorneys to represent them. Within this informal setting, the parties air their differences and try to reach a settlement or resolution without the involvement of independent third parties. Because no third parties are involved and because of the informal setting, negotiation is the simplest form of ADR. Even if a lawsuit has been initiated, the parties may continue to negotiate their differences at any time during the litigation process and attempt to settle their dispute. Less than 10 percent of all corporate lawsuits, for example, end up in trial—the rest are settled beforehand.

PREPARATION FOR NEGOTIATION   In spite of the informality of negotiation, each party must carefully prepare his or her side of the case. The elements of the dispute should be considered, documents and other evidence should be collected, and witnesses should be prepared to testify. Negotiating from a well-prepared position improves the odds of obtaining a favorable result. Even if a dispute is not resolved through negotiation, preparation for negotiation will reduce the effort required to prepare for the next step in the dispute-resolution process.

ASSISTED NEGOTIATION   To facilitate negotiation, various forms of what might be called "assisted negotiation" have emerged in recent years. Assisted negotation, as the term implies, involves the assistance of a third party. Forms of ADR associated with the negotiation process include mini-trials, early neutral case evaluation, and conciliation. Another form of assisted negotiation—the summary jury trial—will be discussed later in this chapter.

A **mini-trial** is a private proceeding in which each party's attorney briefly argues the party's case before the other party. Typically, a neutral third party, who acts as an adviser and an expert in the area being disputed, is also present. If the parties fail to reach an agreement, the adviser renders an opinion as to how a court would likely decide the issue. The proceeding assists the parties in determining whether they should negotiate a settlement of the dispute or take it to court.

In **early neutral case evaluation,** the parties select a neutral third party (generally an expert in the subject matter of the dispute) to evaluate their respective positions. The parties explain their positions to the case evaluator however they wish. The evaluator then assesses the strengths and weaknesses of the parties' positions, and this evaluation forms the basis for negotiating a settlement.

Disputes may also be resolved in a friendly, nonadversarial manner through **conciliation,** in which a third party assists parties to a dispute in reconciling their differences. The conciliator helps to schedule negotiating sessions and carries offers back and forth between the parties when they refuse to face each other in direct negotiations. Technically, conciliators are not to recommend solutions. In practice, however, they often do. In contrast, a mediator is expected to propose solutions.

MEDIATION

One of the oldest forms of ADR is mediation. In the **mediation** process, the parties themselves attempt to negotiate an agreement, but with the assistance of a neutral third party, called a **mediator.** The mediator need not be a lawyer. The mediator may be a single individual, such as a paralegal, an attorney, or a volunteer from the community. Alternatively, a panel of mediators may be used.

Mediation is essentially a form of assisted negotiation. We treat it separately here because traditionally it has been viewed as an alternative to negotiation. Additionally, a mediator usually plays a more active role than the neutral third parties in negotiation-associated forms of ADR.

ADVANTAGES OF MEDIATION Few procedural rules are involved in the mediation process—far fewer than in a courtroom setting. The proceedings can be tailored to fit the needs of the parties—the mediator can be told to maintain a diplomatic role or be asked to express an opinion about the dispute, lawyers can be excluded from the proceedings, and the exchange of a few documents can replace the more expensive and time-consuming process of pretrial discovery. Disputes are often settled far more quickly in mediation than in formal litigation.[1]

There are other benefits. Because the parties reach agreement by mutual consent, the bitterness that often flows from the winner-take-all outcome of a formal trial decision is avoided. Hard feelings are also minimized by the less stressful environment provided by mediation; the absence of the formal rules and adversarial tone of courtroom proceedings lessens the hostility the parties may feel toward one another. Minimizing hard feelings can be very important when the parties have to go on working together while the controversy is being resolved or after it has been settled. This is frequently the case when two businesses—say, a supplier and a purchaser—have a long-standing, mutually beneficial relationship that they would like to preserve despite their controversy. Similar considerations are found in the context of management and labor disputes; employee disciplinary matters and grievances are subjects that invite mediation as an alternative to formal litigation.

Another important benefit of mediation is that the mediator is selected by the parties. In litigation, the parties have no control over the selection of a judge. In mediation, the parties may select a mediator on the basis of expertise in a particular field as well as for fairness and impartiality. To the degree that the mediator has these attributes, he or she will more effectively aid the parties in reaching an agreement over their dispute.

DISADVANTAGES OF MEDIATION Mediation is not without disadvantages. A mediator is likely to charge a fee. (This can be split between the parties, though, and thus may represent less expense than would both sides' hiring lawyers.)

Informality and the absence of a third party referee can also be disadvantageous. (Remember that a mediator can only help the parties reach a decision, not make a decision for them.) Without a deadline hanging over the parties' heads, and without the threat of sanctions if they fail to negotiate in good faith, they may be less willing to make concessions or otherwise strive honestly and diligently to reach a settlement. This can slow the process or even cause it to fail.

SECTION 3 | Arbitration

A third method of dispute resolution combines the advantages of third party decision making—as provided by judges and juries in formal litigation—with the speed and flexibility offered by rules of procedure and evidence that are less rigid than those governing courtroom litigation. This is the process of **arbitration**—the settling of a dispute by an impartial third party (other than a court) who renders a decision. The third party who renders the decision is called an **arbitrator.** The key difference between arbitration and the forms of ADR just discussed is that in arbitration, the third party's decision may be legally binding on the parties.

When a dispute arises, the parties can agree to settle their differences informally through arbitration rather than formally through the court system. Alternatively, the parties may agree ahead of time that, if a dispute should arise, they will submit to arbitration rather than bring a lawsuit. If the parties agree that the arbitrator's decision will be legally binding, they are obligated to abide by the arbitrator's decision regardless of whether or not they agree with it.

The federal government and many state governments favor arbitration over litigation. The federal policy favoring arbitration is embodied in the Federal

---

1. In Florida alone, as many as fifty thousand disputes that might have ended up in court are instead resolved through mediation each year.

Arbitration Act (FAA) of 1925.[2] The FAA requires that courts give deference to all voluntary arbitration agreements in cases governed by federal law. Virtually any dispute can be the subject of arbitration. A voluntary agreement to arbitrate a dispute normally will be enforced by the courts if the agreement does not compel an illegal act or contravene public policy.

THE FEDERAL ARBITRATION ACT

The Federal Arbitration Act does not establish a set arbitration procedure. The parties themselves must agree on the manner of resolving their dispute. The FAA provides the means for enforcing the arbitration procedure that the parties have established for themselves.

Section 4 allows a party to petition a federal district court for an order compelling arbitration under an agreement to arbitrate a dispute. If the judge is "satisfied that the making of the agreement for arbitration or the failure to comply therewith is not in issue, the court shall make an order directing the parties to proceed with arbitration in accordance with the terms of the agreement."

Under Section 9 of the FAA, the parties to the arbitration may agree to have the arbitrator's decision confirmed in a federal district court. Through confirmation,

one party obtains a court order directing another party to comply with the terms of the arbitrator's decision. Section 10 establishes the grounds by which the arbitrator's decision may be set aside (canceled). The grounds for setting aside a decision are limited to misconduct, fraud, corruption, or abuse of power in the arbitration process itself; a court will not review the merits of the dispute or the arbitrator's judgment.

The FAA covers any arbitration clause in a contract that involves interstate commerce. Business activities that have even remote connections or minimal effects on commerce between two or more states are considered to be included. Thus, arbitration agreements involving transactions only slightly connected to the flow of interstate commerce may fall under the FAA, even if the parties, at the time of contracting, did not expect their arbitration agreement to involve interstate commerce.[3]

In the following case, an employer asked a court to issue an order compelling an ex-employee to submit to arbitration under an arbitration agreement that the parties had signed. Under that agreement, it was the employer's responsibility to establish the procedure and the rules for the arbitration. Those rules were the focus of the court's consideration of the employer's request.

---

2. 9 U.S.C. Sections 1–15.

3. *Allied-Bruce Terminix Cos., Inc. v. Dobson*, 513 U.S. 265, 115 S.Ct. 834, 130 L.Ed.2d 753 (1995).

CASE 3.1

United States Court of Appeals, Fourth Circuit, 1999. 173 F.3d 933. http://www.law. emory.edu/4circuit[a]

Hooters of America, Inc. v. Phillips

COMPANY PROFILE *The first Hooters restaurant was opened in Clearwater, Florida, in 1983, by six friends, all of whom had business experience but none of whom had restaurant experience. The following year, they sold the rights to expand the business under the Hooters name to Hooters of America, Inc. (**http://www.hooters.com**). Today, Hooters of America owns or licenses more than two hundred restaurants in forty-two states, as well as Argentina, the Bahamas, Canada, Mexico, the United Kingdom, and other countries. The menu includes spicy chicken wings and sandwiches.*

BACKGROUND AND FACTS *In 1989, Annette Phillips was hired by Hooters of Myrtle Beach (HOMB), a franchisee of Hooters of America, Inc., to work as a bartender at a Hooters restaurant in Myrtle Beach, South Carolina. Five years later, Hooters implemented an alternative dispute-resolution program. The company conditioned eligibility for raises, transfers, and promotions on an employee's signing an "agreement to arbitrate employment-related disputes," which specifically included claims of sexual harassment. The agreement stated that the arbitration was subject to "the company's rules and procedures for alternative resolution of employment-related disputes, as promulgated by the company from time to time." The employees were not given a copy of these rules. Phillips signed the agreement. In June 1996, Gerald Brooks, a Hooters official and the brother of HOMB's principal owner, allegedly sexually harassed Phillips by grabbing and slapping her buttocks. After appealing to*

---

a. In the "Listing by Month of Decision" section, in the "1999 Decisions," click on "April." On that page, scroll down the list of cases to the name of the case, and click on it to access the opinion.

CONTINUED ▶

CASE 3.1 | Continued *her manager for help and being told to "let it go," she quit her job. Phillips threatened to sue, claiming that the attack and the restaurant's failure to address it violated her rights.* [b] *Hooters responded that she was required to submit her claim to arbitration. Phillips refused. Hooters filed a suit in a federal district court against Phillips to compel arbitration under Section 4 of the FAA. The court denied Hooters' request. The company appealed to the U.S. Court of Appeals for the Fourth Circuit.*

IN THE LANGUAGE OF THE COURT

WILKINSON, Chief Judge.

* * * *

Hooters and Phillips agreed to settle any disputes between them not in a judicial forum, but in another neutral forum—arbitration. Their agreement provided that Hooters was responsible for setting up such a forum by promulgating arbitration rules and procedures. * * *

The Hooters rules when taken as a whole, however, are so one-sided that their *only possible purpose is to undermine the neutrality of the proceeding.* The rules require the employee to provide the company notice of her claim at the outset, including "the nature of the Claim" and "the specific act(s) or omissions(s) which are the basis of the Claim." Hooters, on the other hand, is not required to file any responsive pleadings or to notice its defenses. Additionally, at the time of filing this notice, the employee must provide the company with a list of all fact witnesses with a brief summary of the facts known to each. The company, however, is not required to reciprocate. [Emphasis added.]

The Hooters rules also provide a mechanism for selecting a panel of three arbitrators that is crafted to ensure a biased decision maker. The employee and Hooters each select an arbitrator, and the two arbitrators in turn select a third. Good enough, except that the employee's arbitrator and the third arbitrator must be selected from a list of arbitrators created exclusively by Hooters. This gives Hooters control over the entire panel and places no limits whatsoever on whom Hooters can put on the list. Under the rules, Hooters is free to devise lists of partial arbitrators who have existing relationships, financial or familial, with Hooters and its management. In fact, the rules do not even prohibit Hooters from placing its managers themselves on the list. Further, nothing in the rules restricts Hooters from punishing arbitrators who rule against the company by removing them from the list. Given the unrestricted control that one party (Hooters) has over the panel, the selection of an impartial decision maker would be a surprising result.

* * * *

In addition, the rules provide that upon 30 days notice Hooters, but not the employee, may cancel the agreement to arbitrate. Moreover, Hooters reserves the right to modify the rules, "in whole or in part," whenever it wishes and "without notice" to the employee. Nothing in the rules even prohibits Hooters from changing the rules in the middle of an arbitration proceeding.

DECISION AND REMEDY *The U.S. Court of Appeals for the Fourth Circuit held that Hooters' issuance of "so many biased rules" created "a sham system unworthy even of the name of arbitration," in violation of the parties' contract to arbitrate. The court affirmed the judgment of the lower court.*

---

b. Phillips claimed specifically that Hooters violated her rights under Title VII of the Civil Rights Act of 1964. This law will be discussed more fully in Chapter 21.

STATE ARBITRATION STATUTES

Virtually all states follow the federal approach to voluntary arbitration. Most of the states and the District of Columbia have adopted the Uniform Arbitration Act, which was drafted by the National Conference of Commissioners on Uniform State Laws in 1955. Those states that have not adopted the uniform act nonetheless follow many of the practices specified in it.

Under the uniform act, the basic approach is to give full effect to voluntary agreements to arbitrate disputes between private parties. The act supplements private arbitration agreements by providing explicit procedures and remedies for enforcing arbitration agreements. The uniform act does not, however, dictate the terms of the agreement. Moreover, under both federal and state statutes, the parties are afforded considerable latitude in deciding the subject matter of the arbitration and the methods for conducting the arbitration process. In the absence of a controlling statute, the rights and duties of the parties are established and limited by their agreement.

THE ARBITRATION PROCESS

The arbitration process begins with a *submission*. **Submission** is the act of referring a dispute to an arbitrator. The next step is the *hearing,* in which evidence and arguments are presented to the arbitrator. The process culminates in an *award*, which is the decision of the arbitrator.

The right to appeal the award to a court of law is limited. If the award was made under a voluntary arbitration agreement, a court normally will not set it aside even if it was the result of an erroneous determination of fact or an incorrect interpretation of law by the arbitrator.

This limitation is based on at least two grounds. First, if an award is not treated as final, then rather than speeding up the dispute-resolution process, arbitration would merely add one more layer to the process of litigation. Second, the basis of arbitration—the freedom of parties to agree among themselves how to settle a controversy—supports treating an award as final. Having had the opportunity to frame the issues and to set out the manner for resolving the dispute, one party should not complain if the result was not what that party had hoped it would be.

SUBMISSION   The parties may agree to submit questions of fact, questions of law, or both to the arbitrator. The parties may even agree to leave the interpretation of the arbitration agreement to the arbitrator. In the case of an existing agreement to arbitrate, the clause itself is the submission to arbitration.

The submission typically states the identities of the parties, the nature of the dispute to be resolved, the monetary amounts involved in the controversy, the location at which the arbitration is to take place, and the intention of the parties to be bound by the arbitrator's award. Exhibit 3–1 on the next page contains a sample submission form.

Most states require that an agreement to submit a dispute to arbitration be in writing. Moreover, because the goal of arbitration is speed and efficiency in resolving controversies, most states require that matters be submitted within a definite period of time, generally six months from the date on which the dispute arises.

THE HEARING   Because the parties are free to construct the method by which they want their dispute resolved, they must state the issues that will be submitted and the powers that the arbitrator will exercise. The arbitrator may be given power at the outset of the process to establish rules that will govern the proceedings. Typically, these rules are much less restrictive than those governing formal litigation. Regardless of who establishes the rules, the arbitrator will apply them during the course of the hearing.

Restrictions on the kind of evidence and the manner in which it is presented may be less rigid in arbitration, partly because the arbitrator is likely to be an expert in the subject matter involved in the controversy. Restrictions may also be less stringent because there is less fear that the arbitrator will be swayed by improper evidence. In contrast, evidence in a jury trial must sometimes be presented twice: once to the judge, outside the presence of the jury, to determine if the evidence may be heard by the jury, and—depending on the judge's ruling—again, to the jury.

In the typical hearing format, the parties begin as they would at trial by presenting opening arguments to the arbitrator and stating what remedies should or should not be granted. After the opening statements have been made, evidence is presented. Witnesses may be called and examined by both sides. After all the evidence has been presented, the parties give their closing arguments. On completion of the closing arguments, the arbitrator closes the hearing.

THE AWARD   After each side has had an opportunity to present evidence and to argue its case, the arbitrator reaches a decision. The final decision of the arbitrator is referred to as an **award,** even if no money is conferred on a party as a result of the proceedings. Under most statutes, the arbitrator must render an award within thirty days of the close of the hearing.

In most states, the award need not state the arbitrator's findings regarding factual questions in the case. Nor must the award state the conclusions that the arbitrator reached on any questions of law that may have been presented. All that is required for the award to be valid is that it completely resolve the controversy.

EXHIBIT 3-1 Sample Submission Form

American Arbitration Association

SUBMISSION TO DISPUTE RESOLUTION

The named parties hereby submit the following dispute for resolution, under the rules of the American Arbitration Association:

Rules Selected: ☐ Commercial ☐ Construction
☐ Other _____
(describe)

Procedure Selected: ☐ Binding arbitration ☐ Mediation
☐ Other _____
(describe)

Nature of the Dispute (attach additional sheets if necessary):

Amount of Monetary Claim or Nature of Non-Monetary Claim:

Type of Business: Claimant _____ Respondent _____

Place of Hearing: _____

We agree that, if arbitration is selected, we will abide by and perform any award rendered hereunder and that a judgment may be entered on the award.

To be completed and signed by all parties
(attach additional sheets if necessary, please remember to obtain signatures)

Name of Party	Name of Party
Address	Address
City, State, and Zip Code	City, State, and Zip Code
(____) _____ Telephone Fax	(____) _____ Telephone Fax
Name of the Party's Attorney or Representative	Name of the Party's Attorney or Representative
Name of Firm (if applicable)	Name of Firm (if applicable)
Address	Address
City, State, and Zip Code	City, State, and Zip Code
(____) _____ Telephone Fax	(____) _____ Telephone Fax
Signed† (may be signed by a representative) Title	Signed† (may be signed by a representative) Title
Date: _____	Date: _____

Please file two signed copies and the non-refundable filing fee with the AAA.
For additional information, please visit our Web site at www.adr.org

† Signatures of all parties are required.

Form G1A-3/03

Most states do, however, require that the award be in writing, regardless of whether any conclusions of law or findings of fact are included. If the arbitrator does state his or her legal conclusions and factual findings, then a letter or an opinion will be drafted containing the basis for the award. Even when there is no statutory requirement that the arbitrator state the factual and legal basis for the award, the parties may impose the requirement in their submission or in their predispute agreement to arbitrate.

ENFORCEMENT OF AGREEMENTS TO SUBMIT TO ARBITRATION

The role of the courts in the arbitration process is limited. One important role is played at the prearbitration stage. A court may be called on to order one party to an arbitration agreement to submit to arbitration under the terms of the agreement. The court in this role is essentially interpreting a contract. The court must determine what the parties have committed themselves to before ordering that they submit to arbitration.

THE ISSUE OF ARBITRABILITY When a dispute arises as to whether or not the parties have agreed in an arbitration clause to submit a particular matter to arbitration, one party may file suit to compel arbitration. The court before which the suit is brought will not decide the basic controversy but must decide the issue of arbitrability—that is, whether the issue is one that must be resolved through arbitration. If the court finds that the subject matter in controversy is covered by the agreement to arbitrate, then a party may be compelled to arbitrate the dispute involuntarily.

Although the parties may agree to submit the issue of arbitrability to an arbitrator, the agreement must be explicit; a court will never *infer* an agreement to arbitrate. Unless a court finds an *explicit* agreement to have the arbitrator decide whether a dispute is arbitrable, the court will decide the issue. This is an important initial determination, because no party will be ordered to submit to arbitration unless the court is convinced that the party has consented to do so.

MANDATORY ARBITRATION IN THE EMPLOYMENT CONTEXT A significant question in the last several years has concerned mandatory arbitration clauses in employment contracts. Many claim that employees' rights are not sufficiently protected when they are forced, as a condition of being hired, to agree to arbitrate all disputes and thus waive their rights under statutes specifically designed to protect employees. The United States Supreme Court, however, has held that mandatory arbitration clauses in employment contracts are generally enforceable.[4]

Compulsory arbitration agreements often spell out the rules for a mandatory proceeding. For example, an agreement may address in detail the amount and payment of filing fees and other expenses. Some courts have overturned provisions in employment-related agreements that require the parties to split the costs when an individual worker lacks the ability to pay. The court in the following case took this reasoning a step further.

---

4. For a landmark decision on this issue, see *Gilmer v. Interstate/Johnson Lane Corp.*, 500 U.S. 20, 111 S.Ct. 1647, 114 L.Ed.2d 26 (1991).

CASE 3.2 — Morrison v. Circuit City Stores, Inc.

United States
Court of Appeals,
Sixth Circuit, 2003.
317 F.3d 646.
http://pacer.ca6.uscourts.gov/opinions/main.php [a]

KAREN NELSON MOORE, Circuit Judge.

     * * * *

     * * * Plaintiff-Appellant Morrison, an African-American female with a bachelor's degree in engineering from the U.S. Air Force Academy and a master's degree in administration from Central Michigan University, submitted an application for a managerial position at a Circuit City store in Cincinnati, Ohio. As part of the application process, Morrison was required to sign a * * * "Dispute Resolution Agreement." This document contained an arbitration clause that required resolution of all disputes or controversies arising out of

---

a. This is a page within the Web site of the U.S. Court of Appeals for the Sixth Circuit. In the left-hand column, click on "Opinions Search." In the "Short Title contains" box, type "Morrison" and click "Submit Query." In the "Opinion" box corresponding to the name of the case, click on the number to access the opinion.

CONTINUED ➤

CASE 3.2 | Continued

employment with Circuit City in an arbitral forum. * * * Circuit City would not consider any application for employment unless the arbitration agreement was signed * * * .
* * * *

Pursuant to [the agreement] each party is required to pay one-half of the costs of arbitration following the issuance of an arbitration award * * * . In addition, * * * if an employee is able to pay her share of the arbitration costs within [ninety days], her costs (not including attorney fees) are then limited to the greater of either five hundred dollars or three percent of her most recent annual compensation.
* * * *

* * * Morrison began her employment at Circuit City on or about December 1, 1995. Two years later, on December 12, 1997, she was terminated. Morrison alleges that her termination was the result of race and sex discrimination.[b] She filed this lawsuit * * * in Ohio state court, alleging federal and state claims of race and sex discrimination * * * . Circuit City removed the case to federal court and then moved to compel arbitration and to dismiss Morrison's claims. The district court granted Circuit City's motion * * * .

* * * Morrison's appeal followed.
* * * *

We hold that *potential litigants must be given an opportunity, prior to arbitration on the merits, to demonstrate that the potential costs of arbitration are great enough to deter them and similarly situated individuals from seeking to vindicate [assert] their federal statutory rights in the arbitral forum.* * * * Thus, in order to protect the statutory rights at issue, the reviewing court must look to more than just the interests and conduct of a particular plaintiff. * * * [A] court considering whether a cost-splitting provision is enforceable should consider similarly situated potential litigants, for whom costs will loom as a larger concern, because it is, in large part, their presence in the system that will deter discriminatory practices. [Emphasis added.]

For this reason, *if the reviewing court finds that the cost-splitting provision would deter a substantial number of similarly situated potential litigants, it should refuse to enforce the cost-splitting provision in order to serve the underlying functions of the federal statute.* * * * [Emphasis added.]
* * * *

This analysis will yield different results in different cases. It will find, in many cases, that high-level managerial employees and others with substantial means can afford the costs of arbitration, thus making cost-splitting provisions in such cases enforceable. In the case of other employees, however, this standard will render cost-splitting provisions unenforceable in many, if not most, cases.

* * * Circuit City argues that Morrison could have avoided having to pay half of the cost of the arbitration * * * if she could have arranged to pay the greater of $500 or 3 percent of her annual salary (in this case, 3 percent of $54,060, or $1,622) within ninety days of the arbitrator's award. * * *

In the abstract, this sum may not appear prohibitive, but it must be considered from the vantage point of the potential litigant in a case such as this. Recently terminated, the potential litigant must continue to pay for housing, utilities, transportation, food, and the other necessities of life in contemporary society despite losing her primary, and most likely only, source of income. * * *

The provision reducing the (former) employee's exposure to the greater of $500 or three percent of her annual compensation presents a closer issue. However, a potential litigant considering arbitration would still have to arrange to pay three percent of her most recent salary, in this case, $1,622, within a three-month period, or risk incurring her full half of the costs * * * . Faced with this choice—which really boils down to risking one's scarce resources in the hopes of an uncertain benefit—it appears to us that a substantial number of similarly situated persons would be deterred from seeking to vindicate their statutory rights under these circumstances.[c]

---

b. Employment discrimination will be discussed in detail in Chapter 21.
c. The court also concluded that the provision could be severed from the agreement, which meant that the rest of the agreement could be enforced. Because the arbitration in this case had already occurred, and Morrison had not been required to pay any share of the costs, the court affirmed the lower court's order compelling arbitration, "on these different grounds."

CASE 3.2 | Continued

Based on this reasoning, we hold that Morrison has satisfied her burden in the present case in demonstrating that * * * the cost-splitting provision in the agreement was unenforceable with respect to her claims.

QUESTIONS

1. On what argument did Morrison base her appeal of the court's order to arbitrate her employment-discrimination claims?
2. Why did the U.S. Court of Appeals for the Sixth Circuit hold in Morrison's case that the arbitration agreement's cost-splitting provision was unenforceable?

SETTING ASIDE AN ARBITRATION AWARD

After the arbitration has been concluded, the losing party may appeal the arbitrator's award to a court, or the winning party may seek a court order compelling the other party to comply with the award. The scope of review in either situation is much more restricted than in an appellate court's review of a trial court decision. The court does not look at the merits of the underlying dispute, and the court will not add to or subtract from the remedies provided by the award. The court's role is limited to determining whether there exists a valid award. If so, the court will order the parties to comply with the terms. The general view is that because the parties were free to frame the issues and set the powers of the arbitrator at the outset, they cannot complain about the result.

FACT FINDINGS AND LEGAL CONCLUSIONS The
arbitrator's fact findings and legal conclusions are normally final. That the arbitrator may have erred in a ruling during the hearing or made an erroneous fact finding is normally no basis for setting aside an award: the parties agreed that the arbitrator would be the judge of the facts. Similarly, no matter how obviously the arbitrator was mistaken in a conclusion of law, the award is normally nonetheless binding: the parties agreed to accept the arbitrator's interpretation of the law. A court will not look at the merits of the dispute, the sufficiency of the evidence presented, or the arbitrator's reasoning in reaching a particular decision.

This approach is consistent with the underlying view of all voluntary arbitration—that its basis is really contract law. If the parties freely contract with one another, courts will not interfere simply because one side feels that it received a bad bargain. Any party challenging an award must face the presumption that a final award is valid. But is an award final or binding if the parties did not agree that it would be?

PUBLIC POLICY AND ILLEGALITY In keeping with
contract law principles, no award will be enforced if compliance with the award would result in the commission of a crime or would conflict with some greater social policy mandated by statute. A court will not overturn an award, however, simply because the arbitrator was called on to resolve a dispute involving a matter of significant public concern. For an award to be set aside, it must call for some action on the part of the parties that would conflict with or in some way undermine public policy.[5]

DEFECTS IN THE ARBITRATION PROCESS There
are some bases for setting aside an award when there is a defect in the arbitration process. These bases are typified by those set forth in the Federal Arbitration Act. Section 10 of the act provides four grounds on which an arbitration award may be set aside:

1. The award was the result of corruption, fraud, or other "undue means."
2. The arbitrator exhibited bias or corruption.
3. The arbitrator refused to postpone the hearing despite sufficient cause, refused to hear evidence pertinent and material to the dispute, or otherwise acted to substantially prejudice the rights of one of the parties.
4. The arbitrator exceeded his or her powers or failed to use them to make a mutual, final, and definite award.

The first three bases for setting aside the award include actions or decisions that are more than simply mistakes in judgment. Each requires some "bad faith" on the part of the arbitrator. Bad faith actions or decisions are ones that affect the integrity of the arbitration process. The honesty and impartiality, rather than the judgment, of the arbitrator are called into question.

---

5. See, for example, *Meehan v. Nassau Community College*, 647 N.Y.S.2d 865 (App.Div. 2 Dept. 1996).

Sometimes it is difficult to make the distinction between honest mistakes in judgment and actions or decisions made in bad faith. A bribe is clearly the kind of "undue means" included in the first basis for setting aside an award. Letting only one side argue its case is likewise a clear violation of the second basis.

Meetings between the arbitrator and one party outside the presence of the other party also taint the arbitration process. Although meetings might not involve the kind of corruption that results from taking a bribe, they do affect the integrity of the process; the third basis for setting aside an award is meant to protect against this.

Not every refusal by an arbitrator to admit certain evidence is grounds for setting aside an award under the third basis. As noted, to provide a basis for over-

turning an award, the arbitrator's decision must be more than an error in judgment, no matter how obviously incorrect that judgment might appear to another observer. The decision must be so obviously wrong or unfair as to imply bias or corruption. Otherwise, the decision normally cannot be a basis for setting aside an award.

The fourth basis for setting aside an award is that the arbitrator exceeded his or her powers in arbitrating the dispute. This issue involves the question of arbitrability. An arbitrator exceeds his or her powers and authority by attempting to resolve an issue that is not covered by the agreement to submit to arbitration.

In the following case, a party to an arbitration proceeding asked a court to set aside the award.

CASE 3.3 | Major League Baseball Players Association v. Garvey

Supreme Court of the United States, 2001.
532 U.S. 1015,
121 S.Ct. 1724,
149 L.Ed.2d 740.
http://straylight.
law.cornell.edu/
supct/index.php[a]

BACKGROUND AND FACTS *In 1986, 1987, and 1988, the Major League Baseball Players Association complained that the Major League Baseball Clubs had engaged in collusion to underpay some of the players. The grievance was submitted to arbitration before a panel chaired by Thomas Roberts. During a hearing in 1986, Ballard Smith, the president of the San Diego Padres, testified that there had been no collusion. Roberts's panel rejected this testimony as false. The Association and the Clubs entered into a settlement agreement, under which the Clubs set up a fund of $280 million to be distributed to players who suffered losses due to the collusion and the Association established a framework for evaluating each player's claim. A player could challenge the Association's recommendation in binding arbitration. Steve Garvey, who had played for the Padres between 1983 and 1987 under a contract, filed a claim for damages, alleging that the Padres would have extended his contract for the 1988 and 1989 seasons but for the collusion. Roberts, the arbitrator in Garvey's case, denied the claim. Roberts cited Smith's testimony in the 1986 hearing that the Padres were not interested in extending Garvey's contract. Roberts rejected Smith's admission, in a 1996 letter, that he had not told the truth during those hearings and that he had made Garvey an offer that was withdrawn due to the collusion. Garvey filed a suit in a federal district court against Roberts and the association to have the arbitrator's award set aside. The court ruled in the defendants' favor. Garvey appealed to the U.S. Court of Appeals for the Ninth Circuit, which reversed the ruling of the lower court and remanded the case with directions to set aside the arbitrator's award. The defendants appealed to the United States Supreme Court.*

IN THE LANGUAGE OF THE COURT

PER CURIAM [By the whole court].

*   *   *   *

* * * Courts are not authorized to review the arbitrator's decision on the merits despite allegations that the decision rests on factual errors or misinterprets the parties' agreement. * * * [I]f an arbitrator is even arguably construing or applying the contract and acting within the scope of his authority, the fact that a court is convinced he committed serious error does not suffice to overturn his decision. It is only when the arbitrator strays from interpretation and application of the agreement and effectively dispenses his own brand of * * * justice that his decision may be unenforceable. * * *

* * * Even in the very rare instances when an arbitrator's procedural aberrations rise to the level of affirmative misconduct, as a rule the court must not foreclose further pro-

---

a. In the "Search" box, type "Garvey." In the pull-down menu, select "Current decisions only," and click on "submit." In the result, click on the first item that includes the name of the case to access the opinion. The Legal Information Institute of Cornell Law School in Ithaca, New York, maintains this Web site.

CASE 3.3 | Continued   ceedings by settling the merits according to its own judgment of the appropriate result. That step * * * would improperly substitute a judicial determination for the arbitrator's decision that the parties bargained for in their agreement. Instead, the court should simply vacate the award, thus leaving open the possibility of further proceedings if they are permitted under the terms of the agreement.

To be sure, the Court of Appeals here recited these principles, but its application of them is nothing short of baffling. The substance of the Court's discussion reveals that it overturned the arbitrator's decision because it disagreed with the arbitrator's factual findings, particularly those with respect to credibility. The Court of Appeals, it appears, would have credited Smith's 1996 letter, and found the arbitrator's refusal to do so at worst irrational and at best bizarre. But even serious error on the arbitrator's part does not justify overturning his decision, where, as here, he is construing a contract and acting within the scope of his authority.

* * * [The court] both rejected the arbitrator's findings and went further, resolving the merits of the parties' dispute based on the court's assessment of the record before the arbitrator. For that reason, the court found further arbitration proceedings inappropriate. But again, established law ordinarily precludes a court from resolving the merits of the parties' dispute on the basis of its own factual determinations, no matter how erroneous the arbitrator's decision. Even when the arbitrator's award may properly be vacated, the appropriate remedy is to remand the case for further arbitration proceedings. * * * The Court of Appeals usurped the arbitrator's role by resolving the dispute and barring further proceedings.

DECISION AND REMEDY *The United States Supreme Court reversed the judgment of the lower court and remanded the case for further proceedings. The Court held that the appellate court "usurped the arbitrator's role" when the court rejected the arbitrator's findings and resolved the dispute on the basis of its own assessment of the record.*

WAIVER Although a defect in the arbitration process is sufficient grounds for setting aside an award, a party sometimes forfeits the right to challenge an award by failing to object to the defect in a timely manner. The party must object when he or she learns of the problem. After making the objection, the party can still proceed with the arbitration process and still challenge the award in court after the arbitration proceedings have concluded. If, however, a party makes no objection and proceeds with the arbitration process, then a later court challenge to the award may be denied on the ground that the party *waived* the right to challenge the award on the basis of the defect.

Frequently, this occurs when a party fails to object that an arbitrator is exceeding his or her powers in resolving a dispute because the subject matter is not arbitrable or because the party did not agree to arbitrate the dispute. The question of arbitrability is one for the courts to decide. If a party does not object on this issue at the first demand for arbitration, however, a court may consider the objection waived.

CONFLICTS OF LAW Parties are afforded wide latitude in establishing the manner in which their disputes will be resolved. Nevertheless, an agreement to arbitrate may be governed by the Federal Arbitration Act (FAA) or one of the many state arbitration acts, even though the parties do not refer to a statute in their agreement. Recall that the FAA covers any arbitration clause in a contract that involves interstate commerce. Frequently, however, transactions involving interstate commerce also have substantial connections to particular states, which may in turn have their own arbitration acts. In such situations, unless the FAA and state arbitration law are nearly identical, the acts may conflict. How are these conflicts to be resolved?

As a general principle, the supremacy clause and the commerce clause of the U.S. Constitution are the bases for giving federal law preeminence; when there is a conflict, state law is preempted by federal law. Thus, in cases of arbitration, the strong federal policy favoring arbitration can override a state's laws that might be more favorable to normal litigation.

CHOICE OF LAW Notwithstanding federal preemption of conflicting state laws, the Federal Arbitration Act has been interpreted as allowing the parties to choose a particular state law to govern their arbitration agreement. The parties may choose to have the laws of a specific state govern their agreement by including in the agreement a *choice-of-law clause*. The

FAA does not mandate any particular set of rules that parties must follow in arbitration; the parties are free to agree on the manner best suited to their needs. Consistent with this view that arbitration is at heart a contractual matter between private parties, the United States Supreme Court has upheld arbitration agreements containing choice-of-law provisions.

DISADVANTAGES OF ARBITRATION

Arbitration has some disadvantages. The result in any particular dispute can be unpredictable, in part because arbitrators do not need to follow any previous cases in rendering their decisions. Unlike judges, arbitrators do not have to issue written opinions or facilitate a participant's appeal to a court. Arbitrators must decide disputes according to whatever rules have been provided by the parties, regardless of how unfair those rules may be. In some cases, arbitration can be nearly as expensive as litigation. In part, this is because both sides must prepare their cases for presentation before a third party decision maker, just as they would have to do to appear in court. Discovery is usually not available in arbitration, however, which means that during the hearing the parties must take the time to question witnesses whom, in a lawsuit, they would not need to call.

SECTION 4 | The Integration of ADR and Formal Court Procedures

Increasingly, courts are requiring that parties attempt to settle their differences through some form of ADR before proceeding to trial. For example, several federal district courts encourage nonbinding arbitration for cases involving amounts less than $100,000. Less than 10 percent of the cases referred for arbitration ever go to trial. Today, about half of all federal courts have adopted formal rules regarding the use of ADR, and many other courts without such rules use ADR procedures.

Most states have adopted programs that allow them to refer certain types of cases for negotiation, mediation, or arbitration. Typically—as in California and Hawaii—court systems have adopted mandatory mediation or nonbinding arbitration programs for certain types of disputes, usually involving less than a specified threshold dollar amount. Only if the parties fail to reach an agreement, or if one of the parties dis-

agrees with the decision of a third party mediating or arbitrating the dispute, will the case be heard by a court. South Carolina was the first state to institute a voluntary arbitration program at the appellate court level. In the South Carolina system, litigants must waive a court hearing when requesting arbitration. All decisions by the arbitrators are final and binding.

COURT-ANNEXED ARBITRATION

Court-annexed arbitration differs significantly from the voluntary arbitration process discussed above. There are some disputes that courts will not allow to go to arbitration. Most states, for example, do not allow court-annexed arbitration in disputes involving title to real estate or in cases in which a court's equity powers are involved.

A FUNDAMENTAL DIFFERENCE The fundamental difference between voluntary arbitration and court-annexed arbitration is the finality and reviewability of the award. With respect to court-annexed arbitration, either party may reject the award for any reason. In the event that one of the parties does reject the award, the case will proceed to trial, and the court will hear the case *de novo*—that is, the court will reconsider all the evidence and legal questions as though no arbitration had occurred.

Everyone who has a recognizable cause of action or against whom such an action is brought is entitled to have the issue decided in a court of law. Because court-annexed arbitration is not voluntary, there must be some safeguard against using it in a way that denies an individual his or her day in court. This safeguard is provided by permitting either side to reject the award regardless of the reason for so doing.

The party rejecting the award may be penalized, however. Many statutes providing for court-annexed arbitration impose court costs and fees on a party who rejects an arbitration award but does not improve his or her position by going to trial. Thus, for example, if a party rejects an arbitration award, and the award turns out to be more favorable to that party than the subsequent jury verdict, the party may be compelled to pay the costs of the arbitration or some fee for the costs of the trial.

In court-annexed arbitration, discovery of evidence occurs before the hearing. After the hearing has commenced, a party seeking to discover new evidence must usually secure approval from the court that mandated the arbitration. This is intended to prevent the parties from using arbitration as a means of previewing each other's cases and then rejecting the arbitrator's award.

THE ROLE OF THE ARBITRATOR Notwithstanding the differences between voluntary and court-annexed arbitration, the role of the arbitrator is essentially the same in both types of proceedings. The arbitrator determines issues of both fact and law. The arbitrator also makes all decisions concerning applications of the rules of procedure and evidence during the hearing.

WHICH RULES APPLY Regarding the rules of evidence, there are differences among the states. Most states impose the same rules of evidence on an arbitration hearing as on a trial. Other states, such as New Jersey, allow all evidence relevant to the dispute regardless of whether the evidence would be admissible at trial. Still other jurisdictions, such as Washington, leave it to the arbitrator to decide what evidence is admissible.

WAIVER Once a court directs that a dispute is to be submitted to court-annexed arbitration, the parties must proceed to arbitration. As noted above, either side may reject the award that results from the arbitration for any reason. If a party fails to appear at, or participate in, the arbitration proceeding as directed by the court, however, that failure constitutes a waiver of the right to reject the award.

COURT-RELATED MEDIATION

Mediation is proving to be more popular than arbitration as a court-related method of ADR, and mediation programs continue to increase in number in both federal and state courts. Today, more court systems offer or require mediation, rather than arbitration, as an alternative to litigation.

Mediation is often used in disputes relating to employment law, environmental law, product liability, and franchises. One of the most important business advantages of mediation is its lower cost, which can be 25 percent (or less) of the expense of litigation. Another advantage is the speed with which a dispute can go through mediation (possibly one or two days) compared with arbitration (possibly months) or litigation (possibly years).

Part of the popularity of mediation is that its goal, unlike that of litigation and some other forms of ADR, is for opponents to work out a resolution that benefits both sides. The rate of participants' satisfaction with the outcomes in mediated disputes is high. In New Hampshire, for example, where mediation is mandatory for all civil cases in most state trial courts, as many as 70 percent of the participants report satisfaction with the results.

SUMMARY JURY TRIALS

Another means by which the courts have integrated alternative dispute-resolution methods into the traditional court process is through the use of summary jury trials. A **summary jury trial** is a mock trial that occurs in a courtroom before a judge and jury. Evidence is presented in an abbreviated form, along with each side's major contentions. The jury then presents a verdict.

The fundamental difference between a traditional trial and a summary jury trial is that in the latter, the jury's verdict is only advisory. The goal of a summary jury trial is to give each side an idea of how it would fare in a full-blown jury trial with a more elaborate and detailed presentation of evidence and arguments. At the end of the summary jury trial, the presiding judge meets with the parties and may encourage them to settle their dispute without going through a standard jury trial.

SECTION 5 | ADR Forums and Services

Services facilitating dispute resolution outside the courtroom are provided by both government agencies and private organizations.

NONPROFIT ORGANIZATIONS

The major source of private arbitration services is the American Arbitration Association (AAA). Most of the largest law firms in the nation are members of this association. Founded in 1926, the AAA now settles more than 200,000 disputes a year and has offices in every state. Cases brought before the AAA are heard by an expert or a panel of experts—of whom usually about half are lawyers—in the area relating to the dispute. To cover its costs, this nonprofit organization charges a fee, paid by the party filing the claim. In addition, each party to the dispute pays a price for each hearing day, as well as a special additional fee in cases involving personal injuries or property loss.

In addition to the AAA, hundreds of other state and local nonprofit organizations provide arbitration services. For example, the Arbitration Association of

Florida provides ADR services in that state. The Better Business Bureau offers ADR programs to aid in the resolution of certain types of disagreements. Many industries—including the insurance, automobile, and securities industries—also now have mediation or arbitration programs to facilitate timely and inexpensive settlement of claims.

FOR-PROFIT ORGANIZATIONS

Those who seek to settle their disputes quickly can turn to private, for-profit organizations to act as mediators or arbitrators. The leading firm in this private system of justice is JAMS/Endispute, which is based in Santa Ana, California. The private system of justice includes hundreds of firms throughout the country offering dispute-resolution services by hired judges.

Procedures in these private courts are fashioned to meet the desires of the clients seeking their services. For example, the parties might decide on the date of the hearing, the presiding judge, whether the judge's decision will be legally binding, and the site of the hearing—which could be a conference room, a law school office, or a leased courtroom complete with flag and Bible. The judges may follow procedures similar to those of the federal courts and use similar rules. Each party to the dispute may pay a filing fee and a designated fee for a half-day hearing session or a special, one-hour settlement conference.

CONCEPT SUMMARY 3.1	Alternative Dispute Resolution (ADR)	
TYPE OF ADR	**DESCRIPTION**
NEGOTIATION	The parties come together, with or without attorneys to represent them, and try to reach a settlement.
MEDIATION	The parties themselves reach an agreement with the help of a third party, called a mediator, who plays an active role in the dispute settlement. The mediator has discussions with the parties individually and jointly, assists the parties in evaluating their positions, and proposes possible solutions. Mediation is usually the preferred method of ADR in cases involving ongoing or long-term relationships.
ARBITRATION	In this more formal method of ADR, the parties submit their dispute to a neutral third party, the arbitrator, who renders a decision. The decision is binding unless the parties (or a court, in court-related arbitration) specify otherwise. Arbitration awards may be appealed to a court, but only in special circumstances (such as if the award is contrary to public policy) will a court set aside an arbitrator's award. If there is a question concerning the arbitrability of a certain type of claim, a court must decide the issue.

SECTION 6 | Online Dispute Resolution

An increasing number of companies and organizations are offering dispute-resolution services using the Internet. The settlement of disputes in these online forums is known as **online dispute resolution (ODR).** To date, the disputes resolved in these forums have most commonly involved disagreements over the rights to domain names (Web site addresses—see Chapter 14) and disagreements over the quality of goods sold via the Internet, including goods sold through Internet auction sites.

Currently, ODR may be best for resolving small- to medium-sized business liability claims, which may not be worth the expense of litigation or even traditional methods of alternative dispute resolution. Rules being developed in online forums, however, may ultimately become a code of conduct for everyone who does business in cyberspace. Most online forums do not automatically apply the law of any specific jurisdiction. Instead, results are often based on general, more universal legal principles. As with offline methods of dispute resolution, any party may appeal to a court at any time.

NEGOTIATION AND MEDIATION SERVICES

The online negotiation of a dispute is generally simpler and more practical than litigation. Typically, one party files a complaint, and the other party is notified by e-mail. Password-protected access is possible twenty-four hours a day, seven days a week. Fees are sometimes nominal and otherwise low (often 2 to 4 percent, or less, of the disputed amount).

Other Web-based firms, such as CyberSettle.com, Inc., offer online forums for negotiating monetary settlements. The parties to a dispute may agree to submit offers; if the offers fall within a previously agreed range, they will end the dispute, and the parties will split the difference. Special software keeps secret any offers that are not within the range. If there is no agreed-on range, typically an offer includes a deadline within which the other party must respond before the offer expires. The parties can drop the negotiations at any time.

Mediation providers are also resolving disputes online. SquareTrade, one of the mediation providers that has been used by eBay, the online auction site, mediates disputes involving $100 or more between eBay customers, for no charge. SquareTrade, which also resolves disputes among other parties, uses Web-based software that walks participants through a four-step e-resolution process. Negotiation between the parties occurs on a secure page within SquareTrade's Web site. If the parties prefer, they may consult a mediator. The entire process takes as little as ten to fourteen days, and there is no fee unless the parties use a mediator.

Arbitration Programs

There are a number of organizations and companies that offer online arbitration programs. The Internet Corporation for Assigned Names and Numbers (ICANN), a nonprofit corporation that the federal government set up to oversee the distribution of domain names, has issued special rules for the resolution of domain name disputes.[6] ICANN has also authorized several organizations to arbitrate domain name disputes in accordance with its rules. Additionally, the American Arbitration Association announced that it would be launching technology-based arbitration services as well.

Resolution Forum, Inc. (RFI), a nonprofit organization associated with the Center for Legal Responsibility at South Texas College of Law, offers arbitration services through its CAN-WIN conferencing system. Using standard browser software and an

RFI password, the parties to a dispute access an online conference room. When multiple parties are involved, private communications and breakout sessions are possible via private messaging facilities. RFI also offers mediation services.

The Virtual Magistrate Project (VMAG) is affiliated with the American Arbitration Association, Chicago-Kent College of Law, the Cyberspace Law Institute, the National Center for Automated Information Research, and other organizations. VMAG offers arbitration for disputes involving users of online systems; victims of wrongful messages, postings, and filings; and system operators subject to complaints or similar demands. VMAG also arbitrates intellectual property, personal property, real property, and tort disputes related to online contracts. VMAG attempts to resolve a dispute within seventy-two hours. The proceedings occur in a password-protected online newsgroup setting, and private e-mail among the participants is possible. A VMAG arbitrator's decision is issued in a written opinion. A party may appeal the outcome to a court.

SECTION 7 | International Dispute Resolution

Businesspersons who engage in international business transactions normally take special precautions to protect themselves in the event that a party with whom they are dealing in another country breaches an agreement. Often, parties to international contracts include special clauses in their contracts providing for how any disputes arising under the contracts will be resolved.

Forum-Selection and Choice-of-Law Clauses

Parties to international contracts often include *forum-selection clauses*. These clauses designate the jurisdiction (court or country) in which any dispute arising under the contract will be litigated and the nation's law that will be applied. Choice-of-law clauses, which were discussed earlier in this chapter, are also frequently included in international contracts. If no forum and choice-of-law clauses have been included in an international contract, however, legal proceedings will be more complex and attended by much more uncertainty. For example, litigation may take place in two or more countries, with each country applying its own national law to the particular transactions.

---

6. ICANN's Rules for Uniform Domain Name Dispute Resolution Policy are online at **http://www.icann.org/dndr/udrp/uniform-rules.htm**. Domain names will be discussed in more detail in Chapter 14, in the context of trademark law.

Furthermore, even if a plaintiff wins a favorable judgment in a lawsuit litigated in the plaintiff's country, there is no guarantee that the court's judgment will be enforced by judicial bodies in the defendant's country. As will be discussed in Chapter 8, for reasons of courtesy, the judgment may be enforced in the defendant's country, particularly if the defendant's country is the United States and the foreign court's decision is consistent with U.S. national law and policy. Other nations, however, may not be as accommodating as the United States, and the plaintiff may be left empty-handed.

ARBITRATION CLAUSES

In an attempt to prevent such problems, parties to international contracts often include arbitration clauses in their contracts, requiring that any contract disputes be decided by a neutral third party. In international arbitration proceedings, the third party may be a neutral entity (such as the International Chamber of Commerce), a panel of individuals representing both parties' interests, or some other group or organization. The United Nations Convention on the Recognition and Enforcement of Foreign Arbitral Awards[7]—which has been implemented in more than fifty countries, including the United States—assists in the enforcement of arbitration clauses, as do provisions in specific treaties among nations. The American Arbitration Association provides arbitration services for international as well as domestic disputes.

---

7. June 10, 1958, 21 U.S.T. 2517, T.I.A.S. No. 6997 (the "New York Convention").

REVIEWING ALTERNATIVE AND ONLINE DISPUTE RESOLUTION

Adrian Reese, a resident of New York, owned a strip mall located in Ohio, which he leased out to different businesses. The tenants in the building had complained that the two public restrooms were substandard and in need of repair. Reese therefore contracted with Lyle Copeland, a licensed contractor in Ohio, to remodel the bathrooms and fix the outdated plumbing. Copeland began the work on the date promised but progressed very slowly. Then, while ripping out the existing pipes, Copeland accidentally broke the main pipe, which caused flooding and water damage to the building. Several of the tenants immediately vacated the property after the incident. Reese claimed that Copeland was legally responsible for $300,000 in property damage because his actions were reckless and incompetent. Copeland maintained that it was an accident and refused to pay for the damage. Using the information presented in the chapter, answer the following questions.

1. | Under what circumstances would the parties decide to use negotiation to settle this dispute?

2. | In what way might the parties use mediation?

3. | Does the fact that the parties reside in different jurisdictions have any effect on whether they might try mediation or negotiation?

4. | Why would the parties wish to use some method of alternative dispute resolution (ADR) rather than filing a traditional lawsuit?

5. | Suppose that one of the parties rejects any attempt at using ADR and instead files a lawsuit in a federal district court. That court happens to require that this dispute be arbitrated prior to any trial on the matter. Explain whether this arbitration is likely to be legally binding on the parties.

TERMS AND CONCEPTS TO REVIEW

alternative dispute
    resolution (ADR) 65

arbitration 66

arbitrator 66

award 69

conciliation 65

early neutral case evaluation 65

mediation 66

mediator 66

mini-trial 65

negotiation 65

online dispute
    resolution (ODR) 78

submission 69

summary jury trial 77

QUESTIONS AND CASE PROBLEMS

3–1. In an arbitration proceeding, the arbitrator need not be a judge or even a lawyer. How, then, can the arbitrator's decision have the force of law and be binding on the parties involved?

3–2. QUESTION WITH SAMPLE ANSWER

Two private U.S. corporations enter into a joint-venture agreement to conduct mining operations in the newly formed Middle Eastern nation of Euphratia. As part of the agreement, the companies include an arbitration clause and a choice-of-law provision. The first states that any controversy arising out of the performance of the agreement will be settled by arbitration. The second states that the agreement is to be governed by the laws of the location of the venture, Euphratia. A dispute arises, and the parties discontinue operations. One of the parties claims sole ownership to the Euphratian mines and orders the other party to remove its equipment from the mines. The other party disputes the claim of sole ownership and seeks an order from a U.S. federal court compelling the parties to submit to arbitration over the ownership issue and alleged breaches of the joint-venture agreement. How should the court rule if the laws of Euphratia state that, whereas arbitration agreements are to be enforced generally, matters of ownership of natural resources can only be resolved in a Euphratian court of law? Does it matter that two U.S. companies engaged in international commerce would be governed by the Federal Arbitration Act?

For a sample answer to this question, go to Appendix I at the end of this text.

3–3. Two brothers, both of whom are certified public accountants (CPAs), form a professional association to provide tax-accounting services to the public. They also agree, in writing, that any disputes that arise between them over matters concerning the association will be submitted to an independent arbitrator, whom they designate to be their father, who is also a CPA. A dispute arises, and the matter is submitted to the father for arbitration. During the course of arbitration, which occurs over several weeks, the father asks the older brother, who is visiting one evening, to explain a certain entry in the brothers' association accounts. The younger brother learns of the discussion at the next meeting for arbitration; he says nothing about it, however. The arbitration is concluded in favor of the older brother, who seeks a court order compelling the younger brother to comply with the award. The younger brother seeks to set aside the award, claiming that the arbitration process was tainted by bias because "Dad always liked my older brother best." The younger brother also seeks to have the award set aside on the basis of improper conduct in that matters subject to arbitration were discussed between the father and older brother without the younger brother's being present. Should a court confirm the award or set it aside? Why?

3–4. After resolving their dispute, the two brothers encountered in Case Problem 3–3 decide to resume their tax-accounting practice according to the terms of their original agreement. Again a dispute arises, and again it is decided by the father (now retired except for numerous occasions on which he acts as an arbitrator) in favor of the older brother. The older brother files a petition to enforce the award. The younger brother seeks to set aside the award and offers evidence that the father, as arbitrator, made a gross error in calculating the accounts that were material to the dispute being arbitrated. If the court is convinced that the father erred in the calculations, should the award be set aside? Why?

3–5. CASE PROBLEM WITH SAMPLE ANSWER

In 1981, AT&T laid off seventy-nine workers in the Chicago area, purportedly because of a slowdown in economic activity. The Communications Workers of America, a union representing some AT&T workers, argued that there was no lack of work and objected to the layoffs as violations of the terms of a collective bargaining agreement between the union and AT&T. The agreement provided that "differences arising with respect to the interpretation of this contract or the performance of any obligation" under the agreement would be resolved through arbitration. The agreement reserved to AT&T the free exercise of managerial functions such as hiring and firing employees. The agreement conditioned such decision making on compliance with the terms of the contract but expressly excluded disputes over those decisions from arbitration. AT&T relied on this exclusion to avoid the union's demand for arbitration over the layoffs. The union sought a court order to compel arbitration. The court held that the issue of whether the dispute over the layoffs was subject to arbitration should be decided by the arbitrator and ordered the parties to submit the question to the arbitrator. An appellate court affirmed the holding, and AT&T appealed to the United States Supreme Court. How should the Court rule? Discuss fully. [*AT&T Technologies v. Communications Workers of America*, 475 U.S. 643, 106 S.Ct. 1415, 89 L.Ed.2d 648 (1990)]

To view a sample answer for this case problem, go to this book's Web site at http://wleb.westbuslaw.com, select "Chapter 3," and click on "Case Problem with Sample Answer."

3–6. ARBITRATION. Phillip Beaudry, who suffered from mental illness, worked in the Department of Income Maintenance for the state of Connecticut. Beaudry was fired from his job when it was learned that he had misappropriated approximately $1,640 in state funds. Beaudry filed a complaint with his union, Council 4 of the American Federation of State, County, and Municipal Employees (AFSCME), and eventually the dispute was submitted to an arbitrator. The arbitrator concluded that Beaudry had been dismissed without "just cause," because Beaudry's acts were caused by his mental illness and "were not willful or volitional or within his capacity to control." Because Beaudry was disabled, the employer was required, under state law, to transfer him to a position that he was competent to hold. The arbitrator awarded Beaudry reinstatement, back pay, seniority, and other benefits. The state appealed the decision to a court. What public policies must the court weigh in making its decision? How should the court rule? [*State v. Council 4, AFSCME*, 27 Conn.App. 635, 608 A.2d 718 (1992)]

3-7. ARBITRATION. Randall Fris worked as a seaman on an Exxon Shipping Co. oil tanker for eight years without incident. One night, he boarded the ship for duty while intoxicated, in violation of company policy. This policy also allowed Exxon to discharge employees who were intoxicated and thus unfit for work. Exxon discharged Fris. Under a contract with Fris's union, the discharge was submitted to arbitration. The arbitrators ordered Exxon to reinstate Fris on an oil tanker. Exxon filed a suit against the union, challenging the award as contrary to public policy, which opposes having intoxicated persons operate seagoing vessels. Can a court set aside an arbitration award on the ground that the award violates public policy? Should the court set aside the award in this case? Explain. [*Exxon Shipping Co. v. Exxon Seamen's Union*, 11 F.3d 1189 (3d Cir. 1993)]

3-8. ARBITRATION. Stephanie Prince was an employee of Coca-Cola Bottling Co. of New York, Inc. (CNY), and a member of the Soft Drink and Brewery Workers Union. An agreement between CNY and the Union set out a procedure to follow in the event of a dispute between an employee and CNY relating to "any matter whatsoever including, the meaning, interpretation, application or violation of this Agreement." In this context, the agreement mentioned some employment laws but did not mention federal discrimination laws. After the Union was notified, and if the grievance was not resolved within thirty days, the dispute was to be submitted to arbitration. Prince reported to the Union, which told CNY, that she was being sexually harassed by her supervisors, Michael Drake and Leonard Erlanger. When no action was taken and Prince was subject to retaliatory behavior by Drake and Erlanger, she filed a complaint with the Equal Employment Opportunity Commission. The supervisors retaliated again by ordering her to leave the workplace and "stay home." Prince filed a suit in a federal district court against CNY and the supervisors, alleging, among other things, violations of federal discrimination law. CNY responded that its agreement with the Union required Prince to submit her claim to arbitration. Is CNY right? In whose favor should the court rule? Why? [*Prince. v. Coca-Cola Bottling Co. of New York, Inc.*, 37 F.Supp.2d 289 (S.D.N.Y. 1999)]

3-9. ARBITRATOR'S AUTHORITY. In 1999, Michael Steinmetz agreed to buy espresso equipment and the training to use it from Malted Mousse, Inc. (MM), in Tacoma, Washington. Steinmetz gave MM a $5,000 deposit, but later believing that MM misrepresented the condition of the equipment and the extent of the training, he stopped payment on the check. MM filed a suit in a Washington state court against Steinmetz to recover the amount of the deposit. Under the rules of the court, the parties submitted their dispute to arbitration. The arbitrator issued an award in favor of Steinmetz, who asked for attorneys' fees on the basis of a state statute that required their award in cases involving less than $10,000. The arbitrator declared that the statute was unconstitutional and denied Steinmetz's request. Steinmetz appealed this denial to the court, arguing that the arbitrator exceeded his authority. Should the court reverse the arbitrator's award on the issue of the fees? Explain. [*Malted Mousse, Inc. v. Steinmetz*, 113 Wash.App. 157, 52 P.3d 555 (Div. 2, 2002)]

3-10. ARBITRATION. Alexander Little worked for Auto Stiegler, Inc., an automobile dealership in Los Angeles County, California, eventually becoming the service manager. While employed, Little signed an arbitration agreement that required the submission of all employment-related disputes to arbitration. The agreement also provided that any award over $50,000 could be appealed to a second arbitrator. Little was later demoted and terminated. Alleging that these actions were in retaliation for investigating and reporting warranty fraud and thus were in violation of public policy, Little filed a suit in a California state court against Auto Stiegler. The defendant filed a motion with the court to compel arbitration. Little responded that the arbitration agreement should not be enforced in part because the appeal provision was unfairly one sided. Is this provision enforceable? Should the court grant Auto Stiegler's motion? Why or why not? [*Little v. Auto Stiegler, Inc.*, 29 Cal.4th 1064, 63 P.3d 979, 130 Cal.Rptr.2d 892 (2003)]

3-11. A QUESTION OF ETHICS

Linda Bender, in her application for registration as a stockbroker with A. G. Edwards & Sons, Inc., agreed to submit any disputes with her employer to arbitration. Bender later sued her supervisor and employer (the defendants) for sexual harassment in violation of Title VII of the Civil Rights Act of 1964, which prohibits, among other things, employment discrimination based on gender. The defendants requested the court to compel arbitration. The district court judge denied the motion, holding that Bender could not be forced to waive her right to adjudicate Title VII claims in federal court. The appellate court reversed, ruling that Title VII claims are arbitrable. The court held that compelling Bender to submit her claim for arbitration did not deprive her of the right to a judicial forum, because if the arbitration proceedings were somehow legally deficient, she could still take her case to a federal court for review. [*Bender v. A. G. Edwards & Sons, Inc.*, 971 F.2d 698 (11th Cir. 1992)]

(a) Does the right to a postarbitration judicial forum equate to the right to initial access to a judicial forum in employment disputes? Should the defendants' request be granted? Why or why not?

(b) Should the fact that reviewing courts rarely set aside arbitrators' awards have any bearing on the arbitra-

bility of certain types of claims, such as those brought under Title VII?

LAW | on the Web

For updated links to resources available on the Web, as well as a variety of other materials, visit this text's Web site at http://wleb.westbuslaw.com.

For information on alternative dispute resolution, go to the American Arbitration Association's Web site at

http://www.adr.org

To learn more about online dispute resolution, go to the following Web sites:

http://www.mediate.com

http://cybersettle.com

http://SquareTrade.com

LEGAL RESEARCH EXERCISES ON THE WEB

Go to http://wleb.westbuslaw.com, the Web site that accompanies this text. Select "Chapter 3" and click on "Internet Exercises." There you will find the following Internet research exercises that you can perform to learn more about topics covered in this chapter.

Activity 3–1: **LEGAL PERSPECTIVE**
Alternative Dispute Resolution

Activity 3–2: **MANAGEMENT PERSPECTIVE**
Resolve a Dispute Online

CHAPTER 4
Ethics and Business Decision Making

During the early part of the 2000s, the American public was shocked as one business ethics scandal after another became headline news. Each scandal involved serious consequences. Certainly, those responsible for grossly inflating the reported profits at WorldCom, Inc., ended up not only destroying shareholder value in the company but also facing possible prison terms. Those officers and directors at Enron Corporation who utilized a system of complicated off-the-books transactions to inflate current earnings saw their company go bankrupt—the largest bankruptcy in U.S. history at that time. They harmed not only their employees and shareholders but also the communities in which they worked—and themselves (some of them were sentenced to prison). The misdeeds of officers and directors at Tyco International landed that company and its shareholders in similar trouble.

In response to the public's outrage over these scandals, Congress passed the Sarbanes-Oxley Act of 2002, which will be explained in more detail in Chapter 28. This act generally imposed various requirements on corporations in an effort to deter unethical behavior and encourage corporate accountability in the future. Nevertheless, new allegations of unethical business conduct continue to surface. For example, after the popular painkiller Vioxx was recalled in 2004 because of increased risk of heart attack and stroke, evidence surfaced that its maker, Merck & Company, knew about these dangers and allowed the drug to remain on the market. If these allegations are true, Merck's failure to recall the drug could potentially have adversely affected the health of thousands of patients—as well as exposing the company to years of litigation, investigations by the Justice Department and Congress, and a significant loss in market value.

Business ethics, the focus of this chapter, is not just theory. It is practical, useful, and essential. While a good understanding of the legal environment of business is critical, it is not enough. Understanding how one should act in her or his business dealings is equally—if not more—important in today's business arena.

SECTION 1 | Business Ethics

Before we look at business ethics, we need to discuss what is meant by ethics generally. **Ethics** can be defined as the study of what constitutes right or wrong behavior. It is the branch of philosophy that focuses on morality and the way in which moral principles are derived or the way in which a given set of moral principles applies to one's conduct in daily life. Ethics has to do with questions relating to the fairness, justness, rightness, or wrongness of an action. What is fair? What is just? What is the right thing to do in this situation? These are essentially ethical questions.

WHAT IS BUSINESS ETHICS?

Business ethics focuses on what constitutes right or wrong behavior in the business world and on how moral and ethical principles are applied by businesspersons to situations that arise in their daily activities in the workplace. Note that business ethics is not a separate kind of ethics. The ethical standards that guide our behavior as, say, mothers, fathers, or students apply equally well to our activities as businesspersons. Business decision makers, though, must often address more complex ethical issues and conflicts in the workplace than they face in their personal lives.

WHY IS BUSINESS ETHICS IMPORTANT?

Why is business ethics important? The answer to this question is clear from this chapter's introduction. An in-depth understanding of business ethics is important to the long-run viability of a corporation. A thorough knowledge of business ethics is also important to the well-being of the individual officers and directors of the corporation, as well as to the welfare of the firm's employees. Certainly, corporate decisions and activities can significantly affect not only those who own, operate, or work for the company but also such groups as suppliers, the community, and society as a whole.

Throughout this text you will be exposed to a series of ethical issues at the end of every unit. These special *Focus on Ethics* features allow you to examine and apply the various concepts of business ethics that we present in this chapter.

Note that questions concerning ethical and responsible behavior are not confined to the corporate context. Business ethics applies to *all* businesses, regardless of their organizational forms. In a business partnership, for example, partners owe a *fiduciary duty* (a duty of trust and loyalty) to each other and to their firm. This duty can sometimes conflict with what a partner sees as his or her own best interest. Partners who act solely in their own interests may violate their duties to the other partners and the firm, however. By violating this duty, they may end up paying steep penalties—as the following case illustrates.

CASE 4.1 — Time Warner Entertainment Co. v. Six Flags Over Georgia, L.L.C.

Georgia Court
of Appeals, 2002.
254 Ga.App. 598,
563 S.E.2d 178.

BACKGROUND AND FACTS *The Six Flags Over Georgia theme park in Atlanta, Georgia, was developed in 1967 as a limited partnership known as Six Flags Over Georgia, L.L.C. (Flags). The sole limited partner was Six Flags Fund, Limited (Fund). The general partner was Six Flags Over Georgia, Inc. (SFOG). In 1991, Time Warner Entertainment Company (TWE) became the majority shareholder of SFOG. The next year, TWE secretly bought 13.7 acres of land next to the park, limiting the park's expansion opportunities. Over the next couple of years, using confidential business information from the park, TWE began plans to develop a competing park. Meanwhile, TWE installed no major new attractions at the park, deferred basic maintenance, withheld financial information from Fund (the limited partner), and began signing future employment contracts with SFOG officers. TWE also charged Flags for unrelated expenses, including over $4 million for lunches in New York City and luxury automobiles for TWE officers. Flags and Fund filed a suit in a Georgia state court against TWE and SFOG, alleging, among other things, breach of fiduciary duty. A jury awarded the plaintiffs $197,296,000 in compensatory damages and $257,000,000 in punitive damages. TWE appealed to a state intermediate appellate court, alleging in part that the amount of the punitive damages was excessive.*

IN THE LANGUAGE OF THE COURT

ELLINGTON, Judge.

* * * *

We begin our analysis by examining the degree of reprehensibility [wrongfulness] of appellants' conduct in this case. *In examining the degree of reprehensibility of a defendant's conduct, [there are] a number of aggravating factors [to consider], including whether the harm was more than purely economic in nature, and whether the defendant's behavior evinced indifference to or reckless disregard for the health and safety of others.* Here, although the harm to Flags and Fund was primarily economic, it was caused by conduct we find especially reprehensible. Appellants' intentional breach of its fiduciary duty revealed a callous indifference to the financial well-being of its limited partners and their individual investors. [Emphasis added.]

* * * [T]he evidence [presented] supported the jury's conclusion that appellants acted in concert to breach SFOG's fiduciary duty to its business partners. * * * [T]his evidence clearly and convincingly supported an award of punitive damages * * * because the evidence showed that the appellants withheld vital business information from Fund and Flags, undertook to compete with them, took money belonging to them, and carried out a plan to depress the value of their investment, the Six Flags Over Georgia Park. Moreover, the jury found a specific intent to cause harm * * * .

CONTINUED ▶

CASE 4.1 | Continued

Appellants' conduct toward its partners and those who invested in the limited partnership was part of a premeditated plan surreptitiously [secretly] executed over a period of years. Appellants' conduct was deceitful, self-serving, and financially damaging. More importantly, however, appellants' conduct was a breach of fiduciary duty, a violation of a confidential relationship of trust requiring the utmost in good faith. * * * Appellants' conduct was, in short, the kind of behavior we find deserving of reproof [disapproval], rebuke, or censure; blameworthy—the very definition of reprehensible. * * * *Trickery and deceit are reprehensible wrongs, especially when done intentionally through affirmative acts of misconduct.* * * * [Emphasis added.]

* * * *

In this case, the ratio of compensatory to punitive damages is 1 to 1.3. We see no shocking disparity inherent in this figure. Nor does it appear to approach that fuzzy line suggesting the bounds of constitutional impropriety. More importantly, however, given the amount of intentional economic damage inflicted by the appellants, corporate entities with collective assets measured in billions of dollars, we believe the award of punitive damages was reasonably calculated to punish them and to deter such conduct in the future.

DECISION AND REMEDY *The state intermediate appellate court affirmed the judgment of the lower court, finding that the award of punitive damages was not excessive, considering the defendants' financial status and "reprehensible" conduct toward the plaintiffs.*

WHAT IF THE FACTS WERE DIFFERENT? *If TWE had proceeded with its plans to build a competing park but had not otherwise acted "reprehensibly" with regard to Flags and Fund, how might the decision in this case have been different?*

SECTION 2 | Setting the Right Ethical Tone

Many unethical business decisions are made simply because they *can* be made. In other words, the decision makers not only have the opportunity to make such decisions but also are not too concerned about being seriously sanctioned for their unethical actions. Perhaps one of the most difficult challenges for business leaders today is to create the right "ethical tone" in their workplaces so as to deter unethical conduct.

THE IMPORTANCE OF ETHICAL LEADERSHIP

Talking about ethical business decision making means nothing if management does not set standards. Moreover, managers must apply those standards to themselves and to the employees in the company.

ATTITUDE OF TOP MANAGEMENT One of the most important factors in creating and maintaining an ethical workplace is the attitude of top management. Managers who are not totally committed to maintaining an ethical workplace will rarely succeed in creating one. Surveys of business executives indicate that management's behavior, more than anything else, sets the ethical tone of a firm. In other words, employees take their cues from management. If a firm's managers adhere to obvious ethical norms in their business dealings, employees will likely follow their lead. In contrast, if managers act unethically, employees will see no reason to behave any differently. For example, an employee who observes a manager cheating on her expense account quickly learns that such behavior is acceptable.

Managers can also reduce the probability that employees will act unethically by setting realistic production or sales goals. If a sales quota, for example, can be met only through high-pressure, unethical sales tactics, employees trying to act "in the best interests of the firm" may think that management is implicitly asking them to behave unethically.

LOOKING THE OTHER WAY A manager who looks the other way when she or he knows about an employee's unethical behavior also sets an example—one indicating that ethical transgressions will be accepted. Managers must show that they will not tolerate unethical business behavior. Although this may seem harsh, managers have found that discharging even one employee for ethical reasons has a tremendous impact as a deterrent to unethical behavior in the workplace. The following case illustrates what can happen when managers look the other way.

CASE 4.2

United States District Court, District of Alaska, 2004. 296 F.Supp.2d 1071.

In re the *Exxon Valdez*

HOLLAND, District Judge.

* * * *

* * * On Good Friday, March 24, 1989, the oil tanker *Exxon Valdez* was run aground on Bligh Reef in Prince William Sound, Alaska.

On March 24, 1989, * * * Joseph Hazelwood was in command of the *Exxon Valdez*. * * *

* * * *

Defendant Exxon Shipping [Company] owned the *Exxon Valdez*. Exxon employed Captain Hazelwood, and kept him employed knowing that he had an alcohol problem. The captain had supposedly been rehabilitated, but Exxon knew better before March 24, 1989. Hazelwood had sought treatment for alcohol abuse in 1985 but had "fallen off the wagon" by the spring of 1986. * * * Yet, Exxon continued to allow Hazelwood to command a supertanker carrying a hazardous cargo. Because Exxon did nothing despite its knowledge that Hazelwood was once again drinking, Captain Hazelwood was *the* person in charge of a vessel as long as three football fields and carrying 53 million gallons of crude oil. * * *

* * * *

The best available estimate of the crude oil lost from the *Exxon Valdez* into Prince William Sound is about 11 million gallons. * * *

* * * Commercial fisheries throughout this area were totally disrupted, with entire fisheries being closed for the 1989 season. * * * Subsistence fishing by residents of Prince William Sound and Lower Cook Inlet villages was also disrupted. * * * Shore-based businesses dependent upon the fishing industry were also disrupted as were the resources of cities such as Cordova.

* * * Exxon undertook a massive cleanup effort. Approximately $2.1 billion was ultimately spent in efforts to remove the spilled crude oil from the waters and beaches of Prince William Sound, Lower Cook Inlet, and Kodiak Island. Also * * * , Exxon undertook a voluntary claims program, ultimately paying out $303 million, principally to fishermen whose livelihood was disrupted * * * .

* * * *

[Lawsuits] (involving thousands of plaintiffs) were ultimately * * * consolidated into this case. * * *

* * * *

* * * The jury awarded a breathtaking $5 billion in punitive damages against * * * Exxon * * * .

* * * *

Exxon appealed * * * the amount of punitive damages [to the U.S. Court of Appeals for the Ninth Circuit]. * * *

* * * *

* * * [T]he Ninth Circuit Court of Appeals in this case reiterated the * * * guideposts * * * for use in determining whether punitive damages are * * * grossly excessive [including] * * * the reprehensibility of the defendant's conduct * * * . The court of appeals remanded the case [and] * * * unequivocally told this court that "[t]he $5 billion punitive damages award is too high * * * " and "[i]t must be reduced."

CONTINUED ▶

CASE 4.2 | Continued

* * * *

* * * [T]he question before us is whether, under the circumstances of this case, an award of $5 billion in punitive damages is grossly excessive * * * .

* * * *

* * * [T]he reprehensibility of the defendant's conduct is the most important *indicium* [indication] of the reasonableness of a punitive damages award * * * . In determining whether a defendant's conduct is reprehensible, the court considers whether:

> the harm caused was physical as opposed to economic; the tortious conduct evinced an indifference to or a reckless disregard of the health or safety of others; the target of the conduct had financial vulnerability; the conduct involved repeated actions or was an isolated incident; and the harm was the result of intentional malice, trickery, or deceit, or mere accident. * * *

* * * *

The reprehensibility of a party's conduct, like truth and beauty, is subjective. One's view of the quality of an actor's conduct is the result of complex value judgments. The evaluation of a victim will vary considerably from that of a person not affected by an incident. Courts employ disinterested, unaffected lay jurors in the first instance to appraise the reprehensibility of a defendant's conduct. Here, the jury heard about what Exxon knew, and what its officers did and what they failed to do. Knowing what Exxon knew and did through its officers, the jury concluded that Exxon's conduct was highly reprehensible.

* * * *

* * * *Punitive damages should reflect the enormity of the defendant's offense.* * * * Exxon's conduct did not simply cause economic harm to the plaintiffs. Exxon's decision to leave Captain Hazelwood in command of the *Exxon Valdez* demonstrated reckless disregard for a broad range of legitimate Alaska concerns: the livelihood, health, and safety of the residents of Prince William Sound, the crew of the *Exxon Valdez*, and others. Exxon's conduct targeted some financially vulnerable individuals, namely subsistence fishermen. Plaintiffs' harm was not the result of an isolated incident but was the result of Exxon's repeated decisions, over a period of approximately three years, to allow Captain Hazelwood to remain in command despite Exxon's knowledge that he was drinking and driving again. Exxon's bad conduct as to Captain Hazelwood and his operation of the *Exxon Valdez* was intentionally malicious. [Emphasis added.]

* * * Exxon's conduct was many degrees of magnitude more egregious [flagrant] [than defendant's conduct in other cases]. For approximately three years, Exxon management, with knowledge that Captain Hazelwood had fallen off the wagon, willfully permitted him to operate a fully loaded crude oil tanker in and out of Prince William Sound—a body of water which Exxon knew to be highly valuable for its fisheries resources. Exxon's argument that its conduct in permitting a relapsed alcoholic to operate an oil tanker should be characterized as less reprehensible than [in other cases] suggests that Exxon, even today, has not come to grips with the opprobrium [disgracefulness] which society rightly attaches to drunk driving. * * * Based on the foregoing, the court finds Exxon's conduct highly reprehensible.

* * * *

* * * [T]he court reduces the punitive damages award to $4.5 billion as the means of resolving the conflict between its conclusion and the directions of the court of appeals.

* * * *

* * * [T]here is no just reason to delay entry of a final judgment in this case. The court's judgment as to the $4.5 billion punitive damages award is deemed final * * * .

QUESTIONS

1. What might Exxon have done to avoid the tragic consequences in this case?
2. Are there situations in which a business's conduct would be more reprehensible than Exxon's behavior in this case? Explain.

PERIODIC EVALUATION Some companies require their managers to meet individually with employees and to grade them on their ethical (or unethical) behavior. One company, for example, asks its employees to fill out ethical checklists each week and return them to their supervisors. This practice serves two purposes: First, it demonstrates to employees that ethics matters. Second, employees have an opportunity to reflect on how well they have measured up in terms of ethical performance.

CREATING ETHICAL CODES OF CONDUCT

One of the most effective ways to set a tone of ethical behavior within an organization is to create an ethical code of conduct. A well-written code of ethics explicitly states a company's ethical priorities and demonstrates the company's commitment to ethical behavior. The code should set forth guidelines for ethical conduct, establish procedures that employees can follow if they have questions or complaints, and inform employees why these ethics policies are important to the company. A well-written code also might provide appropriate examples to clarify what the company considers to be acceptable and unacceptable conduct.

COSTCO—AN EXAMPLE Within this chapter is a pull-out exhibit showing a code of ethics created by Costco Wholesale Corporation, a large warehouse-club retailer with over 35 million members. This code of conduct indicates Costco's commitment to legal compliance, as well as to the welfare of its members (those who purchase its goods), its employees, and its suppliers. The code also details some specific ways in which the interests and welfare of these different groups will be protected. If you look closely at this exhibit, you will also see that Costco acknowledges that by protecting these groups' interests, it will realize its "ultimate goal"—rewarding its shareholders with maximum shareholder value.

PROVIDING ETHICS TRAINING TO EMPLOYEES For an ethical code to be effective, its provisions must be clearly communicated to employees. Most large companies have implemented ethics training programs, in which management discusses with employees on a face-to-face basis the firm's policies and the importance of ethical conduct. Some firms hold periodic ethics seminars during which employees can openly discuss any ethical problems that they may be experiencing and learn how the firm's ethical policies apply to those specific problems. Smaller firms should also offer some form of ethics training to employees, because this is one factor that courts will consider if the firm is later accused of an ethics violation.

JOHNSON & JOHNSON—AN EXAMPLE OF WEB-BASED ETHICS TRAINING Creating a code of conduct and implementing it are two different activities. In many companies, codes of conduct are simply documents that have very little relevance to day-to-day operations. When Johnson & Johnson wanted to "do better" than other companies with respect to ethical business decision making, it created a Center for Legal and Credo Awareness. (Its code of ethical conduct is called its credo.)

The center created a Web-based set of instructions designed to enhance the corporation's efforts to train employees in the importance of its code of conduct. Given that Johnson & Johnson has over 110,000 employees in fifty-seven countries around the world, reinforcing its code of conduct and its values has not been easy, but Web-based training has helped. The company established a Web-based legal and compliance center, which consists of a set of interactive modules to train employees in areas of law and ethics. The curriculum is tailored to the individual employee based on his or her activities and job responsibilities. Moreover, employees can participate in the training right from their desks whenever they have the time, and the company can track the employees' progress. The Web-based courses are then integrated into an ethical training program that also involves face-to-face classes. This comprehensive program has contributed to Johnson & Johnson's receiving an award from the *Wall Street Journal* for having the best corporate reputation in America.

CORPORATE COMPLIANCE PROGRAMS

In large corporations, ethical codes of conduct are usually just one part of a comprehensive corporate compliance program. Other components of such a program, some of which were already mentioned, include a corporation's ethics committee, ethical training programs, and internal audits to monitor compliance with applicable laws and the company's standards of ethical conduct.

THE SARBANES-OXLEY ACT AND WEB-BASED REPORTING SYSTEMS   The Sarbanes-Oxley Act of 2002[1] requires that companies set up confidential systems so that employees and others may "raise red flags" about suspected illegal or unethical auditing and accounting practices. The act required publicly traded companies to have such systems in place by April 2003.

Some companies have created online reporting systems to accomplish this goal. In one such system, employees can click on an icon on their computers that anonymously links them with Ethicspoint, an organization based in Vancouver, Washington. Through Ethicspoint, employees may report suspicious accounting practices, sexual harassment, and other possibly unethical behavior. Ethicspoint, in turn, alerts management personnel or the audit committee at the designated company to the potential problem. Those who have used the system say that it is less inhibiting than calling a company's toll-free number.

CORPORATE GOVERNANCE PRINCIPLES   Implementation of the Sarbanes-Oxley Act has prompted many companies to create new rules of *corporate governance*. Corporate governance refers to the inter-

nal principles establishing the rights and responsibilities of a corporation's management, board of directors, shareholders, and *stakeholders* (those affected by corporate decisions, including employees, customers, suppliers, and creditors, for example). Corporate governance principles usually go beyond what is required to comply with existing laws. The goal is to set up a system of fair procedures and accurate disclosures that keeps all parties well informed and accountable to one another and provides a mechanism for the corporation to resolve any problems that arise.

COMPLIANCE PROGRAMS MUST BE INTEGRATED   To be effective, a corporate compliance program must be integrated throughout the firm. For large corporations, ethical policies and programs need to be coordinated and monitored by a committee that is separate from the various corporate departments. Otherwise, unethical behavior in one department can easily escape the attention of those in control of the corporation or the corporate officials responsible for implementing and monitoring the company's compliance program.

The following case illustrates what happens when ethical behavior is not practiced in a corporate setting and how such occurrences might be avoided through the widespread implementation of ethics policies and programs.

---

1. H.R. 3762. This act became effective on August 29, 2002.

United States
District Court,
Southern District
of New York, 2003.
273 F.Supp.2d 431.

CASE 4.3   Securities and Exchange Commission v. WorldCom, Inc.

BACKGROUND AND FACTS   *Corporate officers and others supposedly acting on behalf of WorldCom, Inc., committed perhaps the largest accounting fraud in history. The loss to WorldCom's shareholders alone is estimated to be as much as $100 billion. At the time of this writing, the individuals who allegedly perpetrated the fraud have been charged with crimes or are being investigated by the U.S. Department of Justice. WorldCom's creditors are seeking repayment in a federal bankruptcy court. Shareholders and employees have filed suits in federal district courts to recover what they can. Meanwhile, in another suit, the Securities and Exchange Commission (the Commission), which enforces federal securities laws (see Chapter 28), sought something different:*

—not just to clean house but to put the company on a new and positive footing;
—not just to enjoin future violations but to create models of corporate governance and internal compliance for this and other companies to follow;
*—not just to impose penalties but to help stabilize and reorganize the company and thereby help preserve more than 50,000 jobs * * * .*

With these goals in mind, the Commission and the company's new management submitted to the court for its approval an agreement for the payment of a penalty of $750 million—seventy-five times greater than any previous such penalty.

IN THE LANGUAGE OF THE COURT

RAKOFF, District Judge.
      This case raises fundamental questions about how market regulators, and the courts, should respond when criminals use the vehicle of a public company to commit a massive fraud. While the persons who perpetrated the fraud can be criminally prose-

CASE 4.3 | Continued

cuted, the exposure of the fraud often creates * * * pressures that can drive the company into bankruptcy, leaving * * * creditors with little and shareholders with nothing. Innocent employees may find their jobs in jeopardy, and, if the company is very large, entire segments of the market may be disrupted. In a situation where immense financial suffering is therefore likely, is there nothing government regulators can do to restore equilibrium?

* * * *

The first step in this journey, taken at the very outset of the litigation, was the joint decision of the parties to have the Court appoint a Corporate Monitor to oversee the proposed transformation. * * *

Under the Corporate Monitor's watchful eye, the company has replaced its entire board of directors, hired a new and dynamic chief executive officer and begun recruiting other senior managers from without, fired or accepted the resignation of every employee accused * * * of having participated in the fraud, and terminated even those employees who, while not accused of personal misconduct, are alleged to have been insufficiently attentive in preventing the fraud. In this connection, the company has already spent more than $50 million of its own money to fund unrestricted investigations * * * , and their detailed reports have been given wide publicity.

The company has also consented to a permanent injunction authorizing the Corporate Monitor to undertake a complete overhaul of the company's corporate governance and authorizing a group of highly qualified independent consultants to ascertain that the company has fully eliminated the many defects in the company's internal controls detected after a comprehensive review by the company's new outside auditors. The new corporate governance strictures will, among much else, mandate an active, informed, and highly independent board, prohibit related-party transactions and conflicts of interest, require a unique shareholder role in the nomination of directors, and impose significant restrictions on executive compensation packages. Moreover, even though not all of the specific changes in corporate governance and internal controls have yet been formulated, the company has committed in advance to adopt and adhere to all corporate governance and internal control recommendations made by the Corporate Monitor and the independent consultants, subject only to appeal to this Court. * * *

The permanent injunction also requires the company to provide a large segment of its employees with specialized training in accounting principles, public reporting obligations, and business ethics, in accordance with programs being specially developed for the company by New York University and the University of Virginia. At the behest of the Corporate Monitor, the Court also obtained from the new Chief Executive Officer a sworn "Ethics Pledge," requiring, on pain of dismissal, a degree of transparency well beyond [the Commission's] requirements. The company has since required its senior management to sign a similar pledge, and has plans to obtain similar pledges from virtually all employees.

The Court is aware of no large company accused of fraud that has so rapidly and so completely divorced itself from the misdeeds of the immediate past and undertaken such extraordinary steps to prevent such misdeeds in the future. While the Court, at the parties' express request, will continue to retain jurisdiction for however long it takes to make certain that these new controls and procedures are fully implemented and secured, the Court is satisfied that the steps already taken have gone a very long way toward making the company a good corporate citizen.

* * * *

[With respect to the agreement] *the Court is satisfied that the Commission has carefully reviewed all relevant considerations and has arrived at a penalty that, while taking adequate account of the magnitude of the fraud and the need for punishment and deterrence, fairly and reasonably reflects the realities of this complex situation.* Undoubtedly the settlement will be criticized by, among others, those shareholders unfamiliar with the severe limits imposed on their recovery by the bankruptcy laws, those competitors whose own self-interest blinds them to the broader range of public policies that such a settlement implicates, and those professed pundits [commentators] and ideologues for whom anything less than a corporate death penalty constitutes an "outrage." But the Court is convinced, for the reasons already outlined above, that the proposed settlement is not only fair and reasonable but as good an outcome as anyone could reasonably expect in these difficult circumstances. [Emphasis added.]

CONTINUED ▶

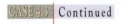 Continued **DECISION AND REMEDY** *The court approved the agreement between the company's new management and the Securities and Exchange Commission to settle the "monetary penalty phase of this litigation" and issued a judgment to that effect. The parties agreed to pay $500 million in cash and $250 million in the company's new stock to be distributed to "qualifying claimants" (creditors).*

CONFLICTS AND TRADE-OFFS

Management constantly faces ethical trade-offs, some of which may lead to legal problems. As mentioned earlier, firms have implied ethical (and legal) duties to a number of groups, including shareholders and employees.

When a company decides to reduce costs by downsizing and restructuring, the decision may benefit shareholders, but it will harm those employees who are laid off or fired. When downsizing occurs, which employees should be laid off first? Cost-cutting considerations might dictate firing the most senior employees, who generally have higher salaries, and retaining less senior employees, whose salaries are much lower. A company does not necessarily act illegally when it does so. Yet the decision to be made by management clearly involves an important ethical question: Which group's interests—those of the shareholders or those of employees who have been loyal to the firm for a long period of time—should take priority in this situation?

In one case, for example, an employer facing a dwindling market and decreasing sales decided to reduce its costs by eliminating some of its obligations to its employees. The company established a subsidiary corporation that it expected to fail and transferred a number of its employees, and the administration of their retirement benefits, to that entity. When the subsidiary failed, several individuals who were left without retirement benefits sued the company for breaching its fiduciary duty under a federal law governing employer-provided pensions. Ultimately, the United States Supreme Court agreed with the plaintiffs, reasoning that "[l]ying is inconsistent with the duty of loyalty owed by all fiduciaries."[2]

SECTION 3 | Companies That Defy the Rules

One of the best ways to learn the ethical responsibilities inherent in operating a business is to look at the mistakes made by other companies. In the following

subsections, we describe some of the ethical failures of companies that have raised public awareness of corporate misconduct and highlighted the need for ethical leadership in business.

ENRON'S GROWTH AND DEMISE IN A NUTSHELL

The Enron Corporation was one of the first companies to benefit from the deregulated electricity market. By 1998, Enron was the largest energy trader in the market. When competition in energy trading increased, Enron diversified into water, power plants, and eventually high-speed Internet and fiber optics (the value of which soon became negligible). Because Enron's managers received bonuses based on whether they met earnings goals, they had an incentive to inflate the anticipated earnings on energy contracts, which they did. Enron included these anticipated earnings in its current earnings profits reports, which vastly overstated the company's actual profit. Then, to artificially maintain and even increase its reported earnings, Enron created a complex network of subsidiaries that enabled it to move losses to its subsidiaries and hide its debts.

The overall effect of these actions was to increase Enron's apparent net worth. These "off-the-books" transactions were also frequently carried out in the Cayman Islands to avoid paying federal income taxes. In addition, Enron's chief executive officer engaged in a pattern of self-dealing by doing business with companies owned by his son and daughter. Enron's management was informed about these incidents of misconduct on numerous occasions, yet the company concealed the financial improprieties for several years—until Enron was bankrupt.

THE ENRON LEGACY

Deceptive accounting practices were at the heart of the Enron debacle, which led to one of the largest bankruptcies in the history of U.S. business. For years to come, the Enron scandal will remain a symbol of the cost of unethical behavior to management, employees, suppliers, shareholders, the community, society, and indeed the world. Enron's shareholders

---

2. *Varity Corp. v. Howe,* 516 U.S. 489, 116 S.Ct. 1065, 134 L.Ed.2d 130 (1996).

lost $62 billion of value in a very short period of time in the early 2000s as a result of management's deceptive accounting practices, conflicts of interest, and deviation from accepted ethical standards of business.

MERCK & COMPANY— A BRIEF HISTORY OF VIOXX

In 1999, Merck & Company, Inc., the maker of Vioxx, received approval from the U.S. Food and Drug Administration (FDA) to market Vioxx as a painkiller. The FDA gave Vioxx a six-month priority review because it was thought that Vioxx caused fewer gastrointestinal side effects, such as bleeding, than other painkillers (including ibuprofen and aspirin). Merck spent millions of dollars persuading physicians and consumers to use Vioxx for pain, especially arthritis pain, instead of less expensive alternatives, which could cause stomach bleeding. Many people who used Vioxx found that it provided more effective short-term relief for pain, particularly from athletic injuries, than any other painkiller on the market at the time. At its peak, Vioxx had more than 20 million users.

Shortly after the drug's debut, however, troubling signs began to appear. In March 2000, Merck reported the results of a study of eight thousand people who had used Vioxx. The study compared the gastrointestinal effects of Vioxx to naproxen, another popular painkiller. Although the study ultimately found that patients taking Vioxx had less stomach bleeding than those taking naproxen, the study also indicated that patients taking Vioxx for eight months or longer had up to four times as many heart attacks and strokes as patients using naproxen. These results occurred even though the study had excluded patients with heart disease risks.

Independent studies of the drug—conducted in 2001, 2002, and 2004—all suggested correlations between Vioxx and increased risk of heart attack. Finally, Merck's own study revealed that Vioxx increased cardiovascular risks after eighteen months of daily use. Shortly after that, in September 2004, Merck voluntarily removed Vioxx from the worldwide market in the largest drug recall in history.

MERCK'S AWARENESS OF THE RISKS OF VIOXX

As mentioned, the initial 2000 study on Vioxx and naproxen showed that patients taking Vioxx for an extended period had up to four times as many heart attacks and strokes as those who took naproxen.

Because the drug was often prescribed on a long-term basis for arthritis patients, this was a significant finding. Merck attributed the result to naproxen's strong protective effect on the heart. Merck never tested this theory, however, and scientists outside the company who found this explanation unlikely began to conduct independent studies of the drug.

In 2001, a cardiologist proposed to Merck a study of Vioxx in patients with severe chest pain, but Merck declined. When a 2002 study found that patients who took high doses of Vioxx had significantly more heart attacks and strokes than similar patients, Merck stated that it still had confidence in the drug's safety. Merck maintained this stance even after receiving a warning letter from the FDA in 2001 reprimanding the company for minimizing the drug's potentially serious cardiovascular effects. The FDA required Merck to send letters to physicians across the country to correct false or misleading impressions and information.

MERCK'S CHOICE

In May 2000, Merck's top research and marketing executives met to consider ways to defend Vioxx against allegations that it posed cardiovascular risks. One suggestion was to develop a study that would directly test whether Vioxx posed these risks. That idea was rejected. Merck's marketing executives were apparently afraid that conducting a study would send the wrong signal about the company's faith in Vioxx. The company's position over the following years stayed the same: Vioxx was safe unless proved otherwise. In August 2005, Merck lost its first Vioxx lawsuit, in which the jury awarded $253 million (reduced to $25 million due to Texas's cap on punitive damages) to Carol Ernst, widow of Robert Ernst. Numerous other state and federal suits against the company had already been filed by that time.

THE DEBATE CONTINUES

The debate over the safety of Vioxx and whether Merck's conduct was ethical poses an interesting question—at what point does a corporation have an ethical duty to act when presented with evidence that its product may be harmful? Various studies estimate that as many as 139,000 people who used Vioxx suffered injury or death. This figure may seem large, but it accounts for less than 1 percent of Vioxx's total users. Some would argue that even one death is too many and that Merck should be responsible for compensating all those who were injured. Others would counter that there are risks involved in the use of any drug and that Merck did nothing wrong by waiting for conclusive evidence of harm before recalling Vioxx. It is likely that the outcome of the hundreds of lawsuits that have already been filed—which could ultimately cost Merck up to $18 billion in damages—and the litigation still to come will decide whether Merck's conduct was ethical. What is clear is that Merck's shareholders lost billions of dollars in value after the company recalled Vioxx and suspicions arose about Merck's conduct.

Shortly after Vioxx was recalled in 2004, questions were posed about the safety of two other drugs—Celebrex and Bextra—in the same class, called COX-2 inhibitors, which were made by different companies and competed with Vioxx. Concerns over drug safety, unethical practices by pharmaceutical companies, and mass consumer advertising of new medications have prompted many to criticize the FDA and recommend an overhaul of its drug-approval system. Even if the FDA eventually adopts revised procedures, however, questions remain over what exactly a corporation must do to fulfill its ethical duties with regard to notifying the public about the potential risks of using a product.

SECTION 4 | Business Ethics and the Law

Today, legal compliance is normally regarded as a **moral minimum**—the minimum acceptable standard for ethical business behavior. Had Enron Corporation strictly complied with existing laws and generally accepted accounting practices, very likely the Enron scandal, which came to light in the early 2000s, would never have happened. Simply obeying the law does not fulfill all business ethics obligations, however, as illustrated by the controversy surrounding the safety of the drug Vioxx. In the interest of preserving personal freedom, as well as for practical reasons, the law does not—and cannot—codify all ethical requirements. No law says, for example, that it is illegal to lie to one's family, but it may be unethical to do so.

It may seem that determining the legality of a given action should be simple. Either something is legal or it is not. In fact, one of the major challenges businesspersons face is that the legality of a particular action is not always clear. In part, this is because there are so many laws regulating business that it is possible

to violate one of them without realizing it. The law also contains numerous "gray areas," making it difficult to predict with certainty how a court will apply a given law to a particular action.

LAWS REGULATING BUSINESS

Today's business firms are subject to extensive government regulation. As mentioned in Chapter 1, virtually every action a firm undertakes—from the initial act of going into business, to hiring and firing personnel, to selling products in the marketplace—is subject to statutory law and to numerous rules and regulations issued by administrative agencies. Furthermore, these rules and regulations are changed or supplemented frequently.

Determining whether a planned action is legal thus requires that decision makers keep abreast of the law. Normally, large business firms have attorneys on their staffs to assist them in making key decisions. Small firms must also seek legal advice before making important business decisions because the consequences of just one violation of a regulatory rule may be costly.

Ignorance of the law will not excuse a business owner or manager from liability for violating a statute or regulation. In one case, for example, the court imposed criminal fines, as well as imprisonment, on a company's supervisory employee for violating a federal environmental act—even though the employee was completely unaware of what was required under the provisions of that act.[3]

"GRAY AREAS" IN THE LAW

In many situations, business firms can predict with a fair amount of certainty whether a given action would be legal. For example, firing an employee solely because of that person's race or gender would clearly violate federal laws prohibiting employment discrimination. In some situations, though, the legality of a particular action may be less clear.

For example, suppose that a firm decides to launch a new advertising campaign. How far can the firm go in making claims for its products or services? Federal and state laws prohibit firms from engaging in "deceptive advertising." At the federal level, the test for deceptive advertising normally used by the Federal Trade Commission is whether an advertising claim

---

3. *United States v. Hanousek*, 176 F.3d 1116 (9th Cir. 1999).

would deceive a "reasonable consumer."[4] At what point, though, would a reasonable consumer be deceived by a particular ad?

In addition, many rules of law require a court to determine what is "foreseeable" or "reasonable" in a particular situation. Because a business has no way of predicting how a specific court will decide these issues, decision makers need to proceed with caution and evaluate an action and its consequences from an ethical perspective. The same problem often occurs in cases involving the Internet when it is often unclear how a court will apply existing laws in the context of cyberspace. Generally, if a company can demonstrate that it acted in good faith and responsibly in the circumstances, it has a better chance of successfully defending its action in court or before an administrative law judge.

SECTION 5 | Approaches to Ethical Reasoning

Each individual, when faced with a particular ethical dilemma, engages in **ethical reasoning**—that is, a reasoning process in which the individual examines the situation at hand in light of her or his moral convictions or ethical standards. Businesspersons do likewise when making decisions with ethical implications.

How do business decision makers decide whether a given action is the "right" one for their firms? What ethical standards should be applied? Broadly speaking, ethical reasoning relating to business traditionally has been characterized by two fundamental approaches. One approach defines ethical behavior in terms of duty, which also implies certain rights. The other approach determines what is ethical in terms of the consequences, or outcome, of any given action. We examine each of these approaches here.

DUTY-BASED ETHICS

Duty-based ethical standards often are derived from revealed truths, such as religious precepts. They can also be derived through philosophical reasoning.

RELIGIOUS ETHICAL STANDARDS In the Judeo-Christian tradition, which is the dominant religious tradition in the United States, the Ten Commandments

of the Old Testament establish fundamental rules for moral action. Other religions have their own sources of revealed truth. Religious rules generally are absolute with respect to the behavior of their adherents. For example, the commandment "Thou shalt not steal" is an absolute mandate for a person who believes that the Ten Commandments reflect revealed truth. Even a benevolent motive for stealing (such as Robin Hood's) cannot justify the act because the act itself is inherently immoral and thus wrong.

Ethical standards based on religious teachings also involve an element of *compassion*. Therefore, for example, even though it might be profitable for a firm to lay off a less productive employee, if that employee's family would suffer as a result, a religious person might give this potential suffering substantial weight. Compassionate treatment of others is also mandated to some extent by the "Golden Rule" ("Do unto others as you would have them do unto you"), which most religions follow.

KANTIAN ETHICS Duty-based ethical standards may also be derived solely from philosophical reasoning. The German philosopher Immanuel Kant (1724–1804), for example, identified some general guiding principles for moral behavior based on what he believed to be the fundamental nature of human beings. Kant believed that human beings are qualitatively different from other physical objects and are endowed with moral integrity and the capacity to reason and conduct their affairs rationally. Therefore, a person's thoughts and actions should be respected. When human beings are treated merely as a means to an end, they are being treated as the equivalent of objects and are being denied their basic humanity.

A central theme in Kantian ethics is that individuals should evaluate their actions in light of the consequences that would follow if *everyone* in society acted in the same way. This **categorical imperative** can be applied to any action. For example, suppose that you are deciding whether to cheat on an examination. If you have adopted Kant's categorical imperative, you will decide *not* to cheat because if everyone cheated, the examination (and the entire education system) would be meaningless.

THE PRINCIPLE OF RIGHTS Because a duty cannot exist without a corresponding right, duty-based ethical standards imply that human beings have basic rights. For example, the commandment "Thou shalt not kill" implies that individuals have a right to live.

---

4. See Chapter 23 for a discussion of the Federal Trade Commission's role in regulating deceptive trade practices, including misleading advertising.

Additionally, religious ethics may involve a rights component because of the belief—characteristic of many religions—that an individual is "made in the image of God." This belief confers on the individual great dignity as a person. For one who holds this belief, not to respect that dignity—and the rights and status that flow from it—would be morally wrong.

The principle that human beings have certain fundamental rights (to life, freedom, and the pursuit of happiness, for example) is deeply embedded in Western culture. As discussed in Chapter 1, the natural law tradition embraces the concept that certain actions (such as killing another person) are morally wrong because they are contrary to nature (the natural desire to continue living). Those who adhere to this **principle of rights,** or "rights theory," believe that a key factor in determining whether a business decision is ethical is how that decision affects the rights of others. These others include the firm's owners, its employees, the consumers of its products or services, its suppliers, the community in which it does business, and society as a whole.

WHICH RIGHTS ARE MOST IMPORTANT? A potential dilemma for those who support rights theory, however, is that they may disagree on which rights are most important. When considering all those affected by a business decision, for example, how much weight should be given to employees relative to shareholders, customers relative to the community, or employees relative to society as a whole?

In general, rights theorists believe that whichever right is stronger in a particular circumstance takes precedence. For example, suppose that a firm can either shut down a plant to avoid dumping pollutants in a river, which would affect the health of thousands of people, or save the jobs of the twelve workers in the plant. In this situation, a rights theorist can easily choose which group to favor. (Not all choices are so clear-cut, however.)

OUTCOME-BASED ETHICS: UTILITARIANISM

"The greatest good for the greatest number" is a paraphrase of the major premise of the utilitarian approach to ethics. **Utilitarianism** is a philosophical theory developed by Jeremy Bentham (1748–1832) and modified by John Stuart Mill (1806–1873)—both British philosophers. In contrast to duty-based ethics, utilitarianism is outcome oriented. It focuses on the conse-

quences of an action, not on the nature of the action itself or on any set of preestablished moral values or religious beliefs.

Under a utilitarian model of ethics, an action is morally correct, or "right," when, among the people it affects, it produces the greatest amount of good for the greatest number. When an action affects the majority adversely, it is morally wrong. Applying the utilitarian theory thus requires (1) a determination of which individuals will be affected by the action in question; (2) a **cost-benefit analysis,** which involves an assessment of the negative and positive effects of alternative actions on these individuals; and (3) a choice among alternative actions that will produce maximum societal utility (the greatest positive net benefits for the greatest number of individuals).

The utilitarian approach to decision making commonly is employed by businesses, as well as by individuals. Weighing the consequences of a decision in terms of its costs and benefits for everyone affected by it is a useful analytical tool in the decision-making process. Utilitarianism is often criticized, however, because it tends to reduce the welfare of human beings to plus and minus signs on a cost-benefit worksheet and to "justify" human costs that many find totally unacceptable.

SECTION 6 | Business Ethics on a Global Level

Given the various cultures and religions throughout the world, conflicts in ethics frequently arise between foreign and U.S. businesspersons. For example, in certain countries the consumption of alcohol and specific foods is forbidden for religious reasons. Under such circumstances, it would be thoughtless and imprudent for a U.S. businessperson to invite a local business contact out for a drink.

The role played by women in other countries may also present some difficult ethical problems for firms doing business internationally. Equal employment opportunity is a fundamental public policy in the United States, and Title VII of the Civil Rights Act of 1964 prohibits discrimination against women in the employment context (see Chapter 21). Some other countries, however, offer little protection for women against gender discrimination in the workplace, including sexual harassment.

We look here at how laws governing workers in other countries, particularly developing countries, have created some especially difficult ethical problems for U.S. sellers of goods manufactured in foreign nations. We also examine some of the ethical ramifications of laws prohibiting bribery and the expansion of ethics programs in the global community.

MONITORING THE EMPLOYMENT PRACTICES OF FOREIGN SUPPLIERS

Many U.S. businesses now contract with companies in developing nations to produce goods, such as shoes and clothing, because the wage rates in those nations are significantly lower than in the United States. Yet what if a foreign company hires women and children at below-minimum-wage rates, for example, or requires its employees to work long hours in a workplace full of health hazards? What if the company's supervisors routinely engage in workplace conduct that is offensive to women?

Given today's global communications network, few companies can assume that their actions in other nations will go unnoticed by "corporate watch" groups that discover and publicize unethical corporate behavior. As a result, U.S. businesses today usually take steps to avoid such adverse publicity—either by refusing to deal with certain suppliers or by arranging to monitor their suppliers' workplaces to make sure that the employees are not being mistreated.

THE FOREIGN CORRUPT PRACTICES ACT

Another ethical problem in international business dealings has to do with the legitimacy of certain side payments to government officials. In the United States, the majority of contracts are formed within the private sector. In many foreign countries, however, government officials make the decisions on most major construction and manufacturing contracts because of extensive government regulation and control over trade and industry. Side payments to government officials in exchange for favorable business contracts are not unusual in such countries, nor are they considered to be unethical. In the past, U.S. corporations doing business in these nations largely followed the dictum, "When in Rome, do as the Romans do."

In the 1970s, however, the U.S. press, and government officials as well, uncovered a number of business scandals involving large side payments by U.S. corpo-

rations to foreign representatives for the purpose of securing advantageous international trade contracts. In response to this unethical behavior, in 1977 Congress passed the Foreign Corrupt Practices Act (FCPA), which prohibits U.S. businesspersons from bribing foreign officials to secure beneficial contracts.

PROHIBITION AGAINST THE BRIBERY OF FOREIGN OFFICIALS The first part of the FCPA applies to all U.S. companies and their directors, officers, shareholders, employees, and agents. This part prohibits the bribery of most officials of foreign governments if the purpose of the payment is to get the official to act in his or her official capacity to provide business opportunities.

The FCPA does not prohibit payment of substantial sums to minor officials whose duties are ministerial. These payments are often referred to as "grease," or facilitating payments. They are meant to accelerate the performance of administrative services that might otherwise be carried out at a slow pace. Thus, for example, if a firm makes a payment to a minor official to speed up an import licensing process, the firm has not violated the FCPA. Generally, the act, as amended, permits payments to foreign officials if such payments are lawful within the foreign country. The act also does not prohibit payments to private foreign companies or other third parties unless the U.S. firm knows that the payments will be passed on to a foreign government in violation of the FCPA.

ACCOUNTING REQUIREMENTS In the past, bribes were often concealed in corporate financial records. Thus, the second part of the FCPA is directed toward accountants. All companies must keep detailed records that "accurately and fairly" reflect their financial activities. In addition, all companies must have accounting systems that provide "reasonable assurance" that all transactions entered into by the companies are accounted for and legal. These requirements assist in detecting illegal bribes. The FCPA further prohibits any person from making false statements to accountants or false entries in any record or account.

PENALTIES FOR VIOLATIONS In 1988, the FCPA was amended to provide that business firms that violate the act may be fined up to $2 million. Individual officers or directors who violate the FCPA may be fined up to $100,000 (the fine cannot be paid by the company) and may be imprisoned for up to five years.

OTHER NATIONS DENOUNCE BRIBERY

For twenty years, the FCPA was the only law of its kind in the world, despite attempts by U.S. political leaders to convince other nations to pass similar legislation. That situation is now changing. In 1997, the Organization for Economic Cooperation and Development created a convention (treaty) that made the bribery of foreign public officials a serious crime. By 2004, at least thirty-five countries had adopted the convention, which obligates them to enact legislation within their nations in accordance with the treaty. In addition, other international institutions, including the European Union, the Organization of American States, and the United Nations, have either passed or are in the process of negotiating rules against bribery in business transactions.

FOREIGN ETHICS CENTERS

The Ethics Resource Center, a nonprofit organization devoted to promoting ethics since 1922, has been instrumental in providing ethics-related training programs to business organizations in other nations. Since 1995, the center, which is located in Washington, D.C., has worked with ethics groups in different parts of the world to establish institutes for ethics training, including centers in Korea, Russia, South Africa, and Turkey. In 2004, the Ethics Resource Center worked with the United Arab Emirates to establish the Gulf Center for Excellence in Ethics (GCEE). The goal of the GCEE is to bring organizational ethics and corporate governance programs to business and government organizations throughout the Gulf and Arab world.

REVIEWING ETHICS AND BUSINESS DECISION MAKING

Isabel Arnett was promoted to chief executive officer (CEO) of Naturelles, Inc., a company that manufactures and sells herbal supplements. Before the board of directors appointed Arnett CEO, she had managed the company's production department, where she earned a reputation as a "slave driver" who routinely refused to provide raises, benefits, and time off for long-term employees. As CEO, she continued her aggressive management style.

In April 2006, company researchers distilled a natural substance that radically increased the body's metabolism, causing significant weight loss without any change in diet or exercise habits. Although the researchers were reluctant to market the product, called Naturolean, without further study, Arnett initiated a massive marketing campaign and began distributing the supplement. Sales soared, shareholders profited, and the company gained value. Two years later, it was discovered that Naturolean caused irreparable brain damage to fetuses in women who had taken it just before or during pregnancy. Using the information presented in the chapter, answer the following questions.

1. | Do employers have an ethical responsibility to give their employees raises, benefits, or time off under duty-based ethical standards? What about under a utilitarian model of ethics? Explain.

2. | If the board of directors knew how Arnett treated company employees, was it unethical of them to promote her to CEO? Why or why not?

3. | Suppose that Naturelles did have an ethical code of conduct and that Arnett's conduct in promoting Naturolean did not violate that code. Would that affect the determination of whether her conduct was ethical? Why or why not?

4. | How might the presence of an ethics code affect a court's determination of whether the company's conduct was ethical?

TERMS AND CONCEPTS TO REVIEW

business ethics 84

categorical imperative 95

cost-benefit analysis 96

ethical reasoning 95

ethics 84

moral minimum 94

principle of rights 96

utilitarianism 96

QUESTIONS AND CASE PROBLEMS

4-1. Some business ethicists maintain that whereas personal ethics has to do with "right" or "wrong" behavior, business ethics is concerned with "appropriate" behavior. In other words, ethical behavior in business has less to do with moral principles than with what society deems to be appropriate behavior in the business context. Do you agree with this distinction? Do personal and business ethics ever overlap? Should personal ethics play any role in business ethical decision making?

4-2. **QUESTION WITH SAMPLE ANSWER**

If a firm engages in "ethical" behavior solely for the purpose of gaining profits from the goodwill it generates, the "ethical" behavior is essentially a means toward a self-serving end (profits and the accumulation of wealth). In this situation, is the firm acting unethically in any way? Should motive or conduct carry greater weight on the ethical scales in this situation?

For a sample answer to this question, go to Appendix I at the end of this text.

4-3. Susan Whitehead serves on the city planning commission. The city is planning to build a new subway system, and Susan's brother-in-law, Jerry, who owns the Custom Transportation Co., has submitted the lowest bid for the system. Susan knows that Jerry could complete the job for the estimated amount, but she also knows that once Jerry finishes this job, he will probably sell his company and retire. Susan is concerned that Custom Transportation's subsequent management might not be as easy to work with if revisions need to be made on the subway system after its completion. She is torn as to whether she should tell the city about the potential changes in Custom Transportation's management. If the city knew about the instability of Custom Transportation, it might prefer to give the contract to one of Jerry's competitors, whose bid was only slightly higher than Jerry's. Does Susan have an ethical obligation to disclose the information about Jerry to the city planning commission? How would you apply duty-based ethical standards to this question? What might be the outcome of a utilitarian analysis? Discuss fully.

4-4. Assume that you are a high-level manager for a shoe manufacturer. You know that your firm could increase its profit margin by producing shoes in Indonesia, where you could hire women for $40 a month to assemble them. You also know, however, that human rights advocates recently accused a competing shoe manufacturer of engaging in exploitative labor practices because the manufacturer sold shoes made by Indonesian women working for similarly low wages. You personally do not believe that paying $40 a month to Indonesian women is unethical because you know that in their impoverished country, $40 a month is a better-than-average wage rate. Assuming that the decision is yours to make, should you have the shoes manufactured in Indonesia and make higher profits for your company? Or should you avoid the risk of negative publicity and the consequences of that publicity for the firm's reputation and subsequent profits? Are there other alternatives? Discuss fully.

4-5. Shokun Steel Co. owns many steel plants. One of its plants is much older than the others. Equipment at the old plant is outdated and inefficient, and the costs of production at that plant are now twice as high as at any of Shokun's other plants. Shokun cannot increase the price of its steel because of competition, both domestic and international. The plant is located in Twin Firs, Pennsylvania, which has a population of about forty-five thousand, and currently employs over a thousand workers. Shokun is contemplating whether to close the plant. What factors should the firm consider in making its decision? Will the firm violate any ethical duties if it closes the plant? Analyze these questions from the two basic perspectives on ethical reasoning discussed in this chapter.

4-6. ETHICAL CONDUCT. Richard and Suzanne Weinstein owned Elm City Cheese Co. Elm City sold its products to three major customers that used the cheese as a "filler" to blend into their cheeses. In 1982, Mark Federico, a certified public accountant, became Elm City's accountant and the Weinsteins' personal accountant. The Weinsteins had known Federico since he was seven years old, and even before he became their accountant, he knew the details of Elm City's business. Federico's duties went beyond typical accounting work, and when the Weinsteins were absent, he was put in charge of operations. In 1992, Federico was made a vice president of the company, and a year later he was placed in charge of day-to-day operations. He also continued to serve as Elm City's accountant. The relationship between Federico and the Weinsteins deteriorated, and in 1995, he resigned as Elm City's employee and as its accountant. Less than two years later, Federico opened Lomar Foods, Inc., to make the same products as Elm City by the same process and to sell the products to the same customers. Federico located Lomar close to Elm City's suppliers. Elm City filed a suit in a Connecticut state court against Federico and Lomar, alleging, among other things, misappropriation of trade secrets. Elm City argued that it was entitled to punitive damages because Federico's conduct was "willful and malicious." Federico responded in part that he did not act willfully and maliciously because he did not know that Elm City's business details were trade secrets. Were Federico's actions "willful and malicious"? Were they ethical? Explain. [*Elm City Cheese Co. v. Federico*, 251 Conn. 59, 752 A.2d 1037 (1999)]

4-7. ⚖ **CASE PROBLEM WITH SAMPLE ANSWER**
Eden Electrical, Ltd., owned twenty-five appliance
stores throughout Israel, at least some of which sold
refrigerators made by Amana Co. Eden bought the
appliances from Amana's Israeli distributor, Pan El
A/Yesh Shem, which approached Eden about taking
over the distributorship. Eden representatives met with
Amana executives. The executives made assurances
about Amana's good faith, its hope of having a long-
term business relationship with Eden, and its willingness
to have Eden become its exclusive distributor in Israel.
Eden signed a distributorship agreement and paid
Amana $2.4 million. Amana failed to deliver this
amount in inventory to Eden, continued selling refrigerators to other entities for the Israeli market, and represented to others that it was still looking for a long-term
distributor. Less than three months after signing the
agreement with Eden, Amana terminated it, without
explanation. Eden filed a suit in a federal district court
against Amana, alleging fraud. The court awarded Eden
$12.1 million in damages. Is this amount warranted?
Why or why not? How does this case illustrate why business ethics is important? [*Eden Electrical, Ltd. v. Amana
Co.*, 370 F.3d 824 (8th Cir. 2004)]

**To view a sample answer for this case problem, go to
this book's Web site at http://wleb.westbuslaw.com,
select "Chapter 4," and click on "Case Problem with
Sample Answer."**

4-8. ETHICAL CONDUCT. Richard Fraser was an
"exclusive career insurance agent" under a contract with
Nationwide Mutual Insurance Co. Fraser leased computer hardware and software from Nationwide for his
business. During a dispute between Nationwide and
the Nationwide Insurance Independent Contractors
Association, an organization representing Fraser and
other exclusive career agents, Fraser prepared a letter to
Nationwide's competitors asking whether they were
interested in acquiring the represented agents' policy-
holders. Nationwide obtained a copy of the letter and
searched its electronic file server for e-mail indicating
that the letter had been sent. It found a stored e-mail
that Fraser had sent to a co-worker indicating that the
letter had been sent to at least one competitor. The
e-mail was retrieved from the co-worker's file of already
received and discarded messages stored on the server.
When Nationwide canceled its contract with Fraser, he
filed a suit in a federal district court against the firm,
alleging, among other things, violations of various federal laws that prohibit the interception of electronic
communications during transmission. In whose favor
should the court rule, and why? Did Nationwide act ethically in retrieving the e-mail? Explain. [*Fraser v.
Nationwide Mutual Insurance Co.*, 352 F.3d 107 (3d Cir.
2004)]

4-9. ETHICAL CONDUCT. Unable to pay more than
$1.2 billion in debt, Big Rivers Electric Corp. filed a peti-
tion to declare bankruptcy in a federal bankruptcy court
in September 1996. Big Rivers' creditors included Bank
of New York (BONY), Chase Manhattan Bank, Mapco
Equities, and others. The court appointed J. Baxter
Schilling to work as a "disinterested" (neutral) party with
Big Rivers and the creditors to resolve their disputes and
set an hourly fee as Schilling's compensation. Schilling
told Chase, BONY, and Mapco that he wanted them to
pay him an additional percentage fee based on the
"success" he attained in finding "new value" to pay Big
Rivers' debts. Without such a deal, he told them, he
would not perform his mediation duties. Chase agreed;
the others disputed the deal, but no one told the court. In
October 1998, Schilling asked the court for nearly $4.5
million in compensation, including the hourly fees,
which totaled about $531,000, and the percentage fees.
Big Rivers and others asked the court to deny Schilling
any fees on the basis that he had improperly negotiated
"secret side agreements." How did Schilling violate his
duties as a "disinterested" party? Should he be denied
compensation? Why or why not? [*In re Big Rivers Electric
Corp.*, 355 F.3d 415 (6th Cir. 2004)]

4-10. VIDEO QUESTION

Go to this text's Web site at http://wleb.westbuslaw.com
and select "Chapter 4." Click on "Video Questions" and
view the video titled *Ethics: Business Ethics an
Oxymoron?* Then answer the following questions.

(a) According to the instructor in the video, what is the
primary reason why businesses act ethically?

(b) Which of the two approaches to ethical reasoning
that were discussed in the chapter seems to have
had more influence on the instructor in the discussion of how business activities are related to societies? Explain your answer.

(c) The instructor asserts that "[i]n the end, it is the
unethical behavior that becomes costly, and conversely ethical behavior creates its own competitive
advantage." Do you agree with this statement? Why
or why not?

LAW | on the Web

For updated links to resources available on the Web, as well as a variety of other materials, visit this text's Web site at http://wleb.westbuslaw.com.

West's Legal Studies in Business offers an in-depth "Inside Look" at the Enron debacle at

http://insidelook.westbuslaw.com

You can find articles on issues relating to shareholders and corporate accountability at the Corporate Governance Web site. Go to

http://www.corpgov.net

For an example of an online group that focuses on corporate activities from the perspective of corporate social responsibility, go to

http://www.corpwatch.org

Global Exchange offers information on global business activities, including some of the ethical issues stemming from those activities, at

http://www.globalexchange.org

LEGAL RESEARCH EXERCISES ON THE WEB

Go to http://wleb.westbuslaw.com, the Web site that accompanies this text. Select "Chapter 4" and click on "Internet Exercises." There you will find the following Internet research exercises that you can perform to learn more about topics covered in this chapter.

Activity 4–1: LEGAL PERSPECTIVE
Ethics in Business

Activity 4–2: MANAGEMENT PERSPECTIVE
Environmental Self-Audits

The Foundations

In Chapter 4, we examined the importance of ethical standards in the business context. We also offered suggestions on how business decision makers can create an ethical workplace. Certainly, it is not wrong for a businessperson to try to increase his or her firm's profits. But there are limits, both ethical and legal, to how far businesspersons can go. In preparing for a career in business, you will find that a background in business ethics and a commitment to ethical behavior are just as important as a knowledge of the specific laws that are covered in this text. Of course, no textbook can give an answer to each and every ethical question that arises in the business environment. Nor can it anticipate the types of ethical questions that will arise in the future, as technology continues to transform the workplace and business relationships.

The most we can do is examine the types of ethical issues that businesspersons have faced in the past and that they are facing today. In the *Focus on Ethics* sections in this book, we provide examples of specific ethical issues that have arisen in various areas of business activity.

In this initial *Focus on Ethics* feature, we look first at the relationship between business ethics and business law. We then discuss various obstacles to ethical behavior in the business context. We conclude the feature with an examination of corporate social responsibility, which is a significant element of today's legal environment of business.

Business Ethics and Business Law

Business ethics and business law are closely intertwined because ultimately the law rests on social beliefs about right and wrong behavior in the business world. Thus, businesspersons, by complying with the law, are acting ethically. Mere legal compliance (the "moral minimum" in terms of business ethics), however, is often not enough. This is because the law does not—and cannot—provide the answers for all ethical questions.

In the business world, numerous actions may be unethical but not necessarily illegal. Consider an example. Suppose that a pharmaceutical company is banned from marketing a particular drug in the United States because of the drug's possible adverse side effects. Yet no law prohibits the company from selling the drug in foreign markets—even though some consumers in those markets may suffer serious health problems as a result of using the drug. At issue here is not whether it would be legal to market the drug in other countries but whether it would be *ethical* to do so. In other words, the law has its limits—it cannot make all ethical decisions for us. Rather, the law assumes that those in business will behave ethically in their day-to-day dealings. If they do not, the courts will not come to their assistance.

Obstacles to Ethical Business Behavior

People sometimes behave unethically in the business context, just as they do in their private lives. Some businesspersons knowingly engage in unethical behavior because they think that they can "get away with it"—that no one will ever learn of their unethical actions.

Examples of this kind of unethical behavior include padding expense accounts, casting doubts on the integrity of a rival co-worker to gain a job promotion, stealing company supplies or equipment, and so on. Obviously, these acts are unethical, and many of them are illegal as well. In some situations, however, businesspersons who would choose to act ethically may be deterred from doing so because of situational circumstances or external pressures.

Ethics and the Corporate Environment Individuals in their personal lives normally are free to decide ethical issues as they wish and to follow through on those decisions. In the business world, and particularly in the corporate environment, rarely is such a decision made by *one* person. If you are an officer or a manager of a large company, for example, you will find that the decision as to what is right or wrong for the company is not totally yours to make. Your input may weigh in the decision, but ultimately a corporate decision is a collective undertaking.

Additionally, collective decision making, because it places emphasis on consensus and unity of opinion, tends to hinder individual ethical assertiveness. For example, suppose that a director has ethical misgivings about a planned corporate venture that promises to be highly profitable. If the other directors have no such misgivings, the director who does may be swayed by the others' enthusiasm for the project and downplay her or his own criticisms.

Furthermore, just as no one person makes a collective decision, so no one person (normally) is held accountable for the decision. The corporate enterprise thus tends to shield corporate personnel from both individual exposure to the consequences of their decisions (such as direct experience with someone who suffers harm from a corporate product) and personal accountability for those decisions.

Ethics and Management Much unethical business behavior occurs simply because management does not always make clear what ethical standards and behaviors are expected of the firm's employees. Although most firms now issue ethical policies or codes of conduct, these policies and codes are not always effective in creating an ethical workplace. At times, this is because the firm's ethical policies are not communicated clearly to employees or do not bear on the real ethical issues confronting decision makers. Additionally, particularly in a large corporation, unethical behavior in one corporate department may simply escape the attention of those in control of the corporation or the corporate officials responsible for implementing and monitoring the company's ethics program.

Unethical behavior may also occur when corporate management, by its own conduct, indicates that ethical considerations take a backseat. If management makes no attempt to deter unethical behavior—through reprimands or employment terminations, for example—it will be obvious to employees that management is not all that serious about ethics. Likewise, if a company gives promotions or salary increases to those who consistently use unethical tactics to increase the firm's profits, then employees who do not resort to such tactics will be at a disadvantage. An employee in this situation may decide that because "everyone else does it," he or she might as well do it too.

Of course, an even stronger encouragement to unethical behavior exists when employers engage in blatantly unethical or illegal conduct and expect their employees to do so as well. An employee in this situation faces two options, neither of which is satisfactory: participate in the conduct or "blow the whistle" on (inform authorities of) the employer's actions—and, of course, risk being fired. (See Chapter 20 for a more detailed discussion of this ethical dilemma and its consequences for employees.)

Corporate Social Responsibility

At one time, businesses faced few ethical requirements other than complying with the law. Generally, if an action was legal, it was regarded as ethical. By the 1960s, however, this attitude had begun to change significantly. Groups concerned with civil rights, employee safety and welfare, consumer protection, environmental preservation, and other causes began to pressure corporate America to behave in a more responsible manner with respect to these causes. Thus was born the concept of *corporate social responsibility*—the idea that corporations can and should act ethically and be accountable to society for their actions.

Just what constitutes corporate social responsibility has been debated for some time. Clearly, though, corporations that go too far in an attempt to increase their profits at the expense of individuals and groups affected by their decisions ultimately may face public outrage and government remedial action—as Enron, WorldCom, and other companies learned in the early 2000s.

Generally, the debate over corporate social responsibility has to do less with whether corporations *should* be responsible than with *how* and *to whom* they should be responsible. Today, there are a number of views on this issue, including those discussed next.

Profit Maximization Corporate directors and officers have a duty to act in the shareholders' interest. Because of the nature of the relationship between corporate directors and officers and the shareholder-owners, the law holds directors and officers to a high standard of care in business decision making (see Chapter 18). Traditionally, it was perceived that this duty to shareholders took precedence over all other corporate duties and that the primary goal of corporations should be profit maximization. Milton Friedman, the Nobel Prize–winning economist and a proponent of the profit-maximization view, saw "one and only one" social responsibility of a corporation: "to use its resources and engage in activities designed to increase its profits, so long as it stays within the rules of the game, which is to say, engages in open and free competition without deception and fraud."[1]

Those who accept this position argue that a firm can best contribute to society by generating profits. Society benefits because a firm realizes profits only when it markets products or services that are desired by society. These products and services enhance the standard of living, and the profits accumulated by successful businesses generate national wealth. Our laws and court decisions promoting trade and commerce reflect the public policy that the fruits of commerce (income and wealth) are desirable and good. Because our society regards income and wealth as ethical goals, corporations, by contributing to income and wealth, automatically are acting ethically.

The Stakeholder Approach Another view of corporate social responsibility stresses that a corporation's duty to its shareholders should be weighed against its duties to other groups affected by corporate decisions. Corporate decision makers should consider not only the welfare of shareholders but also that of *stakeholders*—employees, customers, suppliers, communities, and any group that has a stake in the corporation. The reasoning behind this "stakeholder view" of corporate social responsibility is that in some circumstances, one or more of these groups may have a greater stake in company decisions than do the shareholders.

Consider an example. A heavily indebted corporation is facing imminent bankruptcy. The shareholder-investors have little to lose in this situation because their stock is already next to worthless. The corporation's creditors will be first in line for any corporate assets remaining. Because in this situation it is the creditors who have the greatest "stake" in the corporation, under the stakeholder view, corporate

---

1. Milton Friedman, "Does Business Have Social Responsibility?" *Bank Administration*, April 1971, pp. 13–14.

directors and officers should give greater weight to the creditors' interests than to those of the shareholders.

Corporate Citizenship Another theory of social responsibility argues that corporations should actively promote goals that society deems worthwhile and take positive steps toward solving social problems. Because so much of the wealth and power of this country is controlled by business, business in turn has a responsibility to society to use that wealth and power in socially beneficial ways. To be sure, since the nineteenth century and the emergence of large business enterprises in America, corporations have generally contributed some of their shareholders' wealth to meet social needs. Indeed, virtually all large corporations today have established nonprofit foundations for this purpose. Yet corporate citizenship requires more than just making donations to worthwhile causes. Under a corporate citizenship view of social responsibility, companies are also judged on how they conduct their affairs with respect to employment discrimination, human rights, environmental concerns, and so on.

Critics of this view believe that it is inappropriate to use the power of the corporate business world to fashion society's goals by promoting social causes. Determinations as to what exactly is in society's best interest involve questions that are essentially political; therefore, the public, through the political process, should have a say in making those determinations. The legislature—not the corporate boardroom—is thus the appropriate forum for such decisions.

It Pays to Be Ethical

Most corporations today have learned that it pays to be ethically responsible—even if this means less profit in the short run (and it often does). Today's corporations are subject to more intensive scrutiny—by both government agencies and the public—than corporations of the past. "Corporate watch" groups monitor the activities of U.S. corporations, including activities conducted in foreign countries. With the availability of the Internet, complaints about a corporation's practices can easily be disseminated to a worldwide audience. Similarly, dissatisfied customers and employees can voice their complaints about corporate policies, products, or services in Internet chat rooms and other online forums. Thus, if a corporation fails to conduct its operations ethically or to respond quickly to an ethical crisis, its goodwill and reputation (and future profits) will likely suffer as a result.

There are other reasons as well for a corporation to behave ethically. For example, companies that demonstrate a commitment to ethical behavior—by implementing ethical programs, complying with environmental regulations, and promptly investigating product complaints, for example—often receive more lenient treatment from government agencies and the courts. Additionally, investors may shy away from a corporation's stock if the corporation is perceived to be socially irresponsible. Finally, unethical (and/or illegal) corporate behavior may result in government action, such as new laws imposing further requirements on corporate entities.

DISCUSSION QUESTIONS

1. What might be some other deterrents to ethical behavior in the business context, besides those discussed in this *Focus on Ethics* feature?

2. Can you think of a situation in which a business firm may be acting ethically but not in a socially responsible manner? Explain.

3. Why are consumers and the public generally more concerned with ethical and socially responsible business behavior today than they were, say, fifty years ago?

4. Perceptions of social responsibility differ among countries. Discuss some of the ethical implications of these differences for American firms that do business abroad.

5. Suppose that an automobile manufacturing company has to choose between two alternatives: contributing $1 million annually to the United Way or reinvesting the $1 million in the company. In terms of ethics and social responsibility, which is the better choice?

UNIT TWO
The Public and International Environment

CONTENTS

CHAPTER 5
Constitutional Law

The U.S. Constitution is the supreme law in this country.[1] As mentioned in Chapter 1, neither Congress nor any state may pass a law that conflicts with the Constitution. Laws that govern business have their origin in the lawmaking authority granted by this document.

In this chapter, we examine some basic constitutional concepts and clauses and their significance for businesspersons. We then look at certain freedoms guaranteed by the first ten amendments to the Constitution—the Bill of Rights—and discuss how these freedoms affect business activities.

SECTION 1 | The Constitutional Powers of Government

Following the Revolutionary War, the states created a *confederal form of government*. The Articles of Confederation, which went into effect in 1781, established a confederation of independent states and a central government of very limited powers. The central government could handle only those matters of common concern expressly delegated to it by the member states, and the national congress had no authority to make laws directly applicable to individuals unless the member states explicitly supported such laws. In short, the *sovereign power*[2] to govern rested essentially with the states. The Articles of Confederation clearly reflected the central tenet of the American Revolution—that a national government should not have unlimited power.

PROBLEMS WITH THE CONFEDERATION

The confederation, however, faced serious problems. For one thing, laws passed by the various states hampered national commerce and foreign trade by preventing the free movement of goods and services across state borders. By 1784, the nation faced a seri-

ous economic depression. Many who could not pay their debts were thrown into "debtors' prisons." By 1786, a series of uprisings by farmer debtors were proving difficult to control because the national government did not have the authority to raise revenues (by levying taxes, for example) to support a militia.

Because of these problems, a national convention was called to **amend** (change, alter) the Articles of Confederation. Instead of amending the Articles, however, the delegates to the convention, now called the Constitutional Convention, created the Constitution and a completely new type of government. Many of the provisions of the Constitution, including those discussed in the following pages, were shaped by the delegates' experiences during the confederal era (1781–1789).

A FEDERAL FORM OF GOVERNMENT

The new government created by the Constitution reflected a series of compromises made by the convention delegates on various issues. Some delegates wanted sovereign power to remain with the states; others wanted the national government alone to exercise sovereign power. The end result was a compromise—a **federal form of government** in which the national government and the states *share* sovereign power.

The Constitution sets forth specific powers that can be exercised by the national government and provides that the national government has the implied power to undertake actions necessary to carry out its

---

1. See Appendix B for the full text of the U.S. Constitution.
2. *Sovereign power* refers to that supreme power to which no other authority is superior or equal.

106

expressly designated powers. All other powers are retained by the states. According to the language of the Tenth Amendment to the Constitution, "The powers not delegated to the United States by the Constitution, nor prohibited by it to the States, are reserved to the States respectively, or to the people."

NATIONAL POWERS VERSUS STATE POWERS—AN ONGOING DEBATE The broad language of the Constitution has left much room for debate over the specific nature and scope of the respective powers of the states and the national government. Generally, it has been the task of the courts to determine where the boundary line between state and national powers should lie—and that line changes over time. For most of the twentieth century, for example, the national government met little resistance from the courts when extending its regulatory authority over broad areas of social and economic life. Today, in contrast, the courts, and particularly the United States Supreme Court, are more willing to interpret the Constitution in such a way as to curb the national government's regulatory powers and bolster the rights of state governments.

RELATIONS AMONG THE STATES The Constitution also includes provisions concerning relations among the states in our federal system. Particularly important are the privileges and immunities clause and the full faith and credit clause.

—The Privileges and Immunities Clause. Article IV, Section 2, of the Constitution provides that the "Citizens of each State shall be entitled to all Privileges and Immunities of Citizens in the several States." This clause is often referred to as the interstate **privileges and immunities clause.**[3] When a citizen of one state engages in basic and essential activities in another state (the "foreign state"), the foreign state must have a *substantial reason* for treating the nonresident differently from its own residents. Basic activities include transferring property, seeking employment, or accessing the court system. The foreign state must also establish that its reason for the discrimination is substantially related to the state's ultimate purpose in adopting the legislation or activity.[4] The idea is to generally prevent any state from discriminating against citizens of other states in favor of its own.

Charging nonresidents $2,500 for a shrimp-fishing license, for example, when residents are charged only $25 for the same license, may be considered unconstitutional discrimination against nonresidents who are pursuing the essential activity of making a living.[5] Similarly, attempting to limit the practice of law to residents only (on the premise that it would help reduce the state's unemployment rate) may unconstitutionally restrict a nonresident's professional pursuit without substantial justification.[6]

—The Full Faith and Credit Clause. Article IV, Section 1, of the Constitution provides that "Full Faith and Credit shall be given in each State to the public Acts, Records, and judicial Proceedings of every other State." This clause, which is referred to as the **full faith and credit clause,** applies only to civil matters. It ensures that rights established under deeds, wills, contracts, and the like in one state will be honored by other states. It also ensures that any judicial decision with respect to such property rights will be honored and enforced in all states.

The full faith and credit clause originally was included in the Articles of Confederation to promote mutual friendship among the people of the various states. In fact, it has contributed to the unity of American citizens because it protects their legal rights as they move about from state to state. It also protects the rights of those to whom they owe obligations, such as a person who is awarded money damages by a court. This is extremely important for the conduct of business in a country with a very mobile citizenry.

THE SEPARATION OF NATIONAL GOVERNMENT POWERS

To prevent the possibility that the national government might use its power arbitrarily, the Constitution provided for three branches of government. The legislative branch makes the laws, the executive branch enforces the laws, and the judicial branch interprets the laws. Each branch performs a separate function, and no branch may exercise the authority of another branch.

---

3. Interpretations of this clause commonly use the terms *privilege* and *immunity* synonymously. Generally, the terms refer to certain rights, benefits, or advantages enjoyed by individuals.

4. *Supreme Court of New Hampshire v. Piper,* 470 U.S. 274, 105 S.Ct. 1272, 84 L.Ed.2d 205 (1985).

5. *Toomer v. Witsell,* 334 U.S. 385, 68 S.Ct. 1156, 92 L.Ed. 1460 (1948).

6. *Hicklin v. Orbeck,* 437 U.S. 518, 98 S.Ct. 2482, 57 L.Ed.2d 397 (1978).

Each branch, however, has some power to limit the actions of the other two branches. Congress, for example, can enact legislation relating to spending and commerce, but the president can veto that legislation. The executive branch is responsible for foreign affairs, but treaties with foreign governments require the advice and consent of members of the Senate. Although Congress determines the jurisdiction of the federal courts, the federal courts have the power to hold acts of the other branches of the federal government unconstitutional.[7] Thus, with this system of **checks and balances,** no one branch of government can accumulate too much power.

THE COMMERCE CLAUSE

To prevent states from establishing laws and regulations that would interfere with trade and commerce among the states, the Constitution expressly delegated to the national government the power to regulate interstate commerce. Article I, Section 8, of the U.S. Constitution expressly permits Congress "[t]o regulate Commerce with foreign Nations, and among the several States, and with the Indian Tribes." This clause, referred to as the **commerce clause,** has had a greater impact on business than any other provision in the Constitution. The commerce clause provides the basis for the national government's extensive regulation of state and even local affairs.

One of the early questions raised by the commerce clause was whether the word *among* in the phrase "among the several States" meant *between* the states or *between and within* the states. For some time, the courts interpreted the commerce clause to apply only to commerce between the states (*interstate* commerce) and not commerce within the states (*intrastate* commerce). In 1824, however, in *Gibbons v. Ogden,*[8] the United States Supreme Court held that commerce within the states could also be regulated by the national government as long as the commerce *substantially affected* commerce involving more than one state.

THE EXPANSION OF NATIONAL POWERS UNDER THE COMMERCE CLAUSE In *Gibbons v. Ogden,* the commerce clause was expanded to cover activities that "substantially affect interstate commerce." As the

nation grew and faced new kinds of problems, the commerce clause became a vehicle for the additional expansion of the national government's regulatory powers. Even activities that seemed purely local in nature came under the regulatory reach of the national government if those activities were deemed to substantially affect interstate commerce.

In a 1942 case,[9] for example, the Supreme Court held that wheat production by an individual farmer intended wholly for consumption on his own farm was subject to federal regulation. In *Heart of Atlanta Motel v. United States,*[10] a landmark case decided in 1964, the Supreme Court upheld the federal government's authority to prohibit racial discrimination nationwide in public facilities, including local motels, based on its powers under the commerce clause. The Court noted that "if it is interstate commerce that feels the pinch, it does not matter how local the operation that applies the squeeze." In *McLain v. Real Estate Board of New Orleans, Inc.,*[11] a 1980 case, the Supreme Court acknowledged that the commerce clause had "long been interpreted to extend beyond activities actually in interstate commerce to reach other activities, while wholly local in nature, which nevertheless substantially affect interstate commerce."

THE COMMERCE POWER TODAY Today, at least theoretically, the power over commerce authorizes the national government to regulate all commercial enterprises in the United States. The breadth of the commerce clause permits the national government to legislate in areas in which Congress has not explicitly been granted power. In the last decade, however, the Supreme Court has begun to curb somewhat the national government's regulatory authority under the commerce clause. In 1995, the Court held—for the first time in sixty years—that Congress had exceeded its regulatory authority under the commerce clause. The Court struck down an act that banned the possession of guns within one thousand feet of any school because the act attempted to regulate an area that had "nothing to do with commerce."[12] Subsequently, the Court invalidated key portions of two other federal acts—the Brady Handgun Violence

---

7. As discussed in Chapter 2, the power of judicial review was established by the United States Supreme Court in *Marbury v. Madison,* 5 U.S. (1 Cranch) 137, 2 L.Ed. 60 (1803).

8. 22 U.S. (9 Wheat.) 1, 6 L.Ed. 23 (1824).

9. *Wickard v. Filburn,* 317 U.S. 111, 63 S.Ct. 82, 87 L.Ed. 122 (1942).

10. 379 U.S. 241, 85 S.Ct. 348, 13 L.Ed.2d 258 (1964).

11. 444 U.S. 232, 100 S.Ct. 502, 62 L.Ed.2d 441 (1980).

12. The United States Supreme Court held the Gun-Free School Zones Act of 1990 to be unconstitutional in *United States v. Lopez,* 514 U.S. 549, 115 S.Ct. 1624, 131 L.Ed.2d 626 (1995).

Prevention Act of 1993 and the Violence Against Women Act of 1994—on the ground that they exceeded Congress's commerce clause authority.[13]

MEDICAL MARIJUANA AND THE COMMERCE CLAUSE The current trend of not allowing the federal government to regulate noncommercial activities that take place wholly within a state's borders has led to some controversial decisions in the lower courts. In 2003, for example, a federal appellate court decided a case involving marijuana use on commerce clause grounds. Eight states, including California, have adopted "medical marijuana" laws—legalizing marijuana for medical purposes. Marijuana possession, however, is illegal under the federal Controlled Substances Act (CSA).[14] Two seriously ill California women filed a suit in a federal district court after the federal government seized the marijuana that they were using on the advice of their physicians. The women argued that it is unconstitutional for the federal act to prohibit them from using marijuana for medical purposes that are legal within the state. The federal appellate court agreed, reasoning that the marijuana in this situation would never enter the stream of commerce, but the Supreme Court overturned that decision in 2005.[15]

THE REGULATORY POWERS OF THE STATES As part of their inherent sovereignty, state governments have the authority to regulate affairs within their borders. This authority stems in part from the Tenth Amendment to the Constitution, which reserves all powers not delegated to the national government to the states or to the people. State regulatory powers are often referred to as **police powers.** The term does not relate solely to criminal law enforcement but rather refers to the broad right of state governments to regulate private activities to protect or promote the public order, health, safety, morals, and general welfare. Fire and building codes, antidiscrimination laws, parking regulations, zoning restrictions, licensing requirements, and thousands of other state statutes covering virtually every aspect of life have been enacted pur-

suant to states' police powers. Local governments, including cities, also exercise police powers.[16] Generally, state laws enacted pursuant to a state's police powers carry a strong presumption of validity.

STATE ACTIONS AND THE "DORMANT" COMMERCE CLAUSE The United States Supreme Court has interpreted the commerce clause to mean that the national government has the *exclusive* authority to regulate commerce that substantially affects trade and commerce among the states. This express grant of authority to the national government, which is often referred to as the "positive" aspect of the commerce clause, implies a negative aspect—that the states do *not* have the authority to regulate interstate commerce. This negative aspect of the commerce clause is often referred to as the "dormant" (implied) commerce clause.

The dormant commerce clause comes into play when state regulations impinge on interstate commerce. In this situation, the courts normally weigh the state's interest in regulating a certain matter against the burden that the state's regulation places on interstate commerce. For example, in one case, the United States Supreme Court invalidated state regulations that, in the interest of promoting traffic safety, limited the length of trucks traveling on the state's highways. The Court concluded that the regulations imposed a "substantial burden on interstate commerce" yet failed to "make more than the most speculative contribution to highway safety."[17] Because courts balance the interests involved, it is extremely difficult to predict the outcome in a particular case.

THE SUPREMACY CLAUSE AND FEDERAL PREEMPTION

Article VI of the U.S. Constitution, commonly referred to as the **supremacy clause,** provides that the Constitution, laws, and treaties of the United States are "the supreme Law of the Land." When there is a direct conflict between a federal law and a state law, the state law is rendered invalid. Because some powers are *concurrent* (shared by the federal government and

13. See, for example, *Printz v. United States,* 521 U.S. 898, 117 S.Ct. 2365, 138 L.Ed.2d 914 (1997), involving the Brady Handgun Violence Prevention Act of 1993; and *United States v. Morrison,* 529 U.S. 598, 120 S.Ct. 1740, 146 L.Ed.2d 658 (2000), concerning the federal Violence Against Women Act of 1994.
14. 21 U.S.C. Sections 801 *et seq.*
15. *Gonzales v. Raich,* __ U.S. __, 125 S.Ct. 2195, 162 L.Ed.2d 1 (2005).

16. Local governments derive their authority to regulate their communities from the state, because they are creatures of the state. In other words, they cannot come into existence unless authorized by the state to do so.
17. *Raymond Motor Transportation, Inc. v. Rice,* 434 U.S. 429, 98 S.Ct. 787, 54 L.Ed.2d 664 (1978).

the states), however, it is necessary to determine which law governs in a particular circumstance.

Preemption occurs when Congress chooses to act exclusively in an area in which the federal government and the states have concurrent powers. In this circumstance, a valid federal statute or regulation will take precedence over a conflicting state or local law or regulation on the same general subject. Often, it is not clear whether Congress, in passing a law, intended to preempt an entire subject area against state regulation. In these situations, it is left to the courts to determine whether Congress intended to exercise exclusive power over a given area. No single factor is decisive as to whether a court will find preemption. Generally, congressional intent to preempt will be found if a federal law regulating an activity is so pervasive, comprehensive, or detailed that the states have no room to regulate in that area. Also, when a federal statute creates an agency—such as the National Labor Relations Board—to enforce the law, matters that may come within the agency's jurisdiction will likely preempt state laws.

THE TAXING AND SPENDING POWERS

Article I, Section 8, provides that Congress has the "Power to lay and collect Taxes, Duties, Imposts, and Excises." Section 8 further provides that "all Duties, Imposts and Excises shall be uniform throughout the United States." The requirement of uniformity refers to uniformity among the states, and thus Congress may not tax some states while exempting others.

Traditionally, if Congress attempted to regulate indirectly, by taxation, an area over which it had no authority, the courts would invalidate the tax. Today, however, if a tax measure is reasonable, it is generally held to be within the national taxing power. Moreover, the expansive interpretation of the commerce clause almost always provides a basis for sustaining a federal tax.

Under Article I, Section 8, Congress has the power "to pay the Debts and provide for the common Defence and general Welfare of the United States." Through the spending power, Congress disposes of the revenues accumulated from the taxing power. Congress can spend revenues not only to carry out its expressed powers but also to promote any objective it deems worthwhile, so long as it does not violate the Bill of Rights. For example, Congress could not condition welfare payments on the recipients' agreement to refrain from criticizing government policies. The spending power necessarily involves policy choices, with which taxpayers may disagree.

SECTION 2 | Business and the Bill of Rights

The importance of a written declaration of the rights of individuals eventually caused the first Congress of the United States to submit twelve amendments to the Constitution to the states for approval. The first ten of these amendments, commonly known as the **Bill of Rights,** were adopted in 1791 and embody a series of protections for the individual against various types of interference by the federal government.[18] The protections guaranteed by these ten amendments are summarized in Exhibit 5–1.[19] Some of these constitutional protections apply to business entities as well. For example, corporations exist as separate legal entities, or *legal persons*, and enjoy many of the same rights and privileges as *natural persons* do.

LIMITS ON BOTH FEDERAL AND STATE GOVERNMENTAL ACTIONS

As originally intended, the Bill of Rights limited only the powers of the national government. Over time, however, the United States Supreme Court "incorporated" most of these rights into the protections against state actions afforded by the Fourteenth Amendment to the Constitution. That amendment, passed in 1868 after the Civil War, provides in part that "[n]o State shall . . . deprive any person of life, liberty, or property, without due process of law." Starting in 1925, the Supreme Court began to define various rights and liberties guaranteed in the U.S. Constitution as constituting "due process of law," which was required of state governments under the Fourteenth Amendment. Today, most of the rights and liberties set forth in the Bill of Rights apply to state governments as well as the national government. In other words, neither the federal government nor state governments can deprive persons of those rights and liberties.

---

18. Another of these proposed amendments was ratified 203 years later (in 1992) and became the Twenty-seventh Amendment to the Constitution. See Appendix B.

19. See the Constitution in Appendix B for the complete text of each amendment.

EXHIBIT 5-1 **Protections Guaranteed by the Bill of Rights**

First Amendment: Guarantees the freedoms of religion, speech, and the press and the rights to assemble peaceably and to petition the government.

Second Amendment: States that the right of the people to keep and bear arms shall not be infringed.

Third Amendment: Prohibits, in peacetime, the lodging of soldiers in any house without the owner's consent.

Fourth Amendment: Prohibits unreasonable searches and seizures of persons or property.

Fifth Amendment: Guarantees the rights to indictment by grand jury, to due process of law, and to fair payment when private property is taken for public use; prohibits compulsory self-incrimination and double jeopardy (being tried again for an alleged crime for which one has already stood trial).

Sixth Amendment: Guarantees the accused in a criminal case the right to a speedy and public trial by an impartial jury and with counsel. The accused has the right to cross-examine witnesses against him or her and to solicit testimony from witnesses in his or her favor.

Seventh Amendment: Guarantees the right to a trial by jury in a civil case involving at least twenty dollars.[a]

Eighth Amendment: Prohibits excessive bail and fines, as well as cruel and unusual punishment.

Ninth Amendment: Establishes that the people have rights in addition to those specified in the Constitution.

Tenth Amendment: Establishes that those powers neither delegated to the federal government nor denied to the states are reserved to the states and to the people.

a. Twenty dollars was forty days' pay for the average person when the Bill of Rights was written.

The rights secured by the Bill of Rights are not absolute. As you can see in Exhibit 5–1, many of the rights guaranteed by the first ten amendments are described in very general terms. For example, the Fourth Amendment prohibits *unreasonable* searches and seizures, but it does not define what constitutes an unreasonable search or seizure. Similarly, the Eighth Amendment prohibits excessive bail or fines, but no definition of *excessive* is contained in that amendment. Ultimately, it is the United States Supreme Court, as the final interpreter of the Constitution, that defines our rights and determines their boundaries.

FREEDOM OF SPEECH

A democratic form of government cannot survive unless people can freely voice their political opinions and criticize government actions or policies. Freedom of speech, particularly political speech, is thus a prized right, and traditionally the courts have protected this right to the fullest extent possible.

Symbolic speech—gestures, movements, articles of clothing, and other forms of expressive conduct—is also given substantial protection by the courts. For example, in a 1989 case, *Texas v. Johnson*,[20] the

United States Supreme Court ruled that state laws that prohibited the burning of the American flag as part of a peaceful protest violated the freedom of expression protected by the First Amendment. Congress responded by passing the Flag Protection Act of 1989, which was ruled unconstitutional by the Supreme Court in 1990.[21] Similarly, participating in a hunger strike or wearing a black armband would be protected as symbolic speech.

Expression—oral, written, or symbolized by conduct—is subject to reasonable restrictions. For example, on the campus of a public high school, certain rights may be circumscribed or denied, in part to protect minors from predatory adults and to protect adults and others from predatory minors. A balance must be struck, however, between a government's obligation to protect its citizens and those citizens' exercise of their rights. These competing interests were at issue in the following case.

20. 491 U.S. 397, 109 S.Ct. 2533, 105 L.Ed.2d 342 (1989).

21. *United States v. Eichman*, 496 U.S. 310, 110 S.Ct. 2804, 110 L.Ed.2d 287 (1990).

CASE 5.1

United States
Court of Appeals,
Seventh Circuit, 2004.
355 F.3d 1048.

Hodgkins v. Peterson

ROVNER, Circuit Judge.
* * * *

Shortly after 11:00 P.M. on August 26, 1999, Colin Hodgkins and his three friends [all of whom were minors] left a Steak 'n Shake restaurant in Marion County, Indiana, where they had stopped to eat after attending a school soccer game. As they left the restaurant, police arrested and handcuffed them for violating Indiana's curfew regulation. The police took Colin and his friends to a curfew sweep processing site where he was given a breathalyser test and * * * tested for drugs. * * *

* * * At the time of Colin's arrest, the Indiana statute set a curfew of 11 P.M. on weekday nights [with a few exceptions].
* * * *

* * * Nancy Hodgkins is * * * the mother of * * * Colin * * * . Ms. Hodgkins would like to allow her children to participate in * * * activities protected by the * * * First Amendment * * * , however, she is concerned that if they do so, they will be subject to arrest. * * *

* * * She seeks [an] * * * injunction against defendants Bart Peterson, in his official capacity as Mayor of the City of Indianapolis and [other local government officials], barring them from enforcing the * * * curfew law. * * *
* * * *

* * * [T]he court found * * * only an incidental burden on minors' First Amendment rights. * * * The plaintiffs filed a timely appeal [to the U.S. Court of Appeals for the Seventh Circuit].
* * * *

The strength of our democracy depends on a citizenry that knows and understands its freedoms, exercises them responsibly, and guards them vigilantly. Young adults are not suddenly granted the full panoply [array] of constitutional rights on the day they attain the age of majority. We not only permit but expect youths to exercise those liberties—to learn to think for themselves, to give voice to their opinions, to hear and evaluate competing points of view—so that they might attain the right to vote at age eighteen with the tools to exercise that right. A juvenile's ability to worship, associate, and speak freely is therefore not simply a privilege that benefits her as an individual, but a necessary means of allowing her to become a fully enfranchised [endowed with the privileges of citizenship, especially voting rights] member of democratic society. * * *

[The Hodgkinses] assert that the consequences of violating the curfew law are so burdensome and intrusive that, rather than risk arrest, they will be discouraged from participating in expressive activity during curfew hours. In other words, the plaintiffs claim that the curfew regulation creates a "chill" that imposes on their First Amendment rights. * * *
* * * *

* * * The government claims that plaintiffs cannot mount a * * * challenge to the curfew law * * * because they have not demonstrated either that the curfew law imposes a disproportionate burden on those engaged in First Amendment activities or that it regulates conduct with an expressive element.

We agree that the Indiana curfew ordinance does not disproportionately impact First Amendment rights. As Colin Hodgkins can attest, it burdens minors who want to attend soccer games as much as it burdens those who wish to speak at a political rally. On the other hand, the curfew ordinance regulates minors' abilities to engage in some of the purest and most protected forms of speech and expression. [A] wide range of First Amendment activities occur during curfew hours, including political events, death penalty protests, late-night sessions of the Indiana General Assembly, and neighborhood association meetings or nighttime events. A number of religions mark particular days or events with late-night services, prayers, or other activities: many Christians, for example, commemorate the birth of Christ with a midnight service on Christmas Eve and the Last Supper with an all-night vigil on Holy Thursday; Jews observe the first night of Shavuot by studying Torah all through the night; and

CASE 5.1 | Continued

throughout the month of Ramadan, Muslims engage in late-evening prayer. Late-night or all-night marches, rallies, and sleep-ins are often held to protest government action or inaction. And it is not unusual for political campaigns, particularly in the whirlwind final hours before an election, to hold rallies in the middle of the night. Thus, during the last weeks of the 1960 presidential campaign, then-Senator John F. Kennedy addressed a group of University of Michigan students at 2:00 A.M. on the steps of the Michigan Union. In unprepared remarks, he asked the students whether they would be willing to devote a few years of their lives working in underdeveloped countries in order to foster better relations between the people of those nations and the United States. The students responded with a petition calling for the creation of the Peace Corps, which came into being the following year. These are but a few examples. *The curfew ordinance regulates access to almost every form of public expression during the late-night hours. The effect on the speech of the plaintiffs is significant.* [Emphasis added.]

* * * *

* * * Any juvenile who chooses to participate in a late-night religious or political activity thus runs the risk that he will be arrested if a police officer stops him en route to or from that activity and he cannot prove to the officer's satisfaction that he is out after hours in order to exercise his First Amendment rights.

* * * *

* * * The prospect of an arrest is intimidating in and of itself; but one should also have in mind what else might follow from the arrest. * * * We have no doubt that the authorities are well meaning in administering the drug and alcohol testing and in questioning the minor and his parents about his friends and family life. But these are also rather serious intrusions upon one's personal and familial privacy, and they represent a substantial price for a minor to have to pay in order to take part in a late-night political or religious event. *The chill that the prospect of arrest imposes on a minor's exercise of his or her First Amendment rights is patent [evident].* [Emphasis added.]

* * * *

In sum, we hold that the curfew law * * * is not narrowly tailored to serve a significant governmental interest and fails to allow for ample alternative channels for expression. The statute restricts a minor's access to any public forum during curfew hours * * * . The concrete possibility of arrest * * * makes clear that the statute unduly chills the exercise of a minor's First Amendment rights. * * * Consequently, we reverse the judgment and remand with directions to enjoin [prevent] the enforcement of Indiana's curfew until such time as the State's legislature removes the chill that the statute places on the exercise of First Amendment rights by minors.

QUESTIONS

1. Why is it unfair to require minors to engage in protected activity only during noncurfew hours, during curfew hours accompanied by an authorized adult, or from the minors' homes by phone or over the Internet?
2. How might a curfew law be written to protect both the fundamental constitutional rights of minors and the safety of all citizens?

CORPORATE POLITICAL SPEECH Political speech by corporations also falls within the protection of the First Amendment. For example, in *First National Bank of Boston v. Bellotti*,[22] national banking associations and business corporations asked the United States Supreme Court to review a Massachusetts statute that prohibited corporations from making political contributions or expenditures that individuals were permitted to make. The Court ruled that the statute was unconstitutional because it violated the right of corporations to freedom of speech. Similarly, the Supreme Court has held that a law forbidding a corporation from placing inserts in its billing to express its views on controversial issues violates the First Amendment.[23] Although in 1990 the Supreme Court reversed this

---

22. 435 U.S. 765, 98 S.Ct. 1407, 55 L.Ed.2d 707 (1978).

23. *Consolidated Edison Co. v. Public Service Commission*, 447 U.S. 530, 100 S.Ct. 2326, 65 L.Ed.2d 319 (1980).

trend somewhat,[24] corporate political speech continues to be given significant protection under the First Amendment.

COMMERCIAL SPEECH The courts also give substantial protection to *commercial speech*, which consists of communications—primarily advertising and marketing—made by business firms that only involve their commercial interests. The protection given to commercial speech under the First Amendment is not as extensive as that afforded to noncommercial speech, however. A state may restrict certain kinds of advertising, for example, in the interest of preventing consumers from being misled by the advertising practices. States also have a legitimate interest in the beau-

tification of roadsides, and this interest allows states to place restraints on billboard advertising. For example, in one Florida case, the court found that a law preventing a nude dancing establishment from billboard advertising was constitutionally permissible because it directly advanced a substantial government interest in highway beautification and safety.[25]

Generally, a restriction on commercial speech will be considered valid as long as it meets the following three criteria: (1) it must seek to implement a substantial government interest, (2) it must directly advance that interest, and (3) it must go no further than necessary to accomplish its objective. The court in the following case applied these principles to determine the constitutionality of a county ordinance that regulated video games based on their content—the ordinance applied only to "graphically violent" video games.

---

24. See *Austin v. Michigan Chamber of Commerce*, 494 U.S. 652, 110 S.Ct. 1391, 108 L.Ed.2d 652 (1990), in which the Supreme Court upheld a state law prohibiting corporations from using general corporate funds for independent expenditures in state political campaigns.

25. *Café Erotica v. Florida Department of Transportation*, 830 So.2d 181 (Fla.App. 1 Dist. 2002); review denied, *Café Erotica/We Dare to Bare v. Florida Department of Transportation*, 845 So.2d 888 (Fla. 2003).

CASE 5.2 — Interactive Digital Software Association v. St. Louis County, Missouri

United States
Court of Appeals,
Eighth Circuit. 2003.
329 F.3d 954.

BACKGROUND AND FACTS *St. Louis County, Missouri, passed an ordinance that made it unlawful for any person knowingly to sell, rent, or make available "graphically violent" video games to minors, or to "permit the free play of" such games by minors, without a parent or guardian's consent.[a] Interactive Digital Software Association, and others that create or provide the public with video games and related software, filed a suit against the county in a federal district court. The plaintiffs asserted that the ordinance violated the First Amendment and filed a motion for summary judgment. The county argued that the ordinance forwarded the compelling state interest of protecting the "psychological well-being of minors" by reducing the harm suffered by children who play violent video games. A psychologist, a high school principal, and others offered their conclusions that playing violent video games leads to aggressive behavior, but the county did not provide proof of a link between the games and psychological harm. The court denied the plaintiffs' motion and dismissed the case. The plaintiffs appealed to the U.S. Court of Appeals for the Eighth Circuit.*

IN THE LANGUAGE OF THE COURT

MORRIS SHEPPARD ARNOLD, Circuit Judge.

* * * *

* * * If the first amendment is versatile enough to shield the painting of Jackson Pollock, music of Arnold Schoenberg, or Jabberwocky verse of Lewis Carroll, we see no reason why the pictures, graphic design, concept art, sounds, music, stories, and narrative present in video games are not entitled to a similar protection. The mere fact that they appear in a novel medium is of no legal consequence. Our review of the record convinces us that these violent video games contain stories, imagery, age-old themes of literature, and messages, even an ideology, just as books and movies do. * * *

We recognize that while children have in the past experienced age-old elemental violent themes by reading a fairy tale or an epic poem, or attending a Saturday matinee, the interac-

---

a. St. Louis County Revised Ordinances Sections 602.425 through 602.460.

CASE 5.2 | **Continued**

tive play of a video game might present different difficulties. The County suggests in fact that with video games, the story lines are incidental and players may skip the expressive parts of the game and proceed straight to the player-controlled action. But the same could be said of action-packed movies like "The Matrix" or "Charlie's Angels"; any viewer with a videocassette or DVD player could simply skip to and isolate the action sequences. * * *

We note, moreover, that *there is no justification for disqualifying video games as speech simply because they are constructed to be interactive;* indeed, literature is most successful when it draws the reader into the story, makes him identify with the characters, invites him to judge them and quarrel with them, to experience their joys and sufferings as the reader's own. In fact, some books, such as the pre-teen oriented "Choose Your Own Nightmare" series (in which the reader makes choices that determine the plot of the story, and which lead the reader to one of several endings, by following the instructions at the bottom of the page) can be every bit as interactive * * * . [Emphasis added.]

Whether we believe the advent of violent video games adds anything of value to society is irrelevant; *guided by the First Amendment, we are obliged to recognize that they are as much entitled to the protection of free speech as the best of literature.* * * * [Emphasis added.]

* * * *

* * * [To] constitutionally restrict the speech at issue here, the County must come forward with empirical support for its belief that violent video games cause psychological harm to minors. In this case, * * * the County has failed to present the substantial supporting evidence of harm that is required before an ordinance that threatens protected speech can be upheld. * * * [T]he County may not simply surmise that it is serving a compelling state interest because "[s]ociety in general believes that continued exposure to violence can be harmful to children." Where First Amendment rights are at stake, the Government must present more than anecdote and supposition.

DECISION AND REMEDY *The U.S. Court of Appeals for the Eighth Circuit reversed the judgment of the lower court and remanded the case for the entry of an injunction preventing the county's enforcement of its ordinance. Video games are entitled to the same First Amendment protection as other types of speech, and the defendants failed to present the required evidence of harm to uphold a law threatening protected speech.*

UNPROTECTED SPEECH The United States Supreme Court has made it clear that certain types of speech will not be protected under the First Amendment. Speech that harms the good reputation of another, or defamatory speech (see Chapter 12), is not protected under the First Amendment. Speech that violates criminal laws (threatening speech and pornography, for example) is not constitutionally protected. Other unprotected speech includes "fighting words" (speech that is likely to incite others to respond violently).

—Obscene Speech. The Supreme Court has also held that the First Amendment does not protect obscene speech. The Court has grappled from time to time with the problem of establishing an objective definition of obscene speech. In a 1973 case, *Miller v. California,*[26] the Supreme Court created a test for legal obscenity, including a set of requirements that must be met for material to be legally obscene. Under this test,

material is obscene if (1) the average person finds that it violates contemporary community standards; (2) the work taken as a whole appeals to a prurient (arousing or obsessive) interest in sex; (3) the work shows patently offensive sexual conduct; and (4) the work lacks serious redeeming literary, artistic, political, or scientific merit.

Because community standards vary widely, the *Miller* test has had inconsistent applications, and obscenity remains a constitutionally unsettled issue. Numerous state and federal statutes make it a crime to disseminate obscene materials, however, and the Supreme Court has often upheld such laws, including laws prohibiting the sale and possession of child pornography.[27]

—Online Obscenity. A significant problem facing the courts and lawmakers today is how to control the dissemination of obscenity and child pornography

---

26. 413 U.S. 15, 93 S.Ct. 2607, 37 L.Ed.2d 419 (1973).

27. For example, see *Osborne v. Ohio,* 495 U.S. 103, 110 S.Ct. 1691, 109 L.Ed.2d 98 (1990).

via the Internet. Congress first attempted to protect minors from pornographic materials on the Internet by passing the Communications Decency Act (CDA) of 1996. The CDA declared it a crime to make available to minors online any "obscene or indecent" message that "depicts or describes, in terms patently offensive as measured by contemporary community standards, sexual or excretory activities or organs."[28] Civil rights groups immediately challenged the act as an unconstitutional restraint on speech, and ultimately the United States Supreme Court ruled that portions of the act were unconstitutional. The Court held that the terms *indecent* and *patently offensive* covered large amounts of nonpornographic material with serious educational or other value.

—Subsequent Attempts to Regulate Online Obscenity. Some of Congress's later attempts to curb pornography on the Internet have also encountered constitutional stumbling blocks. For example, the Child Online Protection Act (COPA) of 1998[29] banned material "harmful to minors" distributed without some kind of age-verification system to separate adult and minor users. In 2002, the Supreme Court upheld a lower court's injunction suspending the COPA.[30] In 2000, Congress enacted the Children's Internet Protection Act (CIPA),[31] which requires public schools and libraries to block adult content from access by children by installing **filtering software.** Such software is designed to prevent persons from viewing certain Web sites by responding to a site's Internet address or its **meta tags,** or key words. The CIPA was also challenged on constitutional grounds, but in 2003 the Supreme Court held that the act does not violate the First Amendment. The Court concluded that because libraries can disable the filters for any patrons who ask, the system is reasonably flexible and does not burden free speech to an unconstitutional extent.[32]

FREEDOM OF RELIGION

The First Amendment states that the government may neither establish any religion nor prohibit the free exercise of religious practices. The first part of this constitutional provision is referred to as the **establishment clause,** which has to do with the separation of church and state. The second part of the provision is known as the **free exercise clause.**

THE ESTABLISHMENT CLAUSE The establishment clause prohibits the government from establishing a state-sponsored religion, as well as from passing laws that promote (aid or endorse) religion or that show a preference for one religion over another. Establishment clause issues often involve such matters as the legality of allowing or requiring school prayers, using state-issued school vouchers to pay for tuition at religious schools, teaching evolutionary versus creationist theory, and giving state and local government aid to religious organizations and schools.

—Sunday Closing Laws. Federal or state laws that do not promote or place a significant burden on religion are constitutional even if they have some impact on religion. "Sunday closing laws," for example, make the performance of some commercial activities on Sunday illegal. These statutes, also known as "blue laws" (from the color of the paper on which an early Sunday law was written), have been upheld on the ground that it is a legitimate function of government to provide a day of rest to promote the health and welfare of workers. Even though closing laws admittedly make it easier for Christians to attend religious services, the courts have viewed this effect as an incidental, not a primary, purpose of Sunday closing laws.

—Religious Displays on Public Property. The First Amendment does not require a complete separation of church and state. On the contrary, it affirmatively mandates accommodation of all religions and forbids hostility toward any.[33] An ongoing challenge for the courts is determining the extent to which governments can accommodate a religion without appearing to promote that religion, which would violate the establishment clause. For example, in *Lynch v. Donnelly,*[34] the United States Supreme Court held that a municipality could include religious symbols, such as a Nativity scene, or crèche, in its annual holiday display as long as the religious symbols constituted just one part of a display in which other, nonreligious symbols (such as reindeer and candy-striped poles) were also featured. The Supreme Court applied this

---

28. 47 U.S.C. Section 223(a)(1)(B)(ii).

29. 47 U.S.C. Section 231.

30. *Ashcroft v. American Civil Liberties Union,* 535 U.S. 564, 122 S.Ct. 1700, 152 L.Ed.2d 771 (2002). Also see *American Civil Liberties Union v. Ashcroft,* 322 F.3d 240 (3d Cir. 2003).

31. 17 U.S.C. Sections 1701–1741.

32. *United States v. American Library Association,* 539 U.S. 194, 123 S.Ct. 2297, 156 L.Ed.2d 221 (2003).

33. *Zorach v. Clauson,* 343 U.S. 306, 72 S.Ct. 679, 96 L.Ed. 954 (1952).

34. 465 U.S. 668, 104 S.Ct. 1355, 79 L.Ed.2d 604 (1984).

same reasoning in subsequent cases involving similar issues.[35] Nevertheless, disputes continue to arise involving religious monuments—particularly those depicting the Ten Commandments—on city or county property.[36]

THE FREE EXERCISE CLAUSE The free exercise clause guarantees that no person can be compelled to do something that is contrary to his or her religious beliefs. For this reason, if a law or policy is contrary to a person's religious beliefs, exemptions are often made to accommodate those beliefs. When, however, religious practices work against public policy and the public welfare, the government can act. For example, regardless of a child's or parent's religious beliefs, the government can require certain types of vaccinations.

Additionally, public school students can be required to study from textbooks chosen by school authorities.

For business firms, an important issue involves the accommodation that businesses must make for the religious beliefs of their employees. For example, if an employee's religion prohibits her or him from working on a certain day of the week or at a certain type of job, the employer must make a *reasonable* attempt to accommodate these religious requirements. Employers must reasonably accommodate an employee's religious belief even if the belief is not based on the tenets or dogma of a particular church, sect, or denomination. The only requirement is that the belief be religious in nature and sincerely held by the employee.[37] (See Chapter 21 for a further discussion of religious freedom in the employment context.)

The following case focused on a state scholarship program for college and university students. The case involved this question: Is the free exercise clause violated when the state bans students from using the scholarships to pursue degrees in theology?

---

35. See, for example, *County of Allegheny v. American Civil Liberties Union*, 492 U.S. 573, 109 S.Ct. 3086, 106 L.Ed.2d 472 (1989); and *Capitol Square Review and Advisory Board v. Pinette*, 515 U.S. 753, 115 S.Ct. 2440, 132 L.Ed.2d 650 (1995).
36. See, for example, *Van Orden v. Perry*, 351 F.3d 265 (4th Cir. 2001); *Summum, a Corporate Sole and Church v. Duchesne City*, 340 F.Supp.2d 1223 (D. Utah 2004); and *Modrovich v. Allegheny County, Pennsylvania*, 385 F.3d 397 (3d Cir. 2004).

37. *Frazee v. Illinois Department of Employment Security*, 489 U.S. 829, 109 S.Ct. 1514, 103 L.Ed.2d 914 (1989).

CASE 5.3 — Locke v. Davey

Supreme Court of the
United States, 2004.
540 U.S. 712,
124 S.Ct. 1307,
158 L.Ed.2d 1.
http://www.findlaw.com/
casecode/supreme.html[a]

BACKGROUND AND FACTS *In 1999, the state of Washington created the "Promise Scholarship Program" to assist students with postsecondary education expenses. Those who meet the academic, income, and enrollment requirements can spend the funds on any education-related expense. Under the state constitution, however, students cannot use the scholarships to seek degrees in "devotional theology." A state statute refers to degrees that are "devotional in nature or designed to induce religious faith," but the schools, not the state, determine whether students' majors are "devotional." Joshua Davey was awarded a Promise Scholarship and chose to attend Northwest College, a private Christian college affiliated with the Assemblies of God denomination. When Davey decided to pursue a double major in pastoral ministries and business management/administration, he was denied the scholarship. Davey filed a suit in a federal district court against state officials, arguing in part that this denial violated the free exercise clause. The court issued a judgment in favor of the state. Davey appealed to the U.S. Court of Appeals for the Ninth Circuit, which ruled that the scholarship program was unconstitutional. The state appealed to the United States Supreme Court.*

IN THE LANGUAGE OF THE COURT

Chief Justice *REHNQUIST* delivered the opinion of the Court.

* * * *

* * * [T]he Establishment Clause and the Free Exercise Clause are frequently in tension. Yet we have long said that there is room for play in the joints between them. In other words, *there are some state actions permitted by the Establishment Clause but not required by the Free Exercise Clause*. [Emphasis added.]

---

a. In the "Browsing" section, click on "2004 Decisions." When that page opens, click on the name of the case to access the opinion.

CONTINUED ▶

CASE 5.3 | Continued

This case involves that play in the joints as described above. * * * [T]here is no doubt that the State could, consistent with the Federal Constitution, permit Promise Scholars to pursue a degree in devotional theology, and the State does not contend otherwise. The question before us, however, is whether Washington, pursuant to its own constitution, * * * can deny them such funding without violating the Free Exercise Clause.

Davey urges us to answer that question in the negative. He contends that * * * the program is * * * unconstitutional because it is not * * * neutral with respect to religion. We reject his claim * * * . [T]he State's disfavor of religion (if it can be called that) is of a far milder kind [than in other cases]. It imposes neither criminal nor civil sanctions on any type of religious service or rite. It does not deny to ministers the right to participate in the political affairs of the community. And it does not require students to choose between their religious beliefs and receiving a government benefit. The State has merely chosen not to fund a distinct category of instruction.

* * * *

* * * Because the Promise Scholarship Program funds training for all secular [lay, or nonreligious] professions, [it is contended that] the State must also fund training for religious professions. But training for religious professions and training for secular professions are not fungible [interchangeable]. Training someone to lead a congregation is an essentially religious endeavor. Indeed, majoring in devotional theology is akin to a religious calling as well as an academic pursuit. And *the subject of religion is one in which both the United States and state constitutions embody distinct views—in favor of free exercise, but opposed to establishment—that find no counterpart with respect to other callings or professions. That a State would deal differently with religious education for the ministry than with education for other callings is a product of these views, not evidence of hostility toward religion.* [Emphasis added.]

* * * *

Far from evincing [demonstrating] * * * hostility toward religion * * * , we believe that the entirety of the Promise Scholarship Program goes a long way toward including religion in its benefits. The program permits students to attend pervasively religious schools, so long as they are accredited. As Northwest advertises, its "concept of education is distinctly Christian in the evangelical sense." It prepares *all* of its students, "through instruction, through modeling, [and] through [its] classes, to use * * * the Bible as their guide, as the truth," no matter their chosen profession. And under the Promise Scholarship Program's current guidelines, students are still eligible to take devotional theology courses. * * *

In short, we find neither in the history or text of * * * the Washington Constitution, nor in the operation of the Promise Scholarship Program, anything that suggests *animus* [hostility] towards religion. Given the historic and substantial state interest at issue, we therefore cannot conclude that the denial of funding for vocational religious instruction alone is inherently constitutionally suspect.

* * * The State's interest in not funding the pursuit of devotional degrees is substantial and the exclusion of such funding places a relatively minor burden on Promise Scholars. If any room exists between the two Religion Clauses, it must be here. We need not venture further into this difficult area in order to uphold the Promise Scholarship Program as currently operated by the State of Washington.

DECISION AND REMEDY   *The United States Supreme Court reversed the decision of the lower court. The Supreme Court held that Washington's "exclusion from an otherwise inclusive aid program" of students pursuing degrees in devotional theology "does not violate the Free Exercise Clause of the First Amendment." This exclusion furthers the state's interest in prohibiting the use of tax funds to support the ministry without suggesting hostility toward religion or imposing more than a minor burden on the program's participants.*

WHAT IF THE FACTS WERE DIFFERENT?   *Suppose that the state constitution had allowed the scholarship to be given to students seeking degrees in Christian theology but not to students studying other religious theories. How might this have affected the Supreme Court's decision?*

SEARCHES AND SEIZURES

The Fourth Amendment protects the "right of the people to be secure in their persons, houses, papers, and effects." Before searching or seizing private property, law enforcement officers must obtain a **search warrant**—an order from a judge or other public official authorizing the search or seizure.

SEARCH WARRANTS AND PROBABLE CAUSE

To obtain a search warrant, law enforcement officers must convince a judge that they have reasonable grounds, or probable cause, to believe a search will reveal a specific illegality. To establish **probable cause,** the officers must have trustworthy evidence that would convince a reasonable person that the proposed search or seizure is more likely justified than not. Furthermore, the Fourth Amendment prohibits *general* warrants. It requires a particular description of whatever is to be searched or seized. General searches through a person's belongings are impermissible. The search cannot extend beyond what is described in the warrant.

The requirement for a search warrant has several exceptions. One exception applies when it is likely that the items sought will be removed before a warrant can be obtained. For example, if a police officer has probable cause to believe that an automobile contains evidence of a crime and that the vehicle will likely be unavailable by the time a warrant is obtained, the officer can search the vehicle without a warrant.

SEARCHES AND SEIZURES IN THE BUSINESS CONTEXT

Constitutional protection against unreasonable searches and seizures is important to businesses and professionals. As federal and state regulation of commercial activities increased, frequent and unannounced government inspections were conducted to ensure compliance with the regulations. Such inspections were at times extremely disruptive. In *Marshall v. Barlow's, Inc.*,[38] the United States Supreme Court held that government inspectors do not have the right to enter business premises without a warrant, although the standard of probable cause is not the same as that required in nonbusiness contexts. The existence of a general and neutral enforcement plan will justify issuance of the warrant.

—Business Records. Lawyers and accountants frequently possess the business records of their clients, and inspecting these documents while they are out of the hands of their true owners also requires a warrant. A warrant is not required, however, for the seizure of spoiled or contaminated food. In addition, warrants are not required for searches of businesses in such highly regulated industries as liquor, guns, and strip mining. General manufacturing is not considered to be one of these highly regulated industries, however.

—Employee Safety. Of increasing concern to many government employers is how to maintain a safe and efficient workplace without jeopardizing the Fourth Amendment rights of employees "to be secure in their persons." Requiring government employees to undergo random drug tests, for example, may be held to violate the Fourth Amendment. In Chapter 20, we will discuss Fourth Amendment issues in the employment context, as well as employee privacy rights in general, in greater detail.

SELF-INCRIMINATION

The Fifth Amendment guarantees that no person "shall be compelled in any criminal case to be a witness against himself." Thus, in any federal proceeding, an accused person cannot be compelled to give testimony that might subject him or her to any criminal prosecution. Nor can an accused person be forced to testify against himself or herself in state courts because the due process clause of the Fourteenth Amendment (discussed in the next section) incorporates the Fifth Amendment provision against self-incrimination.

The Fifth Amendment's guarantee against self-incrimination extends only to natural persons. Because a corporation is a legal entity and not a natural person, the privilege against self-incrimination does not apply to it. Similarly, the business records of a partnership do not receive Fifth Amendment protection.[39] When a partnership is required to produce these records, it must do so even if the information provided incriminates the persons who constitute the business entity. In contrast, sole proprietors and sole practitioners (those who fully own their businesses) who have not incorporated cannot be compelled to produce their business records. These individuals have full protection against self-incrimination because they function in only one capacity; there is no separate business entity.

---

38. 436 U.S. 307, 98 S.Ct. 1816, 56 L.Ed.2d 305 (1978).

39. The privilege has been applied to some small family partnerships. See *United States v. Slutsky,* 352 F.Supp. 1105 (S.D.N.Y. 1972).

SECTION 3 | Due Process and Equal Protection

Other constitutional guarantees of great significance to Americans are mandated by the *due process clauses* of the Fifth and Fourteenth Amendments and the *equal protection clause* of the Fourteenth Amendment.

DUE PROCESS

Both the Fifth and Fourteenth Amendments provide that no person shall be deprived "of life, liberty, or property, without due process of law." The **due process clause** of these constitutional amendments has two aspects—procedural and substantive. Note that the due process clause applies to "legal persons" (that is, corporations), as well as to individuals.

PROCEDURAL DUE PROCESS *Procedural* due process requires that any government decision to take life, liberty, or property must be made equitably. For example, fair procedures must be used in determining whether a person will be subjected to punishment or have some burden imposed on her or him. Fair procedure has been interpreted as requiring that the person have at least an opportunity to object to a proposed action before an impartial, neutral decision maker (which need not be a judge). Thus, for example, if a driver's license is construed as a property interest, some sort of opportunity to object to its suspension or termination by the state must be provided.

SUBSTANTIVE DUE PROCESS *Substantive* due process focuses on the content, or substance, of legislation. It generally requires that the government have an appropriate justification or goal in enacting the law and that the law, as applied, sufficiently furthers that goal.

—When Fundamental Rights Are Involved. If a law or other governmental action limits a *fundamental right*, it will be held to violate substantive due process unless it promotes a *compelling* or *overriding state interest*. Fundamental rights include interstate travel, privacy, voting, and all First Amendment rights. Compelling state interests could include, for example, the public's safety. Thus, even though laws designating speed limits affect interstate travel, they may be upheld if they are shown to reduce highway fatalities, because the state has a compelling interest in protecting the lives of its citizens.

Suppose that a state legislature enacted a law imposing a fifteen-year term of imprisonment without a trial on all businesspersons who appeared in their own television commercials. This law would be unconstitutional on both substantive and procedural grounds. Substantive review would invalidate the legislation because it abridges freedom of speech, a fundamental right. Procedurally, the law is constitutionally invalid because it imposes a penalty without giving the accused a chance to defend his or her actions.

—When No Fundamental Rights Are Involved. In situations not involving fundamental rights, a law or action does not violate substantive due process if it *rationally relates* to any *legitimate government purpose*. It is almost impossible for a law or action to fail this "rational basis" test. Under this test, virtually any business regulation will be upheld as reasonable—the United States Supreme Court has upheld insurance regulations, price and wage controls, banking controls, and controls of unfair competition and trade practices against substantive due process challenges.

EQUAL PROTECTION

Under the Fourteenth Amendment, a state may not "deny to any person within its jurisdiction the equal protection of the laws." The United States Supreme Court has used the due process clause of the Fifth Amendment to make the **equal protection clause** applicable to the federal government. Equal protection means that the government must treat similarly situated individuals in a similar manner.

Both substantive due process and equal protection require review of the substance of the law or other governmental action rather than review of the procedures used. When a law or action limits the liberty of all persons to do something, it may violate substantive due process; when a law or action limits the liberty of some persons but not others, it may violate the equal protection clause. Thus, for example, if a law prohibits all advertising on the sides of trucks, it raises a substantive due process question; if it makes an exception to allow truck owners to advertise their businesses, it raises an equal protection issue.

In an equal protection inquiry, when a law or action distinguishes between or among individuals, the basis for the distinction—that is, the classification—is examined by the courts. The courts may use one of three standards: strict scrutiny, intermediate scrutiny, or the "rational basis" test.

STRICT SCRUTINY If a law or action prohibits or inhibits some persons from exercising a fundamental right, the law or action will be subject to "strict scrutiny" by the courts. Under this standard, the classification must be necessary to promote a *compelling state interest*. Also, if the classification is based on a *suspect trait*—such as race, national origin, or citizenship status—the classification must be necessary to promote a compelling state interest. Compelling state interests include remedying past unconstitutional or illegal discrimination but do not include correcting the general effects of "society's" discrimination. Thus, for example, if a city gives preference to minority applicants in awarding construction contracts, the city normally must identify the past unconstitutional or illegal discrimination against minority construction firms that it is attempting to correct. Generally, few laws or actions survive strict-scrutiny analysis by the courts.

INTERMEDIATE SCRUTINY Another standard, that of "intermediate scrutiny," is applied in cases involving discrimination based on gender or legitimacy. Laws using these classifications must be *substantially related to important government objectives*.

For example, an important government objective is preventing illegitimate teenage pregnancies. Therefore, because males and females are not similarly situated in this regard—only females can become pregnant—a law that punishes men but not women for statutory rape will be upheld, even though it treats men and women unequally.

The state also has an important objective in establishing time limits (called *statutes of limitation*) for how long after an event a particular type of action can be brought. Such limits prevent persons from bringing fraudulent and stale (outdated) claims. Nevertheless, the limitation period must be substantially related to the important objective. For example, suppose that a state law requires illegitimate children to file a paternity action within six years of their birth in order to seek support from their biological fathers. This law will fail if legitimate children can seek support from their fathers at any time because distinguishing between support claims on the basis of legitimacy has no relation to the objective of preventing fraudulent or stale claims.

THE "RATIONAL BASIS" TEST In matters of economic or social welfare, the classification will be considered valid if there is any conceivable *rational basis* on which the classification might relate to a legitimate government interest. As mentioned previously, it is almost impossible for a law or action to fail the rational basis test. Thus, for example, a city ordinance that in effect prohibits all pushcart vendors, except a specific few, from operating in a particular area of the city will be upheld if the city provides a rational basis—such as reducing the traffic in the particular area—for the ordinance. In contrast, a law that provides unemployment benefits only to people over six feet tall would clearly fail the rational basis test because it could not further any legitimate government objective.

SECTION 4 | Privacy Rights

The U.S. Constitution does not explicitly mention a general right to privacy, and only relatively recently have the courts regarded the right to privacy as a constitutional right. In a 1928 Supreme Court case, *Olmstead v. United States*,[40] Justice Louis Brandeis stated in his dissent that the right to privacy is "the most comprehensive of rights and the right most valued by civilized men." The majority of the justices at that time did not agree, and it was not until the 1960s that a majority on the Supreme Court endorsed the view that the Constitution protects individual privacy rights. In a landmark 1965 case, *Griswold v. Connecticut*,[41] the Supreme Court held that a constitutional right to privacy was implied by the First, Third, Fourth, Fifth, and Ninth Amendments.

FEDERAL STATUTES AFFECTING PRIVACY RIGHTS

In the last several decades, Congress has enacted a number of statutes that protect the privacy of individuals in various areas of concern. In the 1960s, Americans were sufficiently alarmed by the accumulation of personal information in government files that they pressured Congress to pass laws permitting individuals to access their files. Congress responded in 1966 with the Freedom of Information Act, which allows any person to request copies of any information on her or him contained in federal government files. In 1974, Congress passed the Privacy Act, which also gives persons the right to access such information. Since then, Congress has passed numerous other laws protecting individuals' privacy rights with respect to

---

40. 277 U.S. 438, 48 S.Ct. 564, 72 L.Ed. 944 (1928).
41. 381 U.S. 479, 85 S.Ct. 1678, 14 L.Ed.2d 510 (1965).

financial transactions, electronic communications, and other activities in which personal information may be gathered and stored by organizations.

MEDICAL INFORMATION Responding to the growing need to protect the privacy of individuals' health records—particularly computerized records—Congress passed the Health Insurance Portability and Accountability Act (HIPAA) of 1996.[42] The HIPAA requires health-care providers and health-care plans, including certain employers who sponsor health plans, to inform patients of their privacy rights and of how their personal medical information may be used. The act also generally states that a person's medical records may not be used for purposes unrelated to health care—such as marketing, for example—or disclosed to others without the individual's permission. Covered entities must formulate written privacy policies, designate privacy officials, limit access to computerized health data, physically secure medical records with lock and key, train employees and volunteers on their privacy policies, and sanction those who violate the policies. These protections are intended to assure individuals that their health information, including genetic information, will be properly protected and not used for purposes that the patient did not know about or authorize.

THE PATRIOT ACT In the wake of the terrorist attacks of September 11, 2001, Congress passed legislation, commonly referred to as the USA Patriot Act, which gives increased authority to government officials to monitor Internet activities (such as e-mail and Web site visits) and to gain access to personal financial information and student information.[43] Using technology, law enforcement officials can track the telephone and e-mail conversations of one party to find out the identity of the other party or parties. The government must certify that the information likely to be obtained is relevant to an ongoing criminal investigation but does not need proof of any wrongdoing to gain access to this information. Privacy advocates argue that this law adversely affects the constitutional rights of all Americans, and it has been widely criticized in the media, fueling the public debate over how to secure privacy rights in an electronic age.

OTHER LAWS AFFECTING PRIVACY

State constitutions and statutes also protect individuals' privacy rights, often to a significant degree. Privacy rights are also protected under tort law (see Chapter 12). Additionally, the Federal Trade Commission has played an active role in protecting the privacy rights of online consumers (see Chapter 23). The protection of employees' privacy rights, particularly with respect to electronic monitoring practices, is an area of growing concern (see Chapter 20).

---

42. The HIPAA was enacted as Pub. L. No. 104-191 (1996) and is codified in 29 U.S.C.A. Sections 1181 *et seq.*

43. Uniting and Strengthening America by Providing Appropriate Tools Required to Intercept and Obstruct Terrorism Act of 2001, also known as the USA Patriot Act, was enacted as Pub. L. No. 107-56 (2001).

REVIEWING CONSTITUTIONAL LAW

A state legislature enacted a statute that required any motorcycle operator or passenger on the state's highways to wear a protective helmet. Jim Alderman, a licensed motorcycle operator, sued the state to block enforcement of the law. Alderman asserted that the statute violated the equal protection clause because it placed requirements on motorcyclists that were not imposed on other motorists. Using the information presented in the chapter, answer the following questions.

1. | Why does this statute raise equal protection issues instead of substantive due process concerns?

2. | What are the three levels of scrutiny that the courts use in determining whether a law violates the equal protection clause?

3. | What type of government interest must be served to justify discriminatory classifications under each of these three standards of scrutiny?

4. | Which standard, or test, would apply to this situation? Why?

5. | Applying this standard, or test, is the helmet statute constitutional? Why or why not?

TERMS AND CONCEPTS TO REVIEW

amend 106

Bill of Rights 110

checks and balances 108

commerce clause 108

due process clause 120

equal protection clause 120

establishment clause 116

federal form of government 106

filtering software 116

free exercise clause 116

full faith and credit clause 107

meta tags 116

police powers 109

preemption 110

privileges and immunities
  clause 107

probable cause 119

search warrant 119

supremacy clause 109

symbolic speech 111

QUESTIONS AND CASE PROBLEMS

5–1. A Georgia state law requires the use of contoured rear-fender mudguards on trucks and trailers operating within Georgia state lines. The statute further makes it illegal for trucks and trailers to use straight mudguards. In approximately thirty-five other states, straight mudguards are legal. Moreover, in Florida, straight mudguards are explicitly required by law. There is some evidence suggesting that contoured mudguards might be a little safer than straight mudguards. Discuss whether this Georgia statute violates any constitutional provisions.

5–2. ⚖ QUESTION WITH SAMPLE ANSWER

Thomas worked in the nonmilitary operations of a large firm that produced both military and nonmilitary goods. When the company discontinued the production of non-military goods, Thomas was transferred to a plant producing military equipment. Thomas left his job, claiming that it violated his religious principles to participate in the manufacture of goods to be used in destroying life. In effect, he argued, the transfer to the war-materials plant forced him to quit his job. He was denied unemployment compensation by the state because he had not been effectively "discharged" by the employer but had voluntarily terminated his employment. Did the state's denial of unemployment benefits to Thomas violate the free exercise clause of the First Amendment? Explain.

For a sample answer to this question, go to Appendix I at the end of this text.

5–3. A business has a backlog of orders, and to meet its deadlines, management decides to run the firm seven days a week, eight hours a day. One of the employees, Abe Placer, refuses to work on Saturday on religious grounds. His refusal to work means that the firm may not meet its production deadlines and may therefore suffer a loss of future business. The firm fires Placer and replaces him with an employee who is willing to work seven days a week. Placer claims that by terminating his employment, his employer has violated his constitutional right to the free exercise of his religion. Do you agree? Why or why not?

5–4. The framers of the Constitution feared the twin evils of tyranny and anarchy. Discuss how specific provisions of the Constitution and the Bill of Rights reflect these fears and protect against both of these extremes.

5–5. EQUAL PROTECTION. With the objectives of preventing crime, maintaining property values, and preserving the quality of urban life, New York City enacted an ordinance to regulate the locations of commercial establishments that featured adult entertainment. The ordinance expressly applied to female, but not male, top-less entertainment. Adele Buzzetti owned the Cozy Cabin, a New York City cabaret that featured female top-less dancers. Buzzetti and an anonymous dancer filed a suit in a federal district court against the city, asking the court to block the enforcement of the ordinance. The plaintiffs argued in part that the ordinance violated the equal protection clause. Under the equal protection clause, what standard applies to the court's consideration of this ordinance? Under this test, how should the court rule? Why? [*Buzzetti v. City of New York,* 140 F.3d 134 (2d Cir. 1998)]

5–6. FREEDOM OF SPEECH. The city of Tacoma, Washington, enacted an ordinance that prohibited the playing of car sound systems at a volume that would be "audible" at a distance greater than fifty feet. Dwight Holland was arrested and convicted for violating the ordinance. The conviction was later dismissed, but Holland filed a civil suit in a Washington state court against the city. He claimed in part that the ordinance violated his freedom of speech under the First Amendment. On what basis might the court conclude that this ordinance is constitutional? (Hint: In playing a sound system, was Holland actually expressing himself?) [*Holland v. City of Tacoma,* 90 Wash.App. 533, 954 P.2d 290 (1998)]

5–7. ⚖ CASE PROBLEM WITH SAMPLE ANSWER

To protect the privacy of individuals identified in information systems maintained by federal agencies, the Privacy Act of 1974 regulates the use of the information. The statute provides for a minimum award of $1,000 for "actual damages sustained" caused by "intentional or willful actions" to the "person entitled to recovery." Buck Doe filed for certain disability benefits with an office of the U.S. Department of Labor (DOL). The application form asked for Doe's Social Security number, which the DOL used to identify his claim on documents sent to groups of claimants, their employers, and the lawyers involved in their cases. This disclosed Doe's Social Security number beyond the limits set by the Privacy Act. Doe filed a suit in a federal district court against the DOL, alleging that he was "torn * * * all to pieces" and "greatly concerned and worried" because of the disclosure of his Social Security number and its potentially "devastating" consequences. He did not offer any proof of actual injury, however. Should damages be awarded in such circumstances solely on the basis of the agency's conduct, or should proof of some actual injury be required? Why? [*Doe v. Chao*, 540 U.S. 614, 124 S.Ct. 1204, 157 L.Ed.2d 1122 (2004)]

To view a sample answer for this case problem, go to this book's Web site at http://wleb.westbuslaw.com, select "Chapter 5," and click on "Case Problem with Sample Answer."

5-8. FREEDOM OF SPEECH. Henry Mishkoff is a Web designer whose firm does business as "Webfeats." When Taubman Co. began building a mall called "The Shops at Willow Bend" near Mishkoff's home, Mishkoff registered the domain name "shopsatwillowbend.com" and created a Web site with that address. The site featured information about the mall, a disclaimer indicating that Mishkoff's site was unofficial, and a link to the mall's official site. Taubman discovered Mishkoff's site and filed a suit in a federal district court against him. Mishkoff then registered various other names, including "taubmansucks.com," with links to a site documenting his battle with Taubman. (A Web name with a "sucks.com" moniker attached to it is known as a "complaint name," and the process of registering and using such names is known as "cybergriping.") Taubman asked the court to order Mishkoff to stop using all of these names. Should the court grant Taubman's request? On what basis might the court protect Mishkoff's use of the names? [*Taubman Co. v. Webfeats*, 319 F.3d 770 (6th Cir. 2003)]

5-9. DUE PROCESS. In 1994, the Board of County Commissioners of Yellowstone County, Montana, created Zoning District 17 in a rural area of the county and a planning and zoning commission for the district. The commission adopted zoning regulations, which provided, among other things, that "dwelling units" could be built only through "on-site construction." Later, county officials were unable to identify any health or safety concerns that were addressed by requiring on-site construction. There was no evidence that homes built off-site would negatively affect property values or cause harm to any other general welfare interest of the community. In December 1999, Francis and Anita Yurczyk bought two forty-acre tracts in District 17. The Yurczyks also bought a modular home and moved it onto the property the following spring. Within days, the county advised the Yurczyks that the home violated the on-site construction regulation and would have to be removed. The Yurczyks filed a suit in a Montana state court against the county, alleging in part that the zoning regulation violated their due process rights. Does the Yurczyks' claim relate to procedural or substantive due process rights? What standard would the court apply to determine whether the regulation is constitutional? How should the court rule? Explain. [*Yurczyk v. Yellowstone County*, 2004 MT 3, 319 Mont. 169, 83 P.3d 266 (2004)]

5-10. 🏛 **A QUESTION OF ETHICS**

In 1999, in an effort to reduce smoking by children, the attorney general of Massachusetts issued comprehensive regulations governing the advertising and sale of tobacco products. Among other things, the regulations banned cigarette advertisements within one thousand feet of any elementary school, secondary school, or public playground and required retailers to post any advertising in their stores at least five feet off the floor, out of the immediate sight of young children. A group of tobacco manufacturers and retailers filed suit against the state, claiming that the regulations were preempted by the federal Cigarette Labeling and Advertising Act (FCLAA) of 1965, as amended. That act sets uniform labeling requirements and bans broadcast advertising for cigarettes. Ultimately, the case reached the United States Supreme Court, which held that the federal law on cigarette ads preempted the cigarette advertising restrictions adopted by Massachusetts. The only portion of the Massachusetts regulatory package to survive was the requirement that retailers had to place tobacco products in an area accessible only by the sales staff. In view of these facts, consider the following questions. [*Lorillard Tobacco Co. v. Reilly*, 533 U.S. 525, 121 S.Ct. 2404, 69 L.Ed.2d 532 (2001)]

(a) Some argue that having a national standard for tobacco regulation is more important than allowing states to set their own standards for tobacco regulation. Do you agree? Why or why not?

(b) According to the Court in this case, the federal law does not restrict the ability of state and local governments to adopt general zoning restrictions that apply to cigarettes, as long as those restrictions are "on equal terms with other products." How would you argue in support of this reasoning? How would you argue against it?

LAW | on the Web

For updated links to resources available on the Web, as well as a variety of other materials, visit this text's Web site at http://wleb.westbuslaw.com.

For an online version of the Constitution that provides hypertext links to amendments and other changes, as well as the history of the document, go to

http://www.constitutioncenter.org

For discussions of current issues involving the rights and liberties contained in the Bill of Rights, go to the Web site of the American Civil Liberties Union at

http://www.aclu.org

For a menu of selected constitutional law decisions by the United States Supreme Court, go to the Web site of Cornell Law School's Legal Information Institute at

http://straylight.law.cornell.edu/supct/index.html

LEGAL RESEARCH EXERCISES ON THE WEB

Go to http://wleb.westbuslaw.com, the Web site that accompanies this text. Select "Chapter 5" and click on "Internet Exercises." There you will find the following Internet research exercises that you can perform to learn more about topics covered in this chapter.

Activity 5–1: LEGAL PERSPECTIVE
Commercial Speech

Activity 5–2: MANAGEMENT PERSPECTIVE
Privacy Rights in Cyberspace

CHAPTER 6

Administrative Law

Government agencies established to administer the law have a tremendous impact on the day-to-day operations of the government and the economy. Administrative agencies issue rules covering virtually every aspect of a business's activities. At the federal level, the Securities and Exchange Commission regulates a firm's capital structure and financing, as well as its financial reporting. The National Labor Relations Board oversees relations between a firm and any unions with which it may deal. The Equal Employment Opportunity Commission also regulates employer-employee relationships. The Environmental Protection Agency and the Occupational Safety and Health Administration affect the way a firm manufactures its products, and the Federal Trade Commission influences the way the firm markets those products.

Added to this layer of federal regulation is a second layer of state regulation that, when not preempted by federal legislation, may cover many of the same activities or regulate independently those activities not covered by federal regulation. Finally, agency regulations at the county or municipal level also affect certain types of business activities.

The rules, orders, and decisions of administrative agencies make up the body of *administrative law*. You were introduced briefly to some of the main principles of administrative law in Chapter 1. In the following pages, we look at these principles in much greater detail.

SECTION 1 | Agency Creation and Powers

Because Congress cannot possibly oversee the actual implementation of all the laws it enacts, it must delegate such tasks to others, particularly when highly technical areas, such as air and water pollution, are involved. By delegating some of its authority to make and implement laws to administrative agencies, Congress can monitor indirectly a particular area in which it has passed legislation without becoming bogged down in the details of enforcement—details that are often best left to specialists.

To create an administrative agency, Congress passes **enabling legislation,** which specifies the name, purposes, functions, and powers of the agency being created. Federal administrative agencies may exercise only those powers that Congress has delegated to them in enabling legislation. Through similar enabling acts, state legislatures create state administrative agencies.

ENABLING LEGISLATION—AN EXAMPLE

Consider the enabling legislation for the Federal Trade Commission (FTC). The enabling statute for this agency is the Federal Trade Commission Act of 1914.[1] The act prohibits unfair methods of competition and deceptive trade practices. It also describes the procedures that the FTC must follow to charge persons or organizations with violations of the act, and it provides for judicial review of agency orders. The act grants the FTC the power to do the following:

1. Create "rules and regulations for the purpose of carrying out the Act."
2. Conduct investigations of business practices.
3. Obtain reports from interstate corporations concerning their business practices.
4. Investigate possible violations of federal antitrust statutes.[2]

---

1. 15 U.S.C. Sections 41–58.
2. The FTC shares enforcement of the Clayton Act with the Antitrust Division of the U.S. Department of Justice.

5. Publish findings of its investigations.
6. Recommend new legislation.
7. Hold trial-like hearings to resolve certain kinds of trade disputes that involve FTC regulations or federal antitrust laws.

AGENCY ORGANIZATION AND STRUCTURE—AN EXAMPLE

The FTC can also serve as an example of the organization and structure of a federal administrative agency. The commission that heads the FTC is composed of five members; each is appointed by the president, with the advice and consent of the Senate, for a term of seven years. The president designates one of the commissioners to be chairperson. Various offices and bureaus within the FTC undertake different administrative activities for the agency. Exhibit 6–1 illustrates the organization of the FTC.

TYPES OF AGENCIES

As discussed in Chapter 1, there are two basic types of administrative agencies: executive agencies and independent regulatory agencies. Federal *executive agencies* include the cabinet departments of the executive branch, which were formed to assist the president in carrying out executive functions, and the subagencies within the cabinet departments. The Occupational Safety and Health Administration, for example, is a subagency within the Department of Labor. Exhibit 6–2 on the next page lists the cabinet departments and some of their most important subagencies.

All administrative agencies are part of the executive branch of government, but *independent regulatory agencies* are outside the major executive departments. The Federal Trade Commission and the Securities and Exchange Commission are examples of independent regulatory agencies. These and other selected independent regulatory agencies, as well as their principal functions, are listed in Exhibit 6–3 on page 129.

The accountability of the regulators is the most significant difference between the two types of agencies. Agencies that are considered part of the executive branch are subject to the authority of the president, who has the power to appoint and remove federal officers. In theory, this power is less pronounced in regard to independent agencies, whose officers serve for fixed terms and cannot be removed without just cause. In practice, however, the president's ability to exert influence over independent agencies is often considerable.

AGENCY POWERS AND THE CONSTITUTION

Administrative agencies occupy an unusual niche in the U.S. legal scheme because they exercise powers that are normally divided among the three branches of government. Notice that in the FTC's enabling legislation, discussed earlier, the FTC's grant of power incorporates functions associated with the legislative branch (rulemaking), the executive branch (enforcement of the rules), and the courts (**adjudication,** or the formal resolution of disputes).

LEGISLATIVE RULES As you learned in Chapter 5, the constitutional principle of checks and balances allows each branch of government to act as a check on the actions of the other two branches. Furthermore,

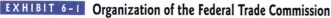

EXHIBIT 6-1 **Organization of the Federal Trade Commission**

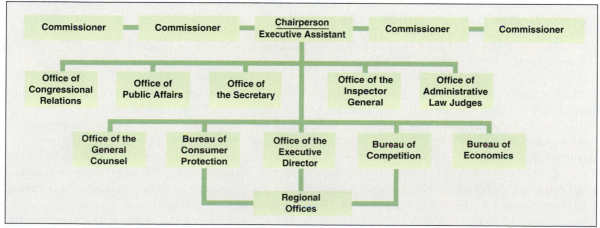

EXHIBIT 6-2 **Executive Departments and Important Subagencies**

DEPARTMENT AND DATE FORMED	SELECTED SUBAGENCIES
State (1789)	Passport Office; Bureau of Diplomatic Security; Foreign Service; Bureau of Human Rights and Humanitarian Affairs; Bureau of Consular Affairs; Bureau of Intelligence and Research
Treasury (1789)	Internal Revenue Service; U.S. Mint
Interior (1849)	U.S. Fish and Wildlife Service; National Park Service; Bureau of Indian Affairs; Bureau of Land Management
Justice (1870)[a]	Federal Bureau of Investigation; Drug Enforcement Administration; Bureau of Prisons; U.S. Marshals Service
Agriculture (1889)	Soil Conservation Service; Agricultural Research Service; Food Safety and Inspection Service; Forest Service
Commerce (1913)[b]	Bureau of the Census; Bureau of Economic Analysis; Minority Business Development Agency; U.S. Patent and Trademark Office; National Oceanic and Atmospheric Administration
Labor (1913)[b]	Occupational Safety and Health Administration; Bureau of Labor Statistics; Employment Standards Administration; Office of Labor-Management Standards; Employment and Training Administration
Defense (1949)[c]	National Security Agency; Joint Chiefs of Staff; Departments of the Air Force, Navy, Army; service academies
Housing and Urban Development (1965)	Office of Community Planning and Development; Government National Mortgage Association; Office of Fair Housing and Equal Opportunity
Transportation (1967)	Federal Aviation Administration; Federal Highway Administration; National Highway Traffic Safety Administration; Federal Transit Administration
Energy (1977)	Office of Civilian Radioactive Waste Management; Office of Nuclear Energy; Energy Information Administration
Health and Human Services (1980)[d]	Food and Drug Administration; Centers for Medicare and Medicaid Services; Centers for Disease Control; National Institutes of Health
Education (1980)[d]	Office of Special Education and Rehabilitation Services; Office of Elementary and Secondary Education; Office of Postsecondary Education; Office of Vocational and Adult Education
Veterans' Affairs (1989)	Veterans Health Administration; Veterans Benefits Administration; National Cemetery System
Homeland Security (2002)	Bureau of Citizenship and Immigration Services; Directorate of Border and Transportation Services; U.S. Coast Guard; Federal Emergency Management Agency

a. Formed from the Office of the Attorney General (created in 1789).
b. Formed from the Department of Commerce and Labor (created in 1903).
c. Formed from the Department of War (created in 1789) and the Department of the Navy (created in 1798).
d. Formed from the Department of Health, Education, and Welfare (created in 1953).

the U.S. Constitution authorizes only the legislative branch to create laws. Yet administrative agencies, to which the Constitution does not specifically refer, make **legislative rules,** or *substantive rules,* that are as legally binding as laws passed by Congress.

THE DELEGATION DOCTRINE Courts generally hold that Article I of the U.S. Constitution authorizes Congress to delegate powers to administrative agencies. In fact, courts generally hold that Article I is the basis for all administrative law. Section 1 of that article grants all legislative powers to Congress and requires Congress to oversee the implementation of all laws. Article I, Section 8, gives Congress the power to make all laws necessary for executing its specified powers. The courts interpret these passages, under what is referred to as the **delegation doctrine,** as granting Congress the power to establish administrative agencies that can create rules for implementing those laws.

EXHIBIT 6-3 **Selected Independent Regulatory Agencies**

Name and Date Formed	Principal Duties
Federal Reserve System Board of Governors (Fed) (1913)	Determines policy with respect to interest rates, credit availability, and the money supply.
Federal Trade Commission (FTC) (1914)	Prevents businesses from engaging in unfair trade practices; stops the formation of monopolies in the business sector; protects consumer rights.
Securities and Exchange Commission (SEC) (1934)	Regulates the nation's stock exchanges, in which shares of stock are bought and sold; enforces the securities laws, which require full disclosure of the financial profiles of companies that wish to sell stock and bonds to the public.
Federal Communications Commission (FCC) (1934)	Regulates all communications by telegraph, cable, telephone, radio, satellite, and television.
National Labor Relations Board (NLRB) (1935)	Protects employees' rights to join unions and bargain collectively with employers; attempts to prevent unfair labor practices by both employers and unions.
Equal Employment Opportunity Commission (EEOC) (1964)	Works to eliminate discrimination in employment based on religion, gender, race, color, disability, national origin, or age; investigates claims of discrimination.
Environmental Protection Agency (EPA) (1970)	Undertakes programs aimed at reducing air and water pollution; works with state and local agencies to help fight environmental hazards. (It has been suggested recently that its status be elevated to that of a department.)
Nuclear Regulatory Commission (NRC) (1975)	Ensures that electricity-generating nuclear reactors in the United States are built and operated safely; regularly inspects operations of such reactors.

The three branches of government exercise certain controls over agency powers and functions, as will be discussed later in this chapter, but in many ways administrative agencies function independently. For this reason, administrative agencies, which constitute the **bureaucracy,** are sometimes referred to as the "fourth branch" of the U.S. government.

SECTION 2 | Administrative Process

The three functions mentioned previously—rulemaking, enforcement, and adjudication—make up what is known as the **administrative process.** Administrative process involves the administration of law by administrative agencies, in contrast to **judicial process,** which comprises the administration of law by the courts.

All federal agencies must follow specific procedural requirements in their rulemaking, adjudication, and other functions. Sometimes Congress specifies certain procedural requirements in an agency's enabling legislation. In the absence of any directives from Congress concerning a particular agency procedure, the Administrative Procedure Act (APA) of 1946[3] applies. The APA is such an integral part of the administrative

process that its application will be considered as we examine the basic functions carried out by administrative agencies. In addition, agency procedures are guided indirectly by the courts' interpretation of APA requirements.

RULEMAKING

A major function of an administrative agency is **rulemaking**—the formulation of new regulations. In an agency's enabling legislation, Congress confers the agency's power to make legislative rules, as already mentioned. For example, the Occupational Safety and Health Act of 1970 authorized the Occupational Safety and Health Administration (OSHA) to develop and issue rules governing safety in the workplace. In formulating any new legislative rule, OSHA must follow specific rulemaking procedures required under the APA.

In addition to making legislative rules, administrative agencies also make *interpretive rules*. These rules are not legally binding on the public but simply indicate how an agency plans to interpret and enforce its statutory authority. For example, the Equal Employment Opportunity Commission periodically issues interpretive rules, usually referred to as enforcement guidelines, indicating how it plans to interpret

---

3. 5 U.S.C. Sections 551–706.

and apply a provision of a certain statute, such as the Americans with Disabilities Act. When making interpretive rules, an agency need not follow the requirements of the APA.

The most commonly used rulemaking procedure is called **notice-and-comment rulemaking.** This procedure involves three basic steps: notice of the proposed rulemaking, a comment period, and the final rule.

NOTICE OF THE PROPOSED RULEMAKING When a federal agency decides to create a new rule, the agency publishes a notice of the proposed rulemaking proceedings in the *Federal Register,* a daily publication of the executive branch that prints government orders, rules, and regulations. The notice states where and when the proceedings will be held, the agency's legal authority for making the rule (usually its enabling legislation), and the terms or subject matter of the proposed rule.

COMMENT PERIOD Following the publication of the notice of the proposed rulemaking proceedings, the agency must allow ample time for persons to comment in writing on the proposed rule. The purpose of this comment period is to give interested parties the oppor-

tunity to express their views on the proposed rule in an effort to influence agency policy. The comments may be in writing or, if a hearing is held, may be given orally.

The agency need not respond to all comments, but it must respond to any significant comments that bear directly on the proposed rule. The agency responds by either modifying its final rule or explaining, in a statement accompanying the final rule, why it did not make any changes. In some circumstances, particularly when the procedure being used in a specific instance is less formal, an agency may accept comments after the comment period is closed. The agency should summarize these *ex parte* (private, "off-the-record") comments in the record for possible review.

THE FINAL RULE After the agency reviews the comments, it drafts the final rule and publishes it in the *Federal Register.* The final rule is later compiled along with the rules and regulations of other federal administrative agencies in the *Code of Federal Regulations* (C.F.R.). Final rules have binding legal effect unless the courts later overturn them.

The court in the following case considered whether to enforce rules that were issued outside of the rulemaking procedure.

CASE 6.1 Hemp Industries Association v. Drug Enforcement Administration

United States
Court of Appeals,
Ninth Circuit, 2004.
357 F.3d 1012.

BACKGROUND AND FACTS *The members of the Hemp Industries Association (HIA) import and distribute sterilized hemp seed and oil and cake derived from hemp seed, and make and sell food and cosmetic products derived from hemp seed and oil. These products contain only nonpsychoactive trace amounts of tetrahydrocannabinol (THC).[a] On October 9, 2001, the U.S. Drug Enforcement Administration (DEA) published an interpretive rule declaring that "any product that contains any amount of THC is a Schedule I controlled substance."[b] On the same day, the DEA proposed two legislative rules. One rule—DEA-205F—amended the listing of THC in "Schedule I" to include natural, as well as synthetic, THC. The second rule—DEA-206F—exempted from control nonpsychoactive hemp products that contain trace amounts of THC not intended to enter the human body. On March 21, 2003, without following formal rulemaking procedures, the DEA declared that these rules were final. This effectively banned the possession and sale of the food products of the HIA's members. The HIA petitioned the U.S. Court of Appeals for the Ninth Circuit to review the rules, asserting that they could not be enforced.*

IN THE LANGUAGE OF THE COURT
BETTY B. FLETCHER, Circuit Judge.
* * * *
* * * Appellants * * * argue that DEA-205F is a scheduling action—placing nonpsychoactive hemp in Schedule I for the first time—that fails to follow the procedures for such actions required by the Controlled Substances Act ("CSA"). * * * *

---

a. A *nonpsychoactive substance* is one that does not affect a person's mind or behavior. Nonpsychoactive hemp is derived from industrial hemp plants grown in Canada and in Europe, the flowers of which contain only a trace amount of the THC contained in marijuana varieties grown for psychoactive use.
b. A *controlled substance* is a drug whose availability is restricted by law.

CASE 6.1 | Continued

* * * *

Under 21 U.S.C. [Section] 811(a) [of the CSA]:

the Attorney General may by rule—
(1) add to * * * a schedule * * * any drug or other substance if he—
* * *

(B) makes with respect to such drug or other substance the findings prescribed by subsection (b) of [S]ection 812 of this title * * * .

Rules of the Attorney General under this subsection shall be made on the record after opportunity for a hearing pursuant to the rulemaking procedures prescribed by [the Administrative Procedure Act (APA)].

* * * *Formal rulemaking requires hearings on the record, and [the APA] invites parties to submit proposed findings and oppose the stated bases of tentative agency decisions, and requires the agency to issue formal rulings on each finding, conclusion, or exception on the record.* We will not reproduce the entirety of the [APA] here; it suffices to say that the DEA did not and does not claim to have followed formal rulemaking procedures. [Emphasis added.]

In addition, the DEA did not comply with [Section] 811(a)(1)(B), because the findings required by [Section] 812(b) were not made. Section 812(b) states:

(b) Placement on schedules; findings required. * * * [A] drug or other substance may not be placed in any schedule unless the findings required for such schedule are made with respect to such drug or other substance.

* * * *

The DEA does not purport to have met the requirements for placement of nonpsychoactive hemp on Schedule I * * * . Instead, the DEA argues that naturally occurring THC in those parts of the hemp plant excluded from the definition of "marijuana" have always been included under the listing for "THC" * * * .

* * * *

Two CSA provisions are relevant to determining whether Appellants' hemp products were banned before [DEA-205F and DEA-206F]: the definition of THC and the definition of marijuana. Both are unambiguous * * * : Appellants' products do not contain the "synthetic" "substances or derivatives" that are covered by the definition of THC, and nonpsychoactive hemp is explicitly excluded from the definition of marijuana.

* * * *

Under 21 U.S.C. [Section] 802(16) [of the CSA]:

The term "marihuana" means all parts of the plant Cannabis sativa L. * * * . Such term does not include the mature stalks of such plant, fiber produced from such stalks, oil or cake made from the seeds of such plant, any other compound, manufacture, salt, derivative, mixture, or preparation of such mature stalks (except the resin extracted therefrom), fiber, oil, or cake, or the sterilized seed of such plant which is incapable of germination.

The nonpsychoactive hemp in Appellants' products is derived from the "mature stalks" or is "oil and cake made from the seeds" of the *Cannabis* plant, and therefore fits within the plainly stated exception to the CSA definition of marijuana.

* * * Congress knew what it was doing, and its intent to exclude nonpsychoactive hemp from regulation is entirely clear.

DECISION AND REMEDY *The U.S. Court of Appeals for the Ninth Circuit held that DEA-205F and DEA-206F "are inconsistent with the unambiguous meaning of the CSA definitions of marijuana and THC," and the DEA did not follow the proper administrative procedures required to schedule a substance. The court issued an injunction against the enforcement of the rules with respect to nonpsychoactive hemp or products containing it.*

WHAT IF THE FACTS WERE DIFFERENT? *Suppose that the statutory definitions of THC and marijuana covered naturally occurring THC and nonpsychoactive hemp. Would the result in this case have been different?*

INVESTIGATION

Administrative agencies conduct investigations of the entities that they regulate. One type of agency investigation occurs during the rulemaking process to obtain information about a certain individual, firm, or industry. The purpose of such an investigation is to ensure that the rule issued is based on a consideration of relevant factors and is not arbitrary and capricious. After final rules are issued, agencies conduct investigations to monitor compliance with those rules. A typical agency investigation of this kind might begin when a citizen reports a possible violation.

INSPECTIONS Many agencies gather information through on-site inspections. Sometimes, inspecting an office, a factory, or some other business facility is the only way to obtain the evidence needed to prove a regulatory violation. Administrative inspections and tests cover a wide range of activities, including safety inspections of underground coal mines, safety tests of commercial equipment and automobiles, and environmental monitoring of factory emissions. An agency may also ask a firm or individual to submit certain documents or records to the agency for examination.

Normally, business firms comply with agency requests to inspect facilities or business records because it is in any firm's interest to maintain a good relationship with regulatory bodies. In some instances, however, such as when a firm thinks an agency's request is unreasonable and may be detrimental to the firm's interest, the firm may refuse to comply with the request. In such situations, an agency may resort to the use of a subpoena or a search warrant.

SUBPOENAS There are two basic types of subpoenas. The subpoena *ad testificandum* ("to testify") is an ordinary subpoena. It is a writ, or order, compelling a witness to appear at an agency hearing. In contrast, the subpoena *duces tecum*[4] ("bring it with you") compels an individual or organization to hand over books, papers, records, or documents to the agency. An administrative agency may use either type of subpoena to obtain testimony or documents.

There are limits on what information an agency can demand. To determine whether an agency is abusing its discretion in its pursuit of information as part of an investigation, a court may consider such factors as the following:

1. The purpose of the investigation. An investigation must have a legitimate purpose. Harassment is an example of an improper purpose. An agency may not issue an administrative subpoena to inspect business records if the agency's motive is to harass or pressure the business into settling an unrelated matter.

2. The relevance of the information being sought. Information is relevant if it reveals that the law is being violated or if it assures the agency that the law is not being violated.

3. The specificity of the demand for testimony or documents. A subpoena must, for example, adequately describe the material being sought.

4. The burden of the demand on the party from whom the information is sought. In responding to a request for information, a party must bear the costs of, for example, copying the documents that must be handed over; a business is generally protected from revealing such information as trade secrets, however.

In addition, a subpoena might not be enforced when the subject matter of an investigation is not within the authority of the agency to investigate. The issue in the following case was whether the subject matter of certain subpoenas issued by the Federal Trade Commission had exceeded the agency's statutory authority.

---

4. Pronounced *doo*-cheez *tee*-kum.

CASE 6.2   Federal Trade Commission v. Ken Roberts Co.

United States
Court of Appeals,
District of Columbia
Circuit, 2001.
276 F.3d 583.

BACKGROUND AND FACTS *Ken Roberts Company, Ken Roberts Institute, Inc., United States Chart Company, and Ted Warren Corporation (collectively, Roberts) sell instructional materials that claim to teach would-be investors how to make money investing. In 1999, the Federal Trade Commission (FTC) began investigating whether a variety of online businesses were engaged in deceptive marketing practices in violation of the Federal Trade Commission Act. Aiming at high-risk, high-yield investment activity and suspicious Internet advertising, the FTC soon focused on Roberts. The FTC issued subpoenas that required Roberts to produce documents and answer written questions relating to the companies' business practices. Roberts refused to respond to most of the requests. The FTC asked a federal district court to enforce the subpoenas. When the court ordered Roberts to comply, Roberts appealed to the U.S. Court of Appeals for the District of Columbia Circuit. Roberts argued that*

CASE 6.2 Continued *its companies were subject only to other federal agencies, whose authority under, in part, the Investment Advisers Act (IAA) preempted the FTC's authority to investigate Roberts's practices.*

IN THE LANGUAGE OF THE COURT

HARRY T. EDWARDS, Circuit Judge:
* * * *

Subpoena enforcement power is not limitless * * * . [A] *subpoena is proper only where the inquiry is within the authority of the agency, the demand is not too indefinite and the information sought is reasonably relevant.* Accordingly, there is no doubt that a court asked to enforce a subpoena will refuse to do so if the subpoena exceeds an express statutory limitation on the agency's investigative powers. Thus, a court must assure itself that the subject matter of the investigation is within the statutory jurisdiction of the subpoena-issuing agency. * * * [Emphasis added.]
* * * *

On its own terms, the FTC Act gives the FTC ample authority to investigate and, if deceptive practices are uncovered, to regulate appellants' advertising practices. Therefore, the FTC is entitled to have its subpoenas enforced unless some other source of law patently [clearly] undermines these broad powers. * * *
* * * *

[Appellants], whose businesses involve securities * * * , assert that the comprehensive scope of the Investment Advisers Act of 1940 preempts the FTC's jurisdiction to regulate the fraudulent practices of "investment advisers" such as themselves. * * *

* * * [T]he IAA contains no express exclusive jurisdiction provision. * * * [But] where intended by Congress, a precisely drawn, detailed statute preempts more general remedies. This can occur either where the two enactments are in irreconcilable conflict or where the latter was clearly meant to serve as a substitute for the former. Appellants contend that the antifraud provision of the IAA, which prohibits investment advisers from engaging "in any transaction, practice, or course of business which operates as a fraud or deceit upon any client or prospective client," stands as just such a specific remedy that displaces the more general coverage of the FTC Act.
* * * *

Because we live in an age of overlapping and concurring regulatory jurisdiction, a court must proceed with the utmost caution before concluding that one agency may not regulate merely because another may. In this case, while it may be true that the IAA and the FTC Act employ different verbal formulae to describe their antifraud standards, it hardly follows that they therefore impose conflicting or incompatible obligations. Undoubtedly, entities in appellants' position can—and of course should—refrain from engaging in both "unfair and deceptive acts or practices" *and* "any transaction, practice, or course of business which operates as a fraud or deceit upon a client or prospective client." The proscriptions of the IAA are not diminished or confused merely because investment advisers must also avoid that which the FTC Act proscribes. And, because these statutes are capable of co-existence, it becomes the *duty* of this court to regard each as effective—at least absent clear congressional intent to the contrary.

Appellants can point to nothing in the background or history of the IAA that demonstrates (or even hints at) a congressional intent to preempt the antifraud jurisdiction of the FTC over those covered by the new statute. Nor does the subsequent case law interpreting these statutes contain such declarations.

DECISION AND REMEDY *The U.S. Court of Appeals for the District of Columbia Circuit affirmed the lower court's decision. The appellate court held that the FTC was entitled to the enforcement of its subpoenas against Roberts. The Investment Advisers Act does not preempt the FTC's authority to investigate possibly deceptive advertising and marketing practices merely because those practices relate to the investment business.*

SEARCH WARRANTS The Fourth Amendment protects against unreasonable searches and seizures by requiring that in most instances a physical search for evidence must be conducted under the authority of a search warrant. An agency's search warrant is an order directing law enforcement officials to search a specific place for a specific item and present it to the agency. Although it was once thought that administrative inspections were exempt from the warrant requirement, the United States Supreme Court held in *Marshall v. Barlow's, Inc.*,[5] that the requirement does apply to the administrative process.

Agencies can conduct warrantless searches in several situations. Warrants are not required to conduct searches in highly regulated industries. Firms that sell firearms or liquor, for example, are automatically subject to inspections without warrants. Sometimes, a statute permits warrantless searches of certain types of hazardous operations, such as coal mines. Also, a warrantless inspection in an emergency situation is normally considered reasonable.

ADJUDICATION

After conducting an investigation of a suspected rule violation, an agency may begin to take administrative action against an individual or organization. Most administrative actions are resolved through negotiated settlements at their initial stages, without the need for formal adjudication.

NEGOTIATED SETTLEMENTS Depending on the agency, negotiations may take the form of a simple conversation or a series of informal conferences. Whatever form the negotiations take, their purpose is to rectify the problem to the agency's satisfaction and eliminate the need for additional proceedings.

Settlement is an appealing option to firms for two reasons: to avoid appearing uncooperative and to avoid the expense involved in formal adjudication proceedings and in possible later appeals. Settlement is also an attractive option for agencies. To conserve their own resources and avert formal actions, administrative agencies devote a great deal of effort to giving advice and negotiating solutions to problems.

FORMAL COMPLAINTS If a settlement cannot be reached, the agency may issue a formal complaint against the suspected violator. If the Environmental Protection Agency (EPA), for example, finds that a factory is polluting groundwater in violation of federal pollution laws, the EPA will issue a complaint against the violator in an effort to bring the plant into compliance with federal regulations. This complaint is a public document, and a press release may accompany it. The factory charged in the complaint will respond by filing an answer to the EPA's allegations. If the fac-

tory and the EPA cannot agree on a settlement, the case will be adjudicated. Recall from Chapter 1 that agency adjudication may involve a trial-like procedure before an **administrative law judge (ALJ).** The administrative adjudication process is described next and illustrated graphically in Exhibit 6–4.

THE ROLE OF THE ADMINISTRATIVE LAW JUDGE
The ALJ presides over the hearing and has the power to administer oaths, take testimony, rule on questions of evidence, and make determinations of fact. Although technically the ALJ works for the agency prosecuting the case (in our example, the EPA), the law requires an ALJ to be an unbiased adjudicator (judge).

Certain safeguards prevent bias on the part of the ALJ and promote fairness in the proceedings. For example, the Administrative Procedure Act (APA) requires that the ALJ be separate from an agency's

EXHIBIT 6-4 **The Process of Formal Administrative Adjudication**

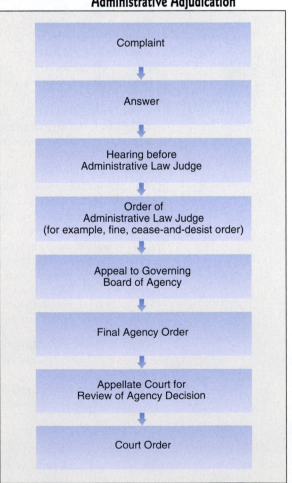

Complaint

↓

Answer

↓

Hearing before Administrative Law Judge

↓

Order of Administrative Law Judge (for example, fine, cease-and-desist order)

↓

Appeal to Governing Board of Agency

↓

Final Agency Order

↓

Appellate Court for Review of Agency Decision

↓

Court Order

---

5. 436 U.S. 307, 98 S.Ct. 1816, 56 L.Ed.2d 305 (1978).

investigative and prosecutorial staff. The APA also prohibits *ex parte* (private) communications between the ALJ and any party to an agency proceeding, such as the EPA or the factory. Finally, provisions of the APA protect the ALJ from agency disciplinary actions unless the agency can show good cause for such an action.

HEARING PROCEDURES Hearing procedures vary widely from agency to agency. Administrative agencies generally exercise substantial discretion over the type of procedure that will be used. Frequently, disputes are resolved through informal adjudication proceedings. For example, the parties, their counsel, and the ALJ may simply meet at a table in a conference room to attempt to settle the dispute.

A formal adjudicatory hearing, in contrast, resembles a trial in many respects. Prior to the hearing, the parties are permitted to undertake extensive discovery (involving depositions, interrogatories, and requests for documents or other information, as described in Chapter 2). During the hearing, the parties may give testimony, present other evidence, and cross-examine adverse witnesses. A significant difference between a trial and an administrative agency hearing, though, is that normally much more information, including hearsay (secondhand information), can be introduced as evidence during an administrative hearing.

AGENCY ORDERS Following a hearing, the ALJ renders an **initial order,** or decision, on the case. Either party can appeal the ALJ's decision to the board or commission that governs the agency. If the factory in the previous example is dissatisfied with the ALJ's decision, it can appeal the decision to the commission that governs the EPA. If the factory is dissatisfied with the commission's decision, it can appeal the decision to a federal court of appeals. If no party appeals the case, the ALJ's decision becomes the **final order** of the agency. The ALJ's decision also becomes final if a party appeals and the commission and the court decline to review the case. If a party appeals and the case is reviewed, the final order comes from the commission's decision or (if that decision is appealed to a federal appellate court) that of the court.

SECTION 3 | Limitations on Agency Powers

Combining the functions normally divided among the three branches of government into an administrative

agency concentrates considerable power in a single organization. Because of this concentration of authority, one of the major policy objectives of the government is to control the risks of arbitrariness and overreaching by administrative agencies without hindering the effective use of agency power to deal with particular problem areas, as Congress intends.

The judicial branch of the government exercises control over agency powers through the courts' review of agency actions. The executive and legislative branches of government also exercise control over agency authority.

JUDICIAL CONTROLS

The Administrative Procedure Act provides for judicial review of most agency decisions, as described above. Agency actions are not automatically subject to judicial review, however.

THE RIPENESS DOCTRINE Under what is known as the *ripeness doctrine*, a court will not review an administrative agency's decision until the case is "ripe for review." Generally, a case is ripe for review if the parties can demonstrate that they have met certain requirements. The party bringing the action must have *standing to sue* the agency (the party must have a direct stake in the outcome of the judicial proceeding), and there must be an *actual controversy* at issue. These are basic judicial requirements that must be met before any court will hear a case, as discussed in Chapter 2. With regard to agency decisions, however, the party must also have *exhausted all possible administrative remedies*. Each agency has its "chain of review," and the party must follow agency appeal procedures before a court will deem that administrative remedies have been exhausted.

The rationale for this doctrine is to prevent courts from entangling themselves in abstract disagreements over administrative policies. The doctrine also protects agencies from judicial interference until an administrative decision has been formalized and its effects are clear. The court can then evaluate both the appropriateness of an issue for judicial decision and the hardship the decision will cause to the challenging party if the court refuses to consider the case.

ISSUES CONSIDERED WHEN REVIEWING AGENCY DECISIONS Recall from Chapter 2 that appellate courts normally defer to the decisions of trial courts on questions of fact. In reviewing administrative actions, the courts show a similar deference to (reluctance to question) the factual findings of agencies.

In reviewing an administrative agency's decision, a court normally will consider the following types of issues:

1. Whether the agency has exceeded its authority under its enabling legislation.
2. Whether the agency has properly interpreted laws applicable to the agency action under review.
3. Whether the agency has violated any constitutional provisions.
4. Whether the agency has acted in accordance with procedural requirements of the law.
5. Whether the agency's actions were arbitrary, capricious, or an abuse of discretion.
6. Whether any conclusions drawn by the agency are not supported by substantial evidence.

The fifth element in the above list is often referred to as the "arbitrary and capricious" test. An agency action will be deemed arbitrary and capricious if it was taken willfully and unreasonably, and without considering the facts of the case.

EXECUTIVE CONTROLS

The executive branch of government exercises control over agencies both through the president's power to appoint federal officers and through the president's veto power. The president may veto enabling legislation presented by Congress or congressional attempts to modify an existing agency's authority.

LEGISLATIVE CONTROLS

Congress also exercises authority over agency powers. Through enabling legislation, Congress gives power to an agency. Of course, an agency may not exceed the power that Congress has delegated to it. Through subsequent legislation, Congress can take away that power or even abolish an agency altogether. Legislative authority is required to fund an agency, and enabling legislation usually sets certain time and monetary limits on the funding of particular programs. Congress can always revise these limits.

In addition to its power to create and fund agencies, Congress has the authority to investigate the implementation of its laws and the agencies that it has created. Individual legislators may also affect agency policy through their "casework" activities, which involve attempts to help their constituents deal with agencies.

Congress also has the power to "freeze" the enforcement of most federal regulations before the regulations take effect. Under the Small Business Regulatory Enforcement Fairness Act of 1996,[6] all federal agencies must submit final rules to Congress before the rules become effective. If, within sixty days, Congress passes a joint resolution of disapproval concerning a rule, enforcement of the regulation is frozen while the rule is reviewed by congressional committees.

Another legislative check on agency actions is the Administrative Procedure Act, discussed earlier in this chapter. Additionally, the laws discussed in the next section provide certain checks on the actions of administrative agencies.

SECTION 4 | Public Accountability

As a result of growing public concern over the powers exercised by administrative agencies, Congress passed several laws to make agencies more accountable through public scrutiny. We discuss here the most significant of these laws.

FREEDOM OF INFORMATION ACT

Enacted in 1966, the Freedom of Information Act (FOIA)[7] requires the federal government to disclose certain "records" to "any person" on request, even if no reason is given for the request. The FOIA exempts certain types of records. For other records, though, a request that complies with the FOIA procedures need only contain a reasonable description of the information sought (see Exhibit 6–5). An agency's failure to comply with a request may be challenged in a federal district court. The media, industry trade associations, public-interest groups, and even companies seeking information about competitors rely on these FOIA provisions to obtain information from government agencies.

Under a 1996 amendment to the FOIA, all federal government agencies now must make their records available electronically—on the Internet, on CD-ROMs, and in other electronic formats. As of November 1, 1996, any document created by an

---

6. 5 U.S.C. Sections 801–808.
7. 5 U.S.C. Section 552.

EXHIBIT 6-5 Sample Letter Requesting Information from an Executive Department or Agency

Agency Head [or Freedom of Information Act Officer]   Date _____
Name of Agency
Address of Agency
City, State, Zip Code

Re: Freedom of Information Act Request

Dear _____ :

This is a request under the Freedom of Information Act.

I request that a copy of the following documents [or documents containing the following information] be provided to me: [identify the documents or information as specifically as possible].

In order to help to determine my status for purposes of determining the applicability of any fees, you should know that I am [insert a suitable description of the requester and the purpose of the request].

[Optional] I am willing to pay fees for this request up to a maximum of $XX. If you estimate that the fees will exceed this limit, please inform me first.

[Optional] I request a waiver of all fees for this request. Disclosure of the requested information to me is in the public interest because it is likely to contribute significantly to public understanding of the operations or activities of the government and is not primarily in my commercial interest. [Include specific details, including how the requested information will be disseminated by the requester for public benefit.]

[Optional] I request that the information I seek be provided in electronic format, and I would like to receive it on a personal computer disk [or a CD-ROM].

[Optional] I ask that my request receive expedited processing because XXXX. [Include specific details concerning your "compelling need," such as being someone "primarily engaged in disseminating information" and specifics concerning your "urgency to inform the public concerning actual or alleged Federal Government activity."]

[Optional] I also include a telephone number at which I can be contacted during the hours of XXXX, if necessary, to discuss any aspect of my request.

Thank you for your consideration of this request.

Sincerely,
[Signature]
Name
Address
City, State, Zip Code
Telephone number [Optional]

Source: U.S. Congress, House Committee on Government Reform, *A Citizen's Guide on How to Use the Freedom of Information Act and the Privacy Act Requesting Government Documents*, 106th Congress, 1st session, H.R. 106–50, 1999.

agency must be accessible by computer within a year after its creation. Agencies must also provide a clear index to all of their documents.

GOVERNMENT IN THE SUNSHINE ACT

Congress passed the Government in the Sunshine Act,[8] or open meeting law, in 1976. It requires that "every portion of every meeting of an agency" be open to "public observation." The act also requires the establishment of procedures to ensure that the public is provided with adequate advance notice of scheduled meetings and agendas. Like the FOIA, the Sunshine Act contains certain exceptions. Closed meetings are permitted when (1) the subject of the meeting concerns accusing any person of a crime, (2) an open meeting would frustrate the implementation of agency actions, or (3) the subject of the meeting involves matters relating to future litigation or rulemaking. Courts interpret these exceptions to allow open access whenever possible.

_____
8. 5 U.S.C. Section 552b.

REGULATORY FLEXIBILITY ACT

Concern over the effects of regulation on the efficiency of businesses, particularly smaller ones, led Congress to pass the Regulatory Flexibility Act[9] in 1980. Under this act, whenever a new regulation will have a "significant impact upon a substantial number of small entities," the agency must conduct a regulatory flexibility analysis. The analysis must measure the cost that the rule would impose on small businesses and must consider less burdensome alternatives. Additionally, the act contains provisions to alert small businesses—through advertising in trade journals, for example—about forthcoming regulations. The act reduces some record-keeping burdens for small businesses, especially with regard to hazardous waste management.

SMALL BUSINESS REGULATORY ENFORCEMENT FAIRNESS ACT

As mentioned above, the Small Business Regulatory Enforcement Fairness Act (SBREFA) of 1996 allows Congress to review new federal regulations for at least sixty days before they take effect. This period gives opponents of the rules time to present their arguments to Congress.

The SBREFA also authorizes the courts to enforce the Regulatory Flexibility Act. This helps to ensure that federal agencies, such as the Internal Revenue Service and the Occupational Health and Safety Administration, will consider ways to reduce the economic impact of new regulations on small businesses. Federal agencies are required to prepare guides that explain in "plain English" how small businesses can comply with federal regulations.

The SBREFA also set up the National Enforcement Ombudsman at the Small Business Administration to receive comments from small businesses about their dealings with federal agencies. Based on these comments, Regional Small Business Fairness Boards rate the agencies and publicize their findings.

Finally, the SBREFA allows small businesses to recover their expenses and legal fees from the government when an agency makes demands for fines or penalties that a court considers excessive.

---

9. 5 U.S.C. Sections 601–612.

SECTION 5 | State Administrative Agencies

Although most of this chapter deals with federal administrative agencies, state agencies play a significant role in regulating activities within the states. Many of the factors that encouraged the proliferation of federal agencies also fostered the expanded presence of state agencies. For example, one reason for the growth of administrative agencies at all levels of government is the inability of Congress and state legislatures to oversee the implementation of their growing number of laws. Another is the greater technical competence of the agencies.

PARALLEL AGENCIES

Commonly, a state creates an agency as a parallel to a federal agency to provide similar services on a more localized basis. Such parallel agencies include the federal Social Security Administration and the state welfare agency, the Internal Revenue Service and the state revenue department, and the Environmental Protection Agency and the state pollution-control agency. Not all federal agencies have parallel state agencies, however. For example, the Federal Bureau of Investigation and the Nuclear Regulatory Commission have no parallel agencies at the state level.

CONFLICTS BETWEEN PARALLEL AGENCIES

If the actions of parallel state and federal agencies conflict, the actions of the federal agency will prevail. For example, if the Federal Aviation Administration specifies the hours during which airplanes may land at and depart from airports, a state or local government cannot issue inconsistent laws or regulations governing the same activities. The priority of federal laws over conflicting state laws is based on the supremacy clause of the U.S. Constitution. Remember from Chapter 5 that this clause, which is found in Article VI of the Constitution, states that the Constitution and "the Laws of the United States which shall be made in Pursuance thereof . . . shall be the supreme Law of the Land." The following case illustrates this principle.

CASE 6.3

United States District Court, District of Minnesota, 2004. 290 F.Supp.2d 993.

Vonage Holdings Corp. v. Minnesota Public Utilities Commission

DAVIS, District Court Judge.

* * * *

This case illustrates the impact of emerging technologies evolving ahead of the regulatory scheme intended to address them. The issue before the Court is tied to the evolution of the Internet and the expansion of its capability to transmit voice communications. Despite its continued growth and development, the Internet remains in its infancy, and is an uncharted frontier with vast unknowns left to explore. Congress has expressed a clear intent to leave the Internet free from undue regulation so that this growth and exploration may continue. Congress also differentiated between "telecommunications services," which may be regulated, and "information services," which like the Internet, may not.

* * * *

Vonage [Holdings Corporation] markets and sells Vonage DigitalVoice, a service that permits voice communication via a high-speed ("broadband") Internet connection. Vonage's service uses a technology called Voice over Internet Protocol ("VoIP"), which allows customers to place and receive voice transmissions routed over the Internet.

Traditional telephone companies use circuit-switched technology. * * * Voice communication using the Internet has been called Internet Protocol ("IP") telephony, and rather than using circuit switching, it utilizes "packet switching," a process of breaking down data into packets of digital bits and transmitting them over the Internet.

* * * *

Vonage has approximately 500 customers with billing addresses in Minnesota. * * *

The Minnesota Department of Commerce ("MDOC") investigated Vonage's services and on July 15, 2003, filed a complaint with the [Minnesota Public Utilities Commission (MPUC)]. The complaint alleged that Vonage failed to * * * obtain a proper certificate of authority required to provide telephone service in Minnesota * * * .

Vonage then moved to dismiss the MDOC complaint. * * * The MPUC * * * [concluded] that * * * Vonage was required to comply with Minnesota statutes and rules regarding the offering of telephone service. Vonage then filed a complaint with this Court seeking [an] * * * injunction.

* * * *

The issue before the Court is whether Vonage may be regulated under [a] Minnesota law that requires telephone companies to obtain certification authorizing them to provide telephone service. Vonage asserts that the Communications Act of 1934, as amended by the Communications Act of 1996, preempts the state authority upon which the MPUC's order relies. * * * Vonage asserts that * * * its services are "information services," which are not subject to regulation, rather than "telecommunications services," which may be regulated. * * *

The Supremacy Clause of Article VI of the Constitution empowers Congress to preempt state law. Preemption occurs when (1) Congress enacts a federal statute that expresses its clear intent to preempt state law; (2) there is a conflict between federal and state law; (3) compliance with both federal and state law is in effect physically impossible; (4) federal law contains an implicit barrier to state regulation; (5) comprehensive congressional legislation occupies the entire field of regulation; or (6) state law is an obstacle to the accomplishment and execution of the full objectives of Congress. *Moreover, a federal agency acting within the scope of its congressionally delegated authority may preempt state regulation.* [Emphasis added.]

* * * *

Examining the statutory language of the Communications Act, the Court concludes that the VoIP service provided by Vonage constitutes an information service because it offers the "capability for generating, acquiring, storing, transforming, processing, retrieving, utilizing, or making available information via telecommunications." * * * Vonage's services are closely tied to the provision of telecommunications services as defined by Congress, the courts and

CONTINUED

CASE 6.3 | Continued

the [Federal Communications Commission (FCC)], but this Court finds that Vonage *uses* telecommunications services, rather than provides them.

* * * *

* * * The Court acknowledges the attractiveness of the MPUC's simplistic "quacks like a duck" argument, essentially holding that because Vonage's customers make phone calls, Vonage's services must be telecommunications services. However, this simplifies the issue to the detriment of an accurate understanding of this complex question. The Court must follow the statutory intent expressed by Congress, and interpreted by the FCC. Short of explicit statutory language, the Court can find no stronger guidance for determining that Vonage's service is an information service * * * .

* * * *

Where federal policy is to encourage certain conduct, state law discouraging that conduct must be preempted. [Emphasis added.]

* * * *

Accordingly, * * * IT IS HEREBY ORDERED that Vonage's motion for * * * [an] injunction * * * is GRANTED.

QUESTIONS

1. How might upholding the state agency's order in the *Vonage* case have affected Vonage?
2. What other consequences might have followed if the court in this case had held that services such as Vonage's could be subject to state regulations enforced by state agencies?

JUDICIAL REVIEW OF STATE AGENCY ACTIONS

Most state agency decisions are subject to judicial review by state courts, provided that the parties seeking that review first meet certain requirements. Once a petition for review is granted, state courts, like their federal counterparts, consider such issues as whether a state or local agency exceeded its authority.

REVIEWING ADMINISTRATIVE LAW

Assume that the Securities and Exchange Commission (SEC) has a rule that it will enforce statutory provisions prohibiting insider trading only when the insiders make monetary profits for themselves. Then the SEC makes a new rule, declaring that it has the statutory authority to bring an enforcement action against an individual even if she or he does not personally profit from the insider trading. In making the new rule, the SEC does not conduct a rulemaking proceeding but simply announces its new decision. A stockbrokerage firm objects and says that the new rule was unlawfully developed without opportunity for public comment. The brokerage firm challenges the rule in an action that ultimately is reviewed by a federal appellate court. Using the information presented in the chapter, answer the following questions.

1. Is the SEC an executive agency or an independent regulatory agency? What is the difference between these two types of government agencies? Does this difference have any bearing on the outcome of this case? Explain.

2. Should the SEC's new rule be invalidated under the Administrative Procedure Act? Why or why not?

3. Is the SEC's new rule a legislative rule or an interpretive rule? Why is this distinction important to the outcome of this case?

4. Generally, what issues will a court consider when reviewing an agency action?

TERMS AND CONCEPTS TO REVIEW

QUESTIONS AND CASE PROBLEMS

6–1. For decades, the Federal Trade Commission (FTC) resolved fair trade and advertising disputes through individual adjudications. In the 1960s, the FTC began promulgating rules that defined fair and unfair trade practices. In cases involving violations of these rules, the due process rights of participants were more limited and did not include cross-examination. Although anyone found violating a rule would receive a full adjudication, the legitimacy of the rule itself could not be challenged in the adjudication. Any party charged with violating a rule was almost certain to lose the adjudication. Affected parties complained to a court, arguing that their rights before the FTC were unduly limited by the new rules. What will the court examine to determine whether to uphold the new rules?

6–2. QUESTION WITH SAMPLE ANSWER
Assume that the Food and Drug Administration (FDA), using proper procedures, adopts a rule describing its future investigations. This new rule covers all future circumstances in which the FDA wants to regulate food additives. Under the new rule, the FDA is not to regulate food additives without giving food companies an opportunity to cross-examine witnesses. At a subsequent time, the FDA wants to regulate methylisocyanate, a food additive. The FDA undertakes an informal rulemaking procedure, without cross-examination, and regulates methylisocyanate. Producers protest, saying that the FDA promised them the opportunity for cross-examination. The FDA responds that the Administrative Procedure Act does not require such cross-examination and that it is free to withdraw the promise made in its new rule. If the producers challenge the FDA in court, on what basis would the court rule in their favor?
For a sample answer to this question, go to Appendix I at the end of this text.

6–3. RULEMAKING PROCEDURES. The Atomic Energy Commission (AEC) was engaged in rulemaking proceedings for nuclear reactor safety. An environmental group sued the commission, arguing that its proceedings were inadequate. The commission had carefully complied with all requirements of the Administrative Procedure Act. The environmentalists argued, however, that the very hazardous and technical nature of the reactor safety issue required elaborate procedures above and beyond those set forth in the act. A federal court of appeals agreed and overturned the AEC rules. The commission appealed the case to the United States Supreme Court. How should the Court rule? Discuss. [*Vermont Yankee Nuclear Power Corp. v. Natural Resources Defense Council, Inc.*, 435 U.S. 519, 98 S.Ct. 1197, 55 L.Ed.2d 460 (1978)]

6–4. ARBITRARY AND CAPRICIOUS TEST. In 1977, the Department of Transportation (DOT) adopted a passive-restraint standard (known as Standard 208) that required new cars to have either air bags or automatic seat belts. By 1981, it had become clear that all of the major auto manufacturers would install automatic seat belts to comply with this rule. The DOT determined that most purchasers of cars would detach their automatic seat belts, rendering them ineffective. Consequently, the department repealed the regulation. State Farm Mutual Automobile Insurance Co. and other insurance companies sued in the District of Columbia Circuit Court of Appeals for a review of the DOT's repeal of the regulation. That court held that the repeal was arbitrary and capricious because the DOT had reversed its rule without sufficient support. The motor vehicle manufacturers, which initially had wanted to avoid the costs associated with implementing Standard 208, then appealed this decision to the United States Supreme Court. What will result? Discuss fully. [*Motor Vehicle Manufacturers Association v. State Farm Mutual Automobile Insurance Co.*, 463 U.S. 29, 103 S.Ct. 2856, 77 L.Ed.2d 443 (1983)]

6–5. JUDICIAL REVIEW. American Message Centers (AMC) provides answering services to retailers. Calls to a retailer are automatically forwarded to AMC, which pays for the calls. AMC obtains telephone service at a discount from major carriers, including Sprint. Sprint's tariff (a public document setting out rates and rules relating to Sprint's services) states that the "subscriber shall be responsible for the payment of all charges for service." When AMC learned that computer hackers had obtained the access code for its lines and had made nearly $160,000 worth of long-distance calls, it asked Sprint to absorb the cost. Sprint refused. AMC filed a complaint with the Federal Communications Commission (FCC), claiming in part that Sprint's tariff was vague and ambiguous, in violation of the Communications Act of 1934 and FCC rules. These laws require that a carrier's tariff "clearly and definitely" specify any "exceptions or conditions which in any way affect the rates named in the tariff." The FCC rejected AMC's complaint. AMC appealed the FCC's decision to a federal appellate court, claiming that the FCC's decision to reject AMC's complaint was arbitrary and capricious. What should the court decide? Discuss fully. [*American Message Centers v. Federal Communications Commission,* 50 F.3d 35 (D.C.Cir. 1995)]

6-6. RULEMAKING. The Occupational Safety and Health Administration (OSHA) is part of the U.S. Department of Labor. OSHA issued a "Directive" under which each employer in selected industries was to be inspected unless it adopted a "Comprehensive Compliance Program (CCP)"—a safety and health program designed to meet standards that in some respects exceeded those otherwise required by law. The Chamber of Commerce of the United States objected to the Directive and filed a petition for review with the U.S. Court of Appeals for the District of Columbia Circuit. The Chamber claimed, in part, that OSHA did not use proper rulemaking procedures in issuing the Directive. OSHA argued that it was not required to follow those procedures because the Directive itself was a "rule of procedure." OSHA claimed that the rule did not "alter the rights or interests of parties, although it may alter the manner in which the parties present themselves or their viewpoints to the agency." What are the steps of the most commonly used rulemaking procedure? Which steps are missing in this case? In whose favor should the court rule, and why? [*Chamber of Commerce of the United States v. U.S. Department of Labor,* 174 F.3d 206 (D.C.Cir. 1999)]

6-7. ⚖ CASE PROBLEM WITH SAMPLE ANSWER

Riverdale Mills Corp. makes plastic-coated steel wire products in Northbridge, Massachusetts. Riverdale uses a water-based cleaning process that generates acidic and alkaline wastewater. To meet federal clean-water requirements, Riverdale has a system within its plant to treat the water. It then flows through a pipe that opens into a manhole-covered test pit outside the plant in full view of Riverdale's employees. Three hundred feet away, the pipe merges into the public sewer system. In October 1997, the U.S. Environmental Protection Agency (EPA) sent Justin Pimpare and Daniel Granz to inspect the plant. Without a search warrant and without Riverdale's express consent, the agents took samples from the test pit. Based on the samples, Riverdale and James Knott, the company's owner, were charged with criminal violations of the federal Clean Water Act. The defendants filed a suit in a federal district court against the EPA agents and others, alleging violations of the

Fourth Amendment. What right does the Fourth Amendment provide in this context? This right is based on a "reasonable expectation of privacy." Should the agents be held liable? Why or why not? [*Riverdale Mills Corp. v. Pimpare,* 392 F.3d 55 (1st Cir. 2004)]

To view a sample answer for this case problem, go to this book's Web site at http://wleb.westbuslaw.com, select "Chapter 6," and click on "Case Problem with Sample Answer."

6-8. ARBITRARY AND CAPRICIOUS TEST. Lion Raisins, Inc., is a family-owned, family-operated business that grows raisins and markets them to private enterprises. In the 1990s, Lion also successfully bid on more than fifteen contracts awarded by the U.S. Department of Agriculture (USDA). In May 1999, a USDA investigation reported that Lion appeared to have falsified inspectors' signatures, given false moisture content, and changed the grade of raisins on three USDA raisin certificates issued between 1996 and 1998. Lion was subsequently awarded five more USDA contracts. Then, in November 2000, the company was the low bidder on two new USDA contracts for school lunch programs. In January 2001, however, the USDA awarded these contracts to other bidders and, on the basis of the May 1999 report, suspended Lion from participating in government contracts for one year. Lion filed a suit in the U.S. Court of Federal Claims against the USDA, seeking, in part, lost profits on the school lunch contracts on the ground that the USDA's suspension was arbitrary and capricious. What reasoning might the court employ to grant a summary judgment in Lion's favor? [*Lion Raisins Inc. v. United States,* 51 Fed.Cl. 238 (2001)]

6-9. INVESTIGATION. Maureen Droge began working for United Air Lines, Inc. (UAL), as a flight attendant in 1990. In 1995, she was assigned to Paris, France, where she became pregnant. Because UAL does not allow its flight attendants to fly during their third trimester of pregnancy, Droge was placed on involuntary leave. She applied for temporary disability benefits through the French social security system, but her request was denied because UAL does not contribute to the French system on behalf of its U.S.-based flight attendants. Droge filed a charge of discrimination with the U.S. Equal Employment Opportunity Commission (EEOC), alleging that UAL had discriminated against her and other Americans. The EEOC issued a subpoena, asking UAL to detail all benefits received by all UAL employees living outside the United States. UAL refused to provide the information, in part on the grounds that it was irrelevant and compliance would be unduly burdensome. The EEOC filed a suit in a federal district court against UAL. Should the court enforce the subpoena? Why or why not? [*Equal Employment Opportunity Commission v. United Air Lines, Inc.,* 287 F.3d 643 (7th Cir. 2002)]

6-10. JUDICIAL CONTROLS. Under federal law, when accepting bids on a contract, an agency must hold "discussions" with all offerors. An agency may ask a single offeror for "clarification" of its proposal, however, without holding "discussions" with the others. Regulations define *clarifications* as "limited exchanges." In March 2001, the U.S. Air Force asked for bids on a contract. The winning contractor would examine, assess, and develop means of integrating national intelligence assets with the U.S. Department of Defense space systems, to enhance the capabilities of the Air Force's Space Warfare Center. Among the bidders were Information Technology and Applications Corp. (ITAC) and RS Information Systems, Inc. (RSIS).

The Air Force asked the parties for more information on their subcontractors but did not allow them to change their proposals. Determining that there were weaknesses in ITAC's bid, the Air Force awarded the contract to RSIS. ITAC filed a suit in the U.S. Court of Federal Claims against the government, contending that the postproposal requests to RSIS, and its responses, were improper "discussions." Should the court rule in ITAC's favor? Why or why not? [*Information Technology & Applications Corp. v. United States*, 316 F.3d 1312 (Fed. Cir. 2003)]

LAW | on the Web

For updated links to resources available on the Web, as well as a variety of other materials, visit this text's Web site at http://wleb.westbuslaw.com.

To view the text of the Administrative Procedure Act of 1946, go to

http://www.fda.gov/opacom/laws/adminpro.htm

The Internet Law Library contains links to federal and state regulatory materials, including the *Code of Federal Regulations*. This page can be found at

http://www.lawguru.com/ilawlib

LEGAL RESEARCH EXERCISES ON THE WEB

Go to http://wleb.westbuslaw.com, the Web site that accompanies this text. Select "Chapter 6" and click on "Internet Exercises." There you will find the following Internet research exercises that you can perform to learn more about topics covered in this chapter.

Activity 6–1: **LEGAL PERSPECTIVE**
The Freedom of Information Act

Activity 6–2: **MANAGEMENT PERSPECTIVE**
Agency Inspections

CHAPTER 7

Criminal Law and Cyber Crimes

The law imposes various sanctions in attempting to ensure that individuals engaging in business in our society can compete and flourish. These sanctions include those imposed by civil law, such as damages for various types of tortious conduct (to be discussed in Chapters 12 and 13); damages for breach of contract (to be discussed in Chapter 10); and the equitable remedies discussed in Chapter 1. Additional sanctions are imposed under criminal law. Indeed, many statutes regulating business provide for criminal as well as civil penalties. Therefore, criminal law joins civil law as an important element in the legal environment of business.

In this chapter, after examining some essential differences between criminal law and civil law, we look at how crimes are classified, the basic requirements that must be met for criminal liability to be established, the various types of crimes that exist, and the defenses that can be raised to avoid criminal liability. We conclude the chapter with a discussion of crimes that occur in cyberspace, which are often referred to as *cyber crime*. Generally, cyber crime refers more to the way in which particular crimes are committed than to a new category of crimes.

SECTION 1 | Civil Law and Criminal Law

Recall from Chapter 1 that *civil law* pertains to the duties that exist between persons or between persons and their governments. Criminal law, in contrast, has to do with crime. A **crime** can be defined as a wrong against society proclaimed in a statute and punishable by a fine and/or imprisonment—or, in some cases, death. As mentioned in Chapter 1, because crimes are *offenses against society as a whole*, they are prosecuted by a public official, such as a district attorney (D.A.) or an attorney general (A.G.), not by victims.

MAJOR DIFFERENCES BETWEEN CIVIL LAW AND CRIMINAL LAW

Because the state has extensive resources at its disposal when prosecuting criminal cases, there are numerous procedural safeguards to protect the rights of defendants. We look here at one of these safeguards—the higher burden of proof that applies in a criminal case—as well as the harsher sanctions for criminal acts compared with civil wrongs. Exhibit 7–1 summarizes

these and other key differences between civil law and criminal law.

BURDEN OF PROOF In a civil case, the plaintiff usually must prove his or her case by a *preponderance of the evidence*. Under this standard, the plaintiff must convince the court that based on the evidence presented by both parties, it is more likely than not that the plaintiff's allegation is true.

In a criminal case, in contrast, the state must prove its case **beyond a reasonable doubt.** If the jury views the evidence in the case as reasonably permitting either a guilty or a not guilty verdict, then the jury's verdict must be not guilty. In other words, the government (prosecutor) must prove that the defendant has committed every essential element of the offense with which she or he is charged beyond a reasonable doubt. If the jury is not convinced of the defendant's guilt beyond a reasonable doubt, the defendant is not guilty. Note also that in a criminal case, the jury's verdict normally must be unanimous—agreed to by all members of the jury—to convict the defendant. (In a civil trial by jury, in contrast, typically only three-fourths of the jurors need to agree.)

The higher burden of proof in criminal cases reflects a fundamental social value—the belief that it

EXHIBIT 7-1	Key Differences between Civil and Criminal Law	
ISSUE	**CIVIL LAW**	**CRIMINAL LAW**
Party who brings suit	Person who suffered harm	The state
Wrongful act	Causing harm to a person or to a person's property	Violating a statute that prohibits some type of activity
Burden of proof	Preponderance of the evidence	Beyond a reasonable doubt
Verdict	Three-fourths majority (typically)	Unanimous
Remedy	Damages to compensate for the harm or a decree to achieve an equitable result	Punishment (fine, imprisonment, or death)

is worse to convict an innocent individual than to let a guilty person go free. We will look at other safeguards later in the chapter, in the context of criminal procedure.

CRIMINAL SANCTIONS The sanctions imposed on criminal wrongdoers are also harsher than those that are applied in civil cases. The purpose of tort law is to allow persons harmed by the wrongful acts of others to obtain compensation, or money damages, from the wrongdoer or to enjoin (prevent) a wrongdoer from undertaking or continuing a wrongful action. Tortfeasors are rarely subject to punitive damages— damages awarded simply to *punish* the wrongdoer. In contrast, criminal sanctions are designed to punish those who commit crimes in order to deter others from committing similar acts in the future. Criminal sanctions include fines as well as the much harsher penalty of the loss of one's liberty by incarceration in a jail or prison. The harshest criminal sanction is, of course, the death penalty.

CIVIL LIABILITY FOR CRIMINAL ACTS

Some torts, such as assault and battery, provide a basis for a criminal prosecution as well as a civil action in tort. For example, Jonas is walking down the street, minding his own business, when a person attacks him. In the ensuing struggle, the attacker stabs Jonas several times, seriously injuring him. A police officer restrains and arrests the wrongdoer. In this situation, the attacker may be subject both to criminal prosecution by the state and to a tort lawsuit brought by Jonas to obtain compensation for his injuries. Exhibit 7–2 on the following page illustrates how the same wrongful act can result in both a civil (tort) action and a criminal action against the wrongdoer.

SECTION 2 | Classification of Crimes

Depending on their degree of seriousness, crimes are classified as felonies or misdemeanors.

FELONIES

Felonies are serious crimes punishable by death or by imprisonment in a federal or state penitentiary for one year or longer.[1] The Model Penal Code[2] provides for four degrees of felony:

1. Capital offenses, for which the maximum penalty is death.
2. First degree felonies, punishable by a maximum penalty of life imprisonment.
3. Second degree felonies, punishable by a maximum of ten years' imprisonment.
4. Third degree felonies, punishable by up to five years' imprisonment.

Although criminal laws vary from state to state, some general rules apply when grading crimes by degree. For example, most jurisdictions punish a burglary that involves a forced entry into a home at night more harshly than a burglary that takes place during the day and involves a nonresidential building or

---

1. Some states, such as North Carolina, consider felonies to be punishable by incarceration for at least two years.
2. The American Law Institute issued the Official Draft of the Model Penal Code in 1962. The Model Penal Code contains four parts: (1) general provisions, (2) definitions of special crimes, (3) provisions concerning treatment and corrections, and (4) provisions on the organization of correction. The Model Penal Code is not a uniform code, however. Because of our federal structure of government, each state has developed its own set of laws governing criminal acts. Thus, types of crime and prescribed punishments may differ from one jurisdiction to another.

EXHIBIT 7-2 Civil (Tort) Lawsuit and Criminal Prosecution for the Same Act

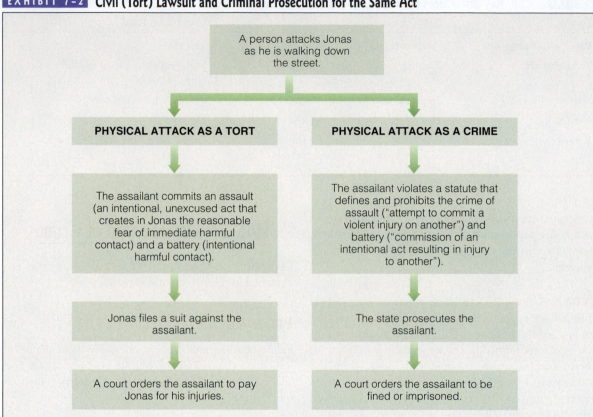

structure. A homicide—the taking of another's life—is classified according to the degree of intent involved.

For example, first degree murder requires that the homicide be premeditated and deliberate, as opposed to a spontaneous act of violence. When no premeditation or deliberation is present but the offender acts with *malice aforethought* (that is, with wanton disregard of the consequences of his or her actions for the victim), the homicide is classified as second degree murder. A homicide that is committed without malice toward the victim is known as *manslaughter*. *Voluntary manslaughter* occurs when the intent to kill may be present, as in a crime committed in the heat of passion, but malice is lacking. A homicide is classified as *involuntary manslaughter* when it results from an act of negligence (such as when a drunk driver causes the death of another person) and there is no intent to kill.

MISDEMEANORS AND PETTY OFFENSES

Under federal law and in most states, any crime that is not a felony is considered a **misdemeanor.** Misde-

meanors are crimes punishable by a fine or by incarceration for up to one year. If confined, the guilty party goes to a local jail instead of a penitentiary. Disorderly conduct and trespass are common misdemeanors. Some states have several classes of misdemeanors. For example, in Illinois, misdemeanors are either Class A (confinement for up to a year), Class B (not more than six months), or Class C (not more than thirty days). Whether a crime is a felony or a misdemeanor can also determine whether the case is tried in a magistrate's court (for example, by a justice of the peace) or a general trial court.

In most jurisdictions, **petty offenses** are considered to be a subset of misdemeanors. Petty offenses are minor violations, such as disturbing the peace and violations of building codes. Even for petty offenses, however, a guilty party can be put in jail for a few days, fined, or both, depending on state law.

Probation and community service are often imposed on those who commit misdemeanors, especially juveniles. Also, most states have decriminalized all but the most serious traffic offenses. These infractions are treated as civil proceedings, and civil fines are imposed. In many states, "points" are assessed against the violator's driving record (and the state will suspend a person's driver's license if too many points are accumulated).

SECTION 3 | The Essentials of Criminal Liability

Two elements must exist for a person to be convicted of a crime: (1) the performance of a prohibited act and (2) a specified state of mind, or intent, on the part of the actor. Additionally, to establish criminal liability, there must be a *concurrence* between the act and the intent. In other words, these two elements must occur together.

For example, suppose that a woman intends to kill her husband by poisoning him. On the day she plans to do so, she is driving her husband home from work and swerves to avoid hitting a cat crossing the road. The car crashes into a tree as a result, killing her husband. Even though she had planned to murder her husband, the woman would not be guilty of murder in this situation because she had not intended to kill him by driving her car into a tree.

THE CRIMINAL ACT

Every criminal statute prohibits certain behavior. Most crimes require an act of *commission*—that is, a person must *do* something in order to be accused of a crime. In criminal law, a prohibited act is referred to as the **actus reus**,[3] or guilty act. In some cases, an act of omission can be a crime, but only when a person has a legal duty to perform the omitted act, such as filing a tax return. For example, in 2005 the federal government filed a criminal action against a former winner of the reality TV show *Survivor* for failing to report more than $1 million in winnings.

The *guilty act* requirement is based on one of the premises of criminal law—that a person should be punished for harm done to society. Thus, for a crime to exist the guilty act must cause some harm to a person or to property. Thinking about killing someone or about stealing a car may be morally wrong, but the thoughts do no harm until they are translated into

action. Of course, a person can be punished for *attempting* murder or robbery, but only if substantial steps toward the criminal objective have been taken. Additionally, the punishment for an attempt to commit a crime is normally less severe than it would be if the act had been completed.

STATE OF MIND

A wrongful mental state **(mens rea)**[4] is also typically required to establish criminal liability. The required mental state, or intent, is indicated in the applicable statute or law. Murder, for example, involves the guilty act of killing another human being, and the guilty mental state is the desire, or intent, to take another's life. For theft, the guilty act is the taking of another person's property, and the mental state involves both the awareness that the property belongs to another and the desire to deprive the owner of it.

A guilty mental state can be attributed to acts of negligence or recklessness as well. *Criminal negligence* involves the mental state in which the defendant deviates from the standard of care that a reasonable person would use under the same circumstances. The defendant is accused of taking an unjustified, substantial, and foreseeable risk that resulted in harm. Under the Model Penal Code, a defendant is negligent even if she or he was not actually aware of the risk but *should have been aware* of it.[5] The Model Penal Code defines *criminal recklessness* as "consciously disregard[ing] a substantial and unjustifiable risk."[6] In other words, a defendant is reckless if he or she is *actually aware* of the risk. A defendant who commits an act *recklessly* is more blameworthy than one who is criminally negligent.

SECTION 4 | Corporate Criminal Liability

As will be discussed in Chapter 18, a corporation is a legal entity created under the laws of a state. Both the corporation as an entity and the individual directors and officers of the corporation are potentially subject to liability for criminal acts.

---

3. Pronounced *ak*-tuhs *ray*-uhs.

4. Pronounced *mehns ray*-uh.
5. Model Penal Code Section 2.02(2)(d).
6. Model Penal Code Section 2.02(2)(c).

LIABILITY OF THE CORPORATE ENTITY

At one time, it was thought that a corporation could not incur criminal liability because, although a corporation is a legal person, it can act only through its agents (corporate directors, officers, and employees). Therefore, the corporate entity itself could not "intend" to commit a crime. Under modern criminal law, however, a corporation may be held liable for crimes. Obviously, corporations cannot be imprisoned, but they can be fined or denied certain legal privileges (such as a license).

The Model Penal Code provides that a corporation may be convicted of a crime in the following situations:

1. The criminal act by the corporation's agent or employee is within the scope of his or her employment, and the purpose of the statute defining the act as a crime is to impose liability on the corporation.
2. The crime consists of a failure to perform a specific affirmative duty imposed on corporations by law.
3. The crime was authorized, requested, commanded, committed, or recklessly tolerated by one of the corporation's high managerial agents.[7]

As implied by the first statement in the above list, corporate criminal liability is vicarious—the corporation as an entity may be liable for the criminal acts of its employees when the acts are committed within the scope of employment. Thus, a corporation that is found to be criminally responsible for an act committed by an employee can be fined for that offense. Through the fine, stockholders and other employees suffer because of the vicarious liability of the corporation. For such criminal liability to be imposed, the prosecutor must show that the corporation could have prevented the act or that there was authorized consent to, or knowledge of, the act by persons in supervisory positions within the corporation.

LIABILITY OF CORPORATE OFFICERS AND DIRECTORS

Corporate directors and officers are personally liable for the crimes they commit, regardless of whether the crimes were committed for their private benefit or on the corporation's behalf. Additionally, corporate directors and officers may be held liable for the actions of employees under their supervision. Under what has become known as the "responsible corporate officer" doctrine, a court may impose criminal liability on a corporate officer regardless of whether he or she participated in, directed, or even knew about a given criminal violation.

For example, in *United States v. Park*,[8] the chief executive officer of a national supermarket chain was held personally liable for sanitation violations in corporate warehouses where food was exposed to contamination by rodents. The United States Supreme Court imposed personal liability on the corporate officer not because he intended the crime or even knew about it but rather because he was in a "responsible relationship" to the corporation and had the power to prevent the violation. Since the *Park* decision, courts have applied this "responsible corporate officer" doctrine on a number of occasions to hold corporate officers liable for their employees' statutory violations, including violations of environmental statutes (discussed in Chapter 24).

SECTION 5 | Types of Crimes

Numerous actions are designated as criminal. Federal, state, and local laws provide for the classification and punishment of hundreds of thousands of different criminal acts. Generally, though, criminal acts can be grouped into five broad categories: violent crime (crimes against persons), property crime, public order crime, white-collar crime, and organized crime. Cyber crime—which consists of crimes committed in cyberspace with the use of computers—is, as mentioned earlier in this chapter, less a category of crime than a new way to commit crime. We will examine cyber crime later in this chapter.

VIOLENT CRIME

Some types of crime are called *violent crimes*, or crimes against persons, because they cause others to suffer harm or death. Murder is a violent crime. So is sexual assault, or rape. Assault and battery, which will be discussed in Chapter 12 in the context of tort law, are also classified as violent crimes. **Robbery**—defined as the taking of money, personal property, or any other article of value from a person by means of force or fear—is also a violent crime. Typically, states have

---

7. Model Penal Code Section 2.07.

8. 421 U.S. 658, 95 S.Ct. 1903, 44 L.Ed.2d 489 (1975).

more severe penalties for *aggravated robbery*—robbery with the use of a deadly weapon.

Each of these violent crimes is further classified by degree, depending on the circumstances surrounding the criminal act. These circumstances include the intent of the person committing the crime, whether a weapon was used, and (in cases other than murder) the level of pain and suffering experienced by the victim.

PROPERTY CRIME

The most common type of criminal activity is property crime, or those crimes in which the goal of the offender is some form of economic gain or the damaging of property. Robbery is a form of property crime, as well as a violent crime, because the offender seeks to gain the property of another. We look here at a number of other crimes that fall within the general category of property crime.

BURGLARY Traditionally, **burglary** was defined as breaking and entering the dwelling of another at night with the intent to commit a felony. Originally, the definition was aimed at protecting an individual's home and its occupants. Most state statutes have eliminated some of the requirements found in the common law definition. The time at which the breaking and entering occurs, for example, is usually immaterial. State statutes frequently omit the element of breaking, and some states do not require that the building be a dwelling. *Aggravated burglary*—which is defined as burglary with the use of a deadly weapon, burglary of a dwelling, or both—incurs a greater penalty.

LARCENY Any person who wrongfully or fraudulently takes and carries away another individual's personal property is guilty of **larceny.** Larceny includes the fraudulent intent to deprive an owner permanently of property. Many business-related larcenies entail fraudulent conduct. Whereas robbery involves force or fear, larceny does not. Therefore, picking pockets is larceny, not robbery. Similarly, taking company products and supplies home for personal use, if one is not authorized to do so, is larceny.

In most states, the definition of property that is subject to larceny statutes has expanded. For example, stealing computer programs may constitute larceny even though the "property" consists of magnetic impulses. Stealing computer time may also be considered larceny. So, too, may the theft of natural gas.

Intercepting cellular phone calls to obtain another's phone-card number—and then using that number to place long-distance calls, often overseas—is a form of property theft. These types of larceny are covered by "theft of services" statutes in many jurisdictions.

The common law distinguishes between grand and petit larceny depending on the value of the property taken. Many states have abolished this distinction, but in those that have not, grand larceny (theft above a certain amount) is a felony and petit larceny is a misdemeanor.

ARSON The willful and malicious burning of a building (and, in some states, personal property) owned by another is the crime of **arson.** At common law, arson applied only to burning down another person's house. The law was designed to protect human life. Today, arson statutes have been extended to cover the destruction of any building, regardless of ownership, by fire or explosion.

Every state has a special statute that covers the burning of a building for the purpose of collecting insurance. If Shaw owns an insured apartment building that is falling apart and sets fire to it himself or pays someone else to do so, he is guilty not only of arson but also of defrauding insurers, which is an attempted larceny. Of course, the insurer need not pay the claim when insurance fraud is proved.

RECEIVING STOLEN GOODS It is a crime to receive stolen goods. The recipient of such goods need not know the true identity of the owner or the thief. All that is necessary is that the recipient knows or should know that the goods are stolen, which implies an intent to deprive the owner of those goods.

FORGERY The fraudulent making or altering of any writing in a way that changes the legal rights and liabilities of another is **forgery.** If, without authorization, Severson signs Bennett's name to the back of a check made out to Bennett, Severson is committing forgery. Forgery also includes changing trademarks, falsifying public records, counterfeiting, and altering a legal document.

OBTAINING GOODS BY FALSE PRETENSES It is a criminal act to obtain goods by false pretenses—for example, to buy groceries with a check, knowing that one has insufficient funds to cover it. Using someone else's credit-card number to obtain goods is another example of obtaining goods by false pretenses. Statutes dealing with such illegal activities vary widely from state to state. For example, in some states an intent to defraud must be proved before a person is criminally liable for writing a bad check.

PUBLIC ORDER CRIME

Historically, societies have always outlawed activities that are considered contrary to public values and morals. Today, the most common public order crimes include public drunkenness, prostitution, gambling, and illegal drug use. These crimes are sometimes referred to as *victimless crimes* because they normally harm only the offender. From a broader perspective, however, they are deemed detrimental to society as a whole because they might create an environment that gives rise to property and violent crimes.

WHITE-COLLAR CRIME

Crimes occurring in the business context are popularly referred to as white-collar crimes. Although there is no official definition of **white-collar crime,** the term is commonly used to mean an illegal act or series of acts committed by an individual or business entity using some nonviolent means to obtain a personal or business advantage. Usually, this kind of crime takes place in the course of a legitimate business occupation. The crimes discussed next normally occur only in the business environment and thus fall into the category of white-collar crimes. Note, though, that certain property crimes, such as larceny and forgery, may also fall into this category if they occur within the business context.

EMBEZZLEMENT When a person entrusted with another person's property or funds fraudulently appropriates that property or those funds, **embezzlement** occurs. Typically, embezzlement involves an employee who steals funds from her or his employer. Banks often face this problem, and so do a number of businesses in which corporate officers or accountants "doctor" the books to cover up the fraudulent conversion of funds for their own benefit. Embezzlement is not larceny because the wrongdoer does not *physically* take the property from the possession of another, and it is not robbery because no force or fear is used.

It does not matter whether the accused takes the funds from the victim or from a third person. If, as the

financial officer of a large corporation, Carlson pockets a certain number of checks from third parties that were given to her to deposit into the corporate account, she is embezzling.

Ordinarily, an embezzler who returns what has been taken will not be prosecuted because the owner usually will not take the time to make a complaint, give depositions, and appear in court. That the accused intended eventually to return the embezzled property does not constitute a sufficient defense to the crime of embezzlement, however.

MAIL AND WIRE FRAUD One of the most potent weapons against white-collar criminals is the Mail Fraud Act of 1990.[9] Under this act, it is a federal crime to use the mails to defraud the public. Illegal use of the mails must involve (1) mailing or causing someone else to mail a writing—something written, printed, or photocopied—for the purpose of executing a scheme to defraud and (2) contemplating or organizing a scheme to defraud by false pretenses. If, for example, Johnson advertises by mail the sale of a cure for cancer that he knows to be fraudulent because it has no medical validity, he can be prosecuted for fraudulent use of the mails.

Federal law also makes it a crime (wire fraud) to use wire, radio, or television transmissions to defraud.[10] Violators may be fined up to $1,000, imprisoned for up to twenty years, or both. If the violation affects a financial institution, the violator may be fined up to $1 million, imprisoned for up to thirty years, or both.

BRIBERY Basically, three types of bribery are considered crimes: (1) commercial bribery, (2) bribery of public officials, and (3) bribery of foreign officials. As an element of the crime of bribery, intent must be present and proved. The bribe can be anything the recipient considers to be valuable. Realize that the *crime of bribery occurs when the bribe is offered.* It does not matter whether the person to whom the bribe is offered accepts the bribe or agrees to perform whatever action is desired by the person offering the bribe. *Accepting a bribe* is a separate crime.

Typically, people make commercial bribes to obtain proprietary information, cover up an inferior product, or secure new business. Industrial espionage sometimes involves commercial bribes. For example, a person in one firm may offer an employee in a competing firm

---

9. 18 U.S.C. Sections 1341–1342.
10. 18 U.S.C. Section 1343.

some type of payoff in exchange for trade secrets or pricing schedules. So-called kickbacks, or payoffs for special favors or services, are a form of commercial bribery in some situations.

Bribing foreign officials to obtain favorable business contracts is a crime. This crime was discussed in detail in Chapter 4, along with the Foreign Corrupt Practices Act of 1977, which was passed to curb the use of bribery by American businesspersons in securing foreign contracts.

BANKRUPTCY FRAUD Today, federal bankruptcy law allows individuals and businesses to be relieved of oppressive debt through bankruptcy proceedings. Numerous white-collar crimes may be committed during the many phases of a bankruptcy action. A creditor, for example, may file a false claim against the debtor, which is a crime. Also, a debtor may fraudulently transfer assets to favored parties before or after the petition for bankruptcy is filed. For example, a company-owned automobile may be "sold" at a bargain price to a trusted friend or relative. Closely related to the crime of fraudulent transfer of property is the crime of fraudulent concealment of property, such as the hiding of gold coins.

INSIDER TRADING An individual who obtains "inside information" about the plans of a publicly listed corporation can often make stock-trading profits by using this information to guide decisions relating to the purchase or sale of corporate securities. *Insider trading* is a violation of securities law and will be considered more fully in Chapter 28. At this point, it may be said that one who possesses inside information and who has a duty not to disclose it to outsiders may not profit from the purchase or sale of securities based on that information until the information is available to the public.

THE THEFT OF TRADE SECRETS As will be discussed in Chapter 14, trade secrets constitute a form of intellectual property that for many businesses can be extremely valuable. The Economic Espionage Act of 1996[11] makes the theft of trade secrets a federal crime. The act also makes it a federal crime to buy or possess another person's trade secrets, knowing that the trade secrets were stolen or otherwise acquired without the owner's authorization.

11. 18 U.S.C. Sections 1831–1839.

Violations of the act can result in steep penalties. The act provides that an individual who violates the act can be imprisoned for up to ten years and fined up to $500,000. If a corporation or other organization violates the act, it can be fined up to $5 million. Additionally, the law provides that any property acquired as a result of the violation or used in the commission of the violation is subject to criminal forfeiture—meaning that the government can take the property. A theft of trade secrets conducted via the Internet, for example, could result in the forfeiture of every computer, printer, or other device used to commit or facilitate the violation.

ORGANIZED CRIME

White-collar crime takes place within the confines of the legitimate business world. Organized crime, in contrast, operates *illegitimately* by, among other things, providing illegal goods and services. Traditionally, the preferred markets for organized crime have been gambling, prostitution, illegal narcotics, and loan sharking (lending funds at higher-than-legal interest rates), along with more recent ventures into counterfeiting and credit-card scams.

MONEY LAUNDERING The profits from organized crime and other illegal activities amount to billions of dollars a year, particularly the profits from illegal drug transactions and, to a lesser extent, from racketeering, prostitution, and gambling. Under federal law, banks, savings and loan associations, and other financial institutions are required to report currency transactions involving more than $10,000. Consequently, those who engage in illegal activities face difficulties in depositing their cash profits from illegal transactions.

As an alternative to storing cash from illegal transactions in a safe-deposit box, wrongdoers and racketeers have invented ways to launder "dirty" money to make it "clean." This **money laundering** is done through legitimate businesses. For example, suppose that Harris, a successful drug dealer, becomes a partner with a restaurateur. Little by little, the restaurant shows an increasing profit. As a partner in the restaurant, Harris is able to report the "profits" of the restaurant as legitimate income on which he pays federal and state taxes. He can then spend those after-tax funds without worrying about whether his lifestyle exceeds the level possible with his reported income.

CONCEPT SUMMARY 7.1 | Types of Crimes

Crime Category	Definitions and Examples
Violent Crime	1. *Definition*—Crimes that cause others to suffer harm or death. 2. *Examples*—Murder, assault and battery, sexual assault (rape), and robbery.
Property Crime	1. *Definition*—Crimes in which the goal of the offender is some form of economic gain or the damaging of property; the most common form of crime. 2. *Examples*—Burglary, larceny, arson, receiving stolen goods, forgery, and obtaining goods by false pretenses.
Public Order Crime	1. *Definition*—Crimes contrary to public values and morals. 2. *Examples*—Public drunkenness, prostitution, gambling, and illegal drug use.
White-Collar Crime	1. *Definition*—An illegal act or series of acts committed by an individual or business entity using some nonviolent means to obtain a personal or business advantage; usually committed in the course of a legitimate occupation. 2. *Examples*—Embezzlement, mail and wire fraud, bribery, bankruptcy fraud, insider trading, and the theft of trade secrets.
Organized Crime	1. *Definition*—A form of crime conducted by groups operating illegitimately to satisfy the public's demand for illegal goods and services (such as gambling and illegal narcotics). 2. *Money laundering*—The establishment of legitimate enterprises through which "dirty" money (obtained through criminal activities, such as illegal drug trafficking) can be "laundered" (made to appear as legitimate income). 3. *RICO*—The Racketeer Influenced and Corrupt Organizations Act (RICO) of 1970 makes it a federal crime to (a) use income obtained from racketeering activity to purchase any interest in an enterprise, (b) acquire or maintain an interest in an enterprise through racketeering activity, (c) conduct or participate in the affairs of an enterprise through racketeering activity, or (d) conspire to do any of the preceding activities. RICO provides for both civil and criminal liability.

The Federal Bureau of Investigation (FBI) estimates that organized crime has invested tens of billions of dollars in as many as a hundred thousand business establishments in the United States for the purpose of money laundering. Globally, it is estimated that $500 billion in illegal money moves through the world banking system every year.

RICO In 1970, in an effort to curb the apparently increasing entry of organized crime into the legitimate business world, Congress passed the Racketeer Influenced and Corrupt Organizations Act (RICO).[12] The statute, which was enacted as part of the Organized Crime Control Act, makes it a federal crime to (1) use income obtained from racketeering activity to purchase any interest in an enterprise, (2) acquire or maintain an interest in an enterprise through racketeering activity, (3) conduct or participate in the affairs of an enterprise through racketeering activity, or (4) conspire to do any of the preceding activities.

Racketeering activity is not a new type of substantive crime created by RICO; rather, RICO incorporates by reference twenty-six separate types of federal crimes and nine types of state felonies[13] and declares that a person who commits two of these offenses is guilty of "racketeering activity." The act provides for both civil and criminal liability.

---

12. 18 U.S.C. Sections 1961–1968.

13. See 18 U.S.C. Section 1961(1)(A). The crimes listed in this section relate to murder, kidnapping, gambling, arson, robbery, bribery, extortion, money laundering, securities fraud, counterfeiting, dealing in obscene matter, dealing in controlled substances (illegal drugs), and a number of others.

—Civil Liability under RICO. The penalties for violations of the RICO statute are harsh. In the event of a violation, the statute permits the government to seek civil penalties, including the divestiture of a defendant's interest in a business (called *forfeiture*) or the dissolution of the business. Perhaps the most controversial aspect of RICO is that in some cases, private individuals are allowed to recover three times their actual losses (treble damages), plus attorneys' fees, for business injuries caused by a violation of the statute.

The broad language of RICO has allowed it to be applied in cases that have little or nothing to do with organized crime, and an aggressive trial attorney may attempt to show that any business fraud constitutes "racketeering activity." In its 1985 decision in *Sedima, S.P.R.L. v. Imrex Co.*,[14] the United States Supreme Court interpreted RICO broadly and set a significant precedent for subsequent applications of the act. Plaintiffs have used the RICO statute in numerous commercial fraud cases because of the inviting prospect of being awarded treble damages if they win. The most frequent targets of civil RICO lawsuits are insurance companies, employment agencies, and commercial banks.

One of the requirements of RICO is that there be more than one offense—there must be a "pattern of racketeering activity." What constitutes a "pattern" has been the subject of much litigation. According to the interpretation of some courts, a pattern must involve, among other things, continued criminal activity. This is known as the "continuity" requirement. Part of this requirement is that the activity occur over a "substantial" period of time.

—Criminal Liability under RICO. Many criminal RICO offenses, such as gambling, arson, and extortion, have little, if anything, to do with normal business activities. But securities fraud (involving the sale of stocks and bonds) and mail and wire fraud may also constitute criminal RICO violations, and RICO has become an effective tool in attacking these white-collar crimes in recent years. Under the criminal provisions of RICO, any individual found guilty of a violation is subject to a fine of up to $25,000 per violation, imprisonment for up to twenty years, or both. Additionally, the statute provides that those who violate RICO may be required to forfeit (give up) any assets, in the form of property or cash, that were acquired as a result of the illegal activity or that were "involved in" or an "instrumentality of" the activity.

SECTION 6 | Defenses to Criminal Liability

In certain circumstances, the law may allow a person to be excused from criminal liability because she or he lacks the required mental state. Criminal defendants may also be relieved of criminal liability if they can show that their criminal actions were justified, given the circumstances. Among the most important defenses to criminal liability are infancy, intoxication, insanity, mistake, consent, duress, justifiable use of force, necessity, entrapment, and the statute of limitations. Additionally, in some cases defendants are given *immunity* from prosecution and thus are relieved, at least in part, of criminal liability for their actions. We look next at each of these defenses.

Note that procedural violations (such as obtaining evidence without a valid search warrant) may also operate as defenses because evidence obtained in violation of a defendant's constitutional rights may not be admitted in court. If the evidence is suppressed, then there may be no basis for prosecuting the defendant.

INFANCY

The term *infant*, as used in the law, refers to any person who has not yet reached the age of majority (see Chapter 9). In all states, certain courts handle cases involving children who allegedly have violated the law. In some states, juvenile courts handle children's cases exclusively. In most states, however, courts that handle children's cases also have jurisdiction over other matters, such as traffic offenses.

Originally, juvenile court hearings were informal, and lawyers were rarely present. Since 1967, however, when the United States Supreme Court ordered that a child charged with delinquency must be allowed to consult with an attorney before being committed to a state institution,[15] juvenile court hearings have become more formal. In most states, a child may be treated as an adult and tried in a regular court if he or she is above a certain age (usually fourteen) and is charged with a felony, such as rape or murder.

---

14. 473 U.S. 479, 105 S.Ct. 3275, 87 L.Ed.2d 346 (1985).

15. *In re Gault*, 387 U.S. 1, 87 S.Ct. 1428, 18 L.Ed.2d 527 (1967).

INTOXICATION

The law recognizes two types of intoxication, whether from drugs or from alcohol: involuntary and voluntary. *Involuntary intoxication* occurs when a person either is physically forced to ingest or inject an intoxicating substance or is unaware that such a substance contains drugs or alcohol. Involuntary intoxication is a defense to a crime if its effect was to make a person incapable of understanding that the act committed was wrong or incapable of obeying the law.

Using voluntary drug or alcohol intoxication as a defense is based on the theory that extreme levels of intoxication may negate the state of mind that a crime requires. Many courts are reluctant to allow *voluntary intoxication* as a defense to a crime, however. After all, the defendant, by definition, voluntarily chose to put herself or himself into an intoxicated state.

INSANITY

Just as a child is often judged incapable of the state of mind required to commit a crime, so also may be someone suffering from a mental illness. Thus, insanity may be a defense to a criminal charge. The courts have had difficulty deciding what standards should be used to measure sanity for the purposes of a criminal trial. One of the oldest standards, or tests, for insanity is the *M'Naghten* test,[16] which is still used in about one-third of the states. Under this test, which is sometimes called the "right-wrong" test, a criminal defendant is not responsible if, at the time of the offense, he or she did not know the nature and quality of the act or did not know that the act was wrong.

Several other jurisdictions use the less restrictive "irresistible-impulse" test to determine sanity. Under this test, a person may be found insane even if she or he was aware that a criminal act was wrong, providing that some "irresistible impulse" resulting from a mental deficiency drove her or him to commit the crime.

Today, almost all federal courts and about half of the states use the relatively liberal standard set forth in the Model Penal Code:

> A person is not responsible for criminal conduct if at the time of such conduct as a result of mental disease or defect he lacks *substantial capacity* either to appreciate the wrongfulness of his conduct or to conform his conduct to the requirements of the law.[17] [Emphasis added.]

This "substantial-capacity" standard is considerably easier to meet than the *M'Naghten* test or the irresistible-impulse test.

Under any of these tests, it is extremely difficult to prove insanity. For this reason, the insanity defense is rarely used. It is raised in only about 1 percent of felony cases and is unsuccessful in about three-fourths of those cases.

MISTAKE

Everyone has heard the saying "Ignorance of the law is no excuse." Ordinarily, ignorance of the law or a mistaken idea about what the law requires is not a valid defense. In some states, however, that rule has been modified. People who claim that they honestly did not know that they were breaking a law may have a valid defense if (1) the law was not published or reasonably made known to the public or (2) the people relied on an official statement of the law that was erroneous.

A *mistake of fact,* as opposed to a *mistake of law,* operates as a defense if it negates the mental state necessary to commit a crime. If, for example, Oliver Wheaton mistakenly walks off with Julie Tyson's briefcase because he thinks it is his, there is no theft. Theft requires knowledge that the property belongs to another.

CONSENT

What if a victim consents to a crime or even encourages the person intending a criminal act to commit it? Ordinarily, **consent** does not operate as a bar to criminal liability. In some rare circumstances, however, the law may allow consent to be used as a defense. In each case, the question is whether the law forbids an act committed against the victim's will or forbids the act without regard to the victim's will. The law forbids murder, prostitution, and drug use whether the victim consents or not. Also, if the act causes harm to a third person who has not consented, there is no escape from criminal liability. Consent or forgiveness given after a crime has been committed is not really a defense, although it can affect the likelihood of prosecution.

Normally, consent is a successful defense only in crimes against property. For example, suppose that Barry gives Phong permission to hunt for deer on Barry's land while staying in Barry's lakeside cabin. After observing Phong carrying a gun into the cabin at night, a neighbor calls the police, and an officer subsequently arrests Phong. If charged with burglary (or

---

16. A rule derived from *M'Naghten's Case,* 8 Eng.Rep. 718 (1843).
17. Model Penal Code Section 4.01.

aggravated burglary, because he had a weapon), Phong can assert the defense of consent and will likely succeed in escaping criminal liability because he had obtained Barry's consent to enter the premises.

DURESS

Duress exists when the *wrongful threat* of one person induces another person to perform an act that he or she would not otherwise have performed. In such a situation, duress is said to negate the mental state necessary to commit a crime. For duress to qualify as a defense, the following requirements must be met:

1. The threat must be of serious bodily harm or death.
2. The harm threatened must be greater than the harm caused by the crime.
3. The threat must be immediate and inescapable.
4. The defendant must have been involved in the situation through no fault of his or her own.

One crime that cannot be excused by duress is murder. It is difficult to justify taking a life as a result of duress even if one's own life is threatened.

JUSTIFIABLE USE OF FORCE

Probably the most well-known defense to criminal liability is **self-defense.** Other situations, however, also justify the use of force: the defense of one's dwelling, the defense of other property, and the prevention of a crime. In all of these situations, it is important to distinguish between deadly and nondeadly force. *Deadly force* is likely to result in death or serious bodily harm. *Nondeadly force* is force that reasonably appears necessary to prevent the imminent use of criminal force.

Generally speaking, people can use the amount of nondeadly force that seems necessary to protect themselves, their dwellings, or other property or to prevent the commission of a crime. Deadly force can be used in self-defense if there is a *reasonable belief* that imminent death or grievous bodily harm will otherwise result, if the attacker is using unlawful force (an example of lawful force would be that exerted by a police officer), and if the defender has not initiated or provoked the attack. Deadly force can be used to defend a dwelling only if the unlawful entry is violent and the person believes deadly force is necessary to prevent imminent death or great bodily harm or—in some jurisdictions—if the person believes deadly force is necessary to prevent the commission of a felony in the dwelling.

NECESSITY

Sometimes criminal defendants can be relieved of liability by showing that a criminal act was necessary to prevent an even greater harm. According to the Model Penal Code, the defense of **necessity** is justifiable if "the harm or evil sought to be avoided by such conduct is greater than that sought to be prevented by the law defining the offense charged."[18] For example, in one case a convicted felon was threatened by an acquaintance with a gun. The felon grabbed the gun and fled the scene, but subsequently he was arrested under a statute that prohibits convicted felons from possessing firearms. In this situation, the necessity defense succeeded because the defendant's crime avoided a "greater evil."[19]

ENTRAPMENT

Entrapment is a defense designed to prevent police officers or other government agents from encouraging crimes in order to apprehend persons wanted for criminal acts. In the typical entrapment case, an undercover agent *suggests* that a crime be committed and somehow pressures or induces an individual to commit it. The agent then arrests the individual for the crime. For entrapment to be considered a defense, both the suggestion and the inducement must take place. The defense is not intended to prevent law enforcement agents from setting a trap for an unwary criminal; rather, the intent is to prevent them from pushing the individual into that trap. The crucial issue is whether a person who committed a crime was predisposed to commit the crime or did so because the agent induced it.

STATUTE OF LIMITATIONS

With some exceptions, such as for the crime of murder, statutes of limitations apply to crimes just as they do to civil wrongs. In other words, the state must initiate criminal prosecution within a certain number of years. If a criminal action is brought after the statutory time period has expired, the accused person can raise the statute of limitations as a defense. The running of the time period in a statute of limitations may be tolled—that is, suspended or stopped temporarily—if the defendant is a minor or is not in the jurisdiction.

---

18. Model Penal Code Section 3.02.
19. *United States v. Paolello*, 951 F.2d 537 (3d Cir. 1991).

When the defendant reaches the age of majority or returns to the jurisdiction, the statute revives—that is, its time period begins to run or to run again.

IMMUNITY

At times, the state may wish to obtain information from a person accused of a crime. Accused persons are understandably reluctant to give information if it will be used to prosecute them, and they cannot be forced to do so. The privilege against self-incrimination is granted by the Fifth Amendment to the Constitution, which reads, in part, "nor shall [any person] be compelled in any criminal case to be a witness against himself." In cases in which the state wishes to obtain information from a person accused of a crime, the state can grant *immunity* from prosecution or agree to prosecute for a less serious offense in exchange for the information. Once immunity is given, the person now has an absolute privilege against self-incrimination and therefore can no longer refuse to testify on Fifth Amendment grounds.

Often, a grant of immunity from prosecution for a serious crime is part of the **plea bargaining** between the defending and prosecuting attorneys. The defendant may be convicted of a lesser offense, while the state uses the defendant's testimony to prosecute accomplices for serious crimes carrying heavy penalties.

SECTION **7** | Criminal Procedures

Criminal law brings the force of the state, with all of its resources, to bear against the individual. Criminal procedures are designed to protect the constitutional rights of individuals and to prevent the arbitrary use of power on the part of the government.

The U.S. Constitution provides specific safeguards for those accused of crimes. The United States Supreme Court has ruled that most of these safeguards apply not only in federal but also in state courts by virtue of the due process clause of the Fourteenth Amendment. These safeguards include the following:

1. The Fourth Amendment protection from unreasonable searches and seizures.
2. The Fourth Amendment requirement that no warrant for a search or an arrest be issued without probable cause.
3. The Fifth Amendment requirement that no one be deprived of "life, liberty, or property without due process of law."

4. The Fifth Amendment prohibition against **double jeopardy** (trying someone twice for the same criminal offense).[20]
5. The Fifth Amendment requirement that no person be required to be a witness against (incriminate) himself or herself.
6. The Sixth Amendment guarantees of a speedy trial, a trial by jury, a public trial, the right to confront witnesses, and the right to a lawyer at various stages in some proceedings.
7. The Eighth Amendment prohibitions against excessive bail and fines and cruel and unusual punishment.

THE EXCLUSIONARY RULE

Under what is known as the **exclusionary rule,** all evidence obtained in violation of the constitutional rights spelled out in the Fourth, Fifth, and Sixth Amendments normally is not admissible at trial. All evidence derived from the illegally obtained evidence is known as the "fruit of the poisonous tree," and such evidence normally must also be excluded from the trial proceedings. For example, if a confession is obtained after an illegal arrest, the arrest is the "poisonous tree," and the confession, if "tainted" by the arrest, is the "fruit."

As you will read shortly, under the *Miranda* rule, suspects must be advised of certain constitutional rights when they are arrested. For example, the Sixth Amendment right to counsel is one of the rights of which a suspect must be advised when he or she is arrested. In many cases, a statement that a criminal suspect makes in the absence of counsel is not admissible at trial unless the suspect has knowingly and voluntarily waived this right. In the following case, the United States Supreme Court considered at what point a suspect's right to counsel is triggered during criminal proceedings.

---

20. The prohibition against double jeopardy means that once a criminal defendant is found not guilty of a particular crime, the government may not reindict the person and retry him or her for the same crime. The prohibition against double jeopardy does not preclude a *civil* suit's being brought against the same person by the crime victim to recover damages. For example, a person found not guilty of assault and battery in a criminal case may be sued by the victim in a civil (tort) case for damages. Additionally, a state's prosecution of a crime will not prevent a separate federal prosecution of the same crime, and vice versa. For example, a defendant found not guilty of violating a state law can be tried in federal court for the same act, if the act is also defined as a crime under federal law.

CASE 7.1 — Fellers v. United States

Supreme Court of the
United States, 2004.
540 U.S. 519,
124 S.Ct. 1019,
157 L.Ed.2d 1016.

Justice *O'CONNOR* delivered the opinion of the Court.

* * * *

On February 24, 2000, after a grand jury indicted petitioner [John J. Fellers] for conspiracy to distribute methamphetamine, Lincoln Police Sergeant Michael Garnett and Lancaster County Deputy Sheriff Jeff Bliemeister went to petitioner's home in Lincoln, Nebraska, to arrest him. The officers knocked on petitioner's door and, when petitioner answered, identified themselves and asked if they could come in. Petitioner invited the officers into his living room.

The officers advised petitioner they had come to discuss his involvement in methamphetamine distribution. They informed petitioner that they had a federal warrant for his arrest and that a grand jury had indicted him for conspiracy to distribute methamphetamine. The officers told petitioner that the indictment referred to his involvement with certain individuals, four of whom they named. Petitioner then told the officers that he knew the four people and had used methamphetamine during his association with them.

After spending about 15 minutes in petitioner's home, the officers transported petitioner to the Lancaster County jail. There, the officers advised petitioner for the first time of his [right to counsel under the Sixth Amendment]. Petitioner and the two officers signed a * * * waiver form, and petitioner then reiterated the inculpatory [incriminating] statements he had made earlier, admitted to having associated with other individuals implicated in the charged conspiracy, and admitted to having loaned money to one of them even though he suspected that she was involved in drug transactions.

Before trial, petitioner moved to suppress the inculpatory statements he made at his home and at the county jail. * * *

The District Court suppressed the "unwarned" statements petitioner made at his house but admitted petitioner's jailhouse statements * * * , concluding petitioner had knowingly and voluntarily waived his * * * rights before making the statements.

Following a jury trial at which petitioner's jailhouse statements were admitted into evidence, petitioner was convicted of conspiring to possess with intent to distribute methamphetamine. Petitioner appealed, arguing that his jailhouse statements should have been suppressed as fruits of the statements obtained at his home in violation of the Sixth Amendment. The [U.S.] Court of Appeals [for the Eighth Circuit] affirmed. * * * [T]he Court of Appeals stated: " * * * [T]he officers did not interrogate [petitioner] at his home." * * * [Fellers appealed to the United States Supreme Court.]

* * * *

The Sixth Amendment right to counsel is triggered at or after the time that judicial proceedings have been initiated * * * whether by way of formal charge, preliminary hearing, indictment, information, or arraignment. We have held that an accused is denied the basic protections of the Sixth Amendment when there is used against him at his trial evidence of his own incriminating words, which federal agents * * * deliberately elicited from him after he had been indicted and in the absence of his counsel. [Emphasis added.]

We have consistently applied the *deliberate-elicitation standard* in * * * Sixth Amendment cases * * * . [Emphasis added.]

The Court of Appeals erred in holding that the absence of an "interrogation" foreclosed petitioner's claim that the jailhouse statements should have been suppressed as fruits of the statements taken from petitioner [Fellers] at his home. First, there is no question that the officers in this case deliberately elicited information from petitioner. Indeed, the officers, upon arriving at petitioner's house, informed him that their purpose in coming was to discuss his involvement in the distribution of methamphetamine and his association with certain charged co-conspirators. Because the ensuing discussion took place after petitioner had been indicted, outside the presence of counsel, and in the absence of any waiver of petitioner's Sixth Amendment rights, the Court of Appeals erred in holding that the officers' actions did not violate the Sixth Amendment standards * * * .

CONTINUED

CASE 7.1 | Continued

Second, because of its erroneous determination that petitioner was not questioned in violation of Sixth Amendment standards, the Court of Appeals improperly conducted its "fruits" analysis * * * . Specifically, it * * * [held] that the admissibility of the jailhouse statements turns solely on whether the statements were knowingly and voluntarily made. The Court of Appeals did not reach the question whether the Sixth Amendment requires suppression of petitioner's jailhouse statements on the ground that they were the fruits of previous questioning conducted in violation of the Sixth Amendment deliberate-elicitation standard. We have not had occasion to decide whether [such statements should be excluded from trial] when a suspect makes incriminating statements after a knowing and voluntary waiver of his right to counsel notwithstanding earlier police questioning in violation of Sixth Amendment standards. We therefore remand to the Court of Appeals to address this issue in the first instance.

Accordingly, the judgment of the Court of Appeals is reversed, and the case is remanded for further proceedings consistent with this opinion.

It is so ordered.

QUESTIONS

1. Why did Fellers argue on appeal that his "jailhouse statements" should have been excluded from his trial?
2. Should Fellers's "jailhouse statements" have been excluded from his trial? Why or why not?

PURPOSE OF THE EXCLUSIONARY RULE The purpose of the exclusionary rule is to deter police from conducting warrantless searches and from engaging in other misconduct. The rule is sometimes criticized because it can lead to injustice. Many a defendant has "gotten off on a technicality" because law enforcement personnel failed to observe procedural requirements based on the above-mentioned constitutional amendments. Even though a defendant may be obviously guilty, if the evidence of that guilt was obtained improperly (without a valid search warrant, for example), it cannot be used against the defendant in court.

EXCEPTIONS TO THE EXCLUSIONARY RULE Over the last several decades, the United States Supreme Court has diminished the scope of the exclusionary rule by creating some exceptions to its applicability. For example, in 1984 the Court held that if illegally obtained evidence would have been discovered "inevitably" and obtained by the police using lawful means, the evidence will be admissible at trial.[21] In another case decided in the same year, the Court held that a police officer who used a technically incorrect search warrant form to obtain evidence had acted in good faith and therefore the evidence was admissible.

The Court thus created the "good faith" exception to the exclusionary rule.[22] Additionally, the courts can exercise a certain amount of discretion in determining whether evidence has been obtained improperly, which somewhat balances the scales.

THE MIRANDA RULE

In regard to criminal procedure, one of the questions many courts faced in the 1950s and 1960s was not whether suspects had constitutional rights—that was not in doubt—but how and when those rights could be exercised. Could the right to be silent (under the Fifth Amendment's prohibition against self-incrimination) be exercised during pretrial interrogation proceedings, or only during the trial? Were confessions obtained from suspects admissible in court if the suspects had not been advised of their right to remain silent and other constitutional rights?

To clarify these issues, the United States Supreme Court issued a landmark decision in 1966 in *Miranda v. Arizona*, which we present here. Today, the procedural rights required by the Court in this case are familiar to virtually every American.

---

21. *Nix v. Williams*, 467 U.S. 431, 104 S.Ct. 2501, 81 L.Ed.2d 377 (1984).

22. *Massachusetts v. Sheppard*, 468 U.S. 981, 104 S.Ct. 3424, 82 L.Ed.2d 737 (1984).

CASE 7.2 — Miranda v. Arizona

Supreme Court of the
United States, 1966.
384 U.S. 436,
86 S.Ct. 1602,
16 L.Ed.2d 694.

BACKGROUND AND FACTS *On March 13, 1963, Ernesto Miranda was arrested at his home for the kidnapping and rape of an eighteen-year-old woman. Miranda was taken to a Phoenix, Arizona, police station and questioned by two officers. Two hours later, the officers emerged from the interrogation room with a written confession signed by Miranda. A paragraph at the top of the confession stated that the confession had been made voluntarily, without threats or promises of immunity, and "with full knowledge of my legal rights, understanding any statement I make may be used against me." Miranda was at no time advised that he had a right to remain silent and a right to have a lawyer present. The confession was admitted into evidence at the trial, and Miranda was convicted and sentenced to prison for twenty to thirty years. Miranda appealed the decision, claiming that he had not been informed of his constitutional rights. The Supreme Court of Arizona held that Miranda's constitutional rights had not been violated and affirmed his conviction. The Miranda case was subsequently reviewed by the United States Supreme Court.*

IN THE LANGUAGE OF THE COURT

Mr. Chief Justice *WARREN* delivered the opinion of the Court.

The cases before us raise questions which go to the roots of our concepts of American criminal jurisprudence; the restraints society must observe consistent with the Federal Constitution in prosecuting individuals for crime. * * *
* * * *

At the outset, if a person in custody is to be subjected to interrogation, he must first be informed in clear and unequivocal terms that he has the right to remain silent. * * *
* * * *

The warning of the right to remain silent must be accompanied by the explanation that anything said can and will be used against the individual in court. This warning is needed in order to make him aware not only of the privilege, *but also of the consequences of forgoing it.* * * * [Emphasis added.]

The circumstances surrounding in-custody interrogation can operate very quickly to overbear the will of one merely made aware of his privilege by his interrogators. Therefore the right to have counsel present at the interrogation is indispensable to the protection of the Fifth Amendment privilege under the system we delineate today.
* * * *

In order fully to apprise a person interrogated of the extent of his rights under this system then, it is necessary to warn him not only that he has the right to consult with an attorney, but also that if he is indigent [without funds] a lawyer will be appointed to represent him. * * * The warning of a right to counsel would be hollow if not couched in terms that would convey to the indigent—the person most often subjected to interrogation—the knowledge that he too has a right to have counsel present.

DECISION AND REMEDY *The Supreme Court held that Miranda could not be convicted of the crime on the basis of his confession because his confession was inadmissible as evidence. For any statement made by a defendant to be admissible, the defendant must be informed of certain constitutional rights prior to police interrogation. If the accused waives his or her rights to remain silent and to have counsel present, the government must demonstrate that the waiver was made knowingly, voluntarily, and intelligently.*

INTERNATIONAL CONSIDERATIONS **The Right to Remain Silent in Great Britain**
The right to remain silent has long been a legal hallmark in Great Britain as well as in the United States. In 1994, however, the British Parliament passed an act that provides that a criminal defendant's silence may be interpreted as evidence of the defendant's guilt. British police officers are now required, when making arrests, to inform the suspects, "You do not have to say anything. But if you do not mention now something which you later use in your defense, the court may decide that your failure to mention it now strengthens the case against you. A record will be made of everything you say, and it may be given in evidence if you are brought to trial."

CONTINUED ▶

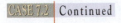 Continued

CONGRESS'S RESPONSE TO THE MIRANDA RULING The Supreme Court's *Miranda* decision was controversial, and two years later Congress attempted to overrule it by enacting Section 3501 of the Omnibus Crime Control and Safe Streets Act of 1968.[23] Essentially, Section 3501 reinstated the rule that had been in effect for 180 years before *Miranda*—namely, that statements by defendants can be used against them as long as the statements are made voluntarily. The U.S. Department of Justice immediately refused to enforce Section 3501, however. Although the U.S. Court of Appeals for the Fourth Circuit attempted to enforce the provision in 1999, its decision was reversed by the United States Supreme Court in 2000. The Supreme Court held that the *Miranda* rights enunciated by the Court in the 1966 case were constitutionally based and thus could not be overruled by a legislative act.[24]

EXCEPTIONS TO THE *MIRANDA* RULE As part of a continuing attempt to balance the rights of accused persons against the rights of society, the Supreme Court has made a number of exceptions to the *Miranda* ruling. In 1984, for example, the Court recognized a "public-safety" exception to the *Miranda* rule. The need to protect the public warranted the admissibility of statements made by the defendant (in this case, indicating where he had placed the gun) as evidence at trial, even though the defendant had not been informed of his *Miranda* rights.[25]

In 1986, the Court held that a confession need not be excluded even though the police failed to inform a suspect in custody that his attorney had tried to reach him by telephone.[26] In an important 1991 decision, the Court stated that a suspect's conviction will not be overturned solely on the ground that the suspect was coerced by law enforcement personnel into making a confession. If the other evidence admitted at trial was strong enough to justify the conviction without the confession, then the fact that the confession was obtained illegally can be, in effect, ignored.[27]

In yet another case, in 1994 the Supreme Court ruled that a suspect must unequivocally and assertively request to exercise his or her right to counsel in order to stop police questioning. Saying, "Maybe I should talk to a lawyer" during an interrogation after being taken into custody is not enough. The Court held that police officers are not required to decipher the suspect's intentions in such situations.[28] In sum, courts today allow confessions that are not unequivocally voluntary to be admitted into evidence against defendants in criminal trials.

RECORDED VIDEO INTERROGATIONS There are no guarantees that *Miranda* will survive indefinitely—particularly in view of the numerous exceptions that are made to the rule. Additionally, law enforcement personnel are increasingly using digital video cameras to record interrogations. According to some scholars, the recording of *all* such interrogations would satisfy the Fifth Amendment's prohibition against coercion and would render the *Miranda* warnings unnecessary.

CRIMINAL PROCESS

As mentioned earlier in this chapter, a criminal prosecution differs significantly from a civil case in several respects. These differences reflect the desire to safeguard the rights of the individual against the state. Exhibit 7–3 summarizes the major steps in processing

23. 42 U.S.C. Section 3789d.

24. *Dickerson v. United States*, 530 U.S. 428, 120 S.Ct. 2326, 147 L.Ed.2d 405 (2000).

25. *New York v. Quarles*, 467 U.S. 649, 104 S.Ct. 2626, 81 L.Ed.2d 550 (1984).

26. *Moran v. Burbine*, 475 U.S. 412, 106 S.Ct. 1135, 89 L.Ed.2d 410 (1986).

27. *Arizona v. Fulminante*, 499 U.S. 279, 111 S.Ct. 1246, 113 L.Ed.2d 302 (1991).

28. *Davis v. United States*, 512 U.S. 452, 114 S.Ct. 2350, 129 L.Ed.2d 362 (1994).

EXHIBIT 7-3 Major Procedural Steps in a Criminal Case

ARREST
Police officer takes suspect into custody. Most arrests are made without a warrant. After the arrest, the officer searches the suspect, who is then taken to the police station.

BOOKING
At the police station, the suspect is searched again, photographed, fingerprinted, and allowed at least one telephone call. After the booking, charges are reviewed, and if they are not dropped, a complaint is filed and a magistrate reviews the case for probable cause.

INITIAL APPEARANCE
The suspect appears before the magistrate, who informs the suspect of the charges and of his or her rights. If the suspect requests a lawyer and cannot afford one, a lawyer is appointed. The magistrate sets bail (conditions under which a suspect can obtain release pending disposition of the case).

GRAND JURY
A grand jury determines if there is probable cause to believe that the defendant committed the crime. The federal government and about half of the states require grand jury indictments for at least some felonies.

PRELIMINARY HEARING
In a court proceeding, a prosecutor presents evidence, and the judge determines if there is probable cause to hold the defendant over for trial.

INDICTMENT
A grand jury formally charges a criminal suspect by issuing an indictment.

INFORMATION
The prosecutor formally charges a criminal suspect by filing an information, or criminal complaint.

ARRAIGNMENT
The suspect is brought before the trial court, informed of the charges, and asked to enter a plea.

PLEA BARGAIN
A plea bargain is a prosecutor's promise to make concessions (or promise to seek concessions) in return for a suspect's guilty plea. Concessions may include a reduced charge or a lesser sentence.

GUILTY PLEA
In many jurisdictions, most cases that reach the arraignment stage do not go to trial but are resolved by a guilty plea, often as a result of a plea bargain. The judge sets the case for sentencing.

TRIAL
Trials can be either jury trials or bench trials. (In a bench trial, there is no jury, and the judge decides questions of fact as well as questions of law.) If the verdict is "guilty," the judge sets the case for sentencing. Everyone convicted of a crime has the right to an appeal.

a criminal case. We now discuss three phases of the criminal process—arrest, indictment or information, and trial—in more detail.

ARREST   Before a warrant for arrest can be issued, there must be probable cause for believing that the individual in question has committed a crime. As discussed in Chapter 5, *probable cause* can be defined as a substantial likelihood that the person has committed or is about to commit a crime. Note that probable cause involves a likelihood, not just a possibility. Arrests may sometimes be made without a warrant if there is no time to get one, but the action of the arresting officer is still judged by the standard of probable cause.

INDICTMENT OR INFORMATION   Individuals must be formally charged with having committed specific crimes before they can be brought to trial. If issued by a grand jury, such a charge is called an **indictment.**[29] A **grand jury** does not determine the guilt or innocence of an accused party; rather, its function is to determine, after hearing the state's evidence, whether a reasonable basis (probable cause) exists for supposing that a crime has been committed and whether a trial ought to be held.

Usually, grand juries are called in cases involving serious crimes, such as murder. For lesser crimes, an individual may be formally charged with a crime by an **information,** or criminal complaint. An information

_____

29. Pronounced in-*dyte*-ment.

will be issued by a government prosecutor if the prosecutor determines that there is sufficient evidence to justify bringing the individual to trial.

TRIAL   At a criminal trial, the accused person does not have to prove anything; the entire burden of proof is on the prosecutor (the state). As discussed at the beginning of this chapter, the burden of proof is higher in a criminal case than in a civil case. The prosecution must show that, based on all the evidence, the defendant's guilt is established *beyond a reasonable doubt.* If there is any reasonable doubt as to whether a criminal defendant did, in fact, commit the crime with which she or he has been charged, then the verdict must be "not guilty." Note that giving a verdict of "not guilty" is not the same as stating that the defendant is innocent; it merely means that not enough evidence was properly presented to the court to prove guilt beyond all reasonable doubt.

Courts have complex rules about what types of evidence may be presented and how the evidence may be brought out in criminal cases, especially in jury trials. These rules are designed to ensure that evidence presented at trials is relevant, reliable, and not prejudicial toward the defendant. For example, under the Sixth Amendment, persons accused of a crime have the right to confront, in open court, the witnesses against them. Is a defendant's Sixth Amendment right to confront witnesses violated when, in a jury trial, witnesses who are reluctant to travel consequently testify by way of two-way video teleconferencing? That was the question in the following case.

CASE 7.3	**United States v. Yates**

United States
Court of Appeals,
Eleventh Circuit. 2004.
391 F.3d 1182.

BACKGROUND AND FACTS   *Anton Pusztai and Anita Yates were involved in operating an Internet pharmacy based in Clanton, Alabama, called the Norfolk Men's Clinic. They were charged in a federal district court with mail fraud and other crimes, including prescription drug–related offenses, in connection with the pharmacy. The government asked the court to allow two witnesses in Australia to testify at Pusztai and Yates's trial by means of a two-way video teleconference. The witnesses—Paul Christian, who allegedly processed customers' Internet payments for Pusztai and Yates, and Dr. Tibor Konkoly, whose name was allegedly used on Internet drug prescriptions—were "essential witnesses," according to the government. But "they are unwilling to travel to the United States" and "they are beyond the government's subpoena powers." Pusztai and Yates argued that allowing the testimony would violate their Sixth Amendment right to confront witnesses. The court allowed the witnesses to testify. A jury found Pusztai and Yates guilty. The defendants appealed to the U.S. Court of Appeals for the Eleventh Circuit.*

CASE 7.3 Continued

IN THE LANGUAGE OF THE COURT

COX, Circuit Judge.
     *   *   *   *

Pusztai and Yates contend that their Sixth Amendment confrontation rights were violated by the admission of testimony by two-way live video teleconference with the witnesses in Australia because it was not necessary to further an important public policy * * * .

     *   *   *   *

The Sixth Amendment provides: "In all criminal prosecutions, the accused shall enjoy the right * * * to be confronted with the witnesses against him." This clause, known as the Confrontation Clause, guarantees the defendant a face-to-face meeting with witnesses appearing before the trier of fact. But this guarantee is not without exception.

* * * [A] Maryland rule of criminal procedure * * * allows child victims of abuse to testify by one-way closed circuit television from outside the courtroom. In such a scenario, the defendant [can] see the testifying child witness on a video monitor, but the child witness [can] not see the defendant. * * * *[A] defendant's right to confront accusatory witnesses may be satisfied absent a physical, face-to-face confrontation at trial only where denial of such confrontation is necessary to further an important public policy * * * .* [Emphasis added.]

     *   *   *   *

In its order, the district court * * * permit[ted] the Australian witnesses to testify by two-way video teleconference before the court in the United States Attorney's Office in Montgomery, Alabama.

* * * [T]he district court ruled that the testimony was necessary to further an important public policy. The court accepted the Government's contention that the testimony would serve the "important public policy of providing the fact-finder with crucial evidence," and found that "the Government also has an interest in expeditiously and justly resolving the case."

We accept the district court's rationale that the witnesses were necessary to the prosecution's case on at least some of the charges, as the record supports the Government's assertion that the testimony was crucial to a successful prosecution of the Defendants and aided expeditious resolution of the case. * * *

But the prosecutor's need for the testimony in order to make a case and expeditiously resolve it are not public policies that are important enough to outweigh a defendant's right to confront an accuser face-to-face. Comparing the public policy behind Maryland's rule—protection of certain children from trauma caused by confronting their attacker—with the policies offered in this case—providing the fact-finder with crucial prosecution evidence and expeditious resolution of the case—leaves us unconvinced that the policy justification in this case meets [the] standard for an important public policy.

The district court made no findings of fact that would support a conclusion that this case is different from any other criminal prosecution in which the Government would find it convenient to present testimony by two-way video teleconference. All criminal prosecutions include at least some evidence crucial to the Government's case, and there is no doubt that many criminal cases could be more expeditiously resolved were it not necessary for witnesses to appear at trial. If we were to approve introduction of testimony in this manner, on this record, every prosecutor could argue that providing crucial prosecution evidence and expeditious resolution of the case are important public policies that support the admission of testimony by two-way video teleconference.

The Sixth Amendment demands more. *The text of the Sixth Amendment does not suggest any open-ended exceptions from the confrontation requirement to be developed by the courts.* We therefore hold that providing the fact-finder with crucial prosecution evidence and expeditious resolution of the case, on the record before us, are not important public policies that justify the denial of actual confrontation between witness and defendant. [Emphasis added.]

CONTINUED ▶

CASE 7.3 | Continued

DECISION AND REMEDY   *The U.S Court of Appeals for the Eleventh Circuit reversed the decision of the lower court to allow the overseas witnesses to testify electronically and remanded the case for a new trial. The appellate court reasoned that the admission of the testimony via a live, two-way video teleconference violated the defendants' Sixth Amendment right to confront witnesses.*

WHAT IF THE FACTS WERE DIFFERENT?   *Suppose that there was only one essential witness in Australia, Paul Christian, who was asked to attend the trial in the United States. Further suppose that Christian was undergoing an intensive course of chemotherapy and was too sick to travel. How might the fact that a witness is unable (as opposed to unwilling) to attend the trial affect the court's opinion on teleconferencing and the Sixth Amendment?*

FEDERAL SENTENCING GUIDELINES

In the past, persons who committed the same crime might receive very different sentences, depending on the judge hearing the case, the jurisdiction in which it was heard, and many other factors. In 1984, however, Congress passed the Sentencing Reform Act. This act created the U.S. Sentencing Commission, which was charged with the task of standardizing sentences for federal crimes. The commission's guidelines, which became effective in 1987, established a range of possible penalties for each federal crime but *required* the judge to select a sentence from within that range. In other words, the guidelines established a mandatory system because judges were not allowed to deviate from the specified sentencing range.

In 2005, the Supreme Court held that certain provisions of the federal sentencing guidelines were unconstitutional. We look at these guidelines in this chapter's *Emerging Trends* feature on pages 166 and 167.

The U.S. Sentencing Commission has also established guidelines, which went into effect in 1991, that encourage stiffer penalties for white-collar crimes, including mail and wire fraud, commercial bribery and kickbacks, and money laundering. In addition, the commission recommended increased penalties for criminal violations of employment laws (see Chapters 20 and 21), securities laws (see Chapter 28), and antitrust laws (see Chapters 26 and 27).[30] The guidelines set forth a number of factors that judges should take into consideration when imposing a sentence for a specified crime. These factors include the defendant company's history of past violations, the extent of management's cooperation with federal investigators, and the extent to which the firm has undertaken spe-cific programs and procedures to prevent criminal activities by its employees.

SECTION 8 | Cyber Crimes

Some years ago, the American Bar Association defined **computer crime** as any act that is directed against computers and computer parts, that uses computers as instruments of crime, or that involves computers and constitutes abuse. Today, because much of the crime committed with the use of computers occurs in cyberspace, many computer crimes fall under the broad label of **cyber crime.**

As we mentioned earlier, most cyber crimes are not "new" crimes. Rather, they are existing crimes in which the Internet is the instrument of wrongdoing. The challenge for law enforcement is to apply traditional laws—which were designed to protect persons from physical harm or to safeguard their physical property—to crimes committed in cyberspace. Here we look at several types of activity that constitute cyber crimes against persons or property. Other cyber crimes will be discussed in later chapters as they relate to particular topics, such as banking or consumer law.

CYBER THEFT

In cyberspace, thieves are not subject to the physical limitations of the "real" world. A thief can steal data stored in a networked computer with Internet access from anywhere on the globe. Only the speed of the connection and the thief's computer equipment limit the quantity of data that can be stolen.

FINANCIAL CRIMES   Computer networks also provide opportunities for employees to commit crimes that can involve serious economic losses. For example, employees of a company's accounting department can

---

30. As required by the Sarbanes-Oxley Act of 2002, the U.S. Sentencing Commission revised its guidelines in 2003 to impose stiffer penalties for corporate securities fraud.

transfer funds among accounts with little effort and often with less risk than would be involved in transactions evidenced by paperwork.

Generally, the dependence of businesses on computer operations has left firms vulnerable to sabotage, fraud, embezzlement, and the theft of proprietary data, such as trade secrets or other intellectual property. The piracy of intellectual property via the Internet is one of the most serious legal challenges facing lawmakers and the courts today.

IDENTITY THEFT A form of cyber theft that has become particularly troublesome in recent years is **identity theft.** Identity theft occurs when the wrongdoer steals a form of identification—such as a name, date of birth, and Social Security number—and uses the information to access the victim's financial resources. This crime existed to a certain extent before the widespread use of the Internet. Thieves would "steal" calling-card numbers by watching people using public telephones, or they would rifle through garbage to find bank account or credit-card numbers. The identity thieves would then use the calling-card or credit-card numbers or would withdraw funds from the victims' accounts.

The Internet, however, has turned identity theft into perhaps the fastest-growing financial crime in the United States. From the identity thief's perspective, the Internet provides those who steal information offline with an easy medium for using items such as stolen credit-card numbers while remaining protected by anonymity. An estimated 10 million Americans are victims of identity theft each year, and annual losses are estimated to exceed $50 billion.

CYBERSTALKING

California enacted the first stalking law in 1990, in response to the murders of six women—including Rebecca Schaeffer, a television star—by men who had harassed them. The law made it a crime to harass or follow a person while making a "credible threat" that puts that person in reasonable fear for his or her safety or the safety of the person's immediate family.[31] Since then, all other states have enacted some form of stalking laws. In about half of the states these laws require a physical act (following the victim).

Cyberstalkers (stalkers who commit their crimes in cyberspace), however, find their victims through Internet chat rooms, Usenet newsgroups or other bulletin boards, or e-mail. To close this "loophole" in existing stalking laws, more than three-fourths of the states now have laws specifically designed to combat cyberstalking and other forms of online harassment.

Note that cyberstalking can be even more threatening than physical stalking in some respects. While it takes a great deal of effort to physically stalk someone, it is relatively easy to harass a victim with electronic messages. Furthermore, the possibility of personal confrontation may discourage a stalker from actually following a victim. This disincentive is removed in cyberspace. Also, there is always the possibility that a cyberstalker will eventually pose a physical threat to her or his target. Finally, the Internet makes it easier to obtain information about the victim, such as where he or she lives or works, because numerous companies provide online investigation and information services.

HACKING

Persons who use one computer to break into another are sometimes referred to as **hackers.** Hackers who break into computers without authorization often commit cyber theft. Sometimes, however, their principal aim is to prove how smart they are by gaining access to others' password-protected computers and causing random data errors or making toll telephone calls for free.[32]

It is difficult to know just how frequently hackers succeed in breaking into databases across the United States. The FBI estimates that only 25 percent of all corporations that suffer such security breaches report the incident to a law enforcement agency. For one thing, corporations do not want it to become publicly known that the security of their data has been breached. For another, admitting to a breach would be admitting to a certain degree of incompetence, which could damage their reputations.

CYBERTERRORISM

Cyberterrorists are also hackers, but rather than trying to gain attention, they strive to remain undetected so that they can exploit computers to achieve harmful impacts. Just as "real" terrorists destroyed the World Trade Center towers and a portion of the Pentagon in

---

31. Ca. Penal Code Section 646.9.

32. The total cost of crime on the Internet is estimated to be several billion dollars annually, but two-thirds of that total is said to consist of unpaid-for toll calls.

The New Advisory Nature of the Federal Sentencing Guidelines

Until 2005, federal judges were required to consult a 1,800-page book that provided *mandatory* federal sentencing guidelines for hundreds of federal crimes. Congress's intent was to impose uniformity in the punishment aspect of the federal criminal justice system. Additionally, over the last several decades, Congress has wanted to appear "tough on crime."

Some federal judges felt uneasy about imposing long prison sentences on certain criminal defendants, particularly on first-time offenders and in illegal-substances cases involving small quantities of drugs. Consider, for example, the punishment of Weldon Angelos. Angelos, a twenty-four-year-old executive of a music company, had no criminal record. Nonetheless, in November 2004 Angelos was sentenced to fifty-five years in federal prison for selling a total of 1.5 pounds of marijuana to a government informant. Judge Paul Cassell of the U.S. District Court for the District of Utah noted that Angelos's sentence was "far in excess of the sentences imposed for such serious crimes as aircraft hijacking, second-degree murder, espionage, kidnapping, aggravated assault, and rape." Cassell went so far as to urge President George W. Bush to commute the sentence, calling it "unjust, cruel, and irrational." The judge was forced to impose it, though, because of mandatory sentencing rules.[a]

FINDING UNCONSTITUTIONALITY IN STATE SENTENCING GUIDELINES

While federal judges both publicly and privately have complained about federal sentencing guidelines for years, it was not until 2004 that the Supreme Court considered the constitutionality of state mandatory sentencing guidelines. In *Blakely v. Washington*,[b] the defendant, Ralph Blakely, pleaded guilty to kidnapping his estranged wife. According to the Washington state sentencing guidelines, his admission alone supported a maximum sentence of fifty-three months. The judge—but not the jury—learned that he had acted with deliberate cruelty. The sentencing judge therefore imposed a ninety-month sentence because of the cruelty issue, which was a statutorily granted reason to depart from the standard sentencing range. Blakely appealed the sentence. He argued that he had a federal constitutional right to have a jury determine beyond a reasonable doubt all of the facts legally essential to his sentence and that this right had been violated. Ultimately, the United States Supreme Court overturned the sentence. The Court relied on its ruling in a previous case in which it had held that "any fact that increases the penalty for a crime beyond the prescribed statutory minimum must be submitted to a jury and proved beyond a reasonable doubt."[c] Interestingly, the Court in the *Blakely* case specifically noted that it was not ruling on the constitutionality of sentencing guidelines at the federal level—a topic it did not address until the following year.

THE SIXTH AMENDMENT AND UNITED STATES V. BOOKER

The Sixth Amendment to the Constitution guarantees a trial by jury. In 2005, in *United States v. Booker*,[d] the United States Supreme Court held that federal sentencing guidelines are subject to the jury trial requirements of the Sixth Amendment. The case involved Freddie Booker, who was arrested with 92.5 grams of crack cocaine in his possession. During questioning by police, he signed a written statement in which he admitted to selling an additional quantity—566 grams of crack cocaine—elsewhere. That statement was not introduced or used at the trial, though.

---

a. *United States v. Angelos*, 345 F.Supp.2d 1227 (D.Utah 2004).
b. 542 U.S. 296, 124 S.Ct. 2531, 159 L.Ed.2d 403 (2004).

c. *Apprendi v. New Jersey*, 530 U.S. 466, 120 S.Ct. 2348, 147 L.Ed.2d 435 (2000).
d. ___U.S.___, 125 S.Ct. 738, 160 L.Ed.2d 621 (2005).

September 2001, cyberterrorists might explode "logic bombs" to shut down central computer systems. Such activities can pose a danger to national security.

Businesses may also be targeted by cyberterrorists. A hacking operation might engage in a wholesale theft of data, such as a merchant's customer files, or monitor a computer to discover a business firm's plans and transactions. A cyberterrorist might also want to insert false codes or data. For example, by hacking into the processing-control system of a food manufacturer, a cyberterrorist might alter the levels of ingredients so that consumers of the food would become ill. A cyberterrorist attack on a major financial institution, such as the New York Stock Exchange or a large bank, could leave securities or money markets in flux and seriously affect the daily lives of millions of citizens. Similarly, any prolonged disruption of computer, cable, satellite, or telecommunications systems due to the actions of expert hackers would have serious repercussions on business operations—and national security—on a

The jury convicted Booker of possessing and distributing more than 50 grams of crack cocaine based solely on the quantity of drugs in his possession at the time of the arrest. Under the federal sentencing guidelines, this offense carried a minimum sentence of ten years in prison and a maximum sentence of life in prison. At the posttrial sentencing hearing, however, the judge concluded that because Booker had admitted to possessing and selling an additional 566 grams of crack cocaine, he should receive an enhanced penalty. Applying the federal sentencing guidelines to this larger quantity of crack cocaine increased Booker's sentence from twenty-two to thirty years in prison.

The question before the Supreme Court was whether it is constitutionally permissible for the judge, instead of the jury, to make a factual determination that enhances the defendant's sentence under the federal sentencing guidelines. The Court ruled that it was not. "It has been settled throughout our history that the Constitution protects every criminal defendant 'against conviction except upon proof beyond a reasonable doubt of every fact necessary to constitute the crime with which he is charged.'"[e] Because the jury did not find beyond a reasonable doubt that Booker had possessed the additional 566 grams of crack, the court could not use this amount to enhance his sentence.

LOOKING TOWARD THE FUTURE

The ruling in *United States v. Booker* (and in a related case, *United States v. Fanfan*[f]) effectively eliminates the requirement that federal judges adhere precisely to the federal sentencing guidelines when setting criminal sentences. In other words, the guidelines are now just that—guidelines. They are

advisory rather than mandatory. Although trial judges must still consider the guidelines when sentencing criminal defendants, the judges now have more discretion. Depending on the circumstances of the case, a trial judge may depart from the guidelines if he or she believes that it is reasonable to do so. If a trial judge's decision is challenged as unreasonable, it will be up to an appellate court to decide the issue.

IMPLICATIONS FOR THE BUSINESSPERSON

1. | Federal sentencing guidelines still exist for criminal violations of employment laws, securities laws, and antitrust laws.

2. | The additional federal sentencing guidelines that went into effect in 1991 with respect to white-collar crimes also still remain on the books. While some federal judges may no longer consider these guidelines in detail, others may continue following them to the letter.

FOR CRITICAL ANALYSIS

1. | Data show that crime rates have fallen since harsher sentences have been imposed at both the federal and state levels. Does this correlation prove that the federal sentencing guidelines have been effective at combating crime?

2. | In all criminal cases, the prosecutor determines the criminal acts with which the defendant will be charged. What, then, is the relationship between a prosecutor's discretionary authority and the federal sentencing guidelines?

RELEVANT WEB SITES

To locate information on the Web concerning the issues discussed in this feature, go to this text's Web site at **http://wleb.westbuslaw.com**, select "Chapter 7," and click on "Emerging Trends."

e. *In re Winship*, 397 U.S. 358, 90 S.Ct. 1068, 25 L.Ed.2d 368 (1970).
f. This case was consolidated with the *Booker* case on appeal before the United States Supreme Court. The lower court's decision in the *Fanfan* case is located at 2004 WL 1723114.

global level. Computer viruses are another tool that can be used by cyberterrorists to cripple communications networks.

PROSECUTING CYBER CRIMES

The "location" of cyber crime (cyberspace) has raised new issues in the investigation of crimes and the prosecution of offenders. A threshold issue is, of course, jurisdiction. A person who commits an act against a business in California, where the act is a cyber crime, might never have set foot in California but might instead reside in New York, or even in Canada, where the act may not be a crime. If the crime was committed via e-mail, the question arises as to whether the e-mail would constitute sufficient "minimum contacts" (see Chapter 2) for the victim's state to exercise jurisdiction over the perpetrator.

Identifying the wrongdoers can also be difficult. Cyber criminals do not leave physical traces, such as fingerprints or DNA samples, as evidence of their crimes. Even electronic "footprints" can be hard to find and follow. For example, e-mail may be sent through a remailer, an online service that guarantees that a message cannot be traced to its source.

For these reasons, laws written to protect physical property are difficult to apply in cyberspace. Nonetheless, governments at both the state and federal levels have taken significant steps toward controlling cyber crime, both by applying existing criminal statutes and by enacting new laws that specifically address wrongs committed in cyberspace.

THE COMPUTER FRAUD AND ABUSE ACT

Perhaps the most significant federal statute specifically addressing cyber crime is the Counterfeit Access Device and Computer Fraud and Abuse Act of 1984 (commonly known as the Computer Fraud and Abuse Act, or CFAA). This act, as amended by the National Information Infrastructure Protection Act of 1996,[33] provides, among other things, that a person who accesses a computer online, without authority, to obtain classified, restricted, or protected data (or attempts to do so) is subject to criminal prosecution. Such data could include financial and credit records, medical records, legal files, military and national security files, and other confidential information in government or private computers. The crime has two elements: accessing a computer without authority and taking the data.

This theft is a felony if it is committed for a commercial purpose or for private financial gain, or if the value of the stolen data (or computer time) exceeds $5,000. Penalties include fines and imprisonment for up to twenty years. A victim of computer theft can also bring a civil suit against the violator to obtain damages, an injunction, and other relief.

---

33. 18 U.S.C. Section 1030.

REVIEWING CRIMINAL LAW AND CYBER CRIMES

Edward Hanousek worked for Pacific & Arctic Railway and Navigation Company (P&A) as a roadmaster of the White Pass & Yukon Railroad in Alaska. Hanousek was responsible "for every detail of the safe and efficient maintenance and construction of track, structures and marine facilities of the entire railroad," including special projects. One project was a rock quarry, known as "6-mile," above the Skagway River. Next to the quarry, and just beneath the surface, ran a high-pressure oil pipeline owned by Pacific & Arctic Pipeline, Inc., P&A's sister company. When the quarry's backhoe operator punctured the pipeline, an estimated 1,000 to 5,000 gallons of oil were discharged into the river. Hanousek was charged with negligently discharging a harmful quantity of oil into a navigable water of the United States in violation of the criminal provisions of the Clean Water Act (CWA). Using the information presented in the chapter, answer the following questions.

1. What are the two elements of criminal liability? Are both elements present in this case? Explain.

2. Under which theory discussed in the chapter might Hanousek be found guilty of a crime?

3. Could the quarry's backhoe operator who punctured the pipeline also be charged with a crime in this situation? Why or why not?

4. Suppose that at trial, Hanousek argued that he could not be convicted because he was not aware of the requirements of the Clean Water Act. Would this defense be successful? Why or why not?

5. If corporate actors were able to avoid responsibility for violations of environmental statutes of which they were unaware, what might result?

6. Based solely on the facts given, are there any defenses to criminal liability that Hanousek could assert? Explain.

TERMS AND CONCEPTS TO REVIEW

QUESTIONS AND CASE PROBLEMS

7–1. The following situations are similar (in all of them, Juanita's television set is stolen), yet three different crimes are described. Identify the three crimes, noting the differences among them.

(a) While passing Juanita's house one night, Sarah sees a portable television set left unattended on Juanita's lawn. Sarah takes the television set, carries it home, and tells everyone she owns it.

(b) While passing Juanita's house one night, Sarah sees Juanita outside with a portable television set. Holding Juanita at gunpoint, Sarah forces her to give up the set. Then Sarah runs away with it.

(c) While passing Juanita's house one night, Sarah sees a portable television set in a window. Sarah breaks the front-door lock, enters, and leaves with the set.

7–2. Which, if any, of the following crimes necessarily involves illegal activity on the part of more than one person?

(a) Bribery.

(b) Forgery.

(c) Embezzlement.

(d) Larceny.

(e) Receiving stolen property.

7–3. **QUESTION WITH SAMPLE ANSWER**

Armington, while robbing a drugstore, shot and seriously injured a drugstore clerk, Jennings. Subsequently, in a criminal trial, Armington was convicted of armed robbery and assault and battery. Jennings later brought a civil (tort) suit against Armington for damages. Armington contended that he could not be tried again

for the same crime, as that would constitute double jeopardy, which is prohibited by the Fifth Amendment to the Constitution. Is Armington correct? Explain.
For a sample answer to this question, go to Appendix I at the end of this text.

7–4. Rafael stops Laura on a busy street and offers to sell her an expensive wristwatch for a fraction of its value. After some questioning by Laura, Rafael admits that the watch is stolen property, although he says he was not the thief. Laura pays for and receives the wristwatch. Has Laura committed any crime? Has Rafael? Explain.

7–5. FIFTH AMENDMENT. The federal government was investigating a corporation and its employees. The alleged criminal wrongdoing, which included the falsification of corporate books and records, occurred between 1993 and 1996 in one corporate division. In 1999, the corporation pled guilty and agreed to cooperate in an investigation of the individuals who might have been involved in the improper corporate activities. "Doe I," "Doe II," and "Doe III" were officers of the corporation during the period in which the illegal activities occurred and worked in the division where the wrongdoing took place. They were no longer employed by the corporation, however, when, as part of the subsequent investigation, the government asked them to provide specific corporate documents in their possession. All three asserted the Fifth Amendment privilege against self-incrimination. The government asked a federal district court to order the three to produce the records. Corporate employees can be compelled to produce corporate records in a criminal proceeding because they hold the records as representatives of the corporation, to which the Fifth Amendment privilege against self-incrimination does not apply. Should *former* employees also be compelled to produce corporate records in their possession? Why or why not? [*In re Three Grand Jury Subpoenas* Duces Tecum *Dated January 29, 1999*, 191 F.3d 173 (2d Cir. 1999)]

7-6. COMPUTER FRAUD. The District of Columbia Lottery Board licensed Soo Young Bae, a Washington, D.C., merchant, to operate a terminal that prints and dispenses lottery tickets for sale. Bae used the terminal to generate tickets with a face value of $525,586, for which he did not pay. The winning tickets among these had a total redemption value of $296,153, of which Bae successfully obtained all but $72,000. Bae pleaded guilty to computer fraud, and the court sentenced him to eighteen months in prison. In sentencing a defendant for fraud, a federal court must make a reasonable estimate of the victim's loss. The court determined that the value of the loss due to the fraud was $503,650—the market value of the tickets less the commission Bae would have received from the lottery board had he sold those tickets. Bae appealed, arguing that "[a]t the instant any lottery ticket is printed," it is worth whatever value the lottery drawing later assigns to it; that is, losing tickets have no value. Bae thus calculated the loss at $296,153, the value of his winning tickets. Should the U.S. Court of Appeals for the District of Columbia Circuit affirm or reverse Bae's sentence? Explain your answer. [*United States v. Bae*, 250 F.3d 774 (D.C.Cir. 2001)]

7-7. ⚖ **CASE PROBLEM WITH SAMPLE ANSWER**

The Sixth Amendment secures to a defendant who faces possible imprisonment the right to counsel at all critical stages of the criminal process, including the arraignment and the trial. In 1996, Felipe Tovar, a twenty-one-year-old college student, was arrested in Ames, Iowa, for operating a motor vehicle while under the influence of alcohol (OWI). Tovar was informed of his right to apply for court-appointed counsel and waived it. At his arraignment, he pled guilty. Six weeks later, he appeared for sentencing, again waived his right to counsel, and was sentenced to two days' imprisonment. In 1998, Tovar was convicted of OWI again, and in 2000, he was charged with OWI for a third time. In Iowa, a third OWI offense is a felony. Tovar asked the court not to use his first OWI conviction to enhance the third OWI charge. He argued that his 1996 waiver of counsel was not "intelligent" because the court did not make him aware of "the dangers and disadvantages of self-representation." What determines whether a person's choice in any situation is "intelligent"? What should determine whether a defendant's waiver of counsel is "intelligent" at critical stages of a criminal proceeding? [*Iowa v. Tovar*, 541 U.S. 77, 124 S.Ct. 1379, 158 L.Ed.2d 209 (2004)]

To view a sample answer for this case problem, go to this book's Web site at http://wleb.westbuslaw.com, select "Chapter 7," and click on "Case Problem with Sample Answer."

7-8. THEFT OF TRADE SECRETS. Four Pillars Enterprise Co. is a Taiwanese company owned by Pin Yen Yang. Avery Dennison, Inc., a U.S. corporation, is one of Four Pillars' chief competitors in the manufacture of adhesives. In 1989, Victor Lee, an Avery employee, met Yang and Yang's daughter Hwei Chen. They agreed to pay Lee $25,000 a year to serve as a consultant to Four Pillars. Over the next eight years, Lee supplied the Yangs with confidential Avery reports, including information that Four Pillars used to make a new adhesive that had been developed by Avery. The Federal Bureau of Investigation (FBI) confronted Lee, and he agreed to cooperate in an operation to catch the Yangs. When Lee next met the Yangs, he showed them documents provided by the FBI. The documents bore "confidential" stamps, and Lee said that they were Avery's confidential property. The FBI arrested the Yangs with the documents in their possession. The Yangs and Four Pillars were charged with, among other crimes, the attempted theft of trade secrets. The defendants argued in part that it was impossible for them to have committed this crime because the documents were not actually trade secrets. Should the court acquit them? Why or why not? [*United States v. Yang*, 281 F.3d 534 (6th Cir. 2002)]

7-9. LARCENY. In February 2001, a homeowner hired Jimmy Smith, a contractor claiming to employ a crew of thirty workers, to build a garage. The homeowner paid Smith $7,950 and agreed to make additional payments as needed to complete the project, up to $15,900. Smith promised to start the next day and finish within eight weeks. Nearly a month passed with no work, while Smith lied to the homeowner that materials were on "back order." During a second month, footings were created for the foundation, and a subcontractor poured the concrete slab, but Smith did not return the homeowner's phone calls. After eight weeks, the homeowner confronted Smith, who promised to complete the job, worked on the site that day until lunch, and never returned. Three months later, the homeowner again confronted Smith, who promised to "pay [him] off" later that day but did not do so. In March 2002, the state of Georgia filed criminal charges against Smith. While his trial was pending, he promised to pay the homeowner "next week" but again failed to refund any of the funds paid. The value of the labor performed before Smith abandoned the project was between $800 and $1,000, the value of the materials was $367, and the subcontractor was paid $2,270. Did Smith commit larceny? Explain. [*Smith v. State of Georgia*, 592 S.E.2d 871 (Ga.App. 2004)]

7-10. VIDEO QUESTION

Go to this text's Web site at **http://wleb.westbuslaw.com** and select "Chapter 7." Click on "Video Questions" and view the video titled *Casino*. Then answer the following questions.

(a) In the video, a casino manager, Ace (Robert DeNiro), discusses how politicians "won their 'comp life' when they got elected." "Comps" are the free gifts that casinos give to high-stakes gamblers to keep their business. If an elected official accepts comps, is he or she committing a crime? If so, what type of crime? Explain your answers.

(b) Assume that Ace committed a crime by giving politicians comps. Can the casino, Tangiers Corporation, be held liable for that crime? Why or why not? How could a court punish the corporation?

(c) Suppose that the Federal Bureau of Investigation wants to search the premises of Tangiers for evidence of criminal activity. If casino management refuses to consent to the search, what constitutional safeguards and criminal procedures, if any, protect Tangiers?

LAW | on the Web

For updated links to resources available on the Web, as well as a variety of other materials, visit this text's Web site at http://wleb.westbuslaw.com.

The Bureau of Justice Statistics in the U.S. Department of Justice offers an impressive collection of statistics on crime at the following Web site:

http://www.ojp.usdoj.gov/bjs

For summaries of famous criminal cases and documents relating to these trials, go to Court TV's Web site at

http://www.courttv.com/index.html

Many state criminal codes are now online. To find your state's code, go to the following home page and select "State" under the link to "Laws: Cases and Codes:"

http://www.findlaw.com

You can learn about some of the constitutional questions raised by various criminal laws and procedures by going to the Web site of the American Civil Liberties Union at

http://www.aclu.org

The following Web site, which is maintained by the U.S. Department of Justice, offers information ranging from the various types of cyber crime to a description of how computers and the Internet are being used to prosecute cyber crime:

http://www.cybercrime.gov

LEGAL RESEARCH EXERCISES ON THE WEB

Go to http://wleb.westbuslaw.com, the Web site that accompanies this text. Select "Chapter 7" and click on "Internet Exercises." There you will find the following Internet research exercises that you can perform to learn more about topics covered in this chapter.

Activity 7–1: **LEGAL PERSPECTIVE**
Revisiting *Miranda*

Activity 7–2: **MANAGEMENT PERSPECTIVE**
Hackers

Activity 7–3: **INTERNATIONAL PERSPECTIVE**
Fighting Cyber Crime Worldwide

CHAPTER 8

International Law

Since ancient times independent peoples and nations have traded their goods and wares with one another. What is new in our day is the dramatic growth in world trade and the emergence of a global business community. Today, nearly every major business considers the potential of international markets for its products or services. It is no longer uncommon for a U.S. corporation to have investments or manufacturing plants in a foreign country or for a foreign corporation to have operations in the United States. Because the exchange of goods, services, and ideas (intellectual property) on a worldwide level is now routine, students of business law should be familiar with the laws pertaining to international business transactions.

Laws affecting the international legal environment of business include both international law and national law. **International law** can be defined as a body of law—formed as a result of international customs, treaties, and organizations—that governs relations among or between nations. International law may be public, creating standards for the nations themselves; or it may be private, establishing international standards for private transactions that cross national borders. **National law** is the law of a particular nation, such as Brazil, Germany, Japan, or the United States. In this chapter, we examine how both international law and national law frame business operations in the international context.

SECTION 1 | International Law

The major difference between international law and national law is that government authorities can enforce national law. What government, however, can enforce international law? By definition, a *nation* is a sovereign entity—which means that there is no higher authority to which that nation must submit. If a nation violates an international law and persuasive tactics fail, other countries or international organizations have no recourse except to take coercive actions—from severance of diplomatic relations and boycotts to, as a last resort, war—against the violating nation.

In essence, international law is the result of centuries-old attempts to reconcile the traditional need of each country to be the final authority over its own affairs with the desire of nations to benefit economically from trade and harmonious relations with one another. Sovereign nations can, and do, voluntarily agree to be governed in certain respects by international law for the purpose of facilitating international trade and commerce, as well as civilized discourse. As a result, a body

of international law has evolved. In this section, we examine the primary sources and characteristics of that body of law, as well as some important legal principles and doctrines that have been developed over time to facilitate dealings among nations.

SOURCES OF INTERNATIONAL LAW

Basically, there are three sources of international law: international customs, treaties and international agreements, and international organizations. We look at each of these sources here.

INTERNATIONAL CUSTOMS   One important source of international law consists of the international customs that have evolved among nations in their relations with one another. Article 38(1) of the Statute of the International Court of Justice refers to an international custom as "evidence of a general practice accepted as law." The legal principles and doctrines that you will read about shortly are rooted in international customs and traditions that have evolved over time in the international arena.

TREATIES AND INTERNATIONAL AGREEMENTS

Treaties and other explicit agreements between or among foreign nations provide another important source of international law. A **treaty** is an agreement or contract between two or more nations that must be authorized and ratified by the supreme power of each nation. Under Article II, Section 2, of the U.S. Constitution, the president has the power "by and with the Advice and Consent of the Senate, to make Treaties, provided two-thirds of the Senators present concur."

A *bilateral* agreement, as the term implies, is an agreement formed by two nations to govern their commercial exchanges or other relations with one another. A *multilateral* agreement is formed by several nations. For example, regional trade associations such as the European Union (EU) and the trading unit established by the North American Free Trade Agreement (NAFTA), both of which are discussed later in this chapter, are the result of multilateral trade agreements. Other regional trade associations that have been created through multilateral agreements include the Association of Southeast Asian Nations (ASEAN) and the Andean Common Market (ANCOM).

INTERNATIONAL ORGANIZATIONS

International organizations and conferences further contribute to international law. In international law, the term **international organization** generally refers to an organization composed mainly of nations' officials and usually established by treaty.

The United States is a member of more than one hundred multilateral and bilateral organizations, including at least twenty through the United Nations (see Exhibit 8–1 on page 175). These organizations adopt resolutions, declarations, and other types of standards that often require nations to behave in a particular manner. The General Assembly of the United Nations, for example, has adopted numerous nonbinding resolutions and declarations that embody principles of international law. Disputes with respect to these resolutions and declarations may be brought before the International Court of Justice. That court, however, normally has authority to settle legal disputes only when nations voluntarily submit to its jurisdiction.

The United Nations Commission on International Trade Law has made considerable progress in establishing uniformity in international law as it relates to trade and commerce. One of the commission's most significant creations to date is the 1980 Convention on Contracts for the International Sale of Goods (CISG). The CISG is designed to settle disputes between parties to sales contracts. It spells out the duties of international buyers and sellers that will apply if the parties have not agreed otherwise in their contracts. The CISG only governs sales contracts between trading partners in nations that have ratified the CISG, however.

International legal disputes also have unique procedural requirements with which parties must be familiar. The following case provides an example of this necessity.

CASE 8.1

Brockmeyer v. May

United States
Court of Appeals,
Ninth Circuit, 2004.
383 F.3d 798.

BACKGROUND AND FACTS *Ronald Brockmeyer owns the trademark <<O>>, under which he distributes adult entertainment media and novelties. He brought a suit against a British company, Marquis Publications, Ltd., in a U.S. district court, alleging that Marquis had violated his trademark rights. Brockmeyer sent the summons and complaint to a post office box in England but received no response. He sent a second letter by first class mail to the post office box, but Marquis again did not respond. The court entered a default judgment for Brockmeyer, awarding him damages of $410,806.12, plus attorneys' fees and costs. Marquis moved to set aside this judgment for failure of service, contending that international service must be made by certified or registered mail. The district court denied the motion, and Marquis appealed.*

IN THE LANGUAGE OF THE COURT

FLETCHER, Circuit Judge

* * * *

   The resolution of this appeal depends on whether Marquis was properly served. Because service of process was attempted abroad, the validity of that service is controlled by [Rule 4(f) of] the Hague Convention. * * *

CONTINUED ▶

CASE 8.1 | **Continued**

* * * *

Today we join the Second Circuit in holding that the Hague Convention allows service of process by international mail. At the same time, we hold that any service by mail in this case was required to be performed in accordance with the requirements of Rule 4(f). Service by international mail is affirmatively authorized by Rule 4(f)(2)(C)(ii), which requires that service be sent by the clerk of the court, using a form of mail requiring a signed receipt. Service by international mail is also affirmatively authorized by Rule 4(f)(3) which requires that the mailing procedure have been specifically directed by the district court. * * * [Plaintiffs] simply dropped the complaint and summons in a mailbox in Los Angeles, to be delivered by ordinary, international first class mail. There is no affirmative authorization for such service in Rule 4(f). The attempted service was therefore ineffective, and the default judgment against Marquis cannot stand.

DECISION AND REMEDY *The U.S. Court of Appeals for the Ninth Circuit reversed the district court's decision and remanded the case to the district court, with instructions to vacate (set aside, treat as void) the judgment against Marquis.*

WHAT IF THE FACTS WERE DIFFERENT? *If Brockmeyer had served Marquis by certified or registered mail, would the result have been different?*

LEGAL PRINCIPLES AND DOCTRINES

Over time, a number of legal principles and doctrines have evolved and have been employed—to a greater or lesser extent—by the courts of various nations to resolve or reduce conflicts that involve a foreign element. The three important legal principles discussed below are based primarily on courtesy and respect and are applied in the interests of maintaining harmonious relations among nations.

THE PRINCIPLE OF COMITY Under what is known as the principle of **comity,** one nation will defer and give effect to the laws and judicial decrees of another country, as long as those laws and judicial decrees are consistent with the law and public policy of the accommodating nation. For example, assume that a Swedish seller and an American buyer have formed a contract, which the buyer breaches. The seller sues the buyer in a Swedish court, which awards damages. The buyer's assets, however, are in the United States and cannot be reached unless the judgment is enforced by a U.S. court of law. In this situation, if a U.S. court determines that the procedures and laws applied in the Swedish court are consistent with U.S. national law and policy, the U.S. court will likely defer to, and enforce, the foreign court's judgment.

One way to understand the principle of comity (and the *act of state doctrine*, which will be discussed shortly) is to consider the relationships among the states in our federal form of government. Each state honors (gives "full faith and credit" to) the contracts, property deeds, wills, and other legal obligations formed in other states, as well as judicial decisions with respect to such obligations. On a worldwide basis, nations similarly attempt to honor judgments rendered in other countries when it is feasible to do so. Of course, a major difference between U.S. federalism and the relationships among nations is that the states within the United States are constitutionally bound to honor other states' actions (see the discussion of the full faith and credit clause in Chapter 5). There is no world constitution, so international doctrines rest primarily on courtesy.

THE ACT OF STATE DOCTRINE The **act of state doctrine** is a judicially created doctrine that provides that the judicial branch of one country will not examine the validity of public acts committed by a recognized foreign government within its own territory. This doctrine is premised on the theory that the judicial branch should not "pass upon the validity of foreign acts when to do so would vex the harmony of our international relations with that foreign nation."

The act of state doctrine can have important consequences for individuals and firms doing business with, and investing in, other countries. For example, this doctrine is frequently employed in cases involving **expropriation,** which occurs when a government seizes a privately owned business or privately owned goods for a proper public purpose and awards just compensation. When a government seizes private property for an illegal purpose and without just compensation, the taking is referred to as a **confiscation.** The line between these two forms of taking is sometimes blurred because of differing interpretations of what is

EXHIBIT 8-1   Selected Multilateral International Organizations in Which the United States Participates

NAME	PURPOSE
Customs Cooperation Council	Established in 1950. Supervises the application and interpretation of an international code classifying goods and customs tariffs.
International Bank for Reconstruction and Development	Popularly known as the World Bank; a specialized agency of the United Nations since 1947. Promotes growth, trade, and balance of trade by facilitating and providing technical assistance, particularly in agriculture, energy, transportation, and telecommunications.
International Civil Aviation Organization	Established in 1947 and became a specialized agency of the United Nations seven months later. Develops international civil aviation by issuing rules and policies for safe and efficient airports and air navigation.
International Court of Justice (World Court)	Established in 1922 and became one of the principal organs of the United Nations in 1945. Jurisdiction comprises all cases that are referred to it. Decides disputes in accordance with the rules of international law.
International Maritime Organization	Established in 1948. Promotes cooperation in the areas of government regulation, practices and technical matters of all kinds affecting shipping in international trade, the adoption of standards of maritime safety and efficiency, and the abolition of discrimination and unnecessary restrictions.
International Telecommunications Satellite Organization	Established in 1964. Operates an international public communications satellite system on a commercial, nondiscriminatory basis.
Permanent Court of Arbitration	Established in 1899 to facilitate the settlement of international disputes. The court has jurisdiction over all cases that it is requested to arbitrate.
World Intellectual Property Organization	Established in 1967 and became a specialized agency of the United Nations in 1974. Promotes protection of intellectual property throughout the world.
World Trade Organization (WTO)	Established in 1994 during the final round of negotiations of the General Agreement on Tariffs and Trade (GATT). The GATT was created in 1947 and was the first global commercial agreement in history. It became the principal instrument for regulating international trade and limiting tariffs and other barriers to world trade on particular commodities and other items. GATT ceased to exist in 1995, when the WTO came into existence to regulate worldwide trade.

illegal and what constitutes just compensation. To illustrate: Tim Flaherty, an American businessperson, owns a mine in Brazil. The government of Brazil seizes the mine for public use and claims that the profits Tim has already realized from the mine constitute just compensation. Tim disagrees, but the act of state doctrine may prevent Tim's recovery in a U.S. court of law. Note that in a case alleging that a foreign government has wrongfully taken the plaintiff's property, the defendant government has the burden of proving that the taking was an expropriation, not a confiscation.

When applicable, both the act of state doctrine and the doctrine of *sovereign immunity*, which we discuss next, tend to shield foreign nations from the jurisdiction of U.S. courts. As a result, firms or individuals who own property overseas generally have little legal protection against government actions in the countries where they operate.

THE DOCTRINE OF SOVEREIGN IMMUNITY When certain conditions are satisfied, the doctrine of **sovereign immunity** exempts foreign nations from the jurisdiction of the U.S. courts. In 1976, Congress codified this rule in the Foreign Sovereign Immunities Act (FSIA).[1] The FSIA also modified previous applications of the doctrine in certain respects by expanding the rights of plaintiff creditors against foreign nations.

The FSIA exclusively governs the circumstances in which an action may be brought in the United

1. 28 U.S.C. Sections 1602–1611.

States against a foreign nation. Section 1605 of the FSIA sets forth the major exceptions to the jurisdictional immunity of a foreign state. A foreign state is not immune from the jurisdiction of U.S. courts when the state has "waived its immunity either explicitly or by implication" or when the state has engaged in actions that are taken "in connection with a commercial activity carried on in the United States by the foreign state" or that have "a direct effect in the United States." The FSIA also contains an exception for torts committed in the United States and for some violations of international law. Generally, because the law is jurisdictional in nature, a plaintiff has the burden of showing that a defendant is not entitled to sovereign immunity.

Questions frequently arise as to whether particular entities fall within the category of foreign state. Under Section 1603 of the FSIA, a *foreign state* is defined to include both a political subdivision of a foreign state and an instrumentality of a foreign state (an agency or entity acting for the state). The specification of a commercial activity has also been the subject of dispute because the act does not spell out the particulars of what constitutes a commercial activity. Rather, it is left to the courts to decide whether a particular activity is governmental or commercial in nature. In the following case, the United States Supreme Court considered whether the principles of the FSIA should apply to a dispute dating back to World War II, before the FSIA had been enacted.

CASE 8.2

Republic of Austria v. Altmann

Supreme Court of the United States, 2004.
541 U.S. 677,
124 S.Ct. 2240,
159 L.Ed.2d 1.

Justice *STEVENS* delivered the opinion of the Court.

In 1998 an Austrian journalist, granted access to the Austrian Gallery's archives [in Vienna, Austria], discovered evidence that certain valuable works in the Gallery's collection had not been donated by their rightful owners but had been seized by the Nazis or expropriated by the Austrian Republic after World War II. The journalist provided some of that evidence to respondent [Maria Altmann], who in turn filed this action [in a U.S. federal district court] to recover possession of six Gustav Klimt paintings. Prior to the Nazi invasion of Austria [in 1938], the paintings had hung in the palatial Vienna home of respondent's uncle, Ferdinand Bloch-Bauer, a Czechoslovakian Jew and patron of the arts. Respondent claims ownership of the paintings under a will executed by her uncle after he fled Austria in 1938. [In the will, he left his estate to Altmann, another niece, and Robert Bentley, a nephew.] She alleges that the Gallery obtained possession of the paintings through wrongful conduct in the years during and after World War II.

The defendants (petitioners here)—the Republic of Austria and the Austrian Gallery (Gallery), an instrumentality of the Republic—filed a motion to dismiss the complaint asserting, among other defenses, a claim of sovereign immunity. [Respondent argued that petitioners are not entitled to immunity because the FSIA exempts from immunity all cases involving "rights in property taken in violation of international law."] The District Court denied the [defendants'] motion, and the [U.S.] Court of Appeals [for the Ninth Circuit] affirmed. We granted *certiorari* limited to the question whether the Foreign Sovereign Immunities Act of 1976 (FSIA or Act) * * * applies to claims that, like respondent's, are based on conduct that occurred before the Act's enactment * * * .

* * * *

To begin with, the preamble of the FSIA expresses Congress' understanding that the Act would apply to all postenactment claims of sovereign immunity. That section provides:

> Claims of foreign states to immunity should henceforth be decided by courts of the United States and of the States in conformity with the principles set forth in this chapter.

* * * [T]his language is unambiguous: Immunity "claims"—not actions protected by immunity, but assertions of immunity to suits arising from those actions—are the relevant conduct regulated by the Act; those claims are "henceforth" to be decided by the courts. * * * [T]his language suggests *Congress intended courts to resolve all such claims "in conformity with the principles set forth" in the Act, regardless of when the underlying conduct occurred.* [Emphasis added.]

The FSIA's overall structure strongly supports this conclusion. Many of the Act's provisions unquestionably apply to cases arising out of conduct that occurred before 1976. * * * [F]or example, * * * whether an entity qualifies as an "instrumentality" of a "foreign state"

CASE 8.2 Continued

for purposes of the FSIA's grant of immunity depends on the relationship between the entity and the state at the time suit is brought rather than when the conduct occurred. * * * [T]here has never been any doubt that the Act's procedural provisions relating to venue, removal, execution, and attachment apply to all pending cases. Thus, the FSIA's preamble indicates that it applies "henceforth," and its body includes numerous provisions that unquestionably apply to claims based on pre-1976 conduct. In this context, *it would be anomalous [irregular, unusual] to presume that an isolated provision (such as the expropriation exception on which respondent relies) is of purely prospective application absent any statutory language to that effect.* [Emphasis added.]

Finally, applying the FSIA to all pending cases regardless of when the underlying conduct occurred is most consistent with two of the Act's principal purposes: clarifying the rules that judges should apply in resolving sovereign immunity claims and eliminating political participation in the resolution of such claims. * * * [T]o accomplish these purposes, Congress established a comprehensive framework for resolving any claim of sovereign immunity: * * * the text and structure of the FSIA demonstrate Congress' intention that the FSIA be the sole basis for obtaining jurisdiction over a foreign state in our courts. * * * *Section 1604 bars federal and state courts from exercising jurisdiction when a foreign state is entitled to immunity, and Section 1330(a) confers jurisdiction on district courts to hear suits brought by United States citizens and by aliens when a foreign state is not entitled to immunity.* * * * [Emphasis added.]

* * * Quite obviously, Congress' purposes in enacting such a comprehensive jurisdictional scheme would be frustrated if, in postenactment cases concerning preenactment conduct, courts were to continue to follow the same ambiguous and politically charged standards that the FSIA replaced.

* * * [W]e affirm the [Court of Appeals'] judgment because the Act * * * clearly applies to conduct, like petitioners' alleged wrongdoing, that occurred prior to 1976 * * * .
* * * *

The judgment of the Court of Appeals is affirmed.
It is so ordered.

QUESTIONS

1. What did the United States Supreme Court hold in this case, and why?
2. How did this case come before the United States Supreme Court, and what is the next step in its journey through the courts?

SECTION 2 | Doing Business Internationally

A U.S. domestic firm can engage in international business transactions in a number of ways. Here, we look at certain aspects of international business transactions, including the ways in which businesspersons typically extend their business operations into the international arena, laws regulating international business activities, and dispute settlement in the international context.

TYPES OF INTERNATIONAL BUSINESS OPERATIONS

Most U.S. companies make the initial foray into international business through exporting. There are several other alternatives, however, including those discussed here.

EXPORTING The simplest way to engage in international business operations is to seek out foreign markets for domestically produced products. In other words, U.S. firms can **export** their goods and services to foreign markets. Exporting can take two forms: direct exporting and indirect exporting. In *direct exporting*, a U.S. company signs a sales contract with a foreign purchaser that provides for the conditions of shipment and payment for the goods. If business expands sufficiently in a foreign country, a U.S. company may develop a specialized marketing organization in that foreign market by appointing a foreign agent or a foreign distributor. This is called *indirect exporting*.

When a U.S. firm wishes to limit its involvement in an international market, it will typically establish an agency relationship with a foreign firm. In an agency relationship, one person (the agent) agrees to act on behalf of, or instead of, another (the principal) (see Chapter 19). The foreign agent is thereby empowered to enter into contracts in the agent's country on behalf of the U.S. principal.

When a substantial market exists in a foreign country, a U.S. firm may wish to appoint a distributor located in that country. The U.S. firm and the distributor enter into a **distribution agreement,** which is a contract between the seller and the distributor setting out the terms and conditions of the distributorship—for example, price, currency of payment, guaranty of supply availability, and method of payment. The terms and conditions primarily involve contract law. Disputes concerning distribution agreements may involve jurisdictional or other issues, however.

MANUFACTURING ABROAD An alternative to direct or indirect exporting is the establishment of foreign manufacturing facilities. Typically, U.S. firms establish manufacturing plants abroad when they believe that by doing so they will reduce costs—particularly for labor, shipping, and raw materials—and thereby be able to compete more effectively in foreign markets. Apple Computer, IBM, General Motors, and Ford are some of the many U.S. companies that have established manufacturing facilities abroad. Foreign firms have done the same in the United States. Sony, Nissan, and other Japanese manufacturers have established U.S. plants to avoid import duties that the U.S. Congress may impose on Japanese products entering this country.

A U.S. firm can conduct manufacturing operations in other countries in several ways. They include licensing and franchising, as well as investing in a wholly owned subsidiary or a joint venture.

—Licensing. A U.S. firm can obtain business from abroad by licensing a foreign manufacturing company to use its copyrighted, patented, or trademarked intellectual property or trade secrets. Like any other licensing agreement, a licensing agreement with a foreign-based firm calls for a payment of royalties on some basis—such as so many cents per unit produced or a certain percentage of profits from units sold in a particular geographic territory. For example, the Coca-Cola Bottling Company licenses firms worldwide to use (and keep confidential) its secret formula for the syrup used in its soft drink, in return for a percentage of the income gained from the sale of Coca-Cola by those firms.

The licensing of intellectual property rights benefits all parties to the transaction. The firm that receives the license can take advantage of an established reputation for quality. The firm that grants the license receives income from the foreign sales of its products and also establishes a global reputation. Also, once a firm's trademark is known worldwide, the demand for other products manufactured or sold by that firm may increase—obviously, an important consideration.

—Franchising. Franchising is a well-known form of licensing. A *franchise* is an arrangement in which the owner of a trademark, trade name, or copyright (the franchisor) licenses another (the franchisee) to use the trademark, trade name, or copyright, under certain conditions or limitations, in the selling of goods or services. In return, the franchisee pays a fee, which is usually based on a percentage of gross or net sales. Examples of international franchises include McDonald's, Holiday Inn, Avis, and Hertz.

—Investing in a Wholly Owned Subsidiary or a Joint Venture. Another way to expand into a foreign market is to establish a wholly owned subsidiary firm in a foreign country. A European subsidiary would likely take the form of a *société anonyme* (S.A.), which is similar to a U.S. corporation. In German-speaking nations, it would be called an *Aktiengesellschaft* (A.G.). When a wholly owned subsidiary is established, the parent company, which remains in the United States, retains complete ownership of all the facilities in the foreign country, as well as total authority and control over all phases of the operation.

A U.S. firm can also expand into international markets through a joint venture. In a joint venture, the U.S. company owns only part of the operation; the rest is owned either by local owners in the foreign country or by another foreign entity. All of the firms involved in a joint venture share responsibilities, as well as profits and liabilities.

THE REGULATION OF INTERNATIONAL BUSINESS ACTIVITIES

International business transactions can affect the economies, foreign policies, domestic politics, and other national interests of the countries involved. For this reason, nations impose laws to restrict or facilitate international business. Controls may also be imposed by international agreements.

INVESTING Firms that invest in foreign nations face the risk that the foreign government may expropriate the investment property. As mentioned earlier in this chapter, expropriation occurs when property is taken and the owner is paid just compensation for what is taken. This does not violate generally observed principles of international law. Such principles are normally violated, however, when property is confiscated by a government without compensation (or without adequate compensation).

Few remedies are available when property is confiscated by a foreign government. Claims are often resolved by lump-sum settlements after negotiations between the United States and the taking nation. For example, investors whose claims arose out of confiscations following the Russian Revolution in 1917 were offered a lump-sum settlement by the Union of Soviet Socialist Republics in 1974. Still outstanding are $2 billion in claims against Cuba for confiscations that occurred in 1959 and 1960.

To counter the deterrent effect that the possibility of confiscation may have on potential investors, many countries guarantee compensation to foreign investors if property is taken. A guaranty can be in the form of national constitutional or statutory laws or provisions in international treaties. As further protection for foreign investments, some countries provide insurance for their citizens' investments abroad.

EXPORT CONTROLS The U.S. Constitution provides in Article I, Section 9, that "No Tax or Duty shall be laid on Articles exported from any State." Thus, Congress cannot impose any export taxes. Congress can, however, use a variety of other devices to restrict or encourage exports. Congress may set export quotas on various items, such as grain being sold abroad.

IMPORT CONTROLS All nations have restrictions on imports, and the United States is no exception. Restrictions include strict prohibitions, quotas, and tariffs. Under the Trading with the Enemy Act of 1917,[2] for example, no goods may be imported from nations that have been designated enemies of the United States. Other laws prohibit the importation of illegal drugs, books that urge insurrection against the United States, and agricultural products that pose dangers to domestic crops or animals.

—Quotas and Tariffs. Limits on the amounts of goods that can be imported are known as **quotas.** At one time, the United States had legal quotas on the number of automobiles that could be imported from Japan. Today, Japan "voluntarily" restricts the number of automobiles exported to the United States. **Tariffs** are taxes on imports. A tariff is usually a percentage of the value of the import, but it can be a flat rate per unit (such as per barrel of oil). Tariffs raise the prices of goods, causing some consumers to purchase less expensive, domestically manufactured goods.

—Antidumping Duties. The United States has specific laws directed at what it sees as unfair international trade practices. **Dumping,** for example, is the sale of imported goods at "less than fair value." *Fair value* is usually determined by the price of those goods in the exporting country. Dumping is designed to undersell U.S. businesses and obtain a larger share of the U.S. market. To prevent this, an extra tariff—known as an *antidumping duty*—may be assessed on the imports.

The procedure for imposing antidumping duties involves two U.S. government agencies: the International Trade Commission (ITC) and the International Trade Administration (ITA). The ITC is an independent agency that assesses the effects of dumping on domestic businesses and then makes recommendations to the president concerning temporary import restrictions. The ITA, which is part of the Department of Commerce, decides whether imports were sold at less than "fair value." The ITA's determination establishes the amount of antidumping duties, which are set to equal the difference between the price charged in the United States and the price charged in the exporting country. A duty may be retroactive to cover alleged past dumping.

INTERNATIONAL AGREEMENTS Over the last decade, countries competing for international trade have become more evenly matched than in earlier years. In part, this is due to the increased use and success of international and regional organizations, such as the World Trade Organization, the European Union, and the North American Free Trade Agreement.

—The World Trade Organization. The origins of the World Trade Organization (WTO) date to 1947, when the General Agreement on Tariffs and Trade (GATT) was formed for the purpose of minimizing

---

2. 12 U.S.C. Section 95a.

trade barriers among nations. In subsequent decades, the GATT became the principal instrument for regulating international trade and, over time, negotiated tariff reductions on a broad range of products.

In 1994, in a final round of GATT negotiations, called the "Uruguay Round," representatives from over one hundred nations signed agreements relating to investment policies, dispute resolution, and other topics. One of these agreements, the Trade-Related Aspects of Intellectual Property Rights Agreement (TRIPS), will be discussed in Chapter 14. The Uruguay Round also established the WTO, which replaced the GATT beginning in 1995. Each member country of the WTO agreed to grant *most-favored-nation status* to other member countries. This status, now referred to as **normal trade relations (NTR) status,** means that each WTO member must treat other WTO members at least as well as it treats the country that receives its most favorable treatment with regard to imports or exports.

—The European Union (EU). The European Union (EU) arose out of the 1957 Treaty of Rome, which created the Common Market, a free trade zone comprising the nations of Belgium, France, West Germany, Italy, the Netherlands, and Luxembourg. Since 1957, more nations have been added. Today, the EU is a single, relatively integrated European trading unit made up of twenty-five European nations.

The EU has its own governing authorities. These include the Council of Ministers, which coordinates economic policies and includes one representative from each nation; a commission, which proposes regulations to the council; and an elected assembly, which oversees the commission. The EU also has its own court, the European Court of Justice, which can review each nation's judicial decisions and is the ultimate authority on EU law.

The EU has gone a long way toward creating a new body of law to govern all of the member nations— although some of its efforts to create uniform laws have been confounded by nationalism. The council and the commission issue regulations, or directives, that define EU law in various areas, and these requirements normally are binding on all member countries. EU directives govern such issues as environmental law, product liability, anticompetitive practices, and laws governing corporations. The EU directive on product liability, for example, states that a "producer of an article shall be liable for damages caused by a defect in the article, whether or not he knew or could have known of the defect." Liability extends to anyone who puts a trademark or other identifying feature on an article, and liability may not be excluded, even by contract.

—The North American Free Trade Agreement (NAFTA). The North American Free Trade Agreement (NAFTA), which was signed in 1993 and became effective on January 1, 1994, created a regional trading unit consisting of Mexico, the United States, and Canada. The primary goal of NAFTA is to eliminate tariffs among these three nations on substantially all goods over a period of fifteen to twenty years.

NAFTA gives the three countries a competitive advantage by retaining tariffs on goods imported from countries outside the NAFTA trading unit. Additionally, NAFTA provides for the elimination of barriers that traditionally have prevented the cross-border movement of services, such as financial and transportation services. For example, NAFTA provides that, with some exceptions, U.S. firms do not have to relocate to Mexico or Canada to provide services in those countries. NAFTA also attempts to eliminate citizenship requirements for the licensing of accountants, attorneys, physicians, and other professionals.

SECTION 3 | National Legal Systems

When doing business in a foreign nation, a company generally will be subject to the jurisdiction and laws of that nation. Therefore, businesspersons will find it helpful to become familiar with the legal systems and laws of foreign nations in which they conduct commercial transactions. In this section, we look at some similarities and differences among national legal systems. We conclude the section with a discussion of international tort law.

Generally, the legal systems of foreign nations differ, in widely varying degrees, from that of the United States. Additionally, a number of nations have specialized commercial law courts to deal with business disputes (in the United States, some jurisdictions are establishing similar courts). France instituted such courts in 1807, and most nations with commercial law codes have done likewise. The United Kingdom also has special commercial courts overseen by judges with expertise in business law.

COMMON LAW AND CIVIL LAW SYSTEMS

Legal systems around the globe generally are divided into *common law* and *civil law* systems.

COMMON LAW SYSTEMS As discussed in Chapter 1, in a common law system, the courts independently develop the rules governing certain areas of law, such as torts and contracts. These common law rules apply to all areas not covered by statutory law. Although the common law doctrine of *stare decisis* obligates judges to follow precedential decisions in their jurisdictions, courts may modify or even overturn precedents when deemed necessary. Additionally, if there is no case law to guide a court, the court may create a new rule of law. Common law systems exist today in countries that were once part of the British Empire (such as Australia, India, and the United States).

CIVIL LAW SYSTEMS In contrast to Great Britain and the other common law countries, most of the European nations base their legal systems on Roman civil law, or "code law." The term *civil law*, as used here, refers not to civil as opposed to criminal law but to *codified* law—an ordered grouping of legal principles enacted into law by a legislature or other governing body. In a **civil law system,** the only official source of law is a statutory code. Courts are required to interpret the code and apply the rules to individual cases, but courts may not depart from the code and develop their own laws. In theory, the law code will set forth all the principles needed for the legal system.

COUNTRIES USING COMMON LAW OR CIVIL LAW SYSTEMS Today, civil law systems are found in most of the continental European countries, as well as in the Latin American, African, and Asian countries that were once colonies of the continental European nations. Japan and South Africa also have civil law systems. The Islamic courts of predominantly Muslim countries also use elements of the civil law system. In the United States, the state of Louisiana, because of its historical ties to France, has, in part, a civil law system. Exhibit 8–2 lists some of the nations that use civil law systems and some that use common law systems.

LEGAL SYSTEMS COMPARED Common law and civil law systems are not wholly distinct. For example, although the United States has a common law system, crimes are defined by statute as in civil law systems. Civil law systems may also allow considerable room for judges to develop law. There is also some variation within common law and civil law systems. The judges of different common law nations have produced differing common law principles. Although the United States and India both derived their legal traditions from England, for example, the common law principles governing contract law vary in some respects between the two countries.

Similarly, the laws of nations that have civil law systems differ considerably. For example, the French code tends to set forth general principles of law, while the German code is far more specific and runs to thousands of sections. In some Middle Eastern countries, codes are grounded in the religious law of Islam, called *sharia*.[3] The religious basis of these codes makes them far more difficult to alter.

JUDGES AND PROCEDURES Judges play similar roles in virtually all countries: their primary function is the resolution of litigation. The characteristics and qualifications of judges, which are typically set forth in the nation's constitution, can vary widely, however. In the United States, the judge normally does not actively participate in a trial, but many foreign judges involve themselves closely in the proceedings, such as by questioning witnesses.

The procedures employed in resolving cases also vary substantially from country to country. A knowledge of a nation's legal procedures is important for a person conducting business transactions in that nation. For example, an American businessperson was

---

3. Pronounced shah-*ree*-uh.

EXHIBIT 8-2 **The Legal Systems of Selected Nations**

CIVIL LAW	COMMON LAW
Argentina	Australia
Austria	Bangladesh
Brazil	Canada
Chile	Ghana
China	India
Egypt	Israel
Finland	Jamaica
France	Kenya
Germany	Malaysia
Greece	New Zealand
Indonesia	Nigeria
Iran	Singapore
Italy	United Kingdom
Japan	United States
Mexico	Zambia
Poland	
South Korea	
Sweden	
Tunisia	
Venezuela	

on trial in Saudi Arabia for assaulting and slandering a co-worker, an offense for which he might have been jailed or deported. He initially was required to present two witnesses to his version of events, but he had only one. Fortunately, he became aware that he could "demand the oath." In this procedure, he swore before God that he had neither kicked nor slandered the complainant. After taking the oath, he was promptly adjudged not guilty, as lying under oath is one of the most serious sins existing under Islamic law. Had he failed to demand the oath, he almost certainly would have been found guilty.

INTERNATIONAL TORTS

The international application of tort liability is growing in significance and controversy. An increasing number of U.S. plaintiffs are suing foreign (or U.S.) entities for torts that these entities have allegedly committed overseas. A number of these cases involve human rights violations by foreign governments. The Alien Tort Claims Act (ATCA),[4] adopted in 1789,

---

4. 28 U.S.C. Section 1350.

allows even foreign citizens to bring civil suits in U.S. courts for injuries caused by violations of the law of nations or a treaty of the United States.

Since 1980, plaintiffs have increasingly used the ATCA to bring actions against companies operating in other countries. In all, over two dozen ATCA cases have been brought against companies doing business in nations such as Colombia, Ecuador, Egypt, Guatemala, India, Indonesia, Nigeria, and Saudi Arabia. Several of these cases have involved alleged environmental destruction. In addition, mineral companies in Southeast Asia have been sued for collaborating with oppressive government regimes, and South African torture victims have filed a multibillion-dollar lawsuit against more than one hundred companies that operated under that nation's apartheid (racially discriminatory) regime. Unocal Corporation recently settled a lawsuit brought because it allowed the army of Myanmar to protect its pipeline through the alleged use of murder and torture.

Of course, U.S. citizens may also file international tort actions in this country, especially when the torts occurred on U.S. soil. The following case addressed litigation arising out of the terrorist attacks of September 11, 2001.

CASE 8.3   **In re Terrorist Attacks on September 11, 2001**

United States District Court, Southern District of New York, 2005. 349 F.Supp.2d 765.

BACKGROUND AND FACTS *Insurance carriers as well as thousands of survivors of victims of the terrorist attacks of September 11, 2001, joined in an action under the ATCA and other legal authorities to recover damages for the attacks. Numerous parties were named as defendants, including the terrorist network al Qaeda, the Kingdom of Saudi Arabia, various foreign government officials, charities, and banks. The complaint claimed that the government officials, charities, and banks had provided material support to Osama bin Laden and the al Qaeda terrorists. The individual defendants were all Saudi Arabian officials, including Prince Sultan, the nation's minister of defense. The defendants moved to dismiss the complaint on multiple grounds, including lack of jurisdiction under the Foreign Sovereign Immunities Act and the plaintiffs' failure to allege a viable tort claim.*

IN THE LANGUAGE OF THE COURT

CASEY, District Judge.
* * * *
* * * Prince Sultan is alleged to have met with Osama bin Laden after Iraq invaded Kuwait in the summer of 1990. * * * Plaintiffs allege that, at the time of the Gulf War, Prince Sultan "took radical stands against Western countries and publicly supported and funded several Islamic charities that were sponsoring Osama bin Laden and al Qaeda operations." * * *

Prince Sultan allegedly made personal contributions, totaling $6,000,000 since 1994, to various Islamic charities that plaintiffs claim sponsor or support al Qaeda. * * * According to plaintiffs, with respect to his alleged donations, "[a]t best, Prince Sultan was grossly negli-

CASE 8.3 | Continued

gent in the oversight and administration of charitable funds, knowing they would be used to sponsor international terrorism." * * *

* * * *

Both Prince Sultan and Prince Turki claim plaintiffs cannot demonstrate their alleged tortious activity caused plaintiffs' injuries. They argue that plaintiffs ignore that Osama bin Laden also targeted the Saudi royal family. * * * Plaintiffs have pleaded al Qaeda's repeated, public targeting of the United States. They have not, however, pleaded facts to support an inference that the Princes were sufficiently close to the terrorists' illegal activities. * * * The court has reviewed the complaints in their entirety and finds no allegations from which it can infer that the Princes knew the charities to which they donated were fronts for al Qaeda. *The court is not ruling as a matter of law that a defendant cannot be liable for contributions to organizations that are not themselves designated terrorists.* But in such a case, there must be some facts presented to support the allegation that the defendant knew the receiving organization to be a solicitor, collector, supporter, front, or launderer for such an entity. [Emphasis added.]

DECISION AND REMEDY *The claims against Prince Sultan and the others were dismissed for failure to state a claim and also for failure to establish personal jurisdiction. Claims were allowed to proceed against some other defendants, including the Saudi National Commercial Bank.*

REVIEWING INTERNATIONAL LAW

Robco, Inc., was a Florida arms dealer. The armed forces of Honduras contracted to purchase weapons from Robco over a six-year period. After the government was replaced and a democracy installed, the Honduran government sought to reduce the size of its military, and its relationship with Robco deteriorated. Honduras refused to go through with the contract and purchase the inventory of arms, which Robco could sell only at a much lower price. Robco filed a suit in a federal district court in the United States to recover damages for this breach of contract by the government of Honduras. Using the information presented in the chapter, answer the following questions.

1. Should the Foreign Sovereign Immunities Act (FSIA) preclude this lawsuit?

2. What exception to the FSIA might apply?

3. If a contract enforcement action had been filed in Honduras, what doctrine of deference would that implicate?

4. Should the act of state doctrine bar this lawsuit?

 ## TERMS AND CONCEPTS TO REVIEW

act of state doctrine 174

civil law system 181

comity 174

confiscation 174

distribution agreement 178

dumping 179

export 177

expropriation 174

international law 172

international organization 173

national law 172

normal trade relations (NTR) status 180

quota 179

sharia 181

sovereign immunity 175

tariff 179

treaty 173

QUESTIONS AND CASE PROBLEMS

8–1. In 1995, France implemented a law making the use of the French language mandatory in certain legal documents. Documents relating to securities offerings, such as prospectuses, for example, must be written in French. So must instruction manuals and warranties for goods and services offered for sale in France. Additionally, all agreements entered into with French state or local authorities, with entities controlled by state or local authorities, and with private entities carrying out a public service (such as providing utilities) must be written in French. What kinds of problems might this law pose for U.S. businesspersons who wish to form contracts with French individuals or business firms?

8–2. ⚖ **QUESTION WITH SAMPLE ANSWER**

As China and formerly Communist nations move toward free enterprise, they must develop a new set of business laws. If you could start from scratch, what kind of business law system would you adopt, a civil law system or a common law system? What kind of business regulations would you impose?

For a sample answer to this question, go to Appendix I at the end of this text.

8–3. ACT OF STATE DOCTRINE. W. S. Kirkpatrick & Co. learned that the Republic of Nigeria was interested in contracting for the construction and equipping of a medical center in Nigeria. Kirkpatrick, with the aid of a Nigerian citizen, secured the contract as a result of bribing Nigerian officials. Nigerian law prohibits both the payment and the receipt of bribes in connection with the awarding of government contracts, and the U.S. Foreign Corrupt Practices Act of 1977 expressly prohibits U.S. firms and their agents from bribing foreign officials to secure favorable contracts. Environmental Tectonics Corp., International (ETC), an unsuccessful bidder for the contract, learned of the bribery and sued Kirkpatrick in a federal district court for damages. The district court granted summary judgment for Kirkpatrick on the ground that resolution of the case in favor of ETC would require imputing to foreign officials an unlawful motivation (the obtaining of bribes) and accordingly might embarrass the Nigerian government or interfere with the conduct of U.S. foreign policy. Was the district court correct in assuming that the act of state doctrine barred ETC's action against Kirkpatrick? What should happen on appeal? Discuss fully. [*W. S. Kirkpatrick & Co. v. Environmental Tectonics Corp., International,* 493 U.S. 400, 110 S.Ct. 701, 107 L.Ed.2d 816 (1990)]

8–4. SOVEREIGN IMMUNITY. Nuovo Pignone, Inc., is an Italian company that designs and manufactures turbine systems. Nuovo sold a turbine system to Cabinda Gulf Oil Co. (CABGOC). The system was manufactured, tested, and inspected in Italy, then sent to Louisiana for mounting on a platform by CABGOC's

contractor. Nuovo sent a representative to consult on the mounting. The platform went to a CABGOC site off the coast of West Africa. Marcus Pere, an instrument technician at the site, was killed when a turbine within the system exploded. Pere's widow filed a suit in a U.S. federal district court against Nuovo and others. Nuovo claimed sovereign immunity on the ground that its majority shareholder at the time of the explosion was Ente Nazionale Idrocaburi, which was created by the government of Italy to lead its oil and gas exploration and development. Is Nuovo exempt from suit under the doctrine of sovereign immunity? Is it subject to suit under the "commercial activity" exception? Why or why not? [*Pere v. Nuovo Pignone, Inc.,* 150 F.3d 477 (5th Cir. 1998)]

8–5. DUMPING. In response to a petition filed on behalf of the U.S. pineapple industry, the U.S. Commerce Department initiated an investigation of canned pineapple fruit imported from Thailand. The investigation concerned Thai producers of the canned fruit, including The Thai Pineapple Public Co. The Thai producers also turned out products, such as pineapple juice and juice concentrate, outside the scope of the investigation. These products use separate parts of the same fresh pineapple, so they share raw material costs. The Commerce Department had to calculate the Thai producers' cost of production, for the purpose of determining fair value and antidumping duties, and in so doing, it had to allocate a portion of the shared fruit costs to the canned fruit. These allocations were based on the producers' own financial records, which were consistent with Thai generally accepted accounting principles. The result was a determination that more than 90 percent of the canned fruit sales were below the cost of production. The producers filed a suit in the U.S. Court of International Trade against the federal government, challenging this allocation. The producers argued that their records did not reflect actual production costs, which instead should be based on the weight of fresh fruit used to make the products. Did the Commerce Department act reasonably in determining the cost of production? Why or why not? [*The Thai Pineapple Public Co. v. United States,* 187 F.3d 1362 (Fed.Cir. 1999)]

8–6. SOVEREIGN IMMUNITY. Tonoga, Ltd., doing business as Taconic Plastics, Ltd., is a manufacturer incorporated in Ireland with its principal place of business in New York. In 1997, Taconic entered into a contract with a German construction company to supply special material for a tent project designed to shelter religious pilgrims visiting holy sites in Saudi Arabia. Most of the material was made in, and shipped from, New York. The company did not pay Taconic and eventually filed for bankruptcy. Another German firm, Werner Voss Architects and Engineers, acting as an agent for the government of Saudi Arabia, guaranteed the payments due Taconic to induce it to complete the project. When Taconic received all but the final payment, the firm filed a suit in a federal district court against the government of Saudi Arabia, claiming a breach of the guaranty and seeking to collect, in part, about $3 million. The defendant filed a motion to dismiss based, in part, on the doctrine of sovereign immunity. Under what circumstances does this doctrine apply? What are its exceptions? Should this suit be dismissed under the "commercial activity" exception? Explain. [*Tonoga, Ltd. v. Ministry of Public Works and Housing of Kingdom of Saudi Arabia*, 135 F.Supp.2d 350 (N.D.N.Y. 2001)]

8–7. ⚖ CASE PROBLEM WITH SAMPLE ANSWER

DaimlerChrysler Corp. makes and markets motor vehicles. DaimlerChrysler assembled the 1993 and 1994 model years of its trucks at plants in Mexico. Assembly involved sheet metal components sent from the United States. DaimlerChrysler subjected some of the parts to a complicated treatment process, which included the application of coats of paint to prevent corrosion, to impart color, and to protect the finish. Under federal law, goods or U.S.-made parts that are assembled abroad can be imported tariff free. A federal statute provides that painting is "incidental" to assembly and does not affect the status of the goods. A federal regulation states that "painting primarily intended to enhance the appearance of an article or to impart distinctive features or characteristics" is not incidental. The U.S. Customs Service levied a tariff on the trucks. DaimlerChrysler filed a suit in the U.S. Court of International Trade, challenging the levy. Should the court rule in DaimlerChrysler's favor? Why or why not? [*DaimlerChrysler Corp. v. United States*, 361 F.3d 1378 (Fed.Cir. 2004)]

To view a sample answer for this case problem, go to this book's Web site at http://wleb.westbuslaw.com, select "Chapter 8," and click on "Case Problem with Sample Answer."

8–8. COMITY. E&L Consulting, Ltd., is a U.S. corporation that sells lumber products in New York, New Jersey, and Pennsylvania. Doman Industries, Ltd., is a Canadian corporation that also sells lumber products, including green hem-fir, a durable product used for home building. Doman supplies over 95 percent of the green hem-fir for sale in the northeastern United States. In 1990, Doman contracted to sell green hem-fir through E&L, which received monthly payments plus commissions. In 1998, Sherwood Lumber Corp., a New York firm and an E&L competitor, approached E&L about a merger. The negotiations were unsuccessful. According to E&L, Sherwood and Doman then conspired to monopolize the green hem-fir market in the United States. When Doman terminated its contract with E&L, the latter filed a suit in a federal district court against Doman, alleging violations of U.S. antitrust law. Doman filed for bankruptcy in a Canadian court and asked the U.S. court to dismiss E&L's suit in part under the principle of comity. What is the "principle of comity"? On what basis would

it apply in this case? What would be the likely result? Discuss. [*E&L Consulting, Ltd. v. Doman Industries, Ltd.*, 360 F.Supp.2d 465 (E.D.N.Y. 2005)]

8–9. IMPORT CONTROL. In 1996, the International Trade Administration (ITA) of the U.S. Department of Commerce assessed antidumping duties against Koyo Seiko Co., NTN Corp., and other companies, on certain tapered roller bearings and their components imported from Japan. In assessing these duties, the ITA requested information from the makers about their home market sales. NTN responded in part that its figures should not include many sample and small-quantity sales, which were made to enable customers to decide whether to buy the products. NTN provided no evidence to support this assertion, however. In calculating the fair market value of the bearings in Japan, the ITA determined, among other things, that sample and small-quantity sales were within the makers' ordinary course of trade. Koyo and others appealed these assessments to the U.S. Court of International Trade. NTN objected in part to the ITA's inclusion of sample and small-quantity sales. On what basis should the ITA make such determinations? Should the court order the ITA to recalculate its assessment on the basis of NTN's objection? Explain. [*Koyo Seiko Co. v. United States*, 186 F.Supp.2d 1332 (CIT [Court of International Trade] 2002)]

8–10. ⚖ A QUESTION OF ETHICS

Ronald Riley, a U.S. citizen, and Council of Lloyd's, a British insurance corporation with its principal place of business in London, entered into an agreement in 1980 that allowed Riley to underwrite insurance through Lloyd's. The agreement provided that if any dispute arose between Lloyd's and Riley, the courts of England would have exclusive jurisdiction, and the laws of England would apply. Over the next decade, some of the parties insured under policies that Riley underwrote experienced large losses, for which they filed claims. Instead of paying his share of the claims, Riley filed a lawsuit in a U.S. district court against Lloyd's and its managers and directors (all British citizens or entities), seeking, among other things, rescission of the 1980 agreement. Riley alleged that the defendants had violated the Securities Act of 1933, the Securities Exchange Act of 1934, and Rule 10b-5. The defendants asked the court to enforce the forum-selection clause in the agreement. Riley argued that if the clause was enforced, he would be deprived of his rights under the U.S. securities laws. The court held that the parties were to resolve their dispute in England. [*Riley v. Kingsley Underwriting Agencies, Ltd.*, 969 F.2d 953 (10th Cir. 1992)]

(a) Did the court's decision fairly balance the rights of the parties? How would you argue in support of the court's decision in this case? How would you argue against it?

(b) Should the fact that an international transaction may be subject to laws and remedies different from or less favorable than those of the United States be a valid basis for denying enforcement of forum-selection and choice-of-law clauses?

(c) All parties to this litigation other than Riley were British. Should the court consider this fact in deciding this case?

LAW | on the Web

For updated links to resources available on the Web, as well as a variety of other materials, visit this text's Web site at http://wleb.westbuslaw.com.

FindLaw, which is now a part of West Group, includes an extensive array of links to international doctrines and treaties, as well as to the laws of other nations, on its Web site. Go to

http://www.findlaw.com

and click on "International Law."

For information on the legal requirements of doing business internationally, a good source is the Internet Law Library's collection of laws of other countries. You can access this source at

http://www.lawguru.com/ilawlib/index.html

LEGAL RESEARCH EXERCISES ON THE WEB

Go to http://wleb.westbuslaw.com, the Web site that accompanies this text. Select "Chapter 8" and click on "Internet Exercises." There you will find the following Internet research exercises that you can perform to learn more about topics covered in this chapter.

Activity 8–1: LEGAL PERSPECTIVE
The World Trade Organization

Activity 8–2: MANAGEMENT PERSPECTIVE
Overseas Business Opportunities

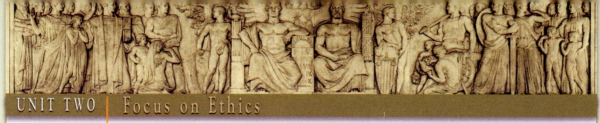

The Public and International Environment

No other areas of law are as dynamic and engender as much controversy as those relating to the public and international environment. All areas of law touch on ethical considerations. But many laws have as their basis practical necessity or commercial need. The law of the public environment, however, concerns issues such as the protection of freedom of speech, the promotion of racial equality, and government regulation of behavior for the public welfare versus individual rights.

The law of the international environment involves such questions as the influence of foreign and international laws, the impact of divergent cultures, and the effect of different legal, political, and economic systems. These issues are in large measure purely ethical in nature. In resolving them, one must rely on basic notions of fairness and justice. Yet conceptions of fairness, justice, and equality differ among individuals and change over time.

Ethical and legal concepts are often closely intertwined. This is because the common law, as it evolved in England and then in America, reflects society's values and customs. This connection between law and ethics is clearly evident in the area of criminal law, which is founded on concepts of right and wrong behavior—although common law concepts governing criminal acts are now expressed in, or replaced by, federal, state, and local criminal statutes. The number of crimes has continued to expand as new ways to commit wrongs have been discovered. In this *Focus on Ethics* feature, we look at the ethical dimensions of selected topics discussed in the preceding chapters, including some issues that are unique to the cyber age.

Free Speech and the Corporation

Free speech is regarded as one of the basic rights of a democratic society. Yet it has never been considered an absolute right. The right of free speech must be balanced against other important rights and the advancement of other important social goals. In that sense, the proper extent of freedom of speech, in its many forms, involves ethical considerations.

Because freedom of speech is not absolute, not all forms of expression are protected. Pornography, for example, is not protected by the First Amendment. Nor are utterances protected that would induce an immediate threat of violence or injury. Even within the context of protected speech, the Supreme Court has historically looked to the nature of the speech involved in determining the extent of the protection afforded.

Commercial speech, for example, is afforded less protection from government restriction than is noncommercial speech.

The lesser degree of protection means in practical terms that it is easier for government to show that the interest it seeks to promote by regulating the speech is more important than protecting the right of speech. But in balancing such conflicting rights and goals, value judgments must be made. For instance, should it make a difference that the speaker is a corporation? Or should the only issue be whether the speech is of a political nature? Is it fair to allow corporations to use their superior economic resources and marketing skills to influence politics? Although it is legal, some argue that it is unethical, particularly when a corporation's decision to allocate funds and influence legislation is motivated by self-interest (profit maximization) rather than by a concern for public welfare.

Privacy Rights in an Online World

Privacy rights are protected under constitutional law, tort law (see Chapter 12), and various federal and state statutes. How to protect privacy rights in an online world, though, has been a recurring question over the last ten years. One problem is that individuals today often cannot even know what kind of information on their personal lives and preferences is being collected by Internet companies and other online users. Nor can they know how that information will be used. "Cookies" installed in computers may allow users' Web movements to be tracked. Furthermore, any person who wants to purchase goods from online merchants or auctions inevitably must reveal some personal information, including (often) a credit-card number.

The Increased Value of Personal Information One of the major concerns of consumers in recent years has been the increasing value of personal information for online marketers, who are willing to pay a high price to those who collect and sell them such information. Because of these concerns—and the possibility of lawsuits based on privacy laws—businesses marketing goods online need to exercise care. Today, it is commonplace for an online business to create and post on its Web site a privacy policy disclosing how any information obtained from its customers will be used.

The Duty of Care and Personal Information Selling data can bolster a company's profits, which may satisfy the firm's duty to its owners, but when the information is personal, its sale may violate an ethical or legal duty. In what circumstances might a party who sells information about someone else have a duty to that other party with respect to the sale of the information?

Gradually, the courts are providing some answers to this question. In one case, for example, a man contacted an

Internet-based investigation and information service and requested information about Amy Boyer. The man provided his name, address, and phone number and paid the fee online using his credit card. In return, the company provided him with Boyer's home address, birth date, Social Security number, and work address. The man then drove to Boyer's workplace and fatally shot her, after which the police discovered that the man maintained a Web site that referred to stalking and killing Boyer. Boyer's mother filed suit against the company for disclosing her daughter's private information without investigating the reason for the request. The state supreme court found that because the threats of stalking and identity theft were sufficiently foreseeable, the company had a duty to exercise reasonable care in disclosing a third person's personal information to a client. [1]

Privacy Rights in the Workplace Another area of concern today is the extent to which employees' privacy rights should be protected in the workplace. Traditionally, employees have been afforded a certain "zone of privacy" in the workplace. For example, the courts have concluded that employees have a reasonable expectation of privacy with respect to personal items contained in their desks or in their lockers. Should this zone of privacy extend to personal e-mail sent via the employer's computer system as well? This question and others relating to employee privacy rights in today's cyber age will be discussed in greater detail in Chapter 20, in the context of employment relationships.

Should Civil Liberties Be Sacrificed to Control Cyber Crime?

Another issue that has come to the forefront in the cyber age is whether it is possible to control cyber crime without sacrificing some civil liberties. Governments in certain countries, such as Russia, have succeeded in controlling Internet crime to some extent by monitoring the e-mail and other electronic transmissions of users of specific Internet service providers. In the United States, however, any government attempt to monitor Internet use to detect criminal conspiracies or terrorist activities does not sit well with the American people. The traditional attitude has been that civil liberties must be safeguarded to the greatest extent feasible.

After the terrorist attacks in September 2001, Congress enacted legislation, including the USA Patriot Act. These statutes gave law enforcement personnel more authority to conduct electronic surveillance, such as monitoring Web sites and e-mail exchanges. For a time, it seemed that the terrorist attacks might have made Americans less reluctant to trade off some of their civil liberties for greater national security. Today,

though, many complain that this legislation has gone too far in curbing traditional civil liberties guaranteed by the U.S. Constitution. As the types of Internet crimes and torts continue to expand, determining the degree to which individuals should sacrifice personal freedoms in exchange for greater protection will likely become even more difficult.

Ethics and the Administrative Process

In Chapter 5 we noted some of the other constitutional protections that apply in the context of business. We looked in Chapter 6 at how some of those protections apply in the administrative process. As noted in Chapter 6, effective governmental regulation necessitates the gathering of relevant information. Often that information can be obtained only by an on-site inspection of business premises or a firsthand examination of business records. When regulatory needs conflict with constitutional principles, not only are legal issues raised, but ethical ones as well.

Recall that the Fourth Amendment protection from unreasonable searches and seizures applies in the context of business. Within the context of administrative law, this protection has been interpreted as requiring that information sought by a regulatory agency be relevant to the matter under scrutiny. Furthermore, any demand for information must be reasonably specific and not unduly burdensome to the business providing the information.

Regulation and Privacy Rights Despite acceptance of the need for regulators to gather information, an inherent conflict exists between the regulatory need for information and the individual's right of privacy. Specifically, how much latitude should be afforded to regulators in gathering information and overseeing private activities?

The United States Supreme Court has attempted to resolve the conflict by balancing the regulators' need to know against individual and corporate expectations of freedom from excessive government prying. An important consideration in resolving the conflict is the less intrusive nature of regulatory searches of businesses: most people simply do not have the same degree of concern about protecting places of business as they do about protecting the family dwelling. As a result, the standards for conducting regulatory investigations and searches are different from those that apply when ordinary police investigations and searches are conducted. For example, even though there may be no suspicion of a regulatory violation, an agency may conduct an investigation or search the premises of a business merely to be assured that no violation is occurring. Within industries subject to a history of extensive regulation, searches may be made even without a warrant. Still, though, as noted in Chapter 6, government is restricted in obtaining private information for regulatory purposes only.

---

1. *Remsburg v. Docusearch, Inc.*, 149 N.H. 148, 816 A.2d 1001 (2003).

The Ethics of Legal Avoidance In the face of an agency investigation, a business may prevent or delay agency efforts by asserting legal challenges to the nature or manner of the investigation. There remains, however, the question of whether—in an ethical rather than legal sense—a business should challenge any such investigation. We would be expected to challenge an unreasonable search of our homes. Regulatory investigations may be somehow different, though.

Most regulatory investigations have as their objective ensuring compliance with existing regulatory schemes or gathering information for future ones. Such schemes are designed to promote the public welfare. Though individuals may disagree about the effectiveness of the scheme or the individual motives of the regulators, society generally accepts the underlying purpose of the regulation—the promotion of public welfare. In such instances, businesses may have an ethical duty not to use legal means to avoid agency action. Indeed, they may have an ethical duty to aid in regulation by compliance, even though they may have a legal right to delay or avoid it.

Ethics and International Transactions

Conducting business internationally involves unique challenges, including, at times, ethical challenges. This is understandable, given that laws and cultures vary from one country to another. Consider the role of women. In the United States, equal employment opportunity is a fundamental public policy. This policy is clearly expressed in Title VII of the Civil Rights Act of 1964 (discussed in Chapter 21), which prohibits discrimination against women in the employment context. Some other countries, however, largely reject any professional role for women, which may cause difficulties for American women conducting business transactions in those countries. For example, when the World Bank sent a delegation that included women to negotiate with the Central Bank of Korea, the Koreans were surprised and offended. They thought that the presence of women meant that the Koreans were not being taken seriously.

There are also some important ethical differences among nations. In Islamic countries, for example, the consumption of alcohol and certain foods is forbidden by the Islamic religion. Thus, it would be thoughtless and imprudent to invite a Saudi Arabian business contact out for a drink. Additionally, in many foreign nations, gift giving is a common practice between contracting companies or between companies and government officials. To Americans, such gift giving may look suspiciously like an unethical (and possibly illegal) bribe. This has been an important source of friction in international business, particularly after the U.S. Congress passed the Foreign Corrupt Practices Act in 1977 (discussed in Chapters 4 and 7). This act prohibits U.S. business firms from offering certain side payments to foreign officials to secure favorable contracts.

DISCUSSION QUESTIONS

1. | You serve as chief executive officer of a large corporation. The state in which your company is headquartered has scheduled a statewide referendum on whether to allow casino gambling to be conducted within the state. Your company is in no way involved in gambling or in the sale of products used in the gaming industry, but you believe that evidence supports the inference that casino gambling, though potentially lucrative for those who operate the casinos, will hurt the state's economy. Some members of the board of directors have expressed similar concerns to you in casual conversation. Should you authorize the use of your company's resources to mount an opposition campaign to the proposal? Why or why not?

2. | What if, in the situation described in question 1, you knew of no conclusive evidence to support or refute the proposition that casino gambling will have an effect on the overall economy of the state? Nevertheless, you had a strong moral conviction that gambling was wrong. How would that change the ethical dimensions of the question of whether you should authorize the use of corporate resources to oppose the gambling initiative?

3. | The United States banned the pesticide DDT, primarily because of its adverse effects on wildlife. In Asia, however, DDT has been a critical component of the mosquito control necessary to combat malaria. Should the ban in the United States prevent U.S. firms from manufacturing DDT and shipping it to an Asian country, where it could be used to save lives? Why or why not?

4. | What are some of the ethical implications for businesspersons doing business internationally? Should a company refuse to send its women employees to represent the company in nations that reject professional roles for women? Should businesspersons traveling abroad always observe the cultural and religious customs of that location? Why or why not?

UNIT THREE
The Commercial Environment

CONTENTS

CHAPTER 9
Contract Formation

The noted legal scholar Roscoe Pound once said that "[t]he social order rests upon the stability and predictability of conduct, of which keeping promises is a large item."[1] Contract law deals with, among other things, the formation and keeping of promises. A **promise** is a person's assurance that the person will or will not do something.

Like other types of law, contract law reflects our social values, interests, and expectations at a given point in time. It shows, for example, to what extent our society allows people to make promises or commitments that are legally binding. It distinguishes between promises that create only *moral* obligations (such as a promise to take a friend to lunch) and promises that are legally binding (such as a promise to pay for merchandise purchased). Contract law also demonstrates what excuses our society accepts for breaking certain types of promises. In addition, it indicates what promises are considered to be contrary to public policy—against the interests of society as a whole—and therefore legally invalid. When the person making a promise is a child or is mentally incompetent, for example, a question will arise as to whether the promise should be enforced. Resolving such questions is the essence of contract law. The common law governs all contracts except when it has been modified or replaced by statutory law, such as the Uniform Commercial Code (UCC),[2] or by administrative agency regulations. Contracts relating to services, real estate, employment, and insurance, for example, generally are governed by the common law of contracts.

Contracts for the sale and lease of goods, however, are governed by the UCC—to the extent that the UCC has modified general contract law. The relationship between general contract law and the law governing sales and leases of goods will be explored in detail in Chapter 11. In the discussion of general contract law that follows, we indicate in footnotes the areas in which the UCC has significantly altered common law contract principles.

SECTION 1 | The Function and Definition of Contract Law

The law encourages competent parties to form contracts for lawful objectives. Indeed, no aspect of modern life is entirely free of contractual relationships. Even the ordinary consumer in his or her daily activities acquires rights and obligations based on contract law. You acquire rights and obligations, for example, when you purchase a DVD or when you borrow funds to buy a house. Contract law is designed to provide stability and predictability, as well as certainty, for both buyers and sellers in the marketplace.

Contract law deals with, among other things, the formation and enforcement of agreements between parties (in Latin, *pacta sunt servanda*—"agreements shall be kept"). By supplying procedures for enforcing private contractual agreements, contract law provides an essential condition for the existence of a market economy. Without a legal framework of reasonably assured expectations within which to plan and venture, businesspersons would be able to rely only on the

---

1. R. Pound, *Jurisprudence*, Vol. 3 (St. Paul: West Publishing Co., 1959), p. 162.
2. See Chapters 1 and 11 for further discussions of the significance and coverage of the UCC. Excerpts from the UCC are presented in Appendix C at the end of this book.

good faith of others. Duty and good faith are usually sufficient to obtain compliance with a promise, but when price changes or adverse economic factors make compliance costly, these elements may not be enough. Contract law is necessary to ensure compliance with a promise or to entitle the innocent party to some form of relief.

A **contract** is "a promise or a set of promises for the breach of which the law gives a remedy, or the performance of which the law in some way recognizes as a duty."[3] Put simply, a contract is a legally binding agreement between two or more parties who agree to perform or to refrain from performing some act now or in the future. Generally, contract disputes arise when there is a promise of future performance. If the contractual promise is not fulfilled, the party who made it is subject to the sanctions of a court (see Chapter 10). That party may be required to pay damages for failing to perform the contractual promise; in limited instances, the party may be required to perform the promised act.

In determining whether a contract has been formed, the element of intent is of prime importance. In contract law, intent is determined by what is called the *objective theory of contracts*, not by the personal or subjective intent, or belief, of a party. The theory is that a party's intention to enter into a legally binding agreement, or contract, is judged by outward, objective facts as interpreted by a *reasonable* person, rather than by the party's own secret, subjective intentions. Objective facts include (1) what the party said when entering into the contract, (2) how the party acted or appeared (intent may be manifested by conduct as well as by oral or written words), and (3) the circumstances surrounding the transaction. We will look further at the objective theory of contracts later in this chapter, in the context of contract formation.

SECTION 2 | Elements of a Contract

The many topics that will be discussed in these chapters on contract law require an understanding of the basic elements of a valid contract and the way in which a contract is created. These topics also require an understanding of the types of circumstances in which even legally valid contracts will not be enforced.

REQUIREMENTS OF A VALID CONTRACT

The following list briefly describes the four requirements that must be met before a valid contract exists. If any of these elements is lacking, no contract will have been formed. (Each requirement will be explained more fully later in this chapter.)

1. *Agreement.* An agreement to form a contract includes an *offer* and an *acceptance.* One party must offer to enter into a legal agreement, and another party must accept the terms of the offer.
2. *Consideration.* Any promises made by the parties to the contract must be supported by legally sufficient and bargained-for *consideration* (something of value received or promised, such as money, to convince a person to make a deal).
3. *Contractual capacity.* Both parties entering into the contract must have the contractual *capacity* to do so; the law must recognize them as possessing characteristics that qualify them as competent parties.
4. *Legality.* The contract's purpose must be to accomplish some goal that is legal and not against public policy.

DEFENSES TO THE ENFORCEABILITY OF A CONTRACT

Even if all of the above-listed requirements are satisfied, a contract may be unenforceable if the following requirements are not met. These requirements typically are raised as *defenses* to the enforceability of an otherwise valid contract.

1. *Genuineness of assent.* The apparent consent of both parties must be genuine. For example, if a contract was formed as a result of fraud, undue influence, mistake, or duress, the contract may not be enforceable.
2. *Form.* The contract must be in whatever form the law requires; for example, some contracts must be in writing to be enforceable.

SECTION 3 | Types of Contracts

There are many types of contracts. In this section, you will learn that contracts can be categorized based on legal distinctions as to formation, performance, and enforceability.

---

3. *Restatement (Second) of Contracts.* The *Restatement of the Law of Contracts* is a nonstatutory, authoritative exposition of the common law of contracts compiled by the American Law Institute in 1932. The *Restatement,* which is now in its second edition (a third edition is being drafted), will be referred to throughout this chapter on contract law.

CONTRACT FORMATION

As you can see in Exhibit 9–1, three classifications, or categories, of contracts are based on how and when a contract is formed. We explain each of these types of contracts in the following subsections.

BILATERAL VERSUS UNILATERAL CONTRACTS

Every contract involves at least two parties. The *offeror* is the party making the offer. The *offeree* is the party to whom the offer is made. Whether the contract is classified as *unilateral* or *bilateral* depends on what the offeree must do to accept the offer and to bind the offeror to a contract.

—Bilateral Contracts. If to accept the offer the offeree must only *promise* to perform, the contract is a *bilateral contract*. Hence, a bilateral contract is a "promise for a promise." No performance, such as payment of money or delivery of goods, need take place for a bilateral contract to be formed. The contract comes into existence at the moment the promises are exchanged.

For example, Jeff offers to buy Ann's digital camera for $200. Jeff tells Ann that he will give her the money for the camera next Friday, when he gets paid. Ann accepts Jeff's offer and promises to give him the camera when he pays her on Friday. Jeff and Ann have formed a bilateral contract.

—Unilateral Contracts. If the offer is phrased so that the offeree can accept the offer only by completing the contract performance, the contract is a *unilateral contract*. Hence, a unilateral contract is a "promise for an act."[4] In other words, the time of contract formation in a unilateral contract is not at the moment when promises are exchanged but when the contract is *performed*. A classic example of a unilateral contract is as follows: O'Malley says to Parker, "If you carry this package across the Brooklyn Bridge, I'll give you $20." Only on Parker's complete crossing with the package does she fully accept O'Malley's offer to pay $20. If she chooses not to undertake the walk, there are no legal consequences.

Contests, lotteries, and other competitions involving prizes are examples of offers to form unilateral contracts. If a person complies with the rules of the contest—such as by submitting the right lottery number at the right place and time—a unilateral contract is formed, binding the organization offering the prize to a contract to perform as promised in the offer.

Can a school's or an employer's letter of tentative acceptance to a prospective student or employee qualify as a unilateral contract? That was the question in the following case.

---

4. Clearly, a contract cannot be "one sided," because by definition, an agreement implies the existence of two or more parties. Therefore, the phrase *unilateral contract*, if read literally, is a contradiction in terms. As traditionally used in contract law, however, the phrase refers to the kind of contract that results when only one promise is being made (the promise made by the offeror in return for the offeree's performance).

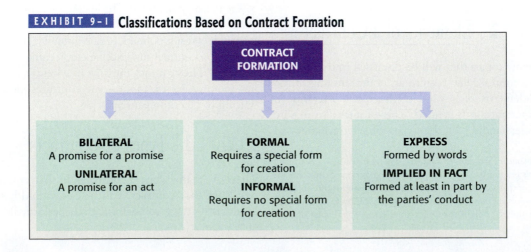

EXHIBIT 9-1 Classifications Based on Contract Formation

CONTRACT FORMATION

BILATERAL
A promise for a promise
UNILATERAL
A promise for an act

FORMAL
Requires a special form for creation
INFORMAL
Requires no special form for creation

EXPRESS
Formed by words
IMPLIED IN FACT
Formed at least in part by the parties' conduct

CASE 9.1

Ardito v. City of Providence

United States
District Court,
District of
Rhode Island, 2003.
263 F.Supp.2d 358.

BACKGROUND AND FACTS *In 2001, the city of Providence, Rhode Island, decided to begin hiring police officers to fill vacancies in its police department. Because only individuals who had graduated from the Providence Police Academy were eligible, the city also decided to conduct two training sessions, the "60th and 61st Police Academies." To be admitted, an applicant had to pass a series of tests and be deemed qualified by members of the department after an interview. The applicants judged most qualified were sent a letter informing them that they had been selected to attend the academy if they successfully completed a medical checkup and a psychological examination. The letter for the applicants to the 61st Academy, dated October 15, stated that it was "a conditional offer of employment." Meanwhile, a new chief of police, Dean Esserman, decided to revise the selection process, which caused some of those who had received the letter to be rejected. Derek Ardito and thirteen other newly rejected applicants—who had all completed the examinations—filed a suit in a federal district court against the city, seeking a halt to the 61st Academy unless they were allowed to attend. They alleged in part that the city was in breach of contract.*

IN THE LANGUAGE OF THE COURT

ERNEST C. TORRES, Chief District Judge.

* * * *

* * * [T]he October 15 letter * * * *is a classic example of an offer to enter into a unilateral contract.* The October 15 letter expressly stated that it was a "conditional offer of employment" and the message that it conveyed was that the recipient would be admitted into the 61st Academy if he or she successfully completed the medical and psychological examinations, requirements that the city could not lawfully impose unless it was making a conditional offer of employment. [Emphasis added.]

Moreover, the terms of that offer were perfectly consistent with what applicants had been told when they appeared [for their interviews]. At that time, [Police Major Dennis] Simoneau informed them that, if they "passed" the [interviews], they would be offered a place in the academy provided that they also passed medical and psychological examinations.

The October 15 letter also was in marked contrast to notices sent to applicants by the city at earlier stages of the selection process. Those notices merely informed applicants that they had completed a step in the process and remained eligible to be considered for admission into the academy. Unlike the October 15 letter, the prior notices did not purport to extend a "conditional offer" of admission.

The plaintiffs accepted the city's offer of admission into the academy by satisfying the specified conditions. Each of the plaintiffs submitted to and passed lengthy and intrusive medical and psychological examinations. In addition, many of the plaintiffs, in reliance on the City's offer, jeopardized their standing with their existing employers by notifying the employers of their anticipated departure, and some plaintiffs passed up opportunities for other employment.

* * * *

The city argues that there is no contract between the parties because the plaintiffs have no legally enforceable right to employment. The city correctly points out that, even if the plaintiffs graduate from the Academy and there are existing vacancies in the department, they would be required to serve a one-year probationary period during which they could be terminated without cause * * * . That argument misses the point. The contract that the plaintiffs seek to enforce is not a contract that they will be appointed as permanent Providence police officers; rather, it is a contract that they would be admitted to the Academy if they passed the medical and psychological examinations.

DECISION AND REMEDY *The court issued an injunction to prohibit the city from conducting the 61st Police Academy unless the plaintiffs were included. The October 15 letter was a unilateral offer that the plaintiffs had accepted by passing the required medical and psychological examinations.*

CONTINUED ▶

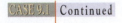 **Continued**

WHAT IF THE FACTS WERE DIFFERENT? *Suppose that the October 15 letter had used the phrase* potential offer of employment *instead of using the word* conditional. *Would the court in this case still have considered the letter to be a unilateral contract? Why or why not?*

—Problems with Unilateral Contracts. A problem arises in unilateral contracts when the *promisor* (the one making the promise) attempts to *revoke* (cancel) the offer after the *promisee* (the one to whom the promise was made) has begun performance but before the act has been completed. The promisee can accept the offer only on full performance, and under traditional contract principles, an offer may be revoked at any time before the offer is accepted. The present-day view, however, is that an offer to form a unilateral contract becomes irrevocable—cannot be revoked—once performance has begun. Thus, even though the offer has not yet been accepted, the offeror is prohibited from revoking it for a reasonable time period.

For instance, in the earlier example involving the Brooklyn Bridge, suppose that Parker is walking across the bridge and has only three yards to go when O'Malley calls out to her, "I revoke my offer." Under traditional contract law, O'Malley's revocation would terminate the offer. Under the modern view of unilateral contracts, however, O'Malley will not be able to revoke his offer because Parker has undertaken performance and walked all but three yards of the bridge. In these circumstances, Parker can finish crossing the bridge and bind O'Malley to the contract.

FORMAL VERSUS INFORMAL CONTRACTS Another classification system divides contracts into formal contracts and informal contracts. *Formal contracts* are contracts that require a special form or method of creation (formation) to be enforceable. One type of formal contract is the *contract under seal,* a formalized writing with a special seal attached. The seal may be actual (made of wax or some other durable substance) or impressed on the paper or indicated simply by the word *seal* or the letters *L.S.* at the end of the document. *L.S.* stands for *locus sigilli* and means "the place for the seal."[5]

A written contract may be considered sealed if the promisor *adopts* a seal already on it. A standard-form contract purchased at the local office supply store, for example, may have the word *seal* (or something else

that qualifies as a seal) printed next to the blanks intended for the signatures. Unless the parties who sign the form indicate a contrary intention, when they sign the form, they adopt the seal.

Informal contracts include all other contracts. Such contracts are also called *simple contracts.* No special form is required (except for certain types of contracts that must be in writing), as the contracts are usually based on their substance rather than their form. Typically, businesspersons put their contracts in writing to ensure that there is some proof of a contract's existence should problems arise.

EXPRESS VERSUS IMPLIED-IN-FACT CONTRACTS
Contracts may also be categorized as *express* or *implied* by the conduct of the parties. We look here at the differences between these two types of contracts.

—Express Contracts. In an *express contract*, the terms of the agreement are fully and explicitly stated in words, oral or written. A signed lease for an apartment or a house is an express written contract. If a classmate calls you on the phone and agrees to buy your textbook from last semester for $45, an express oral contract has been made.

—Implied-in-Fact Contracts. A contract that is implied from the conduct of the parties is called an *implied-in-fact contract* or an implied contract. This type of contract differs from an express contract in that the *conduct* of the parties, rather than their words, creates and defines the terms of the contract. (Note that a contract may be a mixture of an express contract and an implied-in-fact contract. In other words, a contract may contain some express terms, while others are implied.)

—Requirements for Implied-in-Fact Contracts. For an implied-in-fact contract to arise, certain requirements must be met. Normally, if the following conditions exist, a court will hold that an implied contract was formed:

1. The plaintiff furnished some service or property.
2. The plaintiff expected to be paid for that service or property, and the defendant knew or should have known that payment was expected.
3. The defendant had a chance to reject the services or property and did not.

---

5. The contract under seal has been almost entirely abolished under such provisions as UCC 2–203 (Section 2–203 of the UCC). In sales of real estate, however, it is still common to use a seal (or an acceptable substitute).

For example, suppose that you need an accountant to complete your tax return this year. You look through the Yellow Pages and find an accountant at an office in your neighborhood, so you drop by to see her. You go into the accountant's office and explain your problem, and she tells you what her fees are. The next day you return and give her administrative assistant all the necessary information and documents—canceled checks, W-2 forms, and so on. You then walk out the door without saying anything expressly to the assistant. In this situation, you have entered into an implied-in-fact contract to pay the accountant the usual and reasonable fees for her services. The contract is implied by your conduct and by hers. She expects to be paid for completing your tax return, and by bringing in the records she will need to do the work, you have implied an intent to pay her.

CONTRACT PERFORMANCE

Contracts are also classified according to the degree to which they have been performed. A contract that has been fully performed on both sides is called an *executed contract*. A contract that has not been fully performed by the parties is called an *executory contract*. If one party has fully performed but the other has not, the contract is said to be executed on the one side and executory on the other, but the contract is still classified as executory.

For example, assume that you agree to buy ten tons of coal from the Northern Coal Company. Further assume that Northern has delivered the coal to your steel mill, where it is now being burned. At this point, the contract is executed on the part of Northern and executory on your part. After you pay Northern for the coal, the contract will be executed on both sides.

CONTRACT ENFORCEABILITY

A *valid contract* has the elements necessary to entitle at least one of the parties to enforce it in court. Those elements, as mentioned earlier, consist of (1) an agreement consisting of an offer and an acceptance of that offer, (2) supported by legally sufficient consideration, (3) made by parties who have the legal capacity to enter into the contract, and (4) made for a legal purpose. As you can see in Exhibit 9–2, valid contracts may be enforceable, voidable, or unenforceable. Additionally, a contract may be referred to as a *void contract*. We look next at the meaning of the terms *voidable*, *unenforceable*, and *void* in relation to contract enforceability.

VOIDABLE CONTRACTS A *voidable contract* is a valid contract but one that can be avoided at the option of one or both of the parties. The party having the option can elect either to avoid any duty to perform or to *ratify* (make valid) the contract. If the contract is avoided,

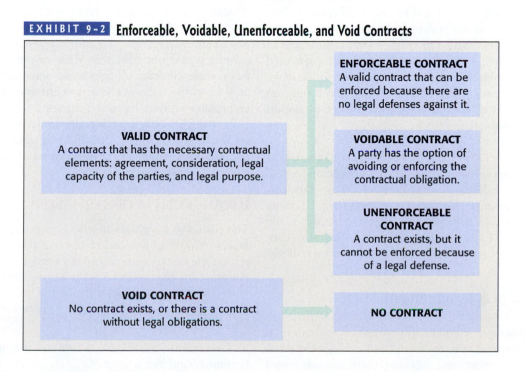

EXHIBIT 9-2 Enforceable, Voidable, Unenforceable, and Void Contracts

VALID CONTRACT
A contract that has the necessary contractual elements: agreement, consideration, legal capacity of the parties, and legal purpose.

ENFORCEABLE CONTRACT
A valid contract that can be enforced because there are no legal defenses against it.

VOIDABLE CONTRACT
A party has the option of avoiding or enforcing the contractual obligation.

UNENFORCEABLE CONTRACT
A contract exists, but it cannot be enforced because of a legal defense.

VOID CONTRACT
No contract exists, or there is a contract without legal obligations.

NO CONTRACT

CONCEPT SUMMARY 9.1 | Types of Contracts

ASPECT	DEFINITION
FORMATION	1. *Bilateral*—A promise for a promise. 2. *Unilateral*—A promise for an act (acceptance is the completed performance of the act). 3. *Formal*—Requires a special form for creation. 4. *Informal*—Requires no special form for creation. 5. *Express*—Formed by words (oral, written, or a combination). 6. *Implied in fact*—Formed by the conduct of the parties.
PERFORMANCE	1. *Executed*—A fully performed contract. 2. *Executory*—A contract not fully performed.
ENFORCEABILITY	1. *Valid*—The contract has the necessary contractual elements: agreement (offer and acceptance), consideration, legal capacity of the parties, and legal purpose. 2. *Voidable*—One party has the option of avoiding or enforcing the contractual obligation. 3. *Unenforceable*—A contract exists, but it cannot be enforced because of a legal defense. 4. *Void*—No contract exists, or there is a contract without legal obligations.

both parties are released from it. If it is ratified, both parties must fully perform their respective legal obligations.

As a general rule, but subject to exceptions, contracts made by minors are voidable at the option of the minor. Contracts entered into under fraudulent conditions are voidable at the option of the defrauded party. In addition, contracts entered into under duress or undue influence are voidable.

UNENFORCEABLE CONTRACTS An *unenforceable contract* is one that cannot be enforced because of certain legal defenses against it. It is not unenforceable because a party failed to satisfy a legal requirement of the contract; rather, it is a valid contract rendered unenforceable by some statute or law. For example, certain contracts must be in writing, and if they are not, they will not be enforceable except in certain exceptional circumstances.

VOID CONTRACTS. A *void contract* is no contract at all. The terms *void* and *contract* are contradictory. A void contract produces no legal obligations on any of the parties. For example, a contract can be void because one of the parties was adjudged by a court to be legally insane (and thus lacked the legal capacity to enter into a contract) or because the purpose of the contract was illegal.

SECTION 4 | Agreement

An essential element for contract formation is **agreement**—that is, the parties must agree on the terms of the contract and manifest their **mutual assent** (agreement) to the same bargain. Ordinarily, agreement is evidenced by two events: an *offer* and an *acceptance*. One party offers a certain bargain to another party, who then accepts that bargain. The agreement does not necessarily have to be in writing. Both parties, however, must manifest their assent to the same bargain. Once an agreement is reached, if the other elements of a contract are present (consideration, capacity, and legality, which will be discussed later in this chapter), a valid contract is formed, generally creating enforceable rights and duties between the parties.

Note that not all agreements are contracts. John and Kevin may agree to play golf on a certain day, but a court would not hold that their agreement is an enforceable contract. A *contractual* agreement arises only when the terms of the agreement impose legally enforceable obligations on the parties.

In today's world, contracts are frequently formed via the Internet. Online offers and acceptances will be discussed in Chapter 11, in the context of electronic contracts, or e-contracts.

REQUIREMENTS OF THE OFFER

The parties to a contract are the *offeror*, the one who makes an offer or proposal to another party, and the *offeree*, the one to whom the offer or proposal is made. An **offer** is a promise or commitment to do or refrain from doing some specified thing in the future. Under the common law, three elements are necessary for an offer to be effective:

1. The offeror must have a serious intention to become bound by the offer.

2. The terms of the offer must be reasonably certain, or definite, so that the parties and the court can ascertain the terms of the contract.

3. The offer must be communicated by the offeror to the offeree, resulting in the offeree's knowledge of the offer.

Once an effective offer has been made, the offeree has the power to accept the offer. If the offeree accepts, an agreement is formed (and thus a contract arises, if other essential elements are present).

INTENTION   The first requirement for an effective offer is a serious intent on the part of the offeror. Serious intent is not determined by the *subjective* intentions, beliefs, and assumptions of the offeror. As discussed in Section 1, courts generally adhere to the *objective theory of contracts* in determining whether a contract has been formed. Under this theory, a party's words and conduct are held to mean whatever a reasonable person in the offeree's position would think they meant.

Offers made in obvious anger, jest, or undue excitement do not meet the intent test because a reasonable person would realize that a serious offer was not being made. Because these offers are not effective, an offeree's acceptance does not create an agreement. For example, suppose that you and three classmates ride to school each day in Davina's new automobile, which has a market value of $20,000. One cold morning, the four of you get into the car, but Davina cannot get the car started. She yells in anger, "I'll sell this car to anyone for $500!" You drop $500 in her lap. Given these facts, a reasonable person, taking into consideration Davina's frustration and the obvious difference in worth between the market value of the car and the proposed purchase price, would declare that her offer was not made with serious intent and that you did not have an agreement.

The concept of intention can be further clarified through an examination of the types of expressions and statements that are *not* offers. We look at these expressions and statements in the subsections that follow. In the classic case of *Lucy v. Zehmer*, presented below, the court considered whether an offer made "after a few drinks" met the serious-intent requirement.

CASE 9.2   ## Lucy v. Zehmer

Supreme Court of
Appeals of Virginia, 1954.
196 Va. 493,
84 S.E.2d 516.

BACKGROUND AND FACTS   *W. O. Lucy and J. C. Lucy, the plaintiffs, filed a suit against A. H. Zehmer and Ida Zehmer, the defendants, to compel the Zehmers to transfer title of their property, known as the Ferguson Farm, to the Lucys for $50,000, as the Zehmers had allegedly agreed to do. Lucy had known Zehmer for fifteen or twenty years and for the last eight years or so had been anxious to buy the Ferguson Farm from Zehmer. One night, Lucy stopped in to visit the Zehmers in the combination restaurant, filling station, and motor court they operated. While there, Lucy tried to buy the Ferguson Farm once again. This time he tried a new approach. According to the trial court transcript, Lucy said to Zehmer, "I bet you wouldn't take $50,000 for that place." Zehmer replied, "Yes, I would too; you wouldn't give fifty." Throughout the evening, the conversation returned to the sale of the Ferguson Farm for $50,000. At the same time, the parties continued to drink whiskey and engage in light conversation. Eventually, Lucy enticed Zehmer to write up an agreement to the effect that Zehmer would sell to Lucy the Ferguson Farm for $50,000. Later, Lucy sued Zehmer to compel him to go through with the sale. Zehmer argued that he had been drunk and that the offer had been made in jest and hence was unenforceable. The trial court agreed with Zehmer, and Lucy appealed.*

IN THE LANGUAGE OF THE COURT

BUCHANAN, J. [Justice] delivered the opinion of the court.
* * * *

In his testimony, Zehmer claimed that he "was high as a Georgia pine," and that the transaction "was just a bunch of two doggoned drunks bluffing to see who could talk the biggest and say the most." That claim is inconsistent with his attempt to testify in great detail as to what was said and what was done. * * *

* * * *

CONTINUED ▶

CASE 9.2 | Continued

The appearance of the contract, the fact that it was under discussion for forty minutes or more before it was signed; Lucy's objection to the first draft because it was written in the singular, and he wanted Mrs. Zehmer to sign it also; the rewriting to meet that objection and the signing by Mrs. Zehmer; the discussion of what was to be included in the sale, the provision for the examination of the title, the completeness of the instrument that was executed, the taking possession of it by Lucy with no request or suggestion by either of the defendants that he give it back, are facts which furnish persuasive evidence that the execution of the contract was a serious business transaction rather than a casual, jesting matter as defendants now contend.

* * * *

In the field of contracts, as generally elsewhere, *[w]e must look to the outward expression of a person as manifesting his intention rather than to his secret and unexpressed intention.* The law imputes to a person an intention corresponding to the reasonable meaning of his words and acts. [Emphasis added.]

* * * *

Whether the writing signed by the defendants and now sought to be enforced by the complainants was the result of a serious offer by Lucy and a serious acceptance by the defendants, or was a serious offer by Lucy and an acceptance in secret jest by the defendants, in either event it constituted a binding contract of sale between the parties.

DECISION AND REMEDY *The Supreme Court of Virginia determined that the writing was an enforceable contract and reversed the ruling of the lower court. The Zehmers were required by court order to follow through with the sale of the Ferguson Farm to the Lucys.*

WHAT IF THE FACTS WERE DIFFERENT? *Suppose that the day after Lucy purchased the farm, he decided that he didn't want it after all, and Zehmer sued Lucy to perform the contract. Would this change in the facts alter the court's decision that Lucy and Zehmer had created an enforceable contract?*

IMPACT OF THIS CASE ON TODAY'S LAW

This is a classic case in contract law because it illustrates so clearly the objective theory of contracts with respect to determining whether a serious offer was intended. Today, the objective theory of contracts continues to be applied by the courts, and *Lucy v. Zehmer* is routinely cited as a significant precedent in this area.

—Expressions of Opinion. An expression of opinion is not an offer. It does not evidence an intention to enter into a binding agreement. Consider an example. Hawkins took his son to McGee, a physician, and asked McGee to operate on the son's hand. McGee said that the boy would be in the hospital three or four days and that the hand would *probably* heal a few days later. The son's hand did not heal for a month, but the father did not win a suit for breach of contract. The court held that McGee had not made an offer to heal the son's hand in a few days. He had merely expressed an opinion as to when the hand would heal.[6]

—Statements of Future Intent. If Arif says, "I *plan* to sell my stock in Novation, Inc., for $150 per

share," a contract is not created if John "accepts" and tenders the $150 per share for the stock. Arif has merely expressed his intention to enter into a future contract for the sale of the stock. If John accepts and tenders the $150 per share, no contract is formed because a reasonable person would conclude that Arif was only *thinking about* selling his stock, not *promising* to sell it.

—Preliminary Negotiations. A request or invitation to negotiate is not an offer. It only expresses a willingness to discuss the possibility of entering into a contract. Included are statements such as "Will you sell Blythe Estate?" or "I wouldn't sell my car for less than $5,000." A reasonable person in the offeree's position would not conclude that these statements evidenced an intention to enter into a binding obliga-

---

6. *Hawkins v. McGee*, 84 N.H. 114, 146 A. 641 (1929).

tion. Likewise, when the government or private firms require construction work, they invite contractors to submit bids. The *invitation* to submit bids is not an offer, and a contractor does not bind the government or private firm by submitting a bid. (The bids that the contractors submit are offers, however, and the government or private firm can bind the contractor by accepting the bid.)

—**Agreements to Agree.** During preliminary negotiations, the parties may form an agreement to agree to a material term of a contract at some future date. Traditionally, such "agreements to agree" were not considered to be binding contracts. More recent cases illustrate the view that agreements to agree serve valid commercial purposes and can be enforced if the parties clearly intended to be bound by such agreements.

For example, suppose Zahn Consulting leases office space from Leon Properties, Inc. Their lease agreement includes a clause permitting Zahn to extend the lease at an amount of rent to be agreed on at the time the lease is extended. Under the traditional rule, because the amount of rent is not specified in the lease clause itself, the clause would be too indefinite in its terms to enforce. Under the current view, a court could hold that the parties intended the future rent to be a reasonable amount and could enforce the clause.[7] In other words, under the modern view, the emphasis is on the parties' intent rather than on form. (For a further discussion of this issue, see this chapter's *Emerging Trends* feature on pages 204 and 205.)

—**Advertisements.** In general, advertisements— including representations made in mail-order catalogues, price lists, and circulars—are treated not as offers to contract but as invitations to negotiate. Suppose that Loeser advertises a used paving machine. The ad is mailed to hundreds of firms and reads, "Used Loeser Construction Co. paving machine. Builds curbs and finishes cement work all in one process. Price: $42,350." If Star Paving calls Loeser and says, "We accept your offer," no contract is formed. Any reasonable person would conclude that Loeser was not promising to sell the paving machine but rather was soliciting offers to buy it. If such an ad were held to constitute a legal offer, and fifty people accepted the offer, there would be no

way for Loeser to perform all fifty of the resulting contracts. He would have to breach forty-nine contracts. Obviously, the law seeks to avoid such unfairness.

Price lists are another form of invitation to negotiate or trade. A seller's price list is not an offer to sell at that price; it merely invites the buyer to offer to buy at that price. In fact, the seller usually puts "prices subject to change" on the price list. Only in rare circumstances will a price quotation be construed as an offer.[8]

Although most advertisements and the like are treated as invitations to negotiate, this does not mean that an advertisement can never be an offer. If the advertisement makes a promise so definite in character that it is apparent that the offeror is binding himself or herself to the conditions stated, the advertisement is treated as an offer.[9]

DEFINITENESS OF TERMS The second requirement for an effective offer involves the definiteness of its terms. An offer must have terms that are reasonably definite so that, if it is accepted and a contract formed, a court can determine if a breach has occurred and can provide an appropriate remedy. The specific terms required depend, of course, on the type of contract. Generally, a contract must include the following terms, either expressed in the contract or capable of being reasonably inferred from it:

1. The identification of the parties.
2. The identification of the object or subject matter of the contract (also the quantity, when appropriate), including the work to be performed, with specific identification of such items as goods, services, and land.
3. The consideration to be paid.
4. The time of payment, delivery, or performance.

An offer may invite an acceptance to be worded in such specific terms that the contract is made definite. For example, suppose that Marcus Business Machines contacts your corporation and offers to sell "from one to ten MacCool copying machines for $1,600 each; state number desired in acceptance." Your corporation agrees to buy two copiers. Because the quantity is specified in the acceptance, the terms are definite, and the contract is enforceable.

Courts sometimes are willing to supply a missing term in a contract when the parties have clearly

---

7. *Restatement (Second) of Contracts*, Section 33. See also Sections 2–204 and 2–305 of the UCC.

8. See, for example, *Fairmount Glass Works v. Crunden-Martin Woodenware Co.*, 106 Ky. 659, 51 S.W. 196 (1899).

9. See, for example, *Lefkowitz v. Great Minneapolis Surplus Store, Inc.*, 251 Minn. 188, 86 N.W.2d 689 (1957).

manifested an intent to form a contract. If, in contrast, the parties have attempted to deal with a particular term of the contract but their expression of intent is too vague or uncertain to be given any precise meaning, the court will not supply a "reasonable" term because to do so might conflict with the intent of the parties. In other words, the court will not rewrite the contract.[10] The following case illustrates this point.

10. See Chapter 11 and UCC 2–204. Article 2 of the UCC specifies different rules relating to the definiteness of terms used in a contract for the sale of goods. In essence, Article 2 modifies general contract law by requiring less specificity.

CASE 9.3   Baer v. Chase

United States
Court of Appeals,
Third Circuit, 2004.
392 F.3d 609.

GREENBERG, Circuit Judge.
* * * *
[David] Chase, who originally was from New Jersey, but relocated to Los Angeles in 1971, is the creator, producer, writer and director of *The Sopranos*. Chase has numerous credits for other television productions as well. * * * Chase had worked on a number of projects involving organized crime activities based in New Jersey, including a script for "a mob boss in therapy," a concept that, in part, would become the basis for *The Sopranos*.

In 1995, Chase was producing and directing a *Rockford Files* "movie-of-the-week" when he met Joseph Urbancyk who was working on the set as a camera operator and temporary director of photography. * * *

[Through Urbancyk, Chase met Robert] Baer, * * * a New Jersey attorney [who] recently had left his employment in the Union County Prosecutor's Office in Elizabeth, New Jersey, where he had worked for the previous six years.
* * * *
Chase, Urbancyk, and Baer met for lunch on June 20, 1995 * * *, with Baer describing his experience as a prosecutor. Baer also pitched the idea to shoot "a film or television shows about the New Jersey Mafia." At that time Baer was unaware of Chase's previous work involving mob activity premised in New Jersey. At the lunch there was no reference to any payment that Chase might make to Baer for the latter's services * * *.

In October 1995, Chase visited New Jersey for three days. During this "research visit" Baer arranged meetings for Chase with Detective Thomas Koczur, Detective Robert A. Jones, and Tony Spirito who provided Chase with information, material, and personal stories about their experiences with organized crime. * * * Baer does not dispute that virtually all of the ideas and locations that he "contributed" to Chase existed in the public record.

After returning to Los Angeles, Chase sent Baer a copy of a draft of a *Sopranos* screenplay that he had written, which was dated December 20, 1995. Baer asserts that after he read it he called Chase and made various comments with regard to it. Baer claims that the two spoke at least four times during the following year and that he sent a letter to Chase dated February 10, 1997, discussing *The Sopranos* script. * * *
* * * *
Baer asserts that he and Chase orally agreed on three separate occasions that if the show became a success, Chase would "take care of" Baer, and "remunerate Baer in a manner commensurate to the true value of his services." * * *

Baer claims that on each of these occasions the parties had the same conversation in which Chase offered to pay Baer, stating "you help me; I pay you." Baer always rejected Chase's offer, reasoning that Chase would be unable to pay him "for the true value of the services Baer was rendering." Each time Baer rejected Chase's offer he did so with a counteroffer, "that I would perform the services while assuming the risk that if the show failed Chase would owe me nothing. If, however, the show succeeded he would remunerate me in a manner commensurate to the true value of my services." Baer acknowledges that this counteroffer * * * always was oral and did not include any fixed term of duration or price. * * * In fact, Chase has not paid Baer for his services.

CASE 9.3 | Continued

On or about May 15, 2002, Baer filed a * * * complaint against Chase in [a federal] district court * * * [claiming among other things] * * * breach of implied contract. Eventually Chase brought a motion for summary judgment * * * . Chase claimed that the alleged contract * * * [was] too vague, ambiguous and lacking in essential terms to be enforced * * * .

The district court granted Chase's motion * * * .
* * * *

Baer predicates [bases] his contract claim on this appeal on an implied-in-fact contract * * * . The issue with respect to the implied-in-fact contract claim concerns whether Chase and Baer entered into an enforceable contract for services Baer rendered that aided in the creation and production of *The Sopranos*. * * *
* * * *

* * * [A] contract arises from offer and acceptance, and must be sufficiently definite so that the performance to be rendered by each party can be ascertained with reasonable certainty. Therefore parties create an enforceable contract when they agree on its essential terms and manifest an intent that the terms bind them. *If parties to an agreement do not agree on one or more essential terms of the purported agreement, courts generally hold it to be unenforceable.* [Emphasis added.]
* * * *

* * * [The] law deems the price term, *i.e.*, the amount of compensation, an essential term of any contract. An agreement lacking definiteness of price, however, is not unenforceable if the parties specify a practicable method by which they can determine the amount. However, *in the absence of an agreement as to the manner or method of determining compensation the purported agreement is invalid.* Additionally, *the duration of the contract is deemed an essential term and therefore any agreement must be sufficiently definitive to allow a court to determine the agreed upon length of the contractual relationship.* [Emphasis added.]
* * * *

The * * * question with respect to Baer's contract claim, therefore, is whether his contract is enforceable in light of the traditional requirement of definitiveness * * * . A contract may be expressed in writing, or orally, or in acts, or partly in one of these ways and partly in others. There is a point, however, at which interpretation becomes alteration. In this case, even when all of the parties' verbal and non-verbal actions are aggregated and viewed most favorably to Baer, we cannot find a contract that is distinct and definitive enough to be enforceable.

Nothing in the record indicates that the parties agreed on how, how much, where, or for what period Chase would compensate Baer. The parties did not discuss who would determine the "true value" of Baer's services, when the "true value" would be calculated, or what variables would go into such a calculation. There was no discussion or agreement as to the meaning of "success" of *The Sopranos*. There was no discussion how "profits" were to be defined. There was no contemplation of dates of commencement or termination of the contract. And again, nothing in Baer's or Chase's conduct, or the surrounding circumstances of the relationship, shed light on, or answers, any of these questions. The district court was correct in its description of the contract between the parties: "The contract as articulated by the Plaintiff lacks essential terms, and is vague, indefinite and uncertain; no version of the alleged agreement contains sufficiently precise terms to constitute an enforceable contract." We therefore will affirm the district court's rejection of Baer's claim to recover under a theory of implied-in-fact contract.

QUESTIONS

1. Why must the terms of a contract be "sufficiently definite" before a court will enforce the contract?
2. What might a court consider when looking for a "sufficiently definite meaning" to make a contract term enforceable?

The Enforcement of Preliminary Agreements

Suppose that during protracted contract negotiations, but before a formal contract is drawn up, the parties proclaim that they have "made a deal." Does their agreement mean that an enforceable contract has been formed even though the parties have not signed a formal contract? Or does their agreement simply mean that they have agreed to agree to a contract in the future?

How a court might interpret such a situation can, of course, have significant consequences for the parties. Fluorogas, Ltd., learned this when a federal court held that its preliminary agreement with Fluorine On Call, Ltd., was a binding contract. In that case, executives of the two companies had enjoyed a weekend of yachting in the Florida keys. During the trip, the executives drew up a brief handwritten document stating that Fluorogas would sell to Fluorine the exclusive rights to a technology to build and sell sophisticated semiconductor equipment. When Fluorogas refused to transfer the patents and intellectual property at issue to Fluorine, Fluorine sued for breach of contract. Was there a contract? Yes, according to the court. Because the essential terms of the agreement were included in the handwritten document, the document constituted a contract, not an agreement to agree to form a contract at some point in the future.[a]

THE TEXACO CASE

An important case challenging the traditional notion that preliminary contracts do not bind the parties was *Texaco, Inc. v.*

Pennzoil Co.[b] When the Pennzoil Company discussed with the Getty Oil Company the possible purchase of Getty's stock, a "memorandum of agreement" was drafted to reflect the terms of the conversations. After more negotiations over the price, both companies issued press releases announcing an agreement in principle on the terms of the memorandum. The next day, Texaco, Inc., offered to buy all of Getty's stock at a higher price. Getty accepted Texaco's offer, and the two firms signed a merger agreement. When Pennzoil sued Texaco for tortious (wrongful) interference with its "contractual" relationship with Getty, a jury concluded that Getty and Pennzoil had intended a binding contract before Texaco made its offer and that only the details were left to be worked out. Texaco was held liable for interfering with this contract and had to pay damages in the hundreds of millions of dollars.

TWO TYPES OF PRELIMINARY AGREEMENTS EMERGE

In *Adjustrite Systems v. GAB Business Services,*[c] the U.S. Court of Appeals for the Second Circuit set forth some helpful guidelines for distinguishing between an agreement to agree and an enforceable contract. The court pointed out that when the parties contemplate further negotiations and the execution of a formal instrument, a preliminary agreement ordinarily does not create a binding contract. If the parties do not

---

a. *Fluorine On Call, Ltd. v. Fluorogas Limited,* No. 01-CV-186 (W.D. Tex. 2002). A federal appellate court later affirmed the district court's holding on the contract issue but reversed the award of damages. *Fluorine On Call, Ltd. v. Fluorogas Limited,* 380 F.3d 849 (5th Cir. 2004).

b. 729 S.W.2d 768 (Tex.App.—Houston [1st Dist.] 1987; writ ref'd n.r.e.). (Generally, a complete Texas Court of Appeals citation includes a writ-of-error history showing the Texas Supreme Court's disposition of the case. In this case, *writ ref'd n.r.e.* is an abbreviation for "writ refused, no reversible error," which means that Texas's highest court refused to grant the appellant's request to review the case because the court did not consider there to be any reversible error.) Note that after the *Texaco* decision, Texas enacted legislation that superseded portions of the court's ruling regarding damages.

c. 145 F.3d 543 (2d Cir. 1998).

COMMUNICATION A third requirement for an effective offer is communication of the offer to the offeree, resulting in the offeree's knowledge of the offer. Ordinarily, one cannot agree to a bargain without knowing that it exists. Suppose that Estrich advertises a reward for the return of his lost dog. Hoban, not knowing of the reward, finds the dog and returns it to Estrich. Hoban cannot recover the reward, because she did not know it had been offered.[11]

---

11. A few states allow recovery of the reward, but not on contract principles. Because Estrich wanted his dog to be returned and Hoban returned it, these few states would allow Hoban to recover on the basis that it would be unfair to deny her the reward just because she did not know it had been offered.

intend to be bound by an agreement until it is in writing and signed, then there is no contract until that event occurs. The Second Circuit recognized, though, that in some circumstances preliminary agreements can create binding obligations. These "binding preliminary agreements" fall into one of two categories—Type I agreements or Type II agreements.

A Type I preliminary agreement is one in which all essential terms have been agreed on and no disputed issues remain to be resolved, as in the Getty-Pennzoil memorandum of agreement. This type of agreement is preliminary only in form and is fully binding. The formal contract to follow is simply that—a writing to satisfy formalities. A Type II preliminary agreement is created when the parties agree on certain major terms but leave other terms open for further negotiation. A Type II preliminary agreement is binding only in the sense that the parties have committed themselves to "negotiate together in good faith in an effort to reach final agreement." A party to a Type II preliminary agreement has no right to demand performance of the proposed contract.

OTHER FACTORS THAT COURTS CONSIDER

The courts have also developed a series of factors to be considered in determining whether the parties to a preliminary agreement intended to be bound in the absence of a final, executed agreement. The first and most important factor is whether the parties expressly stated that they would not be bound by the agreement in the absence of a formal writing.

Another factor to be considered is whether the agreement has been partially performed by either party. Normally, the agreement will be considered partially performed only if one of the parties has given the other something of value and the other party has accepted it. A third factor is whether all of the terms of the alleged contract have been agreed on. If any material terms have not been agreed on, then the third factor is not satisfied. Finally, the courts will consider whether the

agreement at issue is the type of contract that is usually committed to writing. In other words, they will look to what is customary when similar agreements are formed.[d]

IMPLICATIONS FOR THE BUSINESSPERSON

1. When engaging in preliminary negotiations, businesspersons should be aware that if all material terms are agreed on, they may be bound in contract even though they have not yet drawn up a formal contract.

2. Businesspersons should always keep in mind that in determining contractual intent, a court will consider what they say and do during preliminary negotiations—and *not* their subjective intentions.

FOR CRITICAL ANALYSIS

1. In deciding whether an agreement to agree or an enforceable contract has been formed, would it matter whether the parties are experienced business executives or relatively inexperienced businesspersons?

2. Is it fair for a court to hold that parties are bound in contract even though one of the parties claims that he or she did not intend to form a contract? Generally, should the courts give more weight to subjective intent in determining whether a contract has been formed?

RELEVANT WEB SITES

To locate information on the Web concerning the issues discussed in this feature, go to this text's Web site at **http://wleb.westbuslaw.com**, select "Chapter 9," and click on "Emerging Trends."

---

d. For examples of cases in which preliminary agreements did not satisfy these factors, or requirements, see *Novecon, Ltd. v. Bulgarian-American Enterprise Fund*, 190 F.3d 556 (D.C. Cir. 1999); and *Rappaport v. Buske*, 2000 WL 1224828 (S.D.N.Y. 2000).

TERMINATION OF THE OFFER

The communication of an effective offer to an offeree gives the offeree the power to transform the offer into a binding, legal obligation (a contract) by an acceptance. This power of acceptance, however, does not continue forever. It can be terminated either by the action of the parties or by operation of law.

TERMINATION BY ACTION OF THE PARTIES An offer can be terminated by the action of the parties in any of three ways: by revocation, by rejection, or by counteroffer.

—Revocation of the Offer by the Offeror. The offeror's act of withdrawing (revoking) an offer is known as **revocation.** Unless an offer is irrevocable

(irrevocable offers will be discussed shortly), the offeror usually can revoke the offer (even if he or she has promised to keep it open) as long as the revocation is communicated to the offeree before the offeree accepts. Revocation may be accomplished by express repudiation of the offer (for example, with a statement such as "I withdraw my previous offer of October 17") or by performance of acts that are inconsistent with the existence of the offer and are made known to the offeree.

The general rule followed by most states is that a revocation becomes effective when the offeree or the offeree's agent (a person acting on behalf of the offeree) actually receives it. Therefore, a letter of revocation mailed on April 1 and delivered at the offeree's residence or place of business on April 3 becomes effective on April 3.

An offer made to the general public can be revoked in the same manner that the offer was originally communicated. Suppose that a department store offers a $10,000 reward to anyone providing information leading to the apprehension of the persons who burglarized the store's downtown branch. The offer is published in three local papers and four papers in neighboring communities. To revoke the offer, the store must publish the revocation in all of the seven papers in which it published the offer. The revocation is then accessible to the general public, even if some particular offeree does not know about it.

—*Irrevocable Offers.* Although most offers are revocable, some can be made irrevocable—that is, they cannot be revoked, or canceled. An option contract involves one type of irrevocable offer. Increasingly, courts also refuse to allow an offeror to revoke an offer when the offeree has changed position because of justifiable reliance on the offer. (An offer for the sale of goods may also be considered irrevocable if the merchant-offeror gives assurances in a signed writing that the offer will remain open—see the discussion of the "merchant's firm offer" in Chapter 11.)

An *option contract* is created when an offeror promises to hold an offer open for a specified period of time in return for a payment (consideration) given by the offeree. An option contract takes away the offeror's power to revoke the offer for the period of time specified in the option. If no time is specified, then a reasonable period of time is implied. For example, suppose that you are in the business of writing movie scripts. Your agent contacts the head of development at New Line Cinema and offers to sell New Line your latest movie script. New Line likes your script and agrees to pay you $10,000 for a six-month option. In this situation, you (through your agent) are the offeror, and New Line is the offeree. You cannot revoke your offer to sell New Line your script for the next six months. If after six months no contract has been formed, however, New Line loses the $10,000, and you are free to sell the script to another firm.

When the offeree justifiably relies on an offer to her or his detriment, the court may hold that this *detrimental reliance* makes the offer irrevocable. For example, assume that Angela has rented commercial property from Jake for the past thirty-three years under a series of five-year leases. Under business conditions existing as their seventh lease nears its end, the rental property market is more favorable for tenants than for landlords. Angela tells Jake that she is going to look at other, less expensive properties as possible sites for her business. Wanting Angela to remain a tenant, Jake promises to reduce the rent in their next lease. In reliance on the promise, Angela continues to occupy and do business on Jake's property and does not look at other sites. When they sit down to negotiate a new lease, however, Jake says he has changed his mind and will increase the rent. Can he effectively revoke his promise?

Normally he cannot, because Angela has been relying on his promise to reduce the rent. Had the promise not been made, she would have relocated her business. This is a case of detrimental reliance on a promise, which therefore cannot be revoked. In this situation, the doctrine of **promissory estoppel** comes into play. To *estop* means to bar, impede, or preclude someone from doing something. Thus, promissory estoppel means that the promisor (the offeror) is barred from revoking the offer, in this case because the offeree has already changed her actions in reliance on the offer.

—*Rejection of the Offer by the Offeree.* The offer may be rejected by the offeree, in which case the offer is terminated. Any subsequent attempt by the offeree to accept will be construed as a new offer, giving the original offeror (now the offeree) the power of acceptance. A rejection is ordinarily accomplished by words or conduct evidencing an intent not to accept the offer. As with revocation, rejection of an offer is effective only when it is actually received by the offeror or the offeror's agent.

Merely inquiring about an offer does not constitute rejection. Suppose that a friend offers to buy your CD-ROM library for $300, and you respond, "Is that your best offer?" or "Will you pay me $375 for it?" A reasonable person would conclude that you had not rejected the offer but had merely made an inquiry for further consideration of the offer. You can still accept and bind your friend to the $300 purchase price. When the offeree merely inquires as to the firmness of the offer, there is no reason to presume that he or she intends to reject it.

—Counteroffer by the Offeree. A **counteroffer** occurs when the offeree rejects the original offer and simultaneously makes a new offer. Suppose that Duffy offers to sell her Picasso lithograph to Wong for $4,500. Wong responds, "Your price is too high. I'll offer to purchase your lithograph for $4,000." Wong's response is a counteroffer, because it terminates Duffy's offer to sell at $4,500 and creates a new offer by Wong to purchase at $4,000.

At common law, the **mirror image rule** requires the offeree's acceptance to match the offeror's offer exactly—to mirror the offer. Any material change in, or addition to, the terms of the original offer automat-

ically terminates that offer and substitutes the counteroffer. The counteroffer, of course, need not be accepted; but if the original offeror does accept the terms of the counteroffer, a valid contract is created.[12]

TERMINATION BY OPERATION OF LAW The power of the offeree to transform the offer into a binding, legal obligation can be terminated by operation of law through the occurrence of any of the following events:

1. Lapse of time.
2. Destruction of the specific subject matter of the offer.
3. Death or incompetence of the offeror or the offeree.
4. Supervening illegality of the proposed contract.

---

12. The mirror image rule has been greatly modified in regard to sales contracts. Section 2–207 of the UCC provides that a contract is formed if the offeree makes a definite expression of acceptance (such as signing the form in the appropriate location), even though the terms of the acceptance modify or add to the terms of the original offer.

CONCEPT SUMMARY 9.2 | Methods by Which an Offer Can Be Terminated

METHODS OF TERMINATION	BASIC RULES
BY ACTION OF THE PARTIES	
REVOCATION	1. An offer can be revoked at any time before acceptance without liability unless the offer is irrevocable. 2. Option contracts, merchants' firm offers, and, in some circumstances, the promissory estoppel theory render offers irrevocable. 3. Except for public offers, revocation is not effective until received by the offeree or the offeree's authorized agent.
REJECTION	1. Rejection of an offer is accomplished by words or actions that demonstrate a clear intent not to accept the offer or further consider the offer. Inquiries about an offer do not constitute a rejection. 2. A rejection is not effective until received by the offeror or an authorized agent of the offeror.
COUNTEROFFER	A counteroffer is a rejection of the original offer and the making of a new offer.
BY OPERATION OF LAW	
LAPSE OF TIME	1. If a time period for acceptance is stated in the offer, the offer ends at the stated time. 2. If no time period for acceptance is stated, the offer terminates at the end of a reasonable period.
DESTRUCTION	Destruction of the specific subject matter of the offer terminates the offer.
DEATH OR INCOMPETENCE	Death or incompetence of either the offeror or the offeree terminates an offer, unless the offer is irrevocable.
ILLEGALITY	Supervening illegality terminates an offer.

An offer terminates automatically by law when the period of time specified in the offer has passed. For example, suppose Alejandro offers to sell his camper to Kelly if she accepts within twenty days. Kelly must accept within the twenty-day period, or the offer will lapse (terminate). The time period specified in an offer normally begins to run when the offer is actually received by the offeree, not when it is sent or drawn up. When the offer is delayed (through the misdelivery of mail, for example), the period begins to run from the date the offeree would have received the offer, but only if the offeree knows or should know that the offer is delayed.

If the offer does not specify a time for acceptance, the offer terminates at the end of a *reasonable* period of time. What constitutes a reasonable period of time depends on the subject matter of the contract, business and market conditions, and other relevant circumstances. An offer to sell farm produce, for example, will terminate sooner than an offer to sell farm equipment because farm produce is perishable and subject to greater fluctuations in market value.

ACCEPTANCE

Acceptance is a voluntary act (either words or conduct) by the offeree that shows assent (agreement) to the terms of an offer. The acceptance must be unequivocal and must be communicated to the offeror.

UNEQUIVOCAL ACCEPTANCE To exercise the power of acceptance effectively, the offeree must accept unequivocally. This is the *mirror image rule* previously discussed. If the acceptance is subject to new conditions or if the terms of the acceptance *materially* change the original offer, the acceptance may be deemed a counteroffer that implicitly rejects the original offer. An acceptance may be unequivocal even though the offeree expresses dissatisfaction with the contract. For example, "I accept the offer, but I wish I could have gotten a better price" is an effective acceptance. So, too, is "I accept, but can you shave the price?" In contrast, the statement "I accept the offer but only if I can pay on ninety days' credit" is not an unequivocal acceptance and operates as a counteroffer, rejecting the original offer.

Certain terms, when added to an acceptance, will not qualify the acceptance sufficiently to constitute rejection of the offer. Suppose that in response to an offer to sell a piano, the offeree replies, "I accept; please send a written contract." The offeree is requesting a written contract but is not making it a condition for acceptance. Therefore, the acceptance is effective without the written contract. If the offeree replies, "I accept if you send a written contract," however, the acceptance is expressly conditioned on the request for a writing, and the statement is not an acceptance but a counteroffer. (Notice how important each word is!)[13]

SILENCE AS ACCEPTANCE Ordinarily, silence cannot constitute acceptance, even if the offeror states, "By your silence and inaction, you will be deemed to have accepted this offer." This general rule applies because an offeree should not be obligated to act affirmatively to reject an offer when no consideration has passed to the offeree to impose such a duty.

In some instances, however, the offeree does have a duty to speak, in which case her or his silence or inaction will operate as an acceptance. For example, silence may be an acceptance when an offeree takes the benefit of offered services even though he or she had an opportunity to reject them and knew that they were offered with the expectation of compensation. Suppose that Sayre watches while a stranger rakes his leaves, even though the stranger has not been asked to rake the yard. Sayre knows the stranger expects to be paid and does nothing to stop her. Here, his silence constitutes an acceptance, and an implied-in-fact contract is created. He is bound to pay a reasonable value for the stranger's work. This rule normally applies only when the offeree has received a benefit from the goods or services rendered.

—Prior Dealings and Acceptance by Silence. Silence can also operate as acceptance when the offeree has had prior dealings with the offeror. Suppose that a merchant routinely receives shipments from a certain supplier and always notifies the supplier when defective goods are rejected. In this situation, silence regarding a shipment will constitute acceptance.

—Acceptance by Silence of Solicited Offers. Additionally, if a person solicits an offer specifying that certain terms and conditions are acceptable, and the offeror makes the offer in response to the solicitation, the offeree has a duty to reject—that is, a duty to tell the offeror that the offer is not acceptable. In

---

13. In regard to sales contracts, the UCC provides that an acceptance may still be valid even if some terms are added. The new terms are simply treated as proposed additions to the contract.

this situation, failure to reject (silence) operates as an acceptance.

COMMUNICATION OF ACCEPTANCE

Whether the offeror must be notified of the acceptance depends on the nature of the contract. In a bilateral contract, communication of acceptance is necessary because acceptance is in the form of a promise (not performance) and the contract is formed when the promise is made (rather than when the act is performed). The offeree must communicate the acceptance to the offeror. Communication of acceptance is not necessary, however, if the offer dispenses with the requirement. Additionally, if the offer can be accepted by silence, no communication is necessary.

Because a unilateral contract calls for the full performance of some act, acceptance is usually evident, and notification is therefore unnecessary. Exceptions do exist, however. When the offeror requests notice of acceptance or has no adequate means of determining whether the requested act has been performed, or when the law requires notice of acceptance, then notice is necessary.

MODE AND TIMELINESS OF ACCEPTANCE

In bilateral contracts, acceptance must be timely. The general rule is that acceptance in a bilateral contract is timely if it is made before the offer is terminated. Problems arise, however, when the parties involved are not dealing face to face. In such cases, acceptance takes effect, thus completing formation of the contract, at the time the acceptance is communicated via the mode expressly or impliedly authorized by the offeror. According to the *Restatement (Second) of Contracts*, unless the offeror provides otherwise, "an acceptance made in a manner and by a medium invited by an offer is operative and completes the manifestation of mutual assent as soon as put out of the offeree's possession, without regard to whether it ever reaches the offeror."[14]

This rule traditionally has been referred to as the **mailbox rule,** also called the "deposited acceptance rule," because once an acceptance has been deposited in a mailbox, it is "out of the offeree's possession." Under this rule, if the authorized mode of communication is the mail, then an acceptance becomes valid when it is dispatched by mail (even if it is never received by the offeror). Thus, whereas a revocation becomes effective only when it is received by the

offeree, an acceptance becomes effective on *dispatch*, providing that an *authorized* means of communication is used.

—*Authorized Means of Acceptance.* An authorized means of communication may be either expressly authorized—that is, expressly stipulated in the offer—or impliedly authorized by the facts and circumstances surrounding the situation or by law. When an offeror specifies how acceptance should be made (for example, by overnight delivery), *express authorization* is said to exist, and the contract is not formed unless the offeree uses that specified mode of acceptance. Moreover, both offeror and offeree are bound in contract the moment this means of acceptance is employed. If overnight delivery is expressly authorized as the only means of acceptance, a contract is created as soon as the offeree delivers the message to the express delivery company. The contract would still exist even if the delivery company failed to deliver the message.

—**When the Preferred Means of Acceptance Is Not Indicated.** Many offerors, for one reason or another, do not indicate their preferred method of acceptance. When the offeror does not specify expressly that the offeree is to accept by a certain means, or that the acceptance will be effective only when received, acceptance of an offer may be made by any medium that is *reasonable under the circumstances*. When two parties are at a distance, for example, mailing is impliedly authorized because it is a customary mode of dispatch.

Several factors determine whether the acceptance was reasonable: the nature of the circumstances existing at the time the offer was made, the means used by the offeror to transmit the offer to the offeree, and the reliability of the offer's delivery. If, for example, an offer was sent by FedEx overnight delivery because an acceptance was urgently required, then the offeree's use of first class mail (which may take three days or more to deliver) might not be deemed reasonable.

—**When the Authorized Means of Acceptance Is Not Used.** An acceptance sent by means not expressly or impliedly authorized is normally not effective *until it is received by the offeror*. If an acceptance is timely sent and timely received, however, despite the means by which it is transmitted, it is considered to have been effective on its dispatch. If, in the previous example, the acceptance that was sent by first class mail was actually delivered to the offeror the next day

---

14. *Restatement (Second) of Contracts*, Section 63(a).

(the same as FedEx overnight delivery), then the court would recognize the acceptance as operative.

TECHNOLOGY AND ACCEPTANCE RULES   Clearly, some of the traditional rules governing acceptance do not seem to apply to an age in which acceptances are commonly delivered via e-mail, fax, or other delivery system, such as FedEx or DHL. For example, the mailbox rule does not apply to online acceptances, which typically are communicated instantaneously to the offeror. Nonetheless, the traditional rules—and the principles that underlie those rules—provide a basis for understanding what constitutes a valid acceptance in today's online environment. This is because, as in other areas of the law, much of the law governing online offers and acceptances has been adapted from traditional law to a new context.

While online offers are not significantly different from traditional offers contained in paper documents, online acceptances have posed some unusual problems for the court.

SECTION 5 | Consideration

The fact that a promise has been made does not mean the promise can or will be enforced. Under Roman law, a promise was not enforceable without some sort of *causa*—that is, a reason for making the promise that was also deemed to be a sufficient reason for enforcing it. Under the common law, a primary basis for the enforcement of promises is consideration. **Consideration** is usually defined as the value (such as cash) given in

return for a promise (such as the promise to sell a stamp collection on receipt of payment) or in return for a performance.

Often, consideration is broken down into two parts: (1) something of *legally sufficient value* must be given in exchange for the promise; and (2) usually, there must be a *bargained-for* exchange.

LEGAL VALUE

The "something of legally sufficient value" may consist of (1) a promise to do something that one has no prior legal duty to do, (2) the performance of an action that one is otherwise not obligated to undertake, or (3) the refraining from an action that one has a legal right to undertake (called a *forbearance*). Consideration in bilateral contracts normally consists of a promise in return for a promise, as explained earlier. For example, suppose that in a contract for the sale of goods, the seller promises to ship specific goods to the buyer, and the buyer promises to pay for those goods when they are received. Each of these promises constitutes consideration for the contract.

In contrast, unilateral contracts involve a promise in return for a performance. Suppose that Anita says to her neighbor, "When you finish painting the garage, I will pay you $100." Anita's neighbor paints the garage. The act of painting the garage is the consideration that creates Anita's contractual obligation to pay her neighbor $100.

What if, in return for a promise to pay, a person refrains from pursuing harmful habits (a forbearance),

CONCEPT SUMMARY 9.3	Effective Time of Acceptance	
ACCEPTANCE	**TIME EFFECTIVE**
BY AUTHORIZED MEANS OF COMMUNICATION	Effective at the time communication is sent (deposited in a mailbox or delivered to a courier service) via the mode expressly or impliedly authorized by the offeror (mailbox rule). *Exceptions:* 1. If the acceptance is not properly dispatched, it will not be effective until received by the offeror. 2. If the offeror specifically conditioned the offer on receipt of acceptance, it will not be effective until received by the offeror. 3. If acceptance is sent after rejection, whichever is received first is given effect.
BY UNAUTHORIZED MEANS OF COMMUNICATION	Effective on receipt of acceptance by the offeror (if timely received, it is considered to have been effective on dispatch).

such as the use of tobacco and alcohol? Does such forbearance constitute legally sufficient consideration? That was the question before the court in the following case, which is one of the classics in contract law with respect to consideration.

CASE 9.4

Court of Appeals
of New York,
Second Division, 1891.
124 N.Y. 538,
27 N.E. 256.

Hamer v. Sidway

BACKGROUND AND FACTS *William E. Story, Sr., was the uncle of William E. Story II. In the presence of family members and guests invited to a family gathering, the elder Story promised to pay his nephew $5,000 ($72,000 in today's dollars) if he would refrain from drinking, using tobacco, swearing, and playing cards or billiards for money until he reached the age of twenty-one. (Note that in 1869, when this contract was formed, it was legal in New York to drink and play cards for money prior to the age of twenty-one.) The nephew agreed and fully performed his part of the bargain. When he reached the age of twenty-one, he wrote and told his uncle that he had kept his part of the agreement and was therefore entitled to $5,000. The uncle replied that he was pleased with his nephew's performance, writing, "I have no doubt but you have, for which you shall have five thousand dollars, as I promised you. I had the money in the bank the day you was twenty-one years old that I intend for you, and you shall have the money certain. . . . P.S. You can consider this money on interest." The nephew received his uncle's letter and thereafter consented that the money should remain with his uncle according to the terms and conditions of the letter. The uncle died about twelve years later without having paid his nephew any part of the $5,000 and interest. The executor of the uncle's estate (Sidway, the defendant in this action) claimed that there had been no valid consideration for the promise and therefore refused to pay the $5,000 (plus interest) to Hamer, a third party to whom the nephew had transferred his rights in the note. The court reviewed the case to determine whether the nephew had given valid consideration under the law.*

IN THE LANGUAGE OF THE COURT

PARKER, J. [Justice]
* * * *
* * * Courts will not ask whether the thing which forms the consideration does in fact benefit the promisee or a third party, or is of any substantial value to any one. It is enough that something is promised, done, forborne, or suffered by the party to whom the promise is made as consideration for the promise made to him. *In general a waiver of any legal right at the request of another party is a sufficient consideration for a promise.* Any damage, or suspension, or forbearance of a right will be sufficient to sustain a promise. * * * Now, applying this rule to the facts before us, the promisee used tobacco, occasionally drank liquor, and he had a legal right to do so. That right he abandoned for a period of years upon the strength of the promise of the testator [his uncle] that for such forbearance he would give him $5,000. We need not speculate on the effort which may have been required to give up the use of those stimulants. It is sufficient that he restricted his lawful freedom of action within certain prescribed limits upon the faith of his uncle's agreement * * * . [Emphasis added.]

DECISION AND REMEDY *The court ruled that the nephew had provided legally sufficient consideration by giving up smoking, drinking, swearing, and playing cards or billiards for money until he reached the age of twenty-one and was therefore entitled to the money.*

WHAT IF THE FACTS WERE DIFFERENT? *If the nephew had not had a legal right to engage in the behavior that he agreed to forgo, would the result in this case have been different?*

IMPACT OF THIS CASE ON TODAY'S LAW
Although this case was decided over a century ago, the principles enunciated in the case remain applicable to contracts formed today, including online contracts. For a contract to be valid and binding, consideration must be given, and that consideration must be something of legally sufficient value.

BARGAINED-FOR EXCHANGE

The second element of consideration is that it must provide the basis for the bargain struck between the contracting parties. The promise given by the promisor (offeror) must induce the promisee (offeree) to offer a return promise, a performance, or a forbearance, and the promisee's promise, performance, or forbearance must induce the promisor to make the promise.

This element of bargained-for exchange distinguishes contracts from gifts. For example, suppose that Arlene says to her son, "In consideration of the fact that you are not as wealthy as your brothers, I will pay you $500." The fact that the word *consideration* is used does not, by itself, mean that consideration has been given. Indeed, this is not an enforceable promise because the son need not do anything in order to receive the promised $500.[15] The son need not give Arlene something of legal value in return for her promise, and the promised $500 does not involve a bargained-for exchange. Rather, Arlene has simply stated her motive for giving her son a gift.

ADEQUACY OF CONSIDERATION

Legal sufficiency of consideration involves the requirement that consideration be something of legally sufficient value in the eyes of the law. Adequacy of consideration involves "how much" consideration is given. Essentially, adequacy of consideration concerns the fairness of the bargain. On the surface, fairness would appear to be an issue when the items exchanged are of unequal value. In general, however, a court will not question the adequacy of consideration if the consideration is legally sufficient. Under the doctrine of freedom of contract, parties are normally free to bargain as they wish. If people could sue merely because they had entered into an unwise contract, the courts would be overloaded with frivolous suits.

In extreme cases, a court may consider the adequacy of consideration in terms of its amount or worth because inadequate consideration may indicate that fraud, duress, or undue influence was involved or that the element of bargained-for exchange was lacking. It may also reflect a party's incompetence (for example, an individual might have been too intoxicated or simply too young to make a contract). Suppose that Dylan has a house worth $100,000 and sells it for $50,000. A

$50,000 sale could indicate that the buyer unduly pressured Dylan into selling the house at that price or that Dylan was defrauded into selling the house at far below market value. (Of course, it might also indicate that Dylan was in a hurry to sell and that the amount was legally sufficient.)

AGREEMENTS THAT LACK CONSIDERATION

Sometimes, one of the parties (or both parties) to an agreement may think that consideration has been exchanged when in fact it has not. Here, we look at some situations in which the parties' promises or actions do not qualify as contractual consideration.

PREEXISTING DUTY   Under most circumstances, a promise to do what one already has a legal duty to do does not constitute legally sufficient consideration.[16] The preexisting legal duty may be imposed by law or may arise out of a previous contract. A sheriff, for example, cannot collect a reward for providing information leading to the capture of a criminal if the sheriff already has a legal duty to capture the criminal.

Likewise, if a party is already bound by contract to perform a certain duty, that duty cannot serve as consideration for a second contract. For example, suppose that Bauman-Bache, Inc., begins construction on a seven-story office building and after three months demands an extra $75,000 on its contract. If the extra $75,000 is not paid, Bauman-Bache will stop working. The owner of the land, having no one else to complete the construction, agrees to pay the extra $75,000. The agreement is unenforceable because it is not supported by legally sufficient consideration; Bauman-Bache was under a preexisting contract to complete the building.

UNFORESEEN DIFFICULTIES   The rule regarding preexisting duty is meant to prevent extortion and the so-called holdup game. What happens, though, when an honest contractor who has contracted with a landowner to construct a building runs into extraordinary difficulties that were totally unforeseen at the time the contract was formed? In the interests of fairness and equity, the courts sometimes allow exceptions to the preexisting duty rule. In the example just mentioned, if the landowner agrees to pay extra compen-

---

15. See *Fink v. Cox*, 18 Johns. 145, 9 Am.Dec. 191 (N.Y. 1820).

16. See *Foakes v. Beer*, 9 App.Cas. 605 (1884).

sation to the contractor for overcoming unforeseen difficulties, the court may refrain from applying the preexisting duty rule and enforce the agreement. When the "unforeseen difficulties" that give rise to a contract modification involve the types of risks ordinarily assumed in business, however, the courts will usually assert the preexisting duty rule.

RESCISSION AND NEW CONTRACT The law recognizes that two parties can mutually agree to rescind, or cancel, their contract, at least to the extent that it is executory (still to be carried out). *Rescission* is defined as the unmaking of a contract so as to return the parties to the positions they occupied before the contract was made. When rescission and the making of a new contract take place at the same time, but the duties of both parties remain the same as in their rescinded contract, the courts frequently are given a choice of applying the preexisting duty rule or allowing rescission and letting the new contract stand.

PAST CONSIDERATION Promises made in return for actions or events that have already taken place are unenforceable. These promises lack consideration in that the element of bargained-for exchange is missing. In short, you can bargain for something to take place now or in the future but not for something that has already taken place. Therefore, **past consideration** is no consideration.

Suppose, for example, that Elsie, a real estate agent, does her friend Judy a favor by selling Judy's house and not charging any commission. Later, Judy says to Elsie, "In return for your generous act, I will pay you $3,000." This promise is made in return for past consideration and is thus unenforceable; in effect, Judy is stating her intention to give Elsie a gift.

Is a party's suggestion that a professional athlete use a certain nickname for marketing products sufficient consideration for the athlete's later promise to pay the party a portion of the profits? That was the question in the following case.

CASE 9.5 Blackmon v. Iverson

United States
District Court,
Eastern District of
Pennsylvania, 2003.
324 F.Supp.2d 602.

BACKGROUND AND FACTS *Jamil Blackmon became friends with Allen Iverson in 1987 when Iverson was a high school student who showed tremendous promise as an athlete. Blackmon began to provide financial and other support to Iverson and his family. One evening in 1994, Blackmon suggested that Iverson use "The Answer" as a nickname in the summer league basketball tournaments. Blackmon said that Iverson would be "The Answer" to all of the National Basketball Association's woes. Later that night, Iverson said that he would give Blackmon 25 percent of any proceeds from the merchandising of products that used "The Answer" as a logo or a slogan. Blackmon invested time, money, and effort in refining the concept of "The Answer." In 1996, just before Iverson was drafted by the Philadelphia 76ers, Iverson told Blackmon that Iverson intended to use "The Answer" under a contract with Reebok. In 1997, Reebok began to sell, and continues to sell, products bearing "The Answer" slogan. None of the products uses any of Blackmon's designs, however, and Iverson does not share any of his profits with Blackmon. In 1998, Iverson persuaded Blackmon to move to Philadelphia. Blackmon subsequently filed a suit in a federal district court against Iverson, alleging breach of contract, among other things. Iverson filed a motion for summary judgment.*

IN THE LANGUAGE OF THE COURT
MCLAUGHLIN, District Judge.
* * * *

The plaintiff claims that he entered into an express contract with the defendant pursuant to which he was to receive twenty-five percent of the proceeds that the defendant received from marketing products with "The Answer" on them. The defendant argues that there was not a valid contract because * * * there was no consideration alleged.
* * * *

Under [the] law, a plaintiff must present clear and precise evidence of an agreement in which both parties manifested an intent to be bound, for which both parties gave consideration, and which contains sufficiently definite terms.

CONTINUED ▶

Consideration confers a benefit upon the promisor or causes a detriment to the promisee and must be an act, forbearance, or return promise bargained for and given in exchange for the original promise. Under [the] law, past consideration is insufficient to support a subsequent promise. [Emphasis added.]

* * * *

The plaintiff has argued that, in exchange for the defendant's promise to pay the twenty-five percent, the plaintiff gave three things as consideration: (1) the plaintiff's idea to use "The Answer" as a nickname to sell athletic apparel; (2) the plaintiff's assistance to and relationship with the defendant and his family; and (3) the plaintiff's move to Philadelphia.

According to the facts alleged by the plaintiff, he made the suggestion that the defendant use "The Answer" as a nickname and for product merchandising one evening in 1994. This was before the defendant first promised to pay; according to the plaintiff, the promise to pay was made later that evening. The disclosure of the idea also occurred before the defendant told the plaintiff that he was going to use the idea in connection with the Reebok contract in 1996, and before the sales of goods bearing "The Answer" actually began in 1997.

Regardless of whether the contract was formed in 1994, 1996, or 1997, the disclosure of "The Answer" idea had already occurred and was, therefore, past consideration insufficient to create a binding contract.

* * * *

According to the complaint, the plaintiff's relationship and support for the defendant, * * * began in 1987, seven years before the first alleged promise to pay was made. There is no allegation that the plaintiff began engaging in this conduct because of any promise by the defendant, or that the plaintiff continued his gratuitous conduct in 1994, 1996, or 1997 in exchange for the promise to pay. These actions are not valid consideration.

The plaintiff also alleged at oral argument that his move to Philadelphia during the 1997–1998 season was consideration for the promise to pay. If the parties reached a mutual agreement in 1994, the plaintiff has not properly alleged that the move was consideration because there is no allegation that the parties anticipated that the plaintiff would move to Philadelphia three or four years later, or that the plaintiff promised to do so in exchange for the defendant's promise to pay.

Nor is there any allegation that the move was part of the terms of any contract created in 1996 or 1997. The complaint states only that the defendant "persuaded" him to move to Philadelphia to "begin seeking the profits from his ideas." Even when the complaint is construed broadly, there is no allegation that the move was required in exchange for any promise by the defendant to pay. In the absence of valid consideration, the plaintiff has no claim for breach of an express contract.

DECISION AND REMEDY *The court granted Iverson's motion to dismiss Blackmon's complaint. The alleged contract between the parties was not supported by sufficient consideration. The disclosure of the idea for the use of "The Answer" as a marketing tool occurred before the formation of a promise to pay for the use of the idea.*

WHAT IF THE FACTS WERE DIFFERENT? *Suppose that only five minutes had elapsed between Blackmon's suggesting that Iverson use "The Answer" as a marketing slogan and Iverson's promising to give Blackmon a percentage of the proceeds. Would the court's ruling in this case have been any different? Why or why not?*

PROMISSORY ESTOPPEL

Under the doctrine of *promissory estoppel* (also called *detrimental reliance*), a person who has reasonably and substantially relied on the promise of another may be able to obtain some measure of recovery. This doctrine is applied in a wide variety of contexts in which a promise is otherwise unenforceable, such as when a promise is not supported by consideration. Under this doctrine, a court may enforce an otherwise unenforceable promise to avoid the injustice that would otherwise result. For the doctrine to be applied, the following elements are required:

1. There must be a clear and definite promise.
2. The promisee must justifiably rely on the promise.

CONCEPT SUMMARY 9.4 | Consideration

CONCEPT	DESCRIPTION
ELEMENTS OF CONSIDERATION	Consideration is the value given in exchange for a promise. A contract cannot be formed without sufficient consideration. Consideration is often broken down into two elements: 1. *Legal value*—Something of legally sufficient value must be given in exchange for a promise. This may consist of a promise, an act, or a forbearance. 2. *Bargained-for exchange*—There must be a bargained-for exchange.
ADEQUACY OF CONSIDERATION	Adequacy of consideration relates to how much consideration is given and whether a fair bargain was reached. Courts will inquire into the adequacy of consideration (if the consideration is legally sufficient) only when fraud, undue influence, duress, or the lack of a bargained-for exchange may be involved.
AGREEMENTS THAT LACK CONSIDERATION	Consideration is lacking in the following situations: 1. *Preexisting duty*—Consideration is not legally sufficient if one is either by law or by contract under a *preexisting duty* to perform the action being offered as consideration for a new contract. 2. *Past consideration*—Actions or events that have already taken place do not constitute legally sufficient consideration.

3. The reliance normally must be of a substantial and definite character.

4. Justice will be better served by enforcement of the promise.

If these requirements are met, a promise may be enforced even though it is not supported by consideration. In essence, the promisor will be *estopped* (prevented) from asserting the lack of consideration as a defense. For example, suppose that your uncle tells you, "I'll pay you $150 a week so you won't have to work anymore." In reliance on your uncle's promise, you quit your job, but your uncle refuses to pay you. Under the doctrine of promissory estoppel, you may be able to enforce such a promise.[17]

SECTION 6 | Capacity

In addition to agreement and consideration, for a contract to be deemed valid the parties to the contract must have *contractual capacity*—the legal ability to enter into a contractual relationship. Courts generally presume the existence of contractual capacity, but there are some situations in which capacity is lacking or may be questionable. For example, in many situations, a minor has the capacity to enter into a contract but also has the right to avoid liability under it.

Historically, the law has given special protection to those who bargain with the inexperience of youth or those who lack the degree of mental competence required by law. A person *adjudged by a court* to be mentally incompetent, for example, cannot form a legally binding contract with another party. In other situations, a party may have the capacity to enter into a valid contract but also have the right to avoid liability under it. For example, minors—or *infants,* as they are commonly referred to in legal terminology—usually are not legally bound by contracts. In this section, we look at the effect of youth, intoxication, and mental incompetence on contractual capacity.

MINORS

Today, in virtually all states, the *age of majority* (when a person is no longer a minor) for contractual purposes is eighteen years.[18] In addition, some states provide for the termination of minority on marriage. Minority status may also be terminated by a minor's *emancipation,* which occurs when a child's parent or legal guardian relinquishes the legal right to exercise control over the child. Normally, a minor who leaves home to support himself or herself is considered emancipated. Several jurisdictions permit minors to petition a court for emancipation themselves. For business purposes, a minor may petition a court to be treated as an adult.

---

17. *Ricketts v. Scothorn,* 57 Neb. 51, 77 N.W. 365 (1898).

18. The age of majority may still be twenty-one for other purposes, such as the purchase and consumption of alcohol.

The general rule is that a minor can enter into any contract that an adult can, provided that the contract is not one prohibited by law for minors (for example, the sale of tobacco or alcoholic beverages). A contract entered into by a minor, however, is voidable at the option of that minor, subject to certain exceptions. To exercise the option to avoid a contract, a minor need only manifest an intention not to be bound by it. The minor "avoids" the contract by disaffirming it.

The technical definition of *disaffirmance* is the legal avoidance, or setting aside, of a contractual obligation. To disaffirm, a minor must express his or her intent, through words or conduct, not to be bound to the contract. The minor must disaffirm the entire contract, not merely a portion of it. For example, the minor cannot decide to keep part of the goods purchased under a contract and return the remaining goods.

INTOXICATION

Intoxication is a condition in which a person's normal capacity to act or think is inhibited by alcohol or some other drug. A contract entered into by an intoxicated person can be either voidable or valid (and thus enforceable). If the person was sufficiently intoxicated to lack mental capacity, then the transaction may be voidable at the option of the intoxicated person even if the intoxication was purely voluntary. For the contract to be voidable, the person must prove that the intoxication impaired her or his reason and judgment so severely that she or he did not comprehend the legal consequences of entering into the contract.

MENTAL INCOMPETENCE

If a court has previously determined that a person is mentally incompetent and has appointed a guardian to represent the individual, any contract made by the mentally incompetent person is *void*—no contract exists. Only the guardian can enter into binding legal obligations on the incompetent person's behalf.

SECTION 7 | Legality

For a contract to be valid and enforceable, it must be formed for a legal purpose. A contract to do something that is prohibited by federal or state statutory law is illegal and, as such, void from the outset and thus unenforceable. Also, a contract that calls for a tortious act or an action contrary to public policy is illegal and

unenforceable. It is important to note that a contract or a clause in a contract may be illegal even in the absence of a specific statute prohibiting the action promised by the contract.

Although contracts involve private parties, some are not enforceable because of the negative impact they would have on society. Contracts in restraint of trade (anticompetitive agreements) usually adversely affect the public (which favors competition in the economy) and typically violate one or more federal or state statutes.[19] Many such contracts involve a type of restraint called a *covenant not to compete*, or a restrictive covenant. Basically, a restriction on competition must be reasonable—that is, not any greater than necessary to protect a legitimate business interest.

SECTION 8 | Genuineness of Assent

A contract has been entered into by two parties, each with full legal capacity and for a legal purpose. The contract is also supported by consideration. The contract thus meets the four requirements for a valid contract that were specified previously. Nonetheless, the contract may be unenforceable if the parties have not genuinely assented to its terms. As stated earlier, lack of **genuineness of assent** (voluntary consent) can be used as a defense to the contract's enforceability. Genuineness of assent may be lacking because of a mistake, misrepresentation, undue influence, or duress—in other words, because there is no true "meeting of the minds." In this section, we examine problems relating to genuineness of assent.

MISTAKES

We all make mistakes, and it is therefore not surprising that mistakes are made when contracts are formed. It is important to distinguish between *mistakes of fact* and *mistakes of value or quality*. Only a mistake of fact may allow a contract to be avoided.

MISTAKES OF FACT   Mistakes of fact occur in two forms—*bilateral* and *unilateral*. A bilateral, or mutual, mistake is made by both of the contracting parties. A unilateral mistake is made by only one of the parties. We look next at these two types of mistakes and illustrate them graphically in Exhibit 9–3.

---

19. The federal statutes include the Sherman Act, the Clayton Act, and the Federal Trade Commission Act (see Chapters 26 and 27).

EXHIBIT 9-3 Mistakes of Fact

```
                          ┌─────────────────────┐       ┌─────────────────────┐
                          │  BILATERAL MISTAKE  │──────▶│   CONTRACT CAN      │
                          │ Both parties mistaken│       │  BE RESCINDED BY    │
                          └─────────────────────┘       │   EITHER PARTY      │
  ┌──────────┐                                          └─────────────────────┘
  │ MATERIAL │                                          ┌─────────────────────┐
  │ MISTAKE  │─────┐                                    │     CONTRACT        │
  │ OF FACT  │     │                                    │ ENFORCEABLE UNLESS— │
  └──────────┘     │                                    │ ● Other party knew or│
                   │     ┌─────────────────────┐        │   should have known that│
                   └────▶│  UNILATERAL MISTAKE │───────▶│   mistake was made or │
                         │  One party mistaken │        │ ● Mistake was due to  │
                         └─────────────────────┘        │   substantial mathematical│
                                                        │   error, made inadvertently│
                                                        │   and without gross  │
                                                        │   negligence         │
                                                        └─────────────────────┘
```

—Bilateral (Mutual) Mistakes of Fact. A bilateral, or mutual, mistake occurs when both parties are mistaken as to some *material fact*—that is, a fact important to the subject matter of the contract. When a bilateral mistake occurs, the contract can be rescinded, or canceled, by either party. For example, Keeley buys a landscape painting from Umberto's art gallery. Both Umberto and Keeley believe that the painting is by the artist Vincent van Gogh. Later, Keeley discovers that the painting is a very clever fake. Because neither Umberto nor Keeley was aware of this material fact when they made their deal, Keeley can rescind the contract and recover the purchase price of the painting.

A word or term in a contract may be subject to more than one reasonable interpretation. In that situation, if the parties to the contract attach materially different meanings to the term, their mutual mistake of fact may allow the contract to be rescinded because there has been no "meeting of the minds," or true assent, which is required for a contract to arise.

The classic case on bilateral mistake is *Raffles v. Wichelhaus*,[20] which was decided by an English court in 1864. The defendant, Wichelhaus, paid for a shipment of Surat cotton from the plaintiff, Raffles, "to arrive 'Peerless' from Bombay." Wichelhaus expected the goods to be shipped on the *Peerless*, a ship sailing from Bombay, India, in October. Raffles expected to ship the goods on a different *Peerless*, which sailed from Bombay in December. When the goods arrived and Raffles tried to deliver them, Wichelhaus refused to accept them. The court held for Wichelhaus, concluding that no mutual assent existed because the parties had attached materially different meanings to an essential term of the written contract (the ship that was to transport the goods).

In the following case, an injured worker sought to set aside a settlement agreement entered into with his employer, arguing that a physician's mistaken diagnosis of the worker's injury was a mutual mistake of fact on which the agreement was based.

---

20. 159 Eng.Rep. 375 (1864).

CASE 9.6  ## Roberts v. Century Contractors, Inc.

Court of Appeals of
North Carolina, 2004.
162 N.C.App. 688,
592 S.E.2d 215.
http://www.aoc.state.nc.
us/www/public/html/
opinions.htm[a]

BACKGROUND AND FACTS *Bobby Roberts was an employee of Century Contractors, Inc., when a pipe struck him in a work-related accident in July 1993, causing trauma to his neck and back. Dr. James Markworth of Southeastern Orthopaedic Clinic diagnosed Roberts's injuries. After surgery and treatment, Markworth concluded that Roberts was at maximum medical improvement (MMI) and stopped treating him. Roberts agreed with Century to accept $125,000 and payment of related medical expenses, and to waive any right to make further claims in regard to his injury. In June 1998, still experiencing pain, Roberts saw Dr. Allen Friedman, who determined that Roberts was*

---

a. Click on "2004" under "Court of Appeals Opinions." In the result, scroll down to "17 February 2004" and click on the name of the case to access the opinion. The North Carolina Administrative Office of the Courts maintains this Web site.

CONTINUED ▶

CASE 9.6 | Continued *not at MMI. Markworth then admitted that his diagnosis was a mistake. Roberts filed a claim for workers' compensation (see Chapter 40), seeking compensation and medical benefits for his injury. He alleged that his agreement with Century should be set aside due to a mutual mistake of fact. The North Carolina state administrative agency authorized to rule on workers' compensation claims awarded Roberts what he sought. Century appealed to a state intermediate appellate court.*

IN THE LANGUAGE OF THE COURT

LEVINSON, Judge.
* * * *

* * * Compromise settlement agreements, including mediated settlement agreements in Workers' Compensation cases, are governed by general principles of contract law.

It is a well-settled principle of contract law that a valid contract exists only where there has been a meeting of the minds as to all essential terms of the agreement. Therefore, where a mistake is common to both parties and concerns a material past or presently existing fact, such that there is no meeting of the minds, a contract may be avoided. [Emphasis added.]

To afford relief, the mistake must be of a certain nature. The fact about which the parties are mistaken must be an existing or past fact. The mistaken fact must also be material * * *. It must be as to a fact which enters into and forms the basis of the contract, or in other words it must be of the essence of the agreement, the *sine qua non,* or, as is sometimes said, the efficient cause of the agreement, and must be such that it animates and controls the conduct of the parties.

Additionally, relief from a contract due to mistake of fact will be had only where *both* parties to an agreement are mistaken. Thus, as a general rule relief will be denied where the party against whom it is sought was ignorant that the other party was acting under a mistake and the former's conduct in no way contributed thereto. Likewise, a party who assumed the risk of a mistaken fact cannot avoid a contract.

A party bears the risk of a mistake when

(a) the risk is allocated to him by agreement of the parties, or
(b) he is aware, at the time the contract is made that he has only limited knowledge with respect to the facts to which the mistake relates but treats his limited knowledge as sufficient, or
(c) the risk is allocated to him by the court on the ground that it is reasonable in the circumstances to do so.

* * * *

* * * The x-rays [examined by Dr. Friedman] after Dr. Markworth or Southern Orthopaedic Clinic had last treated plaintiff [Roberts], indicated Dr. Markworth's diagnosis of maximum medical improvement * * * was a mistake. Dr. Markworth testified * * * that advising plaintiff that he was at maximum medical improvement at that time was a mistake.

* * * *

* * * [T]he finding of maximum medical improvement and the impairment rating given by Dr. Markworth were material to the settlement of this claim and * * * both parties relied on this information in entering into settlement negotiations.

* * * *

* * * [T]he parties believed that plaintiff had reached maximum medical improvement and, further, * * * they materially relied upon this fact in reaching a settlement. Defendants' essential argument on appeal is that because plaintiff either knew that there was a possibility that [he had not reached MMI] or was negligent in not declining to sign the settlement agreement, mutual mistake is a legal impossibility in this case. As the facts * * * support a contrary conclusion, we do not agree.

* * * The plaintiff testified that he based his decision to sign the settlement agreement on Dr. Markworth's diagnosis and that he would not have settled his case if Dr. Friedman had told him that [he had not reached MMI]. Thus, there is competent record evidence to support the * * * findings that the parties were mistaken as to whether plaintiff had reached maximum medical improvement and that this mistaken fact was material. * * *

CASE 9.6 | Continued **DECISION AND REMEDY** *The state intermediate appellate court affirmed the award of compensation and medical benefits to Roberts. The agreement between Roberts and Century was set aside on the basis of a mutual mistake of fact. Markworth's MMI diagnosis was "material to the settlement of this claim and * * * both parties relied on this information." In fact, however, "plaintiff was not at maximum medical improvement."*

—Unilateral Mistakes of Fact. A unilateral mistake occurs when only one of the contracting parties makes a mistake as to some material fact. The general rule is that a unilateral mistake does not afford the mistaken party any right to relief from the contract. For example, DeVinck intends to sell his motor home for $17,500. When he learns that Benson is interested in buying a used motor home, DeVinck faxes Benson an offer to sell the vehicle to him. When typing the fax, however, DeVinck mistakenly keys in the price of $15,700. Benson immediately sends DeVinck a fax accepting DeVinck's offer. Even though DeVinck intended to sell his motor home for $17,500, his unilateral mistake falls on him. He is bound in contract to sell the motor home to Benson for $15,700.

There are at least two exceptions to this general rule.[21] First, if the *other* party to the contract knows or should have known that a mistake of fact was made, the contract may not be enforceable. In the above example, if Benson knew that DeVinck intended to sell his motor home for $17,500, then DeVinck's unilateral mistake (stating $15,700 in his offer) may render the resulting contract unenforceable. The second exception arises when a unilateral mistake of fact was due to a mathematical mistake in addition, subtraction, division, or multiplication and was made inadvertently and without gross (extreme) negligence. If a contractor's bid was significantly low because he or she made a mistake in addition when totaling the estimated costs, any contract resulting from the bid may be rescinded, or canceled. Of course, in both situations, the mistake must still involve some material fact.

MISTAKES OF VALUE If a mistake concerns the future market value or quality of the object of the contract, the mistake is one of *value*, and either party can normally enforce the contract. Mistakes of value can be bilateral or unilateral; but either way, they do not serve as a basis

for avoiding a contract. For example, suppose that Chi buys a violin from Bev for $250. Although the violin is very old, neither party believes that it is extremely valuable. An antiques dealer later informs the parties, however, that the violin is rare and worth thousands of dollars. Although a mutual mistake has been made, the mistake is not a mistake of *fact* that warrants contract rescission. Similarly, a unilateral mistake of value will not serve as the basis for avoiding a contract.

The reason that mistakes of value or quality have no legal significance is that value is variable. Depending on the time, place, and other circumstances, the same item may be worth considerably different amounts. When parties form a contract, their agreement establishes the value of the object of their transaction—for the moment. Each party is considered to have assumed the risk that the value will change in the future or prove to be different from what he or she thought. Without this rule, almost any party who did not receive what she or he considered a fair bargain could argue mistake.

FRAUDULENT MISREPRESENTATION

In the context of contract law, fraud affects the genuineness of the innocent party's consent to the contract. Thus, the transaction is not voluntary in the sense of involving "mutual assent." When an innocent party is fraudulently induced to enter into a contract, the contract normally can be avoided because that party has not *voluntarily* consented to its terms. Normally, the innocent party can either rescind (cancel) the contract and be restored to his or her original position or enforce the contract and seek damages for any injuries resulting from the fraud.

The word *fraudulent* means many things in the law. Generally, fraudulent misrepresentation refers only to misrepresentation that is consciously false and is intended to mislead another. The perpetrator of the fraudulent misrepresentation knows or believes that the assertion is false or knows that she or he does not

---

21. The *Restatement (Second) of Contracts*, Section 153, liberalizes the general rule to take into account the modern trend of allowing avoidance even though only one party has been mistaken.

have a basis (stated or implied) for the assertion. Typically, fraudulent misrepresentation consists of the following elements:

1. A misrepresentation of a material fact must occur.
2. There must be an intent to deceive.
3. The innocent party must justifiably rely on the misrepresentation.

To collect damages, a party must also have been injured. To obtain rescission of a contract, or to defend against the enforcement of a contract on the basis of fraudulent misrepresentation, in most states a party need not have suffered an injury.

For a person to recover damages caused by fraud, proof of an injury is universally required. The measure of damages is ordinarily equal to the property's value had it been delivered as represented, less the actual price paid for the property. In actions based on fraud, courts often award *punitive damages,* or *exemplary damages,* which are granted to a plaintiff over and above the proved, actual compensation for the loss.[22] As will be discussed in Chapter 12, punitive damages are based on the public-policy consideration of punishing the defendant or setting an example to deter similar wrongdoing by others.

NONFRAUDULENT MISREPRESENTATION

If a plaintiff seeks to rescind a contract on the ground of *fraudulent* misrepresentation, the plaintiff must prove that the defendant had the intent to deceive. Most courts also allow rescission in cases involving *nonfraudulent* misrepresentation—that is, innocent or negligent misrepresentation—if all of the other elements of misrepresentation exist.

INNOCENT MISREPRESENTATION
If a person makes a statement that he or she believes to be true but that actually misrepresents material facts, the person is guilty only of an *innocent misrepresentation,* not of fraud. If an innocent misrepresentation occurs, the aggrieved party can rescind the contract but usually cannot seek damages. For example, Parris tells Roberta that a tract contains 250 acres. Parris is mistaken—the tract of land contains only 215 acres—but Parris does not know that. Roberta is induced by the statement to make a contract to buy the land. Even though the misrepresentation is innocent, Roberta can avoid the contract if the misrepresentation is material.

---

22. See, for example, *Alexander v. Meduna,* 47 P.3d 206 (Wyo. 2002).

NEGLIGENT MISREPRESENTATION
Sometimes a party will make a misrepresentation through carelessness, believing the statement is true. This misrepresentation is negligent if the person fails to exercise reasonable care in uncovering or disclosing the facts or does not use the skill and competence that her or his business or profession requires. For example, an operator of a weight scale certifies the weight of Sneed's commodity, even though the scale's accuracy has not been checked in more than a year. In this situation, the scale operator's lack of action could constitute *negligent misrepresentation.*

In virtually all states, such negligent misrepresentation is equal to *scienter,* or knowingly making a misrepresentation. In effect, negligent misrepresentation is treated as fraudulent misrepresentation, even though the misrepresentation was not purposeful. In negligent misrepresentation, culpable ignorance of the truth supplies the intention to mislead, even if the defendant can claim, "I didn't know."

UNDUE INFLUENCE

Undue influence arises from special kinds of relationships in which one party can greatly influence another party, thus overcoming that party's free will. A contract entered into under excessive or undue influence lacks genuine assent and is therefore voidable.

As mentioned, undue influence arises from relationships in which one party may dominate another party, thus unfairly influencing him or her. Minors and elderly people, for example, are often under the influence of guardians (persons who are legally responsible for another). If a guardian induces a young or elderly ward (the person whom the guardian looks after) to enter into a contract that benefits the guardian, undue influence may have been exerted. Undue influence can arise from a number of confidential or fiduciary relationships: attorney-client, physician-patient, guardian-ward, parent-child, husband-wife, or trustee-beneficiary. The essential feature of undue influence is that the party being taken advantage of does not, in reality, exercise free will in entering into a contract.

DURESS

Assent to the terms of a contract is not genuine if one of the parties is *forced* into the agreement. Forcing a party to do something, including entering into a contract, through fear created by threats is legally defined as *duress.* In addition, blackmail or extortion to induce consent to a contract constitutes duress. Duress is both a defense to the enforcement of a contract and a ground for the rescission of a contract.

THE THREATENED ACT MUST BE WRONGFUL OR ILLEGAL Generally, for duress to occur the threatened act must be wrongful or illegal. Threatening to exercise a legal right, such as the right to sue someone, ordinarily is not illegal and usually does not constitute duress. For example, suppose that Joan injures Olin in an auto accident. The police are not called. Joan has no automobile insurance, but she has substantial assets. Olin wants to settle the potential claim out of court for $3,000, but Joan refuses. After much arguing, Olin loses his patience and says, "If you don't pay me $3,000 right now, I'm going to sue you for $35,000." Joan is frightened and gives Olin a check for $3,000. Later in the day, Joan stops payment on the check, and Olin later sues her for the $3,000. Although Joan argues that she was the victim of duress, the threat of a civil suit normally is not considered duress. Therefore, a court would not allow Joan to use duress as a defense to the enforcement of her settlement agreement with Olin.

ECONOMIC DURESS Economic need is generally not sufficient to constitute duress, even when one party exacts a very high price for an item that the other party needs. If the party exacting the price also creates the need, however, *economic duress* may be found.

For example, suppose that the Internal Revenue Service (IRS) assesses a large tax and penalty against Weller. Weller retains Eyman, the accountant who had filed the tax returns on which the assessment was based, to resist the assessment. Two days before the deadline for filing a reply with the IRS, Eyman declines to represent Weller unless he signs a very high contingency-fee agreement for the services. This agreement would be unenforceable. Although Eyman had threatened only to withdraw his services, something that he was legally entitled to do, he was responsible for delaying the withdrawal until the last days before the deadline. Because it would have been impossible at that late date to obtain adequate representation elsewhere, Weller was forced either to sign the contract or to lose his right to challenge the IRS assessment.

ADHESION CONTRACTS AND UNCONSCIONABILITY

Questions concerning genuineness of assent may arise when the terms of a contract are dictated by a party with overwhelming bargaining power and the signer must agree to those terms or go without the commodity or service in question. Such contracts are often referred to as *adhesion contracts*. An adhesion contract is written *exclusively* by one party (the dominant party, usually the seller or the creditor) and presented to the other party (the adhering party, usually the buyer or the borrower) on a take-it-or-leave-it basis. In other words, the adhering party has no opportunity to negotiate the terms of the contract.

STANDARD-FORM CONTRACTS Standard-form contracts often contain fine-print provisions that shift a risk naturally borne by one party to the other. A variety of businesses use such contracts. Life insurance policies, residential leases, loan agreements, and employment agency contracts are often standard-form contracts. To avoid enforcement of the contract or of a particular clause, the aggrieved party must show that the parties had substantially unequal bargaining positions and that enforcement would be manifestly unfair or oppressive. If the required showing is made, the contract or particular term is deemed *unconscionable* and is not enforced.

UNCONSCIONABILITY AND THE COURTS Technically, unconscionability under Section 2–302 of the Uniform Commercial Code (UCC) applies only to contracts for the sale of goods. Many courts, however, have broadened the concept and applied it in other situations.

It is important to note here that the UCC gives courts a great degree of discretion to invalidate or strike down a contract or clause as being unconscionable. As a result, some states have not adopted Section 2–302 of the UCC. In those states, the legislature and the courts prefer to rely on traditional notions of fraud, undue influence, and duress.

SECTION 9 | The Statute of Frauds

At early common law, parties to a contract were not allowed to testify. This led to the practice of hiring third party witnesses. As early as the seventeenth century, the English recognized the many problems presented by this practice and enacted a statute to help deal with it. The statute, passed by the English Parliament in 1677, was known as "An Act for the Prevention of Frauds and Perjuries." The act established that certain types of contracts, to be enforceable, had to be evidenced by a writing and signed by the party against whom enforcement was sought.

MODERN STATUTES OF FRAUDS

Today, almost every state has a statute, modeled after the English act, that stipulates what types of contracts must be in writing. Although the statutes vary slightly from state to state, all states require certain types of contracts to be in writing or evidenced by a written memorandum signed by the party against whom enforcement is sought, unless certain exceptions apply. In this text, we refer to these statutes collectively as the **Statute of Frauds.** The actual name of the Statute of Frauds is misleading because it neither applies to fraud nor invalidates any type of contract. Rather, it denies *enforceability* to certain contracts that do not comply with its requirements. The following types of contracts are said to fall "within" or "under" the Statute of Frauds and therefore require a writing:

1. Contracts involving interests in land.
2. Contracts that cannot by their terms be performed within one year from the date of formation.
3. Collateral, or secondary, contracts, such as promises to answer for the debt or duty of another and promises by the administrator or executor of an estate to pay a debt of the estate personally—that is, out of his or her own pocket.
4. Promises made in consideration of marriage.
5. Under the UCC, contracts for the sale of goods priced at $500 or more ($5,000 or more under the 2003 amendments to the UCC).

PROMISSORY ESTOPPEL AND THE STATUTE OF FRAUDS

In some states, an oral contract that would otherwise be unenforceable under the Statute of Frauds may be enforced under the doctrine of promissory estoppel, based on detrimental reliance. Section 139 of the *Restatement (Second) of Contracts* provides that in these circumstances, an oral promise can be enforceable notwithstanding the Statute of Frauds if the reliance was foreseeable to the person making the promise and if injustice can be avoided only by enforcing the promise.

SECTION 10 | Third Party Rights

Once it has been determined that a valid and legally enforceable contract exists, attention can turn to the rights and duties of the parties to the contract. A contract is a private agreement between the parties who have entered into it, and traditionally these parties alone have rights and liabilities under the contract. This principle is referred to as *privity of contract*. A *third party*—one who is not a direct party to a particular contract—normally does not have rights under that contract.

There are exceptions to the rule of privity of contract. One exception allows a party to a contract to transfer the rights or duties arising from the contract to another person through an *assignment* (of rights) or a *delegation* (of duties). Another exception involves a *third party beneficiary contract*—a contract in which the parties to the contract intend that the contract benefit a third party.

ASSIGNMENTS

In a bilateral contract, the two parties have corresponding rights and duties. One party has a *right* to require the other to perform some task, and the other has a *duty* to perform it. The transfer of contractual *rights* to a third party is known as an **assignment.** When rights under a contract are assigned unconditionally, the rights of the *assignor* (the party making the assignment) are extinguished. The third party (the *assignee*, or party receiving the assignment) has a right to demand performance from the other original party to the contract. The assignee takes only those rights that the assignor originally had.

As a general rule, all rights can be assigned. Exceptions are made, however, in some circumstances. If a statute expressly prohibits assignment of a particular right, that right cannot be assigned. When a contract is *personal* in nature, the rights under the contract cannot be assigned unless all that remains is a money payment. A right cannot be assigned if assignment will materially increase or alter the risk or duties of the obligor (the other original party owing performance under the contract).[23] If a contract stipulates that a right cannot be assigned, then *ordinarily* the right cannot be assigned.

There are several exceptions to the rule that a contract can, by its terms, prohibit any assignment of the contract. These exceptions are as follows:

1. A contract cannot prevent an assignment of the right to receive money. This exception exists to encourage the free flow of money and credit in modern business settings.
2. The assignment of rights in real estate often cannot be prohibited, because such a prohibition is contrary to public policy. Prohibitions of this kind are called restraints against *alienation* (transfer of land ownership).

---

23. UCC 2–210(2).

3. The assignment of *negotiable instruments* (which include checks and promissory notes) cannot be prohibited.

4. In a contract for the sale of goods, the right to receive damages for breach of contract or for payment of an account owed may be assigned even though the sales contract prohibits such assignment.

DELEGATIONS

Just as a party can transfer rights through an assignment, a party can also transfer duties. The transfer of contractual *duties* to a third party is known as a **delegation.** Normally, a delegation of duties does not relieve the party making the delegation (the *delegator*) of the obligation to perform in the event that the party to whom the duty has been delegated (the *delegatee*) fails to perform. No special form is required to create a valid delegation of duties. As long as the delegator expresses an intention to make the delegation, it is effective; the delegator need not even use the word *delegate.*

As a general rule, any duty can be delegated. Delegation is prohibited, however, in the following circumstances:

1. When special trust has been placed in the obligor.
2. When performance depends on the personal skill or talents of the *obligor* (the person contractually obligated to perform).
3. When performance by a third party will vary materially from that expected by the obligee (the one to whom performance is owed) under the contract.
4. When the contract expressly prohibits delegation.

If a delegation of duties is enforceable, the *obligee* (the one to whom performance is owed) must accept performance from the *delegatee* (the one to whom the duties have been delegated). The obligee can legally refuse performance from the delegatee only if the duty is one that cannot be delegated.

A valid delegation of duties does not relieve the delegator of obligations under the contract. Thus, if the delegatee fails to perform, the delegator is still liable to the obligee.

THIRD PARTY BENEFICIARIES

Another exception to the doctrine of privity of contract exists when the original parties to the contract intend at the time of contracting that the contract performance directly benefit a third person. In this situation, the third person becomes a **third party beneficiary** of the contract. As an **intended beneficiary** of the contract, the third party has legal rights and can sue the promisor directly for breach of the contract.

The benefit that an **incidental beneficiary** receives from a contract between two parties is unintentional. Because the benefit is *unintentional,* an incidental beneficiary cannot sue to enforce the contract. For example, suppose that Bollow contracts with Coolidge to build a recreational facility on Coolidge's land. Once the facility is constructed, it will greatly enhance the property values in the neighborhood. If Bollow subsequently refuses to build the facility, Tran, Coolidge's neighbor, cannot enforce the contract against Bollow, because Tran is an incidental beneficiary.

REVIEWING CONTRACT FORMATION

Grant Borman, who was engaged in a construction project, leased a crane from Allied Equipment and hired Crosstown Trucking Co. to deliver the crane to the construction site. Crosstown, while the crane was in its possession and without permission from either Borman or Allied Equipment, used the crane to install a transformer for a utility company, which paid Crosstown for the job. Crosstown then delivered the crane to Borman's construction site at the appointed time of delivery. When Allied Equipment learned of the unauthorized use of the crane by Crosstown, it sued Crosstown for damages, seeking to recover the rental value of Crosstown's use of the crane. Using the information presented in the chapter, answer the following questions.

1. What are the four requirements of a valid contract?

2. Did Crosstown have a valid contract with Borman concerning the use of the crane? If so, was it a bilateral or a unilateral contract? Explain.

3. What are the requirements of an implied-in-fact contract? Can Allied Equipment obtain damages from Crosstown based on an implied-in-fact contract? Explain.

4. Does the Statute of Frauds apply to this contractual situation? Why or why not?

TERMS AND CONCEPTS TO REVIEW

acceptance 208	genuineness of assent 216	past consideration 213
agreement 198	incidental beneficiary 224	promise 192
assignment 223	intended beneficiary 224	promissory estoppel 206
consideration 210	mailbox rule 209	revocation 205
contract 193	mirror image rule 207	Statute of Frauds 222
counteroffer 207	mutual assent 198	third party beneficiary 223
delegation 223	offer 198	

QUESTIONS AND CASE PROBLEMS

9-1. Suppose that Everett McCleskey, a local business-person, is a good friend of Al Miller, the owner of a local candy store. Every day on his lunch hour, McCleskey goes into Miller's candy store and spends about five minutes looking at the candy. After examining Miller's candy and talking with Miller, McCleskey usually buys one or two candy bars. One afternoon, McCleskey goes into Miller's candy shop, looks at the candy, and picks up a $1 candy bar. Seeing that Miller is very busy, he catches Miller's eye, waves the candy bar at Miller without saying a word, and walks out. Is there a contract? If so, classify it within the categories presented in this chapter.

9-2. **QUESTION WITH SAMPLE ANSWER**

Janine was hospitalized with severe abdominal pain and placed in an intensive care unit. Her doctor told the hospital personnel to order around-the-clock nursing care for Janine. At the hospital's request, a nursing services firm, Nursing Services Unlimited, provided two weeks of in-hospital care and, after Janine was sent home, an additional two weeks of at-home care. During the at-home period of care, Janine was fully aware that she was receiving the benefit of the nursing services. Nursing Services later billed Janine $4,000 for the nursing care, but Janine refused to pay on the ground that she had never contracted for the services, either orally or in writing. In view of the fact that no express contract was ever formed, can Nursing Services recover the $4,000 from Janine? If so, under what legal theory? Discuss.
For a sample answer to this question, go to Appendix I at the end of this text.

9-3. Ball writes Sullivan and inquires how much Sullivan is asking for a specific forty-acre tract of land Sullivan owns. In a letter received by Ball, Sullivan states, "I will not take less than $60,000 for the forty-acre tract as specified." Ball immediately sends Sullivan a telegram stating, "I accept your offer for $60,000 for

the forty-acre tract as specified." Discuss whether Ball can hold Sullivan to a contract for the sale of the land.

9-4. After Kira had had several drinks one night, she sold Charlotte a diamond necklace worth thousands of dollars for just $100. The next day, Kira offered the $100 to Charlotte and requested the return of her necklace. Charlotte refused to accept the $100 or return the necklace, claiming that there was a valid contract of sale. Kira explained that she had been intoxicated at the time the bargain was made and thus the contract was voidable at her option. Was Kira correct? Explain.

9-5. TYPES OF CONTRACTS. Professor Dixon was an adjunct professor at Tulsa Community College (TCC) in Tulsa, Oklahoma. Each semester, near the beginning of the term, the parties executed a written contract that always included the following provision: "It is agreed that this agreement may be cancelled by the Administration or the instructor at anytime before the first class session." In the spring semester of Dixon's seventh year, he filed a complaint with TCC alleging that one of his students, Meredith Bhuiyan, had engaged in disruptive classroom conduct. He gave her an "incomplete" grade and asked TCC to require her to apologize as a condition of receiving a final grade. TCC later claimed, and Dixon denied, that he was told to assign Bhuiyan a grade if he wanted to teach in the fall. Toward the end of the semester, Dixon was told which classes he would teach in the fall, but the parties did not sign a written contract. The Friday before classes began, TCC terminated him. Dixon filed a suit in an Oklahoma state court against TCC and others, alleging breach of contract. Did the parties have a contract? If so, did TCC breach it? Explain. [*Dixon v. Bhuiyan*, 10 P.3d 888 (Okla. 2000)]

9-6. INTENTION. Music that is distributed on compact discs and similar media generates income in the form of "mechanical" royalties. Music that is publicly performed, such as when a song is played on a radio, used in a movie or commercial, or sampled in another song, produces "performance" royalties. Each of these types of royalties is divided between the songwriter and the song's publisher. Vincent Cusano is a musician and songwriter who performed under the name "Vinnie Vincent" as a guitarist with the group KISS in the early 1980s. Cusano co-wrote three songs—entitled "Killer," "I Love It Loud," and "I Still Love You"—that KISS recorded and released in 1982 on an album titled *Creatures of the Night*. Cusano left KISS in 1984. Eight years later, Cusano sold to Horipro Entertainment Group "one hundred (100%) percent undivided interest" of his rights in the songs "other than Songwriter's share of performance income." Later, Cusano filed a suit in a federal district court against Horipro, claiming in part that he never intended to sell the writer's share of the mechanical royalties. Horipro filed a motion for summary judgment. Should the court grant the motion? Explain. [*Cusano v. Horipro Entertainment Group*, 301 F.Supp.2d 272 (S.D.N.Y. 2004)]

9–7. ⚖ CASE PROBLEM WITH SAMPLE ANSWER

As a child, Martha Carr once visited her mother's 108-acre tract of unimproved land in Richland County, South Carolina. In 1968, Betty and Raymond Campbell leased the land. Carr, a resident of New York, was diagnosed as having schizophrenia and depression in 1986, was hospitalized five or six times, and subsequently took prescription drugs for the illnesses. In 1996, Carr inherited the Richland property and, two years later, contacted the Campbells about selling the land to them. Carr asked Betty about the value of the land, and Betty said that the county tax assessor had determined that the land's *agricultural value* was $54,000. The Campbells knew at the time that the county had assessed the total property value at $103,700 for tax purposes. A real estate appraiser found that the *real market value* of the property was $162,000. On August 6, Carr signed a contract to sell the land to the Campbells for $54,000. Believing the price to be unfair, however, Carr did not deliver the deed. The Campbells filed a suit in a South Carolina state court against Carr, seeking specific performance of the contract. At trial, an expert real estate appraiser testified that the real market value of the property was $162,000 at the time of the contract. Under what circumstances will a court examine the adequacy of consideration? Are those circumstances present in this case? Should the court enforce the contract between Carr and the Campbells? Explain. [*Campbell v. Carr*, 361 S.C. 258, 603 S.E.2d 625 (App. 2004)]

To view a sample answer for this case problem, go to this book's Web site at http://wleb.westbuslaw.com, select "Chapter 9," and click on "Case Problem with Sample Answer."

9–8. DURESS.
The law firm of Traystman, Coric and Keramidas represented Andrew Daigle in a divorce in Norwich, Connecticut. Scott McGowan, an attorney with the firm, handled the two-day trial. After the first day of the trial, McGowan told Daigle to sign a promissory note in the amount of $26,973, which represented the amount that Daigle then owed to the firm, or McGowan would withdraw from the case, and Daigle would be forced to get another attorney or to continue the trial by himself. Daigle said that he wanted another attorney, Martin Rutchik, to see the note. McGowan urged Daigle to sign it and assured him that a copy would be sent to Rutchik. Feeling that he had no other choice, Daigle signed the note. When he did not pay, the law firm filed a suit in a Connecticut state court against him. Daigle asserted that the note was unenforceable because he had signed it under duress. What are the requirements for the use of duress as a defense to a contract? Are the requirements met here? What might the law firm argue in response to Daigle's assertion? Explain. [*Traystman, Coric and Keramidas v. Daigle*, 84 Conn.App. 843, 855 A.2d 996 (2004)]

9–9. THIRD PARTY BENEFICIARY.
The National Collegiate Athletic Association (NCAA) regulates intercollegiate amateur athletics among the more than 1,200 colleges and universities with whom it contracts. Among other things, the NCAA maintains rules of eligibility for student participation in intercollegiate athletic events. Jeremy Bloom, a high school football and track star, was recruited to play football at the University of Colorado (CU). Before enrolling, he competed in Olympic and professional World Cup skiing events, becoming the World Cup champion in freestyle moguls. During the Olympics, Bloom appeared on MTV and was offered other paid entertainment opportunities, including a chance to host a show on Nickelodeon. Bloom was also paid to endorse certain ski equipment and contracted to model clothing for Tommy Hilfiger. On Bloom's behalf, CU asked the NCAA to waive its rules restricting student-athlete endorsement and media activities. The NCAA refused, and Bloom quit the activities to play football for CU. He filed a suit in a Colorado state court against the NCAA, however, asserting breach of contract on the ground that its rules permitted these activities if they were needed to support a professional athletic career. The NCAA responded that Bloom did not have standing to pursue this claim. What contract has allegedly been breached in this case? Is Bloom a party to this contract? If not, is he a third party beneficiary of it, and if so, is his status intended or incidental? Explain. [*Bloom v. National Collegiate Athletic Association*, 93 P.3d 621 (Colo.App. 2004)]

9–10. REQUIREMENTS OF THE OFFER.
The Pittsburgh Board of Public Education in Pittsburgh, Pennsylvania, as required by state law, keeps lists of eligible teachers in order of their rank or standing. According to an "Eligibility List" form made available to applicants, no one may be hired to teach whose name is not within the top 10 percent of the names on the list. In 1996, Anna Reed was in the top 10 percent. She was not hired that year, although four other applicants who

placed lower on the list—and not within the top 10 percent—were hired. In 1997 and 1998, Reed was again in the top 10 percent, but she was not hired until 1999. Reed filed a suit in a federal district court against the board and others. She argued in part that the state's requirement that the board keep a list constituted an offer, which she accepted by participating in the process to be placed on that list. She claimed that the board breached this contract by hiring applicants who ranked lower than she did. The case was transferred to a Pennsylvania state court. What are the requirements of an offer? Do the circumstances in this case meet those requirements? Why or why not? [*Reed v. Pittsburgh Board of Public Education*, 862 A.2d 131 (Pa.Cmwlth. 2004)]

9-11. BILATERAL VERSUS UNILATERAL CONTRACTS. D.L. Peoples Group (D.L.) placed an ad in a Missouri newspaper to recruit admissions representatives, who were hired to recruit Missouri residents to attend D.L.'s college in Florida. Donald Hawley responded to the ad, his interviewer recommended him for the job, and he signed, in Missouri, an "Admissions Representative Agreement," which was mailed to D.L.'s president, who signed it in his office in Florida. The agreement provided in part that Hawley would devote exclusive time and effort to the business in his assigned territory in Missouri and that D.L. would pay Hawley a commission if he successfully recruited students for the school. While attempting to make one of his first calls on his new job, Hawley was accidentally shot and killed. On the basis of his death, a claim was filed in Florida for workers' compensation. (Under Florida law, when an accident occurs outside Florida, workers' compensation benefits are payable only if the employment contract was made in Florida.) Is this admissions representative agreement a bilateral or a unilateral contract? What are the consequences of the distinction in this case? Explain. [*D.L. Peoples Group, Inc. v. Hawley*, 804 So.2d 561 (Fla.App. 1 Dist. 2002)]

9-12. NEGLIGENT MISREPRESENTATION. Cleveland Chiropractic College (CCC) promised prospective students that CCC would provide clinical training and experience—a critical part of a chiropractic education and a requirement for graduation and obtaining a license to practice. Specifically, CCC expressly promised that it would provide an ample variety of patients. CCC knew, however, that it did not have the ability to provide sufficient patients, as evidenced by its report to the Council on Chiropractic Education, an accreditation body through which chiropractic colleges monitor and certify themselves. In that report, CCC said that patient recruitment was the "joint responsibility" of the college and the student. During the 1990s, most of the "patients" that students saw were healthy persons whom the students recruited to be stand-in patients. After graduating and obtaining licenses to practice, Michael Troknya and nineteen others filed a suit in a federal district court against CCC, alleging, among other things, negligent misrepresentation. What are the elements of this cause of action? Are they satisfied in this case? Why or why not? [*Troknya v. Cleveland Chiropractic Clinic*, 280 F.3d 1200 (8th Cir. 2002)]

9-13. VIDEO QUESTION

Go to this text's Web site at http://wleb.westbuslaw.com and select "Chapter 9." Click on "Video Questions" and view the video titled *Mistake*. Then answer the following questions.

(a) What kind of mistake is involved in the dispute shown in the video (mutual or unilateral, mistake of fact or mistake of value)?

(b) According to the chapter, in what two situations would the supermarket be able to rescind a contract to sell peppers to Melnick at the incorrectly advertised price?

(c) Does it matter if the price that was advertised was a reasonable price for the peppers? Why or why not?

LAW | on the Web

For updated links to resources available on the Web, as well as a variety of other materials, visit this text's Web site at http://wleb.westbuslaw.com.

The 'Lectric Law Library provides information on contract law, including a definition of a contract, the elements required for a contract, and so on. Go to

http://www.lectlaw.com/lay.html

A good way to learn more about how the courts decide such issues as whether consideration was lacking for a particular contract is to look at relevant case law. To find recent cases on contract law decided by the United States Supreme Court and the federal appellate courts, access Cornell University's School of Law site at

http://www.law.cornell.edu/topics/contracts.html

The *New Hampshire Consumer's Sourcebook* provides information on contract law, including consideration, from a consumer's perspective. You can access this site at

http://www.doj.nh.gov/consumer/sourcebook

LEGAL RESEARCH EXERCISES ON THE WEB

Go to http://wleb.westbuslaw.com, the Web site that accompanies this text. Select "Chapter 9" and click on "Internet Exercises." There you will find the following Internet research exercises that you can perform to learn more about topics covered in this chapter.

Activity 9–1: HISTORICAL PERSPECTIVE
Contracts in Ancient Mesopotamia

Activity 9–2: ETHICAL PERSPECTIVE
Offers and Advertisements

Activity 9–3: SOCIAL PERSPECTIVE
Online Gambling

CHAPTER 10
Contract Performance, Breach, and Remedies

Just as rules are necessary to determine when a legally enforceable contract exists, so also are they required to determine when one of the parties can justifiably say, "I have fully performed, so I am now discharged from my obligations under this contract." Additionally, the parties to a contract need to know what remedies are available to them if the contract is breached.

SECTION 1 | Performance and Discharge

The most common way to **discharge,** or terminate, one's contractual duties is by the **performance** of those duties. For example, a buyer and seller have a contract for the sale of a 2006 Buick for $34,000. This contract will be discharged on the performance by the parties of their obligations under the contract—the buyer's payment of $34,000 to the seller and the seller's transfer of possession of the Buick to the buyer.

The duty to perform under a contract may be *conditioned* on the occurrence or nonoccurrence of a certain event, or the duty may be *absolute*. In the first part of this section, we look at conditions of performance and the degree of performance required. We then examine some other ways in which a contract can be discharged, including discharge by agreement of the parties and discharge by operation of law.

CONDITIONS

In most contracts, promises of performance are not expressly conditioned or qualified. Instead, they are *absolute promises*. They must be performed, or the parties promising the acts will be in breach of contract. For example, Jerome contracts to sell Alfonso a painting for $3,000. The parties' promises—Jerome's transfer of the painting to Alfonso and Alfonso's payment of $3,000 to Jerome—are unconditional. The payment does not have to be made if the painting is not transferred.

In some situations, however, performance is contingent on the occurrence or nonoccurrence of a certain event. A **condition** is a possible future event, the occurrence or nonoccurrence of which will trigger the performance of a legal obligation or terminate an existing obligation under a contract.[1] If this condition is not satisfied, the obligations of the parties are discharged. Suppose that Alfonso, in the previous example, offers to purchase Jerome's painting only if an independent appraisal indicates that it is worth at least $3,000. Jerome accepts Alfonso's offer. Their obligations (promises) are conditioned on the outcome of the appraisal. Should the condition not be satisfied (for example, if the appraiser deems the value of the painting to be only $1,500), the parties' obligations to each other are discharged and cannot be enforced.

DISCHARGE BY PERFORMANCE

The great majority of contracts are discharged by performance. The contract comes to an end when both parties fulfill their respective duties by performing the acts they have promised. Performance can also be accomplished by *tender*. Therefore, a seller who places goods at the disposal of a buyer has tendered delivery and can demand payment. A buyer who offers to pay for goods has tendered payment and can demand

---

1. The *Restatement (Second) of Contracts*, Section 224, defines a *condition* as "an event, not certain to occur, which must occur, unless its nonoccurrence is excused, before performance under a contract becomes due."

delivery of the goods. Once performance has been tendered, the party making the tender has done everything possible to carry out the terms of the contract. If the other party then refuses to perform, the party making the tender can sue for breach of contract.

There are two basic types of performance—*complete performance* and *substantial performance*. A contract may stipulate that performance must meet the personal satisfaction of either the contracting party or a third party. Such a provision must be considered in determining whether the performance rendered satisfies the contract.

COMPLETE PERFORMANCE When a party performs exactly as agreed, there is no question as to whether the contract has been performed. When a party's performance is perfect, it is said to be complete.

Normally, conditions expressly stated in a contract must be fully satisfied for complete performance to take place. For example, most construction contracts require the builder to meet certain specifications. If the specifications are conditions, complete performance is required to avoid material breach (material breach will be discussed shortly). If the conditions are met, the other party to the contract must then fulfill her or his obligation to pay the builder. If the specifications are not conditions and if the builder, without the other party's permission, fails to comply with the specifications, performance is not complete. What effect does such a failure have on the other party's obligation to pay? The answer is part of the doctrine of *substantial performance*.

SUBSTANTIAL PERFORMANCE A party who in good faith performs substantially all of the terms of a contract can enforce the contract against the other

party under the doctrine of substantial performance. Note that good faith is required. Intentionally failing to comply with the terms is a breach of the contract.

—Confers Most Benefits Promised in the Contract. Generally, to qualify as substantial, the performance must not vary greatly from the performance promised in the contract, and it must create substantially the same benefits as those promised in the contract. If the omission, variance, or defect in performance is unimportant and can easily be compensated for by awarding damages, a court is likely to hold that the contract has been substantially performed.

Courts decide whether the performance was substantial on a case-by-case basis, examining all of the facts of the particular situation. For example, in a construction contract, a court would look at the intended purpose of the structure and the expense required to bring the structure into complete compliance with the contract. Thus, the exact point at which performance is considered substantial varies.

—Entitles Other Party to Damages. Because substantial performance is not perfect, the other party is entitled to damages to compensate for the failure to comply with the contract. The measure of the damages is the cost to bring the object of the contract into compliance with its terms, if that cost is reasonable under the circumstances. If the cost is unreasonable, the measure of damages is the difference in value between the performance that was rendered and the performance that would have been rendered if the contract had been performed completely.

The following classic case emphasizes that there is no exact formula for deciding when a contract has been substantially performed.

CASE 10.1   **Jacob & Youngs v. Kent**

Court of Appeals
of New York, 1921.
230 N.Y. 239,
129 N.E. 889.

CARDOZO, J. [Judge]

The plaintiff built a country residence for the defendant at a cost of upwards of $77,000, and now sues to recover a balance of $3,483.46, remaining unpaid. The work of construction ceased in June, 1914, and the defendant then began to occupy the dwelling. There was no complaint of defective performance until March, 1915. One of the specifications for the plumbing work provides that—

> All wrought-iron pipe must be well galvanized, lap welded pipe of the grade known as "standard pipe" of Reading manufacture.

The defendant learned in March, 1915, that some of the pipe, instead of being made in Reading, was the product of other factories. The plaintiff was accordingly directed by the

CONTINUED

CASE 10.1 Continued

architect to do the work anew. The plumbing was then encased within the walls except in a few places where it had to be exposed. Obedience to the order meant more than the substitution of other pipe. It meant the demolition at great expense of substantial parts of the completed structure. The plaintiff left the work untouched, and asked for a certificate that the final payment was due. Refusal of the certificate was followed by this suit [in a New York state court].

The evidence sustains a finding that the omission of the prescribed brand of pipe was neither fraudulent nor willful. It was the result of the oversight and inattention of the plaintiff's subcontractor. Reading pipe is distinguished from Cohoes pipe and other brands only by the name of the manufacturer stamped upon it at intervals of between six and seven feet. Even the defendant's architect, though he inspected the pipe upon arrival, failed to notice the discrepancy. The plaintiff tried to show that the brands installed, though made by other manufacturers, were the same in quality, in appearance, in market value, and in cost as the brand stated in the contract—that they were, indeed, the same thing, though manufactured in another place. The evidence was excluded, and a verdict directed for the defendant. The [state intermediate appellate court] reversed, and granted a new trial.

We think the evidence, if admitted, would have supplied some basis for the inference that the defect was insignificant in its relation to the project. The courts never say that one who makes a contract fills the measure of his duty by less than full performance. They do say, however, that *an omission, both trivial and innocent, will sometimes be atoned for by allowance of the resulting damage, and will not always be the breach of a condition * * *.* [Emphasis added.]

* * * Where the line is to be drawn between the important and the trivial cannot be settled by a formula. In the nature of the case precise boundaries are impossible. The same omission may take on one aspect or another according to its setting. Substitution of equivalents may not have the same significance in fields of art on the one side and in those of mere utility on the other. Nowhere will change be tolerated, however, if it is so dominant or pervasive as in any real or substantial measure to frustrate the purpose of the contract. There is no general license to install whatever, in the builder's judgment, may be regarded as "just as good." The question is one of degree, to be answered, if there is doubt, by the triers of the facts, and, if the inferences are certain, by the judges of the law. *We must weigh the purpose to be served, the desire to be gratified, the excuse for deviation from the letter, the cruelty of enforced adherence. Then only can we tell whether literal fulfillment is to be implied by law as a condition.* * * * [Emphasis added.]

In the circumstances of this case, we think the measure of the allowance is not the cost of replacement, which would be great, but the difference in value, which would be either nominal or nothing. Some of the exposed sections might perhaps have been replaced at moderate expense. The defendant did not limit his demand to them, but treated the plumbing as a unit to be corrected from cellar to roof. In point of fact, the plaintiff never reached the stage at which evidence of the extent of the allowance became necessary. The trial court had excluded evidence that the defect was unsubstantial, and in view of that ruling there was no occasion for the plaintiff to go farther with an offer of proof. We think, however, that the offer, if it had been made, would not of necessity have been defective because directed to difference in value. It is true that in most cases the cost of replacement is the measure. The owner is entitled to the money which will permit him to complete, unless the cost of completion is grossly and unfairly out of proportion to the good to be attained. When that is true, the measure is the difference in value. * * * The rule that gives a remedy in cases of substantial performance with compensation for defects of trivial or inappreciable importance has been developed by the courts as an instrument of justice. The measure of the allowance must be shaped to the same end.

The order should be affirmed, and judgment absolute directed in favor of the plaintiff upon the stipulation, with costs in all courts.

QUESTIONS

1. The New York Court of Appeals found that Jacob & Youngs had substantially performed the contract. To what, if any, remedy is Kent entitled?
2. A requirement of substantial performance is good faith. Do you think that Jacob & Youngs substantially performed all of the terms of the contract in good faith? Why or why not?

CASE 10.1 Continued

IMPACT OF THIS CASE ON TODAY'S LAW
At the time of the *Jacob* case, some courts did not apply the doctrine of substantial performance to disputes involving breaches of contract. This landmark decision contributed to a developing trend toward equity and fairness in those circumstances. Today, an unintentional and trivial omission or deviation from the terms of a contract will not prevent its enforcement but will permit an adjustment in the value of (and hence the price paid for) its performance.

PERFORMANCE TO THE SATISFACTION OF ONE OF THE PARTIES Contracts often state that completed work must personally satisfy one of the parties. The question then arises whether this satisfaction becomes a condition precedent, requiring actual personal satisfaction or approval for discharge, or whether the test of satisfaction is an absolute promise requiring such performance as would satisfy a *reasonable person* (substantial performance).

—Personal-Service Contracts. When the subject matter of the contract is personal, a contract to be performed to the satisfaction of one of the parties is conditioned, and performance must actually satisfy that party. For example, contracts for portraits, works of art, medical or dental work, and tailoring are considered personal. Therefore, only the personal satisfaction of the party will be sufficient to fulfill the condition.

To illustrate: Suppose that Williams agrees to paint a portrait of Hirshon's daughter for $750. The contract provides that Hirshon must be satisfied with the portrait. If Hirshon is not, she will not be required to pay for it. The only requirement imposed on Hirshon is that she behave honestly and in good faith. If Hirshon expresses dissatisfaction only to avoid paying for the portrait, the condition of satisfaction is excused, and her duty to pay becomes absolute. (Of course, the jury, or the judge acting as a jury, will have to decide whether she is acting honestly.)[2]

—All Other Contracts. Contracts that involve mechanical fitness, utility, or marketability need only be performed to the satisfaction of a *reasonable* person. For example, construction contracts and manufacturing contracts are usually *not* considered to be personal, so the party's personal satisfaction is normally irrele-

vant. As long as the performance will satisfy a reasonable person, the contract is fulfilled.[3]

PERFORMANCE TO THE SATISFACTION OF A THIRD PARTY At times, contracts may require performance to the satisfaction of a third party (not a party to the contract). To illustrate: Assume that you contract to pave several city streets. The contract provides that the work will be done "to the satisfaction of Phil Hopper, the supervising engineer." In this situation, the courts are divided.

A few courts require the personal satisfaction of the third party—in this example, Phil Hopper. If Hopper is not satisfied, you will not be paid, even if a reasonable person would be satisfied. Again, the personal judgment must be made honestly, or the condition will be excused.

A majority of courts, however, require the work to be satisfactory to a reasonable person. Thus, even if Hopper is dissatisfied with the paving work, you will be paid, as long as a qualified supervising engineer would have been satisfied. All of the above examples demonstrate the necessity for *clear, specific wording in contracts*.

MATERIAL BREACH OF CONTRACT A **breach of contract** is the nonperformance of a contractual duty. The breach is *material* when performance is not at least substantial. If there is a material breach, then the nonbreaching party is excused from the performance of contractual duties and has a cause of action to sue for damages resulting from the breach. If the breach is *minor* (not material), the nonbreaching party's duty to perform can sometimes be suspended until the breach has been remedied, but the duty to perform is not entirely excused. Once the minor breach has been

---

2. For a classic case illustrating this principle, see *Gibson v. Cranage*, 39 Mich. 49 (1878).

3. If, however, the contract specifically states that it is to be fulfilled to the "personal" satisfaction of one or more of the parties, and the parties so intended, the outcome will probably be different.

cured, the nonbreaching party must resume performance of the contractual obligations undertaken.

Any breach entitles the nonbreaching party to sue for damages, but only a material breach discharges the nonbreaching party from the contract. The policy underlying these rules allows contracts to go forward when only minor problems occur but allows them to be terminated if major difficulties arise.

Under what circumstances is an employer excused from further performance under a contract with an employee? That was the question in the following case.

CASE 10.2 **Shah v. Cover-It, Inc.**

Appellate Court of Connecticut, 2004. 86 Conn.App. 71, 859 A.2d 959.

BACKGROUND AND FACTS *In November 1997, Cover-It, Inc., hired Khalid Shah to work as its structural engineering manager. Shah agreed to work a flexible schedule of thirty-five hours per week. In exchange, he would receive an annual salary of $70,000 for five years, a 2 percent commission on the sales of products that he designed, three weeks of paid vacation after one year, a company car, time off to attend to prior professional obligations, and certain other benefits. Either party could terminate the contract with ninety days' written notice, but if Cover-It terminated it, Shah would receive monthly payments for the rest of the five-year term.[a] In June 1998, Shah went on vacation and did not return until September. In mid-October, Brian Goldwitz, Cover-It's owner and president, terminated Shah's contract. Shah filed a suit in a Connecticut state court against Cover-It and others. The court determined that Shah had breached the contract and rendered a judgment in the defendants' favor. Shah appealed to a state intermediate appellate court.*

IN THE LANGUAGE OF THE COURT

SCHALLER, J. [Judge]

* * * *

On appeal, the plaintiff claims that the court improperly found that he had breached the contract or, in the alternative, that any breach was not material. Specifically, the plaintiff argues that the court failed to identify an express term or condition that was breached and instead merely found that certain acts, considered together, demonstrated a material breach prior to the termination of his employment. Therefore, according to the plaintiff, the defendants were not relieved of their obligations, under the terms of the contract, to pay his full salary for ninety days and to pay his post-termination salary pursuant to the schedule set forth in the contract. * * *

* * * *

It is a general rule of contract law that a total breach of the contract by one party relieves the injured party of any further duty to perform further obligations under the contract. [Emphasis added.]

* * * Section 241 of the *Restatement (Second) of Contracts* provides:

In determining whether a failure to render or to offer performance is material, the following circumstances are significant: (a) the extent to which the injured party will be deprived of the benefit which he reasonably expected; (b) the extent to which the injured party can be adequately compensated for the part of that benefit of which he will be deprived; (c) the extent to which the party failing to perform or to offer to perform will suffer forfeiture; (d) the likelihood that the party failing to perform or to offer to perform will cure his failure, taking account of all the circumstances including any reasonable assurances; [and] (e) the extent to which the behavior of the party failing to perform or to offer to perform comports with standards of good faith and fair dealing.

The standards of materiality are to be applied in the light of the facts of each case in such a way as to further the purpose of securing for each party his expectation of an exchange of performances. Section 241 therefore states circumstances, not rules, which are to be considered in determining whether a particular failure is material. [Emphasis added.]

In the present case, the court found that the plaintiff took a ten-week vacation, which exceeded the time authorized. After the plaintiff returned, he reported for work only two or

a. The contract provided that for up to two years of service, Shah would be paid $20,000 per year; for three years of service, $30,000 per year; and for four years of service, $40,000 per year.

CASE 10.2 Continued three days per week and spent long periods of time visiting Internet Web sites that were unrelated to his professional duties. Additionally, after being instructed by [Cover-It's] human resources manager to document his attendance by use of a time clock, the plaintiff refused and simply marked his time sheets with a "P" for present. Last, the court found that when Goldwitz asked when certain designs would be completed, the plaintiff responded that he was not sure and that he would take his time in completing them. When reviewing those findings in light of the factors set forth in [Section] 241 of the *Restatement (Second) of Contracts*, we conclude that the court's finding of a material breach was not clearly erroneous.

It is clear from the court's findings that the plaintiff failed to perform under the obligations of the employment contract. * * * One cannot recover upon a contract unless he has fully performed his own obligation under it, has tendered performance or has some legal excuse for not performing. As a result of the material breach by the plaintiff, the defendants were excused from further performance under the contract, and were relieved of the obligation to pay the plaintiff his full salary for ninety days and to pay his post-termination salary pursuant to the schedule set forth in the contract.

DECISION AND REMEDY *The state intermediate appellate court affirmed the judgment of the lower court. The appellate court held that Shah had materially breached his contract with Cover-It and that this breach excused Cover-It from further performance of its contractual duties, relieving the defendant of any obligation to continue paying Shah's salary.*

WHAT IF THE FACTS WERE DIFFERENT? *Suppose that during his ten-week absence Shah was fulfilling prior professional obligations and that on his return he met Cover-It's hours and time-keeping requirements. Further suppose that Shah responded to Goldwitz's questions about his projects with reasonable estimates. Would the outcome of the case have been different? Why or why not?*

DISCHARGE BY AGREEMENT

Any contract can be discharged by agreement of the parties. The agreement can be contained in the original contract, or the parties can form a new contract for the express purpose of discharging the original contract.

DISCHARGE BY RESCISSION As mentioned in previous chapters, *rescission* is the process by which a contract is canceled or terminated and the parties are returned to the positions they occupied prior to forming it. For **mutual rescission** to take place, the parties must make another agreement that also satisfies the legal requirements for a contract. There must be an *offer*, an *acceptance*, and *consideration*. Ordinarily, if the parties agree to rescind the original contract, their promises not to perform the acts stipulated in the original contract will be legal consideration for the second contract (the rescission).

Agreements to rescind executory contracts (in which neither party has performed) are generally enforceable, even if the agreement is made orally and even if the original agreement was in writing. An exception applies under the Uniform Commercial Code (UCC) to agreements rescinding a contract for the sale of goods, regardless of price, when the contract requires a written rescission. Also, agreements to rescind contracts involving transfers of realty must be evidenced by a writing.

When one party has fully performed, an agreement to cancel the original contract normally will not be enforceable. Because the performing party has received no consideration for the promise to call off the original bargain, additional consideration is necessary.

DISCHARGE BY NOVATION A contractual obligation may also be discharged through novation. A **novation** occurs when both of the parties to a contract agree to substitute a third party for one of the original parties. The requirements of a novation are as follows:

1. A previous valid obligation.
2. An agreement by all the parties to a new contract.
3. The extinguishing of the old obligation (discharge of the prior party).
4. A new contract that is valid.

For example, suppose that Union Corporation contracts to sell its pharmaceutical division to British Pharmaceuticals, Ltd. Before the transfer is completed, Union, British Pharmaceuticals, and a third company,

Otis Chemicals, execute a new agreement to transfer all of British Pharmaceutical's rights and duties in the transaction to Otis Chemicals. As long as the new contract is supported by consideration, the novation will discharge the original contract (between Union and British Pharmaceuticals) and replace it with the new contract (between Union and Otis Chemicals).

A novation expressly or impliedly revokes and discharges a prior contract. The parties involved may expressly state in the new contract that the old contract is now discharged. If the parties do not expressly discharge the old contract, it will be impliedly discharged if the new contract's terms are inconsistent with the old contract's terms.

DISCHARGE BY SUBSTITUTED AGREEMENT
A *compromise*, or settlement agreement, that arises out of a genuine dispute over the obligations under an existing contract will be recognized at law. Such an agreement will be substituted as a new contract, and it will either expressly or impliedly revoke and discharge the obligations under any prior contract. In contrast to a novation, a substituted agreement does not involve a third party. Rather, the two original parties to the contract form a different agreement to substitute for the original one.

DISCHARGE BY ACCORD AND SATISFACTION
For a contract to be discharged by accord and satisfaction, the parties must agree to accept performance that is different from the performance originally promised. An *accord* is a contract to perform some act to satisfy an existing contractual duty. The duty has not yet been discharged. A *satisfaction* is the performance of the accord agreement. An accord and its satisfaction discharge the original contractual obligation.

Once the accord has been made, the original obligation is merely suspended. The obligor (the one owing the obligation) can discharge the obligation by performing either the obligation agreed to in the accord or the original obligation. If the obligor refuses to perform the accord, the obligee (the one to whom performance is owed) can bring action on the original obligation or seek a decree compelling specific performance on the accord.

For example, suppose that Frazer has a judgment against Ling for $8,000. Later, both parties agree that the judgment can be satisfied by Ling's transfer of his automobile to Frazer. This agreement to accept the auto in lieu of $8,000 in cash is the accord. If Ling transfers the car to Frazer, the accord is fully per-

formed, and the debt is discharged. If Ling refuses to transfer the car, the accord is breached. Because the original obligation is merely suspended, Frazer can sue Ling to enforce the original judgment for $8,000 in cash or bring an action for breach of the accord.

DISCHARGE BY OPERATION OF LAW

Under certain circumstances, contractual duties may be discharged by operation of law. These circumstances include material alteration of the contract, the running of the statute of limitations, bankruptcy, and the impossibility or impracticability of performance.

ALTERATION OF THE CONTRACT
To discourage parties from altering written contracts, the law operates to allow an innocent party to be discharged when the other party has materially altered a written contract without consent. For example, contract terms such as quantity or price might be changed without the knowledge or consent of all parties. If so, the party who was not involved in the alteration can treat the contract as discharged or terminated.[4]

STATUTES OF LIMITATIONS
As mentioned earlier in this text, statutes of limitations restrict the period during which a party can sue on a particular cause of action. After the applicable limitations period has passed, a suit can no longer be brought. For example, the limitations period for bringing suits for breach of oral contracts is usually two to three years; for written contracts, four to five years; and for recovery of amounts awarded in judgments, ten to twenty years, depending on state law. Suits for breach of a contract for the sale of goods generally must be brought within four years after the cause of action has accrued. By their original agreement, the parties can reduce this four-year period to not less than one year, but they cannot agree to extend it.

Technically, the running of a statute of limitations bars access only to *judicial* remedies; it does not extinguish the debt or the underlying obligation. The statute of limitations precludes access to the courts for collection. If, however, the party who owes the debt or obligation agrees to perform (that is, makes a new

---

4. The contract is voidable, and the innocent party can also treat the contract as in effect, either on the original terms or on the terms as altered. A buyer who discovers that a seller altered the quantity of goods in a sales contract from 100 to 1,000 by secretly inserting a zero can purchase either 100 or 1,000 of the items.

promise to perform), the cause of action barred by the statute of limitations will be revived. For the old agreement to be restored by a new promise in this manner, many states require that the promise be in writing or that there be evidence of partial performance.

BANKRUPTCY A proceeding in bankruptcy attempts to allocate the assets the debtor owns to the creditors in a fair and equitable fashion. Once the assets have been allocated, the debtor receives a *discharge in bankruptcy*. A discharge in bankruptcy will ordinarily bar enforcement of most of the debtor's contracts by the creditors. Partial payment of a debt *after* discharge in bankruptcy will not revive the debt. (Bankruptcy will be discussed in detail in Chapter 15.)

IMPOSSIBILITY OR IMPRACTICABILITY OF PERFORMANCE After a contract has been made, performance may become impossible in an objective sense. This is known as **impossibility of performance** and may discharge a contract.

—*Objective Impossibility of Performance.* *Objective impossibility* ("It can't be done") must be distinguished from *subjective impossibility* ("I'm sorry, I simply can't do it"). Examples of subjective impossibility include the situation in which goods cannot be delivered on time because of freight car shortages and the situation in which payment cannot be made on time because the bank is closed. In effect, the party in each of these situations is saying, "It is impossible for me to perform," not "It is impossible for anyone to perform." Accordingly, such excuses do not discharge a contract, and the nonperforming party is normally held in breach of contract. Three basic types of situations, however, generally qualify as grounds for the discharge of contractual obligations based on impossibility of performance:[5]

1. *When one of the parties to a personal contract dies or becomes incapacitated prior to performance.* For example, Fred, a famous dancer, contracts with Ethereal Dancing Guild to play a leading role in its new ballet. Before the ballet can be performed, Fred becomes ill and dies. His personal performance was essential to the completion of the contract. Thus, his death discharges the contract and his estate's liability for his nonperformance.

2. *When the specific subject matter of the contract is destroyed.* For example, A-1 Farm Equipment agrees to sell Gudgel the green tractor on its lot and promises to have it ready for Gudgel to pick up on Saturday. On Friday night, however, a truck veers off the nearby highway and smashes into the tractor, destroying it beyond repair. Because the contract was for this specific tractor, A-1's performance is rendered impossible owing to the accident.

3. *When a change in law renders performance illegal.* For example, a contract to build an apartment building becomes impossible to perform when the zoning laws are changed to prohibit the construction of residential rental property at the planned location.

—*Commercial Impracticability.* Courts may excuse parties from their performance obligations when the performance becomes much more difficult or expensive than originally contemplated at the time the contract was formed. For someone to invoke the doctrine of **commercial impracticability** successfully, however, the anticipated performance must become *extremely* difficult or costly.[6] The added burden of performing not only must be extreme but also *must not have been known by the parties when the contract was made.*

—*Frustration of Purpose.* A theory closely allied with the doctrine of commercial impracticability is the doctrine of **frustration of purpose.** In principle, a contract will be discharged if supervening circumstances make it impossible to attain the purpose both parties had in mind when making the contract.

The origins of the doctrine lie in the old English "coronation cases." A coronation procession was planned for Edward VII when he became king of England following the death of his mother, Queen Victoria. Hotel rooms along the coronation route were rented at exorbitant prices for that day. When the king became ill and the procession was canceled, a flurry of lawsuits resulted. Hotel and building owners sought to enforce the room-rent bills against would-be parade observers, and would-be parade observers sought to be reimbursed for rental monies paid in advance on the rooms. Would-be parade observers were excused from their duty of payment because the purpose of the room contracts had been "frustrated."

---

5. *Restatement (Second) of Contracts*, Sections 262–266; UCC 2–615.

6. *Restatement (Second) of Contracts*, Section 264.

—Temporary Impossibility. An occurrence or event that makes performance temporarily impossible operates to suspend performance until the impossibility ceases. Then, ordinarily, the parties must perform the contract as originally planned. If, however, the lapse of time and the change in circumstances surrounding the contract make it substantially more burdensome for the parties to perform the promised acts, the contract is discharged.

The leading case on the subject, *Autry v. Republic Productions,*[7] involved an actor who was drafted into the army in 1942. Being drafted rendered the actor's contract temporarily impossible to perform, and it was suspended until the end of the war. When the actor got out of the army, the value of the dollar had so changed that performance of the contract would have been substantially burdensome to the actor. Therefore, the contract was discharged.

Exhibit 10–1 graphically illustrates the ways in which a contract can be discharged.

SECTION 2 | Breach of Contract and Remedies

When one party breaches a contract, the other party—the nonbreaching party—can choose one or more of several remedies. A *remedy* is the relief provided for an innocent party when the other party has breached the contract. It is the means employed to enforce a right or to redress an injury.

The most common remedies available to a nonbreaching party include damages, rescission and restitution, specific performance, and reformation. As discussed in Chapter 1, a distinction is made between *remedies at law* and *remedies in equity.* Today, the remedy at law is normally money damages, which are discussed in the first part of this section. Equitable remedies include rescission and restitution, specific performance, and reformation, all of which will be examined later in this section. Usually, a court will not award an equitable remedy unless the remedy at law is inadequate. Special legal doctrines and concepts relating to remedies will be discussed in the final pages of this chapter.

DAMAGES

A breach of contract entitles the nonbreaching party to sue for money (damages). Damages are designed to compensate a party for harm suffered as a result of

another's wrongful act. In the context of contract law, damages compensate the nonbreaching party for the loss of the bargain. Often, courts say that innocent parties are to be placed in the position they would have occupied had the contract been fully performed.[8]

Realize at the outset, though, that to collect damages through a court judgment means litigation, which can be expensive and time consuming. Also keep in mind that court judgments are often difficult to enforce, particularly if the breaching party does not have sufficient assets to pay the damages awarded (as discussed in Chapter 2). For these reasons, the majority of actions for damages (or other remedies) are settled by the parties before trial.

TYPES OF DAMAGES There are basically four broad categories of damages:

1. Compensatory (to cover direct losses and costs).
2. Consequential (to cover indirect and foreseeable losses).
3. Punitive (to punish and deter wrongdoing).
4. Nominal (to recognize wrongdoing when no monetary loss is shown).

We look here at compensatory and consequential damages.

COMPENSATORY DAMAGES Damages compensating the nonbreaching party for the *loss of the bargain* are known as *compensatory damages.* These damages compensate the injured party only for damages actually sustained and proved to have arisen directly from the loss of the bargain caused by the breach of contract. They simply replace what was lost because of the wrong or damage. The standard measure of compensatory damages is the difference between the value of the breaching party's promised performance under the contract and the value of her or his actual performance. This amount is reduced by any loss that the injured party has avoided, however.

To illustrate: Wilcox contracts to perform certain services exclusively for Hernandez during the month of March for $4,000. Hernandez cancels the contract and is in breach. Wilcox is able to find another job during the month of March but can earn only $3,000. He can sue Hernandez for breach and recover $1,000 as compensatory damages. Wilcox can also recover

---

7. 30 Cal.2d 144, 180 P.2d 888 (1947).

8. *Restatement (Second) of Contracts,* Section 347; Section 1–106(1) of the Uniform Commercial Code (UCC).

EXHIBIT 10-1 Contract Discharge

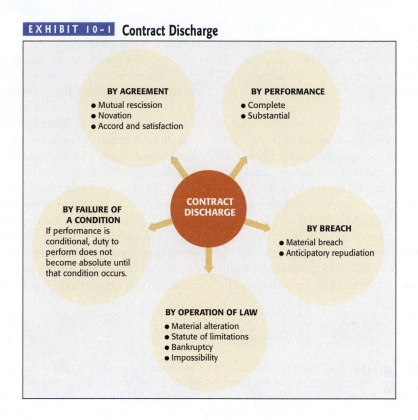

from Hernandez the amount that he spent to find the other job. Expenses that are caused directly by a breach of contract—such as those incurred to obtain performance from another source—are known as *incidental damages*.

The measurement of compensatory damages varies by type of contract. Certain types of contracts deserve special mention. They are contracts for the sale of goods and land contracts.

—Sale of Goods. In a contract for the sale of goods, the usual measure of compensatory damages is an amount equal to the difference between the contract price and the market price.[9] For example, suppose that Chrylon Corporation contracts to buy ten model UTS 400 network servers from an XEXO Corporation dealer for $8,000 each. The dealer, however, fails to deliver the ten servers to Chrylon. The market price of the servers at the time the buyer learns of the breach is $8,150. Chrylon's measure of damages is therefore $1,500 (10 × $150) plus any incidental damages (expenses) caused by the breach. In a situa-

tion in which the buyer breaches and the seller has not yet produced the goods, compensatory damages normally equal lost profits on the sale, not the difference between the contract price and the market price.

—Sale of Land. Ordinarily, because each parcel of land is unique, the remedy for a seller's breach of a contract for a sale of real estate is specific performance—that is, the buyer is awarded the parcel of property for which she or he bargained (specific performance will be discussed more fully later in this chapter). When this remedy is unavailable (for example, when the seller has sold the property to someone else), or when the breach is on the part of the buyer, the measure of damages is ordinarily the same as in contracts for the sale of goods—that is, the difference between the contract price and the market price of the land. The majority of states follow this rule.

A minority of states follow a different rule when the seller breaches the contract and the breach is not deliberate.[10] In this situation, these states allow the

---

9. In other words, the amount is the difference between the contract price and the market price at the time and place at which the goods were to be delivered or tendered. See UCC 2–708 and 2–713.

10. "Deliberate" breaches include the seller's failure to convey the land because the market price has gone up. "Nondeliberate" breaches include the seller's failure to convey the land because an unknown easement (another's right of use over the property) has rendered title unmarketable. See Chapter 25.

prospective purchaser to recover any down payment plus any expenses incurred (such as fees for title searches, attorneys, and escrows). This minority rule effectively places purchasers in the position they occupied prior to the sale.

CONSEQUENTIAL DAMAGES   Foreseeable damages that result from a party's breach of contract are called **consequential damages,** or *special damages*. They differ from compensatory damages in that they are caused by special circumstances beyond the contract itself. They flow from the consequences, or results, of a breach.

For example, if a seller fails to deliver goods, and the seller knows that a buyer is planning to resell these goods immediately, consequential damages will be awarded for the loss of profit from the planned resale. The buyer will also recover compensatory damages for the difference between the contract price and the market price of the goods.

To recover consequential damages, the breaching party must know (or have reason to know) that special circumstances will cause the nonbreaching party to suffer an additional loss. This rule was enunciated in the classic case of *Hadley v. Baxendale*, which is presented next. In reading this decision, it is helpful to understand that it was customary in the mid-1800s in England for large flour mills to have more than one crankshaft in the event that the main crankshaft broke and had to be repaired. Also, in those days it was common knowledge that flour mills did indeed have spare crankshafts. It is against this background that the parties in the case presented here argued their respective positions on whether the damages resulting from the loss of profits while the crankshaft was repaired were reasonably foreseeable.

CASE 10.3   Hadley v. Baxendale

Court of Exchequer, 1854.
156 Eng.Rep. 145.

BACKGROUND AND FACTS   *The Hadleys (the plaintiffs) ran a flour mill in Gloucester. The crankshaft attached to the steam engine in the mill broke, causing the mill to shut down. The shaft had to be sent to a foundry located in Greenwich so that the new shaft could be made to fit the other parts of the engine. Baxendale, the defendant, was a common carrier that transported the shaft from Gloucester to Greenwich. The freight charges were collected in advance, and Baxendale promised to deliver the shaft the following day. It was not delivered for a number of days, however. As a consequence, the mill was closed for several days. The Hadleys sued to recover the profits lost during that time. Baxendale contended that the loss of profits was "too remote" to be recoverable. The court held for the plaintiffs, and the jury was allowed to take into consideration the lost profits. The defendant appealed.*

IN THE LANGUAGE OF THE COURT

ALDERSON, B.

* * * *

* * * Where two parties have made a contract which one of them has broken, the damages which the other party ought to receive in respect of such breach of contract should be such as may fairly and reasonably be considered either arising naturally, *i.e.*, according to the usual course of things, from such breach of contract itself, or such as may reasonably be supposed to have been in the contemplation of both parties, at the time they made the contract, as the probable result of the breach of it. Now, if the special circumstances under which the contract was actually made were communicated by the plaintiffs to the defendants, and thus known to both parties, the damages resulting from the breach of such a contract, *which they would reasonably contemplate*, would be the amount of injury which would ordinarily follow from a breach of contract under these special circumstances so known and communicated. * * * Now, in the present case, if we are to apply the principles above laid down, we find that the only circumstances here communicated by the plaintiffs to the defendants at the time the contract was made, were, that the article to be carried was the broken shaft of a mill, and that the plaintiffs were the millers of that mill. * * * [S]pecial circumstances were here never communicated by the plaintiffs to the defendants. It follows, therefore, that the loss of profits here cannot reasonably be considered such a consequence of the breach of contract as could have been fairly and reasonably contemplated by both the parties when they made this contract. [Emphasis added.]

CASE 10.3 | Continued **DECISION AND REMEDY** *The Court of Exchequer ordered a new trial. According to the court, to collect consequential damages, the plaintiffs would have to have given express notice of the special circumstances that caused the loss of profits.*

IMPACT OF THIS CASE ON TODAY'S LAW

This case established the rule that when damages are awarded, compensation is given only for those injuries that the defendant could reasonably have foreseen as a probable result of the usual course of events following a breach. Today, the rule enunciated by the court in this case still applies. To recover consequential damages, the plaintiff must show that the defendant had reason to know or foresee that a particular loss or injury would occur.

MITIGATION OF DAMAGES In most situations, when a breach of contract occurs, the innocent injured party is held to a duty to mitigate, or reduce, the damages that he or she suffers. Under this doctrine of **mitigation of damages,** the duty owed depends on the nature of the contract.

For example, some states require a landlord to use reasonable means to find a new tenant if a tenant abandons the premises and fails to pay rent. If an acceptable tenant becomes available, the landlord is required to lease the premises to this tenant to mitigate the damages recoverable from the former tenant. The former tenant is still liable for the difference between the amount of the rent under the original lease and the rent received from the new tenant. If the landlord has not used the reasonable means necessary to find a new tenant, presumably a court can reduce the award made by the amount of rent the landlord could have received had such reasonable means been used.

In the majority of states, persons whose employment has been wrongfully terminated owe a duty to mitigate damages suffered because of their employers' breach of the employment contract. In other words, wrongfully terminated employees have a duty to take similar jobs if they are available. If the employees fail to do this, the damages they are awarded will be equivalent to their salaries less the incomes they would have received in similar jobs obtained by reasonable means. The employer has the burden of proving that such a job existed and that the employee could have been hired. Normally, the employee is under no duty to take a job of a different type and rank, however.

LIQUIDATED DAMAGES PROVISIONS A **liquidated damages** provision in a contract specifies that a certain dollar amount is to be paid in the event of a *future* default or breach of contract. (*Liquidated* means determined, settled, or fixed.) For example, a provision requiring a construction contractor to pay $300 for every day he or she is late in completing the construction is a liquidated damages provision. Liquidated damages provisions are frequently used in construction contracts because it is difficult to estimate the amount of damages that would be caused by a delay in completing construction. These clauses are also common in contracts for the sale of goods, and Section 2–718(1) of the Uniform Commercial Code (UCC) specifically authorizes the use of liquidated damages clauses.[11]

—*Liquidated Damages versus Penalties.* When a contract specifies a sum to be paid for nonperformance, the issue becomes whether the amount should be treated as liquidated damages or as a penalty. Liquidated damages provisions are enforceable; penalty provisions are not. Generally, if the amount stated is excessive and the clause is designed to *penalize* the breaching party, a court will consider it a **penalty.** If the amount specified is a reasonable estimation of actual damages, a court may enforce it as a liquidated damages provision.

—*Factors Courts Consider.* To determine if a particular provision is for liquidated damages or for a penalty, two questions must be answered:

1. When the contract was entered into, was it apparent that damages would be difficult to estimate in the event of a breach?
2. Was the amount set as damages a reasonable estimate and not excessive?[12]

---

11. Note that in 2003, this section was amended. Under the revised version of the statute, only in consumer contracts must the amount of damages be difficult to estimate and a reasonable forecast. In contracts between merchants, it is no longer required that the damages be difficult to estimate. See Official Comment 2.
12. *Restatement (Second) of Contracts,* Section 356(1).

If the answers to both questions are yes, the provision normally will be enforced. If either answer is no, the provision normally will not be enforced. For example, in a case involving a sophisticated business contract to lease computer equipment, the court held that a liquidated damages provision that valued computer equipment at more than four times its market value was a reasonable estimate. According to the court, the amount of actual damages was difficult to ascer-

tain at the time the contract was formed because of the "speculative nature of the value of computers at termination of lease schedules."[13]

In the following case, the court considered a liquidated damages provision in the context of an agreement for the lease of a hotel.

13. *Winthrop Resources Corporation v. Eaton Hydraulics, Inc.*, 361 F.3d 465 (8th Cir. 2004).

CASE 10.4   Green Park Inn, Inc. v. Moore

North Carolina
Court of Appeals, 2002.
149 N.C.App. 531,
562 S.E.2d 53.
http://www.nccourts.org[a]

COMPANY PROFILE *Green Park Inn (http://www.greenparkinn.com) is one of the oldest hotels in the United States. Established in 1882 and listed on the National Register of Historic Places, it is located in the Blue Ridge Mountains near Blowing Rock, North Carolina. Eminent guests have included Annie Oakley, Herbert Hoover, Eleanor Roosevelt, Margaret Mitchell, Calvin Coolidge, and John D. Rockefeller. Green Park Inn is a full-service, first class hotel and restaurant.*

BACKGROUND AND FACTS *Allen and Pat McCain own Green Park Inn, Inc., which operates the Green Park Inn. In 1996, they leased the Inn to GMAFCO, LLC, which is owned by Gary and Gail Moore. The lease agreement provided that, in case of a default by GMAFCO, Green Park, Inc., would be entitled to $500,000 as "liquidated damages." GMAFCO defaulted on the February 2000 rent. Green Park Inn, Inc., gave GMAFCO an opportunity to cure the default, but GMAFCO made no further payments and returned possession of the property to the lessor. When Green Park Inn, Inc., sought the "liquidated damages," the Moores refused to pay. Green Park Inn, Inc., filed a suit in a North Carolina state court against the Moores, GMAFCO, and their bank to obtain the $500,000. The defendants contended in part that the lease clause requiring payment of "liquidated damages" was an unenforceable penalty provision. The court ordered the defendants to pay Green Park Inn, Inc. The defendants appealed to a state intermediate appellate court.*

IN THE LANGUAGE OF THE COURT

HUDSON, Judge.
* * * *
The parties agreed to the following in the liquidated damages clause of the Lease Agreement:

Allen and Pat McCain, the only two shareholders of lessor, have actively worked in the day to day operation of the hotel for the past fourteen years, and have steadily built up the clientele, reputation and physical plant of the hotel, and, correspondingly, the revenues/profits of the hotel. In addition, Allen and Pat McCain are 64 and 55 years old respectively, and both retired from the business after this lease was agreed to. The McCains have retired to Florida, and would have to relocate back to Blowing Rock for extended periods of time if they are forced out of retirement to take over operation of the hotel. The parties agree to the following items which will be included in lessor's damages:

(a) restoration of the physical plant;
(b) lost lease payments owed to lessor which will not be paid because of lessee's breach with due consideration having been given to lessor's obligation to mitigate damages;
(c) harm to the reputation of the hotel, which will have to be remedied by lessor;
(d) interruption of business damages caused by the necessity of lessor having to hire new employees to recommence operations.

While some of the items listed in the liquidated damages provision are not indefinite or uncertain, others, such as the harm to the hotel's reputation or the cost to the McCains of

a. Select the link to "Court Opinions," enter "Green Park" in the box labeled "Keywords," and click on "Search." Select the name of the case from the resulting list to access the opinion. The North Carolina Appellate Division Reporter maintains this Web site.

CASE 10.4 | Continued   being forced out of retirement, clearly would have been difficult to ascertain at the time the Lease Agreement was signed. * * *

Whether a liquidated damages amount is a reasonable estimate of the damages that would likely result from a default is a question of fact. * * * [McCain] stated that, after he and his wife were forced out of retirement and back to Blowing Rock to operate the hotel, "[t]he estimate of $500,000.00 as the fair and reasonable estimate to measure the damages suffered by us in the event of default has proven to be just that fair and reasonable." Additionally, the Lease Agreement states that "[t]he parties have agreed that the sum of Five Hundred Thousand Dollars ($500,000.00) represents a fair and reasonable estimate and measure of the damages to be suffered by lessor in the event of default by lessee." Defendants have proffered [offered] no evidence to show the liquidated damages amount was unreasonable. [Emphasis added.]

DECISION AND REMEDY   *The state intermediate appellate court affirmed the decision of the lower court. The lease provision satisfied the two-part test for liquidated damages. The amount of the damages would have been difficult to determine at the time that the lease was signed, and the estimate of the damages was reasonable.*

WHAT IF THE FACTS WERE DIFFERENT?   *If the lease had specified $3 million in damages, would the result in this case have been different? If so, in what way?*

RESCISSION AND RESTITUTION

As discussed earlier in this chapter, *rescission* is essentially an action to undo, or terminate, a contract—to return the contracting parties to the positions they occupied prior to the transaction.[14] When fraud, a mistake, duress, undue influence, misrepresentation, or lack of capacity to contract is present, unilateral rescission is available. Rescission may also be available by statute.[15] The failure of one party to perform entitles the other party to rescind the contract. The rescinding party must give prompt notice to the breaching party.

RESTITUTION   Generally, to rescind a contract, both parties must make **restitution** to each other by returning goods, property, or funds previously conveyed.[16] If the physical property or goods can be returned, they must be. If the goods or property have been consumed, restitution must be made in an equivalent amount of cash.

Essentially, restitution refers to the plaintiff's recapture of a benefit conferred on the defendant through which the defendant has been unjustly enriched. For example, Katie pays $10,000 to Bob in return for Bob's promise to design a house for her. The next day Bob calls Katie and tells her that he has taken a position with a large architectural firm in another state and cannot design the house. Katie decides to hire another architect that afternoon. Katie can obtain restitution of the $10,000.

RESTITUTION IS NOT LIMITED TO RESCISSION CASES   Restitution may be appropriate when a contract is rescinded, but the right to restitution is not limited to rescission cases. Restitution may be sought in actions for breach of contract, tort actions, and other actions at law or in equity. Usually, restitution can be obtained when funds or property has been transferred by mistake or because of fraud. An award in a case may include restitution of funds or property obtained through embezzlement, conversion, theft, copyright infringement, or misconduct by a party in a confidential or other special relationship.

SPECIFIC PERFORMANCE

The equitable remedy of **specific performance** calls for the performance of the act promised in the contract. This remedy is quite attractive to the nonbreaching party for three reasons:

1. The nonbreaching party need not worry about collecting the money damages awarded by a court (see the

---

14. The rescission discussed here is *unilateral* rescission, in which only one party wants to undo the contract. In mutual rescission, both parties agree to undo the contract. Mutual rescission discharges the contract; unilateral rescission is generally available as a remedy for breach of contract.

15. The Federal Trade Commission and many states have rules or statutes allowing consumers to unilaterally rescind contracts made at home with door-to-door salespersons. Rescission is allowed within three days for any reason or for no reason at all. See, for example, California Civil Code Section 1689.5.

16. *Restatement (Second) of Contracts*, Section 370.

discussion in Chapter 2 of some of the difficulties that may arise when trying to enforce court judgments).

2. The nonbreaching party need not spend time seeking an alternative contract.

3. The performance is more valuable than the money damages.

Normally, however, specific performance will not be granted unless the party's legal remedy (money damages) is inadequate.[17] For this reason, contracts for the sale of goods rarely qualify for specific performance. The legal remedy—money damages—is ordinarily adequate in such situations because substantially identical goods can be bought or sold in the market. Only if the goods are unique will a court grant specific performance. For example, paintings, sculptures, or rare books or coins are so unique that money damages will not enable a buyer to obtain substantially identical substitutes in the market.

SALE OF LAND Specific performance is granted to a buyer in a contract for the sale of land. The legal remedy for breach of a land sales contract is inadequate because every parcel of land is considered to be unique. Money damages will not compensate a buyer adequately because the same land in the same location obviously cannot be obtained elsewhere. Only when specific performance is unavailable (for example, when the seller has sold the property to someone else) will money damages be awarded instead.

CONTRACTS FOR PERSONAL SERVICES Personal-service contracts require one party to work personally for another party. Courts normally refuse to grant specific performance of personal-service contracts. If a contract is not deemed personal, the remedy at law may be adequate if substantially identical service (for example, lawn mowing) is available from other persons.

In individually tailored personal-service contracts, courts will not order specific performance by the party who was to be employed because public policy strongly discourages involuntary servitude.[18] Moreover, the courts do not want to have to monitor a continuing service contract if supervision would be difficult—as it would be if the contract required the exercise of per-

sonal judgment or talent. For example, if you contracted with a brain surgeon to perform brain surgery on you and the surgeon refused to perform, the court would not compel (and you certainly would not want) the surgeon to perform under those circumstances. A court cannot ensure meaningful performance in such a situation.[19]

REFORMATION

Reformation is an equitable remedy used when the parties have *imperfectly* expressed their agreement in writing. Reformation allows a court to rewrite the contract to reflect the parties' true intentions.

WHEN FRAUD OR MUTUAL MISTAKE IS PRESENT Reformation occurs most often when fraud or mutual mistake (for example, a clerical error) is present. It is almost always sought so that some other remedy may then be pursued. For example, if Keshan contracts to buy a certain parcel of land from Malboa but their contract mistakenly refers to a parcel of land different from the one being sold, the contract does not reflect the parties' intentions. Accordingly, a court can reform the contract so that it conforms to the parties' intentions and accurately refers to the parcel of land being sold. Keshan can then, if necessary, show that Malboa has breached the contract as reformed. She can at that time request an order for specific performance.

ORAL CONTRACTS AND COVENANTS NOT TO COMPETE There are two other situations in which the courts frequently reform contracts. The first involves two parties who have made a binding oral contract. They further agree to put the oral contract in writing, but in doing so, they make an error in stating the terms. Normally, the courts will allow into evidence the correct terms of the oral contract, thereby reforming the written contract.

The second situation is when the parties have executed a written covenant not to compete (discussed in Chapter 9). If the covenant is for a valid and legitimate purpose (such as the sale of a business) but the area or time restraints of the covenant are unreasonable, some courts will reform the restraints by making them reasonable and will enforce the entire contract

---

17. *Restatement (Second) of Contracts*, Section 359.
18. The Thirteenth Amendment to the U.S. Constitution prohibits involuntary servitude, and thus a court will not order a person to perform under a personal-service contract. A court may grant an order (injunction) prohibiting that person from engaging in similar contracts in the future for a period of time, however.

---

19. Similarly, courts often refuse to order specific performance of construction contracts because courts are not set up to operate as construction supervisors or engineers.

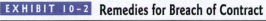

EXHIBIT 10-2 Remedies for Breach of Contract

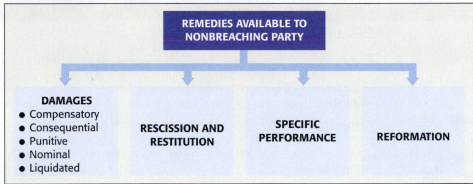

as reformed. Other courts, however, will throw out the entire restrictive covenant as illegal.

Exhibit 10–2 graphically summarizes the remedies, including reformation, that are available to the non-breaching party.

ELECTION OF REMEDIES

In many cases, a nonbreaching party has several remedies available. When the remedies are inconsistent with one another, the common law of contracts requires the party to choose which remedy to pursue. This is called *election of remedies*.

THE PURPOSE OF THE DOCTRINE The purpose of the doctrine of election of remedies is to prevent double recovery. Suppose, for example, that McCarthy agrees in writing to sell his land to Tally. Then McCarthy changes his mind and repudiates the contract. Tally can sue for compensatory damages *or* for specific performance. If Tally could seek compensatory damages in addition to specific performance, she would recover twice for the same breach of contract. The doctrine of election of remedies requires Tally to choose the remedy she wants, and it eliminates any possibility of double recovery. In other words, the election doctrine represents the legal embodiment of the adage "You can't have your cake and eat it, too."

The doctrine has often been applied in a rigid and technical manner, leading to some harsh results. For example, suppose that Beacham is fraudulently induced to buy a parcel of land for $150,000. He spends an additional $10,000 moving onto the land and then discovers the fraud. Instead of suing for damages, Beacham sues to rescind the contract. The court allows Beacham to recover only the purchase price of $150,000 in restitution, but not the additional

$10,000 in moving expenses (because the seller did not receive this money, he or she will not be required to return it). So Beacham suffers a net loss of $10,000 on the transaction. If Beacham had elected to sue for damages instead of seeking the remedy of rescission and restitution, he could have recovered the $10,000 as well as the $150,000.

THE UCC'S REJECTION OF THE DOCTRINE Because of the many problems associated with the doctrine of election of remedies, the UCC expressly rejects it.[20] As will be discussed in Chapter 11, remedies under the UCC are not exclusive but cumulative in nature and include all the available remedies for breach of contract.

PLEADING IN THE ALTERNATIVE Although the parties must ultimately elect which remedy to pursue, modern court procedures do allow plaintiffs to plead their cases "in the alternative" (pleadings were discussed in Chapter 2). In other words, when the plaintiff originally files a lawsuit, he or she can ask the court to order either rescission (and restitution) or damages, for example. Then, as the case progresses to trial, the parties can elect which remedy is most beneficial or appropriate, or the judge can order one remedy and not another. This process still prevents double recovery because the party can only be awarded one of the remedies that was requested.

WAIVER OF BREACH

Under certain circumstances, a nonbreaching party may be willing to accept a defective performance of the contract. This knowing relinquishment of a legal

---

20. See UCC 2–703 and 2–711.

CONCEPT SUMMARY 10.1 | Equitable Remedies

REMEDY	DESCRIPTION
RESCISSION AND RESTITUTION	1. *Rescission*—A remedy whereby a contract is canceled and the parties are restored to the original positions that they occupied prior to the transaction. 2. *Restitution*—When a contract is rescinded, both parties must make restitution to each other by returning the goods, property, or money previously conveyed.
SPECIFIC PERFORMANCE	An equitable remedy calling for the performance of the act promised in the contract. Only available when monetary damages would be inadequate—such as in contracts for the sale of land or unique goods—and never available in personal-service contracts.
REFORMATION	An equitable remedy allowing a contract to be "reformed," or rewritten, to reflect the parties' true intentions. Available when an agreement is imperfectly expressed in writing, such as when a mutual mistake has occurred.

right (that is, the right to require satisfactory and full performance) is called a **waiver.**

CONSEQUENCES OF A WAIVER OF BREACH When a waiver of a breach of contract occurs, the party waiving the breach cannot take any later action on it. In effect, the waiver erases the past breach; the contract continues as if the breach had never occurred. Of course, the waiver of breach of contract extends only to the matter waived and not to the whole contract.

REASONS FOR WAIVING A BREACH Businesspersons often waive breaches of contract to get whatever benefit is still possible out of the contract. For example, a seller contracts with a buyer to deliver to the buyer ten thousand tons of coal on or before November 1. The contract calls for the buyer to pay by November 10 for coal delivered. Because of a coal miners' strike, coal is hard to find. The seller breaches the contract by not tendering delivery until November 5. The buyer may be well advised to waive the seller's breach, accept delivery of the coal, and pay as contracted.

WAIVER OF BREACH AND SUBSEQUENT BREACHES Ordinarily, the waiver by a contracting party will not operate to waive subsequent, additional, or future breaches of contract. This is always true when the subsequent breaches are unrelated to the first breach. For example, an owner who waives the right to sue for late completion of a stage of construction does not waive the right to sue for failure to comply with engineering specifications on the same job. A waiver will be extended to subsequent defective performance, however, if a reasonable person would conclude that

similar defective performance in the future will be acceptable. Therefore, a *pattern of conduct* that waives a number of successive breaches will operate as a continued waiver. To change this result, the non-breaching party should give notice to the breaching party that full performance will be required in the future.

The party who has rendered defective or less-than-full performance remains liable for the damages caused by the breach of contract. In effect, the waiver operates to keep the contract going. The waiver prevents the nonbreaching party from calling the contract to an end or rescinding the contract. The contract continues, but the nonbreaching party can recover damages caused by defective or less-than-full performance.

CONTRACT PROVISIONS LIMITING REMEDIES

A contract may include provisions stating that no damages can be recovered for certain types of breaches or that damages must be limited to a maximum amount. The contract may also provide that the only remedy for breach is replacement, repair, or refund of the purchase price. Provisions stating that no damages can be recovered are called *exculpatory clauses*. Provisions that affect the availability of certain remedies are called *limitation-of-liability clauses*.

Whether these contract provisions and clauses will be enforced depends on the type of breach that is excused by the provision. For example, a provision excluding liability for fraudulent or intentional injury will not be enforced. Likewise, a clause excluding liability for illegal acts or violations of law will not be enforced. A clause excluding liability for negligence may be enforced in certain cases, however. When an exculpatory clause for negligence is contained in a contract made between parties who have roughly equal bargaining positions, the clause usually will be enforced.

REVIEWING CONTRACT PERFORMANCE, BREACH, AND REMEDIES

Val's Foods signs a contract to buy 1,500 pounds of basil from Sun Farms, a small organic herb grower, as long as an independent organization inspects and certifies that the crop contains no pesticide or herbicide residue. Val's has a number of contracts with different restaurant chains to supply pesto and intends to use Sun Farms' basil in its pesto to fulfill these contracts. While Sun Farms is preparing to harvest the basil, an unexpected hailstorm destroys half the crop. Sun Farms attempts to purchase additional basil from other farms, but it is late in the season and the price is twice the normal market price. Sun Farms is too small to absorb this cost and immediately notifies Val's that it will not fulfill the contract. Using the information presented in the chapter, answer the following questions.

1. | Suppose that the basil does not pass the chemical-residue inspection. Which concept discussed in the chapter might allow Val's to refuse to perform the contract in this situation?

2. | Under which legal theory or theories might Sun Farms claim that its obligation under the contract has been discharged by operation of law? Discuss fully.

3. | Suppose that Sun Farms contacts every basil grower in the country and buys the last remaining chemical-free basil anywhere. Nevertheless, Sun Farms is only able to ship 1,475 pounds to Val's. Would this fulfill Sun Farms' obligations to Val's? Why or why not?

4. | Now suppose that Sun Farms sells its operations to Happy Valley Farms. As a part of the sale, all three parties agree that Happy Valley will provide the basil as stated under the original contract. What is this type of agreement called? Does it discharge the obligations of any of the parties? Explain.

TERMS AND CONCEPTS TO REVIEW

breach of contract 231

commercial
  impracticability 235

condition 228

consequential damages 238

discharge 228

frustration of purpose 235

impossibility of
  performance 235

liquidated damages 239

mitigation of damages 239

mutual rescission 233

novation 233

penalty 239

performance 228

reformation 242

restitution 241

specific performance 241

waiver 244

QUESTIONS AND CASE PROBLEMS

10–1. The Caplans own a real estate lot, and they contract with Faithful Construction, Inc., to build a house on it for $60,000. The specifications list "all plumbing bowls and fixtures . . . to be Crane brand." The Caplans leave on vacation, and during their absence Faithful is unable to buy and install Crane plumbing fixtures. Instead, Faithful installs Kohler brand fixtures, an equivalent in the industry. On completion of the building contract, the Caplans inspect the work, discover the substitution, and refuse to accept the house, claiming Faithful has breached the conditions set forth in the specifications. Discuss fully the Caplans' claim.

10-2. ⚖ QUESTION WITH SAMPLE ANSWER

Junior owes creditor Iba $1,000, which is due and payable on June 1. Junior has been in a car accident, has missed a great deal of work, and consequently will not have the funds on June 1. Junior's father, Fred, offers to pay Iba $1,100 in four equal installments if Iba will discharge Junior from any further liability on the debt. Iba accepts. Is this transaction a novation or an accord and satisfaction? Explain.

For a sample answer to this question, go to Appendix I at the end of this text.

10-3. In the following situations, certain events take place after the formation of contracts. Discuss which of these contracts are discharged because the events render the contracts impossible to perform.

(a) Jimenez, a famous singer, contracts to perform in your nightclub. He dies prior to performance.

(b) Raglione contracts to sell you her land. Just before title is to be transferred, she dies.

(c) Oppenheim contracts to sell you one thousand bushels of apples from her orchard in the state of Washington. Because of a severe frost, she is unable to deliver the apples.

(d) Maxwell contracts to lease a service station for ten years. His principal income is from the sale of gasoline. Because of an oil embargo by foreign oil-producing nations, gasoline is rationed, cutting sharply into Maxwell's gasoline sales. He cannot make his lease payments.

10-4. Cohen contracts to sell his house and lot to Windsor for $100,000. The terms of the contract call for Windsor to pay 10 percent of the purchase price as a deposit toward the purchase price, or a down payment. The terms further stipulate that should the buyer breach the contract, the deposit will be retained by Cohen as liquidated damages. Windsor pays the deposit, but because her expected financing of the $90,000 balance falls through, she breaches the contract. Two weeks later Cohen sells the house and lot to Ballard for $105,000. Windsor demands her $10,000 back, but Cohen refuses, claiming that Windsor's breach and the contract terms entitle him to keep the deposit. Discuss who is correct.

10-5. Ken owns and operates a famous candy store and makes most of the candy sold in the store. Business is particularly heavy during the Christmas season. Ken contracts with Sweet, Inc., to purchase ten thousand pounds of sugar to be delivered on or before November 15. Ken has informed Sweet that this particular order is to be used for the Christmas season business. Because of problems at the refinery, the sugar is not tendered to Ken until December 10, at which time Ken refuses it as being too late. Ken has been unable to purchase the quantity of sugar needed to meet his Christmas orders and has had to turn down numerous regular customers, some of whom have indicated that they will purchase candy else-

where in the future. What sugar Ken has been able to purchase has cost him 10 cents per pound above the price contracted for with Sweet. Ken sues Sweet for breach of contract, claiming as damages the higher price paid for sugar from others, lost profits from this year's lost Christmas sales, future lost profits from customers who have indicated that they will discontinue doing business with him, and punitive damages for failure to meet the contracted delivery date. Sweet claims Ken is limited to compensatory damages only. Discuss who is correct, and why.

10-6. ⚖ CASE PROBLEM WITH SAMPLE ANSWER

Train operators and other railroad personnel use signaling systems to ensure safe train travel. Reading Blue Mountain & Northern Railroad Co. (RBMN) and Norfolk Southern Railway Co. entered into a contract for the maintenance of a signaling system that serviced a stretch of track near Jim Thorpe, Pennsylvania. The system included a series of poles, similar to telephone poles, suspending wires above the tracks. The contract provided that "the intent of the parties is to maintain the existing . . . facilities" and split the cost equally. In December 2002, a severe storm severed the wires and destroyed most of the poles. RBMN and Norfolk discussed replacing the old system, which they agreed was antiquated, inefficient, dangerous to rebuild, and expensive, but they could not agree on an alternative. Norfolk installed an entirely new system and filed a suit in a federal district court against RBMN to recover half of the cost. RBMN filed a motion for summary judgment, asserting in part the doctrine of frustration of purpose. What is this doctrine? Does it apply in this case? How should the court rule on RBMN's motion? Explain. [*Norfolk Southern Railway Co. v. Reading Blue Mountain & Northern Railroad Co.*, 364 F.Supp.2d 270 (M.D.Pa. 2004)]

To view a sample answer for this case problem, go to this book's Web site at http://wleb.westbuslaw.com, select "Chapter 10," and click on "Case Problem with Sample Answer."

10-7. SUBSTANTIAL PERFORMANCE. Adolf and Ida Krueger contracted with Pisani Construction, Inc., to erect a metal building as an addition to an existing structure. The two structures were to share a common wall, and the frames and panel heights of the new building were to match those of the existing structure. Shortly before completion of the project, however, it was apparent that the roofline of the new building was approximately three inches higher than that of the existing structure. Pisani modified the ridge caps of the buildings to blend the rooflines. The discrepancy had other consequences, however, including misalignment of the gutters and windows of the two buildings, which resulted in an icing problem in the winter. The Kruegers occupied the new structure, but refused to make the last payment under the contract. Pisani filed a suit in a Connecticut state court to collect. Did Pisani substantially perform its obligations? Should the Kruegers be ordered to pay? Why or why not? [*Pisani Construction, Inc. v. Krueger,* 68 Conn.App. 361, 791 A.2d 634 (2002)]

10-8. LIQUIDATED DAMAGES VERSUS PENALTIES.

Every homeowner in the Putnam County, Indiana, subdivision of Stardust Hills must be a member of the Stardust Hills Owners Association, Inc., and must pay annual dues of $200 for the maintenance of common areas and other community services. Under the association's rules, dues paid more than ten days late "shall bear a delinquent fee at a rate of $2.00 per day." Phyllis Gaddis owned a Stardust Hills lot on which she failed to pay the dues. Late fees began to accrue. Nearly two months later, the association filed a suit in an Indiana state court to collect the unpaid dues and the late fees. Gaddis argued in response that the delinquent fee was an unenforceable penalty. What questions should be considered in determining the status of this fee? Should the association's rule regarding assessment of the fee be enforced? Explain. [*Gaddis v. Stardust Hills Owners Association, Inc.,* 804 N.E.2d 231 (Ind.App. 2004)]

10-9.  A QUESTION OF ETHICS

Julio Garza was employed by the Texas Animal Health Commission (TAHC) as a health inspector in 1981. His responsibilities included tagging cattle, vaccinating and tattooing calves, and working livestock markets. Garza was injured on the job in 1988 and underwent surgery in January 1989. When his paid leave was exhausted, he asked TAHC for light-duty work, specifically the job of tick inspector, but his supervisor refused the request. In September, TAHC notified Garza that he was fired. Garza sued TAHC and others, alleging in part wrongful termination, and an important issue before the court was whether Garza had mitigated his damages. The court found that in the seven years between his termination and his trial date, Garza had held only one job—an unpaid job on his parents' ranch. When asked how often he had looked for work during that time, Garza responded that he did not know, but he had looked in "several" places. The last time he had looked for work

was three or four months before the trial. That effort was merely an informal inquiry to his neighbors about working on their ranch. In view of these facts, consider the following questions. [*Texas Animal Health Commission v. Garza,* 27 S.W.3d 54 (Tex.App.—San Antonio 2000)]

(a) The court in this case stated that the "general rule as to mitigation of damages in breach of employment suits is that the discharged employee must use reasonable diligence to mitigate damages by seeking other employment." In your opinion, did Garza fulfill this requirement? If you were the judge, how would you rule in this case?

(b) Assume for the moment that Garza had indeed been wrongfully terminated. In this situation, would it be fair to Garza to require him to mitigate his damages? Why or why not?

(c) Generally, what are the ethical underpinnings of the rule that employees seeking damages for breach of employment contracts must mitigate their damages?

 ### 10-10. VIDEO QUESTION

Go to this text's Web site at http://wleb.westbuslaw.com and select "Chapter 10." Click on "Video Questions" and view the video titled *Midnight Run.* Then answer the following questions.

(a) In the video, Eddie (Joe Pantoliano) and Jack (Robert DeNiro) negotiate a contract for Jack to find the Duke, a mob accountant who embezzled funds, and bring him back for trial. Assume that the contract is valid. If Jack breaches the contract by failing to bring in the Duke, what kinds of remedies, if any, can Eddie seek? Explain your answer.

(b) Would the equitable remedy of specific performance be available to either Jack or Eddie in the event of a breach? Why or why not?

(c) Now assume that the contract between Eddie and Jack is unenforceable. Nevertheless, Jack performs his side of the bargain (brings in the Duke). Does Jack have any legal recourse in this situation? Why or why not?

LAW | on the Web

For updated links to resources available on the Web, as well as a variety of other materials, visit this text's Web site at http://wleb.westbuslaw.com.

For a summary of how contracts may be discharged and other principles of contract law, go to

http://www.rnoon.com/lawlaymen/contracts/performance.html

For a summary of how contracts may be breached and other information on contract law, go to Lawyers.com's "Business Needs" Web page at

http://www.lawyers.com/lawyers/P~B~General+Business~LDC.html

Then click on "Contracts" and review your options under the "Get Info" section.

The following sites offer information on contract law, including breach of contract and remedies:

http://cori.missouri.edu

http://www.law.cornell.edu/topics/contracts.html

LEGAL RESEARCH EXERCISES ON THE WEB

Go to http://wleb.westbuslaw.com, the Web site that accompanies this text. Select "Chapter 10" and click on "Internet Exercises." There you will find the following Internet research exercises that you can perform to learn more about topics covered in this chapter.

Activity 10–1: LEGAL PERSPECTIVE
Contract Damages and Contract Theory

Activity 10–2: MANAGEMENT PERSPECTIVE
The Duty to Mitigate

Activity 10–3: MANAGEMENT PERSPECTIVE
Commercial Impracticability

CHAPTER 11

Sales, Leases, and E-Contracts

When we turn to contracts for the sale and lease of goods, we move away from common law principles and into the area of statutory law. State statutory law governing sales and lease transactions is based on the Uniform Commercial Code (UCC), which, as mentioned in Chapter 1, has been adopted as law by all states.[1] Relevant sections of the UCC are noted in the following discussion of sales and lease contracts.

As you will read shortly, in 2002 the National Conference of Commissioners on Uniform State Laws approved what became the 2003 amendments to the UCC's Article 2 (on sales) and Article 2A (on leases). Appendix C at the back of this book includes both the existing version of Article 2 and selected provisions from the 2003 amendments to Article 2.

We open this chapter with a look at the scope of Article 2 and Article 2A. Article 2 of the UCC sets out the requirements of sales contracts and how they are formed. It also addresses the sometimes sticky concept of when title passes and who bears the risk of loss for goods in the process of being sold—for example, goods en route from the seller to the buyer—along with the concept of insurable interest. Article 2 regulates performance and obligations required under sales contracts. It also delineates when a breach by either the buyer or the seller occurs and what remedies normally may be sought. A sale of goods usually carries with it at least one type of warranty; sales warranties, express and implied, likewise are governed by the UCC. Article 2A covers similar issues for lease contracts.

In the final section of this chapter, we look at how traditional laws are being applied to contracts formed online. We also examine some new laws that have been created to apply in situations in which traditional laws governing contracts have sometimes been thought inadequate. For example, traditional laws governing signature and writing requirements are not easily adapted to contracts formed in the online environment. Thus, new laws have been created to address these issues.

SECTION 1 | The Scope of Article 2— The Sale of Goods

Article 2 of the UCC governs **sales contracts,** or contracts for the sale of goods. To facilitate commercial transactions, Article 2 modifies some of the common law contract requirements that were discussed in the previous chapters. To the extent that it has not been modified by the UCC, however, the common law of contracts also applies to sales contracts. For example, the common law requirements for a valid contract—agreement (offer and acceptance), consideration, capacity, and legality—that were discussed in Chapter 9 are also applicable to sales contracts. Thus, you should reexamine these common law principles when studying the law of sales.

In general, the rule is that whenever there is a conflict between a common law contract rule and the UCC, the UCC controls. In other words, when a UCC provision addresses a certain issue, the UCC governs; when the UCC is silent, the common law governs.

In regard to Article 2, you should keep in mind two things. First, Article 2 deals with the sale of *goods;* it does not deal with real property (real estate),

---

1. Louisiana has not adopted Articles 2 and 2A, however.

services, or intangible property such as stocks and bonds. Thus, if the subject matter of a dispute is goods, the UCC governs. If it is real estate or services, the common law applies. Second, in some cases, the rules may vary quite a bit, depending on whether the buyer or the seller is a *merchant*. We look now at how the UCC defines a *sale*, *goods*, and *merchant status*.

WHAT IS A SALE?

Section 2–102 of the UCC states that Article 2 "applies to transactions in goods." This implies a broad scope—covering gifts, bailments (temporary deliveries of personal property), and purchases of goods. In this chapter, however, we treat Article 2 as being applicable only to an actual sale (as would most authorities and courts). The UCC defines a **sale** as "the passing of title from the seller to the buyer for a price," where *title* refers to the formal right of ownership of property [UCC 2–106(1)]. The price may be payable in money or in other goods, services, or realty (real estate).

WHAT ARE GOODS?

To be characterized as a *good*, an item of property must be *tangible*, and it must be *movable*. **Tangible property** has physical existence—it can be touched or seen. Intangible property—such as corporate stocks and bonds, patents and copyrights, and ordinary contract rights—has only conceptual existence and thus does not come under Article 2.[2] A *movable* item can be carried from place to place. Hence, real estate is excluded from Article 2.

WHO IS A MERCHANT?

Article 2 governs the sale of goods in general. It applies to sales transactions between all buyers and sellers. In a limited number of instances, however, the UCC presumes that in certain phases of sales transactions involving merchants, special business standards ought to be imposed because of the merchants' relatively high degree of commercial expertise.[3] Such

standards do not apply to the casual or inexperienced seller or buyer ("consumer").

In general, a person is a **merchant** when he or she, acting in a mercantile capacity, possesses or uses an expertise specifically related to the goods being sold. This basic distinction is not always clear-cut. For example, courts in some states have determined that farmers may be merchants, while courts in other states have determined that the drafters of the UCC did not intend to include farmers as merchants.

SECTION 2 | The Scope of Article 2A—Leases

In the past few decades, leases of personal property (goods) have become increasingly common. Consumers and business firms lease automobiles, industrial equipment, items for use in the home (such as floor polishers), and many other types of goods. Until Article 2A was added to the UCC, no specific body of law addressed the legal problems that arose when goods were leased, rather than sold. In cases involving leased goods, the courts generally applied a combination of common law rules, real estate law, and principles expressed in Article 2 of the UCC.

Article 2A of the UCC was created to fill the need for uniform guidelines in this area. Article 2A covers any transaction that creates a lease of goods, as well as subleases of goods [UCC 2A–102, 2A–103(k)]. Article 2A is essentially a repetition of Article 2, except that it applies to leases of goods, rather than sales of goods, and thus varies to reflect differences between sales and lease transactions.

Article 2A defines a **lease agreement** as the bargain of the lessor and lessee, as found in their language and as implied by other circumstances [UCC 2A–103(k)]. A **lessor** is one who sells the right to the possession and use of goods under a lease [UCC 2A–103(p)]. A **lessee** is one who acquires the right to the possession and use of goods under a lease [UCC 2A–103(o)]. Article 2A applies to all types of leases of goods, including commercial leases and consumer leases.

SECTION 3 | The Amendments to Articles 2 and 2A

For the most part, the 2003 amendments to Articles 2 and 2A mark an attempt by the National Conference of Commissioners on Uniform State Laws to update

---

2. The 2003 amendments specifically exclude "information" that is not associated with goods [Amended UCC 2–103(1)(k)]. Nevertheless, Article 2 *may* apply to transactions involving both goods and information when a sale involves "smart goods" (for example, a toy or an automobile that contains computer programs). It is up to the courts to determine whether and to what extent Article 2 should be applied to such transactions.

3. The provisions that apply only to merchants deal principally with the Statute of Frauds, firm offers, confirmatory memoranda, warranties, and contract modification. These special rules reflect expedient business practices commonly known to merchants in the commercial setting. They will be discussed later in this chapter.

the UCC to accommodate electronic commerce. Among other things, the amendments include revised definitions of various terms to make the definitions consistent with those given in the Uniform Electronic Transactions Act (UETA) and the federal Electronic Signatures in Global and National Commerce Act (E-SIGN Act) of 2000—discussed later in this chapter. Throughout the amendments, for example, the word *writing* has been replaced by *record*. The term *sign* has been amended to include electronic signatures. Provisions governing electronic contracts, including contracts formed by electronic agents, have also been added.

In addition, the amendments include a number of new protections for buyers, some of which apply only to buyers who are consumers. Other new or revised provisions relate to contract formation (offer and acceptance), the Statute of Frauds, warranties, and other topics. In this chapter, we refer to the amendments, often in footnotes, whenever the amendments significantly change the existing law under Articles 2 and 2A. As mentioned earlier, we include excerpts from the 2003 amendments to Article 2 in Appendix C for further reference.

SECTION 4 | The Formation of Sales and Lease Contracts

In regard to the formation of sales and lease contracts, the UCC modifies the common law of contracts in several ways. We look here at how Article 2 and Article 2A of the UCC modify common law contract rules. Remember that parties to sales contracts are free to establish whatever terms they wish. The UCC comes into play when the parties have not, in their contract, provided for a contingency that later gives rise to a dispute. The UCC makes this very clear time and again by its use of such phrases as "unless the parties otherwise agree" and "absent a contrary agreement by the parties."

OFFER

In general contract law, the moment a definite offer is met by an unqualified acceptance, a binding contract is formed. In commercial sales transactions, the verbal exchanges, the correspondence, and the actions of the parties may not reveal exactly when a binding contractual obligation arises. The UCC states that an agreement sufficient to constitute a contract can exist even if the moment of its making is undetermined [UCC 2–204(2), 2A–204(2)].

OPEN TERMS According to contract law, an offer must be definite enough for the parties (and the courts) to ascertain its essential terms when it is accepted. The UCC states that a sales or lease contract will not fail for indefiniteness even if one or more terms are left open as long as (1) the parties intended to make a contract and (2) there is a reasonably certain basis for the court to grant an appropriate remedy [UCC 2–204(3), 2A–204(3)].

Although the UCC has radically lessened the requirement of definiteness of terms, keep in mind that if too many terms are left open, a court may find that the parties did not intend to form a contract.

The appendix that follows this chapter shows an actual sales contract used by Starbucks Coffee Company. The contract illustrates many of the terms and clauses that are typically contained in contracts for the sale of goods.

—Open Price Term. If the parties have not agreed on a price, the court will determine a "reasonable price at the time for delivery" [UCC 2–305(1)]. If either the buyer or the seller is to determine the price, the price is to be fixed in good faith [UCC 2–305(2)].

Sometimes the price fails to be fixed through the fault of one of the parties. In that case, the other party can treat the contract as canceled or fix a reasonable price. For example, Johnson and Merrick enter into a contract for the sale of goods and agree that Johnson will fix the price. Johnson refuses to fix the price. Merrick can either treat the contract as canceled or set a reasonable price [UCC 2–305(3)].

—Open Payment Term. When parties do not specify payment terms, payment is due at the time and place at which the buyer is to receive the goods [UCC 2–310(a)]. The buyer can tender payment using any commercially normal or acceptable means, such as a check or credit card. If the seller demands payment in cash, however, the buyer must be given a reasonable time to obtain it [UCC 2–511(2)]. This is especially important when the contract states a definite and final time for performance.

—Open Delivery Term. When no delivery terms are specified, the buyer normally takes delivery at the seller's place of business [UCC 2–308(a)]. If the seller has no place of business, the seller's residence is used. When goods are located in some other place and both parties know it, delivery is made there. If the time for shipment or delivery is not clearly specified in the

sales contract, then the court will infer a "reasonable" time for performance [UCC 2–309(1)].

—*Open Quantity Term.* Normally, if the parties do not specify a quantity, a court will have no basis for determining a remedy. The UCC recognizes two exceptions in requirements and output contracts [UCC 2–306(1)].

In a **requirements contract,** the buyer agrees to purchase—and the seller agrees to sell—all or up to a stated amount of what the buyer *needs* or *requires*. There is implicit consideration in a requirements contract, for the buyer gives up the right to buy from any other seller, and this forfeited right creates a legal detriment. Requirements contracts are common in the business world and are normally enforceable. If, however, the buyer promises to purchase only if the buyer *wishes* to do so, or if the buyer reserves the right to buy the goods from someone other than the seller, the promise is illusory (without consideration) and unenforceable by either party.

In an **output contract,** the seller agrees to sell and the buyer agrees to buy all or up to a stated amount of what the seller *produces*. Again, because the seller essentially forfeits the right to sell goods to another buyer, there is implicit consideration in an output contract.

The UCC imposes a *good faith limitation* on requirements and output contracts. The quantity under such contracts is the amount of requirements or the amount of output that occurs during a *normal* production year. The actual quantity purchased or sold cannot be unreasonably disproportionate to normal or comparable prior requirements or output [UCC 2–306].

MERCHANT'S FIRM OFFER Under regular contract principles, an offer can be revoked at any time before acceptance. The major common law exception is an *option contract*, in which the offeree pays consideration for the offeror's irrevocable promise to keep the offer open for a stated period. The UCC creates a second exception, which applies only to firm offers for the sale or lease of goods made by a merchant (regardless of whether or not the offeree is a merchant). A **firm offer** arises when a merchant-offeror gives assurances *in a signed writing* that the offer will remain open. The merchant's firm offer is irrevocable without the necessity of consideration[4] for the stated period or, if no def-

inite period is stated, a reasonable period (neither to exceed three months) [UCC 2–205, 2A–205].

ACCEPTANCE

Acceptance of an offer to buy, sell, or lease goods generally may be made in any reasonable manner and by any reasonable means. The UCC generally takes the position that if the offeree's response indicates a *definite* acceptance of the offer, a contract is formed, even if the acceptance includes terms additional to, or different from, those contained in the offer [UCC 2–207(1)].

PROMISE TO SHIP OR PROMPT SHIPMENT The UCC permits acceptance of an offer to buy goods "either by a prompt promise to ship or by the prompt or current shipment of conforming or nonconforming goods" [UCC 2–206(1)(b)]. *Conforming* goods accord with the contract's terms; *nonconforming* goods do not. The prompt shipment of *nonconforming goods* constitutes both an *acceptance*, which creates a contract, and a *breach* of that contract. This rule does not apply if the seller seasonably (within a reasonable amount of time) notifies the buyer that the nonconforming shipment is offered only as an *accommodation*, or as a favor. The notice of accommodation must clearly indicate to the buyer that the shipment does not constitute an acceptance and that, therefore, no contract has been formed.

COMMUNICATION OF ACCEPTANCE Under the common law, because a unilateral offer invites acceptance by a performance, the offeree need not notify the offeror of performance unless the offeror would not otherwise know about it. The UCC is more stringent than the common law, stating that when the commencement of the requested performance is a reasonable mode of acceptance, an offeror who is not notified of the performance within a reasonable time may treat the offer as having lapsed before acceptance [UCC 2–206(2), 2A–206(2)].

ADDITIONAL TERMS If the acceptance includes terms additional to, or different from, those contained in the offer and one (or both) of the parties is a *nonmerchant*, the contract is formed according to the terms of the original offer submitted by the original offeror and not according to the additional terms of the acceptance [UCC 2–207(2)]. In contracts *between merchants*, the additional terms automatically become part of the contract unless (1) the original offer expressly limited acceptance to its terms, (2) the new

---

4. If the offeree pays consideration, then an option contract (not a merchant's firm offer) is formed.

or changed terms materially alter the contract, or (3) the offeror objects to the new or changed terms within a reasonable period of time [UCC 2–207(2)].[5]

SECTION 5 | Consideration

The common law rule that a contract requires consideration also applies to sales and lease contracts. Unlike the common law, however, the UCC does not require a contract modification to be supported by new consideration. The UCC states that an agreement modifying a contract for the sale or lease of goods "needs no consideration to be binding" [UCC 2–209(1), 2A–208(1)].

Of course, any contract modification must be made in good faith [UCC 1–203]. For example, Jim agrees to lease certain goods to Louise for a stated price. Subsequently, a sudden shift in the market makes it difficult for Jim to lease the items to Louise at the given price without suffering a loss. Jim tells Louise of the situation, and Louise agrees to pay an additional sum for leasing the goods. Later, Louise reconsiders and refuses to pay more than the original lease price. Under the UCC, Louise's promise to modify the contract needs no consideration to be binding. Hence, Louise is bound by the modified contract.

In this example, a shift in the market is a *good faith* reason for contract modification. What if there really was no shift in the market, however, and Jim knew that Louise needed the goods immediately but refused to deliver them unless Louise agreed to pay an additional sum of money? This sort of extortion of a modification without a legitimate commercial reason would be ineffective, because it would violate the duty of good faith. Jim would not be permitted to enforce the higher price.

SECTION 6 | The Statute of Frauds

As discussed in Chapter 9, the Statute of Frauds requires that certain types of contracts, to be enforceable, must be in writing or evidenced by a writing.

The UCC contains Statute of Frauds provisions covering sales and lease contracts. Under these provisions, sales contracts for goods priced at $500 or more and lease contracts requiring total payments of $1,000 or more must be in writing to be enforceable [UCC 2–201(1), 2A–201(1)].[6]

SUFFICIENCY OF THE WRITING

The UCC has greatly relaxed the requirements for the sufficiency of a writing to satisfy the Statute of Frauds. A writing or a memorandum will be sufficient as long as it indicates that the parties intended to form a contract and as long as it is signed by the party (or agent of the party) against whom enforcement is sought. The contract normally will not be enforceable beyond the quantity of goods shown in the writing, however. All other terms can be proved in court by oral testimony. For leases, the writing must reasonably identify and describe the goods leased and the lease term.

SPECIAL RULES FOR CONTRACTS BETWEEN MERCHANTS

Once again, the UCC provides a special rule for merchants. The rule, however, applies only to sales (under Article 2); there is no corresponding rule that applies to leases (under Article 2A).[7] Merchants can satisfy the requirements of a writing for the Statute of Frauds if, after the parties have agreed orally, one of the merchants sends a signed written confirmation to the other merchant. The communication must indicate the terms of the agreement, and the merchant receiving the confirmation must have reason to know of its contents. Unless the merchant who receives the confirmation gives written notice of objection to its contents within ten days after receipt, the writing is sufficient against the receiving merchant, even though he or she has not signed anything [UCC 2–201(2)].

---

5. The 2003 amendments to UCC Article 2 do not distinguish between merchants and others in setting out rules for the effect of additional terms in contracts for sale, nor do they give a preference to the first or the last terms to be stated. Instead, a court is directed to determine whether (1) the terms appear in the records of both parties, (2) both parties agree to the terms even if they are not in a record, or (3) the terms are supplied or incorporated under another provision of Article 2 [Amended UCC 2–207]. Basically, the amendments give the courts more discretion to include or exclude certain terms.

6. Note that a 2003 amendment significantly increased the price of goods that will fall under the Statute of Frauds. Under the amended UCC 2–201(1), goods must be priced at $5,000 or more to be subject to the record (writing) requirement.

7. According to the comments accompanying UCC 2A–201 (Article 2A's Statute of Frauds), the "between merchants" provision was not included because "the number of such transactions involving leases, as opposed to sales, was thought to be modest."

EXHIBIT 11–1 Major Differences between Contract Law and Sales Law

	CONTRACT LAW	SALES LAW
Contract Terms	Contract must contain all material terms.	Open terms are acceptable if parties intended to form a contract, but contract is not enforceable beyond quantity term.
Acceptance	Mirror image rule applies. If additional terms are added in acceptance, counteroffer is created.	Additional terms will not negate acceptance unless acceptance is expressly conditioned on assent to the additional terms.
Contract Modification	Modification requires consideration.	Modification does not require consideration.
Irrevocable Offers	Option contracts (with consideration).	Merchants' firm offers (without consideration).
Statute of Frauds Requirements	All material terms must be included in the writing.	Writing is required only for sale of goods of $500[a] or more, but contract is not enforceable beyond quantity specified. *Exceptions:* 1. Specially manufactured goods. 2. Admissions by party against whom enforcement is sought. 3. Partial performance. 4. Confirmatory memorandum (between merchants).

a. Under a 2003 amendment to the UCC, a writing (record) is required only for the sale of goods priced at $5,000 or more.

EXCEPTIONS

The UCC defines three exceptions to the writing requirements of the Statute of Frauds. An oral contract for the sale of goods priced at $500 or more ($5,000 or more under the 2003 amendments) or the lease of goods involving total payments of $1,000 or more will be enforceable despite the absence of a writing in the circumstances described in the following subsections [UCC 2–201(3), 2A–201(4)]. These exceptions and other ways in which sales law differs from general contract law are summarized in Exhibit 11–1.

SPECIALLY MANUFACTURED GOODS An oral contract is enforceable if (1) it is for goods that are specially manufactured for a particular buyer or specially manufactured or obtained for a particular lessee, (2) these goods are not suitable for resale or lease to others in the ordinary course of the seller's or lessor's business, and (3) the seller or lessor has substantially started to manufacture the goods or has made commitments for the manufacture or procurement of the goods. In these situations, once the seller or lessor has taken action, the buyer or lessee cannot repudiate the agreement claiming the Statute of Frauds as a defense.

ADMISSIONS An oral contract for the sale or lease of goods is enforceable if the party against whom enforcement is sought admits in pleadings, testimony, or other court proceedings that a sales or lease contract was made.[8] In this situation, the contract will be enforceable even though it was oral, but enforceability will be limited to the quantity of goods admitted.

PARTIAL PERFORMANCE An oral contract for the sale or lease of goods is enforceable if payment has been made and accepted or goods have been received and accepted. This is the "partial performance" exception. The oral contract will be enforced at least to the extent that performance *actually* took place.

SECTION 7 | Title, Risk, and Insurable Interest

Before the creation of the UCC, *title*—the right of ownership—was the central concept in sales law, controlling all issues of rights and remedies of the parties

---

8. Any admission under oath, including one not made in a court, satisfies UCC 2–201(3)(b) and 2A–201(4)(b) under the 2003 amendments to Articles 2 and 2A.

to a sales contract. There were numerous problems with this concept. For example, frequently it was difficult to determine when title actually passed from seller to buyer, and therefore it was also difficult to predict which party a court would decide had title at the time of a loss. Because of such problems, the UCC divorced the question of title as completely as possible from the question of the rights and obligations of buyers, sellers, and third parties (such as subsequent purchasers, creditors, or the tax collector).

In some situations, title is still relevant under the UCC, and the UCC has special rules for locating title. In most situations, however, the UCC has replaced the concept of title with three other concepts: (1) identification, (2) risk of loss, and (3) insurable interest.

In lease contracts, of course, title to the goods is retained by the lessor-owner of the goods. Hence, the UCC's provisions relating to passage of title do not apply to leased goods. Other concepts discussed in this chapter, though, including *identification, risk of loss,* and *insurable interest,* relate to lease contracts as well as to sales contracts.

IDENTIFICATION

Before any interest in specific goods can pass from the seller or lessor to the buyer or lessee, two conditions must prevail:

1. The goods must be in existence.
2. They must be identified as the specific goods designated in the contract.

THE SIGNIFICANCE OF IDENTIFICATION Designating goods as the subject matter of a sales or lease contract is called **identification.** Title and risk of loss cannot pass to the buyer from the seller unless the goods are identified to the contract [UCC 2–105(2)]. (As mentioned, title to leased goods remains with the lessor—or, if the owner is a third party, with that party. The lessee does not acquire title to leased goods.) Identification is significant because it gives the buyer or lessee the right to insure (or obtain an insurable interest in) the goods and the right to recover from third parties who damage the goods.

WHEN IDENTIFICATION TAKES PLACE Once the goods are in existence, the parties can agree in their contract on when identification will take place. If they do not so specify, however, and if the contract calls for the sale or lease of specific and ascertained goods that are already in existence, identification takes place at the time the contract is made.

If a sale involves unborn animals to be born within twelve months after contracting, identification takes place when the animals are conceived. If a lease involves any unborn animals, identification also occurs when the animals are conceived. If a sale involves crops that are to be harvested within twelve months (or the next harvest season occurring after contracting, whichever is longer), identification takes place when the crops are planted or otherwise become growing crops. In a sale or lease of any other future goods, identification occurs when the goods are shipped, marked, or otherwise designated by the seller or lessor as the goods to which the contract refers. Goods that are part of a larger mass are identified when the goods are marked, shipped, or somehow designated by the seller or lessor as the particular goods to pass under the contract.

WHEN TITLE PASSES

Once goods exist and are identified, the provisions of UCC 2–401 apply to the passage of title. Unless an agreement is explicitly made,[9] title passes to the buyer at the time and the place the seller performs the *physical delivery* of the goods [UCC 2–401(2)].

SHIPMENT AND DESTINATION CONTRACTS In the absence of agreement, delivery arrangements can determine when title passes from the seller to the buyer. In a **shipment contract,** the seller is required or authorized to ship goods by carrier, such as a trucking company. Under a shipment contract, the seller is required only to deliver the goods into the hands of a carrier, and title passes to the buyer at the time and place of shipment [UCC 2–401(2)(a)]. *Generally, all contracts are assumed to be shipment contracts if nothing to the contrary is stated in the contract.*

In a **destination contract,** the seller is required to deliver the goods to a particular destination, usually directly to the buyer, although sometimes the buyer designates that the goods should be delivered to another party. Title passes to the buyer when the goods are *tendered* at that destination [UCC 2–401(2)(b)]. A *tender of delivery* is the seller's placing or holding of conforming goods at the buyer's disposition (with any necessary notice), enabling the buyer to take delivery [UCC 2–503(1)].

---

9. In many sections of the UCC, the words "unless otherwise explicitly agreed" appear, meaning that any explicit agreement between the buyer and the seller determines the rights, duties, and liabilities of the parties, including when title passes.

DELIVERY WITHOUT MOVEMENT OF THE GOODS

When the contract of sale does not call for the seller's shipment or delivery of the goods (when the buyer is to pick up the goods), the passage of title depends on whether the seller must deliver a *document of title*, such as a bill of lading or a warehouse receipt, to the buyer. A *bill of lading* is a receipt for goods that is signed by a carrier and that serves as a contract for the transportation of the goods. A *warehouse receipt* is a receipt issued by a warehouser for goods stored in a warehouse.

When a document of title is required, title passes to the buyer *when and where the document is delivered.* Thus, if the goods are stored in a warehouse, title passes to the buyer when the appropriate documents are delivered to the buyer. The goods never move. In fact, the buyer can choose to leave the goods at the same warehouse for a period of time, and the buyer's title to those goods will be unaffected.

When no documents of title are required, and delivery is made without moving the goods, title passes at the time and place the sales contract is made, if the goods have already been identified. If the goods have not been identified, title does not pass until identification occurs. Consider an example. Rogers sells lumber to Bodan. It is agreed that Bodan will pick up the lumber at the yard. If the lumber has been identified (segregated, marked, or in any other way distinguished from all other lumber), title passes to Bodan when the contract is signed. If the lumber is still in general storage bins at the mill, title does not pass to Bodan until the particular pieces of lumber to be sold under this contract are identified [UCC 2–401(3)].

RISK OF LOSS

Under the UCC, risk of loss does not necessarily pass with title. When risk of loss passes from a seller or lessor to a buyer or lessee is generally determined by the contract between the parties. Sometimes, the contract states expressly when the risk of loss passes. At other times, it does not, and a court must interpret the existing terms to ascertain whether the risk has passed.

DELIVERY WITH MOVEMENT OF THE GOODS

When there is no specification in the agreement, the following rules apply to cases involving movement of the goods (so-called carrier cases). In a shipment contract, if the seller or lessor is required or authorized to ship goods by carrier (but not required to deliver them to a particular destination), risk of loss passes to the buyer or lessee when the goods are duly delivered to the carrier [UCC 2–509(1)(a), 2A–219(2)(a)]. In a destination contract, the risk of loss passes to the buyer or lessee when the goods are tendered to the buyer or lessee at the specified destination [UCC 2–509(1)(b), 2A–219(2)(b)].

Specific terms in the contract help determine when risk of loss passes to the buyer. These terms, which are listed and defined in Exhibit 11–2, relate generally to the determination of which party will bear the costs of delivery, as well as which party will bear the risk of loss. Note that the 2003 amendments to UCC Article 2 omit these terms because they are "inconsistent with modern commercial practice." Until most states adopt the amended version of Article 2, however, these terms will remain in use.

—*Shipment Contracts.*   As noted, in a shipment contract, if the seller or lessor is required or authorized to ship goods by carrier (but not required to deliver them to a particular destination), risk of loss passes to the buyer or lessee when the goods are duly delivered to the carrier [UCC 2–509(1)(a), 2A–219(2)(a)].

For example, a seller in Texas sells five hundred cases of grapefruit to a buyer in New York, F.O.B. Houston (free on board in Houston, which means that the buyer pays the transportation charges from Houston—see Exhibit 11–2). The contract authorizes shipment by carrier; it does not require that the seller tender the grapefruit in New York. Risk passes to the buyer when conforming goods are properly placed in the possession of the carrier. If the goods are damaged in transit, the loss is the buyer's. (Actually, buyers have recourse against carriers, subject to certain limitations, and they may insure the goods from the time the goods leave the seller.)

—*Destination Contracts.*   As stated above, in a destination contract, the risk of loss passes to the buyer or lessee when the goods are tendered to the buyer or lessee at the specified destination [UCC 2–509(1)(b), 2A–219(2)(b)]. In the preceding example, if the contract had been a destination contract, F.O.B. New York (see Exhibit 11–2), risk of loss during transit to New York would have been the seller's and would not have passed to the buyer until the carrier tendered the goods to the buyer in New York.

Whether a contract is a shipment contract or a destination contract can have significant consequences for the parties, as illustrated by the following case.

EXHIBIT 11-2 Contract Terms—Definitions

The contract terms listed and defined in this exhibit help to determine which party will bear the costs of delivery and when risk of loss will pass from the seller to the buyer (although the terms will not appear in the UCC once a state has adopted the 2003 amendments).

F.O.B. (free on board)—Indicates that the selling price of goods includes transportation costs to the specific F.O.B. place named in the contract. The seller pays the expenses and carries the risk of loss to the F.O.B. place named [UCC 2–319(1)]. If the named place is the place from which the goods are shipped (for example, the seller's city or place of business), the contract is a shipment contract. If the named place is the place to which the goods are to be shipped (for example, the buyer's city or place of business), the contract is a destination contract.
F.A.S. (free alongside)—Requires that the seller, at his or her own expense and risk, deliver the goods alongside the carrier before risk passes to the buyer [UCC 2–319(2)].
C.I.F. or **C.&F.** (cost, insurance, and freight or just cost and freight)—Requires, among other things, that the seller "put the goods in possession of a carrier" before risk passes to the buyer [UCC 2–320(2)]. (These are basically pricing terms, and the contracts remain shipment contracts, not destination contracts.)
Delivery ex-ship (delivery from the carrying vessel)—Means that risk of loss does not pass to the buyer until the goods are properly unloaded from the ship or other carrier [UCC 2–322].

CASE 11.1   Windows, Inc. v. Jordan Panel Systems Corp.

United States
Court of Appeals,
Second Circuit. 1999.
177 F.3d 114.

LEVAL, Circuit Judge:
* * * *

Windows, Inc. ("Windows" or "the seller") is a fabricator and seller of windows, based in South Dakota. Jordan [Panel] Systems, Inc. ("Jordan" or "the buyer") is a construction subcontractor, which contracted to install window wall panels at an air cargo facility at John F. Kennedy Airport in New York City. Jordan ordered custom-made windows from Windows. The purchase contract specified that the windows were to be shipped properly packaged for cross country motor freight transit and "delivered to New York City."

Windows constructed the windows according to Jordan's specifications. It arranged to have them shipped to Jordan by a common carrier, Consolidated Freightways Corp. ("Consolidated" or "the carrier"), and delivered them to Consolidated intact and properly packaged. During the course of shipment, however, the goods sustained extensive damage. Much of the glass was broken and many of the window frames were gouged and twisted. Jordan's president signed a delivery receipt noting that approximately two-thirds of the shipment was damaged due to "load shift." Jordan, seeking to stay on its contractor's schedule, directed its employees to disassemble the window frames in an effort to salvage as much of the shipment as possible.

Jordan made a claim with Consolidated for damages it had sustained as a result of the casualty, including labor costs from its salvage efforts and other costs from Jordan's inability to perform its own contractual obligations on schedule. Jordan also ordered a new shipment from Windows, which was delivered without incident.

Jordan did not pay Windows for either the first shipment of damaged windows or the second, intact shipment. Windows filed suit to recover payment from Jordan for both shipments in the Supreme Court of the State of New York, Suffolk County. Jordan counterclaimed, seeking incidental and consequential damages resulting from the damaged shipment. Windows then brought a * * * claim against Consolidated, which removed the suit to the United States District Court for the Eastern District of New York.

Windows settled its claims against Consolidated. Windows later withdrew its claims against Jordan. The only remaining claim is Jordan's counterclaim against Windows for incidental and consequential damages.

CONTINUED ▶

CASE 11.1 Continued

The district court granted Windows' motion for summary judgment. [Jordan appealed to the U.S. Court of Appeals for the Second Circuit.] * * *

* * * *

* * * A destination contract is covered by [UCC 2–503(3)]; it arises where "the seller is required to deliver at a particular destination." In contrast, a shipment contract arises [under UCC 2–504] where "the seller is required * * * to send the goods to the buyer and the contract does not require him to deliver them at a particular destination." Under a shipment contract, the seller must "put the goods in the possession of such a carrier and make such a contract for their transportation as may be reasonable having regard to the nature of the goods and other circumstances of the case."

Where the terms of an agreement are ambiguous, there is a strong presumption under the U.C.C. favoring shipment contracts. Unless the parties expressly specify that the contract requires the seller to deliver to a particular destination, the contract is generally construed as one for shipment. [Emphasis added.]

* * * *

To overcome the presumption favoring shipment contracts, the parties must have explicitly agreed to impose on Windows the obligation to effect delivery at a particular destination. The language of this contract does not do so. Nor did Jordan use any commonly recognized industry term indicating that a seller is obligated to deliver the goods to the buyer's specified destination.

Given the strong presumption favoring shipment contracts, and the absence of explicit terms satisfying both requirements for a destination contract, we conclude that the contract should be deemed a shipment contract.

Under the terms of its contract, Windows thus satisfied its obligations to Jordan when it put the goods, properly packaged, into the possession of the carrier for shipment. Upon Windows' proper delivery to the carrier, Jordan assumed the risk of loss, and cannot recover incidental or consequential damages from the seller caused by the carrier's negligence.

This allocation of risk is confirmed by the terms of [UCC 2–509(1)(a)] entitled "Risk of Loss in the Absence of Breach." It provides that where the contract "does not require [the seller] to deliver [the goods] at a particular destination, the risk of loss passes to the buyer when the goods are duly delivered to the carrier." * * * Jordan does not contest the court's finding that Windows duly delivered conforming goods to the carrier. Accordingly, as Windows had already fulfilled its contractual obligations at the time the goods were damaged and Jordan had assumed the risk of loss, there was no "seller's breach" as is required for a buyer to claim incidental and consequential damages. Summary judgment for Windows was therefore proper.

QUESTIONS

1. Under the contract between Windows, Inc., and Jordan, it was Windows' responsibility to pack the windows properly and ship them to New York City. Why was Jordan unable to recover from Windows, Inc., for damage to the windows that occurred in transit?
2. What would be necessary for the court to rule that this contract was a destination contract?

DELIVERY WITHOUT MOVEMENT OF THE GOODS
The UCC also addresses situations in which the seller or lessor is required neither to ship nor to deliver the goods. Frequently, the buyer or lessee is to pick up the goods from the seller or lessor, or the goods are to be held by a bailee. A *bailment* is a temporary delivery of personal property, without passage of title, into the care of another, called a *bailee*. Under the UCC, a bailee is a party who—by a bill of lading, warehouse receipt, or other document of title—acknowledges possession of goods and contracts to deliver them. A warehousing company, for example, or a trucking company that normally issues documents of title for the goods it receives is a bailee.

—Goods Held by the Seller. If the goods are held by the seller, a document of title is usually not used. If the seller is a merchant, risk of loss to goods held by

the seller passes to the buyer when the buyer *actually takes physical possession of the goods* [UCC 2–509(3)]. If the seller is not a merchant, the risk of loss to goods held by the seller passes to the buyer on tender of delivery [UCC 2–509(3)].

In respect to leases, the risk of loss passes to the lessee on the lessee's receipt of the goods if the lessor—or supplier, in a finance lease—is a merchant. Otherwise, the risk passes to the lessee on tender of delivery [UCC 2A–219(c)].[10]

The following case illustrates the consequences of the passage of the risk of loss under these principles.

10. Under the 2003 amendments to UCC 2–509(3) and 2A–219(c), the risk of loss passes to the buyer or the lessee on that party's receipt of the goods regardless of whether the seller or the lessor is a merchant.

CASE 11.2 — Ganno v. Lanoga Corp.

Court of Appeals
of Washington,
Division 2, 2003.
119 Wash.App. 310,
80 P.3d 180.
http://www.legalwa.org[a]

BACKGROUND AND FACTS *Henry Ganno went to the Lumbermen's Building Center store in Fife, Washington, where he bought a twelve-foot beam weighing one hundred pounds. In the lumberyard, a store employee approached Ganno, took his receipt, and used a forklift to place the beam in the open bed of Ganno's truck. The beam projected about four feet from the end of the truck. The employee asked Ganno if he wanted the beam flagged. Ganno said, "Yes," and the employee flagged the beam. The employee did not tie down or otherwise secure the beam, however. A sign in the lumberyard stated Lumbermen's policy not to secure loads for customers. Ganno, who did not get out of the truck or check the load to make sure that it was secure, drove out of the lumberyard onto a public street. When he turned a corner, the beam fell off the truck. As Ganno attempted to retrieve the beam, another vehicle hit it, causing it to strike Ganno's leg and shatter his kneecap. Ganno filed a suit in a Washington state court against Lanogo Corporation, which owned the Fife Lumbermen's store, alleging negligence in failing to secure the beam. The court granted a judgment in Lanoga's favor. Ganno appealed to a state intermediate appellate court.*

IN THE LANGUAGE OF THE COURT

HUNT, C.J. [Chief Judge]

* * * *

Ganno * * * asserts that Lumbermen's duty of care did not end when he drove off Lumbermen's property. * * * [W]e disagree.

[Revised Code of Washington Section 62A.2-509(3), the state of Washington's version of Section 2–509(3)] of the Uniform Commercial Code declares that where the seller is a merchant, the risk of loss passes to the buyer on receipt of goods. Accordingly, Lumbermen's duty of care ended when it placed the beam into Ganno's truckbed.

* * * Ganno received the beam from Lumbermen's in good condition at the merchant's place of business. * * *

In the absence of a legal duty to secure a customer's load, as here, there is no liability to a customer once he is in possession of the goods. The risk of loss passed to Ganno when Lumbermen's loaded the beam into his truck. Again, Lumbermen's is not liable for the ensuing damage after Ganno took possession and left Lumbermen's property.

* * * *

We hold that there are no issues of material fact and that the trial court properly granted Lumbermen's motion for summary judgment as a matter of law. Thus, we affirm.

DECISION AND REMEDY *The state intermediate appellate court affirmed the lower court's judgment, holding that it was Ganno's duty, not Lumbermen's, to make sure the load was secure before Ganno drove onto the public streets. In other words, the risk had passed to Ganno, the buyer, before the loss.*

---

a. Click on the "Washington State Supreme and Appellate Court Decisions" link. Type "Ganno" in the search box, select "Search case titles only," choose "Washington Appellate Reports" in the "Limit search to:" column, and click on "Search." In the result, click on the name of the case to access the opinion. Municipal Research and Services Center of Washington maintains this Web site.

—*Goods Held by a Bailee.*   When a bailee is holding goods for a person who has contracted to sell them and the goods are to be delivered without being moved, the goods are usually represented by a negotiable or nonnegotiable document of title (a bill of lading or a warehouse receipt). Risk of loss passes to the buyer when (1) the buyer receives a negotiable document of title for the goods, (2) the bailee acknowledges the buyer's right to possess the goods, or (3) the buyer receives a nonnegotiable document of title or a writing (record) directing the bailee *and* has had a *reasonable time* to present the document to the bailee and demand the goods. Obviously, if the bailee refuses to honor the document, the risk of loss remains with the seller [UCC 2–503(4)(b), 2–509(2)].

With respect to leases, if goods held by a bailee are to be delivered without being moved, the risk of loss passes to the lessee on acknowledgment by the bailee of the lessee's right to possession of the goods [UCC 2A–219(2)(b)].

CONDITIONAL SALES   Buyers and sellers sometimes form sales contracts that are conditioned either on the buyer's approval of the goods or on the buyer's resale of the goods. Under such contracts, the buyer is in possession of the goods. Sometimes, however, problems arise as to whether the buyer or seller should bear the loss if, for example, the goods are damaged or stolen while in the possession of the buyer.

—*Sale or Return.*   A **sale or return** (sometimes called a *sale and return*) is a type of contract by which the buyer purchases the goods but has a conditional right to return the goods (undo the sale) within a specified time period. When the buyer receives possession at the time of sale, title and risk of loss pass to the buyer. Title and risk of loss remain with the buyer until the buyer returns the goods to the seller within the time period specified. If the buyer fails to return the goods within this time period, the sale is finalized. The return of the goods is made at the buyer's risk and expense. Goods held under a sale-or-return contract are subject to the claims of the buyer's creditors while they are in the buyer's possession.

The UCC treats a **consignment** as a sale or return. Under a consignment, the owner of goods (the *consignor*) delivers them to another (the *consignee*) for the consignee to sell or to keep. If the consignee sells the goods, the consignee must pay the consignor for them. If the consignee does not sell or keep the goods, they may simply be returned to the consignor. While the goods are in the possession of the consignee, the consignee holds title to them, and creditors of the consignee will prevail over the consignor in any action to repossess the goods [UCC 2–326(3)].[11]

—*Sale on Approval.*   Usually, when a seller offers to sell goods to a buyer and permits the buyer to take the goods on a trial basis, a **sale on approval** is made. The term *sale* here is a misnomer, as only an *offer* to sell has been made, along with a bailment created by the buyer's possession.

Therefore, title and risk of loss (from causes beyond the buyer's control) remain with the seller until the buyer accepts (approves) the offer. Acceptance can be made expressly, by any act inconsistent with the *trial* purpose or the seller's ownership, or by the buyer's election not to return the goods within the trial period. If the buyer does not wish to accept, the buyer may notify the seller of that fact within the trial period, and the return is made at the seller's expense and risk [UCC 2–327(1)]. Goods held on approval are not subject to the claims of the buyer's creditors until acceptance.

RISK OF LOSS WHEN A SALES OR LEASE CONTRACT IS BREACHED   There are many ways to breach a sales or lease contract, and the transfer of risk operates differently depending on which party breaches. Generally, the party in breach bears the risk of loss.

—*When the Seller or Lessor Breaches.*   If the goods are so nonconforming that the buyer has the right to reject them, the risk of loss does not pass to the buyer until the defects are *cured* (that is, until the goods are repaired, replaced, or discounted in price by the seller) or until the buyer accepts the goods in spite of their defects (thus waiving the right to reject). For example, a buyer orders blue file cabinets from a seller, F.O.B. seller's plant. The seller ships black file cabinets instead. The black cabinets (nonconforming goods) are damaged in transit. The risk of loss falls on the seller. Had the seller shipped blue cabinets (conforming goods) instead, the risk would have fallen on the buyer [UCC 2–510(2)].

If a buyer accepts a shipment of goods and later discovers a defect, acceptance can be revoked. Revocation allows the buyer to pass the risk of loss back to the seller,

---

11. This provision is omitted from the 2003 amendments to UCC Article 2. Consignments are to be covered by UCC Article 9. See, for example, UCC 9–103(d), 9–109(a)(4), and 9–319.

at least to the extent that the buyer's insurance does not cover the loss [UCC 2–510(2)].

In regard to leases, Article 2A states a similar rule. If the lessor or supplier tenders goods that are so nonconforming that the lessee has the right to reject them, the risk of loss remains with the lessor or the supplier until cure or acceptance [UCC 2A–220(1)(a)]. If the lessee, after acceptance, revokes his or her acceptance of nonconforming goods, the revocation passes the risk of loss back to the seller or supplier, to the extent that the lessee's insurance does not cover the loss [UCC 2A–220(1)(b)].

—*When the Buyer or Lessee Breaches.* The general rule is that when a buyer or lessee breaches a contract, the risk of loss *immediately* shifts to the buyer or lessee. There are three important limitations to this rule [UCC 2–510(3), 2A–220(2)]:

1. The seller or lessor must already have identified the contract goods.
2. The buyer or lessee bears the risk for only a *commercially reasonable time* after the seller or lessor has learned of the breach.
3. The buyer or lessee is liable only to the extent of any deficiency in the seller's or lessor's insurance coverage.

INSURABLE INTEREST

Parties to sales and lease contracts often obtain insurance coverage to protect against damage, loss, or destruction of goods. Any party purchasing insurance, however, must have a sufficient interest in the insured item to obtain a valid policy. Insurance laws—not the UCC—determine sufficiency. The UCC is helpful, however, because it contains certain rules regarding insurable interests in goods.

A buyer or lessee has an **insurable interest** in identified goods. The moment the contract goods are *identified* by the seller or lessor, the buyer or lessee has a special property interest that allows the buyer or lessee to obtain necessary insurance coverage for those goods even before the risk of loss has passed [UCC 2–501(1), 2A–218(1)].

A seller has an insurable interest in goods as long as he or she retains title to the goods. Even after title passes to a buyer, however, a seller who has a security interest in the goods, which is a legal right to secure payment, still has an insurable interest and can insure the goods [UCC 2–501(2)]. Hence, both a buyer and a seller can have an insurable interest in identical goods at the same time. Of course, the buyer or seller must

sustain an actual loss to have the right to recover from an insurance company. In regard to leases, the lessor retains an insurable interest in leased goods until an option to buy has been exercised by the lessee and the risk of loss has passed to the lessee [UCC 2A–218(3)].

SECTION 8 | Performance of Sales and Lease Contracts

To understand the obligations of the parties under a sales or lease contract, it is necessary to know the duties and obligations each party has assumed under the terms of the contract. Keep in mind that "duties and obligations" under the terms of the contract include those specified by the agreement, by custom, and by the UCC.

In the performance of a sales or lease contract, the basic obligation of the seller or lessor is to *transfer and deliver conforming goods*. The basic obligation of the buyer or lessee is to *accept and pay for conforming goods* in accordance with the contract [UCC 2–301, 2A–516(1)]. Overall performance of a sales or lease contract is controlled by the agreement between the parties. When the contract is unclear and disputes arise, the courts look to the UCC.

THE GOOD FAITH REQUIREMENT

The obligations of good faith and commercial reasonableness underlie every sales and lease contract within the UCC. These obligations can form the basis for a suit for breach of contract later on. The UCC's good faith provision, which can never be disclaimed, reads as follows: "Every contract or duty within this Act imposes an obligation of good faith in its performance or enforcement" [UCC 1–203]. Good faith means honesty in fact. In the case of a merchant, it means honesty in fact and the observance of reasonable commercial standards of fair dealing in the trade [UCC 2–103(1)(b)]. In other words, merchants are held to a higher standard of performance or duty than nonmerchants.[12]

OBLIGATIONS OF THE SELLER OR LESSOR

The major obligation of the seller or lessor under a sales or lease contract is to tender conforming goods to the buyer or lessee. **Tender of delivery** requires

---

12. The 2003 amendments to UCC Articles 2 and 2A apply this definition of *good faith* to all parties, merchants and nonmerchants alike [Amended UCC 2–103(1)(j), 2A–103(1)(m)].

that the seller or lessor have and hold *conforming goods* at the disposal of the buyer or lessee and give the buyer or lessee whatever notification is reasonably necessary to enable the buyer or lessee to take delivery [UCC 2–503(1), 2A–508(1)]. **Conforming goods** are goods that conform exactly to the description of the goods in the contract.

Tender must occur at a *reasonable hour* and in a *reasonable manner*. For example, a seller cannot call the buyer at 2:00 A.M. and say, "The goods are ready. I'll give you twenty minutes to get them." Unless the parties have agreed otherwise, the goods must be tendered for delivery at a reasonable hour and kept available for a reasonable period of time to enable the buyer to take possession of them [UCC 2–503(1)(a)].

All goods called for by a contract must be tendered in a single delivery unless the parties agree otherwise [UCC 2–612, 2A–510] or the circumstances are such that either party can rightfully request delivery in lots [UCC 2–307].

PLACE OF DELIVERY   If the contract does not designate the place of delivery for the goods, and the buyer is expected to pick them up, the place of delivery is the *seller's place of business* or, if the seller has none, the *seller's residence* [UCC 2–308]. If the contract involves the sale of *identified goods,* and the parties know when they enter into the contract that these goods are located somewhere other than at the seller's place of business (such as at a warehouse), then the *location of the goods* is the place for their delivery [UCC 2–308].

THE PERFECT TENDER RULE   As previously noted, the seller or lessor has an obligation to ship or tender *conforming goods*, and this entitles the buyer or lessee to accept and pay for the goods according to the terms of the contract. Under the common law, the seller was obligated to deliver goods in conformity with the terms of the contract in every detail. This was called the **perfect tender rule.** The UCC preserves the perfect tender doctrine by stating that if goods or tender of delivery fail *in any respect* to conform to the contract, the buyer or lessee has the right to accept the goods, reject the entire shipment, or accept part and reject part [UCC 2–601, 2A–509].

EXCEPTIONS TO THE PERFECT TENDER RULE   Because of the rigidity of the perfect tender rule, several exceptions to the rule have been created, some of which we discuss here.

—Agreement of the Parties.   Exceptions to the perfect tender rule may be established by agreement. If the parties have agreed, for example, that defective goods or parts will not be rejected if the seller or lessor is able to repair or replace them within a reasonable period of time, the perfect tender rule does not apply.

—Cure.   The UCC does not specifically define the term **cure,** but it refers to the right of the seller or lessor to repair, adjust, or replace defective or nonconforming goods [UCC 2–508, 2A–513]. When any tender of delivery is rejected because of nonconforming goods and the time for performance has not yet expired, the seller or lessor can promptly notify the buyer or lessee of the intention to cure and can then do so *within the contract time for performance* [UCC 2–508(1), 2A–513(1)]. Once the time for performance under the contract has expired, the seller or lessor can still exercise the right to cure if he or she has *reasonable grounds to believe that the nonconforming tender will be acceptable to the buyer or lessee* [UCC 2–508(2), 2A–513(2)].[13]

The right to cure substantially restricts the right of the buyer or lessee to reject goods. For example, if a lessee refuses a tender of goods as nonconforming but does not disclose the nature of the defect to the lessor, the lessee cannot later assert the defect as a defense if the defect is one that the lessor could have cured. Generally, buyers and lessees must act in good faith and state specific reasons for refusing to accept goods [UCC 2–605, 2A–514].

—Substitution of Carriers.   When an agreed-on manner of delivery (such as the use of a particular carrier to transport the goods) becomes impracticable or unavailable through no fault of either party, but a commercially reasonable substitute is available, this substitute performance is sufficient tender to the buyer and must be used [UCC 2–614(1)].

—Commercial Impracticability.   Occurrences unforeseen by either party when a contract was made may make performance commercially impracticable. When this occurs, the rule of perfect tender no longer holds. According to UCC 2–615(a) and 2A–405(a), delay in delivery or nondelivery in whole or in part is not a breach when performance has been made impracticable

---

13. The 2003 amendments to UCC Articles 2 and 2A expressly exempt consumer contracts and consumer leases from these provisions [Amended UCC 2–508, 2A–508]. In other words, cure is not available as a matter of right after a justifiable revocation of acceptance under a consumer contract or lease. The new provisions also abandon the "reasonable grounds to believe" test, thus expanding the seller's right to cure after the time for performance has expired. Although this test has been abandoned, the requirement that the initial tender be made in good faith prevents a seller from deliberately tendering goods that the seller knows the buyer cannot use.

"by the occurrence of a contingency the nonoccurrence of which was a basic assumption on which the contract was made." The seller or lessor must, however, notify the buyer or lessee as soon as practicable that there will be a delay or nondelivery.

Can unanticipated increases in a seller's costs that make performance "impracticable" constitute a valid defense to performance on the basis of commercial impracticability? The court dealt with this question in the following case.

CASE 11.3 — Maple Farms, Inc. v. City School District of Elmira

Supreme Court
of New York, 1974.
76 Misc.2d 1080,
352 N.Y.S.2d 784.

BACKGROUND AND FACTS *On June 15, 1973, Maple Farms, Inc., formed an agreement with the city school district of Elmira, New York, to supply the school district with milk for the 1973–1974 school year. The agreement was in the form of a requirements contract, under which Maple Farms would sell to the school district all the milk the district required at a fixed price—which was the June market price of milk. By December 1973, the price of raw milk had increased by 23 percent over the price specified in the contract. This meant that if the terms of the contract were fulfilled, Maple Farms would lose $7,350. Because it had similar contracts with other school districts, Maple Farms stood to lose a great deal if it was held to the price stated in the contracts. When the school district would not agree to release Maple Farms from its contract, Maple Farms brought an action in a New York state court for a declaratory judgment (a determination of the parties' rights under a contract). Maple Farms contended that the substantial increase in the price of raw milk was an event not contemplated by the parties when the contract was formed and that, given the increased price, performance of the contract was commercially impracticable.*

IN THE LANGUAGE OF THE COURT

CHARLES B. SWARTWOOD, Justice.

* * * *

* * * [The doctrine of commercial impracticability requires that] a contingency—something unexpected—must have occurred. Second, the risk of the unexpected occurrence must not have been allocated either by agreement or by custom. * * *

* * * [H]ere we find that the contingency causing the increase of the price of raw milk was not totally unexpected. The price from the low point in the year 1972 to the price on the date of the award of the contract in June 1973 had risen nearly 10%. And *any businessman should have been aware of the general inflation in this country during the previous years* * * *. [Emphasis added.]

* * * Here the very purpose of the contract was to guard against fluctuation of price of half pints of milk as a basis for the school budget. Surely had the price of raw milk fallen substantially, the defendant could not be excused from performance. We can reasonably assume that the plaintiff had to be aware of escalating inflation. It is chargeable with knowledge of the substantial increase of the price of raw milk from the previous year's low. * * * It nevertheless entered into this agreement with that knowledge. It did not provide in the contract any exculpatory clause to excuse it from performance in the event of a substantial rise in the price of raw milk. On these facts the risk of a substantial or abnormal increase in the price of raw milk can be allocated to the plaintiff.

DECISION AND REMEDY *The New York trial court ruled that inflation and fluctuating prices did not render performance impracticable in this case and granted summary judgment in favor of the school district.*

WHAT IF THE FACTS WERE DIFFERENT? *Suppose that the court had ruled in the plaintiff's favor. How might that ruling have affected the plaintiff's contracts with other parties?*

IMPACT OF THIS CASE ON TODAY'S LAW

This case is a classic illustration of the UCC's commercial impracticability doctrine as courts still apply it today. Under this doctrine, increased cost alone does not excuse performance unless the rise in cost is due to some unforeseen contingency that alters the essential nature of the performance.

—*Destruction of Identified Goods.* Sometimes, an unexpected event, such as a fire, totally destroys goods through no fault of either party and before risk passes to the buyer or lessee. In such a situation, if the *goods were identified at the time the contract was formed,* the parties are excused from performance [UCC 2–613, 2A–221]. If the goods are only partially destroyed, however, the buyer or lessee can inspect them and either treat the contract as void or accept the damaged goods with a reduction of the contract price.

—*Cooperation and Assurance.* Two other exceptions to the perfect tender doctrine apply equally to parties to sales and lease contracts: the duty of cooperation and the right of assurance.

Sometimes the performance of one party depends on the cooperation of the other. The UCC provides that when such cooperation is not forthcoming, the other party can either suspend his or her own performance without liability and hold the uncooperative party in breach or proceed to perform the contract in any reasonable manner [see UCC 2–311(3)(b)].

The UCC provides that if one of the parties to a contract has "reasonable grounds" to believe that the other party will not perform as contracted, he or she may *in writing* "demand adequate assurance of due performance" from the other party. Until such assurance is received, he or she may "suspend" further performance without liability. What constitutes "reasonable grounds" is determined by commercial standards. If such assurances are not forthcoming within a reasonable time (not to exceed thirty days), the failure to respond may be treated as a *repudiation* of the contract [UCC 2–609, 2A–401].

OBLIGATIONS OF THE BUYER OR LESSEE

Once the seller or lessor has adequately tendered delivery, the buyer or lessee is obligated to accept the goods and pay for them according to the terms of the contract.

PAYMENT In the absence of any specific agreements, the buyer or lessee must make payment at the time and place the buyer or lessee *receives* the goods [UCC 2–310(a), 2A–516(1)]. When a sale is made on credit, the buyer is obliged to pay according to the specified credit terms (for example, 60, 90, or 120 days), not when the goods are received. The credit period usually begins on the *date of shipment* [UCC 2–310(d)]. Under a lease contract, a lessee must make the lease payment specified in the contract [UCC 2A–516(1)].

Payment can be made by any means agreed on between the parties—cash or any other method generally acceptable in the commercial world. If the seller demands cash when the buyer offers a check, credit card, or the like, the seller must permit the buyer reasonable time to obtain legal tender [UCC 2–511].

ACCEPTANCE A buyer or lessee can manifest assent to the delivered goods in the following ways, each of which constitutes acceptance:

1. There is an acceptance if the buyer or lessee, after having had a reasonable opportunity to inspect the goods, signifies agreement to the seller or lessor that the goods are either conforming or are acceptable in spite of their nonconformity [UCC 2–606(1)(a), 2A–515(1)(a)].

2. Acceptance is presumed if the buyer or lessee has had a reasonable opportunity to inspect the goods and has failed to reject them within a reasonable period of time [UCC 2–602(1), 2–606(1)(b), 2A–515(1)(b)].

3. In sales contracts, the buyer will be deemed to have accepted the goods if he or she performs any act inconsistent with the seller's ownership. For example, any use or resale of the goods generally constitutes an acceptance. Limited use for the sole purpose of testing or inspecting the goods is not an acceptance, however [UCC 2–606(1)(c)].

If some of the goods delivered do not conform to the contract and the seller or lessor has failed to cure, the buyer or lessee can make a *partial* acceptance [UCC 2–601(c), 2A–509(1)]. The same is true if the nonconformity was not reasonably discoverable before acceptance. A buyer or lessee cannot accept less than a single commercial unit, however. A *commercial unit* is defined by the UCC as a unit of goods that, by commercial usage, is viewed as a "single whole" for purposes of sale, division of which would materially impair the character of the unit, its market value, or its use [UCC 2–105(6), 2A–103(c)]. A commercial unit can be a single article (such as a machine), a set of articles (such as a suite of furniture or an assortment of sizes), a quantity (such as a bale, a gross, or a carload), or any other unit treated in the trade as a single whole.

ANTICIPATORY REPUDIATION

What if, before the time for contract performance, one party clearly communicates to the other the intention not to perform? Such an action is a breach of the contract by *anticipatory repudiation*. When anticipatory repudiation occurs, the nonbreaching party has a choice of two responses. One option is to treat the repudiation as a final breach by pursuing a remedy; the other is to wait and hope that the repudiating party will decide to honor the obligations required by the contract despite the avowed intention to renege [UCC 2–610, 2A–402]. (In either situation, the nonbreaching party may suspend performance.)

Should the second option be pursued, the UCC permits the breaching party (subject to some limitations) to "retract" his or her repudiation. This can be done by any method that clearly indicates an intent to perform. Once retraction is made, the rights of the repudiating party under the contract are reinstated [UCC 2–611, 2A–403].

SECTION 9 | Remedies for Breach of Sales and Lease Contracts

Sometimes, circumstances make it difficult for a person to carry out the performance promised in a contract, in which case the contract may be breached. When breach occurs, the aggrieved party looks for remedies. These remedies range from retaining the goods to requiring the breaching party's performance under the contract. The general purpose of these remedies is to put the aggrieved party "in as good a position as if the other party had fully performed." Remedies under the UCC are *cumulative* in nature. In other words, an innocent party to a breached sales or lease contract is not limited to one, exclusive remedy. (Of course, a party still may not recover twice for the same harm.)

REMEDIES OF THE SELLER OR LESSOR

A buyer or lessee breaches a sales or lease contract by any of the following actions: (1) wrongfully rejecting tender of the goods; (2) wrongfully revoking acceptance of the goods; (3) failing to make payment on or before delivery of the goods; or (4) repudiating the contract. On the buyer's or lessee's breach, the seller or lessor is afforded several distinct remedies under the UCC, including those discussed here.

THE RIGHT TO WITHHOLD DELIVERY In general, sellers and lessors can withhold or discontinue performance of their obligations under sales or lease contracts when the buyers or lessees are in breach. If a buyer or lessee has wrongfully rejected or revoked acceptance of contract goods (rejection and revocation of acceptance will be discussed shortly), failed to make proper and timely payment, or repudiated a part of the contract, the seller or lessor can withhold delivery of the goods in question [UCC 2–703(a), 2A–523(1)(c)]. If the breach results from the buyer's or lessee's insolvency (inability to pay debts as they become due), the seller or lessor can refuse to deliver the goods unless the buyer or lessee pays in cash [UCC 2–702(1), 2A–525(1)].

THE RIGHT TO RESELL OR DISPOSE OF THE GOODS When a buyer or lessee breaches or repudiates the contract while the seller or lessor is still in possession of the goods, the seller or lessor can resell or dispose of the goods, holding the buyer or lessee liable for any loss [UCC 2–703(d), 2–706(1), 2A–523(1)(e), 2A–527(1)].[14]

THE RIGHT TO RECOVER THE PURCHASE PRICE OR LEASE PAYMENTS DUE Under the UCC, an unpaid seller or lessor who is unable to resell or dispose of the goods can bring an action to recover the purchase price or the payments due under the lease contract, plus incidental damages, but only under one of the following circumstances:

1. When the buyer or lessee has accepted the goods and has not revoked acceptance.
2. When conforming goods have been lost or damaged after the risk of loss has passed to the buyer or lessee.
3. When the buyer or lessee has breached after the goods have been identified to the contract and the seller or lessor is unable to resell or otherwise dispose of the goods [UCC 2–709(1), 2A–529(1)].

If a seller or lessor sues under these circumstances, the goods must be held for the buyer or lessee. The seller or lessor can resell or dispose of the goods at any time prior to collection of the judgment from the buyer or lessee, but in that situation the net proceeds

---

14. Under the 2003 amendments to UCC Articles 2 and 2A, this loss includes consequential damages, except that a seller or lessor cannot recover consequential damages from a consumer under a consumer contract or lease [Amended UCC 2–706(1), 2–710, 2A–527(2), 2A–530]. Consequential damages may also be recovered, except from a consumer under a consumer contract or lease, when a seller or lessor has a right to recover the purchase price or lease payments due or to recover other damages [Amended UCC 2–708(1), 2–709(1), 2–710, 2A–528(1), 2A–529(1), 2A–530]. Subtracted from these amounts, of course, would be any expenses saved as a consequence of the buyer's or lessee's breach.

from the sale must be credited to the buyer or lessee. This is an example of the duty to mitigate damages.

THE RIGHT TO RECOVER DAMAGES If a buyer or lessee repudiates a contract or wrongfully refuses to accept the goods, a seller or lessor can maintain an action to recover the damages sustained. Ordinarily, the amount of damages equals the difference between the contract price (or lease payments) and the market price (or lease payments) at the time and place of tender of the goods, plus incidental damages [UCC 2–708(1), 2A–528(1)]. The time and place of tender are frequently given by such terms as F.O.B., F.A.S., C.I.F., and the like (see Exhibit 11–2 on page 257), which determine whether there is a shipment or a destination contract.

If the difference between the contract price (or payments due under the lease contract) and the market price (or payments due under the lease contract) is too small to place the seller or lessor in the position that he or she would have been in if the buyer or lessee had fully performed, the proper measure of damages is the lost profits of the seller or lessor, including a reasonable allowance for overhead and other expenses [UCC 2–708(2), 2A–528(2)].

REMEDIES OF THE BUYER OR LESSEE

A seller or lessor breaches a sales or lease contract by failing to deliver conforming goods or repudiating the contract prior to delivery. On the breach, the buyer or lessee has a choice of several remedies under the UCC, including those discussed here.

THE RIGHT OF COVER In certain situations, buyers and lessees can protect themselves by obtaining **cover**—that is, by buying or leasing substitute goods for those that were due under the contract. This option is available when the seller or lessor repudiates the contract or fails to deliver the goods. It is also available to a buyer or lessee who has rightfully rejected goods or revoked acceptance. Rejection and revocation of acceptance will be discussed shortly.

In obtaining cover, the buyer or lessee must act in good faith and without unreasonable delay [UCC 2–712, 2A–518]. After purchasing or leasing substitute goods, the buyer or lessee can recover from the seller or lessor the difference between the cost of cover and the contract price (or lease payments), plus incidental and consequential damages, less the expenses (such as delivery costs) that were saved as a result of the breach [UCC 2–712, 2–715, 2A–518]. Consequential damages are any losses suffered by the buyer or lessee that the seller or lessor could have foreseen (had reason to know about) at the time of contract formation and any injury to the buyer's or lessee's person or property proximately resulting from the contract's breach [UCC 2–715(2), 2A–520(2)].

Buyers and lessees are not required to cover, and failure to do so will not bar them from using any other remedies available under the UCC. A buyer or lessee who fails to cover, however, risks not being able to collect consequential damages—a situation that could have been avoided had he or she purchased or leased substitute goods.

THE RIGHT TO OBTAIN SPECIFIC PERFORMANCE A buyer or lessee can obtain specific performance when the goods are unique or when the remedy at law is inadequate [UCC 2–716(1), 2A–521(1)]. Ordinarily, an award of money damages is sufficient to place a buyer or lessee in the position he or she would have occupied if the seller or lessor had fully performed. When the contract is for the purchase of a particular work of art or a similarly unique item, however, money damages may not be sufficient. Under these circumstances, equity will require that the seller or lessor perform exactly by delivering the particular goods identified to the contract (a remedy of specific performance).

THE RIGHT TO RECOVER DAMAGES If a seller or lessor repudiates the sales contract or fails to deliver the goods, or if the buyer is justified in rejecting goods that the seller or lessor tenders, then the buyer or lessee has several options under the UCC. The buyer or lessee may cancel the contract and recover as much of the price as has been paid to the seller or lessor. Following cancellation, the buyer or lessee may either (1) cover by obtaining goods from another seller or lessor and seeking reimbursement for the extra costs incurred or (2) recover damages for breach of the contract.

If the buyer or lessee elects to sue for damages, the measure of recovery is the difference between the contract price (or lease payments) and the market price of the goods (or lease payments that could be obtained for the goods) at the time the buyer (or lessee) *learned* of the breach. The market price or market lease payments are determined at the place where the seller or lessor was supposed to deliver the goods. The buyer or lessee can also recover incidental and consequential damages less the expenses that were saved as a result of the breach [UCC 2–713, 2A–519].

THE RIGHT TO REJECT THE GOODS

If either the goods or the tender of the goods by the seller or lessor fails to conform to the contract in any respect, the buyer or lessee can reject the goods. If some of the goods conform to the contract, the buyer or lessee can keep the conforming goods and reject the rest [UCC 2–601, 2A–509]. The buyer or lessee must reject the goods within a reasonable amount of time after delivery or tender of delivery, and the seller or lessor must be notified *seasonably*—that is, in a timely fashion or at the proper time [UCC 2–602(1), 2A–509(2)].

If a *merchant buyer* or *lessee* rightfully rejects goods, and the seller or lessor has no agent or business at the place of rejection, the buyer or lessee is required to follow any reasonable instructions received from the seller or lessor with respect to the goods controlled by the buyer or lessee. The buyer or lessee is entitled to reimbursement for the care and cost entailed in following the instructions [UCC 2–603, 2A–511]. The same requirements hold if the buyer or lessee rightfully revokes his or her acceptance of the goods at some later time [UCC 2–608(3), 2A–517(5)].

If no instructions are forthcoming and the goods are perishable or threaten to decline in value quickly, the buyer or lessee can resell the goods in good faith, taking appropriate reimbursement and a selling commission (not to exceed 10 percent of the gross proceeds) from the proceeds [UCC 2–603(1), (2); 2A–511(1)]. If the goods are not perishable, the buyer or lessee may store them for the seller or lessor or reship them to the seller or lessor [UCC 2–604, 2A–512].

THE RIGHT TO RECOVER DAMAGES FOR ACCEPTED GOODS

A buyer or lessee who has accepted nonconforming goods may also keep the goods and recover for any loss "resulting in the ordinary course of events . . . as determined in any manner which is reasonable" [UCC 2–714(1), 2A–519(3)]. The buyer or lessee, however, must notify the seller or lessor of the breach within a reasonable time after the defect was or should have been discovered.

When the goods delivered are not as warranted, the measure of damages equals the difference between the value of the goods as accepted and their value if they had been delivered as warranted unless special circumstances show proximately caused damages of a different amount, plus incidental and consequential damages [UCC 2–714, 2A–519].

REVOCATION OF ACCEPTANCE

Acceptance of the goods precludes the buyer or lessee from exercising the right of rejection, but it does not necessarily preclude the buyer or lessee from pursuing other remedies. Additionally, in certain circumstances, a buyer or lessee is permitted to *revoke* his or her acceptance of the goods. Acceptance of a lot or a commercial unit can be revoked if the nonconformity *substantially* impairs the value of the lot or unit and if one of the following factors is present:

1. Acceptance was predicated on the reasonable assumption that the nonconformity would be cured, and it has not been cured within a reasonable period of time [UCC 2–608(1)(a), 2A–517(1)(a)].[15]

2. The buyer or lessee did not discover the nonconformity before acceptance, either because it was difficult to discover before acceptance or because assurances made by the seller or lessor that the goods were conforming kept the buyer or lessee from inspecting the goods [UCC 2–608(1)(b), 2A–517(1)(b)].

Revocation of acceptance is not effective until notice is given to the seller or lessor. Notice must occur within a reasonable time after the buyer or lessee either discovers or *should have discovered* the grounds for revocation. Additionally, revocation must occur before the goods have undergone any substantial change (such as spoilage) not caused by their own defects [UCC 2–608(2), 2A–517(4)]. Once acceptance is revoked, the buyer or lessee can pursue remedies, just as if the goods had been rejected.

Is two years after a sale of goods a reasonable time period in which to discover a defect in those goods and notify the seller or lessor of a breach? That was the question in the following case.

---

15. Under the 2003 amendments to UCC 2–508 and 2A–513, cure after a justifiable revocation of acceptance is *not* available as a matter of right in a consumer contract or lease.

CASE 11.4   Fitl v. Strek

Supreme Court
of Nebraska, 2005.
269 Neb. 51,
690 N.W.2d 605.
*http://www.findlaw.com/
11stategov/ne/neca.html*[a]

BACKGROUND AND FACTS *Over the Labor Day weekend in 1995, James Fitl attended a sports-card show in San Francisco, California, where he met Mark Strek, doing business as Star Cards of San Francisco, an exhibitor at the show. Later, on Strek's representation that a certain 1952 Mickey Mantle Topps baseball card was in near-mint condition, Fitl bought the card from Strek for $17,750. Strek delivered it to Fitl in Omaha, Nebraska, where Fitl placed it in a safe-deposit box. In May 1997, Fitl sent the card to Professional Sports Authenticators (PSA), a sports-card grading service. PSA told Fitl that the card was ungradable because it had been discolored and doctored. Fitl complained to Strek, who replied that Fitl should have initiated a return of the card within "a typical grace period for the unconditional return of a card, . . . 7 days to 1 month" of its receipt. In August, Fitl sent the card to ASA Accugrade, Inc. (ASA), another grading service, for a second opinion on its value. ASA also concluded that the card had been refinished and trimmed. Fitl filed a suit in a Nebraska state court against Strek, seeking damages. The court awarded Fitl $17,750, plus his court costs. Strek appealed to the Nebraska Supreme Court.*

IN THE LANGUAGE OF THE COURT

WRIGHT, J. [Justice]
          * * * *
          Strek claims that the [trial] court erred in determining that notification of the defective condition of the baseball card 2 years after the date of purchase was timely pursuant to [UCC] 2–607(3)(a).
          * * * The [trial] court found that Fitl had notified Strek within a reasonable time after discovery of the breach. Therefore, our review is whether the [trial] court's finding as to the reasonableness of the notice was clearly erroneous.
          Section 2–607(3)(a) states: "Where a tender has been accepted * * * the buyer must within a reasonable time after he discovers or should have discovered any breach notify the seller of breach or be barred from any remedy." [Under UCC 1–204(2)] *"[w]hat is a reasonable time for taking any action depends on the nature, purpose, and circumstances of such action."* [Emphasis added.]
          The notice requirement set forth in Section 2–607(3)(a) serves three purposes. * * *
          * * * The most important one is to enable the seller to make efforts to cure the breach by making adjustments or replacements in order to minimize the buyer's damages and the seller's liability. A second policy is to provide the seller a reasonable opportunity to learn the facts so that he may adequately prepare for negotiation and defend himself in a suit. A third policy * * * is the same as the policy behind statutes of limitation: to provide a seller with a terminal point in time for liability.
          * * * *[A] party is justified in relying upon a representation made to the party as a positive statement of fact when an investigation would be required to ascertain its falsity.* In order for Fitl to have determined that the baseball card had been altered, he would have been required to conduct an investigation. We find that he was not required to do so. Once Fitl learned that the baseball card had been altered, he gave notice to Strek. [Emphasis added.]
          * * * [O]ne of the most important policies behind the notice requirement * * * is to allow the seller to cure the breach by making adjustments or replacements to minimize the buyer's damages and the seller's liability. However, even if Fitl had learned immediately upon taking possession of the baseball card that it was not authentic and had notified Strek at that time, there is no evidence that Strek could have made any adjustment or taken any action that would have minimized his liability. In its altered condition, the baseball card was worthless.
          * * * Earlier notification would not have helped Strek prepare for negotiation or defend himself in a suit because the damage to Fitl could not be repaired. Thus, the policies

---

a. In the "Supreme Court Opinions" section, in the "2005" row, click on "January." In the result, click on the appropriate link next to the name of the case to access the opinion.

CASE 11.4 Continued behind the notice requirement, to allow the seller to correct a defect, to prepare for negotiation and litigation, and to protect against stale claims at a time beyond which an investigation can be completed, were not unfairly prejudiced by the lack of an earlier notice to Strek. Any problem Strek may have had with the party from whom he obtained the baseball card was a separate matter from his transaction with Fitl, and an investigation into the source of the altered card would not have minimized Fitl's damages.

DECISION AND REMEDY *The state supreme court affirmed the decision of the lower court. In the circumstances of this case, notice of a defect in the goods two years after their purchase was reasonable. The buyer had reasonably relied on the seller's representation that the goods were "authentic" (which they were not), and when their defects were discovered, the buyer had given a timely notice.*

WHAT IF THE FACTS WERE DIFFERENT? *Suppose that Fitl and Strek had included in their agreement a clause requiring Fitl to give notice of any defect in the card within "7 days to 1 month" of its receipt. Would the result have been different? Why or why not?*

CONTRACTUAL PROVISIONS AFFECTING REMEDIES

The parties to a sales or lease contract can vary their respective rights and obligations by contractual agreement. For example, a seller and buyer can expressly provide for remedies in addition to those provided in the UCC. They can also specifiy remedies in lieu of those provided in the UCC, or they can change the measure of damages. The seller can stipulate that the buyer's only remedy on the seller's breach be repair or replacement of the item, or the seller can limit the buyer's remedy to return of the goods and refund of the purchase price. In sales and lease contracts, an agreed-on remedy is in addition to those provided in the UCC unless the parties expressly agree that the remedy is exclusive of all others [UCC 2–719(1), 2A–503(1)].

If the parties state that a remedy is exclusive, then it is the sole remedy. When circumstances cause an exclusive remedy to fail in its essential purpose, however, it is no longer exclusive [UCC 2–719(2), 2A–503(2)]. For example, a sales contract that limits the buyer's remedy to repair or replacement fails in its essential purpose if the item cannot be repaired and no replacements are available.

SECTION 10 | Sales and Lease Warranties

Warranty is an age-old concept. In sales and lease law, a warranty is an assurance by one party of the existence of a fact on which the other party can rely. Article 2 and Article 2A of the UCC designate several types of warranties that can arise in a sales or lease contract. These warranties include warranties of title, express warranties, and implied warranties.

Because a warranty imposes a duty on the seller or lessor, a breach of warranty is a breach of the seller's or lessor's promise. If the parties have not agreed to limit or modify the remedies available to the buyer or lessee and if the seller or lessor breaches a warranty, the buyer or lessee can sue to recover damages from the seller or lessor. Under some circumstances, a breach can allow the buyer or lessee to rescind (cancel) the agreement.[16]

WARRANTY OF TITLE

Title warranty arises automatically in most sales contracts. UCC 2–312 imposes three types of warranties of title.

GOOD TITLE In most cases, sellers warrant that they have good and valid title to the goods sold and that transfer of the title is rightful [UCC 2–312(1)(a)].

NO LIENS OR INFRINGEMENTS A second warranty of title provided by the UCC protects buyers who are *unaware* of any encumbrances (claims, charges, or liabilities—usually called *liens*[17]) against goods at the time the contract is made [UCC 2–312(1)(b)]. This warranty protects buyers who, for example, unknowingly purchase goods that are subject to a creditor's security interest (see Chapter 15). If a creditor legally repossesses the goods from a buyer *who had no actual*

---

16. *Rescission* restores the parties to the positions they were in before the contract was made.

17. Pronounced *leens*. Liens will be discussed in detail in Chapter 15.

knowledge of the security interest, the buyer can recover from the seller for breach of warranty. (The buyer who has *actual knowledge of a security interest* has no recourse against a seller.) Article 2A affords similar protection for lessees. Section 2A–211(1) provides that during the term of the lease, no claim of any third party will interfere with the lessee's enjoyment of the leasehold interest.

A merchant seller is also deemed to warrant that the goods delivered are free from any copyright, trademark, or patent claims of a third person [UCC 2–312(3), 2A–211(2)].

DISCLAIMER OF TITLE WARRANTY   In an ordinary sales transaction, the title warranty can be disclaimed or modified only by *specific language* in a contract. For example, sellers may assert that they are transferring only such rights, title, and interest as they have in the goods. In a lease transaction, the disclaimer must "be specific, be by a writing, and be conspicuous" [UCC 2A–214(4)]. In certain cases, the circumstances surrounding the sale are sufficient to indicate clearly to a buyer that no assurances as to title are being made. The classic example is a sheriff's sale, when buyers know that the goods have been seized to satisfy debts and the sheriff cannot guarantee title [UCC 2–312(2)].

EXPRESS WARRANTIES

A seller or lessor can create an **express warranty** by making representations concerning the quality, condition, description, or performance potential of the goods. Under UCC 2–313 and 2A–210, express warranties arise when a seller or lessor indicates any of the following:

1. That the goods conform to any *affirmation or promise of fact* that the seller or lessor makes to the buyer or lessee about the goods. Such affirmations or promises are usually made during the bargaining process. Statements such as "these drill bits will *easily* penetrate stainless steel—and without dulling" are express warranties.[18]

2. That the goods conform to any *description* of them. For example, a label that reads "Crate contains one 150-horsepower diesel engine" or a contract that calls for the delivery of a "wool coat" creates an express warranty that the content of the goods sold conforms to the description.

3. That the goods conform to any *sample or model* of the goods shown to the buyer or lessee.

Express warranties can be found in a seller's or lessor's advertisement, brochure, or promotional materials, in addition to being made orally or in an express warranty provision in a sales or lease contract. To create an express warranty, a seller or lessor does not have to use formal words such as *warrant* or *guarantee*. It is only necessary that a reasonable buyer or lessee would regard the representation as part of the basis of the bargain [UCC 2–313(2), 2A–210(2)].[19]

BASIS OF THE BARGAIN   The UCC requires that for an express warranty to be created, the affirmation, promise, description, or sample must become part of the "basis of the bargain" [UCC 2–313(1), 2A–210(1)]. Just what constitutes the basis of the bargain is difficult to say. The UCC does not define the concept, and it is a question of fact in each case whether a representation was made at such a time and in such a way that it induced the buyer or lessee to enter into the contract. Therefore, if an express warranty is not intended, the marketing agent or salesperson should not promise too much.

STATEMENTS OF OPINION AND VALUE   If the seller or lessor merely makes a statement that relates to the value or worth of the goods, or makes a statement of opinion or recommendation about the goods, the seller or lessor is not creating an express warranty [UCC 2–313(2), 2A–210(2)].

For example, a seller claims that "this is the best used car to come along in years; it has four new tires and a 150-horsepower engine just rebuilt this year." The seller has made several *affirmations of fact* that can create a warranty: the automobile has an engine; it has a 150-horsepower engine; the engine was rebuilt this year; there are four tires on the automobile; and the tires are new. The seller's *opinion* that the

---

18. The 2003 amendments to UCC Article 2 introduce the term *remedial promise*, which is "a promise by the seller to repair or replace the goods or to refund all or part of the price on the happening of a specified event" [Amended UCC 2–103(1)(n), 2–313(4)]. A remedial promise is not an express warranty, so a right of action for its breach accrues not at the time of tender, as with warranties, but if the promise is not performed when due [Amended UCC 2–725(2)(c)].

19. The 2003 amendments to the UCC distinguish between immediate buyers (those who enter into contracts with sellers) and remote purchasers (those who buy or lease goods from immediate buyers) and extend sellers' obligations regarding new goods to remote purchasers. For example, a manufacturer sells packaged goods to a retailer, who resells the goods to a consumer. If a reasonable person in the position of the consumer would believe that a description on the package creates an obligation, the manufacturer is liable for its breach. [See Amended UCC 2–313, 2–313A, and 2–313B.]

vehicle is "the best used car to come along in years," however, is known as *puffery* and creates no warranty. (**Puffery** is an expression of opinion by a seller or lessor that is not made as a representation of fact.) A statement relating to the value of the goods, such as "it's worth a fortune" or "anywhere else you'd pay $10,000 for it," usually does not create a warranty.

—An Exception: Statements of Opinion by Experts. Although an ordinary seller or lessor can give an opinion that is not a warranty, if the seller or lessor is an expert and gives an opinion as an expert to a layperson, then a warranty may be created. For example, Saul is an art dealer and an expert in seventeenth-century paintings. If Saul states to Lauren, a purchaser, that in his opinion a particular painting is a Rembrandt, Saul has warranted the accuracy of his opinion.

—Puffery versus Express Warranties. It is not always easy to determine what constitutes an express warranty and what constitutes puffery. The reasonableness of the buyer's or lessee's reliance appears to be the controlling criterion in many cases. For example, a salesperson's statements that a ladder will "never break" and will "last a lifetime" are so clearly improbable that no reasonable buyer should rely on them. Additionally, the context in which a statement is made may be relevant in determining the reasonableness of a buyer's or lessee's reliance. For example, a reasonable person is more likely to rely on a written statement made in an advertisement than on a statement made orally by a salesperson.

IMPLIED WARRANTIES

An **implied warranty** is one that *the law derives* by inference from the nature of the transaction or the relative situations or circumstances of the parties. Under the UCC, merchants impliedly warrant that the goods they sell or lease are merchantable and, in certain circumstances, fit for a particular purpose. In addition, an implied warranty may arise from a course of dealing or usage of trade. We examine these three types of implied warranties in the following subsections.

IMPLIED WARRANTY OF MERCHANTABILITY An **implied warranty of merchantability** automatically arises in every sale or lease of goods made *by a merchant* who deals in goods of the kind sold or leased [UCC 2–314, 2A–212]. Thus, a merchant who is in the business of selling ski equipment makes an implied warranty of merchantability every time the merchant sells a pair of skis, but a neighbor selling his or her skis at a garage sale does not.

To be *merchantable*, goods must be "reasonably fit for the ordinary purposes for which such goods are used." They must be of at least average, fair, or medium-grade quality. The quality must be comparable to quality that will pass without objection in the trade or market for goods of the same description. To be merchantable, the goods must also be adequately packaged and labeled as provided by the agreement, and they must conform to the promises or affirmations of fact made on the container or label, if any.

It makes no difference whether the merchant knew of, or could have discovered, that a product was defective (not merchantable). Of course, merchants are not absolute insurers against *all* accidents arising in connection with the goods. For example, a bar of soap is not unmerchantable merely because a user could slip and fall by stepping on it.

The UCC recognizes the serving of food or drink to be consumed on or off the premises as a sale of goods subject to the implied warranty of merchantability [UCC 2–314(1)]. *Merchantable food* is food that is fit to eat on the basis of consumer expectations. In the following classic case, the court had to determine whether one should reasonably expect to find a fish bone in fish chowder.

CASE 11.5 — Supreme Judicial Court of Massachusetts, 1964. 347 Mass. 421, 198 N.E.2d 309.

Webster v. Blue Ship Tea Room, Inc.

BACKGROUND AND FACTS *Blue Ship Tea Room, Inc., was located in Boston in an old building overlooking the ocean. Webster, who had been born and raised in New England, went to the restaurant and ordered fish chowder. The chowder was milky in color. After three or four spoonfuls, she felt something lodged in her throat. As a result, she underwent two esophagoscopies; in the second esophagoscopy, a fish bone was found and removed. Webster filed a suit against the restaurant in a Massachusetts state court for breach of the implied warranty of merchantability. The jury rendered a verdict for Webster, and the restaurant appealed to the state's highest court.*

CONTINUED

CASE 11.5 Continued

IN THE LANGUAGE OF THE COURT

REARDON, Justice.

[The plaintiff] ordered a cup of fish chowder. Presently, there was set before her "a small bowl of fish chowder." * * * After 3 or 4 [spoonfuls] she was aware that something had lodged in her throat because she "couldn't swallow and couldn't clear her throat by gulping and she could feel it." This misadventure led to two esophagoscopies [procedures in which a telescope-like instrument is used to look into the throat] at the Massachusetts General Hospital, in the second of which, on April 27, 1959, a fish bone was found and removed. The sequence of events produced injury to the plaintiff which was not insubstantial.

We must decide whether a fish bone lurking in a fish chowder, about the ingredients of which there is no other complaint, constitutes a breach of implied warranty under applicable provisions of the Uniform Commercial Code * * * . As the judge put it in his charge [jury instruction], "Was the fish chowder fit to be eaten and wholesome? * * * [N]obody is claiming that the fish itself wasn't wholesome. * * * But the bone of contention here—I don't mean that for a pun—but was this fish bone a foreign substance that made the fish chowder unwholesome or not fit to be eaten?"

* * * *

[We think that it] is not too much to say that a person sitting down in New England to consume a good New England fish chowder embarks on a gustatory [taste-related] adventure which may entail the removal of some fish bones from his bowl as he proceeds. We are not inclined to tamper with age-old recipes by any amendment reflecting the plaintiff's view of the effect of the Uniform Commercial Code upon them. We are aware of the heavy body of case law involving foreign substances in food, but we sense a strong distinction between them and those relative to unwholesomeness of the food itself, [such as] tainted mackerel, and a fish bone in a fish chowder. * * * [W]e consider that the joys of life in New England include the ready availability of fresh fish chowder. We should be prepared to cope with the hazards of fish bones, the occasional presence of which in chowders is, it seems to us, to be anticipated, and which, in the light of a hallowed tradition, do not impair their fitness or merchantability.

DECISION AND REMEDY   *The Supreme Judicial Court of Massachusetts "sympathized with a plaintiff who has suffered a peculiarly New England injury" but entered a judgment for the defendant, Blue Ship Tea Room. A fish bone in fish chowder is not a breach of the implied warranty of merchantability.*

IMPACT OF THIS CASE ON TODAY'S LAW

This classic case, phrased in memorable language, was an early application of the UCC's implied warranty of merchantability to food products. The case established the rule that consumers should expect to find, on occasion, elements of food products that are natural to the product (such as fish bones in fish chowder). Courts today still apply this rule.

IMPLIED WARRANTY OF FITNESS FOR A PARTICULAR PURPOSE The **implied warranty of fitness for a particular purpose** arises when any *seller or lessor* (merchant or nonmerchant) knows the particular purpose for which a buyer or lessee will use the goods *and* knows that the buyer or lessee is relying on the skill and judgment of the seller or lessor to select suitable goods [UCC 2–315, 2A–213].

A "particular purpose" of the buyer or lessee differs from the "ordinary purpose for which goods are used"

(merchantability). Goods can be merchantable but unfit for a particular purpose. For example, suppose that you need a gallon of paint to match the color of your living room walls—a light shade somewhere between coral and peach. You take a sample to your local hardware store and request a gallon of paint of that color. Instead, you are given a gallon of bright blue paint. Here, the salesperson has not breached any warranty of implied merchantability—the bright blue paint is of high quality and suitable for interior walls—but he or she has breached an implied warranty of fitness for a particular purpose.

A seller or lessor does not need to have actual knowledge of the buyer's or lessee's particular purpose. It is sufficient if a seller or lessor "has reason to know" the purpose. The buyer or lessee, however, must have *relied* on the skill or judgment of the seller or lessor in selecting or furnishing suitable goods for an implied warranty to be created.

For example, Bloomberg leases a computer from Future Tech, a lessor of technical business equipment. Bloomberg tells the clerk that she wants a computer that will run a complicated new engineering graphics program at a realistic speed. Future Tech leases Bloomberg an Architex One computer with a CPU speed of only 2.4 gigahertz, even though a speed of at least 3.8 gigahertz would be required to run Bloomberg's graphics program at a "realistic speed." Bloomberg, after realizing that it takes her forever to run her program, wants her money back. Here, because Future Tech has breached the implied warranty of fitness for a particular purpose, Bloomberg normally will be able to recover. The clerk knew specifically that Bloomberg wanted a computer with enough speed to run certain software. Furthermore, Bloomberg relied on the clerk to furnish a computer that would fulfill this purpose. Because Future Tech did not do so, the warranty was breached.

IMPLIED WARRANTY ARISING FROM COURSE OF DEALING OR TRADE USAGE Implied warranties can also arise (or be excluded or modified) as a result of a course of dealing or usage of trade [UCC 2–314(3), 2A–212(3)]. In the absence of evidence to the contrary, when both parties to a sales or lease contract have knowledge of a well-recognized trade custom, the courts will infer that both parties intended for that custom to apply to their contract. For example, if it is an industry-wide custom to lubricate a new car before it is delivered and a dealer fails to do so, the dealer can be held liable to a buyer for damages resulting from the breach of an implied warranty. (This, of course, would also be negligence on the part of the dealer.)

WARRANTY DISCLAIMERS Because each type of warranty is created in a special way, the manner in which warranties can be disclaimed or qualified by a seller or lessor varies with the type of warranty.

—*Express Warranties.* As already stated, any affirmation of fact or promise, description of the goods, or use of samples or models by a seller or lessor creates an express warranty. Obviously, then, express warranties can be excluded if the seller or lessor carefully refrains from making any promise or affirmation of fact relating to the goods, describing the goods, or using a sample or model.

The UCC does permit express warranties to be negated or limited by specific and unambiguous language, provided that this is done in a manner that protects the buyer or lessee from surprise. Therefore, a written disclaimer in language that is clear and conspicuous, and called to a buyer's or lessee's attention, could negate all oral express warranties not included in the written sales or lease contract [UCC 2–316(1), 2A–214(1)]. This allows the seller or lessor to avoid false allegations that oral warranties were made, and it ensures that only representations made by properly authorized individuals are included in the bargain.

—*Implied Warranties.* Generally speaking, unless circumstances indicate otherwise, the implied warranties of merchantability and fitness are disclaimed by the expressions "as is," "with all faults," and other similar expressions that in common understanding for *both* parties call the buyer's or lessee's attention to the fact that there are no implied warranties [UCC 2–316(3)(a), 2A–214(3)(a)].

The UCC also permits a seller or lessor to specifically disclaim an implied warranty either of fitness or of merchantability [UCC 2–316(2), 2A–214(2)]. To disclaim an implied warranty of fitness for a particular purpose, the disclaimer must be in writing and be conspicuous. The word *fitness* does not have to be mentioned in the writing; it is sufficient if, for example, the disclaimer states, "THERE ARE NO WARRANTIES THAT EXTEND BEYOND THE DESCRIPTION ON THE FACE HEREOF."

A merchantability disclaimer must be more specific; it must mention *merchantability*. It need not be written; but if it is, the writing must be conspicuous [UCC 2–316(2), 2A–214(4)].[20]

SECTION 11 | E-Contracts

The basic principles of contract law evolved over a long period of time. Certainly, they were formed long before cyberspace and electronic contracting became

---

20. Under the 2003 amendments to UCC Articles 2 and 2A, if a consumer contract or lease is set forth in a record (writing), the implied warranty of merchantability can be disclaimed only by language also set forth conspicuously in the record [Amended UCC 2–316(3) and 2A–214(3)].

realities. Therefore, new legal theories, new adaptations of existing laws, and new laws are needed to govern **e-contracts,** or contracts entered into electronically. To date, however, most courts have adapted traditional contract law principles and, when applicable, provisions of the UCC to cases involving e-contract disputes.

ONLINE CONTRACT FORMATION

Today, numerous contracts are being formed online. Although the medium through which these contracts are generated has changed, the age-old problems attending contract formation have not. Disputes concerning contracts formed online continue to center around contract terms and whether the parties voluntarily assented to those terms.

Note that online contracts may be formed not only for the sale of goods and services but also for the purpose of *licensing*. For example, as you will read later in this section, the "sale" of software generally involves a license, or a right to use the software, rather than the passage of title (ownership rights) from the seller to the buyer. As you read through the following pages, keep in mind that although we typically refer to the offeror and offeree as a *seller* and a *buyer*, in many transactions these parties would be more accurately described as a *licensor* and a *licensee*.

ONLINE OFFERS Sellers doing business via the Internet can protect themselves against contract disputes and legal liability by creating offers that clearly spell out the terms that will govern their transactions if the offers are accepted. All important terms should be conspicuous and easily viewed by potential buyers.

An important rule for a seller to keep in mind is that the offeror controls the offer, and thus the resulting contract. Therefore, the seller should anticipate the terms that he or she wants to include in a contract and provide for them in the offer. At a minimum, an online offer should include the following provisions:

1. A provision specifying the remedies available to the buyer if the goods turn out to be defective or if the contract is otherwise breached. Any limitation of remedies should be clearly spelled out.
2. A clause that clearly indicates what will constitute the buyer's agreement to the terms of the offer.
3. A provision specifying how payment for the goods or services and for any applicable taxes must be made.
4. A statement of the seller's refund and return policies.

5. Disclaimers of liability for certain uses of the goods. For example, an online seller of business forms may add a disclaimer that the seller does not accept responsibility for the buyer's reliance on the forms rather than on an attorney's advice.
6. A statement explaining how the seller will use the information gathered about the buyer.

—Dispute-Settlement Provisions. In addition to the above provisions, many online offers include provisions relating to dispute settlement. For example, an arbitration clause might be included, indicating that any dispute arising under the contract will be arbitrated in a specified forum.

Many online contracts also contain a **forum-selection clause**—a clause indicating the forum, or location, for the resolution of any dispute arising under the contract. For a further discussion of forum-selection clauses in online contracts, see this chapter's *Contemporary Legal Debates* feature on pages 276 and 277.

—Displaying the Offer. The seller's Web site should include a hypertext link to a page containing the full contract so that potential buyers are made aware of the terms to which they are assenting. The contract generally must be displayed online in a readable format such as a twelve-point typeface. All provisions should be reasonably clear. For example, if a seller is offering certain goods priced according to a complex price schedule, that schedule must be fully provided and explained.

—Indicating How the Offer Can Be Accepted. An online offer should also include some mechanism by which the customer can accept the offer. Typically, online sellers include boxes containing the words "I agree" or "I accept the terms of the offer" that offerees can click on to indicate acceptance.

ONLINE ACCEPTANCES Section 2–204 of the UCC, the law governing sales contracts, provides that any contract for the sale of goods "may be made in any manner sufficient to show agreement, including conduct by both parties which recognizes the existence of such a contract." The *Restatement (Second) of Contracts*, a compilation of common law contract principles, has a similar provision. It states that parties may agree to a contract "by written or spoken words or by other action or by failure to act."[21]

---

21. *Restatement (Second) of Contracts*, Section 19.

—Click-On Agreements. The courts have used the provisions just discussed to conclude that a binding contract can be created by conduct, including conduct accepting an online offer by clicking on a box indicating "I agree" or "I accept." The agreement resulting from such an acceptance is often called a **click-on agreement.**

Generally, the law governing contracts, including sales and lease contracts under the UCC, does not require that all of the terms in a contract must actually have been read by all of the parties to be effective. Therefore, clicking on a button or box that states "I agree" to certain terms can be enough.[22]

—Browse-Wrap Terms. Like the terms of a click-on agreement, **browse-wrap terms** can occur in a transaction conducted over the Internet. Unlike a click-on agreement, however, browse-wrap terms do not require an Internet user to assent to the terms before, say, downloading or using certain software. In other words, a person can install the software without clicking "I agree" to the terms of a license. Offerors of browse-wrap terms generally assert that the terms are binding without the user's active consent.

Critics contend that browse-wrap terms are not enforceable because they do not satisfy the basic elements of contract formation. It has been suggested that to form a valid contract online, a user must at least be presented with the terms before indicating assent.[23] With a browse-wrap term, this would require that a user navigate past it and agree to it before being able to obtain whatever is being granted.

E-SIGNATURES

In many instances, a contract cannot be enforced unless it is signed by the party against whom enforcement is sought. A significant issue in the context of e-commerce has to do with how electronic signatures, or **e-signatures,** can be created and verified on e-contracts.

E-SIGNATURE TECHNOLOGIES Today, numerous technologies allow electronic documents to be signed. The most prevalent e-signature technology is the

asymmetric cryptosystem, which creates a digital signature using two different (asymmetric) cryptographic "keys," one private and one public. With this system, a person attaches a digital signature to a document using a private key, or code. The key has a publicly available counterpart. Anyone with the appropriate software can use the public key to verify that the digital signature was made using the private key. A *cybernotary,* or legally recognized certification authority, issues the key pair, identifies the owner of the keys, and certifies the validity of the public key. The cybernotary also serves as a repository for public keys. Cybernotaries already are available.

STATE LAWS GOVERNING E-SIGNATURES Most states have laws governing e-signatures. The problem is that state e-signature laws are not uniform. Some states—California is a notable example—prohibit many types of documents from being signed with e-signatures, whereas other states are more permissive.

In an attempt to create more uniformity among the states, in 1999 the National Conference of Commissioners on Uniform State Laws and the American Law Institute promulgated the Uniform Electronic Transactions Act (UETA). To date, the UETA has been adopted, at least in part, by forty-eight states. Among other things, the UETA states that a signature may not be denied legal effect or enforceability solely because it is in electronic form.[24] (We will look more closely at the UETA shortly.)

FEDERAL LAW GOVERNING E-SIGNATURES AND E-DOCUMENTS In 2000, Congress enacted the Electronic Signatures in Global and National Commerce Act (E-SIGN Act),[25] which provides that no contract, record, or signature may be "denied legal effect" solely because it is in an electronic form. In other words, under this law, an e-signature is as valid as a signature on paper, and an e-document can be as enforceable as a paper one.

For an e-signature to be enforceable, the contracting parties must have agreed to use electronic signatures. For an electronic document to be valid, it must be in a form that can be retained and accurately reproduced.

The E-SIGN Act does not apply to all types of documents, however. Contracts and documents that

---

22. See, for example, *i.LANSystems, Inc. v. NetScout Service Level Corp.,* 183 F.Supp.2d 838 (D.Mass. 2002).

23. American Bar Association Committee on the Law of Cyberspace, "Click-Through Agreements: Strategies for Avoiding Disputes on the Validity of Assent" (document presented at the annual American Bar Association meeting in August 2001).

24. The 2003 amendments to UCC Article 2 include a similar provision in UCC 2–211.

25. 15 U.S.C. Sections 7001 *et seq.*

The Enforceability of Forum-Selection Clauses

Parties to contracts frequently include clauses in their contracts indicating how any disputes that arise may be resolved. For example, contracts often contain arbitration clauses stipulating that any dispute will be resolved through arbitration proceedings rather than through litigation. A contract may also include a *forum-selection clause,* specifying the forum (such as the court or jurisdiction) in which the dispute will be resolved.

Forum-selection clauses are routinely included in contracts for the international sale of goods because the parties to such contracts are often quite distant from one another geographically. Determining the forum where any dispute arising under a contract will be settled is thus normally part of the bargaining process when the contract is being formed.

FORUM SELECTION AND ONLINE CONTRACTS

Because parties to contracts formed online may be located at physically distant sites, online sellers of goods and services normally include forum-selection clauses in their contracts. These clauses can help online sellers avoid having to appear in court in many distant jurisdictions when customers are dissatisfied with their purchases. (Recall from Chapter 2 that under a state long arm statute, a state court may exercise jurisdiction over an out-of-state defendant if the defendant has "minimum contacts" with the state.)

For example, suppose that a California buyer purchases defective goods sold online by a company located in New York. Unable to obtain a refund or adequate replacement goods from the seller, the California buyer files suit against the seller in a California state court. If the New York seller meets the "minimum-contacts" requirement for the California court to exercise jurisdiction over the dispute, the New York seller will need to travel to California to defend against the lawsuit. Forum-selection clauses in online contracts offer a way for sellers to avoid this problem.

ARE FORUM-SELECTION CLAUSES FAIR TO ONLINE PURCHASERS?

Clearly, those who market goods and services online benefit from including forum-selection clauses in their contracts. Yet what about the purchasers of these goods and services? Continuing with the above example, suppose that the seller's contract includes a forum-selection clause specifying New York as the forum where any disputes under the contract must be resolved. An individual in California may not have the resources to travel to New York to initiate proceedings against the seller in a New York court. In effect, the clause deprives the buyer of the ability to easily sue the seller in the buyer's home state.

Nonetheless, normally the courts will enforce clauses or contracts to which parties have voluntarily agreed, and this principle extends to forum-selection clauses in online contracts as well. As one court held (in a case challenging the enforceability of the forum-selection clause in Microsoft Network's online agreement), "If a forum-selection clause is clear in its purport and has been presented to the party to be

---

are exempt include court papers, divorce decrees, evictions, foreclosures, health-insurance terminations, prenuptial agreements, and wills. Also, the only agreements governed by the UCC that fall under this law are those covered by Articles 2 and 2A and UCC 1–107 and 1–206.

The E-SIGN Act refers explicitly to the UETA and provides that if a state has enacted the uniform version of the UETA, that law is not preempted by the E-SIGN Act. In other words, if the state has enacted the UETA without modification, state law will govern. The problem is that many states have enacted nonuniform (modified) versions of the UETA, largely for the purpose of excluding other areas of state law from the UETA's terms. The E-SIGN Act specifies that those exclusions will be preempted to the extent that they are inconsistent with the E-SIGN Act's provisions.

THE UNIFORM ELECTRONIC TRANSACTIONS ACT

As noted earlier, the UETA, promulgated in 1999, represents one of the first comprehensive efforts to create uniformity and introduce certainty in state laws pertaining to e-commerce. The primary purpose of the UETA is to remove barriers to e-commerce by

bound in a fair and forthright fashion, no . . . policies or principles have been violated."[a]

FORUM-SELECTION CLAUSES ARE NOT ALWAYS ENFORCED

Depending on the jurisdiction, however, a court may make an exception to the rule that forum-selection clauses in online contracts should be enforced. Consider a case decided by a California appellate court in 2001. The case was brought against America Online, Inc. (AOL), by Al Mendoza and other former AOL subscribers living in California. The plaintiffs, who sought compensatory and punitive damages, claimed that AOL had continued to debit their credit cards for monthly service fees, without authorization, for some time after they had terminated their subscriptions. AOL moved to dismiss the action on the basis of the forum-selection clause in its "Terms of Service" agreement with subscribers. That clause required all lawsuits under the agreement to be brought in Virginia, AOL's home state. At issue in the case was whether the clause was enforceable.

A California trial court held that it was not. The court based its conclusion on the finding that the clause, among other things, was contained in a standard form and was not readily identifiable by subscribers because of its small typeface

and location at the end of the agreement. According to the court, the clause was "unfair and unreasonable," and public policy was best served by denying enforceability to the clause. A California appellate court affirmed the lower court's ruling and also gave another reason why the clause should not be enforced. The appellate court noted that Virginia law provides "significantly less" consumer protection than California law, and therefore enforcing the forum-selection clause would violate the "strong California public policy" expressed in the state's consumer protection statutes.[b]

WHERE DO YOU STAND?

The case just discussed may mark an exception to the rule that forum-selection clauses in online contracts are generally enforceable. Yet different courts have reached different conclusions on this issue, which continues to elicit debate. On the one hand, online sellers do need to protect themselves from the possibility of having to travel to distant states time and again to resolve disputes. Also, it is a general principle of contract law that clauses voluntarily entered into by the parties should be enforced. On the other hand, in some instances forum-selection clauses clearly impose an unfair burden on those who purchase goods or services from online vendors. What is your position on this issue? Can you think of a solution that is fair to all parties and consistent with contract law principles?

---

a. *Caspi v. MSN, Inc.*, 323 N.J.Super. 118, 732 A.2d 528 (1999). For another example, see *DeJohn v. The .TV Corp. International*, 245 F.Supp.2d 913 (2003).

b. *America Online, Inc. v. Superior Court*, 90 Cal.App.4th 1, 108 Cal.Rptr.2d 699 (2001).

---

giving the same legal effect to electronic records and signatures as is currently given to paper documents and signatures. The UETA broadly defines an *e-signature* as "an electronic sound, symbol, or process attached to or logically associated with a record and executed or adopted by a person with the intent to sign the record."[26] A *record* is defined as "information that is inscribed on a tangible medium or that is stored in an electronic or other medium and is retrievable in perceivable [visual] form."[27]

The UETA does not apply to all writings and signatures but only to electronic records and electronic signatures *relating to a transaction*. A *transaction* is defined as an interaction between two or more people relating to business, commercial, or governmental activities.[28] The act specifically does not apply to laws governing wills or testamentary trusts or the UCC (other than Articles 2 and 2A).[29] In addition, the provisions of the UETA allow the states to exclude its application to other areas of law.

---

26. UETA 102(8).
27. UETA 102(15).

28. UETA 2(12) and 3.
29. UETA 3(b).

REVIEWING SALES, LEASES, AND E-CONTRACTS

GFI, Inc., a Hong Kong company, makes audio decoder chips, one of the essential components used in the manufacture of MP3 players. Egan Electronics contracts with GFI to buy 2,500 chips F.O.B. Hong Kong via Air Express. At the time for the delivery, GFI delivers only 2,400 chips but explains to Egan that while the shipment is less than 5 percent short, the chips are of a higher quality than those specified in the contract and are worth 5 percent more than the contract price. Egan accepts the shipment and pays GFI the contract price. Two months later, Egan and GFI form another contract, under which GFI is to ship 2,000 more chips to Egan, again F.O.B. Hong Kong via Air Express. Just after the contract is formed, GFI's major manufacturing plant burns down, and its entire inventory of chips is destroyed. GFI, however, is able to ship Egan 1,000 chips that it had stored in its office at a separate location. While the 1,000 chips are in transit, they are destroyed. Nearly a year later, GFI notifies Egan that the plant has been rebuilt, it is back in business, and it can again supply Egan with chips if Egan is interested. Egan responds with an offer to purchase 2,000 chips, with the same delivery terms, and GFI accepts the offer. Two months later, Egan has neither received the shipment nor heard anything further from GFI. Using the information presented in the chapter, answer the following questions.

1. Suppose that Egan refused to pay for the first shipment and sued GFI for breach of contract. Had GFI breached the contract? What would be GFI's best defense against this claim?

2. Assume that the second shipment of chips had *not* been destroyed in transit. In this situation, would GFI be in breach of contract because it only shipped 1,000 chips, not the contracted-for quantity (2,000 chips)?

3. With respect to the 1,000 chips that were destroyed in transit, which party must bear the loss? Why?

4. Regarding the final contract, does Egan have a right to ask GFI about its intentions to perform the contract? If so, does GFI have an obligation to respond? Explain.

TERMS AND CONCEPTS TO REVIEW

QUESTIONS AND CASE PROBLEMS

11–1. A. B. Zook, Inc., is a manufacturer of washing machines. Over the telephone, Zook offers to sell Radar Appliances one hundred model Z washers at a price of $150 per unit. Zook agrees to keep this offer open for ninety days. Radar tells Zook that the offer appears to be a good one and that it will let Zook know of its acceptance within the next two to three weeks. One week later, Zook sends, and Radar receives, notice that Zook has withdrawn its offer. Radar immediately thereafter telephones Zook and accepts the $150-per-unit offer. Zook claims, first, that no sales contract was ever formed between it and Radar and, second, that if there is a contract, the contract is unenforceable. Discuss Zook's contentions.

11–2. **QUESTION WITH SAMPLE ANSWER**

Flint, a retail seller of television sets, orders one hundred Color-X sets from manufacturer Martin. The order specifies the price and that the television sets are to be shipped by Humming Bird Express on or before October 30. The order is received by Martin on October 5. On October 8, Martin writes Flint a letter indicating that the order was received and that the sets will be shipped as directed, at the specified price. This letter is received by Flint on October 10. On October 28, Martin, in preparing the shipment, discovers it has only ninety Color-X sets in stock. Martin ships the ninety Color-X sets and ten television sets of a different model, stating clearly on the invoice that the ten are being shipped only as an accommodation. Flint claims Martin is in breach of contract. Martin claims the shipment was not an acceptance, and therefore no contract was formed. Explain who is correct and why.

For a sample answer to this question, go to Appendix I at the end of this text.

11–3. On May 1, Sikora goes into Carson's retail clothing store to purchase a suit. Sikora finds a suit he likes for $190 and buys it. The suit needs alteration. Sikora is to pick up the altered suit at Carson's store on May 10. Consider the following separate sets of circumstances:

(a) One of Carson's major creditors obtains a judgment on the debt Carson owes and has the court issue a *writ of execution* (a court order to seize a debtor's property to satisfy a debt) to collect on that judgment all clothing in Carson's possession. Discuss Sikora's rights in the suit under these circumstances.

(b) On May 9, through no fault of Carson's, the store burns down, and all contents are a total loss. Between Carson and Sikora, who suffers the loss of the suit destroyed by fire? Explain.

11–4. McDonald has contracted to purchase five hundred pairs of shoes from Vetter. Vetter manufactures the shoes and tenders delivery to McDonald. McDonald accepts the shipment. Later, on inspection, McDonald discovers

that ten pairs of the shoes are poorly made and will have to be sold to customers as seconds. If McDonald decides to keep all five hundred pairs of shoes, what remedies are available to her? Discuss.

11–5. Kirk has contracted to deliver to Doolittle one thousand cases of Wonder brand beans on or before October 1. Doolittle is to specify the means of transportation twenty days prior to the date of shipment. Payment for the beans is to be made by Doolittle on tender of delivery. On September 10, Kirk prepares the one thousand cases for shipment. Kirk asks Doolittle how he would like the goods to be shipped, but Doolittle does not respond. On September 21, Kirk, in writing, demands assurance that Doolittle will be able to pay on tender of the beans. Kirk asks that the money be placed in escrow prior to October 1 in a bank in Doolittle's city named by Kirk. Doolittle does not respond to any of Kirk's requests, but on October 5 he wants to file suit against Kirk for breach of contract for failure to deliver the beans as agreed. Discuss Kirk's liability for failure to tender delivery on October 1.

11–6. **CASE PROBLEM WITH SAMPLE ANSWER**

Propulsion Technologies, Inc., a Louisiana firm doing business as PowerTech Marine Propellers, markets small steel boat propellers that are made by a unique tooling method. Attwood Corp., a Michigan firm, operated a foundry (a place where metal is cast) in Mexico. In 1996, Attwood offered to produce castings of the propellers. Attwood promised to maintain quality, warrant the castings against defects, and obtain insurance to cover liability. In January 1997, the parties signed a letter that expressed these and other terms—Attwood was to be paid per casting, and twelve months' notice was required to terminate the deal—but the letter did not state a quantity. PowerTech provided the tooling. Attwood produced rough castings, which PowerTech refined by checking each propeller's pitch; machining its interior; grinding, balancing, and polishing the propeller; and adding serial numbers and a rubber clutch. In October, Attwood told PowerTech that the foundry was closing. PowerTech filed a suit in a federal district court against Attwood, alleging in part breach of contract. One of the issues was whether their deal was subject to Article 2 of the Uniform Commercial Code (UCC). What type of transactions does Article 2 cover? Does the arrangement between PowerTech and Attwood qualify? Explain. [*Propulsion Technologies, Inc. v. Attwood Corp.*, 369 F.3d 896 (5th Cir. 2004)]

To view a sample answer for this case problem, go to this book's Web site at http://wleb.westbuslaw.com, select "Chapter 11," and click on "Case Problem with Sample Answer."

11–7. STATUTE OF FRAUDS. Quality Pork International is a Nebraska firm that makes and sells custom pork products. Rupari Food Services, Inc., buys and sells food products from and to retail operations and food brokers. In November 1999, Midwest Brokerage arranged an oral contract between Quality and Rupari, under which Quality would ship three orders to Star Food Processing, Inc., and Rupari would pay for the products. Quality shipped the goods to Star and sent invoices to Rupari. In turn, Rupari billed Star for all three orders but paid Quality only for the first two (for $43,736.84 and $47,467.80, respectively), not for the third. Quality filed a suit in a Nebraska state court against Rupari, alleging breach of contract, to recover $44,051.98, the cost of the third order. Rupari argued that there was nothing in writing, as required by the Uniform Commercial Code (UCC) Section 2–201, and thus there was no enforceable contract. What are the exceptions to the UCC's writing requirement? Do any of those exceptions apply here? Explain. [*Quality Pork International v. Rupari Food Services, Inc.,* 267 Neb. 474, 675 N.W.2d 642 (2004)]

11–8. CONDITIONAL SALES. Corvette Collection of Boston, Inc. (CCB), was a used-Corvette dealership located (despite its name) in Pompano Beach, Florida. In addition to selling used Corvettes, CCB serviced Corvettes and sold Corvette parts. CCB owned some of its inventory and held the rest on consignment, although there were no signs indicating the consignments. In November 2001, CCB filed a petition for bankruptcy in a federal district court. At the time, CCB possessed six Corvettes that were consigned by Chester Finley and The Corvette Experience, Inc. (TCE), neither of which had a security interest in the goods. Robert Furr, on CCB's behalf, asked the court to declare that CCB held the goods under a contract for a sale or return. Finley and TCE asserted that the goods were held under a contract for a sale on approval. What difference does it make? Under what circumstances would the court rule in favor of Finley and TCE? How should the court rule under the facts as stated? Why? [*In re Corvette Collection of Boston, Inc.,* 294 Bankr. 409 (S.D.Fla. 2003)]

11–9. PERFECT TENDER. Advanced Polymer Sciences, Inc. (APS), based in Ohio, makes polymers and resins for use as protective coatings in industrial applications. APS also owns the technology for equipment used to make certain composite fibers. *SAVA gumarska in kemijska industria d.d.* (SAVA), based in Slovenia, makes rubber goods. In 1999, SAVA and APS contracted to form *SAVA Advanced Polymers proizvodno podjetje d.o.o.* (SAVA AP) to make and distribute APS products in Eastern Europe. Their contract provided for, among other things, the alteration of a facility to make the products using specially made equipment to be sold by APS to SAVA. Disputes arose between the parties, and in August 2000, SAVA stopped work on the new facility. APS then notified SAVA that it was halting the manufacture of the equipment and "insist[ed] on knowing what is SAVA's intention towards this venture." In October, SAVA told APS that it was canceling their contract. In subsequent litigation, SAVA claimed that APS had repudiated the contract when it stopped making the equipment. What might APS assert in its defense? How should the court rule? Explain. [*SAVA gumarska in kemijska industria d.d. v. Advanced Polymer Sciences, Inc.,* 128 S.W.3d 304 (Tex.App.—Dallas 2004)]

11–10. SHRINK-WRAP AGREEMENTS AND BROWSE-WRAP TERMS. Mary DeFontes bought a computer and a service contract from Dell Computers Corp. DeFontes was charged $950.51, of which $13.51 was identified on the invoice as "tax." This amount was paid to the state of Rhode Island. DeFontes and other Dell customers filed a suit in a Rhode Island state court against Dell, claiming that Dell was overcharging its customers by collecting a tax on service contracts and transportation costs. Dell asked the court to order DeFontes to submit the dispute to arbitration. Dell cited its "Terms and Conditions Agreement," which provides in part that by accepting delivery of Dell's products or services, a customer agrees to submit any dispute to arbitration. Customers can view this agreement through an *inconspicuous* link at the bottom of Dell's Web site, and Dell encloses a copy with each order when it is shipped. Dell argued that DeFontes accepted these terms by failing to return her purchase within thirty days, although the agreement did not state this. Is DeFontes bound to the "Terms and Conditions Agreement"? Should the court grant Dell's request? Why or why not? [*DeFontes v. Dell Computers Corp.,* __ A.2d __ (R.I. 2004)]

11–11. VIDEO QUESTION

Go to this text's Web site at **http://wleb.westbuslaw.com** and select "Chapter 11." Click on "Video Questions" and view the video titled *E-Contracts: Agreeing Online.* Then answer the following questions.

(a) According to the instructor in the video, what is the key factor in determining whether a particular term in an online agreement is enforceable?

(b) Suppose that you click on "I accept" in order to download software from the Internet. You do not read the terms of the agreement before accepting it, even though you know that such agreements often contain forum-selection and arbitration clauses. The software later causes irreparable harm to your computer system, and you want to sue. When you go to the Web site and view the agreement, however, you discover that a choice-of-law clause in the contract specifies that the law of Nigeria controls. Is this term enforceable? Is it a term that should be reasonably expected in an online contract?

(c) Does it matter what the term actually says if it is a type of term that one could reasonably expect to be in the contract? What arguments can be made for and against enforcing a choice-of-law clause in an online contract?

LAW | on the Web

For updated links to resources available on the Web, as well as a variety of other materials, visit this text's Web site at http://wleb.westbuslaw.com.

For information about the National Conference of Commissioners on Uniform State Laws (NCCUSL) and links to online uniform acts, go to

http://www.nccusl.org

The NCCUSL, in association with the University of Pennsylvania Law School, now offers an official site for in-process and final drafts of uniform and model acts. For an index of in-process drafts, go to

http://www.law.upenn.edu/bll/ulc/ulc.htm

For an index of final drafts, go to

http://www.law.upenn.edu/bll/ulc/ulc_final.htm

Cornell University's Legal Information Institute offers online access to the UCC, as well as to UCC articles as enacted by particular states and proposed revisions to articles, at

http://www.law.cornell.edu/ucc/ucc.table.html

LEGAL RESEARCH EXERCISES ON THE WEB

Go to http://wleb.westbuslaw.com, the Web site that accompanies this text. Select "Chapter 11" and click on "Internet Exercises." There you will find the following Internet research exercises that you can perform to learn more about topics covered in this chapter.

Activity 11–1: **LEGAL PERSPECTIVE**
E-Contract Formation

Activity 11–2: **MANAGEMENT PERSPECTIVE**
A Checklist for Sales Contracts

An Example of a Contract for the International Sale of Coffee

❶ OVERLAND COFFEE IMPORT CONTRACT
OF THE
GREEN COFFEE ASSOCIATION
OF
❷ NEW YORK CITY, INC.*

Contract Seller's No.: __504617__
Buyer's No.: __P9264__
Date: __10/11/07__

SOLD BY: __XYZ Co.__
TO: __Starbucks__

❸ QUANTITY: __Five Hundred__ (__500__) Tons of (Bags) __Mexican__ coffee
weighing about __152.117 lbs.__ per bag.

PACKAGING: Coffee must be packed in clean sound bags of uniform size made of sisal, henequen, jute, burlap, or
❹ similar woven material, without inner lining or outer covering of any material properly sewn by hand
and/or machine.
Bulk shipments are allowed if agreed by mutual consent of Buyer and Seller.

DESCRIPTION: __High grown Mexican Altura__
❺

PRICE: At __Ten/$10.00 dollars__ U.S. Currency, per __1b.__ net, (U.S. Funds)
Upon delivery in Bonded Public Warehouse at __Laredo, TX__
(City and State)

PAYMENT: __Cash against warehouse receipts__
❻

Bill and tender to DATE when all import requirements and governmental regulations have been satisfied,
and coffee delivered or discharged (as per contract terms). Seller is obliged to give the Buyer two (2)
calendar days free time in Bonded Public Warehouse following but not including date of tender.

ARRIVAL: During __December__ via __truck__
❼ (Period) (Method of Transportation)
from __Mexico__ for arrival at __Laredo, TX, USA__
(Country of Exportation) (Country of Importation)
Partial shipments permitted.

ADVICE OF
ARRIVAL: Advice of arrival with warehouse name and location, together with the quantity, description, marks and
place of entry, must be transmitted directly, or through Seller's Agent/Broker, to the Buyer or his Agent/
Broker. Advice will be given as soon as known but not later than the fifth business day following arrival
at the named warehouse. Such advice may be given verbally with written confirmation to be sent the
same day.

❽ WEIGHTS: (1) DELIVERED WEIGHTS: Coffee covered by this contract is to be weighed at location named in
tender. Actual tare to be allowed.
(2) SHIPPING WEIGHTS: Coffee covered by this contract is sold on shipping weights. Any loss in
weight exceeding __1/2__ percent at location named in tender is for account of Seller at contract price.
(3) Coffee is to be weighed within fifteen (15) calendar days after tender. Weighing expenses, if any, for
account of __Seller__ (Seller or Buyer)

MARKINGS: Bags to be branded in English with the name of Country of Origin and otherwise to comply with laws
and regulations of the Country of Importation, in effect at the time of entry, governing marking of import
❾ merchandise. Any expense incurred by failure to comply with these regulations to be borne by
Exporter/Seller.

RULINGS: The "Rulings on Coffee Contracts" of the Green Coffee Association of New York City, Inc., in effect on
the date this contract is made, is incorporated for all purposes as a part of this agreement, and together
herewith, constitute the entire contract. No variation or addition hereto shall be valid unless signed by
the parties to the contract.
Seller guarantees that the terms printed on the reverse hereof, which by reference are made a part hereof,
❿ are identical with the terms as printed in By-Laws and Rules of the Green Coffee Association of New
York City, Inc., heretofore adopted.
Exceptions to this guarantee are:
ACCEPTED: COMMISSION TO BE PAID BY:
__XYZ Co.__ __Seller__

⓫ BY _____ДM_____ Seller
Agent
__Starbucks__
Buyer
⓬ BY _____ __ABC Brokerage__
Agent Broker(s)
When this contract is executed by a person acting for another, such person hereby represents that he is
⓭ fully authorized to commit his principal.

* Reprinted with permission of The Green Coffee Association of New York City, Inc.

1 This is a contract for a sale of coffee to be *imported* internationally. If the parties have their principal places of business located in different countries, the contract may be subject to the United Nations Convention on Contracts for the International Sale of Goods (CISG). If the parties' principal places of business are located in the United States, the contract may be subject to the Uniform Commercial Code (UCC).

2 Quantity is one of the most important terms to include in a contract. Without it, a court may not be able to enforce the contract. See Chapter 11.

3 Weight per unit (bag) can be exactly stated or approximately stated. If it is not so stated, usage of trade in international contracts determines standards of weight.

4 Packaging requirements can be conditions for acceptance and payment. See Chapter 10. Bulk shipments are not permitted without the consent of the buyer.

5 A description of the coffee and the "Markings" constitute express warranties. Warranties in contracts for domestic sales of goods are discussed generally in Chapter 11. International contracts rely more heavily on descriptions and models or samples.

6 Under the UCC, parties may enter into a valid contract even though the price is not set. See Chapter 11. Under the CISG, a contract must provide for an exact determination of the price.

7 The terms of payment may take one of two forms: credit or cash. Credit terms can be complicated. A cash term can be simple, and payment can be made by any means acceptable in the ordinary course of business (for example, a personal check or a letter of credit). If the seller insists on actual cash, the buyer must be given a reasonable time to get it. See Chapter 11.

8 *Tender* means the seller has placed goods that conform to the contract at the buyer's disposition. What constitutes a valid tender is explained in Chapter 11. This contract requires that the coffee meet all import regulations and that it be ready for pickup by the buyer at a "Bonded Public Warehouse." (A *bonded warehouse* is a place in which goods can be stored without paying taxes until the goods are removed.)

9 The delivery date is significant because, if it is not met, the buyer may hold the seller in breach of the contract. Under this contract, the seller can be given a "period" within which to deliver the goods, instead of a specific day, which could otherwise present problems. The seller is also given some time to rectify goods that do not pass inspection (see the "Guarantee" clause on page two of the contract). For a discussion of the remedies of the buyer and seller, see Chapter 11.

10 As part of a proper tender, the seller (or its agent) must inform the buyer (or its agent) when the goods have arrived at their destination. The responsibilities of agents are set out in Chapter 19.

11 In some contracts, delivered and shipped weights can be important. During shipping, some loss can be attributed to the type of goods (spoilage of fresh produce, for example) or to the transportation itself. A seller and buyer can agree on the extent to which either of them will bear such losses. See Chapter 11 for a discussion of the liability of common carriers for loss during shipment.

12 Documents are often incorporated in a contract by reference, because including them word for word can make a contract difficult to read. If the document is later revised, the entire contract might have to be reworked. Documents that are typically incorporated by reference include detailed payment and delivery terms; special provisions; and sets of rules, codes, and standards.

13 In international sales transactions, and for domestic deals involving certain products, brokers are used to form the contracts. When so used, the brokers are entitled to a commission. See Chapter 19.

(Continued)

TERMS AND CONDITIONS

ARBITRATION: All controversies relating to, in connection with, or arising out of this contract, its modification, making or the authority or obligations of the signatories hereto, and whether involving the principals, agents, brokers, or others who actually subscribe hereto, shall be settled by arbitration in accordance with the "Rules of Arbitration" of the Green Coffee Association of New York City, Inc., as they exist at the time of the arbitration (including provisions as to payment of fees and expenses). Arbitration is the sole remedy hereunder, and it shall be held in accordance with the law of New York State, and judgment of any award may be entered in the courts of that State, or in any other court of competent jurisdiction. All notices or judicial service in reference to arbitration or enforcement shall be deemed given if transmitted as required by the aforesaid rules.

GUARANTEE: (a) If all or any of the coffee is refused admission into the country of importation by reason of any violation of governmental laws or acts, which violation existed at the time the coffee arrived at Bonded-Public Warehouse, seller is required, as to the amount not admitted and as soon as possible, to deliver replacement coffee in conformity to all terms and conditions of this contract, excepting only the Arrival terms, but not later than thirty (30) days after the date of the violation notice. Any payment made and expenses incurred for any coffee denied entry shall be refunded within ten (10) calendar days of denial of entry, and payment shall be made for the replacement delivery in accordance with the terms of this contract. Consequently, if Buyer removes the coffee from the Bonded Public Warehouse, Seller's responsibility as to such portion hereunder ceases.
(b) Contracts containing the overstamp "No Pass-No Sale" on the face of the contract shall be interpreted to mean: If any or all of the coffee is not admitted into the country of Importation in its original condition by reason of failure to meet requirements of the government's laws or Acts, the contract shall be deemed null and void as to that portion of the coffee which is not admitted in its original condition. Any payment made and expenses incurred for any coffee denied entry shall be refunded within ten (10) calendar days of denial of entry.

CONTINGENCY: This contract is not contingent upon any other contract.

CLAIMS: Coffee shall be considered accepted as to quality unless within _fifteen_ (15) calendar days after delivery at Bonded Public Warehouse or within _fifteen_ (15) calendar days after all Government clearances have been received, whichever is later, either:
(a) Claims are settled by the parties hereto, or,
(b) Arbitration proceedings have been filed by one of the parties in accordance with the provisions hereof.
(c) If neither (a) nor (b) has been done in the stated period or if any portion of the coffee has been removed from the Bonded Public Warehouse before representative sealed samples have been drawn by the Green Coffee Association of New York City, Inc., in accordance with its rules, Seller's responsibility for quality claims ceases for that portion so removed.
(d) Any question of quality submitted to arbitration shall be a matter of allowance only, unless otherwise provided in the contract.

DELIVERY: (a) No more than three (3) chops may be tendered for each lot of 250 bags.
(b) Each chop of coffee tendered is to be uniform in grade and appearance. All expense necessary to make coffee uniform shall be for account of seller.
(c) Notice of arrival and/or sampling order constitutes a tender, and must be given not later than the fifth business day following arrival at Bonded Public Warehouse stated on the contract.

INSURANCE: Seller is responsible for any loss or damage, or both, until Delivery and Discharge of coffee at the Bonded Public Warehouse in the Country of Importation.

All Insurance Risks, costs and responsibility are for Seller's Account until Delivery and Discharge of coffee at the Bonded Public Warehouse in the Country of Importation.

Buyer's insurance responsibility begins from the day of importation or from the day of tender, whichever is later.

FREIGHT: Seller to provide and pay for all transportation and related expenses to the Bonded Public Warehouse in the Country of Importation.

EXPORT DUTIES/TAXES: Exporter is to pay all Export taxes, duties or other fees or charges, if any, levied because of exportation.

IMPORT DUTIES/TAXES: Any Duty or Tax whatsoever, imposed by the government or any authority of the Country of Importation, shall be borne by the Importer/Buyer.

INSOLVENCY OR FINANCIAL FAILURE OF BUYER OR SELLER: If, at any time before the contract is fully executed, either party hereto shall meet with creditors because of inability generally to make payment of obligations when due, or shall suspend such payments, fail to meet his general trade obligations in the regular course of business, shall file a petition in bankruptcy or, for an arrangement, shall become insolvent, or commit an act of bankruptcy, then the other party may at his option, expressed in writing, declare the aforesaid to constitute a breach and default of this contract, and may, in addition to other remedies, decline to deliver further or make payment or may sell or purchase for the defaulter's account, and may collect damage for any injury or loss, or shall account for the profit, if any, occasioned by such sale or purchase.

This clause is subject to the provisions of (11 USC 365 (e) 1) if invoked.

BREACH OR DEFAULT OF CONTRACT: In the event either party hereto fails to perform, or breaches or repudiates this agreement, the other party shall subject to the specific provisions of this contract be entitled to the remedies and relief provided for by the Uniform Commercial Code of the State of New York. The computation and ascertainment of damages, or the determination of any other dispute as to relief, shall be made by the arbitrators in accordance with the Arbitration Clause herein.

Consequential damages shall not, however, be allowed.

⑭ Arbitration is the settling of a dispute by submitting it to a disinterested party (other than a court) that renders a decision. The procedures and costs can be provided for in an arbitration clause or incorporated through other documents. To enforce an award rendered in an arbitration, the winning party can "enter" (submit) the award in a court "of competent jurisdiction." For a general discussion of arbitration and other forms of dispute resolution (other than courts), see Chapter 3.

⑮ When goods are imported internationally, they must meet certain import requirements before being released to the buyer. Because of this, buyers frequently want a guaranty clause that covers the goods not admitted into the country and that either requires the seller to replace the goods within a stated time or allows the contract for those goods not admitted to be void. See Chapter 10.

⑯ In the "Claims" clause, the parties agree that the buyer has a certain time within which to reject the goods. The right to reject is a right by law and does not need to be stated in a contract. If the buyer does not exercise the right within the time specified in the contract, the goods will be considered accepted. See Chapter 11.

⑰ Many international contracts include definitions of terms so that the parties understand what they mean. Some terms are used in a particular industry in a specific way. Here, the word *chop* refers to a unit of like-grade coffee bean. The buyer has a right to inspect ("sample") the coffee. If the coffee does not conform to the contract, the seller must correct the nonconformity. See Chapter 11.

⑱ The "Delivery," "Insurance," and "Freight" clauses, with the "Arrival" clause on page one of the contract, indicate that this is a destination contract. The seller has the obligation to deliver the goods to the destination, not simply deliver them into the hands of a carrier. Under this contract, the destination is a "Bonded Public Warehouse" in a specific location. The seller bears the risk of loss until the goods are delivered at their destination. Typically, the seller will have bought insurance to cover the risk. See Chapter 11 for a discussion of delivery terms and the risk of loss.

⑲ Delivery terms are commonly placed in all sales contracts. Such terms determine who pays freight and other costs and, in the absence of an agreement specifying otherwise, who bears the risk of loss. International contracts may use these delivery terms or they may use INCOTERMS, which are published by the International Chamber of Commerce. For example, the INCOTERM DDP (delivered duty paid) requires the seller to arrange shipment, obtain and pay for import or export permits, and get the goods through customs to a named destination.

⑳ Exported and imported goods are subject to duties, taxes, and other charges imposed by the governments of the countries involved. International contracts spell out who is responsible for these charges.

㉑ This clause protects a party if the other party should become financially unable to fulfill the obligations under the contract. Thus, if the seller cannot afford to deliver, or the buyer cannot afford to pay, for the stated reasons, the other party can consider the contract breached. This right is subject to "11 USC 365(e)(1)," which refers to a specific provision of the U.S. Bankruptcy Code dealing with executory contracts. Bankruptcy provisions are covered in Chapter 15.

㉒ In the "Breach or Default of Contract" clause, the parties agreed that the remedies under this contract are the remedies (except for consequential damages) provided by the UCC, as in effect in the state of New York. The amount and "ascertainment" of damages, as well as other disputes about relief, are to be determined by arbitration. Breach of contract and contractual remedies in general are explained in Chapter 11. Arbitration is discussed in Chapter 3.

㉓ Three clauses frequently included in international contracts are omitted here. There is no choice-of-language clause designating the official language to be used in interpreting the contract terms. There is no choice-of-forum clause designating the place in which disputes will be litigated, except for arbitration (law of New York State). Finally, there is no *force majeure* clause relieving the sellers or buyers from nonperformance due to events beyond their control.

CHAPTER 12

Torts and Cyber Torts

Part of doing business today—and, indeed, part of everyday life—is the risk of being involved in a lawsuit. The list of circumstances in which businesspersons can be sued is long and varied. A customer who is injured by a security guard at a business establishment, for example, may attempt to sue the business owner, claiming that the security guard's conduct was wrongful. Any time that one party's allegedly wrongful conduct causes injury to another, an action may arise under the law of **torts** (the word *tort* is French for "wrong"). Through tort law, society compensates those who have suffered injuries as a result of the wrongful conduct of others.

Many of the lawsuits brought by or against business firms are based on the tort theories discussed in this chapter. Most torts can occur in any context, but there are a few torts, referred to as **business torts,** that apply only to wrongful interferences with the business rights of others. Included in business torts are such vaguely worded concepts as *unfair competition* and *wrongfully interfering with the business relations of others*. In the concluding pages of this chapter, we look at how the courts have applied traditional tort theories to wrongful actions in the online environment. The torts involved here are often called *cyber torts*. Tort theories also come into play in the context of product liability (liability for defective products), which will be discussed in detail in Chapter 13.

SECTION 1 | The Basis of Tort Law

Two notions serve as the basis of all torts: wrongs and compensation. Tort law is designed to compensate those who have suffered a loss or injury due to another person's wrongful act. In a tort action, one person or group brings a lawsuit against another person or group to obtain compensation (money damages) or other relief for the harm suffered.

THE PURPOSE OF TORT LAW

The basic purpose of tort law is to provide remedies for the invasion of various *protected interests*. Society recognizes an interest in personal physical safety, and tort law provides remedies for acts that cause physical injury or that interfere with physical security and freedom of movement. Society recognizes an interest in protecting property, and tort law provides remedies for acts that cause destruction or damage to property. Society also recognizes an interest in protecting certain intangible interests, such as personal privacy, family relations, reputation, and dignity, and tort law provides remedies for invasion of these interests.

Of course, criminal law also involves wrongful conduct and societal interests. A crime, however, is an act so reprehensible that it is considered a wrong against the state or against society as a whole, as well as against the individual victim. Therefore, the *state* prosecutes and punishes (through fines and/or imprisonment—and possibly death) persons who commit criminal acts. A tort action, in contrast, is a civil suit because it involves only private parties and not the government. Nevertheless, some acts do provide a basis for both a criminal prosecution and a tort action—see Chapter 7.

CLASSIFICATIONS OF TORTS

There are two broad classifications of torts: *intentional torts* and *unintentional torts*. The classification of a tort depends largely on how the tort occurs (intentionally or negligently) and the surrounding circumstances. (Under the doctrine of strict liability, discussed in the following chapter, liability may be imposed regardless of fault.)

SECTION 2 | Intentional Torts against Persons

An **intentional tort,** as the term implies, requires intent. The **tortfeasor** (the one committing the tort) must intend to commit an act, the consequences of which interfere with the personal or business interests of another in a way not permitted by law. An evil or harmful motive is not required—in fact, the actor may even have a beneficial motive for committing what turns out to be a tortious act. In tort law, *intent* means only that the actor intended the consequences of his or her act or knew with substantial certainty that specific consequences would result from the act. The law generally assumes that individuals intend the *normal* consequences of their actions. Thus, forcefully pushing another—even if done in jest and without any evil motive—is an intentional tort (if injury results), because the object of a strong push can ordinarily be expected to go flying.

Intentional torts against persons include assault and battery, false imprisonment, intentional infliction of emotional distress, defamation, invasion of the right to privacy, appropriation, and fraudulent misrepresentation. We discuss these torts in the following subsections.

ASSAULT AND BATTERY

Any intentional, unexcused act that creates in another person a reasonable apprehension or fear of immediate harmful or offensive contact is an **assault.** Note that apprehension is not the same as fear. If a contact is such that a reasonable person would want to avoid it, and if there is a reasonable basis for believing that the contact will occur, then the plaintiff suffers apprehension whether or not she or he is afraid. The interest protected by tort law concerning assault is the freedom from having to expect harmful or offensive contact. The arousal of apprehension is enough to justify compensation.

The *completion* of the act that caused the apprehension, if it results in harm to the plaintiff, is a **battery,** which is defined as an unexcused and harmful or offensive physical contact *intentionally* performed. For example, Ivan threatens Jean with a gun, then shoots her. The pointing of the gun at Jean is an assault; the firing of the gun (if the bullet hits Jean) is a battery. The interest protected by tort law concerning battery is the right to personal security and safety. The contact can be harmful, or it can be merely offensive (such as an unwelcome kiss). Physical injury need not occur. The contact can involve any part of the body or anything attached to it—for example, a hat or other item of clothing, a purse, or a chair or an automobile in which one is sitting. Whether the contact is offensive is determined by the *reasonable person standard.*[1] The contact can be made by the defendant or by some force the defendant sets in motion—for example, a rock thrown, food poisoned, or a stick swung.

COMPENSATION If the plaintiff shows that there was contact, and the jury agrees that the contact was offensive, the plaintiff has a right to compensation. There is no need to establish that the defendant acted out of malice. The underlying motive does not matter, only the intent to bring about the harmful or offensive contact to the plaintiff. In fact, proving a motive is never necessary. A plaintiff may be compensated for the emotional harm or loss of reputation resulting from a battery, as well as for physical harm.

DEFENSES TO ASSAULT AND BATTERY A defendant who is sued for assault, battery, or both can raise any of the following legally recognized defenses:

1. *Consent.* When a person consents to the act that damages her or him, there is generally no liability for the damage done.
2. *Self-defense.* An individual who is defending his or her life or physical well-being can claim self-defense. In a situation of either *real* or *apparent* danger, a person may normally use whatever force is *reasonably* necessary to prevent harmful contact (see Chapter 7 for a more detailed discussion of self-defense).
3. *Defense of others.* An individual can act in a reasonable manner to protect others who are in real or apparent danger.
4. *Defense of property.* Reasonable force may be used in attempting to remove intruders from one's home, although force that is likely to cause death or great bodily injury normally cannot be used just to protect property.

FALSE IMPRISONMENT

False imprisonment is defined as the intentional confinement or restraint of another person's activities without justification. It involves interference with the

---

1. The *reasonable person standard* is an objective test of how a reasonable person would have acted under the same circumstances. See the subsection entitled "The Duty of Care and Its Breach" later in this chapter.

freedom to move without restriction. The confinement can be accomplished through the use of physical barriers, physical restraint, or threats of physical force. Moral pressure does not constitute false imprisonment. Furthermore, it is essential that the person being restrained not comply with the restraint willingly. In other words, the person being restrained must not agree to the restraint.

Businesspersons are often confronted with suits for false imprisonment after they have attempted to confine a suspected shoplifter for questioning. Under the privilege to detain granted to merchants in some states, a merchant can normally use the defense of *probable cause* to justify delaying a suspected shoplifter. Probable cause exists when there is sufficient evidence to support the belief that a person is guilty. Although the laws governing false imprisonment vary from state to state, generally they require that any detention be conducted in a *reasonable* manner and that the detention be for only a *reasonable* length of time.

INTENTIONAL INFLICTION OF EMOTIONAL DISTRESS

The tort of *intentional infliction of emotional distress* can be defined as an intentional act that amounts to extreme and outrageous conduct resulting in severe emotional distress to another. For example, a prankster telephones an individual and says that the individual's spouse has just been in a horrible accident. As a result, the individual suffers intense mental pain or anxiety. The caller's behavior is deemed to be extreme and outrageous conduct that exceeds the bounds of decency accepted by society and is therefore **actionable** (capable of serving as the ground for a lawsuit).

Emotional distress claims pose several problems. One major problem is that such claims must be subject to some limitation, or the courts could be flooded with lawsuits alleging emotional distress. A society in which individuals are rewarded if they are unable to endure the normal emotional stresses of day-to-day living is obviously undesirable. Therefore, the law usually focuses on the nature of the acts that fall under this tort. Indignity or annoyance alone is usually not sufficient to support a lawsuit based on intentional infliction of emotional distress.

Many times, however, repeated annoyances (such as those experienced by a person who is being stalked), coupled with threats, are enough. In a business context, for example, the repeated use of extreme methods to collect an overdue debt may be actionable. Also, an event causing an unusually severe emotional reaction, such as the severe distress of a woman incorrectly informed that her husband and two sons have been killed, may be actionable. Because it is difficult to prove the existence of emotional suffering, a court may require that the emotional distress be evidenced by some physical symptom or illness or by a specific emotional disturbance that can be documented by a psychiatric consultant or other medical professional.

DEFAMATION

As discussed in Chapter 5, the freedom of speech guaranteed by the First Amendment is not absolute. In interpreting the First Amendment, the courts must balance the vital guarantee of free speech against other pervasive and strong social interests, including society's interest in preventing and redressing attacks on reputation.

Defamation of character involves wrongfully hurting a person's good reputation. The law imposes a general duty on all persons to refrain from making false, defamatory *statements of fact* about others. Breaching this duty in writing or other permanent form (such as a digital recording) involves the tort of **libel.** Breaching this duty orally involves the tort of **slander.** The tort of defamation also arises when a false statement of fact is made about a person's product, business, or title to property.

Often at issue in lawsuits alleging defamation (including online defamation, discussed later in this chapter) is whether the defendant's statement was one of fact or a *statement of opinion*. Statements of opinion normally are not actionable in tort because they fall under the protection of the First Amendment.

THE PUBLICATION REQUIREMENT The basis of the tort of defamation is the publication of a statement or statements that hold an individual up to contempt, ridicule, or hatred. *Publication* here means that the defamatory statements are communicated to persons other than the defamed party. If Thompson writes Andrews a private letter falsely accusing him of embezzling funds, the action does not constitute libel. If Peters falsely states that Gordon is dishonest and incompetent when no one else is around, the action does not constitute slander. In neither case was the message communicated to a third party.

The courts have generally held that even dictating a letter to a secretary constitutes publication, although the publication may be privileged (a concept that will be explained shortly). Moreover, if a third party overhears defamatory statements by chance, the courts usually hold that this also constitutes publication. Defamatory statements made via the Internet are actionable as well. Note also that any individual who repeats, or republishes, defamatory statements normally is liable even if that person reveals the source of the statements.

DAMAGES FOR LIBEL Once a defendant's liability for libel is established, *general damages* are presumed as a matter of law. General damages are designed to compensate the plaintiff for nonspecific harms—such as disgrace or dishonor in the eyes of the community, humiliation, injured reputation, and emotional distress, for example—that are difficult to measure. In other words, to recover damages in a libel case, the plaintiff need not prove that he or she was actually injured in any way as a result of the libelous statement.

DAMAGES FOR SLANDER In contrast to cases alleging libel, in a case alleging slander, the plaintiff must prove *special damages* to establish the defendant's liability. The plaintiff must show that the slanderous statement caused the plaintiff to suffer actual economic or monetary losses. Unless this initial hurdle of proving special damages is overcome, a plaintiff alleging slander normally cannot go forward with the suit and recover any damages. This requirement is imposed in cases involving slander because slanderous statements have a temporary quality. In contrast, a libelous (written) statement has the quality of permanence, can be circulated widely, and usually results from some degree of deliberation on the part of the author.

Exceptions to the burden of proving special damages in cases alleging slander are made for certain types of slanderous statements. If a false statement constitutes "slander *per se,*" no proof of special damages is required for it to be actionable. The following four types of utterances are considered to be slander *per se:*

1. A statement that another has a loathsome communicable disease.
2. A statement that another has committed improprieties while engaging in a profession or trade.
3. A statement that another has committed or has been imprisoned for a serious crime.
4. A statement that a woman is unchaste or has engaged in serious sexual misconduct.

DEFENSES TO DEFAMATION Truth is almost always a defense against a defamation charge. In other words,

if a defendant in a defamation case can prove that the allegedly defamatory statement of fact was actually true, normally no tort has been committed. Other defenses to defamation may exist if the speech is privileged or concerns a public figure.

—*Privileged Speech.* In some circumstances, a person will not be liable for defamatory statements because she or he enjoys a **privilege,** or immunity. With respect to defamation, privileged communications are of two types: absolute and qualified.[2] Only in judicial proceedings and certain government proceedings is *absolute* privilege granted. For example, statements made by attorneys and judges in the courtroom during a trial are absolutely privileged. So are statements made by government officials during legislative debate, even if the legislators make such statements maliciously—that is, knowing them to be untrue. An absolute privilege is granted in these situations because judicial and government personnel deal with matters that are so much in the public interest that the parties involved should be able to speak out fully and freely and without restriction.

In other situations, a person will not be liable for defamatory statements because he or she has a *qualified,* or conditional, privilege. For example, statements made in written evaluations of employees are qualifiedly privileged. Generally, if the communicated statements are made in good faith and the publication is limited to those who have a legitimate interest in the communication, the statements fall within the area of qualified privilege. The concept of conditional privilege rests on the common law assumption that in some situations, the right to know or speak is equal in importance to the right not to be defamed. If a communication is conditionally privileged, to recover damages, the plaintiff must show that the privilege was abused.

—*Public Figures.* In general, false and defamatory statements that are made about **public figures** (public officials who exercise substantial governmental power and any persons in the public limelight) and published in the press are privileged if they are made without "actual malice." To be made with **actual malice,** a statement must be made *with either knowledge of falsity or a reckless disregard of the truth.*[3]

---

2. Note that the term *privileged communication* in this context is not the same as privileged communication between a professional, such as an attorney, and his or her client.
3. *New York Times Co. v. Sullivan,* 376 U.S. 254, 84 S.Ct. 710, 11 L.Ed.2d 686 (1964).

Statements made about public figures, especially when they are communicated via a public medium, are usually related to matters of general public interest; they refer to people who substantially affect all of us. Furthermore, public figures generally have some access to a public medium for answering disparaging falsehoods about themselves; private individuals do not. For these reasons, public figures have a greater burden of proof in defamation cases (they must prove actual malice) than do private individuals.

INVASION OF PRIVACY

A person has a right to solitude and freedom from prying public eyes—in other words, to privacy. As mentioned in Chapter 5, the courts have held that certain amendments to the U.S. Constitution imply a right to privacy. Some state constitutions explicitly provide for privacy rights. Additionally, a number of federal and state statutes have been enacted to protect individual privacy rights in specific areas. Tort law also safeguards these rights through the tort of *invasion of privacy*. Four acts qualify as invasions of privacy:

1. *The use of a person's name, picture, or other likeness for commercial purposes without permission.* For example, using without permission someone's picture to advertise a product or someone's name to enhance a company's reputation invades the person's privacy. (This tort, which is usually referred to as the tort of *appropriation*, will be examined shortly.)

2. *Intrusion on an individual's affairs or seclusion.* For example, invading someone's home or illegally searching someone's briefcase is an invasion of privacy. This tort has been held to extend to eavesdropping by wiretap, unauthorized scanning of a bank account, compulsory blood testing, and window peeping.

3. *Publication of information that places a person in a false light.* This could be a story attributing to someone ideas not held or actions not taken by that person. (The publication of such a story could involve the tort of defamation as well.)

4. *Public disclosure of private facts about an individual that an ordinary person would find objectionable.* A newspaper account of a private citizen's sex life or financial affairs could be an actionable invasion of privacy.

APPROPRIATION

The use of another person's name, likeness, or other identifying characteristic, without permission and for the benefit of the user, constitutes the tort of **appropriation.** Under the law, normally an individual's right to privacy includes the right to the exclusive use of his or her identity. For example, in a case involving a Ford Motor Company television commercial in which a Bette Midler "sound-alike" sang a song that Midler had made famous, the court held that Ford "for their own profit in selling their product did appropriate part of her identity."[4]

A court ruled similarly in a case brought by Vanna White, the hostess of the popular television game show *Wheel of Fortune*, against Samsung Electronics America, Inc. Without White's permission, Samsung included in an advertisement for Samsung videocassette recorders a depiction of a robot dressed in a wig, gown, and jewelry, posed in a setting that resembled the *Wheel of Fortune* set, in a stance for which White is famous. The court ruled in White's favor, holding that the tort of appropriation does not require the use of a celebrity's name or likeness. The court stated that Samsung's robot ad left "little doubt" as to the identity of the celebrity that the ad was meant to depict.[5]

Cases of wrongful appropriation, or misappropriation, may also involve the rights of those who invest time and funds in the creation of a special system, such as a method of broadcasting sports events. Commercial misappropriation may also occur when a person takes and uses the property of another for the sole purpose of capitalizing unfairly on the goodwill or reputation of the property owner.

FRAUDULENT MISREPRESENTATION

A misrepresentation leads another to believe in a condition that is different from the condition that actually exists. This is often accomplished through a false or an incorrect statement. Misrepresentations may be innocently made by someone who is unaware of the facts. The tort of **fraudulent misrepresentation,** or *fraud*, however, involves intentional deceit for personal gain.

ELEMENTS OF FRAUD   The tort of fraudulent misrepresentation includes several elements:

1. A misrepresentation of material facts or conditions with knowledge that they are false or with reckless disregard for the truth.

2. An intent to induce another party to rely on the misrepresentation.

---

4. *Midler v. Ford Motor Co.*, 849 F.2d 460 (9th Cir. 1988).
5. *White v. Samsung Electronics America, Inc.*, 971 F.2d 1395 (9th Cir. 1992).

3. A justifiable reliance on the misrepresentation by the deceived party.

4. Damages suffered as a result of that reliance.

5. A causal connection between the misrepresentation and the injury suffered.

FACT VERSUS OPINION For fraud to occur, more than mere *puffery*, or *seller's talk* (see Chapter 11), must be involved. Fraud exists only when a person represents as a fact something he or she knows is untrue. For example, it is fraud to claim that the roof of a building does not leak when one knows that it does. Facts are objectively ascertainable, whereas seller's talk is not. "I am the best architect in town" is seller's talk. The speaker is not trying to represent something as fact because the term *best* is a subjective, not an objective, term.

Normally, the tort of fraudulent misrepresentation occurs only when there is reliance on a *statement of fact*. Sometimes, however, reliance on a *statement of opinion* may involve the tort of fraudulent misrepresentation if the individual making the statement of opinion has a superior knowledge of the subject matter. For example, when a lawyer, in a state in which she or he is licensed to practice, makes a statement of opinion about the law, a court would construe reliance on such a statement to be equivalent to reliance on a statement of fact.

SECTION 3 | Business Torts

Torts involving wrongful interference with another's business rights generally fall into two categories—interference with a contractual relationship and interference with a business relationship.

WRONGFUL INTERFERENCE WITH A CONTRACTUAL RELATIONSHIP

The body of tort law relating to *wrongful interference with a contractual relationship* has increased greatly in recent years. A landmark case in this area involved an opera singer, Joanna Wagner, who was under contract to sing for a man named Lumley for a specified period of years. A man named Gye, who knew of this contract, nonetheless "enticed" Wagner to refuse to carry out the agreement, and Wagner began to sing for Gye. Gye's action constituted a tort because it interfered with the contractual relationship between Wagner and Lumley. (Of course, Wagner's refusal to carry out the agreement also entitled Lumley to sue Wagner for breach of contract.)[6]

---

6. *Lumley v. Gye*, 118 Eng.Rep. 749 (1853).

CONCEPT SUMMARY 12.1 | Intentional Torts against Persons

NAME OF TORT	DESCRIPTION
ASSAULT AND BATTERY	Any unexcused and intentional act that causes another person to be apprehensive of immediate harm is an assault. An assault resulting in physical contact is battery.
FALSE IMPRISONMENT	An intentional confinement or restraint of another person's movement without justification.
INTENTIONAL INFLICTION OF EMOTIONAL DISTRESS	An intentional act that amounts to extreme and outrageous conduct resulting in severe emotional distress to another.
DEFAMATION (LIBEL OR SLANDER)	A false statement of fact, not made under privilege, that is communicated to a third person and that causes damage to a person's reputation. For public figures, the plaintiff must also prove that the statement was made with actual malice.
INVASION OF PRIVACY	Publishing or otherwise making known or using information relating to a person's private life and affairs, with which the public has no legitimate concern, without that person's permission or approval.
APPROPRIATION	The use of another person's name, likeness, or other identifying characteristic, without permission and for the benefit of the user.
FRAUDULENT MISREPRESENTATION (FRAUD)	A false representation made by one party, through misstatement of facts or through conduct, with the intention of deceiving another and on which the other reasonably relies to his or her detriment.

THE INTENT FACTOR   In principle, any lawful contract can be the basis for an action of this type. The plaintiff must prove that the defendant actually knew of the contract's existence and *intentionally induced* the breach of the contractual relationship, not merely that the defendant reaped the benefits of a broken contract.

For example, suppose that Carlin has a contract with Sutter that calls for Sutter to do gardening work on Carlin's large estate every week for fifty-two weeks at a specified price per week. Mellon, who needs gardening services, contacts Sutter and offers to pay Sutter a wage that is substantially higher than that offered by Carlin—although Mellon knows nothing about the Sutter-Carlin contract. Sutter breaches his contract with Carlin so that he can work for Mellon. Carlin cannot sue Mellon because Mellon knew nothing of the Sutter-Carlin contract and was totally unaware that the higher wage he offered induced Sutter to breach that contract.

REQUIRED ELEMENTS   The elements necessary for wrongful interference with a contractual relationship to occur can be summarized as follows:

1. A valid, enforceable contract must exist between two parties.

2. A third party must know that this contract exists.
3. This third party must *intentionally* cause one of the two parties to the contract to breach the contract, and the interference must be for the purpose of advancing the economic interest of the third party.

The interference may involve a contract between a firm and its employees or a firm and its customers, suppliers, competitors, or other parties. Sometimes, a competitor of a firm draws away a key employee. If the original employer can show that the competitor induced the breach of the employment contract—that is, that the employee normally would not have broken the contract—damages can be recovered.

The following case illustrates the elements of the tort of wrongful interference with a contractual relationship in the context of a contract between an independent sales representative and his agent (agency relationships are discussed in Chapter 19). The case was complicated by the existence of a second contract between the sales representative and the third party.

CASE 12.1   Mathis v. Liu

United States
Court of Appeals,
Eighth Circuit, 2002.
276 F.3d 1027.

BACKGROUND AND FACTS   *Ching and Alex Liu own Pacific Cornetta, Inc. In 1997, Pacific Cornetta entered into a contract with Lawrence Mathis, under which Mathis agreed to solicit orders for Pacific Cornetta's products from Kmart Corporation for a commission of 5 percent on net sales. Under the terms, either party could terminate the contract at any time. The next year, Mathis entered into a one-year contract with John Evans, under which Evans agreed to serve as Mathis's agent to solicit orders from Kmart for the product lines that Mathis represented, including Pacific Cornetta, for a commission of 1 percent on net sales. Under the terms of this contract, either party could terminate it only on written notice of six months. A few months later, Pacific Cornetta persuaded Evans to break his contract with Mathis and enter into a contract with Pacific Cornetta to be its sales representative to Kmart. Evans terminated his contract with Mathis without notice. Two days later, Pacific Cornetta terminated its contract with Mathis. Mathis filed a suit in a federal district court against Ching and Alex Liu and Pacific Cornetta, alleging in part wrongful interference with a contractual relationship. The court issued a judgment that included a ruling in Mathis's favor on this claim, but Mathis appealed the amount of damages to the U.S. Court of Appeals for the Eighth Circuit.*

IN THE LANGUAGE OF THE COURT

MORRIS SHEPHARD ARNOLD, Circuit Judge.
* * * *
* * * [A] *defendant is liable for tortious interference only if the defendant's interference with some relevant advantage was improper. [The] courts [look at several considerations] to determine whether a defendant's interference is improper. These considerations include the nature of the actor's conduct[,] * * * the actor's motive[,] * * * the interests of the other with which the actor's conduct interferes[,] * * * the interests sought to be advanced by the actor[,] * * * the social interests in protecting the freedom of action of the actor and the*

CASE 12.1 | Continued

contractual interests of the other[,] * * * the proximity or remoteness of the actor's conduct to the interference[,] and * * * the relations between the parties. [Emphasis added.]

We conclude that Mr. Mathis made out a * * * case on this element of his claim. If Mr. Evans's agency arrangement with Mr. Mathis had been purely at-will [a legal doctrine under which a contractual relationship can be terminated at any time by either party for any or no reason], we do not believe that Pacific Cornetta's successful effort to hire Mr. Evans * * * would have risen to the level of impropriety necessary to make out a case for tortious interference. That is because a party's interference with an at-will contract is primarily an interference with the future relation between the parties, and *when an at-will contract is terminated there is no breach of it*. In such circumstances, the interfering party is free for its own competitive advantage, to obtain the future benefits for itself by causing the termination, provided it uses suitable means. [Emphasis added.]

Mr. Evans's contract with Mr. Mathis, however, did not create a simple at-will arrangement because Mr. Evans could terminate it only after giving Mr. Mathis six months' notice of his intention to do so. In these circumstances, we think that the jury was entitled to conclude that Pacific Cornetta's blandishments [flattering statements] were improper, especially since *inducing a breach of contract absent compelling justification is, in and of itself, improper*. [Emphasis added.]

* * * *

Mr. Mathis asked for damages for the loss of anticipatory profits on his tortious interference claim. He argues that the damages that the jury awarded were supported by Mr. Evans's sales of * * * Pacific Cornetta products to Kmart [after Pacific Cornetta terminated its contract with Mathis].

* * * *

We reject this theory * * * . Mr. Mathis's losses on these sales were a result of Pacific Cornetta exercising its right to terminate its contract with him at will, not Pacific Cornetta's tortious interference, and the losses were therefore not recoverable under a theory of tortious interference.

DECISION AND REMEDY *The U.S. Court of Appeals for the Eighth Circuit affirmed the judgment of the lower court. The appellate court concluded that the defendants had committed wrongful interference with Mathis's contract with Evans. Evans's sales of Pacific Cornetta products after Pacific Cornetta terminated its contract with Mathis could not furnish a basis for an award of damages on this claim, however, because the firm's contract with Mathis was terminable at will.*

WHAT IF THE FACTS WERE DIFFERENT? *Suppose that Mathis's contract with Pacific Cornetta had stated that Mathis could only be terminated for misconduct or with six months' notice. How might that have affected the court's ruling in this case?*

WRONGFUL INTERFERENCE WITH A BUSINESS RELATIONSHIP

Individuals devise countless schemes to attract business, but they are forbidden by the courts to interfere unreasonably with another's business in their attempts to gain a share of the market. There is a difference between *competitive practices* and *predatory behavior*. The distinction usually depends on whether a business is attempting to attract customers in general or to solicit only those customers who have already shown an interest in the similar product or service of a specific competitor.

For example, if a shopping center contains two shoe stores, an employee of Store A cannot be positioned at the entrance of Store B for the purpose of diverting customers to Store A. This type of activity constitutes the tort of wrongful interference with a business relationship, often referred to as interference with a prospective (economic) advantage, and it is commonly considered to be an unfair trade practice. If this type of activity were permitted, Store A would reap the benefits of Store B's advertising.

REQUIRED ELEMENTS Generally, a plaintiff must prove the following elements to recover damages for the tort of wrongful interference with a business relationship:

1. There was an established business relationship.

2. The tortfeasor, by use of predatory methods, intentionally caused this business relationship to end.

3. The plaintiff suffered damages as a result of the tortfeasor's actions.

DEFENSES TO WRONGFUL INTERFERENCE   A person will not be liable for the tort of wrongful interference with a contractual or business relationship if it can be shown that the interference was justified, or permissible. Bona fide competitive behavior is a permissible interference even if it results in the breaking of a contract.

For example, if Jerrod's Meats advertises so effectively that it induces Sam's Restaurant to break its contract with Burke's Meat Company, Burke's Meat Company will be unable to recover against Jerrod's Meats on a wrongful interference theory. After all, the public policy that favors free competition in advertising definitely outweighs any possible instability that such competitive activity might cause in contractual relations. Therefore, although luring customers away from a competitor through aggressive marketing and advertising strategies obviously interferes with the competitor's relationship with its customers, such activity is permitted by the courts.

SECTION 4 | Intentional Torts against Property

Intentional torts against property include trespass to land, trespass to personal property, and conversion. These torts are wrongful actions that interfere with individuals' legally recognized rights with regard to their land or personal property. The law distinguishes real property from personal property (see Chapter 25). *Real property* is land and things permanently attached to the land. *Personal property* consists of all other items, which are basically movable. Thus, a house and lot are real property, whereas the furniture inside a house is personal property. Money and securities are also personal property.

TRESPASS TO LAND

The tort of **trespass to land** occurs anytime a person, without permission, enters onto, above, or below the surface of land that is owned by another; causes anything to enter onto the land; or remains on the land or permits anything to remain on it. Note that actual harm to the land is not an essential element of this tort because the tort is designed to protect the right of

an owner to exclusive possession. Common types of trespass to land include walking or driving on another's land; shooting a gun over another's land; throwing rocks at or spraying water on a building that belongs to someone else; building a dam across a river, thus causing water to back up on someone else's land; and constructing one's building so that it extends onto an adjoining landowner's property.

In the past, the right to land gave exclusive possession of a space that extended from "the center of the earth to the heavens," but this rule has been relaxed. Today, reasonable intrusions are permitted. Thus, aircraft can normally fly over privately owned land. Society's interest in air transportation preempts the individual's interest in the airspace.

TRESPASS CRITERIA, RIGHTS, AND DUTIES Before a person can be a trespasser, the real property owner (or other person in actual and exclusive possession of the property, such as a person who is leasing the property) must establish that person as a trespasser. For example, "posted" trespass signs expressly establish as a trespasser a person who ignores these signs and enters onto the property. Any person who enters onto another's property to commit an illegal act (such as a thief entering a lumberyard at night to steal lumber) is established impliedly as a trespasser, without posted signs.

At common law, a trespasser is liable for damages caused to the property and generally cannot hold the owner liable for injuries that the trespasser sustains on the premises. This common law rule is being abandoned in many jurisdictions, however, in favor of a "reasonable duty" rule that varies depending on the status of the parties. For example, a landowner may have a duty to post a notice that the property is patrolled by guard dogs. Also, under the "attractive nuisance" doctrine, a landowner may be held liable for injuries sustained by young children on the landowner's property if the children were attracted to the premises by some object, such as a swimming pool or an abandoned building. Finally, an owner can remove a trespasser from the premises—or detain a trespasser on the premises for a reasonable time—through the use of reasonable force without being liable for assault and battery or false imprisonment.

DEFENSES AGAINST TRESPASS TO LAND Trespass to land involves wrongful interference with another person's real property rights. If it can be shown that the trespass was warranted, however, as when a trespasser enters to assist someone in danger, a defense exists. Another defense exists when the trespasser can show that he or she had a license to come onto the land. A *licensee* is one who is invited (or allowed to enter) onto the property of another for the licensee's benefit. A person who enters another's property to read an electric meter, for example, is a licensee. When you purchase a ticket to attend a movie or sporting event, you are licensed to go onto the property of another to view that movie or event. Note that licenses to enter onto another's property are *revocable* by the property owner. If a property owner asks a meter reader to leave and the meter reader refuses to do so, the meter reader at that point becomes a trespasser.

TRESPASS TO PERSONAL PROPERTY

Whenever any individual, without consent, harms the personal property of another or otherwise interferes with the personal property owner's right to exclusive possession and enjoyment of that property, **trespass to personal property**—also called *trespass to personalty*—occurs. Trespass to personal property involves intentional meddling. If Kelly takes Ryan's business law book as a practical joke and hides it so that Ryan is unable to find it for several days prior to the final examination, Kelly has engaged in a trespass to personal property.

If it can be shown that trespass to personal property was warranted, then a complete defense exists. Most states, for example, allow automobile repair shops to hold a customer's car when the customer refuses to pay for repairs already completed. Trespass to personal property was one of the allegations in the following case. (For a discussion of whether spamming constitutes trespass to personal property, see the discussion of *cyber torts* later in this chapter.)

CASE 12.2

United States
Court of Appeals,
Second Circuit, 2004.
356 F.3d 393.

Register.com, Inc. v. Verio, Inc.

LEVAL, Circuit Judge.
 *   *   *   *
 *   *   * [Register.com, Inc.] is one of over fifty companies serving as registrars for the issuance of domain names on the World Wide Web. As a registrar, Register issues domain names to persons and entities preparing to establish web sites on the Internet. Web sites are identified and accessed by reference to their domain names.

Register was appointed a registrar of domain names by the Internet Corporation for Assigned Names and Numbers, known by the acronym "ICANN." ICANN *   *   * administer[s] the Internet domain name system. To become a registrar of domain names, Register was required to enter into a standard form agreement with ICANN *   *   *.

Applicants to register a domain name submit to the registrar contact information, including at a minimum, the applicant's name, postal address, telephone number, and electronic mail address. The ICANN Agreement, referring to this registrant contact information under the rubric "WHOIS information," requires the registrar *   *   * to preserve it, update it daily, and provide for free public access to it through the Internet *   *   *.

 *   *   * [T]he ICANN Agreement requires the registrar to permit use of its WHOIS data "for any lawful purposes except to *   *   * support the transmission of mass unsolicited, commercial advertising or solicitations via e-mail (spam) *   *   *."
 *   *   *   *
 *   *   * An entity making a WHOIS query through Register's Internet site *   *   * would receive a reply furnishing the requested WHOIS information, captioned by a legend devised by Register, which stated,

> By submitting a WHOIS query, you agree that you will use this data only for lawful purposes and that under no circumstances will you use this data to *   *   * support the transmission of mass unsolicited, commercial advertising or solicitation via e-mail. *   *   *

 *   *   *   *
The defendant [Verio, Inc.] *   *   * is engaged in the business of selling a variety of web site design, development and operation services. *   *   * To facilitate its pursuit of customers,

CONTINUED ▶

CASE 12.2 | Continued Verio undertook to obtain daily updates of the WHOIS information relating to newly registered domain names. To achieve this, Verio devised an automated software program, or robot, which each day would submit multiple successive WHOIS queries * * * . Upon acquiring the WHOIS information of new registrants, Verio would send them marketing solicitations by e-mail, telemarketing and direct mail. * * *

* * * *

Register wrote to Verio demanding that it cease * * * . Verio * * * refused * * * .

Register brought this suit [in a federal district court] on August 3, 2000 * * * . Register asserted, among other claims, that Verio was * * * trespassing on Register's chattels [personal property] in a manner likely to harm Register's computer systems by the use of Verio's automated robot software programs. On December 8, 2000, the district court entered a preliminary injunction. The injunction barred Verio from * * * [a]ccessing Register.com's computers and computer networks * * * by software programs performing multiple, automated, successive queries * * * .

* * * *

Verio * * * attacks the grant of the preliminary injunction against its accessing Register's computers by automated software programs performing multiple successive queries. This prong of the injunction was premised on Register's claim of trespass to chattels. Verio contends the ruling was in error because Register failed to establish that Verio's conduct resulted in harm to Register's servers and because Verio's robot access to the WHOIS database through Register was "not unauthorized." We believe the district court's findings were within the range of its permissible discretion.

*A trespass to a chattel may be committed by intentionally * * * using or intermeddling with a chattel in the possession of another, where the chattel is impaired as to its condition, quality, or value.* [Emphasis added.]

The district court found that Verio's use of search robots, consisting of software programs performing multiple automated successive queries, consumed a significant portion of the capacity of Register's computer systems. While Verio's robots alone would not incapacitate Register's systems, the court found that if Verio were permitted to continue to access Register's computers through such robots, it was "highly probable" that other Internet service providers would devise similar programs to access Register's data, and that the system would be overtaxed and would crash. We cannot say these findings were unreasonable.

Nor is there merit to Verio's contention that it cannot be engaged in trespass when Register had never instructed it not to use its robot programs. As the district court noted, Register's complaint sufficiently advised Verio that its use of robots was not authorized and, according to Register's contentions, would cause harm to Register's systems.

* * * *

The ruling of the district court is hereby AFFIRMED * * * .

QUESTIONS

1. Why should the use of a robot, or "bot," to initiate "multiple successive queries" have a different legal effect than typing and submitting queries manually?
2. Are there any circumstances under which the use of a bot to initiate "multiple successive queries" could be justified against claims of trespass to personal property?

CONVERSION

Conversion is defined as any act that deprives an owner of personal property without that owner's permission and without just cause. Conversion is the civil side of crimes related to theft. A store clerk who steals merchandise from the store commits a crime and engages in the tort of conversion at the same time. When conversion occurs, the lesser offense of trespass to personal property usually occurs as well. If the initial taking of the property was a trespass, retention of that property is conversion. If the initial taking of the property was permitted by the owner or for some other reason is not a trespass, failure to return it may still be conversion.

CONCEPT SUMMARY 12.2 | Intentional Torts against Property

NAME OF TORT	DESCRIPTION
TRESPASS TO LAND	The invasion of another's real property without consent or privilege. Specific rights and duties apply once a person is expressly or impliedly established as a trespasser.
TRESPASS TO PERSONAL PROPERTY	The intentional interference with an owner's right to use, possess, or enjoy his or her personal property without the owner's consent.
CONVERSION	The wrongful taking and use of another person's personal property for the benefit of the tortfeasor or another.
DISPARAGEMENT OF PROPERTY	Any economically injurious falsehood that is made about another's product or property; an inclusive term for the torts of *slander of quality* and *slander of title*.

Even if a person mistakenly believed that she or he was entitled to the goods, a tort of conversion may still have occurred. In other words, good intentions are not a defense against conversion; in fact, conversion can be an entirely innocent act. Someone who buys stolen goods, for example, has committed the tort of conversion even if he or she did not know the goods were stolen.

A successful defense against the charge of conversion is that the purported owner does not in fact own the property or does not have a right to possess it that is superior to the right of the person in possession of the property. Necessity is another possible defense against conversion. If Abrams takes Mendoza's cat, Abrams is guilty of conversion. If Mendoza sues Abrams, Abrams must return the cat or pay damages. If, however, the cat had rabies and Abrams took the cat to protect the public, Abrams has a valid defense—necessity.

DISPARAGEMENT OF PROPERTY

Disparagement of property occurs when economically injurious falsehoods are made not about another's reputation but about another's product or property. *Disparagement of property* is a general term for torts that can be more specifically referred to as *slander of quality* or *slander of title*.

SLANDER OF QUALITY Publishing false information about another's product, alleging it is not what its seller claims, constitutes the tort of **slander of quality.** This tort has also been given the name **trade libel.** The plaintiff must prove that actual damages proximately resulted from the slander of quality. In other words, the plaintiff must show not only that a third person refrained from dealing with the plaintiff

because of the improper publication but also that the plaintiff suffered damages because the third person refrained from dealing with him or her. The economic calculation of such damages—they are, after all, conjectural—is often extremely difficult.

It is possible for an improper publication to be both a slander of quality and a defamation. For example, a statement that disparages the quality of a product may also, by implication, disparage the character of a person who would sell such a product.

SLANDER OF TITLE When a publication falsely denies or casts doubt on another's legal ownership of property, and when this results in financial loss to the property's owner, the tort of **slander of title** may exist. Usually, this is an intentional tort in which someone knowingly publishes an untrue statement about another's ownership of certain property with the intent of discouraging a third person from dealing with the person slandered. For example, it would be difficult for a car dealer to attract customers after competitors published a notice that the dealer's stock consisted of stolen autos.

SECTION 5 | Negligence

In contrast to intentional torts, in torts involving **negligence,** the tortfeasor neither wishes to bring about the consequences of the act nor believes that they will occur. The actor's conduct merely creates a risk of such consequences. If no risk is created, there is no negligence. Moreover, the risk must be foreseeable; that is, it must be such that a reasonable person engaging in the same activity would anticipate the risk and guard against it. In determining what is reasonable conduct, courts consider the nature of the possible harm. Creating a very slight risk of a dangerous explosion might be unreasonable, whereas creating a distinct possibility of someone's burning his or her fingers on a stove might be reasonable.

To succeed in a negligence action, the plaintiff must prove each of the following:

1. That the defendant owed a duty of care to the plaintiff.
2. That the defendant breached that duty.
3. That the plaintiff suffered a legally recognizable injury.
4. That the defendant's breach caused the plaintiff's injury.

We discuss here each of these four elements of negligence.

THE DUTY OF CARE AND ITS BREACH

Central to the tort of negligence is the concept of a **duty of care.** This concept arises from the notion that if we are to live in society with other people, some actions can be tolerated and some cannot; some actions are right and some are wrong; and some actions are reasonable and some are not. The basic principle underlying the duty of care is that people are free to act as they please so long as their actions do not infringe on the interests of others.

THE REASONABLE PERSON STANDARD   Tort law measures duty by the **reasonable person standard.** In determining whether a duty of care has been breached, for example, the courts ask how a reasonable person would have acted in the same circumstances. The reasonable person standard is said to be (though in an absolute sense it cannot be) objective. It is not necessarily how a particular person *would* act. It is society's judgment of how an ordinarily prudent person *should* act. If the so-called reasonable person existed, he or she would be careful, conscientious, prudent, even tempered, and honest. That individuals are required to exercise a reasonable standard of care in their activities is a pervasive concept in business law, and many of the issues dealt with in subsequent chapters of this text have to do with this duty.

In negligence cases, the degree of care to be exercised varies, depending on the defendant's occupation or profession, her or his relationship with the plaintiff, and other factors. Generally, whether an action constitutes a breach of the duty of care is determined on a case-by-case basis. The outcome depends on how the judge (or jury, if it is a jury trial) decides a reasonable person in the position of the defendant would act in the particular circumstances of the case. In the following subsections, we examine the degree of care typically expected of landowners and professionals.

DUTY OF LANDOWNERS   Landowners are expected to exercise reasonable care to protect individuals coming onto their property from harm. In some jurisdictions, landowners may even have a duty to protect trespassers against certain risks. Landowners who rent or lease premises to tenants are expected to exercise reasonable care to ensure that the tenants and their guests are not harmed in common areas, such as stairways, entryways, and laundry rooms.

Retailers and other firms that explicitly or implicitly invite persons to come onto their premises are usually charged with a duty to exercise reasonable care to protect these **business invitees.** For example, if you entered a supermarket, slipped on a wet floor, and sustained injuries as a result, the owner of the supermarket would be liable for damages if, when you slipped, there was no sign warning that the floor was wet. A court would hold that the business owner was negligent because the owner failed to exercise a reasonable degree of care in protecting the store's customers against foreseeable risks about which the owner knew or *should have known*. That a patron might slip on the wet floor and be injured as a result was a foreseeable risk, and the owner should have taken care to avoid this risk or warn the customer of it.[7]

Some risks, of course, are so obvious that an owner need not warn of them. For example, a business owner does not need to warn customers to open a door before attempting to walk through it. Other risks, however, even though they may seem obvious to a business owner, may not be so in the eyes of another, such as a child. For example, a hardware store owner may not think it is necessary to warn customers that, if climbed, a stepladder leaning against the back wall of the store could fall down and harm them. It is possible, though, that a child could tip the ladder over while climbing it and be hurt as a result.

In the following case, the court had to decide whether a store owner should be held liable for a customer's injury on the premises. The question was whether the owner had notice of the condition that led to the customer's injury.

---

7. A business owner can warn of a risk in a number of ways—for example, by placing a sign, traffic cone, sawhorse, board, or the like near a hole in the business's parking lot. See *Hartman v. Walkertown Shopping Center, Inc.*, 113 N.C.App. 632, 439 S.E.2d 787 (1994).

CASE 12.3   Martin v. Wal-Mart Stores, Inc.

United States
Court of Appeals,
Eighth Circuit, 1999.
183 F.3d 770.
http://www.findlaw.com/
casecode/courts/8th.html[a]

BACKGROUND AND FACTS *Harold Martin was shopping in the sporting goods department of a Wal-Mart store. There was one employee in the department at that time. In front of the sporting goods section, in the store's main aisle (which the employees referred to as "action alley"), there was a large display of stacked cases of shotgun shells. On top of the cases were individual boxes of shells. Shortly after the sporting goods employee walked past the display, Martin did so, but Martin slipped on some loose shotgun shell pellets and fell to the floor. He immediately lost feeling in, and control of, his legs. Sensation and control returned, but during the next week, he lost the use of his legs several times for periods of ten to fifteen minutes. Eventually, sensation and control did not return to the front half of his left foot. Doctors diagnosed the condition as permanent. Martin filed a suit against Wal-Mart in a federal district court, seeking damages for his injury. The jury found in his favor, and the court denied Wal-Mart's motion for a directed verdict. Wal-Mart appealed to the U.S. Court of Appeals for the Eighth Circuit.*

IN THE LANGUAGE OF THE COURT
BEAM, Circuit J. [Judge]
*   *   *   *

*   *   * [T]he traditional rule *   *   * required a plaintiff in a slip and fall case to establish that the defendant store had either actual or constructive notice of the dangerous condition. The defendant store [was] deemed to have actual notice if it [was] shown that an employee created or was aware of the hazard. Constructive notice could be established by showing that the dangerous condition had existed for a sufficient length of time that the defendant should reasonably have known about it.
*   *   *   *

*   *   * [R]etail store operations have evolved since the traditional liability rules were established. In modern self-service stores, customers are invited to traverse the same aisles used by the clerks to replenish stock, they are invited to retrieve merchandise from displays for inspection, and to place it back in the display if the item is not selected for purchase. Further, a customer is enticed to look at the displays, thus reducing the chance that the customer will be watchful of hazards on the floor. *   *   * [C]ustomers may take merchandise into their hands and may then lay articles that no longer interest them down in the aisle. *   *   * The risk of items creating dangerous conditions on the floor, previously created by employees, is now created by other customers as a result of the store's decision to employ the self-service mode of operation. *   *   * *Thus, in slip and fall cases in self-service stores, the inquiry of whether the danger existed long enough that the store should have reasonably known of it (constructive notice) is made in light of the fact that the store has notice that certain dangers arising through customer involvement are likely to occur, and the store has a duty to anticipate them.* [Emphasis added.]
*   *   *   *

Wal-Mart *   *   * claims that Martin *   *   * failed to establish that Wal-Mart had actual or constructive notice of the pellets in the action aisle. We disagree. We find there is substantial evidence of constructive notice in the record. Martin slipped on shotgun shell pellets on the floor which were next to a large display of shotgun shells immediately abutting the sporting goods department. The chance that merchandise will wind up on the floor (or merchandise will be spilled on the floor) in the department in which that merchandise is sold or displayed is exactly the type of foreseeable risk [that is part of the self-service exception to the traditional rule]. Under [this exception], Wal-Mart has notice that merchandise is likely to find its way to the floor and create a dangerous condition, and *it must exercise due care to discover this hazard and warn customers or protect them from the danger.* *   *   * Even assuming

---

a. This URL will take you to a Web site maintained by FindLaw, which is now a part of West Group. When you access the site, enter "Wal-Mart" in the "Party Name Search" box and then click on "Search." Scroll down the list on the page that opens and select the link to "Harold Martin v. Wal-Mart Stores."

CONTINUED ▶

CASE 12.3 | Continued that the hazard was created by a customer, a jury could easily find, given that it had notice that merchandise is often mishandled or mislaid by customers in a manner that can create dangerous conditions, that, had Wal-Mart exercised due care under the circumstances, it would have discovered the shotgun pellets on the floor. [Emphasis added.]

DECISION AND REMEDY *The U.S. Court of Appeals for the Eighth Circuit affirmed the judgment of the lower court. There was sufficient evidence for a jury to find that Wal-Mart had constructive notice of the pellets on the floor in the main aisle.*

WHAT IF THE FACTS WERE DIFFERENT? *Suppose that Harold Martin had been in the store not to shop but only to use the restroom. In this situation, is it likely that Wal-Mart would have been liable for his injury?*

DUTY OF PROFESSIONALS If an individual has knowledge, skill, or intelligence superior to that of an ordinary person, the individual's conduct must be consistent with that status. Professionals—including physicians, dentists, architects, engineers, accountants, and lawyers, among others—are required to have a standard minimum level of special knowledge and ability. Therefore, in determining what constitutes reasonable care in the case of professionals, the court takes their training and expertise into account. In other words, an accountant cannot defend against a lawsuit for negligence by stating, "But I was not familiar with that general principle of accounting."

If a professional violates his or her duty of care toward a client, the client may bring a **malpractice** suit against the professional. For example, a patient might sue a physician for *medical malpractice*. A client might sue an attorney for *legal malpractice*.

NO DUTY TO RESCUE Although the law requires individuals to act reasonably and responsibly in their relations with one another, if a person fails to come to the aid of a stranger in peril, that person will not be considered negligent under tort law. For example, assume that you are walking down a city street and see a pedestrian about to step directly in front of an oncoming bus. You realize that the person has not seen the bus and is unaware of the danger. Do you have a legal duty to warn that individual? No. Although most people would probably concede that in this situation, the observer has an *ethical* duty to warn the other, tort law does not impose a general duty to rescue others in peril. Duties may be imposed in regard to certain types of peril, however. For example, most states require a motorist involved in an automobile accident to stop and render aid. Failure to do so is both a tort and a crime.

THE INJURY REQUIREMENT AND DAMAGES

To recover damages (receive compensation), the plaintiff in a tort lawsuit must prove that she or he suffered a *legally recognizable* injury. In other words, the plaintiff must have suffered some loss, harm, wrong, or invasion of a protected interest. This is true in lawsuits for intentional torts as well as lawsuits for negligence. Essentially, the purpose of tort law is to compensate for legally recognized harms and injuries resulting from wrongful acts. If no harm or injury results from a given negligent action, there is nothing to compensate—and no tort exists.

For example, if you carelessly bump into a passerby, who stumbles and falls as a result, you may be liable in tort if the passerby is injured in the fall. If the person is unharmed, however, there normally can be no suit for damages because no injury was suffered. Although the passerby might be angry and suffer emotional distress, few courts recognize negligently inflicted emotional distress as a tort unless it results in some physical disturbance or dysfunction.

COMPENSATORY DAMAGES ARE THE NORM As already mentioned, the purpose of tort law is not to punish people for tortious acts but to compensate the injured parties for damages suffered. **Compensatory damages** are intended to compensate, or reimburse, a plaintiff for actual losses—to make the plaintiff whole. Compensatory damages compensate the plaintiff for property damage and physical injury, which may include medical expenses, lost wages and benefits, pain and suffering, and sometimes even emotional distress.

PUNITIVE DAMAGES ARE RARE Occasionally, however, punitive damages are also awarded in tort lawsuits. **Punitive damages,** or *exemplary damages,* are intended to punish the wrongdoer and deter others from similar wrongdoing. Punitive damages are rarely awarded in lawsuits for ordinary negligence and usually are given only in cases involving intentional torts. They may be awarded, however, in suits involving *gross negligence,* which can be defined as an intentional failure to perform a manifest duty in reckless disregard of the consequences of such a failure for the life or property of another. The amount of punitive damages awarded must be reasonable, however. The United States Supreme Court has held that punitive damages that exceed reasonable bounds may violate due process requirements (discussed in Chapter 5).[8]

CAUSATION

Another element necessary to a tort is *causation.* If a person breaches a duty of care and someone suffers injury, the wrongful activity must have caused the harm for a tort to have been committed.

CAUSATION IN FACT AND PROXIMATE CAUSE In deciding whether the requirement of causation is met, the court must address two questions:

1. *Is there causation in fact?* Did the injury occur because of the defendant's act, or would it have occurred anyway? If an injury would not have occurred without the defendant's act, then there is causation in fact. **Causation in fact** can usually be determined by use of the *but for* test: "but for" the wrongful act, the injury would not have occurred.
2. *Was the act the proximate cause of the injury?* In the-

ory, causation in fact is limitless. One could claim, for example, that "but for" the creation of the world, a particular injury would not have occurred. Thus, as a practical matter, the law has to establish limits, and it does so through the concept of proximate cause. **Proximate cause,** or *legal cause,* exists when the connection between an act and an injury is strong enough to justify imposing liability. Consider an example. Ackerman carelessly leaves a campfire burning. The fire not only burns down the forest but also sets off an explosion in a nearby chemical plant that spills chemicals into a river, killing all the fish for a hundred miles downstream and ruining the economy of a tourist resort. Should Ackerman be liable to the resort owners? To the tourists whose vacations were ruined? These are questions of proximate cause that a court must decide.

Both questions must be answered in the affirmative for liability in tort to arise. If a defendant's action constitutes causation in fact but a court decides that the action is not the proximate cause of the plaintiff's injury, the causation requirement has not been met—and the defendant normally will not be liable to the plaintiff.

FORESEEABILITY Questions of proximate cause are linked to the concept of foreseeability because it would be unfair to impose liability on a defendant unless the defendant's actions created a foreseeable risk of injury. Probably the most cited case on the concept of foreseeability as a requirement for proximate cause—and as a measure of the extent of the duty of care generally—is the *Palsgraf* case. The question before the court was as follows: Does the defendant's duty of care extend only to those who may be injured as a result of a foreseeable risk, or does it extend also to persons whose injuries could not reasonably be foreseen?

---

8. See *State Farm Mutual Automobile Insurance Co. v. Campbell,* 538 U.S. 408, 123 S.Ct. 1513, 155 L.Ed.2d 585 (2003).

CASE 12.4 | **Palsgraf v. Long Island Railroad Co.**

Court of Appeals
of New York, 1928.
248 N.Y. 339,
162 N.E. 99.

BACKGROUND AND FACTS *The plaintiff, Helen Palsgraf, was waiting for a train on a station platform. A man carrying a package was rushing to catch a train that was moving away from a platform across the tracks from Palsgraf. As the man attempted to jump aboard the moving train, he seemed unsteady and about to fall. A railroad guard on the car reached forward to grab him, and another guard on the platform pushed him from behind to help him board the train. In the process, the man's package, which (unknown to the railroad guards) contained fireworks, fell on the railroad tracks and exploded. There was nothing about the package to indicate its contents. The repercussions of the explosion caused scales at the other end of the train platform to fall on Palsgraf, causing injuries for which she sued the railroad company. At the trial, the jury found that the railroad guards had been*

CONTINUED

negligent in their conduct. The railroad company appealed. The appellate court affirmed the trial court's judgment, and the railroad company appealed to New York's highest state court.

IN THE LANGUAGE OF THE COURT

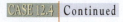

CARDOZO, C.J. [Chief Justice]

* * * *

The conduct of the defendant's guard, if a wrong in its relation to the holder of the package, was not a wrong in its relation to the plaintiff, standing far away. Relatively to her it was not negligence at all. *　*　*

* * * *

*　*　* What the plaintiff must show is "a wrong" to herself; i.e., a violation of her own right, and not merely a wrong to someone else[.] *　*　* *The risk reasonably to be perceived defines the duty to be obeyed[.]* *　*　* Here, by concession, there was nothing in the situation to suggest to the most cautious mind that the parcel wrapped in newspaper would spread wreckage through the station. If the guard had thrown it down knowingly and willfully, he would not have threatened the plaintiff's safety, so far as appearances could warn him. His conduct would not have involved, even then, an unreasonable probability of invasion of her bodily security. Liability can be no greater where the act is inadvertent. [Emphasis added.]

*　*　* One who seeks redress at law does not make out a cause of action by showing without more that there has been damage to his person. If the harm was not willful, he must show that the act as to him had possibilities of danger so many and apparent as to entitle him to be protected against the doing of it though the harm was unintended. *　*　* The victim does not sue *　*　* to vindicate an interest invaded in the person of another. *　*　* He sues for breach of a duty owing to himself.

*　*　* [To rule otherwise] would entail liability for any and all consequences, however novel or extraordinary.

DECISION AND REMEDY *Palsgraf's complaint was dismissed. The railroad had not been negligent toward her because injury to her was not foreseeable. Had the owner of the fireworks been harmed, and had he filed suit, there could well have been a different result.*

INTERNATIONAL CONSIDERATIONS **Differing Standards of Proximate Cause** *The concept of proximate cause is common among nations around the globe, but its application differs from country to country. French law uses the phrase "adequate cause." An event breaks the chain of adequate cause if the event is both unforeseeable and irresistible. England has a "nearest cause" rule that attributes liability based on which event was nearest in time and space. Mexico bases proximate cause on the foreseeability of the harm but does not require that an event be reasonably foreseeable.*

IMPACT OF THIS CASE ON TODAY'S LAW

The *Palsgraf* case established foreseeability as the test for proximate cause. Today, the courts continue to apply this test in determining proximate cause—and thus tort liability for injuries. Generally, if the victim of a harm or the consequences of a harm done are unforeseeable, there is no proximate cause.

SECTION 6 | Defenses to Negligence

The basic defenses to liability in negligence cases are (1) assumption of risk, (2) superseding cause, and (3) contributory and comparative negligence.

ASSUMPTION OF RISK

A plaintiff who voluntarily enters into a risky situation, knowing the risk involved, will not be allowed to recover. This is the defense of **assumption of risk.** For example, a driver entering an automobile race knows there is a risk of being injured or killed in a crash. The driver has assumed the risk of injury. The requirements of this defense are (1) knowledge of the risk and (2) voluntary assumption of the risk.

The risk can be assumed by express agreement, or the assumption of risk can be implied by the plaintiff's knowledge of the risk and subsequent conduct. Of course, the plaintiff does not assume a risk different from or greater than the risk normally carried by the activity. In our example, the race driver assumes the risk of being injured in the race but not the risk that the banking in the curves of the racetrack will give way during the race because of a construction defect.

Risks are not deemed to be assumed in situations involving emergencies. Neither are they assumed when a statute protects a class of people from harm and a member of the class is injured by the harm. For example, courts have generally held that an employee cannot assume the risk of an employer's violation of safety statutes passed for the benefit of employees.

SUPERSEDING CAUSE

An unforeseeable intervening event may break the causal connection between a wrongful act and an injury to another. If so, the intervening event acts as a *superseding cause*—that is, it relieves a defendant of liability for injuries caused by the intervening event. For example, suppose that Derrick, while riding his bicycle, negligently hits Julie, who is walking on the sidewalk. As a result of the impact, Julie falls and fractures her hip. While she is waiting for help to arrive, a small aircraft crashes nearby and explodes, and some of the fiery debris hits her, causing her to sustain severe burns. Derrick will be liable for the damages caused by Julie's fractured hip, but normally he will not be liable for the wounds caused by the plane crash—because the risk of a plane crashing nearby and injuring Julie was not foreseeable.

CONTRIBUTORY AND COMPARATIVE NEGLIGENCE

All individuals are expected to exercise a reasonable degree of care in looking out for themselves. Under the common law doctrine of **contributory negligence,** a plaintiff who was also negligent (failed to exercise a reasonable degree of care) could not recover anything from the defendant. Under this rule, no matter how insignificant the plaintiff's negligence was relative to the defendant's negligence, the plaintiff would be pre-

cluded from recovering any damages. Today, only a few jurisdictions still hold to this doctrine. In the majority of states, the doctrine of contributory negligence has been replaced by a **comparative negligence** standard.

The comparative negligence standard enables both the plaintiff's and the defendant's negligence to be computed and the liability for damages distributed accordingly. Some jurisdictions have adopted a "pure" form of comparative negligence that allows the plaintiff to recover damages even if her or his fault is greater than that of the defendant. Many states' comparative negligence statutes, however, contain a "50 percent" rule, under which the plaintiff recovers nothing if she or he was more than 50 percent at fault. Under this rule, a plaintiff who is 35 percent at fault could recover 65 percent of his or her damages, but a plaintiff who is 65 percent (over 50 percent) at fault could recover nothing.

SECTION 7 | Special Negligence Doctrines and Statutes

A number of special doctrines and statutes relating to negligence are also important. We examine a few of them here.

RES IPSA LOQUITUR

Generally, in lawsuits involving negligence, the plaintiff has the burden of proving that the defendant was negligent. In certain situations, however, the courts may presume that negligence has occurred, in which case the burden of proof rests on the defendant—that is, the defendant must prove that he or she was *not* negligent. The presumption of the defendant's negligence is known as the doctrine of *res ipsa loquitur,*[9] which translates as "the facts speak for themselves."

This doctrine is applied only when the event creating the damage or injury is one that ordinarily does not occur in the absence of negligence. For example, if a person undergoes knee surgery and following the surgery has a severed nerve in the knee area, that person can sue the surgeon under a theory of *res ipsa loquitur*. In this case, the injury would not have occurred but for the surgeon's negligence.[10] For the doctrine of *res ipsa*

---

9. Pronounced *rihz ihp*-suh *low*-kwuh-duhr.

10. See *Edwards v. Boland*, 41 Mass.App.Ct. 375, 670 N.E.2d 404 (1996).

loquitur to apply, the event must have been within the defendant's power to control, and it must not have been due to any voluntary action or contribution on the part of the plaintiff.

NEGLIGENCE *PER SE*

Certain conduct, whether it consists of an action or a failure to act, may be treated as **negligence *per se*** ("in or of itself"). Negligence *per se* may occur if an individual violates a statute or an ordinance providing for a criminal penalty and that violation causes another to be injured. The injured person must prove (1) that the statute clearly sets out what standard of conduct is expected, when and where it is expected, and of whom it is expected; (2) that he or she is in the class intended to be protected by the statute; and (3) that the statute was designed to prevent the type of injury that he or she suffered. The standard of conduct required by the statute is the duty that the defendant owes to the plaintiff, and a violation of the statute is the breach of that duty.

For example, a statute may require a landowner to keep a building in safe condition and may also subject the landowner to a criminal penalty, such as a fine, if the building is not kept safe. The statute is meant to protect those who are rightfully in the building. Thus, if the owner, without a sufficient excuse, violates the statute and a tenant is thereby injured, a majority of courts will hold that the owner's unexcused violation of the statute conclusively establishes a breach of a duty of care—that is, that the owner's violation is negligence *per se*.

"DANGER INVITES RESCUE" DOCTRINE

Under the "danger invites rescue" doctrine, if a person commits an act that endangers another, the person committing the act will be liable not only for any injuries the other party suffers but also for any injuries suffered by a third person in an attempt to rescue the endangered party. For example, suppose that Ludlam, while driving down a street, fails to see a stop sign because he is trying to end a squabble between his two young children in the car's backseat. Salter, on the curb near the stop sign, realizes that Ludlam is about to hit a pedestrian walking across the street at the intersection. Salter runs into the street to push the pedestrian out of the way, and Ludlam's vehicle hits Salter instead. In this situation, Ludlam will be liable for Salter's injury, as well as for any injuries the other pedestrian sustained. Rescuers can injure themselves, or the persons rescued, or even bystanders, but the original wrongdoers will still be liable.

SPECIAL NEGLIGENCE STATUTES

A number of states have enacted statutes prescribing duties and responsibilities in certain circumstances. For example, most states now have what are called **Good Samaritan statutes.**[11] Under these statutes, persons whom others aid voluntarily cannot turn around and sue the "Good Samaritans" for negligence. These laws were passed largely to protect physicians and medical personnel who voluntarily render their services in emergency situations to those in need, such as individuals hurt in car accidents.

Many states have also passed **dram shop acts,** under which a tavern owner or bartender may be held liable for injuries caused by a person who became intoxicated while drinking at the bar or who was already intoxicated when served by the bartender. Some states have statutes that impose liability on *social hosts* (persons hosting parties) for injuries caused by guests who became intoxicated at the hosts' homes. Under these statutes, it is unnecessary to prove that the tavern owner, bartender, or social host was negligent. Sometimes, the definition of a "social host" is broadly fashioned. For example, in a New York case, the court held that the father of a minor who hosted a "bring-your-own-keg" party could be held liable for injuries caused by an intoxicated guest.[12]

SECTION 8 | Cyber Torts

Torts can also be committed in the online environment. Torts committed via the Internet are often called **cyber torts.** One of the tasks of the courts over the last ten years has been deciding how to apply traditional tort law to torts committed in cyberspace. Consider, for example, issues of proof. How can it be proved that an online defamatory remark was "published" (which requires that a third party see or

---

11. These laws derive their name from the Good Samaritan story in the Bible. In the story, a traveler who had been robbed and beaten lay along the roadside, ignored by those passing by. Eventually, a man from the region of Samaria (the "Good Samaritan") stopped to render assistance to the injured person.

12. *Rust v. Reyer*, 91 N.Y.2d 355, 693 N.E.2d 1074, 670 N.Y.S.2d 822 (1998).

hear it)? How can the identity of the person who made the remark be discovered? Can an Internet service provider (ISP) be forced to reveal the source of an anonymous comment? We explore some of these questions in this section, as well as some legal issues that have arisen with respect to bulk e-mail advertising.

DEFAMATION ONLINE

Recall from the discussion of defamation earlier in this chapter that one who repeats or otherwise republishes a defamatory statement is subject to liability as if he or she had originally published it. Thus, publishers generally can be held liable for defamatory contents in the books and periodicals that they publish. Now consider online message forums. These forums allow anyone—customers, employees, or crackpots—to complain about a business firm's personnel, policies, practices, or products. Regardless of whether the complaint is justified and whether it is true, it might have an impact on the firm's business. One of the early questions in the online legal arena was whether the providers of such forums could be held liable, as publishers, for defamatory statements made in those forums.

LIABILITY OF INTERNET SERVICE PROVIDERS

Newspapers, magazines, and television and radio stations may be held liable for defamatory remarks that they disseminate, even if those remarks are prepared or created by others. Prior to the passage of the Communications Decency Act (CDA) of 1996, the courts grappled on several occasions with the question of whether ISPs should be regarded as publishers and thus held liable for defamatory messages made by users of their services. The CDA resolved the issue by stating that "[n]o provider or user of an interactive computer service shall be treated as the publisher or speaker of any information provided by another information content provider."[13]

In a leading case on this issue, decided the year after the CDA was enacted, America Online, Inc. (AOL, now a part of Time Warner, Inc.), was not held liable even though it failed to promptly remove defamatory messages of which it had been made aware. In upholding a district court's ruling in AOL's favor, a federal appellate court stated that the CDA "plainly immunizes computer service providers like AOL from liability for information that originates with third parties." The court explained that the purpose of the statute is "to maintain the robust nature of Internet communication and, accordingly, to keep government interference in the medium to a minimum."[14] The courts have reached similar conclusions in subsequent cases.[15]

Is an Internet dating service liable for a false profile of an actual person—in this case, an actress who has appeared in *Star Trek: Deep Space Nine* and other television shows and movies—posted by an identity thief who provided the content? That was the question in the following case.

---

13. 47 U.S.C. Section 230.
14. *Zeran v. America Online, Inc.*, 129 F.3d 327 (4th Cir. 1997); *cert.* denied, 524 U.S. 937, 118 S.Ct. 2341, 141 L.Ed.2d 712 (1998).
15. See, for example, *Noah v. AOL Time Warner, Inc.*, 261 F.Supp.2d 532 (E.D.Va. 2003).

CASE 12.5 — Carafano v. Metrosplash.com, Inc.

United States Court of Appeals, Ninth Circuit, 2003. 339 F.3d 1119.

BACKGROUND AND FACTS *Matchmaker.com is a commercial Internet dating service. For a fee, members post anonymous profiles and view profiles of other members, contacting them via e-mail sent through Matchmaker. In October 1999, someone posted a profile of Christianne Carafano without her knowledge or consent. Under the stage name Chase Masterson, Carafano has appeared in films and television shows, including* Star Trek: Deep Space Nine *and* General Hospital. *Contacting the profile's e-mail address produced an automatic reply that included Carafano's home address and phone number. She began to receive messages responding to the profile, some of which were threatening. Alarmed, she contacted the police. She felt unsafe in her home and stayed away for several months. Meanwhile, Siouxzan Perry, who handled Carafano's e-mail, learned of the false profile and demanded that Matchmaker remove it immediately. Carafano filed a suit in a California state court against Matchmaker and its owner, Metrosplash.com, Inc., alleging invasion of privacy, appropriation, defamation, and other torts. The case was moved to a federal district court, which issued a summary judgment in the defendants' favor. Carafano appealed to the U.S. Court of Appeals for the Ninth Circuit.*

CONTINUED ▶

IN THE LANGUAGE OF THE COURT

THOMAS, Circuit Judge.

This is a case involving a cruel and sadistic identity theft. In this appeal, we consider to what extent a computer matchmaking service may be legally responsible for false content in a dating profile provided by someone posing as another person. * * *
* * * *

The dispositive [deciding] question in this appeal is whether Carafano's claims are barred by 47 U.S.C. Section 230(c)(1), which states that "[n]o provider or user of an interactive computer service shall be treated as the publisher or speaker of any information provided by another information content provider." Through this provision, Congress granted most Internet services immunity from liability for publishing false or defamatory material so long as the information was provided by another party. *As a result, Internet publishers are treated differently from corresponding publishers in print, television, and radio.* [Emphasis added.]

Congress enacted this provision as part of the Communications Decency Act of 1996 for two basic policy reasons: to promote the free exchange of information and ideas over the Internet and to encourage voluntary monitoring for offensive or obscene material. Congress incorporated these ideas into the text of Section 230 itself, expressly noting that "interactive computer services have flourished, to the benefit of all Americans, with a minimum of government regulation," and that "[i]ncreasingly Americans are relying on interactive media for a variety of political, educational, cultural, and entertainment services." Congress declared it the "policy of the United States" to "promote the continued development of the Internet and other interactive computer services," "to preserve the vibrant and competitive free market that presently exists for the Internet and other interactive computer services," and to "remove disincentives for the development and utilization of blocking and filtering technologies."

In light of these concerns, reviewing courts have treated Section 230(c) immunity as quite robust, adopting a relatively expansive definition of "interactive computer service" and a relatively restrictive definition of "information content provider." *Under the statutory scheme, an "interactive computer service" qualifies for immunity so long as it does not also function as an "information content provider" for the portion of the statement or publication at issue.* [Emphasis added.]

* * * [T]he consensus developing across other [U.S.] courts of appeals [is] that Section 230(c) provides broad immunity for publishing content provided primarily by third parties. * * * Congress made a policy choice * * * not to deter harmful online speech through the separate route of imposing tort liability on companies that serve as intermediaries for other parties' potentially injurious messages. Congress's purpose in providing the Section 230 immunity was thus evident. Interactive computer services have millions of users. The amount of information communicated via interactive computer services is therefore staggering. The specter of tort liability in an area of such prolific speech would have an obvious chilling effect. It would be impossible for service providers to screen each of their millions of postings for possible problems. Faced with potential liability for each message republished by their services, interactive computer service providers might choose to severely restrict the number and type of messages posted. Congress considered the weight of the speech interests implicated and chose to immunize service providers to avoid any such restrictive effect. Under Section 230(c), therefore, so long as a third party willingly provides the essential published content, the interactive service provider receives full immunity regardless of the specific editing or selection process.
* * * *

Thus, despite the serious and utterly deplorable consequences that occurred in this case, we conclude that Congress intended that service providers such as Matchmaker be afforded immunity from suit.

DECISION AND REMEDY *The U.S. Court of Appeals for the Ninth Circuit affirmed the lower court's decision. The appellate court held that under the Communications Decency Act, Matchmaker was not responsible for the "underlying misinformation" that characterized the false profile of Carafano.*

PIERCING THE VEIL OF ANONYMITY A threshold barrier to anyone who seeks to bring an action for online defamation is discovering the identity of the person who posted the defamatory message online. ISPs can disclose personal information about their customers only when ordered to do so by a court. Consequently, businesses and individuals are increasingly resorting to lawsuits against "John Does" (John Doe is a fictitious name that is used when the name of the particular person is not known). Then, using the authority of the courts, they can obtain from the ISPs the identities of the persons responsible for the messages.

In one case, for example, Eric Hvide, a former chief executive of a company called Hvide Marine, sued a number of John Does who had posted allegedly defamatory statements about his company on various online message boards. Hvide, who eventually lost his job, sued the John Does for libel in a Florida court. The court ruled that the ISPs, Yahoo and AOL, had to reveal the identities of the defendant Does.[16]

In some other cases, however, the rights of plaintiffs in such situations have been balanced against the defendants' rights to free speech. For example, a New Jersey court refused to compel Yahoo to disclose the identity of a person who had posted an allegedly defamatory message on Yahoo's message board. The court refused to compel disclosure because, in its view, more than a bare allegation of defamation is required to outweigh an individual's "competing right of anonymity in the exercise of [the] right of free speech."[17]

SPAM

Bulk, unsolicited e-mail ("junk" e-mail) sent to all of the users on a particular e-mailing list is often called **spam.**[18] Typical spam consists of a product ad sent to all of the users on an e-mailing list or all of the members of a newsgroup.

SPAM AS A FORM OF TRESPASS TO PERSONAL PROPERTY Spam can waste user time and network bandwidth (the amount of data that can be transmitted within a certain time). It also imposes a burden on an ISP's equipment as well as on an e-mail recipient's computer system. As a result, some courts have held that spam is a trespass to personal property.

In one case, for example, Cyber Promotions, Inc., sent bulk e-mail to subscribers of CompuServe, Inc., an ISP at that time. CompuServe subscribers complained to the service about the ads, and many canceled their subscriptions. Handling the ads also placed a tremendous burden on CompuServe's equipment. CompuServe told Cyber Promotions to stop using CompuServe's equipment to process and store the ads—in effect, to stop sending the ads to CompuServe subscribers. Ignoring the demand, Cyber Promotions stepped up the volume of its ads. After CompuServe attempted unsuccessfully to block the flow with screening software, it filed a suit against Cyber Promotions in a federal district court, seeking an injunction on the ground that the ads constituted trespass to personal property. The court agreed and ordered Cyber Promotions to stop sending its ads to e-mail addresses maintained by CompuServe.[19]

STATUTORY REGULATION OF SPAM Because of the problems associated with spam, thirty-six states have enacted laws that prohibit or regulate its use. A few states, such as Washington, prohibit unsolicited e-mail that is promoting goods, services, or real estate for sale or lease. In some other states, including Minnesota, an unsolicited e-mail ad must state in its subject line that it is an ad ("ADV"). Many state laws regulating spam require the senders of e-mail ads to instruct the recipients on how they can "opt out" of further e-mail ads from the same source.

The most stringent state law is California's anti-spam law, which went into effect on January 1, 2004. That law follows the "opt-in" model favored by consumer groups and antispam advocates. In other words, the law prohibits any person or business from sending e-mail ads to or from any e-mail address in California unless the recipient has expressly agreed to receive e-mails from the sender. An exemption is made for e-mail sent to consumers with whom the advertiser has a "preexisting or current business relationship."

THE FEDERAL CAN-SPAM ACT In 2003, Congress enacted the Controlling the Assault of Non-Solicited Pornography and Marketing (CAN-SPAM) Act, which took effect on January 1, 2004. The legislation

---

16. *Does v. Hvide,* 770 So.2d 1237 (Fla.App.3d 2000).

17. *Dendrite International, Inc. v. Doe No. 3,* 342 N.J.Super. 134, 775 A.2d 756 (2001).

18. The term *spam* is said to come from a Monty Python song with the lyrics, "Spam spam spam spam, spam spam spam spam, lovely spam, wonderful spam." Like these lyrics, spam online is often considered to be a repetition of worthless text.

19. *CompuServe, Inc. v. Cyber Promotions, Inc.,* 962 F.Supp. 1015 (S.D.Ohio 1997).

applies to any "commercial electronic mail messages" that are sent to promote a commercial product or service. Significantly, the statute preempts state antispam laws except for those provisions in state laws that prohibit false and deceptive e-mailing practices.

—*Requirements.* Generally, the act permits the use of unsolicited commercial e-mail but prohibits certain types of spamming activities, including the use of a false return address and the use of false, misleading, or deceptive information when sending e-mail. The statute also prohibits the use of "dictionary attacks"—sending messages to randomly generated e-mail addresses—and the "harvesting" of e-mail addresses from Web sites through the use of specialized software. Additionally, the law requires senders of commercial e-mail to do the following:

1. Include a return address on the e-mail.
2. Include a clear notification that the message is an ad and provide a valid physical postal address.
3. Provide a mechanism that allows recipients to "opt out" of further e-mail ads from the same source.
4. Take action on a recipient's "opt-out" request within ten days.
5. Label any sexually oriented materials as such.

—*Effect of the CAN-SPAM Act.* Because the federal CAN-SPAM Act preempts state laws, except for certain provisions relating to deceptive e-mailing

practices, stricter provisions in state laws are no longer effective. Thus, it is apparent that the federal act reflects Congress's intent to protect the e-mail marketing industry against state laws, such as California's, that would make e-mail advertising extremely difficult. The federal government also sought to eliminate advertising by peddlers of financial scams and pornography.

Yet critics point out that the new law has done little to reduce the amount of unsolicited e-mail flowing through cyberspace. For one thing, many of the Internet ads being sent today already meet the requirements of the CAN-SPAM Act. For another, because the federal act uses an "opt-out" approach, the burden is placed on e-mail recipients to prevent the delivery of further ads from the same source. Additionally, the act cannot regulate spam sent from foreign servers. A survey conducted shortly after the act went into effect showed almost no noticeable reduction in the amount of spam received through e-mail.[20] Indeed, the volume of spam has actually increased since the CAN-SPAM Act was enacted.

---

20. Pew Internet and American Life Project survey conducted from February 3 to March 1, 2004.

REVIEWING TORTS AND CYBER TORTS

Two sisters, Darla and Irene, are partners in an import business located in a small town in Rhode Island. Irene is married to a well-known real estate developer and is campaigning to be the mayor of their town. Darla is in her midthirties and has never been married. Both sisters travel to other countries to purchase the goods that they sell at their retail store. Irene buys Indonesian goods, and Darla buys goods from Africa. After a tsunami (tidal wave) destroys many of the cities in Indonesia to which Irene usually travels, she phones one of her contacts there and asks him to procure some items and ship them to her. He informs her that it will be impossible to buy these items now because the townspeople are being evacuated due to a water shortage. Irene is angry and tells the man that if he cannot purchase the goods, he should just take them without paying for them after the town has been evacuated. Darla overhears her sister's instructions and is outraged. They have a falling-out, and Darla decides that she no longer wishes to be in business with her sister. Using the information presented in the chapter, answer the following questions.

1. Suppose that Darla tells several of her friends about Irene's instructing the man to take goods without paying for them after the tsunami disaster. Under which intentional tort theory discussed in this chapter might Irene attempt to sue Darla? Would Irene's suit be successful? Why or why not?

REVIEWING TORTS AND CYBER TORTS—Continued

2. Now suppose that Irene wins the election and becomes the city's mayor. Darla then writes a letter to the editor of the local newspaper disclosing Irene's misconduct. What intentional tort might Irene accuse Darla of committing? What defenses could Darla assert?

3. If Irene accepts goods shipped from Indonesia that were wrongfully obtained, has she committed an intentional tort against property? Explain.

4. One day, a customer shopping in Irene and Darla's store enters, without permission, a private room in the back of the store, looking for a restroom. On the door to the room is a large sign stating "Private—Do Not Enter." While in the room, the customer trips over a box on the floor and falls, seriously injuring her hip. A few months later, the customer sues the store, seeking to recover damages. In this situation, will the store be held liable for the customer's injuries? Why or why not?

TERMS AND CONCEPTS TO REVIEW

actionable 288	disparagement of property 297	reasonable person standard 298
actual malice 289	dram shop act 304	*res ipsa loquitur* 303
appropriation 290	duty of care 298	slander 288
assault 287	fraudulent misrepresentation 290	slander of quality 297
assumption of risk 302		slander of title 297
battery 287	Good Samaritan statute 304	spam 307
business invitee 298	intentional tort 287	tort 286
business tort 286	libel 288	tortfeasor 287
causation in fact 301	malpractice 300	trade libel 297
comparative negligence 303	negligence 297	trespass to land 294
compensatory damages 300	negligence *per se* 304	trespass to personal property 295
contributory negligence 303	privilege 289	
conversion 296	proximate cause 301	
cyber tort 304	public figure 289	
defamation 288	punitive damages 301	

QUESTIONS AND CASE PROBLEMS

12–1. Richard is an employee of the Dun Construction Corp. While delivering materials to a construction site, he carelessly backs Dun's truck into a passenger vehicle driven by Green. This is Richard's second accident in six months. When the company owner, Dun, learns of this latest accident, a heated discussion ensues, and Dun fires Richard. Dun is so angry that he immediately writes a letter to the union of which Richard is a member and to all other construction companies in the community, stating that Richard is the "worst driver in the city" and that "anyone who hires him is asking for legal liability." Richard files a suit against Dun, alleging libel on the basis of the statements made in the letters. Discuss the results.

12–2. 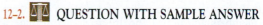 QUESTION WITH SAMPLE ANSWER

Lothar owns a bakery. He has been trying to obtain a long-term contract with the owner of Martha's Tea Salons for some time. Lothar starts a local advertising campaign on radio and television and in the newspaper. This advertising campaign is so persuasive that Martha decides to break the contract she has had with Harley's Bakery so that she can patronize Lothar's bakery. Is Lothar liable to Harley's Bakery for the tort of wrongful interference with a contractual relationship? Is Martha liable for this tort?

For a sample answer to this question, go to Appendix I at the end of this text.

12–3. Gerrit is a former employee of ABC Auto Repair Co. He enters ABC's repair shop, claiming that the company owes him $800 in back wages. Gerrit argues with ABC's general manager, Steward, and Steward orders him off the property. Gerrit refuses to leave, and Steward tells two mechanics to throw him off the property. Gerrit runs to his truck, but on the way, he grabs some tools valued at $800; then he drives away. Gerrit refuses to return the tools.

(a) Discuss whether Gerrit has committed any torts.
(b) If the mechanics had thrown Gerrit off the property, would ABC be guilty of assault and battery? Explain.

12–4. In which of the following situations will the acting party be liable for the tort of negligence? Explain fully.

(a) Shannon goes to the golf course on Sunday morning, eager to try out a new set of golf clubs she has just purchased. As she tees off on the first hole, the head of her club flies off and injures a nearby golfer.
(b) Shannon goes to the golf course on Sunday morning. While she is teeing off at the eleventh hole, her golf ball veers toward a roadway next to the golf course and shatters a car's windshield.
(c) Shannon's physician gives her some pain medication and tells her not to drive after she takes it, as the medication induces drowsiness. In spite of the doctor's warning, Shannon decides to drive to the store while on the medication. Owing to her lack of alertness, she fails to stop at a traffic light and crashes into another vehicle, causing a passenger in that vehicle to be injured.

12–5. Ruth carelessly parks her car on a steep hill, leaving the car in neutral and failing to engage the parking brake. The car rolls down the hill and knocks down an electric line. The sparks from the broken line ignite a grass fire. The fire spreads until it reaches a barn one mile away. The barn houses dynamite, and the burning barn explodes, causing part of the roof to fall on and injure Jim, a passing motorist. Which element of negligence is of the greatest concern here? What legal doctrine resolves this issue? Will Jim be able to recover damages from Ruth?

12–6. TRESPASS TO PROPERTY. America Online, Inc. (AOL), provides services to its customers, or members, including the transmission of e-mail to and from other members and across the Internet. To become a member, a person must agree not to use AOL's computers to send bulk, unsolicited, commercial e-mail (spam). AOL uses filters to block spam, but bulk e-mailers sometimes use other software to thwart the filters. National Health Care Discount, Inc. (NHCD), sells discount optical and dental service plans. To generate leads for NHCD's products, sales representatives, who included AOL members, sent more than 300 million pieces of spam through AOL's computer system. Each item cost AOL an estimated $0.00078 in equipment expenses. Some of the spam used false headers and other methods to hide the source. After receiving more than 150,000 complaints from its members, AOL asked NHCD to stop. When the spam continued, AOL filed a suit in a federal district court against NHCD, alleging in part *trespass to chattels*—an unlawful interference with another's rights to possess personal property. AOL asked the court for a summary judgment on this claim. Did the spamming constitute trespass to chattels? Explain. [*America Online, Inc. v. National Health Care Discount, Inc.*, 121 F.Supp.2d 1255 (N.D.Iowa 2000)]

12–7. ⚖ CASE PROBLEM WITH SAMPLE ANSWER

In 1994, Gary Kremen registered the domain name "sex.com" with Network Solutions, Inc., to the name of Kremen's business, Online Classifieds. Later, Stephen Cohen sent Network Solutions a letter that he claimed to have received from Online Classifieds. It stated that "we have no objections to your use of the domain name sex.com and this letter shall serve as our authorization to the Internet registrar to transfer sex.com to your corporation." Without contacting Kremen, Network Solutions transferred the name to Cohen, who subsequently turned sex.com into a lucrative business. Kremen filed a suit in a federal district court against Cohen and others, seeking the name and Cohen's profits. The court ordered Cohen to return the name to Kremen and pay $65 million in damages. Cohen ignored the order and disappeared. Against whom else might Kremen attempt to obtain relief? Under which theory of intentional torts against property might Kremen be able to file an action? What is the likely result, and why? [*Kremen v. Cohen*, 337 F.3d 1024 (9th Cir. 2003)]

To view a sample answer for this case problem, go to this book's Web site at http://wleb.westbuslaw.com, select "Chapter 12," and click on "Case Problem with Sample Answer."

12–8. NEGLIGENCE. New Hampshire International Speedway, Inc., owned the New Hampshire International Speedway, a racetrack next to Route 106 in Loudon, New Hampshire. In August 1998, on the weekend before the Winston Cup race, Speedway opened part of its parking facility to recreational vehicles (RVs). Speedway voluntarily positioned its employee Frederick Neergaard at the entrance to the parking area as a security guard and to direct traffic. Leslie Wheeler, who was planning to attend the race, drove an RV south on Route 106 toward Speedway. Meanwhile, Dennis Carignan was also driving south on Route 106 on a motorcycle, on which Mary Carignan was a passenger. As Wheeler approached the parking area, he saw Neergaard signaling him to turn left, which he began to do. At the same time, Carignan attempted to pass the RV on its left side, and the two vehicles collided. Mary sustained an injury to her right knee, lacerations on her ankle, and a broken hip. She sued Speedway and others for negligence. Which element of negligence is at the center of this dispute? How is a court likely to rule in this case, and why? [*Carignan v. New Hampshire International Speedway, Inc.*, 858 A.2d 536 (N.H. 2004)]

12-9. DEFAMATION. Lydia Hagberg went to her bank, California Federal Bank, FSB, to cash a check made out to her by Smith Barney (SB), an investment services firm. Nolene Showalter, a bank employee, suspected that the check was counterfeit. Showalter called SB and was told that the check was not valid. As she phoned the police, Gary Wood, a bank security officer, contacted SB again and was informed that its earlier statement was "erroneous" and that the check was valid. Meanwhile, a police officer arrived, drew Hagberg away from the teller's window, spread her legs, patted her down, and handcuffed her. The officer searched her purse, asked her whether she had any weapons or stolen property and whether she was driving a stolen vehicle, and arrested her. Hagberg filed a suit in a California state court against the bank and others, alleging, among other things, slander. Should the absolute privilege for communications made in judicial or other official proceedings apply to statements made when a citizen contacts the police to report suspected criminal activity? Why or why not? [*Hagberg v. California Federal Bank, FSB*, 32 Cal.4th 350, 81 P.3d 244, 7 Cal.Rptr.3d 803 (2004)]

12-10. A QUESTION OF ETHICS

Intel Corporation has an e-mail system for its employees. Ken Hamidi, a former Intel employee, sent a series of six e-mail messages to 35,000 Intel employees over a twenty-one-month period. In the messages, Hamidi criticized the company's labor practices and urged employees to leave the company. Intel sought a court order to stop the e-mail campaign, arguing that Hamidi's actions constituted a trespass to chattels (personal property) because the e-mail significantly interfered with productivity, thus causing economic damage. The state trial court granted Intel's motion for summary judgment and ordered Hamidi to stop sending messages. When the case reached the California Supreme Court, however, the court held that under California law, the tort of tres-

pass to chattels required some evidence of injury to the plaintiff's personal property. Because Hamidi's e-mail had neither damaged Intel's computer system nor impaired its functioning, the court ruled that Hamidi's actions did not amount to a trespass to chattels. The court did not reject the idea that trespass theory could apply to cyberspace. Rather, the court simply held that to succeed in a lawsuit for trespass to chattels, a plaintiff must demonstrate that some concrete harm resulted from the unwanted e-mail. [*Intel Corp. v. Hamidi*, 30 Cal.4th 1342, 71 P.3d 296, 1 Cal.Rptr.3d 32 (2003)]

(a) Should a court require that spam cause actual physical damage or impairment of the computer system (by overburdening it, for example) to establish that a spammer has committed trespass? Why or why not?

(b) The content of Hamidi's messages caused much discussion among employees and managers, diverting workers' time and attention and thus interfering with productivity. Why did the court not consider this disruption to be sufficient evidence of harm? Do you agree with the court?

12-11. VIDEO QUESTION

Go to this text's Web site at **http://wleb.westbuslaw.com** and select "Chapter 12." Click on "Video Questions" and view the video titled *Jaws.* Then answer the following questions.

(a) In the video, the mayor (Murray Hamilton) and a few other men try to persuade Chief Brody (Roy Scheider) not to close the town's beaches. If Brody keeps the beaches open and a swimmer is injured or killed because he failed to warn swimmers about the potential shark danger, has Brody committed the tort of negligence? Explain.

(b) Can Chief Brody be held liable for any injuries or deaths to swimmers under the doctrine of strict liability? Why or why not?

(c) Suppose that Chief Brody goes against the mayor's instructions and warns townspeople to stay off the beach. Nevertheless, several swimmers do not heed his warning and are injured as a result. What defense or defenses could Brody raise under these circumstances if he is sued for negligence?

LAW | on the Web

For updated links to resources available on the Web, as well as a variety of other materials, visit this text's Web site at **http://wleb.westbuslaw.com**.

You can find cases and articles on torts, including business torts, in the tort law section at the following Web site:

http://www.lawmoose.com/internetlawlib/110.htm

LEGAL RESEARCH EXERCISES ON THE WEB

Go to http://wleb.westbuslaw.com, the Web site that accompanies this text. Select "Chapter 12" and click on "Internet Exercises." There you will find the following Internet research exercises that you can perform to learn more about topics covered in this chapter.

Activity 12–1: LEGAL PERSPECTIVE
Negligence and the *Titanic*

Activity 12–2: MANAGEMENT PERSPECTIVE
The Duty to Warn

Activity 12–3: MANAGEMENT PERSPECTIVE
Legal and Illegal Uses of Spam

CHAPTER 13
Strict Liability and Product Liability

The intentional torts and torts of negligence discussed in Chapter 12 involve acts that depart from a reasonable standard of care and cause injuries. In this chapter, we look at another basis for liability in tort—*strict liability*. Under the tort doctrine of **strict liability,** liability for injury is imposed for reasons other than fault. We open this chapter with an examination of this doctrine. We then look at an area of tort law of particular importance to businesspersons—product liability. **Product liability** refers to the liability incurred by manufacturers and sellers of products when product defects cause injury or property damage to consumers, users, or **bystanders** (people in the vicinity of the product).

SECTION 1 | Strict Liability

The modern concept of strict liability traces its origins, in part, to the 1868 English case of *Rylands v. Fletcher*.[1] In the coal-mining area of Lancashire, England, the Rylands, who were mill owners, had constructed a reservoir on their land. Water from the reservoir broke through a filled-in shaft of an abandoned coal mine nearby and flooded the connecting passageways in an active coal mine owned by Fletcher. Fletcher sued the Rylands, and the court held that the defendants (the Rylands) were liable, even though the circumstances did not fit within existing tort liability theories.

In justifying its decision, the court compared the situation to the trespass of dangerous animals: "the true rule of law is, that the person who for his own purposes brings on his land and collects and keeps there anything likely to do mischief if it escapes, must keep it at his peril, and, if he does not do so, is *prima facie* [at first sight; on the face of it] answerable for all the damage which is the natural consequence of its escape."

The doctrine that emerged from *Rylands v. Fletcher* was liberally applied by British courts. Initially, few U.S. courts accepted this doctrine, presumably because the courts were worried about its effect on the expansion of American business. Today, however, the doctrine of strict liability is the norm rather than the exception.

---

1. 3 L.R.—E & I App. [Law Reports—English & Irish Appeal Cases] (H.L. [House of Lords] 1868).

ABNORMALLY DANGEROUS ACTIVITIES

The influence of *Rylands v. Fletcher* can be seen in the strict liability rule for abnormally dangerous activities, which is one application of the strict liability doctrine. Abnormally dangerous activities have three characteristics:

1. The activity involves potential harm, of a serious nature, to persons or property.
2. The activity involves a high degree of risk that cannot be completely guarded against by the exercise of reasonable care.
3. The activity is not commonly performed in the community or area.

Clearly, the primary basis of liability is the creation of an extraordinary risk. For example, even if blasting with dynamite is performed with all reasonable care, there is still a risk of injury. Balancing that risk against the potential for harm, it seems reasonable to ask the person engaged in the activity to pay for any injury it causes. Although there is no fault, there is still responsibility because of the dangerous nature of the undertaking.

OTHER APPLICATIONS OF STRICT LIABILITY

Persons who keep wild animals are strictly liable for any harm inflicted by the animals. The basis for applying strict liability is that wild animals, should they escape from confinement, pose a serious risk of harm to persons in the vicinity. An owner of domestic

Class Actions and Product Liability Lawsuits

Many product liability actions are class actions. A *class action* is a lawsuit in which a single person or a small group of people represents the interests of a larger group. Women allegedly injured by silicone breast implants, for example, sued the manufacturers as a class, as did many of those allegedly injured by asbestos and tobacco. The idea behind class actions is that they allow the average person to participate in complex litigation in an attempt to hold large corporations accountable for their allegedly wrongful acts and harmful products. Because an individual might not have the financial means to pursue the case alone, class actions allow them to pool resources with other injured parties and obtain competent legal counsel to represent them as a group.

Federal procedure has always had specific requirements for maintaining a class action. For example, the class must be so large that individual suits would be impracticable, and there must be legal or factual issues common to all members of the class. Until 2005, however, any state or federal court could hear and decide class actions.

THE CLASS ACTION FAIRNESS ACT OF 2005

The Class Action Fairness Act (CAFA) of 2005[a] significantly changes the way class-action cases are tried. The CAFA was primarily designed to shift large, interstate product liability and tort class-action suits from the state courts to the federal courts (although it affects all class-action claims). The act grants federal courts original, or trial, jurisdiction over any

_____

a. Pub. L. No. 109-2, 119 St. 4 (February 18, 2005).

civil action involving plaintiffs from multiple states in which the damages sought are $5 million or more.

Under the CAFA, a state court can retain jurisdiction over a case *only* if more than two-thirds of the plaintiffs and at least one principal defendant are citizens of the state and the injuries were incurred in the state. If the number of plaintiffs that live in a state is greater than one-third but less than two-thirds, the act gives federal judges the discretion to decide (based on specified considerations) whether the trial should be held in the state or federal court system. The CAFA applies only to actions filed after February 18, 2005.

Another provision in the act increases a defendant's ability to remove (transfer) a case that was filed in a state court to a federal court, even if the defendant also resides in the state where the action was filed. In cases involving multiple defendants, it also allows one defendant to remove the case to federal court without the consent of all defendants (as was previously required). In sum, the act encourages all class actions to be heard by federal court judges, who have historically been less sympathetic to consumers with product liability claims.

GOALS OF THE ACT

One of the main goals of the CAFA is to prevent plaintiffs' lawyers from shopping around for a state court that is predisposed to be sympathetic to their clients' cause. Corporate lawyers and business groups have been complaining for years that the plaintiffs' lawyers shop for local courts in which judges and juries have a reputation for awarding large verdicts in class-action suits. According to proponents, the new law

---

animals (such as dogs, cats, cows, or sheep) may be strictly liable for harm caused by those animals if the owner knew, or should have known, that the animals were dangerous or had a propensity to harm others.

A significant application of strict liability is in the area of product liability—liability of manufacturers and sellers for harmful or defective products. Liability here is a matter of social policy and is based on two factors: (1) the manufacturing company can better bear the cost of injury because it can spread the cost throughout society by increasing prices of goods and services, and (2) the manufacturing company is making a profit from its activities and therefore should bear the cost of injury as an operating expense.

SECTION 2 | Product Liability

Manufacturers, sellers, and lessors of goods can be held liable to consumers, users, and bystanders for physical harm or property damage that is caused by the goods. This is called product liability. Because one particular product may cause harm to a number of consumers, product liability actions are sometimes filed by a group of plaintiffs acting together. (For a discussion of a new law that affects claims filed by a large group of plaintiffs, see this chapter's *Emerging Trends* feature.) We look here at product liability based on negligence and based on misrepresentation.

will prevent such practices and help cut down on frivolous lawsuits, ultimately benefiting the business community. According to President George W. Bush, the act marks a critical step toward ending the "lawsuit culture in our country."[b] The CAFA represents only the first step in the growing trend toward tort reform. Next on the agenda is litigation involving asbestos (a product liability action) and medical malpractice claims.

POTENTIAL PROBLEMS WITH THE ACT

Some claim that the end result of the CAFA will be bad for consumers. According to critics, the practical effect of the CAFA will be that many cases will never make it to court. Litigating in federal court is a costly ordeal, and federal courts have more procedural rules than state courts. For this reason, many plaintiffs' attorneys might leave class-action practice, and injured persons with legitimate claims may not be able to obtain the representation they need. In addition, the federal court system is already overburdened. The number of civil cases filed in the federal courts during 2004 rose substantially, while budget cuts forced a 6 percent reduction in staffing.[c] Some commentators suggest that the federal courts are especially unfamiliar and uncomfortable with consumer and product liability claims. Overall, federal courts are expected to allow fewer large class-action suits to go forward. Also, cer-

tain aspects of the CAFA are likely to complicate its application. For example, how will a court determine whether one-third or two-thirds of the plaintiffs are from a particular state without substantial analysis of the class members?

IMPLICATIONS FOR THE BUSINESSPERSON

1. Product liability actions may still be tried in state courts. The CAFA only applies to class actions in which the plaintiffs seek damages of $5 million or more.

2. Businesspersons should be aware that even when a law appears to change only procedural rules, such as where and how a dispute is litigated, it may have consequences that affect substantive rights, including a party's ability to litigate.

FOR CRITICAL ANALYSIS

1. Do you agree that the CAFA will be effective in curtailing frivolous lawsuits? What other methods can you suggest to stop plaintiffs from filing suits that have no merit?

2. This act was seen as a major victory in the quest for tort reform. Should Congress continue to reform tort law by placing limits on asbestos and malpractice cases? Why or why not?

RELEVANT WEB SITES

To locate information on the Web concerning the issues discussed in this feature, go to this text's Web site at **http://wleb.westbuslaw.com**, select "Chapter 13," and click on "Emerging Trends."

---

b. Presidential press release titled "President Signs Class Action Fairness Act of 2005," February 18, 2005.
c. Administrative Office of the U.S. Courts press release, March 15, 2005.

PRODUCT LIABILITY BASED ON NEGLIGENCE

In Chapter 12, *negligence* was defined as the failure to exercise the degree of care that a reasonable, prudent person would have exercised under the circumstances. If a manufacturer fails to exercise "due care" to make a product safe, a person who is injured by the product may sue the manufacturer for negligence.

DUE CARE MUST BE EXERCISED Due care must be exercised in designing the product, in selecting the materials, in using the appropriate production process, in assembling and testing the product, and in placing

adequate warnings on the label informing the user of dangers of which an ordinary person might not be aware. The duty of care also extends to the inspection and testing of any purchased components that are used in the product sold by the manufacturer.

PRIVITY OF CONTRACT NOT REQUIRED A product liability action based on negligence does not require the injured plaintiff and the negligent defendant-manufacturer to be in **privity of contract.** In other words, the plaintiff and the defendant need not be directly involved in a contractual relationship. A manufacturer is liable for its failure to exercise due care to *any person* who sustains an injury proximately caused by a negligently made (defective) product. Relative to the long history of the common law, this exception to the privity requirement is a fairly recent development, dating to the early part of the twentieth century.[2]

---

2. A landmark case in this respect is *MacPherson v. Buick Motor Co.*, 217 N.Y. 382, 111 N.E. 1050 (1916).

To succeed in a product liability suit against a manufacturer based on negligence, does a plaintiff have to prove the specific defect that caused the plaintiff's injury? That was the question in the following case.

CASE 13.1   Jarvis v. Ford Motor Co.

United States
Court of Appeals,
Second Circuit, 2002.
283 F.3d 33.

COMPANY PROFILE *Henry Ford founded the Ford Motor Company (http://www. ford.com) in Dearborn, Michigan, in 1903 to design and make a mass-produced automobile. Five years later, Ford introduced the Model T, which was made affordable by the company's efficient use of assembly lines. By 1920, 60 percent of all of the vehicles on the road were made by Ford. Today, Ford is the world's largest maker of pickup trucks and the second-largest producer of cars. Ford brand names include Aston Martin, Jaguar, Lincoln, Mercury, and Volvo. Its most popular models are Ford Taurus cars and F-Series pickup trucks. Ford also makes the Aerostar minivan.*

BACKGROUND AND FACTS *In 1991, Kathleen Jarvis bought a new Aerostar. Six days later, she started the van in the driveway of her home in Woodstock, New York. After she turned on the ignition, the engine suddenly revved and the vehicle took off. Jarvis pumped the brake with both feet, but the van would not stop. She steered to avoid people walking in the road before the van entered a ditch and turned over. As a result of the accident, Jarvis suffered a head injury and could not return to her job. She filed a suit in a federal district court against Ford, asserting product liability based, in part, on negligence. Jarvis alleged that a defect in the van had caused the sudden acceleration. Her proof included her testimony, the testimony of other Aerostar owners who had experienced similar problems, and evidence that hundreds of additional Aerostar owners had experienced sudden acceleration. She also presented an expert who theorized that the van's cruise control had malfunctioned and who proposed an inexpensive remedy for this problem. Ford argued that Jarvis had failed to prove the defect that caused the cruise control to malfunction. A jury issued a verdict in Jarvis's favor, but the court granted Ford's motion for judgment as a matter of law. Jarvis appealed to the U.S. Court of Appeals for the Second Circuit.*

IN THE LANGUAGE OF THE COURT

SOTOMAYOR, Circuit Judge.

     *   *   *   *

     *   *   * [A] plaintiff's failure to prove why a product malfunctioned does not necessarily prevent a plaintiff from showing that the product was defective. *   *   * While the burden is upon the plaintiff to prove that the product was defective and that the defect existed while the product was in the manufacturer's possession, [the] plaintiff is not required to prove the specific defect, especially where the product is complicated in nature. *Proof of necessary facts may be circumstantial. Though the happening of the accident is not proof of a defective condition, a defect may be inferred from proof that the product did not perform as intended by the manufacturer* *   *   * . [Emphasis added.]

     *   *   *   *

The district court erred in requiring proof of a specific defect in the Aerostar's cruise control and in not considering Jarvis's circumstantial evidence of a defect. The malfunction in the design of the Aerostar that Jarvis has alleged is that it suddenly accelerated, opening full throttle without Jarvis depressing the accelerator pedal, and that her efforts to stop the vehicle by pumping the brakes were unavailing. If Jarvis's six-day-old Aerostar performed in this manner, a jury could reasonably conclude that it was defective when put on the market by Ford, and that the defect made it reasonably certain that the vehicle would be dangerous when put to normal use, as required [in a cause of action based on] negligent design.

CASE 13.1 | Continued

Although Ford argued that the accident was caused instead by driver error, this theory would have been rejected if the jury had believed Jarvis's testimony that she had her feet on the brake and not on the accelerator, as Ford claimed. * * * Construing the evidence in Jarvis's favor and crediting her version of events, a reasonable jury could find that Ford breached its duty of care. Even accepting as true that sudden acceleration in the 1991 Aerostar would occur, at most, very infrequently when measured against all Aerostar ignition starts [as Ford claimed], the consequences of sudden acceleration could easily be catastrophic, the design of which Jarvis complains has no particular utility to balance its potential for harm, and, according to Jarvis's expert, the malfunction in the cruise control could be avoided by an inexpensive switch that would shut off power to the cruise control when not in use.

DECISION AND REMEDY *The U.S. Court of Appeals for the Second Circuit vacated (set aside, voided) the judgment of the lower court and remanded the case with instructions to reinstate the jury's verdict that Ford was negligent in the design of the cruise control mechanism in the 1991 Aerostar. A plaintiff in a product liability action based on negligence is not required to prove a specific defect when a defect may be inferred from proof that the product did not perform as the manufacturer intended.* [a]

a. This is also the principle in a strict product liability action, according to the *Restatement (Third) of Torts: Products Liability*, which will be discussed later in this chapter.

PRODUCT LIABILITY BASED ON MISREPRESENTATION

When a fraudulent misrepresentation has been made to a user or consumer and that misrepresentation ultimately results in an injury, the basis of liability may be the tort of fraud. In this situation, the misrepresentation must have been made knowingly or with reckless disregard for the facts. For example, the intentional mislabeling of packaged cosmetics and the intentional concealment of a product's defects would constitute fraudulent misrepresentation.

NONFRAUDULENT MISREPRESENTATION Nonfraudulent misrepresentation, which occurs when a merchant *innocently* misrepresents the character or quality of goods, can also provide a basis of liability. In this situation, the plaintiff does not have to prove that the misrepresentation was made knowingly. For example, suppose that a pharmaceutical company innocently indicates to the medical profession that a certain drug that it markets is not physically addictive. The company's statement is supported by fairly extensive studies of the medication, none of which revealed any evidence of addictive qualities. Based on the company's information, a physician prescribes the medication to a patient, who develops an addiction that turns out to be fatal. Even though the addiction was a highly uncommon reaction resulting from the victim's unusual susceptibility to this product, the drug company may still be held liable.

THE MISREPRESENTATION MUST BE OF A MATERIAL FACT Whether fraudulent or nonfraudulent, the misrepresentation must be of a material fact (a fact concerning the quality, nature, or appropriate use of the product on which a normal buyer may be expected to rely). There must also have been an intent to induce the buyer's reliance on the misrepresentation. Misrepresentation on a label or advertisement is enough to show an intent to induce the reliance of anyone who may use the product. In addition, the buyer must have relied on the misrepresentation. If the buyer was not aware of the misrepresentation or if it did not influence the transaction, there is normally no liability.

SECTION 3 | Strict Product Liability

Under the doctrine of *strict liability* (discussed earlier), people may be liable for the results of their acts regardless of their intentions or their exercise of reasonable care. In the 1960s, courts applied the doctrine of strict liability in several landmark cases involving manufactured goods, and it has since become a common method of holding manufacturers liable. Some states, however, including Massachusetts and Virginia, have refused to recognize strict product liability. Additionally, some courts limit the application of the doctrine to cases involving personal injuries (not property damage).

STRICT PRODUCT LIABILITY AND PUBLIC POLICY

The law imposes strict product liability as a matter of public policy. This public policy rests on the threefold assumption that (1) consumers should be protected against unsafe products; (2) manufacturers and distributors should not escape liability for faulty products simply because they are not in privity of contract with the ultimate user of those products; and (3) manufacturers, sellers, and lessors of products are in a better position to bear the costs associated with injuries caused by their products—costs that they can ultimately pass on to all consumers in the form of higher prices.

California was the first state to impose strict product liability in tort on manufacturers. In a landmark 1962 decision, *Greenman v. Yuba Power Products, Inc.*,[3] the California Supreme Court set out the reason for applying tort law rather than contract law (including laws governing warranties) in cases involving consumers who were injured by defective products. According to the *Greenman* court, the "purpose of such liability is to [e]nsure that the costs of injuries resulting from defective products are borne by the manufacturers . . . rather than by the injured persons who are powerless to protect themselves."

THE REQUIREMENTS FOR STRICT PRODUCT LIABILITY

The courts often look to the *Restatements of the Law* for guidance, even though the *Restatements* are not binding authorities. Section 402A of the *Restatement (Second) of Torts*, which was originally issued in 1964, has become a widely accepted statement of the liabilities of sellers of goods (including manufacturers, processors, assemblers, packagers, bottlers, wholesalers, distributors, retailers, and lessors).

The bases for an action in strict liability as set forth in Section 402A of the *Restatement (Second) of Torts*, and as the doctrine came to be commonly applied, can be summarized as a series of six requirements, which are listed here.

1. The product must be in a *defective condition* when the defendant sells it.
2. The defendant must normally be engaged in the *business of selling* (or otherwise distributing) that product.
3. The product must be *unreasonably dangerous* to the user or consumer because of its defective condition (in most states).
4. The plaintiff must incur *physical harm* to self or property by use or consumption of the product.
5. The defective condition must be the *proximate cause* of the injury or damage.
6. The *goods must not have been substantially changed* from the time the product was sold to the time the injury was sustained.

Depending on the jurisdiction, if these requirements were met, a manufacturer's liability to an injured party could be virtually unlimited.

PROVING A DEFECTIVE CONDITION   Under these requirements, in any action against a manufacturer, seller, or lessor the plaintiff need not show why or in what manner the product became defective. The plaintiff does, however, have to prove that the product was defective at the time it left the hands of the seller or lessor and that this defective condition makes it "unreasonably dangerous" to the user or consumer. Unless evidence can be presented that will support the conclusion that it was defective when it was sold or leased, the plaintiff normally will not succeed. If the product was delivered in a safe condition and subsequent mishandling made it harmful to the user, the seller or lessor is not strictly liable.

UNREASONABLY DANGEROUS PRODUCTS   The *Restatement* recognizes that many products cannot possibly be made entirely safe for all uses, and thus only holds sellers or lessors liable for products that are *unreasonably* dangerous. A court could consider a product so defective as to be an **unreasonably dangerous product** in either of the following situations:

1. The product was dangerous beyond the expectation of the ordinary consumer.
2. A less dangerous alternative was *economically* feasible for the manufacturer, but the manufacturer failed to produce it.

As will be discussed next, a product may be unreasonably dangerous due to a flaw in the manufacturing process, a design defect, or an inadequate warning.

---

3. 59 Cal.2d 57, 377 P.2d 897, 27 Cal.Rptr. 697 (1962).

PRODUCT DEFECTS

Because Section 402A of the *Restatement (Second) of Torts* did not clearly define such terms as *defective* and *unreasonably dangerous*, these terms have been subject to different interpretations by different courts. In 1997, to address these concerns, the American Law Institute (ALI) issued the *Restatement (Third) of Torts: Products Liability*. This *Restatement* defines the three types of product defects that have traditionally been recognized in product liability law—manufacturing defects, design defects, and warning defects.

MANUFACTURING DEFECTS   According to Section 2(a) of the *Restatement* concerning product liability, a product "contains a manufacturing defect when the product departs from its intended design even though all possible care was exercised in the preparation and marketing of the product." Basically, a manufacturing defect is a departure from a product unit's design specifications. Defective products include those that are physically flawed, damaged, or incorrectly assembled. A glass bottle that is made too thin and explodes in a consumer's face is an example of a manufacturing defect. Liability is imposed on the manufacturer (and possibly on the wholesaler and retailer) regardless of whether the manufacturer's quality control efforts were "reasonable." The idea behind holding defendants strictly liable for manufacturing defects is to encourage greater investment in product safety and stringent quality control standards.

DESIGN DEFECTS   In contrast to a manufacturing defect (in which the product fails to meet the manufacturer's design specifications), a design defect relates to the product's actual design and to claims that it created an unreasonable risk to the user. A product "is defective in design when the foreseeable risks of harm posed by the product could have been reduced or avoided by the adoption of a reasonable alternative design by the seller or other distributor, or a predecessor in the commercial chain of distribution, and the omission of the alternative design renders the product not reasonably safe."[4]

—Test for Design Defects.   To successfully assert a design defect, a plaintiff has to show that a reasonable alternative design was available and that the defendant's failure to adopt the alternative design rendered

the product not reasonably safe. In other words, a manufacturer or other defendant is liable only when the harm was reasonably preventable. In one case, for example, Gillespie, who cut off several of his fingers while operating a table saw, alleged that the blade guards on the saw were defectively designed. At trial, however, an expert testified that the alternative design for blade guards used for table saws could not have been used for the particular cut that Gillespie was performing at the time he was injured. The court found that Gillespie's claim about defective blade guards must fail because there was no proof that the "better" design of guard would have prevented his injury.[5]

—Factors to Be Considered.   According to the Official Comments accompanying the *Restatement*, a court can consider a broad range of factors, including the magnitude and probability of the foreseeable risks, and the relative advantages and disadvantages of the product as it was designed and as it could have been designed. For example, suppose that four-year-old Andrea suffers serious burns when she gets out of bed one night to go to the bathroom, trips on the electric cord connected to a hot-water vaporizer, and falls on the vaporizer heating unit. Andrea's parents file a suit against the manufacturer alleging that the vaporizer was defectively designed because the top-heating unit is not secured to the jar that holds the hot water.

A court would likely consider the following factors as relevant: (1) the foreseeability that the vaporizer might be accidentally tipped over, (2) the overall safety provided by an alternative design that secures the heating unit to the receptacle holding the water, (3) consumer knowledge or lack of knowledge that the water in the glass jar is scalding hot, (4) the added cost of the safer alternative design, and (5) the relative convenience of a vaporizer with a lift-off cap. If the plaintiff offers sufficient evidence for a reasonable person to conclude that the harm was reasonably preventable, then the manufacturer could be held liable.

WARNING DEFECTS   A product may also be deemed defective because of inadequate instructions or warnings. A product "is defective because of inadequate instructions or warnings when the foreseeable risks of harm posed by the product could have been reduced or avoided by the provision of reasonable instructions or warnings by the seller or other distributor, or a predecessor in the commercial chain of distribution, and the

---

4. *Restatement (Third) of Torts: Products Liability*, Section 2(b).

5. *Gillespie v. Sears, Roebuck & Co.*, 386 F.3d 21 (1st Cir. 2004).

omission of the instructions or warnings renders the product not reasonably safe."[6]

Important factors for a court to consider under the *Restatement (Third) of Torts: Products Liability* include the risks of a product, the "content and comprehensibility" and "intensity of expression" of warnings and instructions, and the "characteristics of expected user groups."[7] For example, children would likely respond readily to bright, bold, simple warning labels, whereas educated adults might need more detailed information.

—Obvious Risks. There is no duty to warn about risks that are obvious or commonly known. Warnings about such risks do not add to the safety of a product and could even detract from it by making other warnings seem less significant. The obviousness of a risk and a user's decision to proceed in the face of that risk may be a defense in a product liability suit based on a warning defect. (Defenses to product liability will be discussed in the next section.)

—Foreseeable Misuses. Generally, a seller must warn those who purchase its product of the harm that can result from the foreseeable misuse of the product as well. The key is the foreseeability of the misuse. According to the Official Comments accompanying the *Restatement (Third) of Torts: Products Liability*, sellers "are not required to foresee and take precautions against every conceivable mode of use and abuse to which their products might be put."

MARKET-SHARE LIABILITY

Generally, in cases involving product liability, a plaintiff must prove that the defective product that caused his or her injury was the product of a specific defendant. In a few situations, however, courts have dropped this requirement when plaintiffs could not prove which of many distributors of a harmful product supplied the particular product that caused the injuries. For example, in one case a plaintiff who was a hemophiliac received injections of a blood protein known as antihemophiliac factor (AHF) concentrate. The plaintiff later tested positive for the AIDS (acquired immune deficiency syndrome) virus. Because it was not known which manufacturer was responsible for the particular AHF received by the plaintiff, the court held that all of the manufacturers of AHF could be held liable under the theory of **market-share liability.**[8] Many jurisdictions, however, do not apply this theory, believing that it deviates too significantly from traditional legal principles.[9]

OTHER APPLICATIONS OF STRICT PRODUCT LIABILITY

Strict product liability also applies to suppliers of component parts. For example, suppose that General Motors buys brake pads from a subcontractor and puts them in Chevrolets without changing their composition. If those pads are defective, both the supplier of the brake pads and General Motors will be held strictly liable for the damages caused by the defects.[10]

Although the drafters of Section 402A of the *Restatement (Second) of Torts* did not take a position on bystanders, all courts extend the strict liability of manufacturers and other sellers to injured bystanders. For example, in one case, an automobile manufacturer was held liable for injuries caused by the explosion of a car's motor. A cloud of steam resulting from the explosion caused multiple collisions because other drivers could not see well.[11]

SECTION 4 | Defenses to Product Liability

Defendants in product liability suits can raise a number of defenses. One defense, of course, is to show that there is no basis for the plaintiff's claim. For example, in a product liability case based on negligence, if a defendant can show that the plaintiff has *not* met the requirements (such as causation) for an action in negligence, generally the defendant will not be liable. In regard to strict product liability, a defendant can claim that the plaintiff failed to meet one of the requirements for an action in strict liability. For example, if the defendant establishes that the goods have been subsequently altered, normally the defendant will not

---

6. *Restatement (Third) of Torts: Products Liability*, Section 2(c).
7. *Restatement (Third) of Torts: Products Liability*, Section 2, Comment h.
8. *Smith v. Cutter Biological, Inc.*, 72 Haw. 416, 823 P.2d 717 (1991). See also *Sutowski v. Eli Lilly & Co.*, 82 Ohio St.3d 347, 696 N.E.2d 187 (1998).
9. For the Illinois Supreme Court's position on market-share liability, see *Smith v. Eli Lilly Co.*, 137 Ill.2d 222, 560 N.E.2d 324 (1990).
10. See *Restatement (Third) of Torts: Products Liability*, Section 5.
11. *Giberson v. Ford Motor Co.*, 504 S.W.2d 8 (Mo. 1974).

be held liable.[12] Defendants may also assert the defenses discussed next.

ASSUMPTION OF RISK

Assumption of risk can sometimes be used as a defense in a product liability action. To establish such a defense, the defendant must show that (1) the plaintiff knew and appreciated the risk created by the product defect and (2) the plaintiff voluntarily assumed the risk, even though it was unreasonable to do so. For example, if a buyer failed to heed a seller's product recall, the buyer may be deemed to have assumed the risk of the product defect that the seller offered to cure.

---

12. Under some state laws, the failure to properly maintain a product may constitute a subsequent alteration. See, for example, *LaPlante v. American Honda Motor Co.*, 27 F.3d 731 (1st Cir. 1994).

PRODUCT MISUSE

Similar to the defense of voluntary assumption of risk is that of **product misuse.** Here, the injured party *does not know that the product is dangerous for a particular use* (contrast this with assumption of risk), but the use is not the one for which the product was designed. The courts have severely limited this defense. For example, even if the injured party does not know about the inherent danger of using the product in a wrong way, if the misuse is reasonably foreseeable, the seller must take measures to guard against it.

Does a manufacturer have a duty to prevent a criminal misuse of its product, particularly if that use is entirely foreign to the purpose for which the product was intended? That was the question in the following case.

CASE 13.2

Ward v. Arm & Hammer

United States District Court, District of New Jersey, 2004. 341 F.Supp.2d 499. http://lawlibrary.rutgers. edu/fed/search.shtml [a]

BACKGROUND AND FACTS *Church & Dwight Company manufactures Arm & Hammer Baking Soda, which features five warnings on its package. George Ward used the baking soda with cocaine to make crack cocaine. After a conviction in March 1995 on criminal charges for distribution of the illegal drug, Ward was sentenced to a two-hundred-month prison term in the low-security Federal Correctional Institution in Petersburg, Virginia. In 2003, Ward filed a suit pro se[b] in a federal district court against Church & Dwight, asserting that the manufacturer failed to include a certain sixth warning on its product's package. According to Ward, the package should have included a description of the consequences of criminally misusing baking soda to make crack cocaine. He argued, "I feel [that] if I was forewarned by this company that I'd never [have] used this product like I was charged with." Church & Dwight filed a motion to dismiss the complaint.*

IN THE LANGUAGE OF THE COURT

CHESLER, District Judge.
* * * *

DISCUSSION

A. *Motion to Dismiss Standard*

In deciding a motion to dismiss * * * all allegations in the complaint must be taken as true and viewed in the light most favorable to the plaintiff. * * * *If, after viewing the allegations in the complaint in the light most favorable to the plaintiff, it appears beyond doubt that no relief could be granted under any set of facts which could prove consistent with the allegations, a court shall dismiss a complaint for failure to state a claim.* [Emphasis added.]

In the case of a *pro se* litigant, the court must find that it is clear beyond doubt that the plaintiff can prove no set of facts in support of his claim which would entitle him to relief.

---

a. In the "Find Decisions by Docket Number" section, select "Civil Case," enter "03-6113" in the "Enter Docket Number" boxes, and click on "Submit Form." In the result, click the appropriate link to access the opinion. Rutgers University Law School in Camden, New Jersey, maintains this Web site.

b. *Pro se* means that Ward filed his suit and argued his case without an attorney.

CONTINUED ▶

CASE 13.2 Continued

B. Duty to Warn of the Consequences of Criminal Misuse of Products

Nowhere in his complaint or response brief does Plaintiff assert that he was unaware that distribution of crack cocaine was unlawful or that ingestion of crack cocaine was harmful. Indeed, Plaintiff in his response brief implies that it is common knowledge that misuse of baking soda with cocaine may be harmful. Furthermore, under [the applicable state] law, citizens are charged with knowledge of the law, including the criminal laws. It follows that Church & Dwight had no duty to warn Plaintiff of that which he knew, and that which the law already charged him with knowing.

Additionally, *the law is clear that manufacturers have no duty to warn of the potential consequences for criminal misuse of their products.* * * * [M]anufacturers have no duty to prevent a criminal misuse of their products which is entirely foreign to the purpose for which the product was intended. Plaintiff himself acknowledges and concedes that "baking soda is not a product that * * * is intended for the production for illegal drug use or distribution." Plaintiff contends, though, that "it cannot be said that the use of this product to make Crack Cocaine is *foreign* anymore, this is well established knowledge * * *." However, * * * the manufacturer of a raw material or component part that is not itself dangerous has no legal duty to prevent a buyer from incorporating the material or part into another device that is or may be dangerous. [Emphasis added.]

To require Church & Dwight to warn customers of potential criminal consequences for the intentional misuse of baking soda would be analogous to requiring that all automobile manufacturers place warnings on their products to the effect that you may be subject to punishment if you use the cars for illegal drag-racing. Although the manufacturers in both instances may be aware of the products' potential for misuse, this itself does not give rise to a duty to warn of the criminal consequences of such unintended activities.

CONCLUSION

Having taken into account the fact that Plaintiff is proceeding in this matter *pro se*, the Court is satisfied nonetheless that it is clear beyond doubt that the plaintiff can prove no set of facts in support of his claim which would entitle him to relief. For the foregoing reasons, the Court will grant Defendant's Motion to Dismiss Plaintiff's claim * * * .

DECISION AND REMEDY *The court granted Church & Dwight's motion to dismiss Ward's complaint. The court held that the manufacturer of Arm & Hammer Baking Soda had no duty to warn that the use of its product with illegal drugs was prohibited and punishable by law.*

WHAT IF THE FACTS WERE DIFFERENT? *Suppose that Ward had not been aware that misuse of baking soda with cocaine is harmful. Would the result in this case have been different?*

COMPARATIVE NEGLIGENCE (FAULT)

Developments in the area of comparative negligence, or fault, have also affected the doctrine of strict liability—the most extreme theory of product liability. Whereas previously the plaintiff's conduct was not a defense to strict liability, today many jurisdictions, when apportioning liability and damages, consider the negligent or intentional actions of both the plaintiff and the defendant. This means that even if the plaintiff misused the products, she or he may nonetheless be able to recover at least some damages for injuries caused by the defendant's defective product. For example, Dan Smith, a mechanic in Alaska, was not wearing a hard hat at work when he was asked to start the diesel engine of an air compressor.

Because the compressor was an older model, he had to prop open a door to start it. When he got the engine started, the door fell from its position and hit Smith's head, which resulted in his suffering from seizures and epilepsy. Smith sued the manufacturer, claiming that the engine was defectively designed. The court ruled that the defendant could raise the plaintiff's ordinary negligence as a defense to reduce proportionally the amount of damages awarded to the plaintiff.[13]

COMMONLY KNOWN DANGERS

The dangers associated with certain products (such as matches and sharp knives) are so commonly known

---

13. *Smith v. Ingersoll-Rand Co.*, 14 P.3d 990 (Alaska 2000).

that, as already mentioned, manufacturers need not warn users of those dangers. If a defendant succeeds in convincing the court that a plaintiff's injury resulted from a *commonly known danger,* the defendant will not be liable.

A classic case on this issue involved a plaintiff who was injured when an elastic exercise rope she had purchased slipped off her foot and struck her in the eye, causing a detachment of the retina. The plaintiff claimed that the manufacturer should be liable because it had failed to warn users that the exerciser might slip off a foot in such a manner. The court stated that to hold the manufacturer liable in these circumstances "would go beyond the reasonable dictates of justice in fixing the liabilities of manufacturers." After all, stated the court, "[a]lmost every physical object can be inherently dangerous or potentially dangerous in a sense. . . . A manufacturer cannot manufacture a knife that will not cut or a hammer that will not mash a thumb or a stove that will not burn a finger. The law does not require [manufacturers] to warn of such common dangers."[14]

A related defense is the *knowledgeable user* defense. If a particular danger is or should be commonly known by particular users of a product, the manufacturer need not warn these users of the danger. In the following case, the plaintiffs alleged that McDonald's, the well-known fast-food chain, should be held liable for failing to warn customers of the adverse health effects of eating large quantities of its food products.

---

14. *Jamieson v. Woodward & Lothrop,* 247 F.2d 23 (D.C. 1957).

CASE 13.3   Pelman v. McDonald's Corp.

United States
District Court,
Southern District
of New York, 2003.
237 F.Supp.2d 512.

SWEET, J. [Judge]

This action presents unique and challenging issues. The plaintiffs have alleged that the practices of [McDonald's Corporation and McDonald's of New York—collectively, McDonald's] in making and selling their products are deceptive and that this deception has caused the minors who have consumed McDonald's products to injure their health by becoming obese. Questions of personal responsibility, common knowledge, and public health are presented * * * .
    *   *   *   *

This opinion is guided by the principle that *legal consequences should not attach to the consumption of hamburgers and other fast food fare unless consumers are unaware of the dangers of eating such food.* * * * [K]nowledge is power. Following from this aphorism, one important principle in assigning legal responsibility is the common knowledge of consumers. If consumers know (or reasonably should know) the potential ill health effects of eating at McDonald's, they cannot blame McDonald's if they, nonetheless, choose to satiate their appetite with a surfeit of supersized McDonald's products. On the other hand, consumers cannot be expected to protect against a danger that was solely within McDonald's knowledge. Thus, one necessary element of any potentially viable claim must be that McDonald's products involve a danger that is not within the common knowledge of consumers. * * * [Emphasis added.]
    * * * Americans now spend more than $110 billion on fast food each year, and on any given day in the United States, almost one in four adults visits a fast food restaurant. * * *
    *   *   *   *

The plaintiffs commenced suit on August 22, 2002, in the State Supreme Court of New York, Bronx County. Defendants removed the action to [the federal district court for] the Southern District of New York on September 30, 2002 * * * .

McDonald's filed [a] motion to dismiss plaintiffs' complaint (the "Complaint") on October 7, 2002. * * *
    *   *   *   *

Ashley Pelman, a minor, and her mother and natural guardian Roberta Pelman are residents of the Bronx, New York.
    *   *   *   *

CONTINUED ▶

CASE 13.3 Continued

[Ashley and other teenagers] are consumers who have purchased and consumed the defendants' products and * * * have become overweight and have developed diabetes, coronary heart disease, high blood pressure, elevated cholesterol intake, and/or other detrimental and adverse health effects * * * .

* * * Ashley and Roberta Pelman purchased and consumed food products at the Bruckner Boulevard [McDonald's] outlet. * * * All products, ingredients, promotions and advertisements sold, provided, utilized, advertised, and promoted by the * * * Bruckner Boulevard [outlet] were authorized by McDonald's Corp. and McDonald's of New York.
* * * *

Obese individuals have a 50 to 100 percent increased risk of premature death from all causes. Approximately 300,000 deaths a year in the United States are currently associated with overweight and obesity. * * * [L]eft unabated, overweight and obesity may soon cause as much preventable disease and death as cigarette smoking.
* * * *

[Among other things, the plaintiffs assert] that McDonald's failed to post nutritional labeling on the products and at points of purchase. * * *
* * * *

* * * Plaintiffs admit that McDonald's has made its nutritional information available online and do not contest that such information is available upon request. Unless McDonald's has specifically promised to provide nutritional information on all its products and at all points of purchase, plaintiffs do not state a claim.
* * * *

[Or] in order to state a claim, the Complaint must allege either that the attributes of McDonald's products are so extraordinarily unhealth[ful] that they are outside the reasonable contemplation of the consuming public or that the products are so extraordinarily unhealth[ful] as to be dangerous in their intended use. The Complaint—which merely alleges that the foods contain high levels of cholesterol, fat, salt, and sugar, and that the foods are therefore unhealth[ful]—fails to reach this bar. It is well-known that fast food in general, and McDonald's products in particular, contain high levels of cholesterol, fat, salt, and sugar, and that such attributes are bad for one.

* * * If a person knows or should know that eating copious orders of supersized McDonald's products is unhealth[ful] and may result in weight gain (and its concomitant [associated] problems) because of the high levels of cholesterol, fat, salt, and sugar, it is not the place of the law to protect them from their own excesses. Nobody is forced to eat at McDonald's. (Except, perhaps, parents of small children who desire McDonald's food, toy promotions, or playgrounds and demand their parents' accompaniment.) Even more pertinent, nobody is forced to supersize their meal or choose less health[ful] options on the menu.

*As long as a consumer exercises free choice with appropriate knowledge, liability * * * will not attach to a manufacturer.* It is only when that free choice becomes but a chimera [illusion]—for instance, by the masking of information necessary to make the choice, such as the knowledge that eating McDonald's with a certain frequency would irrefragably [indisputably] cause harm—that manufacturers should be held accountable. Plaintiffs have failed to allege in the Complaint that their decisions to eat at McDonald's several times a week were anything but a choice freely made and which now may not be pinned on McDonald's. [Emphasis added.]
* * * *

For the foregoing reasons, the Complaint is dismissed in its entirety.

QUESTIONS

1. On what reasoning did the court base its dismissal of the plaintiffs' complaint?
2. What might the plaintiffs have alleged (and substantiated with proof) to succeed in their suit?

STATUTES OF LIMITATIONS AND REPOSE

As discussed in Chapter 1, *statutes of limitations* restrict the time within which an action may be brought. A typical statute of limitations provides that an action must be brought within a specified period of time after the cause of action accrues. Generally, a cause of action is held to accrue when some damage occurs. Sometimes, the running of the prescribed period is *tolled* (that is, suspended) until the party suffering an injury has discovered it or should have discovered it.

Many states have passed laws, called **statutes of repose,** placing outer time limits on some claims so that the defendant will not be left vulnerable to lawsuits indefinitely. These statutes may limit the time within which a plaintiff can file a product liability suit. Typically, a statute of repose begins to run at an earlier date and runs for a longer time than a statute of limitations. For example, a statute of repose may require that claims must be brought within twelve years from the date of sale or manufacture of the defective product. No action can be brought if the injury occurs *after* this statutory period has lapsed. In addition, some of these legislative enactments have limited the application of the doctrine of strict liability to only new goods.

REVIEWING STRICT LIABILITY AND PRODUCT LIABILITY

Shalene Kolchek bought a Great Lakes spa from Val Porter, a dealer who was selling spas at the state fair. Kolchek signed an installment contract; then Porter and Kolchek arranged for the spa to be delivered and installed for her the next day. Three months later, Kolchek left her six-year-old daughter, Litisha, alone in the spa. While exploring the spa's hydromassage jets, Litisha stuck her index finger into one the jet holes and was unable to remove her finger from the jet. Litisha yanked hard, injuring her finger, then panicked and screamed for help. Kolchek was unable to remove Litisha's finger, and the local police and rescue team were called to assist. After a three-hour operation that included draining the spa, sawing out a section of the spa's plastic molding, and slicing the jet casing, Litisha's finger was freed. Following this procedure, the spa was no longer functional. Litisha was taken to the local emergency room, where she was told that a bone in her finger was broken in two places. Using the information presented in the chapter, answer the following questions.

1. Under which theory or theories of product liability can Kolchek sue to recover for Litisha's injuries? Could Kolcheck sue Porter or Great Lakes?

2. Would privity of contract be required for Kolcheck to succeed in a product liability action against Great Lakes?

3. For an action in strict product liability against Great Lakes, what six requirements must Kolchek meet?

4. What type of product defect might Kolchek most effectively claim?

5. What defenses to product liability might Porter or Great Lakes be able to assert?

TERMS AND CONCEPTS TO REVIEW

bystanders 313

market-share liability 320

privity of contract 315

product liability 313

product misuse 321

statute of repose 325

strict liability 313

unreasonably dangerous product 318

QUESTIONS AND CASE PROBLEMS

13–1. Chen buys a television set manufactured by Quality TV Appliance, Inc. She is going on vacation, so she takes the set to her mother's house for her mother to use. Because the set is defective, it explodes, causing her mother to be seriously injured. Chen's mother sues Quality to obtain compensation for her injury and for the damage to her house. Under what theory or theories discussed in this chapter might Chen's mother recover damages from Quality?

13–2. A water pipe burst, flooding a company's switchboard and tripping the switchboard circuit breakers. Company employees assigned to reactivate the switchboard included an electrical technician with twelve years of on-the-job training, a licensed electrician, and an electrical engineer who had studied power engineering in college and had twenty years of experience. The employees attempted to switch one of the circuit breakers back on without testing for short circuits, which they later admitted they knew how to do and should have done. The circuit breaker failed to engage but ignited an explosive fire. The company sued the supplier of the circuit breakers for damages, alleging that the supplier had failed to give adequate warnings and instructions regarding the circuit breakers. How might the supplier defend against this claim? Discuss.

13–3. ⚖ QUESTION WITH SAMPLE ANSWER

Colt manufactures a new pistol. The firing of the pistol depends on an enclosed high-pressure device. The pistol has been thoroughly tested in two laboratories in the Midwest, and its design and manufacture are in accord with current technology. Wayne purchases one of the new pistols from Hardy's Gun and Rifle Emporium. When he uses the pistol in the high altitude of the Rockies, the difference in pressure causes the pistol to misfire, resulting in serious injury to Wayne. Colt can prove that all due care was used in the manufacturing process, and it refuses to pay for Wayne's injuries. Discuss Colt's liability in tort.

For a sample answer to this question, go to Appendix I at the end of this text.

13–4. Gina is standing on a street corner waiting for a ride to work. Gomez has just purchased a new car manufactured by Optimal Motors. He is driving down the street when suddenly the steering mechanism breaks, causing him to run over Gina. Gina suffers permanent injuries. Gomez's total income per year has never exceeded $15,000. Thus, instead of suing Gomez, Gina files suit against Optimal under the theory of strict liability in tort. Optimal claims that it is not liable because (1) due care was used in the manufacture of the car, (2) Optimal is not the manufacturer of the steering mechanism (Smith is), and (3) strict product liability applies only to users or consumers, and Gina is neither. Discuss the validity of the defenses claimed by Optimal.

13–5. Baxter manufactures electric hair dryers. Julie purchases a Baxter dryer from her local Ace Drugstore. Cox, a friend and guest in Julie's home, has taken a shower and wants to dry her hair. Julie tells Cox to use the new Baxter hair dryer that she has just purchased. As Cox plugs in the dryer, sparks fly out from the motor, and sparks continue to fly as she operates it. Despite this, Cox begins drying her hair. Suddenly, the entire dryer ignites into flames, severely burning Cox's scalp. Cox sues Baxter on the basis of negligence and strict liability in tort. Baxter admits that the dryer was defective but denies liability, particularly because Cox was not the person who purchased the dryer. In other words, Cox had no contractual relationship with Baxter. Discuss the validity of Baxter's defense. Are there any other defenses that Baxter might assert to avoid liability? Discuss fully.

13–6. DESIGN DEFECT.   In May 1995, Ms. McCathern and her daughter, together with McCathern's cousin, Ms. Sanders, and her daughter, were riding in Sanders's 1994 Toyota 4Runner. Sanders was driving, McCathern was in the front passenger seat, and the children were in the back-seat. Everyone was wearing a seat belt. While the group was traveling south on Oregon State Highway 395 at a speed of approximately fifty miles per hour, an oncoming vehicle veered into Sanders's lane of travel. When Sanders tried to steer clear, the 4Runner rolled over and landed upright on its four wheels. During the rollover, the roof over the front passenger seat collapsed, and as a result, McCathern sustained serious, permanent injuries. McCathern filed a suit in an Oregon state court against Toyota Motor Corp. and others, alleging in part that the 1994 4Runner "was dangerously defective and unreasonably dangerous in that the vehicle, as designed and sold, was unstable and prone to rollover." What is the test for product liability based on a design defect? What would McCathern have to prove to succeed under that test? [*McCathern v. Toyota Motor Corp.*, 332 Or. 59, 23 P.3d 320 (2001)]

13–7. ⚖ CASE PROBLEM WITH SAMPLE ANSWER

Mary Jane Boerner began smoking in 1945 at the age of fifteen. For a short time, she smoked Lucky Strikes (a brand of cigarettes) before switching to the Pall Mall brand, which she smoked until she quit altogether in 1981. Pall Malls had higher levels of carcinogenic tar than other cigarettes and lacked effective filters, which would have reduced the amount of tar inhaled into the lungs. In 1996, Mary Jane developed lung cancer. She and her husband, Henry Boerner, filed a suit in a federal district court against Brown & Williamson Tobacco Co., the maker of Pall Malls. The Boerners claimed, among other things, that Pall Malls contained a design defect. Mary Jane died in 1999. According to Dr. Peter Marvin, her treating physician, she died from the effects of cigarette smoke. Henry continued the suit, offering evidence that Pall Malls featured a filter that actually increased the amount of tar taken into the body. When is a product defective in design? Does this product meet the requirements? Why or why not? [*Boerner v. Brown & Williamson Tobacco Co.*, 394 F.3d 594 (8th Cir. 2005)]

To view a sample answer for this case problem, go to this book's Web site at <ins>http://wleb.westbuslaw.com</ins>, select "Chapter 13," and click on "Case Problem with Sample Answer."

13-8. LIABILITY TO THIRD PARTIES. Lee Stegemoller was a union member who insulated large machinery between 1947 and 1988. During his career, he worked for a number of different companies. Stegemoller primarily worked with asbestos insulation, which was used on industrial boilers, engines, furnaces, and turbines. After he left a work site, some of the asbestos dust always remained on his clothing. His wife, Ramona, who laundered his work clothes, was also exposed to the dust on a daily basis. Allegedly, as a result of this contact, she was diagnosed with colon cancer, pulmonary fibrosis, and pleural thickening in April 1998. The Stegemollers filed a suit in an Indiana state court against ACandS, Inc., and thirty-three others, contending among other things that the asbestos originated from products attributable to some of the defendants and from the premises of other defendants. Several defendants filed a motion to dismiss the complaint, asserting that Ramona was not a "user or consumer" of asbestos because she was not in the vicinity of the product when it was used. Should the court dismiss the suit on this basis? Explain. [*Stegemoller v. ACandS, Inc.*, 767 N.E.2d 974 (Ind. 2002)]

13-9. PRODUCT LIABILITY. In January 1999, John Clark of Clarksdale, Mississippi, bought a paintball gun. Clark practiced with the gun and knew how to screw in the CO_2 cartridge, pump the gun, and use its safety and trigger. He hunted and had taken a course in hunter safety education. He knew that protective eyewear was available for purchase, but he chose not to buy it. Clark also understood that it was "common sense" not to shoot anyone in the face. Chris Rico, another Clarksdale resident, owned a paintball gun made by Brass Eagle, Inc. Rico was similarly familiar with the gun's use and its risks. At that time and place, Clark, Rico, and their friends played a game that involved shooting paintballs at cars whose occupants also had the guns. One night, while Clark and Rico were cruising with their guns, Rico shot at Clark's car but hit Clark in the eye. Clark filed a suit in a Mississippi state court against Brass Eagle to recover for the injury, alleging in part that its gun was defectively designed. During the trial, Rico testified that his gun "never malfunctioned." In whose favor should the court rule? Why? [*Clark v. Brass Eagle, Inc.*, 866 So.2d 456 (Miss. 2004)]

13-10. A QUESTION OF ETHICS
On July 1, 1993, Gian Luigi Ferri entered the offices of a law firm against which he had a grudge. Using two semi-automatic assault weapons (TEC-9 and TEC-DC9) manufactured and distributed by Navegar, Inc., he killed eight persons and wounded six others before killing himself. The survivors and the families of some of those who had died sued Navegar, based in part on negligence. They claimed that Navegar had a duty not to create risks to the public beyond those inherent in the lawful use of firearms. They offered evidence that Navegar knew or should have known that the assault guns had "no legitimate sporting or self-defense purpose" and that the guns were "particularly well adapted to military-style assault on large numbers of people." They also claimed that the TEC-DC9 advertising "targets a criminal clientele," further increasing the risk of harm. A California trial court granted summary judgment in Navegar's favor. The appellate court reversed, ruling that the case should go to trial. The court stated that "the likelihood that a third person would make use of the TEC-DC9 in the kind of criminal rampage Ferri perpetrated is precisely the hazard that would support a determination that Navegar's conduct was negligent." Navegar appealed the decision to the California Supreme Court. In view of these facts, consider the following questions. [*Merrill v. Navegar, Inc.*, 26 Cal.4th 465, 28 P.3d 116, 110 Cal.Rptr.2d 370 (2001)]

(a) Do you agree with the appellate court that Navegar could be held negligent in marketing the TEC-DC9? What should the California Supreme Court decide? (Before answering this question, you may wish to review the elements of negligence in Chapter 12.)

(b) Should gun manufacturers ever be held liable for deaths caused by nondefective guns? Why or why not?

(c) Generally, do you believe that policy decisions regarding the liability of gun manufacturers should be made by the courts, whose job is to interpret the law, or by Congress and state legislatures, whose job is to make the law?

(d) In your opinion, have Congress and state legislatures gone far enough in regulating the use of firearms, or have they gone too far? Explain.

LAW | on the Web

For updated links to resources available on the Web, as well as a variety of other materials, visit this text's Web site at http://wleb.westbuslaw.com.

For information on the *Restatements of the Law*, including the *Restatement (Second) of Torts* and the *Restatement (Third) of Torts: Products Liability*, go to the Web site of the American Law Institute at

http://www.ali.org

For information on product liability suits against tobacco companies, go to the Web site of the Library & Center for Knowledge Management, which is maintained by the University of California, San Francisco, at

http://library.ucsf.edu/tobacco/litigation

LEGAL RESEARCH EXERCISES ON THE WEB

Go to http://wleb.westbuslaw.com, the Web site that accompanies this text. Select "Chapter 13" and click on "Internet Exercises." There you will find the following Internet research exercises that you can perform to learn more about topics covered in this chapter.

Activity 13–1: LEGAL PERSPECTIVE
Product Liability Litigation

Activity 13–2: MANAGEMENT PERSPECTIVE
The Duty to Warn

CHAPTER 14
Intellectual Property

Most people think of wealth in terms of houses, land, cars, stocks, and bonds. Wealth, however, also includes **intellectual property,** which consists of the products that result from intellectual, creative processes. Although it is an abstract term for an abstract concept, intellectual property is nonetheless wholly familiar to virtually everyone. *Trademarks, service marks, copyrights,* and *patents* are all forms of intellectual property. The book you are reading is copyrighted. The software you use, the movies you see, and the music you listen to are all forms of intellectual property. Exhibit 14–1 on page 331 offers a comprehensive summary of these forms of intellectual property, as well as intellectual property that consists of *trade secrets.* In this chapter, we examine each of these forms in some detail.

Intellectual property has taken on increasing significance in the United States as well as globally. Today, the value of the world's intellectual property probably exceeds the value of physical property, such as machines and houses. For many U.S. companies, ownership rights in intangible intellectual property are more important to their prosperity than are their tangible assets. As you will read in this chapter, a pressing issue for businesspersons today is how to protect these valuable rights in the online world.

The need to protect creative works was voiced by the framers of the U.S. Constitution over two hundred years ago: Article I, Section 8, of the U.S. Constitution authorized Congress "[t]o promote the Progress of Science and useful Arts, by securing for limited Times to Authors and Inventors the exclusive Right to their respective Writings and Discoveries." Laws protecting patents, trademarks, and copyrights are explicitly designed to protect and reward inventive and artistic creativity. Although intellectual property law limits the economic freedom of some individuals, it does so to protect the freedom of others to enjoy the fruits of their labors—in the form of profits.

SECTION 1 | Trademarks and Related Property

A **trademark** is a distinctive mark, motto, device, or implement that a manufacturer stamps, prints, or otherwise affixes to the goods it produces so that they can be identified on the market and their origin made known. In other words, a trademark is a source indicator. At common law, the person who used a symbol or mark to identify a business or product was protected in the use of that trademark. Clearly, by using another's trademark, a business could lead consumers to believe that its goods were made by the other business. The law seeks to avoid this kind of confusion. We examine in this section various aspects of the law governing trademarks.

In the following famous case concerning Coca-Cola, the defendants argued that the Coca-Cola trademark was entitled to no protection under the law because the term did not accurately represent the product.

The Coca-Cola Co. v. The Koke Co. of America

Supreme Court of the
United States, 1920.
254 U.S. 143,
41 S.Ct. 113,
65 L.Ed. 189.
*http://www.findlaw.com/
casecode/supreme.html*[a]

COMPANY PROFILE *John Pemberton, an Atlanta pharmacist, invented a caramel-colored, carbonated soft drink in 1886. His bookkeeper, Frank Robinson, named the beverage "Coca-Cola" after two of the ingredients, coca leaves and kola nuts. Asa Candler bought the Coca-Cola Company (http://www.cocacolacompany.com) in 1891, and within seven years, he made the soft drink available in all of the United States, as well as in parts of Canada and Mexico. Candler continued to sell Coke aggressively and to open up new markets, reaching Europe before 1910. In doing so, however, he attracted numerous competitors, some of which tried to capitalize directly on the Coke name.*

BACKGROUND AND FACTS *The Coca-Cola Company sought to enjoin (prevent) the Koke Company of America and other beverage companies from, among other things, using the word Koke for their products. The Koke Company of America and other beverage companies contended that the Coca-Cola trademark was a fraudulent representation and that Coca-Cola was therefore not entitled to any help from the courts. The Koke Company and the other defendants alleged that the Coca-Cola Company, by its use of the Coca-Cola name, represented that the beverage contained cocaine (from coca leaves), which it no longer did. The trial court granted the injunction against the Koke Company, but the appellate court reversed the lower court's ruling. Coca-Cola then appealed to the United States Supreme Court.*

IN THE LANGUAGE OF THE COURT

Mr. Justice *HOLMES* delivered the opinion of the Court.

* * * *

* * * Before 1900 the beginning of [Coca-Cola's] goodwill was more or less helped by the presence of cocaine, a drug that, like alcohol or caffeine or opium, may be described as a deadly poison or as a valuable [pharmaceutical item, depending on the speaker's purposes]. The amount seems to have been very small,[b] but it may have been enough to begin a bad habit and after the Food and Drug Act of June 30, 1906, if not earlier, long before this suit was brought, it was eliminated from the plaintiff's compound. * * *

* * * Since 1900, the sales have increased at a very great rate corresponding to a like increase in advertising. The name now characterizes a beverage to be had at almost any soda fountain. It means a single thing coming from a single source, and well known to the community. It hardly would be too much to say that the drink characterizes the name as much as the name, the drink. In other words *Coca-Cola probably means to most persons the plaintiff's familiar product to be had everywhere rather than a compound of particular substances.* * * * [B]efore this suit was brought the plaintiff had advertised to the public that it must not expect and would not find cocaine, and had eliminated everything tending to suggest cocaine effects except the name and the picture of [coca] leaves and nuts, which probably conveyed little or nothing to most who saw it. It appears to us that it would be going too far to deny the plaintiff relief against a palpable [readily evident] fraud because possibly here and there an ignorant person might call for the drink with the hope for incipient cocaine intoxication. The plaintiff's position must be judged by the facts as they were when the suit was begun, not by the facts of a different condition and an earlier time. [Emphasis added.]

DECISION AND REMEDY *The district court's injunction was allowed to stand. The competing beverage companies were enjoined (prevented) from calling their products "Koke."*

WHAT IF THE FACTS WERE DIFFERENT? *Suppose that Coca-Cola had been trying to make the public believe that its product contained cocaine. Would the result in this case likely have been different? Why?*

---

a. This URL will take you to a Web site maintained by FindLaw, which is now a part of West Group. In the "Citation Search" section, enter "254" in the left box and "143" in the right box, and click on "Get It" to access the opinion.

b. In reality, until 1903 the amount of active cocaine in each bottle of Coke was equivalent to one "line" of cocaine.

CASE 14.1 Continued

IMPACT OF THIS CASE ON TODAY'S LAW

In this early case, the United States Supreme Court made it clear that trademarks and trade names (and nicknames for those marks and names, such as the nickname "Coke" for "Coca-Cola") that are in common use receive protection under the common law. This holding is significant historically because it is the predecessor to the federal statute later passed to protect trademark rights—the Lanham Act of 1946, to be discussed next. In many ways, this act represented a codification of common law principles governing trademarks.

EXHIBIT 14-1 **Forms of Intellectual Property**

	DEFINITION	HOW ACQUIRED	DURATION	REMEDY FOR INFRINGEMENT
Patent	A grant from the government that gives an inventor the right to exclude others from making, using, and selling an invention.	By filing a patent application with the U.S. Patent and Trademark Office and receiving its approval.	Twenty years from the date of the application; for design patents, fourteen years.	Actual damages, including reasonable royalties or lost profits, *plus* attorneys' fees. Damages may be tripled for willful infringements.
Copyright	The right of an author or originator of a literary or artistic work, or other production that falls within a specified category, to have the exclusive use of that work for a given period of time.	Automatic (once the work or creation is put in tangible form). Only the *expression* of an idea (and not the idea itself) can be protected by copyright.	For authors: the life of the author, plus 70 years. For publishers: 95 years after the date of publication or 120 years after creation.	Actual damages plus profits received by the party who infringed *or* statutory damages under the Copyright Act, *plus* costs and attorneys' fees in either situation.
Trademark (Service Mark and Trade Dress)	Any distinctive word, name, symbol, or device (image or appearance), or combination thereof, that an entity uses to distinguish its goods or services from those of others. The owner has the exclusive right to use that mark or trade dress.	1. At common law, ownership created by use of the mark. 2. Registration with the appropriate federal or state office gives notice and is permitted if the mark is currently in use or will be within the next six months.	Unlimited, as long as it is in use. To continue notice by registration, the owner must renew by filing between the fifth and sixth years and, thereafter, every ten years.	1. Injunction prohibiting the future use of the mark. 2. Actual damages plus profits received by the party who infringed (can be increased under the Lanham Act). 3. Destruction of articles that infringed. 4. *Plus* costs and attorneys' fees.
Trade Secret	Any information that a business possesses and that gives the business an advantage over competitors (including formulas, lists, patterns, plans, processes, and programs).	Through the originality and development of the information and processes that constitute the business secret and are unknown to others.	Unlimited, so long as not revealed to others. Once revealed to others, it is no longer a trade secret.	Money damages for misappropriation (the Uniform Trade Secrets Act also permits punitive damages if willful), *plus* costs and attorneys' fees.

STATUTORY PROTECTION OF TRADEMARKS

Statutory protection of trademarks and related property is provided at the federal level by the Lanham Act of 1946.[1] The Lanham Act was enacted in part to protect manufacturers from losing business to rival companies that used confusingly similar trademarks. The Lanham Act incorporates the common law of trademarks and provides remedies for owners of trademarks who wish to enforce their claims in federal court. Many states also have trademark statutes.

TRADEMARK DILUTION   In 1995, Congress amended the Lanham Act by passing the Federal Trademark Dilution Act,[2] which extended the protection available to trademark owners by creating a federal cause of action for trademark **dilution.** Until the passage of this amendment, federal trademark law prohibited the unauthorized use of the same mark on competing—or on noncompeting but "related"—goods or services only when such use would likely confuse consumers as to the origin of those goods and services. Trademark dilution laws protect "distinctive" or "famous" trademarks (such as Jergens, McDonald's, RCA, and Macintosh) from certain unauthorized uses of the marks *regardless* of a showing of competition or a likelihood of confusion. More than half of the states have also enacted trademark dilution laws.

Although Congress passed the 1995 Federal Trademark Dilution Act in an effort to create uniformity and consistency in dilution cases, until recently, the federal courts were split in the level of proof required to show dilution. Some courts required proof that the defendant's use would cause "actual lessening" of selling power, whereas other courts required only a showing of "likelihood of dilution."

In 2003, the United States Supreme Court resolved this issue in favor of the higher standard (actual lessening of selling power) in the case of *Moseley v. V Secret Catalogue, Inc.*[3] In that case, famous lingerie maker Victoria's Secret brought a trademark dilution action against "Victor's Little Secret," a small retail store that sold adult videos, lingerie, and other items. The lower courts had granted Victoria's Secret an injunction prohibiting the adult store from diluting the trademark. The Supreme Court, however, concluded that likelihood of confusion is not enough and reversed the decision. To establish dilution under the federal act, the Court held that some evidence must establish that the junior user's mark actually reduces the value of the famous mark or lessens its capacity to identify goods and services.

USE OF A SIMILAR MARK MAY CONSTITUTE TRADEMARK DILUTION   In one of the first cases to be decided under the 1995 act's provisions, a federal court held that a famous mark may be diluted not only by the use of an *identical* mark but also by the use of a *similar* mark. The lawsuit was brought by Ringling Bros.—Barnum & Bailey, Combined Shows, Inc., against the state of Utah. Ringling Bros. claimed that Utah's use of the slogan "The Greatest Snow on Earth"—to attract visitors to the state's recreational and scenic resorts—diluted the distinctiveness of the circus's famous trademark "The Greatest Show on Earth." Utah moved to dismiss the suit, arguing that the 1995 provisions protect owners of famous trademarks only against the unauthorized use of identical marks. The court disagreed and refused to grant Utah's motion to dismiss the case.[4]

TRADEMARK REGISTRATION

Trademarks may be registered with the state or with the federal government. To register for protection under federal trademark law, a person must file an application with the U.S. Patent and Trademark Office in Washington, D.C. Under current law, a mark can be registered (1) if it is currently in commerce or (2) if the applicant intends to put it into commerce within six months.

In special circumstances, the six-month period can be extended by thirty months, giving the applicant a total of three years from the date of notice of trademark approval to make use of the mark and file the required use statement. Registration is postponed until the mark is actually used. Nonetheless, during this waiting period, any applicant can legally protect his or her trademark against a third party who previously has neither used the mark nor filed an application for it. Registration is renewable between the fifth and sixth years after the initial registration and every ten years thereafter (every twenty years for those trademarks registered before 1990).

---

1. 15 U.S.C. Sections 1051–1128.
2. 15 U.S.C. Section 1125.
3. 537 U.S. 418, 123 S.Ct. 1115, 155 L.Ed.2d 1 (2003).

4. *Ringling Bros.—Barnum & Bailey, Combined Shows, Inc. v. Utah Division of Travel Development,* 935 F.Supp. 763 (E.D.Va. 1996).

TRADEMARK INFRINGEMENT

Registration of a trademark with the U.S. Patent and Trademark Office gives notice on a nationwide basis that the trademark belongs exclusively to the registrant. The registrant is also allowed to use the symbol ® to indicate that the mark has been registered. Whenever that trademark is copied to a substantial degree or used in its entirety by another, intentionally or unintentionally, the trademark has been *infringed* (used without authorization). When a trademark has been infringed, the owner of the mark has a cause of action against the infringer. A person need not have registered a trademark in order to sue for trademark infringement, but registration does furnish proof of the date of inception of the trademark's use.

A central objective of the Lanham Act is to reduce the likelihood that consumers will be confused by similar marks. For that reason, only those trademarks that are deemed sufficiently distinctive from all competing trademarks will be protected.

DISTINCTIVENESS OF MARK

A trademark must be sufficiently distinct to enable consumers to identify the manufacturer of the goods easily and to distinguish between those goods and competing products.

STRONG MARKS Fanciful, arbitrary, or suggestive trademarks are generally considered to be the most distinctive (strongest) trademarks. This is because these types of marks are normally taken from outside the context of the particular product and thus provide the best means of distinguishing one product from another.

Fanciful trademarks include invented words, such as "Xerox" for one manufacturer's copiers and "Kodak" for another company's photographic products. Arbitrary trademarks include actual words used with products that have no literal connection to the words, such as "English Leather" used as a name for an aftershave lotion (and not for leather processed in England). Suggestive trademarks are those that suggest something about a product without describing the product directly. For example, the trademark "Dairy Queen" suggests an association between the products and milk, but it does not directly describe ice cream.

SECONDARY MEANING Descriptive terms, geographic terms, and personal names are not inherently distinctive and do not receive protection under the law until they acquire a secondary meaning. A secondary meaning may arise when customers begin to associate a specific term or phrase (such as London Fog) with specific trademarked items (coats with "London Fog" labels). Whether a secondary meaning becomes attached to a term or name usually depends on how extensively the product is advertised, the market for the product, the number of sales, and other factors. Once a secondary meaning is attached to a term or name, a trademark is considered distinctive and is protected. The United States Supreme Court has held that even a shade of color can qualify for trademark protection, once customers associate the color with the product.[5]

GENERIC TERMS Generic terms that refer to an entire class of products, such as *bicycle* and *computer*, receive no protection, even if they acquire secondary meanings. A particularly thorny problem arises when a trademark acquires generic use. For example, *aspirin* and *thermos* were originally the names of trademarked products, but today the words are used generically. Other examples are *escalator, trampoline, raisin bran, dry ice, lanolin, linoleum, nylon,* and *corn flakes*.

Note that a generic term will not be protected under trademark law even if the term has acquired a secondary meaning. In one case, for example, America Online, Inc. (AOL), sued AT&T Corporation, claiming that AT&T's use of "You Have Mail" on its WorldNet Service infringed AOL's trademark rights in the same phrase. The court ruled, however, that because each of the three words in the phrase was a generic term, the phrase as a whole was generic. Although the phrase had become widely associated with AOL's e-mail notification service, and thus might have acquired a secondary meaning, this issue was of no significance in the case. The court stated that it would not consider whether the mark had acquired any secondary meaning because "generic marks with secondary meaning are still not entitled to protection."[6]

TRADE DRESS

The term **trade dress** refers to the image and overall appearance of a product—for example, the distinctive

---

5. *Qualitex Co. v. Jacobson Products Co.*, 514 U.S. 159, 115 S.Ct. 1300, 131 L.Ed.2d 248 (1995).
6. *America Online, Inc. v. AT&T Corp.*, 243 F.3d 812 (4th Cir. 2001).

decor, menu, layout, and style of service of a particular restaurant. Trade dress is a broad concept and can include either all or part of the total image or overall impression created by a product or its packaging. It can include such things as the cover of a book or magazine, the layout and appearance of a mail-order catalogue, the use of a lighthouse as part of the design of a golf hole, the fish shape of a cracker, or the G-shaped design of a Gucci watch.

Basically, trade dress is subject to the same protection as trademarks. In cases involving trade dress infringement, as in trademark infringement cases, a major consideration is whether consumers are likely to be confused by the allegedly infringing use.

SERVICE, CERTIFICATION, AND COLLECTIVE MARKS

A **service mark** is essentially a trademark that is used to distinguish the services of one person or company from those of another rather than its products. For example, each airline has a particular mark or symbol associated with its name. United Air Lines uses its slogan "Fly the Friendly Skies" as a service mark. Titles and character names used in radio and television are frequently registered as service marks.

Other marks protected by law include certification marks and collective marks. A **certification mark** is used by one or more persons other than the owner to certify the region, materials, mode of manufacture, quality, or accuracy of the owner's goods or services. When used by members of a cooperative, association, or other organization, it is referred to as a **collective mark.** Examples of certification marks are the phrases "Good Housekeeping Seal of Approval" and "UL Tested." Collective marks appear at the end of motion picture credits to indicate the various associations and organizations that participated in the making of the films.

TRADE NAMES

Trademarks apply to *products.* The term **trade name** is used to indicate part or all of a business's name, whether the business is a sole proprietorship, a partnership, or a corporation. Generally, a trade name is directly related to a business and its goodwill. A trade name may be protected as a trademark if the trade name is also the name of the company's trademarked product—for example, Pepsi-Cola. Unless also used as a trademark or service mark, a trade name cannot be registered with the federal government. Trade names are protected under the common law, however. As

with trademarks, words must be unusual or fancifully used if they are to be protected as trade names. The word *Safeway,* for example, was held by the courts to be sufficiently fanciful to obtain protection as a trade name for a food-store chain.[7]

SECTION 2 | Cyber Marks

In cyberspace, trademarks are sometimes referred to as **cyber marks.** We turn now to a discussion of issues in cyberspace relating to trademarks and how new laws and the courts are addressing these issues. One concern relates to the rights of a trademark's owner to use the mark as part of a domain name (Internet address). Other issues have to do with domain names and cybersquatting, meta tags, and trademark dilution on the Web. The use of licensing as a way to avoid liability for infringing on another's intellectual property rights in cyberspace will also be discussed.

DOMAIN NAMES

In the real world, one business can often use the same name as another without causing any conflict, particularly if the businesses are small, their goods or services are different, and the geographic areas in which they do business are distinctly separate. In the online world, however, there is only one geographic area of business—cyberspace. Thus, disputes between parties over which one has the right to use a particular domain name have become common.

A **domain name** is the core part of an Internet address—for example, "westlaw.com." It includes at least two parts. The top level domain (TLD) is the part of the name to the right of the period, such as *com* or *gov.* The second level domain (the part of the name to the left of the period) is chosen by the business entity or individual registering the domain name.

CONFLICTS OVER DOMAIN NAMES Conflicts over rights to domain names emerged during the 1990s as e-commerce expanded on a worldwide scale. The *.com* TLD came to be widely used by businesses on the Web. Competition among firms with identical or similar names and products for the second level domains preceding the *.com* TLD led, understandably, to numerous disputes over domain name rights. By using the same, or a similar, domain name, parties have attempted to profit from the goodwill of a competitor, to sell pornog-

---

7. *Safeway Stores v. Suburban Foods,* 130 F.Supp. 249 (E.D.Va. 1955).

raphy, to offer for sale another party's domain name, and to otherwise infringe on others' trademarks.

DISPUTE RESOLUTION THROUGH ONLINE ARBITRATION
The federal government set up the Internet Corporation for Assigned Names and Numbers (ICANN), a nonprofit corporation, to oversee the distribution of domain names. ICANN has also played a leading role in facilitating the settlement of domain name disputes worldwide. Since January 2000, ICANN has been operating an online arbitration system to resolve domain name disputes. Now, if trademark infringement involves a domain name, a party may submit a complaint to an ICANN-approved dispute-resolution provider instead of (or in addition to) filing a lawsuit. By 2006, ICANN-approved online arbitration providers were handling well over one thousand disputes annually.

ANTICYBERSQUATTING LEGISLATION

Cybersquatting occurs when a person registers a domain name that is the same as, or confusingly similar to, the trademark of another and then offers to sell the domain name back to the trademark owner. During the 1990s, cybersquatting became a contentious issue and led to much litigation. Often at issue in these cases was whether cybersquatting constituted a commercial use of the mark so as to violate federal trademark law. In 1999, Congress addressed this problem by passing the Anticybersquatting Consumer Protection Act (ACPA),[8] which amended the Lanham Act—the federal law protecting trademarks, discussed earlier in this chapter.

PROVISIONS OF THE ACPA
The ACPA makes it illegal for a person to "register, traffic in, or use" a

8. 15 U.S.C.A. Section 1129.

domain name (1) if the name is identical or confusingly similar to the trademark of another and (2) if the one registering, trafficking in, or using the domain name has a "bad faith intent" to profit from that trademark. The act lists several factors that courts can consider in deciding whether bad faith exists. These factors include the trademark rights of the other person, whether there is an intent to divert consumers in a way that could harm the goodwill represented by the trademark, whether there is an offer to transfer or sell the domain name to the trademark owner, and whether there is an intent to use the domain name to offer goods and services.

APPLICABILITY OF THE ACPA AND SANCTIONS UNDER THE ACT
The ACPA applies to all domain name registrations, even domain names registered before the passage of the act. Successful plaintiffs in suits brought under the act can collect actual damages and profits, or they can elect to receive statutory damages ranging from $1,000 to $100,000.

META TAGS

Search engines compile their results by looking through a Web site's key-word field. **Meta tags,** or key words, may be inserted into this field to increase the site's inclusion in search engine results, even though the site may have nothing to do with the inserted words. Using this same technique, one site may appropriate the key words of other sites with more frequent hits so that the appropriating site will appear in the same search engine results as the more popular sites. Using another's trademark in a meta tag without the owner's permission, however, normally constitutes trademark infringement.

In some situations, using another's trademark as a meta tag may be practically unavoidable. In those situations, the court must determine whether the particular use is permissible or impermissible. One such use of meta tags was at issue in the following case.

CASE 14.2

Playboy Enterprises, Inc. v. Welles

United States
Court of Appeals,
Ninth Circuit, 2002.
279 F.3d 796.

T.G. NELSON, Circuit Judge.
* * * *

Terri Welles was on the cover of *Playboy* in 1981 and was chosen to be the Playboy Playmate of the Year for 1981. Her use of the title "Playboy Playmate of the Year 1981," and her use of other trademarked terms on her website are at issue in this suit. During the relevant time period, Welles' website offered information about and free photos of Welles, advertised photos for sale, advertised memberships in her photo club, and promoted her services as a spokesperson. A biographical section described Welles' selection as Playmate of the Year in 1981 and her years modeling for [Playboy Enterprises, Inc. (PEI)]. After the lawsuit began,

CASE 14.2 | Continued

Welles included discussions of the suit and criticism of PEI on her website and included a note disclaiming any association with PEI.

PEI complains of * * * [Welles's use of] the terms "Playboy" and "Playmate" in the meta tags of the website * * * . PEI claimed [in part] that these uses of its marks constituted trademark infringement [and] dilution * * * . The [federal] district court [that heard the suit] granted defendants' [Welles and her "webmasters," Steven Huntington and Michael Mihalko] motion for summary judgment. PEI appeals the grant of summary judgment on its infringement and dilution claims * * *

* * * *

* * * [W]e conclude that Welles' uses of PEI's trademarks are permissible, nominative uses.[a] They imply no current sponsorship or endorsement by PEI. Instead, they serve to identify Welles as a past PEI "Playmate of the Year."

* * * *

* * * [The] test for nominative use [of a trademark is]:

First, the product or service in question must be one not readily identifiable without use of the trademark; second, only so much of the mark or marks may be used as is reasonably necessary to identify the product or service; and third, the user must do nothing that would, in conjunction with the mark, suggest sponsorship or endorsement by the trademark holder. * * *

* * * *

Welles includes the terms "playboy" and "playmate" in her meta tags. Meta tags describe the contents of a website using keywords. Some search engines search meta tags to identify websites relevant to a search. Thus, when an Internet searcher enters "playboy" or "playmate" into a search engine that uses meta tags, the results will include Welles' site. Because Welles' meta tags do not repeat the terms extensively, her site will not be at the top of the list of search results. Applying the three-factor test for nominative use, we conclude that the use of the trademarked terms in Welles' meta tags is nominative.

* * * Welles has no practical way of describing herself without using trademarked terms. In the context of meta tags, we conclude that she has no practical way of identifying the content of her website without referring to PEI's trademarks.

A large portion of Welles' website discusses her association with Playboy over the years. Thus, the trademarked terms accurately describe the contents of Welles' website, in addition to describing Welles. Forcing Welles and others to use absurd turns of phrase in their meta tags, such as those necessary to identify Welles, would be particularly damaging in the Internet search context. *Searchers would have a much more difficult time locating relevant websites if they could do so only by correctly guessing the long phrases necessary to substitute for trademarks.* We can hardly expect someone searching for Welles' site to imagine the same phrase proposed by the district court to describe Welles without referring to Playboy—"the nude model selected by Mr. Hefner's organization * * * ." Yet if someone could not remember her name, that is what they would have to do. Similarly, someone searching for critiques of Playboy on the Internet would have a difficult time if Internet sites could not list the object of their critique in their meta tags. [Emphasis added.]

There is simply no descriptive substitute for the trademarks used in Welles' meta tags. *Precluding their use would have the unwanted effect of hindering the free flow of information on the Internet, something which is certainly not a goal of trademark law.* Accordingly, the use of trademarked terms in the meta tags meets the first part of the test for nominative use. [Emphasis added.]

We conclude that the meta tags satisfy the second and third elements of the test as well. The meta tags use only so much of the marks as reasonably necessary and nothing is done in conjunction with them to suggest sponsorship or endorsement by the trademark holder. We note that our decision might differ if the meta tags listed the trademarked term so repeatedly that Welles' site would regularly appear above PEI's in searches for one of the trademarked terms.

* * * *

---

a. A *nominative use* of a trademark is one that does not imply sponsorship or endorsement of a product because the product's mark is used only to describe the thing, rather than to identify its source. See *New Kids on the Block v. News America Publishing, Inc.*, 971 F.2d 302 (9th Cir. 1992).

CASE 14.2 | Continued

Dilution works its harm not by causing confusion in consumers' minds regarding the source of a good or service, but by creating an association in consumers' minds between a mark and a different good or service. * * *

Uses that do not create an improper association between a mark and a new product but merely identify the trademark holder's products should be excepted from the reach of the [Federal Trademark Dilution Act]. Such uses cause no harm. The anti-dilution statute recognizes this principle and specifically excepts users of a trademark who compare their product in "commercial advertising or promotion to identify the competing goods or services of the owner of the famous mark."

For the same reason uses in comparative advertising are excepted from anti-dilution law, we conclude that nominative uses are also excepted. A nominative use, by definition, refers to the trademark holder's product. It does not create an improper association in consumers' minds between a new product and the trademark holder's mark.

When Welles refers to her title, she is in effect referring to a product of PEI's. She does not dilute the title by truthfully identifying herself as its one-time recipient any more than Michael Jordan would dilute the name "Chicago Bulls" by referring to himself as a former member of that team, or the two-time winner of an Academy Award would dilute the award by referring to him or herself as a "two-time Academy Award winner." Awards are not diminished or diluted by the fact that they have been awarded in the past. Similarly, they are not diminished or diluted when past recipients truthfully identify themselves as such. It is in the nature of honors and awards to be identified with the people who receive them. * * *
* * * *

For the foregoing reasons, we affirm the district court's grant of summary judgment as to PEI's claims for trademark infringement and trademark dilution * * * .

QUESTIONS

1. Welles also used the PEI marks in the headlines on her Web site and in the banner advertisements that could be transferred to other sites and linked to hers. Should these uses be permitted as nominative? Why or why not?
2. Why would PEI encourage its models to use its marks outside cyberspace but attempt to block such uses within cyberspace?

DILUTION IN THE ONLINE WORLD

As discussed earlier, trademark *dilution* occurs when a trademark is used, without authorization, in a way that diminishes the distinctive quality of the mark. Unlike trademark infringement, a dilution cause of action does not require proof that consumers are likely to be confused by a connection between the unauthorized use and the mark. For this reason, the products involved need not be similar.

In the first case alleging dilution on the Web, a court precluded the use of "candyland.com" as the URL for an adult site. The court held that the use of the URL would dilute the value of the "Candyland" mark owned by the maker of the "Candyland" children's game.[9] In another case, a court issued an injunction on the ground that spamming under another's

logo is trademark dilution. In that case, Hotmail Corporation provided e-mail services and worked to dissociate itself from spam. Van$ Money Pie, Inc., and others spammed thousands of e-mail customers, using the free e-mail Hotmail as a return address. The court ordered the defendants to stop.[10]

LICENSING

One way to make use of another's trademark or other form of intellectual property, while avoiding litigation, is to obtain a license to do so. A license in this context is essentially an agreement permitting the use of a trademark, copyright, patent, or trade secret for certain purposes. For example, a licensee (the party obtaining the license) might be allowed to use the trademark of

---

9. *Hasbro, Inc. v. Internet Entertainment Group, Ltd.*, 1996 WL 84853 (W.D. Wash. 1996).

10. *Hotmail Corp. v. Van$ Money Pie, Inc.*, 1998 WL 388389 (N.D.Cal. 1998).

the licensor (the party issuing the license) as part of the name of its company, or as part of its domain name, without otherwise using the mark on any products or services. Often, selling a license to an infringer is an inexpensive solution to the problem, at least when compared with the costs associated with litigation.

SECTION 3 | Patents

A **patent** is a grant from the government that gives an inventor the right to exclude others from making, using, and selling an invention for a period of twenty years from the date of filing the application for a patent. Patents for designs, as opposed to inventions, are given for a fourteen-year period. The applicant must demonstrate to the satisfaction of the U.S. Patent and Trademark Office that the invention, discovery, process, or design is genuine, novel, useful, and not obvious in light of current technology. A patent holder gives notice to all that an article or design is patented by placing on it the word *Patent* or *Pat.*, plus the patent number. In contrast to patent law in other countries, in the United States patent protection is given to the first person to invent a product or process, even though someone else may have been the first to file for a patent on that product or process.

A significant development relating to patents is the availability online of the world's patent databases. The Web site of the U.S. Patent and Trademark Office (see the *Law on the Web* section at the end of this chapter for its URL) provides searchable databases covering U.S. patents granted since 1976. The Web site of the European Patent Office maintains databases covering all patent documents in sixty-five nations and the legal status of patents in twenty-two of those countries.

PATENT INFRINGEMENT

If a firm makes, uses, or sells another's patented design, product, or process without the patent owner's permission, the tort of patent infringement occurs. Patent infringement may arise even though the patent owner has not put the patented product in commerce. Patent infringement may also occur even though not all features or parts of an invention are identical, provided that the features are equivalent to those used in the patented invention.

Patent infringement litigation can be very costly. Often, rather than pursue litigation, the patent holder will offer to sell to the infringer a license to use the patented design, product, or process. Indeed, in many situations, licensing is the best option because the costs of detection, prosecution, and monitoring infringement are prohibitively high.

PATENTS FOR SOFTWARE

At one time, it was difficult for developers and manufacturers of software to obtain patent protection because many software products simply automate procedures that can be performed manually. In other words, the computer programs do not meet the "novel" and "not obvious" requirements previously mentioned. Also, the basis for software is often a mathematical equation or formula, which is not patentable. In 1981, however, the United States Supreme Court held that it is possible to obtain a patent for a process that incorporates a computer program—providing, of course, that the process itself is patentable.[11] Subsequently, many patents have been issued for software-related inventions.

PATENTS FOR BUSINESS PROCESSES

In a landmark 1998 case, *State Street Bank & Trust Co. v. Signature Financial Group, Inc.*,[12] the U.S. Court of Appeals for the Federal Circuit ruled that only three categories of subject matter will always remain unpatentable: (1) the laws of nature, (2) natural phenomena, and (3) abstract ideas.

After this decision, numerous technology firms applied for business process patents. Walker Digital applied for a business process patent for its "Dutch auction" system, which allowed consumers to make offers for airline tickets on the Internet and led to the creation of Priceline.com. About.com obtained a patent for its "Elaborative Internet Data Mining System," which extracts and pulls together the Web content of a large range of topics onto a single Web site. Amazon.com obtained a business process patent for its "one-click" ordering system, a method of processing credit-card orders securely without asking for the customer's card number or other personal information, such as the customer's name and address, more than once. Indeed, after the *State Street* decision, the number of Internet-related patents issued by the U.S. Patent and Trademark Office initially increased dramatically.

---

11. *Diamond v. Diehr*, 450 U.S. 175, 101 S.Ct. 1048, 67 L.Ed.2d 155 (1981).
12. 149 F.3d 1368 (Fed. Cir. 1998).

SECTION 4 | Copyrights

A **copyright** is an intangible property right granted by federal statute to the author or originator of a literary or artistic production of a specified type. Today, copyrights are governed by the Copyright Act of 1976,[13] as amended. Works created after January 1, 1978, are automatically given statutory copyright protection for the life of the author, plus 70 years. For copyrights owned by publishing houses, the copyright expires 95 years from the date of publication or 120 years from the date of creation, whichever is first. For works by more than one author, the copyright expires 70 years after the death of the last surviving author.

These time periods reflect the extensions of the length of copyright protection enacted by Congress in the Copyright Term Extension Act of 1998.[14] Critics challenged this act as overstepping the bounds of Congress's power and violating the constitutional requirement that copyrights endure for only a limited time. In 2003, however, the United States Supreme Court upheld the act in *Eldred v. Ashcroft*.[15] This holding obviously favored copyright holders by preventing copyrighted works from the 1920s and 1930s from losing protection and falling into the public domain for an additional two decades.

Copyrights can be registered with the U.S. Copyright Office in Washington, D.C. A copyright owner no longer needs to place the symbol © or the term *Copr.* or *Copyright* on the work, however, to have the work protected against infringement. Chances are that if somebody created it, somebody owns it.

WHAT IS PROTECTED EXPRESSION?

Works that are copyrightable include books, records, films, artworks, architectural plans, menus, music videos, product packaging, and computer software. To obtain protection under the Copyright Act, a work must be original and fall into one of the following categories: (1) literary works (including newspaper and magazine articles, computer and training manuals, catalogues, brochures, and print advertisements); (2) musical works and accompanying words (including advertising jingles); (3) dramatic works and accompanying music; (4) pantomimes and choreographic works (including ballets and other forms of dance); (5) pictorial, graphic, and sculptural works (including cartoons, maps, posters, statues, and even stuffed animals); (6) motion pictures and other audiovisual works (including multimedia works); (7) sound recordings; and (8) architectural works. To be protected, a work must be "fixed in a durable medium" from which it can be perceived, reproduced, or communicated. Protection is automatic. Registration is not required.

SECTION 102 EXCLUSIONS Section 102 of the Copyright Act specifically excludes copyright protection for any "idea, procedure, process, system, method of operation, concept, principle, or discovery, regardless of the form in which it is described, explained, illustrated, or embodied." Note that it is not possible to copyright an *idea*. The underlying ideas embodied in a work may be freely used by others. What is copyrightable is the particular way in which an idea is expressed. Whenever an idea and an expression are inseparable, the expression cannot be copyrighted. Generally, anything that is not an original expression will not qualify for copyright protection. Facts widely known to the public are not copyrightable. Page numbers are not copyrightable because they follow a sequence known to everyone. Mathematical calculations are not copyrightable.

COMPILATIONS OF FACTS *Compilations* of facts are copyrightable. Section 103 of the Copyright Act defines a compilation as "a work formed by the collection and assembling of preexisting materials or data that are selected, coordinated, or arranged in such a way that the resulting work as a whole constitutes an original work of authorship." The key requirement in the copyrightability of a compilation is originality. Therefore, the white pages of a telephone directory do not qualify for copyright protection when the information that makes up the directory (names, addresses, and telephone numbers) is not selected, coordinated, or arranged in an original way.[16] In one case, even the Yellow Pages of a telephone directory did not qualify for copyright protection.[17]

---

13. 17 U.S.C. Sections 101 *et seq.*
14. 17 U.S.C.A. Section 302.
15. 537 U.S. 186, 123 S.Ct. 769, 154 L.Ed.2d 683 (2003).

16. *Feist Publications, Inc. v. Rural Telephone Service Co.*, 499 U.S. 340, 111 S.Ct. 1282, 113 L.Ed.2d 358 (1991).
17. *Bellsouth Advertising & Publishing Corp. v. Donnelley Information Publishing, Inc.*, 999 F.2d 1436 (11th Cir. 1993).

COPYRIGHT INFRINGEMENT

Whenever the form or expression of an idea is copied, an infringement of copyright has occurred. The reproduction does not have to be exactly the same as the original, nor does it have to reproduce the original in its entirety. If a substantial part of the original is reproduced, there is copyright infringement.

DAMAGES FOR COPYRIGHT INFRINGEMENT

Those who infringe copyrights may be liable for damages or criminal penalties. These range from actual damages or statutory damages, imposed at the court's discretion, to criminal proceedings for willful violations. Actual damages are based on the harm caused to the copyright holder by the infringement, while statutory damages, not to exceed $150,000, are provided for under the Copyright Act. Criminal proceedings may result in fines and/or imprisonment.

THE "FAIR USE" EXCEPTION

An exception to liability for copyright infringement is made under the "fair use" doctrine. In certain circumstances, a person or organization can reproduce copyrighted material without paying royalties (fees paid to the copyright holder for the privilege of reproducing the copyrighted material). Section 107 of the Copyright Act provides as follows:

> [T]he fair use of a copyrighted work, including such use by reproduction in copies or phonorecords or by any other means specified by [Section 106 of the Copyright Act], for purposes such as criticism, comment, news reporting, teaching (including multiple copies for classroom use), scholarship, or research, is not an infringement of copyright. In determining whether the use made of a work in any particular case is a fair use the factors to be considered shall include–
>
> (1) the purpose and character of the use, including whether such use is of a commercial nature or is for nonprofit educational purposes;
> (2) the nature of the copyrighted work;
> (3) the amount and substantiality of the portion used in relation to the copyrighted work as a whole; and
> (4) the effect of the use upon the potential market for or value of the copyrighted work.

Because these guidelines are very broad, the courts determine whether a particular use is fair on a case-by-case basis. Thus, anyone who reproduces copyrighted material may still be committing a violation. In determining whether a use is fair, courts have often considered the fourth factor to be the most important.

COPYRIGHT PROTECTION FOR SOFTWARE

In 1980, Congress passed the Computer Software Copyright Act, which amended the Copyright Act of 1976 to include computer programs in the list of creative works protected by federal copyright law.[18] The 1980 statute, which classifies computer programs as "literary works," defines a computer program as a "set of statements or instructions to be used directly or indirectly in a computer in order to bring about a certain result."

The unique nature of computer programs, however, has created many problems for the courts in applying and interpreting the 1980 act. Generally, the courts have held that copyright protection extends not only to those parts of a computer program that can be read by humans, such as the "high-level" language of a source code, but also to the binary-language object code, which is readable only by the computer.[19] Additionally, such elements as the overall structure, sequence, and organization of a program were deemed copyrightable.[20] The courts have disagreed on the issue of whether the "look and feel"—the general appearance, command structure, video images, menus, windows, and other screen displays—of computer programs should also be protected by copyright. The courts have tended, however, not to extend copyright protection to look-and-feel aspects of computer programs.

SECTION 5 | Copyrights in Digital Information

Copyright law is probably the most important form of intellectual property protection on the Internet. This is because much of the material on the Internet consists of works of authorship (including multimedia presentations, software, and database information), which are the traditional focus of copyright law. Copyright law is also important because the nature of the Internet requires that data be "copied" to be transferred online. Copies are a significant part of the traditional controversies arising in this area of the law.

---

18. Pub. L. No. 96-517 (1980), amending 17 U.S.C.A. Sections 101, 117.
19. See *Stern Electronics, Inc. v. Kaufman*, 669 F.2d 852 (2d Cir. 1982); and *Apple Computer, Inc. v. Franklin Computer Corp.*, 714 F.2d 1240 (3d Cir. 1983).
20. *Whelan Associates, Inc. v. Jaslow Dental Laboratory, Inc.*, 797 F.2d 1222 (3d Cir. 1986).

THE COPYRIGHT ACT OF 1976

When Congress drafted the principal U.S. law governing copyrights, the Copyright Act of 1976, cyberspace did not exist for most of us. At that time, the rights of copyright owners were threatened not by computer technology but by unauthorized *tangible* copies of works and the sale of rights to movies, television, and other media.

Some issues that were unimagined when the Copyright Act was drafted have posed thorny questions for the courts. For example, to sell a copy of a work, permission of the copyright holder is necessary. Because of the nature of cyberspace, however, one of the early controversies involved determining at what point an intangible, electronic "copy" of a work has been made. The courts have held that loading a file or program into a computer's random access memory, or RAM, constitutes the making of a "copy" for purposes of copyright law.[21] RAM is a portion of a computer's memory into which a file, for example, is loaded so that it can be accessed (read or written over). Thus, a copyright is infringed when a party downloads software into RAM without owning the software or otherwise having a right to download it.[22]

Today, technology has vastly increased the potential for copyright infringement. The question in the following case was whether a musician commits copyright infringement when he or she copies any part—even as little as two seconds—of a copyrighted sound recording without the permission of the copyright's owner.

---

21. *MAI Systems Corp. v. Peak Computer, Inc.*, 991 F.2d 511 (9th Cir. 1993).
22. *DSC Communications Corp. v. Pulse Communications, Inc.*, 170 F.3d 1354 (Fed. Cir. 1999).

CASE 14.3

United States
Court of Appeals,
Sixth Circuit, 2003.
383 F.3d 390.
*http://www.findlaw.com/
casecode/courts/6th.html*[b]

Bridgeport Music, Inc. v. Dimension Films[a]

BACKGROUND AND FACTS *Bridgeport Music, Inc., is in the business of music publishing and using musical composition copyrights. Westbound Records, Inc., is in the business of recording and distributing sound recordings. Bridgeport and Westbound own the composition and recording copyrights to "Get Off Your Ass and Jam" by George Clinton, Jr., and the Funkadelics. The recording "Get Off" opens with a three-note solo guitar riff that lasts four seconds. The rap song "100 Miles and Runnin" contains a two-second sample from the guitar solo, at a lower pitch, looped and extended to sixteen beats, in five places in the song, with each looped segment lasting about seven seconds. "100 Miles" was included in the sound track of the movie* I Got the Hook Up, *which was distributed by No Limit Films. Bridgeport, Westbound, and others filed a suit in a federal district court against No Limit and others, alleging copyright infringement. No Limit did not dispute that it had digitally sampled a copyrighted sound recording. The court found, however, that no reasonable juror, even one familiar with the works of George Clinton, would recognize the source of the sample and issued a summary judgment in the defendants' favor. Plaintiffs appealed the judgment to the U.S. Court of Appeals for the Sixth Circuit.*

IN THE LANGUAGE OF THE COURT

RALPH B. GUY, JR., Circuit Judge.

* * * *

* * * The copyright laws attempt to strike a balance between protecting original works and stifling further creativity. The provisions, for example, for compulsory licensing make it possible for "creators" to enjoy the fruits of their creations, but not to fence them off from the world at large. Although musical compositions have always enjoyed copyright

---

a. Initially, Dimension Films was also a defendant in this case. The claims against this company were dismissed pursuant to a settlement prior to trial.
b. This URL will take you to a Web site maintained by FindLaw, which is now a part of West Group. In the "Docket Number Search" box, type "02-6521" and click on "Get It" to access the opinion.

CONTINUED ➤

CASE 14.3 Continued

protection, it was not until 1971 that sound recordings were subject to a separate copyright. If one were to analogize to a book, it is not the book, *i.e.*, the paper and binding, that is copyrightable, but its contents. There are probably any number of reasons why the decision was made by Congress to treat a sound recording differently from a book even though both are the media in which an original work is fixed rather than the creation itself. Not the least of [these reasons] certainly were advances in technology which made the "pirating" of sound recordings an easy task. The balance that was struck was to give sound recording copyright holders the exclusive right to duplicate the sound recording in the form of phonorecords or copies that directly or indirectly recapture the actual sounds fixed in the recording. This means that *the world at large is free to imitate or simulate the creative work fixed in the recording so long as an actual copy of the sound recording itself is not made.* That leads us directly to the issue in this case. If you cannot pirate the whole sound recording, can you "lift" or "sample" something less than the whole? Our answer to that question is in the negative. [Emphasis added.]

Section 114(b) [of the Copyright Act] provides that "[t]he exclusive right of the owner of copyright in a sound recording under clause (2) of Section 106 is limited to the right to prepare a derivative work in which the actual sounds fixed in the sound recording are rearranged, remixed, or otherwise altered in sequence or quality." In other words, *a sound recording owner has the exclusive right to "sample" his own recording.* We find much to recommend this interpretation. [Emphasis added.]

To begin with, there is ease of enforcement. Get a license or do not sample. We do not see this as stifling creativity in any significant way. It must be remembered that if an artist wants to incorporate a "riff" from another work in his or her recording, he is free to duplicate the sound of that "riff" in the studio. Second, the market will control the license price and keep it within bounds. The sound recording copyright holder cannot exact a license fee greater than what it would cost the person seeking the license to just duplicate the sample in the course of making the new recording. Third, sampling is never accidental. It is not like the case of a composer who has a melody in his head, perhaps not even realizing that the reason he hears this melody is that it is the work of another which he had heard before. When you sample a sound recording you know you are taking another's work product.

This analysis admittedly raises the question of why one should, without infringing, be able to take three notes from a musical composition, for example, but not three notes by way of sampling from a sound recording. * * * Our first answer to this question is what we have earlier indicated. We think this result is dictated by the applicable statute. Second, *even when a small part of a sound recording is sampled, the part taken is something of value.* No further proof of that is necessary than the fact that the producer of the record or the artist on the record intentionally sampled because it would (1) save costs, or (2) add something to the new recording, or (3) both. For the sound recording copyright holder, it is not the "song" but the sounds that are fixed in the medium of his choice. When those sounds are sampled, they are taken directly from that fixed medium. It is a physical taking rather than an intellectual one. [Emphasis added.]

DECISION AND REMEDY *The U.S. Court of Appeals for the Sixth Circuit reversed the lower court's summary judgment on the plaintiff's claims against No Limit and remanded the case. The appellate court held that digitally sampling a copyrighted sound recording of any length is copyright infringement.*

WHAT IF THE FACTS WERE DIFFERENT? *Suppose that instead of a sound recording, this case had involved three seconds of a copyrighted movie, which the defendants pirated off the Internet and incorporated as background in a music video production. Would this court's holding be different? Why or why not?*

FURTHER DEVELOPMENTS IN COPYRIGHT LAW

In the last several years, Congress has enacted legislation designed specifically to protect copyright holders in a digital age. Particularly significant are the No Electronic Theft Act of 1997[23] and the Digital Millennium Copyright Act of 1998.[24]

THE NO ELECTRONIC THEFT ACT Prior to 1997, criminal penalties could be imposed under copyright law only if unauthorized copies were exchanged for financial gain. Yet much piracy of copyrighted materials was "altruistic" in nature; that is, unauthorized copies were made and distributed not for financial gain but simply for reasons of generosity—to share the copies with others. To combat altruistic piracy and for other reasons, Congress passed the No Electronic Theft (NET) Act of 1997.

NET extends criminal liability for the piracy of copyrighted materials to persons who exchange unauthorized copies of copyrighted works, such as software, even though they realize no profit from the exchange. The act also imposes penalties on those who make unauthorized electronic copies of books, magazines, movies, or music for *personal* use, thus altering the traditional "fair use" doctrine. The criminal penalties for violating the act are relatively severe; they include fines as high as $250,000 and incarceration for up to five years.

THE DIGITAL MILLENNIUM COPYRIGHT ACT OF 1998 The passage of the Digital Millennium Copyright Act (DMCA) of 1998 gave significant protection to owners of copyrights in digital information.[25] Among other things, the act established civil and criminal penalties for anyone who circumvents (bypasses, or gets around—by using a special decryption program, for example) encryption software or other technological antipiracy protection. Also prohibited are the manufacture, import, sale, and distribution of devices or services for circumvention.

The DMCA provides for exceptions to fit the needs of libraries, scientists, universities, and others. In general, the law does not restrict the "fair use" of circumvention methods for educational and other noncommercial purposes. For example, circumvention is allowed to test computer security, to conduct encryption research, to protect personal privacy, and to enable parents to monitor their children's use of the Internet. The exceptions are to be reconsidered every three years.

The DMCA also limits the liability of Internet service providers (ISPs). Under the act, an ISP is not liable for any copyright infringement by its customer *unless* the ISP is aware of the subscriber's violation. An ISP may be held liable only if it fails to take action to shut the subscriber down after learning of the violation. A copyright holder must act promptly, however, by pursuing a claim in court, or the subscriber has the right to be restored to online access.

MP3 AND FILE-SHARING TECHNOLOGY

Soon after the Internet became popular, a few enterprising programmers created software to compress large data files, particularly those associated with music. The reduced file sizes make transmitting music over the Internet feasible. The most widely known compression and decompression system is MP3, which enables music fans to download songs or entire compact discs (CDs) onto their computers or onto portable listening devices, such as Rio or iPod. The MP3 system also made it possible for music fans to access other music fans' files by engaging in file-sharing via the Internet.

PEER-TO-PEER (P2P) NETWORKING File-sharing via the Internet is accomplished through what is called **peer-to-peer (P2P) networking.** The concept is simple. Rather than going through a central Web server, P2P networking uses numerous personal computers (PCs) that are connected to the Internet. Files stored on one PC can be accessed by others who are members of the same network. Sometimes this is called a **distributed network** because parts of the network are distributed all over the country or the world. File-sharing offers an unlimited number of uses for distributed networks. Currently, for example, thousands of researchers simultaneously allow their home computers' computing power to be accessed through file-sharing software so

---

23. Pub. L. No. 105-147 (1997). Codified at 17 U.S.C.A. Sections 101, 506; 18 U.S.C.A. Sections 2311, 2319, 2319A, 2320; and 28 U.S.C.A. Sections 994 and 1498.

24. 17 U.S.C. Sections 512, 1201–1205, 1301–1332; and 28 U.S.C. Section 4001.

25. This act implemented the World Intellectual Property Organization (WIPO) Copyright Treaty of 1996, which will be discussed later in this chapter.

that very large mathematical problems can be solved quickly. Additionally, persons scattered throughout the country or the world can work together on the same project by using file-sharing programs.

SHARING STORED MUSIC FILES File-sharing clearly offers many advantages. When file-sharing is used to download others' stored music files, however, copyright issues arise. Recording artists and their labels stand to lose large amounts of royalties and revenues if relatively few CDs are purchased and then made available on distributed networks, from which everyone can get them for free. In the following widely publicized case, several firms in the recording industry sued Napster, Inc., the owner of the then-popular Napster Web site. The firms alleged that Napster was contributing to copyright infringement by those who downloaded CDs from other computers in the Napster file-sharing system. At issue was whether Napster could be held vicariously liable for the infringement.[26]

---

26. *Vicarious* (substitute) *liability* exists when one person is subject to liability for another's actions. A common example occurs in the employment context, when an employer is held vicariously liable by third parties for torts committed by employees in the course of their employment.

CASE 14.4 — A&M Records, Inc. v. Napster, Inc.

United States
Court of Appeals,
Ninth Circuit, 2001.
239 F.3d 1004.
http://www.findlaw.com/
casecode/courts/9th.html [a]

HISTORICAL AND TECHNOLOGICAL SETTING *In 1987, the Moving Picture Experts Group set a standard file format for the storage of audio recordings in a digital format called MPEG-3, abbreviated as "MP3." Digital MP3 files are created through a process called "ripping." Ripping software allows a computer owner to copy an audio compact disc (CD) directly onto a computer's hard drive by compressing the audio information on the CD into the MP3 format. The MP3's compressed format allows for rapid transmission of digital audio files from one computer to another by e-mail or any other file-transfer protocol.*

BACKGROUND AND FACTS *Napster, Inc. (http://www.napster.com), facilitated the transmission of MP3 files among the users of its Web site through a process called "peer-to-peer" file-sharing. Napster allowed users to transfer exact copies of the contents of MP3 files from one computer to another via the Internet. This was made possible by Napster's MusicShare software, available free of charge from Napster's site, and Napster's network servers and server-side software. Napster also provided technical support. A&M Records, Inc., and others engaged in the commercial recording, distribution, and sale of copyrighted musical compositions and sound recordings, filed a suit in a federal district court against Napster, alleging copyright infringement. The court issued a preliminary injunction ordering Napster to stop "facilitating others in copying, downloading, uploading, transmitting, or distributing plaintiffs' copyrighted musical compositions and sound recordings, * * * without express permission of the rights owner." Napster appealed to the U.S. Court of Appeals for the Ninth Circuit.*

IN THE LANGUAGE OF THE COURT

BEEZER, Circuit Judge.

* * * *

* * * In the context of copyright law, vicarious liability extends * * * to cases in which a defendant has the right and ability to supervise the infringing activity and also has a direct financial interest in such activities.

* * * *

The ability to block infringers' access to a particular environment for any reason whatsoever is evidence of the right and ability to supervise. Here, plaintiffs have demonstrated that Napster retains the right to control access to its system. Napster has an express reservation of rights policy, stating on its website that it expressly reserves the "right to refuse service and terminate accounts in [its] discretion, including, but not limited to, if Napster believes that

---

a. This URL will take you to a Web site maintained by FindLaw, which is now a part of West Group. When you access the site, enter "Napster" in the "Party Name Search" box and then click on "Search." Select the *Napster* case dated "02/12/2001" from the list on the page that opens.

CASE 14.4 **Continued** user conduct violates applicable law * * * or for any reason in Napster's sole discretion, with or without cause."

To escape imposition of vicarious liability, the reserved right to police must be exercised to its fullest extent. *Turning a blind eye to detectable acts of infringement for the sake of profit gives rise to liability.* [Emphasis added.]

The district court correctly determined that Napster had the right and ability to police its system and failed to exercise that right to prevent the exchange of copyrighted material. * * *

Napster * * * has the ability to locate infringing material listed on its search indices, and the right to terminate users' access to the system. The file name indices, therefore, are within the "premises" that Napster has the ability to police. We recognize that the files are user-named and may not match copyrighted material exactly (for example, the artist or song could be spelled wrong). For Napster to function effectively, however, file names must reasonably or roughly correspond to the material contained in the files, otherwise no user could ever locate any desired music. As a practical matter, Napster, its users, and the record company plaintiffs have equal access to infringing material by employing Napster's "search function."

Our review of the record requires us to accept the district court's conclusion that plaintiffs have demonstrated a likelihood of success on the merits of the vicarious copyright infringement claim. Napster's failure to police the system's "premises," combined with a showing that Napster financially benefits from the continuing availability of infringing files on its system, leads to the imposition of vicarious liability.

DECISION AND REMEDY *The U.S. Court of Appeals for the Ninth Circuit affirmed the lower court's decision that Napster was obligated to police its own system and had likely infringed the plaintiffs' copyrights. Holding that the injunction was "overbroad," however, the appellate court remanded the case for a clarification of Napster's responsibility to determine whether music on its Web site was copyrighted.* **b**

---

b. Napster later filed for bankruptcy but today offers a for-fee music downloading service. The case against *Napster* has not yet been fully resolved; however, the district court in 2005 did rule in the defendants' favor on one of the plaintiff's claims. __ F.Supp.2d __ (N.D.Cal. 2005).

NEW FILE-SHARING TECHNOLOGIES   In the wake of the *Napster* decision, other companies developed new technologies that allow P2P network users to share stored music files, without paying a fee, more quickly and efficiently than ever. Today's file-sharing software is decentralized and does not use search indices. Thus, the companies have no knowledge or control over which music (or other media files) their users are exchanging. Unlike the Napster system, in which the company played a role in connecting people who were downloading and uploading songs, the new systems are designed to work without the company's input.

Software such as Morpheus and KaZaA, for example, provides users with an interface that is similar to a Web browser. This technology is very different from that used by Napster. Instead of the company locating songs for users on other members' computers, the software automatically annotates files with descriptive information so that the music can easily be categorized and cross-referenced (by artist and title, for instance). When a user performs a search, the software is able to locate a list of peers that have the file available for downloading. Also, to expedite the P2P transfer and ensure that the complete file is received, the software distributes the download task over the entire list of peers simultaneously. By downloading even one file, the user becomes a point of distribution for that file, which is then automatically shared with others on the network.

How will the courts decide the legality of these new digital technologies? The *Contemporary Legal Debates* feature on the next two pages discusses this issue.

SECTION 6 | Trade Secrets

Some business processes and information that are not, or cannot be, patented, copyrighted, or trademarked are nevertheless protected against appropriation by competitors as trade secrets. **Trade secrets** consist of customer lists, plans, research and development, pricing information, marketing methods, production techniques, and generally anything that makes an

New Technology and Copyright Infringement

Nearly 20 million Americans downloaded music from the Internet in 2004. Worldwide, it is estimated that 85 million songs and roughly half a million movies are downloaded from the Internet every day—90 percent of which constitute copyright infringement.[a] Clearly, any person who downloads copyrighted music or movies without permission from the copyright holder is liable for copyright infringement. But what about the companies that provide the software that enables users to exchange copyrighted materials? In what circumstances should these companies be held liable? Courts have had difficulty applying the traditional doctrines of contributory and vicarious copyright liability to new technologies.

THE GROKSTER CASE

Consider, for example, the situation faced by the court in *Metro-Goldwyn-Mayer Studios, Inc. v. Grokster, Ltd.*[b] In that case, organizations in the music and film industry (the plaintiffs) sued several companies that distribute file-sharing software used in P2P networks. The defendants included Grokster, Ltd., and StreamCast Networks, Inc. The plaintiffs claimed that the companies were contributorily and vicariously liable for the infringement of their end users. The federal district court examined the technology involved and concluded that the defendants were not liable for contributory infringement because they lacked the requisite level of knowledge. According to the court, it was not enough that the defendants *generally*

knew that the software they provided might be used to infringe on copyrights; they also had to have *specific knowledge* of the infringement "at a time when they can use that knowledge to stop the particular infringement." Here, the companies had distributed free software. They had no specific knowledge of whether users were exchanging copyrighted files and had no ability to stop users from infringing activities. The court also held that the defendants could not be held vicariously liable for the infringement because they did not monitor, control, or supervise the software's use and had no duty to police infringements.

The district court's decision was affirmed on appeal.[c] The appellate court, relying on an earlier Supreme Court precedent, reasoned that the level of knowledge required depends on whether the product was "capable of substantial" or "commercially significant noninfringing uses."[d] Because file-sharing software is capable of commercially significant noninfringing uses, the appellate court held that the defendants must have reasonable knowledge of specific instances of infringement to be held liable.

THE UNITED STATES SUPREME COURT TAKES UP THE ISSUE

In June 2005, the United States Supreme Court unanimously overturned the appellate court's decision in the *Grokster* case and remanded the case for further proceedings. The Court held

a. Gregory G. Garre, "Copyright Bandits at Large," *Internet Law & Strategy,* Vol. 3, No. 1, January 2005.

b. 243 F.Supp.2d 1073 (C.D.Cal. 2003).

c. *Metro-Goldwyn-Mayer Studios, Inc. v. Grokster, Ltd.*, 380 F.3d 1154 (9th Cir. 2004).

d. See *Sony Corp. of America v. Universal City Studios, Inc.*, 464 U.S. 417, 104 S.Ct. 774, 78 L.Ed.2d 574 (1984).

individual company unique and that would have value to a competitor.

Unlike copyright and trademark protection, protection of trade secrets extends both to ideas and to their expression. (For this reason, and because a trade secret involves no registration or filing requirements, trade secret protection may be well suited for software.) Of course, the secret formula, method, or other information must be disclosed to some persons, particularly to key employees. Businesses generally attempt to protect their trade secrets by having all

employees who use the process or information agree in their contracts, or in confidentiality agreements, never to divulge it.

STATE AND FEDERAL LAW ON TRADE SECRETS

Under Section 757 of the *Restatement of Torts,* "One who discloses or uses another's trade secret, without a privilege to do so, is liable to the other if (1) he [or she] discovered the secret by improper means, or (2) his [or

that "one who distributes a device [software] with the object of promoting its use to infringe copyright, as shown by clear expression or other affirmative steps taken to foster infringement, is liable for the resulting acts of infringement by third parties."[e] The Court did not, however, specify what kind of "affirmative steps" are necessary to establish liability.

According to Justice Souter, who delivered the Court's opinion, there was ample evidence in the record that the defendants acted with the intent to cause copyright violations by use of their software. What was lacking, according to the Court, was evidence that the defendants "communicated an inducing message to their software users." The decision therefore left it up to the lower court on remand to determine if the defendants had actually induced their users to commit infringement.

The Supreme Court's decision in the *Grokster* case shifts the focus in secondary copyright infringement cases away from specific knowledge of acts of infringement to inducing or promoting infringement. Essentially, this means that file-sharing companies that have taken affirmative steps to promote copyright infringement can be held secondarily liable for the millions of infringing acts that their users commit daily. Nevertheless, because the Court did not define exactly what is necessary to impose liability, there is significant room for debate.

THE DEBATE CONTINUES

Many were hoping that the Supreme Court would spell out in the *Grokster* case exactly what is and is not legal in P2P and

file-sharing networks, but the decision failed to clarify that point. Thus, the future of P2P networks and file-sharing services remains unclear.

Critics claim that the Supreme Court's decision in the *Grokster* case creates a great deal of legal uncertainty and will stifle American innovation. Because the decision establishes a new theory of copyright liability that is based on whether the manufacturer created the technology with the intent of inducing infringement, critics claim it will unleash a barrage of litigation against technological innovators. Technology firms will have a harder time convincing banks, investors, and courts that their products are legal. The threat of legal costs and potential damage awards may ultimately lead many technological companies to modify their software and products to please the entertainment industry (copyright holders) rather than consumers.

WHERE DO YOU STAND?

The entertainment industry maintains that providers of the file-sharing services used to swap copyrighted files should be held liable because they know about and encourage their users' acts of infringement. Other groups, however, including the defendants in the *Grokster* case, compare the providers of file-sharing services to companies that sell copy machines. The courts do not hold Xerox Corporation liable when people use its copy machines to make infringing copies of copyrighted materials. Which side of this debate do you support? Is it possible for the courts to determine whether a company has promoted or induced copyright infringement? What is the best way to address the problem of music and movie piracy?

---

e. *Metro-Goldwyn-Mayer Studios, Inc. v. Grokster, Ltd.*, __ U.S. __, 125 S.Ct. 2764, __ L.Ed.2d __ (2005).

---

her] disclosure or use constitutes a breach of confidence reposed in him [or her] by the other in disclosing the secret to him [or her]." The theft of confidential business data by industrial espionage, as when a business taps into a competitor's computer, is a theft of trade secrets without any contractual violation and is actionable in itself.

Until about twenty-five years ago, virtually all law with respect to trade secrets was common law. In an effort to reduce the unpredictability of the common law in this area, a model act, the Uniform Trade

Secrets Act, was presented to the states for adoption in 1979. Parts of the act have been adopted in more than thirty states. Typically, a state that has adopted parts of the act has adopted only those parts that encompass its own existing common law. Additionally, in 1996 Congress passed the Economic Espionage Act,[27] which made the theft of trade secrets a federal crime. We examined the provisions and significance of this act in Chapter 7, in the context of crimes related to business.

---

27. 18 U.S.C. Sections 1831–1839.

TRADE SECRETS IN CYBERSPACE

New computer technology is undercutting a business firm's ability to protect its confidential information, including trade secrets.[28] For example, a dishonest employee could e-mail trade secrets in a company's computer to a competitor or a future employer. If e-mail is not an option, the employee might simply walk out with the information on a computer disk.

SECTION 7 | International Protection for Intellectual Property

For many years, the United States has been a party to various international agreements relating to intellectual property rights. For example, the Paris Convention of 1883, to which about ninety countries are signatory, allows parties in one country to file for patent and trademark protection in any of the other member countries. We look next at the Berne Convention and another international agreement relating to intellectual property.

THE BERNE CONVENTION

Under the Berne Convention (an international copyright agreement) of 1886, as amended, if an American writes a book, every country that has signed the convention must recognize the American author's copyright in the book. Also, if a citizen of a country that has not signed the convention first publishes a book in a country that has signed, all other countries that have signed the convention must recognize that author's copyright. Copyright notice is not needed to gain protection under the Berne Convention for works published after March 1, 1989.

Currently, the laws of many countries, as well as international laws, are being updated to reflect changes in technology and the expansion of the Internet. Copyright holders and other owners of intellectual property generally agree that changes in the law are needed to stop the increasing international piracy of their property. The World Intellectual Property Organization (WIPO) Copyright Treaty of 1996, a spe-

cial agreement under the Berne Convention, attempts to update international law governing copyright protection to include more safeguards against copyright infringement via the Internet. The United States signed the WIPO treaty in 1996 and implemented its terms in the Digital Millennium Copyright Act of 1998, which was discussed earlier in this chapter.

The Berne Convention and other international agreements have given some protection to intellectual property on a global level. Another significant worldwide agreement to increase such protection is the Trade-Related Aspects of Intellectual Property Rights agreement—or, more simply, the TRIPS agreement.

THE TRIPS AGREEMENT

Representatives from more than one hundred nations signed the TRIPS agreement in 1994. It was one of several documents that were annexed to the agreement that created the World Trade Organization, or WTO, in 1995. The TRIPS agreement established, for the first time, standards for the international protection of intellectual property rights, including patents, trademarks, and copyrights for movies, computer programs, books, and music.

IMPORTANT PROVISIONS OF THE AGREEMENT

Prior to the TRIPS agreement, one of the difficulties faced by U.S. sellers of intellectual property in the international market was that another country might either lack laws to protect intellectual property rights or fail to enforce what laws it had. To address this problem, the TRIPS agreement provides that each member country must include in its domestic laws broad intellectual property rights and effective remedies (including civil and criminal penalties) for violations of those rights.

Generally, the TRIPS agreement provides that member nations must not discriminate (in terms of the administration, regulation, or adjudication of intellectual property rights) against foreign owners of such rights. In other words, a member nation cannot give its own nationals (citizens) favorable treatment without offering the same treatment to nationals of all member countries. For example, if a U.S. software manufacturer brings a suit for the infringement of intellectual property rights under Japan's national laws, the U.S. manufacturer is entitled to receive the same treatment as a Japanese domestic manufacturer. Each member nation must also ensure that legal procedures are available for

---

28. Note that in at least one case, a court has held that customers' e-mail addresses may constitute trade secrets. See *T-N-T Motorsports, Inc. v. Hennessey Motorsports, Inc.*, 965 S.W.2d 18 (Tex.App.—Hous. [1 Dist.] 1998); rehearing overruled (1998); petition dismissed (1998).

parties who wish to bring actions for infringement of intellectual property rights. Additionally, as part of the agreement creating the WTO, a mechanism for settling disputes among member nations was established.

TYPES OF INTELLECTUAL PROPERTY COVERED BY THE AGREEMENT

Particular provisions of the TRIPS agreement refer to patent, trademark, and copyright protection for intellectual property. The agreement specifically provides copyright protection for computer programs by stating that compilations of data, databases, and other materials are "intellectual creations" and are to be protected as copyrightable works. Other provisions relate to trade secrets and the rental of computer programs and cinematographic works.

THE MADRID PROTOCOL

In the past, one of the difficulties in protecting U.S. trademarks internationally was the time and expense involved in applying for trademark registration in foreign countries. The filing fees and procedures for trademark registration vary significantly from country to country. The Madrid Protocol, which President George W. Bush signed into law in 2003, may help to resolve these problems. The Madrid Protocol is an international treaty that has been signed by sixty-one countries. Under its provisions, a U.S. company wishing to register its trademark abroad can submit a single application and designate other member countries in which the U.S. company would like to register its mark. The treaty is designed to reduce the costs of international trademark protection by more than 60 percent, according to proponents.

Although the Madrid Protocol may simplify and reduce the cost of trademark registration in foreign countries, it remains to be seen whether it will provide significant benefits to trademark owners. Even assuming that the registration process will be easier, there is still the issue of whether member countries will enforce the law and protect the mark.

REVIEWING INTELLECTUAL PROPERTY

Two computer science majors, Trent and Xavier, have an idea for a new video game, which they propose to call "Hallowed." They form a business and begin developing their idea. Several months later, Trent and Xavier run into a problem with their design and consult with a friend, Brad, who is an expert in creating computer source codes. Before Hallowed is marketed, however, the video game Halo 2 is released for both the Xbox and Game Cube systems. Halo 2 uses source codes similar to those of Hallowed and imitates Hallowed's overall look and feel. Using the information presented in the chapter, answer the following questions.

1. Is an idea for a video game patentable? Why or why not?

2. Suppose that Trent and Xavier did not file an application for a patent. Does that mean that they do not have a right to exclude others from making the game? Explain.

3. If Trent and Xavier did hold the patent on Hallowed, would the release of Halo 2 infringe on their patent? Why or why not?

4. Is an idea for a video game copyrightable? Is a video game copyrightable? At what point does copyright protection apply?

5. Based only the facts described above, could Trent and Xavier sue the makers of Halo 2 for copyright infringement? Why or why not?

6. Would the name "Hallowed" receive protection as a trademark or as trade dress?

7. Suppose that Trent and Xavier discover that Brad took the idea of Hallowed and sold it to the company that produced Halo 2. Which type of intellectual property issue does this raise?

TERMS AND CONCEPTS TO REVIEW

certification mark 334

collective mark 334

copyright 339

cyber mark 334

cybersquatting 335

dilution 332

distributed network 343

domain name 334

intellectual property 329

meta tag 335

patent 338

peer-to-peer (P2P)
    networking 343

service mark 334

trade dress 333

trade name 334

trade secret 345

trademark 329

QUESTIONS AND CASE PROBLEMS

14-1. Professor Wise is teaching a summer seminar in business torts at State University. Several times during the course, he makes copies of relevant sections from business law texts and distributes them to his students. Wise does not realize that the daughter of one of the textbook authors is a member of his seminar. She tells her father about Wise's copying activities, which have taken place without her father's or his publisher's permission. Her father sues Wise for copyright infringement. Wise claims protection under the fair use doctrine. Who will prevail? Explain.

14-2. **QUESTION WITH SAMPLE ANSWER**

In which of the following situations would a court likely hold Ursula liable for copyright infringement?

(a) From a scholarly journal at the library, Ursula photocopies ten pages relating to a topic on which she is writing a term paper.

(b) Ursula makes blouses, dresses, and other clothes and sells them in her small shop. She advertises some of the outfits as Guest items, hoping that customers might mistakenly assume that they were made by Guess, the well-known clothing manufacturer.

(c) Ursula teaches Latin American history at a small university. She has a VCR and frequently tapes television programs relating to Latin America. She then takes the videos to her classroom so that her students can watch them.

For a sample answer to this question, go to Appendix I at the end of this text.

14-3. One day during algebra class, Diedra, an enterprising fourteen-year-old student, began drawing designs on her shoelaces. By the end of the class, Diedra had decorated her shoelaces with the name of the school, Broadson Junior High, written in blue and red (the school colors), and with pictures of bears, the school's mascot. After class, she showed the designs to her teacher, Mrs. Laxton.

When Diedra got home that night, she wrote about her idea in her diary, in which she also drew her shoelace design. Mrs. Laxton had been trying to think of a way to build school spirit. She thought about Diedra's shoelaces and decided to go into business for herself. She called her business Spirited Shoelaces and designed shoelaces for each of the local schools, decorating the shoelaces in each case with the school's name, mascot, and colors. The business became tremendously profitable. Even though Diedra never registered her idea with the U.S. Patent and Trademark Office or the U.S. Copyright Office, does she nonetheless have intellectual property rights in the shoelace design? Will her diary account be sufficient proof that she created the idea? Discuss.

14-4. TRADEMARK INFRINGEMENT. Elvis Presley Enterprises, Inc. (EPE), owned all of the trademarks of the Elvis Presley estate. None of these marks was registered for use in the restaurant business. Barry Capece registered "The Velvet Elvis" as a service mark for a restaurant and tavern with the U.S. Patent and Trademark Office. Capece opened a nightclub called "The Velvet Elvis" with a menu, decor, advertising, and promotional events that evoked Elvis Presley and his music. EPE filed a suit in a federal district court against Capece and others, claiming, among other things, that "The Velvet Elvis" service mark infringed on EPE's trademarks. During the trial, witnesses testified that they thought the bar was associated with Elvis Presley. Should Capece be ordered to stop using "The Velvet Elvis" mark? Why or why not? [*Elvis Presley Enterprises, Inc. v. Capece,* 141 F.3d 188 (5th Cir. 1998)]

14-5. TRADEMARK INFRINGEMENT. A&H Sportswear Co., a swimsuit maker, obtained a trademark for its MIRACLESUIT in 1992. The MIRACLESUIT design makes the wearer appear slimmer. The MIRACLESUIT, which was widely advertised and discussed in the media, was also sold for a brief time in the Victoria's Secret (VS) catalogue, which is published by Victoria's Secret

Catalogue, Inc. In 1993, Victoria's Secret Stores, Inc., began selling a cleavage-enhancing bra, which was named THE MIRACLE BRA and for which a trademark was obtained. The next year, THE MIRACLE BRA swimwear debuted in the VS catalogue and stores. A&H filed a suit in a federal district court against VS Stores and VS Catalogue, alleging in part that THE MIRACLE BRA mark, when applied to swimwear, infringed on the MIRACLESUIT mark. A&H argued that there was a "possibility of confusion" between the marks. The VS entities contended that the appropriate standard was "likelihood of confusion" and that, in this case, there was no likelihood of confusion. In whose favor will the court rule, and why? [*A&H Sportswear, Inc. v. Victoria's Secret Stores, Inc.*, 166 F.3d 197 (3d Cir. 1999)]

14-6. DOMAIN NAME DISPUTES. In 1999, Steve and Pierce Thumann and their father, Fred, created Spider Webs, Ltd., a partnership, to, according to Steve, "develop Internet address names." Spider Webs registered nearly two thousand Internet domain names at an average cost of $70 each, including the names of cities, the names of buildings, names related to a business or trade (such as air conditioning or plumbing), and the names of famous companies. It offered many of the names for sale on its Web site and through eBay.com. Spider Webs registered the domain name "ERNESTANDJULIOGALLO.COM" in Spider Webs' name. E. & J. Gallo Winery filed a suit against Spider Webs, alleging, in part, violations of the Anticybersquatting Consumer Protection Act. Gallo asked the court for, among other things, statutory damages. Gallo also sought to have the domain name at issue transferred to Gallo. During the suit, Spider Webs published anticorporate articles and negative opinions about Gallo, as well as discussions of the suit and of the risks associated with alcohol use, at the URL ERNESTANDJULIOGALLO.COM. Should the court rule in Gallo's favor? Why or why not? [*E. & J. Gallo Winery v. Spider Webs, Ltd.*, 129 F.Supp.2d 1033 (S.D.Tex. 2001)]

14-7. ⚖ CASE PROBLEM WITH SAMPLE ANSWER

Gateway, Inc., sells computers, computer products, computer peripherals, and computer accessories throughout the world. By 1988, Gateway had begun its first national advertising campaign using black-and-white cows and black-and-white cow spots. By 1991, black-and-white cows and spots had become Gateway's symbol. The next year, Gateway registered a black-and-white cow-spot design in association with computers and computer peripherals as its trademark. Companion Products, Inc. (CPI), sells stuffed animals trademarked as "Stretch Pets." Stretch Pets have an animal's head and an elastic body that can wrap around the edges of computer monitors, computer cases, or televisions. CPI produces sixteen Stretch Pets, including a polar bear, a moose, several dogs, and a penguin. One of CPI's top-selling products is a black-and-white cow that CPI identifies as "Cody Cow," which was first sold in 1999. Gateway filed a suit in a federal district court against CPI, alleging trade dress infringement and related claims. What is trade dress? What is the major factor in cases involving trade dress infringement? Does that factor exist in this case? Explain. [*Gateway, Inc. v. Companion Products, Inc.*, 384 F.3d 503 (8th Cir. 2004)]

To view a sample answer for this case problem, go to this book's Web site at http://wleb.westbuslaw.com, select "Chapter 14," and click on "Case Problem with Sample Answer."

14-8. FAIR USE DOCTRINE. Leslie Kelly is a professional photographer who has copyrighted many of his images of the American West. Some of the images can be seen on Kelly's Web site or other sites with which Kelly has a contract. Arriba Soft Corp. operates an Internet search engine that displays its results in the form of small pictures (thumbnails) rather than text. The thumbnails consist of images copied from other sites and reduced in size. By clicking on one of the thumbnails, a user can view a large version of the picture within the context of an Arriba Web page. Arriba displays the large picture by inline linking (importing the image from the other site without copying it onto Arriba's site). When Kelly discovered that his photos were displayed through Arriba's site without his permission, he filed a suit in a federal district court against Arriba, alleging copyright infringement. Arriba claimed that its use of Kelly's images was a "fair use." Considering the factors courts use to determine whether a use is fair, do Arriba's thumbnails qualify? Does Arriba's use of the larger images infringe on Kelly's copyright? Explain. [*Kelly v. Arriba Soft Corp.*, 280 F.3d 934 (9th Cir. 2002)]

14-9. PATENT INFRINGEMENT. As a cattle rancher in Nebraska, Gerald Gohl used handheld searchlights to find and help calving animals (cows giving birth) in harsh blizzard conditions. Gohl thought that it would be more helpful to have a portable searchlight mounted on the outside of a vehicle and remotely controlled. He and Al Gebhardt developed and patented practical applications of this idea—the Golight and the wireless, remote-controlled Radio Ray, which could rotate 360 degrees—and formed Golight, Inc., to make and market these products. In 1997, Wal-Mart Stores, Inc., began selling a portable, wireless, remote-controlled searchlight that was identical to the Radio Ray except for a stop piece that prevented the light from rotating more than 351 degrees. Golight sent Wal-Mart a letter claiming that its device infringed Golight's patent. Wal-Mart sold its remaining inventory of the devices and stopped carrying the product. Golight filed a suit in a federal district court against Wal-Mart, alleging patent infringement. How should the court rule? Explain. [*Golight, Inc. v. Wal-Mart Stores, Inc.*, 355 F.3d 1327 (Fed. Cir. 2004)]

14-10. VIDEO QUESTION

Go to this text's Web site at http://wleb.westbuslaw.com and select "Chapter 14." Click on "Video Questions" and view the video titled *The Jerk*. Then answer the following questions.

(a) In the video, Navin (Steve Martin) creates a special handle for Mr. Fox's (Bill Macy's) glasses. Can Navin obtain a patent or a copyright protecting his invention? Explain your answer.

(b) Suppose that after Navin legally protects his idea, Fox steals it and decides to develop it for himself, without Navin's permission. Has Fox committed infringement? If so, what kind: trademark, patent, or copyright?

(c) Suppose that after Navin legally protects his idea, he realizes he doesn't have the funds to mass-produce the special handle. Navin therefore agrees to allow Fox to manufacture the product. Has Navin granted Fox a license? Explain.

(d) Assume that Navin is able to manufacture his invention. What might Navin do to ensure that his product is identifiable and can be distinguished from other products on the market?

LAW | on the Web

For updated links to resources available on the Web, as well as a variety of other materials, visit this text's Web site at http://wleb.westbuslaw.com.

An excellent overview of the laws governing various forms of intellectual property is available at FindLaw's Web site. Go to

http://profs.lp.findlaw.com

You can find answers to frequently asked questions (FAQs) about trademark and patent law—and links to registration forms, statutes, international patent and trademark offices, and numerous other related materials—at the Web site of the U.S. Patent and Trademark Office. Go to

http://www.uspto.gov

To perform patent searches and to access information on the patenting process, go to

http://www.bustpatents.com

You can also access information on patent law at the following Internet site:

http://www.patents.com

For information on copyrights, go to the U.S. Copyright Office at

http://www.loc.gov/copyright

You can find extensive information on copyright law—including United States Supreme Court decisions in this area and the texts of the Berne Convention and other international treaties on copyright issues—at the Web site of the Legal Information Institute at Cornell University's School of Law. Go to

http://www.law.cornell.edu/topics/copyright.html

Law.com's Web site offers articles, case decisions, and other information concerning intellectual property at

http://www.law.com/jsp/pc/iplaw.jsp

LEGAL RESEARCH EXERCISES ON THE WEB

Go to http://wleb.westbuslaw.com, the Web site that accompanies this text. Select "Chapter 14" and click on "Internet Exercises." There you will find the following Internet research exercises that you can perform to learn more about topics covered in this chapter.

Activity 14–1:   **LEGAL PERSPECTIVE**
Unwarranted Legal Threats

Activity 14–2:   **MANAGEMENT PERSPECTIVE**
Protecting Intellectual Property across Borders

Activity 14–3:   **TECHNOLOGICAL PERSPECTIVE**
File-Sharing

CHAPTER 15
Creditor-Debtor Relations and Bankruptcy

Normally, creditors have no problem collecting the debts owed to them. When disputes arise over the amount owed, however, or when the debtor simply cannot or will not pay, what happens? What remedies are available to creditors when a debtor **defaults** (fails to pay as promised)? In this chapter, we first focus on some basic laws that assist the debtor and creditor in resolving their dispute. We then examine the process of bankruptcy as a last resort in resolving debtor-creditor problems. We specifically include changes resulting from the 2005 Bankruptcy Reform Act.

SECTION 1 | Laws Assisting Creditors

Both the common law and statutory laws create various rights and remedies for creditors. We discuss here some of these rights and remedies, including liens, garnishment, and mortgage foreclosure.

LIENS

A **lien** is a claim against a debtor's property that must be satisfied before the property (or its proceeds) is available to satisfy the claims of other creditors. As mentioned, liens may arise under the common law or under statutory law. Statutory liens include *mechanic's liens*. Liens created at common law include *artisan's liens*. *Judicial liens* include those that represent a creditor's efforts to collect on a debt before or after a judgment is entered by a court. Liens are a very important tool for creditors because they generally take priority over other claims against the same property.

MECHANIC'S LIENS When a person contracts for labor, services, or materials to be furnished for the purpose of making improvements on real property but does not immediately pay for the improvements, the creditor can place a **mechanic's lien** on the property. This creates a special type of debtor-creditor relationship in which the real estate itself becomes security for the debt.

For example, a painter agrees to paint a house for a homeowner for an agreed-on price to cover labor and materials. If the homeowner cannot pay or pays only a portion of the charges, a mechanic's lien against the property can be created. The painter is the lienholder, and the real property is encumbered with a mechanic's lien for the amount owed. If the homeowner does not pay the lien, the property can be sold to satisfy the debt. Notice of the *foreclosure* (the enforcement of the lien) must be given to the debtor in advance, however.

Note that state law governs the procedures that must be followed to create a mechanic's lien. Generally, the lienholder has to file a written notice of lien against the particular property involved. The notice of lien must be filed within a specific time period, measured from the last date on which materials or labor were provided (usually within 60 to 120 days). If the property owner fails to pay the debt, the lienholder is entitled to foreclose on the real estate on which the improvements were made and to sell it to satisfy the amount of the debt. Of course, as mentioned, the lienholder is required by statute to give notice to the owner of the property prior to foreclosure and sale. The sale proceeds are used to pay the debt and the costs of the legal proceedings; the surplus, if any, is paid to the former owner.

ARTISAN'S LIENS An **artisan's lien** is a device created at common law through which a creditor can recover payment from a debtor for labor and materials furnished in the repair of personal property. For example, Whitney leaves her diamond ring at the jewelry shop to be repaired and to have her initials engraved on the band. In the absence of an agreement, the jeweler can keep the ring until Whitney pays for the services that the jeweler provides. Should Whitney fail to pay, the jeweler has a lien on Whitney's ring for the amount of the bill and can sell the ring in satisfaction of the lien.

—*A Possessory Lien.* In contrast to a mechanic's lien, an artisan's lien is *possessory*. The lienholder ordinarily must have retained possession of the property and have expressly or impliedly agreed to provide the services on a cash, not a credit, basis. The lien remains in existence as long as the lienholder maintains possession, and the lien is terminated once possession is voluntarily surrendered—unless the surrender is only temporary. With a temporary surrender, there must be an agreement that the property will be returned to the lienholder. Even with such an agreement, if a third party obtains rights in that property while it is out of the possession of the lienholder, the lien is lost.

—*Notice of Foreclosure and Sale Required.* Modern statutes permit the holder of an artisan's lien to foreclose and sell the property subject to the lien to satisfy payment of the debt. As with a mechanic's lien, the lienholder is required to give notice to the owner of the property prior to foreclosure and sale. In some states, holders of artisan's liens must give notice to title lienholders of automobiles prior to foreclosure. The sale proceeds are used to pay the debt and the costs of the legal proceedings, and the surplus, if any, is paid to the former owner. An artisan's lien has priority over both a filed statutory lien and a bailee's lien.

JUDICIAL LIENS When a debt is past due, a creditor can bring a legal action against the debtor to collect the debt. If the creditor is successful in the action, the court awards the creditor a judgment against the debtor (usually for the amount of the debt plus any interest and legal costs incurred in obtaining the judgment). Frequently, however, the creditor is unable to collect the awarded amount.

To ensure that a judgment in the creditor's favor will be collectible, creditors are permitted to request that certain nonexempt property of the debtor be seized to satisfy the debt. If the court orders the debtor's property to be seized prior to a judgment in the creditor's favor, the court's order is referred to as a *writ of attachment*. If the court orders the debtor's property to be seized following a judgment in the creditor's favor, the court's order is referred to as a *writ of execution*.

—*Attachment.* In the context of judicial liens, **attachment** refers to a court-ordered seizure and taking into custody of property prior to the securing of a judgment for a past-due debt. Normally, attachment is a *prejudgment* remedy, occurring either at the time a lawsuit is filed or immediately thereafter. In order to attach *before* a judgment, a creditor must comply with the specific state's statutory restrictions and the requirements of the due process clause of the Fourteenth Amendment to the U.S. Constitution.

The creditor must have an enforceable right to payment of the debt under law and must follow certain procedures. Otherwise, the creditor can be liable for damages for wrongful attachment. Typically, the creditor must file with the court an *affidavit* (a written or printed statement, made under oath or sworn to) stating that the debtor has failed to pay and delineating the statutory grounds under which attachment is sought. The creditor must also post a bond to cover at least the court costs, the value of the loss of use of the good suffered by the debtor, and the value of the property attached. When the court is satisfied that all the requirements have been met, it issues a **writ of attachment,** which directs the sheriff or other officer to seize nonexempt property. If the creditor prevails at trial, the seized property can be sold to satisfy the judgment.

—*Writ of Execution.* If a creditor obtains a judgment against the debtor and the debtor will not or cannot pay the judgment, the creditor is entitled to go back to the court and request a *writ of execution*. A **writ of execution** is an order that directs the sheriff to seize (levy) and sell any of the debtor's nonexempt real or personal property that is within the court's geographic jurisdiction (usually the county in which the courthouse is located). The proceeds of the sale are used to pay off the judgment, accrued interest, and the costs of the sale. Any excess is paid to the debtor.

The debtor can pay the judgment and redeem the nonexempt property at any time before the sale takes place. Because of exemption laws and bankruptcy laws (discussed later in this chapter), however, many judgments are virtually uncollectible.

GARNISHMENT

An order for **garnishment** permits a creditor to collect a debt by seizing property of the debtor that is being held by a third party. In a garnishment proceeding, the third party—the person or entity on whom the garnishment judgment is served—is called the *garnishee*. Typically, a garnishee is the debtor's employer. A creditor may seek a garnishment judgment against the debtor's employer so that part of the debtor's usual paycheck will be paid to the creditor. In some situations, however, the garnishee is a third party that holds funds belonging to the debtor (such as a bank) or a third party who has possession of, or exercises control over, funds or other types of property belonging to the debtor. Almost all types of property can be garnished, including tax refunds, pensions, and trust funds—so long as the property is not exempt from garnishment and is in the possession of a third party.

GARNISHMENT PROCEEDINGS   The legal proceeding for a garnishment action is governed by state law. As a result of a garnishment proceeding, as noted, a third party (such as the debtor's employer) is ordered by the court to turn over property owned by the debtor (such as wages) to pay the debt. Garnishment can be a prejudgment remedy, requiring a hearing before a court, or a postjudgment remedy. According to the laws in some states, the judgment creditor needs to obtain only one order of garnishment, which will then continuously apply to the judgment debtor's weekly wages until the entire debt is paid. In other states, the judgment creditor must go back to court for a separate order of garnishment for each pay period.

LAWS LIMITING THE AMOUNT OF WAGES SUBJECT TO GARNISHMENT   Both federal and state laws limit the amount that can be taken from a debtor's weekly take-home pay through garnishment proceedings.[1] Federal law provides a minimal framework to protect debtors from losing all their income to pay judgment debts.[2] State laws also provide dollar exemptions, and these amounts are often larger than those provided by federal law. State and federal statutes can be applied together to create a pool of funds sufficient to enable a debtor to continue to provide for family needs while also paying the judgment debt in a reasonable manner. Under federal law, an employer cannot dismiss an employee because his or her wages are being garnished for one indebtedness.

In the following case, the issue was whether, for purposes of a garnishment order, an employee's wages included the tips that the employee received directly from her employer's customers.

---

1. A few states (for example, Texas) do not permit garnishment of wages by private parties except under a child-support order.
2. For example, the federal Consumer Credit Protection Act, 15 U.S.C. Sections 1601–1693r, provides that a debtor can retain either 75 percent of his or her disposable earnings per week or the sum equivalent to thirty hours of work paid at federal minimum wage rates, whichever is greater.

CASE 15.1   Shanks v. Lowe

Court of Appeals
of Maryland, 2001.
364 Md. 538,
774 A.2d 411.

BACKGROUND AND FACTS   *Laura Shanks won a judgment in a Maryland state court against Susan Lowe for $6,000. Shanks obtained a garnishment order and served it on Lowe's employer, Kibby's Restaurant & Lounge, which was ordered to withhold her attachable wages to pay the judgment and other costs. Exempt, under Maryland statutes, was one of two amounts, whichever was greater: (1) $154.50 multiplied by the number of weeks in which wages due were earned or (2) 75 percent of disposable wages ("the part of wages that remain after deduction of any amount required to be withheld by law").*[a] *Kibby's responded that Lowe's gross wages averaged $95 per week and that her "disposable income average per week is approx $35–$40," which was less than the allowable exemption of $154.50. Kibby's added that Lowe also earned tips, which Kibby's included in her wages for tax purposes,*[b] *but claimed that the tips were not wages for garnishment purposes because they were never in Kibby's possession—restaurant patrons paid them directly to Lowe. The court agreed and dismissed the garnishment. Shanks appealed to a state intermediate*

---

a. See Maryland Code Sections 15–601 through 15–607.
b. For example, in one week, Kibby's reported to the federal and state governments $92.44 in wages due to Lowe and $153.50 in tips, for total taxable wages of $245.94. From that amount, Kibby's deducted $29.25 in federal taxes, $18.82 in Social Security taxes, and $13.87 in state taxes, leaving $30.50 owed to Lowe over the amount of her tips.

 **Continued** *appellate court, which affirmed the dismissal. Shanks appealed to the Maryland Court of Appeals, the state's highest court.*

IN THE LANGUAGE OF THE COURT

WILNER, Judge:
The issue before us is whether tips earned by a waitress (or other person who earns tips) constitute "wages" for purposes of the Maryland wage garnishment law * * *. Principally at issue is whether tips fall within the definition of "wages" in [Maryland Code Section] 15–601(c): "all monetary remuneration paid to any employee for his employment." * * *

* * * *

* * * Maryland Code [Section] 3–413(1) * * * requires each employer in Maryland to pay its employees the minimum wage required by the Federal Fair Labor Standards Act. The term "wage" is defined in [Section] 3–401(e) as "all compensation that is due to an employee for employment" * * *. Section 3–419 takes specific account of tips and, as to any employee who regularly receives more than $30/month in tips, * * * provides, in relevant part, that an employer may include, "as part of the wage of an employee to whom this section applies," an amount that the employer sets to represent the tips of the employee, up to $2.77/hour. This is consistent with the Federal law, which defines a "tipped employee" as an employee engaged in an occupation in which he or she customarily and regularly receives more than $30/month in tips and, in relevant part, calculates the required minimum wage for such an employee as the actual cash wage paid by the employer plus an additional amount on account of tips equal to the difference between that actual cash wage and the minimum wage * * *. Thus, for purposes of the State and Federal minimum wage laws, tips are regarded as part of wages.

Significantly, tips are included within the meaning of wages for purposes of the unemployment insurance and workers' compensation laws, each of which provide benefits based on the employee's wages. Were Ms. [Lowe] to file a claim for either unemployment insurance or workers' compensation benefits, any benefits to which she might be entitled would be determined on the basis of the aggregate amounts she received from both Kibby's and its customers.

* * * *

These statutes illustrate a consistent view by the General Assembly [Maryland's legislature] that, in using terms such as "wage" or "wages," it intended to include all forms of remuneration, whether or not paid directly by the employer, except to the extent specifically excluded. When it desired to limit the scope of a statute to the remuneration paid in the form of a salary or other periodic payment by an employer, it made that intent clear.

DECISION AND REMEDY *The Maryland Court of Appeals reversed the judgment of the lower court and remanded the case for further proceedings. The state's highest court held that under state law, for purposes of a garnishment order, tips constitute "monetary remuneration paid to any employee for his employment" and are therefore part of the employee's wages.*

WHAT IF THE FACTS WERE DIFFERENT? *Suppose that the dispute in this case had involved a bonus that Lowe received from her employer rather than the amount she received in tips. Would the court still have concluded the bonus was part of Lowe's wages? Why or why not?*

CREDITORS' COMPOSITION AGREEMENTS

Creditors may contract with the debtor for discharge of the debtor's liquidated debts (debts that are definite, or fixed, in amount) on payment of a sum less than that owed. These agreements are referred to as *composition agreements* or **creditors' composition** agreements and are usually held to be enforceable unless they are formed under duress.

MORTGAGES

A **mortgage** is a written instrument giving a creditor an interest in (lien on) the debtor's real property as security for the payment of a debt. Financial institutions grant

CONCEPT SUMMARY 15.1 | Remedies Available to Creditors

REMEDY	DESCRIPTION

LIENS	1. *Mechanic's lien*—A lien filed on an owner's real estate for labor, services, or materials furnished for improvements made to the realty.
	2. *Artisan's lien*—A lien on an owner's personal property for labor performed or value added to the personal property.
	3. *Judicial liens*—
	   a. Attachment—A court-ordered seizure of property prior to a court's final determination of the creditor's rights to the property. Creditors must strictly comply with applicable state statutes to obtain a writ of attachment.
	   b. Writ of execution—A court order directing the sheriff to seize (levy) and sell a debtor's nonexempt real or personal property to satisfy a court's judgment in the creditor's favor.

GARNISHMENT	A collection remedy that allows the creditor to attach a debtor's funds (such as wages owed or bank accounts) and property that are held by a third person.
MORTGAGE FORECLOSURE	On the debtor's default, the entire mortgage debt is due and payable, allowing the creditor to foreclose on the realty by selling it to satisfy the debt.

mortgage loans for the purchase of property—usually a dwelling (real property will be discussed in Chapter 25). Given the relatively large sums that many individuals borrow to purchase a home, defaults are not uncommon. Mortgages are recorded with the county in the state where the property is located. Recording ensures that the creditor is officially on record as holding an interest in the property. As a further precaution, most creditors require mortgage insurance for debtors who do not pay at least 20 percent of the purchase price as a down payment at the time of the transaction.

MORTGAGE FORECLOSURE Mortgage holders have the right to foreclose on mortgaged property in the event of a debtor's default. The usual method of foreclosure is by judicial sale of the property, although the statutory methods of foreclosure vary from state to state. If the proceeds of the foreclosure sale are sufficient to cover both the costs of the foreclosure and the mortgaged debt, any surplus goes to the debtor. If the sale proceeds are insufficient to cover the foreclosure costs and the mortgaged debt, however, the **mortgagee** (the creditor-lender) can seek to recover the difference from the **mortgagor** (the debtor) by obtaining a *deficiency judgment* representing the difference between the mortgaged debt plus foreclosure costs and the amount actually received from the proceeds of the foreclosure sale.

The creditor obtains a deficiency judgment in a separate legal action that is pursued subsequent to the foreclosure action. The deficiency judgment entitles the creditor to recover from other property owned by the debtor. Some states do not permit deficiency judgments for some types of real estate interests.

REDEMPTION RIGHTS Before the foreclosure sale, a defaulting mortgagor can redeem the property by paying the full amount of the debt, plus any interest and costs that have accrued. This right is known as the **equity of redemption.** In some states, a mortgagor may even redeem the property within a certain period of time—called a **statutory period of redemption**—after the sale. In these states, the deed to the property usually is not delivered to the purchaser until the statutory period has expired.

SECTION 2 | Suretyship and Guaranty

When a third person promises to pay a debt owed by another in the event the debtor does not pay, either a *suretyship* or a *guaranty* relationship is created. The third person's credit becomes the security for the debt owed.

SURETYSHIP

A contract of strict **suretyship** is a promise made by a third person to be responsible for the debtor's obligation. It is an express contract between the **surety** and the creditor. The surety in the strictest sense is primarily liable for the debt of the principal. The creditor can demand payment from the surety from the moment that the debt is due. A suretyship contract is not a form of indemnity; that is, it is not merely a promise to make good any loss that a creditor may incur as a result of the debtor's failure to pay. The creditor need not exhaust all legal remedies against the principal debtor before holding the surety responsible for payment. Moreover, a surety agreement does not have to be in writing to be enforceable, although usually such agreements are in writing.

For example, Jason Oller wants to borrow funds from the bank to buy a used car. Because Jason is still in college, the bank will not lend him the funds unless his father, Stuart Oller, who has dealt with the bank before, will cosign the note (add his signature to the note, thereby becoming jointly liable for payment of the debt). When Mr. Oller cosigns the note, he becomes primarily liable to the bank. On the note's due date, the bank can seek payment from Jason Oller, Stuart Oller, or both jointly.

GUARANTY

A guaranty contract is similar to a suretyship contract in that it includes a promise to answer for the debt or default of another. There are some significant differences between these two types of contracts, however.

SURETYSHIP VERSUS GUARANTY With a suretyship arrangement, the surety is *primarily* liable for the debtor's obligation. With a guaranty arrangement, the **guarantor**—the third person making the guaranty—is *secondarily* liable. The guarantor can be required to pay the obligation only after the principal debtor defaults, and usually only after the creditor has made an attempt to collect from the debtor.

For example, a corporation, BX Enterprises, needs to borrow money to meet its payroll. The bank is skeptical about the creditworthiness of BX and requires Dawson, its president, who is a wealthy businessperson and owner of 70 percent of BX Enterprises, to sign an agreement making himself personally liable for payment if BX does not pay off the loan. As a guarantor of the loan, Dawson cannot be held liable until BX Enterprises is in default.

Another difference between suretyship and guaranty has to do with the Statute of Frauds. Whereas a surety agreement can be oral, the Statute of Frauds generally requires that a contract between a guarantor and a creditor be in writing to be enforceable.

In the following case, the issue was whether a guaranty of a lease signed by the officer of a corporation was enforceable against the officer personally even though he claimed to have signed the guaranty only as a representative of the corporation.

CASE 15.2	**JSV, Inc. v. Hene Meat Co., Inc.**

Court of Appeals
of Indiana, 2003.
794 N.E.2d 555.

BARNES, Judge.
 * * * *

On August 30, 1999, JSV, Inc. ("JSV") signed a lease to rent a portion of a building in Indianapolis from Hene [Meat Company. Mark] Kennedy signed the lease on behalf of JSV as one of that corporation's officers. In addition, Kennedy signed a document simply denominated [described] "GUARANTY." The document indicated that it was "an absolute and unconditional guaranty" of the lease's performance by JSV * * * . Kennedy's printed name and signature on the document are not followed by any corporate officer designation.

JSV stopped paying rent to Hene in September 2000. On June 5, 2001, Hene sued both JSV under the lease and Kennedy under the guaranty [in an Indiana state court]. * * *

On April 16, 2002, Hene moved for summary judgment. * * * On September 9, 2002, * * * the trial court * * * granted Hene's summary judgment motion and entered judgment against both JSV and Kennedy personally for the sum of $75,041.07. Kennedy alone now appeals.
 * * * *

The * * * argument of Kennedy's that we address is whether the trial court erred in granting summary judgment in favor of Hene on its claim that Kennedy was personally liable under the guaranty he executed. * * *

The interpretation of a guaranty is governed by the same rules applicable to other contracts. *Absent ambiguity, the terms of a contract will be given their plain and ordinary meaning and*

CONTINUED ▶

CASE 15.2 | **Continued**

will not be considered ambiguous solely because the parties dispute the proper interpretation of the terms. * * * [Emphasis added.]

We conclude that the guaranty Kennedy executed was unambiguously a personal guaranty * * * . It is axiomatic [clear] under Indiana law that a guaranty agreement must consist of three parties: the obligor, the obligee, and the surety or guarantor. Here, Hene as landlord under the lease was the obligee and JSV as the tenant was the obligor; the disputed issue is the identity of the guarantor. Kennedy claims he signed both the lease *and* the guaranty as an officer of JSV.

However, *there would have been no point in Hene's obtaining Kennedy's guaranty of the lease if he was doing so only in his official capacity as an officer of JSV.* Such an action would have been equivalent to JSV guaranteeing JSV's performance of the lease and to JSV being both the obligor under the lease and the guarantor under the guaranty. * * * [S]uch a result would be paradoxical and untenable. In [a different case] we concluded that where a corporate officer executed a guaranty with respect to credit extended to the corporation, the guaranty was a personal one and the officer personally was the guarantor despite the fact that the officer placed his corporate title after his signature on the guaranty. We further concluded that this was apparent as a matter of law and summary judgment on the issue was appropriate. In this case, the guaranty is even more clearly a personal one * * * because Kennedy's signature thereon is not followed by any corporate officer designation. The trial court did not err in concluding that the guaranty Kennedy executed was a personal one as a matter of law and in granting summary judgment against Kennedy personally. [Emphasis added.]
* * * *

The trial court * * * properly concluded that Kennedy was personally liable to Hene on the guaranty he executed for any breach of the underlying lease by JSV. We affirm.

QUESTIONS

1. How significant should the court have found the omission of the word *personal* from the guaranty?
2. What effect might it have had on the result in this case if Hene had misled Kennedy into believing he was signing the guaranty only in his capacity as an officer of JSV?

THE EXTENT AND TIME OF THE GUARANTOR'S LIABILITY The guaranty contract terms determine the extent and time of the guarantor's liability. For example, the guaranty can be *continuing,* designed to cover a series of transactions by the debtor. Also, the guaranty can be *unlimited* or *limited* as to time and amount. In addition, the guaranty can be *absolute* or *conditional.* With a conditional guaranty, the guarantor becomes liable only on the happening of a certain event. When a guaranty is absolute, the guarantor becomes liable immediately on the debtor's default.

DEFENSES OF THE SURETY AND THE GUARANTOR

The defenses of the surety and the guarantor are basically the same. Therefore, the following discussion applies to both, although it refers only to the surety.

ACTIONS RELEASING THE SURETY Some actions will release the surety from the obligation. For example, making any material modification in the terms of the original contract between the principal debtor and the creditor, including the awarding of a binding extension of time for making payment, without first obtaining the consent of the surety will discharge a gratuitous surety (one who receives no consideration in return for acting as a surety) completely. A surety who is compensated will be discharged to the extent that the surety suffers a loss.

Naturally, if the principal obligation is paid by the debtor or by another person on behalf of the debtor, the surety is discharged from the obligation. Similarly, if valid tender of payment is made, and the creditor for some reason rejects it with knowledge of the surety's existence, then the surety is released from any obligation on the debt.

DEFENSES OF THE PRINCIPAL DEBTOR Generally, any defenses available to the principal debtor can be used by the surety to avoid liability on the obligation to the creditor. Defenses available to the principal debtor that the surety *cannot* use include the principal debtor's incapacity or bankruptcy and the statute of limitations. The ability of the surety to assert any defenses the debtor may have against the creditor is the most important concept in suretyship, because most of the defenses available to the surety are also those of the debtor.

SURRENDER OR IMPAIRMENT OF COLLATERAL In addition, if a creditor surrenders or impairs the debtor's collateral while knowing of the surety and without the surety's consent, the surety is released to the extent of any loss suffered from the creditor's actions. The primary reason for this is to protect the surety who agreed to become obligated only because the debtor's collateral was in the possession of the creditor.

OTHER DEFENSES Obviously, a surety may also have his or her own defenses—for example, incapacity or bankruptcy. If the creditor fraudulently induced the surety to guarantee the debt, the surety can assert fraud as a defense. In most states, the creditor has a legal duty to inform the surety, prior to the formation of the suretyship contract, of material facts known by the creditor that would substantially increase the surety's risk. Failure to so inform is fraud and makes the suretyship obligation voidable.

RIGHTS OF THE SURETY AND THE GUARANTOR

Generally, when the surety or guarantor pays the debt owed to the creditor, the surety or guarantor is entitled to certain rights. Because the rights of the surety and the guarantor are basically the same, the following discussion applies to both.

THE RIGHT OF SUBROGATION First, the surety has the legal **right of subrogation.** Simply stated, this means that any right the creditor had against the debtor now becomes the right of the surety. Included are creditor rights in bankruptcy, rights to collateral possessed by the creditor, and rights to judgments obtained by the creditor. In short, the surety now stands in the shoes of the creditor and may pursue any remedies that were available to the creditor against the debtor.

THE RIGHT OF REIMBURSEMENT Second, the surety has a right to be reimbursed by the debtor. This **right of reimbursement** may stem either from the suretyship contract or from equity. Basically, the surety is entitled to receive from the debtor all outlays made on behalf of the suretyship arrangement. Such outlays can include expenses incurred, as well as the actual amount of the debt paid to the creditor.

THE RIGHT OF CONTRIBUTION Third, in the case of **co-sureties** (two or more sureties on the same obligation owed by the debtor), the **right of contribution** allows a surety who pays more than his or her proportionate share on a debtor's default to recover from the co-sureties the amount paid above the surety's obligation. Generally, a co-surety's liability either is determined by agreement or, in the absence of agreement, is set at the maximum liability under the suretyship contract.

For example, assume that two co-sureties are obligated under a suretyship contract to guarantee the debt of a debtor. Together, the sureties' maximum liability is $25,000. Surety A's maximum liability is $15,000, and surety B's is $10,000. The debtor owes $10,000 and is in default. Surety A pays the creditor the entire $10,000. In the absence of agreement, surety A can recover $4,000 from surety B ($10,000/$25,000 × $10,000 = $4,000, surety B's obligation).

SECTION 3 | Protection for Debtors

The law protects debtors, as well as creditors. Certain property of the debtor, for example, is exempt under state law from creditors' actions. Consumer protection statutes (see Chapter 23) also protect debtors' rights. Of course, bankruptcy laws, which will be discussed later in this chapter, are designed specifically to assist debtors in need of help.

In most states, certain types of real and personal property are exempt from execution or attachment. State exemption statutes usually include both real and personal property.

EXEMPTED REAL PROPERTY

Probably the most familiar exemption is the **homestead exemption.** Each state permits the debtor to retain the family home, either in its entirety or up to a specified dollar amount, free from the claims of unsecured creditors or trustees in bankruptcy. (As of 2005, new federal bankruptcy laws override state exemptions for debtors in bankruptcy and place limitations and restrictions on debtors seeking to use state homestead exemptions.) Suppose that Beere owes Veltman $40,000. The debt is the subject of a lawsuit, and the court awards Veltman a judgment of $40,000 against Beere. Beere's homestead is valued at around $50,000, and the homestead exemption is $25,000. There are no outstanding mortgages or other liens on his homestead. To satisfy the judgment debt, Beere's family home is sold at public auction for $45,000. The proceeds of the sale are distributed as follows:

1. Beere is given $25,000 as his homestead exemption.
2. Veltman is paid $20,000 toward the judgment debt, leaving a $20,000 deficiency judgment (that is, "leftover debt") that can be satisfied from any other nonexempt property (personal or real) that Beere may own, if allowed by state law.

In a few states, statutes allow the homestead exemption only if the judgment debtor has a family. The policy behind this type of statute is to protect the family; if a judgment debtor does not have a family, a creditor may be entitled to collect the full amount realized from the sale of the debtor's home.

EXEMPTED PERSONAL PROPERTY

Personal property that is most often exempt from satisfaction of judgment debts includes the following:

1. Household furniture up to a specified dollar amount.
2. Clothing and certain personal possessions, such as family pictures or a Bible.
3. A vehicle (or vehicles) for transportation (at least up to a specified dollar amount).
4. Certain classified animals, usually livestock but including pets.
5. Equipment that the debtor uses in a business or trade, such as tools or professional instruments, up to a specified dollar amount.

SECTION 4 | Bankruptcy and Reorganization

We look now at another significant right of debtors: the right to petition for bankruptcy relief under federal law. Article I, Section 8, of the U.S. Constitution gave Congress the power to establish "uniform Laws on the subject of Bankruptcies throughout the United States."

Bankruptcy law in the United States has two goals—to protect a debtor by giving him or her a fresh start, free from creditors' claims, and to ensure equitable treatment to creditors who are competing for a debtor's assets. Federal bankruptcy legislation was first enacted in 1898 and has undergone several modifications since that time.

Bankruptcy law prior to 2005 was based on the Bankruptcy Reform Act of 1978, as amended—hereinafter called the Bankruptcy Code, or more simply, the Code (not to be confused with the Uniform Commercial Code, which is also sometimes called the Code). In 2005, Congress enacted a new Bankruptcy Reform Act, which became effective six months after President George W. Bush signed the act into law. The 2005 act significantly overhauled certain provisions of the Bankruptcy Code—for the first time in twenty-five years. One of the major goals of the new act is to require consumers to pay as many of their debts as they possibly can instead of having those debts fully discharged in bankruptcy. The law was passed, in part, in response to businesses' concerns about the rise in personal bankruptcy filings, which have increased every year since 1980 (from fewer than 300,000 to over 1.6 million per year).

BANKRUPTCY PROCEEDINGS

Bankruptcy proceedings are held in federal bankruptcy courts, which are under the authority of the U.S. district courts, and rulings from bankruptcy courts can be appealed to the district courts. Although bankruptcy law is federal law, state laws on secured transactions, liens, judgments, and exemptions also play a role in federal bankruptcy proceedings.

TYPES OF BANKRUPTCY RELIEF

Title 11 of the *United States Code* encompasses the Bankruptcy Code, which has eight chapters. Chapters 1, 3, and 5 of the Code contain general definitional provisions, as well as provisions governing case administration, creditors, the debtor, and the estate. These three chapters apply generally to all kinds of bankruptcies. The next five chapters of the Code set forth the different types of relief that debtors may seek. Chapter 7 provides for **liquidation** proceedings (the selling of all nonexempt assets and the distribution of the proceeds to the debtor's creditors). Chapter 9 governs the adjustment of a municipality's debts. Chapter 11 governs reorganizations. Chapters 12 and 13 provide for the adjustment of debts by parties with regular incomes (family farmers and family fishermen under Chapter 12 and individuals under Chapter 13).[3] A debtor (except for a municipality) need not be insolvent[4] to file for bankruptcy relief under any chapter of the Bankruptcy Code. Anyone obligated to a creditor can declare bankruptcy.

SPECIAL TREATMENT OF CONSUMER-DEBTORS

To fully inform a consumer-debtor of the various types of relief available, the Code requires that the clerk of the court provide certain information to all consumer-debtors prior to the commencement of a bankruptcy filing. (A **consumer-debtor** is a debtor whose debts result primarily from the purchase of goods for personal, family, or household use.) First, the clerk must give consumer-debtors written notice of the general purpose, benefits, and costs of each chapter of the Bankruptcy Code under which they might proceed. Second, under the 2005 act, the clerk must provide consumer-debtors with informational materials on the types of services available from credit counseling agencies.

SECURED VERSUS UNSECURED CREDITORS

Throughout the Bankruptcy Code, a distinction is made between secured and unsecured creditors. A secured creditor is one who holds a *security interest*—an interest in personal property or fixtures that secures, or serves as collateral for, payment of a debt. Unsecured creditors do not have a security interest in property that serves as collateral to the underlying debt.

Even though a creditor may have a security interest in certain personal property, additional steps must be taken to ensure that the creditor's security interest

in collateral takes *priority* over claims made on the collateral by third parties, such as other secured or general creditors, trustees in bankruptcy, and later purchasers of the collateral. A secured creditor establishes priority over such third party claims by taking steps to *perfect* the security interest. Although there are other means of perfecting a security interest, the most common one is by filing with an appropriate public office a *financing statement,* signed by the debtor, describing the collateral and giving the names and addresses of the debtor and the creditor.[5] As will be seen, because bankruptcy generally occurs when the debtor's obligations exceed the debtor's assets, the priority of claims to the available assets is frequently crucial to the outcome of a bankruptcy proceeding.

The remaining sections in this chapter deal with the most frequently used bankruptcy plans allowed under the various chapters of the Bankruptcy Code: Chapter 7 liquidations, Chapter 11 reorganizations, and Chapter 13 plans. The latter two chapters are sometimes referred to as *rehabilitation chapters.* As you read the following sections on bankruptcy, be sure to keep in mind that references to Chapter 7, Chapter 11, and Chapter 13 are references to chapters contained in the Bankruptcy Code.

SECTION 5 | Chapter 7 Liquidation

Liquidation under Chapter 7 of the Bankruptcy Code is generally the most familiar type of bankruptcy proceeding and is often referred to as an *ordinary,* or *straight, bankruptcy.* Put simply, a debtor in a liquidation bankruptcy turns all assets over to a **trustee.** The trustee sells the nonexempt assets and distributes the proceeds to creditors. With certain exceptions, the remaining debts are then **discharged** (extinguished), and the debtor is relieved of the obligation to pay the debts.

Any "person"—defined as including individuals, partnerships, and corporations[6]—may be a debtor in

---

3. There are no Chapters 2, 4, 6, 8, or 10 in Title 11. Such "gaps" are not uncommon in the *United States Code.* This is because chapter numbers (or other subdivisional unit numbers) are sometimes reserved for future use when a statute is enacted. (A gap may also appear if a law has been repealed.)
4. The inability to pay debts as they become due is known as *equitable* insolvency. A *balance sheet* insolvency, which exists when a debtor's liabilities exceed assets, is not the test. Thus, it is possible for debtors to voluntarily petition for bankruptcy or to be thrown into involuntary bankruptcy even though their assets far exceed their liabilities. This may occur when a debtor's cash flow problems become severe.

---

5. There are basically three methods of perfection. First, the debtor may transfer possession of the collateral to the secured creditor. Second, the security interest may be perfected automatically at the time of a credit sale (that is, at the moment the security interest is created under a written security agreement). Third, and most commonly, a security interest may be perfected by the creditor's filing a financing statement.
6. The definition of *corporation* includes unincorporated companies and associations. It also covers labor unions.

a liquidation proceeding. Railroads, insurance companies, banks, savings and loan associations, investment companies licensed by the Small Business Administration, and credit unions cannot be debtors in a liquidation bankruptcy, however. Other chapters of the Bankruptcy Code or federal or state statutes apply to them.

A straight bankruptcy may be commenced by the filing of either a voluntary or an involuntary **petition in bankruptcy**—the document that is filed with a bankruptcy court to initiate bankruptcy proceedings. If a debtor files the petition, it is a voluntary bankruptcy. If one or more creditors file a petition to force the debtor into bankruptcy, it is called an involuntary bankruptcy. We discuss both voluntary and involuntary bankruptcy proceedings under Chapter 7 in the following subsections.

Voluntary Bankruptcy

To bring a voluntary petition in bankruptcy, the debtor files official forms designated for that purpose in the bankruptcy court. The Bankruptcy Reform Act of 2005 specifies that before debtors can file a petition, they must receive credit counseling from an approved nonprofit agency within the 180-day period preceding the date of filing. The act provides detailed criteria for the *U.S. Trustee* to approve nonprofit budget and counseling agencies and requires that a list of approved agencies be made publicly available.[7] A debtor filing a Chapter 7 petition must include a certificate proving that he or she received an individual or group briefing from an approved counseling agency within the last 180 days (roughly six months).

The Code requires a consumer-debtor who has opted for liquidation bankruptcy proceedings to confirm the accuracy of the petition's contents. The debtor must also state in the petition, at the time of filing, that he or she understands the relief available under other chapters of the Code and has chosen to proceed under Chapter 7. If an attorney is representing the consumer-debtor, the attorney must file an affidavit stating that she or he has informed the debtor of the relief available under each chapter of the Bankruptcy Code. In addition, the 2005 act requires the attorney to reasonably attempt to verify the accuracy of the consumer-debtor's petition and

schedules (described below). Failure to do so is considered perjury.

CHAPTER 7 SCHEDULES The voluntary petition must contain the following schedules:

1. A list of both secured and unsecured creditors, their addresses, and the amount of debt owed to each.
2. A statement of the financial affairs of the debtor.
3. A list of all property owned by the debtor, including property that the debtor claims is exempt.
4. A list of current income and expenses.
5. A certificate from an approved credit counseling agency (as discussed previously).
6. Proof of payments received from employers within sixty days prior to the filing of the petition.
7. A statement of the amount of monthly income, itemized to show how the amount is calculated.
8. A copy of the debtor's federal income tax return (or a transcript of such a return) for the most recent year ending immediately before the filing of the petition.

The official forms must be completed accurately, sworn to under oath, and signed by the debtor. To conceal assets or knowingly supply false information on these schedules is a crime under the bankruptcy laws.

—Additional Information May Be Required. At the request of the court, the **U.S. Trustee** (a government official who performs appointment and other administrative tasks that a bankruptcy judge would otherwise have to perform), or any party in interest, the debtor must file tax returns at the end of each tax year while the case is pending and provide copies to the court. This requirement also applies to Chapter 11 and 13 bankruptcies (discussed later in this chapter). Also, if requested by the U.S. Trustee or bankruptcy trustee, the debtor must provide a photo document establishing his or her identity (such as a driver's license or passport) or other personal identifying information.

—Time Period for Filing Schedules. With the exception of tax returns, failure to file the required schedules within forty-five days after the filing of the petition (unless an extension of up to forty-five days is granted) will result in an automatic dismissal of the petition. The debtor has up to seven days before the date of the first creditors' meeting to provide a copy of the most recent tax returns to the trustee.

SUBSTANTIAL ABUSE Prior to 2005, a bankruptcy court could dismiss a Chapter 7 petition for relief (discharge of debts) if the use of Chapter 7 would constitute a "substantial abuse" of that chapter. The Bankruptcy Reform Act of 2005 established a new

---

7. The Bankruptcy Reform Act of 2005 also required the director of the Executive Office for the U.S. Trustees to develop a curriculum for financial-management training and create materials that can be used to educate individual debtors on how to better manage their finances.

system of "means testing" (the debtor's income) to determine whether a debtor's petition is presumed to be a "substantial abuse" of Chapter 7.

—*When Abuse Will Be Presumed.* If the debtor's family income is greater than the median family income in the state in which the petition is filed, the trustee or any party in interest (such as a creditor) can bring a motion to dismiss the Chapter 7 petition. State median incomes vary from state to state and are calculated and reported by the U.S. Bureau of the Census.

The debtor's current monthly income is calculated using the last six months' average income, less certain "allowed expenses" reflecting the basic needs of the debtor. The monthly amount is then multiplied by twelve. If the resulting income exceeds the state median income by $6,000 or more,[8] abuse is presumed, and the trustee or any creditor can file a motion to dismiss the petition. A debtor can rebut (refute) the presumption of abuse "by demonstrating special circumstances that justify additional expenses or adjustments of current

monthly income for which there is no reasonable alternative." (One example might be anticipated medical costs not covered by health insurance.) These additional expenses or adjustments must be itemized and their accuracy attested to under oath by the debtor.

—*When Abuse Will Not Be Presumed.* If the debtor's income is below the state median (or if the debtor has successfully rebutted the means-test presumption), abuse will not be presumed. In these situations, the court may still find substantial abuse, but the creditors will not have standing (see Chapter 2) to file a motion to dismiss. Basically, this leaves intact the prior law on substantial abuse, allowing the court to consider such factors as the debtor's bad faith or circumstances indicating substantial abuse. The following case illustrates how a court determined whether granting a Chapter 7 discharge to the debtor would constitute substantial abuse by applying the "totality-of-the-circumstances" test. Although the case was decided before the 2005 reforms were enacted, a court could take the same approach under the new law (if, for example, the means test did not require substantial abuse to be presumed).

---

8. This amount ($6,000) is the equivalent of $100 per month for five years, indicating that the debtor could pay at least $100 per month under a Chapter 13 five-year repayment plan.

CASE 15.3 — In re Lamanna

United States
Court of Appeals,
First Circuit, 1998.
153 F.3d 1.
http://www.law.
emory.edu/1circuit[a]

BACKGROUND AND FACTS *In 1996, Richard Lamanna was living with his parents. For this reason, his monthly expenses were only $580. His monthly income was $1,350.96, leaving a difference of $770.96, the amount of his disposable income.[b] He had no plans to move out of his parents' house. During four weeks in October and November, he charged $9,994.45 on credit cards. In February 1997, when his total unsecured debt was $15,911.96, he filed a voluntary petition in a federal bankruptcy court to declare bankruptcy under Chapter 7 of the Bankruptcy Code. The court noted that Lamanna was capable of paying all of his debts under a Chapter 13 repayment plan and dismissed the case. The U.S. Bankruptcy Appellate Panel (BAP)[c] for the First Circuit affirmed the dismissal, and Lamanna appealed to the U.S. Court of Appeals for the First Circuit. Lamanna argued in part that if he did not live with his parents, he would not have as much disposable income, and that thus he was being penalized for living with his parents.*

IN THE LANGUAGE OF THE COURT

LYNCH, Circuit Judge.
* * * *
    The question of whether allowing Lamanna's bankruptcy petition would constitute "substantial abuse" of Chapter 7 under Section 707(b) contains two components: first,

---

a. In the "Listing by Month of Decision" section, click on "August" in the row for "1998" cases. When the list of cases appears, click on the case name to access the opinion. This Web site is maintained by Emory University School of Law.

b. *Disposable income* is income "not reasonably necessary to be expended for the maintenance or support of the debtor or a dependent of the debtor," according to 11 U.S.C. Section 1325(b)(2).

c. A *bankruptcy appellate panel* has jurisdiction, with the consent of the parties, to hear appeals from final judgments, orders, and decrees of bankruptcy judges.

CONTINUED ►

CASE 15.3 | Continued

the proper test by which "substantial abuse" is measured; second, whether, applying that test, the BAP [Bankruptcy Appellate Panel] correctly decided the issue. * * *

* * * *

* * * Although tests employed by various courts of appeals do not employ precisely the same language, they share common elements. First and foremost, it is agreed that *a consumer debtor's ability to repay his debts out of future disposable income is strong evidence of "substantial abuse."* * * * In determining whether to apply Section 707(b) to an individual debtor, * * * a court should ascertain from the totality of the circumstances whether he is merely seeking an advantage over his creditors, or is "honest," * * * and whether he is "needy" in the sense that his financial predicament warrants the discharge of his debts in exchange for liquidation of his assets. * * * [T]he "totality of the circumstances" test demands a comprehensive review of the debtor's current and potential financial situation. [Emphasis added.]

* * * *

Applying the "totality of the circumstances" test to Lamanna's case results in affirmance of the dismissal of his Chapter 7 petition for "substantial abuse." Lamanna's schedules showed that he has sufficient disposable income to repay his debts under a Chapter 13 repayment plan in three to five years. There is no evidence that Lamanna's living situation was unstable or likely to change in the near future. There is no evidence of other factors that cast doubt on the stability of Lamanna's future income and expenses. Although Lamanna's expenses are particularly low because he lives with his parents, this state of affairs, as the BAP noted, "is not artificial; it is actual." The court properly based its decision on the current and foreseeable facts. If Lamanna's circumstances dramatically change, he is free to seek relief anew.

Lamanna's argument that the court penalized him for living with his parents (and thus having exceptionally low monthly expenses) boils down to the notion that Section 707 requires the bankruptcy court to impute a minimum cost of living to a debtor and then measure the debtor's actual income against the higher of the imputed minimum and the debtor's actual expenses. Section 707 does not contain such an implicit requirement, and this court will not write such a requirement into the statute.

DECISION AND REMEDY *The U.S. Court of Appeals for the First Circuit affirmed the decision of the lower court and held that granting Lamanna's petition would constitute substantial abuse of Chapter 7. The appellate court looked at the "totality of the circumstances" to reach its conclusion.*

WHAT IF THE FACTS WERE DIFFERENT? *If the debtor in this case had not been able to pay his debts as they came due, would the result in the case have been different?*

ADDITIONAL GROUNDS FOR DISMISSAL As noted, a debtor's voluntary petition for Chapter 7 relief may be dismissed for substantial abuse or for failing to provide the necessary documents (such as schedules and tax returns) within the specified time. In addition, a motion to dismiss a Chapter 7 filing might be granted in two other situations under the Bankruptcy Reform Act of 2005. First, if the debtor has been convicted of a violent crime or a drug-trafficking offense, the victim can file a motion to dismiss the voluntary petition.[9] Second, if the debtor fails to pay postpetition

domestic-support obligations (which include child and spousal support), the court may dismiss the debtor's Chapter 7 petition.

ORDER FOR RELIEF If the voluntary petition for bankruptcy is found to be proper, the filing of the petition will itself constitute an *order for relief*. (An **order for relief** is a court's grant of assistance to a complainant.) Once a consumer-debtor's voluntary petition has been filed, the clerk of the court or other appointee must give the trustee and creditors notice of the order for relief by mail not more than twenty days after entry of the order. A husband and wife may file jointly for bankruptcy under a single petition.

9. Note that the court may not dismiss a case on this ground if the debtor's bankruptcy is necessary to satisfy a claim for a domestic-support obligation.

INVOLUNTARY BANKRUPTCY

An involuntary bankruptcy occurs when the debtor's creditors force the debtor into bankruptcy proceedings. An involuntary case cannot be commenced against a farmer[10] or a charitable institution. For an involuntary action to be filed against other debtors, the following requirements must be met: If the debtor has twelve or more creditors, three or more of these creditors having unsecured claims totaling at least $12,300 must join in the petition. If a debtor has fewer than twelve creditors, one or more creditors having a claim of $12,300 may file.

If the debtor challenges the involuntary petition, a hearing will be held, and the bankruptcy court will enter an order for relief if it finds either of the following:

1. The debtor is generally not paying debts as they become due.
2. A general receiver, assignee, or custodian took possession of, or was appointed to take charge of, substantially all of the debtor's property within 120 days before the filing of the petition.

If the court grants an order for relief, the debtor will be required to supply the same information in the bankruptcy schedules as in a voluntary bankruptcy.

An involuntary petition should not be used as an everyday debt-collection device, and the Code provides penalties for the filing of frivolous petitions against debtors. Judgment may be granted against the petitioning creditors for the costs and attorneys' fees incurred by the debtor in defending against an involuntary petition that is dismissed by the court. If the petition is filed in bad faith, damages can be awarded for injury to the debtor's reputation. Punitive damages may also be awarded.

AUTOMATIC STAY

The moment a petition, either voluntary or involuntary, is filed, an **automatic stay,** or suspension, of virtually all actions by creditors against the debtor or the debtor's property normally goes into effect. In other words, once a petition has been filed, creditors cannot contact the debtor by phone or mail or start any legal proceedings to recover debts or to repossess property. A secured creditor or other party in interest, however, may petition the bankruptcy court for relief from the automatic stay. The Code provides that if a creditor knowingly violates the automatic stay (a willful violation), any party injured, including the debtor, is entitled to recover actual damages, costs, and attorneys' fees and may be entitled to recover punitive damages as well.

Underlying the Code's automatic-stay provision for a secured creditor is a concept known as *adequate protection*. The **adequate protection doctrine,** among other things, protects secured creditors from losing their security as a result of the automatic stay. The bankruptcy court can provide adequate protection by requiring the debtor or trustee to make periodic cash payments or a one-time cash payment (or to provide additional collateral or replacement liens) to the extent that the stay may actually cause the value of the property to decrease. Alternatively, the court may grant other relief that protects the secured party's interest in the property, such as a guaranty by a solvent third party to cover losses suffered by the secured party as a result of the stay.

EXCEPTIONS TO THE AUTOMATIC STAY The 2005 Bankruptcy Reform Act provides several exceptions to the automatic stay. A new exception is created for domestic-support obligations, which include any debt owed to or recoverable by a spouse, former spouse, child of the debtor, a child's parent or guardian, or a governmental unit. In addition, proceedings against the debtor related to divorce, child custody or visitation, domestic violence, and support enforcement are not stayed. Also excepted are investigations by a securities regulatory agency, the creation or perfection of statutory liens for property taxes or special assessments on real property, eviction actions on judgments obtained prior to filing the petition, and withholding from the debtor's wages for repayment of a retirement account loan.

LIMITATIONS ON THE AUTOMATIC STAY Under the new Code, if a creditor or other party in interest requests relief from the stay, the stay will automatically terminate sixty days after the request, unless the court grants an extension[11] or the parties agree otherwise.

---

10. The definition of *farmer* includes persons who receive more than 50 percent of their gross income from farming operations, such as tilling the soil, dairy farming, ranching, or the production or raising of crops, poultry, or livestock. Corporations and partnerships may qualify under certain conditions.

---

11. The court might grant an extension, for example, on a motion by the trustee that the property is of value to the estate.

If two or more bankruptcy petitions were dismissed during the prior year, the Code presumes bad faith and the automatic stay does not go into effect until the court determines that the filing was made in good faith. In addition, if the petition is subsequently dismissed because the debtor failed to file the required documents within thirty days of filing, for example, the stay is terminated. Finally, the automatic stay on secured property terminates forty-five days after the creditors' meeting (to be discussed shortly) unless the debtor redeems or reaffirms certain debts (reaffirmation will be discussed later in this chapter). In other words, the debtor cannot keep the secured property (such as a financed automobile), even if she or he continues to make payments on it, without reinstating the rights of the secured party to collect on the debt.

PROPERTY OF THE ESTATE

On the commencement of a liquidation proceeding under Chapter 7, an *estate in property* is created. The estate consists of all the debtor's legal and equitable interests in property currently held, wherever located, together with community property, property transferred in a transaction voidable by the trustee, proceeds and profits from the property of the estate, and certain after-acquired property. Interests in certain property—such as gifts, inheritances, property settlements (from divorce), and life insurance death proceeds—to which the debtor becomes entitled *within 180 days after filing* may also become part of the estate. Under the 2005 act, withholdings for employee benefit plan contributions are excluded from the estate. Generally, though, the filing of a bankruptcy petition fixes a dividing line: property acquired prior to the filing of the petition becomes property of the estate, and property acquired after the filing of the petition, except as just noted, remains the debtor's.

CREDITORS' MEETING AND CLAIMS

Within a reasonable time after the order for relief has been granted (not less than twenty days or more than forty days), the trustee must call a meeting of the creditors listed in the schedules filed by the debtor. The bankruptcy judge does not attend this meeting.

DEBTOR'S PRESENCE REQUIRED The debtor is required to attend the meeting (unless excused by the court) and to submit to examination under oath by the creditors and the trustee. Failing to appear when required or making false statements under oath may result in the debtor's being denied a discharge in bankruptcy. At the meeting, the trustee ensures that the debtor is aware of the potential consequences of bankruptcy and of his or her ability to file for bankruptcy under a different chapter of the Bankruptcy Code.

CREDITORS' CLAIMS To be entitled to receive a portion of the debtor's estate, each creditor normally files a *proof of claim* with the bankruptcy court clerk within ninety days of the creditors' meeting.[12] The proof of claim lists the creditor's name and address, as well as the amount that the creditor asserts is owed to the creditor by the debtor. A creditor need not file a proof of claim if the debtor's schedules list the creditor's claim as liquidated (exactly determined) and the creditor does not dispute the amount of the claim. A proof of claim is necessary if there is any dispute concerning the claim. If a creditor fails to file a proof of claim, the bankruptcy court or trustee may file the proof of claim on the creditor's behalf but is not obligated to do so.

Generally, any legal obligation of the debtor is a claim (except claims for breach of employment contracts or real estate leases for terms longer than one year). When a claim is disputed, or unliquidated, the bankruptcy court will set the value of the claim. Any creditor holding a debtor's obligation can file a claim against the debtor's estate. These claims are automatically allowed unless contested by the trustee, the debtor, or another creditor. A creditor who files a false claim commits a crime.

EXEMPTIONS

The trustee takes control over the debtor's property, but an individual debtor is entitled to exempt certain property from the bankruptcy. The Bankruptcy Code exempts the following property:[13]

1. Up to $18,450 in equity in the debtor's residence and burial plot (the homestead exemption).
2. Interest in a motor vehicle up to $2,950.
3. Interest, up to $475 for a particular item, in household goods and furnishings, wearing apparel,

---

12. This ninety-day rule applies in Chapter 13 bankruptcies as well.
13. The dollar amounts stated in the Bankruptcy Code are adjusted automatically every three years on April 1 based on changes in the Consumer Price Index. The adjusted amounts are rounded to the nearest $25. The amounts stated in this chapter are in accordance with those computed on April 1, 2004.

appliances, books, animals, crops, and musical instruments (the aggregate total of all items is limited, however, to $9,850).

4. Interest in jewelry up to $1,225.

5. Interest in any other property up to $975, plus any unused part of the $18,450 homestead exemption up to $9,250.

6. Interest in any tools of the debtor's trade up to $1,850.

7. Any unmatured life insurance contract owned by the debtor.

8. Certain interests in accrued dividends and interest under life insurance contracts owned by the debtor, not to exceed $9,850.

9. Professionally prescribed health aids.

10. The right to receive Social Security and certain welfare benefits, alimony and support, certain retirement funds and pensions, and education savings accounts held for specific periods of time.

11. The right to receive certain personal-injury and other awards up to $18,450.

Individual states have the power to pass legislation precluding debtors from using the federal exemptions within the state; a majority of the states have done this. In those states, debtors may use only state, not federal, exemptions. In the rest of the states, an individual debtor (or a husband and wife filing jointly) may choose either the exemptions provided under state law or the federal exemptions.[14]

Note also that the 2005 Bankruptcy Reform Act clarified specifically what is included in "household goods and furnishings" (referred to in number 3 in the above list). For example, the category includes one computer, one radio, one television, one videocassette recorder, educational materials or equipment primarily for use by minor dependent children, and furniture that is used exclusively by a minor dependent (or by an elderly or disabled dependent). Other items, such as works of art; electronic entertainment equipment with a fair market value of over $500; antiques and jewelry (except wedding rings) valued at more than $500; and motor vehicles, tractors, lawn mowers, watercraft, and aircraft are *not* included in household goods.

THE HOMESTEAD EXEMPTION

The 2005 Bankruptcy Reform Act significantly changed the law for those debtors seeking to use state homestead exemption statutes. In six states, among them Florida and Texas, homestead exemptions allow debtors petitioning for bankruptcy to shield unlimited amounts of equity in their homes from creditors. The prior Bankruptcy Code required that the debtor must have been domiciled in the state for at least six months to apply any of the state exemptions. Under the 2005 act, however, the domicile period is now two years. In other words, the debtor must have lived in the state for two years prior to filing the petition to be able to use the state homestead exemption.

In addition, if the homestead is acquired within three and a half years preceding the date of filing, the maximum equity exempted is $125,000, even if the state law would permit a higher amount. (This does not apply to equity that has been rolled over during the specified period from the sale of a previous homestead in the same state.) Also, if the debtor owes a debt arising from a violation of securities law or if the debtor committed certain criminal or tortious acts in the previous five years that indicate the filing was substantial abuse, the debtor may not exempt any amount of equity.[15]

THE TRUSTEE

Promptly after the order for relief in the liquidation proceeding has been entered, an interim, or provisional, trustee is appointed by the U.S. Trustee. The interim, or provisional, trustee presides over the debtor's property until the first meeting of creditors. At this first meeting, either a permanent trustee is elected, or the interim trustee becomes the permanent trustee.

The basic duty of the trustee is to collect the debtor's available estate and reduce it to cash for distribution, preserving the interests of both the debtor and unsecured creditors. This requires that the trustee be accountable for administering the debtor's estate. To enable the trustee to accomplish this duty, the Code gives the trustee certain powers, stated in both

---

14. State exemptions may or may not be limited with regard to value. Under state exemption laws, a debtor may enjoy an unlimited value exemption on a motor vehicle, for example, even though the federal bankruptcy scheme exempts a vehicle only up to a value of $2,950. A state's law may also define the property coming within an exemption differently than the federal law or may exclude, or except, specific items from an exemption, making it unavailable to a debtor who fits within the exception.

15. Specifically, the debtor may not claim the homestead exemption if the debtor has committed any criminal act, intentional tort, or willful or reckless misconduct that caused serious physical injury or death to another individual in the preceding five years. Also, if the debtor has been convicted of a felony, he or she may not be able to claim the exemption.

general and specific terms. These powers must be exercised within two years of the order for relief.

NEW DUTIES UNDER THE 2005 ACT   The Bankruptcy Reform Act of 2005 imposes new duties on trustees (and bankruptcy administrators) with regard to means-testing all debtors who file Chapter 7 petitions. Under the new law, the U.S. Trustee or bankruptcy administrator is required to promptly review all materials filed by the debtor. Not later than ten days after the first meeting of the creditors, the trustee must file a statement as to whether the case is presumed to be an abuse under the means test. The trustee must then provide a copy of this statement concerning abuse to all creditors within five days. Not later than forty days after the first creditors' meeting, the trustee must either file a motion to dismiss the petition (or convert it to a Chapter 13 case) or file a statement setting forth the reasons why the motion would not be appropriate.

The trustee also has new duties under the 2005 act designed to protect domestic-support creditors (those to whom a domestic-support obligation is owed). The trustee is required to provide written notice of the bankruptcy to the claim holder (a former spouse who is owed child support, for example). The notice must also include certain information, such as the debtor's address, the name and address of the debtor's last known employer, and the address and phone number of the state child-support enforcement agency. (Note that these requirements are not limited to Chapter 7 bankruptcies, and the trustee may have additional duties in other types of bankruptcy to collect assets for distribution to the domestic-support creditor.)

THE TRUSTEE'S POWERS   The general powers of the trustee are described by the statement that the trustee occupies a position *equivalent* in rights to that of certain other parties. For example, the trustee has the same rights as a *lien creditor* who could have obtained a judicial lien on the debtor's property or who could have levied execution on the debtor's property. This means that a trustee has priority over an unperfected secured party to the debtor's property. This right of a trustee, equivalent to that of a lien creditor, is known as the *strong-arm power*. A trustee also has power equivalent to that of a *bona fide purchaser* of real property from the debtor.

Nevertheless, in most states a creditor with what is known as a purchase-money security interest may prevail against a trustee if the creditor files within ten days (twenty days, in many states) of the debtor's receipt of the collateral, even if the bankruptcy petition is filed before the creditor perfects. For example, Baker loaned Newbury $20,000 on January 1, taking a security interest in the machinery that Newbury purchased with the $20,000 and that was delivered on that same date. On January 27, before Baker had perfected her security interest, Newbury filed for bankruptcy. The trustee can invalidate Baker's security interest because it was unperfected when Newbury filed the bankruptcy petition. Baker can assert a claim only as an unsecured creditor. But if Newbury had filed for bankruptcy on January 7, and Baker had perfected her security interest on January 8, she would have prevailed, because she would have perfected her security interest within ten days of Newbury's receipt of the machinery.

THE RIGHT TO POSSESSION OF THE DEBTOR'S PROPERTY   The trustee has the power to require persons holding the debtor's property at the time the petition is filed to deliver the property to the trustee. (A trustee usually does not take actual possession of a debtor's property. Instead, a trustee's possession is constructive. For example, to obtain control of a debtor's business inventory, a trustee might change the locks on the doors to the business and hire a security guard.)

AVOIDANCE POWERS   The trustee also has specific powers of *avoidance*—that is, the trustee can set aside a sale or other transfer of the debtor's property, taking it back as a part of the debtor's estate. These powers include any voidable rights available to the debtor, preferences, certain statutory liens, and fraudulent transfers by the debtor. Each of these powers is discussed in more detail below.

The debtor shares most of the trustee's avoidance powers. Thus, if the trustee does not take action to enforce one of the rights mentioned above, the debtor in a liquidation bankruptcy can nevertheless enforce that right.[16]

Note that under the 2005 act, the trustee no longer has the power to avoid any transfer that was a bona fide payment of a domestic-support debt.

VOIDABLE RIGHTS   A trustee steps into the shoes of the debtor. Thus, any reason that a debtor can use to obtain the return of her or his property can be used by

---

16. Under a Chapter 11 bankruptcy (to be discussed later), for which no trustee other than the debtor generally exists, the debtor has the same avoidance powers as a trustee under Chapter 7. Under Chapters 13 (also to be discussed later), a trustee must be appointed.

the trustee as well. These grounds include fraud, duress, incapacity, and mutual mistake.

For example, Ben sells his boat to Tara. Tara gives Ben a check, knowing that she has insufficient funds in her bank account to cover the check. Tara has committed fraud. Ben has the right to avoid that transfer and recover the boat from Tara. Once an order for relief under Chapter 7 of the Code has been entered for Ben, the trustee can exercise the same right to recover the boat from Tara, and the boat becomes a part of the debtor's estate.

PREFERENCES A debtor is not permitted to transfer property or to make a payment that favors—or gives a **preference** to—one creditor over others. The trustee is allowed to recover payments made both voluntarily and involuntarily to one creditor in preference over another. If a **preferred creditor** (one who has received a preferential transfer from the debtor) has sold the property to an innocent third party, the trustee cannot recover the property from the innocent party. The preferred creditor, however, generally can be held accountable for the value of the property.

To have made a preferential payment that can be recovered, an *insolvent* debtor generally must have transferred property, for a *preexisting* debt, within *ninety days* prior to the filing of the petition in bankruptcy. The transfer must give the creditor more than the creditor would have received as a result of the bankruptcy proceedings. The trustee need not prove insolvency, as the Code provides that the debtor is presumed to be insolvent during this ninety-day period.

—Preferences to Insiders. Sometimes, the creditor receiving the preference is an **insider**—an individual, a partner, a partnership, a corporation, or an officer or a director of a corporation (or a relative of one of these) who has a close relationship with the debtor. In this situation, the avoidance power of the trustee is extended to transfers made within *one year* before filing; however, the *presumption* of insolvency is confined to the ninety-day period. Therefore, the trustee must prove that the debtor was insolvent at the time of a transfer that occurred prior to the ninety-day period.

—Transfers That Do Not Constitute Preferences. Not all transfers are preferences. To be a preference, the transfer must be made for something other than current consideration. Most courts generally assume that payment for services rendered within ten to fifteen days prior to the payment of the current consideration is not a preference. If a creditor receives

payment in the ordinary course of business from an individual or business debtor, such as payment of last month's telephone bill, the payment cannot be recovered by the trustee in bankruptcy. To be recoverable, a preference must be a transfer for an antecedent (preexisting) debt, such as a year-old printing bill. In addition, the Code permits a consumer-debtor to transfer any property to a creditor up to a total value of $5,000, without the transfer's constituting a preference (this amount was increased from $600 to $5,000 by the 2005 act). Payment of domestic-support debts does not constitute a preference. Also, transfers that were made as part of an alternative repayment schedule negotiated by an approved credit counseling agency are not preferences.

LIENS ON DEBTOR'S PROPERTY The trustee has the power to avoid certain statutory liens against the debtor's property, such as a landlord's lien for unpaid rent. The trustee can avoid statutory liens that first became effective against the debtor when the bankruptcy petition was filed or when the debtor became insolvent. The trustee can also avoid any lien against a bona fide purchaser that was not perfected or enforceable on the date of the bankruptcy filing.

FRAUDULENT TRANSFERS The trustee may avoid fraudulent transfers or obligations if they are made within two years of the filing of the petition or if they are made with actual intent to hinder, delay, or defraud a creditor. Transfers made for less than a reasonably equivalent consideration are also vulnerable if by making them, the debtor became insolvent, was left engaged in business with an unreasonably small amount of capital, or intended to incur debts that he or she could not pay. When a fraudulent transfer is made outside the Code's two-year limit, creditors may seek alternative relief under state laws. State laws often allow creditors to recover for transfers made up to three years prior to the filing of a petition.

DISTRIBUTION OF PROPERTY

The Code provides specific rules for the distribution of the debtor's property to secured and unsecured creditors. (We will examine these distributions shortly.) If any amount remains after the priority classes of creditors have been satisfied, it is turned over to the debtor. Exhibit 15–1 on the following page illustrates graphically the collection and distribution of property in most voluntary bankruptcies.

EXHIBIT 15-1 Collection and Distribution of Property in Most Voluntary Bankruptcies

This exhibit illustrates the property that might be collected in a debtor's voluntary bankruptcy and how it might be distributed to creditors. Involuntary bankruptcies and some voluntary bankruptcies could include additional types of property and other creditors.

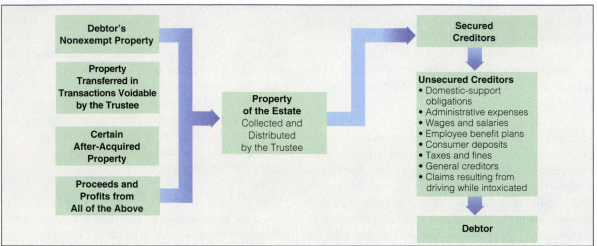

In a bankruptcy case in which the debtor has no assets,[17] creditors are notified of the debtor's petition for bankruptcy but are instructed not to file a claim. In such a case, the unsecured creditors will receive no payment, and most, if not all, of these debts will be discharged.

DISTRIBUTION TO SECURED CREDITORS The rights of perfected secured creditors were discussed earlier in this chapter. The Code provides that a consumer-debtor, either within thirty days of filing a liquidation petition or before the date of the first meeting of the creditors (whichever is first), must file with the clerk a statement of intention with respect to the secured collateral. The statement must indicate whether the debtor will redeem the collateral (make a single payment equal to the current value of the property), reaffirm the debt (continue making payments on the debt), or surrender the property to the secured party.[18] The trustee is obligated to enforce the debtor's statement within forty-five days after the meeting of the creditors. As noted previously, failure of the debtor to redeem or reaffirm within forty-five days terminates the automatic stay.

If the collateral is surrendered to the perfected secured party, the secured creditor can enforce the security interest either by accepting the property in full satisfaction of the debt or by foreclosing on the collateral and using the proceeds to pay off the debt. Thus, the perfected secured party has priority over unsecured parties as to the proceeds from the disposition of the collateral. Indeed, the Code provides that if the value of the collateral exceeds the perfected secured party's claim and if the security agreement so provides, the secured party also has priority as to the proceeds in an amount that will cover reasonable fees and costs incurred because of the debtor's default. Fees include reasonable attorneys' fees. Any excess over this amount is used by the trustee to satisfy the claims of unsecured creditors. Should the collateral be insufficient to cover the secured debt owed, the secured creditor becomes an unsecured creditor for the difference.

DISTRIBUTION TO UNSECURED CREDITORS Bankruptcy law establishes an order of priority for classes of debts owed to *unsecured* creditors, and they are paid in the order of their priority. Each class must be fully paid before the next class is entitled to any of the remaining proceeds. If there are insufficient proceeds to pay fully all the creditors in a class, the proceeds are distributed *proportionately* to the creditors in that class, and classes lower in priority receive nothing. The new bankruptcy law elevated domestic-support obligations to the highest priority of unsecured claims. The order

17. This type of bankruptcy is called a "no-asset" case.
18. Also, if applicable, the debtor must specify whether the collateral will be claimed as exempt property.

of priority among classes of unsecured creditors is as follows:

1. Claims for domestic-support obligations, such as child support and alimony (subject to the priority of the administrative costs that the trustee incurred in administering assets to pay the obligations).

2. Administrative expenses including court costs, trustee fees, and attorneys' fees.

3. In an involuntary bankruptcy, expenses incurred by the debtor in the ordinary course of business from the date of the filing of the petition up to the appointment of the trustee or the court's issuance of an order for relief.

4. Unpaid wages, salaries, and commissions earned within ninety days prior to the filing of the petition, limited to $4,925 per claimant. Any claim in excess of $4,925 or earned before the ninety-day period is treated as a claim of a general creditor (listed as item 10 below).

5. Unsecured claims for contributions to be made to employee benefit plans, limited to services performed during the 180-day period prior to the filing of the bankruptcy petition and $4,925 per employee.

6. Claims by farmers and fishermen, up to $4,925, against debtor-operators of grain storage or fish storage or processing facilities.

7. Consumer deposits of up to $2,225 given to the debtor before the petition was filed in connection with the purchase, lease, or rental of property or purchase of services that were not received or provided. Any claim in excess of $2,225 is treated as a claim of a general creditor (listed as item 10 below).

8. Certain taxes and penalties due to government units, such as income and property taxes.

9. Claims for death or personal injury resulting from the operation of a motor vehicle or vessel if such operation was unlawful because the debtor was intoxicated as a result of using alcohol, a drug, or another substance. (This provision was added by the 2005 act.)

10. Claims of general creditors.

DISCHARGE

From the debtor's point of view, the primary purpose of liquidation is to obtain a fresh start through a discharge of debts.[19] As mentioned earlier, once the debtor's assets have been distributed to creditors as permitted by the Code, the debtor's remaining debts

are then discharged, meaning that the debtor is not obligated to pay them. Certain debts, however, are not dischargeable in bankruptcy. Also, certain debtors may not qualify to have all debts discharged in bankruptcy. These situations are discussed below.

EXCEPTIONS TO DISCHARGE Discharge of a debt may be denied because of the nature of the claim or the conduct of the debtor. Claims that are not dischargeable in a liquidation bankruptcy include the following:

1. Claims for back taxes accruing within two years prior to bankruptcy.

2. Claims for amounts borrowed by the debtor to pay federal taxes or any nondischargeable taxes.

3. Claims against property or funds obtained by the debtor under false pretenses or by false representations.

4. Claims by creditors who were not notified and did not know of the bankruptcy; these claims did not appear on the schedules the debtor was required to file.

5. Claims based on fraud or misuse of funds by the debtor while he or she was acting in a fiduciary capacity or claims involving the debtor's embezzlement or larceny.

6. Domestic-support obligations and property settlements as provided for in a separation agreement or divorce decree.

7. Claims for amounts due on a retirement account loan.

8. Claims based on willful or malicious conduct by the debtor toward another or the property of another.

9. Certain government fines and penalties, which under the 2005 act also include penalties imposed under federal election laws.

10. Certain student loans or obligations to repay funds received as an educational benefit, scholarship, or stipend—unless payment of the loans imposes an undue hardship on the debtor and the debtor's dependents.

11. Consumer debts of more than $500 for luxury goods or services owed to a single creditor incurred within ninety days of the order for relief. (Prior to the passage of the 2005 act, the amount was $1,150 and the period was sixty days.) This denial of discharge is a rebuttable presumption (that is, the denial may be challenged by the debtor), however, and any debts reasonably incurred to support the debtor or dependents are not classified as luxuries.

12. Cash advances totaling more than $750 that are extensions of open-end consumer credit obtained by the debtor within seventy days of the order for relief.

---

19. Discharges are granted under Chapter 7 only to individuals, not to corporations or partnerships. The latter may use Chapter 11, or they may terminate their existence under state law.

(The prior law allowed $1,150 in cash advances that were obtained within sixty days.) A denial of discharge of these debts is also a rebuttable presumption.

13. Judgments or consent decrees against a debtor as a result of the debtor's operation of a motor vehicle or any vessel or aircraft while intoxicated.

14. Fees or assessments arising from a lot in a homeowners' association, as long as the debtor retained an interest in the lot.

15. Failure of the debtor to provide required or requested tax documents. (This exception to discharge also applies to Chapter 11 and Chapter 13 bankruptcies.)

In the following case, the court considered whether to order the discharge of a debtor's student loan obligations. Is it "undue hardship" if, to repay the loans, a debtor has to forgo her son's private school tuition?

CASE 15.4   ## In re Savage

United States
Bankruptcy
Appellate Panel,
First Circuit, 2004.
311 Bankr. 835.

BACKGROUND AND FACTS *Brenda Savage attended college in the mid-1980s—taking out five student loans—but she did not graduate. In 2003, at the age of forty-one, single, and in good health, she lived with her fifteen-year-old son in an apartment in Boston, Massachusetts. Her son attended Boston Trinity Academy, a private school. Savage worked 37.5 hours per week for Blue Cross/Blue Shield of Massachusetts. Her monthly gross wages were $3,079.79. Her employment provided health insurance, dental insurance, life insurance, a retirement savings plan, and paid vacations and personal days. She also received monthly child-support income of $180.60. After deductions, her total net monthly income was $2,030.72. Her monthly expenses included, among other things, $607 for rent, $221 for utilities, $76 for phone, $23.99 for an Internet connection, $430 for food, $75 for clothing, $12.50 for laundry and dry cleaning, $23 for medical expenses, $95.50 for transportation, $193.50 for charitable contributions, $43 for entertainment, $277.50 for her son's tuition, and $50 for his books. In February, Savage filed a petition in bankruptcy, seeking to discharge her student loan obligations to Educational Credit Management Corporation (ECMC). At the time, she owed $32,248.45. The court ordered a discharge of all but $3,120. ECMC appealed to the U.S. Bankruptcy Appellate Panel for the First Circuit.*

IN THE LANGUAGE OF THE COURT

HAINES, Bankruptcy Judge.

*   *   *   *

Under 11 U.S.C. Section 523(a)(8), debtors are not permitted to discharge educational loans unless excepting the loans from discharge will impose an undue hardship on the debtor and the debtor's dependents. *   *   *

*   *   *   *

Under "totality of the circumstances" analysis, a debtor seeking discharge of student loans must prove by a preponderance of evidence that (1) her past, present, and reasonably reliable future financial resources; (2) her and her dependents' reasonably necessary living expenses, and; (3) other relevant facts or circumstances unique to the case prevent her from paying the student loans in question while still maintaining a minimal standard of living, even when aided by a discharge of other pre-petition debts.

*   *   *   *

The debtor must show not only that her current income is insufficient to pay her student loans, but also that her prospects for increasing her income in the future are too limited to afford her sufficient resources to repay the student loans and provide herself and her dependents with a minimal (but fair) standard of living. [Emphasis added.]

Ms. Savage has not demonstrated that her current level of income and future prospects warrant discharge of her loans. Her present income may be insufficient to pay her student loans and still maintain precisely the standard of living she now has. But *   *   * it would enable her to repay the loans without undue hardship. Moreover, the record plainly establishes that her prospects for a steady increase in income over time are promising. She has been steadily employed at the same job and regularly receives annual raises. Nothing indicates change is in the wind. Moreover, Ms. Savage currently works 37½ hours a week, leaving time for some part-time work (or longer hours at her present job) *   *   * .

CASE 15.4 | Continued

* * * *

To prove undue hardship for purposes of Section 523(a)(8), a debtor must show that her necessary and reasonable expenses leave her with too little to afford repayment. * * * [Emphasis added.]

* * * *

Private school tuition is not *generally* considered a reasonably necessary expense in bankruptcy cases * * * . Although compelling circumstances may distinguish a given case, the [courts] uniformly hold that a debtor's mere preference for private schooling is insufficient to qualify the attendant expense as necessary and reasonable.

Ms. Savage did not demonstrate a satisfactory reason why her son needs to attend private school at a monthly cost of $277.50 (plus $50 for books). When asked to explain why she did so, she testified:

> There were a lot of fights, a lot of swearing, a lot of other things going on. I mean he would wake up every morning crying because he didn't want to go to school. * * * So I had to find a school to put him in * * * where he was going to—I mean, he didn't do well that whole year. I had to keep going down to the school several times. He was just a mess the whole school year. * * * So I had to find another school.

Although we understand why Ms. Savage prefers that her son attend private school, she has not demonstrated that the public school system cannot adequately meet her son's educational needs. Her preference appears sincere, but that alone is not sufficient to sustain the bankruptcy court's implicit conclusion that forgoing this expense would constitute undue hardship * * * .

* * * *

Given the fact that at least $322.50 (private school tuition and books) in expense can be eliminated from Ms. Savage's budget without creating undue hardship, her student loans cannot be discharged under Section 523(a)(8). It is worth noting, as well, that Ms. Savage's son will reach majority in just a few years, a consequence that will reduce her required expenses considerably.

DECISION AND REMEDY *The U.S. Bankruptcy Appellate Panel for the First Circuit reversed the order of the bankruptcy court and remanded the case for the entry of a judgment in ECMC's favor. The appellate panel was "satisfied" that "Ms. Savage has now (and will increasingly have) the ability to repay her five student loans without undue hardship."*

WHAT IF THE FACTS WERE DIFFERENT? *Suppose that Savage's son had a learning disability that only a private school could accommodate and treat. Would the result in this case have been different?*

OBJECTIONS TO DISCHARGE In addition to the exceptions to discharge previously listed, a bankruptcy court may also deny the discharge of the *debtor* (as opposed to the debt). In the latter situation, the assets of the debtor are still distributed to the creditors, but the debtor remains liable for the unpaid portion of all claims. Grounds for the denial of discharge of the debtor include the following:

1. The debtor's concealment or destruction of property with the intent to hinder, delay, or defraud a creditor.

2. The debtor's fraudulent concealment or destruction of financial records.

3. The granting of a discharge to the debtor within eight years of the filing of the petition. (This period was increased from six to eight years by the 2005 act.)

4. Failure of the debtor to complete the required consumer education course (unless such a course is unavailable). (This ground for denial was provided for by the 2005 act and also applies to Chapter 13 petitions.)

5. Proceedings in which the debtor could be found guilty of a felony (basically, the 2005 act states that a court may not discharge any debt until the completion of felony proceedings against the debtor).

The purpose of denying a discharge on these or other grounds is to prevent a debtor from avoiding, through bankruptcy, the consequences of his or her wrongful conduct.

EFFECT OF DISCHARGE The primary effect of a discharge is to void any judgment on a discharged debt and enjoin any action to collect a discharged debt. A discharge does not affect the liability of a co-debtor.

REVOCATION OF DISCHARGE On petition by the trustee or a creditor, the bankruptcy court can, within one year, revoke the discharge decree. The discharge decree will be revoked if it is discovered that the debtor acted fraudulently or dishonestly during the bankruptcy proceedings. The revocation renders the discharge void, allowing creditors not satisfied by the distribution of the debtor's estate to proceed with their claims against the debtor.

REAFFIRMATION OF DEBT

An agreement to pay a debt dischargeable in bankruptcy is called a **reaffirmation agreement.** A debtor may wish to pay a debt—such as, for example, a debt owed to a family member, physician, bank, or some other creditor—even though the debt could be discharged in bankruptcy. Also, as noted previously, under the new Code a debtor cannot retain secured property while continuing to pay without entering into a reaffirmation agreement.

To be enforceable, reaffirmation agreements must be made before the debtor is granted a discharge. The agreement must be signed and filed with the court (along with the original disclosure documents, as you will read shortly). Court approval is required unless the debtor is represented by an attorney during the negotiation of the reaffirmation and submits the proper documents and certifications. Nevertheless, court approval may be required even if the debtor is represented by an attorney when it appears that the reaffirmation will result in undue hardship on the debtor. When court approval is required, a separate hearing will take place. The court will approve the reaffirmation only if it finds that the agreement will not result in undue hardship to the debtor and that the reaffirmation is consistent with the debtor's best interests.

PRESUMPTION OF UNDUE HARDSHIP   Under the provisions of the 2005 act, if the debtor's monthly income minus the debtor's monthly expenses as shown on her or his completed and signed statement is less than the scheduled payments on the reaffirmed debt, undue hardship will be presumed. A presumption of undue hardship can be rebutted, however. The debtor can file a written statement with the court that includes an explanation identifying additional sources of funds from which to make the agreed-on payments. If the court is not satisfied with the written explanation, it may disapprove of the reaffirmation or hold a hearing. The debtor may also rebut the presumption of undue hardship by explaining to the court in person at the hearing how she or he will be able to make future payments on the debt.

If the debtor has an attorney, the attorney must certify in writing that he or she has fully advised the debtor of the legal effect and consequences of reaffirmation. In addition, to rebut the presumption of undue hardship, the attorney must certify that, in the attorney's opinion, the debtor is able to make the payments.

NEW REAFFIRMATION DISCLOSURES   To discourage creditors from engaging in abusive reaffirmation practices, the 2005 act added new requirements for reaffirmation. The Code now provides the specific language for several pages of disclosures that must be given to debtors entering reaffirmation agreements.[20] Among other things, these disclosures explain that the debtor is not required to reaffirm any debt, but that liens on secured property, such as mortgages and cars, will remain in effect even if the debt is not reaffirmed. The reaffirmation agreement must disclose the amount of the debt reaffirmed, the rates of interest, the date payments begin, and the right to rescind. The disclosures also caution the debtor, "Only agree to reaffirm a debt if it is in your best interest. Be sure you can afford the payments you agree to make." The original disclosure documents must be signed by the debtor, certified by the debtor's attorney, and filed with the court at the same time as the reaffirmation agreement. A reaffirmation agreement that is not accompanied by the original signed disclosures will not be effective.

If the debtor is represented by an attorney and no presumption of undue hardship arises, then the reaffirmation becomes effective immediately on filing with the court. If the debtor is not represented, the reaffirmation is not effective until the court approves it. The debtor can rescind, or cancel, the agreement at any time before the court enters a discharge order, or within sixty days of the filing of the agreement, whichever is *later.*

SECTION 6 | Chapter 11 Reorganization

The type of bankruptcy proceeding most commonly used by corporate debtors is the Chapter 11 *reorganization.* In a reorganization, the creditors and the debtor formulate a plan under which the debtor pays a portion of the debts and is discharged of the remainder. The debtor is allowed to continue in business. Although this type of bankruptcy is generally a corpo-

---

20. Note that credit unions are exempted from these disclosure requirements.

rate reorganization, any debtors (including individuals but excluding stockbrokers and commodities brokers)[21] who are eligible for Chapter 7 relief are eligible for relief under Chapter 11.[22] In 1994, Congress established a "fast-track" Chapter 11 procedure for small-business debtors whose liabilities do not exceed $2 million and who do not own or manage real estate. This allows for bankruptcy proceedings without the appointment of committees and can save time and costs.

The same principles that govern the filing of a liquidation (Chapter 7) petition apply to reorganization (Chapter 11) proceedings. The case may be brought either voluntarily or involuntarily. The same guidelines govern the entry of the order for relief. The automatic-stay and adequate protection provisions are applicable in reorganizations as well. The 2005 Bankruptcy Reform Act's exceptions to the automatic stay also apply to Chapter 11 proceedings, as do the new provisions regarding substantial abuse and additional grounds for dismissal (or conversion) of bankruptcy petitions. Also, the 2005 act contains specific rules and limitations for individual debtors who file a Chapter 11 petition. For example, an individual debtor's postpetition acquisitions and earnings become the property of the bankruptcy estate.

MUST BE IN THE BEST INTERESTS OF THE CREDITORS

Under Section 305(a) of the Bankruptcy Code, a court, after notice and a hearing, may dismiss or suspend all proceedings in a case at any time if dismissal or suspension would better serve the interests of the creditors. Section 1112 also allows a court, after notice and a hearing, to dismiss a case under reorganization "for cause." Cause includes the absence of a reasonable likelihood of rehabilitation, the inability to effect a plan, and an unreasonable delay by the debtor that is prejudicial to (may harm the interests of) creditors.[23]

WORKOUTS

In some instances, creditors may prefer private, negotiated adjustments of creditor-debtor relations, also known as **workouts,** to bankruptcy proceedings.

Often, these out-of-court workouts are much more flexible and thus more conducive to a speedy settlement. Speed is critical because delay is one of the most costly elements in any bankruptcy proceeding. Another advantage of workouts is that they avoid the various administrative costs of bankruptcy proceedings.

DEBTOR IN POSSESSION

On entry of the order for relief, the debtor generally continues to operate the business as a **debtor in possession (DIP).** The court, however, may appoint a trustee (often referred to as a *receiver*) to operate the debtor's business if gross mismanagement of the business is shown or if appointing a trustee is in the best interests of the estate.

The DIP's role is similar to that of a trustee in a liquidation. The DIP is entitled to avoid prepetition preferential payments made to creditors and prepetition fraudulent transfers of assets. The DIP has the power to decide whether to cancel or assume prepetition executory contracts (those that are not yet performed) or unexpired leases.

CREDITORS' COMMITTEES

As soon as practicable after the entry of the order for relief, a creditors' committee of unsecured creditors is appointed. If the debtor has filed a plan accepted by the creditors, however, the trustee may decide not to call a meeting of the creditors. The committee may consult with the trustee or the DIP concerning the administration of the case or the formulation of the plan. Additional creditors' committees may be appointed to represent special interest creditors. Under the 2005 act, a court may order the trustee to change the membership of a committee or to increase the number of committee members to include a small-business concern if the court deems it necessary to ensure adequate representation of the creditors.

Orders affecting the estate generally will be entered only with the consent of the committee or after a hearing in which the judge is informed of the position of the committee. As mentioned earlier, businesses with debts of less than $2 million that do not own or manage real estate can avoid creditors' committees. In these cases, orders can be entered without a committee's consent.

THE REORGANIZATION PLAN

A reorganization plan to rehabilitate the debtor is a plan to conserve and administer the debtor's assets in the hope of an eventual return to successful operation and solvency.

21. In *Toibb v. Radloff*, 501 U.S. 157, 111 S.Ct. 2197, 115 L.Ed.2d 145 (1991), the United States Supreme Court ruled that a nonbusiness debtor may petition for relief under Chapter 11.
22. In addition, railroads are eligible for Chapter 11 relief.
23. See 11 U.S.C. Section 1112(b). Debtors are not prohibited from filing successive petitions, however. A debtor whose petition is dismissed, for example, can file a new Chapter 11 petition (which may be granted unless it is filed in bad faith).

FILING THE PLAN Only the debtor may file a plan within the first 120 days after the date of the order for relief. Under the 2005 act, the 120-day period may be extended but not beyond 18 months from the date of the order for relief. If the debtor does not meet the 120-day deadline or obtain an extension, and if the debtor fails to procure the required creditor consent (discussed below) within 180 days, any party may propose a plan up to 20 months from the date of the order for relief. (In other words, the 180-day period cannot be extended beyond 20 months past the date of the order for relief.) For a small-business debtor, the time for the debtor's filing is 180 days.

The plan must be fair and equitable and must do the following:

1. Designate classes of claims and interests.
2. Specify the treatment to be afforded the classes. (The plan must provide the same treatment for all claims in a particular class.)
3. Provide an adequate means for execution. (The 2005 Bankruptcy Reform Act requires individual debtors to utilize postpetition assets as necessary to execute the plan.)
4. Provide for payment of tax claims over a five-year period.

ACCEPTANCE AND CONFIRMATION OF THE PLAN

Once the plan has been developed, it is submitted to each class of creditors for acceptance. Each class must accept the plan unless the class is not adversely affected by it. A class has accepted the plan when a majority of the creditors, representing two-thirds of the amount of the total claim, vote to approve it. Confirmation is conditioned on the debtor certifying that all postpetition domestic-support obligations have been paid in full. For small-business debtors, if the plan meets the listed requirements, the court must confirm the plan within forty-five days (unless this period is extended).

Even when all classes of creditors accept the plan, the court may refuse to confirm it if it is not "in the best interests of the creditors."[24] A former spouse or child of the debtor can block the plan if it does not provide for payment of her or his claims in cash. Under the 2005 act, if an unsecured creditor objects to the plan, specific rules apply to the value of property to be distributed under the plan. The plan can also be modified on the request of the debtor, trustee, U.S.

Trustee, or holder of the unsecured claim. Tax claims must be paid over a five-year period.

Even if only one class of creditors has accepted the plan, the court may still confirm the plan under the Code's so-called **cram-down provision.** In other words, the court may confirm the plan over the objections of a class of creditors. Before the court can exercise this right of cram-down confirmation, it must be demonstrated that the plan does not discriminate unfairly against any creditors and that the plan is fair and equitable.

DISCHARGE The plan is binding on confirmation; however, the Bankruptcy Reform Act of 2005 provides that confirmation of a plan does not discharge an individual debtor. For individual debtors, plan completion is required prior to discharge, unless the court orders otherwise. For all other debtors, the court may order discharge at any time after the plan is confirmed. The debtor is given a reorganization discharge from all claims not protected under the plan. This discharge does not apply to any claims that would be denied discharge under liquidation.

SECTION 7 | Bankruptcy Relief under Chapter 13

In addition to bankruptcy relief through liquidation and reorganization, the Code also provides for individuals' repayment plans (Chapter 13). As noted previously, the 2005 Bankruptcy Reform Act includes provisions for converting Chapter 7 bankruptcies into Chapter 13 repayment plans. It is therefore likely that there will be an increase in Chapter 13 bankruptcies as a result, because those debtors who have some ability to pay their obligations will file under Chapter 13. There has been a great deal of controversy over the practical effect of the 2005 act. This chapter's *Contemporary Legal Debates* feature on pages 380 and 381 provides details on some of the issues in dispute.

Chapter 13 of the Bankruptcy Code provides for "Adjustment of Debts of an Individual with Regular Income." Individuals (not partnerships or corporations) with regular income who owe fixed unsecured debts of less than $307,675 or fixed secured debts of less than $922,975 may take advantage of bankruptcy repayment plans. Among those eligible are salaried employees; sole proprietors; and individuals who live on welfare, Social Security, fixed pensions, or investment income. Many small-business debtors have a choice of filing a plan for reorganization or for repay-

---

24. The plan need not provide for full repayment to unsecured creditors. Instead, creditors receive a percentage of each dollar owed to them by the debtor.

ment. Repayment plans offer several advantages, however. One benefit is that they are less expensive and less complicated than reorganization proceedings or, for that matter, even liquidation proceedings.

FILING THE PETITION

A repayment plan case can be initiated only by the filing of a voluntary petition by the debtor or by the conversion of a Chapter 7 petition (because of a finding of substantial abuse under the means test, for example). Certain liquidation and reorganization cases may be converted to repayment plan cases with the consent of the debtor.[25] A trustee, who will make payments under the plan, must be appointed. On the filing of a repayment plan petition, the automatic stay previously discussed takes effect. Although the stay applies to all or part of the debtor's consumer debt, it does not apply to any business debt incurred by the debtor. The automatic stay also does not apply to domestic-support obligations.

THE REPAYMENT PLAN

A plan of rehabilitation by repayment must provide for the following:

1. The turnover to the trustee of such future earnings or income of the debtor as is necessary for execution of the plan.
2. Full payment in deferred cash payments of all claims entitled to priority.[26]
3. Identical treatment of all claims within a particular class. (The Code permits the debtor to list co-debtors, such as guarantors or sureties, as a separate class.)

FILING THE PLAN Only the debtor may file for a repayment plan. This plan may provide either for payment of all obligations in full or for payment of a lesser amount.[27] Prior to the 2005 act, the time for repayment was usually three years unless the court approved an extension for up to five years. Under the new Code, the length of the payment plan (three or five years) is deter-

mined by the debtor's median family income. If the debtor's family income is greater than the state median family income under the means test (previously discussed), the proposed plan must be for five years.[28] The term may not exceed five years, however.

The Code requires the debtor to make "timely" payments from the debtor's disposable income, and the trustee must ensure that the debtor commences these payments. The plan cannot materially alter terms of repayment on a retirement loan account, however. These payment amounts must take into consideration the scheduled payments to lessors of personal property, and must provide adequate protection to secured creditors of personal property. Proof of adequate insurance on personal property is required. The debtor must begin making payments under the proposed plan within thirty days after the plan has been *filed*.

If the plan has not been confirmed, the trustee is instructed to retain the payments until the plan is confirmed and then distribute them accordingly. If the plan is denied, the trustee will return the payments to the debtor less any costs. Failure of the debtor to make timely payments or to commence payments within the thirty-day period will allow the court to convert the case to a liquidation bankruptcy or to dismiss the petition.

CONFIRMATION OF THE PLAN After the plan is filed, the court holds a confirmation hearing, at which interested parties (such as creditors) may object to the plan. Under the 2005 act, the hearing must be held at least twenty days, but no more than forty-five days, after the meeting of the creditors. Confirmation of the plan is dependent on the debtor's certification that postpetition domestic-support obligations have been paid in full, and all prepetition tax returns have been filed. The court will confirm a plan with respect to each claim of a secured creditor under any of the following circumstances:

1. If the secured creditors have accepted the plan.
2. If the plan provides that secured creditors retain their liens until there is payment in full or until the debtor receives a discharge.
3. If the debtor surrenders the property securing the claims to the creditors.

In addition, for confirmation, the plan must provide that a creditor with a so-called purchase-money security interest (PMSI) retains its lien until payment of

---

25. A Chapter 13 case may be converted to a Chapter 7 case either at the request of the debtor or, under certain circumstances, "for cause" by a creditor. A Chapter 13 case may be converted to a Chapter 11 case after a hearing.
26. As with a Chapter 11 reorganization plan, full repayment of all claims is not always required.
27. Under the 2005 act, a plan under Chapter 13 or Chapter 12 (for farmers) might propose to pay less than 100 percent of prepetition domestic-support obligations that had been assigned, but only if disposable income is dedicated to a five-year plan. Disposable income is also redefined to exclude the amounts reasonably necessary to pay current domestic-support obligations.

28. See 11 U.S.C. Section 1322(d) for details on when the court will find that the Chapter 13 plan should extend to a five-year period.

Who Benefits from the 2005 Bankruptcy Reform Act?

When Congress enacted the Bankruptcy Reform Act of 1978, many claimed that the new act made it too easy for debtors to file for bankruptcy protection. Certainly, the facts cannot be denied: from 1978 to 2005, personal bankruptcy filings increased ninefold, reaching a peak of 1,613,097 in the year ending June 30, 2003. By the early 2000s, various business groups—including credit-card companies, banks, and firms providing loans for automobile purchases—were claiming that the bankruptcy process was being abused and that reform was necessary. As Mallory Duncan of the National Retail Federation put it, bankruptcy had gone from being a "stigma" to a "financial planning tool" for many.[a] Not surprisingly, the 2005 Bankruptcy Reform Act's full title is the Bankruptcy Abuse Prevention and Consumer Protection Act.

While lenders in general supported the bankruptcy reform bill, consumer groups fought it. According to Travis B. Plunkett, legislative director of the Consumer Federation of America, "The big winners under the new law will be the special interests that literally wrote it, particularly the credit-card industry. This is particularly ironic because reckless and abusive lending practices by credit-card companies have driven many Americans to the brink of bankruptcy."[b]

As with all contemporary legal debates, both sides have strong supporting arguments. In this feature, we examine a few of the major points of controversy.

HAS THE RISE IN BANKRUPTCIES BEEN DUE TO RISING MEDICAL COSTS?

Those who contend that the Bankruptcy Reform Act is anticonsumer and "mean spirited" point to several studies that link rising bankruptcy rates to high medical costs. Researchers at Harvard's medical and law schools conducted extensive interviews of almost two thousand bankruptcy filers in California, Illinois, Pennsylvania, Tennessee, and Texas. Illness and medical bills were cited as a cause in 46.2 percent of the personal bankruptcies under study. The lead author of the study, Dr. David Himmelstein, stated, "Most of the medical bankruptcies [involved] average Americans who happened to get sick."[c]

Judge Richard Posner of the U.S. Court of Appeals for the Seventh Circuit offers an alternative view about so-called medical bankruptcies. He points out that "[w]hether one is forced into bankruptcy by a medical expense (or by an interruption of employment as a result of a medical problem) depends on one's other borrowing. If one has already borrowed to the hilt, an unexpected medical expense may indeed force one over the edge. But knowing that medical expenses are a risk in our society, prudent people avoid loading themselves to the hilt with non-medical debt."[d]

CREATING MORE HARDSHIPS FOR THE POOR

Prior to the Bankruptcy Reform Act of 2005, only about 20 percent of personal bankruptcies were filed under Chapter 13.

---

a. As cited in Nedra Pickler, "Bush Signs Big Rewrite of Bankruptcy Law," *The Los Angeles Times*, April 20, 2005.

b. "Statement of Travis B. Plunkett, Legislative Director of the Consumer Federation of America, on the New Bankruptcy Law," press release by the Consumer Federation of America, April 20, 2005.

c. David Himmelstein *et al.*, "Illness and Injury as Contributors to Bankruptcy," *Health Affairs*, February 2, 2005.

d. Richard Posner, "The Bankruptcy Reform Act," March 27, 2005. You can access this article online by going to **http://www.becker-posner-blog.com** and selecting "March 2005" in the "Archives" column.

---

the entire debt for a motor vehicle purchased within 910 days before filing the petition. For PMSIs on other personal property, the payment plan must cover debts incurred within a one-year period preceding the filing.

OBJECTION TO THE PLAN   Unsecured creditors do not have the power to confirm a repayment plan, but they can object to it. The court can approve a plan over the objection of the trustee or any unsecured creditor only in either of the following situations:

1. When the value of the property (replacement value as of the date of filing) to be distributed under the plan is at least equal to the amount of the claims.

2. When all of the debtor's projected disposable income to be received during the plan period will be applied to making payments. Disposable income is all income received less amounts needed to pay domestic-support obligations and/or amounts needed to meet ordinary expenses to continue the operation of a business. The 2005 act also excludes from disposable income charitable contributions up to 15 percent of the debtor's gross income, and the reasonable and necessary costs for health insurance for the debtor and his or her dependents.

MODIFICATION OF THE PLAN   Prior to completion of payments, the plan may be modified at the request

ORM A MORE PERFECT UNION · ESTABLISH JUSTICE · INSURE DOMESTIC TRANQUILITY · PROMOTE THE GENERAL WELFARE

ional t Law Puffery · Jurisdiction Internet Electronic Free Speech Prenuptial Filing Agreements Advice of Counsel · Issues Internet Sales Contracts and the over Commerce War Clause Terror Privacy Debate AIDS · Private Who Owns the Engagement Ring? Enforceability Forum-Selection Clauses Developments Using "Takings" Internet · PATRIOT ACT · Exclusive Territorial Rig Environmenta Takings Commer

The remaining bankruptcies were filed under Chapter 7. The distinction has been important for all creditors. Given that most individuals who declared personal bankruptcy had few durable assets, Chapter 7 essentially "stiffed" the bankrupt's creditors. Under the new law, as previously indicated in this chapter, whenever a debtor has an annual income in excess of the mean income in that debtor's state of residence, the debtor may be forced into a Chapter 13 plan and make periodic payments over a period of five years to his or her creditors.

Critics of the 2005 Bankruptcy Reform Act point out that it will be more costly to declare personal bankruptcy in the future than it has been in the past. In part, this is because a much higher percentage of bankruptcy petitioners will now have to agree to a Chapter 13 repayment plan—and thus repay a portion of their debts. Additionally, the new law requires that each debtor's attorney certify the accuracy of all factual allegations in the bankruptcy petition and schedules or be subject to sanctions. Further, the bankruptcy attorney may also be responsible for the legal fees of the trustee or bankruptcy administrator who contests a Chapter 7 discharge. Finally, the debtor's attorney must certify the debtor's ability to make payments under any reaffirmation agreement. As a result, many bankruptcy attorneys have indicated that the certification requirements will force them to hire private investigators, appraisers, and auditors. According to attorney Mark Stern, the certification requirements will drive up the cost of filing a bankruptcy when using a lawyer.[e]

WILL CREDITORS REALLY BENEFIT?

Interestingly, forcing more debtors into Chapter 13 plans may not be all that beneficial to creditors. Consider that not all debtors who have filed under Chapter 13 actually complete their plans. According to David Stone, president of Nevada Association Services (a collection agency for about one thousand homeowners' associations statewide), about 80 percent of debtors default on their Chapter 13 plans. "In theory, if everyone complied with their Chapter 13 plans, [the new law] would be an improvement. But the fact of the matter is that most people fail to comply with Chapter 13 plans and therefore the case is dismissed," he asserts.[f]

WHERE DO YOU STAND?

The Bankruptcy Reform Act of 2005 subjects a large class of individuals in the United States to increased financial risk. Supporters of the new law contend that it will curb abuse by deterring financially troubled debtors from looking at bankruptcy as a mere "planning tool" instead of as a last resort. Critics of the act argue that the reform legislation will make it difficult for debtors to obtain a "fresh start" financially—one of the goals of bankruptcy law in the United States. What is your position on this issue? Do you believe that the 2005 act adequately balances the interests of creditors and debtors? Why or why not?

---

e. As cited in Marcia Coyle, "Debtor's Attorneys See Red in Senate Bill: Bankruptcy Judges More Burdened Also," *The National Law Journal,* March 14, 2005.

f. Steven Mihailovich, "Bankruptcy Law Could Make Problems in Nevada," *Las Vegas Business Press,* May 5, 2005.

---

of the debtor, the trustee, or an unsecured creditor. If any interested party objects to the modification, the court must hold a hearing to determine whether the modified plan will be approved.

DISCHARGE

After completion of all payments, the court grants a discharge of all debts provided for by the repayment plan. Except for allowed claims not provided for by the plan, certain long-term debts provided for by the plan, certain tax claims, payments on retirement accounts, and claims for domestic-support obligations, all other debts are dischargeable. Under prior law, a discharge of

debts under a Chapter 13 repayment plan was sometimes referred to as a "superdischarge" because it allowed the discharge of fraudulently incurred debt and claims resulting from malicious or willful injury.

The 2005 Bankruptcy Reform Act, however, deleted most of the "superdischarge" provisions, especially for debts based on fraud. Today, debts for trust fund taxes, taxes for which returns were never filed or filed late (within two years of filing), domestic-support payments, student loans, and injury or property damage from driving under the influence of alcohol or drugs are nondischargeable. The new law also excludes fraudulent tax obligations, criminal fines and restitution, fraud by a person acting in a fiduciary capacity, and restitution for willfully and maliciously causing personal injury or death.

Even if the debtor does not complete the plan, a hardship discharge may be granted if failure to complete the plan was due to circumstances beyond the debtor's control and if the value of the property distributed under the plan was greater than what would have been paid in a liquidation. A discharge can be revoked within one year if it was obtained by fraud.

REVIEWING CREDITOR-DEBTOR RELATIONS AND BANKRUPTCY

Three months ago, Janet Hart's husband of twenty years died of cancer. Although he had medical insurance, he left Janet with outstanding medical bills of more than $50,000. Janet has worked at the local library for the past ten years, earning $1,700 per month. Since her husband's death, Janet also receives $1,500 in Social Security benefits and $1,100 in life insurance proceeds every month, which leaves her with a monthly income of $4,300. After she pays the monthly mortgage payment of $1,500 and the monthly amounts due on other debts, Janet barely has enough left over to buy groceries for her family. (She has two teenaged daughters at home.) She decides to file for Chapter 7 bankruptcy, hoping for a fresh start. Using the information presented in the chapter, answer the following questions.

1. Under the Bankruptcy Code after the enactment of the 2005 revisions, what must Janet do prior to filing a petition for relief under Chapter 7?

2. What schedules must Janet include with her voluntary petition, and how long does she have to file these schedules? Must anyone verify the information contained in these schedules? Explain.

3. Assume that Janet files a petition under Chapter 7. Further assume that the median family income in the state in which Janet lives is $49,300. Describe the steps a court would take to determine whether Janet's petition is presumed to be "substantial abuse" using the means test.

4. Suppose that the court determines that no *presumption* of substantial abuse applies in Janet's case. Nevertheless, the court finds that Janet does have the ability to repay at least a portion of the amount due on the medical bills out of her disposable income. What would the court likely order in that situation?

TERMS AND CONCEPTS TO REVIEW

QUESTIONS AND CASE PROBLEMS

15-1. Sylvia takes her car to Caleb's Auto Repair Shop. A sign in the window states that all repairs must be paid for in cash unless credit is approved in advance. Sylvia and Caleb agree that Caleb will repair Sylvia's car engine and put in a new transmission. No mention is made of credit. Because Caleb is not sure how much engine repair will be necessary, he refuses to give Sylvia an estimate. He repairs the engine and puts in a new transmission. When Sylvia comes to pick up her car, she learns that the bill is $2,500. Sylvia is furious, refuses to pay Caleb that amount, and demands possession of her car. Caleb insists on payment. Discuss the rights of both parties in this matter.

15-2. **QUESTION WITH SAMPLE ANSWER**

Kanahara is employed by the Cross-Bar Packing Corp. and earns take-home pay of $400 per week. He is $2,000 in debt to the Holiday Department Store for goods purchased on credit over the past eight months. Most of this property is nonexempt and is currently located in Kanahara's apartment. Kanahara is in default on his payments to Holiday. Holiday learns that Kanahara has a girlfriend in another state and that he plans on giving her most of this property for Christmas. Discuss what actions are available and should be taken by Holiday to collect the debt owed by Kanahara.

For a sample answer to this question, go to Appendix I at the end of this text.

15-3. Natalie is a student at Slippery Stone University. In need of funds to pay for tuition and books, she asks West Bank for a short-term loan. The bank agrees to make a loan if Natalie will have someone who is financially responsible guarantee the loan payments. Sheila, a well-known businessperson and a friend of Natalie's family, calls the bank and agrees to pay the loan if Natalie cannot. Because of Sheila's reputation, the loan is made. Natalie is making the payments, but because of illness she is unable to work for one month. She requests that West Bank extend the loan for three months. West Bank agrees, raising the interest rate for the extended period. Sheila is not notified of the extension (and thus does not consent to it). One month later, Natalie drops out of school. All attempts to collect from Natalie fail. West Bank wants to hold Sheila liable. Discuss the validity of West Bank's claim against Sheila.

15-4. Peaslee is not known for his business sense. He started a greenhouse and nursery business two years ago, and because of his lack of experience, he soon was in debt to a number of creditors. On February 1, Peaslee borrowed $5,000 from his father to pay some of these creditors. On May 1, Peaslee paid back the $5,000, depleting his entire working capital. One creditor, the Cool Springs Nursery Supply Corp., extended credit to Peaslee on numerous purchases. Cool Springs pressured

Peaslee for payment, and on July 1, Peaslee paid Cool Springs half the money owed. On September 1, Peaslee voluntarily petitioned himself into bankruptcy. The trustee in bankruptcy claimed that both Peaslee's father and Cool Springs must turn over to the debtor's estate the amounts Peaslee paid to them. Discuss fully the trustee's claims.

15-5. **CASE PROBLEM WITH SAMPLE ANSWER**

Karen and Gerald Baldwin owned property in Rapid City, South Dakota, which they leased to Wyoming Alaska Corp. (WACO) for use as a gas station and convenience store. The lease obligated the Baldwins to maintain the property, but WACO was authorized to make necessary repairs. After seventeen years, the property had become dilapidated; the store's customers were tripping over chunks of concrete in the parking lot, and an underground gasoline storage tank was leaking. The store's manager hired Duffield Construction, Inc., to install a new tank and make other repairs. The Baldwins saw the new tank sitting on the property before the work began. When WACO paid only a small portion of the cost of the repairs, Duffield filed a mechanic's lien and asked a South Dakota state court to foreclose on the property. The Baldwins disputed the lien, arguing that they had not requested the work. What is the purpose of a mechanic's lien? Should property owners who do not contract for improvements be liable for the financial obligations under such a lien? How might property owners protect themselves against a lien for work that they do not request? Explain. [*Duffield Construction, Inc. v. Baldwin*, 679 N.W.2d 477 (S.D. 2004)]

To view a sample answer for this case problem, go to this book's Web site at http://wleb.westbuslaw.com, select "Chapter 15," and click on "Case Problem with Sample Answer."

15-6. GARNISHMENT. Susan Guinta is a real estate salesperson. Smythe Cramer Co. obtained in an Ohio state court a garnishment order to attach Guinta's personal earnings. The order was served on Russell Realtors to attach sales commissions that Russell owed to Guinta. Russell objected, arguing that commissions are not personal earnings and are therefore exempt from attachment under a garnishment of personal earnings. An Ohio statute defines *personal earnings* as "money, or any other consideration or thing of value, that is paid or due to a person in exchange for work, labor, or personal services provided by the person to an employer." An *employer* is "a person who is required to withhold taxes out of payments of personal earnings made to a judgment debtor." Russell does not withhold taxes from its salespersons' commissions. Under a federal statute, *earnings* means "compensation paid or payable for personal services, whether denominated as wages, salary, commission, bonus, or otherwise." Where the federal definition is more restrictive and results in a smaller garnishment, that definition is controlling. Property other than personal earnings may be subject to garnishment without limits. How should the court rule regarding Russell's objection? Why? [*Smythe Cramer Co. v. Guinta*, 762 N.E.2d 1083 (Ohio Mun. 2001)]

15–7. DISCHARGE IN BANKRUPTCY. Jon Goulet attended the University of Wisconsin in Eau Claire and Regis University in Denver, Colorado, from which he earned a bachelor's degree in history in 1972. Over the next ten years, he worked as a bartender and restaurant manager. In 1984, he became a life insurance agent and his income ranged from $20,000 to $30,000. In 1989, however, his agent's license was revoked for insurance fraud, and he was arrested for cocaine possession. From 1991 to 1995, Goulet was again at the University of Wisconsin, working toward, but failing to obtain, a master's degree in psychology. To pay for his studies, he took out student loans totaling $76,000. Goulet then returned to bartending and restaurant management and tried real estate sales. His income for the year 2000 was $1,490, and his expenses, excluding a child-support obligation, were $5,904. When the student loans came due, Goulet filed a petition for bankruptcy. On what ground might the loans be dischargeable? Should the court grant a discharge on this ground? Why or why not? [*Goulet v. Educational Credit Management Corp.*, 284 F.3d 773 (7th Cir. 2002)]

15–8. AUTOMATIC STAY. On January 22, 2001, Marlene Moffett bought a used 1998 Honda Accord from Hendrick Honda in Woodbridge, Virginia. Moffett agreed to pay $20,024.25, with interest, in sixty monthly installments, and Hendrick retained a security interest in the car. (Hendrick thus had the right to repossess the car in the event of default, subject to Moffett's right of redemption.) Hendrick assigned its rights under the sales agreement to Tidewater Finance Co., which perfected its security interest. The car was Moffett's only means of traveling the forty miles from her home to her workplace. In March and April 2002, Moffett missed two monthly payments. On April 25, Tidewater repossessed the car.

On the same day, Moffett filed a Chapter 13 plan in a federal bankruptcy court. Moffett asked that the car be returned to her, in part under the Bankruptcy Code's automatic-stay provision. Tidewater asked the court to terminate the automatic stay so that it could sell the car. How can the interests of both the debtor and the creditor be fully protected in this case? What should the court rule? Explain. [*In re Moffett*, 356 F.3d 518 (4th Cir. 2004)]

15–9. ⚖ **A QUESTION OF ETHICS**

Herpel, Inc., agreed to make a stone fireplace mantel for a house owned by Straub Capital Corp. When the mantel was first delivered, Straub was not satisfied, so Herpel took the mantel back, refinished it, and redelivered it five weeks later. The mantel was installed, but Straub did not pay. Herpel filed a mechanic's lien 113 days after the first delivery but less than 90 days after the second delivery. Herpel then filed an action in a Florida district court to foreclose on the lien. The trial court ruled in favor of Straub because the lien had been filed more than 90 days from the time the mantel was first delivered. The appellate court reversed, noting that although the time for filing a lien is not extended by repair, corrective, or warranty work, "work done in fulfillment of the contract will extend the time for filing of the claim of lien." In view of these events, consider the following questions. [*Herpel, Inc. v. Straub Capital Corp.*, 682 So.2d 661 (S.D.Fla. 1996)]

(a) The court's ruling hinges on the fact that Herpel took the fireplace mantel back, attempted to cure the alleged defects, and then offered it again for acceptance by Straub. Do you agree that this work was "in fulfillment of the contract," rather than to correct the defects?

(b) Would the outcome of this case have been different if the fireplace mantel had been left with the buyer at the time of delivery and the seller had attempted to make repairs to it while it was in the buyer's possession? Why or why not?

(c) Generally, do you think that it is fair for the court to consider who was in possession of the mantel at the time of repair when determining whether the lien was filed within the statutory time period?

LAW | on the Web

For updated links to resources available on the Web, as well as a variety of other materials, visit this text's Web site at http://wleb.westbuslaw.com.

The Legal Information Institute at Cornell University offers a collection of law materials concerning debtor-creditor relationships, including federal statutes and recent Supreme Court decisions on this topic, at

http://www.law.cornell.edu/topics/debtor_creditor.html

The U.S. Department of Labor's Web site contains a page on garnishment and employees' rights in relation to garnishment proceedings at

http://www.dol.gov/asp/programs/handbook/garnish.htm

The U.S. Bankruptcy Code is online at

http://www.law.cornell.edu:80/uscode/11

For information and news on bankruptcy reform legislation, go to the site maintained by Bankruptcy Media at

http://www.bankruptcyfinder.com/bankruptcyreformnews.html

Another good resource for bankruptcy information is the American Bankruptcy Institute (ABI) at

http://www.abiworld.org

LEGAL RESEARCH EXERCISES ON THE WEB

Go to http://wleb.westbuslaw.com, the Web site that accompanies this text. Select "Chapter 15" and click on "Internet Exercises." There you will find the following Internet research exercises that you can perform to learn more about topics covered in this chapter.

Activity 15–1: **LEGAL PERSPECTIVE**
Debtor-Creditor Relations

Activity 15–2: **MANAGEMENT PERSPECTIVE**
Bankruptcy Alternatives

The Commercial Environment

Many aspects of the commercial environment lend themselves to ethical analysis. Businesspersons certainly face ethical questions when they deal with the application of black-letter law to contracts. (*Black-letter law* is an informal term for the principles of law that courts generally accept or that are embodied in statutes.) Courts, for example, generally will not inquire into the adequacy of the consideration given in a contract. In other words, a court will not reevaluate a contract to determine whether what each party gave is equivalent to what that party received.

Ethical questions are also at the core of many principles of the law of sales. Many of the provisions of the Uniform Commercial Code (UCC), such as good faith and commercial reasonableness, though designed to meet the practical needs of business dealings, express ethical standards as well. Product liability also involves ethics. Many of the principles of product liability are based on principles designed to aid individuals injured, without extensive inquiry into issues of fault.

The areas of law covered in the previous unit constitute an important part of the legal environment of business. In each of these areas, new legal (and ethical) challenges have emerged as a result of developments in technology. Today, we are witnessing some of the challenges posed by the use of new communications networks, particularly the Internet. In this *Focus on Ethics* feature, we look at the ethical dimensions of selected topics discussed in the preceding chapters, including some issues that are unique to the cyber age.

Ethics and Freedom of Contract

In Chapter 4, we pointed out the importance of ethical business behavior. But what does acting ethically mean in the area of contracts? If an individual with whom you enter into a contract fails to look after his or her own interests, is that your fault, and should you therefore be doing something about it? If the contract happens to be to your advantage and therefore to the other party's detriment, do you have a responsibility to correct the situation?

The answer to this question is not simple. On the one hand, a common ethical assumption in our society is that individuals should be held responsible for the consequences of their own actions, including their contractual promises. This principle is expressed in the legal concept of freedom of contract.

On the other hand, there are times when courts will hold that the principle of freedom *of* contract should give way to the principle of freedom *from* contract, a principle based on the assumption that people should not be harmed by the actions of others. We look below at some examples of how parties to contracts may be excused from performance under their contracts if that is the only way injustice can be prevented.

Unconscionability

The doctrine of unconscionability represents a good example of how the law attempts to enforce ethical behavior. Under this doctrine, a contract may be deemed to be so unfair to one party as to be unenforceable—even though that party voluntarily agreed to the contract's terms. Unconscionable action, like unethical action, is incapable of precise definition. Information about the particular facts and specific circumstances surrounding the contract is essential. For example, a contract with a marginally literate consumer might be seen as unfair and unenforceable, whereas the same contract with a major business firm would be upheld by the courts.

Section 2–302 of the UCC, which incorporates the common law concept of unconscionability, similarly does not define the concept with any precision. Rather, it leaves it to the courts to determine when a contract is so one sided and unfair to one party as to be unconscionable and thus unenforceable.

Usually, courts will do all they can to save contracts rather than render them unenforceable. Thus, only in extreme situations, as when a contract or clause is so one sided as to "shock the conscience" of the court, will a court hold that a contract or contractual clause is unconscionable.

Ethics and Sales: Good Faith and Commercial Reasonableness

Good faith and commercial reasonableness are two key concepts that permeate the UCC and help to prevent unethical behavior by businesspersons. These two concepts are read into every contract and impose certain duties on all parties. Section 2–311(1) of the UCC indicates that when parties leave the particulars of performance to be specified by one of the parties, "[a]ny such specification must be made in good faith and within limits set by commercial reasonableness."

Bad Faith Not Required A party can breach the obligation of good faith under the UCC even if the party did not show "bad faith"—that is, even when there is no proof that the party was dishonest. For example, in one case a large manufacturer of recreational boats, Genmar Holdings, Inc., purchased Horizon, a small company that produced a particular type of "deep-V" fishing boat. Genmar bought Horizon to expand into the southern boat market and to prevent Horizon from becoming a potential future competitor. At the time of the sale, Genmar executives promised that Horizon boats would be the "champion" of the facility and vowed to keep Horizon's key employees (including the founder and his family) on as managers. The contract required Genmar to pay Horizon a lump sum in cash as well as paying "earn-out consideration" under a specified formula for five years. The "earn-out" amount depended on the number of Horizon brand boats sold and on the annual gross revenues of the facility.

One year after the sale, Genmar renamed the Horizon brand of boats "Nova" and told employees at the facility to give priority to producing the original Genmar brand of boats over the Nova boats. Because the Genmar boats were more difficult and time consuming to make than the Nova boats, the facility's gross revenues and production decreased, and Genmar was not required to pay the "earn-out" amounts. Eventually, Genmar fired the former Horizon employees and stopped manufacturing the Nova brand of boats entirely. The former employees filed a suit alleging that Genmar had breached the implied covenant of good faith and fair dealing. The defendants argued that they could not have violated good faith because there was no proof that they had engaged in fraud, deceit, or misrepresentation. The court held for the plaintiffs, however, and the decision was affirmed on appeal.[1] It is possible for a party to breach its good faith obligations under the UCC even if the party did not engage in fraud, deceit, or misrepresentation.

Commercial Reasonableness The requirement of commercial reasonableness means that the term subsequently supplied by one party should not come as a surprise to the other. The party filling in the missing term may not take advantage of the opportunity to add a contractual term that will be beneficial to himself or herself (and detrimental to the other party) and then demand contractual performance of the other party that was totally unanticipated. Under the UCC, the party filling in the missing term may not deviate from what is commercially reasonable in the context of the transaction. Courts frequently look to course of dealing, usage of trade, and the surrounding circumstances in determining what is commercially reasonable in a given situation.

Oral Contracts and Promissory Estoppel

Oral contracts are made every day. Many—if not most—of them are carried out, and no problems arise. Occasionally, however, oral contracts are not performed, and one party decides to sue the other. Sometimes, to prevent injustice, the courts will enforce oral contracts under the theory of promissory estoppel if detrimental reliance can be shown. The court may even use this theory to remove a contract from the Statute of Frauds—that is, render the oral contract enforceable.

In addition, ethical standards certainly underlie the doctrine of *promissory estoppel,* under which a person who has reasonably relied on the promise of another to his or her detriment can often obtain some measure of recovery. Essentially, promissory estoppel allows a variety of promises to be enforced even though they lack what is formally regarded as consideration.

An oral promise made by an insurance agent to a business owner, for example, may be binding if the owner relies on that promise to her or his detriment. Employees who rely to their detriment on an employer's promise may be able to recover under the doctrine of promissory estoppel.[2] A contractor who, when bidding for a job, relies on a subcontractor's promise to perform certain construction work at a certain price may be able to recover, on the basis of promissory estoppel, any damages sustained because of the subcontractor's failure to perform. These are but a few of the many examples in which the courts, in the interests of fairness and justice, have estopped a promisor from denying that a contract existed.

Do Gun Makers Have a Duty to Warn?

One of the issues facing today's courts is how tort law principles apply to harms caused by guns. Across the nation, many plaintiffs have filed negligence actions against gun manufacturers claiming that gun makers have a duty to warn users of their products of the dangers associated with gun use. Would it be fair to impose such a requirement on gun manufacturers? Some say no, because such dangers are "open and obvious." (Recall from Chapter 13 that manufacturers and sellers do not have a duty to warn of open and obvious dangers.) Others contend that warnings could prevent numerous gun accidents.

State courts addressing this issue have generally ruled that manufacturers have no duty to warn users of the obvious risks associated with gun use. For example, New York's highest court has held that a gun manufacturer's duty of care does not extend to those who are injured by the illegal use of handguns.[3] Several state courts also have found that makers of BB guns and air rifles have no duty to warn users of the risks.[4] Some courts, however, have held that gun makers whose marketing or sales practices cause a large influx of guns into the illegal secondary market could be liable under a public nuisance theory.[5]

---

1. *O'Tool v. Genmar Holdings, Inc.,* 387 F.3d 1188 (10th Cir. 2004).

2. Note, though, at least one court has held that an employer's oral promise not to fire an at-will employee was not enforceable under the doctrine of promissory estoppel. *Balmer v. Elan Corp.,* 278 Ga. 227, 599 S.E.2d 158 (2004).

3. *Hamilton v. Beretta U.S.A. Corp.,* 96 N.Y.2d 222, 750 N.E.2d 1055, 727 N.Y.S.2d 7 (2001).

4. *Abney v. Crosman Corp.,* ___ So.2d ___ (Ala. 2005); *Marzullo v. Crosman Corp.,* 289 F.Supp.2d 1337 (M.D.Fla. 2003).

5. *City of New York v. Beretta U.S.A. Corp.,* F.Supp.2d 256 (E.D.N.Y. 2004); *Johnson v. Bryco Arms,* 304 F.Supp.2d 383 (E.D.N.Y. 2004); *City of Gary ex rel. King v. Smith & Wessen Corp.,* 801 N.E.2d 1222 (Ind. 2003); *Ileto v. Glock, Inc.,* 349 F.3d 1191 (9th Cir. 2003).

Should the Courts Cancel Existing Trademarks That Are Disparaging?

The Lanham Act prohibits the U.S. Patent and Trademark Office from registering trademarks that are immoral, scandalous, or disparaging (demeaning). Trademark examiners review new proposals and reject any new trademarks that are disparaging by today's standards. But what happens when a trademark that was registered some time ago is perceived as disparaging to a group of people today? Can that registration be canceled? According to a federal district court in 2003, the answer is no. The case involved the Washington Redskins, a professional football team, and six Native Americans (the plaintiffs) who claimed that the term *Redskins* was the most derogatory one used for native people and the trademark should be canceled.

The federal district court held that the plaintiffs had not presented enough evidence to prove that the mark was disparaging. According to the court, the test is not whether the term is disparaging to Native Americans today but whether it was disparaging at the time it was originally registered. At trial, the plaintiffs presented evidence that a number of Native Americans found the term insulting today. The plaintiffs also presented some evidence, including survey results and the testimony of historians and linguists, to suggest that the mark was disparaging when it was first registered in 1967. The court found that this evidence was insufficient, however, and held that the plaintiffs had waited too long to complain about the trademark.[6] Given that what society considers disparaging often changes over time, some have contended that this ruling is unfair.

Trademark Protection versus Free Speech Rights

Another legal issue involving questions of fairness pits the rights of trademark owners against the right to free speech. The issue—so-called cybergriping—is unique to the cyber age.

Cybergriping Cybergripers are individuals who complain in cyberspace about corporate products, services, or activities. For trademark owners, the issue becomes particularly thorny when cybergriping sites add the word *sucks* or *stinks* or some other disparaging term to the domain name of the mark's owners. These sites, sometimes referred to collectively as "sucks" sites, are established solely for the purpose of criticizing the products or services sold by the owners of the marks.

The Question of Trademark Infringement A number of companies have sued the owners of such sites for trademark infringement in the hope that a court or an arbitrating panel will order the site owner to cease using the domain name. Generally, however, the courts have been reluctant to hold that the use of a business's domain name in a "sucks" site infringes on the trademark owner's rights. After all, one of the primary reasons trademarks are protected under U.S. law is to prevent customers from becoming confused over the origins of the goods for sale—and a cybergriping site would certainly not create such confusion. Furthermore, American courts give extensive protection to free speech rights, including the right to express opinions about companies and their products.[7]

Ethics and Bankruptcy

The first goal of bankruptcy law is to provide relief and protection to debtors who have "gotten in over their heads." Society has generally concluded that everyone should be given the chance to start over again. But how far should society go in letting debtors avoid obligations that they voluntarily incurred?

Consider the concept of bankruptcy from the point of view of the creditor. The creditor has extended a transfer of purchasing power from himself or herself to the debtor. That transfer of purchasing power represents a transfer of an asset for an asset. The debtor obtains the asset of money, goods, or services, and the creditor obtains the asset called a secured or unsecured legal obligation to pay. Once the debtor is in bankruptcy, voluntarily or involuntarily, the asset that the creditor owns most often has a diminished value. Indeed, in many circumstances, that asset has no value. Yet the easier it becomes for debtors to hide behind bankruptcy laws, the greater will be the incentive for debtors to use such laws to avoid payment of legally owed sums of money.

Clearly, bankruptcy law is a balancing act between providing a second chance and ensuring that creditors are given "a fair shake." Understandably, ethical issues arise in the process.

The Consequences of Bankruptcy

Under the 2005 Bankruptcy Reform Act, filing for personal bankruptcy (particularly under Chapter 7) has become more difficult. Although it is true that there is less of a stigma attached to bankruptcy today than there once was, bankruptcy is never easy for debtors. Many debtors feel a sense of shame and failure when they petition for bankruptcy. After all, bankruptcy is a matter of public record, and there is no way to avoid a certain amount of publicity. In one case, for example, a couple who filed for Chapter 7 bankruptcy wanted to use their attorney's mailing address in another town on their bankruptcy schedules in an effort to prevent an elderly parent and one of their employers from learning about the bankruptcy. The court, however, held that debtors are not

---

6. *Pro-Football, Inc. v. Harjo*, 284 F.Supp.2d 96 (D.D.C. 2003).

7. Many businesses have concluded that while they cannot control what people say about them, they can make it more difficult for it to be said. Today, businesses commonly register such insulting domain names before the cybergripers themselves can register them.

entitled to be protected from publicity surrounding the filing of their cases.[8]

Bankruptcy also has other consequences for debtors, including blemished credit ratings for up to ten years and higher interest charges for new debts, such as those incurred through the purchase of cars or homes. Some private employers may even refuse to hire a job applicant who has filed for bankruptcy. The courts provide little relief for applicants who are denied a job for this reason.[9]

Thus, bankruptcy can have adverse effects for both debtors and creditors. Because of the consequences of bankruptcy, debtors do not always get the fresh start promised by bankruptcy law. At the same time, creditors rarely are able to recover all of the money owed them once a debtor petitions for bankruptcy.

---

8. *In the Matter of Laws*, 223 Bankr. 714 (D.Neb. 1998).
9. See, for example, *Pastore v. Medford Savings Bank*, 186 Bankr. 553 (D.Mass. 1995).

DISCUSSION QUESTIONS

1. Suppose that you contract to purchase steel at a fixed price per ton. A lengthy steelworkers' strike causes the price of steel to triple from the price specified in the contract. If you demand that the supplier fulfill the contract, the supplier will go out of business. What are your ethical obligations in this situation? What are your legal rights?

2. How can a court objectively measure good faith and commercial reasonableness?

3. In your opinion, should gun manufacturers have a duty to warn gun users of the dangers of using guns? Would such a warning be effective in preventing gun-related accidents?

4. Do you think that the law favors debtors at the expense of creditors, or vice versa? Is there any way a better balance between creditors' and debtors' interests could be achieved?

CHAPTER 16

Sole Proprietorships, Franchises, and Partnerships

A basic question facing anyone who wishes to start a business is which of the several forms of business organization available will be most appropriate for the business endeavor. Traditionally, entrepreneurs have used three forms to structure their business enterprises—the sole proprietorship, the partnership, and the corporation. In this chapter, we examine sole proprietorships as well as franchises. Although the franchise is not really a business organizational form, it is widely used today by entrepreneurs seeking to make profits. Then we examine the second traditional business form, the partnership.

SECTION 1 | Sole Proprietorships

The simplest form of business is a **sole proprietorship.** In this form, the owner is the business; thus, anyone who does business without creating a separate business organization has a sole proprietorship. Over two-thirds of all American businesses are sole proprietorships. They are usually small enterprises—about 99 percent of the sole proprietorships in the United States have revenues of less than $1 million per year. Sole proprietors can own and manage any type of business from an informal, home-office undertaking to a large restaurant or construction firm.

ADVANTAGES OF THE SOLE PROPRIETORSHIP

A major advantage of the sole proprietorship is that the proprietor receives all of the profits (because she or he assumes all of the risk). In addition, it is often easier and less costly to start a sole proprietorship than to start any other kind of business, as few legal formalities are involved. This type of business organization also provides more flexibility than does a partnership or a corporation. The sole proprietor is free to make any decision he or she wishes concerning the business— whom to hire, when to take a vacation, what kind of business to pursue, and so on. A sole proprietor pays only personal income taxes on the business's profits, which are reported as personal income on the proprietor's personal income tax return. Sole proprietors are

also allowed to establish tax-exempt retirement accounts in the form of Keogh plans.[1]

DISADVANTAGES OF THE SOLE PROPRIETORSHIP

The major disadvantage of the sole proprietorship is that, as sole owner, the proprietor alone bears the burden of any losses or liabilities incurred by the business enterprise. In other words, the sole proprietor has unlimited liability, or legal responsibility, for all obligations that arise in doing business. This unlimited liability is a major factor to be considered in choosing a business form. The sole proprietorship also has the disadvantage of lacking continuity on the death of the proprietor. When the owner dies, so does the business—it is automatically dissolved. If the business is transferred to family members or other heirs, a new proprietorship is created.

Another disadvantage is that the proprietor's opportunity to raise capital is limited to personal funds and the funds of those who are willing to make loans to him or her. If the owner wishes to expand the business significantly, one way to raise more capital to finance the expansion is to join forces with another entrepreneur and establish a partnership or form a corporation.

---

1. A *Keogh plan* is a retirement program designed for self-employed persons. A person can contribute a certain percentage of income to the plan, and interest earnings will not be taxed until funds are withdrawn from the plan.

The Internet has expanded the ability of sole proprietorships to market their products worldwide without greatly increasing their costs. Does this mean that sole proprietorships should now, for some purposes, be considered the equivalent of corporations and other associational business forms? That was the question in the following case.

CASE 16.1 Hsin Ten Enterprise USA, Inc. v. Clark Enterprises

United States
District Court,
Southern District
of New York, 2000.
138 F.Supp.2d 449.

BACKGROUND AND FACTS *Clark Enterprises is a Kansas company with its only established offices in Salina, Kansas. Clark is a sole proprietorship owned and operated by Clifford Clark, who lives in Salina. Through representatives and trade shows, Clark sells "The Exercise Machine," an aerobic exercise device. The Exercise Machine can also be purchased through Clark's Web site. Clark markets the Exercise Machine in direct competition with "The Chi Machine," another aerobic exercise product. The Chi Machine is manufactured and sold by Hsin Ten Enterprise USA, Inc., a corporation with its principal place of business in Farmingdale, New York. Hsin Ten also makes and sells other products under the "Chi" trademark, which it owns. One of Clark's Web sites uses the name "Chi Exerciser 2000" to promote Clark's Exercise Machine, and the term Chi is frequently used on the Web site to refer to the product. Hsin Ten filed a suit in a federal district court in New York against Clark, asserting trademark infringement and other claims. Clark filed a motion to dismiss the trademark claim in part on the ground that the court did not have venue under 28 U.S.C. Section 1391(c), the applicable statute.[a] That section provides, "For purposes of venue . . . , a defendant that is a corporation shall be deemed to reside in any judicial district in which it is subject to personal jurisdiction." Hsin Ten argued that although Clark is an unincorporated sole proprietorship with its offices in Kansas, it should be deemed a "corporation" for venue purposes.*

IN THE LANGUAGE OF THE COURT
SCHEINDLIN, D.J. [District Judge]
* * * *

On its face, Section 1391(c) applies only to corporations. However, the [United States] Supreme Court has held that it also applies to unincorporated associations. Since then, other courts have held that Section 1391(c) is applicable to partnerships and foreign trusts.

* * * [C]ourts have been unwilling to expand the definition of "corporation" beyond [these] general categories * * * . In fact, at least two other federal courts have declined to extend Section 1391(c) to include sole proprietorships such as Clark.

Hsin Ten argues that Clark is unlike other sole proprietorships because it does business in forty-seven states. Plaintiff contends that Clark "resembles a national corporation in all respects except its choice of legal structure * * * . An entity such as Clark * * * , which obviously enjoys the benefits of doing business on a national scale, should not be granted preferential treatment in venue determinations simply because it chose not to incorporate." Plaintiff's argument is unconvincing.

First, broad geographic distribution does not convert a small sole proprietorship into a corporation. With the advent of the Internet and e-commerce, a sole proprietorship can distribute its products throughout the United States with only a relatively minor investment of resources. Moreover, although Clark does business in forty-seven states, it still is not the type of unincorporated business entity that has been included in the definition of corporation. For instance, * * * [t]he defendant partnership in [one case] was one of only four snowmobile manufacturers in the world [and] had annual sales of over $240 million * * * . By contrast, between July 8, 1999 and October 17, 2000, Clark sold 1,855 Exercise Machines. Although this is impressive for a sole proprietorship, it is hardly remarkable. Nor does it convert Clark to the functional equivalent of a corporation.

a. As explained in Chapter 2, *venue* concerns the most appropriate location for a trial.

CONTINUED

CASE 16.1 | Continued

Second, expanding the definition of "corporation" would greatly burden sole proprietors. Unlike corporations, partnerships and unincorporated associations—all of which are associations of two or more persons—a sole proprietorship is owned and controlled by a single person. *Venue is primarily a question of convenience for litigants and witnesses and venue provisions should be treated in practical terms.* In practical terms, expanding the definition of "corporation" to include sole proprietorships would be overly burdensome and inconvenient to sole proprietors, most of whom would be unable to afford the expense of litigating in distant states. [Emphasis added.]

DECISION AND REMEDY *The court agreed with Clark that it should not be deemed a "corporation" for venue purposes. The court denied Clark's motion to dismiss other parts of Hsin Ten's complaint, however, and ordered the case to proceed to trial.*

SECTION 2 | Franchises

A **franchise** is defined as any arrangement in which the owner of a trademark, a trade name, or a copyright licenses others to use the trademark, trade name, or copyright in the selling of goods or services. A **franchisee** (a purchaser of a franchise) is generally legally independent of the **franchisor** (the seller of the franchise). At the same time, the franchise is economically dependent on the franchisor's integrated business system. In other words, a franchisee can operate as an independent businessperson but still obtain the advantages of a regional or national organization. Today, it is estimated that franchising companies and their franchisees account for about 40 percent of all retail sales in this country. Well-known franchises include McDonald's, 7-Eleven, and Burger King.

TYPES OF FRANCHISES

Because the franchising industry is so extensive and so many different kinds of businesses sell franchises, it is difficult to summarize the many types of franchises that now exist. Generally, though, franchises fall into one of the following three classifications: distributorships, chain-style business operations, and manufacturing or processing-plant arrangements.

DISTRIBUTORSHIP A *distributorship* arises when a manufacturing concern (franchisor) licenses a dealer (franchisee) to sell its product. Often, a distributorship covers an exclusive territory. An example is an automobile dealership.

CHAIN-STYLE BUSINESS OPERATION In a *chain-style business operation*, a franchise operates under a franchisor's trade name and is identified as a member of a select group of dealers that engage in the franchisor's business. The franchisee is generally required to follow standardized or prescribed methods of operation. Often, the franchisor insists that the franchisee maintain certain standards of performance. In addition, sometimes the franchisee is obligated to deal exclusively with the franchisor to obtain materials and supplies. Examples of this type of franchise are McDonald's and most other fast-food chains.

MANUFACTURING OR PROCESSING-PLANT ARRANGEMENT With a *manufacturing* or *processing-plant arrangement*, the franchisor transmits to the franchisee the essential ingredients or formula to make a particular product. The franchisee then markets the product either at wholesale or at retail in accordance with the franchisor's standards. Examples of this type of franchise are Coca-Cola and other soft-drink bottling companies.

LAWS GOVERNING FRANCHISING

Because a franchise relationship is primarily a contractual relationship, it is governed by contract law. If the franchise exists primarily for the sale of products manufactured by the franchisor, the law governing sales contracts as expressed in Article 2 of the Uniform Commercial Code applies (see Chapter 11). Additionally, the federal government and most states have enacted laws governing certain aspects of franchising. Generally, these laws are designed to protect prospective franchisees from dishonest franchisors and to prohibit franchisors from terminating franchises without good cause.

FEDERAL PROTECTION FOR FRANCHISEES Automobile dealership franchisees are protected from automobile manufacturers' bad faith termination of their franchises by the Automobile Dealers' Franchise Act—also known as the Automobile Dealers' Day in Court Act—of 1965.[2] If a manufacturer-franchisor terminates a franchise because of a dealer-franchisee's failure to comply with unreasonable demands (for example, failure to attain an unrealistically high sales quota), the manufacturer may be liable for damages.

Another federal statute is the Petroleum Marketing Practices Act (PMPA) of 1979,[3] which prescribes the grounds and conditions under which a franchisor may terminate or decline to renew a gasoline station franchise. Federal antitrust laws (discussed in Chapters 26 and 27), which prohibit certain types of anticompetitive agreements, may also apply in certain circumstances.

Additionally, the Franchise Rule of the Federal Trade Commission (FTC) requires franchisors to disclose material facts that a prospective franchisee needs to make an informed decision concerning the purchase of a franchise. The rule was designed to enable potential franchisees to weigh the risks and benefits of an investment. The rule requires numerous written disclosures, plus a personal meeting between the franchisor and the prospective franchisee at least ten business days before the franchise agreement is signed or any payment is made in connection with the purchase of the franchise.[4]

STATE PROTECTION FOR FRANCHISEES State legislation tends to be similar to federal statutes and the FTC regulations. For example, to protect franchisees, a state law might require the disclosure of information that is material to making an informed decision regarding the purchase of a franchise. This could include such information as the actual costs of operation, recurring expenses, and profits to be earned, along with facts substantiating these figures. State deceptive trade practices acts may also prohibit certain types of actions on the part of franchisors.

For example, the Illinois Franchise Disclosure Act prohibits any untrue statement of a material fact in connection with the offer or sale of any franchise. If Miyamoto, a franchisor of bagel stores, underestimates the start-up cost and exaggerates the anticipated yearly profits from operating a bagel shop to a franchisee, he has violated state law.[5]

In response to the need for a uniform franchise law, the National Conference of Commissioners on Uniform State Laws drafted a model law that standardizes the various state franchise regulations. Because the uniform legislation represents a compromise of so many diverse interests, however, it has not been adopted as law by many states.

THE FRANCHISE CONTRACT

The franchise relationship is defined by a contract between the franchisor and the franchisee. The franchise contract specifies the terms and conditions of the franchise and spells out the rights and duties of the franchisor and the franchisee. If either party fails to perform its contractual duties, that party may be subject to a lawsuit for breach of contract. Furthermore, if a franchisee is induced to enter into a franchise contract by the franchisor's fraudulent misrepresentation, the franchisor may be liable for damages. Generally, the statutory law and the case law governing franchising tend to emphasize the importance of good faith and fair dealing in franchise relationships.

Because each type of franchise relationship has its own characteristics, it is difficult to describe the broad range of details a franchising contract may include. We look next at some of the major issues that typically are addressed in a franchise contract.

PAYMENT FOR THE FRANCHISE The franchisee ordinarily pays an initial fee or lump-sum price for the franchise license (the privilege of being granted a franchise). This fee is separate from the various products that the franchisee purchases from or through the franchisor. In some industries, the franchisor relies heavily on the initial sale of the franchise for realizing a profit. In other industries, the continued dealing between the parties brings profit to both. In most situations, the franchisor will receive a stated percentage of the annual sales or annual volume of business done by the franchisee. The franchise agreement may also require the franchisee to pay a percentage of the franchisor's advertising costs and certain administrative expenses.

BUSINESS PREMISES The franchise agreement may specify whether the premises for the business must be leased or purchased outright. In some cases, a building must be constructed to meet the terms of the agreement. Certainly, the agreement will specify whether the franchisor supplies equipment and furnishings for the premises or whether this is the responsibility of the franchisee.

---

2. 15 U.S.C. Sections 1221 *et seq.*
3. 15 U.S.C. Sections 2801 *et seq.*
4. 16 C.F.R. Section 436.1.
5. *Bixby's Food Systems, Inc. v. McKay,* 193 F.Supp.2d 1053 (N.D. Ill. 2002).

Exclusive Territorial Rights and the Internet

Many franchise lawsuits involve disputes over territorial rights—an aspect of franchising that often involves an implied covenant of good faith and fair dealing. For example, suppose that the franchise contract does not give the franchisee exclusive territorial rights or is silent on the issue. If the franchisor allows a competing franchise to be established nearby, the franchisee may suffer a significant loss in profits. In this situation, a court may hold that the franchisor's actions breached an implied covenant of good faith and fair dealing.

If, in contrast, the franchisee has been given exclusive territorial rights to serve a specific area, then the matter is more straightforward. If the franchisor allows a competing franchise to be established in the vicinity, the contract has been breached. Yet how do these rules apply in a cyber age, when a franchisor may offer its products for sale via its Web site?

ENTER THE INTERNET

With the growth of inexpensive and easy online marketing, it was inevitable that cyberturf conflicts would eventually arise between franchisors and franchisees. Suppose, for example,

that a franchise contract does grant to the franchisee exclusive rights to sell the franchised product within a certain territory. What happens if the franchisor then begins to sell the product from its Web site to anyone anywhere in the world, including in the franchisee's territory? Does this constitute a breach of the franchise contract?

This is a relatively new issue to come before the courts, and how the question is resolved has important implications for both franchisors and franchisees. From the franchisor's perspective, it would seem unfair to deprive it of the ability to market its goods, efficiently and inexpensively, from its Web site. From the franchisee's perspective, it would seem only fair (and consistent with the franchise contract's guarantee of exclusive territorial rights) to have the exclusive right to market the franchisor's product within its area.

DRUG EMPORIUM'S "ELECTRONIC ENCROACHMENT"

The issue of "electronic encroachment" came before a panel of arbitrators in an American Arbitration Association (AAA) proceeding. (As you learned in Chapter 3, the AAA is a

---

LOCATION OF THE FRANCHISE   Typically, the franchisor will determine the territory to be served. Some franchise contracts will give the franchisee exclusive rights, or "territorial rights," to a certain geographic area. Other franchise contracts, while they define the territory allotted to a particular franchise, either specifically state that the franchise is nonexclusive or are silent on the issue of territorial rights.

In today's online world, franchisees face a problem when franchisors attempt to sell their products themselves via their Web sites. For a discussion of this issue, see this chapter's *Contemporary Legal Debates* feature.

BUSINESS ORGANIZATION   The business organization of the franchisee is of great concern to the franchisor. Depending on the terms of the franchise agreement, the franchisor may specify particular requirements for the form and capital structure of the business. The franchise agreement may also provide that standards of operation—relating to such aspects of the business as sales quotas, quality, and record

keeping—be met by the franchisee. Furthermore, a franchisor may wish to retain stringent control over the training of personnel involved in the operation and over administrative aspects of the business.

QUALITY CONTROL   Although the day-to-day operation of the franchise business is normally left up to the franchisee, the franchise agreement may provide for the amount of supervision and control agreed on by the parties. When the franchise is a service operation, such as a motel, the contract often provides that the franchisor will establish certain standards for the facility to protect the franchise's name and reputation. Typically, the contract will state that the franchisor is permitted to make periodic inspections to ensure that the standards are being maintained.

As a general rule, the validity of a provision permitting the franchisor to establish and enforce certain quality standards is unquestioned. Because the franchisor has a legitimate interest in maintaining the quality of the product or service to protect its name and reputation, it can exercise greater control in this

leading provider of arbitration services.) The proceeding involved franchise contracts between Drug Emporium, Inc., and several of its franchisees. The contracts provided that each franchisee had the exclusive right to conduct business in a specific geographic area. The franchisees claimed that Drug Emporium had breached its contractual obligation to honor their territories by using its Web site to sell directly to customers within the franchisees' territories.

Ultimately, in what is believed to be the first ruling by a court or arbitrating panel on the issue of electronic encroachment, the arbitrating panel decided in favor of the franchisees. The panel ordered Drug Emporium to cease marketing its goods from its Web site to potential customers who were physically located within the franchisees' territories.[a]

WHERE DO YOU STAND?

Although the AAA panel held in favor of the franchisees, there is no way to know how other arbitrating panels or courts will

decide this issue.[b] On the one hand, a valid contract that grants exclusive territorial rights to a franchisee deserves to be enforced, just as any contract does if the parties have voluntarily agreed to its terms. On the other hand, the Internet offers franchisors an inexpensive marketing vehicle, which, according to some, they should be able to utilize. If franchisors are prevented from any direct competition with their franchisees via the Web, franchisors may stop granting exclusive territorial rights to any of their franchisees—which, of course, could also be detrimental to franchisees. Where do you stand on this issue? Should a franchisor be able to market goods on the Internet, even though customers in its franchisees' exclusive territories may purchase the goods directly from the franchisor's Web site? Why or why not?

---

a. *Emporium Drug Mart, Inc. of Shreveport v. Drug Emporium, Inc.*, No. 71-114-0012600 (American Arbitration Association, September 2, 2000).

b. For an article discussing two subsequent arbitrations involving similar facts and issues, but in which the arbitrator concluded that the franchisor's sales activities over the Internet did not violate the franchise contract, see Rupert M. Barkoff, "Encroachment Issues Persist," *The National Law Journal*, April 19, 2004.

---

area than would otherwise be tolerated. Increasingly, however, franchisors are finding that if they exercise too much control over the operations of their franchisees, they may incur vicarious (indirect) liability under agency theory for the acts of their franchisees'

employees. The actual exercise of control, or at least the right to control, is the key consideration. If the franchisee controls the day-to-day operations of the business to a significant degree, the franchisor may be able to avoid liability, as the following case illustrates.

CASE 16.2 | Kerl v. Dennis Rasmussen, Inc.

Wisconsin Supreme Court, 2004.
273 Wis.2d 106,
682 N.W.2d 328.

DIANE S. SYKES, J. [Justice]
* * * *

* * * [On June 11, 1999] Harvey Pierce ambushed and shot Robin Kerl and her fiancé David Jones in the parking lot of a Madison [Wisconsin] Wal-Mart where Kerl and Jones worked. Kerl was seriously injured in the shooting, and Jones was killed. Pierce, who was Kerl's former boyfriend, then shot and killed himself. At the time of the shooting, Pierce was a work-release inmate at the Dane County jail who was employed at a nearby Arby's [Inc.] restaurant operated by Dennis Rasmussen, Inc. ("DRI"). Pierce had left work without permission at the time of the attempted murder and murder/suicide.

Kerl and Jones' estate sued DRI and Arby's, Inc. [in a Wisconsin state court.] * * * [T]he plaintiffs alleged that Arby's is vicariously liable, as DRI's franchisor, for DRI's negligent supervision of Pierce. The * * * court granted summary judgment in favor of Arby's,

CONTINUED

concluding that there was no basis for vicarious liability. The [state intermediate] court of appeals affirmed. [The plaintiffs appealed to the Wisconsin Supreme Court.]

Vicarious liability under the doctrine of *respondeat superior* depends upon the existence of a master/servant agency relationship. Vicarious liability under *respondeat superior* is a form of liability without fault—the imposition of liability on an innocent party for the tortious conduct of another based upon the existence of a particularized agency relationship. As such, it is an exception to our fault-based liability system, and is imposed only where the principal has control or the right to control the physical conduct of the agent such that a master/servant relationship can be said to exist.

A franchise is a business format typically characterized by the franchisee's operation of an independent business pursuant to a license to use the franchisor's trademark or trade name. A franchise is ordinarily operated in accordance with a detailed franchise or license agreement designed to protect the integrity of the trademark by setting uniform quality, marketing, and operational standards applicable to the franchise.

The rationale for vicarious liability becomes somewhat attenuated [weak] when applied to the franchise relationship, and vicarious liability premised upon the existence of a master/servant relationship is conceptually difficult to adapt to the franchising context. If the operational standards included in the typical franchise agreement for the protection of the franchisor's trademark were broadly construed as capable of meeting the "control or right to control" test that is generally used to determine *respondeat superior* liability, then franchisors would almost always be exposed to vicarious liability for the torts of their franchisees. We see no justification for such a broad rule of franchisor vicarious liability. If vicarious liability is to be imposed against franchisors, a more precisely focused test is required. [Emphasis added.]

* * * *

Applying these principles here, we conclude that Arby's did not have control or the right to control the day-to-day operation of the specific aspect of DRI's business that is alleged to have caused the plaintiffs' harm, that is, DRI's supervision of its employees. We note first that the license agreement between Arby's and DRI contains a provision that disclaims any agency relationship. * * *

The license agreement contains a plethora [a large number] of general controls on the operation of DRI's restaurant * * *.

These provisions in the license agreement are consistent with the quality and operational standards commonly contained in franchise agreements to achieve product and marketing uniformity and to protect the franchisor's trademark. They are insufficient to establish a master/servant relationship. More particularly, they do not establish that Arby's controlled or had the right to control DRI's hiring and supervision of employees, which is the aspect of DRI's business that is alleged to have caused the plaintiffs' harm.

The agreement's provisions regarding the specific issue of personnel are broad and general. * * *

By the terms of this agreement, DRI has sole control over the hiring and supervision of its employees. Arby's could not step in and take over the management of DRI's employees. * * * Accordingly, we agree with the court of appeals and the [trial] court that there is no genuine issue of material fact as to whether DRI is Arby's servant for purposes of the plaintiffs' *respondeat superior* claim against Arby's: clearly it is not. Arby's cannot be held vicariously liable for DRI's alleged negligent supervision of Pierce.

* * * *

We conclude that the quality, marketing, and operational standards and inspection and termination rights commonly included in franchise agreements do not establish the close supervisory control or right of control over a franchisee necessary to support imposing vicarious liability against the franchisor for all purposes or as a general matter. We hold that *a franchisor may be subject to vicarious liability for the tortious conduct of its franchisee only if the franchisor had control or a right of control over the daily operation of the specific aspect of the franchisee's business that is alleged to have caused the harm.* Because Arby's did not have control or a right of control over DRI's supervision of its employees, there was no master/servant relationship between

CASE 16.2 | Continued Arby's and DRI for purposes of the plaintiffs' *respondeat superior* claim against Arby's. Arby's cannot be held vicariously liable for DRI's negligent supervision of Pierce. [Emphasis added.] The decision of the court of appeals is affirmed.

QUESTIONS

1. Should a franchisor be allowed to control the operation of its franchisee without liability for the franchisee's conduct? Explain your answer.
2. What would constitute the "right to control" under a franchise contract?

PRICING ARRANGEMENTS Franchises provide the franchisor with an outlet for the firm's goods and services. Depending on the nature of the business, the franchisor may require the franchisee to purchase certain supplies from the franchisor at an established price.[6] A franchisor cannot, however, set the prices at which the franchisee will resell the goods because such price setting may be a violation of state or federal antitrust laws, or both. A franchisor can suggest retail prices but cannot mandate them.

FRANCHISE TERMINATION The duration of the franchise is a matter to be determined between the parties. Generally, a franchise relationship starts with a short trial period, such as a year, so that the franchisee and the franchisor can determine whether they want to stay in business with one another. Usually, the franchise agreement specifies that termination must be "for cause," such as the death or disability of the franchisee, insolvency of the franchisee, breach of the franchise agreement, or failure to meet specified sales quotas. Most franchise contracts provide that notice of termination must be given. If no set time for termination is specified, then a reasonable time, with notice, is implied. A franchisee must be given reasonable time to wind up the business—that is, to do the accounting and return the copyright or trademark or any other property of the franchisor.

—*Wrongful Termination.* Because a franchisor's termination of a franchise often has adverse consequences for the franchisee, much franchise litigation

involves claims of wrongful termination. Generally, the termination provisions of contracts are more favorable to the franchisor than the franchisee. This means that the franchisee, who normally invests a substantial amount of time and financial resources in the franchise operation to make it successful, may receive little or nothing for the business on termination. The franchisor owns the trademark and hence the business.

It is in this area that statutory and case law become important. The federal and state laws discussed earlier attempt, among other things, to protect franchisees from the arbitrary or unfair termination of their franchises by the franchisors. Generally, both statutory and case law emphasize the importance of good faith and fair dealing in terminating a franchise relationship.

—*The Importance of Good Faith and Fair Dealing.* In determining whether a franchisor has acted in good faith when terminating a franchise agreement, the courts generally try to balance the rights of both parties. If a court perceives that a franchisor has arbitrarily or unfairly terminated a franchise, the franchisee will be provided with a remedy for wrongful termination. If a franchisor's decision to terminate a franchise was made in the normal course of the franchisor's business operations, however, and reasonable notice of termination was given to the franchisee, normally a court will not consider the termination wrongful.

SECTION 3 | Partnerships

A **partnership** arises from an agreement, express or implied, between two or more persons to carry on a business for a profit. Partners are co-owners of a business and have joint control over its operation and the right to share in its profits.

---

6. Although a franchisor can require franchisees to purchase supplies from it, requiring a franchisee to purchase exclusively from the franchisor may violate federal antitrust laws (see Chapters 26 and 27). For two landmark cases in these areas, see *United States v. Arnold, Schwinn & Co.*, 388 U.S. 365, 87 S.Ct. 1956, 18 L.Ed.2d 1249 (1967); and *Fortner Enterprises, Inc. v. U.S. Steel Corp.*, 394 U.S. 495, 89 S.Ct. 1252, 22 L.Ed.2d 495 (1969).

AGENCY CONCEPTS AND PARTNERSHIP LAW

When two or more persons agree to do business as partners, they enter into a special relationship with one another. To an extent, their relationship is similar to an agency relationship because each partner is deemed to be the agent of the other partners and of the partnership. The agency concepts that you will read about in Chapter 19 thus apply—specifically, the imputation of knowledge of, and responsibility for, acts carried out within the scope of the partnership relationship. In their relationship to one another, partners are also bound by the fiduciary ties that bind an agent and principal under agency law.

Partnership law is distinct from agency law in one significant way, however. A partnership is based on a voluntary contract between two or more competent persons who agree to place some or all of their funds or other assets, labor, and skills in a business with the understanding that profits and losses will be shared. In a nonpartnership agency relationship, the agent usually does not have an ownership interest in the business, nor is he or she obligated to bear a portion of ordinary business losses.

THE UNIFORM PARTNERSHIP ACT

The Uniform Partnership Act (UPA) governs the operation of partnerships *in the absence of express agreement* and has done much to reduce controversies in the law relating to partnerships. Except for Louisiana, all of the states, as well as the District of Columbia, have adopted the UPA. The majority of states have enacted the most recent version of the UPA, which was adopted in 1994 and amended in 1997 to provide limited liability for partners in a limited liability partnership.[7] Excerpts from the latest version of the UPA, including the 1997 amendments, are presented in Appendix E.

DEFINITION OF PARTNERSHIP

Parties commonly find themselves in conflict over whether their business enterprise is a legal partnership,

especially in the absence of a formal, written partnership agreement. The UPA defines the term *partnership* as "an association of two or more persons to carry on as co-owners a business for profit" [UPA 101(6)]. The *intent* to associate is a key element of a partnership, and one cannot join a partnership unless all other partners consent [UPA 401(i)].

PARTNERSHIP STATUS In resolving disputes over whether partnership status exists, courts usually look for the following three essential elements of partnership implicit in the UPA's definition:

1. A sharing of profits or losses.
2. A joint ownership of the business.
3. An equal right in the management of the business.

If the evidence in a particular case is insufficient to establish all three factors, the UPA provides a set of guidelines to be used. For example, the sharing of profits and losses from a business creates a presumption that a partnership exists. No presumption is made, however, if the profits were received as payment of any of the following [UPA 202(c)(3)]:

1. A debt by installments or interest on a loan.
2. Wages of an employee or for the services of an independent contractor.
3. Rent to a landlord.
4. An annuity to a surviving spouse or representative of a deceased partner.
5. A sale of the goodwill of a business or property.

To illustrate: Suppose that a debtor owes a creditor $5,000 on an unsecured debt. To repay the debt, the debtor agrees to pay (and the creditor, to accept) 10 percent of the debtor's monthly business profits until the loan with interest has been paid. Although the creditor is sharing profits from the business, the debtor and creditor are not presumed to be partners.

When one of the parties disputes whether a partnership was created, the courts frequently look to other factors, such as the conduct of the parties, to determine partnership status. In the following case, the parties met and discussed buying and developing a commercial site. Using some of one party's funds, another party bought the site solely in the name of his business. The buyer refused to share ownership of the property, claiming that he had entered only into an unenforceable agreement to form a partnership and was not a partner.

---

7. At the time this book went to press, over half of the states had adopted the UPA with the 1997 amendments, including the District of Columbia, Puerto Rico, and the U.S. Virgin Islands. We therefore base our discussion of the UPA on the 1997 version of the act and refer to older versions of the UPA in footnotes if necessary.

CASE 16.3

Cap Care Group, Inc. v. McDonald

North Carolina
Court of Appeals, 2002.
149 N.C.App. 817,
561 S.E.2d 578.
http://www.aoc.state.nc.
us/www/public/html/
opinions.htm[a]

BACKGROUND AND FACTS *Cap Care Group, Inc., PWPP Partners, and C & M Investments of High Point, Inc., buy and develop commercial real estate. Ronnel Parker is president of Cap Care and PWPP. Wayne McDonald owns and controls C & M. In November 1996, Parker and Daniel Greene, another Cap Care officer, met McDonald to discuss buying and renovating a commercial site in High Point, North Carolina. Cap Care later claimed that at the meeting the parties (Parker on behalf of Cap Care and PWPP, and McDonald on behalf of C & M) agreed that they would be partners in the purchase and development of the property, and that McDonald would make an offer to the seller on the partnership's behalf. In February 1997, McDonald signed a contract to buy the site, using PWPP funds as half of the earnest money.[b] McDonald and Greene (of Cap Care) then discussed jointly owning the property as partners. In March, McDonald bought the property in the name of C & M only. Cap Care demanded that McDonald contribute the property to the partnership, but he refused. Cap Care filed a suit in a North Carolina state court against McDonald and C & M, alleging in part breach of contract. McDonald argued that he and Parker had merely entered into an unenforceable agreement to form a partnership. The court awarded Cap Care $477,511, plus interest and fees. The defendants appealed to a state intermediate appellate court.*

IN THE LANGUAGE OF THE COURT

THOMAS, Judge.

* * * *

* * * [D]efendants argue the trial court should have granted their motions for directed verdict and judgment notwithstanding the verdict on the issue of the breach of an agreement to enter into a partnership. We disagree.

* * * *

A partnership is defined as an association of two or more persons to carry on as co-owners a business for profit. *A partnership can be formed orally or implied by the parties' conduct.* [Emphasis added.]

McDonald's wife, Wendy McDonald, who is also an officer of C & M, testified that she knew McDonald had a deal with plaintiffs and that Parker had agreed to fund half of the earnest money to get the property. McDonald himself testified that his account would have been overdrawn had he not deposited Parker's checks and that the $20,000 earnest money was part of the purchase price of the property. There was substantial evidence that the parties had reached an agreement to jointly purchase and develop the property. Further, defendants never informed plaintiffs that they were not acting as partners until after the purchase of the property.

An enforceable agreement requires an offer, acceptance, and consideration.

Here, the offer to form a partnership is not contested. Defendants argue they never accepted the offer. However, defendants did accept the consideration of $10,000 from plaintiffs to pay for the property. They also precisely carried out the joint plan of the parties until *after* the purchase of the property. There was never any indication during that process that the parties were not operating in unison, as partners. The general law of partnership applies to a partnership formed for the purpose of dealing in land. *An acceptance by conduct is a valid acceptance.* [Emphasis added.]

Defendants contend there was no meeting of the minds because how the property would be managed was not clear. However, it is well established * * * that a failure to agree on some issues does not invalidate the underlying agreement.

We therefore hold that there was a valid agreement among the parties to form a partnership to purchase the property and that defendants breached that agreement.

---

a. In the "Court of Appeals Opinions" section, click on "2002." On the next page, scroll to the "16 April 2002" section and click on the name of the case to access the opinion.
b. *Earnest money* is a deposit of funds that usually accompanies an offer to buy real estate to show that the offer is earnest, or serious.

CONTINUED ▶

  DECISION AND REMEDY *The state intermediate appellate court affirmed the lower court's judgment. The defendants had entered into, and breached, an oral partnership contract to buy real estate, as evidenced by the parties' discussions, the defendants' acceptance of a partner's funds, and the defendants' acting according to the parties' plan until after the purchase of the property.*

JOINT PROPERTY OWNERSHIP AND PARTNERSHIP STATUS Joint ownership of property, obviously, does not in and of itself create a partnership. Therefore, the fact that, say, MacPherson and Bunker own real property as joint tenants or as tenants in common (a form of joint ownership) does not by itself establish a partnership. In fact, the sharing of gross returns and even profits from such ownership "does not by itself establish a partnership" [UPA 202(c)(1) and (2)]. Thus, if MacPherson and Bunker jointly own a piece of rural property and lease the land to a farmer for a share of the profits from the farming operation in lieu of set rental payments, the sharing of the profits ordinarily will not make MacPherson, Bunker, and the farmer partners.

Note, though, that although the sharing of profits from ownership of property does not prove the existence of a partnership, sharing *both profits and losses* usually does. For example, two sisters, Zoe and Cienna, buy a restaurant together, open a joint bank account from which they pay for supplies and expenses, and share the proceeds that the restaurant generates. Zoe manages the restaurant and Cienna handles the bookkeeping. After eight years, Cienna stops keeping the books and does no other work for the restaurant. Zoe, who is now operating the restaurant by herself, no longer wants to share the profits with Cienna. She offers to buy her sister out, but the two cannot agree on a fair price. When Cienna files a lawsuit, a question arises as to whether the two sisters were partners in the restaurant. In this situation, a court would find that a partnership existed because the sisters shared management responsibilities, had joint accounts, and shared the profits and the losses of the restaurant equally.

ENTITY VERSUS AGGREGATE A partnership is sometimes called a *company* or a *firm*, terms that suggest that the partnership is an entity separate and apart from its aggregate members. The law of partnership recognizes the independent entity for most purposes but may treat the partnership as a composite of its individual partners for some purposes.

—*Partnership as an Entity.* At common law, a partnership was never treated as a separate legal entity. Thus, a common law suit could never be brought by or against the firm in its own name; each individual partner had to sue or be sued. Today, most states provide specifically that a partnership can be treated as an entity for certain purposes. These usually include the capacity to sue or be sued, to collect judgments, and to have all accounting procedures carried out in the name of the partnership. In addition, the UPA clearly states, "A partnership is an entity" and "A partnership may sue and be sued in the name of the partnership" [UPA 201 and 307(a)]. As an entity, a partnership may hold the title to real or personal property in its name rather than in the names of the individual partners. Finally, federal procedural laws frequently permit a partnership to be treated as an entity in such matters as lawsuits in federal courts, bankruptcy proceedings, and the filing of federal information tax returns.

—*Partnership as an Aggregate.* In one circumstance, the partnership is not regarded as a separate legal entity, but is treated as an aggregate of the individual partners. For federal income tax purposes, a partnership is not a taxpaying entity. The income and losses it incurs are "passed through" the partnership framework and attributed to the partners on their individual tax returns. The partnership itself has no tax liability and is responsible only for filing an **information return** with the Internal Revenue Service. In other words, the firm itself pays no taxes. A partner's profit from the partnership (whether distributed or not) is taxed as individual income to the individual partner.

PARTNERSHIP FORMATION

As a general rule, agreements to form a partnership can be *oral, written,* or *implied by conduct.* Some partnership agreements, however, must be in writing to be legally enforceable within the Statute of Frauds (see Chapter 9 for details). For example, a partnership agreement that authorizes the partners to deal in transfers of real property must be evidenced by a sufficient writing (or record).

THE PARTNERSHIP AGREEMENT A partnership agreement, called **articles of partnership,** can include virtually any terms that the parties wish, unless they are illegal or contrary to public policy or statute [UPA 103]. The terms commonly included in a partnership agreement are listed in Exhibit 16–1. (Notice that this list includes an arbitration clause, which is often included in a partnership agreement.)

DURATION OF THE PARTNERSHIP The partnership agreement can specify the duration of the partnership by stating that it will continue until a designated date or until the completion of a particular project. This is called a *partnership for a term*. If this type of partnership is dissolved (broken up) without the consent of all the partners prior to the expiration of the partnership term, the dissolution constitutes a breach of the agreement. The responsible partner can be held liable for any resulting losses.

If no fixed duration is specified, the partnership is a *partnership at will*. Any partner can dissolve this type of partnership at any time without violating the agreement and without incurring liability for losses to other partners that result from the termination.

A CORPORATION AS PARTNER In a general partnership, the partners are personally liable for the debts incurred by the partnership. If one of the general partners is a corporation, however, what does personal liability mean? Basically, the capacity of corporations to contract is a question of corporate law. At one time, many states had restrictions on corporations becoming partners, although such restrictions have become less common over the years.

The Revised Model Business Corporation Act (see Appendix G) allows corporations generally to make contracts and incur liabilities. The UPA specifically permits a corporation to be a partner. By definition, "a partnership is an association of two or more persons," and the UPA defines *person* as including corporations [UPA 101(10)].

PARTNERSHIP BY ESTOPPEL Persons who are not partners may nevertheless hold themselves out as partners and make representations that third parties rely on in dealing with them. In such a situation, a court

EXHIBIT 16-1 Terms Commonly Included in a Partnership Agreement

Basic Structure	1. Name of the partnership. 2. Names of the partners. 3. Location of the business and the state law under which the partnership is organized. 4. Purpose of the partnership. 5. Duration of the partnership.
Capital Contributions	1. Amount of capital that each partner is contributing. 2. The agreed-on value of any real or personal property that is contributed instead of cash. 3. How losses and gains on contributed capital will be allocated, and whether contributions will earn interest.
Sharing of Profits and Losses	1. Percentage of the profits and losses of the business that each partner will receive. 2. When distributions of profit will be made and how net profit will be calculated.
Management and Control	1. How management responsibilities will be divided among the partners. 2. Name of the managing partner or partners, and whether other partners have voting rights.
Accounting and Partnership Records	1. Name of the bank in which the partnership will maintain its business and checking accounts. 2. Statement that an accounting of partnership records will be maintained and that any partner or her or his agent can review these records at any time. 3. The dates of the partnership's fiscal year and when the annual audit of the books will take place.
Dissolution	1. Events that will dissolve the partnership, such as the retirement, death, or incapacity of any partner. 2. How partnership property will be valued and apportioned on dissolution. 3. Whether an arbitrator will determine the value of partnership property on dissolution and whether that determination will be binding.
Miscellaneous	Whether arbitration is required for any dispute relating to the partnership agreement.

may conclude that a **partnership by estoppel** exists and impose liability—but not partnership *rights*—on the alleged partner or partners.

—*Two Aspects of Liability.*   There are two aspects of liability under a theory of partnership by estoppel. The person representing that she or he is a partner in an actual or alleged partnership is liable to any third person who extends credit in good faith reliance on such representations. Similarly, a person who expressly or impliedly consents to the misrepresentation of an alleged partnership relationship is also liable to third parties who extend credit in good faith reliance. When this occurs, the nonpartner is regarded as an agent whose acts are binding on the partnership [UPA 308].

For example, Moreno owns a small shop. Knowing that Midland Bank will not make a loan on his credit alone, Moreno represents that Loman, a financially secure businessperson, is a partner in Moreno's business. Loman knows of Moreno's misrepresentation but fails to correct it. Midland Bank, relying on the strength of Loman's reputation and credit, extends a loan to Moreno. Moreno will be liable to the bank for the loan repayment. In many states, Loman would also be held liable to the bank. Loman has impliedly consented to the misrepresentation and will normally be estopped from denying that she is Moreno's partner. She will be regarded as if she were in fact a partner in Moreno's business insofar as this loan is concerned.

—*When a Nonpartner Is Represented as a Member of an Existing Partnership.*   When a real partnership exists and a partner represents that a nonpartner is a member of the firm, the nonpartner is regarded as an agent whose acts are binding on the partner (but normally *not* on the partnership). For example, Middle Earth Movers has three partners—Jansen, Mahar, and Harran. Mahar represents to the business community that Tully is also a partner. If Tully negotiates a contract in the name of Middle Earth Movers, the contract will be binding on Mahar but normally not on Jansen and Harran (unless, of course, they knew about, and consented to, Mahar's representation about Tully). Again, partnership by estoppel requires that a third person reasonably and detrimentally rely on the representation that a person was part of the partnership.

PARTNERSHIP OPERATION

The rights and duties of partners are governed largely by the specific terms of their partnership agreement. In the absence of provisions to the contrary in the partnership agreement, the law imposes the rights and duties discussed in the following subsections. The character and nature of the partnership business generally influence the application of these rights and duties.

RIGHTS OF PARTNERS   The rights of partners in a partnership relate to the following areas: management, interest in the partnership, compensation, inspection of books, accounting, and property.

—*Management.*   In a general partnership, "All partners have equal rights in the management and conduct of partnership business" [UPA 401(f)]. Unless the partners agree otherwise, each partner has one vote in management matters *regardless of the proportional size of his or her interest in the firm*. Often, in a large partnership partners will agree to delegate daily management responsibilities to a management committee made up of one or more of the partners.

The majority rule controls decisions on ordinary matters connected with partnership business, unless otherwise specified in the agreement. Decisions that significantly affect the nature of the partnership or that are not apparently for carrying on the ordinary course of the partnership business, or business of the kind, however, require the *unanimous* consent of the partners [UPA 301(2), 401(i), 401(j)]. Unanimous consent is likely to be required for a decision to undertake any of the following actions:[8]

1. To alter the essential nature of the firm's business as expressed in the partnership agreement or to alter the capital structure of the partnership.
2. To admit new partners or to engage in a completely new business.
3. To assign partnership property to a trust for the benefit of creditors.
4. To dispose of the partnership's goodwill.
5. To confess judgment against the partnership or submit partnership claims to arbitration. (A **confession of judgment** is an act by a debtor permitting a judgment to be entered against him or her by a creditor, for an agreed sum, without the institution of legal proceedings.)

---

8. The previous version of the UPA specifically listed most of these actions as requiring unanimous consent. The current version of the UPA omits the list entirely to allow the courts more flexibility. The Official Comments explain that most of these acts, except for submitting a claim to arbitration, will likely still remain outside the apparent authority of an individual partner.

6. To undertake any act that would make further conduct of partnership business impossible.

7. To amend the terms of the partnership agreement.

—*Interest in the Partnership.* Each partner is entitled to the proportion of business profits and losses that is designated in the partnership agreement. If the agreement does not apportion profits (indicate how the profits will be shared), the UPA provides that profits will be shared equally. If the agreement does not apportion losses, losses will be shared in the same ratio as profits [UPA 401(b)].

For example, assume that Rico and Brett form a partnership. The partnership agreement provides for capital contributions of $60,000 from Rico and $40,000 from Brett, but it is silent as to how they will share profits or losses. In this situation, they will share both profits and losses equally. If their partnership agreement had provided that they would share profits in the same ratio as capital contributions, however, 60 percent of the profits would go to Rico, and 40 percent of the profits would go to Brett. If the agreement was silent as to losses, losses would be shared in the same ratio as profits (60 percent/40 percent).

—*Compensation.* Devoting time, skill, and energy to partnership business is a partner's duty and generally is not a compensable service. Partners can, of course, agree otherwise. For example, the managing partner of a law firm often receives a salary in addition to her or his share of profits for performing special administrative duties in office and personnel management.

UPA 401(h) provides that a partner is entitled to compensation for services in winding up partnership affairs (and reimbursement for expenses incurred in the process) above and apart from his or her share in the partnership profits.

—*Inspection of Books.* Partnership books and records must be kept accessible to all partners. Each partner has the right to receive (and the corresponding duty to produce) full and complete information concerning the conduct of all aspects of partnership business [UPA 403]. Each firm retains books for recording and securing such information. Partners contribute the information, and a bookkeeper typically has the duty to preserve it. The books must be kept at the firm's principal business office (unless the partners agree otherwise). Every partner, whether active or inactive, is entitled to inspect all books and records on demand and can make copies of the mate-

rials. The personal representative of a deceased partner's estate has the same right of access to partnership books and records that the decedent would have had [UPA 403].

—*Actions for Accounting against the Partnership and among the Partners.* An accounting of partnership assets or profits is required to determine the value of each partner's share in the partnership. An accounting can be performed voluntarily, or it can be compelled by court order. Under UPA 405(b), a partner has the right to bring an action for an accounting during the term of the partnership, as well as on the firm's dissolution and winding up.[9] A partner also has the right to bring an action against the partnership or another partner, with or without a formal accounting, in the following situations:

1. To enforce the partner's rights under the partnership agreement.

2. To enforce the partner's rights under the UPA.

3. To enforce the partner's rights and interests arising independently of the partnership relationship.

—*Property Rights.* A partner has two basic property rights. First, a partner has an interest in the partnership (which includes a share of the profits and losses and the right to participate in management). Second, a partner has a right in specific partnership property. Note, however, that a partner is not the co-owner of partnership property and cannot transfer his or her interest in partnership property, either voluntarily or involuntarily [UPA 501].

—*Partner's Interest in the Firm.* A partner's interest in the firm is a personal asset consisting of a proportionate share of the profits earned [UPA 502] and a return of capital on the partnership's termination. A partner's interest is subject to assignment or to a judgment creditor's lien (a lien obtained through the judicial process). Judgment creditors can attach a partner's interest by petitioning the court that entered the judgment to grant the creditors a **charging order.** This order entitles the judgment creditors to the profits of the partner and to any assets available to the partner on dissolution [UPA 504]. Neither an assignment nor

---

9. Under the previous version of the UPA, a partner could bring an action for an accounting only if the partnership agreement provided for it, the partner was wrongfully excluded from the business or its property or books, another partner was in breach of his or her fiduciary duty, or other circumstances rendered it "just and reasonable."

a court's charging order will cause the dissolution of the firm [UPA 503].

—Partnership Property. Property acquired *by* a partnership is the property of the partnership and not of the partners individually [UPA 203]. Property acquired *in the name of* the partnership or a partner is partnership property if the person's capacity as a partner or the existence of the partnership is indicated in the instrument transferring title. If the transferring instrument refers to neither of these, the property is still presumed to be partnership property when it is acquired with partnership funds [UPA 204].[10]

In all other circumstances, the property is presumed to be the property of an individual partner, even if it is used in the partnership business. Ultimately, in those situations, it is the intention of the partners that determines whether property belongs to the partnership or to a partner in his or her individual capacity [UPA 204(d)].

A partner may use or possess partnership property only on behalf of the partnership [UPA 401(g)]. A partner is not a co-owner of partnership property and has no interest in the property that can be transferred, either voluntarily or involuntarily [UPA 501]. In other words, partnership property is owned by the partnership as an entity and not by the individual partners.[11]

DUTIES AND LIABILITIES OF PARTNERS The duties and liabilities of partners that we examine here are basically derived from agency law. Each partner is an agent of every other partner and acts as both a principal and an agent in any business transaction within the scope of the partnership agreement. Each partner is also a general agent of the partnership in carrying out the usual business of the firm "or business of the kind carried on by the partnership" [UPA 301(1)]. Thus, every act of a partner concerning partnership business and "business of the kind" and every contract signed in the partnership's name bind the firm. The UPA affirms general principles of agency

law that pertain to the authority of a partner to bind a partnership in contract or tort.

—Fiduciary Duties. The only fiduciary duties a partner owes to the partnership and the other partners are the duty of loyalty and the duty of care, according to UPA 404(a). A partner's duty of loyalty is limited to accounting to the partnership for "any property, profit, or benefit" derived by the partner in the conduct of the partnership business or from a use of its property, and to refrain from dealing with the firm as an adverse party or competing with it in the conduct of partnership business [UPA 404(b)]. A partner's duty of care is limited to refraining from "grossly negligent or reckless conduct, intentional misconduct, or a knowing violation of law" [UPA 404(c)].[12]

These duties may not be waived or eliminated in the partnership agreement, and in fulfilling them each partner must act consistently with the obligation of good faith and fair dealing, which applies to all contracts, including partnership agreements [UPA 103(b) and 404(d)].

A partner may pursue his or her own interests, however, without automatically violating these duties [UPA 404(e)]. For example, a partner who owns a shopping mall may vote against a partnership proposal to open a competing mall.

—Authority of Partners. The UPA affirms general principles of agency law that pertain to the authority of a partner to bind a partnership in contract. Under the same principles, a partner may also subject a partnership to liability in tort. When a partner is apparently carrying on partnership business or business of the kind with third parties in the usual way, both the partner and the firm share liability. The partnership will not be liable, however, if the third parties *know* that the partner has no such authority. For example, Patricia, a partner in the partnership of Heise, Green, and Stevens, applies for a loan on behalf of the partnership without authorization from the other partners. The bank manager knows that Patricia has no authority to do so. If the bank manager grants the loan, Patricia will be personally bound, but the firm will not be liable.

Under UPA 105 and 303, a partnership may file in a designated state office a "statement of partnership

---

10. *Partnership property* was defined in the previous version of the UPA as "all property originally brought into the partnership's stock or subsequently acquired, by purchase or otherwise, on account of the partnership" [UPA 8(1)]. This definition, unlike the one in the current UPA, did not provide any guidance concerning when property is "acquired by" a partnership.

11. Under the previous version of the UPA, partners were *tenants in partnership.* This meant that every partner was a co-owner with all other partners of the partnership property. The current UPA does not recognize this concept.

---

12. The previous version of the UPA touched only briefly on the duty of loyalty and left the details of the partners' fiduciary duties to be developed under the law of agency.

authority" to limit the capacity of a partner to act as the firm's agent or transfer property on its behalf. Any limit on a partner's authority, however, does not affect a third party who does not know about the statement—unless the statement of partnership authority is filed with the appropriate state office that records real property transfers (see Chapter 25). Statements limiting the partners' authority to transfer real property that are filed with the appropriate state records office will bind third parties, regardless of their knowledge of the limitation.

—Liability of Partners.

One significant disadvantage associated with a traditional partnership is that partners are *personally* liable for the debts of the partnership. Moreover, the liability is essentially unlimited, because the acts of one partner in the ordinary course of business subject the other partners to personal liability [UPA 305]. The following subsections explain the rules on a partner's liability.

—Joint Liability.

Under the prior version of the UPA, which is still in effect in some states, partners were subject to **joint liability** on partnership debts and contracts, but not on partnership debts arising from torts. Joint liability means the liability is shared between the partners, but each partner is liable for the full amount. If, for example, a third party sues a partner on a partnership contract, the partner has the right to demand that the other partners be sued with her or him. In fact, if the third party does not sue all of the partners, those partners sued cannot be required to pay a judgment, and the assets of the partnership cannot be used to satisfy the judgment. (Similarly, a third party's release of one partner releases all partners.) In other words, to bring a successful claim against the partnership on a debt or contract, a plaintiff must name all of the partners as defendants.

—Joint and Several Liability.

In the majority of the states, under UPA 306(a), partners are jointly and severally (separately, or individually) liable for partnership obligations, including contracts, torts, and breaches of trust. **Joint and several liability** means that a third party may sue all of the partners together (jointly) or one or more of the partners separately (severally) or at his or her option. This is true even if the partner did not participate in, ratify, or know about whatever it was that gave rise to the cause of action.

Generally, under UPA 307(d), however, a creditor cannot bring an action to collect a partnership debt from any partner of a nonbankrupt partnership without first attempting to collect from the partnership, or convincing a court that the attempt would be unsuccessful.

A judgment against one partner on her or his several (separate) liability does not extinguish the others' liability. (Similarly, a release of one partner does not discharge the partners' several liability.) Thus, those not sued in the first action may be sued subsequently. The first action, however, may have been conclusive on the question of liability. If, for example, in an action against one partner, the court held that the partnership was in no way liable, the third party cannot bring an action against another partner and succeed on the issue of the partnership's liability.

If the third party is successful in a suit against a partner or partners, he or she may collect on the judgment only against the assets of those partners named as defendants. A partner who commits a tort is required to indemnify (reimburse) the partnership for any damages it pays. The question in the following case was whether a partnership must indemnify a partner for liability that results from negligent conduct occurring in the ordinary course of the partnership's business.

CASE 16.4   Moren v. Jax Restaurant

Minnesota Court of Appeals, 2004.
679 N.W.2d 165.
http://www.lawlibrary.state.mn.us/archive/cap1st.html[a]

BACKGROUND AND FACTS *"Jax Restaurant" is a partnership that operates Jax Restaurant in Foley, Minnesota. One afternoon in October 2000, Nicole Moren, one of the partners, finished her shift at the restaurant at 4:00 P.M. and picked up her two-year-old son Remington from day care. About 5:30 P.M., Moren returned to the restaurant with Remington after Amy Benedetti, the other partner and Moren's sister, asked for help. Moren's husband, Martin, offered to pick up Remington in twenty minutes. Because Moren did not want Remington running around the restaurant, she brought him into the kitchen with her, set him on top of the counter, and began rolling out pizza dough using a dough-pressing machine. While she was making pizzas, Remington reached his hand into the*

a. In the "Published" section, click on "M–O." On that page, scroll to the name of the case and click on the docket number to access the opinion. The Minnesota State Law Library maintains this Web site.

CONTINUED ▶

CASE 16.4 | Continued *dough press. His hand was crushed, causing permanent injuries. Through his father, Remington filed a suit in a Minnesota state court against the partnership, alleging negligence. The partnership filed a complaint against Moren, arguing that it was entitled to indemnity (compensation or reimbursement) from Moren for her negligence. The court issued a summary judgment in favor of Moren on the complaint. The partnership appealed this judgment to a state intermediate appellate court.*

IN THE LANGUAGE OF THE COURT

CRIPPEN, Judge

*　*　*　*

Under Minnesota's Uniform Partnership Act [the most recent version of the UPA], a partnership is an entity distinct from its partners, and as such, a partnership may sue and be sued in the name of the partnership. [Under the UPA] *"[a] partnership is liable for loss or injury caused to a person *　*　* as a result of a wrongful act or omission, or other actionable conduct, of a partner acting in the ordinary course of business of the partnership or with authority of the partnership."* Accordingly, a "partnership shall *　*　* indemnify [reimburse] a partner for liabilities incurred by the partner in the ordinary course of the business of the partnership *　*　*." Stated conversely, an "act of a partner which is not apparently for carrying on in the ordinary course the partnership business or business of the kind carried on by the partnership binds the partnership only if the act was authorized by the other partners." Thus, under the plain language of the UPA, *a partner has a right to indemnity from the partnership, but the partnership's claim of indemnity from a partner is not authorized or required.* [Emphasis added.]

The [lower] court correctly concluded that Nicole Moren's conduct was in the ordinary course of business of the partnership and, as a result, indemnity by the partner to the partnership was inappropriate. It is undisputed that one of the cooks scheduled to work that evening did not come in, and that Moren's partner asked her to help in the kitchen. It also is undisputed that Moren was making pizzas for the partnership when her son was injured. Because her conduct at the time of the injury was in the ordinary course of business of the partnership, under the UPA, her conduct bound the partnership and it owes indemnity to her for her negligence.

*　*　*　*

Appellant *　*　* claims that because Nicole Moren's action of bringing Remington into the kitchen was partly motivated by personal reasons, her conduct was outside the ordinary course of business. Because it has not been previously addressed, there is no Minnesota authority regarding this issue. *　*　* [W]e conclude that the conduct of Nicole Moren was no less in the ordinary course of business because it also served personal purposes. It is undisputed that Moren was acting for the benefit of the partnership by making pizzas when her son was injured, and even though she was simultaneously acting in her role as a mother, her conduct remained in the ordinary course of the partnership business.

DECISION AND REMEDY *The state intermediate appellate court affirmed the lower court's judgment. "Minnesota law requires a partnership to indemnify its partners for the result of their negligence." The appellate court also reasoned that "the conduct of a partner may be partly motivated by personal reasons and still occur in the ordinary course of business of the partnership." Thus "[l]iability for Nicole Moren's negligence rested with the partnership, even if the partner's conduct partly served her personal interests."*

WHAT IF THE FACTS WERE DIFFERENT? *Suppose that Moren's predominant motive in bringing her son to the restaurant had been to benefit herself because she wanted to feed him free pizza. Would the result have been different? Why or why not?*

—*Liability of Incoming Partners.* A partner newly admitted to an existing partnership normally has limited liability for whatever debts and obligations the partnership incurred prior to the new partner's admission. The new partner's liability can be satisfied only from partnership assets [UPA 306(b)]. This means that the new partner usually has no personal liability for these debts and obligations, but any capital contribution that he or she made to the partnership is subject to these debts.

PARTNERSHIP DISSOCIATION

Dissociation occurs when a partner ceases to be associated in the carrying on of the partnership business. Dissociation normally entitles the partner to have his or her interest purchased by the partnership, and terminates his or her authority to act for the partnership and to participate with the partners in running the business. Otherwise, the partnership continues to do business without the dissociating partner.[13]

EVENTS CAUSING DISSOCIATION Under UPA 601, a partner can be dissociated from a partnership in any of the following ways:

1. By voluntarily giving notice of "express will to withdraw."
2. By the occurrence of an event agreed to in the partnership agreement.
3. By a unanimous vote of the other partners under certain circumstances, such as when a partner transfers substantially all of his or her interest in the partnership, or when it becomes unlawful to carry on partnership business with that partner.
4. By order of a court or arbitrator if the partner has engaged in wrongful conduct that affects the partnership business, breached the partnership agreement or violated a duty owed to the partnership or the other partners, or engaged in conduct that makes it "not reasonably practicable to carry on the business in partnership with the partner" [UPA 601(5)].
5. By declaring bankruptcy, assigning his or her interest in the partnership for the benefit of creditors, becoming physically or mentally incapacitated, or by death. Note that although the bankruptcy or death of a partner represents that partner's "dissociation" from the partnership, it is not an *automatic* ground for the partnership's dissolution (dissolution will be discussed shortly).

WRONGFUL DISSOCIATION A partner has the power to dissociate from a partnership at any time, but a partner's dissociation can be wrongful in a few circumstances [UPA 602]. For example, if dissociation is in breach of a partnership agreement, it is wrongful. Also, in the case of a partnership for a definite term or a particular undertaking, dissociation that occurs before the expiration of the term or the completion of

the undertaking can be wrongful if the partner withdraws by express will, is expelled by a court or an arbitrator, or declares bankruptcy.

A partner who wrongfully dissociates is liable to the partnership and to the other partners for damages caused by the dissociation. This liability is in addition to any other obligation of the partner to the partnership or to the other partners. For example, a dissociating partner would be liable for any damage caused by a breach of a partnership agreement. The partner would also be liable to the partnership for costs incurred to replace the partner's expertise or obtain new financing.

EFFECTS OF DISSOCIATION Dissociation terminates some of the rights of the dissociated partner, creates a mandatory duty for the partnership, and alters the liability of both parties to third parties.

—Rights and Duties. On a partner's dissociation, his or her right to participate in the management and conduct of the partnership business terminates [UPA 603]. The partner's duty of loyalty also ends. A partner's other fiduciary duties, including the duty of care, continue only with respect to events that occurred before dissociation, unless the partner participates in winding up the partnership's business (discussed later in this chapter). Thus, a partner who leaves an accounting firm, for example, may immediately compete with the firm for new clients, but must exercise care in completing ongoing client transactions and must account to the firm for any fees received from the old clients on account of those transactions.

After a partner's dissociation, his or her interest in the partnership must be purchased according to the rules in UPA 701. The **buyout price** is based on the amount that would have been distributed to the partner if the partnership were wound up on the date of dissociation. Offset against the price are amounts owed by the partner to the partnership, including damages for wrongful dissociation.

—Liability to Third Parties. For two years after a partner dissociates from a continuing partnership, the partnership may be bound by the acts of the dissociated partner based on apparent authority [UPA 702]. In other words, the partnership may be liable to a third party with whom a dissociated partner enters into a transaction if the third party reasonably believed that the dissociated partner was still a partner. Similarly, a dissociated partner may be liable for partnership obligations entered into during a two-year period following dissociation [UPA 703].

---

13. Under the previous version of the UPA, when a partner withdrew from a partnership, the partnership was considered dissolved, its business had to be wound up, and the proceeds had to be distributed to creditors and among partners. The new UPA provisions dramatically change the law governing partnership breakups and dissolution by no longer requiring that the partnership end if one partner dissociates.

To avoid this possible liability, a partnership should notify its creditors, and customers or clients, of a partner's dissociation and file a statement of dissociation in the appropriate state office to limit the partner's authority to ninety days after the filing [UPA 704]. A dissociated partner should also file a statement of dissociation with the state to limit his or her potential liability to ninety days.

PARTNERSHIP TERMINATION

Some changes in the relations of the partners that demonstrate unwillingness or inability to carry on the partnership business dissolve the partnership, resulting in termination [UPA 801]. If any partner wishes to continue the business, she or he is free to reorganize into a new partnership with the remaining partners.

The termination of a partnership has two stages—*dissolution* and *winding up*. Both stages must take place before termination is complete. **Dissolution** occurs when any partner (or partners) initiates proceedings to terminate the partnership or when an event specified in the partnership agreement occurs. **Winding up** is the actual process of collecting and distributing the partnership's assets. When winding up is complete, the partnership's *legal* existence is terminated.

Dissolution of a partnership can be brought about by acts of the partners, by operation of law, or by judicial decree.

DISSOLUTION BY ACTS OF THE PARTNERS Dissolution of a partnership may come about through the acts of the partners in several ways. First, any partnership can be dissolved by the partners' agreement. For example, when a partnership agreement states a fixed term or a particular business objective to be accomplished, the passing of the date or the accomplishment of the objective dissolves the partnership.

Second, because a partnership at will is a voluntary association, a partner has the power to dissociate himself or herself from the partnership at any time and perhaps dissolve the partnership by giving notice of "express will to withdraw" [UPA 801(1)]. If, after dissolution, none of the partners, including the withdrawing partner, wants the partnership wound up, the remaining partners may continue the business [UPA 802(b)].[14]

Third, a partnership for a definite term or a particular undertaking can be dissolved if, within ninety days of a partner's dissociation caused by bankruptcy, incapacity, or death, at least half of the remaining partners decide in favor of dissolution [UPA 801(2)].

DISSOLUTION BY OPERATION OF LAW Any event that makes it unlawful for the partnership to continue its business will result in dissolution [UPA 801(4)]. Note, however, that if the illegality of the partnership business is a cause for dissolution, within ninety days, the partners can decide to change the nature of their business and continue in the partnership.[15]

DISSOLUTION BY JUDICIAL DECREE A partner can request a court to dissolve a partnership by judicial decree. A court may dissolve the partnership if it determines that the partnership can only be operated at a loss, if one partner has perpetrated a fraud on the other partners, or when dissension among the partners undermines the ability of the partnership to conduct business [UPA 801(5)].

NOTICE OF DISSOLUTION A partner must communicate her or his intent to dissolve or to withdraw from the firm to each of the other partners. A partner can express this notice of intent by either words (*actual notice*) or actions (*constructive notice*). All partners will share liability for the acts of any partner who continues to conduct business for the firm without knowledge that the partnership has been dissolved.

For example, suppose that Alzor, Jennifer, and Carla have a partnership. Alzor tells Jennifer of her intent to withdraw. Before Carla learns of Alzor's intentions, she enters into a contract with a third party. The contract is equally binding on Alzor, Jennifer, and Carla. Unless the other partners have notice, the withdrawing partner will continue to be bound as a partner to all contracts created for the firm.

To avoid liability for obligations a partner incurs after dissolution of a partnership, the firm must give notice to all affected third parties [UPA 804(2)]. After dissolution, one of the partners can file a statement of dissolution with the appropriate state office, declaring that the partnership has dissolved and is winding up its business. Ninety days after this statement is filed, creditors and other nonpartners are deemed to have notice of the dissolution [UPA 805].

---

14. Any change in a partnership caused by the withdrawal of a partner or the admission of a new partner resulted in dissolution under the previous version of the UPA. If the remaining or new partners continued the firm's business, a new partnership arose.

15. A partner's death or bankruptcy, or an event that made it illegal for the partner to carry on, also dissolved the partnership by operation of law under the previous version of the UPA.

WINDING UP AND DISTRIBUTION OF ASSETS

Once dissolution has occurred and the partners have been notified, they cannot create new obligations on behalf of the partnership. Their only authority is to complete transactions begun but not finished at the time of dissolution and to wind up the business of the partnership [UPA 803, 804(1)]. Winding up includes collecting and preserving partnership assets, discharging liabilities (paying debts), and accounting to each partner for the value of his or her interest in the partnership.

Both creditors of the partnership and creditors of the individual partners can make claims on the partnership's assets. In general, partnership creditors share proportionately with the partners' individual creditors in the assets of the partners' estates, which include their interests in the partnership. A partnership's assets are distributed according to the following priorities [UPA 807]:

1. Payment of debts, including those owed to partner and nonpartner creditors.

2. Return of capital contributions and distribution of profits to partners.[16]

If the partnership's liabilities are greater than its assets, the partners bear the losses—in the absence of a contrary agreement—in the same proportion in which they shared the profits (rather than, for example, in proportion to their contributions to the partnership's capital). Partners continue in their fiduciary relationship until the winding-up process is completed.

---

16. Under the previous version of the UPA, creditors of the partnership had priority over creditors of the individual partners. Also, in distributing partnership assets, third party creditors were paid before partner creditors, and capital contributions were returned before profits.

REVIEWING SOLE PROPRIETORSHIPS, FRANCHISES, AND PARTNERSHIPS

Carlos Del Rey decided to open a Mexican fast-food restaurant and signed a franchise contract with a national chain called *La Grande Enchilada*. The contract required the franchisee to strictly follow the franchisor's operating manual and stated that failure to do so would be grounds for terminating the franchise contract. The manual set forth detailed operating procedures and safety standards, and provided that a *La Grande* representative would inspect the restaurant monthly to ensure compliance. Nine months after Del Rey began operating his restaurant, a spark from the grill ignited an oily towel in the kitchen. No one was injured, but by the time firefighters were able to put out the fire, the kitchen had sustained extensive damage. The cook told the fire department that the towel was "about two feet from the grill" when it caught fire, which was in compliance with the franchisor's manual that required towels to be placed at least one foot from the grills. Nevertheless, the next day *La Grande* notified Del Rey that his franchise would terminate in thirty days for failure to follow the prescribed safety procedures. Using the information presented in the chapter, answer the following questions.

1. What type of franchise was Del Rey's *La Grande Enchilada* restaurant?

2. The franchise agreement stipulates that Del Rey will purchase the building and that *La Grande* will supply the equipment. Del Rey operates the restaurant as a sole proprietorship. Who bears the loss for the damaged kitchen? Explain.

3. Assume that Del Rey operates the restaurant as a sole proprietorship. In the event of his death, can his daughter take over the business? Why or why not?

4. Now assume that Del Rey files a lawsuit against *La Grande*, claiming that his franchise was wrongfully terminated. What factors would a court consider in determining whether the franchise was wrongfully terminated? How would a court be likely to rule?

5. Suppose that it turns out that the fire was actually caused by a defective grill supplied by *La Grande* (rather than by a spark igniting a towel). Would this affect a court's decision on wrongful termination? Should it? Explain.

TERMS AND CONCEPTS TO REVIEW

articles of partnership 402

buyout price 409

charging order 405

confession of judgement 404

dissociation 409

dissolution 410

franchise 394

franchisee 394

franchisor 394

information return 402

joint and several liability 407

joint liability 407

partnership 399

partnership by estoppel 404

sole proprietorship 392

winding up 410

QUESTIONS AND CASE PROBLEMS

16-1. Maria, Pablo, and Vicky are recent college graduates who would like to go into business for themselves. They are considering purchasing a franchise. If they enter into a franchising arrangement, they would have the support of a large company that could answer any questions they might have. Also, a firm that has been in business for many years would be experienced in dealing with some of the problems that novice businesspersons might encounter. These and other attributes of franchises can lessen some of the risks of the marketplace. What other aspects of franchising—positive and negative—might Maria, Pablo, and Vicky want to consider before committing themselves to a particular franchise?

16-2. **QUESTION WITH SAMPLE ANSWER**

National Foods, Inc., sells franchises to its fast-food restaurants, known as Chicky-D's. Under the franchise agreement, franchisees agree to hire and train employees strictly according to Chicky-D's standards. Chicky-D's regional supervisors are required to approve all job candidates before they are hired and all general policies affecting those employees. Chicky-D's reserves the right to terminate a franchise for violating the franchisor's rules. In practice, however, Chicky-D's regional supervisors routinely approve new employees and individual franchisees' policies. After several incidents of racist comments and conduct by Tim, a recently hired assistant manager at a Chicky-D's, Sharon, a counterperson at the restaurant, resigns. Sharon files a suit in a federal district court against National. National files a motion for summary judgment, arguing that it is not liable for harassment by franchise employees. Will the court grant National's motion? Why or why not?

For a sample answer to this question, go to Appendix I at the end of this text.

16-3. Omega Computers, Inc., is a franchisor that grants exclusive physical territories to its franchisees with retail locations, including Pete's Digital Products. Omega sells over two hundred franchises before establishing an interactive Web site. On the site, a customer can order Omega's products directly from the franchisor. When Pete's sets up a Web site through which a customer can also order Omega's products, Omega and Pete's file suits against each other, each alleging that the other is in violation of the franchise relationship. To decide this issue, what factors should the court consider? How might the parties have avoided this conflict? Discuss.

16-4. Daniel is the owner of a chain of shoe stores. He hires Rubya to be the manager of a new store, which is to open in Grand Rapids, Michigan. Daniel, by written contract, agrees to pay Rubya a monthly salary and 20 percent of the profits. Without Daniel's knowledge, Rubya represents himself to Classen as Daniel's partner, showing Classen the agreement to share profits. Classen extends credit to Rubya. Rubya defaults. Discuss whether Classen can hold Daniel liable as a partner.

16-5. Meyer, Knapp, and Cavanna establish a partnership to operate a window-washing service. Meyer contributes $10,000 to the partnership, and Knapp and Cavanna contribute $1,000 each. The partnership agreement is silent as to how profits and losses will be shared. One month after the partnership begins operation, Knapp and Cavanna vote, over Meyer's objection, to purchase another truck for the firm. Meyer believes that because he contributed $10,000, the partnership cannot make any major commitment to purchase over his objection. In addition, Meyer claims that in the absence of any provision in the agreement, profits must be divided in the same ratio as capital contributions. Discuss Meyer's contentions.

16-6. **CASE PROBLEM WITH SAMPLE ANSWER**

Walik Elkhatib, a Palestinian Arab, emigrated to the United States in 1971 and became an American citizen. Eight years later, Elkhatib bought a Dunkin' Donuts, Inc., franchise in Bellwood, Illinois. Dunkin' Donuts began offering breakfast sandwiches with bacon, ham, or sausage through its franchises in 1984, but Elkhatib refused to sell these items at his store on the ground that his religion forbade the handling of pork. In 1995, Elkhatib opened a second franchise in Berkeley, Illinois, at which he also refused to sell pork products. The next year, at both locations, Elkhatib began selling meatless sandwiches. In 1998, Elkhatib opened a third franchise in Westchester, Illinois. When he proposed to relocate this franchise, Dunkin' Donuts refused to approve the new location and added that it would not renew any of his franchise agreements because he did not carry the full sandwich line. Elkhatib filed a suit in a federal district court against Dunkin' Donuts and others. The defendants filed a motion for summary judgment. Did Dunkin' Donuts act in good faith in its relationship with Elkhatib? Explain. [*Elkhatib v. Dunkin' Donuts, Inc.*, __ F.Supp.2d __ (N.D.Ill. 2004)]

To view a sample answer for this case problem, go to this book's Web site at http://wleb.westbuslaw.com, select "Chapter 16," and click on "Case Problem with Sample Answer."

16-7. THE FRANCHISE CONTRACT. On August 23, 1995, Climaco Guzman entered into a commercial janitorial services franchise agreement with Jan-Pro Cleaning Systems, Inc., in Rhode Island for a franchise fee of $3,285. In the agreement, Jan-Pro promised to furnish Guzman with "one (1) or more customer account(s) . . . amounting to $8,000.00 gross volume per year. . . . No portion of the franchise fee is refundable except and to the extent that the Franchisor, within 120 business days following the date of execution of the Franchise Agreement, fails to provide accounts." By February 19, Guzman had not received any accounts and demanded a full refund. Jan-Pro then promised "two accounts grossing $12,000 per year in income." Despite its assurances, Jan-Pro did not have the ability to furnish accounts that met the stated requirements. In September, Guzman filed a suit in a Rhode Island state court against Jan-Pro, alleging in part fraudulent misrepresentation. Should the court rule in Guzman's favor? Why or why not? [*Guzman v. Jan-Pro Cleaning Systems, Inc,.* 839 A.2d 504 (R.I. 2003)]

16-8. INDICATIONS OF PARTNERSHIP. In August 1998, Jea Yu contacted Cameron Eppler, president of Design88, Ltd., to discuss developing a Web site that would cater to investors and provide services to its members for a fee. Yu and Patrick Connelly invited Eppler and Ha Tran, another member of Design88, to a meeting to discuss the site. The parties agreed that Design88 would perform certain Web design, implementation, and maintenance functions for 10 percent of the profits from the site, which would be called "The Underground Trader." They signed a "Master Partnership Agreement," which was later amended to include Power Uptik Productions, LLC (PUP). The parties often referred to themselves as partners. From Design88's offices in Virginia, Design88 designed and hosted the site, solicited members through Internet and national print campaigns, processed member applications, provided technical support, monitored access to the site, and negotiated and formed business alliances on the site's behalf. When relations among the parties soured, PUP withdrew. Design88 filed a suit against PUP and the others. Did a partnership exist among these parties? Explain. [*Design88 Ltd. v. Power Uptik Productions, LLC,* 133 F.Supp.2d 873 (W.D.Va. 2001)]

16-9. ELEMENTS OF A PARTNERSHIP. At least six months before the 1996 Summer Olympic Games in Atlanta, Georgia, Stafford Fontenot, Steve Turner, Mike Montelaro, Joe Sokol, and Doug Brinsmade agreed to sell Cajun food at the Games and began making preparations. Calling themselves "Prairie Cajun Seafood Catering of Louisiana," on May 19 the group applied for a license with the Fulton County, Georgia, Department of Public Health–Environmental Health Services. Later, Ted Norris received for the sale of a mobile kitchen an $8,000 check drawn on the "Prairie Cajun Seafood Catering of Louisiana" account and two promissory notes, one for $12,000 and the other for $20,000. The notes, which were dated June 12, listed only Fontenot "d/b/a [doing business as] Prairie Cajun Seafood" as the maker. On July 31, Fontenot and his friends signed a partnership agreement, which listed specific percentages of profits and losses. They drove the mobile kitchen to Atlanta, but business was "disastrous." When the notes were not paid, Norris filed a suit in a Louisiana state court against Fontenot, seeking payment. What are the elements of a partnership? Was there a partnership among Fontenot and the others? Who is liable on the notes? Explain. [*Norris v. Fontenot,* 867 So.2d 179 (La.App. 3 Cir. 2004)]

16-10. FIDUCIARY DUTIES. Charles Chaney and Lawrence Burdett were equal partners in a partnership in Georgia known as BMW Partners. Their agreement was silent as to the effect of a partner's death on the firm. The partnership's sole asset was real property, which the firm leased in 1987 to a corporation that the partners co-owned. Under the lease, the corporation was to pay the partnership $8,000 per month, but after a few years, the corporation began paying $9,000 per month. Chaney died on April 15, 1998. Burdett wanted to continue the partnership business and offered to buy Chaney's estate's interest in it. Meanwhile, claiming that the real property's fair rental value was $4,500 (not $9,000) and that the corporation had overpaid the rent by $80,000, Burdett adjusted the rental payments to recoup this amount. Bonnie Chaney, Charles's widow and his estate's legal representative, filed a suit in a Georgia state court against Burdett, alleging in part that he had breached his fiduciary duty by adjusting the amount of the rent. Did Burdett's fiduciary duty expire on Chaney's death? Explain. [*Chaney v. Burdett,* 274 Ga. 805, 560 S.E.2d 21 (2002)]

16-11. PARTNERSHIP STATUS. Charlie Waugh owned and operated an auto parts junkyard in Georgia. Charlie's son, Mack, started working in the business part-time as a child and full-time when he left school at the age of sixteen. Mack oversaw the business's finances, depositing the profits in a bank. Charlie gave Mack a one-half interest in the business, telling him that if "something happened" to Charlie, the entire business would be his. In 1994, Charlie and his wife, Alene, transferred to Mack the land on which the junkyard was located. Two years later, however, Alene and her daughters, Gail and Jewel, falsely convinced Charlie, whose mental competence had deteriorated, that Mack had cheated him. Mack was ordered off the land. Shortly thereafter, Charlie died. Mack filed a suit in a Georgia state court against the rest of the family, asserting in part that he and Charlie had been partners and that he was entitled to Charlie's share of the business. Was the relationship between Charlie and Mack a partnership? Is Mack entitled to Charlie's "share"? Explain. [*Waugh v. Waugh*, 265 Ga.App. 799, 595 S.E.2d 647 (2004)]

16–12. ⚖ **A QUESTION OF ETHICS**

Sandra Lerner was one of the original founders of Cisco Systems. When she sold her interest in Cisco, she received a substantial amount of money, which she invested, and she became extremely wealthy. Patricia Holmes met Lerner at Holmes's horse training facility, and they became friends. One evening in Lerner's mansion, while applying nail polish, Holmes layered a raspberry color over black to produce a new color, which Lerner liked. Later, the two created other colors with names such as "Bruise," "Smog," and "Oil Slick," and titled their concept "Urban Decay." Lerner and Holmes started a firm to produce and market the polishes but never discussed the sharing of profits and losses. They agreed to build the business and then sell it. Together, they did market research, experimented with colors, worked on a logo and advertising, obtained capital from an investment firm, and hired employees. Then Lerner began working to edge Holmes out of the firm. Several months later, when Holmes was told not to attend meetings of the firm's officers, she filed a suit in a California state court against Lerner, claiming, among other things, a breach of their partnership agreement. [*Holmes v. Lerner*, 74 Cal.App.4th 442, 88 Cal.Rptr.2d 130 (1 Dist. 1999)]

(a) Lerner claimed that there was no partnership agreement because there was no agreement to divide profits. Was Lerner right? Why or why not? How should the court rule?

(b) Suppose that Lerner, but not Holmes, had contributed a significant amount of personal funds to developing and marketing the new nail polish. Would this entitle Lerner to receive more of the profits? Should it? Explain.

(c) What ethical considerations are involved in the rule that partners have a fiduciary duty to be loyal to one another and to account for all partnership profits? Did Lerner violate her fiduciary duty in this case?

LAW | on the Web

For updated links to resources available on the Web, as well as a variety of other materials, visit this text's Web site at http://wleb.westbuslaw.com.

To learn how the U.S. Small Business Administration assists in forming, financing, and operating businesses, go to

http://www.sbaonline.sba.gov

For information about FTC regulations on franchising, as well as state laws regulating franchising, go to

http://www.ftc.gov/bcp/franchise/netfran.htm

A good source of information on the purchase and sale of franchises is Franchising.org, which is online at

http://www.franchising.org

For some of the advantages and disadvantages of doing business as a partnership, go to the following page, which is part of the U.S. Small Business Administration's Web site. Then scroll down to "Partnerships."

http://www.sba.gov/starting_business/legal/forms.html

LEGAL RESEARCH EXERCISES ON THE WEB

Go to http://wleb.westbuslaw.com, the Web site that accompanies this text. Select "Chapter 16" and click on "Internet Exercises." There you will find the following Internet research exercises that you can perform to learn more about topics covered in this chapter.

Activity 16–1: **LEGAL PERSPECTIVE**
            Liability of Dissociated Partners

Activity 16–2: **MANAGEMENT PERSPECTIVE**
            Franchises

CHAPTER 17
Limited Liability Companies and Limited Partnerships

In the preceding chapters, we have examined sole proprietorships, franchises, and general partnerships. Before we move on to discuss corporations, one of the most prevalent business forms, we pause to examine a relatively new form of business organization called the *limited liability company*, as well as business forms designed to limit the liability of partners. The **limited liability company (LLC)** is a hybrid form that combines the limited liability aspects of the corporation and the tax advantages of a partnership. Increasingly, LLCs are becoming an organizational form of choice among businesspersons—a trend encouraged by state statutes permitting their use.

In this chapter, we begin by examining the LLC. We then look at a similar type of entity that is also relatively new—the *limited liability partnership* (LLP). The chapter concludes with a discussion of the *limited partnership* (LP), a special type of traditional partnership in which some of the partners have limited liability, and the *limited liability limited partnership* (LLLP).

SECTION 1 | Limited Liability Companies

Limited liability companies (LLCs) are governed by state LLC statutes. These laws vary, of course, from state to state. In an attempt to create more uniformity among the states in this respect, in 1995 the National Conference of Commissioners on Uniform State Laws issued the Uniform Limited Liability Company Act (ULLCA). To date, less than one-fourth of the states have adopted the ULLCA, and thus the law governing LLCs remains far from uniform. Some provisions are common to most state statutes, however, and we base our discussion of LLCs in this section on these common elements.

EVOLUTION OF THE LLC

In 1977, Wyoming became the first state to pass legislation authorizing the creation of an LLC. Although LLCs emerged in the United States only in 1977, they have been in existence for over a century in other areas, including several European and South American nations. For example, the South American *limitada* is a form of business organization that operates more or less as a partnership but provides limited liability for the owners.

TAXATION OF THE LLC   In the United States, after Wyoming's adoption of an LLC statute, it still was not known how the Internal Revenue Service (IRS) would treat the LLC for tax purposes. In 1988, however, the IRS ruled that Wyoming LLCs would be taxed as partnerships instead of corporations, providing that certain requirements were met. Prior to this ruling, only one other state—Florida, in 1982—had authorized LLCs. The 1988 ruling encouraged other states to enact LLC statutes, and in less than a decade, all states had done so.

IRS rules that went into effect on January 1, 1997, also encouraged more widespread use of LLCs in the business world. These rules provide that any unincorporated business will automatically be taxed as a partnership unless it indicates otherwise on the tax form. The exceptions involve publicly traded companies, companies formed under a state incorporation statute, and certain foreign-owned companies. If a business chooses to be taxed as a corporation, it can indicate this preference by checking a box on the IRS form.

FOREIGN ENTITIES MAY BE LLC MEMBERS   Part of the impetus behind creating LLCs in this country is that foreign investors are allowed to become LLC members. Generally, in an era increasingly characterized by global business efforts and investments, the LLC offers U.S. firms and potential investors from other countries flexibility and opportunities that allow for limited liability and increased tax benefits.

THE NATURE OF THE LLC

LLCs share many characteristics with corporations. Like corporations, LLCs are creatures of the state. In other words, they must be formed and operated in compliance with state law. Like shareholders in a corporation, members of an LLC enjoy limited liability [ULLCA 303]. Also like corporations, LLCs are legal entities apart from their owners, who are called

members. As a legal person, the LLC can sue or be sued, enter into contracts, and hold title to property [ULLCA 201]. The terminology used to describe LLCs formed in other states or nations is also similar to that used in corporate law. For example, an LLC formed in one state but doing business in another state is referred to in the second state as a *foreign LLC*.

On occasion, the courts will disregard the corporate entity ("pierce the corporate veil") and hold a shareholder personally liable for corporate obligations. At issue in the following case was whether this same principle should be extended to an LLC. Could the managing member of an LLC be held personally liable for property damage caused by the LLC?

CASE 17.1 — Kaycee Land and Livestock v. Flahive

Wyoming Supreme
Court, 2002.
2002 WY 73,
46 P.3d 323.

BACKGROUND AND FACTS *Roger Flahive is the managing member of Flahive Oil & Gas, LLC. To exercise mineral rights beneath certain real property, Flahive Oil & Gas entered into a contract with Kaycee Land and Livestock in Johnson County, Wyoming, allowing Flahive Oil & Gas to use the surface of Kaycee's land. Later, alleging environmental contamination to its property, Kaycee filed a suit in a Wyoming state court against Flahive and his LLC. On discovering that Flahive Oil & Gas had no assets as of the time of the suit, Kaycee asked the court to disregard the LLC entity and hold Flahive personally liable for the contamination. Before issuing a judgment in the case, the court submitted this question to the Wyoming Supreme Court: "[I]s a claim to pierce the Limited Liability entity veil or disregard the Limited Liability Company entity in the same manner as a court would pierce a corporate veil or disregard a corporate shield, an available remedy" against an LLC? Unlike some states' statutes, Wyoming's LLC provisions do not address this issue.*

IN THE LANGUAGE OF THE COURT

KITE, Justice.

* * * *

* * * Every state that has enacted LLC piercing legislation has chosen to follow corporate law standards and not develop a separate LLC standard. Statutes [that] create corporations and LLCs have the same basic purpose—to limit the liability of individual investors with a corresponding benefit to economic development. Statutes created the legal fiction of the corporation being a completely separate entity which could act independently from individual persons. If the corporation were created and operated in conformance with the statutory requirements, the law would treat it as a separate entity and shelter the individual shareholders from any liability caused by corporate action, thereby encouraging investment. However, courts throughout the country have consistently recognized certain unjust circumstances can arise if immunity from liability shelters those who have failed to operate a corporation as a separate entity. *Consequently, when corporations fail to follow the statutorily mandated formalities, co-mingle funds, or ignore the restrictions in their articles of incorporation regarding separate treatment of corporate property, the courts deem it appropriate to disregard the separate identity and do not permit shareholders to be sheltered from liability to third parties for damages caused by the corporations' acts.* [Emphasis added.]

We can discern no reason, in either law or policy, to treat LLCs differently than we treat corporations. If the members and officers of an LLC fail to treat it as a separate entity as con-

CASE 17.1 | **Continued**

templated by statute, they should not enjoy immunity from individual liability for the LLC's acts that cause damage to third parties. * * *

Certainly, the various factors which would justify piercing an LLC veil would not be identical to the corporate situation for the obvious reason that many of the organizational formalities applicable to corporations do not apply to LLCs. The LLC's operation is intended to be much more flexible than a corporation's. Factors relevant to determining when to pierce the corporate veil have developed over time in a multitude of cases. It would be inadvisable in this case * * * to attempt to articulate all the possible factors to be applied to LLCs in Wyoming in the future. For guidance, we direct attention to commentators who have opined on the appropriate factors to be applied in the LLC context.

DECISION AND REMEDY *The Wyoming Supreme Court held that the LLC entity could be disregarded. The court concluded that there was no reason to treat an LLC differently than a corporation when considering whether to disregard the legal entity and hold its members personally liable. The court remanded the case for a determination as to whether piercing the LLC veil was appropriate under these circumstances.*

WHAT IF THE FACTS WERE DIFFERENT? *Suppose that Flahive had scrupulously followed all statutorily mandated formalities, had not commingled personal and LLC funds, and had always treated LLC property as separate and distinct from his personal property. Would the decision in this case likely have been different? Why or why not?*

LLC FORMATION

To form an LLC, **articles of organization** must be filed with a central state agency—usually the secretary of state's office [ULLCA 202]. Typically, the articles are required to include such information as the name of the business, the business's principal address, the name and address of a registered agent, the names of the owners, and information on how the LLC will be managed [ULLCA 203]. The business's name must include the words *Limited Liability Company* or the initials *LLC* [ULLCA 105(a)]. In addition to filing the articles of organization, a few states require that a notice of the intention to form an LLC be published in a local newspaper.

About one-fourth of the states specifically require LLCs to have at least two owners, or members. The rest of the states usually permit one-member LLCs, although some LLC statutes are silent on this issue.

JURISDICTIONAL REQUIREMENTS

One of the significant differences between LLCs and corporations has to do with federal jurisdictional requirements. The federal jurisdiction statute provides that a corporation is deemed to be a citizen of the state where it is incorporated and maintains its principal place of business. The statute does not mention the state citizenship of partnerships, LLCs, and other unincorporated associations, but the courts have tended to regard these entities as citizens of every state in which their members are citizens.

The state citizenship of LLCs may come into play when a party sues an LLC based on diversity of citizenship. Remember from Chapter 2 that in some circumstances, such as when parties to a lawsuit are from different states, a federal court can exercise diversity jurisdiction in cases in which the amount in controversy exceeds $75,000. *Total* diversity of citizenship must exist, however. For example, Fong is a citizen of New York who wishes to bring suit against Skycel, an LLC formed under the laws of Connecticut. One of Skycel's members also lives in New York. Fong will not be able to bring a suit against Skycel in federal court on the basis of diversity jurisdiction because the defendant LLC is also a citizen of New York. The same would be true if Fong was bringing suit against multiple defendants and one of the defendants lived in New York.

ADVANTAGES AND DISADVANTAGES OF THE LLC

Although the LLC offers many advantages to businesspersons, it also has some disadvantages. We look now at some of the advantages and disadvantages of the LLC.

ADVANTAGES OF THE LLC A key advantage of the LLC is that the liability of members is limited to the amount of their investments. Another advantage is the flexibility that the LLC offers in regard to business operations and management (as will be discussed shortly).

An additional benefit is that an LLC with two or more members can choose to be taxed either as a partnership or as a corporation. As will be discussed in Chapter 18, a corporate entity must pay income taxes on its profits, and the shareholders pay personal income taxes on profits distributed as dividends. An LLC that wants to distribute profits to the members may prefer to be taxed as a partnership to avoid the "double taxation" characteristic of the corporate entity. Unless an LLC indicates that it wishes to be taxed as a corporation, the IRS automatically taxes it as a partnership. This means that the LLC as an entity pays no taxes; rather, as in a partnership, profits are "passed through" the LLC to the members, who then personally pay taxes on the profits. If LLC members want to reinvest profits in the business, however, rather than distribute the profits to members, they may prefer to be taxed as a corporation. Corporate income tax rates may be lower than personal tax rates. Part of the attractiveness of the LLC is this flexibility with respect to taxation.

For federal income tax purposes, one-member LLCs are automatically taxed as sole proprietorships unless they indicate that they wish to be taxed as corporations. With respect to state taxes, most states follow the IRS rules.

DISADVANTAGES OF THE LLC The disadvantages of the LLC are relatively few. Although initially there was uncertainty over how LLCs would be taxed, that disadvantage no longer exists. One remaining drawback is that state LLC statutes are not yet uniform. Until all of the states have adopted the ULLCA, an LLC in one state will have to check the rules in the other states in which the firm does business to ensure that it retains its limited liability. Generally, though, most—if not all—states apply to a foreign LLC (an LLC formed in another state) the law of the state where the LLC was formed.

Still another disadvantage is the lack of case law dealing with LLCs. How the courts interpret statutes provides important guidelines for businesses. Given the relative newness of the LLC as a business form in the United States, there is not, as yet, a substantial body of case law to provide this kind of guidance.

SECTION **2** | Management and Operation of an LLC

As mentioned, one of the advantages of the LLC form of business is that it provides a substantial degree of flexibility in terms of operation and management. The members get to choose who will participate in the management and operation of their business, and how other issues will be resolved. We discuss the various options available to members in the following subsections.

THE LLC OPERATING AGREEMENT

In an LLC, the members themselves can decide how to operate the many aspects of the business by forming an **operating agreement** [ULLCA 103(a)]. Operating agreements typically contain provisions relating to management, how profits will be divided, the transfer of membership interests, whether the LLC will be dissolved on the death or departure of a member, and other important issues.

An operating agreement need not be in writing and indeed need not even be formed for an LLC to exist. Generally, though, LLC members should protect their interests by forming a written operating agreement. As with any business arrangement, disputes may arise over any number of issues. If there is no agreement covering the topic under dispute, such as how profits will be divided, the state LLC statute will govern the outcome. For example, most LLC statutes provide that if the members have not specified how profits will be divided, they will be divided equally among the members.

Generally, when an issue is not covered by an operating agreement or by an LLC statute, the principles of partnership law are applied. The following case illustrates what can happen in the absence of a written operating agreement when one of the members of the LLC has a "bad intent."

CASE 17.2   Kuhn v. Tumminelli

Superior Court
of New Jersey,
Appellate Division, 2004.
366 N.J.Super. 431,
841 A.2d 496.
*http://lawlibrary.rutgers.
edu/search.shtml#party*[a]

BACKGROUND AND FACTS *Clifford Kuhn, Jr., and Joseph Tumminelli formed Touch of Class Limousine Service under the New Jersey Limited Liability Company Act in 1999, doing business as Touch of Elegance Limousine Service. They did not sign a written operating agreement, but orally agreed that Kuhn would provide the financial backing and procure customers, and Tumminelli would manage the day-to-day operations of the company. Tumminelli embezzled $283,000 from the company after cashing customers' checks at Quick Cash, Inc., a local check-cashing service. Quick Cash deposited the checks in its bank account with First Union National Bank, N.A., which collected on the checks from the drawee banks, Bank of America Corporation and Chase Manhattan Bank, N.A. Kuhn filed a suit in a New Jersey state court against Tumminelli, the banks, and others to recover the embezzled funds. The court ordered Tumminelli to pay Kuhn and to transfer his interest in Touch of Class to Kuhn, but issued a summary judgment in favor of the other defendants. Kuhn appealed to a state intermediate appellate court, arguing in part that Quick Cash and the banks were liable because Tumminelli did not have the authority to cash the company's checks and convert the funds.*

IN THE LANGUAGE OF THE COURT

LEFELT, J.A.D. [Judge, Appellate Division]

* * * *

New Jersey enacted the Limited Liability Company Act in 1994. Its purpose was to enable members and managers of LLCs to take advantage of both the limited liability afforded to shareholders and directors of corporations and the pass-through tax advantages available to partnerships.

Under the LLC Act, *when a limited liability company is managed by its members, unless otherwise provided in the operating agreement, each member shall have the authority to bind the limited liability company.* Moreover, except as otherwise provided in an operating agreement, a member or manager may lend money to, borrow money from, act as a surety, guarantor, or endorser for, * * * an LLC. [Emphasis added.]

In the absence of a written operating agreement providing to the contrary, Tumminelli as a 50% owner of the LLC had broad authority to bind the LLC * * * and specific authority * * * to endorse and presumably cash checks payable to the LLC. If more limited authority was desired, Kuhn and Tumminelli had to so provide in a written operating agreement.

* * * *

* * * [T]he LLC Act contemplates that its provisions will control unless the members agree otherwise in an operating agreement. *When executing an operating agreement, which must be written if the LLC has more than one member, the members are free to structure the company in a variety of ways and are free to restrict and expand the rights, responsibilities, and authority of its managers and members.* [Emphasis added.]

The LLC Act is, therefore, quite flexible and permits the LLC members great discretion to establish the company structure and procedures, with the statute controlling in the absence of a contrary operating agreement. The legislative intent is revealed by the directive that the LLC Act is to be liberally construed to give the maximum effect to the principle of freedom of contract and to the enforceability of operating agreements.

* * * *

Tumminelli was authorized under the LLC Act to endorse the checks. In fact, considering Tumminelli's position at the LLC, his responsibilities, and daily functions along with the

---

a. In the "Which courts do you want to search?" section, click on the small box next to "Appellate Division." In the "Enter Names Here" section, in the "First Name:" box, type "Kuhn"; in the "Second Name:" box, type "Tumminelli"; then click on "Submit Form." In the result, click on the appropriate link to access the opinion. Rutgers University School of Law in Camden, New Jersey, maintains this Web site.

CONTINUED ▶

CASE 17.2 Continued

statutory grant of authority, it can be inferred that Tumminelli had actual authority to receive the checks, endorse the checks, and cash them at Quick Cash, especially because Kuhn knew that Tumminelli was paying business expenses in cash.

* * * Under Kuhn's argument, even if a person had been authorized to endorse and cash a check, if that person converts the funds to an unauthorized use, a depository bank would be liable, as if the check had been paid on a forged endorsement. * * *

We disagree that an authorized endorsement can become unauthorized by a subsequent unauthorized use of the funds. Rather, we view the circumstances as constituting two acts, the endorsement necessary to obtain the funds and the subsequent use of the funds. These acts are not inseparable. *The misappropriation of the funds is unauthorized, but does not convert an authorized endorsement into a forgery.* [Emphasis added.]

It defies reason to allow an event that occurs after the endorsement to affect the validity of the endorsement. The use to which the agent later puts the check does not affect the agent's authorization to endorse it. The validity of an endorsement does not depend upon the agent's subjective motivation at the time of the endorsement. * * * [H]ow can a bank or anyone else protect themselves against someone's bad intent?

If the agent is otherwise authorized * * * the fact that the agent had an improper purpose in making or endorsing the instrument in the authorized form does not prevent a bona fide purchaser in due course, or a subsequent transferee from one, from having the same rights in the instrument and against the principal as if the agent's act were authorized.

DECISION AND REMEDY *The state intermediate appellate court affirmed the lower court's judgment in favor of Quick Cash and the banks. Tumminelli had the authority to accept, indorse, and cash checks on behalf of Touch of Class, under the LLC Act and in the absence of a written operating agreement, which might have specified otherwise. His "bad intent" to convert the funds to his own use did not affect this authority.*

WHAT IF THE FACTS WERE DIFFERENT? *Suppose that Kuhn and Tumminelli had signed a written operating agreement that required both members' indorsements when cashing customers' checks. Assuming that Quick Cash would have known of this requirement, would the result in this case have been different?*

MANAGEMENT OF AN LLC

Basically, the members have two options for managing an LLC—the members may decide in their operating agreement to be either a "member-managed" LLC or a "manager-managed" LLC. Most LLC statutes and the ULLCA provide that unless the articles of organization specify otherwise, an LLC is assumed to be member managed [ULLCA 203(a)(6)].

PARTICIPATION IN MANAGEMENT In a *member-managed* LLC, all of the members participate in management, and decisions are made by majority vote [ULLCA 404(a)]. In a *manager-managed* LLC, the members designate a group of persons to manage the firm. The management group may consist of only members, both members and nonmembers, or only nonmembers. Managers in a manager-managed LLC owe fiduciary duties to the LLC and its members, including the duty of loyalty and the duty of care

[ULLCA 409(a), 409(h)], just as corporate directors and officers owe fiduciary duties to the corporation and its shareholders.

OPERATING PROCEDURES The members of an LLC can include provisions governing decision-making procedures in their operating agreement. For example, the agreement can include procedures for choosing or removing managers. Although most LLC statutes are silent on this issue, the ULLCA provides that members may choose and remove managers by majority vote [ULLCA 404(b)(3)]. The members can also include in the agreement provisions designating when and for what purposes members' meetings will be held, although in contrast to corporate laws, most state LLC statutes do not require formal meetings.

Members may also specify in their agreement how voting rights will be apportioned. If they do not, LLC statutes in most states provide that voting rights are apportioned according to each member's capital contributions. Some states provide that, in the absence of an agreement to the contrary, each member has one vote.

SECTION 3 | Limited Liability Partnerships

The **limited liability partnership (LLP)** is a hybrid form of business designed mostly for professionals who normally do business as partners in a partnership. The major advantage of the LLP is that it allows a partnership to continue as a pass-through entity for tax purposes but limits the personal liability of the partners.

The first state to enact an LLP statute was Texas, in 1991. Other states quickly followed suit, and by 1997, virtually all of the states had enacted LLP statutes. LLPs must be formed and operated in compliance with state statutes, which may include provisions of the UPA. The appropriate form must be filed with a central state agency, usually the secretary of state's office, and the business's name must include either "Limited Liability Partnership" or "LLP" [UPA 1001, 1002]. In addition, LLPs must file annual reports with the state to remain qualified as an LLP in that state [UPA 1003]. In most states, it is relatively easy to convert a traditional partnership into an LLP because the firm's basic organizational structure remains the same. Additionally, all of the statutory and common law rules governing partnerships still apply (apart from those modified by the LLP statute). Normally, LLP statutes are simply amendments to a state's already existing partnership law.

The LLP is especially attractive for two categories of enterprises: professional services and family businesses. Professional service firms include law firms and accounting firms. *Family limited liability partnerships* (discussed later in this chapter) are basically business organizations in which the majority of the partners are related to each other.

LIABILITY IN AN LLP

Many professionals, such as attorneys and accountants, work together using the partnership business form. As stated in Chapter 16, a major disadvantage of the general partnership is the unlimited personal liability of its owner-partners. Partners are also subject to joint and several (individual) liability for partnership obligations. For example, suppose that a group of accountants is operating as a general partnership. A client sues one of the accountants for malpractice and wins a large judgment, and the firm's malpractice insurance is insufficient to cover the obligation. When the accountant's personal assets are exhausted, the personal assets of the other, innocent partners can be used to satisfy the judgment.

The LLP allows professionals to avoid personal liability for the malpractice of other partners. Although LLP statutes vary from state to state, generally each state statute limits the liability of partners in some way. For example, Delaware law protects each innocent partner from the "debts and obligations of the partnership arising from negligence, wrongful acts, or misconduct." In North Carolina, Texas, and Washington, D.C., the statutes protect innocent partners from obligations arising from "errors, omissions, negligence, incompetence, or malfeasance." The UPA more broadly exempts partners from personal liability for any partnership obligation, "whether arising in contract, tort, or otherwise" [UPA 306(c)]. Although the language of these statutes may seem to apply specifically to attorneys, virtually any group of professionals can use the LLP.

Questions remain, however, concerning the exact limits of this exemption from liability. One issue is whether limits on liability apply outside the state in which the LLP was formed. Another inquiry involves whether liability should be imposed to some extent on a negligent partner's supervising partner.

LIABILITY OUTSIDE THE STATE OF FORMATION Some states require that when an LLP formed in one state wants to do business in another state, the LLP must first register in the other state—for example, by filing a statement of foreign qualification [UPA 1102]. Because state LLP statutes are not uniform, a question arises in this situation. If the LLP statutes in the two states provide different liability protection, which law applies? Most states apply the law of the state in which the LLP was formed, even when the firm does business in another state, which is also the rule under UPA 1101.

SUPERVISING PARTNER'S LIABILITY A partner who commits a wrongful act, such as negligence, is liable for the results of the act. Also liable is the partner who supervises the party who commits a wrongful act. This is generally true for all types of partners and partnerships, including LLPs.

When the partners are members of an LLP and more than one member is negligent, there is a question as to how liability is to be shared. Is each partner jointly and severally liable for the entire result, as a general partner would be in most states? Some states provide for proportionate liability—that is, for separate determinations of the negligence of the partners.[1] The American Institute of Certified Public Accountants supports the enactment of proportionate liability statutes.[2]

For example, suppose that accountants Don and Jane are partners in an LLP, with Don supervising Jane. Jane negligently fails to file tax returns for their client, Centaur Tools. Centaur files a suit against Don and Jane. In a state that does not allow for proportionate liability, Don can be held liable for the entire loss. Under a proportionate liability statute, Don will be liable for no more than his portion of the responsibility for the missed tax deadline. (Even if Jane settles the case quickly, Don will still be liable for his portion.)

FAMILY LIMITED LIABILITY PARTNERSHIPS

A **family limited liability partnership (FLLP)** is a limited liability partnership in which the majority of the partners are persons related to each other—spouses, parents, or siblings, for example. A person acting in a fiduciary capacity for persons so related can also be a partner. All of the partners must be natural persons (as opposed to legal persons, such as corporations) or persons acting in a fiduciary capacity for the benefit of natural persons.

Probably the most significant use of the FLLP form of business organization is in agriculture. Family-owned farms sometimes find this form to their benefit. The FLLP offers the same advantages as other LLPs with certain additional advantages—such as, in Iowa, an exemption from real estate transfer taxes when partnership real estate is transferred among partners.[3]

SECTION 4 | Limited Partnerships

We now look at a business organizational form that limits the liability of *some* of its owners—the **limited partnership (LP).** Limited partnerships originated in medieval Europe and have been existence in the

United States since the early 1800s. In many ways, limited partnerships are like the general partnerships discussed in Chapter 16, but they differ from general partnerships in several ways. Because of this, they are sometimes referred to as *special partnerships*.

A limited partnership consists of at least one **general partner** and one or more **limited partners.** A general partner assumes management responsibility for the partnership and thus has full responsibility for the partnership and for all its debts. A limited partner contributes cash or other property and owns an interest in the firm but does not undertake any management responsibilities and is not personally liable for partnership debts beyond the amount of his or her investment. A limited partner can forfeit limited liability by taking part in the management of the business. A comparison of the characteristics of general partnerships and limited partnerships appears in Exhibit 17–1.[4]

Until 1976, the law governing limited partnerships in all states except Louisiana was the Uniform Limited Partnership Act (ULPA). Since 1976, most states and the District of Columbia have adopted the revised version of the ULPA, known as the Revised Uniform Limited Partnership Act (RULPA). Because the RULPA is the dominant law governing limited partnerships in the United States, we will refer to the RULPA in the following discussion.

FORMATION OF A LIMITED PARTNERSHIP

In contrast to the informal, private, and voluntary agreement that usually suffices for a general partnership, the formation of a limited partnership is a public and formal proceeding that must follow statutory requirements.[5] In this regard, a limited partnership resembles a corporation more than it does a general partnership. A limited partnership must have at least one general partner and one limited partner, as mentioned previously. Additionally, the partners must sign a **certificate of limited partnership,** which requires information similar to that found in a corporate charter (see Chapter 18). The certificate must be filed with

1. See, for example, Colorado Revised Statutes Annotated Section 13-21-111.5(1) and Utah Code Annotated Section 78-27-39.
2. Public Oversight Board of the SEC Practice Section, AICPA, *In the Public Interest: Issues Confronting the Accounting Profession* (New York: AICPA, March 5, 1993), Recommendation I-1.
3. Iowa Statutes Section 428A.2.

4. Under the UPA, a general partnership can be converted into a limited partnership and vice versa [UPA 902, 903]. The UPA also provides for the merger of a general partnership with one or more general or limited partnerships [UPA 905].
5. For a case illustrating the importance of complying with these statutory requirements, see *Miller v. Department of Revenue, State of Oregon,* 327 Or. 129, 958 P.2d 833 (1998).

EXHIBIT 17-1 A Comparison of General Partnerships and Limited Partnerships

CHARACTERISTIC	GENERAL PARTNERSHIP (UPA)	LIMITED PARTNERSHIP (RULPA)
Creation	By agreement of two or more persons to carry on a business as co-owners for profit.	By agreement of two or more persons to carry on a business as co-owners for profit. Must include one or more general partners and one or more limited partners. Filing of a certificate with the secretary of state is required.
Sharing of Profits and Losses	By agreement; or, in the absence of agreement, profits are shared equally by the partners, and losses are shared in the same ratio as profits.	Profits are shared as required in the certificate of limited partnership, and losses are shared likewise, up to the amount of the limited partners' capital contributions. In the absence of a provision in the certificate, profits and losses are shared on the basis of percentages of capital contributions.
Liability	Unlimited personal liability of all partners.	Unlimited personal liability of all general partners; limited partners liable only to the extent of their capital contributions.
Capital Contribution	No minimum or mandatory amount; set by agreement.	Set by agreement.
Management	By agreement; or, in the absence of agreement, all partners have an equal voice.	General partner or partners only. Limited partners have no voice or else are subject to liability as general partners (but only if a third party has reason to believe that the limited partner is a general partner). A limited partner may act as an agent or employee of the partnership and vote on amending the certificate or on the sale or dissolution of the partnership.
Duration	Terminated by agreement of the partners, but (in many states) can continue to do business even when a partner dissociates from the partnership.	By agreement in the certificate or by retirement, death, or mental incompetence of a general partner in the absence of the right of the other general partners to continue the partnership. Death of a limited partner, unless he or she is the only remaining limited partner, does not terminate the partnership.
Distribution of Assets on Liquidation— Order of Priorities	1. Payment of debts, including those owed to partner and nonpartner creditors. 2. Return of capital contributions and distribution of profit to partners.	1. Outside creditors and partner creditors. 2. Partners and former partners entitled to distributions of partnership assets. 3. Unless otherwise agreed, return of capital contributions and distribution of profit to partners.

the designated state official—under the RULPA, the secretary of state. The certificate is usually open to public inspection.

RIGHTS AND LIABILITIES OF PARTNERS

General partners, unlike limited partners, are personally liable to the partnership's creditors; thus, at least one general partner is necessary in a limited partnership so that someone has personal liability. This policy can be circumvented in states that allow a corporation to be the general partner in a partnership. Because the corporation has limited liability by virtue of corporation statutes, if a corporation is the general partner, no one in the limited partnership has personal liability.

RIGHTS OF LIMITED PARTNERS Subject to the limitations that will be discussed shortly, limited partners have essentially the same rights as general partners, including the right of access to partnership books and the right to other information regarding partnership business. On dissolution of the partnership, limited partners are entitled to a return of their contributions in accordance with the partnership certificate [RULPA 201(a)(10)]. They can also assign their interests subject to the certificate [RULPA 702, 704].

The RULPA provides that a limited partner has the right to sue an outside party on behalf of the firm if the general partners with authority to do so have refused to file suit [RULPA 1001].[6] In addition, investor protection legislation, such as securities laws (discussed in Chapter 28), may give some protection to limited partners.

LIABILITIES OF LIMITED PARTNERS In contrast to the personal liability of general partners, the liability of a limited partner is limited to the capital that she or he contributes or agrees to contribute to the partnership [RULPA 502].

A limited partnership is formed by good faith compliance with the requirements for signing and filing the certificate, even if it is incomplete or defective. When a limited partner discovers a defect in the formation of the limited partnership, he or she can avoid future liability by causing an appropriate amendment or certificate to be filed or by renouncing an interest in the profits of the partnership [RULPA 304]. If the limited partner takes neither of these actions on discovery of the defect, however, the partner can be held personally liable by the firm's creditors. Liability for false statements in a partnership certificate runs in favor of persons relying on the false statements and against partners who know of the falsity but still sign the certificate [RULPA 207].

LIMITED PARTNERS AND MANAGEMENT Limited partners enjoy limited liability so long as they do not participate in management [RULPA 303]. A limited partner who participates in management will be just as liable as a general partner to any creditor who transacts business with the limited partnership and believes, based on the limited partner's conduct, that the limited partner is a general partner [RULPA 303]. How much actual review and advisement a limited partner can engage in before being exposed to liability is an unsettled question.[7] A limited partner who knowingly permits his or her name to be used in the name of the limited partnership is liable to creditors who extend credit to the limited partnership without knowledge that the limited partner is not a general partner [RULPA 102, 303(d)].

Although limited partners cannot participate in management, this does not mean that the general partners are totally free of restrictions in running the business. The general partners in a limited partnership have fiduciary obligations to the partnership and to the limited partners, as the following case illustrates.

---

6. For a case from a jurisdiction that does *not* follow the RULPA in this respect, see *Energy Investors Fund, L.P. v. Metric Constructors, Inc.*, 351 N.C. 331, 525 S.E.2d 441 (2000).

7. The question is unsettled partly because state laws differ on this issue. Factors to be considered under the RULPA are listed in RULPA 303(b), (c).

CASE 17.3   Smith v. Fairfax Realty, Inc.

Supreme Court
of Utah, 2003.
82 P.3d 1064.

PARRISH, Justice:

*   *   *   *

*   *   * In 1984, Price [Development Company] purchased a thirty-three-acre parcel of property in Clovis, New Mexico, from [Armand and Virginia Smith]. As part of the transaction, the Smiths received a 15% limited partnership interest in each of two partnerships formed to build and operate [the North Plains Mall] on the property. Price became the general partner *   *   * .

*   *   *   *

In July 1993, Price informed the Smiths that *   *   * [it] wanted to include the North Plains Mall in [a real estate investment trust (REIT)] and told the Smiths that if the mall were included, the Smiths would have three distinct options for handling their 15% interest in the mall.

*   *   * Then, without further communication with the Smiths on the matter, Price proceeded to *   *   * transfer the mall property into the REIT, despite provisions in the partnership agreements that required the Smiths' consent for such transactions. *   *   *

CASE 17.3 | Continued

In the ensuing months, the Smiths repeatedly requested information regarding the status of their interests in the mall, but Price failed to disclose its unilateral decision to contribute the mall property to the REIT. Instead, Price fielded the Smiths' questions regarding the three options previously given to the Smiths, leading them to believe the options were still open, even though Price knew that its unilateral action had left the Smiths with no options. When the Smiths inquired as to the possible value of their holdings should the mall be included in the REIT, Price sent various conflicting estimates * * * .

* * * *

The Smiths brought suit [in a Utah state court] against Price * * * .

* * * [T]he jury reached a verdict in favor of the Smiths, finding that Price had breached * * * its fiduciary duty to the Smiths * * * . The jury awarded the Smiths $410,000 in compensatory damages, * * * $690,000 * * * in prejudgment interest * * * [and] punitive damages in the sum of $5,500,000 against Price [now doing business as Fairfax Realty, Inc. Price appealed to the Utah Supreme Court].

* * * *

* * * [We] analyze Price's misconduct in terms of maliciousness, reprehensibility, and wrongfulness. * * * [C]ertain wrongdoings are more egregious and blameworthy than others so as to justify larger awards. Deliberate false statements, acts of affirmative misconduct, and concealment of evidence of improper motive support more substantial awards, as do acts involving trickery and deceit. * * * *[E]conomic injury, especially when done intentionally through affirmative acts of misconduct, or when the target is financially vulnerable, can warrant a substantial penalty.* [Emphasis added.]

* * * [The trial] court detailed Price's prolonged, deliberate failure to inform the Smiths of the execution of the [transfer] agreements and the resulting unavailability of the three options that Price originally gave the Smiths regarding how their interests could be handled in the REIT transaction. The court also detailed Price's conflicting and "intentionally misleading" calculations of the value of the Smiths' interests in the mall property in the REIT. The calculations given to the Smiths differed significantly from the company's own calculations, which the company did not reveal until six years of litigation had ensued. Additionally, the court detailed Price's acts of financial misconduct, including payment of excessive fees to itself as general partner, commingling funds from different Price-owned properties, and accruing interest to itself on its own capital contributions while denying the Smiths interest on their contributions.

We agree with the trial court that Price's actions amount to affirmative misconduct showing deliberate misrepresentation and disregard of the rights of the Smiths. Price's actions accordingly support a substantial award * * * .

* * * *

* * * Throughout the creation of the REIT, Price was aware of its fiduciary obligations to the Smiths and of the consent clause written into the partnership agreements. Price consciously disregarded its obligations.

* * * *

With respect to Price's failure to disclose its dealings with the partnership property to the Smiths, Price asserts without elaboration that it avoided responding to the Smiths' inquiries on the advice of legal counsel. * * * [S]ubstantial evidence was presented at trial that Price did not want the Smiths to interfere with the REIT's formation by filing an adverse claim or a lawsuit * * * . Thus, Price's self-interested actions, made in the face of known fiduciary obligations, support a substantial * * * award.

* * * *

* * * *The fiduciary relationship of a general partner to a limited partner is one of loyalty, trust, disclosure, and confidence, calling for the utmost good faith and permitting no unfair benefits to the general partner as against the limited partner.* * * * [Emphasis added.]

Price failed as a fiduciary to deal fairly with the Smiths and their partnership interests. * * * The Smiths rightly expected a greater degree of candor and loyalty than they received. * * *

* * * *

We affirm * * * the jury's award * * * . We remand to the [lower] court for a determination of the proper amount of the [interest on the award and of the costs and attorneys' fees required by the partnership agreements].

CONTINUED ▶

CASE 17.3 | Continued

QUESTIONS

1. Why does the law impose fiduciary obligations on general partners?
2. What is the motivation for a general partner to breach its fiduciary obligations to the limited partners?

DISSOLUTION

A limited partnership is dissolved in much the same way as an ordinary partnership (see Chapter 16). The retirement, death, or mental incompetence of a general partner can dissolve the partnership, but not if the business can be continued by one or more of the other general partners in accordance with their certificate or by the consent of all of the members [RULPA 801]. The death or assignment of interest of a limited partner does not dissolve the limited partnership [RULPA 702, 704, 705]. A limited partnership can be dissolved by court decree [RULPA 802].

Bankruptcy or the withdrawal of a general partner dissolves a limited partnership. Bankruptcy of a limited partner, however, does not dissolve the partnership unless it causes the bankruptcy of the limited partnership. The retirement of a general partner causes a dissolution unless the members consent to a continuation by the remaining general partners or unless this contingency is provided for in the certificate.

On dissolution, creditors' rights, including those of partners who are creditors, take first priority. After that, partners and former partners receive unpaid distributions of partnership assets and, except as otherwise agreed, amounts representing returns on their contributions and amounts proportionate to their shares of the distributions [RULPA 804].

LIMITED LIABILITY LIMITED PARTNERSHIPS

A **limited liability limited partnership (LLLP)** is a type of limited partnership. An LLLP differs from a limited partnership in that a general partner in an LLLP has the same liability as a limited partner; that is, the liability of all partners is limited to the amount of their investments in the firm.

A few states provide expressly for LLLPs.[8] In states that do not provide for LLLPs but do allow for limited partnerships and limited liability partnerships, a limited partnership should probably still be able to register with the state as an LLLP.

---

8. See, for example, Colorado Revised Statutes Annotated Section 7-62-109. Other states that provide expressly for limited liability limited partnerships include Delaware, Florida, Missouri, Pennsylvania, Texas, and Virginia.

REVIEWING LIMITED LIABILITY COMPANIES AND LIMITED PARTNERSHIPS

The city of Papagos, Arizona, had a deteriorating bridge in need of repair on a prominent public roadway. The city posted notices seeking proposals for an artistic bridge design and reconstruction. Davidson Masonry, LLC, which was owned and managed by Carl Davidson and his wife, Marilyn Rowe, decided to submit a bid for a decorative concrete project that incorporated artistic metalwork. They contacted Shana Lafayette, a local sculptor who specialized in large-scale metal designs, to help them design the bridge. The city selected their bridge design and awarded them the contract for a commission of $184,000. Davidson Masonry and Lafayette then entered into an agreement to work together on the bridge project. Davidson Masonry agreed to install and pay for concrete and structural work, and Lafayette agreed to install the metalwork at her expense. They agreed that overall profits would be split, with 25 percent to Lafayette and 75 percent to Davidson Masonry. Lafayette designed numerous metal sculptures of salmon that were incorporated into colorful decorative concrete forms designed by Rowe, while Davidson performed the structural engineering. The group worked together successfully until the project was completed. Using the information presented in the chapter, answer the following questions.

REVIEWING LIMITED LIABILITY COMPANIES AND LIMITED PARTNERSHIPS—Continued

1. Would Davidson Masonry automatically be taxed as a partnership or a corporation?

2. What are the advantages and disadvantages of the limited liability company business form?

3. Is Davidson Masonry member managed or manager managed?

4. What principles that apply to partnerships would not apply to the business arrangement between Davidson Masonry and Lafayette?

TERMS AND CONCEPTS TO REVIEW

articles of organization 417

certificate of limited partnership 422

family limited liability partnership (FLLP) 422

general partner 422

limited liability company (LLC) 415

limited liability limited partnership (LLLP) 426

limited liability partnership (LLP) 421

limited partner 422

limited partnership (LP) 422

member 416

operating agreement 418

QUESTIONS AND CASE PROBLEMS

17-1. Giovanni, Lesa, and Tabir form a limited liability company. John contributes 60 percent of the capital, and Lesa and Tabir each contribute 20 percent. Nothing is decided about how profits will be divided. John assumes that he will be entitled to 60 percent of the profits, in accordance with his contribution. Lesa and Tabir, however, assume that the profits will be divided equally. A dispute over the issue arises, and ultimately a court has to decide the issue. What law will the court apply? In most states, what will result? How could this dispute have been avoided in the first place? Discuss fully.

17-2. Asher and Breem form a limited partnership with Asher as the general partner and Breem as the limited partner. Breem puts up $15,000, and Asher contributes some office equipment that he owns. A certificate of limited partnership is properly filed, and business is begun. One month later, Asher becomes ill. Instead of hiring someone to manage the business, Breem takes over complete management responsibilities. While Breem is in control, he makes a contract with Thaler involving a large sum of money. Asher returns to work. Because of other commitments, Asher and Breem breach the Thaler contract. Thaler contends that Asher and Breem will be personally liable for damages caused by the breach if the damages cannot be satisfied out of the assets of the limited partnership. Discuss this contention.

17-3. **QUESTION WITH SAMPLE ANSWER**

Dorinda, Luis, and Elizabeth form a limited partnership. Dorinda is a general partner, and Luis and Elizabeth are limited partners. Consider each of the separate events below, and discuss fully which event(s) constitute(s) a dissolution of the limited partnership.

(a) Luis assigns his partnership interest to Ashley.

(b) Elizabeth is petitioned into involuntary bankruptcy.

(c) Dorinda dies.

For a sample answer to this question, go to Appendix I at the end of this text.

17-4. Joe, a resident of New Jersey, wants to open a restaurant. He asks his friend Kay, an experienced attorney and a New Yorker, for her business and legal advice in exchange for a 20 percent ownership interest in the restaurant. Kay helps Joe negotiate a lease for the restaurant premises and advises Joe to organize the business as a limited liability company (LLC). Joe forms Café Olé, LLC, and with Kay's help, obtains financing. Then, the night before the restaurant opens, Joe tells Kay that he is "cutting her out of the deal." The restaurant proves to be a success. Kay wants to file a suit in a federal district court against Joe and the LLC. Can a federal court exercise jurisdiction over the parties based on diversity of citizenship? Explain.

17–5. LIABILITY OF GENERAL PARTNERS. Val Somers, Pat McGowan, and Brent Roberson were general partners in Vermont Place, a limited partnership formed to construct duplexes on a tract of land in Fort Smith, Arkansas. In 1984, the partnership mortgaged the property so that it could build there. McGowan owned a separate company, Advance Development Corp., which was hired by the partnership to develop the project. On September 3, 1984, Somers and Roberson discovered that McGowan had not been paying the suppliers to the project, including National Lumber Co., and had not been making the mortgage payments. The suppliers and the bank sued the partnership and the general partners individually. Discuss whether Somers and Roberson could be held individually liable for the debts incurred by McGowan. [*National Lumber Co. v. Advance Development Corp.*, 293 Ark. 1, 732 S.W.2d 840 (1987)]

17–6. FOREIGN LIMITED LIABILITY COMPANIES. Page, Scrantom, Sprouse, Tucker & Ford, a Georgia law firm, entered into a lease of office equipment in Georgia. The lessor assigned the lease to Danka Funding Co. (DFC), a New York limited liability company (LLC) with its principal place of business in New Jersey. DFC was registered as a foreign LLC in New Jersey for almost two years before the registration lapsed or was withdrawn. Under the applicable statute, a foreign LLC "may not maintain any action . . . in this State until it has registered." When Page defaulted on the lease, DFC filed a complaint in a New Jersey state court against Page for more than $100,000. In its response, Page pointed out that DFC was not registered as a foreign LLC. DFC reregistered. Asserting that DFC had not been registered when it filed its suit, Page asked a federal district court to dismiss the suit. Should the court grant this request? Why or why not? [*Danka Funding, L.L.C. v. Page, Scrantom, Sprouse, Tucker & Ford, P.C.*, 21 F.Supp.2d 465 (D.N.J. 1998)]

17–7. LIMITED LIABILITY PARTNERSHIPS. Mudge Rose Guthrie Alexander & Ferdon, a law firm, was organized as a general partnership but converted into a limited liability partnership (LLP). Mudge's principal place of business was New York, where it was organized, but some of its members were citizens of Maryland. The firm filed a suit in a federal district court to recover unpaid legal fees from Robert Pickett and other citizens of Maryland. The defendants filed a motion to dismiss on the ground that there was not complete diversity of citizenship, because some of the LLP members were Maryland citizens as well. Mudge argued that an LLP was like a corporation, and therefore the citizenship of the firm's members was irrelevant. How should the court rule? Explain. [*Mudge Rose Guthrie Alexander & Ferdon v. Pickett*, 11 F.Supp.2d 449 (S.D.N.Y. 1998)]

17–8. CASE PROBLEM WITH SAMPLE ANSWER

Westbury Properties, Inc., and others (collectively, the Westbury group) owned, managed, and developed real property. Jerry Stoker and The Stoker Group, Inc. (the Stokers), also developed real property. The Westbury group entered into agreements with the Stokers concerning a large tract of property in Houston County, Georgia. The parties formed limited liability companies (LLCs), including Bellemeade, LLC (the LLC group), to develop various parcels of the tract for residential purposes. The operating agreements provided that "no Member shall be accountable to the [LLC] or to any other Member with respect to [any other] business or activity even if the business or activity competes with the [LLC's] business." The Westbury group entered into agreements with other parties to develop additional parcels within the tract in competition with the LLC group. The Stokers filed a suit in a Georgia state court against the Westbury group, alleging, among other things, breach of fiduciary duty. What duties do the members of an LLC owe to each other? Under what principle might the terms of an operating agreement alter these duties? In whose favor should the court rule? Discuss. [*Stoker v. Bellemeade, LLC*, 272 Ga.App. 817, 165 S.E.2d 1 (2005)]

To view a sample answer for this case problem, go to this book's Web site at http://wleb.westbuslaw.com, select "Chapter 17," and click on "Case Problem with Sample Answer."

17–9. FOREIGN LIMITED LIABILITY COMPANIES. Walter Matjasich and Cary Hanson organized Capital Care, LLC, in Utah. Capital Care operated, and Matjasich and Hanson managed, Heartland Care Center in Topeka, Kansas. LTC Properties, Inc., held a mortgage on the Heartland facilities. When Heartland failed as a business, its residents were transferred to other facilities. Heartland employees who provided care to the residents for five days during the transfers were not paid wages. The employees filed claims with the Kansas Department of Human Resources for the unpaid wages. Kansas state law provides that a *corporate* officer or manager may be liable for a firm's unpaid wages, but protects limited liability company (LLC) members from personal liability generally and states that an LLC cannot be construed as a corporation. Under Utah state law, the members of an LLC can be personally liable for wages due the LLC's employees, however. Should Matjasich and Hanson be held personally liable for the unpaid wages? Explain. [*Matjasich v. State, Department of Human Resources*, 271 Kan. 246, 21 P.3d 985 (2001)]

17–10. LIMITED LIABILITY COMPANIES. Michael Collins entered into a three-year employment contract with E-Magine, LLC. In business for only a brief time, E-Magine lost a considerable sum of money. In terminating operations, which ceased before the term of the contract with Collins expired, E-Magine also terminated Collins's services. Collins signed a "final payment agreement," which purported to be a settlement of any claims that he might have against E-Magine in exchange for a payment of $24,240. Collins filed a suit in a New York state court against E-Magine, its members and managers, and others, alleging, among other things, breach of his employment contract. Collins claimed that signing the "final payment agreement" was the only means for him to obtain what he was owed for past sales commissions and asked the court to impose personal liability on the members and managers of E-Magine for breach of contract. Should the court grant this request? Why or why not? [*Collins v. E-Magine, LLC,* 291 A.D.2d 350, 739 N.Y.S.2d 121 (1 Dept. 2002)]

LAW | on the Web

For updated links to resources available on the Web, as well as a variety of other materials, visit this text's Web site at http://wleb.westbuslaw.com.

In the "Business & Human Resources" section of its home page, Nolo Press provides information on LLCs and limited partnerships. Go to

http://www.nolo.com

You can find information on filing fees for LLCs at

http://www.bizcorp.com

LEGAL RESEARCH EXERCISES ON THE WEB

Go to http://wleb.westbuslaw.com, the Web site that accompanies this text. Select "Chapter 17" and click on "Internet Exercises." There you will find the following Internet research exercises that you can perform to learn more about topics covered in this chapter.

Activity 17–1: **LEGAL PERSPECTIVE**
Limited Liability Companies

Activity 17–2: **MANAGEMENT PERSPECTIVE**
Limited Partnerships and Limited Liability Partnerships

CHAPTER 18

Corporations

The *corporation* is a creature of statute. A **corporation** is an artificial being, existing in law only and neither tangible nor visible. Its existence depends generally on state law, although some corporations, especially public organizations, can be created under federal law. Each state has its own body of corporate law, and these laws are not entirely uniform.

The Model Business Corporation Act (MBCA) is a codification of modern corporation law that has been influential in the codification of state corporation statutes. Today, the majority of state statutes are guided by the most recent version of the MBCA, often referred to as the Revised Model Business Corporation Act (RMBCA). You should keep in mind, however, that there is considerable variation among the regulations of the states that have used the MBCA or the RMBCA as a basis for their statutes, and several states do not follow either act. Because of this, individual state corporation laws should be relied on to determine corporate law rather than the MBCA or RMBCA.

In this chapter, we examine the corporate form of business enterprise. Under modern law, except as limited by charters, statutes, or constitutions, *a corporation can engage in any act and enter into any contract available to a natural person in order to accomplish the purposes for which it was created.* When a corporation is created, the express and implied powers necessary to achieve its purpose also come into existence.

SECTION 1 | The Nature of the Corporation

A corporation can consist of one or more *natural* persons (as opposed to the artificial "legal person" of the corporation) identified under a common name. The corporation substitutes itself for its shareholders in conducting corporate business and in incurring liability, yet its authority to act and the liability for its actions are separate and apart from the individuals who own it. (In certain limited situations, the "corporate veil" can be pierced—that is, liability for the corporation's obligations can be extended to shareholders, a topic to be discussed later in this chapter.)

CORPORATE PERSONNEL

Responsibility for the overall management of the corporation is entrusted to a board of directors, which is elected by the shareholders. The board of directors hires corporate officers and other employees to run the daily business operations of the corporation.

When an individual purchases a share of stock in a corporation, that person becomes a shareholder and an owner of the corporation. Unlike the members in a partnership, the body of shareholders can change constantly without affecting the continued existence of the corporation. A shareholder can sue the corporation, and the corporation can sue a shareholder. Additionally, under certain circumstances, a shareholder can sue on behalf of a corporation. The rights and duties of all corporate personnel will be examined later in this chapter.

CORPORATE TAXATION

Corporate profits are taxed by various levels of government. Corporations can do one of two things with corporate profits—retain them or pass them on to shareholders in the form of dividends. The corporation receives no tax deduction for dividends distributed to shareholders. Dividends are again taxable (except when they represent distributions of capital) as ordinary income to the shareholder receiving them. This double-taxation feature of the corporation is one of its major disadvantages.

NEW DIVIDEND RULE   The Jobs Growth Tax Relief Reconciliation Act of 2003[1] mitigates this double-taxation feature of corporations to some extent. Under this law, certain qualified dividends receive preferential federal tax treatment because the dividends are taxed at the same rate as a person's net long-term capital gains (ranging from 5 to 15 percent) rather than being taxed at the higher rate of the shareholder's ordinary income (up to 35 percent in 2005). To qualify for this reduced rate, the stock on which the dividends are paid must have been held for more than 60 days during the 120-day period beginning 60 days before the dividend is paid.[2] This rule does not apply to certain dividends from foreign corporations, dividends from tax-exempt entities, and dividends that do not satisfy the holding-period requirement. In addition, the law contains "sunset provisions" stipulating that the reduced tax rates will not be available on dividends paid after 2008.

RETAINED EARNINGS   Profits that are not distributed are retained by the corporation. These **retained earnings,** if invested properly, will yield higher corporate profits in the future and thus cause the price of the company's stock to rise. Individual shareholders can then reap the benefits of the retained earnings in the capital gains they receive when they sell their shares.

SECTION 2 | Classification of Corporations

Corporations can be classified in several ways. The classification of a corporation normally depends on its location, purpose, and ownership characteristics.

DOMESTIC, FOREIGN, AND ALIEN CORPORATIONS

A corporation is known as a *domestic corporation* in its home state (the state in which it incorporates). A corporation that is formed in one state but is doing business in another is referred to in that other state as a *foreign corporation*. A corporation formed in another country (say, Mexico) but doing business in the United States is referred to in the United States as an *alien corporation*.

A corporation does not have an automatic right to locate a business in a state other than its state of incorporation. A corporation normally is required to obtain a *certificate of authority* in any state in which it plans to do business. Once the certificate has been issued, the powers conferred on the corporation by its home state generally can be exercised in the other state. Should a foreign corporation do business without obtaining a certificate of authority, the state can fine the corporation; deny it the privilege of using state courts; and even hold its officers, directors, or agents personally liable for corporate obligations, including contractual obligations, incurred in that state.[3]

PUBLIC AND PRIVATE CORPORATIONS

A public corporation is one formed by the government to meet some political or governmental purpose. Cities and towns that incorporate are common examples. In addition, many federal government organizations, such as the U.S. Postal Service, the Tennessee Valley Authority, and AMTRAK, are public corporations.

Private corporations, in contrast, are created either wholly or in part for private benefit. Most corporations are private. Although they may serve a public purpose, as a public utility does, they are owned by private persons rather than by the government.

Note that private corporations whose stock is traded on stock exchanges or over the counter are often called *public companies*. This designation does not alter the fact that such corporations are privately owned.

NONPROFIT CORPORATIONS

Corporations formed for purposes other than making a profit are called *nonprofit* or *not-for-profit* corporations. Nonprofit corporations are usually (although not necessarily) private corporations. Private hospitals, educational institutions, charities, religious organizations, and the like are frequently organized as

---

1. Pub. L. No. 108-27, May 28, 2003, codified at 26 U.S.C.A. Sections 1, 24, 55, 57 note, 63, 163, 168, 179, 301, 306, 341, 338, 467, 531, 541, 584, 702, 854, 1255, 1257, 1400, 1445, 6429, 7518; and at 42 U.S.C.A. Sections 801, 1396d.
2. 26 U.S.C.A. Section 1(h)(11).

3. Note that most state statutes specify certain activities, such as soliciting orders via the Internet, that are not considered doing business within the state. Thus, a certificate of authority is not normally required for a foreign corporation to sell goods or services via the Internet or by mail.

nonprofit corporations. The nonprofit corporation is a convenient form of organization that allows various groups to own property and to form contracts without the individual members' being personally exposed to liability.

CLOSE CORPORATIONS

A **close corporation** is one whose shares are held by members of a family or by relatively few persons. Close corporations are also referred to as *closely held, family,* or *privately held* corporations. Usually, the members of the small group constituting a close corporation are personally known to one another. Because the number of shareholders is so small, there is no trading market for the shares. In practice, a close corporation is often operated like a partnership. Some states recognize this similarity and have enacted special statutory provisions that cover close corporations. These provisions expressly permit close corporations to depart significantly from certain formalities required by traditional corporation law.[4]

Additionally, Section 7.32 of the RMBCA—a provision added to the RMBCA in 1991 and adopted in several states—gives close corporations a substantial amount of flexibility in determining the rules by which they will operate. Under Section 7.32, if all of the shareholders of a corporation agree in writing, the corporation can operate without directors, bylaws, annual or special shareholders' or directors' meetings, stock certificates, or formal records of shareholders' or directors' decisions.[5]

MANAGEMENT OF CLOSE CORPORATIONS The close corporation has a single shareholder or a closely knit group of shareholders, who usually hold the positions of directors and officers. Management of a close corporation resembles that of a sole proprietorship or a partnership. As a corporation, however, the firm must meet whatever specific legal requirements are set forth in state statutes.

To prevent a majority shareholder from dominating a close corporation, the corporation may specify that action can be taken by the board only on approval of more than a simple majority of the directors. Typically, this would not be required for ordinary business decisions but only for extraordinary actions, such as changing the amount of dividends or dismissing an employee-shareholder. Additionally, in some cases, courts have held that majority shareholders owe a fiduciary duty to minority shareholders (discussed later in this chapter).

TRANSFER OF SHARES IN CLOSE CORPORATIONS
By definition, a close corporation has a small number of shareholders. The transfer of one shareholder's shares to someone else can thus cause serious management problems. The other shareholders may find themselves required to share control with someone they do not know or like.

Consider an example. Three brothers, Terry, Damon, and Henry Johnson, are the only shareholders of Johnson's Car Wash, Inc. Henry wants to sell his shares to an unknown third person. Terry and Damon object to Henry's idea, and a dispute ensues. What could they have done to avoid this situation?

—Restrictions in the Articles of Incorporation. The *articles of incorporation* could have restricted the transferability of shares to outside persons by stipulating that shareholders offer their shares to the corporation or other shareholders before selling them to an outside purchaser. In fact, a few states have statutes under which close corporation shares cannot be transferred unless certain persons—including shareholders, family members, and the corporation—are first given the opportunity to purchase the shares for the same price.

—Restrictions through a Shareholder Agreement. Another way that control of a close corporation can be stabilized is through the use of a shareholder agreement. A shareholder agreement can provide that when one of the original shareholders dies, her or his shares of stock in the corporation will be divided in such a way that the proportionate holdings of the survivors, and thus their proportionate control, will be maintained. Courts are generally reluctant to interfere with private agreements, including shareholder agreements. The effect of a close corporation's stock transfer restriction was at the heart of the following case.

---

4. For example, in some states (such as Maryland), the close corporation need not have a board of directors.
5. Shareholders cannot agree, however, to eliminate certain rights of shareholders, such as the right to inspect corporate books and records or the right to bring derivative actions (lawsuits on behalf of the corporation will be discussed later in this chapter).

CASE 18.1

United States
Court of Appeals,
Tenth Circuit, 2003.
320 F.3d 1081.
*http://www.kscourts.org/
ca10/wordsrch.htm*[a]

Salt Lake Tribune Publishing Co. v. AT&T Corp.

EBEL, Circuit Judge:

* * * *

* * * *The Salt Lake Tribune* was owned by the Kearns-Tribune Corporation, the principal shareholders of which were members of the Kearns-McCarthey family. * * * In April 1997, * * * the shareholders * * * decided to sell Kearns-Tribune Corporation to cable company Tele-Communications, Inc. ("TCI"), while receiving an option to repurchase the assets of *The Tribune* at a later date. [The family formed Salt Lake Tribune Publishing Company (Tribune Publishing) to own the option.] * * *

* * * *

* * * In 1999, TCI merged with AT&T Corporation, giving AT&T control over Kearns-Tribune Corporation [which became Kearns-Tribune Limited Liability Company, or KTLLC]. * * * Tribune Publishing * * * [filed] a complaint against AT&T in the United States District Court for the District of Utah in December 2000 [to enforce the option]. * * *

* * * *

* * * Tribune Publishing moved for a preliminary injunction * * * . The district court denied that motion * * * . Tribune Publishing [appealed to the U.S. Court of Appeals for the Tenth Circuit] * * * .

* * * *

In 1952, Deseret News and the predecessor in interest of KTLLC entered into the Joint Operating Agreement ("JOA"), the purpose of which was to share overhead expenses related to the production of *The Salt Lake Tribune* and the *Deseret News*. The JOA created the Newspaper Agency Corporation (NAC) to be the agent of KTLLC and Deseret News. * * * KTLLC and Deseret News each own 50% of the stock in the NAC * * * .

* * * [T]he JOA * * * [prohibits] the transfer by KTLLC or Deseret News of their ownership of the NAC stock to anyone else. * * *

* * * *

* * * [T]he district court * * * ruled that the stock transfer restriction is an obstacle to Tribune Publishing's claim for specific performance of the Option Agreement * * * .

* * * *

* * * Section 16-10a-627 of the Utah Code states:

* * * [A] corporation may impose restrictions on the transfer or registration of transfer of shares of the corporation * * * for any * * * reasonable purpose.

* * * Through the statute, Utah plainly embraces the validity of stock transfer restrictions. * * * *The only issue we must resolve * * * is whether the stock transfer restriction contained in * * * the JOA is designed to serve a reasonable purpose.* [Emphasis added.]

* * * *

The desire to limit the participation of outsiders in a close corporation like the NAC has long been recognized as a reasonable purpose for a share transfer restriction. * * * The particular significance of the "close" character of a corporation * * * lies very clearly in the fact that such a share transfer restriction is inherently more "reasonable" when applied to the stock of a corporation having only a few shareholders who are generally active in the business * * * than when imposed upon the stock of a corporation which has numerous shareholders who * * * do not participate actively in the day-to-day management and conduct of the corporation's affairs. [Emphasis added.]

* * * *

a. Type "Salt Lake Tribune Publishing Co." in the box and click on "Search." In the result, scroll to the name of the case and click on it to access the opinion. Washburn University School of Law Library in Topeka, Kansas, maintains this Web site.

CONTINUED

CASE 18.1 | Continued

Finding unpersuasive Tribune Publishing's arguments that * * * the JOA is invalid, we conclude that the stock transfer restriction is valid and enforceable.

* * * *

With regard to ownership of the Tribune Assets, we disagree with and reverse the district court's ruling * * * .

* * * The district court concluded that Tribune Publishing had a clear entitlement under the Option Agreement to receive "all, and not less than all" of the Tribune Assets upon exercise of the option. It felt, however, that it could not fashion the relief requested by Tribune Publishing: a decree of specific performance requiring the transfer of all of the Tribune Assets.

We find that the district court read too narrowly the relief sought by Tribune Publishing in its complaint. * * * We read Tribune Publishing's complaint as seeking whatever combination of equitable and legal relief the court may award to remedy a refusal by KTLLC to perform under the Option Agreement, including a failure to transfer to Tribune Publishing the NAC stock. It is a venerable [long-standing and respected] principle of our law that *for the violation of every right there should be a remedy,* and we should not lightly put down our obligation to determine whether appropriate remedies exist. [Emphasis added.]

* * * *

Accordingly, the district court's order denying Tribune Publishing's motion for a preliminary injunction is **AFFIRMED** in part and **REVERSED** in part and the matter **REMANDED** for further proceedings.

QUESTIONS

1. What is the relationship between NAC and its shareholders, and how is that relationship different from the usual relationship between a corporation and its shareholders?
2. The plaintiff in this case argued in part that the stock transfer restriction was a "restraint on alienation (transfer of ownership)," constituting "an unreasonable incursion on the free flow of commerce." How do the facts of this case show that this is not a valid argument?

S CORPORATIONS

A close corporation that meets the qualifying requirements specified in Subchapter S of the Internal Revenue Code can operate as an **S corporation.** If a corporation has S corporation status, it can avoid the imposition of income taxes at the corporate level while retaining many of the advantages of a corporation, particularly limited liability.

QUALIFICATION REQUIREMENTS FOR S CORPORATIONS Among the numerous requirements for S corporation status, the following are the most important:

1. The corporation must be a domestic corporation.
2. The corporation must not be a member of an affiliated group of corporations.
3. The shareholders of the corporation must be individuals, estates, or certain trusts. Nonqualifying trusts and partnerships cannot be shareholders. Corporations can be shareholders under certain circumstances.

4. The corporation must have no more than one hundred shareholders.
5. The corporation must have only one class of stock, although not all shareholders need have the same voting rights.
6. No shareholder of the corporation may be a nonresident alien.

BENEFITS OF S CORPORATIONS At times, it is beneficial for a regular corporation to elect S corporation status. Benefits include the following:

1. When the corporation has losses, the S election allows the shareholders to use the losses to offset other income.
2. When the stockholder's tax bracket is lower than the tax bracket for regular corporations, the S election causes the corporation's entire income to be taxed in the shareholder's bracket (because it is taxed as personal income), whether or not it is distributed. This is particularly attractive when the corporation

wants to accumulate earnings for some future business purpose.

Because of these tax benefits, many close corporations opted for S corporation status in the past. Today, however, the limited liability partnership and the limited liability company (discussed in Chapter 17) offer similar advantages plus additional benefits, including more flexibility in forming and operating the business. Hence, the S corporation is losing some of its significance.

PROFESSIONAL CORPORATIONS

Professionals such as physicians, lawyers, dentists, and accountants can incorporate. Professional corporations are typically identified by the letters *P.C.* (professional corporation), *S.C.* (service corporation), or *P.A.* (professional association). In general, the laws governing professional corporations are similar to those governing ordinary business corporations, but there are a few differences with regard to liability that deserve mention.

First, there is generally no limitation on liability for acts of malpractice or obligations incurred because of a breach of duty to a client or patient of the professional corporation. In other words, each shareholder in a professional corporation can be held liable for any malpractice liability incurred by the others within the scope of the corporate business. The reason for this rule is that professionals, in contrast to shareholders in other types of corporations, should not be allowed to avoid liability for their wrongful acts simply by virtue of incorporating. Second, under many states' statutes, professional persons are fully liable not only for their own negligent or wrongful acts, but also for the misconduct of any person under their direct supervision who is rendering professional services on behalf of the corporation. Third, a shareholder in a professional corporation is generally protected from contractual liability and liability arising from the tortious acts of other professionals that are unrelated to malpractice or breach of a duty to clients or patients.

SECTION 3 | Corporate Formation

Corporations generally come into existence through two steps: (1) preliminary organizational and promotional undertakings (particularly, obtaining capital for the future corporation) and (2) the legal process of incorporation.

PROMOTIONAL ACTIVITIES

Before a corporation becomes a reality, people invest in the proposed corporation as subscribers, and contracts are frequently made by *promoters* on behalf of the future corporation. **Promoters** are those who, for themselves or others, take the preliminary steps in organizing a corporation. One of the tasks of the promoter is to issue a **prospectus,** which is a document required by federal or state securities laws (see Chapter 28) that describes the financial operations of the corporation, thus allowing an investor to make an informed decision. The promoter also secures the corporate charter.

In addition, a promoter may purchase or lease property with a view toward selling it to the corporation when the corporation is formed. A promoter may also enter into contracts with attorneys, accountants, architects, and other professionals whose services will be needed in planning for the proposed corporation. Finally, a promoter induces people to purchase stock in the corporation.

PROMOTER'S LIABILITY As a general rule, a promoter is held personally liable on preincorporation contracts. Courts simply hold that promoters are not agents when a corporation has yet to come into existence. If, however, the promoter secures the contracting party's agreement to hold only the corporation (not the promoter) liable on the contract, the promoter will not be liable in the event of any breach.

Once the corporation is formed, the promoter remains personally liable until the corporation assumes the preincorporation contract by *novation.* Novation releases the promoter and makes the corporation liable for performing the contractual obligations. In some cases, the corporation adopts the promoter's contract by undertaking to perform it. Most courts hold that adoption in and of itself does not discharge the promoter from contractual liability. A corporation normally cannot ratify a preincorporation contract, as no principal was in existence at the time the contract was made.

SUBSCRIBERS AND SUBSCRIPTIONS Prior to the actual formation of the corporation, the promoter can contact potential individual investors, and they can agree to purchase shares of stock in the future corporation. This agreement is often referred to as a *subscription agreement,* and the potential investor is called a *subscriber.* Depending on state law, subscribers become shareholders as soon as the corporation is formed or as soon as the corporation accepts the agreement. This way, if corporation X becomes insolvent, the trustee in bankruptcy (see Chapter 15) can collect the consideration for any unpaid stock from a preincorporation subscriber.

Most courts view preincorporation subscriptions as continuing offers to purchase corporate stock. On or after its formation, the corporation can choose to accept the offer to purchase stock. Many courts also treat a subscription as a contract between the subscribers, making it irrevocable except with the consent of all of the subscribers. Under the RMBCA, a subscription is irrevocable for a period of six months unless the subscription agreement provides otherwise or unless all the subscribers agree to the revocation of the subscription. In other jurisdictions, the preincorporation subscriber can revoke the offer to purchase before acceptance without liability, however.

INCORPORATION PROCEDURES

The exact procedures for incorporation differ among the states, but the basic requirements are similar.

STATE CHARTERING   The first step in the incorporation procedure is to select a state in which to incorporate. Because state incorporation laws differ, individuals may look for the states that offer the most advantageous tax or incorporation provisions. Delaware has historically had the least restrictive laws. Consequently, many corporations, including a number of the largest, have incorporated there. Delaware's statutes permit firms to incorporate in Delaware and carry out their business and locate their operating headquarters elsewhere. (Most other states now permit this as well.) Closely held corporations, however, particularly those of a professional nature, generally incorporate in the state in which their principal stockholders live and work.

ARTICLES OF INCORPORATION   The primary document needed to begin the incorporation process is called the **articles of incorporation.** The articles include basic information about the corporation and serve as a primary source of authority for its future organization and business functions. The person or persons who execute the articles are called *incorporators* and will be discussed shortly. Generally, the information indicated below should be included in the articles of incorporation.

—*Corporate Name.*   The choice of a corporate name is subject to state approval to ensure against duplication or deception. State statutes usually require that the secretary of state run a check on the proposed name in the state of incorporation. Some states require the incorporators to run a check on the proposed name at their own expense. Once cleared, a name can be reserved for a short time (for a fee), pending the completion of the articles of incorporation. All corporate statutes require the corporation name to include the word *Corporation*, *Incorporated*, *Company*, or *Limited* or an abbreviation of one of these terms.

The new corporation's name may not be the same as, or deceptively similar to, the name of an existing corporation doing business in the state. For example, if an existing corporation is named General Dynamics, Inc., the state will not allow another corporation to be called General Dynamic, Inc., because that name is deceptively similar to the first and would impliedly transfer part of the goodwill established by the first corporate user to the second corporation. (See the discussion of trade names in Chapter 14.)

—*Nature and Purpose.*   The articles must specify the intended business activities of the corporation, and naturally, these activities must be lawful. Stating a general corporate purpose is usually sufficient to give rise to all of the powers necessary or convenient to the purpose of the organization. The articles can state, for example, that the corporation is organized "to engage in the production and sale of agricultural products." There is a trend toward allowing *corporate charters* (to be discussed shortly) to state that the corporation is organized for "any legal business," with no mention of specifics, to avoid the need for future amendments to the corporate articles.

Some states prohibit certain licensed professionals, such as physicians or lawyers, from forming a general business corporation and require them instead to incorporate as a professional corporation (discussed previously).[6] Also, in some states, businesses in certain industries—such as banks, insurance companies, or public utilities—cannot be operated in the general corporate form and are governed by special incorporation statutes.

---

6. See, for example, New Jersey Statutes Annotated Title 14A:17-1 *et seq.*

—Duration. A corporation can have perpetual existence under the corporate statutes of most states. A few states, however, prescribe a maximum duration, after which the corporation must formally renew its existence.

—Capital Structure. The articles generally set forth the capital structure of the corporation. A few state statutes require a very small capital investment for ordinary business corporations but a greater capital investment for those engaged in insurance or banking. The articles must also indicate the number of shares of stock the corporation is authorized to issue and may include other information, such as the valuation of the shares and the types or classes of stock authorized for issuance.

—Internal Organization. The articles should describe the internal management structure of the corporation, although this can be included in bylaws adopted after the corporation is formed. The articles of incorporation commence the corporation; the bylaws are formed after commencement by the board of directors. Bylaws are subject to, and cannot conflict with, the incorporation statute or the corporation's charter.

Under the RMBCA, the shareholders may amend or repeal bylaws. The board of directors may also amend or repeal bylaws unless the articles of incorporation or provisions of the incorporation statute reserve that power to the shareholders exclusively. Typical bylaw provisions describe voting procedures and requirements for shareholders, the election of the board of directors, the methods of replacing directors, and the manner and scheduling of shareholders' meetings and board meetings (these procedures will be discussed later in this chapter).

—Registered Office and Agent. The corporation must indicate the location and address of its registered office within the state. Usually, the registered office is also the principal office of the corporation. The corporation must give the name and address of a specific person who has been designated as an agent and who can receive legal documents on behalf of the corporation. These legal documents include service of process (the delivery of a court order requiring an appearance in court).

—Incorporators. Each incorporator must be listed by name and must also indicate an address. An incorporator is a person—often, the corporate promoter—who applies to the state on behalf of the corporation to obtain its corporate charter. The incorporator need not be a subscriber and need not have any interest at all in the corporation. Many states do not impose residency or age requirements for incorporators. States vary as to the required number of incorporators; it can be as few as one or as many as three. Incorporators are required to sign the articles of incorporation when they are submitted to the state; often, this is the incorporators' only duty. In some states, they participate at the first organizational meeting of the corporation.

CERTIFICATE OF INCORPORATION Once the articles of incorporation have been prepared, signed, and authenticated by the incorporators, they are sent to the appropriate state official, usually the secretary of state, along with the appropriate filing fee. In many states, the secretary of state will then issue a **certificate of incorporation** representing the state's authorization for the corporation to conduct business. (This may also be called the **corporate charter**.) The certificate and a copy of the articles are returned to the incorporators. The incorporators then hold the initial organizational meeting, which completes the details of incorporation.

FIRST ORGANIZATIONAL MEETING The first organizational meeting is often provided for in the articles of incorporation but is not held until after the charter is actually granted. At this meeting, the incorporators elect the first board of directors and complete the routine business of incorporation (pass bylaws, issue stock, and so forth). Sometimes, the meeting is held after the election of the board of directors, and the business to be transacted depends on the requirements of the state's incorporation statute, the nature of the business, the provisions made in the articles, and the desires of the promoters.

Adoption of bylaws—the internal rules of management for the corporation—is probably the most important function of the first organizational meeting. The shareholders, directors, and officers must abide by the bylaws in conducting corporate business. Corporate employees and third persons dealing with the corporation are not bound by the bylaws, however, unless they have reason to be familiar with them.

SECTION 4 | Improper Incorporation

The procedures for incorporation are very specific. If they are not followed precisely, others may be able to challenge the existence of the corporation. Errors in incorporation procedures can become important when, for example, a third person who is attempting to enforce a contract or bring suit for a tort injury fortuitously learns of them. On the basis of improper incorporation, the plaintiff could seek to make the would-be shareholders personally liable. Also, when the corporation attempts to enforce a contract against a defaulting party, if the defaulting party learns of a defect in the incorporation procedures, he or she may be able to avoid liability on that ground.

To prevent injustice, the courts will sometimes attribute corporate existence to an improperly formed corporation by holding it to be a *de jure* corporation or a *de facto* corporation, as discussed below. In some circumstances, corporation by estoppel may also occur.

DE JURE AND DE FACTO CORPORATIONS

In the event of substantial compliance with all conditions precedent to incorporation, a corporation is said to have *de jure* existence in law. In most states and under RMBCA 2.03(b), the certificate of incorporation is viewed as conclusive evidence that all mandatory statutory provisions have been met. This means that the corporation is properly formed, and only the state, not a third party, can attack its existence. If, for example, an incorporator's address was incorrectly listed, the corporation was improperly formed. The law, however, does not regard such inconsequential procedural defects as detracting from substantial compliance, and courts will uphold the *de jure* status of the corporate entity.

Sometimes, there is a defect in complying with statutory mandates—for example, the corporate charter may have expired. Under these circumstances, the corporation may have *de facto* status, meaning that its existence cannot be challenged by third parties (except the state). The following elements are required for *de facto* status:

1. There must be a state statute under which the corporation can be validly incorporated.
2. The parties must have made a good faith attempt to comply with the statute.

3. The enterprise must already have undertaken to do business as a corporation.

CORPORATION BY ESTOPPEL

If an association that is neither an actual corporation nor a *de facto* or *de jure* corporation holds itself out as being a corporation, it will be estopped from denying corporate status in a lawsuit by a third party. This situation usually arises when a third party contracts with a business entity that claims to be a corporation but does not hold a certificate of incorporation. When justice requires, the courts treat an alleged corporation as if it were an actual corporation for the purpose of determining the rights and liabilities in particular circumstances. Corporation by estoppel is thus determined by the situation. The recognition of corporate status does not extend beyond the resolution of the problem at hand.

SECTION 5 | Disregarding the Corporate Entity

Occasionally, the owners use a corporate entity to perpetrate a fraud, circumvent the law, or in some other way accomplish an illegitimate objective. In these situations, the court will ignore the corporate structure and **pierce the corporate veil,** thus exposing the shareholders to personal liability. In other words, when the facts show that great injustice would result from the use of a corporation to avoid individual responsibility, a court will look behind the corporate structure to the individual stockholder.

The following are some of the factors that frequently cause the courts to pierce the corporate veil:

1. A party is tricked or misled into dealing with the corporation rather than the individual.
2. The corporation is set up never to make a profit or always to be insolvent, or it is too "thinly" capitalized—that is, it has insufficient capital at the time it is formed to meet its prospective debts or potential liabilities.
3. Statutory corporate formalities, such as holding required corporation meetings, are not followed.
4. Personal and corporate interests are mixed together, or **commingled,** to the extent that the corporation has no separate identity.

As the next case illustrates, sometimes more than one of these factors is present.

CASE 18.2

In re Flutie New York Corp.

BACKGROUND AND FACTS *In 1990, Michael Flutie created MFME Model Management Company (MFME), doing business as "Company Management," to represent fashion models for all purposes, including the entertainment business. MFME's offices were in New York City, New York. In 1995, Michael transferred MFME's assets to Flutie New York Corporation (Flutie N.Y.), a company that Michael and his mother Victoria had created one year earlier. Flutie N.Y. performed the same services for the same models at the same address, and also did business as Company Management. Michael's father, Albert, was the sole shareholder and president of Flutie N.Y., but Michael was responsible for all major decisions involving the company. Flutie N.Y. did not follow any corporate formalities—there were no board meetings, shareholders' meetings, or shareholder votes—but did pay Albert's and Michael's personal expenses. In 2001, Michael transferred the assets of Flutie N.Y. to Flutie Media Corporation, a firm that he and Albert had created in 1999. The next year, Flutie N.Y. filed a petition in a federal bankruptcy court to declare bankruptcy. David Kittay, the court-appointed trustee, filed a suit against Michael, in part seeking to pierce the corporate veil and hold him liable for all of Flutie N.Y.'s debts, including more than $2.7 million in creditors' claims.*

IN THE LANGUAGE OF THE COURT

BURTON R. LIFLAND, Bankruptcy Judge.

* * * *

Here, the elements present warrant a finding of individual liability under [a theory that personal and corporate business were commingled] against Michael Flutie. Evidence reflects that Michael Flutie was using Flutie N.Y. and then later Flutie Media, to suit his own needs, and was using corporate funds for his own personal use. It is clear that Michael Flutie had exclusive control over the operations of Flutie N.Y., and with this control he committed wrongful acts which resulted in significant losses by Flutie N.Y.

* * * I find that the transfers to Michael Flutie, as well as the transfers to Albert Flutie on behalf of Michael, were made without fair consideration to Flutie N.Y. The facts are clear that Michael Flutie abused the corporate form and thereby, harmed Flutie N.Y.

Further, there is sufficient evidence that Flutie Media acted as the alter ego of Flutie N.Y. Flutie N.Y. fraudulently transferred model management contracts and/or its arrangements for the services of the models it represented to Flutie Media for no consideration. Flutie Media, under the control of Michael Flutie, continued to operate a modeling agency, continued to represent themselves to the public as Company Management, and continued to earn commissions on the work performed by the former Flutie N.Y. models.

Sufficient factors are also present to warrant the piercing of the corporate veil and a finding that Michael Flutie is liable for any and all damages suffered by Flutie N.Y. It is clear from the evidence adduced [provided] during discovery that no corporate formalities were followed. There were no board of directors' meetings, no board meetings or votes, and stock certificates were never issued.

Several entities shared common office space with Flutie N.Y. without paying rent, including Flutie Media * * * .

Another factor to consider when determining whether to pierce the corporate veil is inadequate capitalization. It is clear from the books and records of Flutie N.Y. that from at least December 31, 1997, through December 31, 2000, the company's liabilities exceeded its assets. In addition, the company had income losses on its income statements in 1995, 1996, 1997, 1998, and 2000. These factors illustrate that from the beginning of the corporation, the business was undercapitalized. [Emphasis added.]

Michael Flutie looted Flutie N.Y. and used the corporate veil as a sham through which to engage in conduct intended to deprive the Debtor's legitimate creditors of assets of the Debtor. * * *

* * * *

CONTINUED

CASE 18.2 | Continued Based on the facts alleged, the Trustee has provided the Court with the requisite proof to support a claim for alter ego against Michael Flutie, and Michael Flutie is, therefore, personally responsible for all of the debts of the Debtor's Estate.

DECISION AND REMEDY *The court pierced the corporate veil and held Michael liable for all of Flutie N.Y.'s debts. The firm was too thinly capitalized, failed to follow corporate formalities, and was used as a "sham" to deprive its creditors of amounts that they were owed. Michael behaved as though the firm's assets were his, and ignored the effect of his actions on the firm and its creditors.*

WHAT IF THE FACTS WERE DIFFERENT? *If the corporation had observed corporate formalities, including board meetings, shareholders' meetings, and shareholder votes, would the result have been different? Explain.*

THE COMMINGLING OF PERSONAL AND CORPORATE ASSETS

To elaborate on the fourth factor in the preceding list, consider a close corporation that is formed according to law by a single person or by a few family members. In such a situation, the corporate entity and the sole stockholder (or family-member stockholders) must carefully preserve the separate status of the corporation and its owners. Certain practices invite trouble for the one-person or family-owned corporation: the commingling of corporate and personal funds; the failure to remit taxes, including payroll and sales taxes; and the shareholders' continuous personal use of corporate property (for example, vehicles).

LOANS TO THE CORPORATION

Corporation laws usually do not specifically prohibit a stockholder from lending funds to her or his corporation. When an officer, director, or majority shareholder lends the corporation funds and takes back security in the form of corporate assets, however, the courts will scrutinize the transaction closely. Any such transaction must be made in good faith and for fair value.

PERSONAL LIABILITY TO CREDITORS

When the corporate privilege is abused for personal benefit and the corporate business is treated in such a careless manner that the corporation and the shareholder in control are no longer separate entities, the court usually will require the shareholder to assume personal liability to creditors for the corporation's debts.

SECTION 6 | Directors, Officers, and Shareholders

Corporate directors, officers, and shareholders all play different roles within the corporate entity. Sometimes, actions that may benefit the corporation as a whole do not coincide with the separate interests of the individuals making up the corporation. In such situations, it is important to know the rights and duties of all participants in the corporate enterprise. The following sections focus on these rights and duties and the ways in which conflicts among corporate participants are resolved.

ROLE OF DIRECTORS

Every corporation is governed by a board of directors. A director occupies a position of responsibility unlike that of other corporate personnel. Directors are sometimes inappropriately characterized as *agents* because they act on behalf of the corporation. No individual director, however, can act as an agent to bind the corporation; and as a group, directors collectively control the corporation in a way that no agent is able to control a principal. Directors are sometimes incorrectly characterized as *trustees* because they occupy positions of trust and control over the corporation. Unlike trustees, however, they do not own or hold title to property for the use and benefit of others.

Few legal requirements exist concerning directors' qualifications. Only a handful of states impose minimum age and residency requirements. A director is sometimes a shareholder, but this is not a necessary qualification—unless, of course, statutory provisions or corporate articles or bylaws require ownership.

ELECTION OF DIRECTORS Subject to statutory limitations, the number of directors is set forth in the corporation's articles or bylaws. Historically, the minimum number of directors has been three, but today many states permit fewer. Indeed, the RMBCA permits corporations with fewer than fifty shareholders to eliminate the board of directors.

—Initial Board of Directors. The first board of directors is normally appointed by the incorporators on the creation of the corporation, or directors are named by the corporation itself in the articles. The initial board serves until the first annual shareholders' meeting. Subsequent directors are elected by a majority vote of the shareholders.

—Term of Office. The term of office for a director is usually one year—from annual meeting to annual meeting. Longer and staggered terms are permissible under most state statutes. A common practice is to elect one-third of the board members each year for a three-year term. In this way, there is greater management continuity.

—Removal of Directors. A director can be removed *for cause* (that is, for failing to perform a required duty), either as specified in the articles or bylaws or by shareholder action. Even the board of directors itself may be given power to remove a director for cause, subject to shareholder review. In most states, unless the shareholders have reserved the right at the time of election, a director cannot be removed without cause.

—Vacancies on the Board of Directors. Vacancies can occur on the board of directors because of death or resignation or when a new position is created through amendment of the articles or bylaws. In these situations, either the shareholders or the board itself can fill the position, depending on state law or on the provisions of the bylaws.

BOARD OF DIRECTORS' MEETINGS The board of directors conducts business by holding formal meetings with recorded minutes. The date on which regular meetings are held is usually established in the articles or bylaws or by board resolution, and no further notice is customarily required. Special meetings can be called, with notice sent to all directors.

Quorum requirements can vary among jurisdictions. (A **quorum** is the minimum number of members of a body of officials or other group that must be present in order for business to be validly transacted.) Many states leave the decision as to quorum requirements to the corporate articles or bylaws. In the absence of specific state statutes, most states provide that a quorum is a majority of the number of directors authorized in the articles or bylaws. Voting is normally done in person (unlike voting at shareholders' meetings, which can be done by proxy, as will be discussed later in this chapter).[7] The rule is one vote per director. Ordinary matters generally require a simple majority vote; certain extraordinary issues may require a greater-than-majority vote.

RIGHTS OF DIRECTORS A director of a corporation has a number of rights, including the rights of participation, inspection, compensation, and indemnification.

—Participation and Inspection. A corporate director must have certain rights to function properly in that position. The main right is one of participation—meaning that the director must be notified of board of directors' meetings so as to participate in them. As just pointed out, regular board meetings are usually established by the bylaws or by board resolution, and no notice of these meetings is required. If special meetings are called, however, notice is required unless waived by the director.

A director must have access to all of the corporate books and records to make decisions and to exercise the necessary supervision over corporate officers and employees. This right of inspection is virtually absolute and cannot be restricted.

—Compensation and Indemnification. Nominal sums are often paid as honorariums to directors. In many corporations, directors are also chief corporate officers (president or chief executive officer, for example) and receive compensation in their managerial positions. Most directors also gain through indirect benefits, such as business contacts, prestige, and other rewards. There is a trend toward providing more than nominal compensation for directors, especially in large corporations in which directorships can be

---

7. One state, Louisiana, allows a director to vote by proxy under certain circumstances. Most states, including California, Delaware, New York, and Texas, expressly permit companies to hold board meetings by conference call or similar means, as long as all participants can hear one another. Section 8.20 of the RMBCA also allows directors' meetings to be held by telephone conference. California permits a board of directors to conduct meetings via electronic video screens, as long as certain conditions are satisfied.

burdensome in terms of time, work, effort, and risk. Many states permit the corporate articles or bylaws to authorize compensation for directors, and in some cases the board can set its own compensation unless the articles or bylaws provide otherwise.

Corporate directors may become involved in lawsuits by virtue of their positions and their actions as directors. Most states permit a corporation to indemnify (guarantee reimbursement to) a director for legal costs, fees, and judgments involved in defending corporation-related suits. Many states specifically permit a corporation to purchase liability insurance for the directors and officers to cover indemnification. When the statutes are silent on this matter, the authority to purchase such insurance is usually considered to be part of the corporation's implied power.

DIRECTORS' MANAGEMENT RESPONSIBILITIES

Directors have responsibility for all policymaking decisions necessary to the management of all corporate affairs. The directors must act as a body in carrying out routine corporate business. One director has one vote, and customarily the majority rules. The general areas of responsibility of the board of directors include the following:

1. Authorization for major corporate policy decisions—for example, the initiation of proceedings for the sale or lease of corporate assets outside the regular course of business, the determination of new product lines, and the oversight of major contract negotiations and major management-labor negotiations.
2. Appointment, supervision, and removal of corporate officers and other managerial employees and determination of their compensation.
3. Financial decisions, such as the declaration and payment of dividends to shareholders and the issuance of authorized shares and bonds.

Most states permit the board of directors to elect an executive committee from among the directors to handle the interim management decisions between board of directors' meetings, as provided in the bylaws. The executive committee is limited to making management decisions about ordinary business matters.

The board of directors can delegate some of its functions to an executive committee or to corporate officers. In doing so, the board is not relieved of its overall responsibility for directing the affairs of the corporation, but corporate officers and managerial personnel are empowered to make decisions relating to ordinary, daily corporate affairs within well-defined guidelines.

ROLE OF CORPORATE OFFICERS AND EXECUTIVES

Officers and other executive employees are hired by the board of directors or, in rare instances, by the shareholders. In addition to carrying out the duties articulated in the bylaws, corporate and managerial officers act as agents of the corporation, and the ordinary rules of agency (as will be discussed in Chapter 19) normally apply to their employment. The qualifications required of officers and executive employees are determined at the discretion of the corporation and are included in the articles or bylaws. In most states, a person can hold more than one office and can be both an officer and a director of the corporation.

The rights of corporate officers and other high-level managers are defined by employment contracts, because these persons are employees of the company. Corporate officers, though, can normally be removed by the board of directors at any time with or without cause and regardless of the terms of the employment contracts—although in such cases the corporation may be liable for breach of contract. The duties of corporate officers are the same as those of directors, because both groups are involved in decision making and are in similar positions of control. Hence, officers and directors are viewed as having the same fiduciary duties of care and loyalty in their conduct of corporate affairs, a subject to which we now turn.

FIDUCIARY DUTIES OF DIRECTORS AND OFFICERS

Directors and officers are deemed fiduciaries of the corporation, because their relationship with the corporation and its shareholders is one of trust and confidence. As fiduciaries, directors and officers owe ethical—and legal—duties to the corporation and the shareholders. These fiduciary duties include the duty of care and the duty of loyalty.

DUTY OF CARE Directors and officers must exercise due care in performing their duties. The standard of *due care* has been variously described in judicial decisions and codified in many corporation codes. Generally, a director or officer is expected to act in good faith, to exercise the care that an ordinarily prudent person would exercise in similar circumstances, and to act in what he or she considers to be the best interests of the corporation. Directors and officers who have not exercised the required duty of care can be held liable for the harms suffered by the corporation as a result of their negligence.

—Duty to Make Informed and Reasonable Decisions.

Directors and officers are expected to be informed on corporate matters. To be informed, a director or officer must do what is necessary to become informed: attend presentations, ask for information from those who have it, read reports, review other written materials such as contracts—in other words, carefully study a situation and its alternatives. Depending on the nature of the business, directors and officers are often expected to act in accordance with their own knowledge and training. Most states and Section 8.30(b) of the RMBCA, however, allow a director to make decisions in reliance on information furnished by competent officers or employees, professionals such as attorneys and accountants, and even an executive committee of the board without being accused of acting in bad faith or failing to exercise due care if such information turns out to be faulty.

Directors are also expected to make reasonable decisions. For example, a director should not accept a *tender offer* (an offer to purchase shares in the company that is made by another company directly to the shareholders) with only a moment's consideration based solely on the market price of the corporation's shares.

—Duty to Exercise Reasonable Supervision.

Directors are expected to exercise a reasonable amount of supervision when they delegate work to corporate officers and employees. For example, suppose that a corporate bank director fails to attend any board of directors' meetings for five years, never inspects any of the corporate books or records, and generally neglects to supervise the efforts of the bank president and the loan committee. Meanwhile, a corporate officer, the bank president, makes various improper loans and permits large overdrafts. In this situation, the corporate director may be held liable to the corporation for losses resulting from the unsupervised actions of the bank president and the loan committee.

—Dissenting Directors.

Directors are expected to attend board of directors' meetings, and their votes should be entered into the minutes of corporate meetings. Unless a dissent is entered, the director is presumed to have assented. Directors who dissent are rarely held individually liable for mismanagement of the corporation. For this reason, a director who is absent from a given meeting sometimes registers with the secretary of the board a dissent to actions taken at the meeting.

DUTY OF LOYALTY *Loyalty* can be defined as faithfulness to one's obligations and duties. In the corporate context, the duty of loyalty requires directors and officers to subordinate their personal interests to the welfare of the corporation.

For example, directors may not use corporate funds or confidential corporate information for personal advantage. Similarly, they must refrain from putting their personal interests above those of the corporation. For instance, a director should not oppose a transaction that is in the corporation's best interest simply because its acceptance may cost the director her or his position.

Cases dealing with fiduciary duty typically involve one or more of the following:

1. Competing with the corporation.
2. Usurping (taking personal advantage of) a corporate opportunity.
3. Having an interest that conflicts with the interest of the corporation.
4. Engaging in insider trading—that is, using information that is not public to make a profit trading securities (as will be discussed in Chapter 28).
5. Authorizing a corporate transaction that is detrimental to minority shareholders.
6. Selling control over the corporation.

CONFLICTS OF INTEREST Corporate directors often have many business affiliations, and a director can sit on the board of more than one corporation. Of course, directors are precluded from entering into or supporting businesses that operate in direct competition with corporations on whose boards they serve. Their fiduciary duty requires them to make a full disclosure of any potential conflicts of interest that might arise in any corporate transaction.

—Disclosure Requirements.

Sometimes a corporation enters into a contract or engages in a transaction in which an officer or director has a personal interest. The director or officer must make a *full disclosure* of that interest and must abstain from voting on the proposed transaction. For example, Ballo Corporation needs office space. Stephan Colson, one of its five directors, owns the building adjoining the corporation's headquarters. He negotiates a lease with Ballo for the space, making a full disclosure to Ballo and the other four board directors. The lease arrangement is fair and reasonable, and it is unanimously approved by the other members of the corporation's board of directors. In such a case, the contract is valid.

The rule is one of reason; otherwise, directors would be prevented from ever giving financial assistance to the corporations they serve.

State statutes contain varying standards, but a contract will generally not be voidable if it was fair and reasonable to the corporation at the time it was made, if there was a full disclosure of the interest of the officers or directors involved in the transaction, and if the contract was approved by a majority of the disinterested directors or shareholders.

—Corporations with Common Directors. Often, contracts are negotiated between corporations having one or more directors who are members of both boards. Such transactions require great care, as they are closely scrutinized by the courts. (As will be discussed in Chapter 27, in certain circumstances—if two large corporations are competing with each other, for example—it may constitute a violation of antitrust laws for a director to sit on the boards of both companies.)

LIABILITY OF DIRECTORS AND OFFICERS

Directors and officers are exposed to liability on many fronts. Corporate directors and officers may be held liable for crimes and torts committed by themselves or by corporate employees under their supervision. Additionally, shareholders may perceive that the corporate directors are not acting in the best interests of the corporation and may sue the directors, in what is called a *shareholder's derivative suit*, on behalf of the corporation. (This type of action will be discussed later in this chapter, in the context of shareholders' rights.) Directors and officers are expected to exercise due care and to use their best judgment in guiding corporate management; if they do not, they may be held liable to the corporation for any resulting damages.

THE BUSINESS JUDGMENT RULE   Under the so-called **business judgment rule,** a corporate director or officer may be able to avoid liability to the corporation or to its shareholders for exercising poor business judgment. After all, directors and officers are not insurers of business success, and honest mistakes of judgment and poor business decisions on their part do not automatically make them liable to the corporation. The business judgment rule generally immunizes directors and officers from liability for the consequences of a decision that is within managerial authority, as long as the decision complies with management's fiduciary duties and as long as acting on the decision is within the powers of the corporation. Consequently, if there is a reasonable basis for a business decision, it is unlikely that the court will interfere with that decision, even if the corporation suffers as a result.

REQUIREMENTS FOR THE BUSINESS JUDGMENT RULE TO APPLY   To benefit from the business judgment rule, directors and officers must act in good faith, in what they consider to be the best interests of the corporation, and with the care that an ordinarily prudent person in a similar position would exercise in like circumstances. This requires an informed decision, with a rational basis, and with no conflict between the decision maker's personal interest and the interest of the corporation.

THE ROLE OF SHAREHOLDERS

The acquisition of a share of stock makes a person an owner and shareholder in a corporation. Shareholders thus own the corporation. Although they have no legal title to corporate property vested in the corporation, such as buildings and equipment, they do have an *equitable* (ownership) interest in the firm.

As a general rule, shareholders have no responsibility for the daily management of the corporation, although they are ultimately responsible for choosing the board of directors, which does have such control. Ordinarily, corporate officers and other employees owe no direct duty to individual stockholders. Their duty is to the corporation as a whole. A director, however, is in a fiduciary relationship to the corporation and therefore serves the interests of the shareholders in general. Ordinarily, there is no legal relationship between shareholders and creditors of the corporation. Shareholders can, in fact, be creditors of the corporation and have the same rights of recovery against the corporation as any other creditor.

In this section, we look at the powers, rights, and liabilities of shareholders, which may be established in the articles of incorporation and under the state's general incorporation law.

SHAREHOLDERS' POWERS   Shareholders must approve fundamental changes affecting the corporation before the changes can be implemented. Hence, shareholders are empowered to amend the articles of incorporation (charter) and bylaws, approve a merger or the dissolution of the corporation, and approve the sale of all or substantially all of the corporation's assets. Some of these powers are subject to prior board approval.

Election and removal of the board of directors are accomplished by a vote of the shareholders. The first board of directors is either named in the articles of incorporation or chosen by the incorporators to serve until the first shareholders' meeting. From that time on, selection and retention of directors are exclusively shareholder functions.

Directors usually serve their full terms; if they are not satisfactory, they are simply not reelected. Shareholders have the inherent power, however, to remove a director from office *for cause* (breach of duty or misconduct) by a majority vote.[8] Some state statutes even permit removal of directors without cause by the vote of a majority of the holders of outstanding shares entitled to vote.[9] Some corporate charters also expressly provide that shareholders, by majority vote, can remove a director at any time without cause.

SHAREHOLDERS' MEETINGS Shareholders' meetings must occur at least annually, and in addition, special meetings can be called to take care of urgent matters. Shareholders are notified of the date and hour of a shareholders' meeting in a written announcement that is sent a reasonable length of time prior to the date of the meeting.[10] Notices of special meetings must include a statement of the purpose of the meeting; business transacted at a special meeting is limited to that purpose.

SHAREHOLDER VOTING Shareholders exercise ownership control through the power of their votes.

—Quorum Requirements. For shareholders to act during a meeting, a quorum must be present. Generally, this condition is met when shareholders holding more than 50 percent of the outstanding shares are present. Corporate business matters are presented in the form of resolutions, which shareholders vote to approve or disapprove. If a state statute sets forth specific voting requirements, the corporation's articles or bylaws must be consistent with these statutory limitations. Some states provide that obtaining the unanimous written consent of shareholders is a permissible alternative to holding a shareholders' meeting.

Once a quorum is present, voting can proceed. A majority vote of the shares represented at the meeting is usually required to pass resolutions. Assume that Novo Pictures, Inc., has 10,000 outstanding shares of voting stock. Its articles of incorporation set the quorum at more than 50 percent of outstanding shares and provide that a majority vote of the shares present is necessary to pass on ordinary matters. Therefore, for this firm, at the shareholders' meeting, a quorum of stockholders representing more than 5,000 outstanding shares must be present to conduct business. If 6,000 shares are represented, a vote of 3,001 will be necessary, and so forth.

At times, more than a simple majority vote will be required either by statute or by corporate charter. Extraordinary corporate matters, such as a merger, a consolidation, or the dissolution of the corporation, require approval by a higher percentage of the representatives of all corporate shares entitled to vote, not just a majority of those present at that particular meeting.

—Voting Lists. A voting list is prepared by the corporation prior to each shareholders' meeting. Persons whose names appear on the corporation's stockholder records as owners are the ones ordinarily entitled to vote.[11] The voting list contains the name and address of each shareholder as shown on the corporate records on a given cutoff date, or *record date*. (The record date may be as much as seventy days before the meeting.) The voting list also includes the number of voting shares held by each owner. The list is usually kept at the corporate headquarters and is available for shareholder inspection.

—Cumulative Voting. Most states permit or require shareholders to elect directors by *cumulative voting*, a method of voting designed to allow minority shareholders representation on the board of directors.[12] When cumulative voting is used, the number of members

---

8. A director can often demand court review of removal for cause.
9. Most states allow *cumulative voting* (which will be discussed shortly) for directors. If cumulative voting is authorized, a director cannot be removed if the number of votes sufficient to elect him or her under cumulative voting is voted against his or her removal. See, for example, California Corporate Code Section 303A. See also Section 8.08(c) of the RMBCA.
10. The shareholder can waive the requirement of written notice by signing a waiver form. A shareholder who does not receive written notice but who learns of the meeting and attends without protesting the lack of notice is said to have waived notice by such conduct. State statutes and corporate bylaws typically set forth the time within which notice must be sent, what methods can be used, and what the notice must contain.
11. When the legal owner is deceased, bankrupt, incompetent, or in some other way under a legal disability, his or her vote can be cast by a person designated by law to control and manage the owner's property.
12. See, for example, California Corporate Code Section 708. Under the RMBCA, however, no cumulative voting rights exist unless the articles of incorporation so provide.

EXHIBIT 18-1 **Results of Cumulative Voting**

BALLOT	MAJORITY SHAREHOLDER VOTES			MINORITY SHAREHOLDER VOTES	DIRECTORS ELECTED
	Alomon	Beasley	Caravel	Dovrik	
1	10,000	10,000	1,000	9,000	Alomon, Beasley, Dovrik
2	9,001	9,000	2,999	9,000	Alomon, Beasley, Dovrik
3	6,000	7,000	8,000	9,000	Beasley, Caravel, Dovrik

of the board to be elected is multiplied by the total number of voting shares. The result equals the number of votes a shareholder has, and this total can be cast for one or more nominees for director. All nominees stand for election at the same time. When cumulative voting is not used, the entire board can be elected by a majority of shares at a shareholders' meeting.

Suppose, for example, that a corporation has 10,000 shares issued and outstanding. The minority shareholders hold only 3,000 shares, and the majority shareholders hold the other 7,000 shares. Three members of the board are to be elected. The majority shareholders' nominees are Alomon, Beasley, and Caravel. The minority shareholders' nominee is Dovrik. Can Dovrik be elected to the board by the minority shareholders?

If cumulative voting is allowed, the answer is yes. The minority shareholders have 9,000 votes among them (the number of directors to be elected times the number of shares equals 3 times 3,000, which equals 9,000 votes). All of these votes can be cast to elect Dovrik. The majority shareholders have 21,000 votes (3 times 7,000 equals 21,000 votes), but these votes have to be distributed among their three nominees. The principle of cumulative voting is that no matter how the majority shareholders cast their 21,000 votes, they will not be able to elect all three directors if the minority shareholders cast all of their 9,000 votes for Dovrik, as illustrated in Exhibit 18–1.

—Other Voting Techniques. A group of shareholders can agree in writing prior to a shareholders' meeting, in a *shareholder voting agreement*, to vote their shares together in a specified manner. Such agreements usually are held to be valid and enforceable. A shareholder can also appoint a voting agent and vote by proxy. A **proxy** is a written authorization to cast the shareholder's vote, and a person can solicit proxies from a number of shareholders in an attempt to concentrate voting power.

Another technique is for shareholders to enter into a **voting trust,** which is an agreement (a trust contract) under which legal title (recorded ownership on the corporate books) is transferred to a trustee who is responsible for voting the shares. The agreement can specify how the trustee is to vote, or it can allow the trustee to use his or her discretion. The trustee takes physical possession of the stock certificate and in return gives the shareholder a *voting trust certificate*. The shareholder retains all of the rights of ownership (for example, the right to receive dividend payments) except for the power to vote the shares.

RIGHTS OF SHAREHOLDERS

Shareholders possess numerous rights. A significant right—the right to vote their shares—has already been discussed. In addition to voting rights, a shareholder has the rights, based on ownership of stock, to receive stock certificates (depending on the jurisdiction), to purchase newly issued stock, to receive dividends, to inspect corporate records, to transfer shares (with some exceptions), to receive a proportionate share of corporate assets on corporate dissolution, and to file suit on behalf of the corporation. These rights will be discussed in the following subsections.

STOCK CERTIFICATES   A **stock certificate** is a certificate issued by a corporation that evidences ownership of a specified number of shares in the corporation. In jurisdictions that require the issuance of stock certificates, shareholders have the right to demand that the corporation issue certificates and record their names and addresses in the corporate stock record books. In most states, boards of directors may provide that shares of stock be uncertificated (that is, that no actual, physical stock certificates need be issued). In that circumstance, the corporation may be required to send the holders of uncertificated shares letters or some other form of notice containing the same information required to be included on the face of stock certificates.

Stock is intangible personal property, and the ownership right exists independently of the certificate itself. A stock certificate may be lost or destroyed, but ownership is not destroyed with it. A new certificate can be issued to replace one that has been lost or destroyed.[13] Notice of shareholders' meetings, dividends, and operational and financial reports are all distributed according to the recorded ownership listed in the corporation's books, not on the basis of possession of the certificate.

PREEMPTIVE RIGHTS   A **preemptive right** is a common law concept under which a preference is given to a shareholder over all other purchasers to subscribe to or purchase a prorated share of a new issue of stock. This allows the shareholder to maintain his or her portion of control, voting power, or financial interest in the corporation. Most statutes either (1) grant preemptive rights but allow them to be negated in the corporation's articles or (2) deny preemptive rights except to the extent that they are granted in the articles. The result is that the articles of incorporation determine the existence and scope of preemptive rights. Generally, preemptive rights apply only to additional, newly issued stock sold for cash and must be exercised within a specified time period (such as thirty days). In addition, they do not apply to **treasury shares**—shares that are authorized but that have not been issued.

For example, Tron Corporation authorizes and issues 1,000 shares of stock, and Omar Loren purchases 100 shares, making him the owner of 10 percent of the company's stock. Subsequently, Tron, by vote of its shareholders, authorizes the issuance of another 1,000 shares (amending the articles of incorporation). This increases its capital stock to a total of 2,000 shares. If preemptive rights have been provided, Loren can purchase one additional share of the new stock being issued for each share currently owned—or 100 additional shares. Thus, he can own 200 of the 2,000 shares outstanding, and his relative position as a shareholder will be maintained. If preemptive rights are not reserved, his proportionate control and voting power will be diluted from that of a 10 percent shareholder to that of a 5 percent shareholder because of the issuance of the additional 1,000 shares.

Preemptive rights can be very important for shareholders in close corporations. This is because of the relatively small number of shares and the substantial interest that each shareholder controls in a close corporation. Without preemptive rights, it would be possible for a shareholder to lose his or her proportionate control over the firm.

STOCK WARRANTS   Usually, when preemptive rights exist and a corporation is issuing additional shares, each shareholder is given **stock warrants,** which are transferable options to acquire a given number of shares from the corporation at a stated price. Warrants are often publicly traded on securities exchanges. When the warrant option is for a short period of time, the stock warrants are usually referred to as *rights*.

DIVIDENDS   A **dividend** is a distribution of corporate profits or income *ordered by the directors* and paid to the shareholders in proportion to their respective shares in the corporation. Dividends can be paid in cash, property, stock of the corporation that is paying the dividends, or stock of other corporations.[14]

State laws vary, but every state determines the general circumstances and legal requirements under which dividends are paid. State laws also control the sources of revenue to be used; only certain funds are legally available for paying dividends. Once declared, a cash dividend becomes a corporate debt enforceable at law like any other debt. Depending on state law, dividends may be paid from the following sources:

1. *Retained earnings*. All state statutes allow dividends to be paid from the undistributed net profits earned by the corporation, including capital gains from the sale of fixed assets. The undistributed net profits are called retained earnings.
2. *Net profits*. A few state statutes allow dividends to be issued from current net profits without regard to deficits in prior years.
3. *Surplus*. A number of state statutes allow dividends to be paid out of any kind of surplus.

—*Illegal Dividends.*   Sometimes dividends are improperly paid from an unauthorized account, or their payment causes the corporation to become insolvent. Generally, in such cases, shareholders must return illegal dividends only if they knew that the dividends were illegal when they received them. A dividend paid

---

13. For a lost or destroyed certificate to be reissued, a shareholder normally must furnish an *indemnity bond* (a guaranty of payment) to protect the corporation against potential loss should the original certificate reappear at some future time in the hands of a bona fide purchaser [UCC 8–302, 8–405(2)].

14. Technically, dividends paid in stock are not dividends. They maintain each shareholder's proportional interest in the corporation. On one occasion, a distillery declared and paid a "dividend" in bonded whiskey.

while the corporation is insolvent is automatically an illegal dividend, and shareholders may be liable for returning the payment to the corporation or its creditors. In all cases of illegal and improper dividends, the board of directors can be held personally liable for the amount of the payment. When directors can show that a shareholder knew a dividend was illegal when it was received, however, the directors are entitled to reimbursement from the shareholder.

—Directors' Failure to Declare a Dividend.   When directors fail to declare a dividend, shareholders can ask a court of equity for an injunction to compel the directors to meet and to declare a dividend. For the injunction to be granted, it must be shown that the directors have acted so unreasonably in withholding the dividend that their conduct is an abuse of their discretion.

Often, large cash reserves are accumulated for a bona fide purpose, such as expansion, research, or some other legitimate corporate use. The mere fact that sufficient corporate earnings or surpluses are available to pay a dividend is not enough to compel directors to distribute funds that, in the board's opinion, should not be distributed. The courts are hesitant to interfere with corporate operations and will not compel directors to declare dividends unless abuse of discretion is clearly shown.

INSPECTION RIGHTS   Shareholders in a corporation enjoy both common law and statutory inspection rights. The shareholder's right of inspection is limited, however, to the inspection and copying of corporate books and records for a *proper purpose*, provided the request is made in advance. Either the shareholder can inspect in person, or an attorney, accountant, or other type of assistant can do so as the shareholder's agent. The RMBCA requires the corporation to maintain an alphabetical voting list of shareholders with addresses and number of shares owned; this list must be kept open at the annual meeting for inspection by any shareholder of record.

The power of inspection is fraught with potential abuses, and the corporation is allowed to protect itself from them. For example, a shareholder can properly be denied access to corporate records to prevent harassment or to protect trade secrets or other confidential corporate information. Some states require that a shareholder must have held his or her shares for a minimum period of time immediately preceding the demand to inspect or must hold a minimum number of outstanding shares. The RMBCA provides that every shareholder is entitled to examine specified corporate records. A shareholder who is denied the right of inspection can seek a court order to compel the inspection.

The question in the following case was whether a shareholder who obtains access to corporate books and records that the company regards as confidential should be free to publicly disseminate information in those documents.

CASE 18.3   Disney v. Walt Disney Co.

Court of
Chancery of
Delaware. 2004.
857 A.2d 444.

BACKGROUND AND FACTS   *Roy Disney is a shareholder of Walt Disney Company, a Delaware corporation with its principal offices in Burbank, California. Disney was a director of the company until he resigned in November 2003. After his resignation, Roy Disney began a campaign to encourage other shareholders to vote "no" on the reelection of Michael Eisner and three other members of the board of directors at the company's March 2004 annual meeting. As part of this effort, in January, Disney sought access to corporate books and records related to compensation for the company's five senior executives. Before honoring this request, the company designated some of the information "confidential" and asked Disney not to publicly disseminate it. He agreed only to hold it in "strict confidence." On review of the material, however, Disney objected to the confidentiality designation. He filed a suit in a Delaware state court against the company, asking the court to order that the designation of the information as "confidential" was inappropriate.*

IN THE LANGUAGE OF THE COURT

LAMB, Vice Chancellor
* * * *
* * * Section 220 of the Delaware General Corporation Law provides every stockholder of a Delaware corporation acting for a proper purpose a powerful right to inspect the company's books and records. * * *

CASE 18.3 Continued

* * * *

* * * [T]he production of nonpublic corporate books and records to a stockholder making a demand pursuant to Section 220 should be conditioned upon a reasonable confidentiality order. * * * Counterposed to the duty to protect the rights of the stockholder, the court has the duty to safeguard the rights and legitimate interests of the corporation. * * * It follows that *the Court of Chancery is empowered to protect the corporation's legitimate interests and to prevent possible abuse of the shareholder's right of inspection by placing such reasonable restrictions and limitations as its deems proper on the exercise of the right.* * * * In fact, it is often the case that the Court of Chancery will condition its judgment in Section 220 cases on the entry of a reasonable confidentiality order to prevent the dissemination of confidential business information to "curiosity seekers." [Emphasis added.]

* * * *

Mr. Disney argues eloquently and forcefully for a * * * novel use of a Section 220 books and records demand—that of ferreting out [extracting] information for use in an ongoing public relations campaign challenging the truthfulness or completeness of a corporation's routine public disclosures, especially its disclosures relating to executive compensation. He argues that disclosure of the information at issue here will serve the best interests of the Company's stockholders "who, given the supposedly incomplete and misleading disclosures made by the Company, have under Delaware law an important right to receive a full and fair disclosure of facts." This is particularly true, he stresses, "where, as here, the disclosure pertains to the bases for a compensation committee's decisions to award enormous compensation packages to a public company's top executives."

In support of this argument, Mr. Disney * * * suggests that the stockholders' need to "know the whole truth" is especially urgent in this case because "there exists a 'crisis of confidence' in executive compensation in the United States that reflects a 'mistrust of the system.'" Thus, he argues, "requiring disclosure of the bases for senior executive compensation decisions in the context of a Section 220 case promotes good public policy."

* * * *

The court is unable to accept this expansive reading of Section 220. To begin with, despite Mr. Disney's invitation to do so, there is no basis in the language of the statute to limit the proposed use of Section 220 to executive compensation issues. Instead, the court would have to recognize a right to make a books and records demand for the purpose of investigating any well-grounded suspicion of mismanagement and then publicly disclosing information discovered from that investigation. In addition, the expansion for which Mr. Disney argues would extend equally to any single stockholder, not only to those thought to adequately represent the interests of the corporation or the stockholders as a whole. Moreover, a stockholder seeking to disclose non-public information in those circumstances would not be under the same fiduciary obligation as the corporation to make complete or candid disclosures. Instead, as is evident in this case, the disclosure sought to be made would likely relate to snippets of information gleaned from a few e-mails or internal memoranda that the stockholder contends are inconsistent with the corporation's public disclosures. Undoubtedly, any decision that permitted the public disclosure of that information would lead the corporation to disclose even more otherwise non-public information in order to put the stockholder's disclosures in what the corporation believes to be the proper context. All in all, this is not a process that promises to advance the best interests of the corporation or its stockholders.

DECISION AND REMEDY *The court denied Roy Disney's request to remove the confidentiality designation from the documents on which the company had imposed it, and dismissed the case. Opening the confidentiality limit in this case would lead to the disclosure of nonpublic information in other cases, which would not "advance the best interests of the corporation or its stockholders."*

WHAT IF THE FACTS WERE DIFFERENT? *If the information that Disney sought to disseminate publicly—via a Web site, for example—had been previously disclosed in a limited manner (such as in a company newsletter), would the result have been different?*

TRANSFER OF SHARES Corporate stock represents an ownership right in intangible personal property. The law generally recognizes the right of an owner to transfer property to another person unless there are valid restrictions on its transferability. Although stock certificates are negotiable and freely transferable by indorsement and delivery, transfer of stock in closely held corporations is generally restricted by the bylaws, by a restriction stamped on the stock certificate, or by a shareholder agreement. The existence of any restrictions on transferability must always be noted on the face of the stock certificate, and these restrictions must be reasonable.

Sometimes, corporations or their shareholders restrict transferability by reserving the option to purchase any shares offered for resale by a shareholder. This **right of first refusal** remains with the corporation or the shareholders for only a specified time or a reasonable period of time. Variations on the purchase option are possible. For example, a shareholder might be required to offer the shares to other shareholders or to the corporation first.

When shares are transferred, a new entry is made in the corporate stock book to indicate the new owner. Until the corporation is notified and the entry is complete, voting rights, notice of shareholders' meetings, dividend distribution, and so forth are all held by the current record owner.

RIGHTS ON DISSOLUTION When a corporation is dissolved and its outstanding debts and the claims of its creditors have been satisfied, the remaining assets are distributed on a pro rata basis among the shareholders. If no preferences in distribution of assets on liquidation are given to any class of stock, then all of the stockholders share the remaining assets.

Shareholders also have the right to petition the court to dissolve the corporation. Suppose that a minority shareholder knows that the board of directors is mishandling corporate assets or is permitting a deadlock to threaten or irreparably injure the corporation's finances. The minority shareholder is not powerless to intervene. He or she can petition a court to appoint a receiver and to liquidate the business assets of the corporation.

The RMBCA permits any shareholder to initiate such an action in any of the following circumstances:

1. The directors are deadlocked in the management of corporate affairs, shareholders are unable to break that deadlock, and irreparable injury to the corporation is being suffered or threatened.

2. The acts of the directors or those in control of the corporation are illegal, oppressive, or fraudulent.
3. Corporate assets are being misapplied or wasted.
4. The shareholders are deadlocked in voting power and have failed, for a specified period (usually two annual meetings), to elect successors to directors whose terms have expired or would have expired with the election of successors.

THE SHAREHOLDER'S DERIVATIVE SUIT When those in control of a corporation—the corporate directors—fail to sue in the corporate name to redress a wrong suffered by the corporation, shareholders are permitted to do so "derivatively" in what is known as a **shareholder's derivative suit.** Some wrong must have been done to the corporation, and before a derivative suit can be brought, the shareholders must first state their complaint to the board of directors. Only if the directors fail to solve the problem or to take appropriate action can the derivative suit go forward.

The right of shareholders to bring a derivative action is especially important when the wrong suffered by the corporation results from the actions of corporate directors. This is because the directors and officers would probably be unwilling to take any action against themselves.

The shareholder's derivative suit is singular in that those suing are not pursuing rights or benefits for themselves personally but are acting as guardians of the corporate entity. Therefore, any damages recovered by the suit normally go into the corporation's treasury, not to the shareholders personally.

LIABILITY OF SHAREHOLDERS

One of the hallmarks of the corporate organization is that shareholders are not personally liable for the debts of the corporation. If the corporation fails, shareholders can lose their investments, but that is generally the limit of their liability. In certain instances of fraud, undercapitalization, or careless observance of corporate formalities, a court will pierce the corporate veil (disregard the corporate entity) and hold the shareholders individually liable. But these situations are the exception, not the rule.

Although rare, there are certain other instances in which a shareholder can be personally liable. One relates to illegal dividends, which were discussed previously. Two others relate to *stock subscriptions* and *watered stock.*

STOCK-SUBSCRIPTION AGREEMENTS Sometimes, stock-subscription agreements—written contracts by which one agrees to buy capital stock of a corporation—exist prior to incorporation. Normally, these agreements are treated as continuing offers and are irrevocable (for up to six months under the RMBCA). Once the corporation has been formed, it can sell shares to investors. In either case, once the subscription agreement or stock offer is accepted, a binding contract is formed. Any refusal to pay constitutes a breach resulting in the personal liability of the shareholder.

WATERED STOCK   Shares of stock can be paid for with property or services rendered instead of cash. (Shares cannot be purchased with promissory notes, however.) The general rule is that for **par-value shares** (that is, shares that have a specific face value, or formal cash-in value, written on them, such as one penny or one dollar), the corporation must receive a value at least equal to the par-value amount. For **no-par shares** (that is, shares without a par value), the corporation must receive the value of the shares as determined by the board or the shareholders.

For either par-value or no-par shares, the setting of the value is based on the same factors: tax rates, whether the corporation needs capital surplus, and what the corporation will receive for the shares (money, property, or services). When shares are issued by the corporation for less than these stated values, the shares are referred to as **watered stock.**[15] In most cases, the shareholder who receives watered stock must pay the difference to the corporation (the shareholder is personally liable). In some states, the shareholder who receives watered stock may be liable to creditors of the corporation for unpaid corporate debts.

To illustrate the concept of watered stock: Suppose that during the formation of a corporation,

Gomez, as one of the incorporators, transfers his property, Sunset Beach, to the corporation for 10,000 shares of stock at a par value of $100 per share for a total price of $1 million. After the property is transferred and the shares are issued, Sunset Beach is carried on the corporate books at a value of $1 million. On appraisal, it is discovered that the market value of the property at the time of transfer was only $500,000. The shares issued to Gomez are therefore watered stock, and he is liable to the corporation for the difference between the value of the shares and the value of the property.

DUTIES OF MAJORITY SHAREHOLDERS

In some cases, a majority shareholder is regarded as having a fiduciary duty to the corporation and to the minority shareholders. This occurs when a single shareholder (or a few shareholders acting in concert) owns a sufficient number of shares to exercise *de facto* (actual) control over the corporation. In these situations, majority shareholders owe a fiduciary duty to minority shareholders.

Consider an example. Three brothers, Alfred, Carl, and Eugene, owned a corporation and had worked for the corporation for most of their adult lives. Each owned a one-third interest. When a dispute arose concerning discrepancies in the corporation's accounting records, Carl and Eugene fired Alfred and told the company's employees that Alfred had had a nervous breakdown, which was not true. Alfred sued Carl and Eugene, alleging, among other things, that they had breached their fiduciary duties. The brothers argued that because there was no diminution in the value of the corporation or the value of Alfred's shares in the company, they had not breached their fiduciary duties. The court, however, held that the brothers' conduct, which was unfairly prejudicial toward Alfred, supported a finding of breach of fiduciary duty.[16]

---

15. The phrase *watered stock* was originally used to describe cattle that—kept thirsty during a long drive—were allowed to drink large quantities of water just prior to their sale. The increased weight of the "watered stock" allowed the seller to reap a higher profit.

16. *Pedro v. Pedro*, 489 N.W.2d 798 (Minn.App. 1992).

REVIEWING CORPORATIONS

David Brock is on the board of directors of Firm Body Fitness, Inc., which owns a string of fitness clubs in New Mexico. Brock owns 15 percent of the Firm Body stock and he is also employed as a tanning technician at one of the fitness clubs. After the January financial report showed that Firm Body's tanning division was operating at a substantial net loss, the board of

(Continued)

REVIEWING CORPORATIONS—Continued

directors, led by Marty Levinson, discussed the possibility of terminating the tanning operations. Brock successfully convinced a majority of the board that the tanning division was necessary to market the clubs' overall fitness package. By April, the tanning division's financial losses had risen. The board hired a business analyst, who conducted surveys and determined that the tanning operations did not significantly increase membership. A shareholder, Diego Peñada, discovered that Brock owned stock in Sunglow, Inc., the company from which Firm Body purchased its tanning equipment. Peñada notified Levinson, who privately reprimanded Brock. Shortly thereafter Brock and Mandy Vail, who owned 37 percent of Firm Body stock and also held shares of Sunglow, voted to replace Levinson on the board of directors. Using the information presented in the chapter, answer the following questions.

1. | What duties did Brock, as a director, owe to Firm Body? Has Brock breached any of these duties? Explain.

2. | Does the fact that Brock owned shares in Sunglow establish a conflict of interest? Why or why not? What would the law require Brock to do in this situation?

3. | Discuss whether Peñada could bring a shareholder's derivative suit based on these facts.

4. | Suppose that Firm Body brought an action against Brock claiming that he had breached the duty of loyalty by not disclosing his interest in Sunglow to the other directors. What theory might Brock use in his defense?

5. | Did Brock and Vail do anything wrong when they voted to replace Levinson as director? Why or why not?

TERMS AND CONCEPTS TO REVIEW

articles of incorporation 436	par-value share 451	S corporation 434
business judgment rule 444	pierce the corporate veil 438	shareholder's derivative suit 450
certificate of incorporation 437	preemptive rights 447	stock certificate 446
close corporation 432	promoter 435	stock warrant 447
commingled 438	prospectus 435	treasury share 447
corporate charter 437	proxy 446	voting trust 446
corporation 430	quorum 441	watered stock 451
dividend 447	retained earnings 431	
no-par share 451	right of first refusal 450	

QUESTIONS AND CASE PROBLEMS

18–1. Jonathan, Gary, and Rob are active members of a partnership called Swim City. The partnership manufactures, sells, and installs outdoor swimming pools in the states of Texas and Arkansas. The partners want to continue to be active in management and to expand the business into other states as well. They are concerned about rather large recent judgments entered against swimming pool companies throughout the United States. Based on these facts only, discuss whether the partnership should incorporate.

18–2. QUESTION WITH SAMPLE ANSWER

Cummings, Okawa, and Taft are recent college graduates who want to form a corporation to manufacture and sell personal computers. Peterson tells them he will set in motion the formation of their corporation. First, Peterson makes a contract with Owens for the purchase of a piece of land for $20,000. Owens does not know of the prospective corporate formation at the time the contract is signed. Second, Peterson makes a contract with

Babcock to build a small plant on the property being purchased. Babcock's contract is conditional on the corporation's formation. Peterson secures all necessary subscription agreements and capitalization, and he files the articles of incorporation. A charter is issued.

(a) Discuss whether the newly formed corporation, Peterson, or both are liable on the contracts with Owens and Babcock.

(b) Discuss whether the corporation is automatically liable to Babcock on formation.

For a sample answer to this question, go to Appendix I at the end of this text.

18–3. Ott Corp. is negotiating with the Wick Construction Co. for the renovation of the Ott corporate headquarters. Wick, owner of the Wick Construction Co., is also one of the five members of the board of directors of Ott. The contract terms are standard for this type of contract. Wick has previously informed two of the other directors of his interest in the construction company. The contract is approved by Ott's board on a three-to-two vote, with Wick voting with the majority. Discuss whether this contract is binding on the corporation.

18–4. Lucia has acquired one share of common stock of a multimillion-dollar corporation with over 500,000 shareholders. Lucia wants to know whether this one share entitles her to (1) attend and vote at shareholders' meetings, (2) inspect the corporate books, and (3) receive yearly dividends. Discuss Lucia's rights in these three matters.

18–5. Riddle has made a preincorporation subscription agreement to purchase 500 shares of a newly formed corporation. The shares have a par value of $100 per share. The corporation is formed, and Riddle's subscription is accepted by the corporation. Riddle transfers a piece of land he owns to the corporation, and the corporation issues 250 shares for it. One year later, with the corporation in serious financial difficulty, the board declares and pays a dividend of $5 per share. It is now learned that the land transferred by Riddle had a market value of $18,000 at the time of transfer. Discuss any liability that shareholder Riddle has to the corporation or to creditors of the corporation.

18–6. S CORPORATIONS. James, Randolph, and Judith Agley and Michael and Nancy Timmis were shareholders in F & M Distributors, Inc., Venture Packaging, Inc., and Diamond Automations, Inc. James Agley was also a shareholder in Middletown Aerospace. All of the firms were S corporations organized and located in Michigan and doing business in Ohio. None of the shareholders was a resident of Ohio, and none of them personally did business in Ohio. Between 1988 and 1992, the Agleys and the Timmises included their prorated share of the S corporations' income on Ohio personal income tax returns. They believed, however, that an out-of-state shareholder should not be taxed in Ohio on the income that he or she receives from an S corporation doing business in Ohio. They contended it is the S corporation that earns the income, not the shareholder.

They also emphasized that none of them personally did business in the state. Finally, they asked the Ohio Tax Commissioner for refunds for those years. Should the state grant their request? Why or why not? [*Agley v. Tracy*, 87 Ohio St.3d 265, 719 N.E.2d 951 (1999)]

18–7. BUSINESS JUDGMENT RULE. Charles Pace and Maria Fuentez were shareholders of Houston Industries, Inc. (HII), and employees of Houston Lighting & Power, a subsidiary of HII, when they lost their jobs because of a company-wide reduction in its workforce. Pace, as a shareholder, three times wrote to HII, demanding that the board of directors terminate certain HII directors and officers and file a suit to recover damages for breach of fiduciary duty. Three times, the directors referred the charges to board committees and an outside law firm, which found that the facts did not support the charges. The board also received input from federal regulatory authorities about the facts behind some of the charges. The board notified Pace that it would refuse his demands. In response, Pace and Fuentez filed a shareholder's derivative suit against Don Jordan and the other HII directors, contending that the board's investigation was inadequate. The defendants moved for summary judgment, arguing that the suit was barred by the business judgment rule. How should the court rule? Why? [*Pace v. Jordan*, 999 S.W.2d 615 (Tex.App.—Houston [1 Dist.] 1999)]

18–8. ⚖ **CASE PROBLEM WITH SAMPLE ANSWER**

In 1978, David Brandt and Dean Somerville incorporated Posilock Puller, Inc. (PPI), to make and market bearing pullers. Each received half of the stock. Initially operating out of McHenry, North Dakota, PPI moved to Cooperstown, North Dakota, in 1984 into a building owned by Somerville. After the move, Brandt's participation in PPI diminished, and Somerville's increased. In 1998, Somerville formed PL MFG as his own business to make components for the bearing pullers and sell the parts to PPI. The start-up costs included a $450,000 loan from Sheyenne Valley Electric Cooperative. PPI executed the loan documents and indorsed the check. The proceeds were deposited into an account for PL MFG, which did not sign a promissory note payable to PPI until 2000. When Brandt learned of PL MFG and the loan, he filed a suit in a North Dakota state court against Somerville, alleging in part a breach of fiduciary duty. What fiduciary duty does a director owe to his or her corporation? What does this duty require? Should the court hold Somerville liable? Why or why not? [*Brandt v. Somerville*, 692 N.W.2d 144, 2005 ND 35 (N.D. 2005)]
To view a sample answer for this case problem, go to this book's Web site at http://wleb.westbuslaw.com, select "Chapter 18," and click on "Case Problem with Sample Answer."

18–9. INSPECTION RIGHTS. Craig Johnson founded Distributed Solutions, Inc. (DSI), in 1991 to make software and provide consulting services, including payroll services for small companies. Johnson was the sole officer and director and the majority shareholder. Jeffrey Hagen was a minority shareholder. In 1993, Johnson sold DSI's payroll services to himself and a few others and set up Distributed Payroll Solutions, Inc. (DPSI). In 1996, DSI had revenues of $739,034 and assets of $541,168. DSI's revenues in 1997 were $934,532. Within a year, however, all of DSI's assets were sold, and Johnson told Hagen that he was dissolving the firm because, in part, it conducted no business and had no prospects for future business. Hagen asked for corporate records to determine the value of DSI's stock, DSI's financial condition, and "whether unauthorized and oppressive acts had occurred in connection with the operation of the corporation which impacted the value of" the stock. When there was no response, Hagen filed a suit in an Illinois state court against DSI and Johnson, seeking an order to compel the inspection. The defendants filed a motion to dismiss, arguing that Hagen had failed to plead a proper purpose. Should the court grant Hagen's request? Discuss. [*Hagen v. Distributed Solutions, Inc.*, 328 Ill.App.3d 132, 764 N.E.2d 1141, 262 Ill.Dec. 24 (1 Dist. 2002)]

18–10. DUTY OF LOYALTY. Digital Commerce, Ltd., designed software to enable its clients to sell their products or services over the Internet. Kevin Sullivan served as a Digital vice president until 2000, when he became president. Sullivan was dissatisfied that his compensation did not include stock in Digital, but he was unable to negotiate a deal that included equity (that is, shares of ownership in the company). In May, Sullivan solicited ASR Corp.'s business for Digital while he investigated employment opportunities with ASR for himself. When ASR would not include an "equity component" in a job offer, Sullivan refused to negotiate further on Digital's behalf. A few months later, Sullivan began to form his own firm to compete with Digital, conducting organizational and marketing activities on Digital's time, including soliciting ASR's business. Sullivan had all e-mail pertaining to the new firm deleted from Digital's computers in August, and then resigned. ASR signed a contract with Sullivan's new firm and paid it $400,000 for work through October 2001. Digital filed a suit in a federal district court against Sullivan, claiming that he usurped a corporate opportunity. Did Sullivan breach his fiduciary duty to Digital? Explain. [*In re Sullivan*, 305 Bankr. 809 (W.D.Mich. 2004)]

18–11. ⚖ A QUESTION OF ETHICS

In 1990, American Design Properties, Inc. (ADP), leased premises at 8604 Olive Boulevard in St. Louis County, Missouri. Under the lease agreement, ADP had the right to terminate the lease on 120 days' written notice, but it did not have the right to sublease the premises without the lessor's (landowner's) consent. ADP had no bank account, no employees, and no money. ADP had never filed an income tax return or held a directors' or shareholders'

meeting. In fact, ADP's only business was to collect and pay the exact amount of rent due under the lease. American Design Group, Inc. (ADG), a wholesale distributor of jewelry and other merchandise, actually occupied 8604 Olive Boulevard. J. H. Blum owned ADG and was an officer and director of both ADG and ADP. Blum's husband, Marvin, was an officer of ADG and signed the lease as an officer of ADP. Marvin's former son-in-law, Matthew Smith, was a salaried employee of ADG, an officer of ADG, and an officer and director of ADP. In 1995, Nusrala Four, Inc. (later known as Real Estate Investors Four, Inc.), purchased the property at 8604 Olive Boulevard and became the lessor. No one told Nusrala that ADG was the occupant of the premises leased by ADP. ADP continued to pay the rent until November 1998 when Smith paid with a check drawn on ADG's account. No more payments were made. On February 26, 1999, Marvin sent Nusrala a note that read, "We have vacated the property at 8604 Olive," which, Nusrala discovered, had been damaged. Nusrala filed a suit in a Missouri state court against ADG and ADP, seeking money for the damage. In view of these facts, consider the following questions. [*Real Estate Investors Four, Inc. v. American Design Group, Inc.*, 46 S.W.3d 51 (Mo.App. E.D. 2001)]

(a) Given that ADG had not signed the lease and was not rightfully a sublessee, could ADG be held liable, at least in part, for the damage to the premises? Under what theory might the court ignore the separate corporate identities of ADG and ADP? If you were the judge, how would you rule in this case?

(b) Assuming that ADP had few, if any, corporate assets, would it be fair to preclude Nusrala from recovering money for the damage from ADG?

(c) Is it ever appropriate for a court to ignore the corporate structure? Why or why not?

18–12. VIDEO QUESTION

Go to this text's Web site at http://wleb.westbuslaw.com and select "Chapter 18." Click on "Video Questions" and view the video titled *Corporation or LLC: Which Is Better?* Then answer the following questions.

(a) Compare the liability that Anna and Caleb would be exposed to as shareholders/owners of a corporation versus as members of a limited liability company (LLC).

(b) How are corporations taxed differently than LLCs?

(c) Given that Anna and Caleb conduct their business (Wizard Internet) over the Internet, can you think of any drawbacks to forming an LLC?

(d) If you were in the position of Anna and Caleb, would you choose to create a corporation or an LLC? Why?

LAW | on the Web

For updated links to resources available on the Web, as well as a variety of other materials, visit this text's Web site at http://wleb.westbuslaw.com.

One of the best sources on the Web for information on corporations, including their directors, is the EDGAR database of the Securities and Exchange Commission (SEC) at

http://www.sec.gov/edgar.shtml

Cornell University's Legal Information Institute has links to state corporation statutes at

http://www.law.cornell.edu/topics/state_statutes.html

You can find definitions of terms used in corporate law, as well as court decisions and articles on corporate law topics, at

http://www.law.com

LEGAL RESEARCH EXERCISES ON THE WEB

Go to http://wleb.westbuslaw.com, the Web site that accompanies this text. Select "Chapter 18" and click on "Internet Exercises." There you will find the following Internet research exercises that you can perform to learn more about topics covered in this chapter.

Activity 18–1: **LEGAL PERSPECTIVE**
Liability of Directors and Officers

Activity 18–2: **MANAGEMENT PERSPECTIVE**
Online Incorporation

The Business Environment

In Chapter 4, we examined the importance of ethical standards in the business context. We also offered suggestions on how business decision makers can create an ethical workplace. Here, we look at selected areas in which the relationships within specific business organizational forms may raise ethical issues.

Fiduciary Duties

The law of agency, which will be outlined in Chapter 19, permeates virtually all relationships within any partnership or corporation. An important duty that arises in the law of agency, and applies to all partners and corporate directors, officers, and management personnel, is the duty of loyalty. As caretakers of the shareholders' wealth, corporate directors and officers also have a fiduciary duty to exercise care when making decisions affecting the corporate enterprise.

The Duty of Loyalty

Every individual has his or her own personal interests, which may at times conflict with the interests of the partnership or corporation with which he or she is affiliated. In particular, a partner or a corporate director may face a conflict between personal interests and the interests of the business entity. Corporate officers may find themselves in a position to acquire assets that would also benefit the corporation if acquired in the corporation's name.

In one landmark case, *Guth v. Loft, Inc.,*[1] Charles G. Guth, the president and a director of Loft, Inc., a soft-drink bottling company, negotiated with the Coca-Cola Company for a discount on its syrups. When the negotiations with Coca-Cola failed to result in a discount for Loft, Guth decided to see what Pepsi-Cola would offer. During his investigation of this possibility, Guth set up a new corporation to acquire the secret formula and trademark for the manufacture of Pepsi-Cola. He did so without offering the opportunity to Loft. A shareholder brought a suit against Guth, arguing that the shares of the new corporation should belong to Loft, and not to Guth personally. The shareholder prevailed. The court ruled that Guth had *usurped* a corporate opportunity in violation of his duty of loyalty to the corporation.

The Duty of Care

In addition to the duty of loyalty, every corporate director or officer owes a duty of care, which includes a duty to be informed and to make informed decisions. Traditionally, though, the duty of care did not include a duty to monitor the behavior of corporate employees to detect and prevent wrongdoing unless the directors had some reason to suspect that wrongful acts were in fact occurring.

Since the corporate sentencing guidelines were issued in 1991 (see Chapter 7), however, the courts may impose—and have been imposing fairly regularly—substantial penalties on corporations and corporate directors for criminal wrongdoing. The guidelines allow these penalties to be mitigated, though, if a company can show that it has an effective compliance program in place to detect and prevent wrongdoing by corporate personnel. Furthermore, in 1996 a Delaware chancery (trial) court suggested that corporate directors have a *duty* to implement such programs.

The case involved criminal behavior on the part of a company's middle- and lower-level employees, and the question was whether the directors, who were apparently unaware of this activity, had breached their oversight duties. Under the traditional rule, as mentioned, directors had no duty to detect and "ferret out" wrongdoing. According to the court in this case, however, the corporate sentencing guidelines have changed this standard. The court stated that "a director's obligation includes a duty to attempt in good faith to assure that a corporation information and reporting system, which the board concludes is adequate, exists."[2]

Fiduciary Duties to Creditors It is a long-standing principle that corporate directors ordinarily owe fiduciary duties only to a corporation's shareholders. This is because directors are, in a sense, the trustees of the shareholders' property. The true owners of the corporation—the shareholders—entrust the directors with the control and management of the business. The law thus imposes on directors fiduciary duties to shareholders, including the duty of loyalty and the duty of care. Directors who favor the interests of other corporate "stakeholders," such as creditors, over those of the shareholders have been held liable for breaching these duties.

The picture changes, however, when a corporation approaches insolvency. At this point, the shareholders' equity interests in the corporation may be worthless, while the interests of creditors become paramount. In this situation, do the fiduciary duties of loyalty and care extend to the corporation's creditors as well as to the shareholders? The answer to this question, according to many courts, is yes. In

---

1. 5 A.2d 503 (Del. 1939).

2. *In re Caremark International, Inc., Derivative Litigation,* 1996 WL 549894 (Del.Ch. [Delaware Chancery Court] 1996).

a leading case on this issue, a Delaware court noted that "[t]he possibility of insolvency can do curious things to incentives, exposing creditors to risks of opportunistic behavior and creating complexities for directors." The court held that when a corporation is on the brink of insolvency, the directors assume a fiduciary duty to other stakeholders that sustain the corporate entity, including creditors.[3] Some courts have even found that the directors' duties to creditors apply not only when the corporation is technically insolvent, but also when the corporation operates in the "vicinity or zone of insolvency."[4]

Fiduciary Duties and Departing Partners Law firms that are organized as partnerships face the ongoing problem of departing partners who take their clients with them. Nothing in the ethical rules governing attorney conduct expressly prohibits departing attorneys from soliciting business from clients with whom they have had an ongoing relationship.

As one court noted, departing attorneys are involved in a "delicate venture." On the one hand, common sense dictates that an attorney who is dissatisfied with the existing association should take steps to locate alternative office space and associations—and do so confidentially. The court also noted that it is permissible for departing partners "to inform clients with whom they have a prior professional relationship about their impending withdrawal and new practice, and to remind the client of its freedom to retain counsel of its choice."

On the other hand, departing partners must take care not to breach their fiduciary obligations to the other partners. The court stated that "secretly attempting to lure firm clients . . . to the new association . . . and abandoning the firm on short notice (taking clients and files) would not be consistent with a partner's fiduciary duties."[5]

Family-Owned Corporations

Close corporations that are owned by family members may face severe problems when relations among the family members deteriorate. For example, suppose that two sisters and their brother are equal shareholders in a close corporation. Each shareholder is both a director and an officer of the corporation. Disagreements over how the corporation should be operated arise, and the two sisters, as the majority on the board of directors, vote to oust the brother from his position as corporate president. Although the brother remains a shareholder and a member of the board, he is deprived of his job (and his salary), which may have important economic consequences. Furthermore, he may be prevented by the

corporate articles or by a shareholder agreement from selling his shares and investing his funds elsewhere.

What can the brother do? Often, the only option in this kind of situation is to petition a court to dissolve the corporation or force the majority shareholders to buy the minority shareholder's shares. Although courts generally are reluctant to interfere with corporate decisions, they have held, in several cases, that majority shareholders owe a fiduciary duty to minority shareholders (see Chapter 18). A breach of this duty may cause a court to order the majority shareholders to buy out the minority shareholder's interest in the firm or, as a last resort, to dissolve the corporation.

Franchise Relationships

Franchise relationships present several significant ethical issues. One issue has to do with the franchisor's quality control over the franchisee's activities. On the one hand, if the franchisor ignores the problem of quality control, the reputation of the franchisor's business may suffer. On the other hand, if a franchisor's control over the operations of the franchisee is too extensive, the franchisor may be liable for the torts of the franchisee's employees under agency theory.[6] Even when an independent business entity purchases a franchise and the franchise agreement specifies that no agency relationship exists, the courts may find otherwise.

Another issue today is how to adapt certain protections for franchisees to the online world. This issue has become increasingly important as more and more prospective franchisees are going online to find information about particular franchises.

Franchisees Held to Be Employees In a series of cases over the last decade, courts have even held franchisees to be employees of the franchisor, notwithstanding their franchise contracts. For example, in one case a franchisee of a commercial sanitation company was deemed to be an employee of the company even though he was designated as a franchisee in a franchise contract with the company.[7]

In another case, the National Labor Relations Board ruled that some five hundred drivers for a New York company that provided limousine services should be considered employees for labor law purposes, despite their franchise contracts with the company.[8] In these and other cases, the decisions were based on the extensive control exercised by the companies over the activities of the franchisees.

3. *Credit Lyonnais Bank Nederland N.V. v. Pathe Communications Corp.*, 1991 WL 277613 (Del.Ch. 1991).

4. See, for example, *Gladstone v. Stuart Cinemas, Inc.*, 878 A.2d 214 (Vt. 2005).

5. *Dowd & Dowd v. Gleason*, 181 Ill.2d 460, 693 N.E.2d 358, 230 Ill.Dec. 229 (1998).

6. See, for example, *Parker v. Domino's Pizza, Inc.*, 629 So.2d 1026 (Fla.App. 1993). As a result of several lawsuits brought by plaintiffs who had been injured by Domino's Pizza delivery drivers, Domino's changed some of its policies in regard to its franchisees. In particular, it stopped requiring its franchisees to abide by the "thirty-minute delivery" requirement.

7. *West Sanitation Services, Inc. v. Francis*, 1998 WL 11023 (N.Y.Sup.Ct.App.Div. 1998).

8. *In re Elite Limousine Plus, Inc.*, 324 NLRB No. 182 (November 6, 1997).

Traditional Franchising Rules and the Internet Recall from Chapter 16 that the Franchise Rule of the Federal Trade Commission (FTC) imposes certain disclosure requirements on franchisors. In 1978, when this rule was issued, most people had not even heard of the Internet. Today, adapting the rule to the online environment has proved difficult. For example, suppose that a franchisor has a Web site with downloadable information for prospective franchisees. Is this the equivalent of an offer that requires compliance with the FTC's Franchise Rule? Further, does the franchisor have to comply with fifty different state franchise regulations? Generally, how can the interests of franchisees be protected in the cyber environment?

In view of these problems, the FTC has proposed several changes to its Franchise Rule. One proposed change would require that the franchisor provide a prospective franchisee with a proper disclosure document at least fourteen days before the signing of any franchise agreement or any payment to the franchisor. In addition, to give the franchisee more time to consider the franchise contract, the franchisor would have to provide the franchisee with a copy of the contract five calendar days before the agreement is to be signed.

Another proposed rule would require online franchisors to state very clearly that franchisees would not be entitled to exclusive territorial rights. Notwithstanding these changes, however, one problem would remain: given the speed with which online franchises can be created, it may be difficult—if not impossible—for the FTC to effectively regulate these relationships.

DISCUSSION QUESTIONS

1. Three decades ago, corporations and corporate directors were rarely prosecuted for crimes, and penalties for corporate crime were relatively light. Today, this is no longer true. Under the corporate sentencing guidelines, corporate fines reaching hundreds of millions of dollars are no longer uncommon. In 2002, Congress passed the Sarbanes-Oxley Act, which imposes even stricter penalties for corporate wrongdoing. Do these developments mean that corporations are committing more crimes today than in the past? Will stricter laws be effective in curbing corporate criminal activity? How can a company avoid liability for crimes committed by its employees?

2. Do you agree that when a corporation is approaching insolvency, the directors' fiduciary obligations should extend to the corporation's creditors as well as to the shareholders? In this situation, should the fiduciary duties owed to creditors take priority over the duties to shareholders? Why or why not?

3. As explained, if a franchisor exercises "too much control" over a franchisee's business operations, a court may deem the franchisor to be liable as an employer for the torts committed by the franchisee's employees. How can holding franchisors liable in such circumstances be squared with the doctrine of freedom of contract?

UNIT FIVE
The Employment Environment

CONTENTS

CHAPTER 19
Agency

One of the most common, important, and pervasive legal relationships is that of **agency.** In an agency relationship between two parties, one of the parties, called the *agent,* agrees to represent or act for the other, called the *principal.* The principal has the right to control the agent's conduct in matters entrusted to the agent. By using agents, a principal can conduct multiple business operations simultaneously in various locations. Thus, for example, contracts that bind the principal can be made at different places with different persons at the same time.

A familiar example of an agent is a corporate officer who serves in a representative capacity for the owners of the corporation. In this capacity, the officer has the authority to bind the principal (the corporation) to a contract. Indeed, agency law is essential to the existence and operation of a corporate entity, because only through its agents can a corporation function and enter into contracts.

Most employees are also considered to be agents for their employers. Thus, some of the concepts that you will learn about in Chapters 20 and 21, on employment law, are based on agency law. Generally, agency relationships permeate the business world. For that reason, an understanding of the law of agency is crucial to understanding business law.

SECTION 1 | Agency Relationships

Section 1(1) of the *Restatement (Second) of Agency*[1] defines *agency* as "the fiduciary relation [that] results from the manifestation of consent by one person to another that the other shall act in his [or her] behalf and subject to his [or her] control, and consent by the other so to act." The term **fiduciary** is at the heart of agency law. The term can be used both as a noun and as an adjective. When used as a noun, it refers to a person having a duty created by his or her undertaking to act primarily for another's benefit in matters connected with the undertaking. When used as an adjective, as in the phrase "fiduciary relationship," it means that the relationship involves trust and confidence.

Agency relationships commonly exist between employers and employees. Agency relationships may sometimes also exist between employers and independent contractors who are hired to perform special tasks or services.

EMPLOYER-EMPLOYEE RELATIONSHIPS

Normally, all employees who deal with third parties are deemed to be agents. A salesperson in a department store, for instance, is an agent of the store's owner (the principal) and acts on the owner's behalf. Employment laws (state and federal) apply only to the employer-employee relationship. Statutes governing Social Security, withholding taxes, workers' compensation, unemployment compensation, workplace safety, employment discrimination, and other aspects of employment (see Chapters 20 and 21) are applicable only when an employer-employee relationship exists. *These laws do not apply to an independent contractor.*

---

1. The *Restatement (Second) of Agency* is an authoritative summary of the law of agency and is often referred to by judges in their decisions and opinions.

Because employees may be deemed agents of their employers, agency law and employment law overlap considerably. Agency relationships, though, as will become apparent, can exist outside an employer-employee relationship and thus have a broader reach than employment laws do.

EMPLOYER–INDEPENDENT CONTRACTOR RELATIONSHIPS

Independent contractors are not employees because, by definition, those who hire them have no control over the details of their work performance. Section 2 of the *Restatement (Second) of Agency* defines an **independent contractor** as follows:

> [An independent contractor is] a person who contracts with another to do something for him [or her] but who is not controlled by the other nor subject to the other's right to control with respect to his [or her] physical conduct in the performance of the undertaking. He [or she] may or may not be an agent.

Building contractors and subcontractors are independent contractors, and a property owner does not control the acts of either of these professionals. Truck drivers who own their equipment and hire out on a per-job basis are independent contractors, but truck drivers who drive company trucks on a regular basis are usually employees.

The relationship between a principal and an independent contractor may or may not involve an agency relationship. To illustrate: An owner of real estate who hires a real estate broker to negotiate the sale of her property not only has contracted with an independent contractor (the real estate broker) but also has established an agency relationship for the specific purpose of selling the property. Another example is an insurance agent, who is both an independent contractor and an agent of the insurance company for which he or she sells policies. (Note that an insurance *broker,* in contrast, normally is an agent of the person obtaining insurance and not of the insurance company.)

DETERMINING EMPLOYEE STATUS

The courts are frequently asked to determine whether a particular worker is an employee or an independent contractor. How a court decides this issue can have a significant effect on the rights and liabilities of the parties. For example, employers are required to pay certain taxes, such as Social Security and unemployment taxes, for employees but not for independent contractors.

CRITERIA USED BY THE COURTS In deciding whether a worker is categorized as an employee or an independent contractor, courts often consider the following questions:

1. How much control can the employer exercise over the details of the work? (If an employer can exercise considerable control over the details of the work and the day-to-day activities of the worker, this indicates employee status. This is perhaps the most important factor weighed by the courts in determining employee status.)
2. Is the worker engaged in an occupation or business distinct from that of the employer? (If so, this points to independent-contractor, not employee, status.)
3. Is the work usually done under the employer's direction or by a specialist without supervision? (If the work is usually done under the employer's direction, this indicates employee status.)
4. Does the employer supply the tools at the place of work? (If so, this indicates employee status.)
5. For how long is the person employed? (If the person is employed for a long period of time, this indicates employee status.)
6. What is the method of payment—by time period or at the completion of the job? (Payment by time period, such as once every two weeks or once a month, indicates employee status.)
7. What degree of skill is required of the worker? (If a great degree of skill is required, this may indicate that the person is an independent contractor hired for a specialized job and not an employee.)

Sometimes, it may be advantageous to have independent-contractor status—for tax purposes, for example. At other times, it is advantageous for a worker to have employee status—to take advantage of laws protecting employees, for example. As stated above, federal statutes governing employment discrimination apply only when an employer-employee relationship exists. The question in the following case was whether, for the purpose of applying one of these statutes, a television show's co-host was an employee or an independent contractor.

CASE 19.1

Alberty-Vélez v. Corporación de Puerto Rico

United States
Court of Appeals,
First Circuit, 2004.
361 F.3d 1.
http://www.ca1.
uscourts.gov[a]

BACKGROUND AND FACTS *In July 1993, Victoria Lis Alberty-Vélez (Alberty) began to co-host a new television show, Desde Mi Pueblo, on WIPR, a television station in Puerto Rico. The show profiled Puerto Rican cities and towns. Instead of signing a single contract, Alberty signed a new contract for each episode. Each contract obligated her to work a certain number of days. She was not obliged to do other work for WIPR, and WIPR was not obliged to contract with her for other work. During the filming, Alberty was responsible for providing her own clothing, shoes, accessories, hair-stylist, and other services and materials. She was paid a lump sum, ranging from $400 to $550, for each episode. WIPR did not withhold income or Social Security taxes and did not provide health insurance, life insurance, a retirement plan, paid sick leave, maternity leave, or vacation pay. Alberty became pregnant, and after November 1994, WIPR stopped contracting with her. She filed a suit in a federal district court against WIPR's owner, Corporación de Puerto Rico para la Difusión Pública, alleging in part discrimination on the basis of her pregnancy in violation of a federal statute. The court issued a judgment in the defendant's favor. Alberty appealed to the U.S. Court of Appeals for the First Circuit.*

IN THE LANGUAGE OF THE COURT

HOWARD, Circuit Judge.

  * * * *

  * * * We * * * will apply the common law test to determine whether Alberty was WIPR's employee or an independent contractor.

  Under the common law test, a court must consider * * * the hiring party's right to control the manner and means by which the product is accomplished. Among other factors relevant to this inquiry are the skills required; the source of the instrumentalities and tools; the location of the work; the duration of the relationship between the parties; whether the hiring party has the right to assign additional projects to the hired party; the extent of the hired party's discretion over when and how long to work; the method of payment; * * * whether the work is part of the regular business of the hiring party; whether the hiring party is in business; the provision of employee benefits; and the tax treatment of the hired party. * * * [Emphasis added.]

  * * * *

  Several factors favor classifying Alberty as an independent contractor. First, a television actress is a skilled position requiring talent and training not available on-the-job. In this regard, Alberty possesses a master's degree in public communications and journalism; is trained in dance, singing, and modeling; taught within the drama department at the University of Puerto Rico; and acted in several theater and television productions prior to her affiliation with "Desde Mi Pueblo."

  Second, Alberty provided the tools and instrumentalities necessary for her to perform. Specifically, she provided, or obtained sponsors to provide, the costumes, jewelry, and other image-related supplies and services necessary for her appearance. * * *

  Third, WIPR could not assign Alberty work in addition to filming "Desde Mi Pueblo." * * *

  Fourth, the method of payment favors independent-contractor status. Alberty received a lump sum fee for each episode. Her compensation was based on completing the filming, not the time consumed. If she did not film an episode she did not get paid.

  Fifth, WIPR did not provide Alberty with benefits. * * *

  Sixth, Alberty's tax treatment suggests independent-contractor status. * * *

  Despite these factors favoring independent-contractor status, Alberty argues that she was WIPR's employee because WIPR controlled the manner of her work by directing her during filming, dictated the location of her work by selecting the filming sites, and determined the hours of her work * * * . *While "control" over the manner, location, and hours of work is often critical to the independent contractor/employee analysis, it must be considered in light of the work performed and the industry at issue.* Considering the tasks that an actor performs, we do not believe that the sort of control identified by Alberty necessarily indicates employee status. [Emphasis added.]

a. In the right-hand column, click on "Opinions." When that page opens, under "General Search," type "02-2187" in the "Opinion Number begins with" box, and click on "Submit Query." In the result, click on the appropriate link to access the opinion. The U.S. Court of Appeals for the First Circuit maintains this Web site.

CASE 19.1 | Continued

*   *   *   *

*   *   * Alberty's work on "Desde Mi Pueblo" required her to film at the featured sites at the required times and to follow the instructions of the director. WIPR could only achieve its goal of producing its program by having Alberty follow these directions. Just as an orchestra musician is subject to the control of the conductor during concerts and rehearsals, an actor is subject to the control of the director during filming. *   *   *

*   *   *   *

While no one factor is dispositive [determines the outcome], it is clear, based on the parties' entire relationship, that a reasonable fact finder could only conclude that Alberty was an independent contractor. *   *   * Accordingly, we conclude that Alberty was an independent contractor as a matter of law and therefore cannot maintain [this] action against WIPR.

DECISION AND REMEDY *The U.S. Court of Appeals for the First Circuit affirmed the lower court's judgment in WIPR's favor. The court stated, "The parties structured their relationship through the use of set length contracts that permitted Alberty the freedom to pursue other opportunities and assured WIPR that it would not have to pay Alberty for the weeks that it was not filming. Further, the lack of benefits, the method of payment, and the parties' own description of their relationship in tax documents all indicate independent-contractor status."*

WHAT IF THE FACTS WERE DIFFERENT? *Suppose that Alberty had been a full-time, hourly worker and that such status was common among television hosts, but WIPR had manipulated the benefits and tax-treatment factors to favor independent-contractor status. How might the result have been different?*

CRITERIA USED BY THE IRS Businesspersons should be aware that the Internal Revenue Service (IRS) has established its own criteria for determining whether a worker is an independent contractor or an employee. Although the IRS once considered twenty factors in determining a worker's status, guidelines that took effect in 1997 encourage IRS examiners to look closely at just one of those factors—the degree of control the business exercises over the worker.

The IRS tends to scrutinize closely a firm's classification of a worker as an independent contractor rather than an employee because employers can avoid certain tax liabilities by hiring independent contractors instead of employees. Even when the firm has classified a worker as an independent contractor, if the IRS decides that the worker is actually an employee, then the employer will be responsible for paying any applicable Social Security, withholding, and unemployment taxes. For example, in one widely publicized case, Microsoft Corporation was ordered to pay back payroll taxes for hundreds of temporary workers who had contractually agreed to work for Microsoft as independent contractors.[2]

EMPLOYEE STATUS AND "WORKS FOR HIRE"
Under the Copyright Act of 1976, any copyrighted work created by an employee within the scope of her or his employment at the request of the employer is a "work for hire," and the employer owns the copyright to the work. In contrast, when an employer hires an independent contractor—a freelance artist, writer, or computer programmer, for example—the independent contractor normally owns the copyright. In this situation, the employer can own the copyright only if the parties agree in writing that the work is a "work for hire" and the work falls into one of nine specific categories, including audiovisual and other works.

In one case, for example, Graham marketed CD-ROM discs containing compilations of software programs that are available free to the public. Graham hired James to create a file-retrieval program that allowed users to access the software on the CDs. James built into the final version of the program a notice stating that he was the author of the program and owned the copyright. Graham removed the notice. When James sold the program to another CD-ROM publisher, Graham filed a suit claiming that James's program was a "work for hire" and that Graham owned the copyright to the file-retrieval program. The court, however, decided that James—who was a skilled computer programmer who controlled the manner and method of his work—was an independent contractor and not an employee for hire. Thus, James owned the copyright to the file-retrieval program.[3]

---

2. *Vizcaino v. U.S. District Court for the Western District of Washington,* 173 F.3d 713 (9th Cir. 1999).

3. *Graham v. James,* 144 F.3d 229 (2d Cir. 1998).

SECTION 2 | Formation of the Agency Relationship

Agency relationships normally are *consensual*; in other words, they come about by voluntary consent and agreement between the parties. Generally, the agreement need not be in writing,[4] and consideration is not required.

A principal must have contractual capacity.[5] A person who cannot legally enter into contracts directly should not be allowed to do so indirectly through an agent. Any person can be an agent, however, regardless of whether he or she has the capacity to contract. Because an agent derives the authority to enter into contracts from the principal and because a contract made by an agent is legally viewed as a contract of the principal, it is immaterial whether the agent personally has the legal capacity to make that contract. Thus, even a minor or a person who is legally incompetent can be appointed as an agent.

An agency relationship can be created for any legal purpose. An agency relationship created for a purpose that is illegal or contrary to public policy is unenforceable. If LaSalle (as principal) contracts with Burke (as agent) to sell illegal narcotics, the agency relationship is unenforceable because selling illegal narcotics is a felony and is contrary to public policy. It is also illegal for physicians and other licensed professionals to employ unlicensed agents to perform professional actions.

Generally, an agency relationship can arise in four ways: by agreement of the parties, by ratification, by estoppel, and by operation of law. We look here at each of these possibilities.

AGENCY BY AGREEMENT

Most agency relationships are based on an express or implied agreement that the agent will act for the principal and that the principal agrees to have the agent so act. An agency agreement can take the form of an express written contract. For example, Henchen enters into a written agreement with Vogel, a real estate agent, to sell Henchen's house. An agency relationship exists between Henchen and Vogel for the sale of the house and is detailed in a document that both parties sign.

Many express agency relationships are created by oral agreement and are not based on a written contract. If Henchen asks Grace, a gardener, to contract with others for the care of his lawn on a regular basis, and Grace agrees, an agency relationship exists between Henchen and Grace for the lawn care.

An agency agreement can also be implied by conduct. For example, a hotel expressly allows only Hans Cooper to park cars, but Hans has no employment contract there. The hotel's manager tells Hans when to work, as well as where and how to park the cars. The hotel's conduct amounts to a manifestation of its willingness to have Hans park its customers' cars, and Hans can infer from the hotel's conduct that he has authority to act as a parking valet. It can be inferred that Hans is an agent for the hotel, his purpose being to provide valet parking services for hotel guests.

AGENCY BY RATIFICATION

On occasion, a person who is in fact not an agent may make a contract on behalf of another (a principal). If the principal approves or affirms that contract by word or by action, an agency relationship is created by ratification. *Ratification* involves a question of intent, and intent can be expressed by either words or conduct. The basic requirements for ratification will be discussed later in this chapter.

AGENCY BY ESTOPPEL

When a principal causes a third person to believe that another person is the principal's agent, and the third person acts to his or her detriment in reasonable reliance on that belief, the principal is "estopped to deny" the agency relationship. In such a situation, the principal's actions have created the *appearance* of an agency that does not in fact exist. The third person must prove that he or she *reasonably* believed that an agency relationship existed, however.[6]

---

4. There are two main exceptions to the statement that agency agreements need not be in writing. An agency agreement must be in writing (1) whenever agency authority empowers the agent to enter into a contract that the Statute of Frauds requires to be in writing (this is called the *equal dignity rule*, which will be discussed later in this chapter) and (2) whenever an agent is given power of attorney.
5. Note that some states allow a minor to be a principal. When a minor is permitted to be a principal, however, any resulting contracts will be voidable by the minor principal but *not* by the adult third party.

6. These concepts also apply when a person who is in fact an agent undertakes an action that is beyond the scope of her or his authority, as will be discussed later in this chapter.

CONCEPT SUMMARY 19.1 | Formation of the Agency Relationship

METHOD OF FORMATION	DESCRIPTION
BY AGREEMENT	Agency relationship is formed through express consent (oral or written) or implied by conduct.
BY RATIFICATION	Principal either by act or by agreement ratifies conduct of a person who is not in fact an agent.
BY ESTOPPEL	Principal causes a third person to believe that another person is the principal's agent, and the third person acts to his or her detriment in reasonable reliance on that belief.
BY OPERATION OF LAW	Agency relationship is based on a social duty (such as the need to support family members) or formed in emergency situations when the agent is unable to contact the principal.

Suppose that Jerry accompanies Grant, a seed sales representative, to call on a customer, Palko, who is the proprietor of the Neighborhood Seed Store. Jerry has performed independent sales work but has never signed an employment agreement with Grant. Grant boasts to Palko that he wishes he had three more assistants "just like Jerry." By making this representation, Grant creates the impression that Jerry is his agent and has authority to solicit orders. Palko has reason to believe from Grant's statements that Jerry is an agent for Grant. Palko then places seed orders with Jerry.

If Grant does not correct the impression that Jerry is an agent, Grant will be bound to fill the orders just as if Jerry were really Grant's agent. The acts or declarations of a purported agent in and of themselves do not create an agency by estoppel. Rather, it is the deeds or statements *of the principal* that create an agency by estoppel. If Jerry walked into Palko's store and claimed to be Grant's agent, when in fact he was not, and Grant had no knowledge of Jerry's representations, Grant would not be bound to any deal struck by Jerry and Palko.

AGENCY BY OPERATION OF LAW

The courts may find an agency relationship in the absence of a formal agreement in other situations as well. This may occur in family relationships. For example, suppose one spouse purchases certain basic necessaries (such as food or clothing) and charges them to the other spouse's charge account. The courts will often rule that the latter is liable for payment of the necessaries, either because of a social policy of promoting the general welfare of the spouse or because of a legal duty to supply necessaries to family members.

Agency by operation of law may also occur in emergency situations, when the agent's failure to act outside the scope of her or his authority would cause the principal substantial loss. If the agent is unable to contact the principal, the courts will often grant this emergency power. For example, a railroad engineer may contract on behalf of his or her employer for medical care for an injured motorist hit by the train.

SECTION 3 | Duties of Agents and Principals

Once the principal-agent relationship has been created, both parties have duties that govern their conduct. As discussed previously, the principal-agent relationship is *fiduciary*—one of trust. In a fiduciary relationship, each party owes the other the duty to act with the utmost good faith. In this section, we examine the various duties of agents and principals.

AGENT'S DUTIES TO THE PRINCIPAL

Generally, the agent owes the principal five duties—performance, notification, loyalty, obedience, and accounting.

PERFORMANCE An implied condition in every agency contract is the agent's agreement to use reasonable diligence and skill in performing the work. When an agent fails to perform his or her duties, liability for breach of contract may result. The degree of skill or care required of an agent is usually that expected of a reasonable person under similar circumstances. Generally, this is interpreted to mean ordinary care. If an agent has represented herself or himself as possessing special skills, however, the agent is expected to exercise the degree of skill or skills claimed. Failure to do so constitutes a breach of the agent's duty.

Not all agency relationships are based on contract. In some situations, an agent acts gratuitously—that is, without payment. A gratuitous agent cannot be liable for breach of contract, as there is no contract; he or she is subject only to tort liability. Once a gratuitous agent has begun to act in an agency capacity, he or she has the duty to continue to perform in that capacity in an acceptable manner and is subject to the same standards of care and duty to perform as other agents.

For example, Bower's friend Alcott is a real estate broker. Alcott offers to sell Bower's farm at no charge. If Alcott never attempts to sell the farm, Bower has no legal cause of action to force her to do so. If Alcott does find a buyer, however, but negligently fails to follow through with the sales contract, causing the buyer to seek other property, then Bower can sue Alcott for negligence.

NOTIFICATION   An agent is required to notify the principal of all matters that come to her or his attention concerning the subject matter of the agency. This is the *duty of notification*, or the duty to inform. For example, suppose that Lang, an artist, is about to negotiate a contract to sell a series of paintings to Barber's Art Gallery for $25,000. Lang's agent learns that Barber is insolvent and will be unable to pay for the paintings. Lang's agent has a duty to inform Lang of this knowledge because it is relevant to the subject matter of the agency—the sale of Lang's paintings. Generally, the law assumes that the principal is aware of any information acquired by the agent that is rele-

vant to the agency—regardless of whether the agent actually passes on this information to the principal.

LOYALTY   Loyalty is one of the most fundamental duties in a fiduciary relationship. Basically stated, the agent has the duty to act *solely for the benefit of his or her principal* and not in the interest of the agent or a third party. For example, an agent cannot represent two principals in the same transaction unless both know of the dual capacity and consent to it. The duty of loyalty also means that any information or knowledge acquired through the agency relationship is confidential. It would be a breach of loyalty to disclose such information either during the agency relationship or after its termination. Typical examples of confidential information are trade secrets and customer lists compiled by the principal (see Chapter 14).

In short, the agent's loyalty must be undivided. The agent's actions must be strictly for the benefit of the principal and must not result in any secret profit for the agent. For example, suppose that Remington contracts with Averly, a real estate agent, to sell Remington's property. Averly knows that he can find a buyer who will pay substantially more for the property than Remington is asking. If Averly were to secretly purchase Remington's property, however, and sell it at a profit to another buyer, Averly would breach his duty of loyalty as Remington's agent. Averly has a duty to act in Remington's best interests and can only become the purchaser in this situation with Remington's knowledge and approval.

The following case involved a real estate agent who discovered, while working for a principal, that the property owner would only sell the property as a package deal with another parcel. If the agent buys the property to resell it to the principal, does the agent breach the duty of loyalty? That was one of the issues in the following case.

CASE 19.2   Cousins v. Realty Ventures, Inc.

Court of Appeal
of Louisiana,
Fifth Circuit, 2003.
844 So.2d 860.

MARION F. EDWARDS, Judge.
* * * *

* * * Don Cousins acted as the representative/agent for Eagle Ventures [Inc.] * * * to find a real estate investment for the corporation to purchase. To do so, Mr. Cousins engaged the services of Leo Hodgins, a real estate agent/broker and owner of Realty Ventures, Inc. ("RVI").
* * * *

In March of 1991, Leo Hodgins learned that 3330 Lake Villa Drive, an 8,000-square-foot office building [in Metairie, Louisiana], owned by Westinghouse Credit Corporation, was being sold for $125,000 * * * . In June 1991, Leo Hodgins first brought 3330 Lake Villa to

Mr. Cousins' attention. * * * [Cousins] asked [Hodgins] to submit an offer to Westinghouse on [behalf of] Eagle Ventures, Inc., for $90,000.00 * * * . Mr. Hodgins submitted the offer to Westinghouse * * * .

* * * Westinghouse * * * was unable to sell the property at the time because it was having difficulties with Tonti Management, which was managing some of its local commercial holdings * * * .

In October 1991, Leo Hodgins resubmitted Eagle Ventures' June 1991 offer * * * . Hodgins [learned] that Westinghouse was ready to sell 3330 Lake Villa, but only as part of a package deal with its neighboring property, 4141 Veterans Boulevard * * * .

* * * *

In April 1992, Mr. Hodgins and his brother, Paul, created a * * * partnership, known as 4141 Vets Limited Partnership, to purchase the property * * * . On May 7, 1992, Westinghouse sold 3330 Lake Villa to 4141 Vets Limited Partnership for $65,000.00 and sold 4141 Veterans to the same * * * partnership for $355,000.00. [Hodgins then offered to sell 3330 Lake Villa to Eagle Ventures for $175,000.]

* * * [P]laintiffs, Don Cousins [and others] filed the instant suit against defendants, * * * Realty Ventures, Inc. [and others]. Plaintiffs' suit alleged that defendants breached their fiduciary duties to them * * * .

* * * [T]he jury returned a verdict in favor of plaintiffs * * * and awarded damages in the amount of $1,750,000 * * * .

Defendants filed this * * * appeal. Plaintiffs answered the appeal.

* * * *

The precise duties of a real estate broker must be determined by an examination of the nature of the task the real estate agent undertakes to perform and the agreements he makes with the involved parties. In the instant case, Leo Hodgins accepted Mr. Cousins' request to find commercial real estate for Eagle Ventures to purchase by turning his attention to 3330 Lake Villa. * * * The [common law] * * * sets forth the types of duties expected of a real estate agent. For example, a real estate agent may be found liable where he or she does not timely communicate an offer and that failure to communicate results in damages to the client. *Similarly, a real estate broker has been found to have a duty to communicate to his principal all offers received and may be liable in damages for failure to do so.* Moreover, a [R]ealtor has a duty to relay accurate information about property, a duty which extends to both vendor and purchaser, and may be held liable if such duty is breached. [Emphasis added.]

* * * *

Plaintiffs argued at trial that Leo Hodgins committed a breach of his fiduciary duty to them in several respects [including] * * * failing to communicate Westinghouse's response to their offer * * * . Defendants argue they owed no further duty to plaintiffs after the June purchase offer for 3330 Lake Villa was submitted to Westinghouse. Once Westinghouse responded that it could not sell the property due to the property management agreement * * * , Leo Hodgins relayed this information to Don Cousins. Plaintiffs contend that the agent/client relationship persisted far beyond that point based on Leo Hodgins' resubmission of Eagle Ventures' offer in October. They argue that the information regarding the package sale of 3330 Lake Villa and 4141 Veterans Boulevard constituted a counteroffer by Westinghouse that should have been communicated to Mr. Cousins. * * *

In our opinion, * * * as late as February or March of 1992, Mr. Cousins was still communicating with Leo Hodgins regarding the status of his offer and Leo Hodgins was still discussing Eagle Ventures' offer with Westinghouse as late as January 1992. We believe Mr. Cousins acted consistently with his belief that Leo Hodgins was acting as his agent with Westinghouse at that time, while Leo Hodgins did nothing to dispel that belief. * * * During some of that time, Leo Hodgins was armed with the information that 3330 Lake Villa was only for sale as a package with 4141 Veterans Boulevard and was covertly planning to acquire the property himself. * * * [Hodgins] never told Don Cousins or anyone else associated with Eagle Ventures about Westinghouse's decision to sell the properties together prior to March 1992. *Leo Hodgins' failure to communicate the package sale to plaintiffs the moment he*

CONTINUED ▶

learned of it constituted a breach of his fiduciary duties to them. Leo Hodgins' duty was to give plaintiffs the information that Westinghouse rejected their offer for a single property sale and allow them to decide whether they wished to purchase both properties. [Emphasis added.]

* * * [W]e conclude the jury's finding that the defendants fraudulently breached their fiduciary duty to plaintiffs is not manifestly erroneous.

* * * *

Accordingly, the judgment is * * * affirmed.

QUESTIONS

1. Suppose that the agent was not aware that his actions breached a fiduciary duty owed to his principal. Would the agent's lack of awareness have affected the outcome in this case? Why or why not?
2. Do the facts in the *Cousins* case indicate steps that an investor might want to consider when dealing through an agent?

OBEDIENCE When an agent is acting on behalf of the principal, a duty is imposed on that agent to follow all lawful and clearly stated instructions of the principal. Any deviation from such instructions is a violation of this duty. During emergency situations, however, when the principal cannot be consulted, the agent may deviate from the instructions without violating this duty. Whenever instructions are not clearly stated, the agent can fulfill the duty of obedience by acting in good faith and in a manner reasonable under the circumstances.

ACCOUNTING Unless an agent and a principal agree otherwise, the agent has the duty to keep and make available to the principal an account of all property and funds received and paid out on behalf of the principal. The agent has a duty to maintain separate accounts for the principal's funds and the agent's personal funds, and no intermingling of these accounts is allowed. Whenever a licensed professional (such as an attorney) violates this duty to account, he or she may be subject to disciplinary proceedings carried out by the appropriate regulatory institution (such as the state bar association) in addition to being liable to the principal (the professional's client) for failure to account.

PRINCIPAL'S DUTIES TO THE AGENT

The principal also has certain duties to the agent. These duties relate to compensation, reimbursement and indemnification, cooperation, and safe working conditions.

COMPENSATION In general, when a principal requests certain services from an agent, the agent reasonably expects payment. The principal therefore has a duty to pay the agent for services rendered. For example, when an accountant or an attorney is asked to act as an agent, an agreement to compensate the agent for this service is implied. The principal also has a duty to pay that compensation in a timely manner. Except in a gratuitous agency relationship, in which the agent does not act for money, the principal must pay the agreed-on value for the agent's services. If no amount has been expressly agreed on, then the principal owes the agent the customary compensation for such services.

REIMBURSEMENT AND INDEMNIFICATION Whenever an agent disburses sums of money to fulfill the request of the principal or to pay for necessary expenses in the course of a reasonable performance of her or his agency duties, the principal has the duty to reimburse the agent for these payments.[7] Agents cannot recover for expenses incurred by their own misconduct or negligence, however.

Subject to the terms of the agency agreement, the principal has the duty to *indemnify* (compensate) an agent for liabilities incurred because of authorized and lawful acts and transactions. For example, if the agent, on the principal's behalf, forms a contract with a third party, and the principal fails to perform the contract, the third party may sue the agent for damages. In this situation, the principal is obligated to compensate the agent for any costs incurred by the agent as a result of

---

7. This principle applies to acts by gratuitous agents as well. If a finder of a dog that becomes sick takes the dog to a veterinarian and pays the required fees for the veterinarian's services, the agent is entitled to be reimbursed by the owner of the dog for those fees.

the principal's failure to perform the contract. Additionally, the principal must indemnify the agent for the value of benefits that the agent confers on the principal. The amount of indemnification is usually specified in the agency contract. If it is not, the courts will look to the nature of the business and the type of loss to determine the amount.

COOPERATION A principal has a duty to cooperate with the agent and to assist the agent in performing his or her duties. The principal must do nothing to prevent such performance. For example, when a principal grants an agent an exclusive territory, creating an *exclusive agency*, the principal cannot compete with the agent or appoint or allow another agent to so compete in violation of the exclusive agency. If the principal did so, she or he would be exposed to liability for the agent's lost sales or profits.

SAFE WORKING CONDITIONS The common law requires the principal to provide safe working premises, equipment, and conditions for all agents and employees. The principal has a duty to inspect working areas and to warn agents and employees about any unsafe situations. When the agent is an employee, the employer's liability is frequently covered by state workers' compensation insurance, and federal and state statutes often require the employer to meet certain safety standards (see Chapter 20).

SECTION 4 | Rights and Remedies of Agents and Principals

It is said that every wrong has its remedy. In business situations, disputes between agents and principals may arise out of either contract or tort laws and carry corresponding remedies. These remedies include monetary damages, termination of the agency relationship, injunction, and required accountings.

AGENT'S RIGHTS AND REMEDIES AGAINST THE PRINCIPAL

For every duty of the principal, the agent has a corresponding right. Therefore, the agent has the right to be compensated, reimbursed, and indemnified and to work in a safe environment. An agent also has the right to perform agency duties without interference by the principal.

TORT AND CONTRACT REMEDIES Remedies of the agent for breach of duty by the principal follow normal contract and tort remedies. For example, suppose that Aaron Hart, a builder who has just completed construction on a new house, contracts with a real estate agent, Fran Boller, to sell the house. The contract calls for the agent to have an exclusive, ninety-day listing and to receive 6 percent of the selling price when the home is sold. Boller holds several open houses and shows the home to a number of potential buyers. One month before the ninety-day listing terminates, Hart agrees to sell the house to another buyer—not one to whom Boller has shown the house—after the ninety-day listing expires. Hart and the buyer agree that Hart will reduce the price of the house by 3 percent, because he will sell it directly and thus will not have to pay Boller's commission. In this situation, if Boller learns of Hart's actions, she can terminate the agency relationship and sue Hart for damages—including the 6 percent commission she should have earned on the sale of the house.

DEMAND FOR AN ACCOUNTING An agent can also withhold further performance and demand that the principal give an accounting. For example, a sales agent may demand an accounting if the agent and principal disagree on the amount of commissions the agent should have received for sales made during a specific period of time.

NO RIGHT TO SPECIFIC PERFORMANCE In a situation in which the principal-agent relationship is not contractual, an agent has no right to specific performance. An agent can recover for past services and future damages but cannot force the principal to allow him or her to continue acting as an agent.

PRINCIPAL'S RIGHTS AND REMEDIES AGAINST THE AGENT

In general, a principal has contract remedies for an agent's breach of fiduciary duties. The principal also has tort remedies if the agent commits misrepresentation, negligence, deceit, libel, slander, or trespass. In addition, any breach of a fiduciary duty by an agent may justify the principal's termination of the agency. The main actions available to the principal are constructive trust, avoidance, and indemnification.

CONSTRUCTIVE TRUST Anything that an agent obtains by virtue of the employment or agency relationship belongs to the principal. An agent commits a breach of fiduciary duty if he or she secretly retains benefits or profits that, by right, belong to the principal. For example, Andrews, a purchasing agent, receives cash rebates from a customer. If Andrews keeps the rebates, he violates his fiduciary duty to his principal, Metcalf. On finding out about the cash rebates, Metcalf can sue Andrews and recover them.

An agent is also prohibited from taking advantage of the agency relationship to obtain goods or property that the principal wants to purchase. For example, Peterson (the principal) wants to purchase property in the suburbs. Cox, Peterson's agent, learns that a valuable tract of land has just become available. Cox cannot buy the land for herself. Peterson gets the right of first refusal. If Cox purchases the land for her own benefit, the courts will impose a *constructive trust* on the land; that is, the land will be held for, and on behalf of, the principal despite the fact that the agent attempted to buy it in her own name.

AVOIDANCE   When an agent breaches the agency agreement or agency duties under a contract, the principal has a right to avoid any contract entered into with the agent. This right of avoidance is at the election of the principal.

INDEMNIFICATION   In certain situations, when a principal is sued by a third party for an agent's negligent conduct, the principal can sue the agent for an equal amount of damages. This is called *indemnification*. The same holds true if the agent violates the principal's instructions. For example, Parke (the principal) tells his agent Moore, who is a used-car salesperson, to make no warranties for the used cars. Moore is eager to make a sale to Walters, a third party, and adds a 50,000-mile warranty for the car's engine. Parke may still be liable to Walters for engine failure, but if Walters sues Parke, Parke normally can then sue Moore for indemnification for violating his instructions.

Sometimes, it is difficult to distinguish between instructions of the principal that limit an agent's authority and those that are merely advice. For example, Gutierrez (the principal) owns an office supply company; Logan (the agent) is the manager. Gutierrez tells Logan, "Don't purchase any more inventory this month." Gutierrez goes on vacation. A large order comes in from a local business, and the present inventory is insufficient to meet it. What is Logan to do? In this situation, Logan probably has the inherent authority to purchase more inventory despite Gutierrez's command. It is unlikely that Logan would be required to indemnify Gutierrez in the event that the local business subsequently canceled the order.

SECTION 5 | Scope of Agent's Authority

A principal's liability in a contract with a third party arises from the authority given the agent to enter into legally binding contracts on the principal's behalf. An agent's authority can be either *actual* (express or implied) or *apparent*.

EXPRESS AUTHORITY

Express authority is embodied in that which the principal has engaged the agent to do. Express authority can be given orally or in writing.

THE EQUAL DIGNITY RULE   The **equal dignity rule** in most states requires that if the contract being executed is or must be in writing, then the agent's authority must also be in writing. Failure to comply with the equal dignity rule can make a contract voidable *at the option of the principal*. The law regards the contract at that point as a mere offer. If the principal decides to accept the offer, acceptance must be ratified, or affirmed, in writing.

Assume that Pattberg (the principal) orally asks Austin (the agent) to sell a ranch that Pattberg owns. Austin finds a buyer and signs a sales contract (a contract for an interest in realty must be in writing) on behalf of Pattberg to sell the ranch. The buyer cannot enforce the contract unless Pattberg subsequently ratifies Austin's agency status in writing. Once the contract is ratified, either party can enforce rights under the contract.

Modern business practice allows an exception to the equal dignity rule. An executive officer of a corporation, when acting for the corporation in an ordinary business situation, is not required to obtain written authority from the corporation. In addition, the equal dignity rule does not apply when an agent acts in the presence of a principal or when the agent's act of signing is merely perfunctory. Thus, if Healy (the principal) negotiates a contract but is called out of town the day it is to be signed and orally authorizes Scougall to sign, the oral authorization is sufficient.

POWER OF ATTORNEY Giving an agent a **power of attorney** confers express authority.[8] The power of attorney is a written document and is usually notarized. (A document is notarized when a **notary public**—a public official authorized to attest to the authenticity of signatures—signs and dates the document and imprints it with her or his seal of authority.) Most states have statutory provisions for creating a power of attorney. A power of attorney can be special (permitting the agent to perform specified acts only), or it can be general (permitting the agent to transact all business for the principal). Because of the extensive authority granted to an agent by a general power of attorney (see Exhibit 19–1), it should be used with great caution and usually only in exceptional circumstances. Ordinarily, a power of attorney terminates on the incapacity or death of the person giving the power.[9]

---

8. An agent who holds the power of attorney is called an *attorney-in-fact* for the principal. The holder does not have to be an attorney-at-law (and often is not).

9. A *durable* power of attorney, however, continues to be effective despite the principal's incapacity. An elderly person, for example, might grant a durable power of attorney to provide for the handling of property and investments or specific health-care needs should he or she become incompetent.

EXHIBIT 19–1 **A Sample General Power of Attorney**

GENERAL POWER OF ATTORNEY

Know All Men by These Presents:

That I, _____ , hereinafter referred to as PRINCIPAL, in the County of _____
State of _____ , do(es) appoint _____ as my true and lawful attorney.

In principal's name, and for principal's use and benefit, said attorney is authorized hereby;

(1) To demand, sue for, collect, and receive all money, debts, accounts, legacies, bequests, interest, dividends, annuities, and demands as are now or shall hereafter become due, payable, or belonging to principal, and take all lawful means, for the recovery thereof and to compromise the same and give discharges for the same;

(2) To buy and sell land, make contracts of every kind relative to land, any interest therein or the possession thereof, and to take possession and exercise control over the use thereof;

(3) To buy, sell, mortgage, hypothecate, assign, transfer, and in any manner deal with goods, wares and merchandise, choses in action, certificates or shares of capital stock, and other property in possession or in action, and to make, do, and transact all and every kind of business of whatever nature;

(4) To execute, acknowledge, and deliver contracts of sale, escrow instructions, deeds, leases including leases for minerals and hydrocarbon substances and assignments of leases, covenants, agreements and assignments of agreements, mortgages and assignments of mortgages, conveyances in trust, to secure indebtedness or other obligations, and assign the beneficial interest thereunder, subordinations of liens or encumbrances, bills of lading, receipts, evidences of debt, releases, bonds, notes, bills, requests to reconvey deeds of trust, partial or full judgments, satisfactions of mortgages, and other debts, and other written instruments of whatever kind and nature, all upon such terms and conditions as said attorney shall approve.

GIVING AND GRANTING to said attorney full power and authority to do all and every act and thing whatsoever requisite and necessary to be done relative to any of the foregoing as fully to all intents and purposes as principal might or could do if personally present.

All that said attorney shall lawfully do or cause to be done under the authority of this power of attorney is expressly approved.

Dated: _____   /s/ _____

State of California
    County of _____ } SS.
On _____ , before me, the undersigned, a Notary Public in and for said
State, personally appeared _____

known to me to be the person _____ whose name _____ subscribed
to the within instrument and acknowledged that _____ executed the same.
                                       (Seal) _____
Witness my hand and official seal.   Notary Public in and for said State.

IMPLIED AUTHORITY

Implied authority is conferred by custom, can be inferred from the position the agent occupies, or is implied by virtue of being reasonably necessary to carry out express authority. For example, Carlson is employed by Packard Grocery to manage one of its stores. Packard has not expressly stated that Carlson has authority to contract with third persons. In this situation, though, authority to manage a business implies authority to do what is reasonably required (as is customary or can be inferred from a manager's position) to operate the business. This includes making contracts for hiring personnel, for buying merchandise and equipment, and even for advertising the products sold in the store.

Because implied authority is conferred on the basis of custom, it is important for third persons to be familiar with the custom of the particular trade. Courts have developed rules to determine what authority is implied based on custom or on the agent's position. In general, implied authority is authority customarily associated with the position occupied by the agent or authority that can be inferred from the express authority given to the agent to fully perform his or her duties.

For example, an agent who has authority to solicit orders for goods sold by the principal generally has no authority to collect payments for the goods unless the agent possesses the goods. The test is whether it was reasonable for the agent to believe that she or he had the authority to enter into the contract in question.

APPARENT AUTHORITY AND ESTOPPEL

Actual authority (express or implied) arises from what the principal manifests *to the agent*. An agent has **apparent authority** when the principal, by either word or action, causes a *third party* reasonably to believe that the agent has authority to act, even though the agent has no express or implied authority. If the third party changes his or her position in reliance on the principal's representations, the principal may be *estopped* (prevented) from denying that the agent had authority.

APPARENT AUTHORITY THROUGH A PATTERN OF CONDUCT

When a principal's actions over time lead a third party to believe that an agency relationship exists, an *agency by estoppel* may arise based on apparent authority. For example, assume that Adam is a traveling sales agent for a pesticide company. Adam neither possesses the goods ordered nor delivers them,

and he has no express or implied authority to collect payments from customers. Now assume that a customer, Ling, pays Adam for a solicited order. Adam then takes the payment to the principal's accounting department. An accountant accepts the payment and sends Ling a receipt. This procedure is thereafter followed for other orders solicited by Adam and paid for by Ling. Later, Adam solicits an order, and Ling pays Adam as before. This time, however, Adam absconds with the money.

Can Ling claim that the payment to Adam was authorized and thus, in effect, was a payment to the principal? The answer is yes, because the principal's *repeated* acts of accepting Ling's payments through Adam led Ling reasonably to believe that Adam had authority to receive payments for goods solicited. Although Adam did not have express or implied authority, the principal's conduct gave Adam apparent authority to collect the payments.

APPARENT AUTHORITY THROUGH AN AGENT'S POSSESSION OF PROPERTY

An agency by estoppel may also arise in other situations based on apparent authority. If, for example, the principal has "clothed the agent" with both possession and apparent ownership of the principal's property, the agent has very broad powers and can deal with the property as if she or he were the true owner.

When land is involved, courts have held that possession alone is not a sufficient indication of ownership. If, however, the agent also possesses the deed to the property and sells the property against the principal's wishes to an unsuspecting buyer, the principal normally cannot cancel the sale or assert a claim to the title.

EMERGENCY POWERS

When an unforeseen emergency demands action by the agent to protect or preserve the property and rights of the principal, but the agent is unable to communicate with the principal, the agent has emergency power.

For example, Fulsom is an engineer for Pacific Railroad. While Fulsom is acting within the scope of his employment, he falls under the train many miles from home and is severely injured. Dudley, the conductor, directs Thompson, a physician, to give medical aid to Fulsom and to charge Pacific for the medical services. Dudley, an agent, has no express or implied authority to bind the principal, Pacific Railroad, for

Thompson's services. Because of the emergency situation, however, the law recognizes Dudley as having authority to act appropriately under the circumstances.

RATIFICATION

Ratification occurs when the principal affirms an agent's *unauthorized* act. When ratification occurs the principal is bound to the agent's act, and the act is treated as if it had been authorized by the principal *from the outset.* Ratification can be either express or implied.

If the principal does not ratify the contract, the principal is not bound, and the third party's agreement with the agent is merely an unaccepted offer. Because the third party's agreement is an unaccepted offer, the third party can revoke it any time, without liability, before the principal ratifies the contract. The agent, however, may be liable to the third party for misrepresenting his or her authority.

REQUIREMENTS FOR RATIFICATION The requirements for ratification can be summarized as follows:

1. The agent must act on behalf of an identified principal who subsequently ratifies the action.
2. The principal must affirm the agent's act in its entirety.
3. The principal's affirmance must occur before the third party withdraws from the transaction.
4. The principal must have the legal capacity to authorize the transaction at the time the agent engages in the act and at the time the principal ratifies. The third party must also have the legal capacity to engage in the transaction.
5. The principal must know all of the material facts involved in the transaction.

PRINCIPAL'S KNOWLEDGE OF THE FACTS Regarding the last requirement in the above list, if a principal ratifies a contract *without knowing* all of the facts, the principal can rescind (cancel) the ratification. If the third party has changed position in reliance on the apparent contract, however, the principal can rescind but must reimburse the third party for any costs.

For example, suppose that an agent, without authority, contracts with a third person on behalf of a principal for repair work on the principal's office building. The principal learns of the contract and agrees to "some repair work," thinking that it will involve only patching and painting the building's exterior. In fact, the contract includes resurfacing the parking lot, which the principal

does not want done. On learning of the additional provision, the principal rescinds the contract. If the third party has made preparations to do the work (such as purchasing materials, hiring additional employees, or renting equipment) in reliance on the principal's apparent ratification, the principal must reimburse the third party for the cost of those preparations.

SECTION 6 | Liability for Contracts

Liability for contracts formed by an agent depends on how the principal is classified and on whether the actions of the agent were authorized or unauthorized. Principals are classified as disclosed, partially disclosed, or undisclosed.[10]

A **disclosed principal** is a principal whose identity is known by the third party at the time the contract is made by the agent. A **partially disclosed principal** is a principal whose identity is not known by the third party, but the third party knows that the agent is or may be acting for a principal at the time the contract is made. An **undisclosed principal** is a principal whose identity is totally unknown by the third party, and the third party has no knowledge that the agent is acting in an agency capacity at the time the contract is made.

AUTHORIZED ACTS

If an agent acts within the scope of her or his authority, normally the principal is obligated to perform the contract regardless of whether the principal was disclosed, partially disclosed, or undisclosed. Whether the agent may also be held liable under the contract, however, depends on the disclosed, partially disclosed, or undisclosed status of the principal.

DISCLOSED OR PARTIALLY DISCLOSED PRINCIPAL
A disclosed or partially disclosed principal is liable to a third party for a contract made by the agent. If the principal is disclosed, an agent has no contractual liability for the nonperformance of the principal or the third party. If the principal is partially disclosed, in most states the agent is also treated as a party to the contract, and the third party can hold the agent liable for contractual nonperformance.[11] The following case illustrates the rules that apply to contracts signed by agents on behalf of fully disclosed principals.

10. *Restatement (Second) of Agency,* Section 4.
11. *Restatement (Second) of Agency,* Section 321.

CASE 19.3

Appellate
Court of Illinois,
First District, 2002.
327 Ill.App.3d 992,
765 N.E.2d 51,
262 Ill.Dec. 225.
http://state.il.us/
court/default.htm[a]

McBride v. Taxman Corp.

BACKGROUND AND FACTS *Walgreens Company entered into a lease with Taxman Corporation to operate a drugstore in Kedzie Plaza, a shopping center in Chicago, Illinois, owned by Kedzie Plaza Associates; Taxman was the center's property manager. The lease required the "Landlord" to promptly remove snow and ice from the center's sidewalks. Taxman also signed, on behalf of Kedzie Associates, an agreement with Arctic Snow and Ice Control, Inc., to remove ice and snow from the sidewalks surrounding the Walgreens store. On January 27, 1996, Grace McBride, a Walgreens employee, slipped and fell on snow and ice outside the entrance to the store. McBride filed a suit in an Illinois state court against Taxman and others alleging, among other things, that Taxman had negligently failed to remove the accumulation of ice and snow.[b] Taxman filed a motion for summary judgment in its favor, which the court granted. McBride appealed to a state intermediate appellate court.*

IN THE LANGUAGE OF THE COURT

Justice CERDA delivered the opinion of the court.

* * * *

On October 10, 1995, Taxman signed, on behalf of the owner, Arctic's one-page "Snow Removal Proposal & Contract" (although dated August 7, 1995), for the term November 15, 1995, through April 15, 1996, for the shopping center where this Walgreens store was located. * * *

Also on October 10, 1995, Arctic and Taxman signed a multi-page document dated October 3, 1995, that was apparently drafted by Taxman. The document was not given a title but contained several pages of terms concerning snow removal "per contract(s) attached." * * *

* * * *

Plaintiff argues that the contract between Taxman and Arctic created a duty of Taxman to remove ice and snow for the benefit of plaintiff. * * *

* * * *

The Arctic proposal and contract was signed "Kedzie Associates by the Taxman." The Taxman-drafted portion of the contract contained a line above the signature of Taxman's director of property management stating "The Taxman Corporation, agent for per contracts attached." The latter document specifically stated that the contract was not an obligation of Taxman and that all liabilities were those of the owner and not Taxman. We conclude that Taxman was the management company for the property owner and entered into the two contracts for snow and ice removal only as the owner's agent.

Taxman did not assume a contractual obligation to remove snow or ice; it merely retained Arctic as a contractor on behalf of the owner.

DECISION AND REMEDY *The state intermediate appellate court affirmed the judgment of the lower court. The appellate court held that Taxman entered into the snow removal contracts only as the agent of the owner, whose identity was fully disclosed. As agent for a disclosed principal, Taxman had no liability for the nonperformance of the principal or the third party to the contract.*

WHAT IF THE FACTS WERE DIFFERENT? *Suppose that the Arctic contract had not identified Kedzie as the principal. How might the court's decision in this case have been different?*

---

a. On this page, click on "Appellate Court of Illinois." On the page that opens, in the "Appellate Court Documents" section, click on "Appellate Court Opinions." In the result, in the "Appellate Court" section, click on "2002." On the next page, in the "First District" section, click on "January." Finally, scroll to the bottom of the chart and click on the case name to access the opinion. The state of Illinois maintains this Web site.
b. McBride included in her suit complaints against Walgreens and Kedzie Associates but settled those complaints before trial.

UNDISCLOSED PRINCIPAL When neither the fact of an agency relationship nor the identity of the principal is disclosed, the undisclosed principal is fully bound to perform just as if the principal had been fully disclosed at the time the contract was made.

When a principal's identity is undisclosed and the agent is forced to pay the third party, the agent is entitled to be *indemnified* (compensated) by the principal. The principal had a duty to perform, even though his or her identity was undisclosed, and failure to do so will make the principal ultimately liable. Once the undisclosed principal's identity is revealed, the third party generally can elect to hold either the principal or the agent liable on the contract.

Conversely, the undisclosed principal can require the third party to fulfill the contract, *unless* (1) the undisclosed principal was expressly excluded as a party in the written contract, (2) the contract is a negotiable instrument signed by the agent with no indication of signing in a representative capacity,[12] or (3) the performance of the agent is personal to the contract, allowing the third party to refuse the principal's performance.

UNAUTHORIZED ACTS

If an agent has no authority but nevertheless contracts with a third party, the principal cannot be held liable on the contract. It does not matter whether the principal was disclosed, partially disclosed, or undisclosed. The agent is liable, however. For example, Scammon signs a contract for the purchase of a truck, purportedly acting as an agent under authority granted by Johnson. In fact, Johnson has not given Scammon any such authority. Johnson refuses to pay for the truck, claiming that Scammon had no authority to purchase it. The seller of the truck is entitled to hold Scammon liable for payment.

If the principal is disclosed or partially disclosed, the agent is liable as long as the third party relied on the agency status. The agent's liability here is based on the theory of breach of implied warranty of authority, not on breach of the contract itself.[13] The agent's implied warranty of authority can be breached intentionally or by a good faith mistake.[14] If the third party knows at the time the contract is made that the agent is mistaken about the extent of her or his authority, though, the agent is not liable. Similarly, if the agent

---

12. Under the Uniform Commercial Code (UCC), only the agent is liable if the instrument neither names the principal nor shows that the agent signed in a representative capacity [UCC 3–402(b)(2)].

13. The agent is not liable on the contract because the agent was never intended personally to be a party to the contract.
14. If the agent intentionally misrepresents his or her authority, then the agent can also be liable in tort for fraud.

CONCEPT SUMMARY 19.2 | Authority of Agent to Bind Principal and Third Party

AUTHORITY OF AGENT	DEFINITION	EFFECT ON PRINCIPAL AND THIRD PARTY
EXPRESS AUTHORITY	Authority expressly given by the principal to the agent.	Principal and third party are bound in contract.
IMPLIED AUTHORITY	Authority implied (1) by custom, (2) from the position in which the principal has placed the agent, or (3) because such authority is necessary if the agent is to carry out expressly authorized duties and responsibilities.	Principal and third party are bound in contract.
APPARENT AUTHORITY	Authority created when the conduct of the principal leads a third party to believe that the principal's agent has authority.	Principal and third party are bound in contract.
UNAUTHORIZED ACTS	Acts committed by an agent that are outside the scope of his or her express, implied, or apparent authority.	Principal and third party are not bound in contract—*unless* the principal ratifies prior to the third party's withdrawal.

indicates to the third party *uncertainty* about the extent of the authority, the agent is not personally liable.

ACTIONS BY E-AGENTS

An electronic agent, or **e-agent,** is not a person but a semiautonomous computer program that is capable of executing specific tasks. E-agents used in e-commerce include software that can search through many databases and retrieve only relevant information for the user. Although in the past, standard agency principles have applied only to *human* agents, today these same agency principles are being applied to e-agents.

The Uniform Electronic Transactions Act (UETA), which was discussed in detail in Chapter 11, sets forth provisions relating to the principal's liability for the actions of e-agents. Provisions of the act have been adopted in the majority of the states. Section 15 of the UETA states that e-agents may enter into binding agreements on behalf of their principals. For example, if you place an order over the Internet, the company (principal) whose system took the order via an e-agent cannot claim that it did not receive your order. The UETA establishes that e-agents generally have the authority to bind the principal in contract—at least in those states that have adopted the act.

The UETA also stipulates that if an e-agent does not provide an opportunity to prevent errors at the time of the transaction, the other party to the transaction can avoid the transaction. If an e-agent fails to provide an on-screen confirmation of a purchase or sale, for instance, the other party can avoid the effect of any errors. For example, suppose that Finig wants to purchase three each of three different items (a total of nine items). The e-agent mistakenly records an order for thirty-three of a single item and does not provide an on-screen verification of the order. If thirty-three items are then sent to Finig, he can avoid the contract to purchase them.

SECTION 7 | Liability for Torts and Crimes

Obviously, any person, including an agent, is liable for his or her own torts and crimes. Whether a principal can also be held liable for an agent's torts and crimes depends on several factors, which we examine here. In some situations, a principal may be held liable not only for the torts of an agent but also for the torts committed by an independent contractor.

PRINCIPAL'S TORTIOUS CONDUCT

A principal conducting an activity through an agent may be liable for harm resulting from the principal's own negligence or recklessness. Thus, a principal may be liable for giving improper instructions, authorizing the use of improper materials or tools, or establishing improper rules that result in the agent's committing a tort. For instance, if Jack knows that Lucy cannot drive but nevertheless tells her to use the company truck to deliver some equipment to a customer, he will be liable for his own negligence to anyone injured by her negligent driving.

PRINCIPAL'S AUTHORIZATION OF AGENT'S TORTIOUS CONDUCT

Similarly, a principal who authorizes an agent to commit a tort may be liable to persons or property injured thereby, because the act is considered to be the principal's. For example, Selkow directs his agent, Warren, to cut the corn on specific acreage, which neither of them has the right to do. The harvest is therefore a trespass (a tort), and Selkow is liable to whoever owns the corn.

Note that an agent acting at the principal's direction can be liable as a *tortfeasor* (one who commits a wrong, or tort), along with the principal, for committing the tortious act even if the agent was unaware of the wrongfulness of the act. Assume in the above example that Warren, the agent, did not know that Selkow lacked the right to harvest the corn. Warren can still be held liable to the owner of the field for damages, along with Selkow, the principal.

LIABILITY FOR AGENT'S MISREPRESENTATION

A principal is exposed to tort liability whenever a third person sustains a loss due to the agent's misrepresentation. The principal's liability depends on whether the agent was actually or apparently authorized to make representations and whether such representations were made within the scope of the agency. The principal is always directly responsible for an agent's misrepresentation made within the scope of the agent's authority.

Assume that Bassett is a demonstrator for Moore's products. Moore sends Bassett to a home show to demonstrate the products and to answer questions from consumers. Moore has given Bassett authority to make statements about the products. If Bassett makes only true representations, all is fine; but if he makes false claims, Moore will be liable for any injuries or damages sustained by third parties in reliance on Bassett's false representations.

APPARENT IMPLIED AUTHORITY When a principal has placed an agent in a position of apparent authority—making it possible for the agent to defraud a third party—the principal may also be liable for the agent's fraudulent acts. For example, Frendak is a loan officer at First Security Bank. In the ordinary course of the job, Frendak approves and services loans and has access to the credit records of all customers. Frendak falsely represents to a borrower, McMillan, that the bank feels insecure about McMillan's loan and intends to call it in unless McMillan provides additional collateral, such as stocks and bonds. McMillan gives Frendak numerous stock certificates, which Frendak keeps in her own possession and later uses to make personal investments. The bank is liable to McMillan for losses sustained on the stocks even though the bank was unaware of the fraudulent scheme.

If, in contrast, Frendak had been a recently hired junior bank teller rather than a loan officer when she told McMillan that the bank required additional security for the loan, McMillan would not have been justified in relying on Frendak's representation. In that situation, the bank normally would not be held liable to McMillan for the losses sustained.

The following case focused on a partner's potential liability for claims against the partnership arising from the torts of its manager. The partner argued that he could not be liable because the manager did not have the apparent authority to commit torts. Among those with claims against the firm was the partner's mother.

CASE 19.4 | In re Selheimer & Co.

United States District Court, Eastern District of Pennsylvania, 2005. 319 Bankr. 395.

BACKGROUND AND FACTS *Selheimer & Company was formed as a partnership in 1967 to act as a securities broker-dealer, buying and selling stocks and bonds and providing other financial services, in Pennsylvania. In 1994, during an investigation by the Securities and Exchange Commission (SEC), the firm closed.[a] Perry Selheimer, the managing partner, was charged with various crimes and pleaded guilty to mail fraud. Other partners, including Edward Murphy, and the firm's clients, including Murphy's mother, Jeanne Murphy, filed claims with the Securities Investor Protection Corporation (SIPC) to be reimbursed for their losses. The SIPC advanced over $250,000 to pay these claims. With more than $1 million in claims outstanding, the SIPC petitioned the firm into involuntary bankruptcy in 2002. Because the firm had few assets, the SIPC asked the court to rule that the personal assets of the individual partners could be used to cover the liability. The SIPC filed a motion for summary judgment on this issue. Edward Murphy opposed the request.*

IN THE LANGUAGE OF THE COURT

STEPHEN RASLAVICH, Bankruptcy Judge.

* * * *

* * * [I]n Pennsylvania a partner is jointly and severally liable for certain torts chargeable to the partnership [if those torts are committed within the ordinary course of the partnership business]. * * * [Emphasis added.]

* * * *

Murphy maintains that he is not * * * liable for Selheimer's acts because the record does not show that such conduct was within the ordinary course of business of the partnership * * *.

The record demonstrates that Selheimer & Co. perpetrated its fraud under the guise of operating a brokerage firm. The partnership was a registered securities broker-dealer that accepted money from clients for investment purposes. Instead, Selheimer embezzled those funds. Selheimer's criminal acts were performed within the normal operation of this partnership's business. Put another way, at the time Selheimer was defrauding clients, it was acting in the ordinary course of the partnership's business. The partnership is therefore liable for those

---

a. The SEC is a federal agency that regulates the activities of securities brokers and others. See Chapter 28.

CONTINUED ▶

CASE 19.4 Continued acts of Mr. Selheimer. And if the partnership is liable for those debts, then individual partners, including Murphy, are jointly and severally liable as well.

* * * *

Alternatively, Murphy argues that there is no evidence of partnership liability * * * because there is nothing to indicate that Selheimer was acting within the scope of his apparent authority when defrauding customers. In this Commonwealth, the doctrine of apparent authority has been incorporated into the principles of agency law. Apparent authority has been defined [in the *Restatement (Second) of Agency*, Section 8] as "the power to affect the legal relations of another person by transactions with third persons, professedly as agent for the other, arising from and in accordance with the other's manifestations to third persons." [According to the *Restatement (Second) of Agency*, Section 27, the] general rule governing the creation of apparent authority is:

> Except for the execution of instruments under seal or for the conduct of transactions required by statute to be authorized in a particular way, apparent authority to do an act is created as to a third person by written or spoken words or any other conduct of the principal which, reasonably interpreted, causes the third person to believe that the principal consents to have the act done on his behalf by the person purporting to act for him.

Apparent authority exists when a principal, by words or conduct, leads people with whom the alleged agent deals to believe the principal has granted the agent authority he or she purports to exercise. *Apparent authority may result when a principal permits an agent to occupy a position [in] which, according to the ordinary experience and habits of mankind, it is usual for that occupant to have authority of a particular kind.* The nature and extent of an agent's apparent authority is a question of fact for the fact-finder. [Emphasis added.]

Murphy misinterprets agency law when he argues that Selheimer lacked authority, express or apparent, to defraud clients. His argument operates from the erroneous premise that the record must show that Selheimer & Co., as principal, gave Perry Selheimer, as agent, license to steal. If that were so, then the doctrine of apparent authority would be eviscerated [gutted]. What matters is whether Selheimer & Co. was authorized to accept client funds for investment. And the record shows that it certainly was: Selheimer & Co. was a broker-dealer registered with the SEC. Mr. Selheimer formally admitted—pleaded guilty, in fact—to having committed "an abuse of trust" as to his clients. Client confidence would not have been placed in him unless he held himself out as an honest broker-dealer of financial investments; otherwise, clients simply would have taken their business elsewhere. There is thus sufficient proof to support a finding that Selheimer was acting within his apparent authority when defrauding clients. That, in turn, supports a finding of liability as to the partnership which may by assessed against Murphy.

DECISION AND REMEDY *The court found that "Selheimer & Co. is deficient; that Murphy was a partner of Selheimer & Co.; and that he is indirectly liable under Pennsylvania law for the acts of Perry Selheimer which are chargeable to Selheimer & Co." on a theory of apparent authority. The court issued a summary judgment "in a liquidated amount for the $251,158.12 in claims advanced by [the] SIPC and an additional $840,667 for the customer claim of Jeanne Murphy."*

WHAT IF THE FACTS WERE DIFFERENT? *If Selheimer & Company had not had the authority to accept funds for investment, did not authorize its manager to accept such funds, and did not represent that the manager or the firm had this authority, would the outcome in this case have been different? Explain.*

INNOCENT MISREPRESENTATION Tort liability based on fraud requires proof that a material misstatement was made knowingly and with the intent to deceive. An agent's innocent mistakes occurring in a contract transaction or involving a warranty contained in the contract can provide grounds for the third party's rescission of the contract and the award of damages. Moreover, justice dictates that when a principal knows that an agent is not accurately advised of facts but does not correct either the agent's or the third party's impressions, the principal is directly responsible to the third party for resulting damages. The point is that the principal is always directly responsible for an agent's misrepresentation made within the scope of authority.

LIABILITY FOR AGENT'S NEGLIGENCE

Under the doctrine of **respondeat superior,**[15] the principal-employer is liable for any harm caused to a third party by an agent-employee within the scope of employment. This doctrine imposes **vicarious liability,** or indirect liability, on the employer—that is, liability without regard to the personal fault of the employer for torts committed by an employee in the course or scope of employment.[16] Third persons injured through the negligence of an employee can sue either the employee who was negligent or the employer, if the employee's negligent conduct occurred while the employee was acting within the scope of employment.

RATIONALE UNDERLYING THE DOCTRINE OF RESPONDEAT SUPERIOR At early common law, a servant (employee) was viewed as the master's (employer's) property. The master was deemed to have absolute control over the servant's acts and was held strictly liable for them no matter how carefully the master supervised the servant. The rationale for the doctrine of *respondeat superior* is based on the principle of social duty that requires every person to manage his or her affairs, whether accomplished by the person or through agents, so as not to injure another. Liability is imposed on employers because they are deemed to be in a better financial position to bear the loss. The superior financial position carries with it the duty to be responsible for damages.

Generally, public policy requires that an injured person be afforded effective relief, and recovery from a business enterprise often provides far more effective relief than recovery from an individual employee. Employers normally carry liability insurance to protect themselves against such lawsuits. They are also able to spread the cost of risk over the entire business enterprise.

The doctrine of *respondeat superior,* which the courts have applied for nearly two centuries, continues to have practical implications in all situations involving principal-agent (employer-employee) relationships. Today, the small-town grocer with one clerk and the multinational corporation with thousands of employees are equally subject to the doctrinal demand of "let the master respond."

DETERMINING THE SCOPE OF EMPLOYMENT As mentioned, for the employer to be liable under the doctrine of *respondeat superior,* the employee's injury-causing act must have occurred within the course and scope of her or his employment. The *Restatement (Second) of Agency,* Section 229, outlines the following general factors that courts will consider in determining whether a particular act occurred within the course and scope of employment:

1. Whether the employee's act was authorized by the employer.
2. The time, place, and purpose of the act.
3. Whether the act was one commonly performed by employees on behalf of their employers.
4. The extent to which the employer's interest was advanced by the act.
5. The extent to which the private interests of the employee were involved.
6. Whether the employer furnished the means or instrumentality (for example, a truck or a machine) by which an injury was inflicted.
7. Whether the employer had reason to know that the employee would perform the act in question and whether the employee had done it before.
8. Whether the act involved the commission of a serious crime.

EMPLOYEE TRAVEL TIME An employee going to and from work or to and from meals is usually considered to be outside the scope of employment. In contrast, all travel time of traveling salespersons or others whose jobs require them to travel is normally considered to be within the scope of employment for the duration of the business trip, including the return trip home, unless there is a significant departure from the employer's business.

NOTICE OF DANGEROUS CONDITIONS The employer is charged with knowledge of any dangerous conditions discovered by an employee and pertinent to the employment situation. Suppose that Brad, a maintenance employee in Tartin's apartment building, notices a lead pipe protruding from the ground in the building's courtyard. The employee neglects either to

---

15. Pronounced ree-*spahn*-dee-uht soo-*peer*-ee-your. The doctrine of *respondeat superior* applies not only to employer-employee relationships but also to other principal-agent relationships in which the principal has the right of control over the agent.
16. The theory of *respondeat superior* is similar to the theory of strict liability covered in Chapter 13.

fix it or to inform the employer of the danger. John falls on the pipe and is injured. The employer is charged with knowledge of the dangerous condition regardless of whether Brad actually informed the employer. That knowledge is imputed to the employer by virtue of the employment relationship.

THE DISTINCTION BETWEEN A "DETOUR" AND A "FROLIC" A useful insight into the concept of the "scope of employment" may be gained from Judge Baron Parke's classic distinction between a "detour" and a "frolic" in the case of *Joel v. Morison* (1834).[17] In this case, the English court held that if a servant merely took a detour from his master's business, the master will be responsible. If, however, the servant was on a "frolic of his own" and not in any way "on his master's business," the master will not be liable.

Consider an example. Mandel, a traveling salesperson, while driving the employer's vehicle to call on a customer, decides to stop at the post office—which is one block off his route—to mail a personal letter. As Mandel approaches the post office, he negligently runs into a parked vehicle owned by Chan. In this situation, because Mandel's detour from the employer's business is not substantial, he is still acting within the scope of employment, and the employer is liable. The result would be different, though, if Mandel had decided to pick up a few friends for cocktails in another city and in the process had negligently run his vehicle into Chan's. In that circumstance, the departure from the employer's business would be substantial, and the employer normally would not be liable to Chan for damages. Mandel would be considered to have been on a "frolic" of his own.

LIABILITY FOR AGENT'S INTENTIONAL TORTS

Most intentional torts that employees commit have no relation to their employment; thus, their employers will not be held liable. Nevertheless, under the doctrine of *respondeat superior,* the employer can be liable for intentional torts of the employee that are committed within the course and scope of employment, just as the employer is liable for negligence. For example, an employer is liable when an employee (such as a "bouncer" at a nightclub or a security guard at a department store) commits assault and battery or false

---

17. 6 Car. & P. 501, 172 Eng. Rep. 1338 (1834).

imprisonment while acting within the scope of employment.

In addition, an employer who knows or should know that an employee has a propensity for committing tortious acts is liable for the employee's acts even if they would not ordinarily be considered within the scope of employment. For example, if the employer hires a bouncer knowing that he has a history of arrests for assault and battery, the employer may be liable if the employee viciously attacks a patron in the parking lot after hours.

An employer is also liable for permitting an employee to engage in reckless actions that can injure others. For example, an employer observes an employee smoking while filling containerized trucks with highly flammable liquids. Failure to stop the employee will cause the employer to be liable for any injuries that result if a truck explodes. Needless to say, most employers purchase liability insurance to cover their potential liability for employee conduct in many situations.

LIABILITY FOR INDEPENDENT CONTRACTOR'S TORTS

Generally, an employer is not liable for physical harm caused to a third person by the negligent act of an independent contractor in the performance of the contract. This is because the employer does not have *the right to control* the details of an independent contractor's performance. Exceptions to this rule are made in certain situations, though, such as when unusually hazardous activities are involved. Typical examples of such activities include blasting operations, the transportation of highly volatile chemicals, or the use of poisonous gases. In these situations, an employer cannot be shielded from liability merely by using an independent contractor. Strict liability is imposed on the employer-principal as a matter of law. Also, in some states, strict liability may be imposed by statute.

LIABILITY FOR AGENT'S CRIMES

An agent is liable for his or her own crimes. A principal or employer is not liable for an agent's or employee's crime simply because the agent or employee committed the crime while otherwise acting within the scope of authority or employment. An exception to this rule is made when the principal or employer participated in the crime by conspiracy or other action. In some jurisdictions, under specific statutes, a principal may be liable for an agent's violating, in the course and scope of employment, such regulations as those governing sanitation, prices, weights, and the sale of liquor.

SECTION 8 | Termination of an Agency

Agency law is similar to contract law in that both an agency and a contract may be terminated by an act of the parties or by operation of law. Once the relationship between the principal and the agent has ended, the agent no longer has *actual* authority to bind the principal—that is, she or he lacks the principal's consent to act on the principal's behalf. Generally, however, if the agency is terminated by an act of the parties, the principal can still be bound by the agent's acts if the agent has acted within the scope of his or her *apparent* authority. To terminate the agent's apparent authority, third parties must be notified of the agency termination—as will be discussed later.

TERMINATION BY ACT OF THE PARTIES

An agency relationship may be terminated by act of the parties in a number of ways, including those discussed here.

LAPSE OF TIME An agency agreement may specify the time period during which the agency relationship will exist. If so, the agency ends when that time expires. For example, Akers signs an agreement of agency with Janz "beginning January 1, 2006, and ending December 31, 2007." The agency is automatically terminated on December 31, 2007. Of course, the parties can agree to continue the relationship; if they do, the same terms will apply. If no definite time is stated, then the agency continues for a reasonable time and can be terminated at will by either party. What constitutes a reasonable time depends on the circumstances and the nature of the agency relationship.

PURPOSE ACHIEVED An agent can be employed to accomplish a particular objective, such as the purchase of stock for a cattle rancher. In that situation, the agency automatically ends after the cattle have been purchased. If more than one agent is employed to accomplish the same purpose, such as the sale of real estate, the first agent to complete the sale automatically terminates the agency relationship for all the others.

OCCURRENCE OF A SPECIFIC EVENT An agency can be created to terminate on the happening of a certain event. For example, Janz asks Akers to handle her business affairs while she is away. When Janz returns, the agency automatically terminates.

Sometimes, one aspect of the agent's authority terminates on the occurrence of a particular event, but the agency relationship itself does not terminate. For example, Janz, a banker, permits Akers, the credit manager, to grant a credit line of $5,000 to certain depositors who maintain a balance of $5,000 in a savings account. If any customer's savings account balance falls below $5,000, Akers can no longer make the credit line available to that customer. Akers, however, continues to have the right to extend credit to the other customers maintaining the minimum balance.

MUTUAL AGREEMENT Recall from basic contract law that parties can rescind (cancel) a contract by mutually agreeing to terminate the contractual relationship. The same holds true in agency law, regardless of whether the agency contract is in writing or whether it is for a specific duration. For example, Janz no longer wishes Akers to be her agent, and Akers does not want to work for Janz anymore. Either party can communicate to the other the intent to terminate the relationship. Agreement to terminate effectively relieves each of the rights, duties, and powers inherent in the relationship.

TERMINATION BY ONE PARTY As a *general* rule, either party can terminate the agency relationship. The agent's act is said to be a *renunciation* of authority. The principal's act is a *revocation* of authority. Although both parties may have the *power* to terminate—because agency is a consensual relationship, and thus neither party can be compelled to continue in the relationship—they may not possess the *right* to terminate and may therefore be liable for breach of contract.

—Wrongful Termination. Wrongful termination can subject the canceling party to a suit for damages. For example, Akers has a one-year employment contract with Janz to act as Janz's agent for $35,000. Janz can discharge Akers before the contract period expires (Janz has the *power* to breach the contract). Janz, though, will be liable to Akers for money damages, because Janz has no *right* to breach the contract.

Even in an agency at will (that is, an agency that either party may terminate at any time), the principal who wishes to terminate must give the agent *reasonable* notice—that is, at least sufficient notice to allow the agent to recoup his or her expenses and, in some situations, to make a normal profit.

—Agency Coupled with an Interest. A special rule applies in an *agency coupled with an interest*. This type of agency is not an agency in the usual sense because it is created for the agent's benefit instead of for the principal's benefit. For example, suppose that Julie borrows $5,000 from Rob, giving Rob some of her jewelry and signing a letter authorizing him to sell the jewelry as her agent if she fails to repay the loan. After Julie receives the funds from Rob, she attempts to revoke his authority to sell the jewelry. Julie will not succeed in this attempt because a principal cannot revoke an agency created for the agent's benefit.

An agency coupled with an interest should not be confused with a situation in which the agent merely derives proceeds or profits from the sale of the subject matter. For example, an agent who merely receives a commission from the sale of real property does not have a beneficial interest in the property itself. Likewise, an attorney whose fee is a percentage of the recovery (a *contingency fee*—see Chapter 2) merely has an interest in the proceeds. These agency relationships are revocable by the principal, subject to any express contractual arrangements between the principal and the agent.

NOTICE OF TERMINATION When an agency has been terminated by act of the parties, it is the principal's duty to inform any third parties who know of the existence of the agency that it has been terminated (although notice of the termination may be given by others).

—Agent's Authority Continues until Notified. An agent's authority continues until the agent receives some notice of termination. As previously mentioned, notice to third parties follows the general rule that an agent's *apparent authority* continues until the third party receives notice (from any source of information) that the authority has been terminated. The principal is expected to notify *directly* any third party who the principal knows has dealt with the agent. For third parties who have heard about the agency but have not dealt with the agent, *constructive notice* is sufficient.[18]

—Form of Notice. No particular form is required for notice of termination of the principal-agent rela-

tionship to be effective. The principal can actually notify the agent, or the agent can learn of the termination through some other means. For example, Manning bids on a shipment of steel, and Stone is hired as an agent to arrange transportation of the shipment. When Stone learns that Manning has lost the bid, Stone's authority to make the transportation arrangement terminates.

If the agent's authority is written, it must be revoked in writing, and the writing must be shown to all people who saw the original writing that established the agency relationship. Sometimes, a written authorization (such as a power of attorney) contains an expiration date. If the authorization has expired that will be sufficient notice of termination.

TERMINATION BY OPERATION OF LAW

Certain events will terminate agency authority automatically because their occurrence makes it impossible for the agent to perform or improbable that the principal would continue to want performance. We look at these events here. Note that when an agency terminates by operation of law, there is no duty to notify third persons—unless the agent's authority is coupled with an interest.[19]

DEATH OR INSANITY The general rule is that the death or insanity of either the principal or the agent automatically and immediately terminates an ordinary agency relationship. Knowledge of the death or insanity is not required. For example, Janz sends Arlen to Japan to purchase a rare book. Before Arlen makes the purchase, Janz dies. Arlen's agent status is terminated at the moment of Janz's death, even though Arlen does not know that Janz has died. (Some states, however, have changed the common law by statute to make knowledge of the principal's death a requirement for agency termination.)

An agent's transactions that occur after the death of the principal are not binding on the principal's estate. Assume that Arlen is hired by Janz to collect a debt from Cochran (a third party). Janz dies, but Arlen, not knowing of Janz's death, still collects the debt from Cochran. Cochran's payment to Arlen is no

---

18. With *constructive notice* of a fact, knowledge of the fact is imputed by law to a person if he or she could have discovered the fact by proper diligence. Constructive notice is often accomplished by publication in a newspaper.

19. There is an exception to this rule in banking. UCC 4–405 provides that the bank, as agent, can continue to exercise specific types of authority even after the customer's death or insanity unless it has knowledge of the death or insanity. When the bank has knowledge of the customer's death, it has authority for ten days after the death to pay checks (but not notes or drafts) drawn by the customer unless it receives a stop-payment order from someone who has an interest in the account, such as an heir.

CONCEPT SUMMARY 19.3 | Termination of an Agency

METHOD OF TERMINATION	RULES	NOTICE OF TERMINATION
ACT OF THE PARTIES		
1. Lapse of time	Automatic at end of stated time.	
2. Purpose achieved	Automatic on completion of purpose.	
3. Occurrence of a specific event	Normally automatic on the happening of the event.	**NOTICE TO THIRD PARTIES REQUIRED—**
4. Mutual agreement	Mutual consent required.	1. Direct to those who have dealt with agency.
5. Termination by one party (revocation, if by principal; renunciation, if by agent)	At-will agencies—generally no breach. Specified-time agencies—breach unless there is legal cause. Cannot revoke an agency coupled with an interest.	2. Constructive to all others.
OPERATION OF LAW		
1. Death or insanity	Automatic on death or insanity of either principal or agent (except when agency is coupled with an interest).	
2. Impossibility—destruction of the specific subject matter	Applies any time agency cannot be performed because of event beyond parties' control.	**NO NOTICE REQUIRED—** Automatic on the happening of the event.
3. Changed circumstances	Events so unusual that it would be inequitable to allow agency to continue to exist.	
4. Bankruptcy	Bankruptcy decree (not mere insolvency) usually terminates agency.	
5. War between principal's country and agent's country	Automatically suspends or terminates agency—no way to enforce legal rights.	

longer legally sufficient to discharge the debt to Janz because Arlen no longer has Janz's authority to collect the funds. If Arlen absconds with the funds, Cochran must pay the debt again to Janz's estate.

IMPOSSIBILITY When the specific subject matter of an agency is destroyed or lost, the agency terminates. For example, Janz employs Arlen to sell Janz's house. Prior to any sale, the house is destroyed by fire. Arlen's agency and authority to sell the house terminate. Similarly, when it is impossible for the agent to perform the agency lawfully because of war or a change in the law, the agency terminates.

CHANGED CIRCUMSTANCES When an event occurs that has such an unusual effect on the subject matter of the agency that the agent can reasonably infer that the principal will not want the agency to continue, the agency terminates. Suppose that Janz hires Arlen to sell a tract of land for $40,000.

Subsequently, Arlen learns that there is oil under the land and that the land is therefore worth $1 million. The agency and Arlen's authority to sell the land for $40,000 are terminated.

BANKRUPTCY If either the principal or the agent petitions for bankruptcy, the agency is *usually* terminated. In certain circumstances, as when the agent's financial status is irrelevant to the purpose of the agency, the agency relationship may continue. *Insolvency* (defined as the inability to pay debts when they become due or when liabilities exceed assets), as distinguished from bankruptcy, does not necessarily terminate the relationship.

WAR When the principal's country and the agent's country are at war with each other, the agency is terminated. In this situation, the agency is automatically suspended or terminated because there is no way to enforce the legal rights and obligations of the parties.

REVIEWING AGENCY

James Blatt hired Marilyn Scott to sell insurance for the Massachusetts Mutual Life Insurance Co. Their contract stated, "Nothing in this contract shall be construed as creating the relationship of employer and employee." The contract was terminable at will by either party. Scott financed her own office and staff, was paid according to performance, had no taxes withheld from her checks, and could legally sell products of Massachusetts Mutual's competitors. But when Blatt learned that Scott was simultaneously selling insurance for Perpetual Life Insurance Corp., one of Massachusetts Mutual's fiercest competitors, Blatt withheld client contact information from Scott that would have assisted her insurance sales for Massachusetts Mutual. Scott complained to Blatt that he was inhibiting her ability to sell insurance for Massachusetts Mutual. Blatt subsequently terminated their contract. Scott filed a suit in a New York state court against Blatt and Massachusetts Mutual. Scott claimed that she had lost sales for Massachusetts Mutual—and her commissions—as a result of Blatt's withholding contact information from her. Using the information presented in the chapter, answer the following questions.

1. Who is the principal and who is the agent in this scenario? By which method was an agency relationship formed between Scott and Blatt?

2. What criteria would the court consider to determine whether Scott was an employee or an independent contractor?

3. How would the IRS decide Scott's employee status?

4. What four duties did Blatt owe Scott in their agency relationship? Which, if any, of those duties has been breached?

5. What five duties did Scott owe Blatt? Did Scott breach any of her duties by selling insurance for Perpetual Life? Explain.

TERMS AND CONCEPTS TO REVIEW

agency 460	fiduciary 460	ratification 473
apparent authority 472	implied authority 472	*respondeat superior* 479
disclosed principal 473	independent contractor 461	undisclosed principal 473
e-agent 476	notary public 471	vicarious liability 479
equal dignity rule 470	partially disclosed principal 473	
express authority 470	power of attorney 471	

QUESTIONS AND CASE PROBLEMS

19–1. Paul Gett is a well-known, wealthy financial expert living in the city of Torris. Adam Wade, Gett's friend, tells Timothy Brown that he is Gett's agent for the purchase of rare coins. Wade even shows Brown a local newspaper clipping mentioning Gett's interest in coin collecting. Brown, knowing of Wade's friendship with Gett, contracts with Wade to sell a rare coin valued at $25,000 to Gett. Wade takes the coin and disappears with it. On the payment due date, Brown seeks to collect from Gett, claiming that Wade's agency made Gett liable. Gett does not deny that Wade was a friend, but he claims that Wade was never his agent. Discuss fully whether an agency was in existence at the time the contract for the rare coin was made.

19–2. ⚖ **QUESTION WITH SAMPLE ANSWER**
Peter hires Alice as an agent to sell a piece of property he owns. The price is to be at least $30,000. Alice discovers that because a shopping mall is planned for the area where Peter's property is located, the fair market value of the property will be at least $45,000 and could be higher.

Alice forms a real estate partnership with her cousin Carl, and she prepares for Peter's signature a contract for the sale of the property to Carl for $32,000. Peter signs the contract. Just before closing and passage of title, Peter learns about the shopping mall and the increased fair market value of his property. Peter refuses to deed the property to Carl. Carl claims that Alice, as agent, solicited a price above that agreed on when the agency was created and that the contract is therefore binding and enforceable. Discuss fully whether Peter is bound to this contract.

For a sample answer to this question, go to Appendix I at the end of this text.

19–3. John Paul Corp. made the following contracts:

(a) A contract with Able Construction to build an addition to the corporate office building.

(b) A contract with a certified public accountant (CPA), a recent college graduate, to head the cost-accounting division.

(c) A contract with a salesperson to solicit orders (contracts) for the corporation in a designated territory.

Able contracts with Apex for materials for the addition; the CPA hires an experienced accountant to advise her on certain accounting procedures; and the salesperson contracts to sell a large order to Green, agreeing to deliver the goods in person within twenty days. Later, Able refuses to pick up the materials, the CPA is in default in paying the hired consultant, and the salesperson does not deliver on time. Apex, the accountant, and Green claim John Paul Corp. is liable under agency law. Discuss fully whether an agency relationship was created by John Paul with Able, the CPA, or the salesperson.

19–4. Paula Enterprises hires Able to act as its agent to purchase a 1,000-acre tract of land from Thompson for $1,000 per acre. Paula Enterprises does not wish Thompson to know that it is the principal or that Able is its agent. Paula wants the land for a new country housing development, and Thompson may not sell the land for that purpose or may demand a premium price. Able makes the contract for the purchase, signing only his name as purchaser and not disclosing to Thompson the agency relationship. The closing and transfer of deed are to take place on September 1.

(a) If Thompson learns of Paula's identity on August 1, can Thompson legally refuse to deed the property on September 1? Explain.

(b) Paula gives Able the funds for the closing, but Able absconds with the funds, causing a breach of Able's contract at the date of closing. Thompson then learns of Paula's identity and wants to enforce the contract. Discuss fully Thompson's rights under these circumstances.

19–5. ABC Tire Corp. hires Arnez as a traveling salesperson and assigns him a geographic area and time schedule in which to solicit orders and service customers. Arnez is given a company car to use in covering the territory. One day, Arnez decides to take his personal car to cover part of his territory. It is 11:00 A.M., and Arnez has just finished calling on all customers in the city of Tarrytown. His next appointment is in the city of Austex, twenty miles down the road, at 2:00 P.M. Arnez starts out for Austex, but halfway there he decides to visit a former college roommate who runs a farm ten miles off the main highway. Arnez is enjoying his visit with his former roommate when he realizes that it is 1:45 P.M. and that he will be late for the appointment in Austex. Driving at a high speed down the country road to reach the main highway, Arnez crashes his car into Thomas's tractor, severely injuring Thomas, a farmer. Thomas claims he can hold the ABC Tire Corp. liable for his injuries. Discuss fully ABC's liability in this situation.

19–6. ⚖ **CASE PROBLEM WITH SAMPLE ANSWER**

In 1998, William Larry Smith signed a lease for certain land in Chilton County, Alabama, owned by Sweet Smitherman. The lease stated that it was between "Smitherman, and WLS, Inc., d/b/a [doing business as] S & H Mobile Homes" and the signature line identified the lessee as "WLS, Inc. d/b/a S & H Mobile Homes . . . By: William Larry Smith, President." The amount of the rent was $5,000, payable by the tenth of each month. All of the checks that Smitherman received for the rent identified the owner of the account as "WLS Corporation d/b/a S & H Mobile Homes." Nearly four years later, Smitherman filed a suit in an Alabama state court against William Larry Smith, alleging that he owed $26,000 in unpaid rent. Smith responded in part that WLS was the lessee and that he was not personally responsible for the obligation to pay the rent. Is Smith a principal, an agent, both a principal and an agent, or neither? In any event, in the lease, is the principal disclosed, partially disclosed, or undisclosed? With the answers to these questions in mind, who is liable for the unpaid rent, and why? Discuss. [*Smith v. Smitherman*, 887 So.2d 285 (Ala.Civ.App. 2004)]

To view a sample answer for this case problem, go to this book's Web site at http://wleb.westbuslaw.com, select "Chapter 19," and click on "Case Problem with Sample Answer."

19–7. LIABILITY FOR INDEPENDENT CONTRACTOR'S TORTS. Greif Brothers Corp., a steel drum manufacturer, owned and operated a manufacturing plant in Youngstown, Ohio. In 1987, Lowell Wilson, the plant superintendent, hired Youngstown Security Patrol, Inc. (YSP), a security company, to guard Greif property and "deter thieves and vandals." Some YSP security guards, as Wilson knew, carried firearms. Eric Bator, a YSP security guard, was not certified as an armed guard but nevertheless took his gun, in a briefcase, to work. While working at the Greif plant on August 12, 1991, Bator fired his gun at Derrell Pusey, in the belief that Pusey was an intruder. The bullet struck and killed Pusey. Pusey's mother filed a suit in an Ohio state court against Greif and others, alleging in part that her son's death was the result of YSP's negligence, for which Greif was responsible. Greif filed a motion for a directed verdict. What is the plaintiff's best argument that Greif is responsible for YSP's actions? What is Greif's best defense? Explain. [*Pusey v. Bator*, 94 Ohio St.3d 275, 762 N.E.2d 968 (2002)]

19–8. PRINCIPAL'S DUTIES TO CUSTOMER. Sam and Theresa Daigle decided to build a home in Cameron Parish, Louisiana. To obtain financing, they contacted Trinity United Mortgage Co. At a meeting with Joe Diez on Trinity's behalf, on July 18, 2001, the Daigles signed a temporary loan agreement with Union Planters Bank. Diez assured them that they did not need to make payments on this loan until their house was built and that permanent financing had been secured. Because the Daigles did not make payments on the Union loan, Trinity declined to make the permanent loan. Meanwhile, Diez left Trinity's employ. On November 1, the Daigles moved into their new house. They tried to contact Diez at Trinity but were told that he was unavailable and would get back to them. Three weeks later, Diez came to the Daigles' home and had them sign documents that they believed were to secure a permanent loan but that were actually an application with Diez's new employer. Union filed a suit in a Louisiana state court against the Daigles for failing to pay on its loan. The Daigles paid Union, obtained permanent financing through another source, and filed a suit against Trinity to recover the cost. Who should have told the Daigles that Diez was no longer Trinity's agent? Could Trinity be liable to the Daigles on this basis? Explain. [*Daigle v. Trinity United Mortgage, L.L.C.*, 890 So.2d 583 (La.App. 3 Cir. 2004)]

19–9. PRINCIPAL'S DUTIES TO AGENT. Josef Boehm was an officer and the majority shareholder of Alaska Industrial Hardware, Inc. (AIH), in Anchorage, Alaska. In August 2001, Lincolnshire Management, Inc., in New York, created AIH Acquisition Corp. to buy AIH. The three firms signed a "commitment letter" to negotiate "a definitive stock purchase agreement"

(SPA). In September, Harold Snow and Ronald Braley began to work, on Boehm's behalf, with Vincent Coyle, an agent for AIH Acquisition, to produce an SPA. They exchanged many drafts and dozens of e-mails. Finally, in February 2002, Braley told Coyle that Boehm would sign the SPA "early next week." That did not occur, however, and at the end of March, after more negotiations and drafts, Boehm demanded more money. AIH Acquisition agreed and, following more work by the agents, another SPA was drafted. In April, the parties met in Anchorage. Boehm still refused to sign. AIH Acquisition and others filed a suit in a federal district court against AIH. Did Boehm violate any of the duties that principals owe to their agents? If so, which duty, and how was it violated? Explain. [*AIH Acquisition Corp., LLC v. Alaska Industrial Hardware, Inc.*, __ F.Supp.2d __ (S.D.N.Y. 2004)]

19–10. VIDEO QUESTION

Go to this text's Web site at <u>http://wleb.westbuslaw.com</u> and select "Chapter 19." Click on "Video Questions" and view the video titled *Fast Times at Ridgemont High*. Then answer the following questions.

(a) Recall from the video that Brad (Judge Reinhold) is told to deliver an order of Captain Hook Fish and Chips to IBM. Is Brad an employee or an independent contractor? Why?

(b) Assume that Brad is an employee and agent of Captain Hook Fish and Chips. What duties does he owe Captain Hook Fish and Chips? What duties does Captain Hook Fish and Chips, as principal, owe Brad?

(c) In the video, Brad throws part of his uniform and several bags of the food that he is supposed to deliver out of his car window while driving. Assuming Brad is an agent-employee of Captain Hook Fish and Chips, did these actions violate any of his duties as an agent? Explain.

LAW | on the Web

For updated links to resources available on the Web, as well as a variety of other materials, visit this text's Web site at <u>http://wleb.westbuslaw.com</u>.

An excellent source for information on agency law, including court cases involving agency concepts, is the Legal Information Institute (LII) at Cornell University. You can access the LII's Web page on this topic at

<u>http://www.law.cornell.edu/topics/agency.html</u>

LEGAL RESEARCH EXERCISES ON THE WEB

Go to http://wleb.westbuslaw.com, the Web site that accompanies this text. Select "Chapter 19" and click on "Internet Exercises." There you will find the following Internet research exercises that you can perform to learn more about topics covered in this chapter.

Activity 19–1: LEGAL PERSPECTIVE
                Employees or Independent Contractors?

Activity 19–2: MANAGEMENT PERSPECTIVE
                Problems with Using Independent Contractors

Activity 19–3: MANAGEMENT PERSPECTIVE
                Liability in Agency Relationships

CHAPTER 20
Employment Relationships

In the United States, employment relationships traditionally have been governed primarily by the common law. Before the Industrial Revolution, which had begun about 1750, workers and employers enjoyed relatively equal bargaining power. Today, the workplace is regulated extensively by federal and state statutes. Recall from Chapter 1 that common law doctrines apply only to areas *not* covered by statutory law. Common law doctrines have thus been displaced to a significant extent by statutory law. In this chapter, we look at the most significant laws, including the common law doctrine of *employment at will*, regulating employment relationships. We examine other important laws regulating the workplace—those prohibiting employment discrimination and labor unions—in Chapters 21 and 22.

SECTION 1 | Employment at Will

Traditionally, employment relationships have generally been governed by the common law doctrine of *employment at will*. Other common law rules governing employment relationships—including rules under contract, tort, and agency law—have already been discussed at length in previous chapters of this text.

Given that many employees (those who deal with third parties) are normally deemed agents of an employer, agency concepts are especially relevant in the employment context. The distinction under agency law between employee status and independent-contractor status is also relevant to employment relationships. Generally, the laws discussed in this chapter and in Chapter 21 apply only to the employer-employee relationship; they do not apply to independent contractors.

APPLICATION OF THE EMPLOYMENT-AT-WILL DOCTRINE

Under the **employment-at-will** doctrine, either party may terminate an employment contract at any time and for any reason, unless the contract specifically provides to the contrary. The legal status of the majority of American workers is "employee at will." In other words, this common law doctrine is still in widespread

use, and only one state (Montana) does not apply the doctrine. Nonetheless, as mentioned in the chapter introduction, federal and state statutes governing employment relationships prevent the doctrine from being applied in a number of circumstances. Today, an employer is not permitted to fire an employee if to do so would violate a federal or state employment statute, such as one prohibiting employment termination for discriminatory reasons (see Chapter 21).

EXCEPTIONS TO THE EMPLOYMENT-AT-WILL DOCTRINE

Under the employment-at-will doctrine, as mentioned, an employer may hire and fire employees at will (regardless of the employees' performance) without liability, unless the decision violates the terms of an employment contract or statutory law. Because of the harsh effects of the employment-at-will doctrine for employees, courts have carved out various exceptions to this doctrine. These exceptions are based on contract theory, tort theory, and public policy.

EXCEPTIONS BASED ON CONTRACT THEORY Some courts have held that an *implied* employment contract exists between the employer and the employee. If the employee is fired outside the terms of the implied contract, he or she may succeed in an action for breach of contract even though no written employment contract exists.

For example, an employer's manual or personnel bulletin may state that, as a matter of policy, workers will be dismissed only for good cause. If the employee is aware of this policy and continues to work for the employer, a court may find that there is an implied contract based on the terms stated in the manual or bulletin. Generally, the key consideration in determining whether an employment manual creates an implied contractual obligation is the employee's reasonable expectations.

Oral promises that an employer makes to employees regarding discharge policy may also be considered part of an implied contract. If the employer fires a worker in a manner contrary to what was promised, a court may hold that the employer has violated the implied contract and is liable for damages. Most state courts will consider this claim and judge it by traditional contract standards. In some cases, courts have held that an implied employment contract exists even though employees agreed in writing to be employees at will.[1] A few states have gone further and held that all employment contracts contain an implied covenant of good faith. In those states, if an employer fires an employee for an arbitrary or unjustified reason, the employee can claim that the covenant of good faith was breached and the contract violated.

EXCEPTIONS BASED ON TORT THEORY In some situations, the discharge of an employee may give rise to an action for wrongful discharge under tort theories. Abusive discharge procedures may result in intentional infliction of emotional distress or defamation. In addition, some courts have permitted workers to sue their employers under the tort theory of fraud. Under this theory, an employer may be held liable for making false promises to a prospective employee if the employee detrimentally relies on the employer's representations by taking the job.

For example, suppose that an employer induces a prospective employee to leave a lucrative position and move to another state by offering "a long-term job with a thriving business." In fact, the employer is having significant financial problems. Furthermore, the employer is planning a merger that will result in the elimination of the position offered to the prospective employee. If the employee takes the job in reliance on the employer's representations and is laid off shortly thereafter, the employee may be able to bring an action against the employer for fraud.[2]

EXCEPTIONS BASED ON PUBLIC POLICY The most widespread common law exception to the employment-at-will doctrine is that made on the basis of public policy. Courts may apply this exception when an employer fires a worker for reasons that violate a fundamental public policy of the jurisdiction.

—Requirements for the Public-Policy Exception. Generally, the courts require that the public policy involved be expressed clearly in the statutory law governing the jurisdiction. The public policy against employment discrimination, for example, is expressed clearly in federal and state statutes. Thus, if a worker is fired for discriminatory reasons but has no cause of action under statutory law (because, for example, the workplace has too few employees to be covered by the statute), that worker may succeed in a suit against the employer for wrongful discharge in violation of public policy.[3]

—Whistleblowing. Sometimes, an employer will direct an employee to perform an illegal act and fire the employee if he or she refuses to do so. At other times, employers will fire or discipline employees who "blow the whistle" on the employer's wrongdoing. **Whistleblowing** occurs when an employee tells a government official, upper-management authorities, or the press that her or his employer is engaged in some unsafe or illegal activity. Whistleblowers on occasion have been protected from wrongful discharge for reasons of public policy.

Today, whistleblowers have some protection under statutory law. For example, most states have enacted so-called whistleblower statutes that protect whistleblowers from subsequent retaliation on the part of employers. On the federal level, the Whistleblower Protection Act of 1989[4] protects federal employees who blow the whistle on their employers from their employers' retaliatory actions. Whistleblower statutes may also provide an incentive to disclose information

---

1. See, for example, *Kuest v. Regent Assisted Living, Inc.*, 111 Wash.App. 36, 43 P.3d 23 (2002).

2. See, for example, *Lazar v. Superior Court of Los Angeles Co.*, 12 Cal.4th 631, 909 P.2d 981, 49 Cal.Rptr.2d 377 (1996); and *McConkey v. AON Corp.*, 804 A.2d 572 (N.J.Super.A.D. 2002).
3. See, for example, *Molesworth v. Brandon*, 341 Md. 621, 672 A.2d 608 (1996); and *Wholey v. Sears Roebuck*, 370 Md. 38, 803 A.2d 482 (2002).
4. 5 U.S.C. Section 1201.

by providing the whistleblower with a monetary reward. For example, the federal False Claims Reform Act of 1986[5] requires that a whistleblower who has disclosed information relating to a fraud perpetrated against the U.S. government receive between 15 and 25 percent of the proceeds if the government brings suit against the wrongdoer.

WRONGFUL DISCHARGE

Whenever an employer discharges an employee in violation of an employment contract or a statutory law protecting employees, the employee may bring an action for **wrongful discharge.** If an employer's actions do not violate any express employment contract or statute, then the question is whether the employer may be subject to liability under a common law doctrine, such as a tort theory or agency. For example, suppose that an employer discharges a female employee and publicly discloses private facts about her sex life to her co-workers. In that situation, the employee could bring a wrongful discharge claim against the employer based on the tort of invasion of privacy.

SECTION 2 | Wage-Hour Laws

In the 1930s, Congress enacted several laws regulating the wages and working hours of employees. In 1931, Congress passed the Davis-Bacon Act,[6] which requires the payment of "prevailing wages" to employees of contractors and subcontractors working on government construction projects. In 1936, the Walsh-Healey Act[7] was passed. This act requires that a minimum wage, as well as overtime pay at 1.5 times regular pay rates, be paid to employees of manufacturers or suppliers entering into contracts with agencies of the federal government.

In 1938, with the passage of the Fair Labor Standards Act[8] (FLSA), Congress extended wage-hour requirements to cover all employers engaged in interstate commerce or engaged in the production of goods for interstate commerce. We examine here the FLSA's provisions in regard to child labor, maximum hours, and minimum wages.

CHILD LABOR

The FLSA prohibits oppressive child labor. Children under fourteen years of age are allowed to do certain types of work, such as deliver newspapers, work for their parents, and be employed in the entertainment and (with some exceptions) agricultural areas. Children who are fourteen or fifteen years of age are allowed to work, but not in hazardous occupations. There are also numerous restrictions on how many hours per day and per week they can work. For example, minors under the age of sixteen cannot work during school hours, for more than three hours on a school day (or eight hours on a nonschool day), for more than eighteen hours during a school week (or forty hours during a nonschool week), or before 7 A.M. or after 7 P.M. (9 P.M. during the summer). Most states require persons under sixteen years of age to obtain work permits.

Persons who are between the ages of sixteen and eighteen do not face such restrictions on working times and hours, but they cannot be employed in hazardous jobs or in jobs detrimental to their health and well-being. Those over the age of eighteen are not affected by any of the above-mentioned restrictions.

HOURS AND WAGES

The FLSA provides that a **minimum wage** of a specified amount ($5.15 per hour, as of this writing) must be paid to employees in covered industries. Congress periodically revises the amount of the minimum wage.[9] Under the FLSA, the term *wages* includes the reasonable costs of the employer in furnishing employees with board, lodging, and other facilities if they are customarily furnished by that employer.

Under the FLSA, any employee who agrees to work more than forty hours per week must be paid no less than one and a half times her or his regular pay for all hours over forty. Note that the FLSA overtime provisions apply only after an employee has worked more than forty hours per *week*. Thus, employees who work for ten hours a day, four days per week, are not entitled to overtime pay because they do not work more than forty hours a week.

---

5. 31 U.S.C. Sections 3729–3733. This act amended the False Claims Act of 1863.

6. 40 U.S.C. Sections 276a–276a-5.

7. 41 U.S.C. Sections 35–45.

8. 29 U.S.C. Sections 201–260.

---

9. Note that many state and local governments also have minimum-wage laws; these laws provide for higher minimum-wage rates than that required by the federal government.

OVERTIME EXEMPTIONS

Certain employees are exempt from the overtime provisions of the act. These exemptions typically include employees whose jobs are categorized as executive, administrative, or professional, as well as outside salespersons and computer employees. In the past, to fall into one of these categories, an employee had to earn more than a specified salary threshold and devote a certain percentage of work time to the performance of specific types of duties. Because the salary limits were low and the duties tests were complex and confusing, over the last twenty years some employers have been able to avoid paying overtime wages to their employees. This prompted the U.S. Department of Labor to substantially revise the regulations pertaining to overtime for the first time in over fifty years.

NEW OVERTIME RULES   In August 2004, new rules were implemented that expand the number of workers eligible for overtime by nearly tripling the salary threshold.[10] Under the new provisions, workers earning less than $23,660 a year are guaranteed overtime pay for working more than forty hours per week (the previous ceiling was $8,060). Employers can continue to pay overtime to ineligible employees if they want to do so, but cannot waive or reduce the overtime requirements of the FLSA.

The exemptions to payment of overtime by employers do not apply to manual laborers or other "blue-collar" workers who perform tasks involving repetitive operations with their hands (such as production-line employees who are not part of management, for example). The exemptions also do not apply to police, firefighters, licensed nurses, and other public-safety workers. White-collar workers who earn more than $100,000 a year, computer programmers, dental hygienists, and insurance adjusters are typically exempt—though they must also meet certain other criteria.

JOB TITLES ALONE ARE INSUFFICIENT TO ESTABLISH EXEMPTIONS   Under the new provisions, an employer cannot deny overtime wages to an employee based only on the employee's job title. For example, in one case an employer refused to pay overtime wages to a computer maintenance worker. The court held that the worker, who performed troubleshooting on individual computers but did not engage in systems analysis or design, was not exempt as a "computer professional" under the rules.[11]

SECTION 3 | Worker Health and Safety

Under the common law, employees injured on the job had to rely on tort law or contract law theories in suits they brought against their employers. Additionally, workers had some recourse under the common law governing agency relationships (discussed in Chapter 19), which imposes a duty on a principal-employer to provide a safe workplace for an agent-employee. Today, numerous state and federal statutes protect employees from the risk of accidental injury, death, or disease resulting from their employment. This section discusses the primary federal statute governing health and safety in the workplace, along with state workers' compensation acts.

THE OCCUPATIONAL SAFETY AND HEALTH ACT

At the federal level, the primary legislation protecting employees' health and safety is the Occupational Safety and Health Act of 1970.[12] Congress passed this act in an attempt to ensure safe and healthful working conditions for practically every employee in the country. The act provides for specific standards that employers must meet, plus a general duty to keep workplaces safe.

ENFORCEMENT AGENCIES   Three federal agencies develop and enforce the standards set by the Occupational Safety and Health Act. The Occupational Safety and Health Administration (OSHA) is part of the Department of Labor and has the authority to promulgate standards, make inspections, and enforce the act. OSHA has issued safety standards governing many workplace details, such as the structural stability of ladders and the requirements for railings. OSHA also establishes standards that protect employees against exposure to substances that may be harmful to their health.

The National Institute for Occupational Safety and Health is part of the Department of Health and Human Services. Its main duty is to conduct research on safety and health problems and to recommend standards for OSHA to adopt. Finally, the Occupational Safety and Health Review Commission is an independent agency set up to handle appeals from actions taken by OSHA administrators.

---

10. 29 C.F.R. Section 541.

11. *Martin v. Indiana Michigan Power Co.*, 381 F.3d 574 (6th Cir. 2004).
12. 29 U.S.C. Sections 553, 651–678.

PROCEDURES AND VIOLATIONS OSHA compliance officers may enter and inspect facilities of any establishment covered by the Occupational Safety and Health Act.[13] Employees may also file complaints of violations. Under the act, an employer cannot discharge an employee who files a complaint or who, in good faith, refuses to work in a high-risk area if bodily harm or death might result.

Employers with eleven or more employees are required to keep occupational injury and illness records for each employee. Each record must be made available for inspection when requested by an OSHA inspector. Whenever a work-related injury or disease occurs, employers must make reports directly to OSHA. Whenever an employee is killed in a work-related accident or when five or more employees are hospitalized in one accident, the employer must notify the Department of Labor within forty-eight hours. If the company fails to do so, it will be fined. Following the accident, a complete inspection of the premises is mandatory.

Criminal penalties for willful violation of the Occupational Safety and Health Act are limited. Employers may be prosecuted under state laws, however. In other words, the act does not preempt state and local criminal laws.[14]

STATE WORKERS' COMPENSATION LAWS

State **workers' compensation laws** establish an administrative procedure for compensating workers injured on the job. Instead of suing, an injured worker files a claim with the administrative agency or board that administers the local workers' compensation claims.

EMPLOYEES COVERED BY WORKERS' COMPENSATION Most workers' compensation statutes are similar. No state covers all employees. Typically excluded are domestic workers, agricultural workers, temporary employees, and employees of common carriers (companies that provide shipping and transportation services to the public). Generally, the statutes cover minors. Usually, the statutes allow employers to purchase insurance from a private insurer or a state fund to pay workers' compensation benefits in the event of a claim. Most states also allow employers to be *self-insured*—that is, employers who show an ability to pay claims do not need to buy insurance.

REQUIREMENTS FOR RECEIVING WORKERS' COMPENSATION In general, the right to recover benefits is predicated wholly on the existence of an employment relationship and the fact that the worker's injury was *accidental* and *occurred on the job or in the course of employment*, regardless of fault. Intentionally inflicted self-injury, for example, would not be considered accidental and hence would not be covered. If an injury occurs while an employee is commuting to or from work, it usually will not be considered to have occurred on the job or in the course of employment and hence will not be covered.

An employee must notify his or her employer of an injury promptly (usually within thirty days of the injury's occurrence). Generally, an employee also must file a workers' compensation claim with the appropriate state agency or board within a certain period (sixty days to two years) from the time the injury is first noticed, rather than from the time of the accident.

WORKERS' COMPENSATION VERSUS LITIGATION An employee's acceptance of workers' compensation benefits bars the employee from suing for injuries caused by the employer's negligence. By barring lawsuits for negligence, workers' compensation laws also bar employers from raising common law defenses to negligence, such as contributory negligence. For example, an employer can no longer raise such defenses as contributory negligence or assumption of risk to avoid liability for negligence. A worker may sue an employer who *intentionally* injures the worker, however.

SECTION 4 | Income Security, Pension, and Health Plans

Federal and state governments participate in insurance programs designed to protect employees and their families by covering the financial impact of retirement, disability, death, hospitalization, and unemployment. The key federal law on this subject is the Social Security Act of 1935.[15]

13. In 1978, the United States Supreme Court held that warrantless inspections violated the warrant clause of the Fourth Amendment to the U.S. Constitution. See *Marshall v. Barlow's, Inc.*, 436 U.S. 307, 98 S.Ct. 1816, 56 L.Ed.2d 305 (1978). Although this case has not been overruled, the Supreme Court subsequently indicated that statutory inspection programs can provide a constitutionally adequate substitute for a warrant. See *Donovan v. Dewey*, 452 U.S. 594, 101 S.Ct. 2534, 69 L.Ed.2d 262 (1981).

14. *Pedraza v. Shell Oil Co.*, 942 F.2d 48 (1st Cir. 1991); *cert.* denied, 502 U.S. 1082, 112 S.Ct. 993, 117 L.Ed.2d 154 (1992). See also *In re Welding Fume Products Liability Litigation*, 364 F.Supp.2d 669 (N.D. Ohio 2005).

15. 42 U.S.C. Sections 301–1397e.

SOCIAL SECURITY

The Social Security Act of 1935 provides for old-age (retirement), survivors, and disability insurance. The act is therefore often referred to as OASDI. Both employers and employees must "contribute" under the Federal Insurance Contributions Act (FICA)[16] to help pay for the employees' loss of income on retirement.

The basis for the employee's and the employer's contribution is the employee's annual wage base—the maximum amount of the employee's wages that are subject to the tax. The employer withholds the employee's FICA contribution from the employee's wages and then matches this contribution. The annual wage base increases each year to take into account the rising cost of living. In 2005, employers were required to withhold 6.2 percent of each employee's wages, up to a maximum amount of $90,000, and to match this contribution.

Retired workers are eligible to receive monthly payments from the Social Security Administration, which administers the Social Security Act. Social Security benefits are fixed by statute but increase automatically with increases in the cost of living.

MEDICARE

Medicare, a federal government health-insurance program, is administered by the Social Security Administration for people sixty-five years of age and older and for some under age sixty-five who are disabled. It has two parts, one pertaining to hospital costs and the other to nonhospital medical costs, such as visits to physicians' offices. People who have Medicare hospital insurance can obtain additional federal medical insurance if they pay small monthly premiums, which increase as the cost of medical care rises.

As with Social Security contributions, both the employer and the employee "contribute" to Medicare. For 2005, employees paid 1.45 percent of their income on *all* wages and salaries, and employers contributed a matching percentage (1.45 percent). This resulted in a total contribution to Medicare (from both employer and employee) that is equal to 2.9 percent of the wages of each employee. Persons who were self-employed contributed 2.9 percent of their total income toward Medicare.

Unlike Social Security contributions (which have a limit each year), there is no cap on the amount of wages subject to the Medicare tax. In other words, for the first $90,000 of income (in 2005), both the employer and the employee paid 7.65 percent each in contributions to finance Medicare and Social Security (a combined total of 15.3 percent). After this maximum taxable income, employees and employers only paid the Medicare portion of the total tax.

PRIVATE PENSION PLANS

Significant legislation has been enacted to regulate employee retirement plans set up by employers to supplement Social Security benefits. The major federal act covering these retirement plans is the Employee Retirement Income Security Act (ERISA) of 1974.[17] This statute empowers the Labor Management Services Administration of the Department of Labor to enforce its provisions governing employers who have private pension funds for their employees. ERISA does not require an employer to establish a pension plan. When a plan exists, however, ERISA establishes standards for its management.

A key provision of ERISA concerns vesting. **Vesting** gives an employee a legal right to receive pension benefits at some future date when she or he stops working. Before ERISA was enacted, some employees who had worked for companies for as long as thirty years received no pension benefits when their employment terminated because those benefits had not vested. ERISA establishes complex vesting rules. Generally, however, all employee contributions to pension plans vest immediately, and employee rights to employer pension-plan contributions vest after five years of employment.

In an attempt to prevent mismanagement of pension funds, ERISA has established rules on how they must be invested. Pension managers must be cautious in choosing investments and must diversify the plan's investments in order to minimize the risk of large losses. ERISA also contains detailed record-keeping and reporting requirements.

UNEMPLOYMENT COMPENSATION

To ease the financial impact of unemployment, the United States has a system of unemployment insurance. The Federal Unemployment Tax Act of 1935[18] created a state-administered system that provides unemployment compensation to eligible individuals. Under this system, employers pay into a fund, and the proceeds are paid out to qualified unemployed workers. The FUTA and state laws require employers

---

16. 26 U.S.C. Sections 3101–3125.

17. 29 U.S.C. Sections 1001 *et seq.*
18. 26 U.S.C. Sections 3301–3310.

that fall under the provisions of the act to pay unemployment taxes at regular intervals.

COBRA

Federal legislation also addresses the issue of health insurance for workers whose jobs have been terminated and who are thus no longer eligible for group health-insurance plans. The Consolidated Omnibus Budget Reconciliation Act (COBRA) of 1985[19] prohibits the elimination of a worker's medical, optical, or dental insurance coverage on the voluntary or involuntary termination of the worker's employment. The act applies to most workers who have either lost their jobs or had their hours decreased so that they are no longer eligible for coverage under the employer's health plan. Only workers fired for gross misconduct are excluded from protection.

APPLICATION OF COBRA The worker has sixty days (beginning with the date that the group coverage would stop) to decide whether to continue with the employer's group insurance plan. If the worker chooses to discontinue the coverage, then the employer has no further obligation. If the worker chooses to continue coverage, though, the employer is obligated to keep the policy active for up to eighteen months. If the worker is disabled, the employer must extend coverage for up to twenty-nine months. The coverage provided must be the same as that enjoyed by the worker prior to the termination or reduction of employment. If family members were originally included, for example, COBRA prohibits their exclusion. The worker does not receive a free ride, however. To receive continued benefits, he or she may be required to pay the entire premium, as well as a 2 percent administrative charge.

EMPLOYERS' OBLIGATIONS UNDER COBRA With some exceptions, employers must comply with COBRA if they employ twenty or more workers and provide a benefit plan to those workers. An employer must inform an employee of COBRA's provisions when that worker faces termination or a reduction of hours that would affect her or his eligibility for coverage under the plan. An employer that fails to comply with COBRA risks substantial penalties, such as a tax of up to 10 percent of the annual cost of the group plan or $500,000, whichever is less.

An employer is relieved of the responsibility to provide benefit coverage if the employer completely eliminates its group benefit plan. An employer is also relieved of responsibility when the worker becomes eligible for Medicare, falls under a spouse's health plan, becomes insured under a different plan (with a new employer, for example), or fails to pay the premium.

EMPLOYER-SPONSORED GROUP HEALTH PLANS

The Health Insurance Portability and Accountability Act (HIPAA)[20] contains provisions that affect employer-sponsored group health plans. HIPAA does not require employers to provide health insurance, but it does establish requirements for those that do provide such coverage. For example, under HIPAA, an employer's ability to exclude persons from coverage for "preexisting conditions" is strictly limited to the previous six months. The act defines preexisting conditions as those for which medical advice, diagnosis, care, or treatment was recommended or received within the previous six months (excluding pregnancy).

In addition, employers who are plan sponsors have significant responsibilities regarding the manner in which they collect, use, and disclose the health information of employees and their families. Essentially, the act requires employers to comply with a number of administrative, technical, and procedural safeguards (such as training employees, designating privacy officials, and distributing privacy notices) to ensure that employees' health information is not disclosed to unauthorized parties. Failure to comply with HIPAA regulations can result in civil penalties of up to $100 per person per violation (with a cap of $25,000 per year). The employer is also subject to criminal prosecution for certain types of HIPAA violations and can face up to $250,000 in criminal fines and imprisonment for up to ten years if convicted.

SECTION 5 | Family and Medical Leave

In 1993, Congress passed the Family and Medical Leave Act (FMLA)[21] to protect employees who need time off work for family or medical reasons. A majority of the states also have legislation allowing for a leave from employment for family or medical reasons, and many employers maintain private family-leave plans for their workers.

---

19. 29 U.S.C. Sections 1161–1169.

20. 29 U.S.C.A. Sections 1181 *et seq.*
21. 29 U.S.C. Sections 2601, 2611–2619, 2651–2654.

COVERAGE AND APPLICATION OF THE FMLA

The FMLA requires employers who have fifty or more employees to provide an employee with up to twelve weeks of family or medical leave during any twelve-month period. Generally, an employee may take family leave to care for a newborn baby, an adopted child, or a foster child, and medical leave when the employee or the employee's spouse, child, or parent has a "serious health condition" requiring care.[22] The act does not apply to part-time or newly hired employees (those who have worked for less than one year).

For most absences, the employee must demonstrate that the health condition requires continued treatment by a health-care provider and includes a period of incapacity of more than three days. Employees suffering from certain chronic health conditions such as asthma and diabetes, as well as those who are pregnant, however, may take FMLA leave for their own incapacities that require absences of less than three days.

PROTECTS EMPLOYEE'S JOB AND HEALTH BENEFITS The employer cannot interfere with, restrain, or deny an employee from exercising or attempting to exercise his or her rights under the FMLA, nor can the employer discharge or discriminate against an employee for taking leave. The employer must continue the worker's health-care coverage and guarantee employment in the same or a comparable position when the employee returns to work. In addition, the employer is required to immediately reinstate the employee after the leave, provided that the worker can perform the essential functions of the position.[23]

An important exception to the FMLA, however, allows the employer to avoid reinstating a *key employee*—defined as an employee whose pay falls within the top 10 percent of the firm's workforce. If reinstating a highly paid key employee would cause "substantial and grievous economic injury" to the employer, the employer is not required to restore the employee's position after the leave. The employer must continue to maintain health benefits for the key employee during the leave, however. This exception is to be used only in specified and limited circumstances, and the employer is required to follow certain procedures. For example, the employer must notify the employee of her or his status as a key employee as soon as possible and must offer the employee the option of returning to work immediately rather than risk losing her or his position.

APPLIES TO BOTH PUBLIC- AND PRIVATE-SECTOR EMPLOYERS The FMLA expressly covers private and public (government) employees. Nevertheless, some states argued that public employees could not sue their state employers in federal courts to enforce their FMLA rights unless the states consented to be sued.[24] This argument came before the United States Supreme Court in the following case.

---

22. The foster care must be state sanctioned before such an arrangement falls within the coverage of the FMLA.

23. See, for example, *Hoge v. Honda of America Manufacturing, Inc.*, 384 F.3d 238 (6th Cir. 2004).
24. Under the Eleventh Amendment to the U.S. Constitution, a state is immune from suit in a federal court unless the state agrees to be sued.

CASE 20.1 — Nevada Department of Human Resources v. Hibbs

Supreme Court of the United States, 2003.
538 U.S. 721.
123 S.Ct. 1972.
155 L.Ed.2d 953.

Chief Justice *REHNQUIST* delivered the opinion of the Court.
* * * *

Petitioners include the Nevada Department of Human Resources (Department) * * * . Respondent William Hibbs (hereinafter respondent) worked for the Department's Welfare Division. In April and May 1997, he sought leave under the FMLA to care for his ailing wife, who was recovering from a car accident and neck surgery. The Department granted his request for the full 12 weeks of FMLA leave and authorized him to use the leave intermittently as needed between May and December 1997. Respondent did so until August 5, 1997, after which he did not return to work. In October 1997, the Department informed respondent that he had exhausted his FMLA leave, that no further leave would be granted, and that he must report to work by November 12, 1997. Respondent failed to do so and was terminated.

CONTINUED

CASE 20.1 | Continued

Respondent sued petitioners in [a] United States District Court * * * . The District Court awarded petitioners summary judgment on the grounds that the FMLA claim was barred by the [U.S. Constitution's] Eleventh Amendment * * * . Respondent appealed * * * . The Ninth Circuit reversed.

We granted *certiorari* * * * .

* * * *

The history of the many state laws limiting women's employment opportunities is chronicled in—and, until relatively recently, was sanctioned by—this Court's own opinions. For example, in [previous cases] the Court upheld state laws prohibiting women from practicing law and tending bar * * * . State laws frequently subjected women to distinctive restrictions, terms, conditions, and benefits for those jobs they could take. In [one case] for example, this Court approved a state law limiting the hours that women could work for wages, and observed that 19 States had such laws at the time. Such laws were based on the related beliefs that (1) woman is, and should remain, the center of home and family life, and (2) a proper discharge of a woman's maternal functions—having in view not merely her own health, but the well-being of the race—justifies legislation to protect her from the greed as well as the passion of man. Until [1971] it remained the prevailing doctrine that government, both federal and state, could withhold from women opportunities accorded men so long as any basis in reason—such as the above beliefs—could be conceived for the discrimination.

Congress responded to this history of discrimination by abrogating [revoking] States' sovereign immunity in Title VII of the Civil Rights Act of 1964 * * * .[a] But state gender discrimination did not cease. * * * According to evidence that was before Congress when it enacted the FMLA, States continue[d] to rely on invalid gender stereotypes in the employment context, specifically in the administration of leave benefits. * * *

* * * *

Congress * * * heard testimony that parental leave for fathers * * * is rare. Even * * * where child-care leave policies do exist, men, both in the public and private sectors, receive notoriously discriminatory treatment in their requests for such leave. Many States offered women extended "maternity" leave that far exceeded the typical 4- to 8-week period of physical disability due to pregnancy and childbirth, but very few States granted men a parallel benefit: Fifteen States provided women up to one year of extended maternity leave, while only four provided men with the same. This and other differential leave policies were not attributable to any differential physical needs of men and women, but rather to the pervasive sex-role stereotype that caring for family members is women's work.

* * * *

* * * Because employers continued to regard the family as the woman's domain, they often denied men similar accommodations or discouraged them from taking leave. These mutually reinforcing stereotypes created a self-fulfilling cycle of discrimination that forced women to continue to assume the role of primary family caregiver, and fostered employers' stereotypical views about women's * * * value as employees. * * *

* * * *

By creating an across-the-board, routine employment benefit for all eligible employees, Congress sought to ensure that family-care leave would no longer be stigmatized as an inordinate drain on the workplace caused by female employees, and that employers could not evade leave obligations simply by hiring men. *By setting a minimum standard of family leave for all eligible employees, irrespective of gender, the FMLA attacks the formerly state-sanctioned stereotype that only women are responsible for family caregiving, thereby reducing employers' incentives to engage in discrimination by basing hiring and promotion decisions on stereotypes.* [Emphasis added.]

* * * *

* * * [T]he FMLA is narrowly targeted at the fault line between work and family— precisely where sex-based overgeneralization has been and remains strongest—and affects only one aspect of the employment relationship.

* * * *

---

a. This statute will be discussed in detail in Chapter 21.

 **Continued**

For the above reasons, we conclude that [the FMLA] is congruent [harmonious] and proportional to its remedial object, and can be understood as responsive to, or designed to prevent, unconstitutional behavior. The judgment of the Court of Appeals [holding that the Eleventh Amendment did not bar the plaintiff's suit] is therefore *Affirmed.*

QUESTIONS

1. What did the Court hold with respect to the primary issue in this case?
2. How might a law foster discrimination even when the law is not obviously discriminatory?

REMEDIES FOR VIOLATIONS OF THE FMLA

Remedies for violations of the FMLA include (1) damages for unpaid wages (or salary), lost benefits, denied compensation, and actual monetary losses (such as the cost of providing for care of the family member) up to an amount equivalent to the employee's wages for twelve weeks; (2) job reinstatement; and (3) promotion, if a promotion had been denied. The successful plaintiff is entitled to court costs, attorneys' fees, and—in cases involving bad faith on the part of the employer—double damages. Supervisors may also be subject to personal liability, as employers, for violations of the act.[25]

Department of Labor (DOL) regulations impose additional sanctions on employers who fail to comply with certain rules relating to notice requirements. For example, employers are required to designate leave as FMLA qualifying and to notify the employee of the designation within two business days (absent extenuating circumstances). If an employer fails to provide this notice, then the employer may not be able to count the FMLA leave against the sick leave normally provided by the employer.[26] Note, however, that the United States Supreme Court has held that an employer cannot be sanctioned for failing to provide notice under DOL regulations unless the employee was injured or prejudiced by the lack of notice.[27]

INTERACTION WITH OTHER LAWS

The FMLA does not affect any other federal or state law that prohibits discrimination. Nor does it supersede any state or local law that provides more generous

family- or medical-leave protection. For example, if a California state law allows employees who are disabled by pregnancy to take up to four months of unpaid leave, an employer in California would have to comply with that law (in addition to the provisions of the FMLA). Also, an employer who is obligated to provide greater leave rights under a collective bargaining agreement must do so, regardless of the FMLA.

SECTION 6 | Employee Privacy Rights

In the last twenty-five years, concerns about the privacy rights of employees have arisen in response to the sometimes invasive tactics used by employers to monitor and screen workers. Perhaps the greatest privacy concern in today's employment arena has to do with electronic performance monitoring. Clearly, employers need to protect themselves from liability for their employees' online activities. They also have a legitimate interest in monitoring the productivity of their workers. At the same time, employees expect to have a certain zone of privacy in the workplace. Indeed, many lawsuits have involved allegations that employers' intrusive monitoring practices violate employees' privacy rights.

ELECTRONIC MONITORING IN THE WORKPLACE

According to a survey by the American Management Association, more than two-thirds of employers engage in some form of electronic monitoring of their employees. Types of monitoring include reviewing employees' e-mail and computer files, video recording of employee job performance, and recording and reviewing telephone conversations and voice mail.

A variety of specially designed software products have made it easier for an employer to track employees' Internet use. For example, software is now available that allows an employer to track virtually every move made using the Internet, including the specific Web

25. See, for example, *Rupnow v. TRC, Inc.*, 999 F.Supp. 1047 (N.D. Ohio 1998).
26. See, for example, *Sims v. Schultz*, 305 F.Supp.2d 838 (N.D.Ill. 2004).
27. *Ragsdale v. Wolverine World Wide, Inc.*, 535 U.S. 81, 122 S.Ct. 1155, 152 L.Ed.2d 167 (2002).

sites visited and the time spent surfing the Web. Filtering software, which was discussed in Chapter 5, can also be used to prevent access to certain Web sites, such as sites containing pornographic or sexually explicit images. Other filtering software may be used to screen incoming e-mail for viruses and to block junk e-mail (spam).

Although the use of filtering software by public employers (government agencies) has led to charges that blocking access to Web sites violates employees' rights to free speech, this issue does not arise in private businesses. This is because the First Amendment's protection of free speech applies only to *government* restraints on speech, not restraints imposed in the private sector.

LAWS PROTECTING EMPLOYEE PRIVACY RIGHTS
A number of laws protect privacy rights. We look here at laws that apply in the employment context.

—Protection under Constitutional and Tort Law. Recall from Chapter 5 that the Supreme Court has inferred a personal right to privacy from the constitutional guarantees provided by the First, Third, Fourth, Fifth, and Ninth Amendments to the Constitution. Tort law (see Chapter 12), state constitutions, and a number of state and federal statutes also provide for privacy rights.

—The Electronic Communications Privacy Act. The major statute with which employers must comply is the Electronic Communications Privacy Act (ECPA) of 1986.[28] This act amended existing federal wiretapping law to cover electronic forms of communications, such as communications via cellular telephones or e-mail. The ECPA prohibits the intentional interception of any wire or electronic communication or the intentional disclosure or use of the information obtained by the interception. Excluded from coverage, however, are any electronic communications through devices that are "furnished to the subscriber or user by a provider of wire or electronic communication service" and that are being used by the subscriber or user, or by the provider of the service, "in the ordinary course of its business."

This "business-extension exception" to the ECPA permits an employer to monitor employee electronic communications in the ordinary course of business. It does not, however, permit an employer to monitor employees' personal communications. Under another exception to the ECPA, however, an employer may avoid liability under the act if the employees consent to having their electronic communications intercepted by the employer. Thus, an employer may be able to avoid liability under the ECPA by simply requiring employees to sign forms indicating that they consent to such monitoring.

Although the law clearly allows employers to engage in electronic monitoring in the workplace, there are some limits on how far an employer can go in monitoring employee communications.

FACTORS CONSIDERED BY THE COURTS IN EMPLOYEE PRIVACY CASES When determining whether an employer should be held liable for violating an employee's privacy rights, the courts generally weigh the employer's interests against the employee's reasonable expectation of privacy. Generally, if employees are informed that their communications are being monitored, they cannot reasonably expect those communications to be private. If employees are not informed that certain communications are being monitored, however, the employer may be held liable for invading their privacy.

In one case, for example, an employer secretly recorded conversations among his four employees by placing a tape recorder in their common office. The conversations were of a highly personal nature and included harsh criticisms of the employer. The employer immediately fired two of the employees because of their comments on the tape. In the ensuing suit, the court held that the employees had a reasonable expectation of privacy in these circumstances and granted summary judgment in their favor. The employees clearly would not have criticized their boss if they had not assumed that their conversations were private.[29] (For a discussion of employee privacy rights and e-mail systems, see this chapter's *Contemporary Legal Debates* feature.)

OTHER TYPES OF MONITORING

In addition to monitoring their employees' online activities, employers also engage in other types of employee screening and monitoring practices. The practices discussed on page 500 have often been challenged as violations of employee privacy rights.

---

28. 18 U.S.C. Sections 2510–2521.

29. *Dorris v. Absher,* 179 F.3d 420 (6th Cir. 1999).

CASE 20.2

United States
Court of Appeals,
Third Circuit, 2004.
385 F.3d 809.

CITGO Asphalt Refining Co. v. Paper, Allied-Industrial, Chemical, and Energy Workers International Union Local No. 2-991

BACKGROUND AND FACTS *CITGO Petroleum Corporation (CITGO) operates more than sixty oil-refining facilities, including CITGO Asphalt Refining Company (CARCO) in Paulsboro, New Jersey. Paper, Allied-Industrial, Chemical, and Energy Workers International Union (PACE) represents some of CITGO's workers. Under an agreement between CITGO and PACE, the company has the right to "make and enforce rules for the maintenance of discipline and safety." In December 1998, CITGO implemented a new substance abuse policy, which included a zero-tolerance provision. The local Chapter 2-991 of PACE challenged the policy at CARCO. During arbitration on the dispute, PACE representatives testified that policies at smaller facilities owned by other companies—Motiva and Sun Oil—did not include zero-tolerance provisions. John DeLeon, a CITGO manager, testified that Tosco, Marathon, and Exxon, three major companies in the industry, had zero-tolerance polices. He also testified that CITGO's safety record is the best in the industry. The arbitrator ruled that CITGO should modify its policy to allow a rehabilitation opportunity, or "second chance." CARCO filed a suit in a federal district court against PACE, challenging the arbitrator's ruling. The court issued an order to enforce the award. CARCO appealed to the U.S. Court of Appeals for the Third Circuit.*

IN THE LANGUAGE OF THE COURT

McKEE, Circuit Judge.

* * * *

* * * [T]he only issue before us is the propriety of the arbitrator's determination that CITGO's zero tolerance policy is unreasonable. CITGO * * * contends that the arbitrator's determination that the zero tolerance policy is unreasonable is not supported by the record. * * *

* * * *

The arbitrator relied only on two "facts" to support his determination that the zero tolerance policy was unreasonable. First, the arbitrator noted that neither Motiva nor Sun Oil have zero tolerance policies at their refineries. However, the fact that two companies with safety records that are inferior to CITGO's do not have zero tolerance policies does not establish that CITGO acted unreasonably in adopting a zero tolerance policy. In fact, considering the stipulated catastrophic repercussions of a safety lapse at the Paulsboro plant, and CITGO's superior safety record, one could just as readily conclude that it was unreasonable for Sun Oil and Motiva not to have a zero tolerance policy. Moreover, the arbitrator's finding of the unreasonableness of the zero tolerance policy completely ignores DeLeon's * * * testimony that the three largest companies in the industry—Exxon, Marathon and Tosco—have zero tolerance policies exactly like CITGO's. The undisputed fact that the three largest companies in the industry have zero tolerance policies certainly casts doubt upon the arbitrator's focus on Motiva and Sun Oil, and the arbitrator never explained why he elevated the importance of Motiva and Sun Oil refineries over larger ones with better safety records.

The arbitrator also relied upon provisions of the Omnibus Transportation Employee Testing Act of 1991 and the [U.S.] Department of Transportation regulations promulgated under it. *That Act and its regulations allow employees a second chance for rehabilitation. However, that does not mean that a decision to the contrary is unreasonable.* This is especially true when we consider the hazardous nature of CITGO's facilities, the need for prompt and unimpaired action in the event of an emergency, and the exception for employees who step forward seeking help for a substance abuse problem that CITGO has included in its policy. Indeed, * * * the statute and the regulations at issue leave it to the parties to define appropriate discipline. * * * When promulgating these regulations, DOT decided not to require employers either to provide rehabilitation or to hold a job open for a driver who has tested positive, on the basis that such decisions should be left to management/driver negotiation. That determination reflects basic

CONTINUED ▶

CASE 20.2 | Continued   background labor law principles, which caution against interference with labor-management agreements about appropriate employee discipline. The arbitrator's award here ignores that caution as well as the express reservation of the employer's prerogatives as set forth in [the agreement between CITGO and PACE]. [Emphasis added.]

Thus, the fact that Motiva and Sun Oil do not have zero tolerance policies and the fact that a particular federal statute and its implementing regulations allow a second chance are not sufficient to support a finding that CITGO's zero tolerance policy is unreasonable. This is especially true given the undisputed evidence that the Paulsboro facility is a hazardous work environment susceptible to explosions, Local 2-991 members are employed in safety-sensitive positions there, and that impaired employees pose a threat to co-workers, the work place, the environment and to the public at large.

Since the Managements Rights Clause of the [agreement between CITGO and PACE] expressly gives CITGO the right "to make and enforce rules for the maintenance of discipline and safety" * * *, we are hard-pressed to understand how the arbitrator could have concluded that the zero tolerance policy is unreasonable without substituting his own judgment for CITGO's and ignoring CITGO's expressly reserved right * * *.

DECISION AND REMEDY *The U.S. Court of Appeals for the Third Circuit reversed the lower court's order and remanded the case for an order vacating the arbitrator's award. That other, smaller companies "do not have zero tolerance policies" and that "a particular federal statute and its implementing regulations allow a second chance" are not sufficient to support a finding that CITGO's zero-tolerance policy is unreasonable. The "safety-sensitive positions" of CITGO's workers and the firm's right under its agreement with PACE outweigh these facts.*

WHAT IF THE FACTS WERE DIFFERENT? *Suppose that CITGO's safety record was not the oil-refining industry's "best," but its "worst." Would the result have been different?*

AIDS TESTING A number of employers test their workers for acquired immune deficiency syndrome (AIDS). Some state laws restrict or ban AIDS testing, and federal statutes offer some protection to employees or job applicants who have AIDS or have tested positive for the AIDS virus. The federal Americans with Disabilities Act of 1990[33] (discussed in Chapter 21), for example, prohibits discrimination against persons with disabilities, and the term *disability* has been broadly defined to include those individuals with diseases such as AIDS. HIPAA, which was discussed earlier in this chapter, would also require employers to follow procedures to safeguard a person's protected medical information—the test results—from disclosure to other employees. As a rule, although the law may not prohibit AIDS testing, it may prohibit the discharge of employees based on the results of those tests and prohibit the employer from disclosing the test results to unauthorized parties.

GENETIC TESTING A serious privacy issue arose when some employers began conducting genetic testing

of employees or prospective employees in an effort to identify individuals who might develop significant health problems in the future. To date, however, only a few cases have come before the courts on this matter. In one case, the Lawrence Berkeley Laboratory screened prospective employees for the gene that causes sickle-cell anemia, although the applicants were not informed of this. In a lawsuit subsequently brought by the prospective employees, a federal appellate court held that they had a cause of action for violation of their privacy rights.[34] The case was later settled for $2.2 million.

In another case, the Equal Employment Opportunity Commission (EEOC), the federal agency in charge of administering laws prohibiting employment discrimination, brought an action against a railroad company that had genetically tested its employees. The EEOC contended that the genetic testing violated the Americans with Disabilities Act of 1990. In 2002, this case was settled out of court, also for $2.2 million.[35]

---

33. 42 U.S.C. Sections 12102–12118.

34. *Norman-Bloodsaw v. Lawrence Berkeley Laboratory*, 135 F.3d 1260 (9th Cir. 1998).

35. For a discussion of this settlement, see David Hechler, "Railroad to Pay $2.2 Million over Genetic Testing," *The National Law Journal*, May 13, 2002, p. A22.

SCREENING PROCEDURES Preemployment screening procedures are another area of concern to potential employees. What kinds of questions are permissible on an employment application or a preemployment test? What kinds of questions invade the potential employee's privacy? Is it an invasion of privacy, for example, to ask questions about the potential employee's sexual orientation or religious convictions? Although an employer may believe that such information is relevant to the job, the applicant may feel differently. Generally, questions on an employment application must have a reasonable nexus, or connection, with the job for which an applicant is applying.

SECTION 7 | Employment-Related Immigration Laws

The most important immigration laws governing employment relationships are the Immigration Reform and Control Act of 1986[36] and the Immigration Act of 1990.[37]

---

36. 29 U.S.C. Section 1802.
37. This act amended various provisions of the Immigration and Nationality Act of 1952, 8 U.S.C. Sections 1101 *et seq.*

IMMIGRATION REFORM AND CONTROL ACT

The Immigration Reform and Control Act (IRCA), which is administered by the U.S. Bureau of Citizenship and Immigration Services, prohibits employers from hiring illegal immigrants. Employers must complete a special form—called Form I-9—for each employee and indicate on it that the employer has verified that the employee is either a U.S. citizen or is otherwise entitled to work in this country.

IMMIGRATION ACT

The Immigration Act of 1990 limits the number of legal immigrants entering the United States by capping the number of visas (entry permits) that are issued each year. Under the act, employers recruiting employees from other countries must complete a certification process and satisfy the Department of Labor that there is a shortage of qualified U.S. workers capable of performing the work. The employer must also establish that bringing immigrants into this country will not adversely affect the existing labor market in that particular area. In this way, the act attempts to serve two purposes: encouraging skilled workers to enter this country and at the same time restricting competition for American jobs.

REVIEWING EMPLOYMENT RELATIONSHIPS

Rick Saldona began working as a traveling salesperson for Aimer Winery in 1977. Sales constituted 90 percent of Saldona's work time. Saldona worked an average of fifty hours per week but received no overtime pay. Aimer provided a pension plan to sales staff. In June 2005, Saldona's new supervisor, Ceasar Braxton, claimed that Saldona had been inflating his reported sales calls and required Saldona to submit to a polygraph test. Saldona reported Braxton to the U.S. Department of Labor, which prohibited Aimer from requiring Saldona to take a polygraph test for this purpose. In August 2005, Saldona's wife, Venita, fell from a ladder and sustained a head injury while employed as a full-time agricultural harvester. Saldona delivered to Aimer's Human Resources Department a letter from his wife's physician indicating that she would need daily care for several months, and Saldona took leave until December 2005. Aimer had sixty-three employees at that time. When Saldona returned to Aimer, he was informed that his position had been eliminated because his sales territory had been combined with an adjacent territory. Aimer told Saldona that he would receive no benefits because his pension had not vested. Using the information presented in the chapter, answer the following questions.

1. | What type of state statute may protect Saldona from retaliation against him for reporting the polygraph test requirement?

(Continued)

REVIEWING EMPLOYMENT RELATIONSHIPS—Continued

2. | Would Saldona have been legally entitled to receive overtime pay at a higher rate? Why or why not?

3. | Would Venita have qualified for workers' compensation for her injury? Explain.

4. | Generally, when would Saldona's pension benefits have vested?

5. | What is the maximum length of time Saldona would have been allowed to take leave to care for his injured spouse?

6. | Under what circumstances would Aimer have been allowed to require a polygraph test of an employee?

TERMS AND CONCEPTS TO REVIEW

employment at will 488	vesting 493	workers' compensation law 492
minimum wage 490	whistleblowing 489	wrongful discharge 490

QUESTIONS AND CASE PROBLEMS

20–1. Calzoni Boating Co. is an interstate business engaged in manufacturing and selling boats. The company has five hundred nonunion employees. Representatives of these employees are requesting a four-day, ten-hours-per-day workweek, and Calzoni is concerned that this would require paying time and a half after eight hours per day. Which federal act is Calzoni thinking of that might require this? Will the act in fact require paying time and a half for all hours worked over eight hours per day if the employees' proposal is accepted? Explain.

20–2. **QUESTION WITH SAMPLE ANSWER**

Denton and Carlo were employed at an appliance plant. Their job required them to perform occasional maintenance work while standing on a wire mesh twenty feet above the plant floor. Other employees had fallen through the mesh, and one of them had been killed by the fall. When Denton and Carlo were asked by their supervisor to perform tasks that would likely require them to walk on the mesh, they refused because of their fear of bodily harm or death. Because of their refusal to do the requested work, the two employees were fired from their jobs. Was their discharge wrongful? If so, under what federal employment law? To what federal agency or department should they turn for assistance? **For a sample answer to this question, go to Appendix I at the end of this text.**

20–3. Galvin Strang worked for a tractor company in one of its factories. Near his work station was a conveyor belt that ran through a large industrial oven. Sometimes, the workers would use the oven to heat their meals. Thirty-inch-high flasks containing molds were fixed at regular intervals on the conveyor and were transported into the oven. Strang had to walk between the flasks to get to his work station. One day, the conveyor was not moving, and Strang used the oven to cook a frozen pot pie. As he was removing the pot pie from the oven, the conveyor came on. One of the flasks struck Strang and seriously injured him. Strang sought recovery under the state workers' compensation law. Should he recover? Why or why not?

20–4. WRONGFUL DISCHARGE. Stephen Fredrick, a pilot for Simmons Airlines, Inc., criticized the safety of the aircraft that Simmons used on many of its flights and warned the airline about possible safety problems. Simmons took no action. After one of the planes crashed, Fredrick appeared on the television program *Good Morning America* to discuss his safety concerns. The same day, Fredrick refused to allow employees of Simmons to search his personal bags before a flight that he was scheduled to work. Claiming insubordination, the airline terminated Fredrick. Fredrick filed a suit in a federal district court against Simmons, claiming, among other things, that he had been discharged in retaliation for his public criticism of the safety of Simmons's aircraft and that this discharge violated the public policy of providing for safe air travel. Simmons responded that an employee who "goes public" with his or her concerns should not be protected by the law. Will the court agree with Simmons? Explain. [*Fredrick v. Simmons Airlines Corp.*, 144 F.3d 500 (7th Cir. 1998)]

20-5. HOURS AND WAGES. Richard Ackerman was an advance sales representative and account manager for Coca-Cola Enterprises, Inc. His primary responsibility was to sell Coca-Cola products to grocery stores, convenience stores, and other sales outlets. Coca-Cola also employed merchandisers, who did not sell Coca-Cola products but performed tasks associated with their distribution and promotion, including restocking shelves, filling vending machines, and setting up displays. The account managers, who serviced the smaller accounts themselves, regularly worked between fifty-five and seventy-two hours each week. Coca-Cola paid them a salary, bonuses, and commissions, but it did not pay them—as it did the merchandisers—additional compensation for the overtime. Ackerman and the other account managers filed a suit in a federal district court against Coca-Cola, alleging that they were entitled to overtime compensation. Coca-Cola responded that because of an exemption under the Fair Labor Standards Act, it was not required to pay them overtime. Is Coca-Cola correct? Explain. [*Ackerman v. Coca-Cola Enterprises, Inc.*, 179 F.3d 1260 (10th Cir. 1999)]

20-6. PERFORMANCE MONITORING. Patience Oyoyo worked as a claims analyst in the claims management department of Baylor Healthcare Network, Inc. When questions arose about Oyoyo's performance on several occasions, department manager Debbie Outlaw met with Oyoyo to discuss, among other things, Oyoyo's personal use of a business phone. Outlaw reminded Oyoyo that company policy prohibited excessive personal calls and that these would result in the termination of her employment. Outlaw began to monitor Oyoyo's phone usage, noting lengthy outgoing calls on several occasions, including some long-distance calls. Eventually, Outlaw terminated Oyoyo's employment, and Oyoyo filed a suit in a federal district court against Baylor. Oyoyo asserted in part that in monitoring her phone calls, the employer had invaded her privacy. Baylor asked the court to dismiss this claim. In whose favor should the court rule, and why? [*Oyoyo v. Baylor Healthcare Network, Inc.*, __ F.Supp.2d __ (N.D.Tex. 2000)]

20-7. HOURS AND WAGES. Tradesmen International, Inc., leases skilled tradespersons (field employees) to construction contractors. To receive a job offer through Tradesmen, applicants must either complete an Occupational Safety and Health Administration (OSHA) ten-hour general construction safety course or commit to registering for the course within sixty days and completing it within a reasonable time. The class instruction has no effect on the trade skills of any field employee. The classes are held outside of regular working hours. Employees perform no work in the class and are not compensated for the time spent in the class. Elaine Chao, the U.S. secretary of labor, filed a suit in a federal district court against Tradesmen for failing to pay overtime compensation to those who attend the class. Does Tradesmen's practice—requiring the class as a prerequisite to employment but not paying applicants to attend it—violate the Fair Labor Standards Act? Explain. [*Chao v. Tradesmen International, Inc.*, 310 F.3d 904 (6th Cir. 2002)]

20-8. ⚖ **CASE PROBLEM WITH SAMPLE ANSWER**
The Touch of Class Lounge is in a suburban shopping plaza, or strip mall, in Omaha, Nebraska. Patricia Bauer, the Lounge's owner, does not own the parking lot, which is provided for the common use of all of the businesses in the plaza. Stephanie Zoucha was a bartender at the Lounge. Her duties ended when she locked the door after closing. On June 4, 2001, at 1:15 A.M., Zoucha closed the bar and locked the door from the inside. An hour later, she walked to her car in the parking lot, where she was struck with "[l]ike a tire iron on the back of my head." Zoucha sustained a skull fracture and other injuries, including significant cognitive damage (impairment of speech and thought formation). Her purse, containing her tip money, was stolen. She identified her attacker as William Nunez, who had been in the Lounge earlier that night. Zoucha filed a petition in a Nebraska state court to obtain workers' compensation. What are the requirements for receiving workers' compensation? Should Zoucha's request be granted or denied? Why? [*Zoucha v. Touch of Class Lounge*, 269 Neb. 89, 690 N.W.2d 610 (2005)]

To view a sample answer for this case problem, go to this book's Web site at http://wleb.westbuslaw.com, select "Chapter 20," and click on "Case Problem with Sample Answer."

20-9. ⚖ **A QUESTION OF ETHICS**
Keith Cline worked for Wal-Mart Stores, Inc., as a night maintenance supervisor. When he suffered a recurrence of a brain tumor, he took a leave from work, which was covered by the Family and Medical Leave Act (FMLA) of 1993 and authorized by his employer. When he returned to work, his employer refused to allow him to continue his supervisory job and demoted him to the status of a regular maintenance worker. A few weeks later, the company fired him, ostensibly because he "stole" company time by clocking in thirteen minutes early for a company meeting. Cline sued Wal-Mart, alleging, among other things, that Wal-Mart had violated the FMLA by refusing to return him to his prior position when he returned to work. In view of these facts, answer the following questions. [*Cline v. Wal-Mart Stores, Inc.*, 144 F.3d 294 (4th Cir. 1998)]

(a) Did Wal-Mart violate the FMLA by refusing to return Cline to his prior position when he returned to work?

(b) From an ethical perspective, the FMLA has been viewed as a choice on the part of society to shift to the employer family burdens caused by changing economic and social needs. What "changing" needs does the act meet? In other words, why did Congress feel that workers should have the right to family and medical leave in 1993, but not in 1983, or 1973, or earlier?

(c) "Congress should amend the FMLA, which currently applies to employers with fifty or more employees, so that it applies to employers with twenty-five or more employees." Do you agree with this statement? Why or why not?

20–10. VIDEO QUESTION

Go to this text's Web site at http://wleb.westbuslaw.com and select "Chapter 20." Click on "Video Questions" and view the video titled *Employment at Will.* Then answer the following questions.

(a) In the video, Laura asserts that she can fire Ray "for any reason; for no reason." Is this true? Explain your answer.
(b) What exceptions to the employment-at-will doctrine are discussed in the chapter? Does Ray's situation fit into any of these exceptions?
(c) Would Ray be protected from wrongful discharge under whistleblowing statutes? Why or why not?
(d) Assume that you are the employer in this scenario. What arguments can you make that Ray should not be able to sue for wrongful discharge in this situation?

LAW | on the Web

For updated links to resources available on the Web, as well as a variety of other materials, visit this text's Web site at http://wleb.westbuslaw.com.

A good Web site for information on employee benefits—including the full text of the FMLA, COBRA, other relevant statutes and case law, and current articles—is BenefitsLink. Go to

> http://benefitslink.com/index.html

The Occupational Safety and Health Administration (OSHA) offers information related to workplace health and safety at

> http://www.osha.gov

The Bureau of Labor Statistics provides a wide variety of data on employment, including data on employment compensation, working conditions, and productivity. Go to

> http://www.bls.gov

LEGAL RESEARCH EXERCISES ON THE WEB

Go to http://wleb.westbuslaw.com, the Web site that accompanies this text. Select "Chapter 20" and click on "Internet Exercises." There you will find the following Internet research exercises that you can perform to learn more about topics covered in this chapter.

Activity 20–1: LEGAL PERSPECTIVE
Workers' Compensation

Activity 20–2: MANAGEMENT PERSPECTIVE
Workplace Monitoring and Surveillance

CHAPTER 21

Employment Discrimination

Out of the 1960s civil rights movement to end racial and other forms of discrimination grew a body of law protecting employees against discrimination in the workplace. This protective legislation further eroded the employment-at-will doctrine, which was discussed in Chapter 20. In the past several decades, judicial decisions, administrative agency actions, and legislation have restricted the ability of employers, as well as unions, to discriminate against workers on the basis of race, color, religion, national origin, gender, age, or disability. A class of persons defined by one or more of these criteria is known as a **protected class.**

Several federal statutes prohibit **employment discrimination** against members of protected classes. The most important statute is Title VII of the Civil Rights Act of 1964.[1] Title VII prohibits employment discrimination on the basis of race, color, religion, national origin, and gender. The Age Discrimination in Employment Act of 1967[2] and the Americans with Disabilities Act of 1990[3] prohibit discrimination on the basis of age and disability, respectively. The protections afforded under these laws extend to U.S. citizens who are working abroad for U.S. firms or for companies that are controlled by U.S. firms— *unless* to do so would violate the laws of the countries in which their workplaces are located. This "foreign laws exception" allows employers to avoid being subjected to conflicting laws.

This chapter focuses on the kinds of discrimination prohibited by these federal statutes. Note, however, that discrimination against employees on the basis of any of the above-mentioned criteria may also violate state human rights statutes or other state laws prohibiting discrimination.

SECTION 1 | Title VII of the Civil Rights Act of 1964

Title VII of the Civil Rights Act of 1964 and its amendments prohibit job discrimination against employees, applicants, and union members on the basis of race, color, national origin, religion, and gender at any stage of employment. Title VII applies to employers affecting interstate commerce with fifteen or more employees, labor unions with fifteen or more members, labor unions that operate hiring halls (to which members go regularly to be rationed jobs as they become available), employment agencies, and state and local governing units or agencies. A special section of the act prohibits discrimination in most federal government employment.

1. 42 U.S.C. Sections 2000e–2000e-17.
2. 29 U.S.C. Sections 621–634.
3. 42 U.S.C. Sections 12102–12118.

PROCEDURES UNDER TITLE VII

Compliance with Title VII is monitored by the Equal Employment Opportunity Commission (EEOC). A victim of alleged discrimination, before bringing a suit against the employer, must first file a claim with the EEOC. The EEOC may investigate the dispute and attempt to obtain the parties' voluntary consent to an out-of-court settlement. If voluntary agreement cannot be reached, the EEOC may then file a suit against the employer on the employee's behalf. If the EEOC decides not to investigate the claim, the victim may bring his or her own lawsuit against the employer.

The EEOC does not investigate every claim of employment discrimination; rather, it investigates only "priority cases." Generally, priority cases are cases that affect many workers, cases involving retaliatory discharge (firing an employee in retaliation for submitting a claim with the EEOC), and cases involving types of discrimination that are of particular concern to the EEOC.

INTENTIONAL AND UNINTENTIONAL DISCRIMINATION

Title VII of the Civil Rights Act of 1964 prohibits both intentional and unintentional discrimination.

INTENTIONAL DISCRIMINATION Intentional discrimination by an employer against an employee is known as **disparate-treatment discrimination.** Because intent may sometimes be difficult to prove, courts have established certain procedures for resolving disparate-treatment cases. Suppose that a woman applies for employment with a construction firm and is rejected. If she sues on the basis of disparate-treatment discrimination in hiring, she must show that (1) she is a member of a protected class, (2) she applied and was qualified for the job in question, (3) she was rejected by the employer, and (4) the employer continued to seek applicants for the position or filled the position with a person not in a protected class.

If the woman can meet these relatively easy requirements, she makes out a *prima facie* **case** of illegal discrimination. Making out a *prima facie* case of discrimination means that the plaintiff has met her initial burden of proof and will win in the absence of a legally acceptable employer defense (defenses to claims of employment discrimination will be discussed later in this chapter). The burden then shifts to the employer-defendant, who must articulate a legal reason for not hiring the plaintiff. For example, the employer might say that the plaintiff was not hired because she lacked sufficient experience or training. To prevail, the plaintiff must then show that the employer's reason is a *pretext* (not the true reason) and that discriminatory intent actually motivated the employer's decision.

UNINTENTIONAL DISCRIMINATION Employers often find it necessary to use interviews and testing procedures to choose from among a large number of applicants for job openings. Minimum educational requirements are also common. Employer practices, such as those involving educational requirements, may have an unintended discriminatory impact on a protected class. **Disparate-impact discrimination** occurs when an employer's practices, procedures, or tests, which do not seem to be discriminatory, adversely impact a protected group of people. In a disparate-impact discrimination case, the complaining party must first show statistically that the employer's practices, procedures, or tests are discriminatory in effect. Once the plaintiff has made out a *prima facie* case, the burden of proof shifts to the employer to show that the practices or procedures in question were justified. There are two ways of proving that disparate impact exists, as discussed below.

—Pool of Applicants. A plaintiff can prove a disparate impact by comparing the employer's workforce to the pool of qualified individuals available in the local labor market. The plaintiff must show that, as a result of educational or other job requirements or hiring procedures, an employer's workforce does not reflect the percentage of nonwhites, women, or members of other protected classes that characterizes the pool of qualified individuals available. If a person challenging an employment practice having a discriminatory effect can show a connection between the practice and the disparity, she or he makes out a *prima facie* case and need not provide evidence of discriminatory intent.

—Rate of Hiring. Disparate-impact discrimination can also occur when an educational or other job requirement or hiring procedure excludes members of a protected class from an employer's workforce at a substantially higher rate than nonmembers, regardless of the racial balance in the employer's workforce. This "rates analysis" compares the selection rate for whites with that for nonwhites (or other members of a protected class). It does not require the plaintiff to prove what percentage of qualified nonwhite persons are available in the local labor market.

The EEOC has devised a test, called the "four-fifths rule" or the "80 percent rule," to determine whether an employment examination is discriminatory on its face. Under this rule, a selection rate for protected classes that is less than four-fifths, or 80 percent, of the rate for the group with the highest rate will generally be regarded as evidence of disparate impact. To illustrate: One hundred majority applicants take an employment test, and fifty pass the test and are hired. One hundred minority applicants take the test, and twenty pass the test and are hired. Because twenty is less than four-fifths (80 percent) of fifty, the test would be considered discriminatory under the EEOC guidelines.

DISCRIMINATION BASED ON RACE, COLOR, AND NATIONAL ORIGIN

Title VII prohibits employers from discriminating against employees or job applicants on the basis of race, color, or national origin. This prohibition extends to both intentional (disparate-treatment) and unintentional (disparate-impact) discrimination. If a company's standards or policies for selecting or promoting employees have the effect of discriminating against employees or job applicants on the basis of race, color, or national origin, they are illegal—unless (except for race) they have a substantial, demonstrable relationship to realistic qualifications for the job in question. Discrimination against these protected classes in regard to employment conditions and benefits is also illegal.

Note that victims of racial or ethnic discrimination may also have a cause of action under 42 U.S.C. Section 1981. This section, which was enacted as part of the Civil Rights Act of 1866, prohibits discrimination on the basis of race or ethnicity in the formation or enforcement of contracts. Although Section 1981 remained a "dead letter" on the books for over a century, since the 1970s many plaintiffs have succeeded in Section 1981 cases against their employers. Unlike Title VII, Section 1981 does not place a cap on damages (see the discussion of Title VII remedies later in this chapter). Thus, if an employee can prove that he or she was discriminated against in the formation or enforcement of a contract, the employee may be able to obtain a greater amount of damages under Section 1981 than under Title VII.

DISCRIMINATION BASED ON RELIGION

Title VII of the Civil Rights Act of 1964 also prohibits government employers, private employers, and unions from discriminating against persons because of their religion. An employer must "reasonably accommodate" the religious practices of its employees, unless to do so would cause undue hardship to the employer's business. For example, if an employee's religion prohibits him from working on a certain day of the week or at a certain type of job, the employer must make a reasonable attempt to accommodate these religious requirements. Employers must reasonably accommodate an employee's religious belief even if the belief is not based on the tenets or dogma of a particular church, sect, or denomination. The only requirement is that the belief be sincerely held by the employee.[4]

DISCRIMINATION BASED ON GENDER

Under Title VII, as well as under other federal acts, employers are forbidden from discriminating against employees on the basis of gender. Employers are prohibited from classifying jobs as male or female and from advertising in help-wanted columns that are designated male or female unless the employer can prove that the gender of the applicant is essential to the job. Furthermore, employers cannot have separate male and female seniority lists. Generally, to succeed in a suit for gender discrimination, a plaintiff must demonstrate that gender was a determining factor in the employer's decision to hire, fire, or promote him or her. Typically, this involves looking at all of the surrounding circumstances.

The Pregnancy Discrimination Act of 1978,[5] which amended Title VII, expanded the definition of gender discrimination to include discrimination based on pregnancy. Women affected by pregnancy, childbirth, or related medical conditions must be treated—for all employment-related purposes, including the provision of benefits under employee benefit programs—the same as other persons not so affected but similar in ability to work.

CONSTRUCTIVE DISCHARGE

The majority of Title VII complaints involve unlawful discrimination in decisions to hire or fire employees. In some situations, however, employees who leave their jobs voluntarily can claim that they were "constructively discharged" by the employer. **Constructive discharge** refers to a situation in which the employer causes the employee's working conditions to be so intolerable that a reasonable person in the employee's position would feel compelled to quit.

PROVING CONSTRUCTIVE DISCHARGE The plaintiff must present objective proof of intolerable working conditions, which the employer knew or had reason to know about yet failed to correct within a reasonable time period. Courts generally also require the employee to show causation—that the employer's unlawful discrimination caused the working conditions to be intolerable. Put a different way, the employee's resignation must be a foreseeable result of the employer's discriminatory action.

For example, Khalil, who was born in Iraq, is humiliated in front of his co-workers at the time that his employer informs him that he is being demoted to an inferior position. Co-workers continue to insult and harass Khalil and make derogatory remarks about his national origin. The employer is aware of this

---

4. *Frazee v. Illinois Department of Employment Security*, 489 U.S. 829, 109 S.Ct. 1514, 103 L.Ed.2d 914 (1989).

5. 42 U.S.C. Section 2000e(k).

discriminatory treatment but does nothing to remedy the situation, despite repeated complaints from Khalil. After several months, Khalil quits his job and files a Title VII claim. In this situation, Khalil would likely have sufficient evidence to maintain an action for constructive discharge in violation of Title VII. Although courts weigh the facts on a case-by-case basis, employee demotion is one of the most frequently cited reasons for a finding of constructive discharge, particularly when the employee was subjected to humiliation.

CAN BE APPLIED TO ANY TYPE OF TITLE VII DISCRIMINATION Note that constructive discharge is a theory that plaintiffs can use to establish any type of discrimination claims under Title VII, including race, color, national origin, religion, gender, pregnancy, and sexual harassment. Constructive discharge

has also been successfully used in situations that involve discrimination based on age or disability (both of which will be discussed later in this chapter). Constructive discharge is most commonly asserted in cases involving sexual harassment, however.

When constructive discharge is claimed, the employee can pursue damages for loss of income, including back pay. These damages would not ordinarily be available to an employee who left a job voluntarily.

The following case involved an employee's claim that she was constructively discharged from her job for refusing to participate in a scheme to discriminate against male co-workers and supervisors. The question for the court was whether the employer should have been aware of the employee's mistreatment and purported unbearable working conditions and done something about it.

CASE 21.1   Conway-Jepsen v. Small Business Administration

United States
District Court,
District of Montana. 2004.
303 F.Supp.2d 1155.

LOVELL, Senior District Judge.
* * * *

Plaintiff Mary Conway-Jepsen, an Assistant District Director for the Helena, Montana, office of the United States [Small] Business Administration (the "Helena SBA") from December 26, 1993, to August 6, 1997, complains that she was retaliated against in violation of Title VII * * * .
* * * *

Shortly after August, 1992, Jo Alice Mospan came to Helena, Montana, as the new District Director ("DD") of the Helena SBA. * * *
* * * *

* * * [T]here were no females above a [certain pay level] in the Helena SBA office and * * * most of the senior employees and supervisors were male.
* * * *

Mospan * * * mete[d] out discipline frequently to SBA employees, but particularly to certain male SBA employees. * * * She was described, in today's parlance, as an "in your face" type micro-manager.
* * * *

* * * [Mospan's] express purpose [was] harassing and ultimately firing certain male career SBA employees, * * * so that they could be replaced by females.
* * * *

* * * When Mospan arrived in 1992, the top layer of supervisors and program directors in the Helena SBA office was male * * * . When Mospan left in 2000, none of these men was employed by the SBA. * * *
* * * *

In 1993, Mospan * * * recruited Conway-Jepsen. * * *

In the Fall of 1994, * * * [I]t dawned on Conway-Jepsen that the promotion of women by Mospan would be "on the backs of the guys * * * ".

* * * Conway-Jepsen told Mospan that what she was doing * * * was wrong. * * * In response, Mospan became angry with Conway-Jepsen. * * *
* * * *

Mospan's [subsequent] harassment of Conway-Jepsen ranged from * * * program-irrelevant work assignments * * * [to] counterproductive actions in Plaintiff's projects * * * .

CASE 21.1 Continued

* * * *

* * * [Conway-Jepsen] eventually sought help from her physician, who * * * recommended that she quit her job. * * *

A few months before Plaintiff did resign, however, she * * * request[ed] that she be transferred to another SBA office or program. Notably, [no SBA official] responded to Plaintiff's request for a transfer * * * .

* * * *

Title VII prohibits an employer from discriminating against any employee because he or she has opposed * * * an unlawful employment practice * * * . In order to prove retaliation, Plaintiff must show that (1) she opposed an unlawful employment practice, (2) she suffered an adverse employment action, and (3) a causal connection existed between the adverse employment action and the protected activity or opposition. * * *

Among the unlawful employment practices forbidden by Title VII is the rule that employers must not * * * *discharge any individual, or otherwise* * * * *discriminate against any individual with respect to his compensation, terms, conditions, or privileges of employment, because of such individual's race, color, religion, sex, or national origin.* * * * [Emphasis added.]

* * * *

In order to meet her burden of proving that she was constructively discharged, Plaintiff must show that a reasonable person in her position would have felt compelled to resign because of intolerable working conditions. * * *

In addition, Plaintiff must show that the intolerable working conditions were created by the very conduct that constituted a violation of Title VII (in this case, e.g., the retaliation) and that her resignation resulted from the intolerable working conditions.

* * * *

* * * [T]he Court concludes that Plaintiff reasonably found her hostile working conditions intolerable, that the intolerable working conditions were created by conduct that constituted a violation of Title VII, and that Plaintiff's resignation resulted from the hostile and intolerable working conditions. The Court concludes that Plaintiff was a diligent and competent SBA employee who was constructively discharged from her position by Mospan's lengthy, continuous, and pervasive pattern of retaliatory treatment for the reason that she had objected to employment practices which were unlawful under Title VII.

* * * *

IT IS HEREBY ORDERED AND ADJUDGED * * * as follows:
1. Defendant * * * shall pay to Plaintiff back pay * * * .
2. Defendant * * * shall reinstate Plaintiff in a non-hostile work environment * * * .
3. Defendant * * * shall pay to Plaintiff * * * compensatory damages for emotional pain, suffering, inconvenience, mental anguish, loss of enjoyment of life, and other nonpecuniary losses.
4. Defendant * * * shall pay Plaintiff's reasonable attorney's fee.

QUESTIONS

1. What message does the outcome in this case send to employers covered by Title VII?
2. What conclusion might be drawn from the facts and result in this case with respect to diversity among employees as a goal for employers?

SEXUAL HARASSMENT

Title VII also protects employees against **sexual harassment** in the workplace. Sexual harassment can take two forms: *quid pro quo* harassment and hostile-environment harassment. *Quid pro quo* is a Latin phrase that is often translated to mean "something in exchange for something else." *Quid pro quo* harassment occurs when job opportunities, promotions, salary increases, and the like are given in return for sexual favors. According to the United States Supreme Court, hostile-environment harassment occurs when "the workplace is permeated with discriminatory intimidation, ridicule, and insult, that is sufficiently severe or pervasive to alter the conditions of the victim's employment and create an abusive working environment."[6]

Generally, the courts apply this Supreme Court guideline on a case-by-case basis. Some courts have held that just one incident of sexually offensive conduct—such as a sexist remark by a co-worker or a photo on an employer's desk of his bikini-clad wife—can create a hostile environment.[7] Other courts, however, require more than one instance of sexually offensive conduct to find that an abusive working environment exists. According to some employment specialists, employers should assume that hostile-environment harassment has occurred if an employee claims that it has.

HARASSMENT BY SUPERVISORS What if an employee is harassed by a manager or supervisor of a large firm, and the firm itself (the "employer") is not aware of the harassment? Should the employer be held liable for the harassment nonetheless? For some time, the courts were in disagreement on this issue. Typically, employers were held liable for Title VII violations by the firm's managerial or supervisory personnel in *quid pro quo* harassment cases regardless of whether the employer knew about the harassment. In hostile-environment cases, in contrast, the majority of courts tended to hold employers liable only if the employer knew or should have known of the harassment and failed to take prompt remedial action.

—Tangible Employment Action. For an employer to be held liable for a supervisor's sexual harassment, the supervisor must have taken a *tangible employment action* against the employee. A **tangible employment action** is a significant change in employment status, such as firing or failing to promote an employee; reassigning the employee to a position with significantly different responsibilities; or effecting a significant change in employment benefits.

Only a supervisor, or another person acting with the authority of the employer, can cause this sort of injury. A co-worker can sexually harass another employee, and anyone who has regular contact with an employee can inflict psychological injuries by offensive conduct. A co-worker cannot dock another's pay, demote her or him, or set conditions for continued employment, however.

—Supreme Court Guidelines. In 1998, in two separate cases, the United States Supreme Court issued some significant guidelines relating to the liability of employers for their supervisors' harassment of employees in the workplace. In *Faragher v. City of Boca Raton*,[8] the Court held that an employer (a city) could be held liable for a supervisor's harassment of employees even though the employer was unaware of the behavior. The Court reached this conclusion primarily because, although the city had a written policy against sexual harassment, the policy had not been distributed to city employees. Additionally, the city had not established any procedures that could be followed by employees who felt that they were victims of sexual harassment. In *Burlington Industries, Inc. v. Ellerth*,[9] the Court ruled that a company could be held liable for the harassment of an employee by one of its vice presidents even though the employee suffered no adverse job consequences.

In these two cases, the Court set forth some commonsense guidelines on liability for harassment in the workplace that are helpful to employers and employees alike. On the one hand, employees benefit by the ruling that employers may be held liable for their supervisors' harassment even though the employers were unaware of the actions and even though the employees suffered no adverse job consequences. On the other hand, the Court made it clear in both decisions that employers have an affirmative defense against liability for their supervisors' harassment of employees if the employers can show the following:

1. That they have taken "reasonable care to prevent and correct promptly any sexually harassing behavior" (by establishing effective harassment policies and complaint procedures, for example).
2. That the employee suing for harassment failed to follow these policies and procedures.

In 2004, the Supreme Court further clarified the tangible employment action requirement in the following case. The Court had to decide how the guidelines apply to a state police employee's constructive discharge caused by her supervisors' sexual harassment. Does a constructive discharge count as a tangible employment action and preclude the employer's assertion of the affirmative defense? That was the issue before the Court.

---

6. *Harris v. Forklift Systems*, 510 U.S. 17, 114 S.Ct. 367, 126 L.Ed.2d 295 (1993).

7. For other examples, see *Radtke v. Everett*, 442 Mich. 368, 501 N.W.2d 155 (1993); and *Nadeau v. Rainbow Rugs, Inc.*, 675 A.2d 973 (Me. 1996).

---

8. 524 U.S. 775, 118 S.Ct. 2275, 141 L.Ed.2d 662 (1998).
9. 524 U.S. 742, 118 S.Ct. 2257, 141 L.Ed.2d 633 (1998).

CASE 21.2 — Pennsylvania State Police v. Suders

Supreme Court of the
United States, 2004.
542 U.S. 129,
124 S.Ct. 2342,
159 L.Ed.2d 204.
http://www.findlaw.com/
casecode/supreme.html[a]

BACKGROUND AND FACTS *In March 1998, the Pennsylvania State Police (PSP) hired Nancy Suders to work as a communications operator. Suders's supervisors—Sergeant Eric Easton, Corporal William Baker, and Corporal Eric Prendergast—subjected her to a continuous barrage of sexual harassment. In June, Suders told Officer Virginia Smith-Elliott, whom PSP had designated as its equal employment opportunity officer, that Suders might need help. Two months later, again to Smith-Elliott, Suders reported that she was being harassed and was afraid. Smith-Elliott told Suders to file a complaint, but did not tell her how to obtain the necessary form. Two days later, Suders's supervisors arrested her for the theft of her own computer-skills exam paper, which she had removed after they reported falsely that she had failed the exam. Suders resigned and filed a suit in a federal district court against PSP, alleging, in part, sexual harassment. The court issued a summary judgment in PSP's favor. Suders appealed to the U.S. Court of Appeals for the Third Circuit, which reversed the judgment and remanded the case for trial, holding that the* Ellerth/Faragher *affirmative defense is never available in constructive discharge cases. PSP appealed to the United States Supreme Court.*

IN THE LANGUAGE OF THE COURT

Justice *GINSBURG* delivered the opinion of the Court.

* * * *

This case concerns an employer's liability for * * * constructive discharge resulting from sexual harassment, or hostile work environment, attributable to a supervisor. Our starting point is the framework [the] *Ellerth* and *Faragher* [decisions, discussed previously in this chapter] established to govern employer liability for sexual harassment by supervisors. * * * [T]hose decisions delineate two categories of hostile work environment claims: (1) harassment that culminates in a tangible employment action, for which employers are strictly liable, and (2) harassment that takes place in the absence of a tangible employment action, to which employers may assert an affirmative defense * * * .

* * * *

Suders' claim is of the same genre as the hostile work environment claims the Court analyzed in [the] *Ellerth* and *Faragher* [decisions]. Essentially, Suders presents a "worse case" harassment scenario, harassment ratcheted up to the breaking point. Like the harassment considered in our pathmarking decisions, harassment so intolerable as to cause a resignation may be effected through co-worker conduct, unofficial supervisory conduct, or official company acts. Unlike an actual termination, which is *always* effected through an official act of the company, a constructive discharge need not be. *A constructive discharge involves both an employee's decision to leave and precipitating conduct: The former involves no official action; the latter, like a harassment claim without any constructive discharge assertion, may or may not involve official action.* [Emphasis added.]

To be sure, a constructive discharge is functionally the same as an actual termination in [some] respects. * * * [B]oth end the employer-employee relationship, and both inflict * * * direct economic harm. But when an official act does not underlie the constructive discharge, the *Ellerth* and *Faragher* analysis, we here hold, calls for extension of the affirmative defense to the employer. As those leading decisions indicate, official directions and declarations are the acts most likely to be brought home to the employer, the measures over which the employer can exercise greatest control. Absent an official act of the enterprise as the last straw, the employer ordinarily would have no particular reason to suspect that a resignation is not the typical kind daily occurring in the work force. And as [the] *Ellerth* and *Faragher* [decisions] further point out, an official act reflected in company records—a demotion or a reduction in compensation, for example—shows beyond question that the supervisor has used his managerial or controlling position to the employee's disadvantage. *Absent such an official act, the extent to which the supervisor's misconduct has been aided by the [employment] relation is less*

---

a. In the "Browsing" section, click on "2004 Decisions." When that page opens, click on the name of the case to access the opinion.

CONTINUED ▶

CASE 21.2 Continued

certain. That uncertainty * * * *justifies affording the employer the chance to establish, through the* Ellerth/Faragher *affirmative defense, that it should not be held vicariously liable.* [Emphasis added.]

* * * *

We agree with the Third Circuit that the case, in its current posture, presents genuine issues of material fact concerning Suders' hostile work environment and constructive discharge claims. We hold, however, that the Court of Appeals erred in declaring the affirmative defense described in [the] *Ellerth* and *Faragher* [decisions] never available in constructive discharge cases. Accordingly, we vacate the Third Circuit's judgment and remand the case for further proceedings consistent with this opinion.

DECISION AND REMEDY *The United States Supreme Court vacated the lower court's judgment and remanded the case for further proceedings. To establish constructive discharge, a plaintiff alleging sexual harassment must show that the work environment became so intolerable that resignation was a fitting response. An employer may then assert the* Ellerth/Faragher *affirmative defense unless the plaintiff quit in reasonable response to a tangible employment action.*

WHAT IF THE FACTS WERE DIFFERENT? *If the plaintiff had filed a complaint with the employer's equal employment opportunity officer, how might the result have been different?*

HARASSMENT BY CO-WORKERS AND NON-EMPLOYEES Often, employees alleging harassment complain that the actions of co-workers, not supervisors, are responsible for creating a hostile working environment. In such cases, the employee still has a cause of action against the employer. Generally, though, the employer will be held liable only if it knew or should have known about the harassment and failed to take immediate remedial action.

Employers may also be liable for harassment by *nonemployees* under certain conditions. For example, if a restaurant owner or manager knows that a particular customer repeatedly harasses a waitress and permits the harassment to continue, the restaurant owner may be liable under Title VII even though the customer is not an employee of the restaurant. The issue turns on the control that the employer exerts over a nonemployee. In one case, the owner of a Pizza Hut franchise was held liable for the harassment of a waitress by two male customers because no steps were taken to prevent the harassment.[10]

SAME-GENDER HARASSMENT The courts have also had to address the issue of whether men who are harassed by other men, or women who are harassed by other women, are also protected by laws that prohibit gender-based discrimination in the workplace. For example, what if the male president of a firm demands sexual favors from a male employee? Does this action qualify as sexual harassment? For some time, the courts were widely split on this question. In 1998, in *Oncale*

v. Sundowner Offshore Services, Inc.,[11] the Supreme Court resolved the issue by holding that Title VII protection extends to situations in which individuals are harassed by members of the same gender.

It can be difficult to prove that the harassment in same-gender harassment cases is "based on sex." Suppose that a gay man is harassed by another man at the workplace. The harasser is not a homosexual and does not treat all men with hostility—just this one man. Does the victim in this situation have a cause of action under Title VII? A court may find that this does not qualify as sexual harassment under Title VII because the harasser's conduct was not "because of sex," but because of sexual orientation.[12]

Although Title VII does not prohibit discrimination or harassment based on a person's sexual orientation, a growing number of companies are voluntarily establishing nondiscrimination policies that include sexual orientation. According to one study, at the end of 2004, 410 companies on the Fortune 500 had procedures in place to specifically protect gay, lesbian, bisexual, and transgender (those transitioning from one gender to another) employees from workplace discrimination and harassment.[13]

---

10. *Lockard v. Pizza Hut, Inc.*, 162 F.3d 1062 (10th Cir. 1998).

11. 523 U.S. 75, 118 S.Ct. 998, 140 L.Ed.2d 207 (1998).

12. See, for example, *McCown v. St. John's Health System*, 349 F.3d 540 (8th Cir. 2003); and *Rene v. MGM Grand Hotel, Inc.*, 305 F.3d 1061 (9th Cir. 2002).

13. Amy Joyce, "Workplace Improves for Gay, Transgender Employees, Rights Group Says," *The Washington Post*, June 6, 2005, reporting a study conducted by the Human Rights Campaign Foundation, "The State of the Workplace for Lesbian, Gay, Bisexual, and Transgender Americans 2004."

ONLINE HARASSMENT

Employees' online activities can create a hostile working environment in many ways. Racial jokes, ethnic slurs, or other comments contained in e-mail may become the basis for a claim of hostile-environment harassment or other forms of discrimination. A worker who sees sexually explicit images on a co-worker's computer screen may find the images offensive and claim that they create a hostile working environment.

Nevertheless, employers may be able to avoid liability for online harassment by taking prompt remedial action. For example, in one case Angela Daniels, an employee under contract to WorldCom, received racially harassing e-mailed jokes from another employee. After receiving the jokes, Daniels complained to WorldCom managers. Shortly afterward, the company issued a warning to the offending employee about the proper use of the e-mail system and held two meetings to discuss company policy on the use of the system. In Daniels's suit against WorldCom for racial discrimination, a federal district court concluded that the employer was not liable for its employee's racially harassing e-mails because the employer took prompt remedial action.[14]

REMEDIES UNDER TITLE VII

Employer liability under Title VII may be extensive. If the plaintiff successfully proves that unlawful discrimination occurred, he or she may be awarded reinstatement, back pay, retroactive promotions, and damages.[15] Compensatory damages are available only in cases of intentional discrimination. Punitive damages may be recovered against a private employer only if the employer acted with malice or reckless indifference to an individual's rights. The statute limits the total amount of compensatory and punitive damages that the plaintiff can recover from specific employers (ranging from $50,000 against employers with one hundred or fewer employees to $300,000 against employers with more than five hundred employees).

---

14. *Daniels v. WorldCom Corp.*, 1998 WL 91261 (N.D.Tex. 1998). Also see *Musgrove v. Mobil Oil Corp.*, 2003 WL 21653125 (N.D. Tex. 2003).

15. Damages were not available under Title VII until 1991. The Civil Rights Act of that year amended Title VII to provide for both compensatory and punitive damages, as well as for jury trials.

SECTION 2 | Equal Pay Act of 1963

The Equal Pay Act of 1963 was enacted as an amendment to the Fair Labor Standards Act of 1938. Basically, the act prohibits gender-based discrimination in the wages paid for similar work. For the equal pay requirements to apply, the male and female workers must be employed at the same establishment.

A person alleging wage discrimination in violation of the Equal Pay Act may sue her or his employer. To determine whether the act has been violated, a court will look to the primary duties of the two jobs—it is job content rather than job description that controls in all cases. The jobs of a barber and a beautician, for example, are considered essentially equal. So, too, are those of a tailor and a seamstress. Small differences in job content do not legally justify higher pay for one gender. An employer will *not* be found liable for violating the act if it can show that the wage differential for equal work was based on (1) a seniority system, (2) a merit system, (3) a system that pays according to quality or quantity of production, or (4) any factor other than gender.

SECTION 3 | Discrimination Based on Age

Age discrimination is potentially the most widespread form of discrimination, because anyone—regardless of race, color, national origin, or gender—could be a victim at some point in life. The Age Discrimination in Employment Act (ADEA) of 1967, as amended, prohibits employment discrimination on the basis of age against individuals forty years of age or older. The act also prohibits mandatory retirement for nonmanagerial workers. For the act to apply, an employer must have twenty or more employees, and the employer's business activities must affect interstate commerce. The EEOC administers the ADEA, but the act also permits private causes of action against employers for age discrimination.

PROCEDURES UNDER THE ADEA

The burden-shifting procedure under the ADEA is similar to that under Title VII. If a plaintiff can establish that he or she (1) was a member of the protected age group, (2) was qualified for the position from which he or she was discharged, and (3) was discharged under circumstances that give rise to an inference of discrimination, the plaintiff has established a *prima facie* case of unlawful age discrimination. The burden then shifts to the employer, who must articulate a legitimate reason for the discrimination. If the plaintiff can prove that the employer's reason is only a pretext and that the plaintiff's age was a determining factor in the employer's decision, the employer will be held liable under the ADEA.

REPLACING OLDER WORKERS WITH YOUNGER WORKERS

Numerous cases of alleged age discrimination have been brought against employers who, to cut costs, replaced older, higher-salaried employees with younger, lower-salaried workers. Whether a firing is discriminatory or simply part of a rational business decision to prune the company's ranks is not always clear. Companies generally defend a decision to discharge a worker by asserting that the worker could no longer perform her or his duties or that the worker's skills were no longer needed. The employee must prove that the discharge was motivated, at least in part, by age bias. Proof that qualified older employees are generally discharged before employees who are younger or that co-workers continually made unflattering age-related comments about the discharged worker may be enough. The plaintiff need not prove that she or he was replaced by a person outside the protected class—that is, by a person under the age of forty years.[16] Rather, the issue in all ADEA cases turns on whether age discrimination has, in fact, occurred, regardless of the age of the replacement worker.

A SPECIAL CASE—STATE EMPLOYEES

Under the Eleventh Amendment to the U.S. Constitution, as that amendment has been interpreted by the United States Supreme Court, states are immune from lawsuits brought by private individuals in federal court, unless the state consents to the suit. In a number of age-discrimination cases brought in the late 1990s, state agencies that were sued by state employees for age discrimination sought to have the suits dismissed on this ground.

STATE EMPLOYEES NOT COVERED BY THE ADEA
In two Florida cases, professors and librarians contended that their employers—two Florida state universities—denied them salary increases and other benefits because they were getting old and their successors could be hired at lower cost. The universities

claimed that as agencies of a sovereign state, they could not be sued without the state's consent. Because the courts were rendering conflicting opinions in these cases, the United States Supreme Court agreed to address the issue. In *Kimel v. Florida Board of Regents*,[17] decided in 2000, the Court held that the sovereign immunity granted the states by the Eleventh Amendment precluded suits against them by private parties alleging violations of the ADEA.

STATE IMMUNITY IS NOT ABSOLUTE
In 2004, the Supreme Court clarified that state immunity under the Eleventh Amendment is not absolute. The case was brought under the Americans with Disabilities Act (ADA), which will be discussed shortly, alleging that disabled individuals were denied access to the courts. The Court held that in some situations, such as when fundamental rights are at stake, Congress has the power to abrogate (abolish) state immunity to private suits through legislation that unequivocally shows Congress's intent to subject states to private suits.[18]

Generally, though, the Court has found that state employers are immune from private suits brought by employees under the ADEA (for age discrimination, as noted above), the ADA[19] (for disability discrimination), and the Fair Labor Standards Act[20] (FLSA, which relates to wages and hours—see Chapter 20), but are not immune from the requirements of the Family Medical Leave Act[21] (FMLA—see Chapter 20).

SECTION 4 | Discrimination Based on Disability

The Americans with Disabilities Act (ADA) of 1990 is designed to eliminate discriminatory employment practices that prevent otherwise qualified workers with disabilities from fully participating in the national labor force. Prior to 1990, the major federal law providing protection to those with disabilities was the Rehabilitation Act of 1973. That act protected only federal government employees and those employed

---

16. *O'Connor v. Consolidated Coin Caterers Corp.*, 517 U.S. 308, 116 S.Ct. 1307, 134 L.Ed.2d 433 (1996).

17. 528 U.S. 62, 120 S.Ct. 631, 145 L.Ed.2d 522 (2000).
18. *Tennessee v. Lane*, 541 U.S. 509, 124 S.Ct. 1978, 158 L.Ed.2d 820 (2004).
19. *Board of Trustees of the University of Alabama v. Garrett*, 531 U.S. 356, 121 S.Ct. 955, 148 L.Ed.2d 866 (2001).
20. *Alden v. Maine*, 527 U.S. 706, 119 S.Ct. 2240, 144 L.Ed.2d 636 (1999).
21. *Nevada Department of Human Resources v. Hibbs*, 538 U.S. 721, 123 S.Ct. 1972, 155 L.Ed.2d 953 (2003). This case was presented in Chapter 20 as Case 20.1.

under federally funded programs. The ADA extends federal protection against disability-based discrimination to all workplaces with fifteen or more workers (with the exception of state government employers, who are generally immune under the Eleventh Amendment, as was just discussed). Basically, the ADA requires that employers "reasonably accommodate" the needs of persons with disabilities unless to do so would cause the employer to suffer an "undue hardship."

PROCEDURES UNDER THE ADA

To prevail on a claim under the ADA, a plaintiff must show that he or she (1) has a disability, (2) is otherwise qualified for the employment in question, and (3) was excluded from the employment solely because of the disability. As in Title VII cases, a claim alleging violation of the ADA may be commenced only after the plaintiff has pursued the claim through the EEOC, which administers the provisions of the act relating to disability-based discrimination in the employment context. The EEOC may decide to investigate and perhaps even sue the employer on behalf of the employee. If the EEOC decides not to sue, then the employee is entitled to sue.

Significantly, the United States Supreme Court held in 2002 that the EEOC could bring a suit against an employer for disability-based discrimination even though the employee had agreed to submit any job-related disputes to arbitration (see Chapter 3). The Court reasoned that because the EEOC was not a party to the arbitration agreement, the agreement was not binding on the EEOC.[22]

Plaintiffs in lawsuits brought under the ADA may seek many of the same remedies that are available under Title VII. These include reinstatement, back pay, a limited amount of compensatory and punitive damages (for intentional discrimination), and certain other forms of relief. Repeat violators may be ordered to pay fines of up to $100,000.

WHAT IS A DISABILITY?

The ADA broadly defines *persons with disabilities* as persons with physical or mental impairments that "substantially limit" their everyday activities. More specifically, the ADA defines a *disability* as "(1) a physical or mental impairment that substantially limits one or more of the major life activities of such individuals; (2) a record of such impairment; or (3) being regarded as having such an impairment."

Health conditions that have been considered disabilities under federal law include blindness, alcoholism, heart disease, cancer, muscular dystrophy, cerebral palsy, paraplegia, diabetes, acquired immune deficiency syndrome (AIDS), and morbid obesity (which exists when an individual's weight is more than two times what it should be).[23] In 1998, the Supreme Court held that a person who is infected with the human immunodeficiency virus (HIV) but who has no symptoms of AIDS is protected under the ADA.[24] The ADA excludes from coverage certain conditions, such as kleptomania (the obsessive desire to steal).

In a series of cases decided in the last several years, the courts have been significantly narrowing the scope of the ADA through their interpretation of what constitutes a disability under the act. For a discussion of these cases, see this chapter's *Emerging Trends* feature on the following two pages.

REASONABLE ACCOMMODATION

If a job applicant or an employee with a disability can perform essential job functions with reasonable accommodation, the employer must make the accommodation. Required modifications may include installing ramps for a wheelchair, establishing flexible working hours, creating or modifying job assignments, and designing or improving training materials and procedures.

Generally, employers should give primary consideration to employees' preferences in deciding what accommodations should be made. If an applicant or employee fails to let the employer know how his or her disability can be accommodated, the employer may avoid liability for failing to hire or retain the individual on the ground that the individual has failed to meet the "otherwise qualified" requirement.[25]

Employers should be cautious in making this assumption in situations involving mental illness, though. For example, in one case, an employee was held to have a cause of action against his employer under the ADA even though the employee never explicitly told the employer how his disability could be accommodated.[26]

---

22. *EEOC v. Waffle House, Inc.*, 534 U.S. 279, 122 S.Ct. 754, 151 L.Ed.2d 755 (2002).

23. *Cook v. Rhode Island Department of Mental Health*, 10 F.3d 17 (1st Cir. 1993).

24. *Bragdon v. Abbott*, 524 U.S. 624, 118 S.Ct. 2196, 141 L.Ed.2d 540 (1998).

25. See, for example, *Beck v. University of Wisconsin Board of Regents*, 75 F.3d 1130 (7th Cir. 1996); and *White v. York International Corp.*, 45 F.3d 357 (10th Cir. 1995).

26. *Bultemeyer v. Fort Wayne Community Schools*, 100 F.3d 1281 (7th Cir. 1996).

Narrowing the Definition of "Disability"

The Americans with Disabilities Act (ADA) does not precisely define what constitutes a disability under the act. Thus, deciding which disabilities qualify under the ADA has largely been left to the courts. Clearly, how the courts interpret the act has significant implications for both employers and employees. When a court holds that a person's impairment does not "substantially limit" a major life activity, that person will not be considered to have a disability under the ADA. Employers benefit from such a holding because they will not be required to accommodate persons with similar disabilities. In contrast, of course, individuals suffering from similar disabilities will not be able to obtain the protections afforded by the ADA.

Starting in 1999, the United States Supreme Court has issued a series of decisions narrowing the definition of what constitutes a disability under the act. In other words, the Court's decisions represent a trend toward limiting the scope of the ADA.

CORRECTABLE CONDITIONS

In 1999, in *Sutton v. United Airlines, Inc.,*[a] the Supreme Court reviewed a case raising the issue of whether severe myopia, or nearsightedness, which can be corrected with eyeglasses or contact lenses, qualified as a disability under the ADA. The Supreme Court ruled that it did not. The determination of whether a person is substantially limited in a major life activity is based on how the person functions when taking medication or using corrective devices, not on how the person functions without these measures.

In a similar case in 2002, a federal appellate court held that a pharmacist suffering from diabetes, which could be corrected by insulin, had no cause of action against his employer under the ADA.[b] In other cases decided in the early 2000s, the courts have held that plaintiffs with bipolar disorder, epilepsy, and other such conditions do *not* fall under the ADA's protections if the conditions can be corrected.

THE TOYOTA CASE

In 2002, the Supreme Court further limited the scope of the ADA by its broad interpretation of what constitutes a substantially limiting impairment of a major life activity. The case before the Court involved Ella Williams, an employee of Toyota Motor Manufacturing in Kentucky. Williams's use of tools on an engine fabrication assembly line eventually caused pain in her hands, wrists, and arms. For the following two years, she held modified-duty jobs to avoid repetitive physical activity. Nonetheless, she started to experience pain in her neck and shoulders and was finally placed on a no-work-of-any-kind restriction. Toyota then terminated her employment.

The Supreme Court had to decide whether her condition, generally referred to as carpal tunnel syndrome, constituted a disability under the ADA. The Court unanimously held that it

a. 527 U.S. 471, 119 S.Ct. 2139, 144 L.Ed.2d 450 (1999).

b. *Orr v. Wal-Mart Stores, Inc.,* 297 F.3d 720 (8th Cir. 2002).

UNDUE HARDSHIP Employers who do not accommodate the needs of persons with disabilities must demonstrate that the accommodations would cause *undue hardship*. Generally, the law offers no uniform standards for identifying what is an undue hardship other than the imposition of a "significant difficulty or expense" on the employer.

Usually, the courts decide whether an accommodation constitutes an undue hardship on a case-by-case basis. In one case, the court decided that paying for a parking space near the office for an employee with a disability was not an undue hardship.[27] In another case, the court held that accommodating the request of an employee with diabetes for indefinite leave until his disease was under control would create an undue hard-ship for the employer, because the employer would not know when the employee was returning to work. The court stated that reasonable accommodation under the ADA means accommodation so that the employee can perform the job now or "in the immediate future" rather than at some unspecified distant time.[28]

JOB APPLICATIONS AND PREEMPLOYMENT PHYSICAL EXAMS Employers must modify their job-application process so that those with disabilities can compete for jobs with those who do not have disabilities. A job announcement that has only a phone number, for example, would discriminate against potential job applicants with hearing impairments. Thus, the job announcement must also provide an address.

27. See *Lyons v. Legal Aid Society,* 68 F.3d 1512 (2d Cir. 1995).

28. *Myers v. Hose,* 50 F.3d 278 (4th Cir. 1995).

did not. The Court stated that although the employee could not perform the manual tasks associated with her job, the condition did not constitute a disability under the ADA because it did not "substantially limit" the major life activity of performing manual tasks. For the fired worker, Williams, to prevail, her carpal tunnel syndrome would have had to be so severe that it prevented or severely restricted activities that were of central importance to her daily life, not just work-related activities.[c]

FURTHER LIMITING THE SCOPE OF THE ADA

In a 2001 case, the Supreme Court also limited the applicability of the ADA by holding that lawsuits under the ADA cannot be brought against state government employers. The Court concluded that states, as sovereigns, are immune from lawsuits brought against them by private parties under the federal ADA.[d]

The Court went on to further limit the scope of the ADA by supporting Equal Employment Opportunity Commission regulations that permit an employer to refuse to hire a person when the job would pose a threat to that person's health.[e]

---

c. *Toyota Motor Manufacturing, Kentucky, Inc. v. Williams*, 534 U.S. 184, 122 S.Ct. 681, 151 L.Ed.2d 615 (2002).
d. *Board of Trustees of the University of Alabama v. Garrett*, 531 U.S. 356, 121 S.Ct. 955, 148 L.Ed.2d 866 (2001).
e. *Chevron USA, Inc. v. Echazabal*, 536 U.S. 73, 122 S.Ct. 2045, 153 L.Ed.2d 82 (2002).

IMPLICATIONS FOR THE BUSINESSPERSON

1. If this emerging trend continues, employers will more easily be able to refuse to hire job candidates who suffer from certain impairments that might make it difficult for them to work effectively at a particular task. In other words, if the trend continues, the burden of accommodating persons with disabilities may be lessened.

2. Even though Court decisions have limited the protections available under the ADA, employers must still strive to reasonably accommodate persons with disabilities.

FOR CRITICAL ANALYSIS

1. Prior to 1999, the Supreme Court and other federal courts had tended to interpret the ADA's definition of *disability* expansively, thus enlarging the scope of the act's coverage. Why do you think that the courts have reversed this trend?

2. What are the costs and benefits of the Americans with Disabilities Act?

RELEVANT WEB SITES

To locate information on the Web concerning the issues discussed in this feature, go to this text's Web site at **http://wleb.westbuslaw.com**, select "Chapter 21," and click on "Emerging Trends."

Employers are restricted in the kinds of questions they may ask on job-application forms and during pre-employment interviews. Furthermore, employers cannot require persons with disabilities to submit to preemployment physicals unless such exams are required of all other applicants. Employers can condition an offer of employment on the applicant's successfully passing a medical examination, but can disqualify the applicant only if the medical problems they discover would render the applicant unable to perform the job.

DANGEROUS WORKERS Employers are not required to hire or retain workers who, because of their disabilities, pose a "direct threat to the health or safety" of their co-workers. (As mentioned in this chapter's *Emerging Trends* feature, employers may also refuse to hire persons with disabilities if the job would pose a threat to their own health.)

In the wake of the AIDS epidemic, many employers became concerned about hiring or continuing to employ workers who have AIDS under the assumption that they might pose a direct threat to the health or safety of others in the workplace. Courts have generally held, however, that AIDS is not so contagious as to disqualify employees from most jobs. Therefore, employers must reasonably accommodate job applicants or employees who have AIDS or who test positive for HIV, the virus that causes AIDS.

SUBSTANCE ABUSERS Drug addiction is a disability under the ADA because drug addiction is a substantially limiting impairment. Those who are currently using illegal drugs are not protected by the act, however. The ADA only protects persons with *former* drug addictions—those who have completed a supervised drug-rehabilitation program or who are currently participating in a supervised rehabilitation program. Individuals who have used drugs casually in the past are not protected under the act. They are not considered addicts and therefore do not have a disability (addiction).

People suffering from alcoholism are protected by the ADA. Employers cannot legally discriminate against employees simply because they suffer from alcoholism and must treat them the same way other employees are treated. For example, an employee with alcoholism who comes to work late because she or he was drinking excessively the night before cannot be disciplined any differently than an employee who comes to work late for another reason. Of course, employers have the right to prohibit the use of alcohol in the workplace and can require that employees not be under the influence of alcohol while working. Employers can also fire or refuse to hire a person with alcoholism if he or she poses a substantial risk of harm either to himself or herself or to others and the risk cannot be reduced by reasonable accommodation.

HEALTH-INSURANCE PLANS Workers with disabilities must be given equal access to any health insurance provided to other employees. Employers can exclude from coverage preexisting health conditions and certain types of diagnostic or surgical procedures, however. An employer can also put a limit, or cap, on health-care payments under its particular group health policy as long as the cap is "applied equally to all insured employees" and does not "discriminate on the basis of disability." Whenever a group health-care plan makes a disability-based distinction in its benefits, the plan violates the ADA. The employer must then be able to justify the distinction by proving one of the following:

1. That limiting coverage of certain ailments is required to keep the plan financially sound.

2. That coverage of certain ailments would cause a significant increase in premium payments or their equivalent, making the plan unappealing to a significant number of employees.

3. That the disparate treatment is justified by the risks and costs associated with a particular disability.

HOSTILE-ENVIRONMENT CLAIMS UNDER THE ADA

As discussed earlier in this chapter, under Title VII of the Civil Rights Act of 1964, an employee may base certain types of employment-discrimination causes of action on a hostile-environment theory. Using this theory, a worker may successfully sue her or his employer, even if the worker was not fired or otherwise discriminated against.

Can a worker file a suit founded on a hostile-environment claim under the ADA? The ADA does not expressly provide for such suits, but some courts have allowed them. Others have assumed that the claim was possible without deciding whether the ADA allowed it.[29] To succeed, such a claim would likely have to be based on conduct that a reasonable person would find so offensive that it would change the conditions of the person's employment.

Whether a worker with a disability who was harassed by her co-workers could successfully sue her employer for a hostile environment was the issue in the following case.

29. See, for example, *Steele v. Thiokol Corp.*, 241 F.3d 1248 (10th Cir. 2001).

CASE 21.3

United States
Court of Appeals,
Fifth Circuit, 2001.
247 F.3d 229.
http://www.ca5.uscourts.
gov/opinions.aspx[a]

Flowers v. Southern Regional Physician Services, Inc.

BACKGROUND AND FACTS *Beginning in September 1993, Sandra Flowers worked for Southern Regional Physician Services, Inc., as a medical assistant to Dr. James Osterberger. In March 1995, Margaret Hallmark, Flowers's immediate supervisor, discovered that Flowers was infected with the human immunodeficiency virus (HIV). Suddenly Flowers, who had received only excellent performance reviews, was the subject of several negative disciplinary reports. Also, she was required to take four drug tests in one week. Previously, she had been asked to take only one. Hallmark stopped socializing with Flowers, her co-workers began avoiding her, and the president of the hospital refused to*

---

a. In the "Docket number is:" box, enter "99-31354" and click on "Search." Then click on the docket number again to access the opinion.

CASE 21.3 | Continued *shake her hand. In November 1995, after being put on probation twice, Flowers was fired. She filed a suit in a federal district court against Southern Regional under the ADA, arguing in part that she had been subjected to a hostile environment on the basis of her disability. The court entered a judgment in her favor and awarded her $100,000. Southern Regional appealed to the U.S. Court of Appeals for the Fifth Circuit.*

IN THE LANGUAGE OF THE COURT

KING, Chief Judge:

* * * *

The ADA provides that no employer covered by the Act "shall discriminate against a qualified individual with a disability because of the disability of such individual in regard to * * * *terms, conditions, and privileges of employment.*" In almost identical fashion, Title VII provides that it is unlawful for an employer "to fail or refuse to hire or to discharge any individual, or otherwise to discriminate against any individual with respect to his compensation, *terms, conditions, or privileges of employment,* because of such individual's race, color, religion, sex, or national origin[.]"

It is evident, after a review of the ADA's language, purpose, and remedial framework, that Congress's intent in enacting the ADA was, *inter alia* [among other things], to eradicate disability-based harassment in the workplace. First, as a matter of statutory interpretation, * * * the [United States] Supreme Court interpreted Title VII, which contains language similar to that in the ADA, to provide a cause of action for harassment which is sufficiently severe or pervasive to alter the conditions of the victim's employment and create an abusive working environment * * * because it affects a term, condition, or privilege of employment. We conclude that the language of Title VII and [of] the ADA dictates a consistent reading of the two statutes. Therefore, following the Supreme Court's interpretation of the language contained in Title VII, we interpret the phrase "terms, conditions, and privileges of employment," as it is used in the ADA, to strike at harassment in the workplace.

Not only are Title VII and the ADA similar in their language, they are also alike in their purposes and remedial structures. *Both Title VII and the ADA are aimed at the same evil— employment discrimination against individuals of certain classes.* Moreover, this court has recognized that the ADA is part of the same broad remedial framework as * * * Title VII, and that all the anti-discrimination acts have been subjected to similar analysis. Furthermore, other courts of appeals have noted the correlation between the two statutes. We conclude, therefore, that the purposes and remedial frameworks of the two statutes also command our conclusion that the ADA provides a cause of action for disability-based harassment. [Emphasis added.]

DECISION AND REMEDY *The U.S. Court of Appeals for the Fifth Circuit held that the right to bring a hostile-environment claim can be inferred because the ADA is similar in language, purpose, and "remedial structure" to Title VII. (The court added that Flowers was entitled only to nominal damages, however, because she did not prove that she actually suffered emotional injury.)*

SECTION 5 | Defenses to Employment Discrimination

The first line of defense for an employer charged with employment discrimination is, of course, to assert that the plaintiff has failed to meet his or her initial burden of proof—proving that discrimination in fact occurred. As noted, plaintiffs bringing cases under the ADA may find it difficult to meet this initial burden because they must prove that their alleged disabilities are disabilities covered by the ADA. Furthermore, plaintiffs in ADA cases must prove that they were otherwise qualified for the job.

Once a plaintiff succeeds in proving that discrimination occurred, then the burden shifts to the employer to justify the discriminatory practice. Often, employers attempt to justify the discrimination by claiming that it was the result of a business necessity, a bona fide occupational qualification, a seniority system, or employee misconduct.

BUSINESS NECESSITY

An employer may defend against a claim of *disparate-impact* discrimination by asserting that a practice that has a discriminatory effect is a **business necessity.** If requiring a high school diploma, for example, is shown to have a discriminatory effect, an employer might argue that a high school education is required for workers to perform the job at a required level of competence. If the employer can demonstrate to the court's satisfaction that a definite connection exists between a high school education and job performance, then the employer will succeed in this business necessity defense.

BONA FIDE OCCUPATIONAL QUALIFICATION

Another defense applies when discrimination against a protected class is essential to a job—that is, when a particular trait is a **bona fide occupational qualification (BFOQ).** For example, a women's clothing boutique might legitimately hire only female attendants if part of an attendant's job involves assisting clients in the boutique's dressing rooms. Similarly, the Federal Aviation Administration can legitimately impose age limits for airline pilots.

Race, color, and national origin, however, can never be justified as a BFOQ. Generally, courts have restricted the BFOQ defense to instances in which the employee's gender or religion is essential to the job.

SENIORITY SYSTEMS

An employer with a history of discrimination may have no members of protected classes in upper-level positions. Even if the employer now seeks to be unbiased, it may face a lawsuit seeking an order that members of protected classes be promoted ahead of schedule to compensate for past discrimination. If no present intent to discriminate is shown, however, and if promotions or other job benefits are distributed according to a fair **seniority system** (in which workers with more years of service are promoted first or laid off last), the employer has a good defense against the suit.

According to the United States Supreme Court, this defense may also apply to alleged discrimination under the ADA. If an employee with a disability requests an accommodation (such as an assignment to a particular position) that conflicts with an employer's seniority system, the accommodation will generally not be considered "reasonable" under the act.[30]

AFTER-ACQUIRED EVIDENCE OF EMPLOYEE MISCONDUCT

In some situations, employers have attempted to avoid liability for employment discrimination on the basis of "after-acquired evidence" of an employee's misconduct. For example, suppose that an employer fires a worker, who then sues the employer for employment discrimination. During pretrial investigation, the employer learns that the employee made material misrepresentations on his employment application—misrepresentations that, had the employer known about them, would have served as a ground to fire the individual. Can this after-acquired evidence be used as a defense?

According to the United States Supreme Court, after-acquired evidence of wrongdoing cannot be used to shield an employer entirely from liability for employment discrimination. It may, however, be used to limit the amount of damages for which the employer is liable.[31]

SECTION 6 | Affirmative Action

The laws discussed in this chapter were designed to reduce or eliminate discriminatory practices with respect to hiring, retaining, and promoting employees. **Affirmative action** programs go a step further and attempt to "make up" for past patterns of discrimination by giving members of protected classes preferential treatment in hiring or promotion. During the 1960s, all federal and state government agencies, private companies that contract to do business with the federal government, and institutions that receive federal funding were required to implement affirmative action policies.

Title VII of the Civil Rights Act of 1964 neither requires nor prohibits affirmative action. Thus, most private companies and organizations have not been required to implement affirmative action policies, though many have done so voluntarily.

Affirmative action programs have caused much controversy over the last forty years, particularly when they result in what is frequently called "reverse

---

30. *U.S. Airways, Inc. v. Barnett,* 535 U.S. 391, 122 S.Ct. 1516, 152 L.Ed.2d 589 (2002).
31. *McKennon v. Nashville Banner Publishing Co.,* 513 U.S. 352, 115 S.Ct. 879, 130 L.Ed.2d 852 (1995).

discrimination"—discrimination against "majority" workers, such as white males. At issue is whether affirmative action programs, because of their inherently discriminatory nature, violate employee rights or the equal protection clause of the Fourteenth Amendment to the U.S. Constitution.

THE BAKKE CASE

An early case addressing this issue outside the employment context, *Regents of the University of California v. Bakke*,[32] involved an affirmative action program implemented by the University of California at Davis. Allan Bakke, who had been turned down for medical school at the Davis campus, sued the university for reverse discrimination after he discovered that his academic record was better than the records of some of the minority applicants who had been admitted to the program.

The United States Supreme Court held that affirmative action programs were subject to intermediate scrutiny. Recall from the discussion of the equal protection clause in Chapter 5 that any law or action evaluated under a standard of intermediate scrutiny, to be constitutionally valid, must be substantially related to important government objectives. Applying this standard, the Court held that the university could give favorable weight to minority applicants as part of a plan to increase minority enrollment so as to achieve a more culturally diverse student body. The Court stated, however, that the use of a quota system, in which a certain number of places are explicitly reserved for minority applicants, violated the equal protection clause of the Fourteenth Amendment.

THE ADARAND CASE

Although the *Bakke* case and later court decisions alleviated the harshness of the quota system, today's courts are going even further in questioning the constitutional validity of affirmative action programs. In 1995, in its landmark decision in *Adarand Constructors, Inc. v. Peña*,[33] the United States Supreme Court held that any federal, state, or local affirmative action program that uses racial or ethnic classifications as the basis for making decisions is subject to strict scrutiny by the courts.

In effect, the Court's ruling in *Adarand* means that an affirmative action program is constitutional only if

it attempts to remedy past discrimination and does not make use of quotas or preferences. Furthermore, once such a program has succeeded in the goal of remedying past discrimination, it must be changed or dropped. Since then, other federal courts have followed the Supreme Court's lead by declaring affirmative action programs invalid unless they attempt to remedy past or current discrimination.[34]

THE HOPWOOD CASE

In 1996, in *Hopwood v. State of Texas*,[35] the Court of Appeals for the Fifth Circuit held that an affirmative action program at the University of Texas School of Law in Austin violated the equal protection clause. In that case, two white law school applicants sued the university when they were denied admission. The court decided that the affirmative action policy unlawfully discriminated in favor of minority applicants. In its decision, the court directly challenged the *Bakke* decision by stating that the use of race even as a means of achieving diversity on college campuses "undercuts the Fourteenth Amendment." The United States Supreme Court declined to hear the case, thus letting the lower court's decision stand. Federal appellate court decisions since then have been divided on whether such programs are constitutional.[36]

SUBSEQUENT COURT DECISIONS

In 2003, the United States Supreme Court reviewed two cases involving issues similar to that in the *Hopwood* case. Both cases involved admissions programs at the University of Michigan. In *Gratz v. Bollinger*,[37] two white applicants who were denied undergraduate admission to the university alleged reverse discrimination. The school's policy gave each applicant a score based on a number of factors, including grade point average, standardized test scores, and personal achievements. The system *automatically* awarded every "underrepresented" minority (African American, Hispanic, and Native American) applicant twenty points—one-fifth of the points needed to

---

32. 438 U.S. 265, 98 S.Ct. 2733, 57 L.Ed.2d 750 (1978).
33. 515 U.S. 200, 115 S.Ct. 2097, 132 L.Ed.2d 158 (1995).
34. See, for example, *Taxman v. Board of Education of the Township of Piscataway*, 91 F.3d 1547 (3d Cir. 1996); and *Schurr v. Resorts International Hotel, Inc.*, 196 F.3d 486 (3d Cir. 1999).
35. 84 F.3d 720 (5th Cir. 1996).
36. See, for example, *Johnson v. Board of Regents of the University of Georgia*, 263 F.3d 1234 (11th Cir. 2001); and *Smith v. University of Washington School of Law*, 233 F.3d 1188 (9th Cir. 2000).
37. 539 U.S. 244, 123 S.Ct. 2411, 156 L.Ed.2d 257 (2003).

guarantee admission. The Court held that this policy violated the equal protection clause.

In contrast, in *Grutter v. Bollinger*,[38] the Court held that the University of Michigan Law School's admission policy was constitutional. In that case, the Court concluded that "[u]niversities can, however, consider race or ethnicity more flexibly as a 'plus' factor in the context of individualized consideration of each and every applicant." The significant difference between the two admissions policies, in the Court's view, was that the law school's approach did not apply a mechanical formula giving "diversity bonuses" based on race or ethnicity.

SECTION 7 | State Laws Prohibiting Discrimination

Although the focus of this chapter is on federal legislation, most states also have statutes that prohibit employment discrimination. Generally, the same kinds of discrimination are prohibited under federal and state legislation. In addition, state statutes often provide

---

38. 539 U.S. 306, 123 S.Ct. 2325, 156 L.Ed.2d 304 (2003).

protection for certain individuals who are not protected under federal laws. For example, a New Jersey appellate court held that anyone over the age of eighteen was entitled to sue for age discrimination under the state law, which specified no threshold age limit.[39]

Furthermore, state laws prohibiting discrimination may apply to firms with fewer employees than the threshold number required under federal statutes, thus offering protection to a greater number of workers. Even when companies are too small to be covered by state statutes, state courts may uphold employees' rights against discrimination in the workplace for public-policy reasons.[40] State laws may also provide for additional damages, such as damages for emotional distress, that are not provided for under federal statutes. Finally, some states, such as California and Washington, have passed laws that end affirmative action programs in those states or modify admission policies at state-sponsored universities.

---

39. *Bergen Commercial Bank v. Sisler*, 307 N.J.Super. 333, 704 A.2d 1017 (1998).

40. See, for example, *Roberts v. Dudley, D.V.M.*, 92 Wash.App. 652, 966 P.2d 377 (1998); and *Insignia Residential Corp. v. Ashton*, 359 Md. 560, 755 A.2d 1080 (2000).

REVIEWING EMPLOYMENT DISCRIMINATION

Amaani Lyle, an African American woman, took a job as a scriptwriters' assistant at Warner Brothers Television Productions working for the writers of *Friends*, a popular, adult-oriented television series. One of her essential job duties was to type detailed notes for the scriptwriters during brainstorming sessions in which they discussed jokes, dialogue, and story lines. The writers then combed through Lyle's notes after the meetings for script material. During these meetings, the three male scriptwriters told lewd and vulgar jokes and made sexually explicit comments and gestures. They often talked about their personal sexual experiences and fantasies, and some of these conversations were then used in episodes of *Friends*.

Lyle never complained that she found the writers' conduct during the meetings offensive. After four months, Lyle was fired because she could not type fast enough to keep up with the writers' conversations during the meetings. She filed a suit against Warner Brothers, alleging sexual harassment and claiming that her termination was based on racial discrimination. Using the information presented in the chapter, answer the following questions.

1. Explain whether Lyle's claim of racial discrimination would be for intentional (disparate-treatment) or unintentional (disparate-impact) discrimination.

2. Can Lyle establish a *prima facie* case of racial discrimination? Why or why not?

3. Lyle was told when she was hired that typing speed was extremely important to her position. At the time, she maintained that she could type eighty words per minute, so she was not given a typing test. It later turned out that Lyle could type only fifty words per minute. What impact might typing speed have on Lyle's lawsuit?

(Continued)

REVIEWING EMPLOYMENT DISCRIMINATION—Continued

4. Lyle's sexual-harassment claim is based on the hostile work environment created by the writers' sexually offensive conduct at meetings that she was required to attend. The writers, however, argue that their behavior was essential to the "creative process" of writing for *Friends*, a show that routinely contains sexual innuendos and adult humor. Which defense discussed in the chapter might Warner Brothers assert using this argument?

5. Suppose that Warner Brothers was completely unaware of the writers' sexually explicit banter and conduct during the meetings. Can Lyle still hold Warner Brothers liable for the writers' conduct? Why or why not?

TERMS AND CONCEPTS TO REVIEW

affirmative action 522

bona fide occupational qualification (BFOQ) 522

business necessity 522

constructive discharge 509

disparate-impact discrimination 508

disparate-treatment discrimination 508

employment discrimination 507

prima facie case 508

protected class 507

seniority system 522

sexual harassment 511

tangible employment action 512

QUESTIONS AND CASE PROBLEMS

21-1. Discuss fully whether any of the following actions would constitute a violation of Title VII of the 1964 Civil Rights Act, as amended:

(a) Tennington, Inc., is a consulting firm and has ten employees. These employees travel on consulting jobs in seven states. Tennington has an employment record of hiring only white males.

(b) Novo Films is making a movie about Africa and needs to employ approximately one hundred extras for this picture. Novo advertises in all major newspapers in Southern California for the hiring of these extras. The ad states that only African Americans need apply.

21-2. **QUESTION WITH SAMPLE ANSWER**

Tavo Jones had worked since 1974 for Westshore Resort, where he maintained golf carts. During the first decade, he received positive job evaluations and numerous merit pay raises. He was promoted to the position of supervisor of golf-cart maintenance at three courses. Then a new employee, Ben Olery, was placed in charge of the golf courses. He demoted Jones, who was over the age of forty, to running one of the three cart facilities, and he froze Jones's salary indefinitely. Olery also demoted five other men over the age of forty. Another cart facility was placed under the supervision of Blake Blair. Later, the cart facilities for the three courses were again consolidated, but Blair—not Jones—was put in charge. At the

time, Blair was in his twenties. Jones overheard Blair say that "we are going to have to do away with these . . . old and senile" men. Jones quit and sued Westshore for employment discrimination. Should he prevail? Explain. **For a sample answer to this question, go to Appendix I at the end of this text.**

21-3. DISCRIMINATION BASED ON DISABILITY. When the University of Maryland Medical System Corp. learned that one of its surgeons was HIV positive, the university offered him transfers to positions that did not involve surgery. The surgeon refused, and the university terminated him. The surgeon filed a suit in a federal district court against the university, alleging in part a violation of the Americans with Disabilities Act. The surgeon claimed that he was "otherwise qualified" for his former position. What does he have to prove to win his case? Should he be reinstated? [*Doe v. University of Maryland Medical System Corp.*, 50 F.3d 1261 (4th Cir. 1995)]

21-4. RELIGIOUS DISCRIMINATION. Mary Tiano, a devout Roman Catholic, worked for Dillard Department Stores, Inc. (Dillard's), in Phoenix, Arizona. Dillard's considered Tiano a productive employee because her sales exceeded $200,000 a year. At the time, the store gave its managers the discretion to grant unpaid leave to employees but prohibited vacations or leave during the holiday season (October through December). Tiano felt that she had a "calling" to go on a "pilgrimage" in October 1988 to Medjugorje, Yugoslavia, where some persons claimed to have had visions of the Virgin Mary.

The Catholic Church had not designated the site an official pilgrimage site, the visions were not expected to be stronger in October, and tours were available at other times. The store managers denied Tiano's request for leave, but she had a nonrefundable ticket and left anyway. Dillard's terminated her employment. For a year, Tiano searched for a new job and did not attain the level of her Dillard's salary for four years. She filed a suit in a federal district court against Dillard's, alleging religious discrimination in violation of Title VII. Can Tiano establish a *prima facie* case of religious discrimination? Explain. [*Tiano v. Dillard Department Stores, Inc.,* 139 F.3d 679 (9th Cir. 1998)]

21–5. DISCRIMINATION BASED ON DISABILITY. Vaughn Murphy was first diagnosed with hypertension (high blood pressure) when he was ten years old. Unmedicated, his blood pressure is approximately 250/160. With medication, however, he can function normally and engage in the same activities as anyone else. In 1994, United Parcel Service, Inc. (UPS), hired Murphy to be a mechanic, a position that required him to drive commercial motor vehicles. To get the job, Murphy had to meet a U.S. Department of Transportation (DOT) regulation that a driver have "no current clinical diagnosis of high blood pressure likely to interfere with his/her ability to operate a commercial vehicle safely." At the time, Murphy's blood pressure was measured at 186/124, but he was erroneously certified and started work. Within a month, the error was discovered and he was fired. Murphy obtained another mechanic's job—one that did not require DOT certification—and filed a suit in a federal district court against UPS, claiming discrimination under the Americans with Disabilities Act. UPS filed a motion for summary judgment. Should the court grant UPS's motion? Explain. [*Murphy v. United Parcel Service, Inc.,* 527 U.S. 516, 119 S.Ct. 2133, 144 L.Ed.2d 484 (1999)]

21–6. DISCRIMINATION BASED ON DISABILITY. PGA Tour, Inc., sponsors professional golf tournaments. A player may enter in several ways, but the most common method is to compete successfully in a three-stage qualifying tournament known as the "Q-School." Anyone may enter the Q-School by submitting two letters of recommendation and paying $3,000 to cover greens fees and the cost of a golf cart, which is permitted during the first two stages, but is prohibited during the third stage. The rules governing the events include the "Rules of Golf," which apply at all levels of amateur and professional golf and do not prohibit the use of golf carts, and the "hard card," which applies specifically to the PGA tour and requires the players to walk the course during most of a tournament. Casey Martin is a talented golfer with a degenerative circulatory disorder that prevents him from walking golf courses. Martin entered the Q-School and asked for permission to use a cart during the third stage. PGA refused. Martin filed a suit in a federal district court against PGA, alleging a violation of the Americans with Disabilities Act. Is a golf cart in these circumstances a "reasonable accommodation" under the

ADA? Why or why not? [*PGA Tour, Inc. v. Martin,* 531 U.S. 1049, 121 S.Ct. 652, 148 L.Ed.2d 556 (2001)]

21–7. ⚖ **CASE PROBLEM WITH SAMPLE ANSWER**
Kimberly Cloutier began working at the Costco store in West Springfield, Massachusetts, in July 1997. Cloutier had multiple earrings and four tattoos, but no facial piercings. In June 1998, Costco promoted Cloutier to cashier. Over the next two years, she engaged in various forms of body modification, including facial piercing and cutting. In March 2001, Costco revised its dress code to prohibit all facial jewelry, aside from earrings. Cloutier was told that she would have to remove her facial jewelry. She asked for a complete exemption from the code, asserting that she was a member of the Church of Body Modification and her eyebrow piercing was part of her religion. She was told to remove the jewelry, cover it, or go home. She went home and was later discharged for her absence. Cloutier filed a suit in a federal district court against Costco, alleging religious discrimination in violation of Title VII. Does an employer have any obligation to accommodate its employees' religious practices? If so, to what extent? How should the court rule in this case? Discuss. [*Cloutier v. Costco Wholesale Corp.,* 390 F.3d 126 (1st Cir. 2004)]

To view a sample answer for this case problem, go to this book's Web site at http://wleb.westbuslaw.com, select "Chapter 21," and click on "Case Problem with Sample Answer."

21–8. DISCRIMINATION BASED ON RACE. The hiring policy of Phillips Community College of the University of Arkansas (PCCUA) is to conduct an internal search for qualified applicants before advertising outside the college. Steven Jones, the university's chancellor, determines the application and appointment process for vacant positions, however, and is the ultimate authority in hiring decisions. Howard Lockridge, an African American, was PCCUA's Technical and Industrial Department Chair. Between 1988 and 1998, Lockridge applied for several different positions, some of which were unadvertised, some of which were unfilled for years, and some of which were filled with less qualified persons from outside the college. In 1998, when Jones advertised an opening for the position of Dean of Industrial Technology and Workforce Development, Lockridge did not apply for the job. Jones hired Tracy McGraw, a white male. Lockridge filed a suit in a federal district court against the university under Title VII. The university filed a motion for summary judgment in its favor. What are the elements of a *prima facie* case of disparate-treatment discrimination? Can Lockridge pass this test, or should the court issue a judgment in the university's favor? Explain. [*Lockridge v. Board of Trustees of the University of Arkansas,* 315 F.3d 1005 (8th Cir. 2003)]

21–9. DISCRIMINATION BASED ON AGE. The United Auto Workers (UAW) is the union that represents the employees of General Dynamics Land Systems,

Inc. In 1997, a collective bargaining agreement between UAW and General Dynamics eliminated the company's obligation to provide health insurance to employees who retired after the date of the agreement, except for current workers at least fifty years of age. Dennis Cline and 194 other employees over the age of forty, but under age fifty, objected to this term. They complained to the Equal Employment Opportunity Commission, claiming that the agreement violated the Age Discrimination in Employment Act (ADEA) of 1967. The ADEA forbids discriminatory preference for the "young" over the "old." Does the ADEA also prohibit favoring the old over the young? How should the court rule? Explain. [*General Dynamics Land Systems, Inc. v. Cline*, 540 U.S. 581, 124 S.Ct. 1236, 157 L.Ed.2d 1094 (2004)]

21–10. VIDEO QUESTION

Go to this text's Web site at http://wleb.westbuslaw.com and select "Chapter 21." Click on "Video Questions" and view the video titled *Parenthood*. Then answer the following questions.

(a) In the video, Gil (Steve Martin) threatens to leave his job when he discovers that his boss is promoting another person to partner instead of him. His boss (Dennis Dugan) laughs and tells him that the threat is not realistic because if Gil leaves, he will be competing for positions with workers who are younger than he is and willing to accept lower salaries. If Gil takes his employer's advice and stays in his current position, can he sue his boss for age discrimination based on the boss's statements? Why or why not?

(b) Suppose that Gil leaves his current position and applies for a job at another firm. The prospective employer refuses to hire him based on his age. What would Gil have to prove to establish a *prima facie* case of age discrimination? Explain your answer.

(c) What defenses might Gil's current employer raise if Gil sues for age discrimination?

LAW | on the Web

For updated links to resources available on the Web, as well as a variety of other materials, visit this text's Web site at http://wleb.westbuslaw.com.

An abundance of helpful information on disability-based discrimination, including the text of the Americans with Disabilities Act of 1990, can be found at the following Web site:

http://www.janwvu.edu/links/adalinks.htm

An excellent source for information on various forms of employment discrimination is the Equal Employment Opportunity Commission's Web site at

http://www.eeoc.gov

LEGAL RESEARCH EXERCISES ON THE WEB

Go to http://wleb.westbuslaw.com, the Web site that accompanies this text. Select "Chapter 21" and click on "Internet Exercises." There you will find the following Internet research exercises that you can perform to learn more about topics covered in this chapter.

Activity 21–1: LEGAL PERSPECTIVE
Americans with Disabilities

Activity 21–2: MANAGEMENT PERSPECTIVE
Equal Employment Opportunity

Activity 21–3: SOCIAL PERSPECTIVE
Religious and National-Origin Discrimination

Labor Law

Through the first half of the nineteenth century, most Americans were self-employed, often in agriculture. For those who were employed by others, the employers generally set the terms of employment. The nature of employment changed with the growth of the Industrial Revolution. Fewer Americans were self-employed. Terms of employment were sometimes set through bargaining between employees and employers. Most industrial enterprises were in their infancies, however, and to encourage their development, the government gave employers considerable freedom to hire, fire, and determine other employment conditions in response to changing conditions in the marketplace.

With increasing industrialization, the size of workplaces and the number of workplace hazards increased. Workers came to believe that to counter the power and freedom of their employers and to protect themselves, they needed to organize into unions. Employers discouraged—sometimes forcibly—collective activities such as unions. In support of unionization, Congress enacted such legislation as the Railway Labor Act of 1926.[1] These laws were often restricted to particular industries. Beginning in 1932, Congress enacted a number of statutes that increased employees' rights generally. At the heart of these rights is the right to join unions and engage in *collective bargaining* with management to negotiate working conditions, salaries, and benefits for a group of workers.

This chapter describes the development of labor law and legal recognition of the right to form unions. The laws that govern the management-union relationship are set forth in historical perspective. Then the chapter describes the process of unionizing a company, the collective bargaining required of a unionized employer, the "industrial war" of strikes and lockouts that may result if bargaining fails, and the labor practices that are considered unfair under federal law.

SECTION 1 | Federal Labor Law

Initially, federal labor laws governing union-employer relations were concerned with protecting the rights and interests of workers. Subsequent legislation placed some restraints on unions and granted rights to employers. This section summarizes the four major federal labor law statutes.

NORRIS-LAGUARDIA ACT

Congress protected peaceful strikes, picketing, and boycotts in 1932 in the Norris-LaGuardia Act.[2] The

statute restricted federal courts in their power to issue injunctions against unions engaged in peaceful strikes. The act also provided that contracts limiting an employee's right to join a union were unlawful. Such contracts were known as **yellow dog contracts.** (In the early part of the twentieth century, "yellow dog" meant "coward.") In effect, this act declared a national policy permitting employees to organize.

In the following case, a union threatened to picket an employer unless the employer agreed to subcontract work only to subcontractors who employed the union's members. The court had to decide whether, under the Norris-LaGuardia Act, it could issue an injunction to restrain the union from picketing.

1. 45 U.S.C. Sections 151–188.
2. 29 U.S.C. Sections 101–115.

CASE 22.1

United States
Court of Appeals,
Ninth Circuit, 2000.
203 F.3d 703.
*http://www.ca9.
uscourts.gov*[a]

Burlington Northern Santa Fe Railway Co. v. International Brotherhood of Teamsters Local 174

BACKGROUND AND FACTS *Burlington Northern and Santa Fe Railway Company operates a hub in Seattle, Washington. Burlington terminated a subcontract with Eagle Systems, Inc., for loading and unloading services at the Seattle hub and transferred the work to another subcontractor, Parsec, Inc. As a consequence, fifty-three Eagle employees lost their jobs. International Brotherhood of Teamsters Local 174 represented the Eagle employees who lost their jobs, as well as the employees of other subcontractors who worked under subcontracts with Burlington. Local 174 did not represent the Parsec employees, however. The union was afraid that Burlington's use of other subcontractors who did not employ Local 174's members would cause "substantial economic costs and personal hardship." The union asked Burlington to persuade Parsec to hire the former Eagle employees. Burlington refused. Local 174 asked Burlington to agree not to subcontract in the future any loading and unloading services to any subcontractor whose employees were not represented by Local 174. The union threatened to picket in support of this demand. Burlington filed a suit in a federal district court against Local 174, alleging violations of federal labor law, among other things, and seeking an injunction. The court granted the injunction, restraining Local 174 from "[c]alling, ordering, authorizing, encouraging, inducing, approving, continuing, starting, suffering, permitting, or carrying out any strike, picket, or work stoppage" at Burlington's facilities. The union appealed to the U.S. Court of Appeals for the Ninth Circuit.*

IN THE LANGUAGE OF THE COURT

PREGERSON, Circuit Judge.

* * * *

The Norris-LaGuardia Act deprives federal courts of jurisdiction to issue an injunction to restrain peaceful picketing in "any case involving or growing out of any labor dispute." Norris-LaGuardia defines the term "labor dispute" as

> any controversy concerning terms or conditions of employment, or concerning the association or representation of persons in negotiating, fixing, maintaining, changing, or seeking to arrange terms or conditions of employment, regardless of whether or not the disputants stand in the proximate relation of employer and employee.

We hold that a dispute between a union and a client company (here, Burlington Northern) over whether the client company's subcontractors must employ that union's members is a Norris-LaGuardia labor dispute. Thus, * * * the district court had no power to enjoin Local 174 from picketing Burlington Northern.

* * * *

* * * *The [United States] Supreme Court has consistently characterized Norris-LaGuardia's definition of "labor dispute" as "broad." Equally expansive is the test that the Supreme Court fashioned for determining whether a particular controversy is a labor dispute. Simply, "the employer-employee relationship [must be at] the matrix of the controversy." [Emphasis added.]

It is clear that "the matrix" of Local 174's dispute with Burlington Northern is "the employer-employee relationship." Members of Local 174 lost their jobs because Burlington Northern transferred their work to a subcontractor who did not rehire them and who signed a collective bargaining agreement with a different union. Local 174 feared that Burlington Northern would terminate other subcontracts under which its members worked, leading to more job losses and causing wages and working conditions to deteriorate. Local 174 asked Burlington Northern to guarantee that this process would not occur, but Burlington Northern

---

a. In the left column, click on "Opinions." On that page, click on "Opinions by date" and select "2000." In the expanded list, click on "March." In that list, scroll down to the name of the case and click on it to access the opinion.

CONTINUED ▶

CASE 22.1 | Continued refused. In short, this dispute is about who will perform work at Burlington Northern's Seattle hub, which union will represent the employees of Burlington Northern's subcontractors, and what will be the terms of their employment.

> **DECISION AND REMEDY** *The U.S. Court of Appeals for the Ninth Circuit vacated the lower court's order and remanded with instructions to dismiss the case. The court could not issue an injunction to block Local 174's picketing because the disagreement between Burlington and Local 174 was a "labor dispute" within the meaning of the Norris-LaGuardia Act. Under that act, a federal court cannot issue an injunction to block peaceful picketing that is part of a labor dispute.*

NATIONAL LABOR RELATIONS ACT

The National Labor Relations Act of 1935 (NLRA),[3] also called the Wagner Act, established the right of employees to form unions, the right of those unions to engage in collective bargaining (negotiate contracts for their members), and the right to strike. The act also created the National Labor Relations Board (NLRB) to oversee union elections and to prevent employers from engaging in unfair labor union activities and unfair labor practices.

The purpose of the NLRA was to secure for employees the rights to organize, to bargain collectively through representatives of their own choosing, and to engage in concerted activities for that and other purposes. Section 8(a) of the act specifically defined a number of employer practices as unfair to labor. These unfair labor practices are central to labor law and are discussed throughout the remainder of the chapter.

Another purpose of the act was to promote fair and just settlements of disputes by peaceful processes. The NLRB was granted investigatory powers and was authorized to issue complaints against employers in response to employee charges of unfair labor practices. The NLRB was further empowered to issue cease-and-desist orders—which could be enforced by a federal court of appeals if necessary—when violations were found.

Employers viewed the NLRA as a drastic piece of legislation. Those who opposed the act claimed that the Constitution's commerce clause (Article I, Section 8, Clause 3) did not grant Congress the power to regulate labor relations. They argued that labor was subject to state, not federal, law. Those who were willing to admit that the NLRA did fall under the commerce clause claimed that the NLRA created an undue burden, which rendered it unconstitutional. The constitutionality of the act was tested in 1937 in

NLRB v. Jones & Laughlin Steel Corp.[4] In its decision, the United States Supreme Court held that the act and its application were constitutionally valid.

To be protected under the NLRA, an individual must be an *employee*, as that term is defined in the statute. Courts have long held that job applicants fall within the definition (otherwise, the NLRA's ban on discrimination in regard to hiring would mean nothing). Additionally, the United States Supreme Court has held that individuals who are hired by a union to organize a company are to be considered employees of the company for NLRA purposes.[5]

LABOR-MANAGEMENT RELATIONS ACT

The Labor-Management Relations Act of 1947 (LMRA, or the Taft-Hartley Act)[6] was passed to proscribe certain union practices. The Taft-Hartley Act contained provisions protecting employers as well as employees. The act was bitterly opposed by organized labor groups. It provided a detailed list of unfair labor activities that unions as well as management were now forbidden to practice. In addition, the law gave the president the authority to intervene in labor disputes and delay strikes that would "imperil the national health or safety."

An important provision of the LMRA concerned the **closed shop**—a firm that requires union membership of its workers as a condition of obtaining employment. Closed shops were made illegal under the Taft-Hartley Act. The act preserved the legality of the **union shop,** which does not require membership as a prerequisite for employment but can, and usually does, require that workers join the recognized union after a specified amount of time on the job. The act

---

3. 29 U.S.C. Sections 151–169.

4. 301 U.S. 1, 57 S.Ct. 615, 81 L.Ed. 893 (1937).
5. *National Labor Relations Board v. Town & Country Electric, Inc.,* 516 U.S. 85, 116 S.Ct. 450, 133 L.Ed.2d 371 (1995).
6. 29 U.S.C. Sections 141, 504.

also allowed individual states to pass their own **right-to-work laws**—laws making it illegal for union membership to be required for *continued* employment in any establishment. Thus, union shops are technically illegal in the twenty-three states that have right-to-work laws.

LABOR-MANAGEMENT REPORTING AND DISCLOSURE ACT

The Labor-Management Reporting and Disclosure Act of 1959 (the Landrum-Griffin Act)[7] established an employee bill of rights, as well as reporting requirements for union activities to prevent corruption. The Landrum-Griffin Act strictly regulated internal union business procedures.

Union elections, for example, are regulated by the Landrum-Griffin Act, which requires that regularly scheduled elections of officers occur and that secret ballots be used. Ex-convicts are prohibited from holding union office. Moreover, union officials are made accountable for union property and funds. Members have the right to attend and to participate in union meetings, to nominate officers, and to vote in most union proceedings.

COVERAGE AND PROCEDURES

Coverage of the federal labor laws is broad and extends to all employers whose business activity either involves or affects interstate commerce. Some workers are specifically excluded from these laws. Railroads and airlines are not covered by the NLRA but are covered by a separate act, the Railway Labor Act, which closely parallels the NLRA. Other types of workers, such as agricultural workers and domestic servants, are excluded from the NLRA and have no coverage under separate legislation.

When a union or employee believes that the employer has violated federal labor law (or vice versa), the union or employee files a charge with a regional office of the NLRB. The form for an employee to use to file an unfair labor practice charge against an employer is shown in Exhibit 22–1 on the next page. The charge is investigated, and if it is found worthy, the regional director files a complaint. An *administrative law judge* (ALJ) initially hears the complaint and rules on it (see Chapter 6). The board reviews the ALJ's findings and decision. If the NLRB finds a violation, it may issue remedial orders (including requiring rehiring of dis-

7. 29 U.S.C. Sections 153, 1111.

charged workers). The NLRB decision may be appealed to a U.S. court of appeals.

SECTION 2 | The Decision to Form or Select a Union

The key starting point for labor relations law is the decision by a company's employees to form a union, which is usually referred to in the law as their bargaining representative. Many workplaces have no union, and workers bargain individually with the employer. If the workers decide that they want the added power of collective union representation, they must follow certain steps to have a union certified. Usually, the employer will fight these efforts to unionize.

PRELIMINARY ORGANIZING

Suppose that a national union, such as the American Federation of Labor and Congress of Industrial Organizations (AFL-CIO), wants to organize workers who produce semiconductor chips. The union would visit a manufacturing plant of a company—SemiCo in this example. If some SemiCo workers are interested in joining the union, they must begin organizing. An essential part of the process is to decide exactly which workers will be covered in the planned union. Will all manufacturing workers be covered or just those engaged in a single stage in the manufacturing process?

The first step in forming a union is to get the relevant workers to sign **authorization cards.** These cards usually state that the worker desires to have a certain union, such as the AFL-CIO, represent the workforce. If those in favor of the union can obtain authorization cards from a majority of workers, they may present the cards to the employer and ask the employer, SemiCo, to recognize the union formally. SemiCo is not required to do so, however.

More frequently, authorization cards are obtained to justify an election among workers for unionization. If SemiCo refuses to recognize the union based on authorization cards, an election is necessary to determine whether unionization has majority support among the workers. After the unionizers obtain authorization cards from at least 30 percent of the workers to be represented, the unionizers present these cards to the NLRB regional office with a petition for an election.

This 30 percent support is generally considered a sufficient showing of interest to justify an election on union representation. Union backers are not required

EXHIBIT 22-1 **Unfair Labor Practice Complaint Form**

FORM EXEMPT UNDER 44 U.S.C. 3512

FORM NLRB-501 (11-94)	UNITED STATES OF AMERICA NATIONAL LABOR RELATIONS BOARD **CHARGE AGAINST EMPLOYER**	**DO NOT WRITE IN THIS SPACE**	
		Case	Date Filed

INSTRUCTIONS: File an original and 4 copies of this charge with NLRB Regional Director for the region in which the alleged unfair labor practice occurred or is occurring.

1. EMPLOYER AGAINST WHOM CHARGE IS BROUGHT

a. Name of Employer	b. Number of workers employed

c. Address *(street, city, state, ZIP code)*	d. Employer Representative	e. Telephone No.
		Fax No.

f. Type of Establishment *(factory, mine, wholesaler, etc.)*	g. Identify Principal Product or Service

h. The above-named employer has engaged in and is engaging in unfair labor practices within the meaning of section 8(a), subsections (1) and *(list subsections)* _____ of the National Labor Relations Act, and these unfair labor practices are unfair practices affecting commerce within the meaning of the Act.

2. Basis of the Charge *(set forth a clear and concise statement of the facts constituting the alleged unfair labor practices)*

By the above and other acts, the above-named employer has interfered with, restrained, and coerced employees in the exercise of the rights guaranteed in Section 7 of the Act

3. Full name of party filing charge *(if labor organization, give full name, including local name and number)*

4a. Address *(street and number, city, state, and ZIP code)*	4b. Telephone No.
	Fax No.

5. Full name of national or international labor organization of which it is an affiliate or constituent unit *(to be filled in when charge is filed by a labor organization)*

6. DECLARATION

I declare that I have read the above charge and that the statements are true to the best of my knowledge and belief.

By _____   _____

    (signature of representative or person making charge)   *(Title, if any)*

Address _____   _____   _____

                                                   (Telephone No.)   *(Date)*

WILLFUL FALSE STATEMENTS ON THIS CHARGE CAN BE PUNISHED BY FINE AND IMPRISONMENT (U.S. CODE, TITLE 18, SECTION 1001)

to employ authorization cards but generally must have some evidence that at least 30 percent of the relevant workforce supports a union or an election on unionization.

APPROPRIATE BARGAINING UNIT

The NLRB considers the employees' petition as a basis for calling an election. In addition to a sufficient showing of interest in unionization, the proposed union must represent an **appropriate bargaining unit.**

Not every group of workers can form together into a single union. One key requirement of an appropriate bargaining unit is a *mutuality of interest* among all the workers to be represented. Groups of workers with significantly conflicting interests may not be represented in a single union.

JOB SIMILARITY One factor in determining the mutuality of interest is the *similarity of the jobs* of all the workers to be unionized. The NLRB considers factors such as similar levels of skill and qualifications, similar levels of wages and benefits, and similar working conditions. If represented workers have vastly different working conditions, they are unlikely to have the mutuality of interest necessary to bargain as a single unit with their employer.

One issue of job similarity has involved companies that employ both general industrial workers and craft workers (those with specialized skills, such as electricians). On many occasions, the NLRB has found that industrial and craft workers should be represented by different unions, although this is not an absolute rule.

WORK-SITE PROXIMITY A second factor in determining the appropriate bargaining unit is *geographical*. If workers at only a single manufacturing plant are to be unionized, the geographical factor is not a problem. Even if the workers desire to join a national union, such as the AFL-CIO, they can join together in a single "local" division of that union. Geographical disparity may become a problem if a union is attempting to join workers at many different manufacturing sites together into a single union.

NONMANAGEMENT EMPLOYEES A third factor to be considered is the rule against unionization of *management* employees. The labor laws differentiate between labor and management and preclude members of management from being part of a union. There is no clear-cut definition of *management*, but supervisors are considered management and may not be included in worker unions. A supervisor is an individual who has the discretionary authority, as a representative of the employer, to make decisions such as hiring, suspending, promoting, firing, or disciplining other workers.[8] Professional employees, including legal and medical personnel, may be considered labor rather than management.

MOVING TOWARD CERTIFICATION

A union, then, becomes certified through a procedure that begins with petitioning the NLRB. The proposed union must present authorization cards or other evidence showing an employee interest level of at least 30 percent. The organization must also show that the proposed union represents an appropriate bargaining unit. If the workers are under the NLRA's jurisdiction and if no other union has been certified within the past twelve months for these workers, the NLRB will schedule an election.

SECTION 3 | Union Election

Labor law provides for an election to determine whether employees choose to be represented by a union and, if so, which union. The NLRB supervises this election, ensuring secret voting and voter eligibility. The election is usually held about a month after the NLRB orders the vote (although it may be much longer, if management disputes the composition of an appropriate bargaining unit). If the election is a fair one, and if the proposed union receives majority support, the board certifies the union as the bargaining representative. Otherwise, the board will not certify the union.

Sometimes, a plant with an existing union may attempt to *decertify* (de-unionize) the union. Although this action may be encouraged by management, it must be conducted by the employees. This action also requires a petition to the NLRB, with a showing of 30 percent employee support and no certification within the past year. The NLRB may grant this petition and call for a decertification election.

UNION ELECTION CAMPAIGNS

Union organizers may campaign among workers to solicit votes for unionization. Considerable litigation has arisen over the rights of workers and outside union supporters to conduct such campaigns.

---

8. *Waldau v. Merit Systems Protection Board*, 19 F.3d 1395 (Fed.Cir. 1994).

THE EMPLOYER'S RIGHT TO LIMIT CAMPAIGN ACTIVITIES The employer retains great control over any activities, including unionization campaigns, that take place on company property and company time. Employers may lawfully use this authority to limit the campaign activities of union supporters. For example, management may prohibit all solicitations and distribution of pamphlets on company property as long as it has a legitimate business reason for doing so (such as to ensure safety or to prevent interference with business). The employer may also reasonably limit the places where solicitation occurs (for example, limit it to the lunchroom), limit the times during which solicitation can take place, and prohibit all outsiders from access to the workplace. All these actions are lawful.

Suppose that a union seeks to organize clerks at a department store. Courts have found that an employer can prohibit all solicitation in areas of the store open to the public. Union campaign activities in these circumstances could seriously interfere with the store's business.

RESTRICTIONS ON MANAGEMENT There are some legal restrictions on management regulation of union solicitation. The key restriction is the *nondiscrimination* rule. An employer may prohibit all solicitation during work time or in certain places but may not selectively prohibit union solicitation during work time. If the employer permits political candidates to campaign on the employer's premises, for example, it also must permit union solicitation.[9]

WORKERS' RIGHTS AND OBLIGATIONS Workers have a right to some reasonable opportunity to campaign. For example, the Supreme Court held that employees have a right to distribute a pro-union newsletter in nonworking areas on the employer's property during nonworking time. In this case, management had the burden to show some material harm from this action and could not do so.[10]

Like an employer, a union and its supporters may not engage in unfair labor practices during a union election campaign. In the following case, the court considered the impact of a union proponent's allegedly unfair labor practice on the outcome of an election.

---

9. *Nonemployee* union organizers do not have the right to trespass on an employer's property to organize employees, however. See *Lechmere, Inc. v. NLRB*, 502 U.S. 527, 112 S.Ct. 841, 117 L.Ed.2d 79 (1992).

10. *Eastex, Inc. v. NLRB*, 437 U.S. 556, 98 S.Ct. 2505, 57 L.Ed.2d 428 (1978).

CASE 22.2 — Associated Rubber Co. v. NLRB

United States
Court of Appeals,
Eleventh Circuit, 2002.
296 F.3d 1055.
http://www.law.
emory.edu/11circuit[a]

CARNES, Circuit Judge.

* * * *

On June 14, 1999, the [United Steelworkers of America, AFL-CIO-CLC] filed a petition with the [National Labor Relations] Board seeking certification as the collective bargaining representative of certain maintenance workers, truck drivers, and mechanics employed at [Associated Rubber Company's] three plants in Tallapoosa, Georgia, where the company operates its rubber production facilities. A secret ballot election was held on July 23, 1999, and the union won by a vote of 53 to 50, with one non-determinative challenged ballot. Associated Rubber, however, timely filed objections to the election * * *.

The Board ordered a hearing * * *. At the hearing there was evidence of * * * what the parties refer to as the "Banbury mixer incident."

* * * *

A Banbury mixer is a piece of machinery used to custom mix rubber products. * * *

* * * Less than two weeks before the election, Tim Spears, the first shift mill operator in Plant 2 for Banbury mixer 1's production line, showed his opposition to the union by refusing to accept some literature that a union supporter offered him. Leroy Brown, a union supporter and first shift operator for that Banbury mixer, told Spears he had better accept the literature. When Spears declined, Brown told him that he would "pay" for it * * *.

* * * [W]hile Brown was operating Banbury mixer 1 and Spears was operating the mill below, Brown speeded up the rate at which the heavy, hot batches of compound were falling and had to be handled by Spears. * * *

---

a. In the "Listing by Month of Decision" section, in the "2002" row, click on "July." In the result, click on the name of the case to access the opinion. Emory University School of Law in Atlanta, Georgia, maintains this Web site.

 **Continued**

* * * Spears was sufficiently rattled by the incident to tell the foreman that if the union won the election, he would quit his job out of fear that the incident might reoccur.

It was no secret around the plant that Brown had threatened Spears for refusing to take union literature, and had then carried out the threat. * * * The election was held just three days after it happened.

* * * *

* * * The Board * * * [overruled Associated Rubber's] objections to the validity of the election * * * and certified the union as the unit's exclusive collective bargaining representative. * * *

* * * *

* * * Associated Rubber petitioned this Court for review * * *.

* * * *

When the union itself engages in objectionable misconduct, the Board will overturn the election if the conduct interfered with the employees' exercise of free choice to such an extent that it materially affected the results of the election. If, however, a third party engages in misconduct, the party objecting to the election has the burden of showing that the misconduct was so aggravated as to create a general atmosphere of fear and reprisal rendering a free election impossible. * * *

* * * *

Applying these legal standards to the record in this case convinces us that the Board's conclusion that the Banbury mixer incident did not warrant overturning the election should itself be overturned. To begin with, the record shows that Brown accelerated the mixer in retaliation for Spears' refusal to accept union literature. Brown threatened to make Spears "pay" for refusing to accept union literature, and he did so. Seven or eight days after the threat, and as the election drew near, Brown accelerated the Banbury mixer during Spears' shift as mill operator, causing the hot 450-pound batches of rubber compound to drop at a faster rate, a rate that made things more difficult and more dangerous than would have been the case but for Brown's malicious behavior. * * *

* * * *

* * * No employee ought to be subjected to any increased danger because of his position in a union certification election, and an increased risk of injury can itself be enough to have a chilling effect on the employees' right to freely decide whether they wish to be represented by a union.

* * * *

Importantly, the incident occurred only three days before the election took place. That fact makes the incident worse and increases the impact it had on the election. * * *

* * * *

In sum, the fact that Spears was threatened and then retaliated against in a way that placed him in personal danger would reasonably create fear in the minds of employees who were voting in the certification election. Although there apparently is no evidence that Spears' own vote was affected, at least seven people, including Spears, knew of the incident and connected it to Brown's earlier threat, and the election results turned on two votes. * * *

[For these reasons, the court set aside the Board's order.]

QUESTIONS

1. What did the court hold with respect to the issue in this case?
2. If Brown's conduct in the "Banbury incident" had been motivated by something other than his support for the union and Spears's refusal to accept union literature, would the result in this case have been different?

MANAGEMENT ELECTION CAMPAIGN

Management may also campaign among its workers against the union (or for decertification of an existing union). Campaign tactics, however, are carefully mon-itored and regulated by the NLRB. Otherwise, the economic power of management might allow coercion of the workers.

Management still has many advantages in the campaign. For example, management is allowed to call all workers together during work time and make a speech against unionization. Management need not give the union supporters an equal opportunity for rebuttal. The NLRB does restrict what management may say in such a speech, however.

NO THREATS   In campaigning against the union, the employer may not make threats of reprisals if employees vote to unionize. A supervisor may not state, "If the union wins, you'll all be fired." This would be a threat. Employers must be very careful on this issue. For example, suppose an employer says, "Our competitor's plant in town unionized, and half the workers lost their jobs." The NLRB might consider this to be a veiled threat and therefore unfair.

"LABORATORY CONDITIONS"   Obviously, union election campaigns are not like national political campaigns, when a political party can make almost any claim. The NLRB tries to maintain "laboratory conditions" for a fair election that is unaffected by pressure. In establishing such conditions, the board considers the totality of circumstances in the campaign. The NLRB is especially strict about promises (or threats) made by the employer at the last minute, immediately before the election, because the union lacks an opportunity to respond effectively to these last-minute statements.

There is even a specific rule that prohibits an employer from making any election speech on company time, to massed assemblies of workers, within twenty-four hours of the time for voting. Such last-minute speeches are permitted only if employees attend voluntarily and on their own time.[11]

The employer is also prohibited from taking actions that might intimidate its workers. Employers may not undertake certain types of surveillance of workers or even create the impression of observing workers to identify union sympathizers. Management also is limited in its ability to question individual workers about their positions on unionization. These actions are deemed to contain implicit threats.

NLRB OPTIONS   If the employer issues threats or engages in other unfair labor practices and then wins the election, the NLRB may invalidate the results. The

NLRB may certify the union, even though it lost the election, and direct the employer to recognize the union as the employees' exclusive bargaining representative. Or the NLRB may ask a court to order a new election.

SECTION 4 | Collective Bargaining

If a fair election is held and the union wins, the NLRB will certify the union as the *exclusive bargaining representative* of the workers polled. Unions may provide a variety of services to their members, but the central legal right of a union is to serve as the sole representative of the group of workers in bargaining with the employer over the workers' rights.

The concept of bargaining is at the heart of the federal labor laws. When a union is officially recognized, it may make a demand to bargain with the employer. The union then sits at the table opposite the representatives of management to negotiate contracts for its workers. The terms of employment that result from the negotiations apply to all workers in the bargaining unit, even those who do not choose to belong to the union. This process is known as **collective bargaining.** Such bargaining is like most other business negotiations, and each side uses its economic power to pressure or persuade the other side to grant concessions.

Bargaining does not mean that either side must give in on demands or even that the sides must always compromise. It does mean that a demand must be taken seriously and considered as part of a package to be negotiated. Most important, both sides must bargain in "good faith."

SUBJECTS OF BARGAINING

A common issue in collective bargaining concerns the subjects over which the parties can bargain. The law makes certain subjects mandatory for collective bargaining. These topics cannot be "taken off the table" unilaterally but must be discussed and bargained over.

TERMS AND CONDITIONS OF EMPLOYMENT   The NLRA provides that employers may bargain with workers over wages, hours of work, and other terms and conditions of employment. These are broad terms that cover many employment issues. Suppose that a union wants a contract provision granting all workers four weeks of paid vacation. The company need not give in to this demand but must at least consider it and bargain over it.

---

11. Political party–like electioneering on behalf of a union, on the day of a union election, however, has been held acceptable and does not invalidate the election. See *Overnite Transportation Co. v. NLRB,* 104 F.3d 109 (7th Cir. 1997).

Many other employment issues are also considered appropriate subjects for collective bargaining. These include safety rules, insurance coverage, pension and other employee benefit plans, procedures for employee discipline, and procedures for employee grievances against the company. The Supreme Court has held that an employer must bargain even over the price of food sold in the company cafeteria.[12]

A few subjects are illegal in collective bargaining. Management need not bargain over a provision that would be illegal if included in a contract. Thus, if a union presents a demand for **featherbedding** (the hiring of unnecessary excess workers) or for an unlawful closed shop, management need not respond to these demands.

CLOSING OR RELOCATING A PLANT Management need not bargain with a union over the decision to close a particular facility. Similarly, management need not bargain over a decision to relocate a plant if the move involves a basic change in the nature of the employer's operation.[13] Management may choose to bargain over such decisions, however, to obtain concessions on other bargaining subjects.

Management must bargain over the economic consequences of such decisions. Thus, issues such as **severance pay** (compensation for the termination of employment) in the event of a plant shutdown are appropriate for collective bargaining. Also, if a relocation does *not* involve a basic change in the nature of an operation, management must bargain over the decision unless it can show (1) that the work performed at the new location varies significantly from the work performed at the former plant; (2) that the work performed at the former plant is to be discontinued entirely and not moved to the new location; (3) that the move involves a change in the scope and direction of the enterprise; (4) that labor costs were not a factor in the decision; or (5) that even if labor costs were a factor, the union could not have offered concessions that would have changed the decision to relocate.

PRIVACY ISSUES Employee privacy rights were discussed in Chapter 20. Are these rights, and their potential or real violations, appropriate subjects for collective bargaining? The NLRB has determined that physical examinations, requirements for drug or alcohol testing, and polygraph (lie-detector) testing are mandatory subjects of bargaining. The question in the following case was whether the use of hidden surveillance cameras could also be bargained over.

---

12. *Ford Motor Co. v. NLRB*, 441 U.S. 488, 99 S.Ct. 1842, 60 L.Ed.2d 420 (1979).
13. *Dubuque Packing Co.*, 303 N.L.R.B. No. 386 (1991).

CASE 22.3   National Steel Corp. v. NLRB

United States
Court of Appeals,
Seventh Circuit, 2003.
324 F.3d 928.
http://laws.lp.findlaw.
com/7th/952521.html [a]

BACKGROUND AND FACTS *National Steel Corporation operates a plant in Granite City, Illinois, where it employs approximately three thousand employees, who are represented by ten different unions and covered by seven different collective bargaining agreements. National Steel uses over one hundred video cameras in plain view to monitor areas of the plant and periodically employs hidden cameras to investigate suspected misconduct. In February 1999, National Steel installed a hidden camera to discover who was using a manager's office when the manager was not at work. The camera revealed a union member using the office to make long-distance phone calls. When National Steel discharged the employee, the union asked the company about other hidden cameras and indicated that it wanted to bargain over their use. National Steel refused to supply the information. The union filed a charge with the NLRB, which ordered National Steel to provide the information and bargain over the use of the cameras. National Steel appealed to the U.S. Court of Appeals for the Seventh Circuit.*

IN THE LANGUAGE OF THE COURT

WILLIAMS, Circuit Judge.
* * * *

The [National Labor Relations] Board determined * * * that the use of hidden surveillance cameras is a mandatory subject of collective bargaining because it found the

---

a. This is a page within the Web site maintained by FindLaw (now a part of West Group).

CONTINUED ➤

CASE 22.3 | Continued

installation and use of such cameras "analogous to physical examinations, drug/alcohol testing requirements, and polygraph testing, all of which the Board has found to be mandatory subjects of bargaining." It found that hidden cameras are focused primarily on the "working environment" that employees experience on a daily basis and are used to expose misconduct or violations of the law by employees or others. The Board held that such changes in an employer's methods have "serious implications for its employees' job security." The Board found that the use of such devices "is not entrepreneurial in character [and] is not fundamental to the basic direction of the enterprise." We find the Board's legal conclusion * * * objectively reasonable and wholly supported. * * *

* * * According to National Steel, requiring it to bargain over hidden surveillance cameras, especially as to their locations precludes an employer from meaningfully using such devices because bargaining itself will compromise the secrecy that is required for them to be effective. * * *

* * * [T]he Board acknowledged an employer's need for secrecy if hidden surveillance cameras are to serve a purpose. The Board's order to National Steel preserves those managerial interests while also honoring the union's collective bargaining rights. It only requires National Steel to negotiate with the unions over the company's installation and use of hidden surveillance cameras and * * * does not dictate how the legitimate interests of the parties are to be accommodated in the process. The Board's order does not mandate an outcome of negotiations, nor does it make any suggestion that National Steel must yield any prerogatives, other than yielding the right to proceed exclusive of consultation with the union. * * * *Here, the Board's order is consistent with the [National Labor Relations] Act's requirement that parties resolve their differences through good faith bargaining*; it simply directs National Steel to initiate an accommodation process, and to provide assertedly confidential information in accord with whatever accommodation the parties agree upon (such as a confidentiality agreement * * *). The Board's order does not eliminate National Steel's management right to use hidden cameras and it seeks to preserve the level of confidentiality necessary to allow for the continued effective use of such devices. [Emphasis added.]

DECISION AND REMEDY *The U.S. Court of Appeals for the Seventh Circuit upheld the NLRB's order to National Steel to bargain over the use of hidden surveillance cameras in the workplace. The court emphasized that this order did not prohibit their use, but only made that use a subject of collective bargaining.*

GOOD FAITH BARGAINING

Parties engaged in collective bargaining often claim that the other side is not bargaining in good faith, as required by labor law. Although good faith is a matter of subjective intent, a party's actions are used to evaluate the finding of good or bad faith in bargaining.

Obviously, the employer must be willing to meet with union representatives. Excessive delaying tactics may be proof of bad faith, as is insistence on obviously unreasonable contract terms. Suppose that a company makes a single overall contract offer on a "take-it-or-leave-it" basis and refuses to consider modifications of individual terms. This also is considered bad faith in bargaining.

While bargaining is going on, management may not make unilateral changes in important working conditions, such as wages or hours of employment. These changes must be bargained over. Once bargain-

ing reaches an impasse, management may make such unilateral changes. The law also includes an exception permitting unilateral changes in cases of business necessity.

A series of decisions have found other actions to constitute bad faith in bargaining, including the following:

1. Engaging in a campaign among workers to undermine the union.
2. Constantly shifting positions on disputed contract terms.
3. Sending bargainers who lack authority to commit the company to a contract.

If an employer (or a union) refuses to bargain in good faith without justification, it has committed an unfair labor practice, and the other party may petition the NLRB for an order requiring good faith bargaining. Except in extreme cases, the NLRB does not have authority to require a party to accede to any specific contract terms. The NLRB may require a party to reimburse the other side for its litigation expenses.

SECTION 5 | Strikes

The law does not require parties to reach a contract agreement in collective bargaining. Even when parties have bargained in good faith, they may be unable to reach a final agreement. When extensive collective bargaining has been conducted and the parties still cannot agree, an impasse has been reached.

When bargaining has reached an impasse, the union may call a strike against the employer to pressure it into making concessions. A strike occurs when the unionized workers leave their jobs and refuse to work. The workers also typically picket the plant, standing outside the facility with signs that complain of management's unfairness.

A strike is an extreme action. Striking workers lose their right to be paid. Management loses production and may lose customers, whose orders cannot be filled. Labor law regulates the circumstances and conduct of strikes. Most strikes are "economic strikes," which are initiated because the union wants a better contract. A union may also strike when the employer has engaged in unfair labor practices.

The right to strike is guaranteed by the NLRA, within limits, and strike activities, such as picketing, are protected by the free speech guarantee of the First Amendment to the Constitution. Nonworkers have a right to participate in picketing an employer. The NLRA also gives workers the right to refuse to cross a picket line of fellow workers who are engaged in a lawful strike. Not all strikes are lawful, however.

ILLEGAL STRIKES

An otherwise lawful strike may become illegal because of the conduct of the strikers. Violent strikes (including the threat of violence) are illegal. The use of violence against management employees or substitute workers is illegal. Certain forms of "massed picketing" are also illegal. If the strikers form a barrier and deny management or other nonunion workers access to the plant, the strike is illegal. Similarly, "sit-down" strikes, in which employees simply stay in the plant without working, are illegal.

SECONDARY BOYCOTTS A strike directed against someone other than the strikers' employer, such as the companies that sell materials to the employer, is a **secondary boycott.** Suppose that the unionized workers of SemiCo (our hypothetical semiconductor company) go out on strike. To increase their economic leverage, the workers picket the leading suppliers and customers of SemiCo in an attempt to hurt the company's business. SemiCo is considered the primary employer, and its suppliers and customers are considered secondary employers. Picketing of the suppliers or customers is a secondary boycott, which was made illegal by the Taft-Hartley Act.

—*Common Situs Picketing.* A controversy may arise in a strike when both the primary employer and a secondary employer occupy the same job site. In this situation, it may be difficult to distinguish between lawful picketing of the primary employer and an unlawful strike against a secondary employer. The law permits a union to picket a site occupied by both primary and secondary employers, an act called **common situs picketing.** If evidence indicates that the strike is directed against the secondary employer, however, it may become illegal. For example, if a union sends a threatening letter to the secondary employer about the strike, that fact may show that the picketing includes an illegal secondary boycott.

—*Hot-Cargo Agreements.* In a **hot-cargo agreement,** employers voluntarily agree with unions not to handle, use, or deal in non-union-produced goods of other employers. This particular type of secondary boycott was *not* made illegal by the Taft-Hartley Act, because that act only prevented unions from inducing *employees* to strike or otherwise act to force employers not to handle these goods. The Landrum-Griffin Act addressed this problem:

> It shall be [an] unfair labor practice for any labor organization and any employer to enter into any contract or any agreement . . . whereby such employer . . . agrees to refrain from handling, using, selling, transporting or otherwise dealing in any of the products of any other employer, or to cease doing business with any other person.

Hot-cargo agreements are therefore illegal. Parties injured by an illegal hot-cargo agreement or other secondary boycott may sue the union for damages.

A union may legally urge consumer boycotts of the primary employer, even at the site of a secondary employer. Suppose that a union is on strike against

SemiCo, which manufactures semiconductors that are bought by Intellect, Inc., a distributor of electronic components. Intellect sells SemiCo's semiconductors to computer manufacturers. The striking workers can urge the manufacturers not to buy SemiCo's products. The workers cannot urge a total boycott of Intellect, as that would constitute a secondary boycott.

WILDCAT STRIKES A **wildcat strike** occurs when a minority group of workers, perhaps dissatisfied with a union's representation, calls its own strike. The union is the exclusive bargaining representative of a group of workers, and only the union can call a strike. A wildcat strike, unauthorized by the certified union, is illegal.

STRIKES THAT THREATEN NATIONAL HEALTH OR SAFETY The law also places some restrictions on strikes that threaten national health or safety. The law, however, does not prohibit such strikes, nor does it require the settlement of labor disputes that threaten the national welfare. The Taft-Hartley Act simply provides time to encourage the settlement of these disputes, called the "cooling-off period."

One of the most controversial aspects of the Taft-Hartley Act was the establishment of this **eighty-day cooling-off period**—a provision allowing federal courts to issue injunctions against strikes that would create a national emergency. The president of the United States can obtain a court injunction that will last for eighty days, and presidents have occasionally used this provision. During these eighty days, the president and other government officials can work with the employer and the union to produce a settlement and avoid a strike that may cause a national emergency.

STRIKES THAT CONTRAVENE NO-STRIKE CLAUSES A strike may also be illegal if it contravenes a *no-strike clause*. The previous collective bargaining agreement between a union and an employer may have contained a clause in which the union agreed not to strike (a **no-strike clause**). The law permits the employer to enforce this no-strike clause and obtain an injunction against the strike in some circumstances.

The Supreme Court held that a no-strike clause could be enforced with an injunction if the contract contained a clause providing for arbitration of unresolved disputes.[14] The Court held that the arbitration clause was an effective substitute for the right to strike.

In the absence of an applicable arbitration provision, however, an employer cannot enjoin (forbid) a strike, even if the contract contains a no-strike clause.

REPLACEMENT WORKERS

Suppose that SemiCo's workers go out on strike. SemiCo is not required to shut down its operations but may find substitute workers to replace the strikers, if possible. These substitute workers are often called "scabs" by union supporters. An employer may even give the replacement workers permanent positions with the company.

In the 1930s and 1940s, strikes were powerful in part because employers often had difficulty finding trained replacements to keep their businesses running during strikes. Since the illegal air traffic controller strike in 1981, when President Ronald Reagan successfully hired replacement workers, employers have increasingly used this strategy, with considerable success. Even the National Football League (NFL), when struck by the players in 1987, found replacements to play for the NFL teams. Although some scoffed at the ability of the replacement players, the tactic was largely successful for management, as the strike was called off after only three weeks. An employer can even use an employment agency to recruit replacement workers.[15]

RIGHTS OF STRIKERS AFTER THE STRIKE

An important issue concerns the rights of strikers after the strike ends. In a typical economic strike over working conditions, the strikers have no right to return to their jobs. If satisfactory replacement workers have been found, the strikers may find themselves out of work. The law does prohibit the employer from discriminating against former strikers. Even if the employer fires all the strikers and retains all the replacement workers, former strikers must be rehired to fill any new vacancies. Former strikers who are rehired retain their seniority rights.

Different rules apply when a union strikes because the employer has engaged in unfair labor practices. If an employer is discriminating against a union's workers, they may go out on an unfair labor practice strike. Furthermore, an economic strike may become an unfair labor practice strike if the employer refuses to bargain in

14. *Boys Markets, Inc. v. Retail Clerks Local 770*, 398 U.S. 235, 90 S.Ct. 1583, 26 L.Ed.2d 199 (1970).

15. *Professional Staff Nurses Association v. Dimensions Health Corp.*, 110 Md.App. 270, 677 A.2d 87 (1996).

good faith. In the case of an unfair labor practice strike, the employer may still hire replacements but must give the strikers back their jobs once the strike is over. An employer may, however, refuse to rehire unfair labor practice strikers if the strike was deemed unlawful or if there is simply no longer any work for them to do.

SECTION 6 | Lockouts

Lockouts are the employer's counterpart to the worker's right to strike. A **lockout** occurs when the employer shuts down to prevent employees from working. Lockouts are usually used when the employer believes that a strike is imminent.

Lockouts may be a legal employer response. In the leading Supreme Court case on this issue, a union and an employer had reached a stalemate in collective bargaining. The employer feared that the union would delay a strike until the busy season and thereby cause the employer to suffer more greatly from the strike. The employer called a lockout before the busy season to deny the union this leverage, and the Supreme Court held that this action was legal.[16]

Some lockouts are illegal, however. An employer may not use its lockout weapon as a tool to break the union and pressure employees into decertification. Consequently, an employer must show some economic justification for instituting a lockout.

SECTION 7 | Unfair Labor Practices

The preceding sections have discussed unfair labor practices with respect to union elections, collective bargaining, and strikes. Many unfair labor practices may occur within the normal working relationship as well.

16. *American Ship Building Co. v. NLRB*, 380 U.S. 300, 85 S.Ct. 955, 13 L.Ed.2d 855 (1965).

The most significant of these practices are discussed below. Exhibit 22–2 lists the basic unfair labor practices.

EMPLOYER'S REFUSAL TO RECOGNIZE UNION AND NEGOTIATE

As noted above, once a union has been certified as the exclusive representative of a bargaining unit, an employer must recognize and bargain in good faith with the union over issues affecting all employees who are within the bargaining unit. Failure to do so is an unfair labor practice. Because the NLRA embraces a policy of majority rule, certification of the union as the bargaining unit's representative binds *all* of the employees in that bargaining unit. Thus, the union must fairly represent all the members of the bargaining unit.

PRESUMPTION OF EMPLOYEE SUPPORT Certification does not mean that a union will continue indefinitely as the exclusive representative of the bargaining unit. If the union loses the majority support of those it represents, an employer is not obligated to continue recognition of, or negotiation with, the union. As a practical matter, a newly elected representative needs time to establish itself among the workers and to begin to formulate and implement its programs. Therefore, as a matter of labor policy, a union is immune from attack by employers and from repudiation by the employees for a period of one year after certification. During this period, it is *presumed* that the union enjoys majority support among the employees; the employer cannot refuse to deal with the union as the employees' exclusive representative, even if the employees prefer not to be represented by that union.

Beyond the one-year period, the presumption of majority support continues, but it is *rebuttable*. An employer may rebut (refute) the presumption with objective evidence that a majority of employees do not wish to be represented by the union. If the evidence is

EXHIBIT 22–2 Basic Unfair Labor Practices

EMPLOYERS	UNIONS
1. Refuse to recognize a union and to bargain in good faith.	1. Refuse to bargain in good faith.
2. Interfere with, restrain, or coerce employees in their efforts to form a union and bargain collectively.	2. Picket to coerce unionization without the majority support of the employees.
3. Dominate a union.	3. Demand the hiring of unnecessary excess workers.
4. Discriminate against union workers.	4. Discriminate against nonunion workers.
5. Punish employees for engaging in concerted activity.	5. Agree to participate in a secondary boycott.
	6. Engage in an illegal strike.
	7. Charge excessive membership fees.

sufficient to support a *good faith* belief that the union no longer enjoys majority support among the employees, the employer may refuse to continue to recognize and negotiate with the union.[17]

QUESTIONS OF MAJORITY SUPPORT   A delicate question arises during a strike in which an employer

hires replacement workers. Specifically, should it be *assumed* that the replacement workers do not support the union? If they do not, and if as a result the union no longer has majority support, the employer need not continue negotiating with the union.

Another question arises when two companies merge or consolidate, when one company buys the assets or stock of another, or when, under any other circumstances, one employer steps into the shoes of another. Is a collective bargaining agreement between a union and a predecessor employer binding on the union and the successor employer? That was the question in the following case.

17. An employer cannot agree to a collective bargaining agreement and later refuse to abide by it, however, on the ground of a good faith belief that the union did not have majority support when the agreement was negotiated. See *Auciello Iron Works, Inc. v. NLRB,* 517 U.S. 781, 116 S.Ct. 1754, 135 L.Ed.2d 64 (1996).

CASE 22.4 | Canteen Corp. v. NLRB

United States
Court of Appeals,
Seventh Circuit, 1997.
103 F.3d 1355.

BACKGROUND AND FACTS   *The food service employees at the Medical College of Wisconsin were represented by the Hotel Employees and Restaurant Employees Union. When Canteen Corporation took over the food service, it agreed to negotiate a new contract with the union. Meanwhile, without informing the union, Canteen told the employees that their wages would be cut 20 to 25 percent. The employees resigned. Canteen then recruited employees from other sources and refused to negotiate with the union on the ground that it no longer represented the employees. The union filed an unfair labor practice charge with the National Labor Relations Board (NLRB). The NLRB ordered Canteen to reinstate the employees at their previous wage rates until a new contract could be negotiated. Canteen asked the U.S. Court of Appeals for the Seventh Circuit to review the order.*

IN THE LANGUAGE OF THE COURT

RIPPLE, Circuit Judge.
        *   *   *   *
        *   *   **A new employer must consult with the union when it is clear that the employer intends to hire the employees of its predecessor as the initial workforce. *   *   *
        *   *   *   *
        *   *   * The totality of Canteen's conduct demonstrated that it was perfectly clear that Canteen planned to retain the predecessor employees. *   *   *
        *   *   * Canteen's intention to retain the *   *   * employees was backed by an expectation so strong that it neglected to take serious steps to recruit from other sources until it was informed that [the employees] had rejected job offers. *   *   * Canteen intended from the outset to hire all of the predecessor employees and did not mention in [its] discussions [with the union] the possibility of any other changes in its initial terms and conditions of employment.

DECISION AND REMEDY   *The U.S. Court of Appeals for the Seventh Circuit mandated that the NLRB's order be enforced. The employer was required to reinstate the employees at their previous wage rates until a new contract could be negotiated.*

EMPLOYER'S INTERFERENCE IN UNION ACTIVITIES

The NLRA declares it to be an unfair labor practice for an employer to interfere with, restrain, or coerce employees in the exercise of their rights to form a union and bargain collectively. Unlawful employer interference may take a variety of forms.

Courts have found it an unfair labor practice for an employer to make threats that may interfere with an employee's decision to join a union. Even asking employees about their views on the union may be considered coercive. Employees responding to such questioning must be able to remain anonymous and must receive assurances against employer reprisals. Employers also may not prohibit certain forms of union activity in the workplace. If an employee has a grievance with the company, the employer cannot prevent the union's participation in support of the employee, for example.

If an employer has unlawfully interfered with the operation of a union, the NLRB or a reviewing court may issue a cease-and-desist order halting the practice. The company typically is required to post the order on a bulletin board and renounce its past unlawful conduct.

EMPLOYER'S DOMINATION OF UNION

In the early days of unionization, employers fought back by forming employer-sponsored unions to represent employees. These "company unions" were seldom more than the puppets of management. The NLRA outlawed company unions and any other form of employer domination of workers' unions.

Under the law against employer domination, an employer can have no say in which employees belong to the union or which employees serve as union officers. Nor may supervisors or other management personnel participate in union meetings.

Company actions that support a union may also be considered improper potential domination. For this reason, a company cannot give union workers pay for time spent on union activities, because this is considered undue support for the union. The company may not provide financial aid to a union and may not solicit workers to join a union.

EMPLOYER'S DISCRIMINATION AGAINST UNION EMPLOYEES

The NLRA prohibits employers from discriminating against workers because they are union officers or are otherwise associated with a union. When workers must be laid off, the company cannot consider union participation as a criterion for deciding whom to fire.

The antidiscrimination provisions also apply to hiring decisions. Suppose that certain employees of SemiCo are represented by a union, but the company is attempting to weaken the union's strength. The company cannot require potential new hires to guarantee that they will not join the union.

Discriminatory punishment of union members or officers can be difficult to prove. The company will claim to have good reasons for its action. The NLRB has specified a series of factors to be considered in determining whether an action had an unlawful, discriminatory motivation. These include giving inconsistent reasons for the action, applying rules inconsistently and more strictly against union members, failing to give an expected warning prior to discharge or other discipline, and acting contrary to worker seniority.

The decision to close a facility cannot be made with a discriminatory motive. If a company has several facilities and only one is unionized, the company cannot shut down the union plant simply because of the union. The company could shut down the union plant if it were demonstrably less efficient than the other facilities, however.

UNION'S UNFAIR LABOR PRACTICES

Certain union activities are declared to be unfair labor practices by the Taft-Hartley Act. Secondary boycotts, discussed earlier in this chapter, are one such union unfair labor practice.

COERCION   Another significant union unfair labor practice is coercion or restraint on an employee's decision to participate in or refrain from participating in union activities. Obviously, it is unlawful for a union to threaten an employee or a family with violence for failure to join the union. The law's prohibition includes economic coercion as well. Suppose that a union official declares, "We have a lot of power here; you had better join the union, or you may lose your job." This threat is an unfair labor practice.

The NLRA provides unions with the authority to regulate their own internal affairs, which includes disciplining union members. This discipline cannot be used in an improperly coercive fashion, however. Suppose a disaffected union member feels that the union is no longer providing proper representation for employees and starts a campaign to decertify the union.

The union may expel the employee from membership but may not fine or otherwise discipline the worker.

DISCRIMINATION   Another significant union unfair labor practice is discrimination. A union may not discriminate against workers because they refuse to join. This provision also prohibits a union from using its influence to cause an employer to discriminate against workers who refuse to join the union. A union cannot force an employer to deny promotions to workers who fail to join the union.

OTHER UNFAIR PRACTICES   Other union unfair labor practices include featherbedding, participation in picketing to coerce unionization without majority employee support, and refusal to engage in good faith bargaining with employer representatives.

Unions are allowed to bargain for certain "union security clauses" in contracts. Although closed shops are illegal, a union can bargain for a provision that requires workers to contribute to the union within thirty days after they are hired. This is typically called an *agency shop*, or *union shop*, clause.

The union shop clause can compel workers to begin paying dues to the certified union but cannot require the worker to "join" the union. Dues payment can be required to prevent workers from taking the benefits of union bargaining without contributing to the union's efforts. The clause cannot require workers to contribute their efforts to the union, however, or to go out on strike.

Even a requirement of dues payment has its limits. Excessive initiation fees or dues may be illegal. Unions often use their revenues to contribute to causes or to lobby politicians. A nonunion employee subject to a union shop clause who must pay dues cannot be required to contribute to this sort of union expenditure.

Section 8(a)(3) of the NLRA sets out the right of a union to bargain for a union security clause. The United States Supreme Court has interpreted this statute in several cases and imposed the limits discussed above. In the following case, the Supreme Court was asked to consider whether a union breached its duty of fair representation by negotiating a clause that was phrased in the language of the statute without explaining the Court's interpretation of that language.

CASE 22.5   Marquez v. Screen Actors Guild, Inc.

Supreme Court of the
United States, 1998.
525 U.S. 33,
119 S.Ct. 292,
142 L.Ed.2d 242.
http://straylight.law.
cornell.edu/supct/index.html[a]

BACKGROUND AND FACTS   *The Screen Actors Guild (SAG) is a union that represents performers in the entertainment industry. In 1994, Lakeside Productions signed a collective bargaining agreement with SAG, making SAG the exclusive bargaining agent for the performers that Lakeside hired for its productions. The agreement contained a union security clause, providing that to work under the agreement, any performer who had worked more than thirty days in the industry must be "a member of the Union in good standing." This clause tracked the language of Section 8(a)(3) of the NLRA without explaining that to be a "member," a worker only had to pay certain dues. Naomi Marquez, a part-time actress, was offered a one-line role in an episode of the television series* Medicine Ball, *which was produced by Lakeside. Because she had previously worked in the motion picture industry for more than thirty days, she was told to pay about $500 in union fees before she could begin work for Lakeside. Marquez delayed until SAG agreed to allow her to pay the fees after Lakeside paid her for her work. By this time, however, Lakeside had hired a different actress. Marquez filed a suit in a federal district court against SAG and Lakeside, arguing, among other things, that SAG breached its duty of fair representation by negotiating a union security clause written in the language of the NLRA. She claimed that this was arbitrary and in bad faith. The court granted the defendants' motion for summary judgment, which the U.S. Court of Appeals for the Ninth Circuit affirmed. Marquez appealed to the United States Supreme Court.*

IN THE LANGUAGE OF THE COURT
Justice O'CONNOR delivered the opinion of the Court.
* * * *
   * * * SAG's negotiation of a union security clause with language derived from the NLRA section authorizing such a clause is far from arbitrary. * * *[B]y tracking the

a. In the left column, under "Archive of decisions/by Party," click on "1990–present." In the "1998" row, click on "1st party." On that page, select "M–O" and click on the case name to access the opinon.

statutory language, the clause incorporates all of the refinements that have become associated with that language. * * *[T]he relevant provisions of [Section] 8(a)(3) have become terms of art; the words and phrasing of the section now encompass the rights that we announced in [our decisions]. After we stated that the statutory language incorporates an employee's right not to "join" the union (except by paying fees and dues) and an employee's right to pay for only representational activities, we cannot fault SAG for using this very language to convey these very concepts.

Petitioner [Marquez] also invites us to conclude that the union's conduct in negotiating the union security clause breached the duty of fair representation because it was done in bad faith. * * *. According to petitioner, * * * it is bad faith for a union to use the statutory language in the collective bargaining agreement because such use can only mislead employees. Petitioner's argument fails because it is so broad. It is difficult to conclude that a union acts in bad faith by notifying workers of their rights through more effective means of communication and by using a term of art to describe those rights in a contract workers are unlikely to read. * * *

The second part of petitioner's bad faith argument—that there was no other reason for the union's choice of the statutory language—also fails. *The statutory language, which we have said incorporates all of the refinements associated with the language, is a shorthand description of workers' legal rights.* A union might choose to use this shorthand precisely because it incorporates all of the refinements. Petitioner argues that this reason for failing to explain all of the intricate rights and duties associated with a legal term of art is bad faith. The logic of petitioner's argument has no stopping point; it would require unions (and all other contract drafters) to spell out all the intricacies of every term used in a contract. Contracts would become massive and unwieldy treatises, yet there would be no discernible benefit from the increased mass. * * * Contrary to petitioner's claim, we conclude that it may be perfectly reasonable for a union to use terms of art in a contract. [Emphasis added.]

DECISION AND REMEDY *The Supreme Court affirmed the decision of the lower court. The union's conduct in negotiating a union security clause that tracked the statutory language was not arbitrary or in bad faith. By negotiating this clause, the union did not breach its duty of fair representation.*

SECTION 8 | Rights of Nonunion Employees

Most of labor law involves the formation of unions and associated rights. Even nonunion employees have some similar rights, however. Most workers do not belong to unions, so this issue is significant. The NLRA protects concerted employee action, for example, and does not limit its protection to certified unions.

CONCERTED ACTIVITY

Data from the NLRB indicate that a growing number of nonunion employees are challenging employer barriers to their **concerted action.** Protected concerted action is that taken by employees for their mutual benefit regarding wages, hours, or terms and conditions of employment.

Even an action by a single employee may be protected concerted activity, if that action is taken for the benefit of other employees and if the employee has at least discussed the action with other approving workers. If only a single worker engages in a protest or walkout, the employer will not be liable for an unfair labor practice if it fires the worker unless the employer is aware that this protest or walkout is concerted activity taken with the assent of other workers. Sometimes the mutual interest of other workers should be obvious to the employer, however.

SAFETY

A common circumstance for nonunion activity is concern over workplace safety. The Labor-Management Relations Act authorizes an employee to walk off the job if he or she has a good faith belief that the working conditions are abnormally dangerous. The employer cannot lawfully discharge the employee under these conditions.

Suppose that Knight Company operates a plant building mobile homes. A large ventilation fan at the plant blows dust and abrasive materials into the faces of workers. The workers have complained, but Knight Company has done nothing. The workers finally refuse to work until the fan is modified, and Knight fires them. The NLRB will find that the walkout is a protected activity and can command Knight to rehire the workers with back pay.

To be protected under federal labor law, a safety walkout must be *concerted* activity. If a single worker walks out over a safety complaint, other workers must be affected by the safety issue for the walkout to be protected under the LMRA.

EMPLOYEE COMMITTEES

Personnel specialists note that worker problems are often attributable to a lack of communication between labor and management. In a nonunion workforce, a company may wish to create some institution to communicate with workers and act together with them to improve workplace conditions.

This institution, generally called an **employee committee,** is composed of representatives from both management and labor. The committee meets periodically and has some authority to create rules. The committee gives employees a forum to voice their dissatisfaction with certain conditions and gives management a conduit to inform workers fully of policy decisions.

The creation of an employee committee may be entirely well motivated on the company's part and may serve the interests of workers as well as management. Nevertheless, employee committees are fraught with potential problems under federal labor laws, and management must be aware of these problems.

The central problem with employee committees is that they may become the functional equivalent of unions dominated by management, in violation of the NLRA. Thus, these committees cannot perform union functions. For example, the employee representatives on such a committee should not present a package of proposals on wages and terms of employment, because this is the role of a union negotiating committee.

In the following case, a union complained that an employer had committed an unfair labor practice by maintaining an employee committee.

CASE 22.6   ## In re Simmons Industries, Inc.

National Labor Relations Board, 1996. 321 N.L.R.B. No. 32. http://www.nlrb.gov/ nlrb/legal/decisions[a]

HISTORICAL AND SOCIAL SETTING *In the 1930s and 1940s, after Congress enacted the first laws protecting unions, union membership as a percentage of the workforce grew rapidly, until about a third of all workers belonged to unions. As the size of the workforce continued to grow, however, the number of workers belonging to unions did not increase proportionately. By the mid-1990s, union members made up only about 15 percent of the workforce. Unions, which have sometimes been frustrated by employees' reluctance to organize, often blame unsuccessful attempts to unionize a particular employer's workforce on the employer.*

BACKGROUND AND FACTS *Simmons Industries, Inc., operated chicken processing plants. One of Simmons's customers was Kentucky Fried Chicken (KFC). To satisfy KFC's concerns with quality, Simmons formed at each plant a total quality management (TQM) committee. Simmons appointed managers and employees from a cross section of the plants to serve on the committees and set the committees' agendas, which included such topics as employee bonuses and absences. Later, the United Food and Commercial Workers Union attempted unsuccessfully to organize the employees. The union filed a complaint with the National Labor Relations Board (NLRB), alleging that Simmons had committed unfair labor practices by, among other things, maintaining a TQM committee at its plant in Jay, Oklahoma. The union argued that the committee was a "labor organization" dominated by management in violation of the National Labor Relations Act (NLRA).*

IN THE LANGUAGE OF THE COURT

DECISION AND ORDER
* * * *
* * * [T]he concept of "labor organization" * * * includes very loose, informal, unstructured, and irregular meeting groups. Such a loose organization will meet the [NLRA] defi-

---

a. In the "for term" box, type in "Simmons" and hit "Go." On that page, scroll to the case name ("Simmons Industries") and click on the 321-32 pdf link to read the opinion.

CASE 22.6 | Continued

nition if: (1) employees participate, (2) the organization exists, at least in part, for the purpose of dealing with employers, and (3) these dealings concern conditions of work or concern other statutory subjects such as grievances, labor disputes, wages, rates of pay, or hours of employment.
    *   *   *   *

    *   *   * [E]mployee members were representative of each *   *   * grouping of employees. *   *   * [T]he committee discussed and made proposals solicited by [Simmons] with respect to the formulation and implementation of an incentive bonus pay program, clearly a mandatory bargaining subject. [Simmons] accepted some of the committee's proposal and guided itself by others in formulating the bonus plan. *   *   * Furthermore, the *   *   * Committee continued *   *   * to discuss and make proposals with respect to employee discipline, attendance, and punctuality problems and employee courtesy breaks. On recommendations based in large part on employee member complaints, the plant manager issued a set of rules that clearly affected these conditions of employment and mandatory bargaining subjects. Thus the *   *   * Committee *   *   * effectively constituted a representational employee committee, in effect a labor organization, which was unlawfully dominated, interfered with in operation and administration, and rendered unlawful assistance to by [Simmons] in violation of [the NLRA].

DECISION AND REMEDY *The NLRB ordered Simmons to, among other things, "[i]mmediately disestablish and cease giving assistance or any other support" to its TQM committees.*[b]

---

b. This decision was an application of the principle declared in the leading case in this area, *Electromation, Inc.,* 309 N.L.R.B. 990 (1992).

REVIEWING LABOR LAW

In April 2005, several employees for Javatech, Inc., a computer hardware developer with 250 employees, formed the Javatech Employees Union (JEU). In June, the National Labor Relations Board (NLRB) conducted an election that showed that a majority of Javatech employees supported the union. JEU began bargaining with management over wages and benefits. In January 2006, Javatech management offered JEU a 1 percent annual wage increase to all employees with no other changes in employment benefits. JEU countered by requesting a 3 percent wage increase and an employee health-insurance package. Javatech management responded that the 1 percent wage increase was the company's only offer. JEU petitioned the NLRB for an order requesting good faith bargaining. After meeting with an NLRB representative, Javatech management still refused to consider modifying its position. JEU leaders then became embroiled in a factional dispute about whether it should accept this offer or go on strike. New union leaders were elected in July 2006, and the employer refused to meet with the new JEU representatives, claiming that the union no longer had majority support from employees. In August 2006, a group of seven Javatech engineers began feeling ill while working with a new adhesive used in creating motherboards. The seven engineers discussed going on strike without union support. Before reaching agreement, one of the engineers, Rosa Molina, became dizzy while working with the adhesive and walked out of the workplace. Using the information presented in the chapter, answer the following questions.

1. How many employees must have turned in authorization cards to allow JEU to petition the NLRB for an election?

2. To satisfy the good faith bargaining requirement under labor law, what would Javatech need to change about its bargaining negotiations?

3. Could the seven engineers legally call a strike? What would this be called?

4. Was Javatech in compliance with labor law when the company refused to negotiate with JEU in July 2006? Explain.

5. Would Molina's safety walkout be protected under federal labor law?

TERMS AND CONCEPTS TO REVIEW

appropriate bargaining unit 533	eighty-day cooling-off period 540	right-to-work law 531
authorization card 531	employee committee 546	secondary boycott 539
closed shop 530	featherbedding 537	severance pay 537
collective bargaining 536	hot-cargo agreement 539	union shop 530
common situs picketing 539	lockout 541	wildcat strike 540
concerted action 545	no-strike clause 540	yellow dog contract 528

QUESTIONS AND CASE PROBLEMS

22–1. A group of employees at the Briarwood Furniture Co.'s manufacturing plant were interested in joining a union. A representative of the American Federation of Labor and Congress of Industrial Organizations (AFL-CIO) told the group that her union was prepared to represent the workers and suggested that the group begin organizing by obtaining authorization cards from their fellow employees. After obtaining 252 authorization cards from among Briarwood's 500 nonmanagement employees, the organizers requested that the company recognize the AFL-CIO as the official representative of the employees. The company refused. Has the company violated federal labor laws? What should the organizers do?

22–2. The Briarwood Furniture Co., discussed in the preceding problem, employs 400 unskilled workers and 100 skilled workers in its plant. The unskilled workers operate the industrial machinery used in processing Briarwood's line of standardized plastic office furniture. The skilled workers, who work in an entirely separate part of the plant, are experienced artisans who craft Briarwood's line of expensive wood furniture products. Do you see any problems with a single union's representing all the workers at the Briarwood plant? Explain. Would your answers to Problem 22–1 change if you knew that 51 of the authorization cards had been signed by the skilled workers, with the remainder signed by the unskilled workers?

22–3. QUESTION WITH SAMPLE ANSWER
Suppose that Consolidated Stores is undergoing a unionization campaign. Prior to the election, management says that the union is unnecessary to protect workers. Management also provides bonuses and wage increases to the workers during this period. The employees reject the union. Union organizers protest that the wage increases during the election campaign unfairly prejudiced the vote. Should these wage increases be regarded as an unfair labor practice? Discuss.
For a sample answer to this question, go to Appendix I at the end of this text.

22–4. SimpCo was engaged in ongoing negotiations over a new labor contract with the union representing the company's employees. As the deadline for expiration of the old labor contract drew near, several employees who were involved in union activities were disciplined for being late to work. The union claimed that other employees had not been dealt with as harshly and that the company was discriminating on the basis of union activity. When the negotiations failed to prove fruitful and the old contract expired, the union called a strike. The company claimed that the action was an economic strike to press the union's demands for higher wages. The union contended that the action was an unfair labor practice strike because of the alleged discrimination. What importance does the distinction have for the striking workers and the company?

22–5. CASE PROBLEM WITH SAMPLE ANSWER
The Teamsters Union represented twenty-seven employees of Curtin Matheson Scientific, Inc. When a collective bargaining agreement between the union and the company expired, the company made an offer for a new agreement, which the union rejected. The company locked out the twenty-seven employees, and the union began an economic strike. The company hired replacement workers. When the union ended its strike and offered to accept the company's earlier offer, the company refused. The company also refused to bargain further, asserting doubt that the union was supported by a majority of the employees. The union sought help from the National Labor Relations Board (NLRB), which refused to presume that the replacement workers did not support the union. On the company's appeal, a court overturned the NLRB's ruling. The union appealed to the United States Supreme Court. How should the Court rule? [*NLRB v. Curtin Matheson Scientific, Inc.*, 494 U.S. 775, 110 S.Ct. 1542, 108 L.Ed.2d 801 (1990)]
To view a sample answer for this case problem, go to this book's Web site at http://wleb.westbuslaw.com, select "Chapter 22," and click on "Case Problem with Sample Answer."

22-6. EMPLOYEE COMMITTEES. Electromation, Inc., a manufacturer of electrical components and related products, cut wages, bonuses, and incentive pay and tightened attendance and leave policies. When the employees complained, Electromation set up "action committees," each consisting of employees and management representatives. No employee was involved in drafting the goals of the committees. The committees were told to suggest solutions, which would be implemented if management "believed they were within budget concerns" and "would be acceptable to the employees." Employee committee members were expected to discuss suggestions with their co-workers. The Teamsters Union, which had been seeking to organize the employees, challenged the establishment of the committees as an unfair labor practice and asked the NLRB to order that they be dissolved. On what basis might the NLRB grant the union's request? [*Electromation, Inc.*, 309 N.L.R.B. 990 (1992)]

22-7. SECONDARY BOYCOTTS. For many years, grapefruit was shipped to Japan from Fort Pierce and Port Canaveral, Florida. In 1990, Coastal Stevedoring Co. in Fort Pierce and Port Canaveral Stevedoring, Ltd., in Port Canaveral—nonunion firms—were engaged in a labor dispute with the International Longshoremen's Association (ILA). The ILA asked the National Council of Dockworkers' Unions of Japan to prevent Japanese shippers from using nonunion stevedores in Florida, and the council warned Japanese firms that their workers would not unload fruit loaded in the United States by nonunion labor. The threat caused all citrus shipments from Florida to Japan to go through Tampa, where they were loaded by stevedores represented by the ILA. Coastal, Canaveral, and others complained to the National Labor Relations Board (NLRB), alleging that the ILA's request of the Japanese unions was an illegal secondary boycott. How should the NLRB rule? [*International Longshoremen's Association, AFL-CIO*, 313 N.L.R.B. No. 53 (1993)]

22-8. UNION RECOGNITION. The International Association of Machinists and Aerospace Workers was certified as the exclusive representative of a unit of employees of F & A Food Sales, Inc. The employees were associated with F & A's trucking operations. The parties negotiated a collective bargaining agreement (CBA) that recognized the union as the employees' representative and reserved F & A's right to subcontract work as the company deemed necessary. Five months after negotiating the CBA, F & A subcontracted the services performed by the unit to Ryder Dedicated Logistics, Inc. Ryder operated from the same facility, used the same trucks, and employed substantially the same employees as had F & A. The union did not represent the workers while Ryder employed them. Seventeen months later,

Ryder terminated the subcontract, and F & A resumed its own trucking operations with the same facility, the same trucks, and many of the same employees. The union asserted its right to represent the employees under the CBA. F & A refused to recognize the union. The union filed a charge of unfair labor practice with the NLRB. Is the CBA still in effect? Is the union still the representative of this unit of employees? Explain. [*National Labor Relations Board. v. F & A Food Sales, Inc.*, 202 F.3d 1258 (10th Cir. 2000)]

22-9. UNFAIR LABOR PRACTICE. The New York Department of Education's e-mail policy prohibits the use of the e-mail system for unofficial purposes, except that officials of the New York Public Employees Federation (PEF), the union representing state employees, can use the system for some limited communications, including the scheduling of union meetings and activities. In 1998, Michael Darcy, an elected PEF official, began sending mass, union-related e-mails to employees, including a summary of a union delegates' convention, a union newsletter, a criticism of proposed state legislation, and a criticism of the state governor and the Governor's Office of Employee Relations. Richard Cate, the Department's chief operating officer, met with Darcy and reiterated the Department's e-mail policy. When Darcy refused to stop his use of the e-mail system, Cate terminated his access to it. Darcy filed a complaint with the New York Public Employment Relations Board, alleging an unfair labor practice. Do the circumstances support Cate's action? Why or why not? [*Benson v. Cuevas*, 293 A.D.2d 927, 741 N.Y.S.2d 310 (3 Dept. 2002)]

22-10. COLLECTIVE BARGAINING. Verizon New York, Inc. (VNY), provides telecommunications services. VNY and the Communications Workers of America (CWA) are parties to collective bargaining agreements covering installation and maintenance employees. At one time, VNY supported annual blood drives. VNY, CWA, and charitable organizations jointly set dates, arranged appointments, and adjusted work schedules for the drives. For each drive, about a thousand employees, including managers, spent up to four hours traveling to a donor site, giving blood, recovering, and returning to their jobs. Employees received full pay for the time. In 2001, VNY told CWA that it would no longer allow employees to participate "on Company time," claiming that it experienced problems meeting customer requests for service during the drives. CWA filed a complaint with the National Labor Relations Board (NLRB), asking that VNY be ordered to bargain over the decision. Did VNY commit an unfair labor practice? Should the NLRB grant CWA's request? Why or why not? [*Verizon New York, Inc. v. National Labor Relations Board*, 360 F.3d 206 (D.C. Cir. 2004)]

LAW | on the Web

For updated links to resources available on the Web, as well as a variety of other materials, visit this text's Web site at http://wleb.westbuslaw.com.

The American Federation of Labor and Congress of Industrial Organizations (AFL-CIO) provides links to a broad variety of labor-related resources at

http://www.aflcio.org

The National Labor Relations Board is online at the following URL:

http://www.nlrb.gov

LEGAL RESEARCH EXERCISES ON THE WEB

Go to http://wleb.westbuslaw.com, the Web site that accompanies this text. Select "Chapter 22" and click on "Internet Exercises." There you will find the following Internet research exercises that you can perform to learn more about topics covered in this chapter.

Activity 22–1: LEGAL PERSPECTIVE
The National Labor Relations Board

Activity 22–2: MANAGEMENT PERSPECTIVE
Mail Policies and Union Activity

Activity 22–3: MANAGEMENT PERSPECTIVE
Unions and Labor Laws

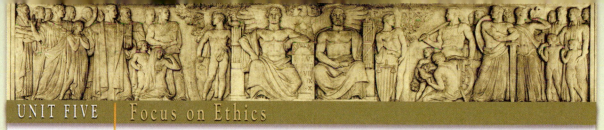

The Employment Environment

Ethical principles—and challenging ethical issues—pervade the employment environment. In part, this is because employment relationships often involve intricate duties of agency. As you read in Chapter 19, when one person agrees to act on behalf of another, as an agent does in an agency relationship, that person assumes certain ethical responsibilities. Similarly, the principal also assumes certain ethical duties. In essence, agency law gives legal force to the ethical duties arising in an agency relationship. Although agency law also focuses on the rights of agents and principals, those rights are framed by the concept of duty—that is, an agent's duty becomes a right for the principal and vice versa.

Employees who deal with third parties are also deemed to be agents and thus share the ethical (and legal) duties imposed under agency law. In the employment context, however, it is not always possible for an employee to negotiate favorable employment terms. Often, an employee who is offered a job either accepts the job on the employer's terms or looks elsewhere for a position. Although numerous federal and state statutes protect employees, in some situations employees still have little recourse against their employers. At the same time, employers complain that statutes regulating employment relationships impose so many requirements that they find it hard to exercise a reasonable amount of control over their workplaces.

In the following pages, we focus on the ethical dimensions of selected issues in agency and employment law.

The Agent's Duty to the Principal

The very nature of the principal-agent relationship is one of trust, which we call a fiduciary relationship. Because of the nature of this relationship, an agent is considered to owe certain duties to the principal. These duties include being loyal and obedient, informing the principal of important facts concerning the agency, accounting to the principal for property or money received, and performing with reasonable diligence and skill.

Thus, ethical conduct would prevent an agent from representing two principals in the same transaction, making a secret profit from the agency relationship, or failing to disclose the interest of the agent in property the principal was purchasing. The expected ethical conduct of the agent has evolved into rules that, if breached, cause the agent to be held legally liable.

But does an agent's obligation extend beyond the duty to the principal and include a duty to society as well? Consider, for example, the situation faced by an employee who knows that her employer is engaging in an unethical—or even illegal—practice, such as marketing an unsafe product. Does the employee's duty to the principal include keeping silent about this practice, which may harm users of the product? Does the employee have a duty to protect consumers by disclosing this information to the public, even if she loses her job as a result? Some scholars have argued that many of the greatest evils in the past thirty years have been accomplished in the name of duty to the principal.

The Principal's Duty to the Agent

Just as agents owe certain fiduciary duties to their principals, so do principals owe ethical duties to their agents, such as compensation and job-related expenses. If an agent incurs expenses or liability while acting on the principal's behalf, for example, it is only fair that the principal should assume responsibility for those expenses or that liability.

Principals also owe their agents a duty of cooperation. One might expect most principals to cooperate with their agents out of self-interest, but this is not universally the case. Suppose that a principal hires an agent on commission to sell a building, and the agent puts considerable time and expense into the process. If the principal changes his mind and decides to retain the building, he might want to prevent the agent from completing a sale. Is such action ethical? Does it violate the principal's duty of cooperation? What alternatives would the principal have?

Although a principal is legally obligated to fulfill certain duties to the agent, these duties do not include any specific duty of loyalty. Some argue that the lack of employer loyalty to employees has resulted in a reduction in employee loyalty to employers. After all, they maintain, why should an employee be loyal to an employer's interests over the years when the employee knows that the employer has no corresponding legal duty to be loyal to the employee's interests? Employers who do show a sense of loyalty to employees—for example, by not laying off longtime, faithful employees when business is slow or when those employees could be replaced by younger workers at lower cost—base that sense of loyalty primarily on ethical, not legal, considerations.

Respondeat Superior

Agency law is designed to enforce the ethical or fiduciary duties that arise once an agency relationship is established. To perhaps an even greater extent, agency law is designed to protect third parties—people outside the agency relationship.

One legal concept that addresses the effect of agency relationships on third parties is the doctrine of *respondeat superior*. The doctrine raises a significant ethical question: Why should innocent employers be required to assume responsibility for the tortious, or wrongful, actions of their agent-employees? The answer has to do with the courts' perception that when one of two innocent parties must suffer a loss, the party in the best position to prevent that loss should bear the burden. In an employment relationship, for example, the employer has more control over the employee's behavior than a third party to the relationship does.

Another reason for retaining the doctrine of *respondeat superior* in our laws is based on the employer's assumed ability to pay any damages that are incurred by a third party. Our collection of shared beliefs suggests that an injured party should be afforded the most effective relief possible. Thus, even though an employer may be absolutely innocent, the employer has "deeper pockets" than the employee and will be more likely to have the funds necessary to make the injured party whole.

Employee versus Independent Contractor

An aspect of agency law that has troubled employers and employees alike on numerous occasions has to do with a worker's declared status as an independent contractor. Not surprisingly, many employers prefer to designate certain workers as independent contractors rather than as employees. Yet, increasingly, the courts are holding that certain workers who are designated as independent contractors are, in fact, employees if the employer exercises a significant degree of control over their performance. It does not matter whether the parties had specified, in written contracts, that the workers were independent contractors.

For example, in one case a group of drivers for a delivery service agreed to work as independent contractors and to use their own cars to make deliveries. Each driver signed a contract explicitly agreeing to work as an independent contractor. Nonetheless, a court held that the workers qualified as employees because they were dependent for their business on the employer. The delivery service "procured the customers, set the delivery prices, made the delivery assignments, billed the customers, set the commission rate, and paid the drivers."[1]

Why Should the Courts Intervene? If a worker agrees to be classified as an independent contractor, why should a court interfere with this decision? The answer is, at least in part, that issues of fairness may be involved. The common law of agency, as developed and applied by the courts, implicitly recognizes these issues.

After all, if a worker is an independent contractor, the worker must pay all Social Security taxes, instead of sharing them with his or her employer. Additionally, the worker will not be entitled to employer-provided benefits—such as group health insurance, pension plans, and stock options—that are available to employees. Furthermore, the worker will not receive the legal protections afforded to employees under such laws as those prohibiting employment discrimination. For example, in one case an independent contractor who worked for a nursing home was fired from her job after she submitted a complaint about the facility to the state inspection department. She sued the employer, contending that she had been fired in retaliation for submitting the complaint. The court, however, held for the nursing home. Because the worker was an independent contractor, she was free to negotiate the terms of her employment, which diminished the need for court-based remedies.[2]

The Disparity in Bargaining Power For some types of work, especially work that requires great expertise, the worker may have sufficient bargaining power to negotiate favorable contract terms with the employer. Often, however, workers lack such power. If an employer states that a worker is being hired as an independent contractor, what can the worker do? Generally, in this situation the worker has only two options—accept the arrangement or forfeit the job. Certainly, that was the choice faced by many workers at Microsoft Corporation when that company, to save costs, required employees to agree to become independent contractors if they wished to continue to work for Microsoft.

Whistleblowing

Many whistleblowing statutes reward employees who report their employers' wrongdoing with a percentage of the funds recovered after a lawsuit. In other words, employees have a strong financial incentive to offer up their employers for civil litigation. But what if the employee is somehow involved in the wrongdoing? Should the employee still receive a share of the proceeds?

Consider, for example, the largest Medicaid fraud settlement in U.S. history, involving a deal between Bayer Corporation and Kaiser Permanente, a health-maintenance organization. As one of Bayer's biggest customers, Kaiser demanded a discount price on Cipro, an antibiotic manufactured by Bayer. By law, however, Bayer could not sell the antibiotic to Kaiser for less than it sold Cipro to the federal government for use in the Medicaid program. (Medicaid helps low-income persons pay for necessary medical services.) If Bayer lowered the price of Cipro to Kaiser, it would have to refund millions of dollars to Medicaid. Therefore, Bayer "privately labeled" the same antibiotic using a different name and sold it to Kaiser at a 40 percent discount. Ironically, the person who blew the whistle on the fraudulent scheme—

---

1. *AFM Messenger Service, Inc. v. The Department of Employment Security*, 198 Ill.2d 380, 763 N.E.2d 272, 261 Ill.Dec. 302 (2001).

2. *Harvey v. Care Initiatives, Inc.*, 634 N.W.2d 681 (Iowa 2001). Note that some courts might have held that a worker's discharge in these circumstances was contrary to public policy.

George Couto—was the marketing manager who actually negotiated the private labeling deal with Kaiser. Although Couto did not initiate the labeling scheme, he was instrumental in its success—despite the fact that he had suspected that the practice was illegal. Even though Couto had been a prime mover in the fraudulent scheme on behalf of Bayer, he was given 24 percent of the government's share of the $257 million settlement.[3]

Whistleblower statutes exist to encourage employees to report the wrongdoing of their employers with the ultimate objective of inhibiting such wrongdoing. But is it fair for an employee who participates in the employer's wrongdoing to benefit financially to such a large degree? Will this practice effectively inhibit, or could it even encourage, wrongful acts?

At-Will Employment

Because of the extensive array of statutory protections for workers, it is easy to lose sight of the fact that the majority of workers in the United States have the legal status of "employees at will" (see Chapter 20). An employer may fire at-will employees for any reason or no reason if they do not have employment contracts—unless, of course, the employees fall under the protection of a state or federal statute.

Statutes Do Not Protect All Employees A problem faced by many at-will employees is that federal and state statutes regulating the workplace do not apply to all employers. As already mentioned, the Family and Medical Leave Act applies only to employers that have fifty or more workers. Additionally, the major federal law prohibiting employment discrimination applies only to firms that have twenty-five or more employees and are engaged in interstate commerce. Similarly, state laws apply only to firms with a threshold number of employees, such as eight or ten employees. Even if an employer is subject to such statutes, these laws do not apply to many types of employment disputes, such as whether an employment contract was formed.

Exceptions to the At-Will Doctrine Sometimes, the only hope for plaintiffs in many employment disputes is that a court will make an exception to the at-will doctrine—on the basis of public policy, for example. The public-policy exception, though, remains just that—an exception. Often, courts are reluctant to make such an exception unless it can be justified by a clearly expressed public policy.

Consider an example. Lewis Kurtzman had worked in the pharmaceutical industry for over twenty years when he was contacted by Applied Analytical Industries, Inc. (AAI). AAI offered Kurtzman a job as director of sales for the company, which was located in Wilmington, North Carolina. AAI

representatives allegedly made such statements as "This is a long-term growth opportunity for you"; "This is a secure position"; and "We're offering you a career position." Relying on these assurances, Kurtzman and his family sold their home in Massachusetts and moved to Wilmington. Seven months after he began working for AAI, he was fired "without cause."

Kurtzman sued AAI, claiming that AAI had breached an implied employment contract under which his employment could not be terminated without some showing of cause. When the case ultimately reached the Supreme Court of North Carolina, however, that court stated that "[t]he employment-at-will doctrine has prevailed in this state for a century. The narrow exceptions to it have been grounded in considerations of public policy." According to the court, the facts in this case did not "present policy concerns of this nature. Rather, they are representative of negotiations and circumstances characteristically associated with traditional at-will employment situations."[4]

Age Discrimination

Today, some older employees face discrimination in the form of age-based harassment. In other words, they are subjected to offensive comments and conduct from their supervisors or co-workers simply because of their age.

An employee who experiences a hostile work environment because of racial or gender discrimination may file a claim against his or her employer under Title VII of the Civil Rights Act of 1964. In contrast, an employee who alleges a hostile work environment based on age has no such recourse—at least, according to many courts—under the Age Discrimination in Employment Act (ADEA) of 1967. Some argue that age-based hostile-environment claims should be recognized under the ADEA because the types of protections offered by the ADEA are so similar to those offered by Title VII. To date, however, only one federal appellate court—the U.S. Court of Appeals for the Sixth Circuit—has squarely addressed the question and concluded that the ADEA extends to hostile-environment age-based discrimination.[5] The other federal appellate courts either have not addressed the question or have dismissed such claims with no real analysis of the issue.

DISCUSSION QUESTIONS

1. How much obedience and loyalty does an agent-employee owe an employer? What if the employer engages in an activity—or requests that the employee engage in an activity—that violates the employee's ethical standards but does not necessarily violate any public policy or law? In such a situation, does an employee's duty to abide by her

---

3. Peter Aronson, "A Rogue to Catch a Rogue," *The National Law Journal,* August 18–25, 2003.

4. *Kurtzman v. Applied Analytical Industries, Inc.,* 347 N.C. 329, 493 S.E.2d 420 (1997).

5. *Crawford v. Medina General Hospital,* 96 F.3d 830 (6th Cir. 1996).

or his own ethical standards override the employee's duty of loyalty to the employer?

2. If an agent injures a third party during the course of employment, under the doctrine of *respondeat superior,* the employer may be held liable for the agent's actions even though the employer did not authorize the action and was not even aware of it. Do you think that it is fair to hold employers liable in such situations? Do you think that it would be more equitable to hold that the employee alone should bear the responsibility for his or her tortious (legally wrongful) actions to third parties, even when the actions are committed within the scope of employment?

3. Should an employee who is involved in but later "blows the whistle" on an employer's wrongdoing be allowed to collect a financial reward under whistleblower statutes? Why or why not?

4. Suppose that a company, as part of its job-benefits package for employees, provides free tuition for those employees who want to continue their education. The company, however, refuses to provide this educational benefit to workers over the age of fifty. Would this be a violation of the ADEA? May a company legally refuse to provide older workers with the same benefits as younger workers?

UNIT SIX
The Regulatory Environment

CONTENTS

CHAPTER 23
Consumer Protection

All statutes, agency rules, and common law judicial decisions that serve to protect the interests of consumers are classified as **consumer law.** Traditionally, in disputes involving consumers, it was assumed that the freedom to contract carried with it the obligation to live by the deal made. Over time, this attitude has changed considerably. Today, myriad federal and state laws protect consumers from unfair trade practices, unsafe products, discriminatory or unreasonable credit requirements, and other problems related to consumer transactions. Nearly every agency and department of the federal government has an office of consumer affairs, and most states have one or more such offices to help consumers. Also, typically the attorney general's office assists consumers at the state level.

In this chapter, we examine some of the major laws and regulations protecting consumers. Because of the wide variation among state consumer protection laws, our primary focus in this chapter is on federal legislation. Exhibit 23–1 indicates some of the types of consumer transactions that are regulated by federal laws.

SECTION 1 | Deceptive Advertising

One of the earliest federal consumer protection laws—and still one of the most important—was the Federal Trade Commission Act of 1914.[1] As mentioned in Chapter 6, the act created the Federal Trade Commission (FTC) to carry out the broadly stated goal of preventing unfair and deceptive trade practices, including deceptive advertising.[2]

DECEPTIVE ADVERTISING DEFINED

Advertising will be deemed deceptive if a consumer would be misled by the advertising claim. Vague generalities and obvious exaggerations are permissible. These claims are known as *puffery*. When a claim takes on the appearance of literal authenticity, however, it may create problems. Advertising that *appears* to be based on factual evidence but in fact is not will be deemed deceptive.

Some advertisements contain "half-truths," meaning that the presented information is true but incomplete and therefore leads consumers to a false conclusion. For example, the makers of Campbell's soups advertised that "most" Campbell's soups were low in fat and cholesterol and thus were helpful in fighting heart disease. What the ad did not say was that Campbell's soups are high in sodium, and high-sodium diets may increase the risk of heart disease. The FTC ruled that Campbell's claims were thus deceptive. Advertising that contains an endorsement by a celebrity may be deemed deceptive if the celebrity does not actually use the product.

BAIT-AND-SWITCH ADVERTISING

The FTC has issued rules that govern specific advertising techniques. One of the most important rules is contained in the FTC's "Guides Against Bait Advertising,"[3] issued in 1968. The rule seeks to prevent **bait-and-switch advertising**—that is, advertising a very low price for a particular item that will likely be unavailable to the consumer, who will then be encouraged to purchase a more expensive item. The low price is the "bait" to lure the consumer into the store. The salesperson is instructed to "switch" the consumer to a

---

1. 15 U.S.C. Sections 41–58.
2. 15 U.S.C. Section 45.

3. 16 C.F.R. Part 238.

EXHIBIT 23-1 Selected Areas of Consumer Law Regulated by Statutes

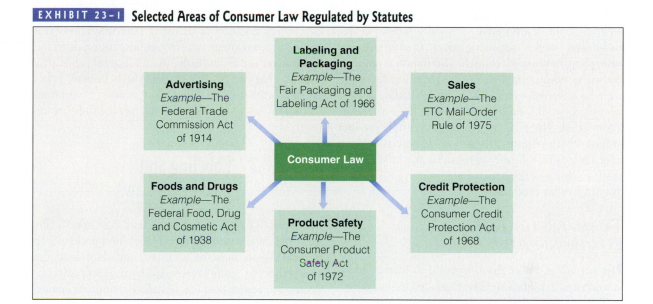

different, more expensive item. Under the FTC guidelines, bait-and-switch advertising occurs if the seller refuses to show the advertised item, fails to have a reasonable quantity of the item in stock, fails to promise to deliver the advertised item within a reasonable time, or discourages employees from selling the item.

ONLINE DECEPTIVE ADVERTISING

Deceptive advertising may occur in the online environment as well. For several years, the FTC has been quite active in monitoring online advertising and has identified hundreds of Web sites that have made false or deceptive advertising claims. These claims have concerned products ranging from medical treatments for various diseases to exercise equipment and weight-loss aids.

In 2000, the FTC issued new guidelines to help online businesses comply with existing laws prohibiting deceptive advertising.[4] The guidelines did not set forth new rules but rather described how existing laws apply to online advertising. Under the rules, generally any ads—online or offline—must be truthful and not misleading, and any claims made in an ad must be substantiated. Additionally, ads cannot be "unfair," defined in the guidelines as "caus[ing] or . . . likely to cause substantial consumer injury that consumers could not reasonably avoid and that is not outweighed by the benefit to consumers or competition."

4. *Advertising and Marketing on the Internet: Rules of the Road*, September 2000.

The guidelines also call for "clear and conspicuous" disclosure of any qualifying or limiting information. The FTC suggests that advertisers should assume that consumers will not read an entire Web page. Therefore, to satisfy the "clear and conspicuous" requirement, online advertisers should place the disclosure as close as possible to the claim being qualified or include the disclosure within the claim itself. If such placement is not feasible, the next-best placement is on a section of the page to which a consumer can easily scroll. Generally, hyperlinks to a disclosure are recommended only for lengthy disclosures or for disclosures that must be repeated in a variety of locations on the Web page.

FTC ACTIONS AGAINST DECEPTIVE ADVERTISING

The FTC receives complaints from many sources, including competitors of alleged violators, consumers, consumer organizations, trade associations, Better Business Bureaus, government organizations, and state and local officials. If enough consumers complain and the complaints are widespread, the FTC will investigate the problem. If the FTC concludes that a given advertisement is unfair or deceptive, it drafts a formal complaint, which is sent to the alleged offender. The company may agree to settle the complaint without further proceedings, or the FTC can conduct a hearing in which the company can present its defense (see Chapter 6).

If the FTC succeeds in proving that an advertisement is unfair or deceptive, it usually issues a **cease-and-desist order** requiring that the challenged advertising be stopped. It might also impose a sanction known as **counteradvertising** by requiring the company to advertise anew—in print, on radio, and on television—to inform the public about the earlier misinformation. The FTC may institute **multiple product orders,** which require a firm to cease and desist from false advertising not only in regard to the product that was the subject of the action but also in regard to all of the firm's other products.

TELEMARKETING AND ELECTRONIC ADVERTISING

The pervasive use of the telephone to market goods and services to homes and businesses led to the passage in 1991 of the Telephone Consumer Protection Act (TCPA).[5] The act prohibits telephone solicitation using an automatic telephone dialing system or a prerecorded voice. Most states also have laws regulating telephone solicitation. The TCPA also makes it illegal to transmit ads via fax without first obtaining the recipient's permission. (Similar issues have arisen with respect to junk e-mail, called *spam*—see Chapter 12.)

The act is enforced by the Federal Communications Commission and also provides for a private right of action. Consumers can recover any actual monetary loss resulting from a violation of the act or receive $500 in damages for each violation, whichever is greater. If a court finds that a defendant willfully or knowingly violated the act, the court has the discretion to treble (triple) the damages awarded.

The Telemarketing and Consumer Fraud and Abuse Prevention Act of 1994[6] directed the FTC to establish rules governing telemarketing and to bring actions against fraudulent telemarketers. The FTC's Telemarketing Sales Rule of 1995[7] requires a telemarketer, before making a sales pitch, to inform the recipient that the call is a sales call and to identify the seller's name and the product being sold. The rule makes it illegal for telemarketers to misrepresent information (including facts about their goods or services, for example). Additionally, telemarketers must inform the people they call of the total cost of the goods being sold, any restrictions on obtaining or using the goods, and whether a sale will be considered to be final and

nonrefundable. A telemarketer must also remove a consumer's name from its list of potential contacts if the customer so requests. An amendment made to the Telemarketing Sales Rule in 2002 established the national Do Not Call Registry, which became effective in October 2003. Telemarketers must refrain from calling those consumers who have placed their names on the list.

SECTION **2** | Labeling and Packaging Laws

A number of federal and state laws deal specifically with the information given on labels and packages. In general, labels must be accurate, and they must use words that are easily understood by the ordinary consumer. For example, a box of cereal cannot be labeled "giant" if that would exaggerate the amount of cereal contained in the box. In some instances, labels must specify the raw materials used in the product, such as the percentage of cotton, nylon, or other fiber used in a garment. In other instances, the product must carry a warning. Cigarette packages and advertising, for example, must include one of several warnings about the health hazards associated with smoking.[8] Some cigar manufacturers also have agreed to put warnings on the cigars they produce that are similar to what appears on cigarette packages.

FEDERAL STATUTES

Federal laws regulating the labeling and packaging of products include the Wool Products Labeling Act of 1939,[9] the Fur Products Labeling Act of 1951,[10] the Flammable Fabrics Act of 1953,[11] the Fair Packaging and Labeling Act of 1966,[12] the Comprehensive Smokeless Tobacco Health Education Act of 1986,[13] and the Nutrition Labeling and Education Act of 1990.[14] The Comprehensive Smokeless Tobacco Health Education Act, for example, requires that producers, packagers, and importers of smokeless tobacco label their product with one of several warnings about the health hazards associated with the use of smokeless

---

5. 47 U.S.C. Sections 227 *et seq.*
6. 15 U.S.C. Sections 6101–6108.
7. 16 C.F.R. Sections 310.1–310.8.

8. 15 U.S.C. Sections 1331–1341.
9. 15 U.S.C. Section 68.
10. 15 U.S.C. Section 69.
11. 15 U.S.C. Section 1191.
12. 15 U.S.C. Sections 1451 *et seq.*
13. 15 U.S.C. Sections 4401–4408.
14. 21 U.S.C. Section 343-1.

tobacco; the warnings are similar to those contained on other tobacco product packages.

FOOD LABELING

The Fair Packaging and Labeling Act requires that products carry labels that identify the product; the net quantity of the contents, as well as the quantity of servings, if the number of servings is stated; the manufacturer; and the packager or distributor. The act also authorizes requirements concerning words used to describe packages, terms that are associated with savings claims, information disclosures for ingredients in nonfood products, and standards for the partial filling of packages.

Food products must bear labels detailing nutritional content, including how much fat the food contains and what kind of fat it is. These restrictions are enforced by the Department of Health and Human Services, as well as the FTC. The Nutrition Labeling and Education Act of 1990 requires standard nutrition facts (including fat content) on food labels; regulates the use of such terms as *fresh* and *low fat*; and, subject to the federal Food and Drug Administration's approval, authorizes certain health claims.

SECTION 3 | Sales

Many of the laws that protect consumers concern the disclosure of certain terms in sales transactions and provide rules governing various forms of sales, such as door-to-door sales, mail-order sales, referral sales, and the unsolicited receipt of merchandise. Much of the federal regulation of sales is conducted by the FTC under its regulatory authority to curb unfair trade practices. Other federal agencies, however, are involved to various degrees. For example, the Federal Reserve Board of Governors has issued **Regulation Z,**[15] which governs credit provisions associated with sales contracts.

Many states have also enacted laws governing consumer sales transactions. Moreover, states have protected consumers to a certain extent through adopting the Uniform Commercial Code and, in a few states, the Uniform Consumer Credit Code.

DOOR-TO-DOOR SALES

Door-to-door sales are singled out for special treatment in the laws of most states, in part because of the nature of the sales transaction. Repeat purchases are not as likely as they are in stores, so the seller has less incentive to cultivate the goodwill of the purchaser. Furthermore, the seller is unlikely to present alternative products and their prices. Thus, a number of states have passed "cooling-off" laws that permit the buyers of goods sold door to door to cancel their contracts within a specified period of time, usually two to three days after the sale.

An FTC regulation also requires sellers to give consumers three days to cancel any door-to-door sale. Because this rule applies in addition to the relevant state statutes, consumers are given the most favorable benefits of the FTC rule and their own state statutes. In addition, the FTC rule requires that consumers be notified in Spanish of this right if the oral negotiations for the sale were in that language.

TELEPHONE AND MAIL-ORDER SALES

Sales made by either telephone or mail order are the greatest source of complaints to the nation's Better Business Bureaus. To a certain extent, consumers are protected under federal laws prohibiting mail fraud, which were discussed in Chapter 7, and under state consumer protection laws that parallel and supplement the federal laws.

The FTC Mail or Telephone Order Merchandise Rule of 1993, which amended the FTC Mail-Order Rule of 1975,[16] provides specific protections for consumers who purchase goods via phone lines or through the mails. The 1993 rule extended the 1975 rule to include sales in which orders are transmitted by computer, fax machine, or some similar means involving telephone lines. Among other things, the rule requires mail-order merchants to ship orders within the time promised in their catalogues or advertisements, to notify consumers when orders cannot be shipped on time, and to issue a refund within a specified period of time when a consumer cancels an order.

In addition, the Postal Reorganization Act of 1970[17] provides that *unsolicited* merchandise sent by U.S. mail may be retained, used, discarded, or disposed of in any manner deemed appropriate, without the recipient's incurring any obligation to the sender.

ONLINE SALES

In recent years, the Internet has become a vehicle for a wide variety of business-to-consumer (B2C) sales transactions. Protecting consumers from fraudulent

---

15. 12 C.F.R. Sections 226.1–226.30.

16. 16 C.F.R. Sections 435.1–435.2.
17. 39 U.S.C. Section 3009.

and deceptive sales practices conducted via the Internet has proved to be a challenging task. Nonetheless, the FTC and other federal agencies have brought a number of enforcement actions against those who perpetrate online fraud. Additionally, the laws mentioned earlier, such as the federal statute prohibiting wire fraud, apply to online transactions.

Some states have amended their consumer protection statutes to cover Internet transactions as well. For example, the California legislature revised its Business and Professions Code to include transactions conducted over the Internet or by "any other electronic means of communication." Previously, that code covered only telephone, mail-order catalogue, radio, and television sales. Now any entity selling over the Internet in California must explicitly create an on-screen notice indicating its refund and return policies, where its business is physically located, its legal name, and a number of other details. Various states are also setting up information sites to help consumers protect themselves.

SECTION 4 | Credit Protection

Because of the extensive use of credit by American consumers, credit protection has become an especially important area regulated by consumer protection legislation. One of the most significant statutes regulating the credit and credit-card industries is Title I of the Consumer Credit Protection Act (CCPA),[18] which is commonly referred to as the Truth-in-Lending Act (TILA).

THE TRUTH-IN-LENDING ACT

The TILA is basically a *disclosure law*. It is administered by the Federal Reserve Board and requires sellers and lenders to disclose credit terms or loan terms so that individuals can shop around for the best financing arrangements. TILA requirements apply only to persons who, in the ordinary course of business, lend funds, sell on credit, or arrange for the extension of credit. Thus, sales or loans made between two consumers do not come under the protection of the act. Additionally, only debtors who are natural persons (as opposed to the artificial "person" of a corporation) are protected by this law; other legal entities are not.

The disclosure requirements are contained in Regulation Z, which, as mentioned earlier in this chapter, was promulgated by the Federal Reserve Board. If the contracting parties are subject to the TILA, the requirements of Regulation Z apply to any transaction involving an installment sales contract in which payment is to be made in more than four installments. Transactions subject to Regulation Z typically include installment loans, retail and installment sales, car loans, home-improvement loans, and certain real estate loans if the amount of financing is less than $25,000.

Under the provisions of the TILA, all of the terms of a credit instrument must be clearly and conspicuously disclosed. The TILA provides for contract rescission (cancellation) if a creditor fails to follow *exactly* the procedures required by the act.[19] TILA requirements are strictly enforced.

EQUAL CREDIT OPPORTUNITY   In 1974, the Equal Credit Opportunity Act (ECOA)[20] was enacted as an amendment to the TILA. The ECOA prohibits the denial of credit solely on the basis of race, religion, national origin, color, gender, marital status, or age. The act also prohibits credit discrimination on the basis of whether an individual receives certain forms of income, such as public-assistance benefits.

Under the ECOA, a creditor may not require the signature of an applicant's spouse, other than as a joint applicant, on a credit instrument if the applicant qualifies under the creditor's standards of creditworthiness for the amount and terms of the credit request. Creditors are permitted to ask for any information from a credit applicant except information that could be used for the type of discrimination covered in the act or its amendments.

CREDIT-CARD RULES   The TILA also contains provisions regarding credit cards. One provision limits the liability of a cardholder to $50 per card for unauthorized charges made before the creditor is notified that the card has been lost. Another provision prohibits a credit-card company from billing a consumer for any unauthorized charges if the credit card was improperly issued by the company; for example, if a consumer receives an unsolicited credit card in the mail and the

---

18. 15 U.S.C. Sections 1601–1693r.

19. Note, however, that amendments to the TILA enacted in 1995 prevent borrowers from rescinding loans because of minor clerical errors in closing documents [15 U.S.C. Sections 1605, 1631, 1635, 1640, and 1641].

20. 15 U.S.C. Sections 1691–1691f.

card is later stolen and used by the thief to make purchases, the consumer to whom the card was sent will not be liable for the unauthorized charges.

Further provisions of the act concern billing disputes related to credit-card purchases. If a debtor thinks that an error has occurred in billing or wishes to withhold payment for a faulty product purchased by credit card, the act outlines specific procedures for both the consumer and the credit-card company to follow in settling the dispute.

CONSUMER LEASES The Consumer Leasing Act (CLA) of 1988[21] amended the TILA to provide protection for consumers who lease automobiles and other goods. The CLA applies to those who lease or arrange to lease consumer goods in the ordinary course of their business. The act applies only if the goods are priced at $25,000 or less and if the lease term exceeds four months. The CLA and its implementing regulation, Regulation M,[22] require lessors to disclose in writing all of the material terms of the lease.

The Fair Credit Reporting Act

In 1970, to protect consumers against inaccurate credit reporting, Congress enacted the Fair Credit Reporting Act (FCRA).[23] The act provides that consumer credit reporting agencies may issue credit reports to users only for specified purposes, including the extension of credit, the issuance of insurance policies, compliance with a court order, and in response to a consumer's request for a copy of his or her own credit report. The act further provides that whenever a consumer is denied credit or insurance on the basis of her or his

credit report, or is charged more than others ordinarily would be for credit or insurance, the consumer must be notified of that fact and of the name and address of the credit reporting agency that issued the credit report.

CONSUMER ACCESS TO INFORMATION Under the FCRA, consumers may request the source of any information being given out by a credit agency, as well as the identity of anyone who has received an agency's report. Consumers are also permitted to access information about them contained in a credit reporting agency's files. If a consumer discovers that an agency's files contain inaccurate information about his or her credit standing, the agency, on the consumer's written request, must investigate the matter and delete any unverifiable or erroneous information within a reasonable period of time.

An agency that fails to comply with the act is liable for actual damages, plus additional damages not to exceed $1,000 and attorneys' fees.[24] Damages are also available from anyone who uses a credit report for an improper purpose, as well as from banks and other companies that report information to credit agencies and do not respond adequately to customer complaints.

REPORTING AGENCY MUST INVESTIGATE DISPUTED INFORMATION The agency's investigation should include contacting the creditor whose information a consumer disputes; the creditor, after receiving notice of the dispute, normally should conduct a "reasonable investigation" of its records to determine whether the disputed information can be verified. The question in the following case was exactly what constitutes a "reasonable investigation" by the creditor.

---

21. 15 U.S.C. Sections 1667–1667e.
22. 12 C.F.R. Part 213.
23. 15 U.S.C. Sections 1681–1681t.

24. 15 U.S.C. Section 1681n.

CASE 23.1	**Johnson v. MBNA America Bank, N.A.**

United States
Court of Appeals,
Fourth Circuit, 2004.
357 F.3d 426.

WILLIAM W. WILKINS, Chief Judge:

MBNA America Bank, N.A. (MBNA) appeals a judgment entered against it following a jury verdict in favor of Linda Johnson in her action alleging that MBNA violated a provision of the Fair Credit Reporting Act (FCRA) by failing to conduct a reasonable investigation of Johnson's dispute concerning an MBNA account appearing on her credit report. * * *
* * * *

The account at issue, an MBNA MasterCard account, was opened in November 1987. The parties disagree regarding who applied for this account and therefore who was legally obligated to pay amounts owed on it. It is undisputed that one of the applicants was Edward N. Slater, whom Johnson married in March 1991. MBNA contends that Johnson was a co-applicant

CASE 23.1 | Continued

with Slater, and thus a co-obligor on the account. Johnson claims, however, that she was merely an authorized user and not a co-applicant.

In December 2000, Slater filed for bankruptcy, and MBNA promptly removed his name from the account. That same month, MBNA contacted Johnson and informed her that she was responsible for the approximately $17,000 balance on the account. * * * Johnson disputed the MBNA account with [consumer] credit reporting agencies. In response, each credit reporting agency [notified] MBNA * * * . In response * * * , MBNA * * * verified that the disputed information was correct. Based on MBNA's responses * * * , the credit reporting agencies continued reporting the MBNA account on Johnson's credit report.

Johnson subsequently sued MBNA [in a federal district court] * * * . [A] jury found that MBNA had negligently failed to comply with the FCRA, and it awarded Johnson $90,300 in actual damages. * * *

* * * *

MBNA argues that the language of [the FCRA] requiring furnishers of credit information to "conduct an investigation" regarding disputed information, imposes only a minimal duty on creditors to briefly review their records to determine whether the disputed information is correct. Stated differently, MBNA contends that this provision does not contain any qualitative component that would allow courts or juries to assess whether the creditor's investigation was reasonable. By contrast, Johnson asserts [the FCRA] requires creditors to conduct a reasonable investigation. * * *

* * * *

The key term at issue here, "investigation," is defined [in dictionaries] as "a detailed inquiry or systematic examination." Thus, the plain meaning of "investigation" clearly requires some degree of careful inquiry by creditors. Further, [the FCRA] uses the term "investigation" in the context of articulating a creditor's duties in the consumer dispute process * * * . It would make little sense to conclude that, in creating a system intended to give consumers a means to dispute—and, ultimately, correct—inaccurate information on their credit reports, Congress used the term "investigation" to include superficial, *un*reasonable inquiries by creditors. We therefore hold that *[the FCRA] requires creditors, after receiving notice of a consumer dispute from a credit reporting agency, to conduct a reasonable investigation of their records to determine whether the disputed information can be verified.* [Emphasis added.]

* * * *

MBNA next contends that even if [the FCRA] requires creditors to conduct reasonable investigations of consumer disputes, no evidence here supports a determination * * * that MBNA's investigation of Johnson's dispute was unreasonable. * * *

* * * MBNA was notified of the specific nature of Johnson's dispute—namely, her assertion that she was not a co-obligor on the account. Yet MBNA's agents testified that their investigation was primarily limited to (1) confirming that the name and address listed on the [correspondence from the credit reporting agencies] were the same as the name and address contained in [MBNA's database] and (2) noting that the [database] contained a code indicating that Johnson was the sole responsible party on the account. The MBNA agents also testified that, in investigating consumer disputes generally, they do not look beyond the information contained in the [database] and never consult underlying documents such as account applications. Based on this evidence, a [court] could reasonably conclude that MBNA acted unreasonably in failing to verify the accuracy of the information contained in the [database].

* * * *

Additionally, MBNA argues that Johnson failed to establish that MBNA's allegedly inadequate investigation was the proximate cause of her damages because there were no other records MBNA could have examined that would have changed the results of its investigation. In particular, MBNA relies on testimony that * * * the original account application was no longer in MBNA's possession. Even accepting this testimony, however, a [court] could reasonably conclude that if the MBNA agents had investigated the matter further and determined that MBNA no longer had the application, they could have at least informed the credit reporting agencies that MBNA could not conclusively verify that Johnson was a co-obligor.

* * * *

For the reasons set forth above, we affirm the judgment of the district court.

 **Continued**

QUESTIONS

1. What should a consumer do, before applying for credit, to avoid disputes such as the confrontation that arose in the *Johnson* case?
2. What costs should be weighed in determining whether a creditor's investigation of a consumer's dispute is reasonable under the FCRA?

FAIR AND ACCURATE CREDIT TRANSACTIONS ACT

In an effort to combat identity theft (discussed in Chapter 7), Congress passed the Fair and Accurate Credit Transactions Act (FACT Act) of 2003.[25] The act established a national fraud alert system so that consumers who suspect that they have been or may be victimized by identity theft can place an alert on their credit files. The act also requires the major credit reporting agencies to provide consumers with a free copy of their own credit report every twelve months. Another provision requires account numbers on credit-card receipts to be shortened ("truncated") so that merchants, employees, or others who may have access to the receipts do not have access to the consumers' names and full credit-card numbers. The act further mandates that financial institutions work with the Federal Trade Commission to identify "red flag" indicators of identity theft and to develop rules on how to dispose of sensitive credit information.

The FACT Act gives consumers who have been victimized by identity theft some assistance in rebuilding their credit reputations. For example, credit reporting agencies must stop reporting allegedly fraudulent account information once the consumer establishes that identify theft has occurred. Business owners and creditors are required to provide consumers with copies of any records that can help the consumer prove that the particular account or transaction is fraudulent (a forged signature, for example). In addition, the act allows consumers to report the accounts affected by identity theft directly to creditors in order to help prevent the spread of erroneous credit information.

THE FAIR DEBT COLLECTION PRACTICES ACT

In 1977, Congress enacted the Fair Debt Collection Practices Act (FDCPA)[26] in an attempt to curb what were perceived to be abuses by collection agencies. The act applies only to specialized debt-collection agencies that regularly attempt to collect debts on behalf of someone else, usually for a percentage of the amount owed. Creditors attempting to collect debts are not covered by the act unless, by misrepresenting themselves, they cause debtors to believe they are collection agencies.

REQUIREMENTS UNDER THE ACT The act explicitly prohibits a collection agency from using any of the following tactics:

1. Contacting the debtor at the debtor's place of employment if the debtor's employer objects.
2. Contacting the debtor during inconvenient or unusual times (for example, calling the debtor at three o'clock in the morning) or at any time if the debtor is being represented by an attorney.
3. Contacting third parties other than the debtor's parents, spouse, or financial adviser about payment of a debt unless a court authorizes such action.
4. Using harassment or intimidation (for example, using abusive language or threatening violence) or employing false or misleading information (for example, posing as a police officer).
5. Communicating with the debtor at any time after receiving notice that the debtor is refusing to pay the debt, except to advise the debtor of further action to be taken by the collection agency.

The FDCPA also requires a collection agency to include a **validation notice** whenever it initially contacts a debtor for payment of a debt or within five days of that initial contact. The notice must state that the debtor has thirty days within which to dispute the debt and to request a written verification of the debt from the collection agency. The debtor's request for debt validation must be in writing.

ENFORCEMENT OF THE ACT The enforcement of the FDCPA is primarily the responsibility of the Federal Trade Commission. The act provides that a debt collector who fails to comply with the act is liable for actual damages, plus additional damages not to exceed $1,000[27] and attorneys' fees.

---

25. Pub. L. No. 108-159, 117 Stat. 1952 (December 4, 2003).
26. 15 U.S.C. Section 1692.

27. According to the U.S. Court of Appeals for the Sixth Circuit, the $1,000 limit on damages applies to each lawsuit, not to each violation. See *Wright v. Finance Service of Norwalk, Inc.*, 22 F.3d 647 (6th Cir. 1994).

Cases brought under the FDCPA often raise questions as to who qualifies as a debt collector or debt-collection agency subject to the act. For example, for several years it was not clear whether attorneys who attempted to collect debts owed to their clients were subject to the FDCPA's provisions. In 1995, the United States Supreme Court addressed this issue to resolve conflicting opinions in the lower courts. The Court held that an attorney who regularly tries to obtain payment of consumer debts through legal proceedings meets the FDCPA's definition of "debt collector."[28]

GARNISHMENT OF WAGES

Despite the increasing number of protections afforded debtors, creditors are not without means of securing payment on debts. One of these is the right to garnish a debtor's wages after the debt has gone unpaid for a prolonged period. Recall from Chapter 15 that *garnishment* is the legal procedure by which a creditor may collect on a debt by directly attaching, or seizing, a portion of the debtor's assets (such as wages) that are in the possession of a third party (such as an employer).

State law provides the basis for a process of garnishment, but the law varies among the states as to how easily garnishment can be obtained. Indeed, a few states, such as Texas, prohibit garnishment of wages except for child support and court-approved spousal maintenance. Constitutional due process and federal legislation under the TILA also provide certain protections against abuse.[29] In general, the debtor is entitled to notice and an opportunity to be heard in a process of garnishment. Moreover, wages cannot be garnished beyond 25 percent of the debtor's after-tax earnings, and the garnishment must leave the debtor with at least a specified minimum income.

SECTION 5 | Consumer Health and Safety

Laws discussed earlier regarding the labeling and packaging of products go a long way toward promoting consumer health and safety. But there is a significant distinction between regulating the information dispensed about a product and regulating the content of the product itself. The classic example is tobacco products. Tobacco products have not been altered by regulation or banned outright despite their obvious hazards. What has been regulated are the warnings that producers are required to give consumers about the hazards of tobacco.[30] This section focuses on laws that regulate the actual products made available to consumers.

THE FEDERAL FOOD, DRUG AND COSMETIC ACT

The first federal legislation regulating food and drugs was enacted in 1906 as the Pure Food and Drugs Act. That law, as amended in 1938, exists currently as the Federal Food, Drug and Cosmetic Act (FFDCA).[31] The act protects consumers against adulterated and misbranded foods and drugs. More recent amendments have added substantive and procedural requirements to the act. In its present form, the act establishes food standards, specifies safe levels of potentially hazardous food additives, and sets classifications of food and food advertising.

Most of these statutory requirements are monitored and enforced by the Food and Drug Administration (FDA). Under an extensive set of procedures established by the FDA, drugs must be shown to be effective as well as safe before they may be marketed to the public, and the use of some food additives suspected of being carcinogenic is prohibited. A 1976 amendment to the FFDCA[32] authorizes the FDA to regulate medical devices, such as pacemakers and other health devices and equipment, and to withdraw from the market any such device that is mislabeled.

THE CONSUMER PRODUCT SAFETY ACT

Consumer product-safety legislation began in 1953 with the passage of the Flammable Fabrics Act, which prohibits the sale of highly flammable clothing or materials. Over the next two decades, Congress enacted legislation regarding the design or composition of specific classes of products. Then, in 1972, Congress, by enacting the Consumer Product Safety Act,[33] created a comprehensive scheme of regulation over matters of consumer safety. The act also established the Consumer Product Safety Commission (CPSC), which has far-reaching authority over consumer safety.

---

28. *Heintz v. Jenkins*, 514 U.S. 291, 115 S.Ct. 1489, 131 L.Ed.2d 395 (1995).
29. 15 U.S.C. Sections 1671–1677.
30. We are ignoring recent civil litigation concerning the liability of tobacco product manufacturers for injuries that arise from the use of tobacco.
31. 21 U.S.C. Sections 301–393.
32. 21 U.S.C. Sections 352(o), 360(j), 360(k), and 360c–360k.
33. 15 U.S.C. Sections 2051–2083.

THE CPSC'S AUTHORITY The CPSC conducts research on the safety of individual consumer products, and it maintains a clearinghouse of information on the risks associated with various products. The Consumer Product Safety Act authorizes the CPSC to set standards for consumer products and to ban the manufacture and sale of any product that it deems to be potentially hazardous to consumers. The CPSC also has authority to remove from the market any products it believes to be imminently hazardous and to require manufacturers to report on any products already sold or intended for sale if the products have proved to be dangerous. The CPSC also has authority to administer other product-safety legislation, such as the Child Protection and Toy Safety Act of 1969[34] and the Federal Hazardous Substances Act of 1960.[35]

The CPSC's authority is sufficiently broad to allow it to ban any product that it believes poses an "unreasonable risk" to consumers. Some of the products that the CPSC has banned include various types of fireworks, cribs, and toys, as well as many products containing asbestos or vinyl chloride.

NOTIFICATION REQUIREMENTS The Consumer Product Safety Act requires the distributors of consumer products to notify immediately the CPSC on receipt of information that a product "contains a defect which . . . creates a substantial risk to the public" or "an unreasonable risk of serious injury or death." The following case illustrates the consequences of failing to fulfill this requirement.

---

34. This act consists of amendments to 15 U.S.C. Sections 1261, 1262, and 1274.
35. 15 U.S.C. Sections 1261–1277.

CASE 23.2 **United States v. Mirama Enterprises, Inc.**

United States
Court of Appeals,
Ninth Circuit, 2004.
387 F.3d 983.

BACKGROUND AND FACTS *Mirama Enterprises, Inc., began operations in 1996 and today does business as Aroma Housewares Company from its headquarters in San Diego, California. Aroma imports a variety of electric kitchen appliances from China and Taiwan and distributes them to retailers in the United States and abroad. From 1996 until 1998, Aroma distributed a juice extractor, or juicer, made by a company in Taiwan, to retail stores throughout the United States. In early January 1998, Aroma received a complaint from a consumer whose juicer had broken. In February, consumer Richard Norton wrote Aroma to report that his juicer had shattered. In capital letters, Norton stated that the juicer*

> *SUDDENLY EXPLODED, THROWING WITH GREAT VIOLENCE PIECES OF THE CLEAR PLASTIC COVER AND SHREDS OF THE RAZOR-SHARP SEPARATOR SCREEN AS FAR AS EIGHT FEET IN MY KITCHEN. * * ***

Over the next months, twenty-three complaints about exploding juicers, some of which caused injuries, were made by consumers including Jan Griffin, who added, "I feel that this juicer should be recalled, as it is very unsafe. The injuries that I suffered could have been a lot worse." In August, consumer Sylvia Mendoza filed a suit against Aroma, alleging injuries caused by a shattering juicer. On November 16, Aroma filed a report with the CPSC, which recalled the juicer on June 30, 1999. The federal government filed a suit against Mirama, seeking damages for its alleged failure to notify the CPSC of the danger earlier. The government filed a motion for summary judgment. The court ruled in the government's favor. Mirama appealed to the U.S. Court of Appeals for the Ninth Circuit.

IN THE LANGUAGE OF THE COURT

KOZINSKI, Circuit Judge:
* * * *
 * * * [T]he [lower] court held that Aroma's failure to report each potentially dangerous product sold or distributed for sale to consumers was a separate offense, bringing the total number of offenses to somewhere between 30,000 and 40,000. The court ordered the company to pay $300,000 * * * .

Aroma does not contest liability; it challenges only the penalty * * * .

CONTINUED

* * * *

* * * Aroma suggests there is a single violation because only one product line is involved, albeit one of which there were numerous identical units sold. Alternatively, Aroma argues that it violated the reporting requirement at most twenty-three times—once for each failure to report a juicer that a consumer claimed had exploded. * * *

Initially, we consider Aroma's suggestion that "consumer product" in [the Consumer Product Safety Act (CPSA)] refers to the juicer model rather than to the individual units sold. This interpretation is problematic in view of the CPSA's penalty scheme, which imposes a small fine for each violation, capped at a much larger amount in the aggregate. The statutory cap necessarily contemplates that a single defect may affect a large number of products: Regardless of adjustments for inflation, the penalty caps out only after 250 violations. Aroma's interpretation would effectively render the cap meaningless. While a few product lines may share a common defect, it is almost inconceivable that 250 separate lines would possess the same defect. We will not presume that Congress adopted a statutory maximum that could never be reached.

Interpreting "consumer product" to refer to the product line also conflicts with the CPSA's definition of consumer product as "any *article*, or component part thereof, produced or distributed" for sale to or use by a consumer. The ordinary meaning of "article" refers to an individual member of a class (such as a unit of Aroma's juicer line), rather than the class (or product line) itself. *[The CPSA] thus requires that distributors report each individual unit about which they receive information that "reasonably supports the conclusion that such product * * * contains a defect which could create a substantial product hazard * * * or * * * creates an unreasonable risk of serious injury or death."* Accordingly [the CPSA's] provision that violations "shall constitute a separate offense with respect to each consumer product involved" means that a company commits a separate offense for every potentially dangerous unit it fails to report. [Emphasis added.]

* * * Aroma received consumer complaints for only twenty-three units. But the fact that some two dozen units malfunctioned in precisely the same way is evidence that those units share a common defect, which may affect each of the thousands of identical units Aroma distributed. Indeed, it would make little sense to focus only on the particular units discovered to be defective rather than those others that may possess the same flaw. * * *

Our interpretation is supported by the fact that consumer complaints are not the only source of information that can trigger [the CPSA's] reporting requirement. [Consumer Product Safety] Commission regulations note that "[s]uch information can include reports from experts, test reports, product liability lawsuits or claims, * * * quality control data, scientific or epidemiological studies, reports of injury, information from other firms or government entities, and other relevant information." Aroma's proposed reading would squeeze much of the juice out of the statute: Companies would have no incentive to report information that they obtained through their own testing or any source other than consumer complaints, even if it clearly suggested a risk of serious injury or death, because they would face no penalties for failing to report.

DECISION AND REMEDY *The U.S. Court of Appeals for the Ninth Circuit affirmed the lower court's judgment. "Aroma was required to report not merely the twenty-three juicers that shattered, but the 30,000 to 40,000 juicers in the stream of commerce that might well pose an unreasonable risk of serious injury to consumers. When it failed to do so, Aroma committed 30,000 to 40,000 reporting offenses."*

SECTION 6 | State Consumer Protection Laws

Thus far, our primary focus has been on federal legislation. State laws, however, often provide more sweeping and significant protections for the consumer than do federal laws. The warranty and unconscionability provisions of the Uniform Commercial Code (UCC—discussed in Chapter 11) offer important protections for consumers against unfair practices on the part of sellers and lessors.

Far less widely adopted than the UCC is the Uniform Consumer Credit Code (UCCC). The

UCCC has provisions concerning truth in lending, maximum credit ceilings, door-to-door sales, fine-print clauses, and other practices affecting consumer transactions.

Virtually all states have specific consumer protection acts, often titled "deceptive trade practices acts." Although these statutes vary widely, a common thread runs through most of them. Typically, state consumer protection laws are directed at deceptive trade practices, such as a seller's provision of false or misleading information to consumers. As just mentioned, some of the legislation provides broad protection for consumers. A prime example is the Texas Deceptive Trade Practices Act of 1973, which forbids a seller from selling to a buyer anything that the buyer does not need or cannot afford.

In California, in the 1950s, unscrupulous promoters were misrepresenting their services to obtain unjustified payments from property owners for real estate transactions. Therefore, in 1959 the state restricted the collection of "advance fees" to those with state-issued licenses, except for "newspapers of general circulation," which were found not to have engaged in any fraud. In the following case, the court considered whether this interpretation could be applied to an out-of-state, Internet-based service.

CASE 23.3   ForSaleByOwner.com v. Zinnemann

United States District Court, Eastern District of California, 2004. 347 F.Supp.2d 868.

BACKGROUND AND FACTS *ForSaleByOwner.com (FSBO) advertises residential real property for sale. FSBO charges a flat fee to owners to advertise their homes. The Web site lists the properties in a nationwide database that prospective buyers can view at no charge. FSBO also provides information about home sales, crime, schools, costs of living in specific locales, mortgage payments, and interest rates. To providers of related services (home-improvement contractors and others), FSBO sells listings in an online directory. FSBO is not a real estate agent, and proclaims on its site that it is "legally prohibited from taking part in the actual sales transaction of any of the properties." Under California Business and Professions Code Section 10130, it is unlawful for any person or company to act as a real estate broker without first obtaining a state license. Sections 10026, 10131, and 10131.2 define* real estate broker *to include anyone—except newspapers—who, for an "advance fee," lists residential real property for sale. FSBO filed a suit in a federal district court against Paula Zinnemann, Commissioner of the California Department of Real Estate, and others, claiming that this statute violated FSBO's rights under the First Amendment to the U.S. Constitution. FSBO filed a motion for summary judgment.*

IN THE LANGUAGE OF THE COURT

ENGLAND, District Judge.

    *   *   *   *

FSBO argues that California's real estate licensing laws *   *   * "single out" publishers of real estate advertising and information, like FSBO, for a burden the state places on no other speech and is directed only at works with a specified content. FSBO contends that publishers of other sales magazines or websites for different products (like automobiles, jewelry or boats, for instance) are not required to be licensed, and even more significantly argues that newspapers *   *   * are exempt from real estate licensing requirements despite the fact that they offer services virtually identical to those provided by FSBO. According to FSBO, this *differential treatment is unconstitutional unless the State's regulation is necessary to serve a compelling state interest and is narrowly drawn to achieve that end.* [Emphasis added.]

FSBO's argument that [the statute] unconstitutionally discriminates based on media type is persuasive. The Court agrees that California's real estate licensing scheme impermissibly differentiates between certain types of publications carrying the same basic content. *   *   * Given the uncontroverted fact that FSBO's activities are virtually identical to those pursued online by California newspapers, the distinction drawn between the two publishing mediums appears wholly arbitrary.

    *   *   *   *

*   *   * Indeed, given the fact that the online newspaper services and the FSBO website are virtually identical, there appears to be no justification whatsoever for any distinction

CONTINUED

CASE 23.3 | Continued

between the two mediums. Even if a distinction was warranted in 1959, when the statute was amended to include the newspaper exemption, that does not mean that the same rationale for exempting newspapers remains viable in 2004, given the vast advances in technology that have occurred in the meantime.

As FSBO points out, if use of the Internet itself justifies state regulation, that would logically suggest that both online newspaper services and websites like FSBO's should be equally restricted. Instead, however, online newspaper advertising for real property is not subject to licensing, whereas the very same information disseminated by FSBO requires a real estate broker's license. That license entails substantial coursework requirements as well as passage of a rigorous broker's exam. Defendants have simply shown no compelling need why such requirements must be satisfied in the case of FSBO but need not be adhered to by newspapers.

* * * Defendants suggest that FSBO accepts fees from mortgage brokers for business generated through a website referral process, despite the fact that no such referral service is even available on the FSBO website for users in California. The only other specific activity targeted by Defendants concerns referral fees paid by FSBO for customers directed through other websites.

Defendants have not demonstrated that these arrangements are improper, or that licensing will do anything to prevent or regulate any resulting improprieties. Defendants make no effort to show how regulating such activities constitutes a compelling state interest, not to mention whether requiring FSBO to obtain a broker's license is a remedy narrowly tailored to address such an interest. Otherwise, while Defendants vaguely attempt to paint newspapers as geographically situated and relatively more stable than Internet companies, they have not established why this should require websites like FSBO's to obtain a California broker's license as a prerequisite to listing properties for sale, when online services doing exactly the same thing are not subject to any licensing requirement so long as they are operated by a "newspaper." Defendants provide no reasonable explanation whatsoever for this differential treatment, let alone a compelling interest to justify it.

DECISION AND REMEDY *The court granted FSBO's motion for summary judgment. The court reasoned that the California statute, as applied to FSBO, was unconstitutional, based on the "disparity of treatment" between newspapers and Web sites such as that of FSBO. The defendants failed to show "any compelling state interest" for requiring FSBO to obtain a broker's license, while identical online services were exempt if newspapers operated them.*

WHAT IF THE FACTS WERE DIFFERENT? *If newspapers published real estate listings only in print and did not provide the same services as FSBO online, would the result have been different?*

REVIEWING CONSUMER PROTECTION

Tonja Sage saw a local motorcycle dealer's newspaper advertisement for a MetroRider EZ electric scooter for $1,699. When she met the salesperson at the dealership, however, she learned that the EZ model had been sold out. The salesperson told Sage that he still had the higher-end MetroRider FX model in stock for $2,199 and would offer her one for $1,999. Sage was disappointed but decided to purchase the FX model. Sage told the sales representative that she wished to purchase the scooter on credit and was directed to the dealer's credit department. As she filled out the credit forms, the clerk told Sage, an African American female, that she would need a cosigner to obtain a loan. Sage could not understand why she would need a cosigner and asked to speak to the store manager. The manager apologized, told her that the clerk was mistaken, and said that he would "speak to"

REVIEWING CONSUMER PROTECTION—Continued

the clerk about that. The manager completed Sage's credit application, and Sage then rode the scooter home. Seven months later, Sage received a letter from the manufacturer informing her that a flaw had been discovered in the scooter's braking system and that the model had been recalled. Using the information presented in the chapter, answer the following questions.

1. Had the dealer engaged in deceptive advertising? If so, what form of deceptive advertising was involved? What may the Federal Trade Commission (FTC) order the dealer to do if the ad proved deceptive?

2. Suppose that Sage had ordered the scooter through the dealer's Web site but the dealer had been unable to deliver it by the date promised. What would the merchant be required to do, and what FTC regulation requires the merchant to do it?

3. Assuming that the clerk had required a cosigner based on Sage's race or gender, what act prohibits such credit discrimination?

4. The safety of the scooter is regulated by what organization? How?

TERMS AND CONCEPTS TO REVIEW

bait-and-switch advertising 556   counteradvertising 558   validation notice 563

cease-and-desist order 558   multiple product orders 558

consumer law 556   Regulation Z 559

QUESTIONS AND CASE PROBLEMS

23-1. Andrew, a resident of California, received an advertising circular in the U.S. mail announcing a new line of regional cookbooks distributed by the Every-Kind Cookbook Co. Andrew didn't want any books and threw the circular away. Two days later, Andrew received in the mail an introductory cookbook entitled *Lower Mongolian Regional Cookbook*, as announced in the circular, on a "trial basis" from Every-Kind. Andrew was not interested but did not go to the trouble to return the cookbook. Every-Kind demanded payment of $20.95 for the *Lower Mongolian Regional Cookbook*. Discuss whether Andrew can be required to pay for the book.

23-2. Maria Ochoa receives two new credit cards on May 1. She had solicited one of them from Midtown Department Store, and the other arrived unsolicited from High-Flying Airlines. During the month of May, Ochoa makes numerous credit-card purchases from Midtown Department Store, but she does not use the High-Flying Airlines card. On May 31, a burglar breaks into Ochoa's home and steals both credit cards, along with other items. Ochoa notifies the Midtown Department Store of the theft on June 2, but she fails to notify High-Flying Airlines. Using the Midtown credit card, the burglar makes a $500 purchase on June 1 and a $200 purchase on June 3. The burglar then charges a vacation flight on the High-Flying Airlines card for $1,000 on June 5. Ochoa receives the bills for these charges and refuses to pay them. Discuss Ochoa's liability in these situations.

23-3. **QUESTION WITH SAMPLE ANSWER**

On June 28, a salesperson for Renowned Books called on the Gonchars at their home. After a very persuasive sales pitch by the agent, the Gonchars agreed in writing to purchase a twenty-volume set of historical encyclopedias from Renowned Books for a total of $299. A down payment of $35 was required, with the remainder of the cost to be paid in monthly payments over a one-year period. Two days later the Gonchars, having second thoughts, contacted the book company and stated that they had decided to rescind the contract. Renowned Books said this would be impossible. Has Renowned Books violated any consumer law by not allowing the Gonchars to rescind their contract? Explain.
For a sample answer to this question, go to Appendix I at the end of this text.

23–4. EQUAL CREDIT OPPORTUNITY. The Riggs National Bank of Washington, D.C., loaned more than $11 million to Samuel Linch and Albert Randolph. To obtain the loan, Linch and Randolph provided personal financial statements. Linch's statement included substantial assets that he owned jointly with his wife, Marcia. As a condition of the loan, Riggs required that Marcia, as well as Samuel and Albert, sign a personal guaranty for repayment. When the borrowers defaulted, Riggs filed a suit in a federal district court to recover its funds, based on the personal guaranties. The court ruled against the borrowers, who appealed. On what basis might the borrowers argue that Riggs violated the Equal Credit Opportunity Act? [*Riggs National Bank of Washington, D.C. v. Linch*, 36 F.3d 370 (4th Cir. 1994)]

23–5. DEBT COLLECTION. Equifax A.R.S., a debt-collection agency, sent Donna Russell a notice about one of her debts. The front of the notice stated that "[i]f you do not dispute this claim (see reverse side) and wish to pay it within the next 10 days we will not post this collection to your file." The reverse side set out Russell's rights under the Fair Debt Collection Practices Act (FDCPA), including that she had thirty days to decide whether to contest the claim. Russell filed a suit in a federal district court against Equifax. The court ruled against Russell, who appealed. On what basis might Russell argue that Equifax violated the FDCPA? [*Russell v. Equifax A.R.S.*, 74 F.3d 30 (2d Cir. 1996)]

23–6. FAIR DEBT COLLECTION. CrossCheck, Inc., provides check-authorization services to retail merchants. When a customer presents a check, the merchant contacts CrossCheck, which estimates the probability that the check will clear the bank. If the check is within an acceptable statistical range, CrossCheck notifies the merchant. If the check is dishonored, the merchant sends it to CrossCheck, which pays it. CrossCheck then attempts to redeposit the check. If this fails, CrossCheck takes further steps to collect the amount. CrossCheck attempts to collect on more than two thousand checks per year and spends $2 million on these efforts, which involve about 7 percent of its employees and 6 percent of its total expenses. William Winterstein took his truck to C&P Auto Service Center, Inc., for a tune-up and paid for the service with a check. C&P contacted CrossCheck and, on its recommendation, accepted the check. When the check was dishonored, C&P mailed it to CrossCheck, which reimbursed C&P and sent a letter to Winterstein requesting payment. Winterstein filed a suit in a federal district court against CrossCheck, asserting that the letter violated the Fair Debt Collection Practices Act. CrossCheck filed a motion for summary judgment. On what ground might the court grant the motion? Explain. [*Winterstein v. CrossCheck, Inc.*, 149 F.Supp.2d 466 (N.D.Ill. 2001)]

23–7. ⚖ CASE PROBLEM WITH SAMPLE ANSWER

Source One Associates, Inc., is based in Poughquag, New York. Peter Easton, Source One's president, is responsible for its daily operations. Between 1995 and 1997, Source One received requests from persons in Massachusetts seeking financial information about individuals and businesses. To obtain this information, Easton first obtained the targeted individuals' credit reports through Equifax Consumer Information Services by claiming that the reports would be used only in connection with credit transactions involving the consumers. From the reports, Easton identified financial institutions at which the targeted individuals held accounts and then called the institutions to learn the account balances by impersonating either officers of the institutions or the account holders. The information was then provided to Source One's customers for a fee. Easton did not know why the customers wanted the information. The state ("Commonwealth") of Massachusetts filed a suit in a Massachusetts state court against Source One and Easton, alleging, among other things, violations of the Fair Credit Reporting Act (FCRA). Did the defendants violate the FCRA? Explain. [*Commonwealth v. Source One Associates, Inc.*, 436 Mass. 118, 763 N.E.2d 42 (2002)]

To view a sample answer for this case problem, go to this book's Web site at http://wleb.westbuslaw.com, select "Chapter 23," and click on "Case Problem with Sample Answer."

23–8. DECEPTIVE ADVERTISING. "Set up & Ready to Make Money in Minutes Guaranteed!" the ads claimed. "The Internet Treasure Chest (ITC) will give you everything you need to start your own exciting Internet business including your own worldwide website all for the unbelievable price of only $59.95." The ITC "contains virtually everything you need to quickly and easily get your very own worldwide Internet business up, running, stocked with products, able to accept credit cards and ready to take orders almost immediately." What ITC's marketers—Damien Zamora and end70 Corp.—did not disclose were the significant additional costs required to operate the business: domain name registration fees, monthly Internet access and hosting charges, monthly fees to access the ITC product warehouse, and other "upgrades." The Federal Trade Commission filed a suit in a federal district court against end70 and Zamora, seeking an injunction and other relief. Are the defendants' claims "deceptive advertising"? If so, what might the court order the defendants to do to correct any misrepresentations? [*Federal Trade Commission v. end70 Corp.*, __ F.Supp.2d __ (N.D.Tex. 2003)]

23–9. ⚖ A QUESTION OF ETHICS

One of the products that McDonald's Corp. sells is the Happy Meal®, which consists of a McDonald's food entree, a small order of French fries, a small drink, and a toy. In the early 1990s, McDonald's began to aim its Happy Meal® marketing at children aged one to three. In 1995, McDonald's began making nutritional information for its food products available in documents known as McDonald's Nutrition Facts. Each document lists each food item that the restaurant serves and provides a nutritional breakdown, but the Happy Meal® is not included. Marc Cohen filed a suit in an Illinois state court against McDonald's, alleging in part that the defendant violated a state law prohibiting consumer fraud and deceptive business practices by failing to adhere to the Nutrition Labeling and Education Act of 1990 (NLEA). The court dismissed the suit, and Cohen appealed to a state intermediate appellate court, which affirmed the dismissal, holding that the NLEA preempted the plaintiff's claims. In view of these facts, consider the following questions. [*Cohen v. McDonald's Corp.*, 347 Ill.App.3d 627, 808 N.E.2d 1, 283 Ill.Dec. 451 (1 Dist. 2004)]

(a) What does the NLEA provide? Under these provisions, the NLEA sets out different requirements for products specifically intended for children under the age of four. Does this make sense? Is this ethical? Why or why not?

(b) Because the federal government has not established certain requirements for children under age four,

there are no regulations under the NLEA for reporting these requirements. Should a state court impose such regulations? Explain.

23–10. VIDEO QUESTION

Go to this text's Web site at http://wleb.westbuslaw.com and select "Chapter 23." Click on "Video Questions" and view the video titled *Advertising Communication Law: Bait and Switch*. Then answer the following questions.

(a) Is the auto dealership's advertisement for the truck in the video deceptive? Why or why not?

(b) Is the advertisement for the truck an offer to which the dealership is bound? Does it matter if Betty detrimentally relied on the advertisement?

(c) Is Tony committed to buying Betty's trade-in truck for $3,000 because that is what he told her over the phone?

LAW | on the Web

For updated links to resources available on the Web, as well as a variety of other materials, visit this text's Web site at http://wleb.westbuslaw.com.

For a government-sponsored Web site containing reports on consumer issues, go to

http://www.consumer.com

The Web site of the Federal Trade Commission (FTC) offers extensive information on consumer protection laws, consumer problems, enforcement issues, and other topics relevant to consumer law. Go to

http://www.ftc.gov

and click on "Consumer Protection."

To learn more about the FTC's "cooling-off" rule, you can access it directly by going to the following URL:

http://www.ftc.gov/bcp/conline/pubs/buying/cooling.htm

LEGAL RESEARCH EXERCISES ON THE WEB

Go to http://wleb.westbuslaw.com, the Web site that accompanies this text. Select "Chapter 23" and click on "Internet Exercises." There you will find the following Internet research exercises that you can perform to learn more about topics covered in this chapter.

Activity 23–1: **LEGAL PERSPECTIVE**
       The Food and Drug Administration

Activity 23–2: **MANAGEMENT PERSPECTIVE**
       Internet Advertising and Marketing

Environmental Law

Concerns over the degradation of the environment have increased over time in response to the environmental effects of population growth, urbanization, and industrialization. Environmental protection is not without a price, however. For many businesses, the costs of complying with environmental regulations are high, and for some they are too high. A constant tension exists between the desire to increase profits and productivity and the need to protect the environment. In this chapter, we discuss **environmental law,** which consists of all laws and regulations designed to protect and preserve our environmental resources.

SECTION 1 | Common Law Actions

Common law remedies against environmental pollution originated centuries ago in England. Those responsible for operations that created dirt, smoke, noxious odors, noise, or toxic substances were sometimes held liable under common law theories of nuisance or negligence. Today, injured individuals continue to rely on the common law to obtain damages and injunctions against business polluters.

NUISANCE

Under the common law doctrine of **nuisance,** persons may be held liable if they use their property in a manner that unreasonably interferes with others' rights to use or enjoy their own property. In these situations, courts commonly balance the equities between the harm caused by the pollution and the costs of stopping it.

Courts have often denied injunctive relief on the ground that the hardships that would be imposed on the polluter and on the community are greater than the hardships suffered by the plaintiff. For example, a factory that causes neighboring landowners to suffer from smoke, dirt, and vibrations may be left in operation if it is the core of a local economy. The injured parties may be awarded only money damages. These damages may include compensation for the decline in the value of their property as a result of the factory's operation.

A property owner may be given relief from pollution if he or she can identify a distinct harm separate from that affecting the general public. This harm is referred to as a "private" nuisance. Under the common law, citizens were denied standing (access to the courts—see Chapter 2) unless they suffered a harm distinct from the harm suffered by the public at large. Some states still require this. For example, in one case a group of individuals who made their living by commercial fishing in a major river in New York filed a suit seeking damages and an injunction against a company that was polluting the river. The New York court found that the plaintiffs had standing because they were particularly harmed by the pollution in the river.[1] A public authority (such as a state's attorney general), however, can sue to abate a "public" nuisance.

NEGLIGENCE AND STRICT LIABILITY

An injured party may sue a business polluter in tort under the negligence and strict liability theories discussed in Chapter 13. The basis for a negligence action is a business's alleged failure to use reasonable care toward a party whose injury was foreseeable and was caused by the lack of reasonable care. For example, employees might sue an employer whose failure to use proper pollution controls contaminated the air, causing the employees to suffer respiratory illnesses. A developing area of tort law involves **toxic torts**—actions against toxic polluters.

---

1. *Lee v. General Electric Co.,* 538 N.Y.S.2d 844, 145 A.D.2d 291 (1989).

Businesses that engage in ultrahazardous activities—such as the transportation of radioactive materials—are strictly liable for whatever injuries the activities cause. In a strict liability action, the injured party need not prove that the business failed to exercise reasonable care.

SECTION 2 | Federal, State, and Local Regulation

All levels of government in the United States regulate some aspect of the environment. In this section, we look at some of the ways in which the federal, state, and local governments control business activities and land use in the interests of environmental preservation and protection.

FEDERAL REGULATION

Congress has passed a number of statutes to control the impact of human activities on the environment. Exhibit 24–1 lists and summarizes the major federal environmental statutes discussed in this chapter. Some of these statutes were passed in an attempt to improve air and water quality. Others specifically regulate toxic chemicals, including pesticides, herbicides, and hazardous wastes.

EXHIBIT 24–1 Major Federal Environmental Statutes

POPULAR NAME	PURPOSE	STATUTE REFERENCE
Rivers and Harbors Appropriations Act (1899)	To prohibit ships and manufacturers from discharging and depositing refuse in navigable waterways.	33 U.S.C. Sections 401–418.
Federal Insecticide, Fungicide, and Rodenticide Act (1947)	To control the use of pesticides and herbicides.	7 U.S.C. Sections 136–136y.
Federal Water Pollution Control Act (1948)	To eliminate the discharge of pollutants from major sources into navigable waters.	33 U.S.C. Sections 1251–1387.
Clean Air Act (1963)	To control air pollution from mobile and stationary sources.	42 U.S.C. Sections 7401–7671q.
National Environmental Policy Act (1969)	To limit environmental harm from federal government activities.	42 U.S.C. Sections 4321–4370d.
Endangered Species Act (1973)	To protect species that are threatened with extinction.	16 U.S.C. Sections 1531–1544.
Safe Drinking Water Act (1974)	To regulate pollutants in public drinking water systems.	42 U.S.C. Sections 300f to 300j-25.
Resource Conservation and Recovery Act (1976)	To establish standards for hazardous waste disposal.	42 U.S.C. Sections 6901–6986.
Toxic Substances Control Act (1976)	To regulate toxic chemicals and chemical compounds.	15 U.S.C. Sections 2601–2692.
Comprehensive Environmental Response, Compensation, and Liability Act (1980)	To regulate the clean-up of hazardous waste–disposal sites.	42 U.S.C. Sections 9601–9675.
Oil Pollution Act (1990)	To establish liability for the clean-up of navigable waters after oil-spill disasters.	33 U.S.C. Sections 2701–2761.
Small Business Liability Relief and Brownfields Revitalization Act (2002)	To allow developers who comply with state voluntary clean-up programs to avoid federal liability for the properties that they decontaminate and develop.	42 U.S.C. Section 9628.

REGULATORY AGENCIES The most well known of the federal agencies regulating environmental law is the Environmental Protection Agency (EPA), which was created in 1970 to coordinate federal environmental responsibilities. Other federal agencies with authority for regulating specific environmental matters include the Department of the Interior, the Department of Defense, the Department of Labor, the Food and Drug Administration, and the Nuclear Regulatory Commission. These regulatory agencies—and all other agencies of the federal government—must take environmental factors into consideration when making significant decisions.

Most federal environmental laws provide that citizens can sue to enforce environmental regulations if government agencies fail to do so—or can sue to protest agency enforcement actions if they believe that these actions go too far. Typically, a threshold hurdle in such suits is meeting the requirements for standing to sue (see Chapter 2).

State and local regulatory agencies also play a significant role in carrying out federal environmental legislation. Typically, the federal government relies on state and local governments to implement federal environmental statutes and regulations such as those regulating air quality.

ENVIRONMENTAL IMPACT STATEMENTS The National Environmental Policy Act (NEPA) of 1969[2] requires that an **environmental impact statement (EIS)** be prepared for every major federal action that significantly affects the quality of the environment. An EIS must analyze (1) the impact on the environment that the action will have, (2) any adverse effects on the environment and alternative actions that might be taken, and (3) irreversible effects the action might generate.

An action qualifies as "major" if it involves a substantial commitment of resources (monetary or otherwise). An action is "federal" if a federal agency has the power to control it. Construction by a private developer of a ski resort on federal land, for example, may require an EIS. Building or operating a nuclear plant, which requires a federal permit, or constructing a dam as part of a federal project requires an EIS. If an agency decides that an EIS is unnecessary, it must issue a statement supporting this conclusion. EISs have become instruments for private citizens, consumer

interest groups, businesses, and others to challenge federal agency actions on the basis that the actions improperly threaten the environment.

STATE AND LOCAL REGULATION

Many states regulate the degree to which the environment may be polluted. Thus, for example, even when state zoning laws permit a business's proposed development, the proposal may have to be altered to lessen the development's impact on the environment. State laws may restrict a business's discharge of chemicals into the air or water or regulate its disposal of toxic wastes. States may also regulate the disposal or recycling of other wastes, including glass, metal, and plastic containers and paper. Additionally, states may restrict the emissions from motor vehicles.

City, county, and other local governments oversee certain aspects of the environment. For instance, local zoning laws control some land use. These laws may be designed to inhibit or direct the growth of cities and suburbs or to protect the natural environment. In the interest of safeguarding the environment, such laws may prohibit certain land uses. One of the issues subject to ongoing debate is whether landowners should be compensated when restrictions are placed on the use of their property.

Other aspects of the environment may also be subject to local regulation. Methods of waste and garbage removal and disposal, for example, can have a substantial impact on a community. The appearance of buildings and other structures, including advertising signs and billboards, may affect traffic safety, property values, or local aesthetics. Noise generated by a business or its customers may be annoying, disruptive, or damaging to its neighbors. The location and condition of parks, streets, and other public uses of land subject to local control affect the environment and can also affect business.

SECTION 3 | Air Pollution

Federal involvement with air pollution goes back to the 1950s, when Congress authorized funds for air-pollution research. In 1963, the federal government passed the Clean Air Act,[3] which focused on multistate air pollution and provided assistance to the states. Various amendments, particularly in 1970,

---

2. 42 U.S.C. Sections 4321–4370d.

3. 42 U.S.C. Sections 7401–7671q.

1977, and 1990, strengthened the government's authority to regulate air quality. These laws provide the basis for issuing regulations to control pollution coming primarily from mobile sources (such as automobiles) and stationary sources (such as electric utilities and industrial plants).

MOBILE SOURCES

Automobiles and other vehicles are referred to as mobile sources of pollution. The EPA has issued regulations specifying standards for mobile sources of pollution, as well as for service stations. The agency periodically updates these standards in light of new developments and data.

MOTOR VEHICLES Regulations governing air pollution from automobiles and other mobile sources specify pollution standards and time schedules for meeting these standards. For example, the 1990 amendments to the Clean Air Act required automobile manufacturers to cut new automobiles' exhaust emissions of nitrogen oxide by 60 percent and emissions of other pollutants by 35 percent. By 1998, all new automobiles had to meet this standard. Regulations that became effective beginning with 2004 model cars called for nitrogen oxide tailpipe emissions to be cut by nearly 10 percent by 2007. For the first time, sport utility vehicles (SUVs) and light trucks were required to meet the same emission standards as automobiles.

UPDATING POLLUTION-CONTROL STANDARDS As mentioned, the EPA attempts to update pollution-control standards when new scientific information becomes available. For example, some studies conducted in the 1990s claimed that very small particles (2.5 microns, or millionths of a meter) of soot affect our health as significantly as larger particles. Based on this evidence, the EPA issued new particulate standards for motor vehicle exhaust systems and other sources of pollution in 1996. The EPA also set a more rigorous acceptable standard for ozone, which is formed when sunlight combines with pollutants from cars and other sources. Ozone is the basic ingredient of smog.

The EPA's particulate standards and ozone standard were challenged in court by a number of business groups. These groups contended that the EPA had exceeded its authority under the Clean Air Act by issuing the stricter rules. Additionally, the groups claimed that the EPA had to take economic costs into

account when developing new regulations. In 2000, however, the United States Supreme Court upheld the EPA's authority under the Clean Air Act to issue the standards. The Court also held that the EPA did not have to take economic costs into account when creating new rules.[4]

STATIONARY SOURCES

The Clean Air Act also authorizes the EPA to establish air-quality standards for stationary sources (such as manufacturing plants) but recognizes that the primary responsibility for implementing these standards rests with state and local governments. The EPA sets primary and secondary levels of ambient standards—that is, the maximum levels of certain pollutants—and the states formulate plans to achieve those standards.

DIFFERENT STANDARDS MAY APPLY Different standards apply to sources of pollution in clean areas and those in polluted ones. Different standards also apply to existing sources of pollution and major new sources. Major new sources include existing sources modified by a change in a method of operation that increases emissions. Performance standards for major sources require use of the *maximum achievable control technology*, or MACT, to reduce emissions from the combustion of fossil fuels (coal and oil). As mentioned, the EPA issues guidelines as to what equipment meets this standard.

CURBING ACID RAIN AND GROUND-LEVEL POLLUTION Under the 1990 amendments to the Clean Air Act, 110 of the oldest coal-burning power plants in the United States had to cut their emissions by 40 percent by the year 2001 to reduce acid rain. Utilities were granted "credits" to emit certain amounts of sulfur dioxide, and those that emit less than the allowed amounts can sell their credits to other polluters. The amendments also required an end to the production of chlorofluorocarbons, carbon tetrachloride, and methyl chloroform, which are used in air-conditioning, refrigeration, and insulation and have been linked to depletion of the ozone layer.

The relationship between the Clean Air Act's 1990 amendments and a New York state law was at issue in the following case.

---

4. *Whitman v. American Trucking Associations,* 531 U.S. 457, 121 S.Ct. 903, 149 L.Ed.2d 1 (2000).

CASE 24.1

Clean Air Markets Group v. Pataki

United States
District Court,
Northern District
of New York, 2002.
194 F.Supp.2d 147.

BACKGROUND AND FACTS *Acid rain consists of atmospheric sulfates and nitrates, which are formed from sulfur dioxide (SO_2) and nitrogen oxides (NOx). By 1999, some scientists were contending that SO_2 emissions at the rates permitted by the Clean Air Act would not allow for the environmental restoration of parts of the state of New York. Additional reductions in SO_2 emissions would be required. George Pataki, the governor of New York, ordered New York utilities to cut SO_2 emissions to half of the amount permitted by the Clean Air Act by January 2, 2007. By doing this, the New York utilities would have additional SO_2 credits to sell. In May 2000, the New York state legislature enacted the Air Pollution Mitigation Law (APML), under which most sums received for the sale or trade of SO_2 allowances to polluters in Upwind States—fourteen midwestern, eastern, and southern states that significantly contributed to acid rain in New York—would be forfeited to the New York Public Service Commission (PSC), which regulates New York utilities. This effectively lowered the market value of credits originating with New York utilities. Clean Air Markets Group (CAMG) filed a suit in a federal district court against Pataki and others, claiming in part that the APML was preempted under the U.S. Constitution's supremacy clause.[a] All parties filed motions for summary judgment.*

IN THE LANGUAGE OF THE COURT

HURD, District Judge.

* * * *

* * * [The APML] creates an obstacle to the accomplishment and execution of the full purposes and objectives of Congress. [The Clean Air Act] provides that SO_2 allowances "may be transferred among designated representatives of the owners or operators of [covered units (utilities)] and any other person who holds such allowances." [The APML's] restrictions on transferring allowances to units in the Upwind States is contrary to the federal provision that allowances be tradeable to any other person. Additionally, Congress considered geographically restricted allowance transfers and rejected it. The EPA, in setting regulations to implement [the Clean Air Act], also considered geographically restricted allowance trading and rejected it * * * . *The rejection of a regionally restricted allowance trading system illustrates the Congressional objective of having a nationwide trading market for SO_2 allowances. New York's regional restrictions on SO_2 allowance trading by New York units [are] an obstacle to the execution of that objective.* [Emphasis added.]

Pataki argues that the Air Pollution Mitigation Law * * * imposes a more stringent requirement for air pollution control or abatement, as expressly permitted. However, * * * the Air Pollution Mitigation Law sets no emissions requirements. It sets no requirements for air pollution control or abatement at all. Rather, the New York law is a state regulation of federally allocated SO_2 allowances. Further, it is a restriction on the nationwide trading system for which the Clean Air Act provides. It is insufficient to merely say that it imposes requirements for air pollution control, or that the goal is air pollution control or abatement. New York's Air Pollution Mitigation Law is preempted because it interferes with the Clean Air Act's method for achieving the goal of air pollution control: a cap and nationwide SO_2 allowance trading system.

In addition to interfering with the nationwide trading of SO_2 allowances, the Air Pollution Mitigation Law would result in decreased availability of SO_2 allowances in the Upwind States. Restricted availability of SO_2 allowances could indirectly reduce emissions in the Upwind States. No doubt the New York legislators had this in mind when the Air Pollution Mitigation Law was enacted. However, the Clean Air Act permits restrictions on emissions by a state in that state, but it does not permit one state to control emissions in

---

a. As explained in Chapter 5, if federal law has not supplanted an entire field of state law, state law is preempted to the extent that it actually conflicts with federal law. A conflict between state and federal law occurs when compliance with both is physically impossible or when the state law is an obstacle to accomplishing the objective of the federal law.

CASE 24.1 | Continued another state. Thus, the inevitable result of laws such as New York's Air Pollution Mitigation Law would be the indirect regulation of allowance trading and emissions in other states, which could not be done directly.

DECISION AND REMEDY *The court granted CAMG's motion for summary judgment, holding that New York's Air Pollution Mitigation Law is preempted, under the supremacy clause, by the Clean Air Act because it interferes with that law's methods for achieving air-pollution control. The court enjoined the enforcement of the state law.*

WHAT IF THE FACTS WERE DIFFERENT? *Suppose that the APML also provided for a subsidy to those who claimed that the value of their pollution credits had been reduced. Would this have affected the outcome of the case?*

HAZARDOUS AIR POLLUTANTS

Hazardous air pollutants are those likely to cause an increase in mortality or in serious irreversible or incapacitating illness. In all, there are 189 of these pollutants, including asbestos, benzene, beryllium, cadmium, mercury, and vinyl chloride. These pollutants may cause cancer as well as neurological and reproductive damage. They are emitted from stationary sources by a variety of business activities, including smelting (melting ore to produce metal), dry cleaning, house painting, and commercial baking. Instead of establishing specific emissions standards for each hazardous air pollutant, the 1990 amendments to the Clean Air Act require industry to use pollution-control equipment that represents the maximum achievable control technology, or MACT, to limit emissions. The EPA issues guidelines as to what equipment meets this standard.

In 1996, the EPA issued a rule to regulate hazardous air pollutants emitted by landfills. The rule required landfills constructed after May 30, 1991, that emit more than a specified amount of pollutants to install landfill gas collection and control systems. The rule also required the states to impose the same requirements on landfills constructed before May 30, 1991, if they accepted waste after November 8, 1987.[5]

VIOLATIONS OF THE CLEAN AIR ACT

For violations of emission limits under the Clean Air Act, the EPA can assess civil penalties of up to $25,000 per day. Additional fines of up to $5,000 per day can be assessed for other violations, such as failing to maintain the required records. To penalize those who find it more cost-effective to violate the act than

to comply with it, the EPA is authorized to impose a penalty equal to the violator's economic benefits from noncompliance. Persons who provide information about violators may be paid up to $10,000. Private citizens can also sue violators.

Those who knowingly violate the act may be subject to criminal penalties, including fines of up to $1 million and imprisonment for up to two years (for false statements or failures to report violations). Corporate officers are among those who may be subject to these penalties.

SECTION 4 | Water Pollution

Water pollution stems mostly from industrial, municipal, and agricultural sources. Pollutants entering streams, lakes, and oceans include organic wastes, heated water, sediments from soil runoff, nutrients (including fertilizers and human and animal wastes), and toxic chemicals and other hazardous substances. We look here at laws and regulations governing water pollution.

NAVIGABLE WATERS

Federal regulations governing water pollution can be traced back to the Rivers and Harbors Appropriations Act of 1899.[6] These regulations prohibited ships and manufacturers from discharging or depositing refuse in navigable waterways. Once limited to waters actually used for navigation, the term *navigable waters* is today interpreted to include intrastate lakes and streams used by interstate travelers and industries, as well as coastal and freshwater wetlands (*wetlands* will be defined shortly).

---

5. 40 C.F.R. Sections 60.750–759.

6. 33 U.S.C. Sections 401–418.

THE CLEAN WATER ACT AND ITS AMENDMENTS

In 1948, Congress passed the Federal Water Pollution Control Act (FWPCA),[7] but its regulatory system and enforcement powers proved to be inadequate. In 1972, amendments to the FWPCA—known as the Clean Water Act—established the following goals: (1) make waters safe for swimming, (2) protect fish and wildlife, and (3) eliminate the discharge of pollutants into the water. The amendments required that municipal and industrial polluters apply for permits before discharging wastes into navigable waters. The Clean Water Act also set specific schedules, which were extended by amendment in 1977 and by the Water Quality Act of 1987.[8] Under these schedules, the EPA establishes limitations for discharges of various types of pollutants based on the technology available for controlling them. The 1972 act also requires municipal and industrial polluters to apply for permits before discharging wastes into navigable waters.

STANDARDS FOR EQUIPMENT Regulations, for the most part, specify that the *best available control technology,* or BACT, be installed. The EPA issues guidelines as to what equipment meets this standard; essentially, the guidelines require the most effective pollution-control equipment available. New sources must install BACT equipment before beginning operations. Existing sources are subject to timetables for the installation of BACT equipment. These sources must immediately install equipment that utilizes the *best practical control technology,* or BPCT. The EPA also issues guidelines as to what equipment meets this standard.

WETLANDS The Clean Water Act prohibits the filling or dredging of wetlands unless a permit is obtained from the Army Corps of Engineers. The EPA defines **wetlands** as "those areas that are inundated or saturated by surface or ground water at a frequency and duration sufficient to support, and that under normal circumstances do support, a prevalence of vegetation typically adapted for life in saturated soil conditions." In recent years, the broad interpretation of what constitutes a wetland subject to the regulatory authority of the federal government has generated substantial controversy.

Perhaps one of the most controversial regulations was the "migratory-bird rule" issued by the Army Corps

of Engineers. Under this rule, any bodies of water that could affect interstate commerce, including seasonal ponds or waters "used or suitable for use by migratory birds" that fly over state borders, were "navigable waters" subject to federal regulation under the Clean Water Act as wetlands. The rule was challenged in a case brought by a group of communities in the Chicago suburbs that wanted to build a landfill in a tract of land northwest of Chicago that had once been used as a strip mine. Over time, areas that were once pits in the mine became ponds used by a variety of migratory birds. The Army Corps of Engineers, claiming that the shallow ponds formed a habitat for migratory birds, refused to grant a permit for the landfill.

Ultimately, the United States Supreme Court held that the Army Corps of Engineers had exceeded its authority under the Clean Water Act. The Court stated that it was not prepared to hold that isolated and seasonable ponds, puddles, and "prairie potholes" become "navigable waters of the United States" simply because they serve as a habitat for migratory birds.[9]

VIOLATIONS OF THE CLEAN WATER ACT Under the Clean Water Act, violators are subject to a variety of civil and criminal penalties. Depending on the violation, civil penalties range from a maximum of $10,000 per day, and not more than $25,000 per violation, to as much as $25,000 per day. Criminal penalties, which apply only if an act was intentional, range from a fine of $2,500 per day and imprisonment for up to one year to a fine of $1 million and fifteen years' imprisonment. Injunctive relief and damages can also be imposed. The polluting party can be required to clean up the pollution or pay for the cost of doing so.

DRINKING WATER

Another statute governing water pollution is the Safe Drinking Water Act.[10] Passed in 1974, this act requires the EPA to set maximum levels for pollutants in public water systems. Operators of public water supply systems must come as close as possible to meeting the EPA's standards by using the best available technology that is economically and technologically feasible. The EPA is particularly concerned with contamination from underground sources. Pesticides and

7. 33 U.S.C. Sections 1251–1387.
8. This act amended 33 U.S.C. Section 1251.
9. *Solid Waste Agency of Northern Cook County v. U.S. Army Corps of Engineers,* 531 U.S. 159, 121 S.Ct. 675, 148 L.Ed.2d 576 (2001).
10. 42 U.S.C. Sections 300f to 300j-25.

wastes leaked from landfills or disposed of in underground injection wells are among the more than two hundred pollutants known to exist in groundwater used for drinking in at least thirty-four states. Many of these substances are associated with cancer and damage to the central nervous system, liver, and kidneys.

The act was amended in 1996 to give the EPA greater flexibility in setting regulatory standards governing drinking water. Prior to the 1996 amendments, the EPA had to set standards for twenty-five different drinking water contaminants every three years, which it had largely failed to do. Under the 1996 amendments, the EPA can move at whatever rate it deems necessary to control the contaminants of greatest concern to the public health. The 1996 amendments also imposed new requirements on suppliers of drinking water. Each supplier must send to every household it provides with water an annual statement describing the source of its water, the level of any contaminants contained in the water, and any possible health concerns associated with the contaminants.

OCEAN DUMPING

The Marine Protection, Research, and Sanctuaries Act of 1972[11] (known popularly as the Ocean Dumping Act) regulates the transportation and dumping of material into ocean waters. (The term *material* is synonymous with the term *pollutant* as used in the Federal Water Pollution Control Act.) The Ocean Dumping Act prohibits entirely the ocean dumping of radiological, chemical, and biological warfare agents and high-level radioactive waste.

The act establishes a permit program for transporting and dumping other materials. There are specific exemptions—materials subject to the permit provisions of other pollution legislation, wastes from structures regulated by other laws (for example, offshore oil exploration and drilling platforms), sewage, and other wastes. The Ocean Dumping Act also authorizes the designation of marine sanctuaries for "preserving or restoring such areas for their conservation, recreational, ecological, or esthetic values."

Each violation of any provision or permit may result in a civil penalty of not more than $50,000 or revocation or suspension of the permit. A knowing violation is a criminal offense that may result in a $50,000 fine, imprisonment for not more than a year, or both. An injunction may also be imposed.

OIL POLLUTION

The Oil Pollution Act of 1990[12] provides that any onshore or offshore oil facility, oil shipper, vessel owner, or vessel operator that discharges oil into navigable waters or onto an adjoining shore may be liable for clean-up costs, as well as damages. The act created a $1 billion oil clean-up and economic compensation fund and decreed that by the year 2011, oil tankers using U.S. ports must be double hulled to limit the severity of accidental spills.

Under the act, damage to natural resources, private property, and the local economy, including the increased cost of providing public services, is compensable. The penalties range from $2 million to $350 million, depending on the size of the vessel and depending on whether the oil spill came from a vessel or an offshore facility. The party held responsible for the clean-up costs can bring a civil suit for contribution from other potentially liable parties.

SECTION 5 | Toxic Chemicals

Originally, most environmental clean-up efforts were directed toward reducing smog and making water safe for fishing and swimming. Over time, however, control of toxic chemicals has become an important part of environmental law.

PESTICIDES AND HERBICIDES

The Federal Insecticide, Fungicide, and Rodenticide Act (FIFRA) of 1947[13] regulates pesticides and herbicides. Under the FIFRA, pesticides and herbicides must be (1) registered before they can be sold, (2) certified and used only for approved applications, and (3) used in limited quantities when applied to food crops. If a substance is identified as harmful, the EPA can cancel its registration after a hearing. If the harm is imminent, the EPA can suspend registration pending the hearing. The EPA, or state officers or employees, may also inspect factories where these chemicals are manufactured.

Under 1996 amendments to the Federal Food, Drug and Cosmetic Act, for a pesticide to remain on the market, there must be a "reasonable certainty of no harm" to people from exposure to the pesticide.[14] This

---

11. 16 U.S.C. Sections 1401–1445.

12. 33 U.S.C. Sections 2701–2761.
13. 7 U.S.C. Sections 136–136y.
14. 21 U.S.C. Section 346a.

means that there must be no more than a one-in-a-million risk to people of developing cancer from exposure in any way, including eating food that contains residues from the pesticide. Nearly all fruits and vegetables and processed foods contain some pesticide residues. Under the 1996 amendments, the EPA must distribute to grocery stores brochures on high-risk pesticides that are in food, and the stores must display these brochures for consumers.

Can a state regulate the sale and use of federally registered pesticides? Tort suits against pesticide manufacturers were common long before the enactment of the FIFRA in 1947 and continued to be a feature of the legal landscape at the time the FIFRA was amended. Until it heard the following case, however, the United States Supreme Court had never considered whether that statute preempts claims arising under state law.

CASE 24.2

Bates v. Dow Agrosciences, LLC

Supreme Court of the
United States, 2005.
__ U.S. __,
125 S.Ct. 1788,
161 L.Ed.2d 687.
http://www.findlaw.com/
casecode/supreme.html [a]

BACKGROUND AND FACTS *The Environmental Protection Agency (EPA) conditionally registered Strongarm, a new weed-killing pesticide, on March 8, 2000.*[b] *Dow Agrosciences, LLC, immediately sold Strongarm to Texas peanut farmers, who normally plant their crops around May 1. The label stated, "Use of Strongarm is recommended in all areas where peanuts are grown." When the farmers applied Strongarm to their fields, the pesticide damaged their crops while failing to control the growth of weeds. After unsuccessfully attempting to negotiate with Dow, the farmers announced their intent to sue Strongarm's maker for violations of Texas state law. Dow filed a suit in a federal district court against the peanut farmers, asserting that the FIFRA preempted their claims. The court issued a summary judgment in Dow's favor. The farmers appealed to the U.S. Court of Appeals for the Fifth Circuit, which affirmed the lower court's judgment. The farmers appealed to the United States Supreme Court.*

IN THE LANGUAGE OF THE COURT

Justice STEVENS delivered the opinion of the Court.
* * * *
Under FIFRA * * * , [a] pesticide is misbranded if its label contains a statement that is false or misleading in any particular, including a false or misleading statement concerning the efficacy of the pesticide. *A pesticide is also misbranded if its label does not contain adequate instructions for use, or if its label omits necessary warnings or cautionary statements.* [Emphasis added.]
* * * *
* * * [Section] 136v provides:

"(a) * * * A State may regulate the sale or use of any federally registered pesticide or device in the State, but only if and to the extent the regulation does not permit any sale or use prohibited by [FIFRA].
"(b) * * * Such State shall not impose or continue in effect any requirements for labeling or packaging in addition to or different from those required under [FIFRA]. * * * "

* * * *
* * * *Nothing in the text of FIFRA would prevent a State from making the violation of a federal labeling or packaging requirement a state offense,* thereby imposing its own sanctions on pesticide manufacturers who violate federal law. The imposition of state sanctions for violating state rules that merely duplicate federal requirements is equally consistent with the text of [Section] 136v. [Emphasis added.]
* * * *
* * * For a particular state rule to be preempted, it must satisfy two conditions. First, it must be a requirement "for labeling or packaging"; rules governing the design of a product, for example, are not preempted. Second, it must impose a labeling or packaging requirement that

---

a. In the "Browsing" section, click on "2005 Decisions." In the result, click on the name of the case to access the opinion.
b. Strongarm might more commonly be called a herbicide, but the FIFRA classifies it as a pesticide.

CASE 24.2 | Continued

is "in addition to or different from those required under [FIFRA]." A state regulation requiring the word "poison" to appear in red letters, for instance, would not be preempted if an EPA regulation imposed the same requirement.

* * * Rules that require manufacturers to design reasonably safe products, to use due care in conducting appropriate testing of their products, to market products free of manufacturing defects, and to honor their express warranties or other contractual commitments plainly do not qualify as requirements for "labeling or packaging." None of these common-law rules requires that manufacturers label or package their products in any particular way. Thus, petitioners' claims for defective design, defective manufacture, negligent testing, and breach of express warranty are not preempted.

* * * *

Dow * * * argues that [this] "parallel requirements" reading of [Section] 136v(b) would "give juries in 50 States the authority to give content to FIFRA's misbranding prohibition, establishing a crazy-quilt of anti-misbranding requirements * * * ." Conspicuously absent from the submissions by Dow * * * is any plausible alternative interpretation of "in addition to or different from" that would give that phrase meaning. Instead, they appear to favor reading those words out of the statute * * * . This amputated version of [Section] 136v(b) would no doubt have clearly and succinctly commanded the preemption of all state requirements concerning labeling. *That Congress added the remainder of the provision is evidence of its intent to draw a distinction between state labeling requirements that are preempted and those that are not.* [Emphasis added.]

* * * *

In sum, under our interpretation, [Section] 136v(b) * * * preempts competing state labeling standards—imagine 50 different labeling regimes prescribing the color, font size, and wording of warnings—that would create significant inefficiencies for manufacturers. The provision also preempts any statutory or common-law rule that would impose a labeling requirement that diverges from those set out in FIFRA * * * . It does not, however, preempt any state rules that are fully consistent with federal requirements.

DECISION AND REMEDY *The United States Supreme Court vacated the lower court's judgment. A state can regulate the sale and use of federally registered pesticides to the extent that it does not permit anything that the FIFRA prohibits, but a state cannot impose any requirements for labeling or packaging in addition to or different from those that the FIFRA requires. The Court remanded the case, however, for further proceedings subject to this standard, concerning certain state law claims "on which we have not received sufficient briefing."*

WHAT IF THE FACTS WERE DIFFERENT? *Suppose that the FIFRA required Strongarm's label to include the word CAUTION, and the Texas peanut farmers filed their claims under a state regulation that required the label to use the word DANGER. Would the result have been different?*

VIOLATIONS OF THE FIFRA It is a violation of the FIFRA to sell a pesticide or herbicide that is unregistered, a pesticide or herbicide with a registration that has been canceled or suspended, or a pesticide or herbicide with a false or misleading label. For example, it is an offense to sell a substance that is adulterated (that has a chemical strength different from the concentration declared on the label). It is also an offense to destroy or deface any labeling required under the act. The act's labeling requirements include directions for the use of the pesticide or herbicide, warnings to protect human health and the environment, a statement of treatment in the case of poisoning, and a list of the ingredients.

A private party can petition the EPA to suspend or cancel the registration of a pesticide or herbicide. If the EPA fails to act, the private party can petition a federal court to review the EPA's lack of action.

PENALTIES FOR VIOLATIONS Penalties for registrants and producers for violating the FIFRA include imprisonment for up to one year and a fine of no more than $50,000. Penalties for commercial dealers include imprisonment for up to one year and a fine of no more than $25,000. Farmers and other private users of pesticides or herbicides who violate the act are subject to a $1,000 fine and incarceration for up to thirty days.

TOXIC SUBSTANCES

The first comprehensive law covering toxic substances was the Toxic Substances Control Act of 1976.[15] The act was passed to regulate chemicals and chemical compounds that are known to be toxic—such as asbestos and polychlorinated biphenyls, popularly known as PCBs—and to institute investigation of any possible harmful effects from new chemical compounds. The regulations authorize the EPA to require that manufacturers, processors, and other organizations planning to use chemicals first determine their effects on human health and the environment. The EPA can regulate substances that may pose an imminent hazard or an unreasonable risk of injury to health or the environment. The EPA may require special labeling, limit the use of a substance, set production quotas, or prohibit the use of a substance altogether.

SECTION 6 | Hazardous Wastes

Some industrial, agricultural, and household wastes pose more serious threats than others. If not properly disposed of, these toxic chemicals may present a substantial danger to human health and the environment. If released into the environment, they may contaminate public drinking water resources.

RESOURCE CONSERVATION AND RECOVERY ACT

In 1976, Congress passed the Resource Conservation and Recovery Act (RCRA)[16] in reaction to an ever-increasing concern about the effects of hazardous waste materials on the environment. The RCRA required the EPA to establish regulations to monitor and control hazardous waste disposal and to determine which forms of solid waste should be considered hazardous and thus subject to regulation. The act authorized the EPA to promulgate various technical requirements for some types of facilities for storage and treatment of hazardous waste. The act also requires all producers of hazardous waste materials to label and package properly any hazardous waste to be transported.

AMENDMENTS TO THE RCRA The RCRA was amended in 1984 and 1986 to decrease the use of land containment in the disposal of hazardous waste. The amendments also require compliance with the act by some generators of hazardous waste—such as those generating less than 1,000 kilograms (2,200 pounds) a month—that had previously been excluded from regulation under the RCRA.

PENALTIES UNDER THE RCRA Under the RCRA, a company may be assessed a civil penalty based on the seriousness of the violation, the probability of harm, and the extent to which the violation deviates from RCRA requirements. The assessment may be up to $25,000 for each violation. Criminal penalties include fines up to $50,000 for each day of violation, imprisonment for up to two years (in most instances), or both. In addition, if a person knowingly violates the RCRA requirements and endangers the life of another, he or she may be imprisoned for up to fifteen years and fined up to $250,000. Criminal fines and the time of imprisonment can also be doubled for certain repeat offenders.

SUPERFUND

In 1980, Congress passed the Comprehensive Environmental Response, Compensation, and Liability Act (CERCLA),[17] commonly known as Superfund. The basic purpose of Superfund is to attempt to regulate the clean-up of disposal sites in which hazardous waste is leaking into the environment. A special federal fund was created for that purpose.

POTENTIALLY RESPONSIBLE PARTIES Superfund provides that when a release or a threatened release of hazardous chemicals from a site occurs, the EPA can clean up the site and recover the cost of the clean-up from the following persons: (1) the person who generated the wastes disposed of at the site, (2) the person who transported the wastes to the site, (3) the person who owned or operated the site at the time of the disposal, or (4) the current owner or operator. A person falling within one of these categories is referred to as a **potentially responsible party (PRP).** In the following case, the issue was the meaning of *disposal* as that term is used in the provision of CERCLA that lists PRPs.

---

15. 15 U.S.C. Sections 2601–2692.
16. 42 U.S.C. Sections 6901–6986.

17. 42 U.S.C. Sections 9601–9675.

CASE 24.3 — Carson Harbor Village, Ltd. v. Unocal Corp.

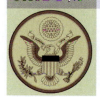

United States
Court of Appeals,
Ninth Circuit, 2001.
270 F.3d 863.

McKEOWN, Circuit Judge:

* * * *

Carson Harbor [Village Limited] owns and operates a mobile home park on seventy acres in the City of Carson, California. From 1977 until 1983, prior to Carson Harbor's ownership, defendant Carson Harbor Village Mobile Home Park, a general partnership controlled by defendants Braley and Smith (the "Partnership Defendants"), owned the property. They, like Carson Harbor, operated a mobile home park on the property. Beginning over thirty years earlier, however, from 1945 until 1983, Unocal Corporation held a leasehold interest in the property and used it for petroleum production, operating a number of oil wells, pipelines, above-ground storage tanks, and production facilities.

An undeveloped open-flow wetlands area covers approximately seventeen acres of the site. * * *

While attempting to refinance the property in 1993, Carson Harbor discovered hazardous substances on the site. The prospective lender commissioned an environmental assessment, which revealed tar-like and slag materials in the wetlands area of the property. Subsequent investigation revealed that the materials were a waste or by-product of petroleum production and that they had been on the property for several decades prior to its development as a mobile home park. * * * The material and surrounding soils contained elevated levels of petroleum hydrocarbons (measured in "total petroleum hydrocarbons" or "TPH") and lead * * * .

* * * *

In 1997, Carson Harbor brought suit [in a federal district court] against the Partnership Defendants [and others] seeking relief under federal environmental statutes, [including] CERCLA * * * . Carson Harbor sought to recover the costs of its cleanup (which totaled approximately $285,000) as well as damages arising from its inability to refinance the property. * * *

* * * The district court granted the defendants' [motion for summary judgment]. * * *

* * * *

Carson Harbor appealed the district court's rulings on the CERCLA claim [to the U.S. Court of Appeals for the Ninth Circuit] * * * .

* * * *

CERCLA defines "disposal" * * * with reference to the definition of "disposal" in RCRA, which in turn defines "disposal" as follows:

The term "disposal" means the discharge, deposit, injection, dumping, spilling, leaking, or placing of any solid waste or hazardous waste into or on any land or water so that such solid waste or hazardous waste or any constituent thereof may enter the environment or be emitted into the air or discharged into any waters, including ground waters.

Under this definition, for the Partnership Defendants to be PRPs [potentially responsible parties], there must have been a "discharge, deposit, injection, dumping, spilling, leaking, or placing" of contaminants on the property during their ownership.

* * * *

Examining the facts of this case, we hold that the gradual passive migration of contamination through the soil that allegedly took place during the Partnership Defendants' ownership was not a "discharge, deposit, injection, dumping, spilling, leaking, or placing" and, therefore, was not a "disposal" within the meaning of [CERCLA]. The contamination on the property included tar-like and slag materials. The tar-like material was highly viscous and uniform, without any breaks or stratification. The slag material had a vesicular structure and was more porous and rigid than the tar-like material. There was some evidence that the tar-like material moved through the soil and that lead and/or TPH may have moved from that material into the soil. If we try to characterize this passive soil migration in plain English, a

CONTINUED ▶

CASE 24.3 | **Continued**   number of words come to mind, including gradual "spreading," "migration," "seeping," "oozing," and possibly "leaching." But certainly none of those words fits within the plain and common meaning of "discharge, * * * injection, dumping, * * * or placing." Although these words generally connote active conduct, even if we were to infuse passive meanings, these words simply do not describe the passive migration that occurred here. Nor can the gradual spread here be characterized as a "deposit," because there was neither a deposit by someone, nor does the term "deposit" encompass the gradual spread of contaminants. The term "spilling" is likewise inapposite. Nothing spilled out of or over anything. Unlike the spilling of a barrel or the spilling over of a holding pond, movement of the tar-like and slag materials was not a spill.

Of the terms defining "disposal," the only one that might remotely describe the passive soil migration here is "leaking." But under the plain and common meaning of the word, we conclude that there was no "leaking." The circumstances here are not like that of the leaking barrel or underground storage tank envisioned by Congress, or a vessel or some other container that would connote "leaking." Therefore, there was no "disposal," and the Partnership Defendants are not PRPs. On this basis, we affirm the district court's grant of summary judgment to the Partnership Defendants on the CERCLA claim.

QUESTIONS

1. Why not interpret the term *disposal* to include all subsoil passive migration of hazardous substances, and thus hold any owner of contaminated property liable for the cost of its clean-up?
2. Is it possible to objectively determine how clean-up costs for hazardous waste sites should be apportioned among the responsible parties?

JOINT AND SEVERAL LIABILITY Liability under Superfund is usually joint and several—that is, a PRP who generated only a fraction of the hazardous waste disposed of at the site may nevertheless be liable for all of the clean-up costs. CERCLA authorizes a party who has incurred clean-up costs to bring a "contribution action" against any other person who is liable or potentially liable for a percentage of the costs.

REVIEWING ENVIRONMENTAL LAW

In the late 1980s, various residents of Lake Caliopa, Minnesota, began noticing an unusually high number of lung ailments among their population. A group of concerned local citizens pooled their resources and commissioned a study of the frequency of these health conditions per capita as compared to national averages. The study concluded that Lake Caliopa had four to seven times the usual frequency of asthma, bronchitis, and emphysema when compared to national data. During the study period, citizens began expressing concerns about the large volumes of smog emitted by the Cotton Design apparel manufacturing plant on the outskirts of town. The plant had opened its production facility two miles east of town beside the Tawakoni River in 1977 and employed seventy full-time workers by 1991. Just downstream on the Tawakoni River, the city of Lake Caliopa operated a public water works facility, which supplied all city residents with water. In August 1991, the Minnesota Pollution Control Agency required Cotton Design to install new equipment to control air and water pollution. In May 1992, thirty citizens brought a class-action lawsuit in a Minnesota state court against Cotton Design for various respiratory ailments allegedly caused or compounded by smog from Cotton Design's factory. Using the information presented in the chapter, answer the following questions.

1. Under the common law, what would each plaintiff be required to identify in order to be given relief by the court?
2. Are air-quality regulations typically overseen by federal, state, or local governments? Which agency establishes these regulations?

REVIEWING ENVIRONMENTAL LAW—Continued

3. The equipment to control air pollution has to meet what standard for limiting emissions from Cotton Design? To what requirements relating to water pollution would Cotton Design be subject?

4. What information must the city send to every household that the city supplies with water?

5. In what ways can the Environmental Protection Agency regulate organizations, such as Cotton Design, that use toxic substances?

TERMS AND CONCEPTS TO REVIEW

environmental impact
  statement (EIS) 574

environmental law 572

nuisance 572

potentially responsible
  party (PRP) 582

toxic tort 572

wetlands 578

QUESTIONS AND CASE PROBLEMS

24–1. Some scientific knowledge indicates that there is no safe level of exposure to a cancer-causing agent. In theory, even one molecule of such a substance has the potential for causing cancer. Section 112 of the Clean Air Act requires that all cancer-causing substances be regulated to ensure a margin of safety. Some environmental groups have argued that all emissions of such substances must be eliminated to attain such a margin of safety. Total elimination would likely shut down many major U.S. industries. Should the Environmental Protection Agency totally forbid all emissions of cancer-causing chemicals? Discuss.

24–2. **QUESTION WITH SAMPLE ANSWER**

Fruitade, Inc., is a processor of a soft drink called Freshen Up. Fruitade uses returnable bottles, which it cleans with a special acid to allow for further beverage processing. The acid is diluted with water and then allowed to pass into a navigable stream. Fruitade crushes its broken bottles and throws the crushed glass into the stream. Discuss fully any environmental laws that Fruitade has violated.
For a sample answer to this question, go to Appendix I at the end of this text.

24–3. Moonbay is a home-building corporation that primarily develops retirement communities. Farmtex owns a number of feedlots in Sunny Valley. Moonbay purchased 20,000 acres of farmland in the same area and began building and selling homes on this acreage. In the meantime, Farmtex continued to expand its feedlot business, and eventually only 500 feet separated the two operations. Because of the odor and flies from the feed-

lots, Moonbay found it difficult to sell the homes in its development. Moonbay wants to enjoin (prevent) Farmtex from operating its feedlot in the vicinity of the retirement home development. Under what common law theory would Moonbay file this action? Has Farmtex violated any federal environmental laws? Discuss.

24–4. **TOXIC CHEMICALS.** The Environmental Protection Agency canceled the registration of the pesticide diazinon for use on golf courses and sod farms because of concerns over the effects of diazinon on birds. The Federal Insecticide, Fungicide, and Rodenticide Act authorizes cancellation of the registration of products that "generally cause unreasonable adverse effects on the environment." The statute further defines "unreasonable adverse effects on the environment" to mean "any unreasonable risk to man or the environment, taking into account the . . . costs and benefits." Thus, in determining whether a pesticide should continue to be used, it is necessary to balance the risks and benefits of the use of the pesticide. Does this mean that, to prohibit the pesticide's use, a judge must find that the pesticide kills birds more often than not, or is it sufficient to find that the use of the pesticide results in recurrent bird kills? [*Ciba-Geigy Corp. v. Environmental Protection Agency*, 874 F.2d 277 (5th Cir. 1989)]

24–5. **WATER POLLUTION.** Taylor Bay Protective Association is a nonprofit corporation established for the purpose of restoring and improving the water quality of Taylor Bay. Local water districts began operating a flood-control project in the area. As part of the project, a pumping station was developed. Testimony at trial revealed that the pumps were operated contrary to the instructions provided in the operation and maintenance manual. The pumps acted as vacuums, sucking up silt and depositing the silt in Taylor Bay. Thus, the project resulted in sedimentation and turbidity (a condition of having dense, stirred-up particles) problems in the downstream watercourse of Taylor Bay. The association sued the local water districts, alleging that the pumping operations created a nuisance. Do the pumping operations qualify as a common law nuisance? Who should be responsible for the clean-up costs? Discuss both questions fully. [*Taylor Bay Protective Association v. Environmental Protection Agency*, 884 F.2d 1073 (8th Cir. 1989)]

24–6. CLEAN WATER ACT. Attique Ahmad owned the Spin-N-Market, a convenience store and gas station. The gas pumps were fed by underground tanks, one of which had a leak at its top that allowed water to enter. Ahmad emptied the tank by pumping its contents into a storm drain and a sewer system. Through the storm drain, gasoline flowed into a creek, forcing the city to clean the water. Through the sewer system, gasoline flowed into a sewage treatment plant, forcing the city to evacuate the plant and two nearby schools. Ahmad was charged with discharging a pollutant without a permit, which is a criminal violation of the Clean Water Act. The act provides that a person who "knowingly violates" the act commits a felony. Ahmad claimed that he had believed he was discharging only water. Did Ahmad commit a felony? Why or why not? Discuss fully. [*United States v. Ahmad*, 101 F.3d 386 (5th Cir. 1996)]

24–7. ⚖ CASE PROBLEM WITH SAMPLE ANSWER
William Gurley was the president and majority stockholder in Gurley Refining Co. (GRC). GRC bought used oil, treated it, and sold it. The refining process created a by-product residue of oily waste. GRC disposed of this waste by dumping it at, among other locations, a landfill in West Memphis, Arkansas. In February 1992, after detecting hazardous chemicals at the site, the Environmental Protection Agency (EPA) asked Gurley about his assets, the generators of the material disposed of at the landfill, site operations, and the structure of GRC. Gurley refused to respond, except to suggest that the EPA ask GRC. In October, the EPA placed the site on its clean-up list and again asked Gurley for information. When he still refused to respond, the EPA filed a suit in a federal district court against him, asking the court to impose a civil penalty. In February 1999, Gurley finally answered the EPA's questions. Under CERCLA, a court may impose a civil penalty "not to exceed $25,000 for each day of noncompliance against any person who unreasonably fails to comply" with an information request. Should the court assess a penalty in this case? Why or why not? [*United States v. Gurley*, 384 F.3d 316 (6th Cir. 2004)]
To view a sample answer for this case problem, go to this book's Web site at http://wleb.westbuslaw.com, select "Chapter 24," and click on "Case Problem with Sample Answer."

24–8. ENVIRONMENTAL IMPACT STATEMENT. Greers Ferry Lake is in Arkansas, and its shoreline is under the management of the U.S. Army Corps of Engineers, which is part of the U.S. Department of Defense (DOD). The Corps's 2000 Shoreline Management Plan (SMP) rezoned numerous areas along the lake, authorized the Corps to issue permits for the construction of new boat docks in the rezoned areas, increased by 300 percent the area around habitable structures that could be cleared of vegetation, and instituted a Wildlife Enhancement Permit to allow limited modifications of the shoreline. In relation to the SMP's adoption, the Corps issued a Finding of No Significant Impact, which declared that no environmental impact statement (EIS) was necessary. The Corps issued thirty-two boat dock construction permits under the SMP before Save Greers Ferry Lake, Inc., filed a suit in a federal district court against the DOD, asking the court to, among other things, stop the Corps from acting under the SMP and order it to prepare an EIS. What are the requirements for an EIS? Is an EIS needed in this case? Explain. [*Save Greers Ferry Lake, Inc. v. Department of Defense*, 255 F.3d 498 (8th Cir. 2001)]

24–9. CERCLA. Beginning in 1926, Marietta Dyestuffs Co. operated an industrial facility in Marietta, Ohio, to make dyes and other chemicals. In 1944, Dyestuffs became part of American Home Products Corp. (AHP), which sold the Marietta facility to American Cyanamid Co. in 1946. In 1950, AHP sold the rest of the Dyestuffs assets and all of its stock to Goodrich Co., which immediately liquidated the acquired corporation. Goodrich continued to operate the dissolved corporation's business, however. Cyanamid continued to make chemicals at the Marietta facility, and in 1993, it created Cytec Industries, Inc., which expressly assumed all environmental liabilities associated with Cyanamid's ownership and operation of the facility. Cytec spent nearly $25 million on clean-up costs and filed a suit in a federal district court against Goodrich to recover, under CERCLA, a portion of the costs attributable to the clean-up of hazardous wastes that may have been discarded at the site between 1926 and 1946. Cytec filed a motion for summary judgment in its favor. Should the court grant Cytec's motion? Explain. [*Cytec Industries, Inc. v. B. F. Goodrich Co.*, 196 F.Supp.2d 644 (S.D. Ohio 2002)]

24–10. ⚖ A QUESTION OF ETHICS
The Endangered Species Act of 1973 makes it unlawful for any person to "take" endangered or threatened species. The act defines *take* to mean to "harass, harm, pursue," "wound," or "kill." The secretary of the interior (Bruce Babbitt) issued a regulation that further defined *harm* to include "significant habitat modification or degradation where it actually kills or injures wildlife." A group of businesses and individuals involved in the timber industry brought an action against the secretary of

the interior and others. The group complained that the application of the "harm" regulation to the red-cockaded woodpecker and the northern spotted owl had injured the group economically because it prevented logging operations (habitat modification) in Pacific Northwest forests containing these species. The group challenged the regulation's validity, contending that Congress did not intend the word *take* to include habitat modification. The case ultimately reached the United States Supreme Court, which held that the secretary reasonably construed Congress's intent when he defined *harm* to include habitat modification. [*Babbitt v. Sweet Home Chapter of Communities for a Great Oregon*, 515 U.S. 687, 115 S.Ct. 2407, 132 L.Ed.2d 597 (1995)]

(a) Traditionally, the term *take* has been used to refer to the capture or killing of wildlife, usually for private gain. Is the secretary's regulation prohibiting habitat modification consistent with this definition?

(b) One of the issues in this case was whether Congress intended to protect existing generations of species or future generations. How do the terms *take* and *habitat modification* relate to this issue?

(c) Three dissenting Supreme Court justices contended that construing the act as prohibiting habitat modification "imposes unfairness to the point of financial ruin—not just upon the rich, but upon the simplest farmer who finds his land conscripted to national zoological use." Should private parties be required to bear the burden of preserving habitats for wildlife?

(d) Generally, should the economic welfare of private parties be taken into consideration when creating and applying environmental statutes and regulations?

LAW | on the Web

For updated links to resources available on the Web, as well as a variety of other materials, visit this text's Web site at http://wleb.westbuslaw.com.

For information on the EPA's standards, guidelines, and regulations, go to the EPA's Web site at

http://www.epa.gov

To learn about the RCRA's "buy-recycled" requirements and other steps that the federal government has taken toward "greening the environment," go to

http://www.epa.gov/cpg

The Law Library of the Indiana University School of Law provides numerous links to online environmental law sources. Go to

http://www.law.indiana.edu/library/services/onl_env.shtml

LEGAL RESEARCH EXERCISES ON THE WEB

Go to http://wleb.westbuslaw.com, the Web site that accompanies this text. Select "Chapter 24" and click on "Internet Exercises." There you will find the following Internet research exercises that you can perform to learn more about topics covered in this chapter.

Activity 24–1: LEGAL PERSPECTIVE
Nuisance Law

Activity 24–2: MANAGEMENT PERSPECTIVE
Complying with Environmental Regulation

Activity 24–3: ETHICAL PERSPECTIVE
Environmental Justice

CHAPTER 25

Land-Use Control and Real Property

Property ownership confers certain rights. An owner generally has the right to possess the property; the right either to use the property or to derive profits from another's use of the property; and the right to *alienate*[1] the property—that is, to sell, bequeath (pass on through a will), or give to others the same rights of ownership. Not all forms of ownership provide such a complete bundle of rights, but one or more of these attributes are normally included when we say that property is "owned."

Even for one who possesses the entire bundle of rights we have delineated, however, ownership is not absolute. The law places restrictions on how property may be used. It also imposes duties on the owners regarding how the land is to be maintained. In addition, individual owners may agree with others to restrict or limit the use of their property. Thus, property owners cannot always do with their property whatever they wish. Nuisance and environmental laws, for example, restrict how people carry out certain types of activities on their own land. Briefly stated, the rights of every property owner are subject to certain conditions and limitations.

In this chapter, we first look at the nature of real property and of ownership rights in real property. We then focus on restrictions on ownership in real property. **Real property** (sometimes called *realty* or *real estate*) means the land and everything permanently attached to the land. When structures are *permanently* attached to the land, then everything attached permanently to the structures is also realty. Everything else is **personal property** (or *personalty*). Although real property includes more than land, it is generally referred to simply as "land." Hence, the control over ownership and use that we examine in this chapter is commonly referred to as **land-use control.**

SECTION 1 | The Nature of Real Property

Real property consists of land and the buildings, plants, and trees that it contains. Whereas personal property is movable, real property is immovable. Real property usually means land (and structures), but it also includes airspace and subsurface rights, plant life and vegetation, and *fixtures* (which will be explained shortly).

LAND

Land includes the soil on the surface of the earth and the natural products or artificial structures that are attached to it. It further includes all the waters contained on or under the earth's surface and the air space above it. In other words, absent a contrary statute or case law, a landowner has the right to everything existing permanently below the surface of his or her property to the center of the earth and above it to the sky (subject to certain qualifications).

AIRSPACE AND SUBSURFACE RIGHTS

The owner of real property has relatively exclusive rights to the airspace above the land, as well as to the soil and minerals underneath it. When no limitations on airspace rights or subsurface rights are indicated on the document transferring title at the time of purchase, a purchaser can generally expect to have an unrestricted right to possession of the property (subject to the limits on ownership rights, which will be examined in detail later in this chapter).

---

1. *Alienate* derives from the Latin word *alienus* (alien), which is from the Latin *alus* (other). In legal terms, alienate means to transfer the title to property.

Cases involving air rights present questions such as the right of commercial and private planes to fly over property and the right of individuals and governments to seed clouds and produce artificial rain. Flights over private land do not normally violate the property owners' rights unless the flights are low and frequent, causing a direct interference with the enjoyment and use of the land.[2]

Ownership of the surface of land can be separated from ownership of its subsurface. Subsurface rights can be extremely valuable when minerals, oil, or natural gas is located beneath the surface. A subsurface owner's rights would be of little value if he or she could not use the surface to exercise those rights. Hence, a subsurface owner will have a right (called a *profit*—discussed later in this chapter) to use the surface of the land to, for example, find and remove minerals. If the owners of the subsurface rights excavate and their excavation causes the surface to subside, however, they may be liable to the owner of the surface rights.

PLANT LIFE AND VEGETATION

Plant life, both natural and cultivated, is also considered to be real property. In many instances, natural vegetation, such as trees, adds greatly to the value of realty. When a parcel of land is sold and the land has growing crops on it, the sale includes the crops, unless otherwise specified in the sales contract. When crops are sold by themselves, however, they are considered to be personal property or goods. Consequently, the sale of crops is a sale of goods, and it is governed by the Uniform Commercial Code (see Chapter 11) rather than by real property law.

FIXTURES

Certain personal property can become so closely associated with the real property to which it is attached that the law views it as real property. Such property is known as a **fixture**—a thing *affixed* to realty. A thing is affixed to realty when it is attached to it by roots; embedded in it; or permanently attached by means of cement, plaster, bolts, nails, or screws. The fixture can be physically attached to real property, can be attached to another fixture, or can even be without any actual physical attachment to the land, as long as the owner *intends* the property to be a fixture.

Fixtures are included in the sale of land if the sales contract does not provide otherwise. The sale of a house includes the land and the house and garage on it, as well as the cabinets, plumbing, and windows. Because these are permanently affixed to the property, they are considered to be a part of it. Unless otherwise agreed, however, the curtains and throw rugs are not included. Items such as drapes and window-unit air conditioners are difficult to classify. Thus, a contract for the sale of a house or commercial realty should indicate which items of this sort are included in the sale. At issue in the following case was whether an agricultural irrigation system qualified as a fixture.

---

2. *United States v. Causby*, 328 U.S. 256, 66 S.Ct. 1062, 90 L.Ed. 1206 (1946).

CASE 25.1	**In re Sand & Sage Farm & Ranch, Inc.**[a]

United States
Bankruptcy Court,
District of Kansas, 2001.
266 Bankr. 507.

BACKGROUND AND FACTS *In 1988, Randolf and Sandra Ardery bought an eighty-acre tract in Edwards County, Kansas. On the land was an eight-tower center-pivot irrigation system. The system consisted of an underground well and pump connected to a pipe that ran to the pivot where the water line was attached to a further system of pipes and sprinklers suspended from the towers, extending over the land in a circular fashion. The system's engine and gearhead were bolted to a concrete slab above the pump and well and were attached to the pipe. To secure a loan to buy the land, the Arderys granted to Farmers State Bank a mortgage that covered "all buildings, improvements, and fixtures." In 1996, the Arderys, and their firm Sand & Sage Farm & Ranch, Inc., granted Ag Services of America a security interest in the farm's "equipment." Nothing in the security agreement or financing statement referred to fixtures.[b] In 2000, the Arderys and Sand &*

---

a. The term *in re* means "in the matter of," "concerning," or "regarding." Case titles that begin with *in re* indicate that the matter before the court did not involve adversarial parties but rather called for some judicial action to be taken—in this case, a determination of who had ownership rights in an irrigation system.

b. Security agreements were discussed in Chapter 15.

CONTINUED ▶

CASE 25.1 | Continued *Sage filed for bankruptcy in a federal bankruptcy court and asked for permission to sell the land, with the irrigation system, to Bohn Enterprises, Limited Partnership. Ag Services claimed that it had priority to the proceeds covering the value of the irrigation system. The bank responded that it had priority because the system was a "fixture."*

IN THE LANGUAGE OF THE COURT

ROBERT E. NUGENT, Bankruptcy Judge.
* * * *

* * * [There is] a three-step judicial test for determining whether personalty attached to real estate is legally a fixture. Paraphrased, the steps are:

(i) how firmly the goods are attached or the ease of their removal (annexation);
(ii) the relationship of the parties involved (intent); and
(iii) how operation of the goods is related to the use of the land (adaptation).

Of the three factors, intent is the controlling factor and is deduced largely from the property-owner's acts and the surrounding circumstances. [Emphasis added.]
* * * *

* * * [The irrigation system] is firmly attached to the realty. The irrigation pipes are connected to the center pivot which is bolted to a cement slab in the center of the irrigation property and connected to the underground well and pump by wires and pipes. Further, the system is not easily removable. The towers must be disassembled in sections and transported separately, and disassembly and removal of the engine, gearhead, and pump would be time-consuming and require the assistance of experienced people. It would also be expensive * * *.

The relationships between the parties involved in each transaction also suggest the shared intent that the irrigation system be a fixture. In 1988, * * * Ardery [bought the land] with the irrigation system included. Ardery, in turn, mortgaged the land, and the fixtures, to the Bank [whose officer] testified that he considered the conveyance of the mortgage to include the system as that was the Bank's custom and practice in Edwards County. Ardery and Bohn clearly intend the system to pass with the land in the sale now before the Court. * * *

The irrigation system is suitably adapted to the land. There can be little dispute concerning the need for pivot irrigation in the semi-arid conditions of southwestern Kansas. All witnesses agreed, and it is well within this Court's common experience, that irrigated units of land are substantially more productive of crops than dryland acres. This alone demonstrates the relation between the operation of the goods and use of the land.

DECISION AND REMEDY *The court concluded that the system was a fixture. The bank was entitled to the proceeds from its sale.*

SECTION 2 | Ownership Interests in Real Property

Ownership of property is an abstract concept that cannot exist independently of the legal system. No one actually possesses or *holds* a piece of land, along with the air above, the earth below, and all the water contained on it. One can only possess *rights* in real property. Numerous rights are involved in real property ownership. One who holds the entire bundle of rights owns in *fee simple absolute*. We look first at the fee simple absolute and then at the various types of limited property interests that exist when an owner

in fee simple absolute parts with some, but not all, of his or her rights in real property.

FEE SIMPLE

In a **fee simple absolute,** the owner has the greatest aggregation of rights, privileges, and power possible. The owner can give the property away, sell the property for a price, or transfer the property by will to another. The fee simple absolute is limited absolutely to a person and his or her heirs and is assigned forever without limitation or condition. The rights that accompany a fee simple absolute include the right to use the land for whatever purpose the owner sees fit, subject to laws that prevent the owner from unreasonably interfering with another person's land and subject to applicable zoning laws. Furthermore, the owner has the right of *exclusive* possession of the property. A fee simple absolute is potentially infinite in duration and can be disposed of by deed or by will (by selling or by giving away). When there is no will, the fee simple absolute passes to the owner's legal heirs.

Ownership in fee simple may become limited when the property is transferred to another *conditionally*. When this occurs, the fee simple is known as a **fee simple defeasible** (the word *defeasible* means capable of being terminated, or annulled). For example, a **conveyance,** or transfer of real property, "to A and his heirs as long as the land is used for charitable purposes" creates a fee simple defeasible, because ownership of the property is conditioned on the land's being used for charitable purposes. The original owner retains a *partial* ownership interest, because if the specified condition does not occur (if the land ceases to be used for charitable purposes), then the land reverts, or returns, to the original owner. If the original owner is not living at the time, the land passes to his or her heirs. The conveyance of a fee simple defeasible usually includes the words as *long as, until, while,* or *during*.

LIFE ESTATES

A **life estate** is an estate that lasts for the life of some specified individual. A conveyance "to A for his life" creates a life estate.[3] In a life estate, the life tenant (the party who holds the estate) has fewer rights of ownership than the holder of a fee simple defeasible, because the rights necessarily cease to exist on the life tenant's death. The life tenant has the right to use the land, provided no *waste* (injury to the land) is committed. In other words, the life tenant cannot injure the land in a manner that would adversely affect its value to the owner of the future interest in it. The life tenant can use the land to harvest crops or, if mines and oil wells are already on the land, can extract minerals and oil from it, but the life tenant cannot exploit the land by creating new wells or mines.

With few exceptions, the owner of a life estate has an exclusive right to possession during his or her lifetime. In addition, the life tenant has the right to

mortgage the life estate and create other interests in the land, but none can extend beyond the life of the tenant.

Along with these rights, the life tenant also has some duties—to keep the property in repair and to pay property taxes. In short, the owner of the life estate has the same rights as a fee simple owner except that he or she must maintain the value of the property during his or her tenancy, less the decrease in value resulting from the normal use of the property allowed by the life tenancy.

FUTURE INTERESTS

When an owner in fee simple absolute conveys the estate conditionally to another (such as with a fee simple defeasible) or for a limited period of time (such as with a life estate), the original owner still retains an interest in the land. The owner retains the right to repossess ownership of the land if the conditions of the fee simple defeasible are not met or when the life of the life-estate holder ends. The residuary (or leftover) interest in the property that the owner retains is called a **future interest,** because if it arises, it will only arise in the future.

If the owner retains ownership of the future interest, then the future interest is a **reversionary interest,** because the property will *revert* to the original owner if the condition specified in the fee simple defeasible fails or when the life tenant dies. If, however, the owner of the future interest transfers ownership rights in that future interest to another, the future interest is a **remainder.** For example, a conveyance "to A for life, then to B" creates a life estate for A and a remainder (future interest) for B. An **executory interest** is a type of future interest very similar to a remainder, but an executory interest does not take effect immediately on the expiration of another interest, such as a life estate. For example, a conveyance "to A for life and one year after A's death to B" creates an executory interest for B.

LEASEHOLD ESTATES

A **leasehold estate** is created when a real property owner or lessor (landlord) agrees to convey the right to possess and use the property to a lessee (tenant) for a certain period of time. The tenant has a *qualified* right to exclusive possession (qualified by the right of the landlord to enter onto the premises to ensure that waste is not being committed). The tenant can use the land—for example,

---

3. A less common type of life estate is created by the conveyance "to A for the life of B." This is known as an estate *pur autre vie,* or an estate for the duration of the life of another.

by harvesting crops—but cannot injure it by such activities as cutting down timber for sale or extracting oil. Here we look at the types of leasehold estates, or tenancies, that can be created when real property is leased.

TENANCY FOR YEARS   A **tenancy for years** is created by an express contract (which can sometimes be oral) by which property is leased for a specified period of time, such as a month, a year, or a period of years. For example, signing a one-year lease to occupy an apartment creates a tenancy for years. At the end of the period specified in the lease, the lease ends (without notice), and possession of the apartment returns to the lessor. The lease may provide for renewal or extension.

PERIODIC TENANCY   A **periodic tenancy** is created by a lease that does not specify how long it is to last but does specify that rent is to be paid at certain intervals. This type of tenancy is automatically renewed for another rental period unless properly terminated. For example, a periodic tenancy is created by a lease that states, "Rent is due on the tenth day of every month." This provision creates a tenancy from month to month. This type of tenancy can also be from week to week or from year to year. A periodic tenancy sometimes arises when a landlord allows a tenant under a tenancy for years to remain in possession after the lease expires and continue paying monthly or weekly rent. At common law, to terminate a periodic tenancy, the landlord or tenant must give one period's notice to the other party. If the tenancy is month to month, for example, one month's notice must be given. State statutes often require a different period for notice of termination in a periodic tenancy, however.

TENANCY AT WILL   Suppose a landlord rents an apartment to a tenant "for as long as both agree." In such a case, the tenant receives a **tenancy at will.** At common law, either party can terminate the tenancy without notice (that is, "at will"). This type of tenancy usually arises when a tenant who has been under a tenancy for years retains possession after the termination date of that tenancy with the landlord's consent. Before the tenancy has been converted into a periodic tenancy (by the periodic payment of rent), it is a tenancy at will, terminable by either party without notice. The death of either party or the voluntary commission of waste by the tenant will terminate a tenancy at will.

TENANCY AT SUFFERANCE   The mere possession of land without right is called a **tenancy at sufferance.** It is not a true tenancy. A tenancy at sufferance is not an estate, because it is created by a tenant's *wrongfully* retaining possession of property. Whenever a life estate, tenancy for years, periodic tenancy, or tenancy at will ends and the tenant continues to retain possession of the premises without the owner's permission, a tenancy at sufferance is created.

CONCURRENT OWNERSHIP

Persons who share ownership rights simultaneously in particular property are said to be *concurrent owners*. There are two principal types of **concurrent ownership:** *tenancy in common* and *joint tenancy*. Concurrent ownership rights can also be held in a *tenancy by the entirety* or as *community property*, although these latter two types of concurrent ownership are less common.

TENANCY IN COMMON   A form of co-ownership in which each of two or more persons owns an undivided portion of the property is a **tenancy in common.** The portions need not be equal. When a tenant in common dies, the property interest passes to his or her heirs. For example, suppose Henri and Luis own equal interests in a rare coin collection as tenants in common. If Henri dies before Luis, one-half of the coin collection will become the property of Henri's heirs. If instead Henri sells his interest to Stella, Stella and Luis will become co-owners as tenants in common. If Stella dies, her interest in the personal property will pass to her heirs, and they in turn will own the property with Luis as tenants in common.

JOINT TENANCY   In a **joint tenancy,** each of two or more persons owns an undivided interest in the whole (personal property), and a deceased joint tenant's interest *passes to the surviving joint tenant or tenants*. Joint tenancy can be terminated at any time before the joint tenant's death by gift or by sale. If no termination occurs, then on the death of a joint tenant, his or her interest transfers to the remaining joint tenants, not to the heirs of the deceased joint tenant. To illustrate: If Henri and Luis from the preceding example are joint tenants and if Henri dies before Luis, the entire collection will become the property of Luis. Henri's heirs will receive absolutely no interest in the collection. If Henri sells his interest to Stella, Stella and Luis will become co-owners. Henri's sale, however, will have terminated the joint tenancy, and Stella and Luis will become owners as tenants in common.

Exhibit 25–1 illustrates the concepts of tenancy in common and joint tenancy.

EXHIBIT 25-1 **Tenancy in Common and Joint Tenancy**

If Henri and Luis own equal interests in a coin collection as tenants in common, and Henri dies, one-half of the coin collection will become the property of Henri's heirs. If instead Henri sells his interest to Stella, Stella and Luis will become co-owners as tenants in common. If Henri and Luis own the coin collection as joint tenants, however, and Henri dies, the entire collection will become the property of Luis. If instead Henri sells his interest to Stella, Luis and Stella will become co-owners as tenants in common.

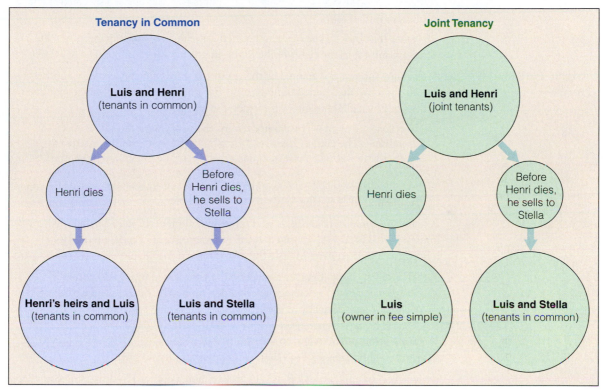

TENANCY BY THE ENTIRETY A **tenancy by the entirety** is created by a *conveyance* (transfer) of real property to a husband and wife. It is distinguished from a joint tenancy by the inability of either spouse to transfer separately his or her interest during his or her lifetime. In states in which statutes give the wife the right to convey her property, tenancy by the entirety has been effectively abolished. A divorce, either spouse's death, or mutual agreement will terminate a tenancy by the entirety.

COMMUNITY PROPERTY A limited number of states[4] allow property to be owned as **community property.** If property is held as community property, each spouse technically owns an *undivided* one-half

interest in it. This type of ownership generally does not apply to property acquired prior to the marriage or to property acquired by gift or inheritance during the marriage.

SECTION 3 | Private Control of Land Use

One source of land-use control is voluntary agreements between private individuals. A landowner's use of his or her property may be limited by another individual's right to, for example, cross the property. Such interests do not depend on the individual's possession of the property but still limit the use of the property. These interests may be created in a deed. Other promises included in a deed, or in an assignment, lease, mortgage, or other instrument

---

4. These states include Alaska, Arizona, California, Idaho, Louisiana, Nevada, New Mexico, Texas, Washington, and Wisconsin, as well as Puerto Rico.

CONCEPT SUMMARY 25.1 | Ownership Interests in Real Property

TYPE OF INTEREST	DESCRIPTION
FEE SIMPLE	1. *Fee simple absolute*—The most complete form of ownership. 2. *Fee simple defeasible*—Ownership in fee simple that can end if a specified event or condition occurs.
LIFE ESTATE	An estate that lasts for the life of a specified individual; ownership rights in a life estate are subject to the rights of the future-interest holder.
FUTURE INTEREST	A residuary interest not granted by the grantor in conveying an estate to another for life, for a specified period of time, or on the condition that a specific event does or does not occur. Future interests include the following: 1. *Reversionary interest*—The grantor retains the residuary interest. 2. *Remainder*—The grantor transfers ownership rights in the future interest to another who will take possession immediately on the expiration of another interest. 3. *Executory interest*—Like a remainder, but it does not take effect immediately on the expiration of another interest.
LEASEHOLD ESTATE	A leasehold interest, or estate, is an interest in real property that is held only for a limited period of time, as specified in the lease agreement. Types of tenancies relating to leased property include the following: 1. *Tenancy for years*—Tenancy for a period of time stated by express contract. 2. *Periodic tenancy*—Tenancy for a period determined by the frequency of rent payments; automatically renewed unless proper notice is given. 3. *Tenancy at will*—Tenancy for as long as both parties agree; no notice of termination is required. 4. *Tenancy at sufferance*—Possession of land without legal right.
CONCURRENT OWNERSHIP	Exists when title to property is held by two or more persons. Co-ownership can take the following forms: 1. *Tenancy in common*—Two or more persons own an undivided interest in property; on one tenant's death, the property interest passes to his or her heirs. 2. *Joint tenancy*—Two or more persons own an undivided interest in property; on the death of a joint tenant, the property interest transfers to the remaining tenant(s), not to the heirs of the deceased. 3. *Tenancy by the entirety*—Between a husband and wife, and similar to a joint tenancy, except that a spouse cannot transfer separately his or her interest during his or her lifetime. 4. *Community property*—Between a husband and wife, and each spouse technically owns an undivided one-half interest in property acquired during the marriage. This type of ownership occurs in only a few states.

relating to real property, may limit a landowner's use of his or her property in other ways. Here, we examine the ways in which private agreements serve as mechanisms for control of land use.

NONPOSSESSORY INTERESTS

Some interests in land do not include any rights of possession. These interests, known as nonpossessory interests, include *easements, profits,* and *licenses.* Because easements and profits are similar, and the same rules apply to both, they will be discussed together.

EASEMENTS AND PROFITS An **easement** is the right of a person to make limited use of another person's real property without taking anything from the property. Suppose Sara, the owner of Whiteacres, has a right to drive her car across Ken's land, Greenacres, which is adjacent to Whiteacres. This right-of-way over Greenacres is an easement. In contrast, a **profit** is the right to go onto land in possession of another and take away some part of the land itself or some product of the land. For example, Chen, the owner of Sea View, gives Loretta the right to go there and remove all the sand and gravel that she needs for her cement business. Loretta has a profit.[5]

—Creation of an Easement or Profit. Easements and profits can be created by *deed* or *will* or by *implication, necessity,* or *prescription.* Creation by deed or will involves simply the delivery of a *deed* or a transfer by a *will,* by the owner of an easement, stating that the grantee (the person receiving the profit or easement) is granted the rights in the easement or profit that the grantor had. An easement or profit is created by *implication* when the circumstances surrounding the division of a parcel of property imply its creation. If

Adrian divides a parcel of land that has only one well for drinking water and conveys the half without a well to Victor, a profit by implication arises, because Victor needs drinking water.

An easement may also be created by *necessity.* An easement by necessity does not require division of property for its existence. A person who rents an apartment, for example, has an easement by necessity in the private road leading up to it. An easement or profit arises by *prescription* when one person exercises an easement, such as a right-of-way, on another person's land without the landowner's consent, and the use is apparent and continues for a period of time equal to the applicable statute of limitations.

—Effect of a Sale of Property. When a parcel of land that is *benefited* by an easement or profit on adjacent land is sold, the property carries the easement or profit along with it. Thus, if Sara sells Whiteacres to MacDonald and includes the right-of-way across her neighbor Ken's land, Greenacres, in the deed to MacDonald, MacDonald will own both the property and the easement that benefits it.

When a parcel of land that has the *burden* of an easement or profit benefiting adjacent land is sold, the new owner must recognize its existence only if he or she knew or should have known of it or if it was recorded in the appropriate office of the county. Thus, if Sara records her easement across Greenacres in the appropriate county office before Ken conveys his land, the new owner of Greenacres will have to allow Sara, or any subsequent owner of Whiteacres, to continue to use the right-of-way across Greenacres.

Whether an easement accompanied a sale of property was at issue in the following case.

---

5. Easements and profits may be *appurtenant* or *in gross.* An easement or profit appurtenant arises when the owner of one piece of land has a right to go onto (or remove things from) an adjacent piece of land owned by another. An easement or profit in gross simply gives the owner of the easement or profit the right to go onto (or remove something from) land owned by another; there is no requirement that the owner of the easement or profit also own land.

CASE 25.2 **Webster v. Ragona**

New York
Supreme Court,
Appellate Division,
Third Department, 2004.
7 A.D.3d 850,
776 N.Y.S.2d 347.

BACKGROUND AND FACTS *Walter Peeters owned two commercial buildings at 26 and 32 Main Street in Oneonta, New York. The tenants at both addresses used a common driveway for access to a parking lot behind the buildings. In 1992, Gerard Webster leased 26 Main Street and opened a restaurant on the premises. The same year, Giacinto and Antoinette Ragona began leasing 32 Main Street to operate a video store. In September 1994, the Ragonas bought their building. The contract of sale conditioned transfer of title on "the granting of any necessary permanent easement for parking in the rear of the premises." The parties signed an agreement to transfer an easement in the driveway, which the Ragonas agreed to insure and to maintain. That winter, they used the driveway, repaired it, and cleared it of snow. In May 1995, Webster bought 26 Main Street, which included the driveway. The deed did not mention the Ragonas' easement. Six years later,*

CONTINUED

CASE 25.2 | Continued

Webster and his associates filed a suit in a New York state court against the Ragonas, arguing in part that their easement in the driveway was extinguished on Peeters's sale of 26 Main Street. The court issued a summary judgment in the defendants' favor. The plaintiffs appealed to a state intermediate appellate court.

IN THE LANGUAGE OF THE COURT

SPAIN, J. [Justice]

* * * *

An easement appurtenant is created when such easement is (1) conveyed in writing, (2) subscribed by the person creating the easement and (3) burdens the servient estate for the benefit of the dominant estate. The easement agreement fulfills all of these elements. Plaintiffs nevertheless argue that an easement appurtenant was not created, relying on the fact that the instrument does not expressly state that the easement is permanent * * * .

While it is true that *whether an easement is appurtenant or merely a personal, non-inheritable and non-assignable right depends upon the intent of the parties to the instrument in which the right-of-way was granted,* as with any contract, where possible such intent should be gleaned solely from the language of the instrument creating the easement. It is only when language used in a conveyance is susceptible of more than one interpretation that the courts will look into surrounding circumstances, the situation of the parties, etc. In our view, the easement agreement at issue here can only be interpreted to convey an easement appurtenant. That the easement did not employ the term "permanent" or include an express reference binding Peeters' heirs and assigns is not dispositive [controlling]. The grant of such an easement need not include language expressly describing the easement as "permanent" because *an easement appurtenant, once created, necessarily runs with the land.* Indeed, the clear purpose of the agreement was to convert an informal right-of-way which was already in existence into a legally binding easement which would burden Peeters' estate at 26 Main Street for the benefit of 32 Main Street, the Ragonas' dominant estate. Significantly, the instrument did not contain any language restricting the easement or retaining any right of revocation. Accordingly, we need not look beyond the easement agreement itself to ascertain that the easement created thereby is binding upon Peeters' successors in interest, provided they had notice of the easement when they took title—which brings us to plaintiffs' remaining contentions. [Emphasis added.]

* * * *

In the complaint, plaintiffs [Webster and his associates] allege that they were unaware, prior to purchasing 26 Main Street, that the property was encumbered by an easement or subject to use by the Ragonas. In their answer, the Ragonas allege that plaintiffs had both actual and constructive notice of their claim to the easement, claiming, among other things, that their conduct in maintaining the disputed property would have caused a reasonable person to inquire about the status of that property. * * *

Notably, plaintiffs have not denied any of the specific allegations which would have put them on notice that the Ragonas were using the property in question * * * . Instead, plaintiffs rely on the claim that they lacked notice that the easement was permanent and binding upon them as subsequent purchasers. [The] Supreme Court correctly found that this claim is insufficient to preclude summary judgment in favor of the Ragonas because plaintiffs' knowledge that the Ragonas were enjoying use of the property was sufficient to charge plaintiffs with the duty to inquire about the nature and status of the right-of-way.

DECISION AND REMEDY   *The state intermediate appellate court affirmed the judgment of the lower court. The Ragonas had a "permanent" easement appurtenant in the driveway between 26 and 32 Main Street. "[A]n easement appurtenant, once created, necessarily runs with the land."*

WHAT IF THE FACTS WERE DIFFERENT?   *What might the result in this case have been if Peeters had told Webster when he bought 26 Main Street that the Ragonas did not have a "permanent" easement in the driveway?*

—Termination of an Easement or Profit. An easement or profit can be terminated or extinguished in several ways. The simplest way is to deed it back to the owner of the land that is burdened by it. Also, if the owner of an easement or profit becomes the owner of the property burdened by it, then it is merged into the property. Another way is to abandon the easement with the intent to relinquish the right to use it.

LICENSES A **license** is the revocable right of a person to come onto another person's land. It is a personal privilege that arises from the consent of the owner of the land and that can be revoked by the owner. A ticket to attend a movie at a theater is an example of a license. The ticket is only a revocable license, not a conveyance of an interest in property.

RESTRICTIVE COVENANTS

A private restriction on the use of land is known as a **restrictive covenant.** If the restriction is binding on the party who purchases the property originally as well as on subsequent purchasers—in other words, if its benefit or obligation passes with the land's ownership—it is said to "run with the land."

COVENANTS RUNNING WITH THE LAND A restrictive covenant that runs with the land goes with the land and cannot be separated from it. Consider an example. Owen is the owner of Grasslands, a twenty-acre estate whose northern half contains a small reservoir. Owen wishes to convey the northern half to Arid City, but before he does, he digs an irrigation ditch connecting the reservoir with the lower ten acres, which he uses as farmland. When Owen conveys the northern ten acres to Arid City, he enters into an agreement with the city. The agreement, which is contained in the deed, states, "Arid City, its heirs and assigns, promises not to remove more than five thousand gallons of water per day from the Grasslands reservoir." Owen has created a restrictive covenant running with the land under which Arid City and all future owners of the northern ten acres of Grasslands are limited as to the amount of water they can draw from its reservoir.

Four requirements must be met for a covenant running with the land to be enforceable. If they are not met, the covenant will apply to the two original par-

ties to a contract only and will not run with the land to future owners. The requirements are as follows:

1. The covenant running with the land must be created in a written agreement (covenant). It is usually contained in the document that conveys the land.
2. The parties must intend that the covenant run with the land. In other words, the instrument that contains the covenant must state not only that the promisor is bound by the terms of the covenant but also that all the promisor's "successors, heirs, or assigns" will be bound.
3. The covenant must touch and concern the land—that is, the limitations on the activities of the owner of the burdened land must have some connection with the land. For example, a purchaser of land cannot be bound by a covenant requiring him or her to drive only Ford pickups, because such a restriction has no relation to the land purchased.
4. The successors to the original parties to the covenant must have notice of the covenant.

To satisfy the last requirement, the notice may be actual or constructive. For example, in the course of developing a fifty-lot suburban subdivision, Levitt records a declaration of restrictions that effectively limits construction on each lot to one single-family house. In each lot's deed is a reference to the declaration with a provision that the purchaser and his or her successors are bound to those restrictions. Thus, each purchaser assumes ownership with notice of the restrictions. If an owner attempts to build a duplex (or any structure that does not comply with the restrictions) on a lot, the other owners may obtain a court order enjoining the construction.

In fact, Levitt might simply have included the restrictions on the subdivision's map, filed the map in the appropriate public office, and included a reference to the map in each deed. In this way, each owner would have been held to have constructive notice of the restrictions.

ILLEGAL RESTRICTIVE COVENANTS Restrictive covenants have sometimes been used to perpetuate neighborhood segregation, and in these cases they have been invalidated by the courts. In the United States Supreme Court case of *Shelley v. Kraemer,*[6] restrictive covenants proscribing resale to minority groups were declared unconstitutional and could no

---

6. 334 U.S. 1, 68 S.Ct. 836, 92 L.Ed. 1161 (1948).

longer be enforced in courts of law. In addition, the Civil Rights Act of 1968 (also known as the Fair Housing Act) prohibits all discrimination based on race, color, religion, gender, familial status, or national origin in the sale and leasing of housing.

SECTION 4 | Public Control of Land Use

Land use is subject to regulation by the state within whose political boundaries the land is located. Most states authorize control over land use through various planning boards and zoning authorities at a city or county level. The federal government does not engage in land-use control under normal circumstances, except with respect to federally owned land.[7] The federal government does influence state and local regulation, however, through the allocation of federal funds. Stipulations on land use may be a condition to the states' receiving such funds.

SOURCES OF PUBLIC CONTROL

The states' power to control the use of land through legislation is derived from their *police power* and the doctrine of *eminent domain*. Under their police power, state governments enact legislation that promotes the health, safety, and welfare of their citizens. This legislation includes land-use controls. The power of **eminent domain** is the government's authority to take private property for public use or purpose without the owner's consent. Typically, this is accomplished through a judicial proceeding to obtain title to the land.

POLICE POWER

As an exercise of its police power,[8] a state can regulate the use of land within its jurisdiction. A few states control land use at the state level. Hawaii, for instance, employs a statewide land-use classification scheme. Some states have a land-permit process that operates in conjunction with local control. Florida, for example, uses such a scheme in certain areas of "critical envi-

ronmental concern" to permit or prohibit development on the basis of available roads, sewers, and so on. Vermont also utilizes a statewide land-permit scheme.

Usually, however, a state authorizes its city or county governments to regulate the use of land within their local jurisdictions. A state confers this power through *enabling legislation*. Enabling legislation normally requires local governments to devise *general plans* before imposing other land-use controls. Enabling acts also typically authorize local bodies to enact *zoning laws* to regulate the use of land and the types of, and specifications for, structures. Local planning boards may regulate the development of subdivisions, in which private developers subdivide large tracts of land and construct commercial or residential units for resale to others. Local governments may also enact growth-management ordinances to control development in their jurisdictions.

GOVERNMENT PLANS Most states require that land-use laws follow a local government's general plan. A **general plan** is a comprehensive, long-term scheme dealing with the physical development, and in some cases redevelopment, of a city or community. It addresses such concerns as types of housing, protection of natural resources, provision of public facilities and transportation, and other issues related to land use. A plan indicates the direction of growth in a community and the contributions that private developers must make toward providing such public facilities as roads. If a proposed use is not authorized by the general plan, the plan may be amended to permit the use. (A plan may also be amended to preclude a proposed use.)

Even when a proposed use complies with a general plan, it may not be allowed. Most jurisdictions have requirements in addition to those in the general plan. These requirements are included in specific plans—also called special, area, or community plans. Specific plans typically pertain to only a portion of a jurisdiction's area. For example, a specific plan may concern a downtown area subject to redevelopment efforts, an area with special environmental concerns, or an area with increased public transportation needs arising from population growth.

ZONING LAWS In addition to complying with a general plan and any specific plans, a particular land use must comply with zoning laws. The term **zoning** refers to the dividing of an area into districts to which specific land-use regulations apply. A typical zoning law consists of a zoning map and a zoning ordinance. The zoning map indicates the characteristics of each parcel

---

7. Federal (and state) laws concerning environmental matters—such as air and water quality, the protection of endangered species, and the preservation of natural wetlands—are also a source of land-use control.

8. As pointed out in Chapter 5, the police power of a state encompasses the right to regulate private activities to protect or promote the public order, health, safety, morals, and general welfare.

of land within an area and divides that area into districts. The zoning ordinance specifies the restrictions on land use within those districts.

Zoning ordinances generally include two types of restrictions. One type pertains to the kind of land use—such as commercial versus residential—to which property within a particular district may be put. The second type dictates the engineering features and architectural design of structures built within that district.

—*Use Restrictions.* Districts are typically zoned for residential, commercial, industrial, or agricultural use. Each district may be further subdivided for degree or intensity of use. For example, a residential district may be subdivided to permit a certain number of apartment buildings and a certain number of units in each building. Commercial and industrial districts are often zoned to permit *heavy* or *light* activity. Heavy activity might include the operation of large factories. Light activity might include the operation of professional office buildings or small retail shops. Zoning that specifies the use to which property may be put is referred to as **use zoning.**

—*Structural Restrictions.* Restrictions known as *bulk regulations* cover such details as minimum floor-space requirements and minimum lot-size restrictions. For example, a particular district's minimum floor-space requirements might specify that a one-story building contain a minimum of 1,240 square feet of floor space, and minimum lot-size restrictions might specify that each single-family dwelling be built on a lot that is at least one acre in size. Referred to collectively as **bulk zoning,** these regulations also dictate *setback* (the distance between a building and a street, sidewalk, or other boundary) and the height of buildings, with different requirements for buildings in different areas.

Restrictions related to structure may also be concerned with such matters as architectural control, the overall appearance of a community, and the preservation of historic buildings. An ordinance may require that all proposed construction be approved by a design review board composed of local architects. A community may restrict the size and placement of outdoor advertising, such as billboards and business signs. A property owner may be prohibited from tearing down or remodeling a historic landmark or building. In challenges against these types of restrictions, the courts have generally upheld the regulations.[9]

—*Variances.* A **zoning variance** allows property to be used or structures to be built in some way that varies from the restrictions of a zoning ordinance. A variance may exempt property from a use restriction to allow, for example, a bakery shop in a residential area. Or, a variance may exempt a building from a height restriction so that, for example, a two-story house can be built in a district in which houses are otherwise limited to one floor. Some jurisdictions do not permit variances from use restrictions.

Variances are normally granted by local adjustment boards. In general, a property owner must meet three criteria to obtain a variance:

1. The owner must find it impossible to realize a reasonable return on the land as currently zoned.
2. The adverse effect of the zoning ordinance must be particular to the party seeking the variance and not have a similar effect on other owners in the same zone.
3. Granting the variance must not substantially alter the essential character of the zoned area.

Courts tend to be rather lenient about the first two requirements. By far the most important criterion in granting a variance is whether it will substantially alter the character of the neighborhood.

In contrast to a "use" provision, an "area" restriction regulates the area, height, density, setback, or sideline attributes of a building or other development on a piece of property. For example, an area provision may dictate the distance between buildings.

SUBDIVISION REGULATIONS When subdividing a parcel of land into smaller plots, a private developer must comply not only with local zoning ordinances but also with local subdivision regulations. Subdivision regulations are different from zoning ordinances, although they may be administered by the same local agencies that oversee the zoning process. In the design of a subdivision, the local authorities may demand, for example, the allocation of space for a public park or school or may require a developer to construct streets to accommodate a specific level of traffic.

GROWTH-MANAGEMENT ORDINANCES To prevent population growth from racing ahead of the community's ability to provide necessary public services, local authorities may enact a growth-management ordinance to limit, for example, the number of residential building permits. A property owner may thus be precluded from constructing a residential building on his or her property even if the area is zoned for the

---

9. See, for example, *Penn Central Transportation Co. v. New York City,* 438 U.S. 104, 98 S.Ct. 2646, 57 L.Ed.2d 631 (1978).

use and the proposed structure complies with all other requirements. A growth-management ordinance may prohibit the issuance of residential building permits for a specific period of time, until the occurrence of a specific event (such as a decline in the total number of residents in the community), or on the basis of the availability of necessary public services (such as the capacity for drainage in the area or the proximity of hospitals and police stations).

LIMITATIONS ON THE EXERCISE OF POLICE POWER The government's exercise of its police power to regulate the use of land is limited in at least three ways. Two of these limitations arise under the Fourteenth Amendment to the Constitution. The third limitation arises under the Fifth Amendment and requires that, under certain circumstances, the government must compensate an owner who is deprived of the use of his or her property.

—Due Process and Equal Protection. A government cannot regulate the use of land in a way that violates either the due process clause or the equal protection clause of the Fourteenth Amendment. A government may be deemed to violate the due process clause if it acts arbitrarily or unreasonably. Thus, there must be a *rational basis* for classifications that are imposed on property. Any classification that is reasonably related to the health or general welfare of the public is deemed to have a rational basis.

Under the equal protection clause, land-use controls cannot be discriminatory. A zoning ordinance is discriminatory if it affects one parcel of land in a way in which it does not affect surrounding parcels and if there is no rational basis for the difference. For example, classifying a single parcel in a way that does not accord with a general plan is discriminatory. Similarly, a zoning ordinance cannot be racially discriminatory. For example, a community may not zone itself to exclude all low-income housing if the intention is to exclude minorities.

As explained in Chapter 5, substantive due process focuses on the substance of governmental action. In the following case, a local zoning board delayed action on a business's proposal to build and operate a multiplex theater complex. The issue before the court was whether a new standard should be applied in a substantive due process challenge to this delay.

CASE 25.3

United Artists Theatre Circuit, Inc. v. Township of Warrington, Pennsylvania

United States
Court of Appeals,
Third Circuit, 2003.
316 F.3d 392.

BACKGROUND AND FACTS *In January 1996, United Artists Theatre Circuit, Inc. (UA), an owner and operator of movie theaters, obtained preliminary approval from the board of supervisors of Warrington Township, Pennsylvania, to build a multiplex theater. The board subsequently changed its approval to require UA to acquire an easement for a left-turn lane and install a signal before construction could begin. UA filed a suit against the township in a Pennsylvania state court, which ultimately ruled that the new requirement was unlawful. Meanwhile, in January 1997, Regal Cinema proposed a competing theater. Because the market could support only one theater, the project that was approved first was likely to be the only one built. The board asked each party to pay an annual "impact" fee of $100,000. Regal agreed. UA refused. The board granted final approval to the Regal proposal in May, but tabled its vote on UA's proposal three times before granting final approval in September. UA filed a suit in a federal district court against the township and each supervisor, claiming in part violations of substantive due process. The defendants filed motions for summary judgment, which the court denied, concluding that each supervisor had an "improper motive" in delaying approval of UA's proposal. The defendants appealed to the U.S. Court of Appeals for the Third Circuit.*

IN THE LANGUAGE OF THE COURT

ALITO, Circuit Judge:
* * * *
In *County of Sacramento v. Lewis*,[a] the [United States] Supreme Court explained the standard that applies when a plaintiff alleges that an action taken by an executive branch

---

a. 523 U.S. 833, 118 S.Ct. 1708, 140 L.Ed.2d 1043 (1998).

CASE 25.3 | Continued

official violated substantive due process. * * * The Court observed that *"the core of the concept" of due process is "protection against arbitrary action"* and that *"only the most egregious official conduct can be said to be arbitrary in the constitutional sense." * * * [T]he cognizable level of executive abuse of power [is] that which shocks the conscience * * *.* [Emphasis added.]

* * * *

* * * United Artists maintains that this case is not governed by the "shocks the conscience" standard, but by the less demanding "improper motive" test that * * * was * * * applied by our court in a line of land-use cases. In these cases, we held that a municipal land-use decision violates substantive due process if it was made for any reason unrelated to the merits or with any improper motive.

* * * *

[But] we see no reason why the present case should be exempted from the *Lewis* shocks-the-conscience test simply because the case concerns a land-use dispute. * * * Since [the *Lewis* case,] our court has applied the "shocks the conscience" standard in a variety of contexts. There is no reason why land-use cases should be treated differently. We thus hold that, in light of *Lewis*, [the "improper motive" test that we applied in previous cases is] no longer good law.

* * * *

Application of the "shocks the conscience" standard in this context also prevents us from being cast in the role of a zoning board of appeals. * * * [E]very appeal by a disappointed developer from an adverse ruling of the local planning board involves some claim of abuse of legal authority, but it is not enough simply to give these state law claims constitutional labels such as "due process" or "equal protection" in order to raise a substantial federal question * * *. Land-use decisions are matters of local concern, and such disputes should not be transformed into substantive due process claims based only on allegations that government officials acted with improper motives.

DECISION AND REMEDY   *The U.S. Court of Appeals for the Third Circuit vacated the lower court's judgment and remanded the case for reconsideration of the defendants' motions for summary judgment under the "shocks the conscience" test.*

—Just Compensation. Under the Fifth Amendment, private property may not be taken for a public purpose without the payment of just compensation.[10] If government restrictions on a landowner's property rights are overly burdensome, the regulation may be deemed a **taking.** A taking occurs when a regulation denies an owner the ability to use his or her property for any reasonable income-producing or private purpose for which it is suited. This requires the government to pay the owner.

Suppose that Perez purchases a large tract of land with the intent to subdivide and develop it into residential properties. At the time of the purchase, there are no zoning laws restricting use of the land. After

Perez has taken significant steps to develop the property, the county attempts to zone the tract "public parkland only." If this prohibits Perez from developing any of the land, it will be deemed a taking. If the county does not fairly compensate Perez, the regulation will be held unconstitutional and void.

The distinction between an ordinance that merely restricts land use and an outright taking is crucial. A restriction is simply an exercise of the state's police power; even though it limits a property owner's land use, the owner generally need not be compensated for the limitation. An ordinance that completely deprives an owner of use or benefit of property, or an outright governmental taking of property, however, must be compensated.

The United States Supreme Court has held that restrictions do not constitute a taking of an owner's property if they "substantially advance legitimate state interests" and do not "den[y] an owner economically

---

10. Although the Fifth Amendment pertains to actions taken by the federal government, the Fourteenth Amendment has been interpreted as extending this limitation to state actions.

viable use of his land."[11] It is not clear, however, exactly what constitutes a "legitimate state interest" or when particular restrictions "substantially advance" that interest. Furthermore, the term "economically viable use" has not yet been clearly defined.

EMINENT DOMAIN

As noted earlier, governments have an inherent power to take property for public use or purpose without the consent of the owner. This is the power of eminent domain, and it is very important in the public control of land use.

Every property owner holds his or her interest in land subject to a superior interest. Just as in medieval England the king was the ultimate landowner, so in the United States the government retains an ultimate ownership right in all land. This right, known as eminent domain, is sometimes referred to as the *condemnation power* of the government to take land for public use. It gives to the government a right to acquire possession of real

property in the manner directed by the Constitution and the laws of the state whenever the public interest requires it. Property may not be taken for private benefit, but only for public use.

For example, when a new public highway is to be built, the government must decide where to build it and how much land to condemn. After the government determines that a particular parcel of land is necessary for public use, it brings a judicial proceeding to obtain title to the land. A property owner whose land is being condemned may oppose the condemnation. Arguing that the government does not need the land is not usually enough, however. The owner must show fraud or some other illegality, such as that the taking is for a private purpose.

Under the Fifth Amendment, although the government may take land for public use, it must pay fair and just compensation for it. Thus, in the previous highway example, after the proceeding to obtain title to the land, there is a second proceeding in which the court determines the *fair value* of the land. Fair value is usually approximately equal to market value.

Can the power of eminent domain be used to further economic development? That was the question in the following case.

---

11. *Agins v. Tiburon*, 447 U.S. 255, 100 S.Ct. 2138, 65 L.Ed.2d 106 (1980).

CASE 25.4 | Kelo v. City of New London, Connecticut

Supreme Court of the United States, 2005. __ U.S. __, 125 S.Ct. 2655, __ L.Ed.2d __. http://www.findlaw.com/ casecode/supreme.html[a]

Justice *STEVENS* delivered the opinion of the Court.
* * * *

The city of New London (hereinafter City) sits at the junction of the Thames River and the Long Island Sound in southeastern Connecticut. Decades of economic decline led a state agency in 1990 to designate the City a "distressed municipality." In 1996, the Federal Government closed the Naval Undersea Warfare Center, which had been located in the Fort Trumbull area of the City and had employed over 1,500 people. In 1998, the City's unemployment rate was nearly double that of the State, and its population of just under 24,000 residents was at its lowest since 1920.

These conditions prompted state and local officials to target New London * * * for economic revitalization. * * * In February [1998] the pharmaceutical company Pfizer, Inc., announced that it would build a $300 million research facility on a site immediately adjacent to Fort Trumbull; local planners hoped that Pfizer would draw new business to the area, thereby serving as a catalyst to the area's rejuvenation. * * *
* * * *

The city council approved [a] plan in January 2000 [to redevelop the area that once housed the federal facility]. The [City] successfully negotiated the purchase of most of the real estate in

---

a. In the "Browsing" section, click on "2005 Decisions." In the result, click on the name of the case to access the opinion.

CASE 25.4 | **Continued**

the 90-acre area, but its negotiations with [some of the property owners] failed. As a consequence, in November 2000, the [City] initiated * * * condemnation proceedings * * *.

* * * *

* * * Susette Kelo has lived in the Fort Trumbull area since 1997. She has made extensive improvements to her house, which she prizes for its water view. * * *

In December 2000 [Kelo and others] brought this action in [a Connecticut state] Court [against the City and others]. They claimed, among other things, that the taking of their properties would violate the "public use" restriction in the [U.S. Constitution's] Fifth Amendment. * * * [T]he * * * Court [issued a ruling partly in favor of both sides].

* * * [B]oth sides took appeals to the Supreme Court of Connecticut. That court held * * * that all of the City's proposed takings were valid. * * *

* * * *

We granted *certiorari* to determine whether a city's decision to take property for the purpose of economic development satisfies the "public use" requirement of the Fifth Amendment.

* * * *

* * * *[T]his Court long ago rejected any literal requirement that condemned property be put into use for the general public.* * * * Not only was the "use by the public" test difficult to administer ([for example,] what proportion of the public need have access to the property? at what price?), but it proved to be impractical given the diverse and always evolving needs of society. Accordingly, * * * this Court * * * *embraced the broader and more natural interpretation of public use as "public purpose."* * * * [Emphasis added.]

The disposition of this case therefore turns on the question whether the City's development plan serves a "public purpose." * * *

* * * *

Viewed as a whole, our jurisprudence has recognized that the needs of society have varied between different parts of the Nation, just as they have evolved over time in response to changed circumstances. * * * For more than a century, our public use jurisprudence has wisely eschewed [avoided] rigid formulas and intrusive scrutiny in favor of affording legislatures broad latitude in determining what public needs justify the use of the takings power.

* * * *

Those who govern the City were not confronted with the need to remove blight in the Fort Trumbull area, but their determination that the area was sufficiently distressed to justify a program of economic rejuvenation is entitled to our deference. The City has carefully formulated an economic development plan that it believes will provide appreciable benefits to the community, including—but by no means limited to—new jobs and increased tax revenue. As with other exercises in urban planning and development, the City is endeavoring to coordinate a variety of commercial, residential, and recreational uses of land, with the hope that they will form a whole greater than the sum of its parts. To effectuate this plan, the City has invoked a state statute that specifically authorizes the use of eminent domain to promote economic development. Given the comprehensive character of the plan, the thorough deliberation that preceded its adoption, and the limited scope of our review, it is appropriate for us * * * to resolve the challenges of the individual owners, not on a piecemeal basis, but rather in light of the entire plan. Because that plan unquestionably serves a public purpose, the takings challenged here satisfy the public use requirement of the Fifth Amendment.

* * * *

The judgment of the Supreme Court of Connecticut is affirmed.

QUESTIONS

1. Why did the United States Supreme Court grant *certiorari* in this case, and what did the Court hold with respect to the principal issue?
2. Considering the impact of the majority's ruling, what are some arguments against this decision?

REVIEWING LAND-USE CONTROL AND REAL PROPERTY

Vern Shoepke purchased a two-story home on a one-acre lot in the town of Roche, Maine, in 2001. The property was adjacent to a public park that included a popular Frisbee™ golf course. (Frisbee golf is a sport similar to golf but using Frisbees.) Wayakichi Creek runs along the north end of the park and along Shoepke's property. The previous owner had entered into a written agreement with the city of Roche under which the city was given the right to use the northern five feet of Schoepke's property as part of a public trail system along the creek. This agreement, or covenant, was contained in Shoepke's deed to the property. After moving into his Roche home, Shoepke signed a lease agreement with Lauren Slater under which Slater agreed to rent the second floor for nine months. Teenagers regularly threw Frisbee golf discs from the trail behind Shoepke's property over his yard to the adjacent park. Shoepke habitually shouted and cursed at the teenagers for throwing objects over his yard. In 2004, the town of Roche passed an ordinance to appropriate all necessary land along the Wayakichi trail to widen the path to ten feet. Roche compensated Shoepke and other property owners along the path according to a city-sponsored land appraisal. Using the information presented in the chapter, answer the following questions.

1. | Would the throwing of Frisbees over Shoepke's land constitute trespass?

2. | Was Slater's nine-month lease a tenancy for years, a periodic tenancy, a tenancy at will, or a tenancy at sufferance?

3. | What is the term for the type of covenant that was contained in Shoepke's deed?

4. | What are the four requirements that must be met for this type of covenant to be enforceable?

5. | What is the term for Roche's power to appropriate Shoepke's property for public use? Was this a restriction or a taking? How may Shoepke best oppose this action?

TERMS AND CONCEPTS TO REVIEW

QUESTIONS AND CASE PROBLEMS

25–1. Glenn is the owner of a lakeside house and lot. He deeds the house and lot to "my wife, Livia, for life, then to my daughter, Sarina." Given these facts, answer the following questions:

(a) Does Glenn have any ownership interest in the lakeside house after making these transfers? Explain.

(b) What is Livia's interest called? Is there any limitation on her rights to use the property as she wishes? Discuss.

(c) What is Sarina's interest called? Explain.

25-2. Murray owns 640 acres of rural land. A new highway is being built nearby by Ajax Corp., Inc. Ajax purchases from Murray the rights to build and use a road across Murray's land for construction vehicles to pass over and to remove sand and gravel required to build the highway. A deed is prepared and filed in the county by Ajax. Later, a dispute arises between Murray and Ajax, and Murray refuses Ajax the right to use the road or to remove sand and gravel. Ajax claims its property rights cannot be revoked by Murray. Discuss fully what property rights Ajax has in this matter.

25-3. ⚖ **QUESTION WITH SAMPLE ANSWER**

The county intends to rezone an area from industrial use to residential use. Land within the affected area is largely undeveloped, but nonetheless it is expected that the proposed action will reduce the market value of the affected land by as much as 50 percent. Will the landowners be successful in suing to have the action declared a taking of their property, entitling them to just compensation?

For a sample answer to this question, go to Appendix I at the end of this text.

25-4. Suppose that as a condition of a developer's receiving approval for constructing a new residential community, the local authorities insist that the developer dedicate, or set aside, land for a new hospital. The hospital would serve not only the proposed residential community but also the rest of the city. If the developer challenges the condition in court, under what standard might the court invalidate the condition?

25-5. To prevent population growth from racing ahead of the local government's ability to provide adequate police and fire protection, as well as road development for the increase in traffic, the local planning board imposes an ordinance limiting the issuance of residential building permits to one thousand per year for the next three years. A property developer who owns several tracts zoned for residential housing and whose development plans comply with all other existing ordinances challenges the ban in court. Will she succeed? Discuss all the relevant issues. What difference would it make if the developer had already expended considerable resources and taken the last step toward approval of the development project?

25-6. ⚖ **CASE PROBLEM WITH SAMPLE ANSWER**

Merton Peterson owned a golf course, a supper club, and the parking lot between them. Both golfers and club patrons always parked in the lot. Peterson sold the club and the lot to the American Legion, which sold them to VBC, Inc. (owned by Richard Beck and others). When VBC demanded rent from Peterson for use of the lot, Peterson filed a suit in a South Dakota state court to determine title. On what basis might the court hold that Peterson has an easement for the use of the lot? Does Peterson have an easement? [*Peterson v. Beck*, 537 N.W.2d 375 (S.Dak. 1995)]

To view a sample answer for this case problem, go to this book's Web site at http://wleb.westbuslaw.com, select "Chapter 25," and click on "Case Problem with Sample Answer."

25-7. TAKING. Richard and Jaquelyn Jackson owned property in a residential subdivision near an airport operated by the Metropolitan Knoxville Airport Authority in Blount County, Tennessee. The Airport Authority considered extending a runway near the subdivision and undertook a study that found that the noise, vibration, and pollution from aircraft using the extension would render the Jacksons' property incompatible with residential use. The airport built the extension, bringing about the predicted results, and the Jacksons filed a suit against the Airport Authority, alleging a taking of their property. The Airport Authority responded that there was no taking because there were no direct flights over the Jacksons' property. In whose favor will the court rule, and why? [*Jackson v. Metropolitan Knoxville Airport Authority*, 922 S.W.2d 860 (Tenn. 1996)]

25-8. EMINENT DOMAIN. The state of Indiana, through its department of transportation, planned to improve U.S. Highway 41 in Parke County, Indiana. To accomplish the improvement, Indiana sought to obtain from Thomas Collom approximately half an acre of his property abutting the east side of the highway and offered him $4,495 for it. When Collom refused to sell, the state filed a suit in an Indiana state court against Collom to obtain the property. Collom denied that his half acre was necessary for the improvement that the state wanted to make to the highway. He asserted that the state did not need his land because the highway would curve west, away from his property, and no drainage ditch was necessary given the existing water flow in the area. The state argued that this was not an appropriate response because a determination of the need for a taking was the responsibility of the state, not the owner of the property that the state was trying to take. In whose favor should the court rule, and why? [*State of Indiana v. Collom*, 720 N.E.2d 737 (Ind.App. 1999)]

25-9. EASEMENTS. In 1988, Gary Dubin began leasing property from Robert Chesebrough at 26011 Bouquet Canyon Road in Los Angeles County, California, to operate Alert Auto, a vehicle repair shop. There was a narrow driveway on one side of the premises, but blocking the widest means of access were crash posts on the adjacent unoccupied property, which Chesebrough also owned. The lease did not mention a means of access, but Dubin's primary customers were to be large trucks and motor homes, which could reach Alert Auto only over the wide driveway. Chesebrough had the posts removed. After his death, the Robert Newhall Chesebrough Trust became the owner of both properties, which Wespac

Management Group, Inc., managed. In 2000, Wespac reinstalled the posts. Dubin filed a suit in a California state court against the Trust and others, alleging that he had an easement, which the posts were obstructing, and sought damages and an injunction. The defendants denied the existence of any easement. Does Dubin have an easement? If so, how was it created? Explain. [*Dubin v. Robert Newhall Chesebrough Trust*, 96 Cal.App.4th 465, 116 Cal.Rptr.2d 872 (2 Dist. 2002)]

25-10. EASEMENTS. The Wallens family owned a cabin on Lummi Island in the state of Washington. A driveway ran from the cabin across their property to South Nugent Road. In 1952, Floyd Massey bought the adjacent lot and built a cabin. To gain access to his property, he used a bulldozer to extend the driveway, without the Wallenses' permission but also without their objection. In 1975, the Wallenses sold their property to Wright Fish Co. Massey continued to use and maintain the driveway without permission or objection. In 1984, Massey sold his property to Robert Drake. Drake and his employees continued to use and maintain the driveway without permission or objection, although Drake knew it was located largely on Wright's property. In 1997, Wright sold its lot to Robert Smersh. The next year, Smersh told Drake to stop using the driveway. Drake filed a suit in a Washington state court against Smersh, claiming an easement by prescription. Does Drake's use of the driveway meet all of the requirements? What should the court rule? Explain. [*Drake v. Smersh*, 122 Wash.App. 147, 89 P.3d 726 (Div. 1 2004)]

LAW | on the Web

For updated links to resources available on the Web, as well as a variety of other materials, visit this text's Web site at http://wleb.westbuslaw.com.

For links to numerous sources relating to real property, go to

http://www.findlaw.com/01topics/33property/index.html

and click on "Property Law & Real Estate."

For information on condemnation procedures and rules under one state's (California's) law, go to

http://www.eminentdomainlaw.net/propertyguide.html

LEGAL RESEARCH EXERCISES ON THE WEB

Go to http://wleb.westbuslaw.com, the Web site that accompanies this text. Select "Chapter 25" and click on "Internet Exercises." There you will find the following Internet research exercises that you can perform to learn more about topics covered in this chapter.

Activity 25–1: LEGAL PERSPECTIVE
Eminent Domain

Activity 25–2: MANAGEMENT PERSPECTIVE
How to Challenge a Condemnation of Property

CHAPTER 26

Antitrust and Monopoly

The environment of business is generally one of competition among rival firms. In free and open competition, businesses attempt to develop and sell products that are more appealing to customers than are the products of rival firms. Competition among sellers therefore promotes the development of appealing products. When products sold by different firms are similar, firms compete by trying to sell at the lowest price possible while still earning enough after costs to make it worthwhile to remain in that particular endeavor. For example, if Acme, Inc., develops a new digital video disc (DVD) drive that has broad appeal among consumers, it will begin to earn profits greater than those of its rivals—profits commensurate with the appeal of its new product. All else being equal, the greater the appeal of Acme's DVD drive, the greater its profits.

The legal environment of business is premised on encouraging innovative, competitive business behavior. The law attempts to prevent and correct conduct that interferes with free and open competition. The law is concerned with two broad categories of behavior: conduct that leads to or tends to produce *monopoly power* and conduct that is an unreasonable *restraint of trade*. In this chapter, we consider the federal laws that deal with individual firms' behavior leading to or tending to create monopolies. In Chapter 27, we discuss in detail the federal laws that regulate activities that restrain competition.

SECTION 1 | Market Power

To encourage innovative behavior, we might feel justified in allowing Acme to have a *monopoly* over the sale of the DVD drive, at least for a while—say, twenty years, which is the duration of a patent. The term **monopoly** is generally used to describe a market in which there is a single seller. In that respect, Acme would be a monopolist, albeit for a limited time, in the DVD drive market. In legal terms, *monopolist* may also describe a firm that, although not the sole seller in the market, can nonetheless substantially ignore rival firms in setting a selling price for its product or can in some way limit rivals from competing in the market (possibly by preventing rivals from entering the market altogether). Acme's monopoly would give it **market power** (the power of a firm to control the market for its product). Acme would have the power during the term of its monopoly to prevent other firms from selling the DVD drive. Acme would be free to charge whatever price it

chose to, and it would choose a price that made its profits as large as possible.

COMPETITIVE BEHAVIOR

Another firm might seek to develop a different type of DVD drive, one with appeal equal to or greater than Acme's DVD drive. If it succeeded, it would draw customers away from Acme. It, too, might seek a legal monopoly over its product. There would then be two monopolies rather than one, but society would have the benefit of two unique and valued products. Moreover, Acme would be concerned that if it charged too high a price for its DVD drive, it would lose customers to its rival. Acme's rival would have the same concern over the price of its product.

Eventually, after the legal monopolies expired, numerous firms would be allowed to market identical products. Each firm would seek to attract customers by charging the lowest price. The only thing that would prevent prices from falling ever lower is that at some point the price of a DVD drive would be so low that new firms would quit trying to enter the market to compete for DVD drive consumers. They would instead devote their efforts and resources to alternative, more profitable ventures. Ultimately, the DVD drive would sell for a competitive price—one that would, of course, cover the costs of production, as well as earn a return equal to that which could be earned by employing the same resources in an alternative industry.

THE GOALS OF ANTITRUST LAW

The scenario described above highlights the benefits to society of having firms develop, produce, and sell goods and services, even though obtaining those benefits may involve conferring a limited monopoly such as that given to Acme. Our scenario should make clear an often overlooked point: market power is not inherently bad. Market power can correlate to high profits, which are the reward for innovation, foresight, and good management. Market power is the prize that motivates firms to benefit society with innovative products and competitive prices.

What is at issue is not market power *per se* but how firms go about acquiring market power and what firms do with that power once they acquire it. **Antitrust law** consists of the statutes and principles that regulate business conduct so as to promote the forms of competition that benefit society while simultaneously seeking to rein in the exercise of market power that often is the fruit of such competition.

SECTION 2 | The Common Law and the Restraint of Trade

Socially beneficial commercial activity involves cooperation, as well as competition. A business firm, for example, may compete with certain firms in some markets but cooperate with other firms in other markets. A firm that sells finished goods directly to the public may itself act as a consumer by purchasing intermediate products from a second firm. In this sense, the two firms act cooperatively rather than competitively, at least vis-à-vis one another. Similarly, two firms may cooperate to develop or market a new product.

PUBLIC POLICY AND CONTRACTS

Any mutual effort that calls for more than a brief period of sustained cooperation requires commitment from all the parties. The principal means of ensuring

such a sustained commitment is through a contract between the parties. Most cooperative efforts among business firms, in fact, are embodied in some form of contract. But a principle of the common law of contracts is that no contract is enforceable if it is against public policy.

ECONOMIC EFFICIENCY   Many contracts between business firms promote competition. Because competition, as noted above, is beneficial to society, such contracts are not against public policy. A contract may provide assurances that one firm will be able to obtain necessary inputs from another on a long-term basis. Similarly, a contract may provide assurances to two firms entering into a joint venture that each will continue fulfilling its obligation on the project beyond the initial investment stage. In both of these instances, the rights and remedies afforded by contract law promote economic efficiency. Such agreements are not against public policy.

RESTRAINTS OF TRADE   Some agreements between business firms, however, may reduce competition. An agreement between two bakers to coordinate their production of bread so as to limit output and charge a uniform, higher price in the market might entirely eliminate competition in the affected market. If the two bakers were the only suppliers in the market, their combining together would in effect create a joint monopoly under which they would share exclusive control over the market. Such an agreement would be condemned under the common law as an *unreasonable restraint of trade*.

Consider, though, a restaurant owner who decides to sell her restaurant to the manager. The manager might demand that, as a condition to the sale, the owner refrain from opening another restaurant across the street. Should such an agreement be condemned as being against public policy? At first glance, it is a restraint of trade: it prevents the local community from benefiting from the restauranting skills of the owner. If the agreement were not enforced, however, the manager, who was willing to pay a price commensurate with the current earnings of the restaurant, would not recover the price; customers would probably follow the owner with the established reputation to her new restaurant across the street from the old one.

If the manager knew beforehand that the agreement would not be enforced, it would be the owner who would suffer, because the manager would not be willing to pay a price reflecting the expectation that the earnings of the restaurant would continue at the current level. Society might consider enforcing such agreements in spite of the restraint of trade so that entrepreneurs who contemplate opening new businesses will be ensured of later being able to sell those businesses at full value. If others know that sellers will be held to the promise not to compete, the sellers can sell their businesses for more than they could if such promises were condemned as being against public policy.

INTERFERENCE WITH FREE TRADE

Compare the two agreements just discussed. Both interfere with free trade. The first involves outright collusion between two competitors (the bakers) to completely eliminate competition between themselves. Their agreement calls for artificially driving prices higher by restricting output. The second agreement (the one between the restaurant owner and the manager) also restrains trade, but the restraint is not the primary purpose of the agreement. The restraint is really the only means of ensuring that both parties to the sale of an established restaurant can reap the full benefit of their bargain: the sale of the restaurant for its highest value. The second agreement thus can be viewed as reasonable given that it is the only means of achieving a legitimate end. It also has offsetting benefits in that it encourages entrepreneurship by allowing the owner to sell her business for its highest value.

SECTION 3 | The Origins of Federal Antitrust Legislation

Despite condemning anticompetitive agreements on the basis of public policy, the common law proved to be an ineffective means of protecting free competition. There are temptations for business firms to agree to limit competition or to harm other rivals. Such agreements, to be sure, are unenforceable, because they are held to be against public policy. But the problem under the common law is that such agreements are left unchallenged unless one of the parties to an agreement refuses to abide by its terms. *Unenforceable* means only that a court will not sanction a party that reneges on its promise; it does not mean that a forum will be provided in which anticompetitive agreements can be challenged by others who are not parties to the agreements. These shortcomings became acutely obvious in the United States during the latter half of the 1800s as a concentrated group of powerful individuals

began to acquire unrivaled market power by combining competing firms under singular control.

THE TREND TOWARD MONOPOLY

After the Civil War ended, the nation renewed its drive westward. With the movement westward came the expansion of the railroads—which soon developed into monopolies—and the further integration of the economy. The growth of national markets also witnessed the efforts of a number of small companies to combine into large business organizations, many of which gained considerable market power. These large organizations became known as **trusts,** the most famous—or infamous—being John D. Rockefeller's Standard Oil Trust. In general, a trust is an arrangement in which some party, referred to as a trustee, holds legal title to property for the benefit of another. As used by Standard Oil and others around the turn of the century, trusts were a device used to amass market power. The participants transferred their stock to a trustee and in return received trust certificates. The trustee then made decisions fixing prices, controlling output, and allocating geographical markets in which specified members could operate without competition from other members.

In some cases, an entire industry was dominated by a single organization. The public perception was that the trusts used their market power to drive small competitors out of business, leaving the trusts free to raise prices virtually at will.[1]

THE FEDERAL RESPONSE

Congress initially dealt with the railroad monopolies, attempting regulation rather than an outright assault on monopoly power. The result was the Interstate Commerce Act of 1887.[2]

Congress next attempted to deal with trusts in a direct, unified way by passing the Sherman Act in 1890.[3] The Sherman Act is a broadly worded pronouncement that prohibits competitors from making agreements that unreasonably restrain trade and condemns conduct leading to or tending to produce monopoly power. Violations of the Sherman Act are criminal offenses, as well as civil ones.

---

1. There is now a considerable amount of literature that questions whether predatory tactics are economically viable and whether they in fact characterize the activities of Rockefeller and the other "robber barons" of the late nineteenth century.
2. 49 U.S.C. Sections 1–22.
3. 15 U.S.C. Sections 1–7.

The Sherman Act, however, failed to end public concerns over monopolies. The United States Supreme Court initially construed the statute too narrowly to give it much effect and subsequently applied it so rigorously as to make the act unworkable. Lackluster enforcement also contributed to the public's dissatisfaction. Concern over the trust problem dominated the 1912 presidential election and eventually, in 1914, led to enactment of the Clayton Act[4] and the Federal Trade Commission Act.[5] This legislation sought to deal with the monopoly problem by proscribing specific acts and providing for more aggressive means of enforcement.

The Clayton Act (as amended by the Robinson-Patman Act in 1936 and the Celler-Kefauver Act of 1950) addresses specific actions that are considered to be anticompetitive. The Federal Trade Commission Act created the Federal Trade Commission and invested it with broad enforcement powers to *prevent*, as well as correct, business behavior broadly defined as *unfair trade practices*.

In the remainder of this chapter, we consider the federal legislation in more detail and examine the means of enforcement. We also examine the narrower area of antitrust law that deals with individual firms' behavior leading to or tending to create monopolies. We reserve for Chapter 27 the broader area of antitrust law that deals with all forms of joint activities that restrain competition.

SECTION 4 | Overview of the Major Federal Antitrust Laws

The major pieces of federal antitrust legislation—the Sherman Act, the Clayton Act, and the Federal Trade Commission Act—are briefly outlined below and discussed in more detail later in this chapter and in Chapter 27.

THE SHERMAN ACT

The main provisions of the Sherman Act are contained in Sections 1 and 2 of the act. Both sections describe illegal conduct in very broad terms. Section 1 prohibits a concerted activity on the part of two or more persons to restrain trade:

> Section 1: Every contract, combination in the form of trust or otherwise, or conspiracy, in restraint of trade or commerce among the several States, or with foreign

4. 15 U.S.C. Sections 12–27.
5. 15 U.S.C. Sections 41–58.

nations, is hereby declared to be illegal [and is a felony punishable by fine or imprisonment].

Section 2 applies to both unilateral and concerted actions:

> Section 2: Every person who shall monopolize, or attempt to monopolize, or combine or conspire with any other person or persons, to monopolize any part of the trade or commerce among the several States, or with foreign nations, shall be deemed guilty of a felony [and is similarly punishable].

Section 1 of the act prohibits concerted activity that unreasonably restrains trade. Section 2 condemns individual anticompetitive behavior that produces, or is intended to produce, monopoly power. Both restraint of trade and monopoly power are fundamental concepts in antitrust law.

A **restraint of trade** is any agreement between firms that has the effect of reducing competition in the marketplace. Some restraints of trade are so blatantly anticompetitive—such as agreements to restrict output or fix prices—that they are condemned without inquiry into any business justification that may be advanced in defense of the agreements. These are known as *per se* violations. Other agreements judge the restraints under a rule of reason (discussed later in this chapter) similar to the common law analysis of the reasonableness of the restraint discussed earlier. Restraints of trade are discussed more completely in the next chapter.

Monopoly power is an extreme amount of market power. Recall our initial discussion of Acme's market power in the hypothetical scenario in which Acme was given, for a time, exclusive control over the DVD drive market; specifically, Acme could ignore the effect of raising its product price on the ability of competitors to enter the DVD drive market. Such extreme market power is an example of monopoly power. Any firm, even if it is not the sole supplier of its product, that is not completely constrained by the potential response of a rival in deciding what price to charge for its product has some degree of market power. Deciding whether such power is great enough to be classified as monopoly power is one of the most difficult tasks encountered in the application of antitrust law.

THE CLAYTON ACT

In contrast to the Sherman Act's broad proscriptions, the Clayton Act's provisions deal with *specific* practices that are not expressly covered by the Sherman Act but that are considered to reduce competition or lead to monopoly power. These practices are divided into four categories—price discrimination, exclusionary practices, corporate mergers, and interlocking directorates. These behaviors violate the Clayton Act only if they substantially tend to lessen competition or create monopoly power. Violations of the Clayton Act are civil, not criminal, violations.

PRICE DISCRIMINATION *Price discrimination* occurs when sellers charge different buyers different prices for identical goods. Section 2 of the Clayton Act prohibits certain classes of price discrimination for reasons other than differences in production or transportation costs. The Clayton Act was amended in 1936 by the Robinson-Patman Act as Congress sought to make it more difficult for businesses to evade the terms of Section 2. To violate Section 2, the seller must be engaged in interstate commerce, and the effect of the price discrimination must be to lessen competition substantially. Under the Robinson-Patman Act, sellers are prohibited from reducing prices to levels substantially below those charged by their competitors unless they can justify the reduction by demonstrating that the lower price was charged "in good faith to meet an equally low price of a competitor."[6]

EXCLUSIONARY PRACTICES Section 3 of the Clayton Act prohibits sellers and lessors from selling or leasing "on the condition, agreement or understanding that the . . . purchaser or lessee thereof shall not use or deal in the goods . . . of a competitor or competitors of the seller." Section 3 in effect prohibits two types of vertical arrangements involving exclusionary tactics: exclusive-dealing contracts and tie-in sales agreements.

An *exclusive-dealing contract* is one in which a seller forbids the buyer from purchasing products from the seller's competitors. For example, imagine that most soft drinks are produced by one firm, that most soft drinks are marketed by one other firm, and that the producer signs an exclusive-dealing contract with the retail seller. Because the retail seller has committed itself to the established producer, any other soft-drink producer that wants to enter the soft-drink market may find it difficult to do so. Such contracts are prohibited under Section 3, mentioned above, if the effect of the contract will "substantially lessen competition or tend to create a monopoly."

In a *tying arrangement*, or *tie-in sales agreement*, the seller conditions the sale of a product (the tying product)

on the buyer's agreeing to purchase another product (the tied product) produced or distributed by the same seller. The legality of such agreements depends on many factors, especially on consideration of the purpose of the arrangement and its likely effect on competition in the relevant markets (consider that there are two markets, because the agreement involves both the tying and the tied product). In the next chapter, we deal in depth with both exclusive-dealing contracts and tying arrangements as part of our analysis of restraints of trade.

CORPORATE MERGERS Under Section 7 of the Clayton Act, a person or business organization is forbidden to hold stock or assets in another business if "the effect . . . may be to substantially lessen competition." This section provides the statutory authorization for the government's challenging corporate mergers that could have an anticompetitive effect. Two crucial considerations are the market shares among firms in the relevant market and barriers to a firm's entry into the market.

INTERLOCKING DIRECTORATES Section 8 of the Clayton Act deals with *interlocking directorates*, which result when individuals serve as directors on the boards of two or more competing companies simultaneously. Specifically, no person may be a director in two or more corporations at the same time if either of the corporations has capital, surplus, or undivided profits aggregating more than $21,327,000 or competitive sales of $2,132,700. The threshold amounts are adjusted upward each year by the Federal Trade Commission (FTC). (The amounts given here are those announced by the FTC in 2005.)

THE FEDERAL TRADE COMMISSION ACT

The Federal Trade Commission Act's sole substantive provision is Section 5. It provides, in part, as follows:

> Unfair methods of competition in or affecting commerce, and unfair or deceptive acts or practices in or affecting commerce are hereby declared illegal.

Notice that whereas the Clayton Act prohibits specific forms of anticompetitive behavior, the FTC Act is a "catchall." Section 5 condemns all forms of anticompetitive behavior that are not covered under other federal antitrust laws.

The FTC Act also created the Federal Trade Commission, an administrative agency with functions that include antitrust enforcement, as well as other duties concerning consumer protection.

---

6. *United States v. United States Gypsum Co.*, 438 U.S. 422, 98 S.Ct. 2864, 5 L.Ed.2d 854 (1978).

SECTION 5 | Enforcement of the Antitrust Laws

Government agencies enforce the federal antitrust laws. In some circumstances, a private party can sue violators for damages. Before the government can prosecute successfully or a private party can win a lawsuit, however, certain jurisdictional requirements must be met.

JURISDICTIONAL REQUIREMENTS

The Sherman Act applies only to conduct that has a significant impact on commerce. Because Congress can regulate only interstate commerce, in principle only interstate commerce is affected by this act.[7] Courts have generally held that any activity that substantially affects interstate commerce falls under the Sherman Act. Courts have construed the meaning of *interstate commerce* more and more broadly each year, bringing even local activities within the regulatory power of the national government.

FEDERAL ENFORCEMENT

The federal agencies that enforce the federal antitrust laws are the Department of Justice (DOJ) and the Federal Trade Commission (FTC). The DOJ can prosecute violations of the Sherman Act as either criminal or civil violations. Violations of the Clayton Act are not crimes, and the DOJ can enforce that statute only through civil proceedings. The various remedies that the DOJ has asked the courts to impose include **divestiture** (making a company give up one or more of its operations) and **dissolution** (making a company end its operating functions). A group of meat packers, for example, can be forced to divest itself of control or ownership of butcher shops.

The FTC enforces the Clayton Act and has sole authority to enforce the only substantive provision of the Federal Trade Commission Act, Section 5. FTC actions are effected through administrative cease-and-desist proceedings, but the FTC can seek court sanctions for violations of its administrative orders. As part of its enforcement of the Clayton Act, the FTC requires certain persons involved in a merger, consolidation, or other acquisition to notify the agency.[8] The first page of the notification form is shown in Exhibit 26–1. Antitrust law as it applies to mergers will be discussed in detail in Chapter 27.

7. See the discussion of the commerce clause in Chapter 5.
8. See 15 U.S.C. Section 18a.

PRIVATE ACTIONS

A private party can sue for **treble damages** (three times what he or she has suffered) and attorneys' fees under Section 4 of the Clayton Act if the party is injured as a result of a violation of any of the federal antitrust laws (except Section 5 of the Federal Trade Commission Act). In some instances, private parties may also seek injunctive relief to prevent antitrust violations. The courts have determined that the ability to sue depends on the directness of the injury suffered by the would-be plaintiff. Thus, a person wishing to sue under the Sherman Act must prove (1) that the antitrust violation either directly caused, or was at least a substantial factor in causing, the injury that was suffered and (2) that the unlawful actions of the accused party affected business activities of the plaintiff that were protected by the antitrust laws.

In recent years, more than 90 percent of all antitrust actions have been brought by private plaintiffs. One reason for this is, of course, that successful plaintiffs recover treble damages as a result of the defendants' antitrust law violations. Such recoveries by private plaintiffs for antitrust violations have been rationalized as encouraging "private attorneys general" who will vigorously pursue antitrust violators on their own initiative. This policy consideration has also prompted the courts to ask, in assessing whether a litigant has standing to sue for an alleged antitrust violation, whether the particular plaintiff is properly suited to fulfill the role of a private attorney general.

SECTION 6 | U.S. Antitrust Laws in the Global Context

U.S. antitrust laws have a broad application. They may subject persons in foreign nations to their provisions as well as protect foreign consumers and competitors from violations committed by U.S. business firms. Consequently, *foreign persons*, a term that by definition includes foreign governments, may sue under U.S. antitrust laws in U.S. courts.

Section 1 of the Sherman Act of 1890 provides for the extraterritorial effect of the U.S. antitrust laws. The United States is a major proponent of free competition in the global economy, and thus any conspiracy that has a substantial effect on U.S. commerce is within the reach of the Sherman Act. The violation may even occur outside the United States, and foreign governments as well as persons can be sued for violation of U.S. antitrust laws. Before U.S. courts will

EXHIBIT 26-1 FTC Notification Form

TRANSACTION NUMBER ASSIGNED

[ ][ ][ ][ ][ ][ ][ ]

16 C.F.R. Part 803 - Appendix
NOTIFICATION AND REPORT FORM FOR CERTAIN MERGERS AND ACQUISITIONS

Approved by OMB
3084-0005
Expires 05/31/2007

THE INFORMATION REQUIRED TO BE SUPPLIED ON THESE ANSWER SHEETS IS SPECIFIED IN THE INSTRUCTIONS

↓ Attach the Affidavit required by § 803.5 to this page.

FEE INFORMATION	TAXPAYER IDENTIFICATION NUMBER _____
	or SOCIAL SECURITY NUMBER of payer _____
AMOUNT PAID $_____	(acquiring person (and payer if different from acquiring person))

In cases where your filing fee would be higher if based on acquisition price or where the acquisition price is undetermined to the extent that it may straddle a filing fee threshold, attach an explanation of how you determined the appropriate fee (acquiring persons only).

Attachment Number _____

CHECK ATTACHED ☐   MONEY ORDER ATTACHED ☐
WIRE TRANSFER ☐   CONFIRMATION NO._____
FROM: NAME OF INSTITUTION _____
NAME OF PAYER (if different from PERSON FILING) _____

IS THIS A CORRECTIVE FILING?   ☐ YES   ☐ NO

IS THIS ACQUISITION SUBJECT TO FOREIGN FILING REQUIREMENTS?   ☐ YES   ☐ NO
If YES, list jurisdictions: (voluntary) _____

IS THIS ACQUISITION A CASH TENDER OFFER?   ☐ YES   ☐ NO | BANKRUPTCY?   ☐ YES   ☐ NO

DO YOU REQUEST EARLY TERMINATION OF THE WAITING PERIOD? (Grants of early termination are published in the Federal Register AND on the FTC web site www.ftc.gov)
☐ YES   ☐ NO

ITEM 1 – PERSON FILING

1(a) NAME and
HEADQUARTERS ADDRESS
of PERSON FILING

1(b) PERSON FILING NOTIFICATION IS
☐ an acquiring person   ☐ an acquired person   ☐ both

1(c) PUT AN "X" IN THE APPROPRIATE BOX TO DESCRIBE PERSON FILING NOTIFICATION
☐ Corporation   ☐ Unincorporated Entity   ☐ Other (Specify): _____

1(d) DATA FURNISHED BY
☐ calendar year   ☐ fiscal year (specify period) _____ (month/year) to _____ (month/year)

THIS FORM IS REQUIRED BY LAW and must be filed separately by each person which, by reason of a merger, consolidation or acquisition, is subject to §7A of the Clayton Act, 15 U.S.C. §18a, as added by Section 201 of the Hart-Scott-Rodino Antitrust Improvements Act of 1976, Pub. L. No. 94-435, 90 Stat. 1390, and rules promulgated thereunder (hereinafter referred to as "the rules" or by section number). The statute and rules are set forth in the Federal Register at 43 FR 33450; the rules may also be found at 16 CFR Parts 801-03. Failure to file this **Notification and Report Form**, and to observe the required waiting period before consummating the acquisition in accordance with the applicable provisions of 15 U.S.C. §18a and the rules, subjects any "person," as defined in the rules, or any individuals responsible for noncompliance, to liability for a penalty of not more than $11,000 for each day during which such person is in violation of 15 U.S.C. §18a.

All information and documentary material filed in or with this Form is confidential. It is exempt from disclosure under the Freedom of Information Act, and may be made public only in an administrative or judicial proceeding, or disclosed to Congress or to a duly authorized committee or subcommittee of Congress.

Filing - Complete and return *two* copies (with one original affidavit and certification and one set of documentary attachments) of this Notification and Report Form to: Premerger Notification Office, Bureau of Competition, Room 303, Federal Trade Commission, 600 Pennsylvania Avenue, N.W., Washington, D.C. 20580. *Three* copies (with one set of documentary attachments) should be sent to: Director of Operations and Merger Enforcement, Antitrust Division, Department of Justice, Patrick Henry Building, 601 D Street, N.W., Room #10013, Washington, D.C. 20530. (For FEDEX airbills to the Department of Justice, do not use the 20530 zip code; use zip code 20004.)

DISCLOSURE NOTICE - Public reporting burden for this report is estimated to vary from 8 to 160 hours per response, with an average of 39 hours per response, including time for reviewing instructions, searching existing data sources, gathering and maintaining the data needed, and completing and reviewing the collection of information. Send comments regarding the burden estimate or any other aspect of this report, including suggestions for reducing this burden to:

Premerger Notification Office,
H-303
Federal Trade Commission
Washington, DC 20580

Office of Information and
Regulatory Affairs,
Office of Management and Budget
Washington, DC 20503

Under the Paperwork Reduction Act, as amended, an agency may not conduct or sponsor, and a person is not required to respond to, a collection of information unless it displays a currently valid OMB control number. That number is 3084-0005, which also appears in the upper right-hand corner of the first page of this form.

EXHIBIT 26-2   Exemptions to Antitrust Enforcement

EXEMPTION	SOURCE AND SCOPE
Labor	Clayton Act—Permits unions to organize and bargain without violating antitrust laws and specifies that strikes and other labor activities do not normally violate any federal law.
Agricultural associations	Clayton Act and Capper-Volstead Act of 1992—Allow agricultural cooperatives to set prices.
Fisheries	Fisheries Cooperative Marketing Act of 1976—Allows the fishing industry to set prices.
Insurance companies	McCarran-Ferguson Act of 1945—Exempts the insurance business in states in which the industry is regulated.
Exporters	Webb-Pomerene Act of 1918—Allows U.S. exporters to engage in cooperative activity to compete with similar foreign associations; Export Trading Company Act of 1982—Permits the Department of Justice to exempt certain exporters.
Professional baseball	The United States Supreme Court has held that professional baseball is exempt because it is not "interstate commerce."[a]
Oil marketing	Interstate Oil Compact of 1935—Allows states to set quotas on oil to be marketed in interstate commerce.

a. *Federal Baseball Club of Baltimore, Inc. v. National League of Professional Baseball Clubs*, 259 U.S. 200, 42 S.Ct. 465, 66 L.Ed. 898 (1922). A federal district court has held that this exemption applies only to the game's reserve system. (Under the reserve system, teams hold players' contracts for the players' entire careers. The reserve system is generally being replaced by the free agency system.) See *Piazza v. Major League Baseball*, 831 F.Supp. 420 (E.D.Pa. 1993).

exercise jurisdiction and apply antitrust laws, it must be shown that the alleged violation had a *substantial effect on* U.S. commerce. U.S. jurisdiction is automatically invoked, however, when a *per se* violation occurs.

If a domestic firm, for example, joins a foreign cartel to control the production, price, or distribution of goods, and this cartel has a *substantial effect* on U.S. commerce, a *per se* violation may exist. Hence, both the domestic firm and the foreign cartel could be sued for violation of the U.S. antitrust laws. Likewise, if foreign firms doing business in the United States enter into a price-fixing or other anticompetitive agreement to control a portion of U.S. markets, a *per se* violation may exist.

In 1982, Congress amended the Sherman Act and the Federal Trade Commission Act of 1914 to limit their application when unfair methods of competition are involved in U.S. export trade or commerce with foreign nations. The acts are not limited, however, when there is a "direct, substantial, and reasonably foreseeable effect" on U.S. domestic commerce that results in a claim for damages.

as labor, insurance, and foreign trade. These exemptions are listed and explained in Exhibit 26–2.

One of the most significant of these exemptions covers joint efforts by businesspersons to obtain legislative, judicial, or executive action. This is often referred to as the **Noerr-Pennington doctrine**.[9] For example, video producers might jointly lobby Congress to change the copyright laws, or some video-rental companies might sue another video-rental firm, without being held liable for attempting to restrain trade. Although selfish rather than purely public-minded conduct is permitted, there is an exception: an action will not be protected if it is clear that the action is "objectively baseless in the sense that no reasonable [person] could reasonably expect success on the merits" and it is an attempt to make anticompetitive use of government processes.[10]

The following case concerns the first exemption in the list of exemptions shown in Exhibit 26–2.

SECTION 7 | Exemptions

There are many legislative and constitutional limitations on antitrust enforcement. Most are statutory and judicially created exemptions that apply in such areas

---

9. See *Eastern Railroad Presidents Conference v. Noerr Motor Freight, Inc.*, 365 U.S. 127, 81 S.Ct. 523, 5 L.Ed.2d 464 (1961), and *United Mine Workers of America v. Pennington*, 381 U.S. 657, 85 S.Ct. 1585, 14 L.Ed.2d 626 (1965).

10. *Professional Real Estate Investors, Inc. v. Columbia Pictures Industries, Inc.*, 508 U.S. 49, 113 S.Ct. 1920, 123 L.Ed.2d 611 (1993).

EXHIBIT 26-2 **Exemptions to Antitrust Enforcement—Continued**

EXEMPTION	SOURCE AND SCOPE
Defense activities	Defense Production Act of 1950—Allows the president to approve, and thereby exempt, certain activities to further the military defense of the United States.
Small businesses' cooperative research	Small Business Administration Act of 1958—Allows small firms to undertake cooperative research.
Joint ventures' research or production	National Cooperative Research Act of 1984 and National Cooperative Production Amendments of 1993—Permit research or production of a product, process, or service by joint ventures consisting of competitors.
State actions	The United States Supreme Court has held that actions by a state are exempt if the state clearly articulates and actively supervises the policy behind its action.[b]
Regulated industries	Industries (such as airlines) are exempt when a federal administrative agency (such as the Federal Aviation Administration) has primary regulatory authority.
Businesspersons' joint efforts to seek government action	Cooperative efforts by businesspersons to obtain legislative, judicial, or executive action are exempt unless it is clear that an effort is "objectively baseless" and is an attempt to make anticompetitive use of government processes.[c]

b. See *Parker v. Brown,* 317 U.S. 341, 63 S.Ct. 307, 87 L.Ed. 315 (1943).

c. *Eastern Railroad Presidents Conference v. Noerr Motor Freight, Inc.,* 365 U.S. 127, 81 S.Ct. 523, 5 L.Ed.2d 464 (1961); and *United Mine Workers of America v. Pennington,* 381 U.S. 657, 89 S.Ct. 1585, 14 L.Ed.2d 626 (1965).

CASE 26.1

United States
Court of Appeals,
Second Circuit. 2004.
369 F.3d 124.

Clarett v. National Football League

SOTOMAYOR, Circuit Judge.

* * * *

[Maurice] Clarett, former running back for Ohio State University ("OSU") and Big Ten Freshman of the Year, is an accomplished and talented amateur football player. After gaining national attention as a high school player, Clarett became the first college freshman since 1943 to open as a starter at the position of running back for OSU. He led that team through an undefeated season, even scoring the winning touchdown in a double-overtime victory in the 2003 Fiesta Bowl to claim the national championship. * * * Clarett is now interested in turning professional by entering the [National Football League ("NFL" or "the League")] draft. Clarett is precluded from so doing, however, under the NFL's current rules governing draft eligibility.

* * * The eligibility rules * * * permit a player to enter the draft three full seasons after that player's high school graduation.

Clarett graduated high school on December 11, 2001, two-thirds of the way through the 2001 NFL season and is a season shy of the three necessary to qualify under the draft's eligibility rules. Unwilling to forgo the prospect of a year of lucrative professional play or run the risk of a career-compromising injury were his entry into the draft delayed until next year, Clarett filed this suit [in a federal district court] alleging that the NFL's draft eligibility rules are an unreasonable restraint of trade in violation of Section 1 of the Sherman Act and Section 4 of the Clayton Act.

* * * [T]he major source of the parties' * * * disputes is the relationship between the challenged eligibility rules and the current collective bargaining agreement governing the terms and conditions of employment for NFL players * * * . The current collective bargaining

CONTINUED

agreement between the NFL and its players union was negotiated between the NFL Management Council ("NFLMC"), which is the NFL member clubs' multi-employer bargaining unit, and the NFL Players Association ("NFLPA"), the NFL players' exclusive bargaining representative. * * *

* * * *

* * * On February 5, 2004, the district court granted summary judgment in favor of Clarett and ordered him eligible to enter this year's draft. * * * [The NFL appealed to this court.]

* * * *

* * * *[T]o accommodate the collective bargaining process, certain concerted activity among and between labor and employers [is] held to be beyond the reach of the antitrust laws.* * * [Emphasis added.]

* * * *

Although the NFL has maintained draft eligibility rules in one form or another for much of its history, the inception of a collective bargaining relationship between the NFL and its players union some thirty years ago irrevocably altered the governing legal regime. * * * [P]rospective players no longer have the right to negotiate directly with the NFL teams over the terms and conditions of their employment. That responsibility is instead committed to the NFL and the players union to accomplish through the collective bargaining process, and throughout that process the NFL and the players union are to have the freedom to craft creative solutions to their differences in light of the economic imperatives of their industry. Furthermore, the NFL teams are permitted to engage in joint conduct with respect to the terms and conditions of players' employment as a multi-employer bargaining unit without risking antitrust liability. * * *

* * * *

Clarett's argument that antitrust law should permit him to circumvent this scheme established by federal labor law starts with the contention that the eligibility rules do not constitute a mandatory subject of collective bargaining and thus cannot fall within the protection of the * * * exemption. * * * [H]owever, we find that the eligibility rules are mandatory bargaining subjects. Though tailored to the unique circumstance of a professional sports league, the eligibility rules for the draft represent a quite literal condition for initial employment and for that reason alone might constitute a mandatory bargaining subject. But moreover, the eligibility rules constitute a mandatory bargaining subject because they have tangible effects on the wages and working conditions of current NFL players. Because the unusual economic imperatives of professional sports raise numerous problems with little or no precedent in standard industrial relations, * * * many of the arrangements in professional sports that, at first glance, might not appear to deal with wages or working conditions are indeed mandatory bargaining subjects. * * *

Furthermore, by reducing competition in the market for entering players, the eligibility rules also affect the job security of veteran players. Because the size of NFL teams is capped, the eligibility rules diminish a veteran player's risk of being replaced by either a drafted rookie or a player who enters the draft and, though not drafted, is then hired as a rookie free agent. Consequently, * * * we find that to regard the NFL's eligibility rules as merely permissive bargaining subjects would ignore the reality of collective bargaining in sports.

* * * *

For the foregoing reasons, the judgment of the district court is REVERSED and the case REMANDED with instructions to enter judgment in favor of the NFL. The order of the district court designating Clarett eligible to enter this year's NFL draft is VACATED [set aside, rendered void].

QUESTIONS

1. Why are the NFL's member clubs permitted to agree that a player will not be hired until three full football seasons after the player's high school graduation?
2. Why couldn't the NFL's eligibility rules be eliminated from the list of mandatory subjects for the parties' collective bargaining agreement?

SECTION 8 | Monopolies

As noted above, the impetus for the initial federal antitrust legislation was concern over monopolies—specifically, concern that in particular markets a single, dominant firm could acquire and use market power to dictate or influence prices and output. Section 2 of the Sherman Act deals broadly with such cases. Section 2 condemns "every person who shall monopolize or attempt to monopolize." (Note that Section 2 applies to activities in the restraint of trade on the part of a single firm or individual. In contrast, Section 1, as described in the next chapter, applies to certain activities in the restraint of trade on the part of more than one individual or firm.) The essence of a single entity's violation of Section 2 is the entity's willful acquisition or maintenance of monopoly power, or its specifically intended *attempt* to do so, provided the attempt has a reasonable chance of success.

In the remainder of this chapter, we focus on single-firm behavior that is intended either to create or to preserve a monopoly within a particular market. Notice that two distinct types of behavior are subject to sanction under Section 2. First, conduct pursued by a firm that is already a monopolist is condemned as *monopolization* if the conduct interferes with free trade and is intended to preserve the firm's monopoly. Second, conduct intended to capture monopoly power is condemned as an *attempt to monopolize*.

Another Section 2 offense is the act of *predatory pricing*. **Predatory pricing** involves an attempt by one firm to drive its competitors from the market by selling its product substantially *below* normal costs of production. Once the competitors are eliminated, the firm will attempt to recapture its losses and go on to earn very high profits by driving up prices far above their competitive levels.

MONOPOLIZATION

In *United States v. Grinnell Corp.*,[11] the United States Supreme Court defined the offense of **monopolization** as involving the following two elements: "(1) the possession of monopoly power in the relevant market and (2) the willful acquisition or maintenance of the power as distinguished from growth or development as a consequence of a superior product, business acumen, or historic accident." A violation of Section 2 requires that both these elements be established.

MONOPOLY POWER The Sherman Act does not define *monopoly*. In economic parlance, monopoly refers to control by a single entity of an entire market. It is well established in antitrust law, however, that a firm may be a monopolist even though it is not the sole seller in a market. Nor is monopoly a function of size alone (for example, a "mom and pop" grocery located in an isolated desert town is a geographical monopolist if it is the only grocery serving that particular market). In theory, size in relation to the market is what matters, because monopoly involves power to affect prices and output.

—*Market Power.* The United States Supreme Court has defined monopoly power as "the power to control prices or exclude competition." This definition is of limited help, though, and most scholars generally consider monopoly power to be simply a *considerable* degree of market power or, otherwise stated, a *significant* degree of freedom from competitive pressure regarding output and pricing decisions. This generally is the way in which the Supreme Court has applied the concept.

As difficult as it is to define market power precisely, it is even more difficult to measure it. As a workable proxy, courts often look to the firm's percentage share of the "relevant market." This is the so-called **market-share test**.[12] The relevant market consists of two elements: (1) a relevant product market and (2) a relevant geographical market. A firm generally is considered to have monopoly power if its share of the relevant market is 70 percent or more. This is not an absolute, however. It is only a loose rule of thumb; in some cases, a smaller share may be held to constitute monopoly power.[13] Next, we discuss examples of the two elements of the market-share test.

—*Product Market.* No doubt the relevant product market should include all products that, although produced by different firms, nonetheless have identical attributes. But in determining the relevant market, it must be remembered that products that are not identical may be substituted for one another. Coffee

---

11. 384 U.S. 563, 86 S.Ct. 1698, 16 L.Ed.2d 778 (1966).

12. Other measures have been devised, but the market-share test is the most widely used.

13. This standard was first articulated by Judge Learned Hand in the famous *Aluminum Co. of America* case that will be discussed later in this chapter. A 90 percent share was held to be clear evidence of monopoly power. Anything less than 64 percent, said Judge Hand, made monopoly power doubtful, and anything less than 30 percent was clearly not monopoly power. This is merely a rule of thumb, however; it is not a binding principle of law.

may substitute for tea, cellophane may substitute for waxed paper, and so on. In defining the relevant product market, the key issue is the degree of interchangeability between products. If one product is a sufficient substitute for another, the two are considered to be part of the same product market.

In *United States v. E. I. du Pont de Nemours & Co.*,[14] du Pont was sued for monopolizing the cellophane market. Du Pont controlled about 75 percent of cellophane production but contended that it had no monopoly power, because the relevant market included not only cellophane but also all other flexible packaging materials. The United States Supreme Court found that there was indeed a sufficient degree of interchangeability between cellophane and alternatives such as waxed paper and aluminum foil. The Court noted, for example, that although 35 percent of the snack-food industry used cellophane, an even larger percentage used some other packaging material. Consequently, the Court concluded that du Pont did not control a share of the relevant market sufficient to constitute monopoly power.

Many times, decisions concerning relevant product markets can be interpreted as arbitrary. For example, the FTC blocked a merger between Staples, Inc., and Office Depot, Inc., on the ground that, in the office supply business, they had only one other competitor, OfficeMax, Inc. To eliminate any of the three, the FTC claimed, would violate antitrust laws. Staples contended, however, that, combined with Office Depot, it would control less than 6 percent of a market that included such giant retailers as Wal-Mart Stores, Inc., warehouse clubs, and national catalogue dealers. In other words, the FTC was looking at the way office supplies are sold, while Staples was arguing that the agency should look at office supplies as a product. Even after Office Depot agreed to sell sixty-three of its stores to OfficeMax, the FTC still refused to approve the merger and asked a federal district court to block it.

—Geographical Market. The second component of the relevant market is the geographical boundaries of the market. For products that are sold nationwide, the geographical boundaries encompass the entire United States. If transportation costs are significant or if a producer and its competitors sell in only a limited area—one in which customers have no access to other sources of the product—then the geographical market is limited to that area. In this sense, a national firm may compete in several distinct areas, having monopoly

power in one but not another. Generally, the geographical market is that section of the country within which a firm can increase its price a bit without attracting new sellers or without losing many customers to alternative suppliers outside that area.

The advent of e-commerce and the Internet is likely to dramatically change the notion of the size and limits of a geographical market. It may become difficult to perceive any geographical market as local, except for such products as concrete.

—Anticompetitive Behavior. Monopoly power is not, in and of itself, illegal. Recall that the monopolization offense has two elements. In addition to monopoly power, there is the requirement of "willful acquisition or maintenance of that power." A dominant market share may be the result of business acumen or the development of a superior product, or it may simply be the result of historical accident. None of these situations should give rise to antitrust concerns. Indeed, it would be counter to society's interest to condemn a firm that had acquired its position on the basis of the first two reasons.

If, however, a firm possesses monopoly power as a result of engaging in some purposeful act to acquire or to maintain that power through anticompetitive means, then the firm is in violation of Section 2. The United States Supreme Court has interpreted this second element as requiring some conduct intended to diminish competition.

Conduct that diminishes competition may not necessarily be anticompetitive. Devising new, low-cost production methods and developing and producing better products all hurt competitors. But they do not injure competition; they are the result of competition. In our initial hypothetical scenario, even if Acme had not received an exclusive monopoly, its DVD drive breakthrough would have given it monopoly power for a period of time until rival firms had had sufficient time to develop and market products that could effectively compete. But ultimately, Acme's innovation would have led to increased competition. Thus, only certain acts are condemned under Section 2, even if the acting firm possesses monopoly power. The hallmark of an action that does violate Section 2 is that, without providing better production or products, the action makes competing in the relevant market more difficult for the acting firm's rivals.

ANTICOMPETITIVE INTENT The qualifier that the sanctioned action must have been "willful" is said to require intent, but the intent requirement is difficult

---

14. 351 U.S. 377, 76 S.Ct. 994, 100 L.Ed.2d 1264 (1956).

to formulate. In most monopolization cases, intent may be inferred from evidence that the firm had monopoly power and engaged in anticompetitive behavior. For example, in *United States v. Aluminum Co. of America*,[15] the seemingly innocent act of expanding the demand for its products ran Alcoa afoul of Section 2. The court found that Alcoa had intentionally and artificially stimulated demand and then increased its own capacity to meet that increased demand.

The Court of Appeals for the Second Circuit[16] relied on the fact that Alcoa clearly possessed a mar-

ket share sufficient to give it monopoly power (90 percent of what the court determined to be the relevant market) and that the only apparent reason for its expansion was to prevent competitors from entering the aluminum market. This factual conclusion is often criticized, but the principle set out is now well established. Market domination that results from legitimate competitive behavior—such as foresight, innovation, skill, and good management—will not be condemned unless that domination is abused or acquired through behavior that harms, rather than flows from, competition.

The following case included an allegation of a violation of Section 2 of the Sherman Act.

---

15. 148 F.2d 416 (2d Cir. 1945).

16. The Second Circuit acted as the court of final appeal in place of the United States Supreme Court because the latter could not muster a quorum of six qualified justices to hear the case. The case was referred to the court of appeals of the circuit from which it had come under a specially drawn statute (28 U.S.C. Section 2109).

CASE 26.2 — United States v. Microsoft Corp.

United States
Court of Appeals,
District of
Columbia Circuit, 2001.
253 F.3d 34.
http://www.cadc.uscourts.gov[a]

HISTORICAL AND TECHNOLOGICAL SETTING *In 1981, Microsoft Corporation released the first version of its Microsoft Disk Operating System (MS-DOS). When International Business Machines Corporation (IBM) selected MS-DOS for preinstallation on its first generation of personal computers (PCs), Microsoft's product became the dominant operating system for Intel-compatible PCs.[b] In 1985, Microsoft began shipping a software package called Windows. Although originally a user-interface on top of MS-DOS, Windows took on more operating-system functionality over time. Throughout the 1990s, Microsoft's share of the market for Intel-compatible operating systems was more than 90 percent.*

BACKGROUND AND FACTS *In 1994, Netscape Communications Corporation began marketing Navigator, the first popular graphical Internet browser. Navigator worked with Java, a technology developed by Sun Microsystems, Inc. Java enabled applications to run on a variety of platforms, which meant that users did not need Windows. Microsoft perceived a threat to its dominance of the operating-system market and developed a competing browser, Internet Explorer (Explorer). Microsoft then began to require computer makers that wanted to install Windows also to install Explorer and exclude Navigator. Meanwhile, Microsoft commingled browser code and other code in Windows so that deleting files containing Explorer would cripple the operating system. Microsoft offered to promote and pay Internet service providers (ISPs) to distribute Explorer and exclude Navigator. Microsoft also developed its own Java code and deceived many independent software sellers into believing that this code would help in designing cross-platform applications when, in fact, it would run only on Windows. The U.S. Department of Justice and a number of state attorneys general filed a suit in a federal district court against Microsoft, alleging, in part, monopolization in violation of Section 2 of the Sherman Act. The court ruled against Microsoft.[c] Microsoft appealed to the U.S. Court of Appeals for the District of Columbia Circuit.*

---

a. On this page, click on "All Opinions." In the section headed "Please select from the following menu to find opinions by date of issue," choose "June" from the "Month" menu, select "2001" from the "Year" menu, and click on "Go!" From the result, scroll to the name of the case and click on the docket number to access the opinion. The U.S. Court of Appeals for the District of Columbia Circuit maintains this Web site.

b. An *Intel-compatible PC* is designed to function with Intel Corporation's 80x86/Pentium families of microprocessors or with compatible microprocessors.

c. The district court ordered, among other things, a structural reorganization of Microsoft, including a separation of its operating-system and applications businesses. See *United States v. Microsoft*, 97 F.Supp.2d 59 (D.D.C. 2000).

CONTINUED ▶

CASE 26.2 | Continued

IN THE LANGUAGE OF THE COURT

PER CURIAM: [By the whole court]
* * * *
* * * Claiming that software competition is uniquely "dynamic," [Microsoft] suggests * * * that monopoly power in the software industry should be proven directly, that is, by examining a company's actual behavior to determine if it reveals the existence of monopoly power. * * *

* * * *
* * * Microsoft's pattern of exclusionary conduct could only be rational if the firm knew that it possessed monopoly power. It is to that conduct that we now turn.

* * * *
* * * [P]rovisions in Microsoft's agreements licensing Windows to [computer makers] * * * reduce usage share of Netscape's browser and, hence, protect Microsoft's operating system monopoly. * * *

* * * *
Therefore, Microsoft's efforts to gain market share in one market (browsers) served to meet the threat to Microsoft's monopoly in another market (operating systems) by keeping rival browsers from gaining the critical mass of users necessary to attract developer attention away from Windows as the platform for software development. * * *

* * * *
* * * [W]e conclude that [Microsoft's] commingling [of browser and nonbrowser code] has an anticompetitive effect; * * * the commingling deters [computer makers] from pre-installing rival browsers, thereby reducing the rivals' usage share and, hence, developers' interest in rivals' [Application Programming Interfaces (APIs)] as an alternative to the API set exposed by Microsoft's operating system.

* * * *
* * * By ensuring that the majority of all [ISP] subscribers are offered [Internet Explorer] either as the default browser or as the only browser, Microsoft's deals with the [ISPs] clearly have a significant effect in preserving its monopoly * * *.

* * * *
* * * Microsoft's exclusive deals with the [Internet software vendors] had a substantial effect in further foreclosing rival browsers from the market * * *.

DECISION AND REMEDY *The U.S. Court of Appeals for the District of Columbia Circuit affirmed the part of the lower court's opinion holding that Microsoft did possess and maintain monopoly power in the market for Intel-compatible operating systems. The appellate court reversed other holdings of the lower court, however, and remanded the case for a reconsideration of the appropriate remedy.*

COMMENTS *The appellate court also concluded that the trial court judge's remarks (to members of the press and others during the trial) "would give a reasonable, informed observer cause to question his impartiality in ordering the company split in two." The appellate court cited this bias as its reason for reversing the order to break up Microsoft and remanding the case to a different trial court judge to reconsider what penalty would be appropriate. Essentially, the appellate court opened the door to a much lighter penalty for Microsoft. Since then, the Department of Justice and nine of the state attorneys general who brought the suit agreed with Microsoft to settle the case. On November 1, 2002, a federal trial court judge approved the settlement. Generally, the settlement gives consumers more choices and allows Microsoft's rivals more flexibility to offer competing software features on computers running Windows.*

PREDATORY PRICING

As mentioned earlier in this chapter, predatory pricing—selling below cost—is a violation of Section 2 of the Sherman Act. In monopolization cases, predatory pricing is one form of conduct that continues to receive considerable attention. One reason for this is that a dominant theme in antitrust cases is the promotion of consumer welfare. But consumers benefit from low prices. If a firm sells a valuable product for a price below cost, then it is the firm that loses, not the consumer. Despite the fact that consumers benefit from the low price, predatory pricing is still condemned.

Condemnation of predatory pricing is based on the fear that although it may benefit consumers in the short term, in the longer term, it will harm competition. The harm feared is that a rich rival, by pricing below its competitors' costs, could drive the competitors out of the market by outlasting them during the phase in which prices were below cost. In the subsequent phase, the rich rival would still be in the market but would no longer face any competitors. The firm would then be free to reap large profits by raising the price far above what it had been when the firm faced market competition.

In any event, there are procompetitive reasons not only for low prices but even for prices below cost. Such pricing may be, for example, the only way in which a new firm can gain a "toehold" in a market populated by established firms, especially if the latter have strong brand-name recognition in the market. To prevent the entry of new competitors into a market by forbidding them from using low prices, perhaps even prices below cost, would hinder rather than promote competition.

Faced with such uncertainty as to the purpose and effect of firms' pricing decisions, courts have struggled to invent a workable standard for judging predatory pricing. Some courts look at market structure in deciding predatory pricing cases. Under this approach, a court looks at the potential for harm to consumers created by a firm's below-cost pricing. If it appears that a firm pricing below cost will be unable to capture

monopoly profits at a later time, the court rejects any attempt to discern intent. The essence of the market approach is that if the firm is unlikely to capture monopoly profits through high prices in the future, intent does not matter.[17] Consumers benefit from the low prices regardless. Moreover, if the firm is pursuing a legitimate objective of trying to gain access to an established market, the efforts should not be hampered by rivals crying foul simply because they lose business to a competitor selling at a lower price.

ATTEMPTS TO MONOPOLIZE

Section 2 also prohibits an **attempt to monopolize** a market. Any action challenged as an attempt to monopolize must have been specifically intended to exclude competitors and garner monopoly power. In addition, the attempt must have had a "dangerous" probability of success; that is, the attempt need not have succeeded but must have posed a *serious* threat of monopolization. A probability cannot be dangerous unless the alleged offender possesses at least some degree of market power. The following case demonstrates how an attempt to monopolize can occur.

17. See, for example, *Brooke Group, Ltd. v. Brown & Williamson Tobacco Corp.*, 509 U.S. 209, 113 S.Ct. 2578, 125 L.Ed.2d 168 (1993), in which the Supreme Court held that a seller's price-cutting policies could not be predatory "[g]iven the market's realities"—the size of the seller's market share, the expanding output by other sellers, and other factors.

CASE 26.3 — Nobody in Particular Presents, Inc. v. Clear Channel Communications, Inc.

United States District Court, District of Colorado, 2004. 311 F.Supp.2d 1048.

BACKGROUND AND FACTS *Nobody in Particular Presents, Inc. (NIPP), is a music concert promoter in the Denver, Colorado, area and has promoted concerts by Beck, Pearl Jam, the Neville Brothers, and many others in a number of cities. Clear Channel Communications (CCC) is one of the largest radio and entertainment conglomerates in the world. Through its wholly owned subsidiaries, Clear Channel has holdings in radio stations, concert venues, and the concert promotions industry. Clear Channel has four rock-format radio stations in the Denver area and is a major area concert promoter, controlling about 47 percent of the local market. Clear Channel's market share in terms of advertising revenue for rock music may be as high as 87.3 percent. NIPP filed an action against Clear Channel, complaining that Clear Channel used its position in rock-format radio to intimidate and coerce rock artists and their record labels into signing with Clear Channel subsidiaries for concert promotion. The defendant (Clear Channel) allegedly informed artists that local radio stations would not play their music or even accept their advertising unless they signed up for Clear Channel promotion. Those who did sign up for Clear Channel concert promotion received additional airtime and free promotions. NIPP alleged that this was an attempt to monopolize the market in violation of Section 2 of the Sherman Act. Clear Channel moved for summary judgment.*

CONTINUED ▶

CASE 26.3 | Continued

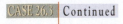

IN THE LANGUAGE OF THE COURT

NOTTINGHAM, J.

* * * *

Here, NIPP has presented sufficient evidence that Clear Channel's refusal to accept paid advertising is founded upon an intention to create monopoly power for itself in the rock concert promotions market. As shown earlier in electronic mail messages, Michael O'Connor asked his station personnel to refuse advertising for promoters competing with SFX/Clear Channel Entertainment and/or Radio festivals. This refusal to deal may not be in the commercial best interest of Clear Channel's radio stations because, as O'Connor himself testified, providing radio advertising and radio promotional support benefits the radio stations. * * * *Assuming that the refusal to deal is not in the best commercial interests of the radio stations, an inference could be made that the refusal supports other, more sinister motives, such as the creation of a monopoly. * * * * Finally, NIPP has demonstrated evidence of marketwide injury by showing an increase in ticket prices and a decreasing market share for all of Clear Channel's competitors in the rock concert market * * * *. [Emphasis added.]

DECISION AND REMEDY *The defendant's motion for summary judgment on attempted monopolization claims was denied, but the court granted the motion on actual monopolization claims, because the defendant did not have a large enough market share of the concert promotion business to qualify as an actual monopolist.*

REVIEWING ANTITRUST AND MONOPOLY

In 1989, Roxanna Leland, who lived in Curio Valley, an isolated town in rural Michigan, began selling fresh pies under the business name Momma Roxie's Heavenly Pies. Leland's business grew as a result of the superior quality of the pies and her willingness to carry fresh pies daily into every Curio Valley shop. Such a local desire for the pies grew that Momma Roxie's eventually garnered 80 percent of the pie sales in Curio Valley. In 1999, Leland sold the business and its name to Arnold Sachmeister under an agreement that Leland would not sell pies in Curio Valley for twenty years. Under Sachmeister, Momma Roxie's began requiring that every pie purchaser buy an "Arnie's Poem of the Day" for $1 along with each pie. In 2006, a new local pie dealer, Crusty Joe, began successfully competing with Momma Roxie's. Momma Roxie's soon began selling all pies at half the price of Crusty Joe. Using the information presented in the chapter, answer the following questions.

1. What is the term for a firm that holds such market power that it can limit rivals from competing in the market?

2. Did the agreement between Leland and Sachmeister constitute a restraint of trade? If so, would this be considered a reasonable or unreasonable restraint?

3. What is the term applicable to the requirement that each buyer purchase a poem along with a pie? Is such a requirement legal?

4. What remedies would Crusty Joe have available if it were injured as a result of Sachmeister's sales of Momma Roxie's pies at reduced prices?

5. If Crusty Joe were to initiate an antitrust action against Momma Roxie's, what two elements must Crusty Joe establish to define the offense of monopolization?

6. To succeed in an action for predatory pricing against Momma Roxie's, what must Crusty Joe demonstrate?

TERMS AND CONCEPTS TO REVIEW

antitrust law 608	market-share test 617	predatory pricing 617
attempt to monopolize 621	monopolization 617	restraint of trade 610
dissolution 612	monopoly 607	treble damages 612
divestiture 612	monopoly power 610	trust 609
market power 607	*Noerr-Pennington* doctrine 614	

QUESTIONS AND CASE PROBLEMS

26–1. The Southern Motor Carriers Rate Conference is a private organization that lobbies regulatory commissions in various southern states on behalf of national and regional private commercial carriers. A new carrier claims that the organization is really in the business of setting rates and controlling the issuance of licenses through its influence over the members of the various regulatory boards. How might the organization violate antitrust laws? If the organization does no more than lobby the various agencies, does it run afoul of the antitrust laws in light of the Supreme Court's enunciation of the *Noerr-Pennington* doctrine?

26–2. A car rental firm specializes in renting automobiles to insurance company customers who need temporary replacements while their cars are being repaired. Several other car rental agencies serve the same geographical area. The specialty agency substantially reduces the daily rental fee on its cars. Other firms in the area contend that the reductions amount to predatory pricing. If an antitrust action is brought against the specialty agency, how should the case be decided? Discuss all factors that must be considered.

26–3. QUESTION WITH SAMPLE ANSWER
Super-Tech Industries presently controls 55 percent of the market for the manufacture and sale of computers. The balance of the market is controlled by five other manufacturers, with Alcan Corp. having 25 percent of the market. Alcan has an innovative research staff, but every time Alcan introduces a faster, more powerful, and more efficient computer into the market, Super-Tech immediately informs its customers of the upcoming development of a competing computer that it will sell at 30 percent below the Alcan price. Alcan claims that these activities on the part of Super-Tech are an antitrust violation. Discuss fully whether this unilateral action by Super-Tech violates antitrust law.
For a sample answer to this question, go to Appendix I at the end of this text.

26–4. Goodfellows, Inc., is a close corporation with only two shareholders. Goodfellows is engaged in the pizza delivery business. Two other such firms serve the same market, but Goodfellows controls a 75 percent share. The two shareholders agree that one will purchase all of the shares that belong to the other. As a condition of the transaction, the shareholder selling the shares agrees not to open a competing pizza delivery business within a seventy-mile radius or become employed by any rival firm within the same designated area. The covenant is to last five years. Is it an unreasonable restraint of trade? Would a court likely declare unenforceable the promise not to compete?

26–5. CASE PROBLEM WITH SAMPLE ANSWER
BTR, Inc., owns the patent rights to sorbothane (an elastic polymer with characteristics that make it useful in a variety of products). In 1980, BTR granted Shirley and Larry McQuillan all distribution rights to sorbothane and exclusive rights to buy sorbothane for use in equestrian products. In 1981, BTR split the distribution rights between the McQuillans and Spectrum Sports, Inc. The next year, BTR asked the McQuillans to relinquish more of their distribution rights, but they refused. A few months later, BTR appointed another company as national distributor for sorbothane equestrian products. In August 1983, BTR refused to accept the McQuillans' orders, and Spectrum replaced them as national distributor of some sorbothane products. The McQuillans' business failed. They sued BTR and Spectrum. Did the defendants violate Section 2 of the Sherman Act? [*Spectrum Sports, Inc. v. McQuillan*, 506 U.S. 884, 113 S.Ct. 884, 122 L.Ed.2d 247 (1993)]
To view a sample answer for this case problem, go to this book's Web site at http://wleb.westbuslaw.com, select "Chapter 26," and click on "Case Problem with Sample Answer."

26–6. ANTITRUST LAWS. Great Western Directories, Inc. (GW), is an independent publisher of telephone directory Yellow Pages. GW buys information for its listings from Southwestern Bell Telephone Co. (SBT). Southwestern Bell Corp. owns SBT and Southwestern Bell Yellow Pages (SBYP), which publishes a directory in competition with GW. In June 1988, in some markets, SBT raised the price for its listing information, and SBYP lowered the price for advertising in its Yellow Pages. GW feared that these companies would do the same thing in other local markets, and it would then be too expensive to compete in those markets. Because of this fear, GW left one market and declined to compete in another. Consequently, SBYP had a monopoly in those markets. GW and another independent publisher filed a suit in a federal district court against Southwestern Bell Corp. What antitrust law, if any, did Southwestern Bell Corp. violate? Should the independent companies be entitled to damages? [*Great Western Directories, Inc. v. Southwestern Bell Telephone Co.*, 74 F.3d 613 (5th Cir. 1996)]

26–7. MONOPOLIES. At one time, all advertisers and advertising agencies sent their ads to newspapers by mail, courier, or some other form of physical delivery. By the mid-1980s, electronic delivery emerged as an alternative. In 1986, AD/SAT, a division of Skylight, Inc., began to deliver ads from New York and Los Angeles to newspapers through AD/SAT's high-speed facsimile system over a satellite network owned and operated by the Associated Press (AP). The AP, a cooperative association whose members include more than 1,500 U.S. newspapers, collects and distributes news and photographs to newspapers. AD/SAT's competitors included DigiFlex, Ad eXpress, AdStar, AdLink, and Business Link. By 1994, forty-eight of the fifty largest papers in the United States were AD/SAT customers, but 80 percent of all ads delivered to newspapers were sent by overnight couriers, such as Federal Express. That year, the AP launched AdSEND to compete in the delivery of ads to newspapers via the AP's satellite network. Unlike AD/SAT, AdSEND handled the delivery of ads using computers and charged only advertisers for the delivery. AD/SAT filed a suit in a federal district court against the AP and others. Did the AP's entry into the ad delivery business violate Section 2 of the Sherman Act? Why or why not? [*AD/SAT, a Division of Skylight, Inc. v. Associated Press*, 181 F.3d 216 (2d.Cir. 1999)]

26–8. ATTEMPTED MONOPOLIZATION. In 1995, to make personal computers (PCs) easier to use, Intel Corp. and other companies developed a standard, called the Universal Serial Bus (USB) specification, to enable the easy attachment of peripherals (printers and other hardware) to PCs. Intel and others formed the Universal Serial Bus Implementers Forum (USB-IF) to promote USB technology and products. Intel, however, makes relatively few USB products and does not make any USB interconnect devices. Multivideo Labs, Inc. (MVL), designed and distributed Active Extension Cables (AECs) to connect peripheral devices to each other or to a PC. The AECs were not USB compliant, a fact that Intel employees told other USB-IF members. Asserting that this caused a "general cooling of the market" for AECs, MVL filed a suit in a federal district court against Intel, claiming in part attempted monopolization in violation of the Sherman Act. Intel filed a motion for summary judgment. How should the court rule, and why? [*Multivideo Labs, Inc. v. Intel Corp.*, __ F.Supp.2d __ (S.D.N.Y. 2000)]

26–9. MONOPOLIZATION. Moist snuff is a smokeless tobacco product sold in small round cans from racks, which include point-of-sale (POS) ads. POS ads are critical because tobacco advertising is restricted and the number of people who use smokeless tobacco products is relatively small. In the moist snuff market in the United States, there are only four competitors, including U.S. Tobacco Co. and its affiliates (USTC) and Conwood Co. In 1990, USTC, which held 87 percent of the market, began to convince major retailers, including Wal-Mart Stores, Inc., to use USTC's "exclusive racks" to display its products and those of all other snuff makers. USTC agents would then destroy competitors' racks. USTC also began to provide retailers with false sales data to convince them to maintain its poor-selling items and drop competitors' less expensive products. Conwood's Wal-Mart market share fell from 12 percent to 6.5 percent. In stores in which USTC did not have rack exclusivity, however, Conwood's market share increased to 25 percent. Conwood filed a suit in a federal district court against USTC, alleging in part that USTC used its monopoly power to exclude competitors from the moist snuff market. Should the court rule in Conwood's favor? What is USTC's best defense? Discuss. [*Conwood Co., L.P. v. U.S. Tobacco Co.*, 290 F.3d 768 (6th Cir. 2002)]

26–10. MONOPOLIZATION. Dentsply International, Inc., is one of a dozen manufacturers of artificial teeth for dentures and other restorative devices. Dentsply sells its teeth to twenty-three dealers of dental products. The dealers supply the teeth to dental laboratories, which fabricate dentures for sale to dentists. There are hundreds of other dealers who compete with one another on the basis of price and service. Some manufacturers sell directly to the laboratories. There are also thousands of laboratories that compete with one another on the basis of price and service. Because of advances in dental medicine, however, artificial tooth manufacturing is marked by low growth potential, and Dentsply dominates the industry. Dentsply's market share is greater than 75 percent and is about fifteen times larger than that of its next-closest competitor. Dentsply prohibits its dealers from marketing competitors' teeth unless they were selling the teeth before 1993. The federal government filed a suit in a federal district court against Dentsply, alleging in part a violation of Section 2 of the Sherman Act. What must the government show to succeed in its suit? Are those elements present in this case? What should the court rule? Explain. [*United States v. Dentsply International, Inc.*, 399 F.3d 181 (3d Cir. 2005)]

LAW | on the Web

For updated links to resources available on the Web, as well as a variety of other materials, visit this text's Web site at http://wleb.westbuslaw.com.

You can access the Antitrust Division of the U.S. Department of Justice online at

http://www.usdoj.gov

To see the American Bar Association's Web page on antitrust law, go to

http://www.abanet.org/antitrust

LEGAL RESEARCH EXERCISES ON THE WEB

Go to http://wleb.westbuslaw.com, the Web site that accompanies this text. Select "Chapter 26" and click on "Internet Exercises." There you will find the following Internet research exercises that you can perform to learn more about topics covered in this chapter.

Activity 26–1: LEGAL PERSPECTIVE
            The Standard Oil Trust

Activity 26–2: MANAGEMENT PERSPECTIVE
            Monopolization

CHAPTER 27
Antitrust and Restraint of Trade

The major thrust of federal antitrust legislation has been directed at anticompetitive agreements between rival firms. Agreements to fix prices, restrict output, divide markets, exclude other competitors, and otherwise impede the dynamics of a free market have all been condemned as violations of federal antitrust laws. Such joint actions have been prosecuted as impermissible restraints of trade under Section 1 of the Sherman Act and, if the firms possess substantial market power, as conspiracies to monopolize under Section 2 of the same act.

Some agreements may be forced on an unwilling firm by another firm possessing substantial market power. Typical of such agreements are *exclusive-dealing contracts* and *tying arrangements*, described in the preceding chapter. Recall that an exclusive-dealing contract conditions one firm's willingness to deal with another on the latter's continued refusal to deal with the former's rivals. Tying arrangements normally require that the purchaser of one product also purchase a second product. Also recall that such agreements violate provisions of the Clayton Act if the contracts or arrangements harm the competitive process or interfere with free trade.

In this chapter, we continue our study of antitrust law by examining in detail the various forms of *concerted behavior* that are condemned as harmful to competition. In particular, we examine how courts attempt to distinguish between those types of trade restrictions that are necessary— perhaps even beneficial—to the competitive process and those that impede competition. We also examine the legal standards for determining whether mergers between firms should be declared illegal on the ground that the result would be to lessen competition.

SECTION 1 | Restraint of Trade: Overview

The underlying assumption of Section 1 of the Sherman Act is that society's welfare is harmed if rival firms are permitted to join in an agreement that consolidates their market power or otherwise restrains competition. Not all agreements between rivals, however, result in enhanced market power or *unreasonably* restrain trade. It is virtually inconceivable that an agreement to fix prices or restrict output could be designed for any purpose other than to diminish interfirm competition. Yet there are numerous instances in which agreements among rivals might actually increase social welfare by making firms more efficient, by making information more readily available, or by creating joint incentives to undertake risky research and development projects.

PER SE VIOLATIONS

Some agreements are considered so blatantly and substantially anticompetitive that they are deemed **per se violations** of Section 1. For example, if two competitors in a concentrated industry agree to set the prices for their products at the same level, their agreement is considered so anticompetitive that it is deemed a *per se* violation. If an agreement is found to be a *per se* violation, a court is precluded from inquiring whether the agreement should be upheld on the ground that it provides benefits that outweigh its anticompetitive effects.

THE RULE OF REASON

If an agreement is not found to be a *per se* violation of Section 1, then the court proceeds to analyze its legality under what is referred to as a **rule of reason,** according to which the court balances the reasons for the agreement against its potentially anticompetitive effects.

In determining whether a specific agreement that is not a *per se* violation should nonetheless be condemned as a Section 1 offense, a court will consider several factors. The court must evaluate the parties' purposes in effecting the agreement, determine whether the parties have power to implement the agreement's purposes, and assess what the effect or potential effect of the agreement is. Some antitrust scholars maintain that case law suggests that courts will also consider a fourth element: whether the parties could have relied on less restrictive means to achieve their goals.

The need for a rule-of-reason analysis of some agreements in restraint of trade is obvious—if the rule of reason had not been developed, virtually any business agreement could conceivably be held to violate the Sherman Act. Justice Louis Brandeis effectively phrased this sentiment in *Chicago Board of Trade v. United States*, a case decided in 1918:

> Every agreement concerning trade, every regulation of trade, restrains. To bind, to restrain, is of their very essence. The true test of legality is whether the restraint imposed is such as merely regulates and perhaps thereby promotes competition or whether it is such as may suppress or even destroy competition.[1]

SECTION 2 | Horizontal Restraints

The term **horizontal restraint** is encountered frequently in antitrust law. A horizontal restraint is any agreement that in some way restrains competition between rival firms competing in the same market. Whenever firms at the same level of operation and in direct competition with one another (for example, retailers of a similar product located in the same geographical market) agree to operate in a way that restricts their market activities, they are said to have imposed a horizontal restraint on trade. Some horizontal restraints are *per se* violations of Section 1, but others may be permissible; those that are not *per se* violations are tested under the rule of reason.

PRICE FIXING

Consider the scenario presented in Chapter 26 involving the introduction of a new digital video disc (DVD) drive. Suppose our hypothetical firm, Acme, had

instead sought large profits by some means other than arduous and financially risky research into innovative DVD drive technology. Assume that advanced DVD drive technology does not yet exist. Acme's managers decide to make life easy for themselves. They go to other DVD drive producers and say, "Let's not work to one another's disadvantage. There's enough demand for DVD drives for all of us to charge higher prices if we don't undercut one another's prices." Acme's plan calls for each producer to charge a price higher than an established minimum. The minimum price is set as the total cost of the least productive producer plus a 10 percent profit margin. More efficient firms (that is, firms that can produce at lower cost) will, of course, enjoy higher profits.

Although not all such schemes are as simple or as blatant as our hypothetical example suggests, they all involve some means of eliminating competition between rivals to sell at the lowest price while still earning a normal profit (that is, one commensurate with the profit that could be earned in some alternative endeavor using the same resources). By eliminating price competition in which firms seek to sell more by charging less than their rivals, firms restrict output. This is the essence of **price fixing.**

PER SE VIOLATION Perhaps the definitive case regarding price-fixing agreements remains the 1940 case of *United States v. Socony-Vacuum Oil Co.*, also known as the *Madison Oil* case.[2] In this case, a group of independent oil producers in Texas and Louisiana were caught between falling demand due to the Great Depression and increasing supply from newly discovered oil fields in the region. In response, a group of the major refining companies agreed to buy "distress" gasoline (excess supplies) from the independents so as to dispose of it in an "orderly manner." Although there was no explicit agreement as to price, it was clear that the purpose of the agreement was to limit the supply of gasoline on the market, thereby raising prices.

There may have been good reasons for such an agreement. The refiners may simply have wanted to avoid a temporary situation that would have driven the independent suppliers out of business, thus making it difficult to secure crude oil supplies later, after the economic climate had improved. Nonetheless, the threats posed by such agreements to open and free competition were deemed significant. The United States Supreme Court recognized these dangers in the

---

1. 246 U.S. 231, 38 S.Ct. 242, 62 L.Ed. 683 (1918).

2. 310 U.S. 150, 60 S.Ct. 811, 84 L.Ed.2d 1129 (1940).

Socony-Vacuum case. The Court held that the asserted reasonableness of a price-fixing agreement is never a defense; any agreement that restricts output or artificially fixes price is a *per se* violation of Section 1. The rationale of the *per se* rule was best stated in what is now the most famous portion of the Court's decision: footnote 59 of Justice William O. Douglas's opinion.

In it, he compared a freely functioning price system to a body's central nervous system, condemning price-fixing agreements as threats to "the central nervous system of the economy."

At issue in the following case was whether an agreement between two pharmaceutical manufacturers constituted a *per se* violation of the Sherman Act.

CASE 27.1

In re Cardizem CD Antitrust Litigation

United States
Court of Appeals,
Sixth Circuit. 2003.
332 F.3d 896.

OBERDORFER, District Judge.

*   *   *   *

*   *   * [Hoescht Marion Roussel, Inc. (HMR)] manufactures and markets Cardizem CD, a brand-name prescription drug which is used for the treatment of angina and hypertension and for the prevention of heart attacks and strokes. *   *   * HMR's patent for [Cardizem CD] expired in November 1992.

*   *   * Andrx [Pharmaceuticals, Inc.] was the first potential generic manufacturer of Cardizem CD *   *   *, entitling it to [a] 180-day exclusivity period [within which to sell the generic without competition from other drug makers] once it received [Food and Drug Administration (FDA)] approval.

*   *   *   *

In January 1996, HMR *   *   * filed a patent infringement suit against Andrx in [a federal district court] *   *   * . [F]iling that complaint automatically triggered [a] thirty-month waiting period during which *   *   * Andrx could not market its generic product. *   *   *

On September 15, 1997, the FDA tentatively approved Andrx's [generic] *   *   * .

Nine days later, on September 24, 1997, HMR and Andrx entered into [an] Agreement. It provided that Andrx would not market a *   *   * generic version of Cardizem CD in the United States until *   *   * Andrx obtain[ed] a favorable, final, and unappealable determination in the patent infringement case *   *   * . In exchange, HMR agreed to make *   *   * payments to Andrx in the amount of $40 million per year *   *   * .

*   *   *   *

*   *   * [Louisiana Wholesale Drug Company and other buyers of Cardizem CD filed a suit in a federal district court against the two firms] under the federal antitrust laws *   *   * . [The court issued a summary judgment in the plaintiffs' favor. The defendants appealed to the U.S. Court of Appeals for the Sixth Circuit.]

*   *   *   *

*   *   * The Agreement guaranteed to HMR that its only potential competitor at that time, Andrx, would, for the price of $10 million per quarter, refrain from marketing its generic version of Cardizem CD even after it had obtained FDA approval, protecting HMR's exclusive access to the market for Cardizem CD throughout the United States *   *   * . Andrx and HMR terminated the Agreement and the payments in June 1999 *   *   * . In the interim, *   *   * from July 1998 through June 1999, Andrx kept its generic product off the market and HMR paid Andrx $89.83 million. By delaying Andrx's entry into the market, the Agreement also delayed the entry of other generic competitors, who could not enter until the expiration of Andrx's 180-day period of marketing exclusivity *   *   * . There is simply no escaping the conclusion that *the Agreement, all of its other conditions and provisions notwithstanding, was, at its core, a horizontal agreement to eliminate competition in the market for Cardizem CD throughout the entire United States, a classic example of a per se illegal restraint of trade.* [Emphasis added.]

None of the defendants' attempts to avoid *per se* treatment is persuasive. *   *   * [T]he Agreement cannot be fairly characterized as merely an attempt to enforce patent rights or an interim settlement of the patent litigation. As the plaintiffs point out, it is one thing to take advantage of a monopoly that naturally arises from a patent, but another thing altogether to

CASE 27.1 | Continued

bolster the patent's effectiveness in inhibiting competitors by paying the only potential competitor $40 million per year to stay out of the market. Nor does the fact that this is a "novel" area of law preclude *per se* treatment. To the contrary, whatever may be its peculiar problems and characteristics, the Sherman Act, so far as price-fixing agreements are concerned, establishes one uniform rule applicable to all industries alike. We see no reason not to apply that rule here, especially when the record does not support the defendants' claim that the district court made "errors" in its analysis. Finally, the defendants' claims that the Agreement lacked anticompetitive effects and had procompetitive benefits are simply irrelevant. * * * *[T]he virtue/vice of the* per se *rule is that it allows courts to presume that certain behaviors as a class are anticompetitive without expending judicial resources to evaluate the actual anticompetitive effects or procompetitive justifications in a particular case.* * * * [Emphasis added.]

The respondents' principal argument is that the *per se* rule is inapplicable because their agreements are alleged to have procompetitive justifications. The argument indicates a misunderstanding of the *per se* concept. The anticompetitive potential inherent in all price-fixing agreements justifies their facial invalidation even if procompetitive justifications are offered for some. Those claims of enhanced competition are so unlikely to prove significant in any particular case that we adhere to the rule of law that is justified in its general application.

Thus, the law is clear that once it is decided that a restraint is subject to *per se* analysis, the claimed lack of any actual anticompetitive effects or presence of procompetitive effects is irrelevant.
* * * *

For the foregoing reasons, we [hold that the lower court properly granted] the plaintiffs' motions for summary judgment that the defendants had committed a *per se* violation of the antitrust laws.

QUESTIONS

1. How were the plaintiffs injured by the agreement between the defendants in this case?
2. What difference should it have had on the outcome that Andrx could have unilaterally, and legally, decided not to bring its generic to market?

IDENTIFYING A PRICE-FIXING ARRANGEMENT

Price-fixing arrangements are not always easy to identify. An otherwise legitimate arrangement may unintentionally result in price fixing. Price fixing also may be difficult to detect because the parties wish to conceal their scheme.

HORIZONTAL MARKET DIVISIONS

Prices can be controlled indirectly through agreements to restrict output, as well as explicitly through agreements to fix prices. Because the former type of agreement operates to decrease the supplies available to consumers, it has the same effect as a direct agreement to raise prices. Efforts to control prices are often effected by **horizontal market divisions**—that is, agreements to divide the market up among rival firms. The allocation may be geographical (for example, letting one firm serve the Midwest, another the East Coast, and so on), or it may be functional, by class of customer (for example, having one firm deal exclusively with retailers and a second firm deal solely with wholesalers).

In some respects, market divisions may have an even greater impact on competition than do price-fixing agreements. Each firm has a monopoly over its allocated share of the market for that particular brand—it is the sole supplier. The sole supplier is free not only from price competition for that brand but also from competition for that brand regarding quality, customer service, and all other dimensions of competition.

Consider once again our hypothetical scenario involving Acme and its rival DVD drive producers. Suppose that, flush with the initial success of their price-fixing agreement, the producers agree that each firm that begins selling DVD drives to dealers in remote communities in which DVD drives have not been available will thereafter have an exclusive right to sell retail or through dealers in that area. Initially, there is intense competition to find such virgin markets. After all the profitable markets have been taken, however, conditions in the exclusive markets may change. Suppliers may begin to limit the warranties they offer. Prices may begin to rise despite the lack of warranties. And service may diminish. Because of such potential effects, agreements like that made by the DVD drive producers are generally treated as *per se* violations of Section 1.

TRADE ASSOCIATIONS

The common interests of firms or individuals within an industry or profession are frequently promoted by trade associations or professional organizations. These organizations may provide for the exchange of information among the members, the enhancement of the public image of the trade or profession, the setting of industry or professional standards, or the pooling of resources to represent the members' interests to various governmental bodies. Some of these activities benefit society, as well as the individual members. Even those activities that benefit the members' general economic well-being may not necessarily be anticompetitive.

For example, lumber producers might be concerned about whether or not they are cutting more trees than expected future demand would warrant given the cutting levels of rival firms. The market for lumber might be widely dispersed over the whole nation, making it especially difficult for small firms to gauge overall demand conditions in the lumber market. Lumber firms might thus decide to form a trade association that could amass data on the output and price levels of its members in various markets. The association would be of economic benefit to lumber firms by reducing the costs of projecting market demand. Such knowledge could also benefit society by making the lumber market function more

smoothly, dampening cycles of oversupply and undersupply of lumber output. Even if it did not make the industry function more smoothly, such knowledge would be unlikely to harm competition in the industry unless the industry was *concentrated*.

CONCENTRATED INDUSTRIES A **concentrated industry** is one in which either a single firm or a small number of firms control a large percentage of market sales. In concentrated industries, trade associations can be, and have been, used as a means to facilitate anticompetitive actions, such as fixing prices, allocating markets, or, as discussed in the next section, conducting boycotts—all with the clear objective of lessening competition. For example, consider again the lumber association. Such an association would provide information that members could use to determine whether a secret agreement to fix prices was being adhered to by the conspirators. Thus, such associations offer possibilities of both great benefit and substantial harm.

RULE OF REASON USUALLY APPLIED In most instances, the rule of reason is applied in evaluating such practices and agreements. If a court finds that a particular practice or agreement that restrains trade involves no apparent intent to fix prices or limit output, and that it benefits the public as well as the association, then the court will weigh those benefits against the harms to competition under the rule of reason. As in other cases, however, if the harm to competition is substantial, a trade association's activities will be condemned as a Section 1 violation. As shown in the following case, not even action undertaken by a health-care professional organization allegedly for the sole purpose of protecting the public will escape scrutiny if it is likely to harm market competition.

CASE 27.2   ## Wilk v. American Medical Association

United States
Court of Appeals,
Seventh Circuit. 1990.
895 F.2d 352.

BACKGROUND AND FACTS *In 1966, the American Medical Association (AMA) passed a resolution labeling chiropractic an unscientific cult. (Chiropractors attempt to cure or relieve bodily ailments by making skeletal adjustments.) In effect, this label prevented physicians from associating with chiropractors, because Principle 3 of the Principles of Medical Ethics—the AMA's code of ethical conduct—provided that a "physician should practice a method of healing founded on a scientific basis; and he should not voluntarily associate with anyone who violates this principle." Medical doctors used Principle 3 to justify their refusal to have anything to do with chiropractors or to allow chiropractors to use hospital diagnostic services or become members of hospital medical staffs. Despite the AMA's efforts, chiropractic became licensed in all fifty states; and in a 1980 revision of the AMA's ethical code, Principle 3 was eliminated. Chester Wilk and four other chiro-*

CASE 27.2 | Continued

practors brought an action against the AMA, claiming that the boycott had violated Section 1 of the Sherman Act and seeking injunctive relief from the boycott's "lingering effects" on chiropractors. The trial court, holding that the AMA had violated Section 1 of the Sherman Act by conducting an illegal boycott in restraint of trade, granted an injunction that, among other things, required the AMA to publish widely the trial court's order. The AMA appealed.

IN THE LANGUAGE OF THE COURT

MANION, Circuit Judge.

* * * *

Despite the fact that * * * the conspiracy ended in 1980, * * * the illegal boycott's "lingering effects" still threatened plaintiffs with current injury * * * . [T]he boycott caused injury to chiropractors' reputations which had not been repaired, and current economic injury to chiropractors. Further, the AMA never affirmatively acknowledged that there are no impediments to professional association and cooperation between chiropractors and medical physicians * * * .

* * * *

* * * Essentially, the AMA argues that * * * health care consumers almost invariably lack sufficient information needed to evaluate the quality of medical services. This increases the risk of fraud and deception on consumers by unscrupulous health care providers * * * . The AMA's conduct, the theory goes on, * * * allowed consumers to be assured that physicians would use only scientifically valid treatments. This in effect * * * provided consumers with essential information * * * .

Getting information to the market is a fine goal, but * * * the AMA was not motivated solely by such altruistic [unselfish] concerns. Indeed, * * * the AMA intended to "destroy a competitor," namely, chiropractors. It is not enough to carry the day to argue that competition should be eliminated in the name of public safety.

DECISION AND REMEDY *The appellate court affirmed both the trial court's ruling that the AMA had violated Section 1 of the Sherman Act by conducting an illegal boycott of chiropractors and the trial court's decision to grant an injunction against the AMA.*

GROUP BOYCOTTS

A **group boycott,** or concerted refusal to deal, is any agreement by which two or more buyers or sellers refuse to engage in any transactions with a particular person or organization, the object of the boycott. An obvious, and indeed frequent, purpose of a boycott is to eliminate or discipline a competitor of the boycotting group. Boycotts are thus a powerful tool for enforcing anticompetitive arrangements among firms.

ANTICOMPETITIVE INTENT Refer again to the DVD drive producers and their hypothetical attempts to fix prices and allocate market territories. After their initial success in obtaining greater profits for the industry, they face at least two problems. The first is how to discipline errant firms that attempt to increase their profits by selling for less than the agreed price or by encroaching on another firm's exclusive territory. The second is how to prevent new firms attracted by the large profits in the DVD drive industry from entering the market and reducing each member's share of profits.

Observe the actions of the group members further. They have now formed the High-Quality DVD Drive Association. The function of the association, at least as stated in its charter, is to "promote the interests of the consumer above all other considerations by ensuring that DVD drives are always manufactured according to the highest possible standards." To facilitate its goals, the association has decided to confer its "seal of approval" on all DVD drive products deemed of worthy quality. In fact, the association has never denied an original producer-member's request for approval except in those instances when the producer happens to have failed to abide by the original price and market-allocation terms the group has set.

Things are not so easy, however, for subsequent arrivals into the DVD drive industry. Alleging that the new firms are able to enter the market and compete only by use of "substandard components," the association refuses to bestow any new seals of approval.

Moreover, the association urges dealers, some of whom have been invited to become members of the association, not to carry or service any products that do not have the association's seal of approval. In concert, the group refuses to have any dealings with any retailers, wholesalers, or other manufacturers who do not exclusively use products carrying the association's seal of approval. This is a group boycott.

PROCOMPETITIVE INTENT Sometimes, however, group boycotts are intended to promote economic efficiency, moral or social causes, or the general well-being of the group, without intending to injure competition. For example, a professional organization or a trade association might seek to promote its public image by sponsoring a program to prevent its members from engaging in deceptive advertising or employing high-pressure sales tactics. A member's failure to abide

by the program guidelines could be punished by expulsion from the organization or association or by denial of the group's endorsement, such as withholding of the association's "seal of approval."

Despite the possibility of a procompetitive intent or some other socially valuable objective, concerted refusals to deal—group boycotts—are generally said to be *per se* violations of Section 1. A more accurate statement is that a court will treat a group boycott as a *per se* violation of Section 1 in cases in which the group possesses market power and the boycott is intended to restrict or exclude a competitor. If, however, these elements are missing, the court may be inclined to weigh the benefits of the group's efforts against the harm inflicted by the boycott. In the following case, the United States Supreme Court emphasizes these principles.

CASE 27.3   NYNEX Corp. v. Discon, Inc.

Supreme Court of the United States, 1998.
525 U.S. 128,
119 S.Ct. 493,
142 L.Ed.2d 510.
http://straylight.law.
cornell.edu/supct/index.html[a]

BACKGROUND AND FACTS *NYNEX Corporation owns New York Telephone Company (NYTel), which provides telephone service to most of New York. NYTel has a monopoly on phone service in the areas that it serves. NYNEX also owns NYNEX Material Enterprises. Material Enterprises obtains removal services for NYTel. These services consist of salvaging and disposing of obsolete equipment. Material Enterprises, which had been using the services of Discon, Inc., switched its business to AT&T Technologies, Inc., which supplied the removal services at inflated prices. Material Enterprises charged the inflated prices to NYTel, which passed the charges onto its customers. Material Enterprises later received secret rebates of the excessive charges from AT&T. (Essentially, Material Enterprises and NYNEX used NYTel's monopoly to obtain increased revenues.) When the scheme was uncovered, NYTel agreed to refund over $35 million to its customers. Discon, Inc., filed a suit in a federal district court against NYNEX and others, alleging, among other things, that as part of their scheme, the defendants had conspired to eliminate Discon from the market in favor of AT&T, because Discon had refused to participate in the rebate scheme. Discon contended that this was an illegal group boycott. The defendants filed a motion to dismiss, which the court granted. Discon appealed to the U.S. Court of Appeals for the Second Circuit, which reversed the lower court's judgment and held that the treatment of Discon could be an illegal group boycott. The defendants appealed to the United States Supreme Court.*

IN THE LANGUAGE OF THE COURT
Justice *BREYER* delivered the opinion of the Court.
* * * *
* * * [T]he specific legal question before us is whether an antitrust court considering an agreement by a buyer to purchase goods or services from one supplier rather than another should (after examining the buyer's reasons or justifications) apply the *per se* rule if it finds no legitimate business reason for that purchasing decision. We conclude no boycott-related *per se* rule applies and that the plaintiff here must allege and prove harm, not just to a single competitor, but to the competitive process, i.e., to competition itself.

---
a. In the left column, under "Archive of decisions/by Party," click on "1990–present." In the "1998" row, click "1st party." On the page that opens, click on "M–O" and select the name of the case to access its opinion.

CASE 27.3 Continued

Our conclusion rests in large part upon precedent, for *precedent limits the* per se *rule* in the boycott context to cases involving horizontal agreements among direct competitors. * * * [Emphasis added.]

* * * [In a previous case] this Court * * * held that a "vertical restraint is not illegal *per se* unless it includes some agreement on price or price levels." This precedent makes the *per se* rule inapplicable, for the case before us concerns only a vertical agreement and a vertical restraint, a restraint that takes the form of depriving a supplier of a potential customer.

Nor have we found any special feature of this case that could distinguish it from the precedent * * * . We concede Discon's claim that the petitioners' behavior hurt consumers by raising telephone service rates. But that consumer injury naturally flowed not so much from a less competitive market for removal services, as from the exercise of market power that is lawfully in the hands of a monopolist, namely, New York Telephone, combined with a deception worked upon the regulatory agency that prevented the agency from controlling New York Telephone's exercise of its monopoly power.

To apply the *per se* rule here—where the buyer's decision, though not made for competitive reasons, composes part of a regulatory fraud—would transform cases involving business behavior that is improper for various reasons, say, cases involving nepotism or personal pique, into treble-damages antitrust cases. And that *per se* rule would discourage firms from changing suppliers—even where the competitive process itself does not suffer harm.

The freedom to switch suppliers lies close to the heart of the competitive process that the antitrust laws seek to encourage. At the same time, other laws, for example, "unfair competition" laws, business tort laws, or regulatory laws, provide remedies for various competitive practices thought to be offensive to proper standards of business morality. Thus, this Court has refused to apply *per se* reasoning in cases involving that kind of activity. [Emphasis added.]

DECISION AND REMEDY *The Supreme Court vacated the decision of the U.S. Court of Appeals for the Second Circuit and remanded the case for further proceedings. A choice by a single buyer to buy from one supplier rather than another is not subject to the* per se *group boycott rule, even if there is no legitimate business reason for that buyer's purchasing decision.*

JOINT VENTURES

A **joint venture** is any undertaking by two or more firms or individuals that, while maintaining their distinct identities, come together for the limited purpose of achieving a specific goal. Antitrust analysis of joint ventures involves two issues: first, whether the joining together is itself a violation of antitrust laws; and second, whether the purpose or means of the joint venture is impermissible. The first issue is covered by Section 7 of the Clayton Act, as well as Section 1 of the Sherman Act. An important consideration is the joint venture's percentage market share. Here we limit our focus to the legality of the joint venture's purpose and actions.

Unlike price-fixing agreements and market divisions, joint ventures are not necessarily anticompetitive. Indeed, many are likely to provide economic efficiencies. For example, it may be beneficial to society, as well as to the individual firms involved, if firms engaging in substantial research and development (R&D) efforts pool their resources. Pooling

R&D resources prevents firms from duplicating one another's efforts. Once the R&D phase has been completed, the firms will compete along other dimensions, such as price, quality, and consumer services. Pooling resources also allows the firms to share the risk that the initial efforts may be fruitless. In some cases, a venture that is desirable from society's point of view involves risks so substantial that no single firm would want to undertake the venture alone. When the risk is spread among many firms, individual risk is reduced, and the venture is more appealing.

If a joint venture does not involve price fixing or market divisions, the agreement will be analyzed under the rule of reason. Whether the venture will then be upheld under Section 1 depends on an overall assessment of the purposes of the venture, a strict analysis of the potential benefits relative to the likely harms, and in some cases an assessment of whether there are less restrictive alternatives for achieving the same goals.

EXHIBIT 27-1   Backward and Forward Vertical Integration

A firm that is integrated backward moves down the chain of production. A firm that is integrated forward moves up the chain of production.

SECTION 3 | Vertical Restraints

Another distinct set of restraints of trade comprises those imposed by the seller on the buyer (or vice versa), as distinct from those imposed *among* sellers or buyers. The latter restraints involve what is termed a vertical relationship. Horizontal relationships occur at the same level of operations. Vertical relationships, by comparison, encompass the entire chain of production: the purchase of inputs, basic manufacturing, distribution to wholesalers, and eventual sale of a product at the retail level. For some products, these distinct phases are carried on by different firms. In other instances, a single firm may carry out two or more of the functional phases. Firms such as the latter are considered to be **vertically integrated firms.**

There are two kinds of vertical integration—backward and forward. A firm that is integrated backward moves down the chain of production toward a supplier. A firm that is integrated forward moves up the chain of production toward the consumer market. For example, if the Red Ball Shoe Manufacturing Company, a shoe manufacturer, owns its source of leather, it is integrated backward; if Red Ball owns its retail outlets, it is integrated forward (see Exhibit 27–1).

Even though firms operating at different functional levels do not directly compete with one another, each does compete with other firms operating at its own level of operation. Thus, agreements between firms standing in a vertical relationship may affect competition. For example, suppose that a contractual agreement between tire manufacturer Firestone and Billy Ray's Automotive Supplies, an independent retailer, conditions Billy Ray's future supply of Firestone tires on its willingness to resell only at a price set by Firestone. This agreement is a form of **vertical restraint**—an anticompetitive agreement between entities operating at different levels of the market structure. Other types of vertical restraints are often encountered, but not all of them necessarily harm competition. Indeed, many are procompetitive.

Marketing decisions within a vertically integrated firm are not subject to attack under Section 1. The legality of certain other classes of vertical restraints is judged under a rule of reason. Still others are deemed *per se* violations of Section 1.

TERRITORIAL OR CUSTOMER RESTRICTIONS

In arranging for the distribution of its product, a manufacturing firm may seek to insulate its dealers or retailers from direct competition with one another. There may be legitimate, procompetitive reasons for doing so. One such reason is to prevent a dealer from cutting costs and undercutting same-brand rivals by providing the product without promotion or customer service, while relying on a nearby same-brand dealer to provide these services. The cost-cutting same-brand dealer could thus enjoy the benefits of the promotional and customer service costs expended by his or her rivals without incurring the associated costs. This is an example of the "free rider" problem.[3] One way of addressing the problem is to restrict same-brand dealers to selling in specific markets or to certain classes of customers. These restrictions are judged under a rule of reason.

The following case, *Continental T.V., Inc. v. GTE Sylvania, Inc.*, overturned the United States Supreme Court's earlier stance, which had been set out in *United States v. Arnold, Schwinn & Co.*[4] In *Schwinn*, the Court had held territorial or customer restrictions to be *per se* violations. The *Continental* case has been heralded as one of the most important antitrust cases since the 1940s. It represents a definite shift away from rigid characterization to a more flexible approach emphasizing economics and efficiency.

---

3. For a discussion of the free rider problem in the context of sports telecasting, see *Chicago Professional Sports Limited Partnership v. National Basketball Association*, 961 F.2d 667 (7th Cir. 1993).

4. 388 U.S. 365, 87 S.Ct. 1856, 18 L.Ed.2d 1249 (1967).

Continental T.V., Inc. v. GTE Sylvania, Inc.

Supreme Court of the
United States, 1977.
433 U.S. 36,
97 S.Ct. 2549,
53 L.Ed.2d 568.
http://www.findlaw.com/
casecode/supreme.html[a]

BACKGROUND AND FACTS *GTE Sylvania, Inc., a manufacturer of television sets, adopted a franchise plan that limited the number of franchises granted in any given geographical area and that required each franchise to sell only Sylvania products from the location or locations at which it was franchised. A franchise did not constitute an exclusive territory, and Sylvania retained sole discretion to increase the number of retailers in an area, depending on the success or failure of existing retailers in developing their market. Continental T.V., Inc., was a retailer under Sylvania's franchise plan. Shortly after Sylvania proposed a new franchise that would compete with Continental, Sylvania terminated Continental's franchise, and a suit was brought in a federal district court for money owed. Continental claimed that Sylvania's vertically restrictive franchise system violated Section 1 of the Sherman Act. The district court ruled in favor of Continental, and Sylvania appealed. The appellate court reversed the trial court's decision. Continental appealed to the United States Supreme Court.*

IN THE LANGUAGE OF THE COURT

Mr. Justice POWELL delivered the opinion of the Court.

* * * *

Vertical restrictions reduce intrabrand competition by limiting the number of sellers of a particular product competing for the business of a given group of buyers. * * *

Vertical restrictions promote interbrand competition by allowing the manufacturer to achieve certain efficiencies in the distribution of his products. * * * Established manufacturers can use them to induce retailers to engage in promotional activities or to provide service and repair facilities necessary to the efficient marketing of their products. * * * The availability and quality of such services affect a manufacturer's goodwill and the competitiveness of his product. * * *

* * * *

* * * When anticompetitive effects are shown to result from particular vertical restrictions, they can be adequately policed under the rule of reason * * * .

DECISION AND REMEDY *The United States Supreme Court upheld the appellate court's reversal of the district court's decision. Sylvania's vertical system, which was not price restrictive, did not constitute a per se violation of Section 1 of the Sherman Act.*

IMPACT OF THIS CASE ON TODAY'S LAW

As noted, this case is generally thought of as one of the most important antitrust cases since the 1940s. It marked a definite shift from rigid characterization of these kinds of vertical restraints to a more flexible, economic analysis of the restraints under the rule of reason. Today's courts still apply the rule of reason to territorial and customer restrictions, following the precedent laid down in this case.

---

a. In the "Citation Search" section, type "433" in the first box, type "36" in the second box, and click "Get It" to access the case.

RESALE PRICE MAINTENANCE AGREEMENTS

Resale price maintenance agreements, also referred to as *fair trade agreements,* occur when a manufacturer seeks to establish a minimum price that a retailer or wholesaler may charge for the manufacturer's product. Under these agreements, the manufacturer conditions sales to the retailer or wholesaler on the latter's reselling only at a price allowed by the manufacturer.

In a 1968 case, *Albrecht v. Herald Co.,*[5] the United States Supreme Court had held that these vertical price-fixing agreements constituted *per se* violations of Section 1 of the Sherman Act. In the following case,

---

5. 390 U.S. 145, 88 S.Ct. 869, 19 L.Ed.2d 998 (1968).

which involved an agreement that set a maximum price for the resale of products supplied by a wholesaler to a dealer, the Supreme Court reevaluated its approach in *Albrecht*. At issue was whether such price-fixing arrangements should continue to be deemed *per se* violations of Section 1 of the Sherman Act or whether the rule of reason should be applied.

CASE 27.5   State Oil Co. v. Khan

Supreme Court of the
United States, 1997.
522 U.S. 3,
118 S.Ct. 275,
139 L.Ed.2d 199.
http://www.findlaw.com/
casecode/supreme.html[a]

BACKGROUND AND FACTS *Barkat Khan leased a gas station under a contract with State Oil Company, which also agreed to supply gas to Khan for resale. Under the contract, State Oil would set a suggested retail price and sell gas to Khan for 3.25 cents per gallon less than that price. Khan could sell the gas at a higher price, but he would then be required to pay State Oil the difference (which would equal the entire profit Khan realized from raising the price). Khan failed to pay some of the rent due under the lease, and State Oil terminated the contract. Khan filed a suit in a federal district court against State Oil, alleging, among other things, price fixing in violation of the Sherman Act. The court granted summary judgment for State Oil. Khan appealed. The U.S. Court of Appeals for the Seventh Circuit reversed this judgment, and State Oil appealed to the United States Supreme Court.*

IN THE LANGUAGE OF THE COURT

Justice O'CONNOR delivered the opinion of the Court.
     * * * *

     * * * Our analysis is * * * guided by our general view that the primary purpose of the antitrust laws is to protect interbrand competition. * * * [C]ondemnation of practices resulting in lower prices to consumers is especially costly because cutting prices in order to increase business often is the very essence of competition.

     * * * [W]e find it difficult to maintain that vertically imposed maximum prices could harm consumers or competition to the extent necessary to justify their *per se* invalidation.
* * *

     * * * *

     * * * [T]he *per se* rule * * * could in fact exacerbate problems related to the unrestrained exercise of market power by monopolist-dealers. Indeed, *both courts and antitrust scholars have noted that [the* per se*] rule may actually harm consumers and manufacturers.* * * * [Emphasis added.]
     * * * *

     * * * [V]ertical maximum price fixing, like the majority of commercial arrangements subject to the antitrust laws, should be evaluated under the rule of reason. In our view, rule-of-reason analysis can effectively identify those situations in which vertical maximum price fixing amounts to anticompetitive conduct.

DECISION AND REMEDY *The United States Supreme Court vacated the decision of the appellate court and remanded the case. The Supreme Court held that vertical price fixing is not a* per se *violation of the Sherman Act but should be evaluated under the rule of reason.*

WHAT IF THE FACTS WERE DIFFERENT? *Suppose that the distributor's price setting had had the effect of undercutting competition. Would this have affected the result in this case?*

INTERNATIONAL CONSIDERATIONS Regulation in Other Countries *Other countries have begun to adopt their own versions of U.S. antitrust laws. For example, the Japan Fair Trade Commission has adopted a set of guidelines to reduce anticompetitive practices by*

---

a. In the "Party Name Search" box, type "Khan" and click "Search." When the results appear, click on the case name to access the opinion. This page, which is part of a Web site maintained by FindLaw, contains links to opinions of the United States Supreme Court.

CASE 27.5 | Continued

Japanese companies. Under the guidelines, manufacturers are prohibited from terminating deal- ers who sell their products for prices below those suggested by the manufacturers. The European Court of Justice has upheld a fine levied against a Dutch company for threatening to engage in below-cost pricing to force a British competitor out of a particular market.[b] And now independent republics that were once part of the Soviet Union have sought the assistance of U.S. economic and technical experts in revamping their centrally planned economies.

b. *AKZO Chemie BV v. Commission of the European Community,* E.C.Ct.Jus., No. C-62/86, July 3, 1991. (The European Community is now called the European Union, or EU.)

REFUSALS TO DEAL

Group boycotts, as mentioned, are subject to sharp scrutiny under Section 1. In contrast, basic freedom of contract has been held to support the rule that manu- facturers, acting unilaterally rather than in concert, as in a group boycott, are free to deal—or not to deal—with whomever they choose. For example, assume that in our hypothetical example, Acme acts alone to set the price for the resale of its DVD drives by refusing to deal with any wholesaler that resells them at a different price. Acme has not violated the Sherman Act; it has only exercised its right to deal with whomever it chooses.

In some instances, however, a refusal to deal will violate antitrust laws. These instances involve offenses proscribed under Section 2 of the Sherman Act and occur only if (1) the firm refusing to deal has, or is likely to acquire, monopoly power and (2) the refusal is likely to have an anticompetitive effect on a partic- ular market.

PRICE DISCRIMINATION

Whenever a seller charges different buyers different prices for identical goods, the seller is engaging in **price discrimination.** Recall from the preceding chapter that such behavior may violate the Robinson-Patman Act, which was enacted in 1936 and amended Section 2 of the Clayton Act. A viola- tion of Section 2 occurs if a seller discriminates in the prices it charges different customers for com- modities of like quality and grade in interstate com- merce and the practice results in injury to competition. The act prohibits indirect discrimina- tion, such as variations in the terms of delivery and differences in sales returns, cash discounts, and the like, as well as direct price discrimination.

CUSTOMER PREFERENCES Although the act appears to embrace the goals of fairness and equality in the marketplace, it has often been criticized as

being economically unrealistic. For instance, a differ- ence in packaging, labeling, or product quality nor- mally does not exempt the pricing of the differing products from scrutiny under the act if the difference is deemed to be *negligible*. Thus, orange juice con- tainers that differ by one-eighth inch are considered to be of like grade and quality, because they are *functionally* identical in terms of performance. Despite functional equivalence, however, customer perceptions may favor one type of container over another.

In the same vein, identical products sold under dif- ferent labels are deemed to be of like quality, though some experts note that many customers exhibit strong preferences for better-known brand names even though the products are physically identical. In *Federal Trade Commission v. Borden Co.*,[6] the United States Supreme Court addressed the issue of a milk producer's charging different prices for milk sold under different labels. Borden sold evaporated milk under the Borden label, a well-known brand, and at the same time, it packed and marketed evaporated milk under private labels owned by its customers. Although the milk was physically indistinguishable, Borden charged a higher price for its brand-labeled milk. In spite of obvious customer prefer- ence for the Borden brand of milk, the Court concluded that the act applied to the pricing difference because the milk was of like quality and grade in terms of phys- ical attributes. The Court held that preferences due to brand-name recognition created through national advertising should not be considered in resolving whether goods are of like grade and quality.

TIME AND COST CONSIDERATIONS Despite these examples, some economic aspects are taken into account in judging the legality of pricing practices under the Robinson-Patman Act. For example, as noted in the preceding chapter, Section 2 is not vio- lated even though the goods sold are identical if the

6. 383 U.S. 637, 86 S.Ct. 1092, 16 L.Ed.2d 153 (1966).

seller can justify the price differential on the basis of differences in cost, such as the cost of transporting the goods to buyers in disparate locations. Similarly, consideration is given to the fact that prices are not static but fluctuate as market conditions change. Thus, price discrimination occurs only if sales at different price levels are made reasonably close together in time.

Closeness in time is determined by the economic circumstances of the sales. For example, sales of products that are not frequently sold and that involve considerable production costs may be considered close in time even if they occur years apart. Conversely, sales of low-cost products sold in high volume may be considered close in time when they occur a day or even a few hours apart. Jet aircraft typify high-cost, low-volume products. Closeness in time for sales of aircraft could be two years or more. In contrast, sales of bakery goods occur on an almost continuous basis. Closeness in time for sales of such products could be several hours or, at most, a day.

EXCLUSIONARY PRACTICES

Recall also from the preceding chapter that Section 3 of the Clayton Act prohibits sellers and lessors from selling or leasing goods, machinery, supplies, and the like "on the condition, agreement or understanding that the . . . purchaser or lessee thereof shall not use or deal in the goods . . . of a competitor or competitors of the seller." Two types of vertical arrangements involving exclusionary tactics—*exclusive-dealing contracts* and *tying arrangements*—are within the reach of Section 3 of the Clayton Act.

EXCLUSIVE-DEALING CONTRACTS Contracts under which a seller forbids the buyer from purchasing products from the seller's competitors are called **exclusive-dealing contracts.** Such contracts are prohibited under Section 3 if the effect of the contract will "substantially lessen competition or tend to create a monopoly."

The leading decision on exclusive-dealing contracts remains the 1949 case of *Standard Oil Co. of California v. United States,*[7] in which the then-largest gasoline seller in the United States was challenged by the government under Section 3 for making exclusive-dealing contracts with independent stations in seven western states.

The United States Supreme Court, in assessing the impact of the exclusive-dealing agreement on competition in the retail market, noted that the "independents" covered under the arrangement constituted 16 percent of all retail outlets and 7 percent of all retail gas sales in the area. The Court also noted that the market was substantially concentrated because the seven largest suppliers all used exclusive-dealing contracts with their independent retailers and together controlled 65 percent of the market. Looking at market conditions after the arrangements were instituted, the Court noted that market shares were extremely stable and entry into the market was apparently restricted. Thus, the Court found that Section 3 had been violated, because competition was "foreclosed in a substantial share" of the relevant market.

TYING ARRANGEMENTS A seller may condition the sale of a product (the tying product) on the buyer's agreeing to purchase another product (the tied product) produced or distributed by the same seller. As noted in the preceding chapter, the legality of such **tying arrangements** depends on factors such as the purpose of the arrangement and its likely effect on competition in the relevant markets. There are two relevant markets, because the agreement involves two distinct products, the tying product and the tied product.

In 1936, the United States Supreme Court held that International Business Machines (IBM) and Remington Rand, by requiring purchase of their own machine cards (the tied product) as a condition of leasing their tabulation machines (the tying product), had violated Section 3 of the Clayton Act. The two firms were the only ones in the market with completely automated tabulation machines, and the Court concluded that each possessed market power sufficient to "substantially lessen competition" through their respective tying arrangements.[8]

The Clayton Act provisions in Section 3 have been held to apply only to commodities, not to services. But tying arrangements also can be considered agreements that restrain trade in violation of Section 1 of the Sherman Act. Cases involving tying arrangements for services have been brought under Section 1 of the Sherman Act. Although the Court continues to state

7. 337 U.S. 293, 69 S.Ct. 1051, 93 L.Ed. 1371 (1949).

8. *International Business Machines Corp. v. United States,* 298 U.S. 131, 56 S.Ct. 701, 80 L.Ed.2d 1085 (1936).

that many tying arrangements are illegal *per se,* it nonetheless has shown a willingness to look at factors that are important in a rule-of-reason analysis.

Most courts today generally judge the legality of tying arrangements involving services or commodities by looking at both the firm's market power in the tying product market and the amount of commerce affected in the tied product market. The firm must have sufficient market power in the tying product to coerce the purchase of the tied product, and the tying arrangement must affect a substantial amount of commerce in the market for the tied product.

MERGERS

Under Section 7 of the Clayton Act, a person or business organization cannot hold stock or assets in another business when "the effect . . . may be to substantially lessen competition." This section is the statutory authority for preventing mergers that could result in monopoly power or a substantial lessening of competition in the marketplace.

A crucial consideration in most merger cases is *market concentration.* **Market concentration** roughly translates into the allocation of percentage market shares among the various firms in the relevant product market. For example, if the four largest grocery stores in Chicago accounted for 80 percent of all retail food sales, the market clearly would be concentrated in those four firms. Competition is not necessarily diminished solely as a result of market concentration, and other factors will be considered, including whether the merger will make it more difficult for *potential* competitors to enter the relevant market.

HORIZONTAL MERGERS Mergers between firms that compete with each other in the same market are called **horizontal mergers.** If a horizontal merger creates an entity with a resulting significant market share, the merger may be presumed illegal. This is because of the United States Supreme Court's interpretation that Congress, in amending Section 7 of the Clayton Act in 1950, intended to prevent mergers that increase market concentration.[9] Three other factors are also considered: overall concentration of the relevant market, the relevant market's history of

tending toward concentration, and whether the apparent design of the merger is to establish market power or restrict competition.

—Market Share and Market Concentration. The Court's intense focus on market share in horizontal merger decisions has made the definition of relevant markets especially critical in most Section 7 cases. As a result, the Federal Trade Commission (FTC) and the Department of Justice (DOJ) have established guidelines indicating which mergers will be challenged.

Under the guidelines, the first factor to be considered in determining whether a merger will be challenged is the degree of concentration in the relevant market. In determining market concentration, the FTC and the DOJ employ what is known as the **Herfindahl-Hirschman index (HHI).** The HHI is computed by summing the squares of the percentage market shares of the firms in the relevant market. For example, if there are four firms with shares of 30 percent, 30 percent, 20 percent, and 20 percent, respectively, then the HHI equals 2,600 (900 + 900 + 400 + 400 = 2,600). If the premerger HHI is less than 1,000, then the market is unconcentrated, and the merger is unlikely to be challenged. If the premerger HHI is between 1,000 and 1,800, the industry is moderately concentrated, and the merger will be challenged only if it increases the HHI by 100 points or more.[10] If the HHI is greater than 1,800, the market is highly concentrated. In a highly concentrated market, a merger that produces an increase in the HHI of between 50 and 100 points raises significant competitive concerns. Mergers that produce an increase in the HHI of more than 100 points in a highly concentrated market are deemed likely to enhance market power.[11] HHI figures were a factor in the following case.

---

9. *Brown Shoe v. United States,* 370 U.S. 294, 82 S.Ct. 1502, 8 L.Ed.2d 510 (1962).

10. Compute the change in the index by doubling the product of the merging firms' premerger market shares. For example, a merger between a firm with a 5 percent share and one with a 6 percent share will increase the HHI by 2 × (5 × 6) = 60. For an analysis of the HHI concentration of companies in the credit-card market, see *SCFC ILC, Inc. v. Visa U.S.A., Inc.,* 819 F.Supp. 956 (D.Utah 1993).

11. See, for example, *United States v. United Tote, Inc.,* 768 F.Supp. 1064 (D.Del. 1991), in which the court ordered the divestiture of a firm whose HHI was 3,940 before a merger and 4,640 after the merger.

CASE 27.6

United States
District Court,
District of
Columbia, 2002.
211 F.Supp.2d 34.

Federal Trade Commission v. Libbey, Inc.

COMPANY PROFILE *Libbey, Inc., is the largest manufacturer and seller of food service glassware in the United States. Libbey's product line consists of various styles of tumblers, stemware, and other products. In particular, Libbey produces and sells soda-lime glassware.*[a] *Libbey's customers include restaurants, such as Outback Steakhouse; hotels, such as Marriott International, Inc.; airlines, such as United Airlines, Inc.; and distributors who resell soda-lime glassware to restaurants, hotels, and other food service establishments.*

BACKGROUND AND FACTS *The food service glassware market generates sales of approximately $270 million a year. Libbey's share of this market is about 72 percent. Arc International, Anchor Hocking Corporation, and Oneida Limited have market shares of 10, 7, and 3 percent, respectively. Nearly 80 percent of glassware purchases are to replace stolen, broken, or otherwise useless items to maintain a consistent stock. Because Libbey dominates the market, most customers must acquire new glassware from Libbey or glassware that resembles its products. More than twenty years ago, Anchor was the first company to produce Libbey look-alike glassware and is currently the leading seller of Libbey look-alikes. In June 2001, Libbey entered into an agreement to buy Anchor from Newell Rubbermaid, Inc. Libbey proposed to merge with Anchor. The Federal Trade Commission (FTC) filed a suit in a federal district court against Libbey to obtain a preliminary injunction to bar the merger until the FTC could determine whether there was a violation of Section 7 of the Clayton Act or other antitrust law. In response, Libbey and Newell eliminated the sale of Anchor's food service glassware business from their deal and argued that this change alleviated any potential anticompetitive effect of the merger.*

IN THE LANGUAGE OF THE COURT

WALTON, District Judge.

* * * *

    * * * [O]ne factor that is an important consideration when analyzing possible anticompetitive effects is whether the acquisition would result in the elimination of a particularly aggressive competitor in a highly concentrated market * * * . The FTC has presented substantial evidence that the proposed merger might effectively eliminate as a competitor in the food service glassware market what is now Anchor * * * .

    The evidence also demonstrates that Anchor has provided effective competition against Libbey in this market as evidenced by the fact that Anchor has been able to secure the business of several former Libbey customers and had the goal of securing more of Libbey's business in the future before the original merger agreement was negotiated. Second, the evidence also shows that Anchor currently offers food service glassware at prices that are frequently 10–20 percent below Libbey's prices. Third, Anchor is the largest seller of Libbey look-alikes, a feature that is essential to a company's ability to compete in this market. Finally, evidence presented by the FTC demonstrated that Anchor's glassware sales have grown annually over the last several years and * * * Anchor was poised to even more aggressively target Libbey customers.

* * * *

    The Court can also determine whether the FTC has established that the amended agreement may substantially lessen competition by an examination of the concentration statistics and the HHI's [Herfindahl-Hirschman indices] * * * within the geographic markets. * * *

* * * *

    * * * [T]he pre-merger HHI in the soda-lime glassware market in the United States of 5,251 indicates a highly concentrated premerger market. The original proposed merger announced on June 17, 2001, would have resulted in an HHI increase of 1,052, thus resulting in a postmerger HHI of 6,241. This is clear evidence that the original merger would have sub-

---

a. Soda-lime glassware is less expensive and less fragile than lead crystal, which is used primarily in fine dining establishments, and unlike plastic drinkware, it does not scratch easily or diminish in clarity with repeated washing.

CASE 27.6 | Continued stantially lessened competition in the market. Defendants do not dispute the FTC's characterization of the impact the original proposed merger would have on the food service glassware market. Instead, they argue that the FTC must make an affirmative showing that the amended proposed merger will substantially harm competition. However, as already discussed above, the FTC's evidence, when considered cumulatively, establishes that the amended agreement would potentially have the same anticompetitive effect as the original agreement.

DECISION AND REMEDY *The court issued the preliminary injunction. The court concluded that like the original merger agreement, the amended agreement could substantially lessen competition in the food service glassware market.*

—Other Factors. The guidelines stress that determining market share and market concentration is only the starting point in analyzing the potential anticompetitive effects of a merger. Before deciding to challenge a merger, the FTC and the DOJ will look at a number of other factors, including the ease of entry into the relevant market, economic efficiency, the financial condition of the merging firms, the nature and price of the product or products involved, and so on. If a firm is a leading one—having at least a 35 percent share and twice that of the next leading firm—any merger with another firm will be closely scrutinized.

—Political Considerations in Defining the Relevant Market. Not considered in the above discussion are the sometimes unfathomable definitions of the relevant market determined by the federal government. To take an example, reconsider the proposed Office Depot–Staples merger that the FTC refused to approve in 1997. Had the two merged as originally planned, they would have accounted for 6 percent of the market for office supplies. When the FTC initially indicated its disapproval, Office Depot agreed to sell sixty-three of its stores to OfficeMax, thereby bringing the proposed merger to only 4 percent of the office supplies market.

The FTC decided that the relevant product market was not office supplies, but rather office supplies sold at large specialty discount stores! It then concluded that the proposed merger would seriously weaken competition in the newly defined market. In other words, the decision was evidently political rather than based on any theory of the economics of antitrust law. After all, office supplies are also sold at Costco, Wal-Mart, Sam's Club, Kmart, and elsewhere. To exclude these obvious competitors from the FTC's analysis was indeed baffling.[12]

VERTICAL MERGERS A **vertical merger** occurs when a company at one stage of production acquires a company at a higher or lower stage of production. Courts in the past have almost exclusively focused on "foreclosure" in assessing vertical mergers. Foreclosure occurs because competitors of the merging firms lose opportunities to either sell or to buy products from the merging firms.

Today, whether a vertical merger will be deemed illegal depends on several factors, including market concentration, barriers to entry into the market, and the apparent intent of the merging parties. Mergers that do not prevent competitors of either of the merging firms from competing in a segment of the market will not be condemned as "foreclosing" competition and are legal.

CONGLOMERATE MERGERS **Conglomerate mergers** are mergers between firms that do not compete with each other because they are in different markets. There are three general types of conglomerate mergers: market-extension, product-extension, and diversification mergers. A market-extension merger occurs when a firm seeks to sell its product in a new market by merging with a firm already established in that market. A product-extension merger occurs when a firm seeks to add a closely related product to its existing line by merging with a firm already producing that product. For example, a manufacturer might seek to extend its product line of household products to include floor wax by acquiring a leading manufacturer of floor wax. Diversification occurs when a firm merges with another firm that offers a product or service wholly unrelated to the first firm's existing activities. An example of a diversification merger would be Google's acquisition of Holiday Inns.

---

12. At the FTC's request, a court blocked the merger on antitrust grounds.

REVIEWING ANTITRUST AND RESTRAINT OF TRADE

The Internet Corporation for Assigned Names and Numbers (ICANN) is a nonprofit entity organizing Internet domain names. It is governed by a board of directors elected by various groups with commercial interests in the Internet. One of ICANN's functions is to authorize an entity as a registry for certain "top level domains" (TLDs). ICANN entered into an agreement with VeriSign to serve as registry for the ".com" TLD to provide registry services in accordance with ICANN's specifications. VeriSign complained that ICANN was restricting the services that it could make available as a registrar and blocking new services, imposing unnecessary conditions on those services, and setting prices at which the services were offered. VeriSign claimed that ICANN's control of the registry services for domain names violated Section 1 of the Sherman Act.

1. Should ICANN's actions be judged under the rule of reason or deemed a *per se* violation of Section 1 of the Sherman Act?
2. Should ICANN's actions be viewed as a horizontal or a vertical restraint of trade?
3. Does it matter that ICANN's leadership is chosen by those with a commercial interest in the Internet?
4. If judged under the rule of reason, what might be ICANN's defense for having a standardized set of registry services that must be used?

TERMS AND CONCEPTS TO REVIEW

concentrated industry 630

conglomerate merger 641

exclusive-dealing contract 638

group boycott 631

Herfindahl-Hirschman index (HHI) 639

horizontal market division 629

horizontal merger 639

horizontal restraint 627

joint venture 633

market concentration 639

per se violation 626

price discrimination 637

price fixing 627

resale price maintenance agreement 635

rule of reason 626

tying arrangement 638

vertical merger 641

vertical restraint 634

vertically integrated firm 634

QUESTIONS AND CASE PROBLEMS

27–1. Most of the egg wholesalers supplying eggs to grocery stores in a particular area sell eggs to the retailers under various credit terms. The credit terms vary among the different buyers and sellers, but all of the wholesalers follow a common practice of reducing by 10 percent the price charged to a retailer if the retailer pays the wholesaler within three days of delivery. The various wholesalers agree that henceforth the 10 percent discount will be discontinued. If the agreement is indeed carried out by the wholesalers and the discount policy is discontinued, have the wholesalers violated any antitrust laws? Explain. If suit is brought against the wholesalers, what—if any—justification could they offer for the agreement?

27–2. Suppose that the wholesale egg suppliers in the preceding problem agree that the three largest suppliers should sell exclusively to the area's large chain-store groceries, leaving the remaining suppliers to sell solely to local individual "mom and pop" stores. Does the agreement violate any antitrust laws? Is it a defense that the larger suppliers, because of their scale of operations, enjoy a cost advantage that allows them to supply the large chain buyers more efficiently?

27–3. **QUESTION WITH SAMPLE ANSWER**
Discuss *fully* whether each of the following situations violates the Sherman Act:

(a) Trujillo Foods, Inc., is the leading seller of frozen Mexican foods in three southwestern states. The various retail outlets that sell Trujillo products are in close competition, and customers are very price conscious. Trujillo has conditioned its sales to retailers with the agreement that the retailers will not sell below a minimum price nor above a maximum price. The retailers are allowed to set any price within these limits.

(b) Franklin, Inc., Green, Inc., and Fill-It, Inc., are competitors in the manufacture and sale of microwave ovens sold primarily east of the Mississippi River. As a patriotic gesture and to assist the unemployed, the three competitors agree to lower their prices on all microwave models by 20 percent for a three-month period that includes the Fourth of July and Labor Day.

(c) Foam Beer, Inc., sells its beer to distributors all over the United States. Foam sends each of its distributors a recommended price list, explaining that past records indicate that selling beer at those prices should ensure the distributor a reasonable rate of return. The price list clearly states that the sale of beer by Foam to the distributor is not conditioned on the distributor's reselling the beer at the recommended price and that the distributor is free to set the price.

For a sample answer to this question, go to Appendix I at the end of this text.

27–4. Mickey's Appliance Store was a new retail seller of appliances in Sunwest City. Mickey's innovative sales techniques and financing caused the appliance department of Luckluster Department Store to lose a great many sales. Luckluster was a large department store and part of a large chain with substantial buying power. Luckluster told a number of appliance manufacturers that if they continued to sell to Mickey's, Luckluster would stop purchasing from them. The manufacturers immediately stopped selling appliances to Mickey's. Mickey's filed suit against Luckluster and the manufacturers, claiming their actions constituted an antitrust violation. Luckluster and the manufacturers could prove that Mickey's was a small retailer with a small portion of the market. Because the relevant market was not substantially affected, they claimed they were not guilty of restraint of trade. Discuss *fully* whether there was an antitrust violation.

27–5. ⚖ **CASE PROBLEM WITH SAMPLE ANSWER**
Thomas Blackburn, Raymond Green, Charles Sweeney, and Daniel Pfeiffer practiced law together as partners, relying on advertising to attract clients. When they came to a disagreement over the use of partnership funds, they split into separate partnerships—one formed by Blackburn and Green and the other by Sweeney and Pfeiffer. After the split, they negotiated and signed an agreement that included a term restricting, for an indefinite time, the geographical area within which each could advertise. Less than a year later, the Blackburn

firm filed a suit in a federal district court against the Sweeney firm, alleging in part that the restriction on advertising was a *per se* violation of the Sherman Act. On what basis might the court hold that the agreement to restrict advertising was a horizontal agreement to divide markets among competitors? [*Blackburn v. Sweeney*, 53 F.3d 825 (7th Cir. 1995)]
To view a sample answer for this case problem, go to this book's Web site at http://wleb.westbuslaw.com, select "Chapter 27," and click on "Case Problem with Sample Answer."

27–6. ROBINSON-PATMAN ACT. The Stelwagon Manufacturing Co. agreed with Tarmac Roofing Systems, Inc., to promote and develop a market for Tarmac's products in the Philadelphia area. In return, Tarmac promised not to sell its products to other area distributors. In 1991, Stelwagon learned that Tarmac had been selling its products to Stelwagon's competitors—the Standard Roofing Co. and the Celotex Corp.—at substantially lower prices. Stelwagon filed a suit against Tarmac in a federal district court. What is the principal factor in determining whether Tarmac violated the Robinson-Patman Act? Did Tarmac violate the act? [*Stelwagon Manufacturing Co. v. Tarmac Roofing Systems, Inc.*, 63 F.3d 1267 (3d Cir. 1995)]

27–7. RESTRAINT OF TRADE. The National Collegiate Athletic Association (NCAA) coordinates the intercollegiate athletic programs of its members by issuing rules and setting standards governing, among other things, the coaching staffs. The NCAA set up a "Cost Reduction Committee" to consider ways to cut the costs of intercollegiate athletics while maintaining competition. The committee included financial aid personnel, intercollegiate athletic administrators, college presidents, university faculty members, and a university chancellor. It was felt that "only a collaborative effort could reduce costs while maintaining a level playing field." The committee proposed a rule to restrict the annual compensation of certain coaches to $16,000. The NCAA adopted the rule. Basketball coaches affected by the rule filed a suit in a federal district court against the NCAA, alleging a violation of Section 1 of the Sherman Antitrust Act. Is the rule a *per se* violation of the Sherman Act, or should it be evaluated under the rule of reason? If it is subject to the rule of reason, is it an illegal restraint of trade? Explain fully. [*Law v. National Collegiate Athletic Association*, 134 F.3d 1010 (10th Cir. 1998)]

27–8. TYING ARRANGEMENT. Public Interest Corp. (PIC) owned and operated television station WTMV-TV in Lakeland, Florida. MCA Television, Ltd., owns and licenses syndicated television programs. The parties entered into a licensing contract with respect to several television shows. MCA conditioned the license on PIC's agreeing to take another show, *Harry and the Hendersons*. PIC agreed to this arrangement, although it would not have chosen to license *Harry* if it did not have to do so to secure the licenses for the other shows. More than two years into the contract, a dispute arose over PIC's payments, and negotiations failed to resolve the dispute. In a letter, MCA suspended PIC's broadcast rights for all of its shows and stated that "[a]ny telecasts of MCA programming by WTMV-TV . . . will be deemed unauthorized and shall constitute an infringement of MCA's copyrights." PIC nonetheless continued broadcasting MCA's programs, with the exception of *Harry*. MCA filed a suit in a federal district court against PIC, alleging breach of contract and copyright infringement. PIC filed a counterclaim, contending in part that MCA's deal was an illegal tying arrangement. Is PIC correct? Explain. [*MCA Television, Ltd. v. Public Interest Corp.*, 171 F.3d 1265 (11th Cir. 1999)]

27-9. RESTRAINT OF TRADE. High fructose corn syrup (HFCS) is a sweetener made from corn and used in food products. There are two grades, HFCS 42 and HFCS 55. The five principal HFCS makers, including Archer Daniels Midland Co. (ADM), account for 90 percent of the sales. In 1988, shortly after Terrence Wilson became the head of ADM's corn-processing division, which was responsible for HFCS and other products, ADM announced that it was raising its price for HFCS 42 to 90 percent of the price of HFCS 55. It cost only 65 percent as much to manufacture HFCS 42, but the other makers followed suit. Over the next seven years, the makers sometimes bought HFCS from each other even when they could have produced the amount at a lower cost, and many sales to other customers were made at prices below the list prices. After Wilson was imprisoned for antitrust violations with regard to other ADM products, HFCS buyers filed a suit in a federal district court against the makers, alleging a *per se* violation of the Sherman Act and seeking billions of dollars in damages. How might the makers have violated antitrust law? What might be their defense? How should the court rule? Discuss. [*In re High Fructose Corn Syrup Antitrust Litigation*, 295 F.3d 651 (7th Cir. 2002)]

27-10. RESTRAINT OF TRADE. Visa U.S.A., Inc., MasterCard International, Inc., American Express (Amex), and Discover are the four major credit- and charge-card networks in the United States. Visa and MasterCard are joint ventures, owned by the thousands of banks that are their members. The banks issue the cards, clear transactions, and collect fees from the merchants who accept the cards. By contrast, Amex and Discover themselves issue cards to customers, process transactions, and collect fees. Since 1995, Amex has asked banks to issue its cards. No bank has been willing to do so, however, because it would have to stop issuing Visa and MasterCard cards under those networks' rules barring member banks from issuing cards on rival networks. The U.S. Department of Justice filed a suit in a federal district court against Visa and MasterCard, alleging in part that the rules were illegal restraints of trade under the Sherman Act. Do the rules harm competition? If so, how? What relief might the court order to stop any anticompetitiveness? [*United States v. Visa U.S.A., Inc.*, 344 F.3d 229 (2d Cir. 2003)]

LAW | on the Web

For updated links to resources available on the Web, as well as a variety of other materials, visit this text's Web site at http://wleb.westbuslaw.com.

The Federal Trade Commission offers an abundance of information on antitrust law, including *A Plain English Guide to Antitrust Laws*, which is available at

http://www.ftc.gov/ftc/bc/compguide/index.html

The Tech Law Journal presents "news, records, and analysis of legislation, litigation, and regulation affecting the computer and Internet industry" in the area of antitrust law at

http://www.techlawjournal.com/atr/default.htm

LEGAL RESEARCH EXERCISES ON THE WEB

Go to http://wleb.westbuslaw.com, the Web site that accompanies this text. Select "Chapter 27" and click on "Internet Exercises." There you will find the following Internet research exercises that you can perform to learn more about topics covered in this chapter.

Activity 27–1: LEGAL PERSPECTIVE
Mergers and Antitrust Law

Activity 27–2: MANAGEMENT PERSPECTIVE
Avoiding Antitrust Problems

CHAPTER 28
Investor Protection and Corporate Governance

The stock market crash of October 29, 1929, and the ensuing economic depression caused the public to focus on the importance of securities markets for the economic well-being of the nation. Congress was pressured to regulate securities trading, and the result was the Securities Act of 1933[1] and the Securities Exchange Act of 1934.[2] Both acts were designed to provide investors with more information to help them make buying and selling decisions about securities—generally defined as any documents evidencing corporate ownership (stock) or debts (bonds)—and to prohibit deceptive, unfair, and manipulative practices in the purchase and sale of securities.

This chapter discusses the nature of federal securities regulation and its effect on the business world. We begin by looking at the federal administrative agency that regulates securities transactions, the Securities and Exchange Commission. Next, we examine the major traditional laws governing securities offerings and trading. We then discuss corporate governance and the Sarbanes-Oxley Act, which was passed by Congress in 2002 and significantly affects certain types of securities transactions. In the concluding pages of this chapter, we look at how securities laws are being adapted to the online environment.

SECTION 1 | The Securities and Exchange Commission

The 1934 act created the Securities and Exchange Commission (SEC) as an independent regulatory agency whose function was to administer the 1933 and 1934 acts. The SEC plays a key role in interpreting the provisions of these acts (and their amendments) and in creating regulations governing the purchase and sale of securities.

THE BASIC FUNCTIONS OF THE SEC

The SEC regulates the securities industry by undertaking the following activities:

1. Requiring disclosure of facts concerning offerings of securities listed on national securities exchanges and offerings of certain securities traded over the counter (OTC).

2. Regulating the trade in securities on the national and regional securities exchanges and in the OTC markets.

3. Investigating securities fraud.

4. Requiring the registration of securities brokers, dealers, and investment advisers and regulating their activities.

5. Supervising activities conducted by mutual funds companies.

6. Recommending administrative sanctions, injunctive remedies, and criminal prosecution in cases involving violations of securities laws. (The Fraud Section of the Criminal Division of the U.S. Department of Justice prosecutes violations of federal securities laws.)

THE EXPANDING REGULATORY POWERS OF THE SEC

Since its creation, the SEC's regulatory functions have gradually been increased by legislation granting it authority in different areas. For example, to further curb securities fraud, the Securities Enforcement

---

1. 15 U.S.C. Sections 77a–77aa.
2. 15 U.S.C. Sections 78a–78mm.

Remedies and Penny Stock Reform Act of 1990[3] allowed SEC administrative law judges to hear many more types of securities violation cases and expanded the SEC's enforcement options. The act also gave courts the power to prevent persons who have engaged in securities fraud from serving as officers and directors of publicly held corporations. The Securities Acts Amendments of 1990 authorized the SEC to seek sanctions against those who violate foreign securities laws.[4] The Market Reform Act of 1990 gave the SEC authority to suspend trading in securities in the event that prices rise and fall excessively in a short period of time.[5]

The National Securities Markets Improvement Act of 1996 allowed the SEC to exempt persons, securities, and transactions from the requirements of the securities laws.[6] The act also limited the authority of the states to regulate certain securities transactions, as well as particular investment advisory firms.[7] The Sarbanes-Oxley Act of 2002,[8] which will be discussed shortly, further expanded the authority of the SEC by directing the agency to issue new rules relating to corporate disclosure requirements and by creating an SEC oversight board.

STREAMLINING THE REGULATORY PROCESS

For years, Congress and the SEC have been attempting to streamline the regulatory process generally. The goal is to make the process more efficient and more relevant to today's securities trading practices. Another goal is to create more oversight over securities transactions and accounting practices. As the number and types of online securities frauds increase, the SEC is trying to keep pace by expanding its online fraud division.

SECTION 2 | The Securities Act of 1933

The Securities Act of 1933 governs initial sales of stock by businesses. The act was designed to prohibit various forms of fraud and to stabilize the securities industry by requiring that all essential information concerning the issuance of securities be made available to the investing public. Basically, the purpose of this act is to require disclosure.

WHAT IS A SECURITY?

Section 2(1) of the Securities Act states that securities include the following:

> [A]ny note, stock, treasury stock, bond, debenture, evidence of indebtedness, certificate of interest or participation in any profit-sharing agreement, collateral-trust certificate, preorganization certificate or subscription, transferable share, investment contract, voting-trust certificate, certificate of deposit for a security, fractional undivided interest in oil, gas, or other mineral rights, or, in general, any interest or instrument commonly known as a "security," or any certificate of interest or participation in, temporary or interim certificate for, receipt for, guarantee of, or warrant or right to subscribe to or purchase, any of the foregoing.[9]

The courts have interpreted the act's definition of what constitutes a *security*[10] to include investment contracts. An investment contract is any transaction in which a person (1) invests (2) in a common enterprise (3) reasonably expecting profits (4) derived *primarily* or *substantially* from others' managerial or entrepreneurial efforts.[11]

For our purposes, it is probably most convenient to think of securities in their most common form—stocks and bonds issued by corporations. Bear in mind, though, that securities can take many forms and have been held to include interests in whiskey, cosmetics, worms, beavers, boats, vacuum cleaners, muskrats, and cemetery lots, as well as investment contracts in condominiums, franchises, limited partnerships, oil or gas or other mineral rights, and farm animals accompanied by care agreements. Businesspersons usually require the advice of an attorney to determine whether a given transaction involves securities.

REGISTRATION STATEMENT

Section 5 of the Securities Act of 1933 broadly provides that if a security does not qualify for an exemption, that security must be *registered* before it is offered

---

3. 15 U.S.C. Section 77g.
4. 15 U.S.C. Section 78a.
5. 15 U.S.C. Section 78i(h).
6. 15 U.S.C. Sections 77z-3, 78mm.
7. 15 U.S.C. Section 80b-3a.
8. H.R. 3762. This act became effective on August 29, 2002.

9. 15 U.S.C. Section 77b(1). Amendments in 1982 added stock options.
10. See 15 U.S.C. Section 77b(a)(1).
11. *SEC v. W. J. Howey Co.*, 328 U.S. 293, 66 S.Ct. 1100, 90 L.Ed. 1244 (1946).

to the public either through the mails or through any facility of interstate commerce, including securities exchanges. Issuing corporations must file a *registration statement* with the SEC. Investors must be provided with a prospectus that describes the security being sold, the issuing corporation, and the risk attaching to the security. In principle, the registration statement and the prospectus supply sufficient information to enable unsophisticated investors to evaluate the financial risk involved.

CONTENTS OF THE REGISTRATION STATEMENT

The registration statement must include the following:

1. A description of the significant provisions of the security offered for sale, including the relationship between that security and the other securities of the registrant. Also, the corporation must disclose how it intends to use the proceeds of the sale.
2. A description of the corporation's properties and business.
3. A description of the management of the corporation; its security holdings; and its remuneration and other benefits, including pensions and stock options. Any interests of directors or officers in any material transactions with the corporation must be disclosed.
4. A financial statement certified by an independent public accounting firm.
5. A description of pending lawsuits.

OTHER REQUIREMENTS Before filing the registration statement and the prospectus with the SEC, the corporation is allowed to obtain an underwriter who will monitor the distribution of the new issue. There is a twenty-day waiting period (which can be accelerated by the SEC) after registration before the sale can take place. During this period, oral offers between interested investors and the issuing corporation concerning the purchase and sale of the proposed securities may take place, and very limited written advertising is allowed. At this time, what is known as a **red herring** prospectus may be distributed. The name comes from the red legend printed across it stating that the registration statement has been filed but has not yet become effective.

After the waiting period, the SEC allows the registration statement to become "effective." The registered securities can then be legally bought and sold. Written advertising is initially allowed in the form of a **tombstone ad,** so named because historically the format resembled a tombstone. Such ads simply tell the investor where and how to obtain a prospectus. Normally, any other type of advertising is prohibited until the registration becomes effective.

EXEMPT SECURITIES

A number of specific securities are exempt from the registration requirements of the Securities Act of 1933. These securities—which can also generally be resold without being registered—include the following:[12]

1. All bank securities sold prior to July 27, 1933.
2. Commercial paper, if the maturity date does not exceed nine months.
3. Securities of charitable organizations.
4. Securities resulting from a corporate reorganization issued for exchange with the issuer's existing security holders and certificates issued by trustees, receivers, or debtors in possession under the bankruptcy laws (bankruptcy was discussed in Chapter 15).
5. Securities issued exclusively for exchange with the issuer's existing security holders, provided no commission is paid (for example, stock dividends and stock splits).
6. Securities issued to finance the acquisition of railroad equipment.
7. Any insurance, endowment, or annuity contract issued by a state-regulated insurance company.
8. Government-issued securities.
9. Securities issued by banks, savings and loan associations, farmers' cooperatives, and similar institutions subject to supervision by governmental authorities.
10. In consideration of the "small amount involved,"[13] an issuer's offer of up to $5 million in securities in any twelve-month period.

For the last exemption, under Regulation A,[14] the issuer must file with the SEC a notice of the issue and an offering circular, which must also be provided to investors before the sale. This is a much simpler and less expensive process than the procedures associated with full registration. Companies are allowed to "test the waters" for potential interest before preparing the offering circular. (To *test the waters* means to determine potential interest without actually selling any securities or requiring any commitment on the part of those who are interested.) Small-business issuers (companies with annual revenues of less than $25 million and less than

---

12. 15 U.S.C. Section 77c.
13. 15 U.S.C. Section 77c(b).
14. 17 C.F.R. Sections 230.251–230.263.

$25 million in outstanding voting stock) can also utilize an integrated registration and reporting system that uses simpler forms than the full registration procedure.

Exhibit 28–1 summarizes the securities and transactions (discussed next) that are exempt from the registration requirements under the Securities Act of 1933 and SEC regulations.

EXEMPT TRANSACTIONS

An issuer of securities that are not exempt under any of the categories listed above can avoid the high cost and complicated procedures associated with registration by taking advantage of certain *exempt transactions*. These exemptions are very broad, and thus many sales occur without registration. Because the exemptions overlap somewhat, an offering may qualify for more than one.

SMALL OFFERINGS—REGULATION D The SEC's Regulation D contains four separate exemptions from registration requirements for limited offers (offers that either involve a small amount of money or are made in a limited manner). Regulation D provides that any of these offerings made during any twelve-month period are exempt from the registration requirements.

—Rule 504. Noninvestment company offerings up to $1 million in any twelve-month period are exempt.[15] In contrast to investment companies

---

15. 17 C.F.R. Section 230.504. Rule 504 is the exemption used by most small businesses, but that could change under the new SEC Rule 1001. This rule permits, under certain circumstances, "testing the waters" for offerings of up to $5 million *per transaction*. These offerings, however, can be made only to "qualified purchasers" (knowledgeable, sophisticated investors).

EXHIBIT 28–1 **Exemptions under the 1933 Act for Securities Offerings by Businesses**

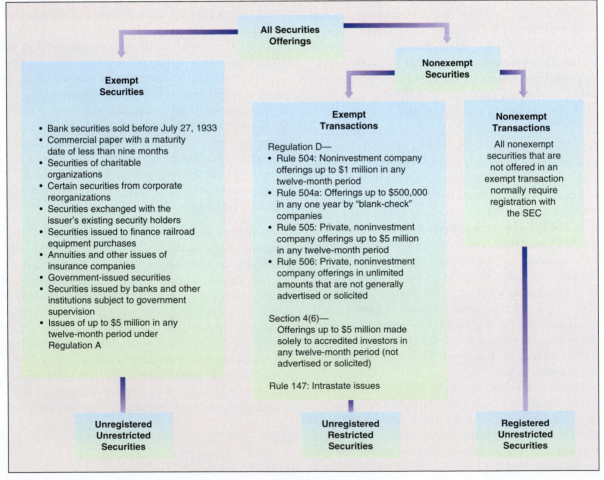

(discussed later in this chapter), noninvestment companies are firms that are not engaged primarily in the business of investing or trading in securities.

—Rule 504a. Offerings up to $500,000 in any one year by so-called blank-check companies—companies with no specific business plans except to locate and acquire as yet unidentified businesses or opportunities—are exempt if no general solicitation or advertising is used; the SEC is notified of the sales; and precaution is taken against nonexempt, unregistered resales.[16] The limits on advertising and unregistered resales do not apply if the offering is made solely in states that provide for registration and disclosure and the securities are sold in compliance with those provisions.[17]

—Rule 505. Private, noninvestment company offerings up to $5 million in any twelve-month period are exempt, regardless of the number of **accredited investors** (banks, insurance companies, investment companies, the issuer's executive officers and directors, and persons whose income or net worth exceeds a certain threshold), so long as there are no more than thirty-five unaccredited investors; no general solicitation or advertising is used; the SEC is notified of the sales; and precaution is taken against nonexempt, unregistered resales. If the sale involves *any* unaccredited investors, *all* investors must be given material information about the offering company, its business, and the securities before the sale. Unlike Rule 506 (discussed next), Rule 505 includes no requirement that the issuer believe each unaccredited investor "has such knowledge and experience in financial and business matters that he [or she] is capable of evaluating the merits and the risks of the prospective investment."[18]

—Rule 506. Private offerings in unlimited amounts that are not generally solicited or advertised are exempt if the SEC is notified of the sales; precaution is taken against nonexempt, unregistered resales; and the issuer believes that each unaccredited investor has sufficient knowledge or experience in financial matters to be capable of evaluating the investment's

merits and risks. There may be no more than thirty-five unaccredited investors, although there may be an unlimited number of accredited investors. If there are any unaccredited investors, the issuer must provide to all purchasers material information about itself, its business, and the securities before the sale.[19]

This exemption is perhaps the most important one for those firms that want to raise funds through the sale of securities without registering them. It is often referred to as the *private placement* exemption because it exempts "transactions not involving any public offering."[20] This provision applies to private offerings to a limited number of persons who are sufficiently sophisticated and able to assume the risk of the investment (and who thus have no need for federal registration protection). It also applies to private offerings to similarly sophisticated institutional investors.

SMALL OFFERINGS—SECTION 4(6) Under Section 4(6) of the Securities Act of 1933, an offer made *solely* to accredited investors is exempt if its amount is not more than $5 million. Any number of accredited investors may participate, but no unaccredited investors may do so. No general solicitation or advertising may be used; the SEC must be notified of all sales; and precaution must be taken against nonexempt, unregistered resales. Precaution is necessary because these are *restricted* securities and may be resold only by registration or in an exempt transaction.[21] (The securities purchased and sold by most people who handle stock transactions are called, in contrast, *unrestricted* securities.)

INTRASTATE ISSUES—RULE 147 Also exempt are intrastate transactions involving purely local offerings.[22] This exemption applies to most offerings that are restricted to residents of the state in which the issuing company is organized and doing business. For nine months after the last sale, virtually no resales may be made to nonresidents, and precautions must be taken against this possibility. These offerings remain subject to applicable laws in the state of issue.

RESALES Most securities can be resold without registration (although some resales may be subject to restrictions, as discussed above in connection with specific exemptions). The Securities Act of 1933 provides exemptions for resales by most persons other

---

16. Precautions to be taken against nonexempt, unregistered resales include asking the investor whether he or she is buying the securities for others; before the sale, disclosing to each purchaser in writing that the securities are unregistered and thus cannot be resold, except in an exempt transaction, without first being registered; and indicating on the certificates that the securities are unregistered and restricted.

17. 17 C.F.R. Section 230.504a.

18. 17 C.F.R. Section 230.505.

19. 17 C.F.R. Section 230.506.

20. 15 U.S.C. Section 77d(2).

21. 15 U.S.C. Section 77d(6).

22. 15 U.S.C. Section 77c(a)(11); 17 C.F.R. Section 230.147.

than issuers or underwriters. The average investor who sells shares of stock need not file a registration statement with the SEC. Resales of restricted securities acquired under Rule 504a, Rule 505, Rule 506, or Section 4(6), however, trigger the registration requirements unless the party selling them complies with Rule 144 or Rule 144A. These rules are sometimes referred to as "safe harbors."

—Rule 144. Rule 144 exempts restricted securities from registration on resale if there is adequate current public information about the issuer, the person selling the securities has owned them for at least one year, they are sold in certain limited amounts in unsolicited brokers' transactions, and the SEC is given notice of the resale.[23] "Adequate current public information" consists of the reports that certain companies are required to file under the Securities Exchange Act of 1934. A person who has owned the securities for at least two years is subject to none of these requirements, unless the person is an affiliate. An *affiliate* is one who controls, is controlled by, or is in common control with the issuer.

23. 17 C.F.R. Section 230.144.

—Rule 144A. Securities that at the time of issue are not of the same class as securities listed on a national securities exchange or quoted in a U.S. automated interdealer quotation system may be resold under Rule 144A.[24] They may be sold only to a qualified institutional buyer (an institution, such as an insurance company, an investment company, or a bank, that owns and invests at least $100 million in securities). The seller must take reasonable steps to ensure that the buyer knows that the seller is relying on the exemption under Rule 144A. A sample restricted stock certificate is shown in Exhibit 28–2.

VIOLATIONS OF THE 1933 ACT

It is a violation of the Securities Act of 1933 to intentionally defraud investors by misrepresenting or omitting facts in a registration statement or prospectus. Liability is also imposed on those who are negligent for not discovering the fraud. Selling securities before the effective date of the registration statement or under an exemption for which the securities do not qualify results in liability.

24. 17 C.F.R. Section 230.144A.

EXHIBIT 28–2 A Sample Restricted Stock Certificate

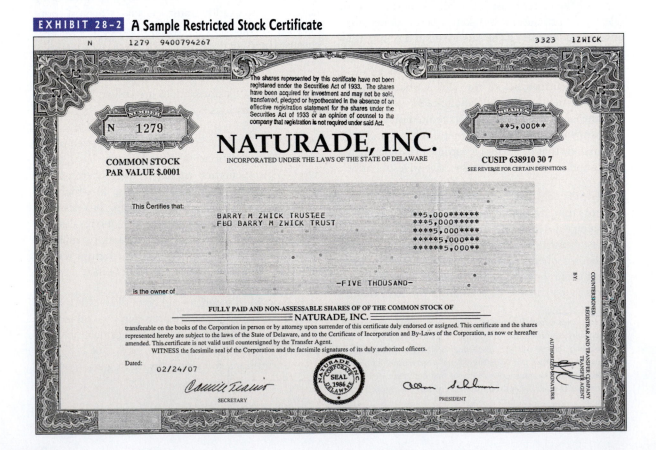

DEFENSES There are three basic defenses to charges of violations under the 1933 act. Even if a statement was not true or a fact was left out of the registration statement, a defendant can avoid liability if he or she can prove that the statement or omission was not material. A defendant can also avoid liability by proving that the plaintiff knew about the misrepresentation and bought the stock anyway.

Any defendant, except the issuer of the stock, can also assert what is called the *due diligence* defense. To make this defense, a person must prove that she or he reasonably believed, at the time the registration statement became effective, that the statements in it were true and there were no omissions of material facts.

CRIMINAL PENALTIES The U.S. Department of Justice brings criminal actions against those who willfully violate the 1933 act. Violators may be penalized by fines up to $10,000, imprisonment up to five years, or both.

CIVIL SANCTIONS The SEC is authorized to impose civil sanctions against those who willfully violate the 1933 act. It can request an injunction to prevent further sales of the securities involved or ask a court to grant other relief, such as ordering a violator to refund profits.

Private parties who purchase securities and suffer harm as a result of false or omitted statements or other violations may bring a suit in a federal court to recover their losses and additional damages. If a registration statement or a prospectus contains material false statements or omissions, for example, damages may be recovered from those who signed the statement or those who provided information used in preparing the statement (such as accountants and other experts).

SECTION 3 | The Securities Exchange Act of 1934

The Securities Exchange Act of 1934 provides for the regulation and registration of securities exchanges, brokers, dealers, and national securities associations, such as the National Association of Securities Dealers. The SEC regulates the markets in which securities are traded by maintaining a continuous disclosure system for all corporations with securities on the national securities exchanges and for those companies that have assets in excess of $10 million and five hundred or more shareholders. These corporations are referred to as Section 12 companies, as they are required to file a registration application with the SEC for their securities under Section 12 of the 1934 act.

The act regulates proxy solicitation for voting (see Chapter 18), and it allows the SEC to engage in market surveillance to regulate certain market practices such as fraud, market manipulation, misrepresentation, and stabilization. (*Stabilization* is a commonly used technique in which securities underwriters bid for securities to stabilize their prices during their issuance.)

SECTION 10(b), SEC RULE 10b-5, AND INSIDER TRADING

Section 10(b) is one of the most important sections of the Securities Exchange Act of 1934. This section prohibits the use of any manipulative or deceptive device in violation of SEC rules and regulations.

One of the major goals of Section 10(b) and SEC Rule 10b-5 is to prevent so-called **insider trading.** Because of their positions, corporate directors and officers often obtain advance inside information that may affect the future market value of the corporate stock. Obviously, their "inside" positions give them a trading advantage over the general public and shareholders. The 1934 Securities Exchange Act defines the term *inside information* and extends liability to officers and directors for taking advantage of such information in their personal transactions when they know that it is unavailable to the persons with whom they are dealing.

Section 10(b) of the 1934 act and SEC Rule 10b-5 cover not only corporate officers, directors, and majority shareholders but also any persons having access to or receiving information of a nonpublic nature on which trading is based.

SEC RULE 10b-5 Among the rules prescribed by the SEC is **SEC Rule 10b-5,** which prohibits the commission of fraud in connection with the purchase or sale of any security. Rule 10b-5 states as follows:

It shall be unlawful for any person, directly or indirectly, by the use of any means or instrumentality of interstate commerce, or of the mails or of any facility of any national securities exchange,

(a) To employ any device, scheme, or artifice to defraud,

(b) To make any untrue statement of a material fact or to omit to state a material fact necessary in order to make the statements made, in the light of the circumstances under which they were made, not misleading, or

(c) To engage in any act, practice, or course of business which operates or would operate as a fraud or deceit upon any person, in connection with the purchase or sale of any security.[25]

APPLICABILITY OF SEC RULE 10b-5
SEC Rule 10b-5 applies in virtually all situations involving the trading of securities, whether on organized exchanges, in over-the-counter markets, or in private transactions. The rule covers notes, bonds, certificates of interest and participation in any profit-sharing agreement, agreements to form a corporation, and joint-venture agreements; in short, the rule covers just about any form of security. Whether a firm has securities registered under the 1933 act has no bearing on whether the 1934 act applies.

SEC Rule 10b-5 is applicable only when the requisites of federal jurisdiction (such as the use of the mails, of stock exchange facilities, or of any instrumentality of interstate commerce) are present. Virtually no commercial transaction, however, can be completed without such contact. In addition, the states have corporate securities laws, many of which include provisions similar to SEC Rule 10b-5.

DISCLOSURE REQUIREMENTS UNDER SEC RULE 10b-5
Any material omission or misrepresentation of material facts in connection with the purchase or sale

---

25. 17 C.F.R. Section 240.10b-5.

---

of a security may violate Section 10(b) and SEC Rule 10b-5. The key to liability (which can be civil or criminal) under this rule is whether the information omitted or misrepresented is *material*.

—Examples of Material Facts Calling for Disclosure.
The following are some examples of material facts calling for disclosure under the rule:

1. Fraudulent trading in the company stock by a broker-dealer.
2. A dividend change (whether up or down).
3. A contract for the sale of corporate assets.
4. A new discovery, a new process, or a new product.
5. A significant change in the firm's financial condition.
6. Potential litigation against the company.

Note that none of these facts, in itself, is *automatically* a material fact. Rather, it will be regarded as a material fact if it is significant enough that it will likely affect an investor's decision to purchase or sell certain securities.

The case that follows is a landmark decision interpreting SEC Rule 10b-5. The SEC sued several of Texas Gulf Sulphur Company's directors, officers, and employees under SEC Rule 10b-5 after they purchased large amounts of the company's stock prior to the announcement of a rich ore discovery by the corporation. At issue was whether the ore discovery was a material fact that had to be disclosed under Rule 10b-5.

CASE 28.1   SEC v. Texas Gulf Sulphur Co.

United States
Court of Appeals,
Second Circuit, 1968.
401 F.2d 833.

BACKGROUND AND FACTS *Texas Gulf Sulphur Company (TGS) conducted aerial geophysical surveys over more than 15,000 square miles of eastern Canada. The operations indicated concentrations of commercially exploitable minerals. At one site near Timmins, Ontario, TGS drilled a hole that appeared to yield a core with an exceedingly high mineral content. TGS kept secret the results of the core sample. Officers and employees of the company made substantial purchases of TGS's stock or accepted stock options after learning of the ore discovery, even though further drilling was necessary to establish whether there was enough ore to be mined commercially. Several months later, TGS announced that the strike was expected to yield at least 25 million tons of ore. Subsequently, the price of TGS stock rose substantially. The Securities and Exchange Commission (SEC) brought a suit against the officers and employees of TGS for violating SEC Rule 10b-5. The officers and employees argued that the information on which they had traded had not been material at the time of their trades because the mine had not then been commercially proved. The trial court held that most of the defendants had not violated SEC Rule 10b-5, and the SEC appealed.*

CASE 28.1 | Continued

IN THE LANGUAGE OF THE COURT
WATERMAN, Circuit Judge.

* * * *

* * * [W]hether facts are material within Rule 10b-5 when the facts relate to a particular event and are undisclosed by those persons who are knowledgeable thereof *will depend at any given time upon a balancing of both the indicated probability that the event will occur and the anticipated magnitude of the event in light of the totality of the company activity.* Here, * * * knowledge of the possibility, which surely was more than marginal, of the existence of a mine of the vast magnitude indicated by the remarkably rich drill core located rather close to the surface (suggesting mineability by the less expensive openpit method) within the confines of a large anomaly (suggesting an extensive region of mineralization) might well have affected the price of TGS stock and would certainly have been an important fact to a reasonable, if speculative, investor in deciding whether he should buy, sell, or hold. [Emphasis added.]

* * * *

* * * [A] major factor in determining whether the * * * discovery was a material fact is the importance attached to the drilling results by those who knew about it. * * * [T]he timing by those who knew of it of their stock purchases * * *—purchases in some cases by individuals who had never before purchased * * * TGS stock—virtually compels the inference that the insiders were influenced by the drilling results.

DECISION AND REMEDY *The appellate court ruled in favor of the SEC. All of the trading by insiders who knew of the mineral find before its true extent had been publicly announced violated SEC Rule 10b-5.*

IMPACT OF THIS CASE ON TODAY'S LAW
This landmark case affirmed the principle that the test of whether information is "material," for SEC Rule 10b-5 purposes, is whether it would affect the judgment of reasonable investors. The corporate insiders' purchases of stock and stock options (rights to purchase stock) indicated that they were influenced by the drilling results and that the information about the drilling results was material. The courts continue to cite this case when applying SEC Rule 10b-5 to cases of alleged insider trading.

—The Private Securities Litigation Reform Act of 1995. Ironically, one of the effects of SEC Rule 10b-5 was to deter disclosure of forward-looking information. To understand why, consider an example. A company announces that its projected earnings in a certain time period will be X amount. It turns out that the forecast is wrong. The earnings are in fact much lower, and the price of the company's stock is affected—negatively. The shareholders then bring a class-action suit against the company, alleging that the directors violated SEC Rule 10b-5 by disclosing misleading financial information.

In an attempt to rectify this problem and promote disclosure, Congress passed the Private Securities Litigation Reform Act of 1995. Among other things, the act provides a "safe harbor" for publicly held companies that make forward-looking statements, such as financial forecasts. Those who make such statements are protected against federal liability for securities

fraud as long as the statements are accompanied by "meaningful cautionary statements identifying important factors that could cause actual results to differ materially from those in the forward-looking statement."[26]

After the 1995 act was passed, a number of class-action suits involving securities were filed in state courts to skirt the requirements of the 1995 federal act. In response to this problem, Congress passed the Securities Litigation Uniform Standards Act of 1998. The act placed stringent limits on the ability of plaintiffs to bring class-action suits in state courts against firms whose securities are traded on national stock exchanges.

OUTSIDERS AND SEC RULE 10b-5 The traditional insider-trading case involves true insiders—corporate

---

26. 15 U.S.C. Sections 77z-2, 78u-5.

officers, directors, and majority shareholders who have access to (and trade on) inside information. Increasingly, however, liability under Section 10(b) of the 1934 act and SEC Rule 10b-5 has been extended to include certain "outsiders"—those who trade on inside information acquired indirectly. Two theories have been developed under which outsiders may be held liable for insider trading: the *tipper/tippee theory* and the *misappropriation theory*.

—Tipper/Tippee Theory. Anyone who acquires inside information as a result of a corporate insider's breach of his or her fiduciary duty can be liable under SEC Rule 10b-5. This liability extends to **tippees** (those who receive "tips" from insiders) and even remote tippees (tippees of tippees).

The key to liability under this theory is that the inside information must be obtained as a result of someone's breach of a fiduciary duty to the corporation whose shares are traded. The tippee is liable under this theory only if (1) there is a breach of a duty not to disclose inside information, (2) the disclosure is in exchange for personal benefit, and (3) the tippee

knows (or should know) of this breach and benefits from it.[27]

—Misappropriation Theory. Liability for insider trading may also be established under the misappropriation theory. This theory holds that if an individual wrongfully obtains (misappropriates) inside information and trades on it for her or his personal gain, then the individual should be held liable because, in essence, the individual stole information rightfully belonging to another.

The misappropriation theory has been controversial because it significantly extends the reach of SEC Rule 10b-5 to outsiders who ordinarily would not be deemed fiduciaries of the corporations in whose stock they trade. In the following case, the United States Supreme Court addressed the issue of whether liability under SEC Rule 10b-5 can be based on the misappropriation theory.

---

27. See, for example, *Chiarella v. United States*, 445 U.S. 222, 100 S.Ct. 1108, 63 L.Ed.2d 348 (1980); and *Dirks v. SEC*, 463 U.S. 646, 103 S.Ct. 3255, 77 L.Ed.2d 911 (1983).

CASE 28.2   United States v. O'Hagan

Supreme Court of the United States, 1997.
521 U.S. 642,
117 S.Ct. 2199,
138 L.Ed.2d 724.
http://straylight.law.cornell.edu/supct/index.htm[a]

BACKGROUND AND FACTS *James O'Hagan was a partner in the law firm of Dorsey & Whitney. Grand Metropolitan PLC (Grand Met) hired Dorsey & Whitney to assist in a takeover of the Pillsbury Company. Before Grand Met made its tender offer, O'Hagan bought shares of Pillsbury stock. When the tender offer was announced, the price of Pillsbury stock increased more than 35 percent. O'Hagan sold his shares for a profit of more than $4 million. The Securities and Exchange Commission (SEC) prosecuted O'Hagan for, among other things, securities fraud in violation of Rule 10b-5 under the misappropriation theory. The SEC contended that O'Hagan breached fiduciary duties he owed to his law firm and Grand Met. When O'Hagan was convicted, he appealed to the U.S. Court of Appeals for the Eighth Circuit, which reversed the conviction. The SEC appealed to the United States Supreme Court.*

IN THE LANGUAGE OF THE COURT

Justice GINSBURG delivered the opinion of the Court.
* * * *
The "misappropriation theory" holds that a person commits fraud "in connection with" a securities transaction, and thereby violates [Section]10(b) * * * , when he misappropriates confidential information for securities trading purposes, in breach of a duty owed to the source of the information. Under this theory, a fiduciary's undisclosed, self-serving use of a principal's information to purchase or sell securities, in breach of a duty of loyalty and confidentiality, defrauds the principal of the exclusive use of that information. *In lieu of premising liability on a fiduciary relationship between company insider and purchaser or seller of the company's stock, the misappropriation theory premises liability on a fiduciary-turned-trader's deception of those who entrusted him with access to confidential information.* [Emphasis added.]

---

a. In the "Search" box, type in the *O'Hagan* case name and click on "Search" to access the Court's opinion.

CASE 28.2 Continued

* * * [M]isappropriation * * * satisfies [Section] 10(b)'s requirement that charge-able conduct involve a "deceptive device or contrivance" used "in connection with" the purchase or sale of securities. * * * [M]isappropriators * * * deal in deception. A fiduciary who pretends loyalty to the principal while secretly converting the principal's information for personal gain dupes or defrauds the principal.

* * * *

* * * [T]he fiduciary's fraud is consummated [brought to fruition, fulfilled] * * * when, without disclosure to his principal, he uses the information to purchase or sell securities. * * *

* * * *

* * * An investor's informational disadvantage vis-à-vis a misappropriator with material, nonpublic information stems from contrivance, not luck; it is a disadvantage that cannot be overcome with research or skill.

DECISION AND REMEDY *The United States Supreme Court held that liability under Rule 10b-5 can be based on the misappropriation theory, reversed the lower court's judgment, and remanded the case.*

WHAT IF THE FACTS WERE DIFFERENT? *Suppose that O'Hagan had disclosed to Dorsey & Whitney and Grand Met that he was going to trade on the nonpublic information. Would he have been liable for misappropriation? Why or why not?*

INSIDER REPORTING AND TRADING—SECTION 16(b)

Officers, directors, and certain large stockholders of Section 12 corporations (stockholders owning 10 percent of the class of equity securities registered under Section 12 of the 1934 act) are required to file reports with the SEC concerning their ownership and trading of the corporation's securities.[28] To discourage such insiders from using nonpublic information about their companies to their personal benefit in the stock market, Section 16(b) of the 1934 act provides for the recapture by the corporation of all profits realized by the insider on any purchase and sale or sale and purchase of the corporation's stock within any six-month period. It is irrelevant whether the insider actually uses inside information; *all such short-swing profits must be returned to the corporation.*

Section 16(b) applies not only to stock but also to warrants, options, and securities convertible into stock. In addition, the courts have fashioned complex rules for determining profits. Note that the SEC exempts a number of transactions under Rule 16b-3.[29] For all of these reasons, corporate insiders are wise to seek specialized counsel prior to trading in the corpo-

ration's stock. Exhibit 28–3 on the next page compares the effects of SEC Rule 10b-5 and Section 16(b).

PROXY STATEMENTS

Section 14(a) of the Securities Exchange Act of 1934 regulates the solicitation of proxies (see Chapter 18) from shareholders of Section 12 companies. The SEC regulates the content of proxy statements, which are statements sent to shareholders by corporate managers and others who are requesting authority to vote on behalf of the shareholders in a particular election on specified issues.

Whoever solicits a proxy must fully and accurately disclose in the proxy statement all of the facts that are pertinent to the matter on which the shareholders are to vote. SEC Rule 14a-9 is similar to the antifraud provisions of SEC Rule 10b-5. Remedies for violations are extensive, ranging from injunctions to prevent a vote from being taken to monetary damages.

VIOLATIONS OF THE 1934 ACT

As mentioned earlier, violations of Section 10(b) and Rule 10b-5 of the Securities Exchange Act of 1934 include insider trading. This is a criminal offense, with criminal penalties. Violators of these laws may also be subject to civil liability. For any sanctions to be imposed, however, there must be *scienter*—the violator

---

28. 15 U.S.C. Section 78*l*. Note that Section 403 of the Sarbanes-Oxley Act of 2002 speeds up the reporting deadlines specified in Section 16(b).

29. 17 C.F.R. Section 240.16b-3.

EXHIBIT 28-3 Comparison of Coverage, Application, and Liability under SEC Rule 10b-5 and Section 16(b)

AREA OF COMPARISON	SEC RULE 10b-5	SECTION 16(b)
What is the subject matter of the transaction?	Any security (does not have to be registered).	Any security (does not have to be registered).
What transactions are covered?	Purchase or sale.	Short-swing purchase and sale or short-swing sale and purchase.
Who is subject to liability?	Virtually anyone with inside information under a duty to disclose—including officers, directors, controlling stockholders, and tippees.	Officers, directors, and certain 10 percent stockholders.
Is omission or misrepresentation necessary for liability?	Yes.	No.
Are there any exempt transactions?	No.	Yes, there are a variety of exemptions.
Is direct dealing with the party necessary?	No.	No.
Who may bring an action?	A person transacting with an insider, the SEC, or a purchaser or seller damaged by a wrongful act.	A corporation or a shareholder by derivative action.

must have had an intent to defraud or knowledge of his or her misconduct. *Scienter* can be proved by showing that a defendant made false statements or wrongfully failed to disclose material facts.

Violations of Section 16(b) include the sale by insiders of stock acquired less than six months before the time of sale. These violations are subject to civil sanctions. Liability under Section 16(b) is strict liability. Neither *scienter* nor negligence is required.

CRIMINAL PENALTIES For violations of Section 10(b) and Rule 10b-5, an individual may be fined up to $5 million, imprisoned for up to twenty years, or both. A partnership or a corporation may be fined up to $25 million. Under Section 807 of the Sarbanes-Oxley Act of 2002, for a willful violation of the 1934 act the violator may, in addition to being subject to a fine, be imprisoned for up to twenty-five years.

In a criminal prosecution under the securities laws, a jury is not allowed to speculate on whether a defendant acted willfully—in other words, there can be no reasonable doubt that the defendant knew he or she was acting wrongfully. The issue in the following case was whether, in light of this principle, there was enough evidence to present to a jury that Martha Stewart, founder of a well-known media and homemaking empire, intended to deceive other investors.

CASE 28.3   United States v. Stewart

United States
District Court,
Southern District
of New York, 2004.
305 F.Supp.2d 368.

CEDARBAUM, District Judge.
* * * *

The criminal charges [in this case] against [Martha] Stewart * * * arose from Stewart's December 27, 2001 sale of 3,928 shares of stock in ImClone Systems, Inc. ("ImClone"). ImClone is a biotechnology company whose then–chief executive officer, Samuel Waksal, was a friend of Stewart's and a client of Stewart's stockbroker * * * [Peter] Bacanovic. On December 28, * * * ImClone announced that the Food and Drug Administration had rejected the company's application for approval of Erbitux, a cancer-fighting drug that ImClone had previously described as its lead product.

CASE 28.3 | Continued

The Indictment alleges that on the morning of December 27, 2001, * * * Bacanovic learned that Waksal * * * [was] selling or attempting to sell * * * ImClone shares. Bacanovic allegedly instructed his assistant, Douglas Faneuil, to inform Stewart of the * * * trading activity, and she sold her shares in response to that information.

According to the Indictment, [Stewart] then lied about the real reason for Stewart's sale in order to cover up what was possibly an illegal trade and to deflect attention from Stewart in the ensuing investigations into suspicious ImClone trading in advance of the Erbitux announcement. [Stewart] claimed that [she] had a standing agreement * * * [to] sell her position in ImClone if the stock fell to $60 per share.

* * * *

* * * [T]he Indictment charges Stewart, the CEO of [Martha Stewart Living Omnimedia (MSLO)] with fraud in connection with the purchase and sale of MSLO securities * * * . The [charge] is based on three repetitive public statements she made in June of 2002 [at a conference attended by investment professionals and investors] after the media began reporting investigations of her ImClone trades * * * .

* * * *

* * * *"[S]cienter," or intent, in the civil securities fraud context, indicates a mental state embracing intent to deceive, manipulate, or defraud, and is a required element of any claim of securities fraud.* In a criminal prosecution, the Government must also prove that the defendant acted willfully, that is, with a realization that she was acting wrongfully. * * * The issue at hand is * * * whether, taking into account the heightened standard of proof in criminal cases, there is sufficient evidence of Stewart's intent to deceive investors to present the matter to the jury. [Emphasis added.]

* * * *

The Government contends that a reasonable jury could draw inferences from the evidence * * * that would permit it to find beyond a reasonable doubt that Stewart intended to deceive investors with her statements. Specifically, the Government argues that the evidence supports the inferences that Stewart was aware of the impact of the negative publicity about her ImClone trade on the market value of MSLO securities * * * and that Stewart deliberately directed her statements to investors in MSLO securities.

* * * I hold that a reasonable juror could not, without resorting to speculation and surmise, find beyond a reasonable doubt that Stewart's purpose was to influence the market in MSLO securities.

* * * *

With respect to the June * * * statement, the Government contends that Stewart's awareness that she was speaking to analysts and investors, her prefatory statement that she was embarking upon a topic about which her audience was "probably interested," and the timing of the statement, which occurred as the stock continued to fall, are sufficient * * * to permit the jury to infer that she intended to deceive investors in MSLO securities when she made the statement.

* * * [T]he fact that the * * * statement was read to an audience of analysts and investors * * * cannot be viewed in isolation—the entire context of the statement must be considered. Thus, any inference to be drawn from the makeup of the audience must also take into account the fact that Stewart was only one of several representatives of MSLO, and that MSLO was only one of several corporations making presentations at the conference. The evidence does not show that the conference was organized by Stewart or her company. There is no evidence that the negative publicity about ImClone influenced Stewart's decision to attend and take advantage of a platform from which to reach investors directly. To the contrary, her statement—a very brief portion of a much longer presentation—indicates otherwise. The Government argues that her statement indicating an awareness that the audience was "probably interested" in what she had to say about the ImClone trade is meaningful. Yet her remarks at the close of the statement—"I have nothing to add on this matter today. And I'm here to talk about our terrific company * * * "—support an inference that she wanted to dispose of the issue and begin to address the subjects of the conference.

* * * *

CONTINUED ▶

 **Continued**   For the foregoing reasons, defendant Stewart's motion for a judgment of acquittal on [this charge] is granted.[a]

1. How does the *scienter*, or intent, requirement in the context of criminal securities fraud differ from its counterpart in the context of civil securities fraud?
2. When a criminal securities fraud case is tried by a jury, as the *Stewart* case was, what is the judge's role with respect to issues to be presented to the jury?

a. Stewart was later convicted on other charges related to her sale of ImClone stock, including obstruction of justice and lying to federal officials, and was sentenced and served five months in prison and five months and three weeks of house arrest. She is appealing the decision in an attempt to clear her name.

CIVIL SANCTIONS The SEC can bring a suit in a federal district court against anyone violating, or aiding in a violation of, the 1934 act or SEC rules by purchasing or selling a security while in the possession of material nonpublic information.[30] The violation must occur on or through the facilities of a national securities exchange or from or through a broker or dealer.[31] The court may assess as a penalty of as much as triple the profits gained or the loss avoided by the guilty party. Profit or loss is defined as "the difference between the purchase or sale price of the security and the value of that security as measured by the trading price of the security at a reasonable period of time after public dissemination of the nonpublic information."[32]

The Insider Trading and Securities Fraud Enforcement Act of 1988 enlarged the class of persons who may be subject to civil liability for insider-trading violations. This act also gave the SEC authority to award **bounty payments** (rewards given by government officials for acts beneficial to the state) to persons providing information leading to the prosecution of insider-trading violations.[33]

Private parties may also sue violators of Section 10(b) and Rule 10b-5. A private party may obtain rescission of a contract to buy securities or damages to the extent of the violator's illegal profits. Those found liable have a right to seek contribution from those who share responsibility for the violations, including accountants, attorneys, and corporations.[34] For violations of Section 16(b), a corporation can bring an action to recover the short-swing profits.

SECTION 4 | Corporate Governance

Corporate governance can be narrowly defined as the relationship between a corporation and its shareholders. The Organization of Economic Cooperation and Development (OECD) provides a broader definition:

> Corporate governance is the system by which business corporations are directed and controlled. The corporate governance structure specifies the distribution of rights and responsibilities among different participants in the corporation, such as the board of directors, managers, shareholders, and other stakeholders, and spells out the rules and procedures for making decisions on corporate affairs.[35]

While this definition has no true legal value, it does set the tone for the ways in which modern corporations should be governed. In other words, effective corporate governance requires more than compliance with laws and regulations.

30. 15 U.S.C. Section 78u(d)(2)(A).

31. Transactions pursuant to a public offering by an issuer of securities are exempted.

32. 15 U.S.C. Section 78u(d)(2)(C).

33. 15 U.S.C. Section 78u-1.

34. The Supreme Court has ruled that no private cause of action can be brought against those who "aid and abet" under Section 10(b) and SEC Rule 10b-5. *Central Bank of Denver, N.A. v. First Interstate Bank of Denver, N.A.*, 511 U.S. 164, 114 S.Ct. 1439, 128 L.Ed.2d 119 (1994). Only the SEC can bring actions against so-called aiders and abettors. Nevertheless, some courts have held accountants and attorneys liable as primary violators under Section 10(b), and a conflict exists in the federal circuit courts on precisely what course of conduct subjects a secondary actor to primary liability.

35. *Governance in the 21st Century: Future Studies*, OECD, 2001.

THE NEED FOR GOOD CORPORATE GOVERNANCE

The need for effective corporate governance arises in large corporations because corporate ownership (by shareholders) is separated from corporate control (by officers and managers). In the real world, officers and managers are tempted to advance their own interests, even when such interests conflict with those of the shareholders. The reason for concern about managerial opportunism can be illustrated by the recent well-publicized scandals in the corporate world.

ATTEMPTS AT ALIGNING THE INTERESTS OF SHAREHOLDERS WITH THOSE OF OFFICERS

Some corporations have sought to align the financial interests of their officers with those of the company's shareholders. Thus, many officers have been provided with **stock options** for the corporation, which could be exercised at a set price and sold for a profit above that per-share price. When a corporation's share value grows, these options become more valuable for the officers, thereby giving them a financial stake in the share price.

Options have turned out to be an imperfect device for controlling governance, however. Executives in some companies have been tempted to "cook" the company's books in order to keep share prices higher so that they could exercise their options for a profit. Executives in other corporations experienced no losses when share prices dropped; instead, some had their options "repriced" so that they did not suffer from the share price decline and could still profit from future increases above the lowered share price. Although stock options theoretically can motivate officers to protect shareholder interests, stock option plans became a way for officers to take advantage of shareholders.

Because of numerous headline-making scandals within major corporations, there has been an outcry for more "outside" directors—the theory is that independent directors will more closely monitor the actions of corporate officers. Today, we see more boards with outside directors (those with no formal employment affiliation with the company). Note, though, that outside directors may not be truly independent of corporate officers; they may be friends or business associates of the leading officers. A study of board appointments found that the best way to

increase one's probability of appointment was to "suck up" to the chief executive officer.[36]

CORPORATE GOVERNANCE AND CORPORATE LAW

Good corporate governance standards are designed to address problems (such as those briefly discussed above) and to motivate officers to make decisions to promote the financial interests of the company's shareholders. Generally, corporate governance entails corporate decision-making structures that monitor employees (particularly officers) to ensure that they are acting for the benefit of the shareholders. Thus, corporate governance involves, at a minimum:

1. The audited reporting of financial conditions at the corporation, so that managers can be evaluated.
2. Legal protections for shareholders, so that violators of the law, who attempt to take advantage of shareholders, can be punished for misbehavior and victims may recover damages for any associated losses.

THE PRACTICAL SIGNIFICANCE OF GOOD CORPORATE GOVERNANCE Effective corporate governance may have considerable practical significance. A study by researchers at Harvard University and the Wharton School of Business found that firms providing greater shareholder rights had higher profits, higher sales growth, higher firm value, and other economic advantages.[37] Better corporate governance in the form of greater accountability to investors may therefore offer the opportunity to enhance considerably institutional wealth.

GOVERNANCE AND CORPORATION LAW Corporate governance is the essential purpose of corporation law in the United States. These statutes set up the legal framework for corporate governance. Under the corporate law of Delaware, where most major companies incorporate, all corporations must have in place certain structures of corporate governance. The key structure of corporate law is, of course, the board of directors. Directors make the most important decisions about the future of the corporation and monitor

---

36. Jennifer Reingold, "Suck Up and Move Fast," *Fast Company*, January 2005, p. 34.
37. Paul A. Gompers, Joy L. Ishii, and Andrew Metrick, "Corporate Governance and Equity Prices," *Quarterly Journal of Economics*, Vol. 118, (2003), p. 107.

the actions of corporate officers. Directors are elected by shareholders to look out for their best interests.

THE BOARD OF DIRECTORS Some argue that shareholder democracy is key to improving corporate governance. If shareholders could vote on major corporate decisions, shareholders could presumably have more control over the corporation. Essential to shareholder democracy is the concept of electing the board of directors, usually at the corporation's annual meeting. Under corporate law, a corporation must have a board of directors elected by shareholders. Virtually anyone can become a director, though some organizations, such as the New York Stock Exchange, require certain standards of service for directors of their listed corporations.

Directors have the responsibility of ensuring that officers are operating wisely and in the exclusive interest of shareholders. Directors receive reports from the officers and give them managerial directions. The board in theory controls the compensation of officers (presumably tied to performance). The reality, though, is that corporate directors devote a relatively small amount of time to monitoring officers.

Ideally, shareholders would monitor the directors' supervision of officers. As one leading board monitor stated, "Boards of directors are like subatomic particles—they behave differently when they are observed." Consequently, monitoring directors, and holding them responsible for corporate failings, can induce the directors to do a better job of monitoring officers and ensuring that the company is being managed in the interest of shareholders. While the directors can be sued for failing to effectively do their jobs, directors are rarely held personally liable.

IMPORTANCE OF THE AUDIT COMMITTEE One crucial board committee is known as the *audit committee*. Members of the audit committee oversee the corporation's accounting and financial reporting processes, including both internal and outside auditors. These audit committee members must, however, have sufficient expertise and be willing to spend the time necessary to examine carefully the corporation's bookkeeping methods. Otherwise, the audit committee may be ineffective.

The audit committee also oversees the corporation's "internal controls." These are the measures taken to ensure that reported results are accurate; they are carried out largely by the company's internal audit-

ing staff. As an example, these controls help to determine whether a corporation's debts are collectible. If the debts are not collectible, it is up to the audit committee to make sure that the corporation's financial officers cannot simply pretend that payment will eventually be made.

THE COMPENSATION COMMITTEE Another important committee of the board of directors is the *compensation committee*. This committee monitors and determines the compensation to be paid to the company's officers. In the process, it has the responsibility for assessing officers' performance, and its members may try to design compensation systems that encourage better performance by officers on behalf of shareholders.

THE SARBANES-OXLEY ACT OF 2002

As discussed in Chapter 4, in 2002, following a series of corporate scandals, Congress passed the Sarbanes-Oxley Act (see Appendix H for excerpts and explanatory comments). The act separately addresses certain issues relating to corporate governance. Generally, the act attempts to increase corporate accountability by imposing strict disclosure requirements and harsh penalties for violations of securities laws. Among other things, the act requires chief corporate executives to take responsibility for the accuracy of financial statements and reports that are filed with the SEC. Chief executive officers (CEOs) and chief financial officers (CFOs) personally must certify that the statements and reports are accurate and complete.

Additionally, the new rules require that certain financial and stock-transaction reports be filed with the SEC earlier than was required under the previous rules. The act also mandates SEC oversight over a new entity, called the Public Company Accounting Oversight Board, that regulates and oversees public accounting firms. Other provisions of the act created new private civil actions and expanded the SEC's remedies in administrative and civil actions.

Because of the importance of this act for those dealing with securities transactions, we present some of the act's key provisions relating to corporate accountability in Exhibit 28–4. We also discuss the act and its effect on corporate governance procedures in this chapter's *Emerging Trends* feature on pages 662 and 663.

EXHIBIT 28-4 **Some Key Provisions of the Sarbanes-Oxley Act of 2002 Relating to Corporate Accountability**

Certification Requirements—Under Section 906 of the Sarbanes-Oxley Act, the chief executive officers (CEOs) and chief financial officers (CFOs) of most major companies listed on public stock exchanges must now certify financial statements that are filed with the SEC. For virtually all filed financial reports, CEOs and CFOs have to certify that such reports "fully comply" with SEC requirements and that all of the information reported "fairly represents in all material respects, the financial conditions and results of operations of the issuer."

Under Section 302 of the act, for each quarterly and annual filing with the SEC, CEOs and CFOs of reporting companies are required to certify that a signing officer reviewed the report and that it contains no untrue statements of material fact. Also, the signing officer or officers must certify that they have established an internal control system to identify all material information, and that any deficiencies in the system were disclosed to the auditors.

Loans to Directors and Officers—Section 402 prohibits any reporting company, as well as any private company that is filing an initial public offering, from making personal loans to directors and executive officers (with a few limited exceptions, such as for certain consumer and housing loans).

Protection for Whistleblowers—Section 806 protects "whistleblowers"—those employees who report ("blow the whistle" on) securities violations by their employers—from being fired or in any way discriminated against by their employers.

Blackout Periods—Section 306 prohibits certain types of securities transactions during "blackout periods"—periods during which the issuer's ability to purchase, sell, or otherwise transfer funds in individual account plans (such as pension funds) is suspended.

Enhanced Penalties for—
- *Violations of Section 906 Certification Requirements*—A CEO or CFO who certifies a financial report or statement filed with the SEC knowing that the report or statement does not fulfill all of the requirements of Section 906 will be subject to criminal penalties of up to $1 million in fines, ten years in prison, or both. *Willful* violators of the certification requirements may be subject to $5 million in fines, twenty years in prison, or both.
- *Violations of the Securities Exchange Act of 1934*—Penalties for securities fraud under the 1934 act were also increased (as discussed earlier in this chapter). Individual violators may be fined up to $5 million, imprisoned for up to twenty years, or both. *Willful* violators may be imprisoned for up to twenty-five years in addition to being fined.
- *Destruction or Alteration of Documents*—Anyone who alters, destroys, or conceals documents or otherwise obstructs any official proceeding will be subject to fines, imprisonment for up to twenty years, or both.
- *Other Forms of White-Collar Crime*—The act stiffened the penalties for certain criminal violations, such as federal mail and wire fraud, and ordered the U.S. Sentencing Commission to revise the sentencing guidelines for white-collar crimes (see Chapter 7).

Statute of Limitations for Securities Fraud—Section 804 provides that a private right of action for securities fraud may be brought no later than two years after the discovery of the violation or five years after the violation, whichever is earlier.

SECTION 5 | Regulation of Investment Companies

Investment companies, and mutual funds in particular, grew rapidly after World War II. **Investment companies** act on behalf of many smaller shareholders/owners by buying a large portfolio of securities and managing that portfolio professionally. A **mutual fund** is a specific type of investment company that continually buys or sells to investors shares of ownership in a portfolio. Such companies are regulated by the Investment Company Act of 1940,[38] which pro-

vides for SEC regulation of their activities. The 1940 act was expanded by the Investment Company Act Amendments of 1970. Further minor changes were made in the Securities Acts Amendments of 1975 and in later years.

DEFINITION OF AN INVESTMENT COMPANY

For the purposes of the act, an *investment company* is defined as any entity that (1) "is . . . engaged primarily . . . in the business of investing, reinvesting, or trading in securities" or (2) is engaged in such business and more than 40 percent of the company's assets consist

---

38. 15 U.S.C. Sections 80a-1 to 80a-64.

Corporate Governance and the Sarbanes-Oxley Act

Traditionally, securities law has not been considered a central part of corporate governance considerations. Rather, securities law primarily requires disclosures of corporate financial results and other corporate actions; it does not directly regulate those actions. Practically, though, securities law may be a valuable tool for enhancing good corporate governance. Securities law is intended to make sure that companies accurately disclose their activities and financial results, such as audited statements. Such accurate disclosure better enables shareholders and directors to monitor the job done by the corporate officers. The securities laws also govern accountants who audit public companies, setting standards for their performance.

THE TREND TOWARD MORE INTERNAL CONTROLS AND ACCOUNTABILITY WITHIN PUBLIC COMPANIES

As already noted, in 2002, Congress passed the Sarbanes-Oxley Act, which was intended to improve corporate governance in the United States. This statute includes some traditional securities law provisions but also introduces direct *federal* corporate governance requirements for public companies (companies whose shares are traded in the public securities markets). The law addresses many of the corporate governance procedures discussed in this chapter and creates new requirements in an attempt to make the system work more effectively. The requirements deal with independent monitoring of company officers by both the board of directors and auditors.

Sections 302 and 404 of Sarbanes-Oxley require high-level managers (the most senior officers) to establish and maintain an effective system of internal controls. Moreover, senior management must reassess the system's effectiveness on an annual basis. Some companies already had strong and effective internal control systems in place before the passage of the act, but others had to take expensive steps to bring their internal controls up to the new federal standard. These include "disclosure controls and procedures" to ensure that company financial reports are accurate and timely. Assessment must involve the documenting of financial results and accounting policies before reporting them. By the end of 2005, hundreds of companies had reported that they had identified and corrected shortcomings in their internal control systems.

THE CERTIFICATION AND MONITORING REQUIREMENTS OF SARBANES-OXLEY

Section 906 requires that chief executive officers (CEOs) and chief financial officers (CFOs) certify that the corporate financial statements "fairly present, in all material respects, the financial condition and results of operation of the issuer." These corporate officers are subject to both civil and criminal penalties for violation of this section. This requirement makes officers directly accountable for the accuracy of their financial reporting and avoids any "ignorance defense" if shortcomings are later discovered.

Sarbanes-Oxley also adopts requirements to improve directors' monitoring of officers' activities. All members of the corporate audit committee for public companies must be

of investment securities. Excluded from coverage by the act are banks, insurance companies, savings and loan associations, finance companies, oil and gas drilling firms, charitable foundations, tax-exempt pension funds, and other special types of institutions, such as closely held corporations.

REGISTRATION AND REPORTING REQUIREMENTS

The 1940 act requires that every investment company register with the SEC by filing a notification of registration. Registered investment companies must also file annual reports with the SEC. To safeguard com-

pany assets, all securities must be held in the custody of a bank or stock exchange member, and that bank or stock exchange member must follow strict procedures established by the SEC.

RESTRICTIONS ON INVESTMENT COMPANIES

The 1940 act also imposes restrictions on the activities of investment companies and persons connected with them. For example, investment companies are not allowed to purchase securities on the margin (pay only part of the total price, borrowing the rest), sell short (sell shares not yet owned), or participate in joint trad-

outside directors. The New York Stock Exchange (NYSE) has a similar rule that also extends to the board's compensation committee. The audit committee must have a written charter that sets out its duties and provides for performance appraisal. At least one "financial expert" must serve on the audit committee, which must hold executive meetings without company officers being present. The audit committee must establish procedures for "whistleblowers." In addition to reviewing the internal controls, the committee also monitors the actions of the outside auditor.

THE SEPARATION OF AUDIT AND NONAUDIT SERVICES

The law includes other provisions to improve accounting accuracy. Auditors are prohibited from providing substantial nonaudit services for a company of any kind that might compromise the auditors' independence. The lead audit partner and reviewing partner must rotate off each assignment every five years. This rotation is aimed at preventing them from establishing unduly close relationships with the management officers they are auditing. Other rules apply to lawyers representing public companies and require them to blow the whistle on their clients when they determine a client is engaged in illegal behavior.

CORPORATE ETHICAL CODES

Sarbanes-Oxley also contains provisions for corporate ethical codes. A company regulated by the SEC must report whether it has established an ethical code governing high-level offi-

cers. The contents of that code must be publicly available. The NYSE similarly requires that each listed company adopt a code of conduct and ethics for its officers and post it on the company's Web site. This code of conduct and ethics must specifically prohibit self-dealing at the expense of shareholders. Of course, the code must also prohibit violations of the law.

IMPLICATIONS FOR THE BUSINESSPERSON

1. As more publicly traded corporations adopt internal control systems, persons working for public companies should be aware that their actions could be subjected to multiple levels of scrutiny, from both inside and outside the corporation.

2. Attorneys hired by public companies now have a duty to report their own clients' illegal conduct.

FOR CRITICAL ANALYSIS

1. Do you believe that audit and compensation committees will be effective in enhancing the directors' ability to monitor officers' actions? Why or why not?

2. How will the new requirements for certified financial disclosures be likely to affect who is selected to be an officer of the corporation?

RELEVANT WEB SITES

To locate information on the Web concerning the issues discussed in this feature, go to this text's Web site at **http://wleb.westbuslaw.com**, select "Chapter 28," and click on "Emerging Trends."

---

ing accounts. Additionally, no dividends may be paid from any source other than accumulated, undistributed net income.

SECTION 6 | State Securities Laws

Today, all states have their own corporate securities laws, or **blue sky laws,** that regulate the offer and sale of securities within individual state borders. (The phrase *blue sky laws* dates to a 1917 United States Supreme Court decision in which the Court declared that the purpose of such laws was to prevent "speculative schemes which have no more basis than

so many feet of 'blue sky.' "[39]) Article 8 of the Uniform Commercial Code, which has been adopted by all of the states, also imposes various requirements relating to the purchase and sale of securities.

REQUIREMENTS UNDER STATE SECURITIES LAWS

Despite some differences in philosophy, all state blue sky laws have certain features. Typically, state laws have disclosure requirements and antifraud provisions,

---

39. *Hall v. Geiger-Jones Co.*, 242 U.S. 539, 37 S.Ct. 217, 61 L.Ed. 480 (1917).

many of which are patterned after Section 10(b) of the Securities Exchange Act of 1934 and SEC Rule 10b-5. State laws also provide for the registration or qualification of securities offered or issued for sale within the state and impose disclosure requirements. Unless an exemption from registration is applicable, issuers must register or qualify their stock with the appropriate state official, often called a *corporations commissioner*. Additionally, most state securities laws regulate securities brokers and dealers. The Uniform Securities Act, which has been adopted in part by several states, was drafted to be acceptable to states with differing regulatory philosophies.

CONCURRENT REGULATION

State securities laws apply mainly to intrastate transactions. Since the adoption of the 1933 and 1934 federal securities acts, the state and federal governments have regulated securities concurrently. Issuers must comply with both federal and state securities laws, and exemptions from federal law are not necessarily exemptions from state laws.

The dual federal and state system has not always worked well, particularly during the early 1990s, when there was considerable expansion of the securities markets. In response, Congress passed the National Securities Markets Improvement Act of 1996, which preempted significant areas of state power to duplicate federal regulation. The National Conference of Commissioners on Uniform State Laws then substantially revised the Uniform Securities Act and recommended it to the states for adoption in 2002. Unlike the previous version of this law, the new act is designed to coordinate state and federal securities regulation and enforcement efforts. Since 2002, nine states have adopted the Uniform Securities Act, and several other states are considering adoption.[40]

SECTION 7 | Online Securities Offerings and Disclosures

The Spring Street Brewing Company, headquartered in New York, made history when it became the first company to attempt to sell securities via the Internet.

Through its online *initial public offering* (IPO), which ended in early 1996, Spring Street raised about $1.6 million—without having to pay any commissions to brokers or underwriters. The offering was made pursuant to Regulation A, which, as mentioned earlier in this chapter, allows small-business issuers to use a simplified registration procedure.

Such online IPOs are particularly attractive to small companies and start-up ventures that may find it difficult to raise capital from institutional investors or through underwriters. By making the offering online under Regulation A, the company can avoid both commissions and the costly and time-consuming filings required for a traditional IPO under federal and state law.

Clearly, technological advances have affected the securities industry—and securities law—just as they have affected other areas of the law. Investors can now use the Internet to access information that can help them make informed decisions. The SEC's EDGAR (Electronic Data Gathering, Analysis, and Retrieval) database includes IPOs, proxy statements, annual corporate reports, registration statements, and other documents that have been filed with the commission. (See this chapter's *Law on the Web* section for instructions on how to access the EDGAR database.)

REGULATIONS GOVERNING ONLINE SECURITIES OFFERINGS

One of the early questions posed by online offerings was whether the delivery of securities *information* via the Internet met the requirements of the 1933 Securities Act, which traditionally were applied to the delivery of paper documents. In an interpretative release issued in 1995, the SEC stated that "[t]he use of electronic media should be at least an equal alternative to the use of paper-based media" and that anything that can be delivered in paper form under the current securities laws might also be delivered in electronic form.[41] For example, a prospectus in downloadable form will meet SEC requirements.

Basically, there has been no change in the substantive law of disclosure; only the delivery vehicle has changed. When the Internet is used to deliver a

---

40. At the time this book went to press, the 2002 version of the Uniform Securities Act had been adopted in Idaho, Iowa, Kansas, Maine, Missouri, Oklahoma, South Carolina, South Dakota, and Vermont, as well as in the U.S. Virgin Islands. Adoption legislation was pending in Alabama, Alaska, Hawaii, and Nebraska. You can find current information on state adoptions at **http://www.nccusl.org**.

41. "Use of Electronic Media for Delivery Purposes," Securities Act Release No. 33-7233 (October 6, 1995). The rules governing the use of electronic transmissions for delivery purposes were subsequently confirmed in Securities Act Release No. 33-7289 (May 9, 1996) and expanded in Securities Act Release No. 33-7856 (April 28, 2000).

prospectus, the same rules apply as for the delivery of a paper prospectus. Once the following three requirements have been satisfied, the prospectus has been successfully delivered.

1. *Timely and adequate notice of the delivery of information is required.* Hosting a prospectus on a Web site does not constitute adequate notice, but separate e-mails or even postcards stating the URL where the prospectus can be viewed will satisfy the SEC's notice requirements.

2. *The online communication system must be easily accessible.* This is very simple to do today because virtually anyone interested in purchasing securities has access to the Web.

3. *Some evidence of delivery must be created.* This requirement is relatively easy to satisfy. Those making online offerings can require an e-mail return receipt verification of any materials sent electronically.

POTENTIAL LIABILITY CREATED BY ONLINE OFFERING MATERIALS

All printed prospectuses indicate that only the information given in the prospectuses can be used to make an investment decision about the securities offered. The same wording, of course, appears on Web-based offerings. Those who create such Web-based offerings may be tempted to go one step further—they may include hyperlinks to other sites that have analyzed the future prospects of the company, the products and services sold by the company, or the offering itself. To avoid potential liability, however, online offerors (the entities making the offerings) need to exercise caution when including such hyperlinks.

Suppose that a hyperlink goes to an analyst's Web page on which there are optimistic statements concerning the financial outlook of the offering company. Further suppose that after the IPO, the stock price falls. By including the hyperlink on its Web site, the offering company is impliedly supporting the information presented on the linked page. In such a situation, the company may be liable under federal securities laws.[42]

Potential problems may also occur with some Regulation D offerings, if the offeror places the offering circular on its Web site for general consumption by anybody on the Internet. Because Regulation D offerings are private placements, general solicitation is restricted. If anyone can have access to the offering circular on the Web, the Regulation D exemption may be disqualified.

ONLINE SECURITIES OFFERINGS BY FOREIGN COMPANIES

Online securities offerings by foreign companies may also present difficulties. Traditionally, foreign companies have been unable to offer new shares to the U.S. public unless they first register them with the SEC. Today, however, anybody in the world can offer shares of stock globally via the Web.

The SEC asks that foreign issuers on the Internet implement measures to warn U.S. investors. For example, a foreign company offering shares of stock on the Internet must include a disclaimer on its Web site stating that it has not gone through the registration procedure in the United States. If the SEC believes that a Web site's offering of foreign securities has been targeted at U.S. residents, it will pursue that company in an attempt to require it to register in the United States.[43]

ONLINE SECURITIES FRAUD

The Internet, of course, has also been used to commit fraud. A major problem facing the SEC today is how to enforce the antifraud provisions of the securities laws in the online environment. In 1999, in the first cases involving illegal online securities offerings, the SEC filed suit against three individuals for illegally offering securities on an Internet auction site.[44] In essence, all three indicated that their companies would soon go public and attempted to sell unregistered securities via the Web auction site. All of these actions were in violation of Sections 5, 17(a)(1), and 17(a)(3) of the 1933 Securities Act. Since then, the SEC has brought a variety of Internet-related fraud cases, including cases involving investment scams and the manipulation of stock prices in Internet chat rooms.

INVESTMENT SCAMS An ongoing concern for the SEC is how to curb investment scams. One fraudulent investment scheme involved twenty thousand investors, who lost, in all, more than $3 million. Some

---

42. See, for example, *In re Syntec Corp. Securities Litigation*, 95 F.3d. 922 (9th Cir. 1996).

43. International Series Release No. 1125 (March 23, 1998).
44. *In re Davis*, SEC Administrative File No. 3-10080 (October 20, 1999); *In re Haas*, SEC Administrative File No. 3-10081 (October 20, 1999); and *In re Sitaras*, SEC Administrative File No. 3-10082 (October 20, 1999).

cases have involved false claims about the earnings potential of home-business programs, such as the claim that one could "earn $4,000 or more each month." Others have concerned claims of "guaranteed credit repair."

USING CHAT ROOMS TO MANIPULATE STOCK PRICES

"Pumping and dumping" occurs when a person who has purchased a particular stock heavily promotes ("pumps up") that stock—thereby creating a great demand for it and driving up its price—and then sells ("dumps") it. The practice of pumping up a stock and then dumping it is quite old. In the online world, however, the process can occur much more quickly and efficiently.

The most famous case in this area involved Jonathan Lebed, a fifteen-year-old stock trader and Internet user from New Jersey. Lebed was the first minor ever charged with securities fraud by the SEC, but he is unlikely to be the last. The SEC charged that Lebed bought thinly traded stocks. After purchasing a stock, he would flood stock-related chat rooms, particularly at Yahoo's finance boards, with messages touting the stock's virtues. He used numerous false names so that no one would know that a single person was posting the messages. He would say that the stock was the most "undervalued stock in history" and that its price would jump by 1,000 percent "very soon." When other investors bought the stock, the price would go up quickly, and Lebed would then sell out. The SEC forced the teenager to repay almost $300,000 in gains plus interest. He was allowed, however, to keep about $500,000 of the profits he made trading small-company stocks that he also touted on the Internet.

The SEC has been bringing an increasing number of cases against those who manipulate stock prices in this way. Consider that in 1995, such fraud resulted in only six SEC cases. By 2005, the SEC had brought over two hundred actions against online perpetrators of fraudulent stock-price manipulation.

REVIEWING INVESTOR PROTECTION AND CORPORATE GOVERNANCE

Dale Emerson served as the chief financial officer for Reliant Electric Co., a distributor of electricity serving portions of Montana and North Dakota. Reliant was in the final stages of planning a takeover of Dakota Gasworks, Inc., a natural gas distributor that operated solely within North Dakota. Emerson went on a weekend fishing trip with his uncle, Ernest Wallace. Emerson mentioned to Wallace that he had been putting in a lot of extra hours at the office planning a takeover of Dakota Gasworks. On returning from the fishing trip, Wallace met with a broker from Chambers Investments and purchased $20,000 of Reliant stock. Three weeks later, Reliant made a tender offer to Dakota Gasworks stockholders and purchased 57 percent of Dakota Gasworks stock. Over the next two weeks, the price of Reliant stock rose 72 percent before leveling out. Wallace then sold his Reliant stock for a gross profit of $14,400. Using the information presented in the chapter, answer the following questions.

1. Would registration with the SEC be required for Dakota Gasworks securities? Why or why not? List three types of transactions that would qualify as exempt from SEC registration.

2. Did Emerson violate any of the laws discussed in this chapter? Why or why not? Did he violate any legal duty? If so, to whom did he owe a duty?

3. Which securities law or laws might Wallace have violated? According to what theory? Explain.

4. Suppose that Reliant's directors chose to offer its stock for sale via the Internet. What would be some advantages of this procedure? How might an investor go about accessing information about Reliant's stock via the Internet?

TERMS AND CONCEPTS TO REVIEW

accredited investor 649

blue sky laws 663

bounty payment 658

corporate governance 658

insider trading 651

investment company 661

mutual fund 661

red herring 647

SEC Rule 10b-5 651

stock options 659

tippee 654

tombstone ad 647

QUESTIONS AND CASE PROBLEMS

28-1. A corporation incorporated and doing business in Florida, Estrada Hermanos, Inc., decides to sell $1 million worth of its no-par-value common stock to the public. The stock will be sold only within the state of Florida. José Estrada, the chairman of the board, says the offering need not be registered with the Securities and Exchange Commission. His brother, Gustavo, disagrees. Who is right? Explain.

28-2. **QUESTION WITH SAMPLE ANSWER**
Huron Corp. has 300,000 common shares outstanding. The owners of these outstanding shares live in several different states. Huron has decided to split the 300,000 shares two for one. Will Huron Corp. have to file a registration statement and prospectus on the 300,000 new shares to be issued as a result of the split? Explain.
For a sample answer to this question, go to Appendix I at the end of this text.

28-3. SEC RULE 10b-5. Louis Ferraro was the chairman and president of Anacomp, Inc. In June 1988, Ferraro told his good friend Michael Maio that Anacomp was negotiating a tender offer for stock in Xidex Corp. Maio passed on the information to Patricia Ladavac, a friend of both Ferraro and Maio. Maio and Ladavac immediately purchased shares in Xidex stock. On the day that the tender offer was announced—an announcement that caused the price of Xidex shares to increase—Maio and Ladavac sold their Xidex stock and made substantial profits (Maio made $211,000 from the transactions, and Ladavac gained $78,750). The Securities and Exchange Commission (SEC) brought an action against the three individuals, alleging that they had violated, among other laws, SEC Rule 10b-5. Maio and Ladavac claimed that they had done nothing illegal. They argued that they had no fiduciary duty either to Anacomp or to Xidex, and therefore they had no duty to disclose or abstain from trading in the stock of those corporations. Had Maio and Ladavac violated SEC Rule 10b-5? Discuss fully. [*SEC v. Maio*, 51 F.3d 623 (7th Cir. 1995)]

28-4. SECTION 10(b). Joseph Jett worked for Kidder, Peabody & Co., a financial services firm owned by General Electric Co. (GE). Over a three-year period, Jett allegedly engaged in a scheme to generate false profits at Kidder, Peabody to increase his performance-based bonuses. When the scheme was discovered, Daniel Chill and other GE shareholders who had bought stock in the previous year filed a suit in a federal district court against GE. The shareholders alleged that GE had engaged in securities fraud in violation of Section 10(b). They claimed that GE's interest in justifying its investment in Kidder, Peabody gave GE "a motive to willfully blind itself to facts casting doubt on Kidder's purported profitability." On what basis might the court dismiss the shareholders' complaint? Discuss fully. [*Chill v. General Electric Co.*, 101 F.3d 263 (2d Cir. 1996)]

28-5. SEC RULE 10b-5. Grand Metropolitan PLC (Grand Met) planned to make a tender offer as part of an attempted takeover of the Pillsbury Company. Grand Met hired Robert Falbo, an independent contractor, to complete electrical work as part of security renovations to its offices to prevent leaks of information concerning the planned tender offer. Falbo was given a master key to access the executive offices. When an executive secretary told Falbo that a takeover was brewing, he used his key to access the offices and eavesdrop on conversations to learn that Pillsbury was the target. Falbo bought thousands of shares of Pillsbury stock for less than $40 per share. Within two months, Grand Met made an offer for all outstanding Pillsbury stock at $60 per share and ultimately paid up to $66 per share. Falbo made over $165,000 in profit. The Securities and Exchange Commission (SEC) filed a suit in a federal district court against Falbo and others for alleged violations of, among other things, SEC Rule 10b-5. Under what theory might Falbo be liable? Do the circumstances of this case meet all of the requirements for liability under that theory? Explain. [*SEC v. Falbo*, 14 F.Supp.2d 508 (S.D.N.Y. 1998)]

28-6. DEFINITION OF A SECURITY. In 1997, Scott and Sabrina Levine formed Friendly Power Co. (FPC) and Friendly Power Franchise Co. (FPC-Franchise). FPC obtained a license to operate as a utility company in California. FPC granted FPC-Franchise the right to pay commissions to "operators" who converted residential customers to FPC. Each operator paid for a "franchise"— a geographic area, determined by such factors as the number of households and competition from other utilities. In exchange for 50 percent of FPC's net profits on sales to residential customers in its territory, each franchise was required to maintain a 5 percent market share of power customers in that territory. Franchises were sold to telemarketing firms, which solicited customers. The telemarketers sold interests in each franchise to between fifty and ninety-four "partners," each of whom invested funds. FPC began supplying electricity to its customers in May 1998. Less than three months later, the Securities and Exchange Commission (SEC) filed a suit in a federal district court against the Levines and others, alleging that the "franchises" were unregistered securities offered for sale to the public in violation of the Securities Act of 1933. What is the definition of a security? Should the court rule in favor of the SEC? Why or why not? [*SEC v. Friendly Power Co., LLC*, 49 F.Supp.2d 1363 (S.D.Fla. 1999)]

28–7. ⚖️ CASE PROBLEM WITH SAMPLE ANSWER

Scott Ginsburg was chief executive officer (CEO) of Evergreen Media Corp., which owned and operated radio stations. In 1996, Evergreen became interested in acquiring EZ Communications, Inc., which also owned radio stations. To initiate negotiations, Ginsburg met with EZ's CEO, Alan Box, on Friday, July 12. Two days later, Scott phoned his brother Mark, who, on Monday, bought 3,800 shares of EZ stock. Mark discussed the deal with their father Jordan, who bought 20,000 EZ shares on Thursday. On July 25, the day before the EZ bid was due, Scott phoned his parents' home, and Mark bought another 3,200 EZ shares. The same routine was followed over the next few days, with Scott periodically phoning Mark or Jordan, both of whom continued to buy EZ shares. Evergreen's bid was refused, but on August 5, EZ announced its merger with another company. The price of EZ stock rose 30 percent, increasing the value of Mark and Jordan's shares by $664,024 and $412,875, respectively. The Securities and Exchange Commission (SEC) filed a civil suit in a federal district court against Scott. What was the most likely allegation? What is required to impose sanctions for this offense? Should the court hold Scott liable? Why or why not? [*SEC v. Ginsburg*, 362 F.3d 1292 (11th Cir. 2004)]

To view a sample answer for this case problem, go to this book's Web site at http://wleb.westbuslaw.com, select "Chapter 28," and click on "Case Problem with Sample Answer."

28–8. VIOLATIONS OF THE 1934 ACT. 2TheMart.com, Inc., was conceived in January 1999 to launch an auction Web site to compete with eBay, Inc. On January 19, 2TheMart announced that its Web site was in its "final development" stages and expected to be active by the end of July as a "preeminent" auction site, and that the company had "retained the services of leading Web site design and architecture consultants to design and construct" the site. Based on the announcement, investors rushed to buy 2TheMart's stock, causing a rapid increase in the price. On February 3, 2TheMart entered into an agreement with IBM to take preliminary steps to plan the site. Three weeks later, 2TheMart announced that the site was "currently in final development." On June 1, 2TheMart signed a contract with IBM to design, build, and test the site, with a target delivery date of October 8. When 2TheMart's site did not debut as announced, Mary Harrington and others who had bought the stock filed a suit in a federal district court against the firm's officers, alleging violations of the Securities Exchange Act of 1934. The defendants responded, in part, that any alleged misrepresentations were not material and asked the court to dismiss the suit. How should the court rule, and why? [*In re 2TheMart.com, Inc. Securities Litigation*, 114 F.Supp.2d 955 (C.D.Ca. 2000)]

28–9. INSIDER REPORTING AND TRADING. Ronald Bleakney, an officer at Natural Microsystems Corp. (NMC), a Section 12 corporation, directed NMC sales in North America, South America, and Europe. In November 1998, Bleakney sold more than 7,500 shares of NMC stock. The following March, Bleakney resigned from the firm, and the next month, he bought more than 20,000 shares of its stock. NMC provided some guidance to employees concerning the rules of insider trading, and with regard to Bleakney's transactions, the corporation said nothing about potential liability. Richard Morales, an NMC shareholder, filed a suit against NMC and Bleakney to compel recovery, under Section 16(b) of the Securities Exchange Act of 1934, of Bleakney's profits from the purchase and sale of his shares. (When Morales died, his executor Deborah Donoghue became the plaintiff.) Bleakney argued that he should not be liable because he relied on NMC's advice. Should the court order Bleakney to disgorge his profits? Explain. [*Donoghue v. Natural Microsystems Corp.*, 198 F.Supp.2d 487 (S.D.N.Y. 2002)]

28–10. VIDEO QUESTION

Go to this text's Web site at http://wleb.westbuslaw.com and select "Chapter 28." Click on "Video Questions" and view the video titled *Mergers and Acquisitions*. Then answer the following questions.

(a) Was the purchase of Onyx Advertising a material fact that the Quigley Company had a duty to disclose under SEC Rule 10b-5? Why or why not?

(b) Does it matter whether Quigley knew about or authorized the company spokesperson's statements? Why or why not?

(c) Which case discussed in the chapter presented issues that are very similar to those presented in the video? Under the holding of that case, would Onyx Advertising be able to maintain a suit against the Quigley Company for violation of SEC Rule 10b-5?

(d) Who else might be able to bring a suit against the Quigley Company for insider trading under SEC Rule 10b-5?

LAW | on the Web

For updated links to resources available on the Web, as well as a variety of other materials, visit this text's Web site at http://wleb.westbuslaw.com.

To access the SEC's EDGAR database, go to

http://www.sec.gov/edgar.shtml

The Center for Corporate Law at the University of Cincinnati College of Law examines many of the laws discussed in this chapter, including the Securities Act of 1933 and the Securities Exchange Act of 1934. Go to

http://www.law.uc.edu/CCL

LEGAL RESEARCH EXERCISES ON THE WEB

Go to http://wleb.westbuslaw.com, the Web site that accompanies this text. Select "Chapter 28" and click on "Internet Exercises." There you will find the following Internet research exercises that you can perform to learn more about topics covered in this chapter.

Activity 28–1: LEGAL PERSPECTIVE
Electronic Delivery

Activity 28–2: MANAGEMENT PERSPECTIVE
The SEC's Role

The Regulatory Environment

If this text had been written a hundred years ago, it would have had little to say about federal government regulation. Today, in contrast, virtually every area of economic activity is regulated by the government.

Essentially, government regulation brings two ethical principles into conflict. On the one hand, deeply embedded in American culture is the idea that the government should play a limited role in directing our lives. Indeed, this nation was founded so that Americans could be free from the "heavy hand of government" experienced by the colonists under British rule. On the other hand, one of the basic functions of government is to protect the welfare of individuals and the environment in which they live.

Ultimately, virtually every law or rule regulating business represents a decision to give up certain rights in order to protect other perceived rights. In this *Focus on Ethics* feature, we look at some of the ethical aspects of government regulation.

Telemarketing and Free Speech

A good example of the conflict between the rights of one group and that of another is the debate over the Do Not Call Registry. As noted in Chapter 23, in 2002 the Federal Trade Commission (FTC) amended the Telemarketing Sales Rule to establish a national "do-not-call" list. The rule became effective in 2003. The do-not-call list offered telephone users the option of registering their names with the FTC to protect themselves from unwanted phone solicitations.

Consumers versus Telemarketers Consumers, who had long complained about receiving unsolicited sales calls, welcomed the Do Not Call Registry and the reduced number of sales calls that they have received as a result. Indeed, respondents in one survey indicated that after the rule was implemented, their unwanted phone calls decreased from an average of thirty calls per month to only six calls per month.

Telemarketers, in contrast, have strongly objected to the new rule. Business has sagged for numerous companies, causing jobs to be lost. Many firms have continued to contact individuals on the registry, making themselves vulnerable to fines of up to $11,000 for each phone number that they dial on the list.

The Free Speech Issue Soon after the do-not-call regulations became effective, a number of telemarketing firms filed lawsuits against the FTC. The firms claimed that the new rules abridged their commercial speech, which is protected under the First Amendment (see Chapter 5). A federal district court judge sided with the telemarketers, ruling that the FTC's rules were unconstitutional on First Amendment grounds.

On appeal, however, the U.S. Court of Appeals for the Tenth Circuit overturned the decision and outlined four reasons why the do-not-call list was consistent with First Amendment requirements. First, the registry restricts only "core commercial speech," such as sales calls. Second, the court stated that an individual's home is a personal sanctuary. Because the do-not-call list specifically targets speech that invades the privacy of the home, there is no breach of First Amendment rights. Third, the registry is an optional program that places the right to restrict commercial speech in the hands of consumers, not the government. Finally, the court concluded that the Do Not Call Registry "materially furthers the government's interests in combating the danger of abusive telemarketing and preventing the invasion of consumer privacy."[1]

Credit Reporting Agencies and "Blacklisting"

Today, some consumer credit reporting agencies will also investigate and report a person's litigation history online. Physicians and landlords frequently use such services to learn whether prospective patients or tenants have a prior history of suing their physicians or their landlords. One service, for example, allows physicians, for a fee, to perform over two hundred online name searches to find out if a person was a plaintiff in a previous malpractice suit.

Users say that these services are an ideal way to screen out undesirable patients and applicants and reduce the risk of being sued. Consumer rights advocates, however, claim that the sale of such information is akin to "blacklisting"— discriminating against potential patients or tenants on the basis of previous litigation history. Moreover, some agencies do not provide consumers with access to the reports. This means that physicians and landlords may obtain information about individuals' involvement in prior court proceedings without allowing the information to be challenged. In the last decade, these practices have led to complaints of unfairness as well as lawsuits against reporting agencies.

By and large, though, consumers have had little recourse if what is being reported about them is accurate. If the information being disseminated about a person by a reporting agency is false, however, that person will likely have a cause of action against the agency. Under the Fair Credit Reporting Act (FCRA) of 1970, companies that sell consumer information

---

1. *Mainstream Marketing Services, Inc. v. Federal Trade Commission,* 358 F.3d 1228 (10th Cir. 2004).

must report the information accurately and must provide a remedy for consumers who seek to dispute the information. If no remedy is provided, the agency will be in violation of the FCRA.[2]

Environmental Law

Questions of fairness inevitably arise in regard to environmental law. Has the government gone too far—or not far enough—in regulating businesses in the interest of protecting the environment? At what point do the costs of environmental regulations become too burdensome for society to bear?

Consider the problem of toxic waste. Although everybody is in favor of cleaning up America's toxic waste dumps, nobody has the slightest idea what this task will ultimately cost. Much of the problem in determining the eventual costs of the Comprehensive Environmental Response, Compensation, and Liability Act (CERCLA), commonly known as Superfund (see Chapter 24), stems from the difficulty of estimating the costs of cleaning up a site. Moreover, there is no agreed-on standard as to how clean a site must be before it no longer poses any threat. Must 100 percent of the contamination be removed, or would removal of some lesser amount achieve a reasonable degree of environmental quality?

Global Environmental Issues

Pollution does not respect geographic borders. Indeed, one of the reasons that the federal government became involved in environmental protection was that state regulation alone apparently could not solve the problem of air or water pollution. Pollutants generated in one state move in the air and water to other states. Neither does pollution respect national borders. Environmental issues, perhaps more than any others, bring home to everyone the fact that the world today is truly a global community. What one country does or does not do with respect to environmental preservation may be felt by citizens in countries thousands of miles away.

Cross-Border Pollution One issue that has come to the fore in recent years is cross-border pollution. On numerous occasions, beaches in San Diego, California, have been closed because of pollution originating in Mexico. Canada has complained for years about air pollution in that nation caused by sulfuric acid generated by coal-burning power plants in the United States. Examples similar to these can be found everywhere in the world. Countries have made various attempts to reduce cross-border pollution through treaties or other agreements, but it remains a challenging issue for virtually all nations.

---

2. See, for example, *Decker v. U.D. Registry, Inc.*, 105 Cal.App.4th 1382, 129 Cal.Rptr.2d 892 (2003).

Global Warming Another challenging—and controversial—issue is potential global warming. The fear is that emissions, largely from combustion of fossil fuels, will remain in the atmosphere and create a "greenhouse effect" by preventing heat from radiating outward. Concerns over this issue have led to many attempts to force all world polluters to "clean up their acts." For example, leaders of 160 nations have already agreed to reduce greenhouse emissions in their respective countries. They did this when they ratified the Kyoto Protocol, which was drawn up at a world summit meeting held in Kyoto, Japan, in 1997. The Kyoto Protocol, which is often referred to as the global warming treaty, established different rates of reduction in greenhouse emissions for different countries or regions. Most nations, however, including the United States, will not meet the treaty's objectives. Indeed, the Bush administration told the world in early 2001 that the treaty was a dead letter because it did not address the problem of curbing greenhouse gases from most of the developing world.

Is Economic Development the Answer? Economists have shown that economic development is the quickest way to reduce pollution worldwide. After a nation reaches a certain per capita income level, the more economic growth the nation experiences, the lower the pollution output. This occurs because richer nations have the resources to pay for pollution reduction. For example, the United States pollutes much less per unit of output than do developing nations—because we are willing to pay for pollution abatement.

Land-Use Regulations and the "Takings Clause"

Regulations to control land use, including environmental regulations, are prevalent throughout the United States. Generally, these laws reflect the public's interest in preserving natural resources and habitats for wildlife. At times, their goal is to enable the public to have access to and enjoy limited natural resources, such as coastal areas. Although few would disagree with the rationale underlying these laws, the owners of the private property directly affected by the laws often feel that they should be compensated for the limitations imposed on their right to do as they wish with their land.

Remember from Chapter 25 that the Fifth Amendment to the U.S. Constitution gives the government the power to "take" private property for public use. The Fifth Amendment attaches an important condition to this power, however: when private land is taken for public use, the landowner must be given "just compensation."

No General Rule In cases alleging that a "regulatory taking" has occurred, the courts have largely decided the issue on a case-by-case basis. In other words, there is no general rule that one can cite to indicate whether a specific situation will be deemed a taking. In one case, the city of Monterey, California, in the interests of protecting various forms of coastal wildlife, would not allow an owner of oceanfront property to build a residential development. In effect, the city's actions meant that the entire property had to be left in its natural state, thus making the owner's planned use of the land impossible. When the landowner challenged the city's action as an unconstitutional taking without compensation, the United States Supreme Court ultimately agreed, and the landowner had to be compensated.[3]

In another case, however, the Supreme Court held for the regulators. In an attempt to curb pollution in Lake Tahoe, located on the California-Nevada border, a regional government planning agency issued a moratorium on (a temporary suspension of) the construction of housing in certain areas around the lake. The moratorium was extended time and again until, some twenty years later, a number of landowners sued the agency. The landowners claimed that a regulatory taking had occurred for which they should be compensated. The Supreme Court disagreed. Because the agency's actions had not deprived the owners of their property for too long a time, no taking had occurred. How long was too long? The Court said that no categorical rule could be stated; the answer always depended on "the facts presented."[4]

A Question of Fairness The question of whether private landowners should be compensated when their land is essentially "taken" for public use by environmental and land-use regulations clearly involves issues of fairness. On the one hand, states, cities, and other local governments want to preserve their natural resources and need some authority to regulate land use to achieve this goal. On the other hand, private property owners complain that they alone should not have to bear the costs of creating a benefit, such as environmental preservation, given that all members of the public enjoy that benefit.

Antitrust Law—The Baseball Exemption

The fact that, until relatively recently, baseball remained totally exempt from antitrust laws not only seemed unfair to many but also defied logic: Why was an exemption made for baseball but not for other professional sports? The answer to this perfectly reasonable question has always been the same: baseball was exempt because the United States Supreme Court, in 1922, said that it was. The Court held that baseball was a sport played only locally by local players. Because the activity purportedly did not involve interstate commerce, it did not meet the requirement for federal jurisdiction.

The exemption was challenged in the early 1970s, but the Supreme Court ruled that it was up to Congress, not the Court, to overturn the exemption. In 1998, Congress did address the issue and passed the Curt Flood Act—named for the St. Louis Cardinals' star outfielder who challenged the exemption in the early 1970s. The act, however, did not invalidate the 1922 Supreme Court decision but only limited some of the effects of baseball's exempt status. Essentially, the act allows players the option of suing team owners for anticompetitive practices if, for example, the owners collude to "blacklist" players, hold down players' salaries, or force players to play for specific teams.

Baseball is still not subject to antitrust laws to the extent that football, basketball, and other professional sports are. Critics of the exemption argue that it should be completely abolished because it makes no sense to continue to treat an enterprise generating revenues of $3 billion a year as a "local" activity.

The Emergence of Corporate Governance

The well-publicized corporate abuses that took place in the last ten years have fueled the impetus for businesspersons to create their own internal rules for corporate governance (discussed in Chapter 28). In a few situations, officers have blatantly stolen from the corporation and its shareholders. More frequently, though, officers receive benefits or "perks" of office that are excessive. To illustrate: Tyco International bought a $6,000 shower curtain and a $15,000 umbrella stand for its CEO's apartment.

Corporate officers may be given numerous benefits that they may or may not deserve. A leading corporate officer can receive compensation of $50 million or more even when her or his company's share price is actually declining. Even if corporate officers are scrupulously honest and have modest personal tastes, their behavior may still raise concerns: they may not be good managers, and they may make incompetent corporate choices. They may be a little lazy and fail to do the hard work necessary to investigate corporate decisions. Alternatively, officers may simply fail to appreciate the concerns of shareholders on certain matters, such as maximizing short-term versus long-term results.

Corporate governance controls are meant to ensure that officers receive only the benefits they earn. Governance monitors the actions taken by officers to make sure they are wise and in the best interests of the company. In this way, the corporation can be confident that it is acting ethically toward its shareholders.

Insider Trading

As you learned in Chapter 28, SEC Rule 10b-5 has broad applicability. The rule covers not only corporate insiders but even "outsiders" who trade on tips received from insiders. Investigating and prosecuting violations of SEC Rule 10b-5 is

---

3. *City of Monterey v. Del Monte Dunes at Monterey, Ltd.*, 526 U.S. 687, 119 S.Ct. 1624, 143 L.Ed.2d 882 (1999). For a more recent case in which a court held that a taking had occurred, see *Vulcan Materials Co. v. The City of Tehuacana*, 369 F.3d 882 (5th Cir. 2004).
4. *Tahoe-Sierra Preservation Council v. Tahoe Regional Planning Agency*, 535 U.S. 302, 122 S.Ct. 1465, 152 L.Ed.2d 517 (2002).

costly, both for the government and for those accused of insider trading. Some people doubt that such extensive regulation is necessary and even contend that insider trading should be legal. Would there be any benefit from the legalization of insider trading?

To evaluate this question, review the facts in *SEC v. Texas Gulf Sulphur Co.* (Case 28.1 in Chapter 28). If insider trading were legal, the discovery of the ore sample would probably have caused many more company insiders to purchase stock. Consequently, the price of Texas Gulf's stock would have increased fairly quickly. These increases presumably would have attracted the attention of outside investors, who would have realized sooner that something positive had happened to the company and would thus have purchased the stock. The higher demand for the stock would have more quickly translated into higher prices for the stock and hence, perhaps, a more efficient capital market. Nonetheless, the SEC and the courts have routinely upheld the rule that insider trading is illegal.

The Sarbanes-Oxley Act and Insider Trading

The attorney-client privilege generally prevents lawyers from disclosing confidential client information—even when the client has committed an unlawful act. The idea is to encourage clients to be open and honest with their attorneys to ensure competent representation. The Sarbanes-Oxley Act of 2002, however, requires attorneys to report any material violations of securities laws to the corporation's highest authority. The act does not require that the lawyer break client confidences, though, because the lawyer is still reporting to officials within the corporation.

In August 2003, the SEC went one step further than the Sarbanes-Oxley Act to mandate a "noisy withdrawal"—that is, the SEC requires attorneys whose corporate clients are violating securities laws to publicly withdraw from representing the corporation and notify the SEC. This rule is controversial and has been the subject of much debate. Should the SEC be able to force lawyers to disclose privileged client information? Is it fair to the corporation? The American Bar Association (ABA) modified its ethics rules in 2003 to allow—but not require—attorneys to break confidence with a client to report possible corporate fraud. Nonetheless, compliance with the SEC rule is mandatory. In the SEC's view, lawyers owe a duty to the corporation and its investors, not to the individual officers and directors.[5]

DISCUSSION QUESTIONS

1. | Assume that removing all asbestos from all public buildings in the nation would save ten lives per year and that the cost of the asbestos removal would be $250 billion (or $25 billion per life saved). Is this too high a price to pay? Should cost ever be a consideration when human lives are at stake?

2. | Will the national Do Not Call Registry affect the way that business is conducted in this country? What types of businesses do you think will be the most adversely affected by the registry in the long run?

3. | Should credit reporting agencies be prohibited from releasing an individual's prior litigation history to a prospective physician or landlord? Even if such information is true and available in public court records, should the government restrict Web access to this information via reporting agencies? Why or why not?

4. | Do you believe that the law strikes a fair balance between the rights of landowners and the right of governments to control land use in the public interest? Why or why not?

5. | Three decades ago, corporations and corporate directors were rarely prosecuted for crimes, and penalties for corporate crimes were relatively light. Today, this is no longer true. Under the corporate sentencing guidelines and the Sarbanes-Oxley Act, corporate wrongdoers can receive strict penalties. Do these developments mean that corporations are committing more crimes today than in the past? Will stricter laws be effective in curbing corporate criminal activity? How can a company avoid liability for crimes committed by its employees?

---

5. See 17 C.F.R. Part 205.

Appendices

CONTENTS

How to Brief Cases and Analyze Case Problems

HOW TO BRIEF CASES

To fully understand the law with respect to business, you need to be able to read and understand court decisions. To make this task easier, you can use a method of case analysis that is called *briefing*. There is a fairly standard procedure that you can follow when you "brief" any court case. You must first read the case opinion carefully. When you feel you understand the case, you can prepare a brief of it.

Although the format of the brief may vary, typically it will present the essentials of the case under headings such as those listed below.

1. Citation. Give the full citation for the case, including the name of the case, the date it was decided, and the court that decided it.

2. Facts. Briefly indicate (a) the reasons for the lawsuit; (b) the identity and arguments of the plaintiff(s) and defendant(s), respectively; and (c) the lower court's decision—if appropriate.

3. Issue. Concisely phrase, in the form of a question, the essential issue before the court. (If more than one issue is involved, you may have two—or even more—questions here.)

4. Decision. Indicate here—with a "yes" or "no," if possible—the court's answer to the question (or questions) in the *Issue* section above.

5. Reason. Summarize as briefly as possible the reasons given by the court for its decision (or decisions) and the case or statutory law relied on by the court in arriving at its decision.

AN EXAMPLE OF A BRIEFED SAMPLE COURT CASE

As an example of the format used in briefing cases, we present here a briefed version of the sample court case that was presented in Chapter 1 in Exhibit 1–6.

D.A.B.E., INC. v. CITY OF TOLEDO
United States Court of Appeals,
Sixth Circuit, 2005.
393 F.3d 692.

FACTS The city of Toledo, Ohio, has regulated smoking in public places since 1987. In 2003, Toledo's city council enacted a new Clean Indoor Air Ordinance. The ordinance restricts the ability to smoke in public places—stores, theaters, courtrooms, libraries, museums, health-care facilities, restaurants, and bars. In enclosed public places, smoking is generally prohibited except in a "separate smoking lounge" that is designated for this purpose. D.A.B.E., Inc., a group consisting of the owners of bars, restaurants, and bowling alleys, filed a suit in a federal district court, claiming that the ordinance constituted a taking of their property in violation of the Fifth Amendment to the U.S. Constitution. The plaintiffs also argued that the ordinance was preempted (prevented from taking effect) by a state statute that regulated smoking "in places of public assembly," excluding restaurants, bowling alleys, and bars. The court ruled in favor of the city. The plaintiffs appealed to the U.S. Court of Appeals for the Sixth Circuit.

ISSUE Does the ordinance deny the plaintiffs "economically viable use of their property," as required to prove a taking? Does a state indoor smoking statute preempt the city ordinance?

DECISION No, to both questions. The U.S. Court of Appeals for the Sixth Circuit affirmed the lower court's ruling. The ordinance did not prevent the beneficial use of the plaintiffs' property, because it did not categorically prohibit smoking, but only regulated it. The state indoor smoking statute did not cover the excluded businesses, and the legislature did not indicate an intent to bar a city from restricting smoking in those places.

REASON The Fifth Amendment provides that private property shall not "be taken for public use, without just compensation." A taking occurs when an ordinance denies an owner economically viable use of his or her property. In this case, the plaintiffs alleged that they lost customers because of the ordinance. The court reasoned that the ordinance's only effect on the plaintiffs' businesses is to restrict the areas in which customers can smoke and the conditions under which smoking is permitted. This might "require some financial investment, but an ordinance does not effect a taking merely because compliance with it requires the expenditure of money." Besides, the owners could elect to make other uses of their property. As for the preemption issue, a state statute takes precedence over a local ordinance when they conflict. In this case, a statute prohibits smoking in certain locations, but "it does not contain the slightest hint that the legislature intended to create a positive right to smoke in all public places where it did not expressly forbid smoking. Nothing in the [statute] is inconsistent with a local jurisdiction's decision to impose greater limits on public smoking."

REVIEW OF SAMPLE COURT CASE

Here we provide a review of the briefed version to indicate the kind of information that is contained in each section.

CITATION The name of the case is *D.A.B.E., Inc. v. City of Toledo*. D.A.B.E. is the plaintiff; Toledo is the defendant. The U.S. Court of Appeals for the Sixth Circuit decided this case in 2005. The citation states that this case can be found in volume 393 the *Federal Reporter, Third Series*, on page 692.

FACTS The *Facts* section identifies the plaintiff and the defendant, describes the events leading up to this suit, the allegations made by the plaintiff in the initial suit, and (because this case is an appellate court decision) the lower court's ruling and the party appealing this ruling. The appellant's contention on appeal is also sometimes included here.

ISSUE The *Issue* section presents the central issue (or issues) decided by the court. In this case, the U.S. Court of Appeals for the Sixth Circuit considers whether the ordinance constitutes a taking in violation of the Fifth Amendment and whether a state statute preempts (or supersedes) the city ordinance.

DECISION The *Decision* section includes the court's decision on the issues before it. The decision reflects the opinion of the judge or justice hearing the case. Decisions by appellate courts are frequently phrased in reference to the lower court's decision; that is, the appellate court may "affirm" the lower court's ruling or "reverse" it. Here, the court determined that the ordinance did not effect a taking because it did not prevent the plaintiffs' beneficial use of their property. The statute did not preempt the ordinance because the legislature did not indicate an intent to prohibit a city from restricting smoking in places excluded from the statute. The court affirmed the lower court's ruling.

REASON The *Reason* section includes references to the relevant laws and legal principles that the court applied in arriving at its conclusion in the case. The relevant law here included the Fifth Amendment, the state indoor smoking statute, and the principles derived from judicial interpretations and applications of those laws. This section also explains the court's application of the law to the facts in this case.

ANALYZING CASE PROBLEMS

In addition to learning how to brief cases, students of business law and the legal environment also find it helpful to know how to analyze case problems. Part of the study of business law and the legal environment usually involves analyzing case problems, such as those included in this text at the end of each chapter.

For each case problem in this book, we provide the relevant background and facts of the lawsuit and the issue before the court. When you are assigned one of these problems, your job will be to determine how the court should decide the issue, and why. In other words, you will need to engage in legal analysis and reasoning. Here we offer some suggestions on how to make this task less daunting. We begin by presenting a sample problem:

> While Janet Lawson, a famous pianist, was shopping in Quality Market, she slipped and fell on a wet floor in one of the aisles. The floor had recently been mopped by one of the store's employees, but there were no signs warning customers that the floor in that area was wet. As a result of the fall, Lawson injured her right arm and was unable to perform piano concerts for the next six months. Had she been able to perform the scheduled concerts, she would have earned approximately $60,000 over that period of time. Lawson sued Quality Market for this amount, plus another $10,000 in medical expenses. She claimed that the store's failure to warn customers of the wet floor constituted negligence and therefore the market was liable for her injuries. Will the court agree with Lawson? Discuss.

UNDERSTAND THE FACTS

This may sound obvious, but before you can analyze or apply the relevant law to a specific set of facts, you must clearly understand those facts. In other words, you should read through the case problem carefully—more than once, if necessary—to make sure you understand the identity of the plaintiff(s) and defendant(s) in the case and the progression of events that led to the lawsuit.

In the sample case just given, the identity of the parties is fairly obvious. Janet Lawson is the one bringing the suit; therefore, she is the plaintiff. Quality Market, against whom she is bringing the suit, is the defendant. Some of the case problems you may work on have multiple plaintiffs or defendants. Often, it is helpful to use abbreviations for the parties. To indicate a reference to a plaintiff, for example, the *pi* symbol—π—is often used, and a defendant is denoted by a *delta*—Δ—a triangle.

The events leading to the lawsuit are also fairly straightforward. Lawson slipped and fell on a wet floor, and she contends that Quality Market should be liable for her injuries because it was negligent in not posting a sign warning customers of the wet floor.

When you are working on case problems, realize that the facts should be accepted as they are given. For example, in our sample problem, it should be accepted that the floor was wet and that there was no sign. In other words, avoid making conjectures, such as "Maybe

the floor wasn't too wet," or "Maybe an employee was getting a sign to put up," or "Maybe someone stole the sign." Questioning the facts as they are presented only adds confusion to your analysis.

LEGAL ANALYSIS AND REASONING

Once you understand the facts given in the case problem, you can begin to analyze the case. Recall from Chapter 1 that the IRAC method is a helpful tool to use in the legal analysis and reasoning process. IRAC is an acronym for Issue, Rule, Application, Conclusion. Applying this method to our sample problem would involve the following steps:

1. First, you need to decide what legal **issue** is involved in the case. In our sample case, the basic issue is whether Quality Market's failure to warn customers of the wet floor constituted negligence. As discussed in Chapter 12, negligence is a *tort*—a civil wrong. In a tort lawsuit, the plaintiff seeks to be compensated for another's wrongful act. A defendant will be deemed negligent if he or she breached a duty of care owed to the plaintiff and the breach of that duty caused the plaintiff to suffer harm.

2. Once you have identified the issue, the next step is to determine what **rule of law** applies to the issue. To make this determination, you will want to review carefully the text of the chapter in which the problem appears to find the relevant rule of law. Our sample case involves the tort of negligence, covered in Chapter 12. The applicable rule of law is the tort law principle that business owners owe a duty to exercise reasonable care to protect their customers ("business invitees"). Reasonable care, in this context, includes either removing—or warning customers of—*foreseeable* risks about which the owner *knew* or *should have known*. Business owners need not warn customers of "open and obvious" risks, however. If a business owner breaches this duty of care (fails to exercise the appropriate degree of care toward customers), and the breach of duty causes a customer to be injured, the business owner will be liable to the customer for the customer's injuries.

3. The next—and usually the most difficult—step in analyzing case problems is the **application** of the relevant rule of law to the specific facts of the case you are studying. In our sample problem, applying the tort law principle just discussed presents few difficulties. An employee of the store had mopped the floor in the aisle where Lawson slipped and fell, but no sign was present indicating that the floor was wet. That a customer might fall on a wet floor is clearly a foreseeable risk. Therefore, the failure to warn customers about the wet floor was a breach of the duty of care owed by the business owner to the store's customers.

4. Once you have completed step 3 in the IRAC method, you should be ready to draw your **conclusion.** In our sample case, Quality Market is liable to Lawson for her injuries, because the market's breach of its duty of care caused Lawson's injuries.

The fact patterns in the case problems presented in this text are not always as simple as those presented in our sample problem. Often, for example, there may be more than one plaintiff or defendant. There also may be more than one issue involved in a case and more than one applicable rule of law. Furthermore, in some case problems the facts may indicate that the general rule of law should not apply. For example, suppose a store employee advised Lawson not to walk on the floor in the aisle because it was wet, but Lawson decided to walk on it anyway. This fact could alter the outcome of the case because the store could then raise the defense of assumption of risk (see Chapter 12). Nonetheless, a careful review of the chapter should always provide you with the knowledge you need to analyze the problem thoroughly and arrive at accurate conclusions.

The Constitution of the United States

PREAMBLE

We the People of the United States, in Order to form a more perfect Union, establish Justice, insure domestic Tranquility, provide for the common defence, promote the general Welfare, and secure the Blessings of Liberty to ourselves and our Posterity, do ordain and establish this Constitution for the United States of America.

ARTICLE I

Section 1. All legislative Powers herein granted shall be vested in a Congress of the United States, which shall consist of a Senate and House of Representatives.

Section 2. The House of Representatives shall be composed of Members chosen every second Year by the People of the several States, and the Electors in each State shall have the Qualifications requisite for Electors of the most numerous Branch of the State Legislature.

No Person shall be a Representative who shall not have attained to the Age of twenty five Years, and been seven Years a Citizen of the United States, and who shall not, when elected, be an Inhabitant of that State in which he shall be chosen.

Representatives and direct Taxes shall be apportioned among the several States which may be included within this Union, according to their respective Numbers, which shall be determined by adding to the whole Number of free Persons, including those bound to Service for a Term of Years, and excluding Indians not taxed, three fifths of all other Persons. The actual Enumeration shall be made within three Years after the first Meeting of the Congress of the United States, and within every subsequent Term of ten Years, in such Manner as they shall by Law direct. The Number of Representatives shall not exceed one for every thirty Thousand, but each State shall have at Least one Representative; and until such enumeration shall be made, the State of New Hampshire shall be entitled to chuse three, Massachusetts eight, Rhode Island and Providence Plantations one, Connecticut five, New York six, New Jersey four, Pennsylvania eight, Delaware one, Maryland six, Virginia ten, North Carolina five, South Carolina five, and Georgia three.

When vacancies happen in the Representation from any State, the Executive Authority thereof shall issue Writs of Election to fill such Vacancies.

The House of Representatives shall chuse their Speaker and other Officers; and shall have the sole Power of Impeachment.

Section 3. The Senate of the United States shall be composed of two Senators from each State, chosen by the Legislature thereof, for six Years; and each Senator shall have one Vote.

Immediately after they shall be assembled in Consequence of the first Election, they shall be divided as equally as may be into three Classes. The Seats of the Senators of the first Class shall be vacated at the Expiration of the second Year, of the second Class at the Expiration of the fourth Year, and of the third Class at the Expiration of the sixth Year, so that one third may be chosen every second Year; and if Vacancies happen by Resignation, or otherwise, during the Recess of the Legislature of any State, the Executive thereof may make temporary Appointments until the next Meeting of the Legislature, which shall then fill such Vacancies.

No Person shall be a Senator who shall not have attained to the Age of thirty Years, and been nine Years a Citizen of the United States, and who shall not, when elected, be an Inhabitant of that State for which he shall be chosen.

The Vice President of the United States shall be President of the Senate, but shall have no Vote, unless they be equally divided.

The Senate shall chuse their other Officers, and also a President pro tempore, in the Absence of the Vice President, or when he shall exercise the Office of President of the United States.

The Senate shall have the sole Power to try all Impeachments. When sitting for that Purpose, they shall be on Oath or Affirmation. When the President of the United States is tried, the Chief Justice shall preside: And no Person shall be convicted without the Concurrence of two thirds of the Members present.

Judgment in Cases of Impeachment shall not extend further than to removal from Office, and disqualification to hold and enjoy any Office of honor, Trust, or Profit under the United States: but the Party convicted shall nevertheless be liable and subject to Indictment, Trial, Judgment, and Punishment, according to Law.

Section 4. The Times, Places and Manner of holding Elections for Senators and Representatives, shall be prescribed in each State by the Legislature thereof; but the Congress may at any time by Law make or alter such Regulations, except as to the Places of chusing Senators.

The Congress shall assemble at least once in every Year, and such Meeting shall be on the first Monday in December, unless they shall by Law appoint a different Day.

Section 5. Each House shall be the Judge of the Elections, Returns, and Qualifications of its own Members, and a Majority of each shall constitute a Quorum to do Business; but a smaller Number may adjourn from day to day, and may be authorized to compel the Attendance of absent Members, in such Manner, and under such Penalties as each House may provide.

Each House may determine the Rules of its Proceedings, punish its Members for disorderly Behavior, and, with the Concurrence of two thirds, expel a Member.

Each House shall keep a Journal of its Proceedings, and from time to time publish the same, excepting such Parts as may in their Judgment require Secrecy; and the Yeas and Nays of the Members of either House on any question shall, at the Desire of one fifth of those Present, be entered on the Journal.

Neither House, during the Session of Congress, shall, without the Consent of the other, adjourn for more than three days, nor to any other Place than that in which the two Houses shall be sitting.

Section 6. The Senators and Representatives shall receive a Compensation for their Services, to be ascertained by Law, and paid out of the Treasury of the United States. They shall in all Cases, except Treason, Felony and Breach of the Peace, be privileged from Arrest during their Attendance at the Session of their respective Houses, and in going to and returning from the same; and for any Speech or Debate in either House, they shall not be questioned in any other Place.

No Senator or Representative shall, during the Time for which he was elected, be appointed to any civil Office under the Authority of the United States, which shall have been created, or the Emoluments whereof shall have been increased during such time; and no Person holding any Office under the United States, shall be a Member of either House during his Continuance in Office.

Section 7. All Bills for raising Revenue shall originate in the House of Representatives; but the Senate may propose or concur with Amendments as on other Bills.

Every Bill which shall have passed the House of Representatives and the Senate, shall, before it become a Law, be presented to the President of the United States; If he approve he shall sign it, but if not he shall return it, with his Objections to the House in which it shall have originated, who shall enter the Objections at large on their Journal, and proceed to reconsider it. If after such Reconsideration two thirds of that House shall agree to pass the Bill, it shall be sent together with the Objections, to the other House, by which it shall likewise be reconsidered, and if approved by two thirds of that House, it shall become a Law. But in all such Cases the Votes of both Houses shall be determined by Yeas and Nays, and the Names of the Persons voting for and against the Bill shall be entered on the Journal of each House respectively. If any Bill shall not be returned by the President within ten Days (Sundays excepted) after it shall have been presented to him, the Same shall be a Law, in like Manner as if he had signed it, unless the Congress by their Adjournment prevent its Return in which Case it shall not be a Law.

Every Order, Resolution, or Vote, to which the Concurrence of the Senate and House of Representatives may be necessary (except on a question of Adjournment) shall be presented to the President of the United States; and before the Same shall take Effect, shall be approved by him, or being disapproved by him, shall be repassed by two thirds of the Senate and House of Representatives, according to the Rules and Limitations prescribed in the Case of a Bill.

Section 8. The Congress shall have Power To lay and collect Taxes, Duties, Imposts and Excises, to pay the Debts and provide for the common Defence and general Welfare of the United States; but all Duties, Imposts and Excises shall be uniform throughout the United States;

To borrow Money on the credit of the United States;

To regulate Commerce with foreign Nations, and among the several States, and with the Indian Tribes;

To establish an uniform Rule of Naturalization, and uniform Laws on the subject of Bankruptcies throughout the United States;

To coin Money, regulate the Value thereof, and of foreign Coin, and fix the Standard of Weights and Measures;

To provide for the Punishment of counterfeiting the Securities and current Coin of the United States;

To establish Post Offices and post Roads;

To promote the Progress of Science and useful Arts, by securing for limited Times to Authors and Inventors the exclusive Right to their respective Writings and Discoveries;

To constitute Tribunals inferior to the supreme Court;

To define and punish Piracies and Felonies committed on the high Seas, and Offenses against the Law of Nations;

To declare War, grant Letters of Marque and Reprisal, and make Rules concerning Captures on Land and Water;

To raise and support Armies, but no Appropriation of Money to that Use shall be for a longer Term than two Years;

To provide and maintain a Navy;

To make Rules for the Government and Regulation of the land and naval Forces;

To provide for calling forth the Militia to execute the Laws of the Union, suppress Insurrections and repel Invasions;

To provide for organizing, arming, and disciplining, the Militia, and for governing such Part of them as may be employed in the Service of the United States, reserving to the States respectively, the Appointment of the Officers, and the Authority of training the Militia according to the discipline prescribed by Congress;

To exercise exclusive Legislation in all Cases whatsoever, over such District (not exceeding ten Miles square) as may, by Cession of particular States, and the Acceptance of Congress, become the Seat of the Government of the United States, and to exercise like Authority over all Places purchased by the Consent of the Legislature of the State in which the Same shall be, for the Erection of Forts, Magazines, Arsenals, dock-Yards, and other needful Buildings;—And

To make all Laws which shall be necessary and proper for carrying into Execution the foregoing Powers, and all other Powers vested by this Constitution in the Government of the United States, or in any Department or Officer thereof.

Section 9. The Migration or Importation of such Persons as any of the States now existing shall think proper to admit, shall not be prohibited by the Congress prior to the Year one thousand eight hundred and eight, but a Tax or duty may be imposed on such Importation, not exceeding ten dollars for each Person.

The privilege of the Writ of Habeas Corpus shall not be suspended, unless when in Cases of Rebellion or Invasion the public Safety may require it.

No Bill of Attainder or ex post facto Law shall be passed.

No Capitation, or other direct, Tax shall be laid, unless in Proportion to the Census or Enumeration herein before directed to be taken.

No Tax or Duty shall be laid on Articles exported from any State.

No Preference shall be given by any Regulation of Commerce or Revenue to the Ports of one State over those of another: nor shall Vessels bound to, or from, one State be obliged to enter, clear, or pay Duties in another.

No Money shall be drawn from the Treasury, but in Consequence of Appropriations made by Law; and a regular Statement and Account of the Receipts and Expenditures of all public Money shall be published from time to time.

No Title of Nobility shall be granted by the United States: And no Person holding any Office of Profit or Trust under them, shall, without the Consent of the Congress, accept of any present, Emolument, Office, or Title, of any kind whatever, from any King, Prince, or foreign State.

Section 10. No State shall enter into any Treaty, Alliance, or Confederation; grant Letters of Marque and Reprisal; coin Money; emit Bills of Credit; make any Thing but gold and silver Coin a Tender in Payment of Debts; pass any Bill of Attainder, ex post facto Law, or Law impairing the Obligation of Contracts, or grant any Title of Nobility.

No State shall, without the Consent of the Congress, lay any Imposts or Duties on Imports or Exports, except what may be absolutely necessary for executing its inspection Laws: and the net Produce of all Duties and Imposts, laid by any State on Imports or Exports, shall be for the Use of the Treasury of the United States; and all such Laws shall be subject to the Revision and Controul of the Congress.

No State shall, without the Consent of Congress, lay any Duty of Tonnage, keep Troops, or Ships of War in time of Peace, enter into any Agreement or Compact with another State, or with a foreign Power, or engage in War, unless actually invaded, or in such imminent Danger as will not admit of delay.

ARTICLE II

Section 1. The executive Power shall be vested in a President of the United States of America. He shall hold his Office during the Term of four Years, and, together with the Vice President, chosen for the same Term, be elected, as follows:

Each State shall appoint, in such Manner as the Legislature thereof may direct, a Number of Electors, equal to the whole Number of Senators and Representatives to which the State may be entitled in the Congress; but no Senator or Representative, or Person holding an Office of Trust or Profit under the United States, shall be appointed an Elector.

The Electors shall meet in their respective States, and vote by Ballot for two Persons, of whom one at least shall not be an Inhabitant of the same State with themselves. And they shall make a List of all the Persons voted for, and of the Number of Votes for each; which List they shall sign and certify, and transmit sealed to the Seat of the Government of the United States, directed to the President of the Senate. The President of the Senate shall, in the Presence of the Senate and House of Representatives, open all the Certificates, and the Votes shall then be counted. The Person having the greatest Number of Votes shall be the President, if such Number be a Majority of the whole Number of Electors appointed; and if there be more than one who have such Majority, and have an equal Number of Votes, then the House of Representatives shall immediately chuse by Ballot one of them for President; and if no Person have a Majority, then from the five highest on the List the said House shall in like Manner chuse the President. But in chusing the President, the Votes shall be taken by States, the Representation from each State having one Vote; A quorum for this Purpose shall consist of a Member or Members from two thirds of the States, and a Majority of all the States shall be necessary to a Choice. In every Case, after the Choice of the President, the Person having the greater Number of Votes of the Electors shall be the Vice President. But if there should remain two or more who have equal Votes, the Senate shall chuse from them by Ballot the Vice President.

The Congress may determine the Time of chusing the Electors, and the Day on which they shall give their Votes; which Day shall be the same throughout the United States.

No person except a natural born Citizen, or a Citizen of the United States, at the time of the Adoption of this Constitution, shall be eligible to the Office of President; neither shall any Person be eligible to that Office who shall not have attained to the Age of thirty five Years, and been fourteen Years a Resident within the United States.

In Case of the Removal of the President from Office, or of his Death, Resignation or Inability to discharge the Powers and Duties of the said Office, the same shall devolve on the Vice President, and the Congress may by Law provide for the Case of Removal, Death, Resignation or Inability, both of the President and Vice President, declaring what Officer shall then act as President, and such Officer shall act accordingly, until the Disability be removed, or a President shall be elected.

The President shall, at stated Times, receive for his Services, a Compensation, which shall neither be increased nor diminished during the Period for which he shall have been elected, and he shall not receive within that Period any other Emolument from the United States, or any of them.

Before he enter on the Execution of his Office, he shall take the following Oath or Affirmation: "I do solemnly swear (or affirm) that I will faithfully execute the Office of President of the United States, and will to the best of my Ability, preserve, protect and defend the Constitution of the United States."

Section 2. The President shall be Commander in Chief of the Army and Navy of the United States, and of the Militia of the several States, when called into the actual Service of the United States; he may require the Opinion, in writing, of the principal Officer in each of the executive Departments, upon any Subject relating to the Duties of their respective Offices, and he shall have Power to grant Reprieves and Pardons for Offenses against the United States, except in Cases of Impeachment.

He shall have Power, by and with the Advice and Consent of the Senate to make Treaties, provided two thirds of the Senators present concur; and he shall nominate, and by and with the Advice and Consent of the Senate, shall appoint Ambassadors, other public Ministers and Consuls, Judges of the supreme Court, and all other Officers of the United States, whose Appointments are not herein otherwise provided for, and which shall be established by Law; but the Congress may by Law vest the Appointment of such inferior Officers, as they think proper, in the President alone, in the Courts of Law, or in the Heads of Departments.

The President shall have Power to fill up all Vacancies that may happen during the Recess of the Senate, by granting Commissions which shall expire at the End of their next Session.

Section 3. He shall from time to time give to the Congress Information of the State of the Union, and recommend to their Consideration such Measures as he shall judge necessary and expedient; he may, on extraordinary Occasions, convene both Houses, or either of them, and in Case of Disagreement between them, with Respect to the Time of Adjournment, he may adjourn them to such Time as he shall think proper; he shall receive Ambassadors and other public Ministers; he shall take Care that the Laws be faithfully executed, and shall Commission all the Officers of the United States.

Section 4. The President, Vice President and all civil Officers of the United States, shall be removed from Office on Impeachment for, and Conviction of, Treason, Bribery, or other high Crimes and Misdemeanors.

ARTICLE III

Section 1. The judicial Power of the United States, shall be vested in one supreme Court, and in such inferior Courts as the Congress may from time to time ordain and establish. The Judges, both of the supreme and inferior Courts, shall hold their Offices during good Behaviour, and shall, at stated Times, receive for their Services a Compensation, which shall not be diminished during their Continuance in Office.

Section 2. The judicial Power shall extend to all Cases, in Law and Equity, arising under this Constitution, the Laws of the United States, and Treaties made, or which shall be made, under their Authority;—to all Cases affecting Ambassadors, other public Ministers and Consuls;—to all Cases of admiralty and maritime Jurisdiction;—to Controversies to which the United States shall be a Party;—to Controversies between two or more States;—between a State and Citizens of another State;—between Citizens of different States;—between Citizens of the same State claiming Lands under Grants of different States, and between a State, or the Citizens thereof, and foreign States, Citizens or Subjects.

In all Cases affecting Ambassadors, other public Ministers and Consuls, and those in which a State shall be a Party, the supreme Court shall have original Jurisdiction. In all the other Cases before mentioned, the supreme Court shall have appellate Jurisdiction, both as to Law and Fact, with such Exceptions, and under such Regulations as the Congress shall make.

The Trial of all Crimes, except in Cases of Impeachment, shall be by Jury; and such Trial shall be held in the State where the said Crimes shall have been committed; but when not committed within any State, the Trial shall be at such Place or Places as the Congress may by Law have directed.

Section 3. Treason against the United States, shall consist only in levying War against them, or, in adhering to their Enemies, giving them Aid and Comfort. No Person shall be convicted of Treason unless on the Testimony of two Witnesses to the same overt Act, or on Confession in open Court.

The Congress shall have Power to declare the Punishment of Treason, but no Attainder of Treason shall work Corruption of Blood, or Forfeiture except during the Life of the Person attainted.

ARTICLE IV

Section 1. Full Faith and Credit shall be given in each State to the public Acts, Records, and judicial Proceedings of every other State. And the Congress may by general Laws prescribe the Manner in which such Acts, Records and Proceedings shall be proved, and the Effect thereof.

Section 2. The Citizens of each State shall be entitled to all Privileges and Immunities of Citizens in the several States.

A Person charged in any State with Treason, Felony, or other Crime, who shall flee from Justice, and be found in another State, shall on Demand of the executive Authority of the State from which he fled, be delivered up, to be removed to the State having Jurisdiction of the Crime.

No Person held to Service or Labour in one State, under the Laws thereof, escaping into another, shall, in Consequence of any Law or Regulation therein, be discharged from such Service or Labour, but shall be delivered up on Claim of the Party to whom such Service or Labour may be due.

Section 3. New States may be admitted by the Congress into this Union; but no new State shall be formed or erected within the Jurisdiction of any other State; nor any State be formed by the Junction of two or more States, or Parts of States, without the Consent of the Legislatures of the States concerned as well as of the Congress.

The Congress shall have Power to dispose of and make all needful Rules and Regulations respecting the Territory or other Property belonging to the United States; and nothing in this Constitution shall be so construed as to Prejudice any Claims of the United States, or of any particular State.

Section 4. The United States shall guarantee to every State in this Union a Republican Form of Government, and shall protect each of them against Invasion; and on Application of the Legislature, or of the Executive (when the Legislature cannot be convened) against domestic Violence.

ARTICLE V

The Congress, whenever two thirds of both Houses shall deem it necessary, shall propose Amendments to this Constitution, or, on the Application of the Legislatures of two thirds of the several States, shall call a Convention for proposing Amendments, which, in either Case, shall be valid to all Intents and Purposes, as part of this Constitution, when ratified by the Legislatures of three fourths of the several States, or by Conventions in three fourths thereof, as the one or the other Mode of Ratification may be proposed by the Congress; Provided that no Amendment which may be made prior to the Year One thousand eight hundred and eight shall in any Manner affect the first and fourth Clauses in the Ninth Section of the first Article; and that no State, without its Consent, shall be deprived of its equal Suffrage in the Senate.

ARTICLE VI

All Debts contracted and Engagements entered into, before the Adoption of this Constitution shall be as valid against the United States under this Constitution, as under the Confederation.

This Constitution, and the Laws of the United States which shall be made in Pursuance thereof; and all Treaties made, or which shall be made, under the Authority of the United States, shall be the supreme Law of the Land; and the Judges in every State shall be bound thereby, any Thing in the Constitution or Laws of any State to the Contrary notwithstanding.

The Senators and Representatives before mentioned, and the Members of the several State Legislatures, and all executive and judicial Officers, both of the United States and of the several States, shall be bound by Oath or Affirmation, to support this Constitution; but no religious Test shall ever be required as a Qualification to any Office or public Trust under the United States.

ARTICLE VII

The Ratification of the Conventions of nine States shall be sufficient for the Establishment of this Constitution between the States so ratifying the Same.

AMENDMENT I [1791]

Congress shall make no law respecting an establishment of religion, or prohibiting the free exercise thereof; or abridging the freedom of speech, or of the press; or the right of the people peaceably to assembly, and to petition the Government for a redress of grievances.

AMENDMENT II [1791]

A well regulated Militia, being necessary to the security of a free State, the right of the people to keep and bear Arms, shall not be infringed.

AMENDMENT III [1791]

No Soldier shall, in time of peace be quartered in any house, without the consent of the Owner, nor in time of war, but in a manner to be prescribed by law.

AMENDMENT IV [1791]

The right of the people to be secure in their persons, houses, papers, and effects, against unreasonable searches and seizures, shall not be violated, and no Warrants shall issue, but upon probable cause, supported by Oath or affirmation, and particularly describing the place to be searched, and the persons or things to be seized.

AMENDMENT V [1791]

No person shall be held to answer for a capital, or otherwise infamous crime, unless on a presentment or indictment of a Grand Jury, except in cases arising in the land or naval forces, or in the Militia, when in actual service in time of War or public danger; nor shall any person be subject for the same offence to be twice put in jeopardy of life or limb; nor shall be compelled in any criminal case to be a witness against himself, nor be deprived of life, liberty, or property, without due process of law; nor shall private property be taken for public use, without just compensation.

AMENDMENT VI [1791]

In all criminal prosecutions, the accused shall enjoy the right to a speedy and public trial, by an impartial jury of the State and district wherein the crime shall have been committed, which district shall have been previously ascertained by law, and to be informed of the nature and cause of the accusation; to be confronted with the witnesses against him; to have compulsory process for obtaining witnesses in his favor, and to have the Assistance of Counsel for his defence.

AMENDMENT VII [1791]

In Suits at common law, where the value in controversy shall exceed twenty dollars, the right of trial by jury shall be preserved, and no fact tried by jury, shall be otherwise re-examined in any Court of the United States, than according to the rules of the common law.

AMENDMENT VIII [1791]

Excessive bail shall not be required, nor excessive fines imposed, nor cruel and unusual punishments inflicted.

AMENDMENT IX [1791]

The enumeration in the Constitution, of certain rights, shall not be construed to deny or disparage others retained by the people.

AMENDMENT X [1791]

The powers not delegated to the United States by the Constitution, nor prohibited by it to the States, are reserved to the States respectively, or to the people.

AMENDMENT XI [1798]

The Judicial power of the United States shall not be construed to extend to any suit in law or equity, commenced or prosecuted against one of the United States by Citizens of another State, or by Citizens or Subjects of any Foreign State.

AMENDMENT XII [1804]

The Electors shall meet in their respective states, and vote by ballot for President and Vice-President, one of whom, at least, shall not be an inhabitant of the same state with themselves; they shall name in their ballots the person voted for as President, and in distinct ballots the person voted for as Vice-President, and they shall make distinct lists of all persons voted for as President, and of all persons voted for as Vice-President, and of the number of votes for each, which lists they shall sign and certify, and transmit sealed to the seat of the government of the United States, directed to the President of the Senate;—The President of the Senate shall, in the presence of the Senate and House of Representatives, open all the certificates and the votes shall then be counted;—The person having the greatest number of votes for President, shall be the President, if such number be a majority of the whole number of Electors appointed; and if no person have such majority, then from the persons having the highest numbers not exceeding three on the list of those voted for as President, the House of Representatives shall choose immediately, by ballot, the President. But in choosing the President, the votes shall be taken by states, the representation from each state having one vote; a quorum for this purpose shall consist of a member or members from two-thirds of the states, and a majority of all states shall be neces-

sary to a choice. And if the House of Representatives shall not choose a President whenever the right of choice shall devolve upon them, before the fourth day of March next following, then the Vice-President shall act as President, as in the case of the death or other constitutional disability of the President.—The person having the greatest number of votes as Vice-President, shall be the Vice-President, if such number be a majority of the whole number of Electors appointed, and if no person have a majority, then from the two highest numbers on the list, the Senate shall choose the Vice-President; a quorum for the purpose shall consist of two-thirds of the whole number of Senators, and a majority of the whole number shall be necessary to a choice. But no person constitutionally ineligible to the office of President shall be eligible to that of Vice-President of the United States.

AMENDMENT XIII [1865]

Section 1. Neither slavery nor involuntary servitude, except as a punishment for crime whereof the party shall have been duly convicted, shall exist within the United States, or any place subject to their jurisdiction.

Section 2. Congress shall have power to enforce this article by appropriate legislation.

AMENDMENT XIV [1868]

Section 1. All persons born or naturalized in the United States, and subject to the jurisdiction thereof, are citizens of the United States and of the State wherein they reside. No State shall make or enforce any law which shall abridge the privileges or immunities of citizens of the United States; nor shall any State deprive any person of life, liberty, or property, without due process of law; nor deny to any person within its jurisdiction the equal protection of the laws.

Section 2. Representatives shall be apportioned among the several States according to their respective numbers, counting the whole number of persons in each State, excluding Indians not taxed. But when the right to vote at any election for the choice of electors for President and Vice President of the United States, Representatives in Congress, the Executive and Judicial officers of a State, or the members of the Legislature thereof, is denied to any of the male inhabitants of such State, being twenty-one years of age, and citizens of the United States, or in any way abridged, except for participation in rebellion, or other crime, the basis of representation therein shall be reduced in the proportion which the number of such male citizens shall bear to the whole number of male citizens twenty-one years of age in such State.

Section 3. No person shall be a Senator or Representative in Congress, or elector of President and Vice President, or hold any office, civil or military, under the United States, or under any State, who having previously taken an oath, as a member of Congress, or as an officer of the United States, or as a member of any State legislature, or as an executive or judicial officer of any State, to support the Constitution of the United States, shall have engaged in insurrection or rebellion against the same, or given aid or comfort to the enemies thereof. But Congress may by a vote of two-thirds of each House, remove such disability.

Section 4. The validity of the public debt of the United States, authorized by law, including debts incurred for payment of pensions and bounties for services in suppressing insurrection or rebellion, shall not be questioned. But neither the United States nor any State shall assume or pay any debt or obligation incurred in aid of insurrection or rebellion against the United States, or any claim for the loss or emancipation of any slave; but all such debts, obligations and claims shall be held illegal and void.

Section 5. The Congress shall have power to enforce, by appropriate legislation, the provisions of this article.

AMENDMENT XV [1870]

Section 1. The right of citizens of the United States to vote shall not be denied or abridged by the United States or by any State on account of race, color, or previous condition of servitude.

Section 2. The Congress shall have power to enforce this article by appropriate legislation.

AMENDMENT XVI [1913]

The Congress shall have power to lay and collect taxes on incomes, from whatever source derived, without apportionment among the several States, and without regard to any census or enumeration.

AMENDMENT XVII [1913]

Section 1. The Senate of the United States shall be composed of two Senators from each State, elected by the people thereof, for six years; and each Senator shall have one vote. The electors in each State shall have the qualifications requisite for electors of the most numerous branch of the State legislatures.

Section 2. When vacancies happen in the representation of any State in the Senate, the executive authority of such State shall issue writs of election to fill such vacancies: *Provided,* That the legislature of any State may empower the executive thereof to make temporary appointments until the people fill the vacancies by election as the legislature may direct.

Section 3. This amendment shall not be so construed as to affect the election or term of any Senator chosen before it becomes valid as part of the Constitution.

AMENDMENT XVIII [1919]

Section 1. After one year from the ratification of this article the manufacture, sale, or transportation of intoxicating liquors within, the importation thereof into, or the exportation thereof from the United States and all territory subject to the jurisdiction thereof for beverage purposes is hereby prohibited.

Section 2. The Congress and the several States shall have concurrent power to enforce this article by appropriate legislation.

Section 3. This article shall be inoperative unless it shall have been ratified as an amendment to the Constitution by the legislatures of the several States, as pro-

vided in the Constitution, within seven years from the date of the submission hereof to the States by the Congress.

AMENDMENT XIX [1920]

Section 1. The right of citizens of the United States to vote shall not be denied or abridged by the United States or by any State on account of sex.

Section 2. Congress shall have power to enforce this article by appropriate legislation.

AMENDMENT XX [1933]

Section 1. The terms of the President and Vice President shall end at noon on the 20th day of January, and the terms of Senators and Representatives at noon on the 3d day of January, of the years in which such terms would have ended if this article had not been ratified; and the terms of their successors shall then begin.

Section 2. The Congress shall assemble at least once in every year, and such meeting shall begin at noon on the 3d day of January, unless they shall by law appoint a different day.

Section 3. If, at the time fixed for the beginning of the term of the President, the President elect shall have died, the Vice President elect shall become President. If the President shall not have been chosen before the time fixed for the beginning of his term, or if the President elect shall have failed to qualify, then the Vice President elect shall act as President until a President shall have qualified; and the Congress may by law provide for the case wherein neither a President elect nor a Vice President elect shall have qualified, declaring who shall then act as President, or the manner in which one who is to act shall be selected, and such person shall act accordingly until a President or Vice President shall have qualified.

Section 4. The Congress may by law provide for the case of the death of any of the persons from whom the House of Representatives may choose a President whenever the right of choice shall have devolved upon them, and for the case of the death of any of the persons from whom the Senate may choose a Vice President whenever the right of choice shall have devolved upon them.

Section 5. Sections 1 and 2 shall take effect on the 15th day of October following the ratification of this article.

Section 6. This article shall be inoperative unless it shall have been ratified as an amendment to the Constitution by the legislatures of three-fourths of the several States within seven years from the date of its submission.

AMENDMENT XXI [1933]

Section 1. The eighteenth article of amendment to the Constitution of the United States is hereby repealed.

Section 2. The transportation or importation into any State, Territory, or possession of the United States for delivery or use therein of intoxicating liquors, in violation of the laws thereof, is hereby prohibited.

Section 3. This article shall be inoperative unless it shall have been ratified as an amendment to the Constitution by conventions in the several States, as provided in the Constitution, within seven years from the date of the submission hereof to the States by the Congress.

AMENDMENT XXII [1951]

Section 1. No person shall be elected to the office of the President more than twice, and no person who has held the office of President, or acted as President, for more than two years of a term to which some other person was elected President shall be elected to the office of President more than once. But this Article shall not apply to any person holding the office of President when this Article was proposed by the Congress, and shall not prevent any person who may be holding the office of President, or acting as President, during the term within which this Article becomes operative from holding the office of President or acting as President during the remainder of such term.

Section 2. This article shall be inoperative unless it shall have been ratified as an amendment to the Constitution by the legislatures of three-fourths of the several States within seven years from the date of its submission to the States by the Congress.

AMENDMENT XXIII [1961]

Section 1. The District constituting the seat of Government of the United States shall appoint in such manner as the Congress may direct:

A number of electors of President and Vice President equal to the whole number of Senators and Representatives in Congress to which the District would be entitled if it were a State, but in no event more than the least populous state; they shall be in addition to those appointed by the states, but they shall be considered, for the purposes of the election of President and Vice President, to be electors appointed by a state; and they shall meet in the District and perform such duties as provided by the twelfth article of amendment.

Section 2. The Congress shall have power to enforce this article by appropriate legislation.

AMENDMENT XXIV [1964]

Section 1. The right of citizens of the United States to vote in any primary or other election for President or Vice President, for electors for President or Vice President, or for Senator or Representative in Congress, shall not be denied or abridged by the United States, or any State by reason of failure to pay any poll tax or other tax.

Section 2. The Congress shall have power to enforce this article by appropriate legislation.

AMENDMENT XXV [1967]

Section 1. In case of the removal of the President from office or of his death or resignation, the Vice President shall become President.

Section 2. Whenever there is a vacancy in the office of the Vice President, the President shall nominate a Vice President who shall take office upon confirmation by a majority vote of both Houses of Congress.

Section 3. Whenever the President transmits to the President pro tempore of the Senate and the Speaker of the House of Representatives his written declaration that he is unable to discharge the powers and duties of his office, and until he transmits to them a written declaration to the contrary, such powers and duties shall be discharged by the Vice President as Acting President.

Section 4. Whenever the Vice President and a majority of either the principal officers of the executive departments or of such other body as Congress may by law provide, transmit to the President pro tempore of the Senate and the Speaker of the House of Representatives their written declaration that the President is unable to discharge the powers and duties of his office, the Vice President shall immediately assume the powers and duties of the office as Acting President.

Thereafter, when the President transmits to the President pro tempore of the Senate and the Speaker of the House of Representatives his written declaration that no inability exists, he shall resume the powers and duties of his office unless the Vice President and a majority of either the principal officers of the executive department or of such other body as Congress may by law provide, transmit within four days to the President pro tempore of the Senate and the Speaker of the House of Representatives their written declaration that the President is unable to discharge the powers and duties of his office. Thereupon Congress shall decide the issue, assembling within forty-eight hours for that purpose if not in session. If the Congress, within twenty-one days after receipt of the latter written declaration, or, if Congress is not in session, within twenty-one days after Congress is required to assemble, determines by two-thirds vote of both Houses that the President is unable to discharge the powers and duties of his office, the Vice President shall continue to discharge the same as Acting President; otherwise, the President shall resume the powers and duties of his office.

AMENDMENT XXVI [1971]

Section 1. The right of citizens of the United States, who are eighteen years of age or older, to vote shall not be denied or abridged by the United States or by any State on account of age.

Section 2. The Congress shall have power to enforce this article by appropriate legislation.

AMENDMENT XXVII [1992]

No law, varying the compensation for the services of the Senators and Representatives, shall take effect, until an election of Representatives shall have intervened.

APPENDIX C
The Uniform Commercial Code (Excerpts)

Article 2
SALES

Part 1 Short Title, General Construction and Subject Matter

§ 2–101. Short Title.

This Article shall be known and may be cited as Uniform Commercial Code—Sales.

§ 2–102. Scope; Certain Security and Other Transactions Excluded From This Article.

Unless the context otherwise requires, this Article applies to transactions in goods; it does not apply to any transaction which although in the form of an unconditional contract to sell or present sale is intended to operate only as a security transaction nor does this Article impair or repeal any statute regulating sales to consumers, farmers or other specified classes of buyers.

§ 2–103. Definitions and Index of Definitions.

(1) In this Article unless the context otherwise requires

    (a) "Buyer" means a person who buys or contracts to buy goods.

    (b) "Good faith" in the case of a merchant means honesty in fact and the observance of reasonable commercial standards of fair dealing in the trade.

    (c) "Receipt" of goods means taking physical possession of them.

    (d) "Seller" means a person who sells or contracts to sell goods.

(2) Other definitions applying to this Article or to specified Parts thereof, and the sections in which they appear are:

"Acceptance". Section 2–606.
"Banker's credit". Section 2–325.
"Between merchants". Section 2–104.
"Cancellation". Section 2–106(4).
"Commercial unit". Section 2–105.
"Confirmed credit". Section 2–325.
"Conforming to contract". Section 2–106.
"Contract for sale". Section 2–106.
"Cover". Section 2–712.
"Entrusting". Section 2–403.
"Financing agency". Section 2–104.
"Future goods". Section 2–105.
"Goods". Section 2–105.
"Identification". Section 2–501.
"Installment contract". Section 2–612.
"Letter of Credit". Section 2–325.
"Lot". Section 2–105.
"Merchant". Section 2–104.
"Overseas". Section 2–323.
"Person in position of seller". Section 2–707.
"Present sale". Section 2–106.
"Sale". Section 2–106.
"Sale on approval". Section 2–326.
"Sale or return". Section 2–326.
"Termination". Section 2–106.

(3) The following definitions in other Articles apply to this Article:

"Check". Section 3–104.
"Consignee". Section 7–102.
"Consignor". Section 7–102.
"Consumer goods". Section 9–109.
"Dishonor". Section 3–507.
"Draft". Section 3–104.

(4) In addition Article 1 contains general definitions and principles of construction and interpretation applicable throughout this Article.

As amended in 1994 and 1999.

§ 2–104. Definitions: "Merchant"; "Between Merchants"; "Financing Agency".

(1) "Merchant" means a person who deals in goods of the kind or otherwise by his occupation holds himself out as having knowledge or skill peculiar to the practices or goods involved in the transaction or to whom such knowledge or skill may be attributed by his employment of an agent or broker or other intermediary who by his occupation holds himself out as having such knowledge or skill.

(2) "Financing agency" means a bank, finance company or other person who in the ordinary course of business makes advances against goods or documents of title or who by arrangement with either the seller or the buyer intervenes in ordinary course to make or collect payment due or claimed under the contract for sale, as by purchasing or paying the seller's draft or making advances against it or by merely taking it for collection whether or not documents of title accompany the draft. "Financing agency" includes also a bank or other person who similarly intervenes between persons who are in the position of seller and buyer in respect to the goods (Section 2–707).

(3) "Between merchants" means in any transaction with respect to which both parties are chargeable with the knowledge or skill of merchants.

§ 2–105. Definitions: Transferability; "Goods"; "Future" Goods; "Lot"; "Commercial Unit".

(1) "Goods" means all things (including specially manufactured goods) which are movable at the time of identification to the contract for sale other than the money in which the price is to be paid, investment securities (Article 8) and things in action. "Goods" also includes the unborn young of animals and growing crops and other identified things attached to realty as described in the section on goods to be severed from realty (Section 2–107).

(2) Goods must be both existing and identified before any interest in them can pass. Goods which are not both existing and identified are "future" goods. A purported present sale of future goods or of any interest therein operates as a contract to sell.

(3) There may be a sale of a part interest in existing identified goods.

(4) An undivided share in an identified bulk of fungible goods is sufficiently identified to be sold although the quantity of the bulk is not determined. Any agreed proportion of such a bulk or any quantity thereof agreed upon by number, weight or other measure may to the extent of the seller's interest in the bulk be sold to the buyer who then becomes an owner in common.

(5) "Lot" means a parcel or a single article which is the subject matter of a separate sale or delivery, whether or not it is sufficient to perform the contract.

(6) "Commercial unit" means such a unit of goods as by commercial usage is a single whole for purposes of sale and division of which materially impairs its character or value on the market or in use. A commercial unit may be a single article (as a machine) or a set of articles (as a suite of furniture or an assortment of sizes) or a quantity (as a bale, gross, or carload) or any other unit treated in use or in the relevant market as a single whole.

§ 2–106. Definitions: "Contract"; "Agreement"; "Contract for Sale"; "Sale"; "Present Sale"; "Conforming" to Contract; "Termination"; "Cancellation".

(1) In this Article unless the context otherwise requires "contract" and "agreement" are limited to those relating to the present or future sale of goods. "Contract for sale" includes both a present sale of goods and a contract to sell goods at a future time. A "sale" consists in the passing of title from the seller to the buyer for a price (Section 2–401). A "present sale" means a sale which is accomplished by the making of the contract.

(2) Goods or conduct including any part of a performance are "conforming" or conform to the contract when they are in accordance with the obligations under the contract.

(3) "Termination" occurs when either party pursuant to a power created by agreement or law puts an end to the contract otherwise than for its breach. On "termination" all obligations which are still executory on both sides are discharged but any right based on prior breach or performance survives.

(4) "Cancellation" occurs when either party puts an end to the contract for breach by the other and its effect is the same as that of "termination" except that the cancelling party also retains any remedy for breach of the whole contract or any unperformed balance.

§ 2–107. Goods to Be Severed From Realty: Recording.

(1) A contract for the sale of minerals or the like (including oil and gas) or a structure or its materials to be removed from realty is a contract for the sale of goods within this Article if they are to be severed by the seller but until severance a purported present sale thereof which is not effective as a transfer of an interest in land is effective only as a contract to sell.

(2) A contract for the sale apart from the land of growing crops or other things attached to realty and capable of severance without material harm thereto but not described in subsection (1) or of timber to be cut is a contract for the sale of goods within this Article whether the subject matter is to be severed by the buyer or by the seller even though it forms part of the realty at the time of contracting, and the parties can by identification effect a present sale before severance.

(3) The provisions of this section are subject to any third party rights provided by the law relating to realty records, and the contract for sale may be executed and recorded as a document transferring an interest in land and shall then constitute notice to third parties of the buyer's rights under the contract for sale.

As amended in 1972.

Part 2 Form, Formation and Readjustment of Contract

§ 2–201. Formal Requirements; Statute of Frauds.

(1) Except as otherwise provided in this section a contract for the sale of goods for the price of $500 or more is not enforceable by way of action or defense unless there is some writing sufficient to indicate that a contract for sale has been made between the parties and signed by the party against whom enforcement is sought or by his authorized agent or broker. A writing is not insufficient because it omits or incorrectly states a term agreed upon but the contract is not enforceable under this paragraph beyond the quantity of goods shown in such writing.

(2) Between merchants if within a reasonable time a writing in confirmation of the contract and sufficient against the sender is received and the party receiving it has reason to know its contents, its satisfies the requirements of subsection (1) against such party unless written notice of objection to its contents is given within ten days after it is received.

(3) A contract which does not satisfy the requirements of subsection (1) but which is valid in other respects is enforceable

(a) if the goods are to be specially manufactured for the buyer and are not suitable for sale to others in the ordinary course of the seller's business and the seller, before notice of repudiation is received and under circumstances which reasonably indicate that the goods are for the buyer, has made either a substantial beginning of their manufacture or commitments for their procurement; or

(b) if the party against whom enforcement is sought admits in his pleading, testimony or otherwise in court that a contract for sale was made, but the contract is not enforceable under this provision beyond the quantity of goods admitted; or

(c) with respect to goods for which payment has been made and accepted or which have been received and accepted (Sec. 2–606).

§ 2–202. Final Written Expression: Parol or Extrinsic Evidence.

Terms with respect to which the confirmatory memoranda of the parties agree or which are otherwise set forth in a writing intended by the parties as a final expression of their agreement with respect to such terms as are included therein may not be contradicted by evidence of any prior agreement or of a contemporaneous oral agreement but may be explained or supplemented

(a) by course of dealing or usage of trade (Section 1–205) or by course of performance (Section 2–208); and

(b) by evidence of consistent additional terms unless the court finds the writing to have been intended also as a complete and exclusive statement of the terms of the agreement.

§ 2–203. Seals Inoperative.

The affixing of a seal to a writing evidencing a contract for sale or an offer to buy or sell goods does not constitute the writing a sealed instrument and the law with respect to sealed instruments does not apply to such a contract or offer.

§ 2–204. Formation in General.

(1) A contract for sale of goods may be made in any manner sufficient to show agreement, including conduct by both parties which recognizes the existence of such a contract.

(2) An agreement sufficient to constitute a contract for sale may be found even though the moment of its making is undetermined.

(3) Even though one or more terms are left open a contract for sale does not fail for indefiniteness if the parties have intended to make a contract and there is a reasonably certain basis for giving an appropriate remedy.

§ 2–205. Firm Offers.

An offer by a merchant to buy or sell goods in a signed writing which by its terms gives assurance that it will be held open is not revocable, for lack of consideration, during the time stated or if no time is stated for a reasonable time, but in no event may such period of irrevocability exceed three months; but any such term of assurance on a form supplied by the offeree must be separately signed by the offeror.

§ 2–206. Offer and Acceptance in Formation of Contract.

(1) Unless other unambiguously indicated by the language or circumstances

(a) an offer to make a contract shall be construed as inviting acceptance in any manner and by any medium reasonable in the circumstances;

(b) an order or other offer to buy goods for prompt or current shipment shall be construed as inviting acceptance either by a prompt promise to ship or by the prompt or current shipment of conforming or nonconforming goods, but such a shipment of non-conforming goods does not constitute an acceptance if the seller seasonably notifies the buyer that the shipment is offered only as an accommodation to the buyer.

(2) Where the beginning of a requested performance is a reasonable mode of acceptance an offeror who is not notified of acceptance within a reasonable time may treat the offer as having lapsed before acceptance.

§ 2–207. Additional Terms in Acceptance or Confirmation.

(1) A definite and seasonable expression of acceptance or a written confirmation which is sent within a reasonable time operates as an acceptance even though it states terms additional to or different from those offered or agreed upon, unless acceptance is expressly made conditional on assent to the additional or different terms.

(2) The additional terms are to be construed as proposals for addition to the contract. Between merchants such terms become part of the contract unless:

> (a) the offer expressly limits acceptance to the terms of the offer;

> (b) they materially alter it; or

> (c) notification of objection to them has already been given or is given within a reasonable time after notice of them is received.

(3) Conduct by both parties which recognizes the existence of a contract is sufficient to establish a contract for sale although the writings of the parties do not otherwise establish a contract. In such case the terms of the particular contract consist of those terms on which the writings of the parties agree, together with any supplementary terms incorporated under any other provisions of this Act.

§ 2–208. Course of Performance or Practical Construction.

(1) Where the contract for sale involves repeated occasions for performance by either party with knowledge of the nature of the performance and opportunity for objection to it by the other, any course of performance accepted or acquiesced in without objection shall be relevant to determine the meaning of the agreement.

(2) The express terms of the agreement and any such course of performance, as well as any course of dealing and usage of trade, shall be construed whenever reasonable as consistent with each other; but when such construction is unreasonable, express terms shall control course of performance and course of performance shall control both course of dealing and usage of trade (Section 1–205).

(3) Subject to the provisions of the next section on modification and waiver, such course of performance shall be relevant to show a waiver or modification of any term inconsistent with such course of performance.

§ 2–209. Modification, Rescission and Waiver.

(1) An agreement modifying a contract within this Article needs no consideration to be binding.

(2) A signed agreement which excludes modification or rescission except by a signed writing cannot be otherwise modified or rescinded, but except as between merchants such a requirement on a form supplied by the merchant must be separately signed by the other party.

(3) The requirements of the statute of frauds section of this Article (Section 2–201) must be satisfied if the contract as modified is within its provisions.

(4) Although an attempt at modification or rescission does not satisfy the requirements of subsection (2) or (3) it can operate as a waiver.

(5) A party who has made a waiver affecting an executory portion of the contract may retract the waiver by reasonable notification received by the other party that strict performance will be required of any term waived, unless the retraction would be unjust in view of a material change of position in reliance on the waiver.

§ 2–210. Delegation of Performance; Assignment of Rights.

(1) A party may perform his duty through a delegate unless otherwise agreed or unless the other party has a substantial interest in having his original promisor perform or control the acts required by the contract. No delegation of performance relieves the party delegating of any duty to perform or any liability for breach.

(2) Except as otherwise provided in Section 9–406, unless otherwise agreed, all rights of either seller or buyer can be assigned except where the assignment would materially change the duty of the other party, or increase materially the burden or risk imposed on him by his contract, or impair materially his chance of obtaining return performance. A right to damages for breach of the whole contract or a right arising out of the assignor's due performance of his entire obligation can be assigned despite agreement otherwise.

(3) The creation, attachment, perfection, or enforcement of a security interest in the seller's interest under a contract is not a transfer that materially changes the duty of or increases materially the burden or risk imposed on the buyer or impairs materially the buyer's chance of obtaining return performance within the purview of subsection (2) unless, and then only to the extent that, enforcement actually results in a delegation of material performance of the seller. Even in that event, the creation, attachment, perfection, and enforcement of the security interest remain effective, but (i) the seller is liable to the buyer for damages caused by the delegation to the extent that the damages could not reasonably by prevented by the buyer, and (ii) a court having jurisdiction may grant other appropriate relief, including cancellation of the contract for sale or an injunction against enforcement of the security interest or consummation of the enforcement.

(4) Unless the circumstnaces indicate the contrary a prohibition of assignment of "the contract" is to be construed as barring only the delegation to the assignee of the assignor's performance.

(5) An assignment of "the contract" or of "all my rights under the contract" or an assignment in similar general terms is an assignment of rights and unless the language or the circumstances (as in an assignment for security) indicate the contrary, it is a delegation of performance of the duties of the assignor and its acceptance by the assignee constitutes a promise by him to perform those duties. This promise is enforceable by either the assignor or the other party to the original contract.

(6) The other party may treat any assignment which delegates performance as creating reasonable grounds for insecurity and may without prejudice to his rights against the assignor demand assurances from the assignee (Section 2–609).

As amended in 1999.

Part 3 General Obligation and Construction of Contract

§ 2–301. General Obligations of Parties.

The obligation of the seller is to transfer and deliver and that of the buyer is to accept and pay in accordance with the contract.

§ 2–302. Unconscionable Contract or Clause.

(1) If the court as a matter of law finds the contract or any clause of the contract to have been unconscionable at the time it was made the court may refuse to enforce the contract, or it may enforce the remainder of the contract without the unconscionable clause, or it may so limit the application of any unconscionable clause as to avoid any unconscionable result.

(2) When it is claimed or appears to the court that the contract or any clause thereof may be unconscionable the parties shall be afforded a reasonable opportunity to present evidence as to its commercial setting, purpose and effect to aid the court in making the determination.

§ 2–303. Allocations or Division of Risks.

Where this Article allocates a risk or a burden as between the parties "unless otherwise agreed", the agreement may not only shift the allocation but may also divide the risk or burden.

§ 2–304. Price Payable in Money, Goods, Realty, or Otherwise.

(1) The price can be made payable in money or otherwise. If it is payable in whole or in part in goods each party is a seller of the goods which he is to transfer.

(2) Even though all or part of the price is payable in an interest in realty the transfer of the goods and the seller's obligations with reference to them are subject to this Article, but not the transfer of the interest in realty or the transferor's obligations in connection therewith.

§ 2–305. Open Price Term.

(1) The parties if they so intend can conclude a contract for sale even though the price is not settled. In such a case the price is a reasonable price at the time for delivery if

(a) nothing is said as to price; or

(b) the price is left to be agreed by the parties and they fail to agree; or

(c) the price is to be fixed in terms of some agreed market or other standard as set or recorded by a third person or agency and it is not so set or recorded.

(2) A price to be fixed by the seller or by the buyer means a price for him to fix in good faith.

(3) When a price left to be fixed otherwise than by agreement of the parties fails to be fixed through fault of one party the other may at his option treat the contract as cancelled or himself fix a reasonable price.

(4) Where, however, the parties intend not to be bound unless the price be fixed or agreed and it is not fixed or agreed there is no contract. In such a case the buyer must return any goods already received or if unable so to do must pay their reasonable value at the time of delivery and the seller must return any portion of the price paid on account.

§ 2–306. Output, Requirements and Exclusive Dealings.

(1) A term which measures the quantity by the output of the seller or the requirements of the buyer means such actual output or requirements as may occur in good faith, except that no quantity unreasonably disproportionate to any stated estimate or in the absence of a stated estimate to any normal or otherwise comparable prior output or requirements may be tendered or demanded.

(2) A lawful agreement by either the seller or the buyer for exclusive dealing in the kind of goods concerned imposes unless otherwise agreed an obligation by the seller to use best efforts to supply the goods and by the buyer to use best efforts to promote their sale.

§ 2–307. Delivery in Single Lot or Several Lots.

Unless otherwise agreed all goods called for by a contract for sale must be tendered in a single delivery and payment is due only on such tender but where the circumstances give either party the right to make or demand delivery in lots the price if it can be apportioned may be demanded for each lot.

§ 2–308. Absence of Specified Place for Delivery.

Unless otherwise agreed

(a) the place for delivery of goods is the seller's place of business or if he has none his residence; but

(b) in a contract for sale of identified goods which to the knowledge of the parties at the time of contracting are in some other place, that place is the place for their delivery; and

(c) documents of title may be delivered through customary banking channels.

§ 2–309. Absence of Specific Time Provisions; Notice of Termination.

(1) The time for shipment or delivery or any other action under a contract if not provided in this Article or agreed upon shall be a reasonable time.

(2) Where the contract provides for successive performances but is indefinite in duration it is valid for a reasonable time but unless otherwise agreed may be terminated at any time by either party.

(3) Termination of a contract by one party except on the happening of an agreed event requires that reasonable notification be received by the other party and an agreement dispensing with notification is invalid if its operation would be unconscionable.

§ 2–310. Open Time for Payment or Running of Credit; Authority to Ship Under Reservation.

Unless otherwise agreed

(a) payment is due at the time and place at which the buyer is to receive the goods even though the place of shipment is the place of delivery; and

(b) if the seller is authorized to send the goods he may ship them under reservation, and may tender the documents of title, but the buyer may inspect the goods after their arrival before payment is due unless such inspection is inconsistent with the terms of the contract (Section 2–513); and

(c) if delivery is authorized and made by way of documents of title otherwise than by subsection (b) then payment is due at the time and place at which the buyer is to receive the documents regardless of where the goods are to be received; and

(d) where the seller is required or authorized to ship the goods on credit the credit period runs from the time of shipment but post-dating the invoice or delaying its dispatch will correspondingly delay the starting of the credit period.

§ 2–311. Options and Cooperation Respecting Performance.

(1) An agreement for sale which is otherwise sufficiently definite (subsection (3) of Section 2–204) to be a contract is not made invalid by the fact that it leaves particulars of performance to be specified by one of the parties. Any such specification must be made in good faith and within limits set by commercial reasonableness.

(2) Unless otherwise agreed specifications relating to assortment of the goods are at the buyer's option and except as otherwise provided in subsections (1)(c) and (3) of Section 2–319 specifications or arrangements relating to shipment are at the seller's option.

(3) Where such specification would materially affect the other party's performance but is not seasonably made or where one party's cooperation is necessary to the agreed performance of the other but is not seasonably forthcoming, the other party in addition to all other remedies

(a) is excused for any resulting delay in his own performance; and

(b) may also either proceed to perform in any reasonable manner or after the time for a material part of his own performance treat the failure to specify or to cooperate as a breach by failure to deliver or accept the goods.

§ 2–312. Warranty of Title and Against Infringement; Buyer's Obligation Against Infringement.

(1) Subject to subsection (2) there is in a contract for sale a warranty by the seller that

(a) the title conveyed shall be good, and its transfer rightful; and

(b) the goods shall be delivered free from any security interest or other lien or encumbrance of which the buyer at the time of contracting has no knowledge.

(2) A warranty under subsection (1) will be excluded or modified only by specific language or by circumstances which give the buyer reason to know that the person selling does not claim title in himself or that he is purporting to sell only such right or title as he or a third person may have.

(3) Unless otherwise agreed a seller who is a merchant regularly dealing in goods of the kind warrants that the goods shall be delivered free of the rightful claim of any third person by way of infringement or the like but a buyer who furnishes specifications to the seller must hold the seller harmless against any such claim which arises out of compliance with the specifications.

§ 2–313. Express Warranties by Affirmation, Promise, Description, Sample.

(1) Express warranties by the seller are created as follows:

(a) Any affirmation of fact or promise made by the seller to the buyer which relates to the goods and becomes part of the basis of the bargain creates an express warranty that the goods shall conform to the affirmation or promise.

(b) Any description of the goods which is made part of the basis of the bargain creates an express warranty that the goods shall conform to the description.

(c) Any sample or model which is made part of the basis of the bargain creates an express warranty that the whole of the goods shall conform to the sample or model.

(2) It is not necessary to the creation of an express warranty that the seller use formal words such as "warrant" or "guarantee" or that he have a specific intention to make a warranty, but an affirmation merely of the value of the goods or a statement purporting to be merely the seller's opinion or commendation of the goods does not create a warranty.

§ 2–314. Implied Warranty: Merchantability; Usage of Trade.

(1) Unless excluded or modified (Section 2–316), a warranty that the goods shall be merchantable is implied in a contract for their sale if the seller is a merchant with respect to goods of that kind. Under this section the serving for value of food or drink to be consumed either on the premises or elsewhere is a sale.

(2) Goods to be merchantable must be at least such as

(a) pass without objection in the trade under the contract description; and

(b) in the case of fungible goods, are of fair average quality within the description; and

(c) are fit for the ordinary purposes for which such goods are used; and

(d) run, within the variations permitted by the agreement, of even kind, quality and quantity within each unit and among all units involved; and

(e) are adequately contained, packaged, and labeled as the agreement may require; and

(f) conform to the promises or affirmations of fact made on the container or label if any.

(3) Unless excluded or modified (Section 2–316) other implied warranties may arise from course of dealing or usage of trade.

§ 2–315. Implied Warranty: Fitness for Particular Purpose.

Where the seller at the time of contracting has reason to know any particular purpose for which the goods are required and that the buyer is relying on the seller's skill or judgment to select or furnish suitable goods, there is unless excluded or modified under the next section an implied warranty that the goods shall be fit for such purpose.

§ 2–316. Exclusion or Modification of Warranties.

(1) Words or conduct relevant to the creation of an express warranty and words or conduct tending to negate or limit warranty shall be construed wherever reasonable as consistent with each other; but subject to the provisions of this Article on parol or extrinsic evidence (Section 2–202) negation or limitation is inoperative to the extent that such construction is unreasonable.

(2) Subject to subsection (3), to exclude or modify the implied warranty of merchantability or any part of it the language must mention merchantability and in case of a writing must be conspicuous, and to exclude or modify any implied warranty of fitness the exclusion must be by a writing and conspicuous. Language to exclude all implied warranties of fitness is sufficient if it states, for example, that "There are no warranties which extend beyond the description on the face hereof."

(3) Notwithstanding subsection (2)

(a) unless the circumstances indicate otherwise, all implied warranties are excluded by expressions like "as is", "with all faults" or other language which in common understanding calls the buyer's attention to the exclusion of warranties and makes plain that there is no implied warranty; and

(b) when the buyer before entering into the contract has examined the goods or the sample or model as fully as he desired or has refused to examine the goods there is no implied warranty with regard to defects which an examination ought in the circumstances to have revealed to him; and

(c) an implied warranty can also be excluded or modified by course of dealing or course of performance or usage of trade.

(4) Remedies for breach of warranty can be limited in accordance with the provisions of this Article on liquidation or limitation of damages and on contractual modification of remedy (Sections 2–718 and 2–719).

§ 2–317. Cumulation and Conflict of Warranties Express or Implied.

Warranties whether express or implied shall be construed as consistent with each other and as cumulative, but if such construction is unreasonable the intention of the parties shall determine which warranty is dominant. In ascertaining that intention the following rules apply:

(a) Exact or technical specifications displace an inconsistent sample or model or general language of description.

(b) A sample from an existing bulk displaces inconsistent general language of description.

(c) Express warranties displace inconsistent implied warranties other than an implied warranty of fitness for a particular purpose.

§ 2–318. Third Party Beneficiaries of Warranties Express or Implied.

Note: If this Act is introduced in the Congress of the United States this section should be omitted. (States to select one alternative.)

Alternative A

A seller's warranty whether express or implied extends to any natural person who is in the family or household of his buyer or who is a guest in his home if it is reasonable to expect that such person may use, consume or be affected by the goods and who is injured in person by breach of the warranty. A seller may not exclude or limit the operation of this section.

Alternative B

A seller's warranty whether express or implied extends to any natural person who may reasonably be expected to use, consume or be affected by the goods and who is injured in person by breach of the warranty. A seller may not exclude or limit the operation of this section.

Alternative C

A seller's warranty whether express or implied extends to any person who may reasonably be expected to use, consume or be affected by the goods and who is injured by breach of the warranty. A seller may not exclude or limit the operation of this section with respect to injury to the person of an individual to whom the warranty extends.

As amended 1966.

§ 2–319. F.O.B. and F.A.S. Terms.

(1) Unless otherwise agreed the term F.O.B. (which means "free on board") at a named place, even though used only in connection with the stated price, is a delivery term under which

(a) when the term is F.O.B. the place of shipment, the seller must at that place ship the goods in the manner provided in this Article (Section 2–504) and bear the expense and risk of putting them into the possession of the carrier; or

(b) when the term is F.O.B. the place of destination, the seller must at his own expense and risk transport the goods to that place and there tender delivery of them in the manner provided in this Article (Section 2–503);

(c) when under either (a) or (b) the term is also F.O.B. vessel, car or other vehicle, the seller must in addition at his own expense and risk load the goods on board. If the term is F.O.B. vessel the buyer must name the vessel and in an appropriate case the seller must comply with the provisions of this Article on the form of bill of lading (Section 2–323).

(2) Unless otherwise agreed the term F.A.S. vessel (which means "free alongside") at a named port, even though used only in connection with the stated price, is a delivery term under which the seller must

(a) at his own expense and risk deliver the goods alongside the vessel in the manner usual in that port or on a dock designated and provided by the buyer; and

(b) obtain and tender a receipt for the goods in exchange for which the carrier is under a duty to issue a bill of lading.

(3) Unless otherwise agreed in any case falling within subsection (1)(a) or (c) or subsection (2) the buyer must seasonably give any needed instructions for making delivery, including when the term is F.A.S. or F.O.B. the loading berth of the vessel and in an appropriate case its name and sailing date. The seller may treat the failure of needed instructions as a failure of cooperation under this Article (Section 2–311). He may also at his option move the goods in any reasonable manner preparatory to delivery or shipment.

(4) Under the term F.O.B. vessel or F.A.S. unless otherwise agreed the buyer must make payment against tender of the required documents and the seller may not tender nor the buyer demand delivery of the goods in substitution for the documents.

§ 2–320. C.I.F. and C. & F. Terms.

(1) The term C.I.F. means that the price includes in a lump sum the cost of the goods and the insurance and freight to the named destination. The term C. & F. or C.F. means that the price so includes cost and freight to the named destination.

(2) Unless otherwise agreed and even though used only in connection with the stated price and destination, the term C.I.F. destination or its equivalent requires the seller at his own expense and risk to

(a) put the goods into the possession of a carrier at the port for shipment and obtain a negotiable bill or bills of lading covering the entire transportation to the named destination; and

(b) load the goods and obtain a receipt from the carrier (which may be contained in the bill of lading) showing that the freight has been paid or provided for; and

(c) obtain a policy or certificate of insurance, including any war risk insurance, of a kind and on terms then current at the port of shipment in the usual amount, in the currency of the contract, shown to cover the same goods covered by the bill of lading and providing for payment of loss to the order of the buyer or for the account of whom it may concern; but the seller may add to the price the amount of the premium for any such war risk insurance; and

(d) prepare an invoice of the goods and procure any other documents required to effect shipment or to comply with the contract; and

(e) forward and tender with commercial promptness all the documents in due form and with any indorsement necessary to perfect the buyer's rights.

(3) Unless otherwise agreed the term C. & F. or its equivalent has the same effect and imposes upon the seller the same obligations and risks as a C.I.F. term except the obligation as to insurance.

(4) Under the term C.I.F. or C. & F. unless otherwise agreed the buyer must make payment against tender of the required documents and the seller may not tender nor the buyer demand delivery of the goods in substitution for the documents.

§ 2–321. C.I.F. or C. & F.: "Net Landed Weights"; "Payment on Arrival"; Warranty of Condition on Arrival.

Under a contract containing a term C.I.F. or C. & F.

(1) Where the price is based on or is to be adjusted according to "net landed weights", "delivered weights", "out turn" quantity or quality or the like, unless otherwise agreed the seller must reasonably estimate the price. The payment due on tender of the documents called for by the contract is the amount so estimated, but after final adjustment of the price a settlement must be made with commercial promptness.

(2) An agreement described in subsection (1) or any warranty of quality or condition of the goods on arrival places upon the seller the risk of ordinary deterioration, shrinkage and the like in transportation but has no effect on the place or time of identification to the contract for sale or delivery or on the passing of the risk of loss.

(3) Unless otherwise agreed where the contract provides for payment on or after arrival of the goods the seller must before payment allow such preliminary inspection as is feasible; but if the goods are lost delivery of the documents and payment are due when the goods should have arrived.

§ 2–322. Delivery "Ex-Ship".

(1) Unless otherwise agreed a term for delivery of goods "ex-ship" (which means from the carrying vessel) or in

equivalent language is not restricted to a particular ship and requires delivery from a ship which has reached a place at the named port of destination where goods of the kind are usually discharged.

(2) Under such a term unless otherwise agreed

(a) the seller must discharge all liens arising out of the carriage and furnish the buyer with a direction which puts the carrier under a duty to deliver the goods; and

(b) the risk of loss does not pass to the buyer until the goods leave the ship's tackle or are otherwise properly unloaded.

§ 2–323. Form of Bill of Lading Required in Overseas Shipment; "Overseas".

(1) Where the contract contemplates overseas shipment and contains a term C.I.F. or C. & F. or F.O.B. vessel, the seller unless otherwise agreed must obtain a negotiable bill of lading stating that the goods have been loaded on board or, in the case of a term C.I.F. or C. & F., received for shipment.

(2) Where in a case within subsection (1) a bill of lading has been issued in a set of parts, unless otherwise agreed if the documents are not to be sent from abroad the buyer may demand tender of the full set; otherwise only one part of the bill of lading need be tendered. Even if the agreement expressly requires a full set

(a) due tender of a single part is acceptable within the provisions of this Article on cure of improper delivery (subsection (1) of Section 2–508); and

(b) even though the full set is demanded, if the documents are sent from abroad the person tendering an incomplete set may nevertheless require payment upon furnishing an indemnity which the buyer in good faith deems adequate.

(3) A shipment by water or by air or a contract contemplating such shipment is "overseas" insofar as by usage of trade or agreement it is subject to the commercial, financing or shipping practices characteristic of international deep water commerce.

§ 2–324. "No Arrival, No Sale" Term.

Under a term "no arrival, no sale" or terms of like meaning, unless otherwise agreed,

(a) the seller must properly ship conforming goods and if they arrive by any means he must tender them on arrival but he assumes no obligation that the goods will arrive unless he has caused the non-arrival; and

(b) where without fault of the seller the goods are in part lost or have so deteriorated as no longer to conform to the contract or arrive after the contract time, the buyer may proceed as if there had been casualty to identified goods (Section 2–613).

§ 2–325. "Letter of Credit" Term; "Confirmed Credit".

(1) Failure of the buyer seasonably to furnish an agreed letter of credit is a breach of the contract for sale.

(2) The delivery to seller of a proper letter of credit suspends the buyer's obligation to pay. If the letter of credit is dishonored, the seller may on seasonable notification to the buyer require payment directly from him.

(3) Unless otherwise agreed the term "letter of credit" or "banker's credit" in a contract for sale means an irrevocable credit issued by a financing agency of good repute and, where the shipment is overseas, of good international repute. The term "confirmed credit" means that the credit must also carry the direct obligation of such an agency which does business in the seller's financial market.

§ 2–326. Sale on Approval and Sale or Return; Rights of Creditors.

(1) Unless otherwise agreed, if delivered goods may be returned by the buyer even though they conform to the contract, the transaction is

(a) a "sale on approval" if the goods are delivered primarily for use, and

(b) a "sale or return" if the goods are delivered primarily for resale.

(2) Goods held on approval are not subject to the claims of the buyer's creditors until acceptance; goods held on sale or return are subject to such claims while in the buyer's possession.

(3) Any "or return" term of a contract for sale is to be treated as a separate contract for sale within the statute of frauds section of this Article (Section 2–201) and as contradicting the sale aspect of the contract within the provisions of this Article or on parol or extrinsic evidence (Section 2–202).

As amended in 1999.

§ 2–327. Special Incidents of Sale on Approval and Sale or Return.

(1) Under a sale on approval unless otherwise agreed

(a) although the goods are identified to the contract the risk of loss and the title do not pass to the buyer until acceptance; and

(b) use of the goods consistent with the purpose of trial is not acceptance but failure seasonably to notify the seller of election to return the goods is acceptance, and if the goods conform to the contract acceptance of any part is acceptance of the whole; and

(c) after due notification of election to return, the return is at the seller's risk and expense but a merchant buyer must follow any reasonable instructions.

(2) Under a sale or return unless otherwise agreed

(a) the option to return extends to the whole or any commercial unit of the goods while in substantially their original condition, but must be exercised seasonably; and

(b) the return is at the buyer's risk and expense.

§ 2–328. Sale by Auction.

(1) In a sale by auction if goods are put up in lots each lot is the subject of a separate sale.

(2) A sale by auction is complete when the auctioneer so announces by the fall of the hammer or in other customary manner. Where a bid is made while the hammer is falling in acceptance of a prior bid the auctioneer may in his discretion reopen the bidding or declare the goods sold under the bid on which the hammer was falling.

(3) Such a sale is with reserve unless the goods are in explicit terms put up without reserve. In an auction with reserve the auctioneer may withdraw the goods at any time until he announces completion of the sale. In an auction without reserve, after the auctioneer calls for bids on an article or lot, that article or lot cannot be withdrawn unless no bid is made within a reasonable time. In either case a bidder may retract his bid until the auctioneer's announcement of completion of the sale, but a bidder's retraction does not revive any previous bid.

(4) If the auctioneer knowingly receives a bid on the seller's behalf or the seller makes or procures such as bid, and notice has not been given that liberty for such bidding is reserved, the buyer may at his option avoid the sale or take the goods at the price of the last good faith bid prior to the completion of the sale. This subsection shall not apply to any bid at a forced sale.

Part 4 Title, Creditors and Good Faith Purchasers

§ 2–401. Passing of Title; Reservation for Security; Limited Application of This Section.

Each provision of this Article with regard to the rights, obligations and remedies of the seller, the buyer, purchasers or other third parties applies irrespective of title to the goods except where the provision refers to such title. Insofar as situations are not covered by the other provisions of this Article and matters concerning title became material the following rules apply:

(1) Title to goods cannot pass under a contract for sale prior to their identification to the contract (Section 2–501), and unless otherwise explicitly agreed the buyer acquires by their identification a special property as limited by this Act. Any retention or reservation by the seller of the title (property) in goods shipped or delivered to the buyer is limited in effect to a reservation of a security interest. Subject to these provisions and to the provisions of the Article on Secured Transactions (Article 9), title to goods passes from the seller to the buyer in any manner and on any conditions explicitly agreed on by the parties.

(2) Unless otherwise explicitly agreed title passes to the buyer at the time and place at which the seller completes his performance with reference to the physical delivery of the goods, despite any reservation of a security interest and even though a document of title is to be delivered at a different time or place; and in particular and despite any reservation of a security interest by the bill of lading

(a) if the contract requires or authorizes the seller to send the goods to the buyer but does not require him to deliver them at destination, title passes to the buyer at the time and place of shipment; but

(b) if the contract requires delivery at destination, title passes on tender there.

(3) Unless otherwise explicitly agreed where delivery is to be made without moving the goods,

(a) if the seller is to deliver a document of title, title passes at the time when and the place where he delivers such documents; or

(b) if the goods are at the time of contracting already identified and no documents are to be delivered, title passes at the time and place of contracting.

(4) A rejection or other refusal by the buyer to receive or retain the goods, whether or not justified, or a justified revocation of acceptance revests title to the goods in the seller. Such revesting occurs by operation of law and is not a "sale".

§ 2–402. Rights of Seller's Creditors Against Sold Goods.

(1) Except as provided in subsections (2) and (3), rights of unsecured creditors of the seller with respect to goods which have been identified to a contract for sale are subject to the buyer's rights to recover the goods under this Article (Sections 2–502 and 2–716).

(2) A creditor of the seller may treat a sale or an identification of goods to a contract for sale as void if as against him a retention of possession by the seller is fraudulent under any rule of law of the state where the goods are situated, except that retention of possession in good faith and current course of trade by a merchant-seller for a commercially reasonable time after a sale or identification is not fraudulent.

(3) Nothing in this Article shall be deemed to impair the rights of creditors of the seller

(a) under the provisions of the Article on Secured Transactions (Article 9); or

(b) where identification to the contract or delivery is made not in current course of trade but in satisfaction of or as security for a pre-existing claim for money, security or the like and is made under circumstances which under any rule of law of the state where the goods are situated would apart from this Article constitute the transaction a fraudulent transfer or voidable preference.

§ 2–403. Power to Transfer; Good Faith Purchase of Goods; "Entrusting".

(1) A purchaser of goods acquires all title which his transferor had or had power to transfer except that a purchaser of a limited interest acquires rights only to the extent of the interest purchased. A person with voidable title has power to transfer a good title to a good faith purchaser for value. When goods have been delivered under a transaction of purchase the purchaser has such power even though

(a) the transferor was deceived as to the identity of the purchaser, or

(b) the delivery was in exchange for a check which is later dishonored, or

(c) it was agreed that the transaction was to be a "cash sale", or

(d) the delivery was procured through fraud punishable as larcenous under the criminal law.

(2) Any entrusting of possession of goods to a merchant who deals in goods of that kind gives him power to transfer all rights of the entruster to a buyer in ordinary course of business.

(3) "Entrusting" includes any delivery and any acquiescence in retention of possession regardless of any condition expressed between the parties to the delivery or acquiescence and regardless of whether the procurement of the entrusting or the possessor's disposition of the goods have been such as to be larcenous under the criminal law.

(4) The rights of other purchasers of goods and of lien creditors are governed by the Articles on Secured Transactions (Article 9), Bulk Transfers (Article 6) and Documents of Title (Article 7).

As amended in 1988.

Part 5 Performance

§ 2–501. Insurable Interest in Goods; Manner of Identification of Goods.

(1) The buyer obtains a special property and an insurable interest in goods by identification of existing goods as goods to which the contract refers even though the goods so identified are non-conforming and he has an option to return or reject them. Such identification can be made at any time and in any manner explicitly agreed to by the parties. In the absence of explicit agreement identification occurs

(a) when the contract is made if it is for the sale of goods already existing and identified;

(b) if the contract is for the sale of future goods other than those described in paragraph (c), when goods are shipped, marked or otherwise designated by the seller as goods to which the contract refers;

(c) when the crops are planted or otherwise become growing crops or the young are conceived if the contract is for the sale of unborn young to be born within twelve months after contracting or for the sale of crops to be harvested within twelve months or the next normal harvest season after contracting whichever is longer.

(2) The seller retains an insurable interest in goods so long as title to or any security interest in the goods remains in him and where the identification is by the seller alone he may until default or insolvency or notification to the buyer that the identification is final substitute other goods for those identified.

(3) Nothing in this section impairs any insurable interest recognized under any other statute or rule of law.

§ 2–502. Buyer's Right to Goods on Seller's Insolvency.

(1) Subject to subsections (2) and (3) and even though the goods have not been shipped a buyer who has paid a part or all of the price of goods in which he has a special property under the provisions of the immediately preceding section may on making and keeping good a tender of any unpaid portion of their price recover them from the seller if:

(a) in the case of goods bought for personal, family, or household purposes, the seller repudiates or fails to deliver as required by the contract; or

(b) in all cases, the seller becomes insolvent within ten days after receipt of the first installment on their price.

(2) The buyer's right to recover the goods under subsection (1)(a) vests upon acquisition of a special property, even if the seller had not then repudiated or failed to deliver.

(3) If the identification creating his special property has been made by the buyer he acquires the right to recover the goods only if they conform to the contract for sale.

As amended in 1999.

§ 2–503. Manner of Seller's Tender of Delivery.

(1) Tender of delivery requires that the seller put and hold conforming goods at the buyer's disposition and give the buyer any notification reasonably necessary to enable him to take delivery. The manner, time and place for tender are determined by the agreement and this Article, and in particular

(a) tender must be at a reasonable hour, and if it is of goods they must be kept available for the period reasonably necessary to enable the buyer to take possession; but

(b) unless otherwise agreed the buyer must furnish facilities reasonably suited to the receipt of the goods.

(2) Where the case is within the next section respecting shipment tender requires that the seller comply with its provisions.

(3) Where the seller is required to deliver at a particular destination tender requires that he comply with subsection (1) and also in any appropriate case tender documents as described in subsections (4) and (5) of this section.

(4) Where goods are in the possession of a bailee and are to be delivered without being moved

(a) tender requires that the seller either tender a negotiable document of title covering such goods or procure acknowledgment by the bailee of the buyer's right to possession of the goods; but

(b) tender to the buyer of a non-negotiable document of title or of a written direction to the bailee to deliver is sufficient tender unless the buyer seasonably objects, and receipt by the bailee of notification of the buyer's rights fixes those rights as against the bailee and all third persons; but risk of loss of the goods and of any failure by the bailee to honor the non-negotiable document of title or to obey the direction remains on the seller until the buyer has had a reasonable time to present the document or direction, and a refusal by the bailee to honor the document or to obey the direction defeats the tender.

(5) Where the contract requires the seller to deliver documents

(a) he must tender all such documents in correct form, except as provided in this Article with respect to bills of lading in a set (subsection (2) of Section 2–323); and

(b) tender through customary banking channels is sufficient and dishonor of a draft accompanying the documents constitutes non-acceptance or rejection.

§ 2–504. Shipment by Seller.

Where the seller is required or authorized to send the goods to the buyer and the contract does not require him to deliver them at a particular destination, then unless otherwise agreed he must

(a) put the goods in the possession of such a carrier and make such a contract for their transportation as may be reasonable having regard to the nature of the goods and other circumstances of the case; and

(b) obtain and promptly deliver or tender in due form any document necessary to enable the buyer to obtain possession of the goods or otherwise required by the agreement or by usage of trade; and

(c) promptly notify the buyer of the shipment.

Failure to notify the buyer under paragraph (c) or to make a proper contract under paragraph (a) is a ground for rejection only if material delay or loss ensues.

§ 2–505. Seller's Shipment under Reservation.

(1) Where the seller has identified goods to the contract by or before shipment:

(a) his procurement of a negotiable bill of lading to his own order or otherwise reserves in him a security interest in the goods. His procurement of the bill to the order of a financing agency or of the buyer indicates in addition only the seller's expectation of transferring that interest to the person named.

(b) a non-negotiable bill of lading to himself or his nominee reserves possession of the goods as security but except in a case of conditional delivery (subsection (2) of Section 2–507) a non-negotiable bill of lading naming the buyer as consignee reserves no security interest even though the seller retains possession of the bill of lading.

(2) When shipment by the seller with reservation of a security interest is in violation of the contract for sale it constitutes an improper contract for transportation within the preceding section but impairs neither the rights given to the buyer by shipment and identification of the goods to the contract nor the seller's powers as a holder of a negotiable document.

§ 2–506. Rights of Financing Agency.

(1) A financing agency by paying or purchasing for value a draft which relates to a shipment of goods acquires to the extent of the payment or purchase and in addition to its own rights under the draft and any document of title securing it any rights of the shipper in the goods including the right to stop delivery and the shipper's right to have the draft honored by the buyer.

(2) The right to reimbursement of a financing agency which has in good faith honored or purchased the draft under commitment to or authority from the buyer is not impaired by subsequent discovery of defects with reference to any relevant document which was apparently regular on its face.

§ 2–507. Effect of Seller's Tender; Delivery on Condition.

(1) Tender of delivery is a condition to the buyer's duty to accept the goods and, unless otherwise agreed, to his duty to pay for them. Tender entitles the seller to acceptance of the goods and to payment according to the contract.

(2) Where payment is due and demanded on the delivery to the buyer of goods or documents of title, his right as against the seller to retain or dispose of them is conditional upon his making the payment due.

§ 2–508. Cure by Seller of Improper Tender or Delivery; Replacement.

(1) Where any tender or delivery by the seller is rejected because non-conforming and the time for performance has not yet expired, the seller may seasonably notify the buyer of his intention to cure and may then within the contract time make a conforming delivery.

(2) Where the buyer rejects a non-conforming tender which the seller had reasonable grounds to believe would be acceptable with or without money allowance the seller may if he seasonably notifies the buyer have a further reasonable time to substitute a conforming tender.

§ 2–509. Risk of Loss in the Absence of Breach.

(1) Where the contract requires or authorizes the seller to ship the goods by carrier

(a) if it does not require him to deliver them at a particular destination, the risk of loss passes to the buyer when the goods are duly delivered to the carrier even though the shipment is under reservation (Section 2–505); but

(b) if it does require him to deliver them at a particular destination and the goods are there duly tendered while in the possession of the carrier, the risk of loss passes to the buyer when the goods are there duly so tendered as to enable the buyer to take delivery.

(2) Where the goods are held by a bailee to be delivered without being moved, the risk of loss passes to the buyer

(a) on his receipt of a negotiable document of title covering the goods; or

(b) on acknowledgment by the bailee of the buyer's right to possession of the goods; or

(c) after his receipt of a non-negotiable document of title or other written direction to deliver, as provided in subsection (4)(b) of Section 2–503.

(3) In any case not within subsection (1) or (2), the risk of loss passes to the buyer on his receipt of the goods if the seller is a merchant; otherwise the risk passes to the buyer on tender of delivery.

(4) The provisions of this section are subject to contrary agreement of the parties and to the provisions of this Article on sale on approval (Section 2–327) and on effect of breach on risk of loss (Section 2–510).

§ 2–510. Effect of Breach on Risk of Loss.

(1) Where a tender or delivery of goods so fails to conform to the contract as to give a right of rejection the risk of their loss remains on the seller until cure or acceptance.

(2) Where the buyer rightfully revokes acceptance he may to the extent of any deficiency in his effective insurance coverage treat the risk of loss as having rested on the seller from the beginning.

(3) Where the buyer as to conforming goods already identified to the contract for sale repudiates or is otherwise in breach before risk of their loss has passed to him, the seller may to the extent of any deficiency in his effective insurance coverage treat the risk of loss as resting on the buyer for a commercially reasonable time.

§ 2–511. Tender of Payment by Buyer; Payment by Check.

(1) Unless otherwise agreed tender of payment is a condition to the seller's duty to tender and complete any delivery.

(2) Tender of payment is sufficient when made by any means or in any manner current in the ordinary course of business unless the seller demands payment in legal tender and gives any extension of time reasonably necessary to procure it.

(3) Subject to the provisions of this Act on the effect of an instrument on an obligation (Section 3–310), payment by check is conditional and is defeated as between the parties by dishonor of the check on due presentment.

As amended in 1994.

§ 2–512. Payment by Buyer Before Inspection.

(1) Where the contract requires payment before inspection non-conformity of the goods does not excuse the buyer from so making payment unless

    (a) the non-conformity appears without inspection; or

    (b) despite tender of the required documents the circumstances would justify injunction against honor under this Act (Section 5–109(b)).

(2) Payment pursuant to subsection (1) does not constitute an acceptance of goods or impair the buyer's right to inspect or any of his remedies.

As amended in 1995.

§ 2–513. Buyer's Right to Inspection of Goods.

(1) Unless otherwise agreed and subject to subsection (3), where goods are tendered or delivered or identified to the contract for sale, the buyer has a right before payment or acceptance to inspect them at any reasonable place and time and in any reasonable manner. When the seller is required or authorized to send the goods to the buyer, the inspection may be after their arrival.

(2) Expenses of inspection must be borne by the buyer but may be recovered from the seller if the goods do not conform and are rejected.

(3) Unless otherwise agreed and subject to the provisions of this Article on C.I.F. contracts (subsection (3) of Section 2–321), the buyer is not entitled to inspect the goods before payment of the price when the contract provides

    (a) for delivery "C.O.D." or on other like terms; or

    (b) for payment against documents of title, except where such payment is due only after the goods are to become available for inspection.

(4) A place or method of inspection fixed by the parties is presumed to be exclusive but unless otherwise expressly agreed it does not postpone identification or shift the place for delivery or for passing the risk of loss. If compliance becomes impossible, inspection shall be as provided in this section unless the place or method fixed was clearly intended as an indispensable condition failure of which avoids the contract.

§ 2–514. When Documents Deliverable on Acceptance; When on Payment.

Unless otherwise agreed documents against which a draft is drawn are to be delivered to the drawee on acceptance of the draft if it is payable more than three days after presentment; otherwise, only on payment.

§ 2–515. Preserving Evidence of Goods in Dispute.

In furtherance of the adjustment of any claim or dispute

    (a) either party on reasonable notification to the other and for the purpose of ascertaining the facts and preserving evidence has the right to inspect, test and sample the goods including such of them as may be in the possession or control of the other; and

    (b) the parties may agree to a third party inspection or survey to determine the conformity or condition of the goods and may agree that the findings shall be binding upon them in any subsequent litigation or adjustment.

Part 6 Breach, Repudiation and Excuse

§ 2–601. Buyer's Rights on Improper Delivery.

Subject to the provisions of this Article on breach in installment contracts (Section 2–612) and unless otherwise agreed under the sections on contractual limitations of remedy (Sections 2–718 and 2–719), if the goods or the tender of delivery fail in any respect to conform to the contract, the buyer may

(a) reject the whole; or

(b) accept the whole; or

(c) accept any commercial unit or units and reject the rest.

§ 2–602. Manner and Effect of Rightful Rejection.

(1) Rejection of goods must be within a reasonable time after their delivery or tender. It is ineffective unless the buyer seasonably notifies the seller.

(2) Subject to the provisions of the two following sections on rejected goods (Sections 2–603 and 2–604),

(a) after rejection any exercise of ownership by the buyer with respect to any commercial unit is wrongful as against the seller; and

(b) if the buyer has before rejection taken physical possession of goods in which he does not have a security interest under the provisions of this Article (subsection (3) of Section 2–711), he is under a duty after rejection to hold them with reasonable care at the seller's disposition for a time sufficient to permit the seller to remove them; but

(c) the buyer has no further obligations with regard to goods rightfully rejected.

(3) The seller's rights with respect to goods wrongfully rejected are governed by the provisions of this Article on Seller's remedies in general (Section 2–703).

§ 2–603. Merchant Buyer's Duties as to Rightfully Rejected Goods.

(1) Subject to any security interest in the buyer (subsection (3) of Section 2–711), when the seller has no agent or place of business at the market of rejection a merchant buyer is under a duty after rejection of goods in his possession or control to follow any reasonable instructions received from the seller with respect to the goods and in the absence of such instructions to make reasonable efforts to sell them for the seller's account if they are perishable or threaten to decline in value speedily. Instructions are not reasonable if on demand indemnity for expenses is not forthcoming.

(2) When the buyer sells goods under subsection (1), he is entitled to reimbursement from the seller or out of the proceeds for reasonable expenses of caring for and selling them, and if the expenses include no selling commission then to such commission as is usual in the trade or if there is none to a reasonable sum not exceeding ten per cent on the gross proceeds.

(3) In complying with this section the buyer is held only to good faith and good faith conduct hereunder is neither acceptance nor conversion nor the basis of an action for damages.

§ 2–604. Buyer's Options as to Salvage of Rightfully Rejected Goods.

Subject to the provisions of the immediately preceding section on perishables if the seller gives no instructions within a reasonable time after notification of rejection the buyer may store the rejected goods for the seller's account or reship them to him or resell them for the seller's account with reimbursement as provided in the preceding section. Such action is not acceptance or conversion.

§ 2–605. Waiver of Buyer's Objections by Failure to Particularize.

(1) The buyer's failure to state in connection with rejection a particular defect which is ascertainable by reasonable inspection precludes him from relying on the unstated defect to justify rejection or to establish breach

(a) where the seller could have cured it if stated seasonably; or

(b) between merchants when the seller has after rejection made a request in writing for a full and final written statement of all defects on which the buyer proposes to rely.

(2) Payment against documents made without reservation of rights precludes recovery of the payment for defects apparent on the face of the documents.

§ 2–606. What Constitutes Acceptance of Goods.

(1) Acceptance of goods occurs when the buyer

(a) after a reasonable opportunity to inspect the goods signifies to the seller that the goods are conforming or that he will take or retain them in spite of their nonconformity; or

(b) fails to make an effective rejection (subsection (1) of Section 2–602), but such acceptance does not occur until the buyer has had a reasonable opportunity to inspect them; or

(c) does any act inconsistent with the seller's ownership; but if such act is wrongful as against the seller it is an acceptance only if ratified by him.

(2) Acceptance of a part of any commercial unit is acceptance of that entire unit.

§ 2–607. Effect of Acceptance; Notice of Breach; Burden of Establishing Breach After Acceptance; Notice of Claim or Litigation to Person Answerable Over.

(1) The buyer must pay at the contract rate for any goods accepted.

(2) Acceptance of goods by the buyer precludes rejection of the goods accepted and if made with knowledge of a nonconformity cannot be revoked because of it unless the acceptance was on the reasonable assumption that the nonconformity would be seasonably cured but acceptance does

not of itself impair any other remedy provided by this Article for non-conformity.

(3) Where a tender has been accepted

(a) the buyer must within a reasonable time after he discovers or should have discovered any breach notify the seller of breach or be barred from any remedy; and

(b) if the claim is one for infringement or the like (subsection (3) of Section 2–312) and the buyer is sued as a result of such a breach he must so notify the seller within a reasonable time after he receives notice of the litigation or be barred from any remedy over for liability established by the litigation.

(4) The burden is on the buyer to establish any breach with respect to the goods accepted.

(5) Where the buyer is sued for breach of a warranty or other obligation for which his seller is answerable over

(a) he may give his seller written notice of the litigation. If the notice states that the seller may come in and defend and that if the seller does not do so he will be bound in any action against him by his buyer by any determination of fact common to the two litigations, then unless the seller after seasonable receipt of the notice does come in and defend he is so bound.

(b) if the claim is one for infringement or the like (subsection (3) of Section 2–312) the original seller may demand in writing that his buyer turn over to him control of the litigation including settlement or else be barred from any remedy over and if he also agrees to bear all expense and to satisfy any adverse judgment, then unless the buyer after seasonable receipt of the demand does turn over control the buyer is so barred.

(6) The provisions of subsections (3), (4) and (5) apply to any obligation of a buyer to hold the seller harmless against infringement or the like (subsection (3) of Section 2–312).

§ 2–608. Revocation of Acceptance in Whole or in Part.

(1) The buyer may revoke his acceptance of a lot or commercial unit whose non-conformity substantially impairs its value to him if he has accepted it

(a) on the reasonable assumption that its nonconformity would be cured and it has not been seasonably cured; or

(b) without discovery of such non-conformity if his acceptance was reasonably induced either by the difficulty of discovery before acceptance or by the seller's assurances.

(2) Revocation of acceptance must occur within a reasonable time after the buyer discovers or should have discovered the ground for it and before any substantial change in condition of the goods which is not caused by their own defects. It is not effective until the buyer notifies the seller of it.

(3) A buyer who so revokes has the same rights and duties with regard to the goods involved as if he had rejected them.

§ 2–609. Right to Adequate Assurance of Performance.

(1) A contract for sale imposes an obligation on each party that the other's expectation of receiving due performance will not be impaired. When reasonable grounds for insecurity arise with respect to the performance of either party the other may in writing demand adequate assurance of due performance and until he receives such assurance may if commercially reasonable suspend any performance for which he has not already received the agreed return.

(2) Between merchants the reasonableness of grounds for insecurity and the adequacy of any assurance offered shall be determined according to commercial standards.

(3) Acceptance of any improper delivery or payment does not prejudice the party's right to demand adequate assurance of future performance.

(4) After receipt of a justified demand failure to provide within a reasonable time not exceeding thirty days such assurance of due performance as is adequate under the circumstances of the particular case is a repudiation of the contract.

§ 2–610. Anticipatory Repudiation.

When either party repudiates the contract with respect to a performance not yet due the loss of which will substantially impair the value of the contract to the other, the aggrieved party may

(a) for a commercially reasonable time await performance by the repudiating party; or

(b) resort to any remedy for breach (Section 2–703 or Section 2–711), even though he has notified the repudiating party that he would await the latter's performance and has urged retraction; and

(c) in either case suspend his own performance or proceed in accordance with the provisions of this Article on the seller's right to identify goods to the contract notwithstanding breach or to salvage unfinished goods (Section 2–704).

§ 2–611. Retraction of Anticipatory Repudiation.

(1) Until the repudiating party's next performance is due he can retract his repudiation unless the aggrieved party has since the repudiation cancelled or materially changed his position or otherwise indicated that he considers the repudiation final.

(2) Retraction may be by any method which clearly indicates to the aggrieved party that the repudiating party intends to perform, but must include any assurance justifiably demanded under the provisions of this Article (Section 2–609).

(3) Retraction reinstates the repudiating party's rights under the contract with due excuse and allowance to the aggrieved party for any delay occasioned by the repudiation.

§ 2–612. "Installment Contract"; Breach.

(1) An "installment contract" is one which requires or authorizes the delivery of goods in separate lots to be sepa-

rately accepted, even though the contract contains a clause "each delivery is a separate contract" or its equivalent.

(2) The buyer may reject any installment which is non-conforming if the non-conformity substantially impairs the value of that installment and cannot be cured or if the non-conformity is a defect in the required documents; but if the non-conformity does not fall within subsection (3) and the seller gives adequate assurance of its cure the buyer must accept that installment.

(3) Whenever non-conformity or default with respect to one or more installments substantially impairs the value of the whole contract there is a breach of the whole. But the aggrieved party reinstates the contract if he accepts a non-conforming installment without seasonably notifying of cancellation or if he brings an action with respect only to past installments or demands performance as to future installments.

§ 2–613. Casualty to Identified Goods.

Where the contract requires for its performance goods identified when the contract is made, and the goods suffer casualty without fault of either party before the risk of loss passes to the buyer, or in a proper case under a "no arrival, no sale" term (Section 2–324) then

(a) if the loss is total the contract is avoided; and

(b) if the loss is partial or the goods have so deteriorated as no longer to conform to the contract the buyer may nevertheless demand inspection and at his option either treat the contract as voided or accept the goods with due allowance from the contract price for the deterioration or the deficiency in quantity but without further right against the seller.

§ 2–614. Substituted Performance.

(1) Where without fault of either party the agreed berthing, loading, or unloading facilities fail or an agreed type of carrier becomes unavailable or the agreed manner of delivery otherwise becomes commercially impracticable but a commercially reasonable substitute is available, such substitute performance must be tendered and accepted.

(2) If the agreed means or manner of payment fails because of domestic or foreign governmental regulation, the seller may withhold or stop delivery unless the buyer provides a means or manner of payment which is commercially a substantial equivalent. If delivery has already been taken, payment by the means or in the manner provided by the regulation discharges the buyer's obligation unless the regulation is discriminatory, oppressive or predatory.

§ 2–615. Excuse by Failure of Presupposed Conditions.

Except so far as a seller may have assumed a greater obligation and subject to the preceding section on substituted performance:

(a) Delay in delivery or non-delivery in whole or in part by a seller who complies with paragraphs (b) and (c) is not a breach of his duty under a contract for sale if performance as agreed has been made impracticable by the occurrence of a contingency the nonoccurrence of which was a basic assumption on which the contract was made or by compliance in good faith with any applicable foreign or domestic governmental regulation or order whether or not it later proves to be invalid.

(b) Where the causes mentioned in paragraph (a) affect only a part of the seller's capacity to perform, he must allocate production and deliveries among his customers but may at his option include regular customers not then under contract as well as his own requirements for further manufacture. He may so allocate in any manner which is fair and reasonable.

(c) The seller must notify the buyer seasonably that there will be delay or non-delivery and, when allocation is required under paragraph (b), of the estimated quota thus made available for the buyer.

§ 2–616. Procedure on Notice Claiming Excuse.

(1) Where the buyer receives notification of a material or indefinite delay or an allocation justified under the preceding section he may by written notification to the seller as to any delivery concerned, and where the prospective deficiency substantially impairs the value of the whole contract under the provisions of this Article relating to breach of installment contracts (Section 2–612), then also as to the whole,

> (a) terminate and thereby discharge any unexecuted portion of the contract; or

> (b) modify the contract by agreeing to take his available quota in substitution.

(2) If after receipt of such notification from the seller the buyer fails so to modify the contract within a reasonable time not exceeding thirty days the contract lapses with respect to any deliveries affected.

(3) The provisions of this section may not be negated by agreement except in so far as the seller has assumed a greater obligation under the preceding section.

Part 7 Remedies

§ 2–701. Remedies for Breach of Collateral Contracts Not Impaired.

Remedies for breach of any obligation or promise collateral or ancillary to a contract for sale are not impaired by the provisions of this Article.

§ 2–702. Seller's Remedies on Discovery of Buyer's Insolvency.

(1) Where the seller discovers the buyer to be insolvent he may refuse delivery except for cash including payment for all goods theretofore delivered under the contract, and stop delivery under this Article (Section 2–705).

(2) Where the seller discovers that the buyer has received goods on credit while insolvent he may reclaim the goods

upon demand made within ten days after the receipt, but if misrepresentation of solvency has been made to the particular seller in writing within three months before delivery the ten day limitation does not apply. Except as provided in this subsection the seller may not base a right to reclaim goods on the buyer's fraudulent or innocent misrepresentation of solvency or of intent to pay.

(3) The seller's right to reclaim under subsection (2) is subject to the rights of a buyer in ordinary course or other good faith purchaser under this Article (Section 2–403). Successful reclamation of goods excludes all other remedies with respect to them.

§ 2–703. Seller's Remedies in General.

Where the buyer wrongfully rejects or revokes acceptance of goods or fails to make a payment due on or before delivery or repudiates with respect to a part or the whole, then with respect to any goods directly affected and, if the breach is of the whole contract (Section 2–612), then also with respect to the whole undelivered balance, the aggrieved seller may

(a) withhold delivery of such goods;

(b) stop delivery by any bailee as hereafter provided (Section 2–705);

(c) proceed under the next section respecting goods still unidentified to the contract;

(d) resell and recover damages as hereafter provided (Section 2–706);

(e) recover damages for non-acceptance (Section 2–708) or in a proper case the price (Section 2–709);

(f) cancel.

§ 2–704. Seller's Right to Identify Goods to the Contract Notwithstanding Breach or to Salvage Unfinished Goods.

(1) An aggrieved seller under the preceding section may

(a) identify to the contract conforming goods not already identified if at the time he learned of the breach they are in his possession or control;

(b) treat as the subject of resale goods which have demonstrably been intended for the particular contract even though those goods are unfinished.

(2) Where the goods are unfinished an aggrieved seller may in the exercise of reasonable commercial judgment for the purposes of avoiding loss and of effective realization either complete the manufacture and wholly identify the goods to the contract or cease manufacture and resell for scrap or salvage value or proceed in any other reasonable manner.

§ 2–705. Seller's Stoppage of Delivery in Transit or Otherwise.

(1) The seller may stop delivery of goods in the possession of a carrier or other bailee when he discovers the buyer to be insolvent (Section 2–702) and may stop delivery of carload, truckload, planeload or larger shipments of express or freight when the buyer repudiates or fails to make a payment due before delivery or if for any other reason the seller has a right to withhold or reclaim the goods.

(2) As against such buyer the seller may stop delivery until

(a) receipt of the goods by the buyer; or

(b) acknowledgment to the buyer by any bailee of the goods except a carrier that the bailee holds the goods for the buyer; or

(c) such acknowledgment to the buyer by a carrier by reshipment or as warehouseman; or

(d) negotiation to the buyer of any negotiable document of title covering the goods.

(3) (a) To stop delivery the seller must so notify as to enable the bailee by reasonable diligence to prevent delivery of the goods.

(b) After such notification the bailee must hold and deliver the goods according to the directions of the seller but the seller is liable to the bailee for any ensuing charges or damages.

(c) If a negotiable document of title has been issued for goods the bailee is not obliged to obey a notification to stop until surrender of the document.

(d) A carrier who has issued a non-negotiable bill of lading is not obliged to obey a notification to stop received from a person other than the consignor.

§ 2–706. Seller's Resale Including Contract for Resale.

(1) Under the conditions stated in Section 2–703 on seller's remedies, the seller may resell the goods concerned or the undelivered balance thereof. Where the resale is made in good faith and in a commercially reasonable manner the seller may recover the difference between the resale price and the contract price together with any incidental damages allowed under the provisions of this Article (Section 2–710), but less expenses saved in consequence of the buyer's breach.

(2) Except as otherwise provided in subsection (3) or unless otherwise agreed resale may be at public or private sale including sale by way of one or more contracts to sell or of identification to an existing contract of the seller. Sale may be as a unit or in parcels and at any time and place and on any terms but every aspect of the sale including the method, manner, time, place and terms must be commercially reasonable. The resale must be reasonably identified as referring to the broken contract, but it is not necessary that the goods be in existence or that any or all of them have been identified to the contract before the breach.

(3) Where the resale is at private sale the seller must give the buyer reasonable notification of his intention to resell.

(4) Where the resale is at public sale

(a) only identified goods can be sold except where there is a recognized market for a public sale of futures in goods of the kind; and

(b) it must be made at a usual place or market for public sale if one is reasonably available and except in the case of goods which are perishable or threaten to decline in value speedily the seller must give the buyer reasonable notice of the time and place of the resale; and

(c) if the goods are not to be within the view of those attending the sale the notification of sale must state the place where the goods are located and provide for their reasonable inspection by prospective bidders; and

(d) the seller may buy.

(5) A purchaser who buys in good faith at a resale takes the goods free of any rights of the original buyer even though the seller fails to comply with one or more of the requirements of this section.

(6) The seller is not accountable to the buyer for any profit made on any resale. A person in the position of a seller (Section 2–707) or a buyer who has rightfully rejected or justifiably revoked acceptance must account for any excess over the amount of his security interest, as hereinafter defined (subsection (3) of Section 2–711).

§ 2–707. "Person in the Position of a Seller".

(1) A "person in the position of a seller" includes as against a principal an agent who has paid or become responsible for the price of goods on behalf of his principal or anyone who otherwise holds a security interest or other right in goods similar to that of a seller.

(2) A person in the position of a seller may as provided in this Article withhold or stop delivery (Section 2–705) and resell (Section 2–706) and recover incidental damages (Section 2–710).

§ 2–708. Seller's Damages for Non-Acceptance or Repudiation.

(1) Subject to subsection (2) and to the provisions of this Article with respect to proof of market price (Section 2–723), the measure of damages for non-acceptance or repudiation by the buyer is the difference between the market price at the time and place for tender and the unpaid contract price together with any incidental damages provided in this Article (Section 2–710), but less expenses saved in consequence of the buyer's breach.

(2) If the measure of damages provided in subsection (1) is inadequate to put the seller in as good a position as performance would have done then the measure of damages is the profit (including reasonable overhead) which the seller would have made from full performance by the buyer, together with any incidental damages provided in this Article (Section 2–710), due allowance for costs reasonably incurred and due credit for payments or proceeds of resale.

§ 2–709. Action for the Price.

(1) When the buyer fails to pay the price as it becomes due the seller may recover, together with any incidental damages under the next section, the price

(a) of goods accepted or of conforming goods lost or damaged within a commercially reasonable time after risk of their loss has passed to the buyer; and

(b) of goods identified to the contract if the seller is unable after reasonable effort to resell them at a reasonable price or the circumstances reasonably indicate that such effort will be unavailing.

(2) Where the seller sues for the price he must hold for the buyer any goods which have been identified to the contract and are still in his control except that if resale becomes possible he may resell them at any time prior to the collection of the judgment. The net proceeds of any such resale must be credited to the buyer and payment of the judgment entitles him to any goods not resold.

(3) After the buyer has wrongfully rejected or revoked acceptance of the goods or has failed to make a payment due or has repudiated (Section 2–610), a seller who is held not entitled to the price under this section shall nevertheless be awarded damages for non-acceptance under the preceding section.

§ 2–710. Seller's Incidental Damages.

Incidental damages to an aggrieved seller include any commercially reasonable charges, expenses or commissions incurred in stopping delivery, in the transportation, care and custody of goods after the buyer's breach, in connection with return or resale of the goods or otherwise resulting from the breach.

§ 2–711. Buyer's Remedies in General; Buyer's Security Interest in Rejected Goods.

(1) Where the seller fails to make delivery or repudiates or the buyer rightfully rejects or justifiably revokes acceptance then with respect to any goods involved, and with respect to the whole if the breach goes to the whole contract (Section 2–612), the buyer may cancel and whether or not he has done so may in addition to recovering so much of the price as has been paid

(a) "cover" and have damages under the next section as to all the goods affected whether or not they have been identified to the contract; or

(b) recover damages for non-delivery as provided in this Article (Section 2–713).

(2) Where the seller fails to deliver or repudiates the buyer may also

(a) if the goods have been identified recover them as provided in this Article (Section 2–502); or

(b) in a proper case obtain specific performance or replevy the goods as provided in this Article (Section 2–716).

(3) On rightful rejection or justifiable revocation of acceptance a buyer has a security interest in goods in his possession or control for any payments made on their price and any expenses reasonably incurred in their inspection, receipt, transportation, care and custody and may hold such goods and resell them in like manner as an aggrieved seller (Section 2–706).

§ 2–712. "Cover"; Buyer's Procurement of Substitute Goods.

(1) After a breach within the preceding section the buyer may "cover" by making in good faith and without unreasonable delay any reasonable purchase of or contract to purchase goods in substitution for those due from the seller.

(2) The buyer may recover from the seller as damages the difference between the cost of cover and the contract price together with any incidental or consequential damages as hereinafter defined (Section 2–715), but less expenses saved in consequence of the seller's breach.

(3) Failure of the buyer to effect cover within this section does not bar him from any other remedy.

§ 2–713. Buyer's Damages for Non-Delivery or Repudiation.

(1) Subject to the provisions of this Article with respect to proof of market price (Section 2–723), the measure of damages for non-delivery or repudiation by the seller is the difference between the market price at the time when the buyer learned of the breach and the contract price together with any incidental and consequential damages provided in this Article (Section 2–715), but less expenses saved in consequence of the seller's breach.

(2) Market price is to be determined as of the place for tender or, in cases of rejection after arrival or revocation of acceptance, as of the place of arrival.

§ 2–714. Buyer's Damages for Breach in Regard to Accepted Goods.

(1) Where the buyer has accepted goods and given notification (subsection (3) of Section 2–607) he may recover as damages for any non-conformity of tender the loss resulting in the ordinary course of events from the seller's breach as determined in any manner which is reasonable.

(2) The measure of damages for breach of warranty is the difference at the time and place of acceptance between the value of the goods accepted and the value they would have had if they had been as warranted, unless special circumstances show proximate damages of a different amount.

(3) In a proper case any incidental and consequential damages under the next section may also be recovered.

§ 2–715. Buyer's Incidental and Consequential Damages.

(1) Incidental damages resulting from the seller's breach include expenses reasonably incurred in inspection, receipt, transportation and care and custody of goods rightfully rejected, any commercially reasonable charges, expenses or commissions in connection with effecting cover and any other reasonable expense incident to the delay or other breach.

(2) Consequential damages resulting from the seller's breach include

(a) any loss resulting from general or particular requirements and needs of which the seller at the time of contracting had reason to know and which could not reasonably be prevented by cover or otherwise; and

(b) injury to person or property proximately resulting from any breach of warranty.

§ 2–716. Buyer's Right to Specific Performance or Replevin.

(1) Specific performance may be decreed where the goods are unique or in other proper circumstances.

(2) The decree for specific performance may include such terms and conditions as to payment of the price, damages, or other relief as the court may deem just.

(3) The buyer has a right of replevin for goods identified to the contract if after reasonable effort he is unable to effect cover for such goods or the circumstances reasonably indicate that such effort will be unavailing or if the goods have been shipped under reservation and satisfaction of the security interest in them has been made or tendered. In the case of goods bought for personal, family, or household purposes, the buyer's right of replevin vests upon acquisition of a special property, even if the seller had not then repudiated or failed to deliver.

As amended in 1999.

§ 2–717. Deduction of Damages From the Price.

The buyer on notifying the seller of his intention to do so may deduct all or any part of the damages resulting from any breach of the contract from any part of the price still due under the same contract.

§ 2–718. Liquidation or Limitation of Damages; Deposits.

(1) Damages for breach by either party may be liquidated in the agreement but only at an amount which is reasonable in the light of the anticipated or actual harm caused by the breach, the difficulties of proof of loss, and the inconvenience or nonfeasibility of otherwise obtaining an adequate remedy. A term fixing unreasonably large liquidated damages is void as a penalty.

(2) Where the seller justifiably withholds delivery of goods because of the buyer's breach, the buyer is entitled to restitution of any amount by which the sum of his payments exceeds

(a) the amount to which the seller is entitled by virtue of terms liquidating the seller's damages in accordance with subsection (1), or

(b) in the absence of such terms, twenty per cent of the value of the total performance for which the buyer is obligated under the contract or $500, whichever is smaller.

(3) The buyer's right to restitution under subsection (2) is subject to offset to the extent that the seller establishes

(a) a right to recover damages under the provisions of this Article other than subsection (1), and

(b) the amount or value of any benefits received by the buyer directly or indirectly by reason of the contract.

(4) Where a seller has received payment in goods their reasonable value or the proceeds of their resale shall be treated as payments for the purposes of subsection (2); but if the seller has notice of the buyer's breach before reselling goods received in part performance, his resale is subject to the conditions laid down in this Article on resale by an aggrieved seller (Section 2–706).

§ **2–719.** **Contractual Modification or Limitation of Remedy.**

(1) Subject to the provisions of subsections (2) and (3) of this section and of the preceding section on liquidation and limitation of damages,

(a) the agreement may provide for remedies in addition to or in substitution for those provided in this Article and may limit or alter the measure of damages recoverable under this Article, as by limiting the buyer's remedies to return of the goods and repayment of the price or to repair and replacement of nonconforming goods or parts; and

(b) resort to a remedy as provided is optional unless the remedy is expressly agreed to be exclusive, in which case it is the sole remedy.

(2) Where circumstances cause an exclusive or limited remedy to fail of its essential purpose, remedy may be had as provided in this Act.

(3) Consequential damages may be limited or excluded unless the limitation or exclusion is unconscionable. Limitation of consequential damages for injury to the person in the case of consumer goods is prima facie unconscionable but limitation of damages where the loss is commercial is not.

§ **2–720.** **Effect of "Cancellation" or "Rescission" on Claims for Antecedent Breach.**

Unless the contrary intention clearly appears, expressions of "cancellation" or "rescission" of the contract or the like shall not be construed as a renunciation or discharge of any claim in damages for an antecedent breach.

§ **2–721.** **Remedies for Fraud.**

Remedies for material misrepresentation or fraud include all remedies available under this Article for non-fraudulent breach. Neither rescission or a claim for rescission of the contract for sale nor rejection or return of the goods shall bar or be deemed inconsistent with a claim for damages or other remedy.

§ **2–722.** **Who Can Sue Third Parties for Injury to Goods.**

Where a third party so deals with goods which have been identified to a contract for sale as to cause actionable injury to a party to that contract

(a) a right of action against the third party is in either party to the contract for sale who has title to or a security interest or a special property or an insurable interest in the goods; and if the goods have been destroyed or converted a right of action is also in the party who either bore the risk of loss under the contract for sale or has since the injury assumed that risk as against the other;

(b) if at the time of the injury the party plaintiff did not bear the risk of loss as against the other party to the contract for sale and there is no arrangement between them for disposition of the recovery, his suit or settlement is, subject to his own interest, as a fiduciary for the other party to the contract;

(c) either party may with the consent of the other sue for the benefit of whom it may concern.

§ **2–723.** **Proof of Market Price: Time and Place.**

(1) If an action based on anticipatory repudiation comes to trial before the time for performance with respect to some or all of the goods, any damages based on market price (Section 2–708 or Section 2–713) shall be determined according to the price of such goods prevailing at the time when the aggrieved party learned of the repudiation.

(2) If evidence of a price prevailing at the times or places described in this Article is not readily available the price prevailing within any reasonable time before or after the time described or at any other place which in commercial judgment or under usage of trade would serve as a reasonable substitute for the one described may be used, making any proper allowance for the cost of transporting the goods to or from such other place.

(3) Evidence of a relevant price prevailing at a time or place other than the one described in this Article offered by one party is not admissible unless and until he has given the other party such notice as the court finds sufficient to prevent unfair surprise.

§ **2–724.** **Admissibility of Market Quotations.**

Whenever the prevailing price or value of any goods regularly bought and sold in any established commodity market is in issue, reports in official publications or trade journals or in newspapers or periodicals of general circulation published as the reports of such market shall be admissible in evidence. The circumstances of the preparation of such a report may be shown to affect its weight but not its admissibility.

§ **2–725.** **Statute of Limitations in Contracts for Sale.**

(1) An action for breach of any contract for sale must be

commenced within four years after the cause of action has accrued. By the original agreement the parties may reduce the period of limitation to not less than one year but may not extend it.

(2) A cause of action accrues when the breach occurs, regardless of the aggrieved party's lack of knowledge of the breach. A breach of warranty occurs when tender of delivery is made, except that where a warranty explicitly extends to future performance of the goods and discovery of the breach must await the time of such performance the cause of action accrues when the breach is or should have been discovered.

(3) Where an action commenced within the time limited by subsection (1) is so terminated as to leave available a remedy by another action for the same breach such other action may be commenced after the expiration of the time limited and within six months after the termination of the first action unless the termination resulted from voluntary discontinuance or from dismissal for failure or neglect to prosecute.

(4) This section does not alter the law on tolling of the statute of limitations nor does it apply to causes of action which have accrued before this Act becomes effective.

Article 2 Amendments (Excerpts)[1]

Part 1 Short Title, General Construction and Subject Matter

*   *   *   *

§ 2–103. Definitions and Index of Definitions.

(1) In this article unless the context otherwise requires

*   *   *   *

(b) "Conspicuous", with reference to a term, means so written, displayed, or presented that a reasonable person against which it is to operate ought to have noticed it. A term in an electronic record intended to evoke a response by an electronic agent is conspicuous if it is presented in a form that would enable a reasonably configured electronic agent to take it into account or react to it without review of the record by an individual. Whether a term is "conspicuous" or not is a decision for the court. Conspicuous terms include the following:

    (i) for a person:

        (A) a heading in capitals equal to or greater in size than the surrounding text, or in contrasting type, font, or color to the surrounding text of the same or lesser size and;

---

1. Additions and new wording are underlined. What follows represents only selected changes made by the 2003 amendments. Although the National Conference of Commissioners on Uniform State Laws and the American Law Institute approved the amendments in May of 2003, as of this writing, they have not as yet been adopted by any state.

        (B) language in the body of a record or display in larger type than the surrounding text, or in contrasting type, font, or color to the surrounding text of the same size, or set off from surrounding text of the same size by symbols or other marks that call attention to the language; and

    (ii) for a person or an electronic agent, a term that is so placed in a record or display that the person or electronic agent cannot proceed without taking action with respect to the particular term.

(c) "Consumer" means an individual who buys or contracts to buy goods that, at the time of contracting, are intended by the individual to be used primarily for personal, family, or household purposes.

(d) "Consumer contract" means a contract between a merchant seller and a consumer.

*   *   *   *

(j) "Good faith" means honesty in fact and the observance of reasonable commercial standards of fair dealing.

(k) "Goods" means all things that are movable at the time of identification to a contract for sale. The term includes future goods, specially manufactured goods, the unborn young of animals, growing crops, and other identified things attached to realty as described in Section 2–107. The term does not include information, the money in which the price is to be paid, investment securities under Article 8, the subject matter of foreign exchange transactions, and choses in action.

*   *   *   *

(m) "Record" means information that is inscribed on a tangible medium or that is stored in an electronic or other medium and is retrievable in perceivable form.

(n) "Remedial promise" means a promise by the seller to repair or replace the goods or to refund all or part of the price upon the happening of a specified event.

*   *   *   *

(p) "Sign" means, with present intent to authenticate or adopt a record,

    (i) to execute or adopt a tangible symbol; or

    (ii) to attach to or logically associate with the record an electronic sound, symbol, or process.

*   *   *   *

Part 2 Form, Formation, Terms and Readjustment of Contract; Electronic Contracting

§ 2–201. Formal Requirements; Statute of Frauds.

(1) A contract for the sale of goods for the price of $5,000 or more is not enforceable by way of action or defense unless there is some record sufficient to indicate that a contract for sale has been made between the parties and signed by the party against which enforcement is sought or by the party's authorized agent or broker. A record is not insufficient

because it omits or incorrectly states a term agreed upon but the contract is not enforceable under this subsection beyond the quantity of goods shown in the record.

(2) Between merchants if within a reasonable time a record in confirmation of the contract and sufficient against the sender is received and the party receiving it has reason to know its contents, it satisfies the requirements of subsection (1) against the recipient unless notice of objection to its contents is given in a record within 10 days after it is received.

(3) A contract which does not satisfy the requirements of subsection (1) but which is valid in other respects is enforceable

> (a) if the goods are to be specially manufactured for the buyer and are not suitable for sale to others in the ordinary course of the seller's business and the seller, before notice of repudiation is received and under circumstances which reasonably indicate that the goods are for the buyer, has made either a substantial beginning of their manufacture or commitments for their procurement; or
>
> (b) if the party against which enforcement is sought admits in the party's pleading, or in the party's testimony or otherwise under oath that a contract for sale was made, but the contract is not enforceable under this paragraph beyond the quantity of goods admitted; or
>
> (c) with respect to goods for which payment has been made and accepted or which have been received and accepted (Sec. 2–606).

(4) A contract that is enforceable under this section is not rendered unenforceable merely because it is not capable of being performed within one year or any other applicable period after its making.

* * * *

§ 2–207. Terms of Contract; Effect of Confirmation.

Subject to Section 2–202, if (i) conduct by both parties recognizes the existence of a contract although their records do not otherwise establish a contract, (ii) a contract is formed by an offer and acceptance, or (iii) a contract formed in any manner is confirmed by a record that contains terms additional to or different from those in the contract being confirmed, the terms of the contract, are:

> (a) terms that appear in the records of both parties;
>
> (b) terms, whether in a record or not, to which both parties agree; and
>
> (c) terms supplied or incorporated under any provision of this Act.

* * * *

Part 3 General Obligation and Construction of Contract

⚹   ⚹   ⚹   ⚹

§ 2–312. Warranty of Title and Against Infringement; Buyer's Obligation Against Infringement.

(1) Subject to subsection (3) there is in a contract for sale a warranty by the seller that

> (a) the title conveyed shall be, good and its transfer rightful and shall not, unreasonably expose the buyer to litigation because of any colorable claim to or interest in the goods; and
>
> (b) the goods shall be delivered free from any security interest or other lien or encumbrance of which the buyer at the time of contracting has no knowledge.

(2) Unless otherwise agreed a seller that is a merchant regularly dealing in goods of the kind warrants that the goods shall be delivered free of the rightful claim of any third person by way of infringement or the like but a buyer that furnishes specifications to the seller must hold the seller harmless against any such claim that arises out of compliance with the specifications.

(3) A warranty under this section may be disclaimed or modified only by specific language or by circumstances that give the buyer reason to know that the seller does not claim title, that the seller is purporting to sell only the right or title as the seller or a third person may have, or that the seller is selling subject to any claims of infringement or the like.

§ 2–313. Express Warranties by Affirmation, Promise, Description, Sample; Remedial Promise.

(1) In this section, "immediate buyer" means a buyer that enters into a contract with the seller.

* * * *

(4) Any remedial promise made by the seller to the immediate buyer creates an obligation that the promise will be performed upon the happening of the specified event.

§ 2–313A. Obligation to Remote Purchaser Created by Record Packaged with or Accompanying Goods.

(1) In this section:

> (a) "Immediate buyer" means a buyer that enters into a contract with the seller.
>
> (b) "Remote purchaser" means a person that buys or leases goods from an immediate buyer or other person in the normal chain of distribution.

(2) This section applies only to new goods and goods sold or leased as new goods in a transaction of purchase in the normal chain of distribution.

(3) If in a record packaged with or accompanying the goods the seller makes an affirmation of fact or promise that relates to the goods, provides a description that relates to the goods, or makes a remedial promise, and the seller reasonably expects the record to be, and the record is, furnished to the remote purchaser, the seller has an obligation to the remote purchaser that:

> (a) the goods will conform to the affirmation of fact, promise or description unless a reasonable person in the position of the remote purchaser would not believe that the affirmation of fact, promise or description created an obligation; and
>
> (b) the seller will perform the remedial promise.

(4) It is not necessary to the creation of an obligation under this section that the seller use formal words such as "warrant" or "guarantee" or that the seller have a specific intention to undertake an obligation, but an affirmation merely of the value of the goods or a statement purporting to be merely the seller's opinion or commendation of the goods does not create an obligation.

(5) The following rules apply to the remedies for breach of an obligation created under this section:

(a) The seller may modify or limit the remedies available to the remote purchaser if the modification or limitation is furnished to the remote purchaser no later than the time of purchase or if the modification or limitation is contained in the record that contains the affirmation of fact, promise or description.

(b) Subject to a modification or limitation of remedy, a seller in breach is liable for incidental or consequential damages under Section 2–715, but not for lost profits.

(c) The remote purchaser may recover as damages for breach of a seller's obligation arising under subsection (2) the loss resulting in the ordinary course of events as determined in any reasonable manner.

(5) An obligation that is not a remedial promise is breached if the goods did not conform to the affirmation of fact, promise or description creating the obligation when the goods left the seller's control.

§ 2–313B. Obligation to Remote Purchaser Created by Communication to the Public.

(1) In this section:

(a) "Immediate buyer" means a buyer that enters into a contract with the seller.

(b) "Remote purchaser" means a person that buys or leases goods from an immediate buyer or other person in the normal chain of distribution.

(2) This section applies only to new goods and goods sold or leased as new goods in a transaction of purchase in the normal chain of distribution.

(3) If in an advertisement or a similar communication to the public a seller makes an affirmation of fact or promise that relates to the goods, provides a description that relates to the goods, or makes a remedial promise, and the remote purchaser enters into a transaction of purchase with knowledge of and with the expectation that the goods will conform to the affirmation of fact, promise, or description, or that the seller will perform the remedial promise, the seller has an obligation to the remote purchaser that:

(a) the goods will conform to the affirmation of fact, promise or description unless a reasonable person in the position of the remote purchaser would not believe that the affirmation of fact, promise or description created an obligation; and

(b) the seller will perform the remedial promise.

(4) It is not necessary to the creation of an obligation under this section that the seller use formal words such as "warrant" or "guarantee" or that the seller have a specific intention to undertake an obligation, but an affirmation merely of the value of the goods or a statement purporting to be merely the seller's opinion or commendation of the goods does not create an obligation.

(5) The following rules apply to the remedies for breach of an obligation created under this section:

(a) The seller may modify or limit the remedies available to the remote purchaser if the modification or limitation is furnished to the remote purchaser no later than the time of purchase. The modification or limitation may be furnished as part of the communication that contains the affirmation of fact, promise or description.

(b) Subject to a modification or limitation of remedy, a seller in breach is liable for incidental or consequential damages under Section 2–715, but not for lost profits.

(c) The remote purchaser may recover as damages for breach of a seller's obligation arising under subsection (2) the loss resulting in the ordinary course of events as determined in any reasonable manner.

(6) An obligation that is not a remedial promise is breached if the goods did not conform to the affirmation of fact, promise or description creating the obligation when the goods left the seller's control.

* * * *

§ 2–316. Exclusion or Modification of Warranties.

* * * *

(2) Subject to subsection (3), to exclude or modify the implied warranty of merchantability or any part of it in a consumer contract the language must be in a record, be conspicuous, and state "The seller undertakes no responsibility for the quality of the goods except as otherwise provided in this contract," and in any other contract the language must mention merchantability and in case of a record must be conspicuous. Subject to subsection (3), to exclude or modify the implied warranty of fitness the exclusion must be in a record and be conspicuous. Language to exclude all implied warranties of fitness in a consumer contract must state "The seller assumes no responsibility that the goods will be fit for any particular purpose for which you may be buying these goods, except as otherwise provided in the contract," and in any other contract the language is sufficient if it states, for example, that "There are no warranties that extend beyond the description on the face hereof." Language that satisfies the requirements of this subsection for the exclusion and modification of a warranty in a consumer contract also satisfies the requirements for any other contract.

(3) Notwithstanding subsection (2):

(a) unless the circumstances indicate otherwise, all

implied warranties are excluded by expressions like "as is", "with all faults" or other language which in common understanding calls the buyer's attention to the exclusion of warranties, makes plain that there is no implied warranty, and in a consumer contract evidenced by a record is set forth conspicuously in the record; and

(b) when the buyer before entering into the contract has examined the goods or the sample or model as fully as desired or has refused to examine the goods after a demand by the seller there is no implied warranty with regard to defects which an examination ought in the circumstances to have revealed to the buyer; and

(c) an implied warranty can also be excluded or modified by course of dealing or course of performance or usage of trade.

* * * *

§ 2–318. Third Party Beneficiaries of Warranties and Obligations.

(1) In this section:

(a) "Immediate buyer" means a buyer that enters into a contract with the seller.

(b) "Remote purchaser" means a person that buys or leases goods from an immediate buyer or other person in the normal chain of distribution.

Alternative A to subsection (2)

(2) A seller's warranty to an immediate buyer, whether express or implied, a seller's remedial promise to an immediate buyer, or a seller's obligation to a remote purchaser under Section 2–313A or 2–313B extends to any natural person who is in the family or household of the immediate buyer or the remote purchaser or who is a guest in the home of either if it is reasonable to expect that the person may use, consume or be affected by the goods and who is injured in person by breach of the warranty, remedial promise or obligation. A seller may not exclude or limit the operation of this section.

Alternative B to subsection (2)

(2) A seller's warranty to an immediate buyer, whether express or implied, a seller's remedial promise to an immediate buyer, or a seller's obligation to a remote purchaser under Section 2–313A or 2–313B extends to any natural person who may reasonably be expected to use, consume or be affected by the goods and who is injured in person by breach of the warranty, remedial promise or obligation. A seller may not exclude or limit the operation of this section.

Alternative C to subsection (2)

(2) A seller's warranty to an immediate buyer, whether express or implied, a seller's remedial promise to an immediate buyer, or a seller's obligation to a remote purchaser

under Section 2–313A or 2–313B extends to any person that may reasonably be expected to use, consume or be affected by the goods and that is injured by breach of the warranty, remedial promise or obligation. A seller may not exclude or limit the operation of this section with respect to injury to the person of an individual to whom the warranty, remedial promise or obligation extends.

* * * *

Part 5 Performance
* * * *

§ 2–502. Buyer's Right to Goods on Seller's Insolvency.

(1) Subject to subsections (2) and (3) and even though the goods have not been shipped a buyer that has paid a part or all of the price of goods in which the buyer has a special property under the provisions of the immediately preceding section may on making and keeping good a tender of any unpaid portion of their price recover them from the seller if:

(a) in the case of goods bought by a consumer, the seller repudiates or fails to deliver as required by the contract; or

(b) in all cases, the seller becomes insolvent within ten days after receipt of the first installment on their price.

(2) The buyer's right to recover the goods under subsection (1) vests upon acquisition of a special property, even if the seller had not then repudiated or failed to deliver.

(3) If the identification creating the special property has been made by the buyer, the buyer acquires the right to recover the goods only if they conform to the contract for sale.

* * * *

§ 2–508. Cure by Seller of Improper Tender or Delivery; Replacement.

(1) Where the buyer rejects goods or a tender of delivery under Section 2–601 or 2–612 or, except in a consumer contract, justifiably revokes acceptance under Section 2–608(1)(b) and the agreed time for performance has not expired, a seller that has performed in good faith, upon seasonable notice to the buyer and at the seller's own expense, may cure the breach of contract by making a conforming tender of delivery within the agreed time. The seller shall compensate the buyer for all of the buyer's reasonable expenses caused by the seller's breach of contract and subsequent cure.

(2) Where the buyer rejects goods or a tender of delivery under Section 2–601 or 2–612 or except in a consumer contract justifiably revokes acceptance under Section 2–608(1)(b) and the agreed time for performance has expired, a seller that has performed in good faith, upon seasonable notice to the buyer and at the seller's own expense, may cure the breach of contract, if the cure is appropriate and timely under the circumstances, by making a tender of conforming goods. The seller shall compensate the buyer for all of the buyer's reasonable

expenses caused by the seller's breach of contract and subsequent cure.

§ 2–509. Risk of Loss in the Absence of Breach.

(1) Where the contract requires or authorizes the seller to ship the goods by carrier

  (a) if it does not require the seller to deliver them at a particular destination, the risk of loss passes to the buyer when the goods are delivered to the carrier even though the shipment is under reservation (Section 2–505); but

  (b) if it does require the seller to deliver them at a particular destination and the goods are there tendered while in the possession of the carrier, the risk of loss passes to the buyer when the goods are there so tendered as to enable the buyer to take delivery.

(2) Where the goods are held by a bailee to be delivered without being moved, the risk of loss passes to the buyer

  (a) on the buyer's receipt of a negotiable document of title covering the goods; or

  (b) on acknowledgment by the bailee to the buyer of the buyer's right to possession of the goods; or

  (c) after the buyer's receipt of a non-negotiable document of title or other direction to deliver in a record, as provided in subsection (4)(b) of Section 2–503.

(3) In any case not within subsection (1) or (2), the risk of loss passes to the buyer on the buyer's receipt of the goods.

(4) The provisions of this section are subject to contrary agreement of the parties and to the provisions of this Article on sale on approval (Section 2–327) and on effect of breach on risk of loss (Section 2–510).

*   *   *   *

§ 2–513. Buyer's Right to Inspection of Goods.

*   *   *   *

(3) Unless otherwise agreed, the buyer is not entitled to inspect the goods before payment of the price when the contract provides

  (a) for delivery on terms that under applicable course of performance, course of dealing, or usage of trade are interpreted to preclude inspection before payment; or

  (b) for payment against documents of title, except where such payment is due only after the goods are to become available for inspection.

*   *   *   *

Part 6 Breach, Repudiation and Excuse

*   *   *   *

§ 2–605. Waiver of Buyer's Objections by Failure to Particularize.

(1) The buyer's failure to state in connection with rejection a particular defect or in connection with revocation of

acceptance a defect that justifies revocation precludes the buyer from relying on the unstated defect to justify rejection or revocation of acceptance if the defect is ascertainable by reasonable inspection

  (a) where the seller had a right to cure the defect and could have cured it if stated seasonably; or

  (b) between merchants when the seller has after rejection made a request in a record for a full and final statement in record form of all defects on which the buyer proposes to rely.

(2) A buyer's payment against documents tendered to the buyer made without reservation of rights precludes recovery of the payment for defects apparent on the face of the documents.

*   *   *   *

§ 2–607. Effect of Acceptance; Notice of Breach; Burden of Establishing Breach After Acceptance; Notice of Claim or Litigation to Person Answerable Over.

*   *   *   *

(3) Where a tender has been accepted

  (a) the buyer must within a reasonable time after the buyer discovers or should have discovered any breach notify the seller. However, failure to give timely notice bars the buyer from a remedy only to the extent that the seller is prejudiced by the failure and

  (b) if the claim is one for infringement or the like (subsection (3) of Section 2–312) and the buyer is sued as a result of such a breach the buyer must so notify the seller within a reasonable time after the buyer receives notice of the litigation or be barred from any remedy over for liability established by the litigation.

*   *   *   *

§ 2–608. Revocation of Acceptance in Whole or in Part.

*   *   *   *

(4) If a buyer uses the goods after a rightful rejection or justifiable revocation of acceptance, the following rules apply:

  (a) Any use by the buyer which is unreasonable under the circumstances is wrongful as against the seller and is an acceptance only if ratified by the seller.

  (b) Any use of the goods which is reasonable under the circumstances is not wrongful as against the seller and is not an acceptance, but in an appropriate case the buyer shall be obligated to the seller for the value of the use to the buyer.

*   *   *   *

§ 2–612. "Installment Contract"; Breach.

*   *   *   *

(2) The buyer may reject any installment which is nonconforming if the non-conformity substantially impairs the

value of that installment to the buyer or if the non-conformity is a defect in the required documents; but if the non-conformity does not fall within subsection (3) and the seller gives adequate assurance of its cure the buyer must accept that installment.

(3) Whenever non-conformity or default with respect to one or more installments substantially impairs the value of the whole contract there is a breach of the whole. But the aggrieved party reinstates the contract if the party accepts a non-conforming installment without seasonably notifying of cancellation or if the party brings an action with respect only to past installments or demands performance as to future installments.

*　*　*　*

Part 7 Remedies

§ 2–702. Seller's Remedies on Discovery of Buyer's Insolvency.

*　*　*　*

(2) Where the seller discovers that the buyer has received goods on credit while insolvent the seller may reclaim the goods upon demand made within a reasonable time after the buyer's receipt of the goods. Except as provided in this subsection the seller may not base a right to reclaim goods on the buyer's fraudulent or innocent misrepresentation of solvency or of intent to pay.

*　*　*　*

§ 2–703. Seller's Remedies in General.

(1) A breach of contract by the buyer includes the buyer's wrongful rejection or wrongful attempt to revoke acceptance of goods, wrongful failure to perform a contractual obligation, failure to make a payment when due, and repudiation.

(2) If the buyer is in breach of contract the seller, to the extent provided for by this Act or other law, may:

(a) withhold delivery of the goods:

(b) stop delivery of the goods under Section 2–705;

(c) proceed under Section 2–704 with respect to goods unidentified to the contract or unfinished;

(d) reclaim the goods under Section 2–507(2) or 2–702(2);

(e) require payment directly from the buyer under Section 2–325(c);

(f) cancel;

(g) resell and recover damages under Section 2–706;

(h) recover damages for nonacceptance or repudiation under Section 2–708(1);

(i) recover lost profits under Section 2–708(2);

(j) recover the price under Section 2–709;

(k) obtain specific performance under Section 2–716;

(l) recover liquidated damages under Section 2–718;

(m) in other cases, recover damages in any manner that is reasonable under the circumstances.

(3) If a buyer becomes insolvent, the seller may:

(a) withhold delivery under Section 2–702(1);

(b) stop delivery of the goods under Section 2–705;

(c) reclaim the goods under Section 2–702(2).

*　*　*　*

§ 2–705. Seller's Stoppage of Delivery in Transit or Otherwise.

(1) The seller may stop delivery of goods in the possession of a carrier or other bailee when the seller discovers the buyer to be insolvent (Section 2–702) or when the buyer repudiates or fails to make a payment due before delivery or if for any other reason the seller has a right to withhold or reclaim the goods.

*　*　*　*

§ 2–706. Seller's Resale Including Contract for Resale.

(1) In an appropriate case involving breach by the buyer, the seller may resell the goods concerned or the undelivered balance thereof. Where the resale is made in good faith and in a commercially reasonable manner the seller may recover the difference between the contract price and the resale price together with any incidental or consequential damages allowed under the provisions of this Article (Section 2–710), but less expenses saved in consequence of the buyer's breach.

*　*　*　*

§ 2–708. Seller's Damages for Non-Acceptance or Repudiation.

(1) Subject to subsection (2) and to the provisions of this Article with respect to proof of market price (Section 2–723)

(a) the measure of damages for non-acceptance by the buyer is the difference between the contract price and the market price at the time and place for tender together with any incidental or consequential damages provided in this Article (Section 2–710), but less expenses saved in consequence of the buyer's breach; and

(b) the measure of damages for repudiation by the buyer is the difference between the contract price and the market price at the place for tender at the expiration of a commercially reasonable time after the seller learned of the repudiation, but no later than the time stated in paragraph (a), together with any incidental or consequential damages provided in this Article (Section 2–710), but less expenses saved in consequence of the buyer's breach.

(2) If the measure of damages provided in subsection (1) or in Section 2–706 is inadequate to put the seller in as good a

position as performance would have done then the measure of damages is the profit (including reasonable overhead) which the seller would have made from full performance by the buyer, together with any incidental or consequential damages provided in this Article (Section 2–710).

§ 2–709. Action for the Price.

(1) When the buyer fails to pay the price as it becomes due the seller may recover, together with any incidental or consequential damages under the next section, the price

(a) of goods accepted or of conforming goods lost or damaged within a commercially reasonable time after risk of their loss has passed to the buyer; and

(b) of goods identified to the contract if the seller is unable after reasonable effort to resell them at a reasonable price or the circumstances reasonably indicate that such effort will be unavailing.

* * * *

§ 2–710. Seller's Incidental and Consequential Damages.

(1) Incidental damages to an aggrieved seller include any commercially reasonable charges, expenses or commissions incurred in stopping delivery, in the transportation, care and custody of goods after the buyer's breach, in connection with return or resale of the goods or otherwise resulting from the breach.

(2) Consequential damages resulting from the buyer's breach include any loss resulting from general or particular requirements and needs of which the buyer at the time of contracting had reason to know and which could not reasonably be prevented by resale or otherwise.

(3) In a consumer contract, a seller may not recover consequential damages from a consumer.

* * * *

§ 2–711. Buyer's Remedies in General; Buyer's Security Interest in Rejected Goods.

(1) A breach of contract by the seller includes the seller's wrongful failure to deliver or to perform a contractual obligation, making of a nonconforming tender of delivery or performance, and repudiation.

(2) If a seller is in breach of contract under subsection (1) the buyer, to the extent provided for by this Act or other law, may:

(a) in the case of rightful cancellation, rightful rejection or justifiable revocation of acceptance recover so much of the price as has been paid;

(b) deduct damages from any part of the price still due under Section 2–717;

(c) cancel;

(d) cover and have damages under Section 2–712 as to all goods affected whether or not they have been iden-

tified to the contract;

(e) recover damages for non-delivery or repudiation under Section 2–713;

(f) recover damages for breach with regard to accepted goods or breach with regard to a remedial promise under Section 2–714;

(g) recover identified goods under Section 2–502;

(h) obtain specific performance or obtain the goods by replevin or similar remedy under Section 7–716;

(i) recover liquidated damages under Section 2–718;

(j) in other cases, recover damages in any manner that is reasonable under the circumstances.

(3) On rightful rejection or justifiable revocation of acceptance a buyer has a security interest in goods in the buyer's possession or control for any payments made on their price and any expenses reasonably incurred in their inspection, receipt, transportation, care and custody and may hold such goods and resell them in like manner as an aggrieved seller (Section 2–706).

* * * *

§ 2–713. Buyer's Damages for Non-Delivery or Repudiation.

(1) Subject to the provisions of this Article with respect to proof of market price (Section 2–723), if the seller wrongfully fails to deliver or repudiates or the buyer rightfully rejects or justifiably revokes acceptance

(a) the measure of damages in the case of wrongful failure to deliver by the seller or rightful rejection or justifiable revocation of acceptance by the buyer is the difference between the market price at the time for tender under the contract and the contract price together with any incidental or consequential damages provided in this Article (Section 2–715), but less expenses saved in consequence of the seller's breach; and

(b) the measure of damages for repudiation by the seller is the difference between the market price at the expiration of a commercially reasonable time after the buyer learned of the repudiation, but no later than the time stated in paragraph (a), and the contract price together with any incidental or consequential damages provided in this Article (Section 2–715), less expenses saved in consequence of the seller's breach.

* * * *

§ 2–725. Statute of Limitations in Contracts for Sale.

(1) Except as otherwise provided in this section, an action for breach of any contract for sale must be commenced within the later of four years after the right of action has accrued under subsection (2) or (3) or one year after the breach was or should have been discovered, but no longer than five years after the right of action accrued. By the orig-

inal agreement the parties may reduce the period of limitation to not less than one year but may not extend it. However, in a consumer contract, the period of limitation may not be reduced.

(2) Except as otherwise provided in subsection (3), the following rules apply:

(a) Except as otherwise provided in this subsection, a right of action for breach of a contract accrues when the breach occurs, even if the aggrieved party did not have knowledge of the breach.

(b) For breach of a contract by repudiation, a right of action accrues at the earlier of when the aggrieved party elects to treat the repudiation as a breach or when a commercially reasonable time for awaiting performance has expired.

(c) For breach of a remedial promise, a right of action accrues when the remedial promise is not performed when performance is due.

(d) In an action by a buyer against a person that is answerable over to the buyer for a claim asserted against the buyer, the buyer's right of action against the person answerable over accrues at the time the claim was originally asserted against the buyer.

(3) If a breach of a warranty arising under Section 2–312, 2–313(2), 2–314, or 2–315, or a breach of an obligation, other than a remedial promise, arising under Section 2–313A or 2–313B, is claimed the following rules apply:

(a) Except as otherwise provided in paragraph (c), a right of action for breach of a warranty arising under Section 2–313(2), 2–314 or 2–315 accrues when the seller has tendered delivery to the immediate buyer, as defined in Section 2–313, and has completed performance of any agreed installation or assembly of the goods.

(b) Except as otherwise provided in paragraph (c), a right of action for breach of an obligation other than a remedial promise arising under Section 2–313A or 2–313B accrues when the remote purchaser, as defined in sections 2–313A and 2–313B, receives the goods.

(c) Where a warranty arising under Section 2–313(2) or an obligation, other than a remedial promise, arising under 2–313A or 2–313B explicitly extends to future performance of the goods and discovery of the breach must await the time for performance the right of action accrues when the immediate buyer as defined in Section 2–313 or the remote purchaser as defined in Sections 2–313A and 2–313B discovers or should have discovered the breach.

(d) A right of action for breach of warranty arising under Section 2–312 accrues when the aggrieved party discovers or should have discovered the breach. However, an action for breach of the warranty of non-infringement may not be commenced more than six years after tender of delivery of the goods to the aggrieved party.

* * * *

Article 2A
LEASES

Part 1 General Provisions

§ 2A–101. Short Title.

This Article shall be known and may be cited as the Uniform Commercial Code—Leases.

§ 2A–102. Scope.

This Article applies to any transaction, regardless of form, that creates a lease.

§ 2A–103. Definitions and Index of Definitions.

(1) In this Article unless the context otherwise requires:

(a) "Buyer in ordinary course of business" means a person who in good faith and without knowledge that the sale to him [or her] is in violation of the ownership rights or security interest or leasehold interest of a third party in the goods buys in ordinary course from a person in the business of selling goods of that kind but does not include a pawnbroker. "Buying" may be for cash or by exchange of other property or on secured or unsecured credit and includes receiving goods or documents of title under a pre-existing contract for sale but does not include a transfer in bulk or as security for or in total or partial satisfaction of a money debt.

(b) "Cancellation" occurs when either party puts an end to the lease contract for default by the other party.

(c) "Commercial unit" means such a unit of goods as by commercial usage is a single whole for purposes of lease and division of which materially impairs its character or value on the market or in use. A commercial unit may be a single article, as a machine, or a set of articles, as a suite of furniture or a line of machinery, or a quantity, as a gross or carload, or any other unit treated in use or in the relevant market as a single whole.

(d) "Conforming" goods or performance under a lease contract means goods or performance that are in accordance with the obligations under the lease contract.

(e) "Consumer lease" means a lease that a lessor regularly engaged in the business of leasing or selling makes to a lessee who is an individual and who takes under the lease primarily for a personal, family, or household purpose [, if the total payments to be made under the lease contract, excluding payments for options to renew or buy, do not exceed $_____].

(f) "Fault" means wrongful act, omission, breach, or default.

(g) "Finance lease" means a lease with respect to which:

(i) the lessor does not select, manufacture or supply the goods;

(ii) the lessor acquires the goods or the right to possession and use of the goods in connection with the lease; and

(iii) one of the following occurs:

(A) the lessee receives a copy of the contract by which the lessor acquired the goods or the right to possession and use of the goods before signing the lease contract;

(B) the lessee's approval of the contract by which the lessor acquired the goods or the right to possession and use of the goods is a condition to effectiveness of the lease contract;

(C) the lessee, before signing the lease contract, receives an accurate and complete statement designating the promises and warranties, and any disclaimers of warranties, limitations or modifications of remedies, or liquidated damages, including those of a third party, such as the manufacturer of the goods, provided to the lessor by the person supplying the goods in connection with or as part of the contract by which the lessor acquired the goods or the right to possession and use of the goods; or

(D) if the lease is not a consumer lease, the lessor, before the lessee signs the lease contract, informs the lessee in writing (a) of the identity of the person supplying the goods to the lessor, unless the lessee has selected that person and directed the lessor to acquire the goods or the right to possession and use of the goods from that person, (b) that the lessee is entitled under this Article to any promises and warranties, including those of any third party, provided to the lessor by the person supplying the goods in connection with or as part of the contract by which the lessor acquired the goods or the right to possession and use of the goods, and (c) that the lessee may communicate with the person supplying the goods to the lessor and receive an accurate and complete statement of those promises and warranties, including any disclaimers and limitations of them or of remedies.

(h) "Goods" means all things that are movable at the time of identification to the lease contract, or are fixtures (Section 2A–309), but the term does not include money, documents, instruments, accounts, chattel paper, general intangibles, or minerals or the like, including oil and gas, before extraction. The term also includes the unborn young of animals.

(i) "Installment lease contract" means a lease contract that authorizes or requires the delivery of goods in sep-

arate lots to be separately accepted, even though the lease contract contains a clause "each delivery is a separate lease" or its equivalent.

(j) "Lease" means a transfer of the right to possession and use of goods for a term in return for consideration, but a sale, including a sale on approval or a sale or return, or retention or creation of a security interest is not a lease. Unless the context clearly indicates otherwise, the term includes a sublease.

(k) "Lease agreement" means the bargain, with respect to the lease, of the lessor and the lessee in fact as found in their language or by implication from other circumstances including course of dealing or usage of trade or course of performance as provided in this Article. Unless the context clearly indicates otherwise, the term includes a sublease agreement.

(*l*) "Lease contract" means the total legal obligation that results from the lease agreement as affected by this Article and any other applicable rules of law. Unless the context clearly indicates otherwise, the term includes a sublease contract.

(m) "Leasehold interest" means the interest of the lessor or the lessee under a lease contract.

(n) "Lessee" means a person who acquires the right to possession and use of goods under a lease. Unless the context clearly indicates otherwise, the term includes a sublessee.

(o) "Lessee in ordinary course of business" means a person who in good faith and without knowledge that the lease to him [or her] is in violation of the ownership rights or security interest or leasehold interest of a third party in the goods, leases in ordinary course from a person in the business of selling or leasing goods of that kind but does not include a pawnbroker. "Leasing" may be for cash or by exchange of other property or on secured or unsecured credit and includes receiving goods or documents of title under a pre-existing lease contract but does not include a transfer in bulk or as security for or in total or partial satisfaction of a money debt.

(p) "Lessor" means a person who transfers the right to possession and use of goods under a lease. Unless the context clearly indicates otherwise, the term includes a sublessor.

(q) "Lessor's residual interest" means the lessor's interest in the goods after expiration, termination, or cancellation of the lease contract.

(r) "Lien" means a charge against or interest in goods to secure payment of a debt or performance of an obligation, but the term does not include a security interest.

(s) "Lot" means a parcel or a single article that is the subject matter of a separate lease or delivery, whether or not it is sufficient to perform the lease contract.

(t) "Merchant lessee" means a lessee that is a merchant with respect to goods of the kind subject to the lease.

(u) "Present value" means the amount as of a date certain of one or more sums payable in the future, discounted to the date certain. The discount is determined by the interest rate specified by the parties if the rate was not manifestly unreasonable at the time the transaction was entered into; otherwise, the discount is determined by a commercially reasonable rate that takes into account the facts and circumstances of each case at the time the transaction was entered into.

(v) "Purchase" includes taking by sale, lease, mortgage, security interest, pledge, gift, or any other voluntary transaction creating an interest in goods.

(w) "Sublease" means a lease of goods the right to possession and use of which was acquired by the lessor as a lessee under an existing lease.

(x) "Supplier" means a person from whom a lessor buys or leases goods to be leased under a finance lease.

(y) "Supply contract" means a contract under which a lessor buys or leases goods to be leased.

(z) "Termination" occurs when either party pursuant to a power created by agreement or law puts an end to the lease contract otherwise than for default.

(2) Other definitions applying to this Article and the sections in which they appear are:

"Accessions". Section 2A–310(1).

"Construction mortgage". Section 2A–309(1)(d).

"Encumbrance". Section 2A–309(1)(e).

"Fixtures". Section 2A–309(1)(a).

"Fixture filing". Section 2A–309(1)(b).

"Purchase money lease". Section 2A–309(1)(c).

(3) The following definitions in other Articles apply to this Article:

"Accounts". Section 9–106.

"Between merchants". Section 2–104(3).

"Buyer". Section 2–103(1)(a).

"Chattel paper". Section 9–105(1)(b).

"Consumer goods". Section 9–109(1).

"Document". Section 9–105(1)(f).

"Entrusting". Section 2–403(3).

"General intangibles". Section 9–106.

"Good faith". Section 2–103(1)(b).

"Instrument". Section 9–105(1)(i).

"Merchant". Section 2–104(1).

"Mortgage". Section 9–105(1)(j).

"Pursuant to commitment". Section 9–105(1)(k).

"Receipt". Section 2–103(1)(c).

"Sale". Section 2–106(1).

"Sale on approval". Section 2–326.

"Sale or return". Section 2–326.

"Seller". Section 2–103(1)(d).

(4) In addition Article 1 contains general definitions and principles of construction and interpretation applicable throughout this Article.

As amended in 1990 and 1999.

§ 2A–104. Leases Subject to Other Law.

(1) A lease, although subject to this Article, is also subject to any applicable:

(a) certificate of title statute of this State: (list any certificate of title statutes covering automobiles, trailers, mobile homes, boats, farm tractors, and the like);

(b) certificate of title statute of another jurisdiction (Section 2A–105); or

(c) consumer protection statute of this State, or final consumer protection decision of a court of this State existing on the effective date of this Article.

(2) In case of conflict between this Article, other than Sections 2A–105, 2A–304(3), and 2A–305(3), and a statute or decision referred to in subsection (1), the statute or decision controls.

(3) Failure to comply with an applicable law has only the effect specified therein.

As amended in 1990.

§ 2A–105. Territorial Application of Article to Goods Covered by Certificate of Title.

Subject to the provisions of Sections 2A–304(3) and 2A–305(3), with respect to goods covered by a certificate of title issued under a statute of this State or of another jurisdiction, compliance and the effect of compliance or noncompliance with a certificate of title statute are governed by the law (including the conflict of laws rules) of the jurisdiction issuing the certificate until the earlier of (a) surrender of the certificate, or (b) four months after the goods are removed from that jurisdiction and thereafter until a new certificate of title is issued by another jurisdiction.

§ 2A–106. Limitation on Power of Parties to Consumer Lease to Choose Applicable Law and Judicial Forum.

(1) If the law chosen by the parties to a consumer lease is that of a jurisdiction other than a jurisdiction in which the lessee resides at the time the lease agreement becomes enforceable or within 30 days thereafter or in which the goods are to be used, the choice is not enforceable.

(2) If the judicial forum chosen by the parties to a consumer lease is a forum that would not otherwise have jurisdiction over the lessee, the choice is not enforceable.

§ 2A–107. Waiver or Renunciation of Claim or Right After Default.

Any claim or right arising out of an alleged default or breach of warranty may be discharged in whole or in part without consideration by a written waiver or renunciation signed and delivered by the aggrieved party.

§ 2A–108. Unconscionability.

(1) If the court as a matter of law finds a lease contract or any clause of a lease contract to have been unconscionable at the time it was made the court may refuse to enforce the lease contract, or it may enforce the remainder of the lease contract without the unconscionable clause, or it may so limit the application of any unconscionable clause as to avoid any unconscionable result.

(2) With respect to a consumer lease, if the court as a matter of law finds that a lease contract or any clause of a lease contract has been induced by unconscionable conduct or that unconscionable conduct has occurred in the collection of a claim arising from a lease contract, the court may grant appropriate relief.

(3) Before making a finding of unconscionability under subsection (1) or (2), the court, on its own motion or that of a party, shall afford the parties a reasonable opportunity to present evidence as to the setting, purpose, and effect of the lease contract or clause thereof, or of the conduct.

(4) In an action in which the lessee claims unconscionability with respect to a consumer lease:

(a) If the court finds unconscionability under subsection (1) or (2), the court shall award reasonable attorney's fees to the lessee.

(b) If the court does not find unconscionability and the lessee claiming unconscionability has brought or maintained an action he [or she] knew to be groundless, the court shall award reasonable attorney's fees to the party against whom the claim is made.

(c) In determining attorney's fees, the amount of the recovery on behalf of the claimant under subsections (1) and (2) is not controlling.

§ 2A–109. Option to Accelerate at Will.

(1) A term providing that one party or his [or her] successor in interest may accelerate payment or performance or require collateral or additional collateral "at will" or "when he [or she] deems himself [or herself] insecure" or in words of similar import must be construed to mean that he [or she] has power to do so only if he [or she] in good faith believes that the prospect of payment or performance is impaired.

(2) With respect to a consumer lease, the burden of establishing good faith under subsection (1) is on the party who exercised the power; otherwise the burden of establishing lack of good faith is on the party against whom the power has been exercised.

Part 2 Formation and Construction of Lease Contract

§ 2A–201. Statute of Frauds.

(1) A lease contract is not enforceable by way of action or defense unless:

(a) the total payments to be made under the lease contract, excluding payments for options to renew or buy, are less than $1,000; or

(b) there is a writing, signed by the party against whom enforcement is sought or by that party's authorized agent, sufficient to indicate that a lease contract has been made between the parties and to describe the goods leased and the lease term.

(2) Any description of leased goods or of the lease term is sufficient and satisfies subsection (1)(b), whether or not it is specific, if it reasonably identifies what is described.

(3) A writing is not insufficient because it omits or incorrectly states a term agreed upon, but the lease contract is not enforceable under subsection (1)(b) beyond the lease term and the quantity of goods shown in the writing.

(4) A lease contract that does not satisfy the requirements of subsection (1), but which is valid in other respects, is enforceable:

(a) if the goods are to be specially manufactured or obtained for the lessee and are not suitable for lease or sale to others in the ordinary course of the lessor's business, and the lessor, before notice of repudiation is received and under circumstances that reasonably indicate that the goods are for the lessee, has made either a substantial beginning of their manufacture or commitments for their procurement;

(b) if the party against whom enforcement is sought admits in that party's pleading, testimony or otherwise in court that a lease contract was made, but the lease contract is not enforceable under this provision beyond the quantity of goods admitted; or

(c) with respect to goods that have been received and accepted by the lessee.

(5) The lease term under a lease contract referred to in subsection (4) is:

(a) if there is a writing signed by the party against whom enforcement is sought or by that party's authorized agent specifying the lease term, the term so specified;

(b) if the party against whom enforcement is sought admits in that party's pleading, testimony, or otherwise in court a lease term, the term so admitted; or

(c) a reasonable lease term.

§ 2A–202. Final Written Expression: Parol or Extrinsic Evidence.

Terms with respect to which the confirmatory memoranda of the parties agree or which are otherwise set forth in a writing intended by the parties as a final expression of their agreement with respect to such terms as are included therein may not be contradicted by evidence of any prior agreement or of a contemporaneous oral agreement but may be explained or supplemented:

(a) by course of dealing or usage of trade or by course of performance; and

(b) by evidence of consistent additional terms unless the court finds the writing to have been intended also as a complete and exclusive statement of the terms of the agreement.

§ 2A–203. Seals Inoperative.

The affixing of a seal to a writing evidencing a lease contract or an offer to enter into a lease contract does not render the writing a sealed instrument and the law with respect to sealed instruments does not apply to the lease contract or offer.

§ 2A–204. Formation in General.

(1) A lease contract may be made in any manner sufficient to show agreement, including conduct by both parties which recognizes the existence of a lease contract.

(2) An agreement sufficient to constitute a lease contract may be found although the moment of its making is undetermined.

(3) Although one or more terms are left open, a lease contract does not fail for indefiniteness if the parties have intended to make a lease contract and there is a reasonably certain basis for giving an appropriate remedy.

§ 2A–205. Firm Offers.

An offer by a merchant to lease goods to or from another person in a signed writing that by its terms gives assurance it will be held open is not revocable, for lack of consideration, during the time stated or, if no time is stated, for a reasonable time, but in no event may the period of irrevocability exceed 3 months. Any such term of assurance on a form supplied by the offeree must be separately signed by the offeror.

§ 2A–206. Offer and Acceptance in Formation of Lease Contract.

(1) Unless otherwise unambiguously indicated by the language or circumstances, an offer to make a lease contract must be construed as inviting acceptance in any manner and by any medium reasonable in the circumstances.

(2) If the beginning of a requested performance is a reasonable mode of acceptance, an offeror who is not notified of acceptance within a reasonable time may treat the offer as having lapsed before acceptance.

§ 2A–207. Course of Performance or Practical Construction.

(1) If a lease contract involves repeated occasions for performance by either party with knowledge of the nature of the performance and opportunity for objection to it by the other, any course of performance accepted or acquiesced in without objection is relevant to determine the meaning of the lease agreement.

(2) The express terms of a lease agreement and any course of performance, as well as any course of dealing and usage of trade, must be construed whenever reasonable as consistent with each other; but if that construction is unreasonable, express terms control course of performance, course of performance controls both course of dealing and usage of trade, and course of dealing controls usage of trade.

(3) Subject to the provisions of Section 2A–208 on modification and waiver, course of performance is relevant to show a waiver or modification of any term inconsistent with the course of performance.

§ 2A–208. Modification, Rescission and Waiver.

(1) An agreement modifying a lease contract needs no consideration to be binding.

(2) A signed lease agreement that excludes modification or rescission except by a signed writing may not be otherwise modified or rescinded, but, except as between merchants, such a requirement on a form supplied by a merchant must be separately signed by the other party.

(3) Although an attempt at modification or rescission does not satisfy the requirements of subsection (2), it may operate as a waiver.

(4) A party who has made a waiver affecting an executory portion of a lease contract may retract the waiver by reasonable notification received by the other party that strict performance will be required of any term waived, unless the retraction would be unjust in view of a material change of position in reliance on the waiver.

§ 2A–209. Lessee under Finance Lease as Beneficiary of Supply Contract.

(1) The benefit of the supplier's promises to the lessor under the supply contract and of all warranties, whether express or implied, including those of any third party provided in connection with or as part of the supply contract, extends to the lessee to the extent of the lessee's leasehold interest under a finance lease related to the supply contract, but is subject to the terms warranty and of the supply contract and all defenses or claims arising therefrom.

(2) The extension of the benefit of supplier's promises and of warranties to the lessee (Section 2A–209(1)) does not: (i) modify the rights and obligations of the parties to the supply contract, whether arising therefrom or otherwise, or (ii) impose any duty or liability under the supply contract on the lessee.

(3) Any modification or rescission of the supply contract by the supplier and the lessor is effective between the supplier and the lessee unless, before the modification or rescission, the supplier has received notice that the lessee has entered into a finance lease related to the supply contract. If the modification or rescission is effective between the supplier and the lessee, the lessor is deemed to have assumed, in addition to the obligations of the lessor to the lessee under the lease contract, promises of the supplier to the lessor and warranties that were so modified or rescinded as they existed and were available to the lessee before modification or rescission.

(4) In addition to the extension of the benefit of the supplier's promises and of warranties to the lessee under subsection (1), the lessee retains all rights that the lessee may

have against the supplier which arise from an agreement between the lessee and the supplier or under other law.
As amended in 1990.

§ 2A–210. Express Warranties.

(1) Express warranties by the lessor are created as follows:

(a) Any affirmation of fact or promise made by the lessor to the lessee which relates to the goods and becomes part of the basis of the bargain creates an express warranty that the goods will conform to the affirmation or promise.

(b) Any description of the goods which is made part of the basis of the bargain creates an express warranty that the goods will conform to the description.

(c) Any sample or model that is made part of the basis of the bargain creates an express warranty that the whole of the goods will conform to the sample or model.

(2) It is not necessary to the creation of an express warranty that the lessor use formal words, such as "warrant" or "guarantee," or that the lessor have a specific intention to make a warranty, but an affirmation merely of the value of the goods or a statement purporting to be merely the lessor's opinion or commendation of the goods does not create a warranty.

§ 2A–211. Warranties Against Interference and Against Infringement; Lessee's Obligation Against Infringement.

(1) There is in a lease contract a warranty that for the lease term no person holds a claim to or interest in the goods that arose from an act or omission of the lessor, other than a claim by way of infringement or the like, which will interfere with the lessee's enjoyment of its leasehold interest.

(2) Except in a finance lease there is in a lease contract by a lessor who is a merchant regularly dealing in goods of the kind a warranty that the goods are delivered free of the rightful claim of any person by way of infringement or the like.

(3) A lessee who furnishes specifications to a lessor or a supplier shall hold the lessor and the supplier harmless against any claim by way of infringement or the like that arises out of compliance with the specifications.

§ 2A–212. Implied Warranty of Merchantability.

(1) Except in a finance lease, a warranty that the goods will be merchantable is implied in a lease contract if the lessor is a merchant with respect to goods of that kind.

(2) Goods to be merchantable must be at least such as

(a) pass without objection in the trade under the description in the lease agreement;

(b) in the case of fungible goods, are of fair average quality within the description;

(c) are fit for the ordinary purposes for which goods of that type are used;

(d) run, within the variation permitted by the lease agreement, of even kind, quality, and quantity within each unit and among all units involved;

(e) are adequately contained, packaged, and labeled as the lease agreement may require; and

(f) conform to any promises or affirmations of fact made on the container or label.

(3) Other implied warranties may arise from course of dealing or usage of trade.

§ 2A–213. Implied Warranty of Fitness for Particular Purpose.

Except in a finance of lease, if the lessor at the time the lease contract is made has reason to know of any particular purpose for which the goods are required and that the lessee is relying on the lessor's skill or judgment to select or furnish suitable goods, there is in the lease contract an implied warranty that the goods will be fit for that purpose.

§ 2A–214. Exclusion or Modification of Warranties.

(1) Words or conduct relevant to the creation of an express warranty and words or conduct tending to negate or limit a warranty must be construed wherever reasonable as consistent with each other; but, subject to the provisions of Section 2A–202 on parol or extrinsic evidence, negation or limitation is inoperative to the extent that the construction is unreasonable.

(2) Subject to subsection (3), to exclude or modify the implied warranty of merchantability or any part of it the language must mention "merchantability", be by a writing, and be conspicuous. Subject to subsection (3), to exclude or modify any implied warranty of fitness the exclusion must be by a writing and be conspicuous. Language to exclude all implied warranties of fitness is sufficient if it is in writing, is conspicuous and states, for example, "There is no warranty that the goods will be fit for a particular purpose".

(3) Notwithstanding subsection (2), but subject to subsection (4),

(a) unless the circumstances indicate otherwise, all implied warranties are excluded by expressions like "as is" or "with all faults" or by other language that in common understanding calls the lessee's attention to the exclusion of warranties and makes plain that there is no implied warranty, if in writing and conspicuous;

(b) if the lessee before entering into the lease contract has examined the goods or the sample or model as fully as desired or has refused to examine the goods, there is no implied warranty with regard to defects that an examination ought in the circumstances to have revealed; and

(c) an implied warranty may also be excluded or modified by course of dealing, course of performance, or usage of trade.

(4) To exclude or modify a warranty against interference or against infringement (Section 2A–211) or any part of it, the language must be specific, be by a writing, and be con-

spicuous, unless the circumstances, including course of performance, course of dealing, or usage of trade, give the lessee reason to know that the goods are being leased subject to a claim or interest of any person.

§ 2A–215. Cumulation and Conflict of Warranties Express or Implied.

Warranties, whether express or implied, must be construed as consistent with each other and as cumulative, but if that construction is unreasonable, the intention of the parties determines which warranty is dominant. In ascertaining that intention the following rules apply:

(a) Exact or technical specifications displace an inconsistent sample or model or general language of description.

(b) A sample from an existing bulk displaces inconsistent general language of description.

(c) Express warranties displace inconsistent implied warranties other than an implied warranty of fitness for a particular purpose.

§ 2A–216. Third-Party Beneficiaries of Express and Implied Warranties.

Alternative A

A warranty to or for the benefit of a lessee under this Article, whether express or implied, extends to any natural person who is in the family or household of the lessee or who is a guest in the lessee's home if it is reasonable to expect that such person may use, consume, or be affected by the goods and who is injured in person by breach of the warranty. This section does not displace principles of law and equity that extend a warranty to or for the benefit of a lessee to other persons. The operation of this section may not be excluded, modified, or limited, but an exclusion, modification, or limitation of the warranty, including any with respect to rights and remedies, effective against the lessee is also effective against any beneficiary designated under this section.

Alternative B

A warranty to or for the benefit of a lessee under this Article, whether express or implied, extends to any natural person who may reasonably be expected to use, consume, or be affected by the goods and who is injured in person by breach of the warranty. This section does not displace principles of law and equity that extend a warranty to or for the benefit of a lessee to other persons. The operation of this section may not be excluded, modified, or limited, but an exclusion, modification, or limitation of the warranty, including any with respect to rights and remedies, effective against the lessee is also effective against the beneficiary designated under this section.

Alternative C

A warranty to or for the benefit of a lessee under this Article, whether express or implied, extends to any person who may reasonably be expected to use, consume, or be affected by the goods and who is injured by breach of the warranty. The operation of this section may not be excluded, modified, or limited with respect to injury to the person of an individual to whom the warranty extends, but an exclusion, modification, or limitation of the warranty, including any with respect to rights and remedies, effective against the lessee is also effective against the beneficiary designated under this section.

§ 2A–217. Identification.

Identification of goods as goods to which a lease contract refers may be made at any time and in any manner explicitly agreed to by the parties. In the absence of explicit agreement, identification occurs:

(a) when the lease contract is made if the lease contract is for a lease of goods that are existing and identified;

(b) when the goods are shipped, marked, or otherwise designated by the lessor as goods to which the lease contract refers, if the lease contract is for a lease of goods that are not existing and identified; or

(c) when the young are conceived, if the lease contract is for a lease of unborn young of animals.

§ 2A–218. Insurance and Proceeds.

(1) A lessee obtains an insurable interest when existing goods are identified to the lease contract even though the goods identified are nonconforming and the lessee has an option to reject them.

(2) If a lessee has an insurable interest only by reason of the lessor's identification of the goods, the lessor, until default or insolvency or notification to the lessee that identification is final, may substitute other goods for those identified.

(3) Notwithstanding a lessee's insurable interest under subsections (1) and (2), the lessor retains an insurable interest until an option to buy has been exercised by the lessee and risk of loss has passed to the lessee.

(4) Nothing in this section impairs any insurable interest recognized under any other statute or rule of law.

(5) The parties by agreement may determine that one or more parties have an obligation to obtain and pay for insurance covering the goods and by agreement may determine the beneficiary of the proceeds of the insurance.

§ 2A–219. Risk of Loss.

(1) Except in the case of a finance lease, risk of loss is retained by the lessor and does not pass to the lessee. In the case of a finance lease, risk of loss passes to the lessee.

(2) Subject to the provisions of this Article on the effect of default on risk of loss (Section 2A–220), if risk of loss is to pass to the lessee and the time of passage is not stated, the following rules apply:

(a) If the lease contract requires or authorizes the goods to be shipped by carrier

(i) and it does not require delivery at a particular destination, the risk of loss passes to the lessee when the goods are duly delivered to the carrier; but

(ii) if it does require delivery at a particular destination and the goods are there duly tendered while in the possession of the carrier, the risk of loss passes to the lessee when the goods are there duly so tendered as to enable the lessee to take delivery.

(b) If the goods are held by a bailee to be delivered without being moved, the risk of loss passes to the lessee on acknowledgment by the bailee of the lessee's right to possession of the goods.

(c) In any case not within subsection (a) or (b), the risk of loss passes to the lessee on the lessee's receipt of the goods if the lessor, or, in the case of a finance lease, the supplier, is a merchant; otherwise the risk passes to the lessee on tender of delivery.

§ 2A–220. Effect of Default on Risk of Loss.

(1) Where risk of loss is to pass to the lessee and the time of passage is not stated:

(a) If a tender or delivery of goods so fails to conform to the lease contract as to give a right of rejection, the risk of their loss remains with the lessor, or, in the case of a finance lease, the supplier, until cure or acceptance.

(b) If the lessee rightfully revokes acceptance, he [or she], to the extent of any deficiency in his [or her] effective insurance coverage, may treat the risk of loss as having remained with the lessor from the beginning.

(2) Whether or not risk of loss is to pass to the lessee, if the lessee as to conforming goods already identified to a lease contract repudiates or is otherwise in default under the lease contract, the lessor, or, in the case of a finance lease, the supplier, to the extent of any deficiency in his [or her] effective insurance coverage may treat the risk of loss as resting on the lessee for a commercially reasonable time.

§ 2A–221. Casualty to Identified Goods.

If a lease contract requires goods identified when the lease contract is made, and the goods suffer casualty without fault of the lessee, the lessor or the supplier before delivery, or the goods suffer casualty before risk of loss passes to the lessee pursuant to the lease agreement or Section 2A–219, then:

(a) if the loss is total, the lease contract is avoided; and

(b) if the loss is partial or the goods have so deteriorated as to no longer conform to the lease contract, the lessee may nevertheless demand inspection and at his [or her] option either treat the lease contract as avoided or, except in a finance lease that is not a consumer lease, accept the goods with due allowance from the rent payable for the balance of the lease term for the deterioration or the deficiency in quantity but without further right against the lessor.

Part 3 Effect of Lease Contract

§ 2A–301. Enforceability of Lease Contract.

Except as otherwise provided in this Article, a lease contract is effective and enforceable according to its terms between the parties, against purchasers of the goods and against creditors of the parties.

§ 2A–302. Title to and Possession of Goods.

Except as otherwise provided in this Article, each provision of this Article applies whether the lessor or a third party has title to the goods, and whether the lessor, the lessee, or a third party has possession of the goods, notwithstanding any statute or rule of law that possession or the absence of possession is fraudulent.

§ 2A–303. Alienability of Party's Interest Under Lease Contract or of Lessor's Residual Interest in Goods; Delegation of Performance; Transfer of Rights.

(1) As used in this section, "creation of a security interest" includes the sale of a lease contract that is subject to Article 9, Secured Transactions, by reason of Section 9–109(a)(3).

(2) Except as provided in subsections (3) and Section 9–407, a provision in a lease agreement which (i) prohibits the voluntary or involuntary transfer, including a transfer by sale, sublease, creation or enforcement of a security interest, or attachment, levy, or other judicial process, of an interest of a party under the lease contract or of the lessor's residual interest in the goods, or (ii) makes such a transfer an event of default, gives rise to the rights and remedies provided in subsection (4), but a transfer that is prohibited or is an event of default under the lease agreement is otherwise effective.

(3) A provision in a lease agreement which (i) prohibits a transfer of a right to damages for default with respect to the whole lease contract or of a right to payment arising out of the transferor's due performance of the transferor's entire obligation, or (ii) makes such a transfer an event of default, is not enforceable, and such a transfer is not a transfer that materially impairs the propsect of obtaining return performance by, materially changes the duty of, or materially increases the burden or risk imposed on, the other party to the lease contract within the purview of subsection (4).

(4) Subject to subsection (3) and Section 9–407:

(a) if a transfer is made which is made an event of default under a lease agreement, the party to the lease contract not making the transfer, unless that party waives the default or otherwise agrees, has the rights and remedies described in Section 2A–501(2);

(b) if paragraph (a) is not applicable and if a transfer is made that (i) is prohibited under a lease agreement or (ii) materially impairs the prospect of obtaining return performance by, materially changes the duty of, or materially increases the burden or risk imposed on, the other party to the lease contract, unless the party not making the transfer agrees at any time to the transfer in the lease contract or otherwise, then, except as limited by contract, (i) the transferor is liable to the party not making the transfer for damages caused by the transfer to the extent that the damages could not reasonably be prevented by the party not making the transfer and (ii) a court having jurisdiction may grant other appropriate relief, including cancellation of the lease contract or an injunction against the transfer.

(5) A transfer of "the lease" or of "all my rights under the lease", or a transfer in similar general terms, is a transfer of rights and, unless the language or the circumstances, as in a transfer for security, indicate the contrary, the transfer is a delegation of duties by the transferor to the transferee. Acceptance by the transferee constitutes a promise by the transferee to perform those duties. The promise is enforceable by either the transferor or the other party to the lease contract.

(6) Unless otherwise agreed by the lessor and the lessee, a delegation of performance does not relieve the transferor as against the other party of any duty to perform or of any liability for default.

(7) In a consumer lease, to prohibit the transfer of an interest of a party under the lease contract or to make a transfer an event of default, the language must be specific, by a writing, and conspicuous.

As amended in 1990 and 1999.

§ 2A–304. Subsequent Lease of Goods by Lessor.

(1) Subject to Section 2A–303, a subsequent lessee from a lessor of goods under an existing lease contract obtains, to the extent of the leasehold interest transferred, the leasehold interest in the goods that the lessor had or had power to transfer, and except as provided in subsection (2) and Section 2A–527(4), takes subject to the existing lease contract. A lessor with voidable title has power to transfer a good leasehold interest to a good faith subsequent lessee for value, but only to the extent set forth in the preceding sentence. If goods have been delivered under a transaction of purchase the lessor has that power even though:

(a) the lessor's transferor was deceived as to the identity of the lessor;

(b) the delivery was in exchange for a check which is later dishonored;

(c) it was agreed that the transaction was to be a "cash sale"; or

(d) the delivery was procured through fraud punishable as larcenous under the criminal law.

(2) A subsequent lessee in the ordinary course of business from a lessor who is a merchant dealing in goods of that kind to whom the goods were entrusted by the existing lessee of that lessor before the interest of the subsequent lessee became enforceable against that lessor obtains, to the extent of the leasehold interest transferred, all of that lessor's and the existing lessee's rights to the goods, and takes free of the existing lease contract.

(3) A subsequent lessee from the lessor of goods that are subject to an existing lease contract and are covered by a certificate of title issued under a statute of this State or of another jurisdiction takes no greater rights than those provided both by this section and by the certificate of title statute.

As amended in 1990.

§ 2A–305. Sale or Sublease of Goods by Lessee.

(1) Subject to the provisions of Section 2A–303, a buyer or sublessee from the lessee of goods under an existing lease contract obtains, to the extent of the interest transferred, the leasehold interest in the goods that the lessee had or had power to transfer, and except as provided in subsection (2) and Section 2A–511(4), takes subject to the existing lease contract. A lessee with a voidable leasehold interest has power to transfer a good leasehold interest to a good faith buyer for value or a good faith sublessee for value, but only to the extent set forth in the preceding sentence. When goods have been delivered under a transaction of lease the lessee has that power even though:

(a) the lessor was deceived as to the identity of the lessee;

(b) the delivery was in exchange for a check which is later dishonored; or

(c) the delivery was procured through fraud punishable as larcenous under the criminal law.

(2) A buyer in the ordinary course of business or a sublessee in the ordinary course of business from a lessee who is a merchant dealing in goods of that kind to whom the goods were entrusted by the lessor obtains, to the extent of the interest transferred, all of the lessor's and lessee's rights to the goods, and takes free of the existing lease contract.

(3) A buyer or sublessee from the lessee of goods that are subject to an existing lease contract and are covered by a certificate of title issued under a statute of this State or of another jurisdiction takes no greater rights than those provided both by this section and by the certificate of title statute.

§ 2A–306. Priority of Certain Liens Arising by Operation of Law.

If a person in the ordinary course of his [or her] business furnishes services or materials with respect to goods subject to a lease contract, a lien upon those goods in the possession of that person given by statute or rule of law for those materials or services takes priority over any interest of the lessor or lessee under the lease contract or this Article unless the lien is created by statute and the statute provides otherwise or unless the lien is created by rule of law and the rule of law provides otherwise.

§ 2A–307. Priority of Liens Arising by Attachment or Levy on, Security Interests in, and Other Claims to Goods.

(1) Except as otherwise provided in Section 2A–306, a creditor of a lessee takes subject to the lease contract.

(2) Except as otherwise provided in subsection (3) and in Sections 2A–306 and 2A–308, a creditor of a lessor takes subject to the lease contract unless the creditor holds a lien that attached to the goods before the lease contract became enforceable.

(3) Except as otherwise provided in Sections 9–317, 9–321, and 9–323, a lessee takes a leasehold interest subject to a security interest held by a creditor of the lessor.

As amended in 1990 and 1999.

§ 2A–308. Special Rights of Creditors.

(1) A creditor of a lessor in possession of goods subject to a lease contract may treat the lease contract as void if as against the creditor retention of possession by the lessor is fraudulent under any statute or rule of law, but retention of possession in good faith and current course of trade by the lessor for a commercially reasonable time after the lease contract becomes enforceable is not fraudulent.

(2) Nothing in this Article impairs the rights of creditors of a lessor if the lease contract (a) becomes enforceable, not in current course of trade but in satisfaction of or as security for a pre-existing claim for money, security, or the like, and (b) is made under circumstances which under any statute or rule of law apart from this Article would constitute the transaction a fraudulent transfer or voidable preference.

(3) A creditor of a seller may treat a sale or an identification of goods to a contract for sale as void if as against the creditor retention of possession by the seller is fraudulent under any statute or rule of law, but retention of possession of the goods pursuant to a lease contract entered into by the seller as lessee and the buyer as lessor in connection with the sale or identification of the goods is not fraudulent if the buyer bought for value and in good faith.

§ 2A–309. Lessor's and Lessee's Rights When Goods Become Fixtures.

(1) In this section:

(a) goods are "fixtures" when they become so related to particular real estate that an interest in them arises under real estate law;

(b) a "fixture filing" is the filing, in the office where a mortgage on the real estate would be filed or recorded, of a financing statement covering goods that are or are to become fixtures and conforming to the requirements of Section 9–502(a) and (b);

(c) a lease is a "purchase money lease" unless the lessee has possession or use of the goods or the right to possession or use of the goods before the lease agreement is enforceable;

(d) a mortgage is a "construction mortgage" to the extent it secures an obligation incurred for the construction of an improvement on land including the acquisition cost of the land, if the recorded writing so indicates; and

(e) "encumbrance" includes real estate mortgages and other liens on real estate and all other rights in real estate that are not ownership interests.

(2) Under this Article a lease may be of goods that are fixtures or may continue in goods that become fixtures, but no lease exists under this Article of ordinary building materials incorporated into an improvement on land.

(3) This Article does not prevent creation of a lease of fixtures pursuant to real estate law.

(4) The perfected interest of a lessor of fixtures has priority over a conflicting interest of an encumbrancer or owner of the real estate if:

(a) the lease is a purchase money lease, the conflicting interest of the encumbrancer or owner arises before the goods become fixtures, the interest of the lessor is perfected by a fixture filing before the goods become fixtures or within ten days thereafter, and the lessee has an interest of record in the real estate or is in possession of the real estate; or

(b) the interest of the lessor is perfected by a fixture filing before the interest of the encumbrancer or owner is of record, the lessor's interest has priority over any conflicting interest of a predecessor in title of the encumbrancer or owner, and the lessee has an interest of record in the real estate or is in possession of the real estate.

(5) The interest of a lessor of fixtures, whether or not perfected, has priority over the conflicting interest of an encumbrancer or owner of the real estate if:

(a) the fixtures are readily removable factory or office machines, readily removable equipment that is not primarily used or leased for use in the operation of the real estate, or readily removable replacements of domestic appliances that are goods subject to a consumer lease, and before the goods become fixtures the lease contract is enforceable; or

(b) the conflicting interest is a lien on the real estate obtained by legal or equitable proceedings after the lease contract is enforceable; or

(c) the encumbrancer or owner has consented in writing to the lease or has disclaimed an interest in the goods as fixtures; or

(d) the lessee has a right to remove the goods as against the encumbrancer or owner. If the lessee's right to remove terminates, the priority of the interest of the lessor continues for a reasonable time.

(6) Notwithstanding paragraph (4)(a) but otherwise subject to subsections (4) and (5), the interest of a lessor of fixtures, including the lessor's residual interest, is subordinate

to the conflicting interest of an encumbrancer of the real estate under a construction mortgage recorded before the goods become fixtures if the goods become fixtures before the completion of the construction. To the extent given to refinance a construction mortgage, the conflicting interest of an encumbrancer of the real estate under a mortgage has this priority to the same extent as the encumbrancer of the real estate under the construction mortgage.

(7) In cases not within the preceding subsections, priority between the interest of a lessor of fixtures, including the lessor's residual interest, and the conflicting interest of an encumbrancer or owner of the real estate who is not the lessee is determined by the priority rules governing conflicting interests in real estate.

(8) If the interest of a lessor of fixtures, including the lessor's residual interest, has priority over all conflicting interests of all owners and encumbrancers of the real estate, the lessor or the lessee may (i) on default, expiration, termination, or cancellation of the lease agreement but subject to the agreement and this Article, or (ii) if necessary to enforce other rights and remedies of the lessor or lessee under this Article, remove the goods from the real estate, free and clear of all conflicting interests of all owners and encumbrancers of the real estate, but the lessor or lessee must reimburse any encumbrancer or owner of the real estate who is not the lessee and who has not otherwise agreed for the cost of repair of any physical injury, but not for any diminution in value of the real estate caused by the absence of the goods removed or by any necessity of replacing them. A person entitled to reimbursement may refuse permission to remove until the party seeking removal gives adequate security for the performance of this obligation.

(9) Even though the lease agreement does not create a security interest, the interest of a lessor of fixtures, including the lessor's residual interest, is perfected by filing a financing statement as a fixture filing for leased goods that are or are to become fixtures in accordance with the relevant provisions of the Article on Secured Transactions (Article 9).

As amended in 1990 and 1999.

§ 2A–310. Lessor's and Lessee's Rights When Goods Become Accessions.

(1) Goods are "accessions" when they are installed in or affixed to other goods.

(2) The interest of a lessor or a lessee under a lease contract entered into before the goods became accessions is superior to all interests in the whole except as stated in subsection (4).

(3) The interest of a lessor or a lessee under a lease contract entered into at the time or after the goods became accessions is superior to all subsequently acquired interests in the whole except as stated in subsection (4) but is subordinate to interests in the whole existing at the time the lease contract was made unless the holders of such interests in the whole have in writing consented to the lease or disclaimed

an interest in the goods as part of the whole.

(4) The interest of a lessor or a lessee under a lease contract described in subsection (2) or (3) is subordinate to the interest of

(a) a buyer in the ordinary course of business or a lessee in the ordinary course of business of any interest in the whole acquired after the goods became accessions; or

(b) a creditor with a security interest in the whole perfected before the lease contract was made to the extent that the creditor makes subsequent advances without knowledge of the lease contract.

(5) When under subsections (2) or (3) and (4) a lessor or a lessee of accessions holds an interest that is superior to all interests in the whole, the lessor or the lessee may (a) on default, expiration, termination, or cancellation of the lease contract by the other party but subject to the provisions of the lease contract and this Article, or (b) if necessary to enforce his [or her] other rights and remedies under this Article, remove the goods from the whole, free and clear of all interests in the whole, but he [or she] must reimburse any holder of an interest in the whole who is not the lessee and who has not otherwise agreed for the cost of repair of any physical injury but not for any diminution in value of the whole caused by the absence of the goods removed or by any necessity for replacing them. A person entitled to reimbursement may refuse permission to remove until the party seeking removal gives adequate security for the performance of this obligation.

§ 2A–311. Priority Subject to Subordination.

Nothing in this Article prevents subordination by agreement by any person entitled to priority.

As added in 1990.

Part 4 Performance of Lease Contract: Repudiated, Substituted and Excused

§ 2A–401. Insecurity: Adequate Assurance of Performance.

(1) A lease contract imposes an obligation on each party that the other's expectation of receiving due performance will not be impaired.

(2) If reasonable grounds for insecurity arise with respect to the performance of either party, the insecure party may demand in writing adequate assurance of due performance. Until the insecure party receives that assurance, if commercially reasonable the insecure party may suspend any performance for which he [or she] has not already received the agreed return.

(3) A repudiation of the lease contract occurs if assurance of due performance adequate under the circumstances of the particular case is not provided to the insecure party within a reasonable time, not to exceed 30 days after receipt of a demand by the other party.

(4) Between merchants, the reasonableness of grounds for insecurity and the adequacy of any assurance offered must be determined according to commercial standards.

(5) Acceptance of any nonconforming delivery or payment does not prejudice the aggrieved party's right to demand adequate assurance of future performance.

§ 2A–402. Anticipatory Repudiation.

If either party repudiates a lease contract with respect to a performance not yet due under the lease contract, the loss of which performance will substantially impair the value of the lease contract to the other, the aggrieved party may:

(a) for a commercially reasonable time, await retraction of repudiation and performance by the repudiating party;

(b) make demand pursuant to Section 2A–401 and await assurance of future performance adequate under the circumstances of the particular case; or

(c) resort to any right or remedy upon default under the lease contract or this Article, even though the aggrieved party has notified the repudiating party that the aggrieved party would await the repudiating party's performance and assurance and has urged retraction. In addition, whether or not the aggrieved party is pursuing one of the foregoing remedies, the aggrieved party may suspend performance or, if the aggrieved party is the lessor, proceed in accordance with the provisions of this Article on the lessor's right to identify goods to the lease contract notwithstanding default or to salvage unfinished goods (Section 2A–524).

§ 2A–403. Retraction of Anticipatory Repudiation.

(1) Until the repudiating party's next performance is due, the repudiating party can retract the repudiation unless, since the repudiation, the aggrieved party has cancelled the lease contract or materially changed the aggrieved party's position or otherwise indicated that the aggrieved party considers the repudiation final.

(2) Retraction may be by any method that clearly indicates to the aggrieved party that the repudiating party intends to perform under the lease contract and includes any assurance demanded under Section 2A–401.

(3) Retraction reinstates a repudiating party's rights under a lease contract with due excuse and allowance to the aggrieved party for any delay occasioned by the repudiation.

§ 2A–404. Substituted Performance.

(1) If without fault of the lessee, the lessor and the supplier, the agreed berthing, loading, or unloading facilities fail or the agreed type of carrier becomes unavailable or the agreed manner of delivery otherwise becomes commercially impracticable, but a commercially reasonable substitute is available, the substitute performance must be tendered and accepted.

(2) If the agreed means or manner of payment fails because of domestic or foreign governmental regulation:

(a) the lessor may withhold or stop delivery or cause the supplier to withhold or stop delivery unless the lessee provides a means or manner of payment that is commercially a substantial equivalent; and

(b) if delivery has already been taken, payment by the means or in the manner provided by the regulation discharges the lessee's obligation unless the regulation is discriminatory, oppressive, or predatory.

§ 2A–405. Excused Performance.

Subject to Section 2A–404 on substituted performance, the following rules apply:

(a) Delay in delivery or nondelivery in whole or in part by a lessor or a supplier who complies with paragraphs (b) and (c) is not a default under the lease contract if performance as agreed has been made impracticable by the occurrence of a contingency the nonoccurrence of which was a basic assumption on which the lease contract was made or by compliance in good faith with any applicable foreign or domestic governmental regulation or order, whether or not the regulation or order later proves to be invalid.

(b) If the causes mentioned in paragraph (a) affect only part of the lessor's or the supplier's capacity to perform, he [or she] shall allocate production and deliveries among his [or her] customers but at his [or her] option may include regular customers not then under contract for sale or lease as well as his [or her] own requirements for further manufacture. He [or she] may so allocate in any manner that is fair and reasonable.

(c) The lessor seasonably shall notify the lessee and in the case of a finance lease the supplier seasonably shall notify the lessor and the lessee, if known, that there will be delay or nondelivery and, if allocation is required under paragraph (b), of the estimated quota thus made available for the lessee.

§ 2A–406. Procedure on Excused Performance.

(1) If the lessee receives notification of a material or indefinite delay or an allocation justified under Section 2A–405, the lessee may by written notification to the lessor as to any goods involved, and with respect to all of the goods if under an installment lease contract the value of the whole lease contract is substantially impaired (Section 2A–510):

   (a) terminate the lease contract (Section 2A–505(2)); or

   (b) except in a finance lease that is not a consumer lease, modify the lease contract by accepting the available quota in substitution, with due allowance from the rent payable for the balance of the lease term for the deficiency but without further right against the lessor.

(2) If, after receipt of a notification from the lessor under Section 2A–405, the lessee fails so to modify the lease agreement within a reasonable time not exceeding 30 days, the lease contract lapses with respect to any deliveries affected.

§ 2A–407. Irrevocable Promises: Finance Leases.

(1) In the case of a finance lease that is not a consumer lease the lessee's promises under the lease contract become irrevocable and independent upon the lessee's acceptance of the goods.

(2) A promise that has become irrevocable and independent under subsection (1):

(a) is effective and enforceable between the parties, and by or against third parties including assignees of the parties, and

(b) is not subject to cancellation, termination, modification, repudiation, excuse, or substitution without the consent of the party to whom the promise runs.

(3) This section does not affect the validity under any other law of a covenant in any lease contract making the lessee's promises irrevocable and independent upon the lessee's acceptance of the goods.

As amended in 1990.

Part 5 Default

A. In General

§ 2A–501. Default: Procedure.

(1) Whether the lessor or the lessee is in default under a lease contract is determined by the lease agreement and this Article.

(2) If the lessor or the lessee is in default under the lease contract, the party seeking enforcement has rights and remedies as provided in this Article and, except as limited by this Article, as provided in the lease agreement.

(3) If the lessor or the lessee is in default under the lease contract, the party seeking enforcement may reduce the party's claim to judgment, or otherwise enforce the lease contract by self-help or any available judicial procedure or nonjudicial procedure, including administrative proceeding, arbitration, or the like, in accordance with this Article.

(4) Except as otherwise provided in Section 1–106(1) or this Article or the lease agreement, the rights and remedies referred to in subsections (2) and (3) are cumulative.

(5) If the lease agreement covers both real property and goods, the party seeking enforcement may proceed under this Part as to the goods, or under other applicable law as to both the real property and the goods in accordance with that party's rights and remedies in respect of the real property, in which case this Part does not apply.

As amended in 1990.

§ 2A–502. Notice After Default.

Except as otherwise provided in this Article or the lease agreement, the lessor or lessee in default under the lease contract is not entitled to notice of default or notice of enforcement from the other party to the lease agreement.

§ 2A–503. Modification or Impairment of Rights and Remedies.

(1) Except as otherwise provided in this Article, the lease agreement may include rights and remedies for default in addition to or in substitution for those provided in this Article and may limit or alter the measure of damages recoverable under this Article.

(2) Resort to a remedy provided under this Article or in the lease agreement is optional unless the remedy is expressly agreed to be exclusive. If circumstances cause an exclusive or limited remedy to fail of its essential purpose, or provision for an exclusive remedy is unconscionable, remedy may be had as provided in this Article.

(3) Consequential damages may be liquidated under Section 2A–504, or may otherwise be limited, altered, or excluded unless the limitation, alteration, or exclusion is unconscionable. Limitation, alteration, or exclusion of consequential damages for injury to the person in the case of consumer goods is prima facie unconscionable but limitation, alteration, or exclusion of damages where the loss is commercial is not prima facie unconscionable.

(4) Rights and remedies on default by the lessor or the lessee with respect to any obligation or promise collateral or ancillary to the lease contract are not impaired by this Article.

As amended in 1990.

§ 2A–504. Liquidation of Damages.

(1) Damages payable by either party for default, or any other act or omission, including indemnity for loss or diminution of anticipated tax benefits or loss or damage to lessor's residual interest, may be liquidated in the lease agreement but only at an amount or by a formula that is reasonable in light of the then anticipated harm caused by the default or other act or omission.

(2) If the lease agreement provides for liquidation of damages, and such provision does not comply with subsection (1), or such provision is an exclusive or limited remedy that circumstances cause to fail of its essential purpose, remedy may be had as provided in this Article.

(3) If the lessor justifiably withholds or stops delivery of goods because of the lessee's default or insolvency (Section 2A–525 or 2A–526), the lessee is entitled to restitution of any amount by which the sum of his [or her] payments exceeds:

(a) the amount to which the lessor is entitled by virtue of terms liquidating the lessor's damages in accordance with subsection (1); or

(b) in the absence of those terms, 20 percent of the then present value of the total rent the lessee was obligated to pay for the balance of the lease term, or, in the case of a consumer lease, the lesser of such amount or $500.

(4) A lessee's right to restitution under subsection (3) is subject to offset to the extent the lessor establishes:

(a) a right to recover damages under the provisions of this Article other than subsection (1); and

(b) the amount or value of any benefits received by the lessee directly or indirectly by reason of the lease contract.

§ 2A–505. Cancellation and Termination and Effect of Cancellation, Termination, Rescission, or Fraud on Rights and Remedies.

(1) On cancellation of the lease contract, all obligations that are still executory on both sides are discharged, but any right based on prior default or performance survives, and the cancelling party also retains any remedy for default of the whole lease contract or any unperformed balance.

(2) On termination of the lease contract, all obligations that are still executory on both sides are discharged but any right based on prior default or performance survives.

(3) Unless the contrary intention clearly appears, expressions of "cancellation," "rescission," or the like of the lease contract may not be construed as a renunciation or discharge of any claim in damages for an antecedent default.

(4) Rights and remedies for material misrepresentation or fraud include all rights and remedies available under this Article for default.

(5) Neither rescission nor a claim for rescission of the lease contract nor rejection or return of the goods may bar or be deemed inconsistent with a claim for damages or other right or remedy.

§ 2A–506. Statute of Limitations.

(1) An action for default under a lease contract, including breach of warranty or indemnity, must be commenced within 4 years after the cause of action accrued. By the original lease contract the parties may reduce the period of limitation to not less than one year.

(2) A cause of action for default accrues when the act or omission on which the default or breach of warranty is based is or should have been discovered by the aggrieved party, or when the default occurs, whichever is later. A cause of action for indemnity accrues when the act or omission on which the claim for indemnity is based is or should have been discovered by the indemnified party, whichever is later.

(3) If an action commenced within the time limited by subsection (1) is so terminated as to leave available a remedy by another action for the same default or breach of warranty or indemnity, the other action may be commenced after the expiration of the time limited and within 6 months after the termination of the first action unless the termination resulted from voluntary discontinuance or from dismissal for failure or neglect to prosecute.

(4) This section does not alter the law on tolling of the statute of limitations nor does it apply to causes of action that have accrued before this Article becomes effective.

§ 2A–507. Proof of Market Rent: Time and Place.

(1) Damages based on market rent (Section 2A–519 or 2A–528) are determined according to the rent for the use of the goods concerned for a lease term identical to the remaining lease term of the original lease agreement and prevailing at the times specified in Sections 2A–519 and 2A–528.

(2) If evidence of rent for the use of the goods concerned for a lease term identical to the remaining lease term of the original lease agreement and prevailing at the times or places described in this Article is not readily available, the rent prevailing within any reasonable time before or after the time described or at any other place or for a different lease term which in commercial judgment or under usage of trade would serve as a reasonable substitute for the one described may be used, making any proper allowance for the difference, including the cost of transporting the goods to or from the other place.

(3) Evidence of a relevant rent prevailing at a time or place or for a lease term other than the one described in this Article offered by one party is not admissible unless and until he [or she] has given the other party notice the court finds sufficient to prevent unfair surprise.

(4) If the prevailing rent or value of any goods regularly leased in any established market is in issue, reports in official publications or trade journals or in newspapers or periodicals of general circulation published as the reports of that market are admissible in evidence. The circumstances of the preparation of the report may be shown to affect its weight but not its admissibility.

As amended in 1990.

B. Default by Lessor

§ 2A–508. Lessee's Remedies.

(1) If a lessor fails to deliver the goods in conformity to the lease contract (Section 2A–509) or repudiates the lease contract (Section 2A–402), or a lessee rightfully rejects the goods (Section 2A–509) or justifiably revokes acceptance of the goods (Section 2A–517), then with respect to any goods involved, and with respect to all of the goods if under an installment lease contract the value of the whole lease contract is substantially impaired (Section 2A–510), the lessor is in default under the lease contract and the lessee may:

(a) cancel the lease contract (Section 2A–505(1));

(b) recover so much of the rent and security as has been paid and is just under the circumstances;

(c) cover and recover damages as to all goods affected whether or not they have been identified to the lease contract (Sections 2A–518 and 2A–520), or recover damages for nondelivery (Sections 2A–519 and 2A–520);

(d) exercise any other rights or pursue any other remedies provided in the lease contract.

(2) If a lessor fails to deliver the goods in conformity to the lease contract or repudiates the lease contract, the lessee may also:

(a) if the goods have been identified, recover them (Section 2A–522); or

(b) in a proper case, obtain specific performance or replevy the goods (Section 2A–521).

(3) If a lessor is otherwise in default under a lease contract, the lessee may exercise the rights and pursue the remedies provided in the lease contract, which may include a right to cancel the lease, and in Section 2A–519(3).

(4) If a lessor has breached a warranty, whether express or implied, the lessee may recover damages (Section 2A–519(4)).

(5) On rightful rejection or justifiable revocation of acceptance, a lessee has a security interest in goods in the lessee's possession or control for any rent and security that has been paid and any expenses reasonably incurred in their inspection, receipt, transportation, and care and custody and may hold those goods and dispose of them in good faith and in a commercially reasonable manner, subject to Section 2A–527(5).

(6) Subject to the provisions of Section 2A–407, a lessee, on notifying the lessor of the lessee's intention to do so, may deduct all or any part of the damages resulting from any default under the lease contract from any part of the rent still due under the same lease contract.

As amended in 1990.

§ 2A–509. Lessee's Rights on Improper Delivery; Rightful Rejection.

(1) Subject to the provisions of Section 2A–510 on default in installment lease contracts, if the goods or the tender or delivery fail in any respect to conform to the lease contract, the lessee may reject or accept the goods or accept any commercial unit or units and reject the rest of the goods.

(2) Rejection of goods is ineffective unless it is within a reasonable time after tender or delivery of the goods and the lessee seasonably notifies the lessor.

§ 2A–510. Installment Lease Contracts: Rejection and Default.

(1) Under an installment lease contract a lessee may reject any delivery that is nonconforming if the nonconformity substantially impairs the value of that delivery and cannot be cured or the nonconformity is a defect in the required documents; but if the nonconformity does not fall within subsection (2) and the lessor or the supplier gives adequate assurance of its cure, the lessee must accept that delivery.

(2) Whenever nonconformity or default with respect to one or more deliveries substantially impairs the value of the installment lease contract as a whole there is a default with respect to the whole. But, the aggrieved party reinstates the installment lease contract as a whole if the aggrieved party accepts a nonconforming delivery without seasonably notifying of cancellation or brings an action with respect only to past deliveries or demands performance as to future deliveries.

§ 2A–511. Merchant Lessee's Duties as to Rightfully Rejected Goods.

(1) Subject to any security interest of a lessee (Section 2A–508(5)), if a lessor or a supplier has no agent or place of business at the market of rejection, a merchant lessee, after rejection of goods in his [or her] possession or control, shall follow any reasonable instructions received from the lessor or the supplier with respect to the goods. In the absence of those instructions, a merchant lessee shall make reasonable efforts to sell, lease, or otherwise dispose of the goods for the lessor's account if they threaten to decline in value speedily. Instructions are not reasonable if on demand indemnity for expenses is not forthcoming.

(2) If a merchant lessee (subsection (1)) or any other lessee (Section 2A–512) disposes of goods, he [or she] is entitled to reimbursement either from the lessor or the supplier or out of the proceeds for reasonable expenses of caring for and disposing of the goods and, if the expenses include no disposition commission, to such commission as is usual in the trade, or if there is none, to a reasonable sum not exceeding 10 percent of the gross proceeds.

(3) In complying with this section or Section 2A–512, the lessee is held only to good faith. Good faith conduct hereunder is neither acceptance or conversion nor the basis of an action for damages.

(4) A purchaser who purchases in good faith from a lessee pursuant to this section or Section 2A–512 takes the goods free of any rights of the lessor and the supplier even though the lessee fails to comply with one or more of the requirements of this Article.

§ 2A–512. Lessee's Duties as to Rightfully Rejected Goods.

(1) Except as otherwise provided with respect to goods that threaten to decline in value speedily (Section 2A–511) and subject to any security interest of a lessee (Section 2A–508(5)):

(a) the lessee, after rejection of goods in the lessee's possession, shall hold them with reasonable care at the lessor's or the supplier's disposition for a reasonable time after the lessee's seasonable notification of rejection;

(b) if the lessor or the supplier gives no instructions within a reasonable time after notification of rejection, the lessee may store the rejected goods for the lessor's or the supplier's account or ship them to the lessor or the supplier or dispose of them for the lessor's or the supplier's account with reimbursement in the manner provided in Section 2A–511; but

(c) the lessee has no further obligations with regard to goods rightfully rejected.

(2) Action by the lessee pursuant to subsection (1) is not acceptance or conversion.

§ 2A–513. Cure by Lessor of Improper Tender or Delivery; Replacement.

(1) If any tender or delivery by the lessor or the supplier is rejected because nonconforming and the time for performance has not yet expired, the lessor or the supplier may seasonably notify the lessee of the lessor's or the supplier's intention to cure and may then make a conforming delivery within the time provided in the lease contract.

(2) If the lessee rejects a nonconforming tender that the lessor or the supplier had reasonable grounds to believe would be acceptable with or without money allowance, the lessor or the supplier may have a further reasonable time to substitute a conforming tender if he [or she] seasonably notifies the lessee.

§ 2A–514. Waiver of Lessee's Objections.

(1) In rejecting goods, a lessee's failure to state a particular defect that is ascertainable by reasonable inspection precludes the lessee from relying on the defect to justify rejection or to establish default:

(a) if, stated seasonably, the lessor or the supplier could have cured it (Section 2A–513); or

(b) between merchants if the lessor or the supplier after rejection has made a request in writing for a full and final written statement of all defects on which the lessee proposes to rely.

(2) A lessee's failure to reserve rights when paying rent or other consideration against documents precludes recovery of the payment for defects apparent on the face of the documents.

§ 2A–515. Acceptance of Goods.

(1) Acceptance of goods occurs after the lessee has had a reasonable opportunity to inspect the goods and

(a) the lessee signifies or acts with respect to the goods in a manner that signifies to the lessor or the supplier that the goods are conforming or that the lessee will take or retain them in spite of their nonconformity; or

(b) the lessee fails to make an effective rejection of the goods (Section 2A–509(2)).

(2) Acceptance of a part of any commercial unit is acceptance of that entire unit.

§ 2A–516. Effect of Acceptance of Goods; Notice of Default; Burden of Establishing Default after Acceptance; Notice of Claim or Litigation to Person Answerable Over.

(1) A lessee must pay rent for any goods accepted in accordance with the lease contract, with due allowance for goods rightfully rejected or not delivered.

(2) A lessee's acceptance of goods precludes rejection of the goods accepted. In the case of a finance lease, if made with knowledge of a nonconformity, acceptance cannot be revoked because of it. In any other case, if made with knowledge of a nonconformity, acceptance cannot be revoked because of it unless the acceptance was on the reasonable assumption that the nonconformity would be seasonably cured. Acceptance does not of itself impair any other remedy provided by this Article or the lease agreement for nonconformity.

(3) If a tender has been accepted:

(a) within a reasonable time after the lessee discovers or should have discovered any default, the lessee shall notify the lessor and the supplier, if any, or be barred from any remedy against the party notified;

(b) except in the case of a consumer lease, within a reasonable time after the lessee receives notice of litigation for infringement or the like (Section 2A–211) the lessee shall notify the lessor or be barred from any remedy over for liability established by the litigation; and

(c) the burden is on the lessee to establish any default.

(4) If a lessee is sued for breach of a warranty or other obligation for which a lessor or a supplier is answerable over the following apply:

(a) The lessee may give the lessor or the supplier, or both, written notice of the litigation. If the notice states that the person notified may come in and defend and that if the person notified does not do so that person will be bound in any action against that person by the lessee by any determination of fact common to the two litigations, then unless the person notified after seasonable receipt of the notice does come in and defend that person is so bound.

(b) The lessor or the supplier may demand in writing that the lessee turn over control of the litigation including settlement if the claim is one for infringement or the like (Section 2A–211) or else be barred from any remedy over. If the demand states that the lessor or the supplier agrees to bear all expense and to satisfy any adverse judgment, then unless the lessee after seasonable receipt of the demand does turn over control the lessee is so barred.

(5) Subsections (3) and (4) apply to any obligation of a lessee to hold the lessor or the supplier harmless against infringement or the like (Section 2A–211).

As amended in 1990.

§ 2A–517. Revocation of Acceptance of Goods.

(1) A lessee may revoke acceptance of a lot or commercial unit whose nonconformity substantially impairs its value to the lessee if the lessee has accepted it:

(a) except in the case of a finance lease, on the reasonable assumption that its nonconformity would be cured and it has not been seasonably cured; or

(b) without discovery of the nonconformity if the lessee's acceptance was reasonably induced either by the lessor's assurances or, except in the case of a finance lease, by the difficulty of discovery before acceptance.

(2) Except in the case of a finance lease that is not a consumer lease, a lessee may revoke acceptance of a lot or commercial unit if the lessor defaults under the lease contract and the default substantially impairs the value of that lot or commercial unit to the lessee.

(3) If the lease agreement so provides, the lessee may revoke acceptance of a lot or commercial unit because of other defaults by the lessor.

(4) Revocation of acceptance must occur within a reasonable time after the lessee discovers or should have discovered the ground for it and before any substantial change in condition of the goods which is not caused by the nonconformity. Revocation is not effective until the lessee notifies the lessor.

(5) A lessee who so revokes has the same rights and duties with regard to the goods involved as if the lessee had rejected them.

As amended in 1990.

§ 2A–518. Cover; Substitute Goods.

(1) After a default by a lessor under the lease contract of the type described in Section 2A–508(1), or, if agreed, after other default by the lessor, the lessee may cover by making any purchase or lease of or contract to purchase or lease goods in substitution for those due from the lessor.

(2) Except as otherwise provided with respect to damages liquidated in the lease agreement (Section 2A–504) or otherwise determined pursuant to agreement of the parties (Sections 1–102(3) and 2A–503), if a lessee's cover is by lease agreement substantially similar to the original lease agreement and the new lease agreement is made in good faith and in a commercially reasonable manner, the lessee may recover from the lessor as damages (i) the present value, as of the date of the commencement of the term of the new lease agreement, of the rent under the new lease agreement applicable to that period of the new lease term which is comparable to the then remaining term of the original lease agreement minus the present value as of the same date of the total rent for the then remaining lease term of the original lease agreement, and (ii) any incidental or consequential damages, less expenses saved in consequence of the lessor's default.

(3) If a lessee's cover is by lease agreement that for any reason does not qualify for treatment under subsection (2), or is by purchase or otherwise, the lessee may recover from the lessor as if the lessee had elected not to cover and Section 2A–519 governs.

As amended in 1990.

§ 2A–519. Lessee's Damages for Non-Delivery, Repudiation, Default, and Breach of Warranty in Regard to Accepted Goods.

(1) Except as otherwise provided with respect to damages liquidated in the lease agreement (Section 2A–504) or otherwise determined pursuant to agreement of the parties (Sections 1–102(3) and 2A–503), if a lessee elects not to cover or a lessee elects to cover and the cover is by lease agreement that for any reason does not qualify for treatment under Section 2A–518(2), or is by purchase or otherwise, the measure of damages for non-delivery or repudiation by the lessor or for rejection or revocation of acceptance by the lessee is the present value, as of the date of the default, of the then market rent minus the present value as of the same date of the original rent, computed for the remaining lease term of the original lease agreement, together with incidental and consequential damages, less expenses saved in consequence of the lessor's default.

(2) Market rent is to be determined as of the place for tender or, in cases of rejection after arrival or revocation of acceptance, as of the place of arrival.

(3) Except as otherwise agreed, if the lessee has accepted goods and given notification (Section 2A–516(3)), the measure of damages for non-conforming tender or delivery or other default by a lessor is the loss resulting in the ordinary course of events from the lessor's default as determined in any manner that is reasonable together with incidental and consequential damages, less expenses saved in consequence of the lessor's default.

(4) Except as otherwise agreed, the measure of damages for breach of warranty is the present value at the time and place of acceptance of the difference between the value of the use of the goods accepted and the value if they had been as warranted for the lease term, unless special circumstances show proximate damages of a different amount, together with incidental and consequential damages, less expenses saved in consequence of the lessor's default or breach of warranty.

As amended in 1990.

§ 2A–520. Lessee's Incidental and Consequential Damages.

(1) Incidental damages resulting from a lessor's default include expenses reasonably incurred in inspection, receipt, transportation, and care and custody of goods rightfully rejected or goods the acceptance of which is justifiably revoked, any commercially reasonable charges, expenses or commissions in connection with effecting cover, and any other reasonable expense incident to the default.

(2) Consequential damages resulting from a lessor's default include:

(a) any loss resulting from general or particular requirements and needs of which the lessor at the time of contracting had reason to know and which could not reasonably be prevented by cover or otherwise; and

(b) injury to person or property proximately resulting from any breach of warranty.

§ 2A–521. Lessee's Right to Specific Performance or Replevin.

(1) Specific performance may be decreed if the goods are unique or in other proper circumstances.

(2) A decree for specific performance may include any terms and conditions as to payment of the rent, damages, or other relief that the court deems just.

(3) A lessee has a right of replevin, detinue, sequestration, claim and delivery, or the like for goods identified to the lease contract if after reasonable effort the lessee is unable to effect cover for those goods or the circumstances reasonably indicate that the effort will be unavailing.

§ 2A–522. Lessee's Right to Goods on Lessor's Insolvency.

(1) Subject to subsection (2) and even though the goods have not been shipped, a lessee who has paid a part or all of the rent and security for goods identified to a lease contract (Section 2A–217) on making and keeping good a tender of any unpaid portion of the rent and security due under the lease contract may recover the goods identified from the lessor if the lessor becomes insolvent within 10 days after receipt of the first installment of rent and security.

(2) A lessee acquires the right to recover goods identified to a lease contract only if they conform to the lease contract.

C. Default by Lessee

§ 2A–523. Lessor's Remedies.

(1) If a lessee wrongfully rejects or revokes acceptance of goods or fails to make a payment when due or repudiates with respect to a part or the whole, then, with respect to any goods involved, and with respect to all of the goods if under an installment lease contract the value of the whole lease contract is substantially impaired (Section 2A–510), the lessee is in default under the lease contract and the lessor may:

(a) cancel the lease contract (Section 2A–505(1));

(b) proceed respecting goods not identified to the lease contract (Section 2A–524);

(c) withhold delivery of the goods and take possession of goods previously delivered (Section 2A–525);

(d) stop delivery of the goods by any bailee (Section 2A–526);

(e) dispose of the goods and recover damages (Section 2A–527), or retain the goods and recover damages (Section 2A–528), or in a proper case recover rent (Section 2A–529)

(f) exercise any other rights or pursue any other remedies provided in the lease contract.

(2) If a lessor does not fully exercise a right or obtain a remedy to which the lessor is entitled under subsection (1), the lessor may recover the loss resulting in the ordinary course of events from the lessee's default as determined in any reasonable manner, together with incidental damages, less expenses saved in consequence of the lessee's default.

(3) If a lessee is otherwise in default under a lease contract, the lessor may exercise the rights and pursue the remedies provided in the lease contract, which may include a right to cancel the lease. In addition, unless otherwise provided in the lease contract:

(a) if the default substantially impairs the value of the lease contract to the lessor, the lessor may exercise the rights and pursue the remedies provided in subsections (1) or (2); or

(b) if the default does not substantially impair the value of the lease contract to the lessor, the lessor may recover as provided in subsection (2).

As amended in 1990.

§ 2A–524. Lessor's Right to Identify Goods to Lease Contract.

(1) After default by the lessee under the lease contract of the type described in Section 2A–523(1) or 2A–523(3)(a) or, if agreed, after other default by the lessee, the lessor may:

(a) identify to the lease contract conforming goods not already identified if at the time the lessor learned of the default they were in the lessor's or the supplier's possession or control; and

(b) dispose of goods (Section 2A–527(1)) that demonstrably have been intended for the particular lease contract even though those goods are unfinished.

(2) If the goods are unfinished, in the exercise of reasonable commercial judgment for the purposes of avoiding loss and of effective realization, an aggrieved lessor or the supplier may either complete manufacture and wholly identify the goods to the lease contract or cease manufacture and lease, sell, or otherwise dispose of the goods for scrap or salvage value or proceed in any other reasonable manner.

As amended in 1990.

§ 2A–525. Lessor's Right to Possession of Goods.

(1) If a lessor discovers the lessee to be insolvent, the lessor may refuse to deliver the goods.

(2) After a default by the lessee under the lease contract of the type described in Section 2A–523(1) or 2A–523(3)(a) or, if agreed, after other default by the lessee, the lessor has the right to take possession of the goods. If the lease contract so provides, the lessor may require the lessee to assemble the goods and make them available to the lessor at a place to be designated by the lessor which is reasonably convenient to both parties. Without removal, the lessor may render unusable any goods employed in trade or business, and may dispose of goods on the lessee's premises (Section 2A–527).

(3) The lessor may proceed under subsection (2) without judicial process if that can be done without breach of the peace or the lessor may proceed by action.

As amended in 1990.

§ 2A–526. Lessor's Stoppage of Delivery in Transit or Otherwise.

(1) A lessor may stop delivery of goods in the possession of a carrier or other bailee if the lessor discovers the lessee to

be insolvent and may stop delivery of carload, truckload, planeload, or larger shipments of express or freight if the lessee repudiates or fails to make a payment due before delivery, whether for rent, security or otherwise under the lease contract, or for any other reason the lessor has a right to withhold or take possession of the goods.

(2) In pursuing its remedies under subsection (1), the lessor may stop delivery until

(a) receipt of the goods by the lessee;

(b) acknowledgment to the lessee by any bailee of the goods, except a carrier, that the bailee holds the goods for the lessee; or

(c) such an acknowledgment to the lessee by a carrier via reshipment or as warehouseman.

(3) (a) To stop delivery, a lessor shall so notify as to enable the bailee by reasonable diligence to prevent delivery of the goods.

(b) After notification, the bailee shall hold and deliver the goods according to the directions of the lessor, but the lessor is liable to the bailee for any ensuing charges or damages.

(c) A carrier who has issued a nonnegotiable bill of lading is not obliged to obey a notification to stop received from a person other than the consignor.

§ 2A–527. Lessor's Rights to Dispose of Goods.

(1) After a default by a lessee under the lease contract of the type described in Section 2A–523(1) or 2A–523(3)(a) or after the lessor refuses to deliver or takes possession of goods (Section 2A–525 or 2A–526), or, if agreed, after other default by a lessee, the lessor may dispose of the goods concerned or the undelivered balance thereof by lease, sale, or otherwise.

(2) Except as otherwise provided with respect to damages liquidated in the lease agreement (Section 2A–504) or otherwise determined pursuant to agreement of the parties (Sections 1–102(3) and 2A–503), if the disposition is by lease agreement substantially similar to the original lease agreement and the new lease agreement is made in good faith and in a commercially reasonable manner, the lessor may recover from the lessee as damages (i) accrued and unpaid rent as of the date of the commencement of the term of the new lease agreement, (ii) the present value, as of the same date, of the total rent for the then remaining lease term of the original lease agreement minus the present value, as of the same date, of the rent under the new lease agreement applicable to that period of the new lease term which is comparable to the then remaining term of the original lease agreement, and (iii) any incidental damages allowed under Section 2A–530, less expenses saved in consequence of the lessee's default.

(3) If the lessor's disposition is by lease agreement that for any reason does not qualify for treatment under subsection (2), or is by sale or otherwise, the lessor may recover from

the lessee as if the lessor had elected not to dispose of the goods and Section 2A–528 governs.

(4) A subsequent buyer or lessee who buys or leases from the lessor in good faith for value as a result of a disposition under this section takes the goods free of the original lease contract and any rights of the original lessee even though the lessor fails to comply with one or more of the requirements of this Article.

(5) The lessor is not accountable to the lessee for any profit made on any disposition. A lessee who has rightfully rejected or justifiably revoked acceptance shall account to the lessor for any excess over the amount of the lessee's security interest (Section 2A–508(5)).

As amended in 1990.

§ 2A–528. Lessor's Damages for Non-acceptance, Failure to Pay, Repudiation, or Other Default.

(1) Except as otherwise provided with respect to damages liquidated in the lease agreement (Section 2A–504) or otherwise determined pursuant to agreement of the parties (Section 1–102(3) and 2A–503), if a lessor elects to retain the goods or a lessor elects to dispose of the goods and the disposition is by lease agreement that for any reason does not qualify for treatment under Section 2A–527(2), or is by sale or otherwise, the lessor may recover from the lessee as damages for a default of the type described in Section 2A–523(1) or 2A–523(3)(a), or if agreed, for other default of the lessee, (i) accrued and unpaid rent as of the date of the default if the lessee has never taken possession of the goods, or, if the lessee has taken possession of the goods, as of the date the lessor repossesses the goods or an earlier date on which the lessee makes a tender of the goods to the lessor, (ii) the present value as of the date determined under clause (i) of the total rent for the then remaining lease term of the original lease agreement minus the present value as of the same date of the market rent as the place where the goods are located computed for the same lease term, and (iii) any incidental damages allowed under Section 2A–530, less expenses saved in consequence of the lessee's default.

(2) If the measure of damages provided in subsection (1) is inadequate to put a lessor in as good a position as performance would have, the measure of damages is the present value of the profit, including reasonable overhead, the lessor would have made from full performance by the lessee, together with any incidental damages allowed under Section 2A–530, due allowance for costs reasonably incurred and due credit for payments or proceeds of disposition.

As amended in 1990.

§ 2A–529. Lessor's Action for the Rent.

(1) After default by the lessee under the lease contract of the type described in Section 2A–523(1) or 2A–523(3)(a) or, if agreed, after other default by the lessee, if the lessor complies with subsection (2), the lessor may recover from the lessee as damages:

(a) for goods accepted by the lessee and not repossessed by or tendered to the lessor, and for conforming goods lost or damaged within a commercially reasonable time after risk of loss passes to the lessee (Section 2A–219), (i) accrued and unpaid rent as of the date of entry of judgment in favor of the lessor (ii) the present value as of the same date of the rent for the then remaining lease term of the lease agreement, and (iii) any incidental damages allowed under Section 2A–530, less expenses saved in consequence of the lessee's default; and

(b) for goods identified to the lease contract if the lessor is unable after reasonable effort to dispose of them at a reasonable price or the circumstances reasonably indicate that effort will be unavailing, (i) accrued and unpaid rent as of the date of entry of judgment in favor of the lessor, (ii) the present value as of the same date of the rent for the then remaining lease term of the lease agreement, and (iii) any incidental damages allowed under Section 2A–530, less expenses saved in consequence of the lessee's default.

(2) Except as provided in subsection (3), the lessor shall hold for the lessee for the remaining lease term of the lease agreement any goods that have been identified to the lease contract and are in the lessor's control.

(3) The lessor may dispose of the goods at any time before collection of the judgment for damages obtained pursuant to subsection (1). If the disposition is before the end of the remaining lease term of the lease agreement, the lessor's recovery against the lessee for damages is governed by Section 2A–527 or Section 2A–528, and the lessor will cause an appropriate credit to be provided against a judgment for damages to the extent that the amount of the judgment exceeds the recovery available pursuant to Section 2A–527 or 2A–528.

(4) Payment of the judgment for damages obtained pursuant to subsection (1) entitles the lessee to the use and possession of the goods not then disposed of for the remaining lease term of and in accordance with the lease agreement.

(5) After default by the lessee under the lease contract of the type described in Section 2A–523(1) or Section 2A–523(3)(a) or, if agreed, after other default by the lessee, a lessor who is held not entitled to rent under this section must nevertheless be awarded damages for non-acceptance under Sections 2A–527 and 2A–528.

As amended in 1990.

§ 2A–530. Lessor's Incidental Damages.

Incidental damages to an aggrieved lessor include any commercially reasonable charges, expenses, or commissions incurred in stopping delivery, in the transportation, care and custody of goods after the lessee's default, in connection with return or disposition of the goods, or otherwise resulting from the default.

§ 2A–531. Standing to Sue Third Parties for Injury to Goods.

(1) If a third party so deals with goods that have been identified to a lease contract as to cause actionable injury to a party to the lease contract (a) the lessor has a right of action against the third party, and (b) the lessee also has a right of action against the third party if the lessee:

(i) has a security interest in the goods;

(ii) has an insurable interest in the goods; or

(iii) bears the risk of loss under the lease contract or has since the injury assumed that risk as against the lessor and the goods have been converted or destroyed.

(2) If at the time of the injury the party plaintiff did not bear the risk of loss as against the other party to the lease contract and there is no arrangement between them for disposition of the recovery, his [or her] suit or settlement, subject to his [or her] own interest, is as a fiduciary for the other party to the lease contract.

(3) Either party with the consent of the other may sue for the benefit of whom it may concern.

§ 2A–532. Lessor's Rights to Residual Interest.

In addition to any other recovery permitted by this Article or other law, the lessor may recover from the lessee an amount that will fully compensate the lessor for any loss of or damage to the lessor's residual interest in the goods caused by the default of the lessee.

As added in 1990.

The United Nations Convention on Contracts for the International Sale of Goods (Excerpts)

Part I. SPHERE OF APPLICATION AND GENERAL PROVISIONS

* * * *

Chapter II—General Provisions

* * * *

Article 8

(1) For the purposes of this Convention statements made by and other conduct of a party are to be interpreted according to his intent where the other party knew or could not have been unaware what that intent was.

(2) If the preceding paragraph is not applicable, statements made by and other conduct of a party are to be interpreted according to the understanding that a reasonable person of the same kind as the other party would have had in the same circumstances.

(3) In determining the intent of a party or the understanding a reasonable person would have had, due consideration is to be given to all relevant circumstances of the case including the negotiations, any practices which the parties have established between themselves, usages and any subsequent conduct of the parties.

Article 9

(1) The parties are bound by any usage to which they have agreed and by any practices which they have established between themselves.

(2) The parties are considered, unless otherwise agreed, to have impliedly made applicable to their contract or its formation a usage of which the parties knew or ought to have known and which in international trade is widely known to, and regularly observed by, parties to contracts of the type involved in the particular trade concerned.

* * * *

Article 11

A contract of sale need not be concluded in or evidenced by writing and is not subject to any other requirement as to form. It may be proved by any means, including witnesses.

* * * *

Part II. FORMATION OF THE CONTRACT

Article 14

(1) A proposal for concluding a contract addressed to one or more specific persons constitutes an offer if it is sufficiently definite and indicates the intention of the offeror to be bound in case of acceptance. A proposal is sufficiently definite if it indicates the goods and expressly or implicitly fixes or makes provision for determining the quantity and the price.

(2) A proposal other than one addressed to one or more specific persons is to be considered merely as an invitation to make offers, unless the contrary is clearly indicated by the person making the proposal.

Article 15

(1) An offer becomes effective when it reaches the offeree.

(2) An offer, even if it is irrevocable, may be withdrawn if the withdrawal reaches the offeree before or at the same time as the offer.

Article 16

(1) Until a contract is concluded an offer may be revoked if the revocation reaches the offeree before he has dispatched an acceptance.

(2) However, an offer cannot be revoked:

(a) If it indicates, whether by stating a fixed time for acceptance or otherwise, that it is irrevocable; or

(b) If it was reasonable for the offeree to rely on the offer as being irrevocable and the offeree has acted in reliance on the offer.

Article 17

An offer, even if it is irrevocable, is terminated when a rejection reaches the offeror.

Article 18

(1) A statement made by or other conduct of the offeree indicating assent to an offer is an acceptance. Silence or inactivity does not in itself amount to acceptance.

(2) An acceptance of an offer becomes effective at the moment the indication of assent reaches the offeror. An acceptance is not effective if the indication of assent does not reach the offeror within the time he has fixed or, if no time is fixed, within a reasonable time, due account being taken of the circumstances of the transaction, including the rapidity of the means of communication employed by the offeror. An oral offer must be accepted immediately unless the circumstances indicate otherwise.

(3) However, if, by virtue of the offer or as a result of practices which the parties have established between themselves or of usage, the offeree may indicate assent by performing an act, such as one relating to the dispatch of the goods or payment of the price, without notice to the offeror, the acceptance is effective at the moment the act is performed, provided that the act is performed within the period of time laid down in the preceding paragraph.

Article 19

(1) A reply to an offer which purports to be an acceptance but contains additions, limitations or other modifications is a rejection of the offer and constitutes a counter-offer.

(2) However, a reply to an offer which purports to be an acceptance but contains additional or different terms which do not materially alter the terms of the offer constitutes an acceptance, unless the offeror, without undue delay, objects orally to the discrepancy or dispatches a notice to that effect. If he does not so object, the terms of the contract are the terms of the offer with the modifications contained in the acceptance.

(3) Additional or different terms relating, among other things, to the price, payment, quality and quantity of the goods, place and time of delivery, extent of one party's liability to the other or the settlement of disputes are considered to alter the terms of the offer materially.

* * * *

Article 22

An acceptance may be withdrawn if the withdrawal reaches the offeror before or at the same time as the acceptance would have become effective.

* * * *

Part III.   SALE OF GOODS
Chapter I—General Provisions

Article 25

A breach of contract committed by one of the parties is fundamental if it results in such detriment to the other party as substantially to deprive him of what he is entitled to expect under the contract, unless the party in breach did not foresee and a reasonable person of the same kind in the same circumstances would not have foreseen such a result.

* * * *

Article 28

If, in accordance with the provisions of this Convention, one party is entitled to require performance of any obligation by the other party, a court is not bound to enter a judgment for specific performance unless the court would do so under its own law in respect of similar contracts of sale not governed by this Convention.

Article 29

(1) A contract may be modified or terminated by the mere agreement of the parties.

(2) A contract in writing which contains a provision requiring any modification or termination by agreement to be in writing may not be otherwise modified or terminated by agreement. However, a party may be precluded by his conduct from asserting such a provision to the extent that the other party has relied on that conduct.

* * * *

Chapter II—Obligations of the Seller

* * * *

Section II. Conformity of the Goods and Third Party Claims

Article 35

(1) The seller must deliver goods which are of the quantity, quality and description required by the contract and which are contained or packaged in the manner required by the contract.

(2) Except where the parties have agreed otherwise, the goods do not conform with the contract unless they:

(a) Are fit for the purposes for which goods of the same description would ordinarily be used;

(b) Are fit for any particular purpose expressly or impliedly made known to the seller at the time of the conclusion of the contract, except where the circumstances show that the buyer did not rely, or that it was unreasonable for him to rely, on the seller's skill and judgment;

(c) Possess the qualities of goods which the seller has held out to the buyer as a sample or model;

(d) Are contained or packaged in the manner usual for such goods or, where there is no such manner, in a manner adequate to preserve and protect the goods.

(3) The seller is not liable under subparagraphs (a) to (d) of the preceding paragraph for any lack of conformity of the goods if at the time of the conclusion of the contract the buyer knew or could not have been unaware of such lack of conformity.

*   *   *   *

Article 64

(1) The seller may declare the contract avoided:

(a) If the failure by the buyer to perform any of his obligations under the contract or this Convention amounts to a fundamental breach of contract; or

(b) If the buyer does not, within the additional period of time fixed by the seller in accordance with paragraph (1) of article 63, perform his obligation to pay the price or take delivery of the goods, or if he declares that he will not do so within the period so fixed.

(2) However, in cases where the buyer has paid the price, the seller loses the right to declare the contract avoided unless he does so:

(a) In respect of late performance by the buyer, before the seller has become aware that performance has been rendered; or

(b) In respect of any breach other than late performance by the buyer, within a reasonable time:

(i) After the seller knew or ought to have known of the breach; or

(ii) After the expiration of any additional period of time fixed by the seller in accordance with paragraph (1) of article 63, or after the buyer has declared that he will not perform his obligations within such an additional period.

*   *   *   *

Chapter IV—Passing of Risk

*   *   *   *

Article 67

(1) If the contract of sale involves carriage of the goods and the seller is not bound to hand them over at a particular place, the risk passes to the buyer when the goods are handed over to the first carrier for transmission to the buyer in accordance with the contract of sale. If the seller is bound to hand the goods over to a carrier at a particular place, the risk does not pass to the buyer until the goods are handed over to the carrier at that place. The fact that the seller is authorized to retain documents controlling the disposition of the goods does not affect the passage of the risk.

(2) Nevertheless, the risk does not pass to the buyer until the goods are clearly identified to the contract, whether by markings on the goods, by shipping documents, by notice given to the buyer or otherwise.

*   *   *   *

Chapter V—Provisions Common to the Obligations of the Seller and of the Buyer

Section I. Anticipatory Breach and Instalment Contracts

Article 71

(1) A party may suspend the performance of his obligations if, after the conclusion of the contract, it becomes apparent that the other party will not perform a substantial part of his obligations as a result of:

(a) A serious deficiency in his ability to perform or in his creditworthiness; or

(b) His conduct in preparing to perform or in performing the contract.

(2) If the seller has already dispatched the goods before the grounds described in the preceding paragraph become evident, he may prevent the handing over of the goods to the buyer even though the buyer holds a document which entitles him to obtain them. The present paragraph relates only to the rights in the goods as between the buyer and the seller.

(3) A party suspending performance, whether before or after dispatch of the goods, must immediately give notice of the suspension to the other party and must continue with performance if the other party provides adequate assurance of his performance.

Article 72

(1) If prior to the date for performance of the contract it is clear that one of the parties will commit a fundamental breach of contract, the other party may declare the contract avoided.

(2) If time allows, the party intending to declare the contract avoided must give reasonable notice to the other party in order to permit him to provide adequate assurance of his performance.

(3) The requirements of the preceding paragraph do not apply if the other party has declared that he will not perform his obligations.

Article 73

(1) In the case of a contract for delivery of goods by instalments, if the failure of one party to perform any of his obligations in respect of any instalment constitutes a fundamental breach of contract with respect to that instalment, the other party may declare the contract avoided with respect to that instalment.

(2) If one party's failure to perform any of his obligations in respect of any instalment gives the other party good grounds to conclude that a fundamental breach of contract

will occur with respect to future instalments, he may declare the contract avoided for the future, provided that he does so within a reasonable time.

(3) A buyer who declares the contract avoided in respect of any delivery may, at the same time, declare it avoided in respect of deliveries already made or of future deliveries if, by reason of their interdependence, those deliveries could not be used for the purpose contemplated by the parties at the time of the conclusion of the contract.

Section II. Damages

Article 74

Damages for breach of contract by one party consist of a sum equal to the loss, including loss of profit, suffered by the other party as a consequence of the breach. Such damages may not exceed the loss which the party in breach foresaw or ought to have foreseen at the time of the conclusion of the contract, in the light of the facts and matters of which he then knew or ought to have known, as a possible consequence of the breach of contract.

Article 75

If the contract is avoided and if, in a reasonable manner and within a reasonable time after avoidance, the buyer has bought goods in replacement or the seller has resold the goods, the party claiming damages may recover the difference between the contract price and the price in the substitute transaction as well as any further damages recoverable under article 74.

Article 76

(1) If the contract is avoided and there is a current price for the goods, the party claiming damages may, if he has not made a purchase or resale under article 75, recover the difference between the price fixed by the contract and the current price at the time of avoidance as well as any further damages recoverable under article 74. If, however, the party claiming damages has avoided the contract after taking over the goods, the current price at the time of such taking over shall be applied instead of the current price at the time of avoidance.

(2) For the purposes of the preceding paragraph, the current price is the price prevailing at the place where delivery of the goods should have been made or, if there is no current price at that place, the price at such other place as serves as a reasonable substitute, making due allowance for differences in the cost of transporting the goods.

Article 77

A party who relies on a breach of contract must take such measures as are reasonable in the circumstances to mitigate the loss, including loss of profit, resulting from the breach. If he fails to take such measures, the party in breach may claim a reduction in the damages in the amount by which the loss should have been mitigated.

The Uniform Partnership Act (Excerpts)

(The Uniform Partnership Act was amended in 1997 to provide limited liability for partners in a limited liability partnership. Over half the states, including District of Columbia, Puerto Rico, and the U.S. Virgin Islands, have adopted this latest version of the UPA.)

Article 1
GENERAL PROVISIONS

SECTION 101. Definitions In this [Act]:

*   *   *   *

(6) "Partnership" means an association of two or more persons to carry on as co-owners a business for profit formed under Section 202, predecessor law, or comparable law of another jurisdiction.

(7) "Partnership agreement" means the agreement, whether written, oral, or implied, among the partners concerning the partnership, including amendments to the partnership agreement.

(8) "Partnership at will" means a partnership in which the partners have not agreed to remain partners until the expiration of a definite term or the completion of a particular undertaking.

(9) "Partnership interest" or "partner's interest in the partnership" means all of a partner's interests in the partnership, including the partner's transferable interest and all management and other rights.

(10) "Person" means an individual, corporation, business trust, estate, trust, partnership, association, joint venture, government, governmental subdivision, agency, or instrumentality, or any other legal or commercial entity.

*   *   *   *

SECTION 103. Effect of Partnership Agreement; Nonwaivable Provisions.

(a) Except as otherwise provided in subsection (b), relations among the partners and between the partners and the partnership are governed by the partnership agreement. To the extent the partnership agreement does not otherwise provide, this [Act] governs relations among the partners and between the partners and the partnership.

(b) The partnership agreement may not:

(1) vary the rights and duties under Section 105 except to eliminate the duty to provide copies of statements to all of the partners;

(2) unreasonably restrict the right of access to books and records under Section 403(b);

(3) eliminate the duty of loyalty under Section 404(b) or 603(b)(3), but:

(i) the partnership agreement may identify specific types or categories of activities that do not violate the duty of loyalty, if not manifestly unreasonable; or

(ii) all of the partners or a number or percentage specified in the partnership agreement may authorize or ratify, after full disclosure of all material facts, a specific act or transaction that otherwise would violate the duty of loyalty;

(4) unreasonably reduce the duty of care under Section 404(c) or 603(b)(3);

(5) eliminate the obligation of good faith and fair dealing under Section 404(d), but the partnership agreement may prescribe the standards by which the performance of the obligation is to be measured, if the standards are not manifestly unreasonable;

(6) vary the power to dissociate as a partner under Section 602(a), except to require the notice under Section 601(1) to be in writing;

(7) vary the right of a court to expel a partner in the events specified in Section 601(5);

*   *   *   *

SECTION 105. Execution, Filing, and Recording of Statements.

(a) A statement may be filed in the office of [the Secretary of State]. A certified copy of a statement that is filed in an office in another State may be filed in the office of [the Secretary of State]. Either filing has the effect provided in this [Act] with respect to partnership property located in or transactions that occur in this State.

(b) A certified copy of a statement that has been filed in the office of the [Secretary of State] and recorded in the office for recording transfers of real property has the effect provided for recorded statements in this [Act]. A recorded statement that is not a certified copy of a statement filed in the office of the [Secretary of State] does not have the effect provided for recorded statements in this [Act].

*   *   *   *

SECTION 106. Governing Law.

(a) Except as otherwise provided in subsection (b), the law of the jurisdiction in which a partnership has its chief executive office governs relations among the partners and between the partners and the partnership.

(b) The law of this State governs relations among the partners and between the partners and the partnership and the liability of partners for an obligation of a limited liability partnership.

*   *   *   *

Article 2
NATURE OF PARTNERSHIP

SECTION 201. Partnership as Entity.

(a) A partnership is an entity distinct from its partners.

(b) A limited liability partnership continues to be the same entity that existed before the filing of a statement of qualification under Section 1001.

SECTION 202. Formation of Partnership.

*   *   *   *

(c) In determining whether a partnership is formed, the following rules apply:

(1) Joint tenancy, tenancy in common, tenancy by the entireties, joint property, common property, or part ownership does not by itself establish a partnership, even if the co-owners share profits made by the use of the property.

(2) The sharing of gross returns does not by itself establish a partnership, even if the persons sharing them have a joint or common right or interest in property from which the returns are derived.

(3) A person who receives a share of the profits of a business is presumed to be a partner in the business, unless the profits were received in payment:

(i) of a debt by installments or otherwise;

(ii) for services as an independent contractor or of wages or other compensation to an employee;

(iii) of rent;

(iv) of an annuity or other retirement or health benefit to a beneficiary, representative, or designee of a deceased or retired partner;

(v) of interest or other charge on a loan, even if the amount of payment varies with the profits of the business, including a direct or indirect present or future ownership of the collateral, or rights to income, proceeds, or increase in value derived from the collateral; or

(vi) for the sale of the goodwill of a business or other property by installments or otherwise.

SECTION 203. Partnership Property.

Property acquired by a partnership is property of the partnership and not of the partners individually.

SECTION 204. When Property is Partnership Property.

*   *   *   *

(d) Property acquired in the name of one or more of the partners, without an indication in the instrument transferring title to the property of the person's capacity as a partner or of the existence of a partnership and without use of partnership assets, is presumed to be separate property, even if used for partnership purposes.

Article 3
RELATIONS OF PARTNERS TO PERSONS DEALING WITH PARTNERSHIP

SECTION 301. Partner Agent of Partnership.

Subject to the effect of a statement of partnership authority under Section 303:

(1) Each partner is an agent of the partnership for the purpose of its business. An act of a partner, including the execution of an instrument in the partnership name, for apparently carrying on in the ordinary course the partnership business or business of the kind carried on by the partnership binds the partnership, unless the partner had no authority to act for the

partnership in the particular matter and the person with whom the partner was dealing knew or had received a notification that the partner lacked authority.

(2) An act of a partner which is not apparently for carrying on in the ordinary course the partnership business or business of the kind carried on by the partnership binds the partnership only if the act was authorized by the other partners.

* * * *

SECTION 303. Statement of Partnership Authority.

(a) A partnership may file a statement of partnership authority, which:

(1) must include:

(i) the name of the partnership;

(ii) the street address of its chief executive office and of one office in this State, if there is one;

(iii) the names and mailing addresses of all of the partners or of an agent appointed and maintained by the partnership for the purpose of subsection (b); and

(iv) the names of the partners authorized to execute an instrument transferring real property held in the name of the partnership; and

(2) may state the authority, or limitations on the authority, of some or all of the partners to enter into other transactions on behalf of the partnership and any other matter.

* * * *

(d) Except as otherwise provided in subsection (g), a filed statement of partnership authority supplements the authority of a partner to enter into transactions on behalf of the partnership as follows:

(1) Except for transfers of real property, a grant of authority contained in a filed statement of partnership authority is conclusive in favor of a person who gives value without knowledge to the contrary, so long as and to the extent that a limitation on that authority is not then contained in another filed statement. A filed cancellation of a limitation on authority revives the previous grant of authority.

(2) A grant of authority to transfer real property held in the name of the partnership contained in a certified copy of a filed statement of partnership authority recorded in the office for recording transfers of that real property is conclusive in favor of a person who gives value without knowledge to the contrary, so long as and to the extent that a certified copy of a filed statement containing a limitation on that authority is not then of record in the office for recording transfers of that real property. The recording in the office for recording transfers of that real property of a certified copy of a

filed cancellation of a limitation on authority revives the previous grant of authority.

(e) A person not a partner is deemed to know of a limitation on the authority of a partner to transfer real property held in the name of the partnership if a certified copy of the filed statement containing the limitation on authority is of record in the office for recording transfers of that real property.

(f) Except as otherwise provided in subsections (d) and (e) and Sections 704 and 805, a person not a partner is not deemed to know of a limitation on the authority of a partner merely because the limitation is contained in a filed statement.

* * * *

SECTION 305. Partnership Liable for Partner's Actionable Conduct.

(a) A partnership is liable for loss or injury caused to a person, or for a penalty incurred, as a result of a wrongful act or omission, or other actionable conduct, of a partner acting in the ordinary course of business of the partnership or with authority of the partnership.

(b) If, in the course of the partnership's business or while acting with authority of the partnership, a partner receives or causes the partnership to receive money or property of a person not a partner, and the money or property is misapplied by a partner, the partnership is liable for the loss.

SECTION 306. Partner's Liability.

(a) Except as otherwise provided in subsections (b) and (c), all partners are liable jointly and severally for all obligations of the partnership unless otherwise agreed by the claimant or provided by law.

(b) A person admitted as a partner into an existing partnership is not personally liable for any partnership obligation incurred before the person's admission as a partner.

(c) An obligation of a partnership incurred while the partnership is a limited liability partnership, whether arising in contract, tort, or otherwise, is solely the obligation of the partnership. A partner is not personally liable, directly or indirectly, by way of contribution or otherwise, for such an obligation solely by reason of being or so acting as a partner. This subsection applies notwithstanding anything inconsistent in the partnership agreement that existed immediately before the vote required to become a limited liability partnership under Section 1001(b).

SECTION 307. Actions by and Against Partnership and Partners.

(a) A partnership may sue and be sued in the name of the partnership.

* * * *

(d) A judgment creditor of a partner may not levy execution against the assets of the partner to satisfy a judgment based on a claim against the partnership unless the partner is personally liable for the claim under Section 306 and:

(1) a judgment based on the same claim has been obtained against the partnership and a writ of execution on the judgment has been returned unsatisfied in whole or in part;

(2) the partnership is a debtor in bankruptcy;

(3) the partner has agreed that the creditor need not exhaust partnership assets;

(4) a court grants permission to the judgment creditor to levy execution against the assets of a partner based on a finding that partnership assets subject to execution are clearly insufficient to satisfy the judgment, that exhaustion of partnership assets is excessively burdensome, or that the grant of permission is an appropriate exercise of the court's equitable powers; or

(5) liability is imposed on the partner by law or contract independent of the existence of the partnership.

(e) This section applies to any partnership liability or obligation resulting from a representation by a partner or purported partner under Section 308.

SECTION 308. Liability of Purported Partner.

(a) If a person, by words or conduct, purports to be a partner, or consents to being represented by another as a partner, in a partnership or with one or more persons not partners, the purported partner is liable to a person to whom the representation is made, if that person, relying on the representation, enters into a transaction with the actual or purported partnership. If the representation, either by the purported partner or by a person with the purported partner's consent, is made in a public manner, the purported partner is liable to a person who relies upon the purported partnership even if the purported partner is not aware of being held out as a partner to the claimant. If partnership liability results, the purported partner is liable with respect to that liability as if the purported partner were a partner. If no partnership liability results, the purported partner is liable with respect to that liability jointly and severally with any other person consenting to the representation.

(b) If a person is thus represented to be a partner in an existing partnership, or with one or more persons not partners, the purported partner is an agent of persons consenting to the representation to bind them to the same extent and in the same manner as if the purported partner were a partner, with respect to persons who enter into transactions in reliance upon the representation. If all of the partners of the existing partnership consent to the representation, a partnership act or obligation results. If fewer than all of the partners of the existing partnership consent to the representation, the person acting and the partners consenting to the representation are jointly and severally liable.

* * * *

Article 4
RELATIONS OF PARTNERS TO EACH OTHER AND TO PARTNERSHIP

SECTION 401. Partner's Rights and Duties.

* * * *

(b) Each partner is entitled to an equal share of the partnership profits and is chargeable with a share of the partnership losses in proportion to the partner's share of the profits.

* * * *

(f) Each partner has equal rights in the management and conduct of the partnership business.

(g) A partner may use or possess partnership property only on behalf of the partnership.

(h) A partner is not entitled to remuneration for services performed for the partnership, except for reasonable compensation for services rendered in winding up the business of the partnership.

(i) A person may become a partner only with the consent of all of the partners.

(j) A difference arising as to a matter in the ordinary course of business of a partnership may be decided by a majority of the partners. An act outside the ordinary course of business of a partnership and an amendment to the partnership agreement may be undertaken only with the consent of all of the partners.

* * * *

SECTION 403. Partner's Rights and Duties with Respect to Information.

(a) A partnership shall keep its books and records, if any, at its chief executive office.

(b) A partnership shall provide partners and their agents and attorneys access to its books and records. It shall provide former partners and their agents and attorneys access to books and records pertaining to the period during which they were partners. The right of access provides the opportunity to inspect and copy books and records during ordinary business hours. A partnership may impose a reasonable charge, covering the costs of labor and material, for copies of documents furnished.

* * * *

SECTION 404. General Standards of Partner's Conduct.

(a) The only fiduciary duties a partner owes to the partnership and the other partners are the duty of loyalty and the duty of care set forth in subsections (b) and (c).

(b) A partner's duty of loyalty to the partnership and the other partners is limited to the following:

(1) to account to the partnership and hold as trustee for it any property, profit, or benefit derived by the partner in the conduct and winding up of the partnership business or derived from a use by the partner of partnership property, including the appropriation of a partnership opportunity;

(2) to refrain from dealing with the partnership in the conduct or winding up of the partnership business as or on behalf of a party having an interest adverse to the partnership; and

(3) to refrain from competing with the partnership in the conduct of the partnership business before the dissolution of the partnership.

(c) A partner's duty of care to the partnership and the other partners in the conduct and winding up of the partnership business is limited to refraining from engaging in grossly negligent or reckless conduct, intentional misconduct, or a knowing violation of law.

(d) A partner shall discharge the duties to the partnership and the other partners under this [Act] or under the partnership agreement and exercise any rights consistently with the obligation of good faith and fair dealing.

(e) A partner does not violate a duty or obligation under this [Act] or under the partnership agreement merely because the partner's conduct furthers the partner's own interest.

* * * *

SECTION 405. Actions by Partnership and Partners.

(a) A partnership may maintain an action against a partner for a breach of the partnership agreement, or for the violation of a duty to the partnership, causing harm to the partnership.

(b) A partner may maintain an action against the partnership or another partner for legal or equitable relief, with or without an accounting as to partnership business, to:

(1) enforce the partner's rights under the partnership agreement;

(2) enforce the partner's rights under this [Act], including:

(i) the partner's rights under Sections 401, 403, or 404;

(ii) the partner's right on dissociation to have the partner's interest in the partnership purchased pursuant to Section 701 or enforce any other right under [Article] 6 or 7; or

(iii) the partner's right to compel a dissolution and winding up of the partnership business under or enforce any other right under [Article] 8; or

(3) enforce the rights and otherwise protect the interests of the partner, including rights and interests arising independently of the partnership relationship.

* * * *

Article 5
TRANSFEREES AND CREDITORS OF PARTNER

SECTION 501. Partner Not Co-Owner of Partnership Property.

A partner is not a co-owner of partnership property and has no interest in partnership property which can be transferred, either voluntarily or involuntarily.

SECTION 502. Partner's Transferable Interest in Partnership.

The only transferable interest of a partner in the partnership is the partner's share of the profits and losses of the partnership and the partner's right to receive distributions. The interest is personal property.

SECTION 503. Transfer of Partner's Transferable Interest.

(a) A transfer, in whole or in part, of a partner's transferable interest in the partnership:

(1) is permissible;

(2) does not by itself cause the partner's dissociation or a dissolution and winding up of the partnership business; and

(3) does not, as against the other partners or the partnership, entitle the transferee, during the continuance of the partnership, to participate in the management or conduct of the partnership business, to require access to information concerning partnership transactions, or to inspect or copy the partnership books or records.

* * * *

SECTION 504. Partner's Transferable Interest Subject to Charging Order.

(a) On application by a judgment creditor of a partner or of a partner's transferee, a court having jurisdiction may charge the transferable interest of the judgment debtor to satisfy the judgment. The court may appoint a receiver of the share of the distributions due or to become due to the judgment debtor in respect of the partnership and make all other orders, directions, accounts, and inquiries the judgment debtor might have made or which the circumstances of the case may require.

* * * *

Article 6
PARTNER'S DISSOCIATION

SECTION 601. Events Causing Partner's Dissociation.

A partner is dissociated from a partnership upon the occurrence of any of the following events:

(1) the partnership's having notice of the partner's express will to withdraw as a partner or on a later date specified by the partner;

(2) an event agreed to in the partnership agreement as causing the partner's dissociation;

(3) the partner's expulsion pursuant to the partnership agreement;

(4) the partner's expulsion by the unanimous vote of the other partners if:

  (i) it is unlawful to carry on the partnership business with that partner;

  (ii) there has been a transfer of all or substantially all of that partner's transferable interest in the partnership, other than a transfer for security purposes, or a court order charging the partner's interest, which has not been foreclosed;

  (iii) within 90 days after the partnership notifies a corporate partner that it will be expelled because it has filed a certificate of dissolution or the equivalent, its charter has been revoked, or its right to conduct business has been suspended by the jurisdiction of its incorporation, there is no revocation of the certificate of dissolution or no reinstatement of its charter or its right to conduct business; or

  (iv) a partnership that is a partner has been dissolved and its business is being wound up;

(5) on application by the partnership or another partner, the partner's expulsion by judicial determination because:

  (i) the partner engaged in wrongful conduct that adversely and materially affected the partnership business;

  (ii) the partner willfully or persistently committed a material breach of the partnership agreement or of a duty owed to the partnership or the other partners under Section 404; or

  (iii) the partner engaged in conduct relating to the partnership business which makes it not reasonably practicable to carry on the business in partnership with the partner;

(6) the partner's:

  (i) becoming a debtor in bankruptcy;

  (ii) executing an assignment for the benefit of creditors;

  (iii) seeking, consenting to, or acquiescing in the appointment of a trustee, receiver, or liquidator of that partner or of all or substantially all of that partner's property; or

  (iv) failing, within 90 days after the appointment, to have vacated or stayed the appointment of a trustee, receiver, or liquidator of the partner or of all or substantially all of the partner's property obtained without the partner's consent or acquiescence, or failing within

90 days after the expiration of a stay to have the appointment vacated;

(7) in the case of a partner who is an individual:

  (i) the partner's death;

  (ii) the appointment of a guardian or general conservator for the partner; or

  (iii) a judicial determination that the partner has otherwise become incapable of performing the partner's duties under the partnership agreement;

*   *   *   *

SECTION 602. Partner's Power to Dissociate; Wrongful Dissociation.

(a) A partner has the power to dissociate at any time, rightfully or wrongfully, by express will pursuant to Section 601(1).

(b) A partner's dissociation is wrongful only if:

  (1) it is in breach of an express provision of the partnership agreement; or

  (2) in the case of a partnership for a definite term or particular undertaking, before the expiration of the term or the completion of the undertaking:

    (i) the partner withdraws by express will, unless the withdrawal follows within 90 days after another partner's dissociation by death or otherwise under Section 601(6) through (10) or wrongful dissociation under this subsection;

    (ii) the partner is expelled by judicial determination under Section 601(5);

    (iii) the partner is dissociated by becoming a debtor in bankruptcy; or

    (iv) in the case of a partner who is not an individual, trust other than a business trust, or estate, the partner is expelled or otherwise dissociated because it willfully dissolved or terminated.

(c) A partner who wrongfully dissociates is liable to the partnership and to the other partners for damages caused by the dissociation. The liability is in addition to any other obligation of the partner to the partnership or to the other partners.

SECTION 603. Effect of Partner's Dissociation.

(a) If a partner's dissociation results in a dissolution and winding up of the partnership business, [Article] 8 applies; otherwise, [Article] 7 applies.

(b) Upon a partner's dissociation:

  (1) the partner's right to participate in the management and conduct of the partnership business terminates, except as otherwise provided in Section 803;

  (2) the partner's duty of loyalty under Section 404(b)(3) terminates; and

  (3) the partner's duty of loyalty under Section 404(b)(1) and (2) and duty of care under Section 404(c) continue

only with regard to matters arising and events occurring before the partner's dissociation, unless the partner participates in winding up the partnership's business pursuant to Section 803.

Article 7
PARTNER'S DISSOCIATION WHEN BUSINESS NOT WOUND UP

SECTION 701. Purchase of Dissociated Partner's Interest.

(a) If a partner is dissociated from a partnership without resulting in a dissolution and winding up of the partnership business under Section 801, the partnership shall cause the dissociated partner's interest in the partnership to be purchased for a buyout price determined pursuant to subsection (b).

(b) The buyout price of a dissociated partner's interest is the amount that would have been distributable to the dissociating partner under Section 807(b) if, on the date of dissociation, the assets of the partnership were sold at a price equal to the greater of the liquidation value or the value based on a sale of the entire business as a going concern without the dissociated partner and the partnership were wound up as of that date. Interest must be paid from the date of dissociation to the date of payment.

(c) Damages for wrongful dissociation under Section 602(b), and all other amounts owing, whether or not presently due, from the dissociated partner to the partnership, must be offset against the buyout price. Interest must be paid from the date the amount owed becomes due to the date of payment.

* * * *

SECTION 702. Dissociated Partner's Power to Bind and Liability to Partnership.

(a) For two years after a partner dissociates without resulting in a dissolution and winding up of the partnership business, the partnership, including a surviving partnership under [Article] 9, is bound by an act of the dissociated partner which would have bound the partnership under Section 301 before dissociation only if at the time of entering into the transaction the other party:

(1) reasonably believed that the dissociated partner was then a partner;

(2) did not have notice of the partner's dissociation; and

(3) is not deemed to have had knowledge under Section 303(e) or notice under Section 704(c).

(b) A dissociated partner is liable to the partnership for any damage caused to the partnership arising from an obligation

incurred by the dissociated partner after dissociation for which the partnership is liable under subsection (a).

SECTION 703. Dissociated Partner's Liability to Other Persons.

(a) A partner's dissociation does not of itself discharge the partner's liability for a partnership obligation incurred before dissociation. A dissociated partner is not liable for a partnership obligation incurred after dissociation, except as otherwise provided in subsection (b).

(b) A partner who dissociates without resulting in a dissolution and winding up of the partnership business is liable as a partner to the other party in a transaction entered into by the partnership, or a surviving partnership under [Article] 9, within two years after the partner's dissociation, only if the partner is liable for the obligation under Section 306 and at the time of entering into the transaction the other party:

(1) reasonably believed that the dissociated partner was then a partner;

(2) did not have notice of the partner's dissociation; and

(3) is not deemed to have had knowledge under Section 303(e) or notice under Section 704(c).

* * * *

SECTION 704. Statement of Dissociation.

(a) A dissociated partner or the partnership may file a statement of dissociation stating the name of the partnership and that the partner is dissociated from the partnership.

(b) A statement of dissociation is a limitation on the authority of a dissociated partner for the purposes of Section 303(d) and (e).

(c) For the purposes of Sections 702(a)(3) and 703(b)(3), a person not a partner is deemed to have notice of the dissociation 90 days after the statement of dissociation is filed.

* * * *

Article 8
WINDING UP PARTNERSHIP BUSINESS

SECTION 801. Events Causing Dissolution and Winding Up of Partnership Business.

A partnership is dissolved, and its business must be wound up, only upon the occurrence of any of the following events:

(1) in a partnership at will, the partnership's having notice from a partner, other than a partner who is dissociated under Section 601(2) through (10), of that partner's express will to withdraw as a partner, or on a later date specified by the partner;

(2) in a partnership for a definite term or particular undertaking:

    (i) within 90 days after a partner's dissociation by death or otherwise under Section 601(6) through (10) or wrongful dissociation under Section 602(b), the express will of at least half of the remaining partners to wind up the partnership business, for which purpose a partner's rightful dissociation pursuant to Section 602(b)(2)(i) constitutes the expression of that partner's will to wind up the partnership business;

    (ii) the express will of all of the partners to wind up the partnership business; or

    (iii) the expiration of the term or the completion of the undertaking;

(3) an event agreed to in the partnership agreement resulting in the winding up of the partnership business;

(4) an event that makes it unlawful for all or substantially all of the business of the partnership to be continued, but a cure of illegality within 90 days after notice to the partnership of the event is effective retroactively to the date of the event for purposes of this section;

(5) on application by a partner, a judicial determination that:

    (i) the economic purpose of the partnership is likely to be unreasonably frustrated;

    (ii) another partner has engaged in conduct relating to the partnership business which makes it not reasonably practicable to carry on the business in partnership with that partner; or

    (iii) it is not otherwise reasonably practicable to carry on the partnership business in conformity with the partnership agreement; or

*   *   *   *

SECTION 802. Partnership Continues after Dissolution.

(a) Subject to subsection (b), a partnership continues after dissolution only for the purpose of winding up its business. The partnership is terminated when the winding up of its business is completed.

(b) At any time after the dissolution of a partnership and before the winding up of its business is completed, all of the partners, including any dissociating partner other than a wrongfully dissociating partner, may waive the right to have the partnership's business wound up and the partnership terminated. In that event:

    (1) the partnership resumes carrying on its business as if dissolution had never occurred, and any liability incurred by the partnership or a partner after the dissolution and before the waiver is determined as if dissolution had never occurred; and

    (2) the rights of a third party accruing under Section 804(1) or arising out of conduct in reliance on the dis-

solution before the third party knew or received a notification of the waiver may not be adversely affected.

SECTION 803. Right to Wind Up Partnership.

(a) After dissolution, a partner who has not wrongfully dissociated may participate in winding up the partnership's business, but on application of any partner, partner's legal representative, or transferee, the [designate the appropriate court], for good cause shown, may order judicial supervision of the winding up.

(b) The legal representative of the last surviving partner may wind up a partnership's business.

(c) A person winding up a partnership's business may preserve the partnership business or property as a going concern for a reasonable time, prosecute and defend actions and proceedings, whether civil, criminal, or administrative, settle and close the partnership's business, dispose of and transfer the partnership's property, discharge the partnership's liabilities, distribute the assets of the partnership pursuant to Section 807, settle disputes by mediation or arbitration, and perform other necessary acts.

SECTION 804. Partner's Power to Bind Partnership After Dissolution.

Subject to Section 805, a partnership is bound by a partner's act after dissolution that:

(1) is appropriate for winding up the partnership business; or

(2) would have bound the partnership under Section 301 before dissolution, if the other party to the transaction did not have notice of the dissolution.

SECTION 805. Statement of Dissolution.

(a) After dissolution, a partner who has not wrongfully dissociated may file a statement of dissolution stating the name of the partnership and that the partnership has dissolved and is winding up its business.

(b) A statement of dissolution cancels a filed statement of partnership authority for the purposes of Section 303(d) and is a limitation on authority for the purposes of Section 303(e).

(c) For the purposes of Sections 301 and 804, a person not a partner is deemed to have notice of the dissolution and the limitation on the partners' authority as a result of the statement of dissolution 90 days after it is filed.

*   *   *   *

SECTION 807. Settlement of Accounts and Contributions among Partners.

(a) In winding up a partnership's business, the assets of the partnership, including the contributions of the partners required by this section, must be applied to discharge its obligations to creditors, including, to the extent permitted by law, partners who are creditors. Any surplus must be applied to pay in cash the net amount distributable to partners in accordance with their right to distributions under subsection (b).

(b) Each partner is entitled to a settlement of all partnership accounts upon winding up the partnership business. In settling accounts among the partners, profits and losses that result from the liquidation of the partnership assets must be credited and charged to the partners' accounts. The partnership shall make a distribution to a partner in an amount equal to any excess of the credits over the charges in the partner's account. A partner shall contribute to the partnership an amount equal to any excess of the charges over the credits in the partner's account but excluding from the calculation charges attributable to an obligation for which the partner is not personally liable under Section 306.

* * * *

(d) After the settlement of accounts, each partner shall contribute, in the proportion in which the partner shares partnership losses, the amount necessary to satisfy partnership obligations that were not known at the time of the settlement and for which the partner is personally liable under Section 306.

* * * *

Article 10
LIMITED LIABILITY PARTNERSHIP

SECTION 1001. Statement of Qualification.

(a) A partnership may become a limited liability partnership pursuant to this section.

(b) The terms and conditions on which a partnership becomes a limited liability partnership must be approved by the vote necessary to amend the partnership agreement except, in the case of a partnership agreement that expressly considers obligations to contribute to the partnership, the vote necessary to amend those provisions.

(c) After the approval required by subsection (b), a partnership may become a limited liability partnership by filing a statement of qualification. The statement must contain:

(1) the name of the partnership;

(2) the street address of the partnership's chief executive office and, if different, the street address of an office in this State, if any;

(3) if the partnership does not have an office in this State, the name and street address of the partnership's agent for service of process;

(4) a statement that the partnership elects to be a limited liability partnership; and

(5) a deferred effective date, if any.

* * * *

SECTION 1002. Name.

The name of a limited liability partnership must end with "Registered Limited Liability Partnership", "Limited Liability Partnership", "R.L.L.P.", "L.L.P.", "RLLP," or "LLP".

SECTION 1003. Annual Report.

(a) A limited liability partnership, and a foreign limited liability partnership authorized to transact business in this State, shall file an annual report in the office of the [Secretary of State] which contains:

(1) the name of the limited liability partnership and the State or other jurisdiction under whose laws the foreign limited liability partnership is formed;

(2) the street address of the partnership's chief executive office and, if different, the street address of an office of the partnership in this State, if any; and

(3) if the partnership does not have an office in this State, the name and street address of the partnership's current agent for service of process.

(b) An annual report must be filed between [January 1 and April 1] of each year following the calendar year in which a partnership files a statement of qualification or a foreign partnership becomes authorized to transact business in this State.

* * * *

Article 11
FOREIGN LIMITED LIABILITY PARTNERSHIP

SECTION 1101. Law Governing Foreign Limited Liability Partnership.

(a) The law under which a foreign limited liability partnership is formed governs relations among the partners and between the partners and the partnership and the liability of partners for obligations of the partnership.

* * * *

SECTION 1102. Statement of Foreign Qualification.

(a) Before transacting business in this State, a foreign limited liability partnership must file a statement of foreign qualification. The statement must contain:

(1) the name of the foreign limited liability partnership which satisfies the requirements of the State or other jurisdiction under whose law it is formed and ends with "Registered Limited Liability Partnership", "Limited Liability Partnership", "R.L.L.P.", "L.L.P.", "RLLP," or "LLP";

(2) the street address of the partnership's chief executive office and, if different, the street address of an office of the partnership in this State, if any;

(3) if there is no office of the partnership in this State, the name and street address of the partnership's agent for service of process; and

(4) a deferred effective date, if any.

*   *   *   *

SECTION 1104. Activities Not Constituting Transacting Business.

(a) Activities of a foreign limited liability partnership which do not constitute transacting business for the purpose of this [article] include:

(1) maintaining, defending, or settling an action or proceeding;

(2) holding meetings of its partners or carrying on any other activity concerning its internal affairs;

(3) maintaining bank accounts;

(4) maintaining offices or agencies for the transfer, exchange, and registration of the partnership's own securities or maintaining trustees or depositories with respect to those securities;

(5) selling through independent contractors;

(6) soliciting or obtaining orders, whether by mail or through employees or agents or otherwise, if the orders require acceptance outside this State before they become contracts;

(7) creating or acquiring indebtedness, with or without a mortgage, or other security interest in property;

(8) collecting debts or foreclosing mortgages or other security interests in property securing the debts, and holding, protecting, and maintaining property so acquired;

(9) conducting an isolated transaction that is completed within 30 days and is not one in the course of similar transactions; and

(10) transacting business in interstate commerce.

(b) For purposes of this [article], the ownership in this State of income-producing real property or tangible personal property, other than property excluded under subsection (a), constitutes transacting business in this State.

*   *   *   *

The Revised Uniform Limited Partnership Act (Excerpts)

Article 1
GENERAL PROVISIONS

Section 101. Definitions.

As used in this [Act], unless the context otherwise requires:

(1) "Certificate of limited partnership" means the certificate referred to in Section 201, and the certificate as amended or restated.

(2) "Contribution" means any cash, property, services rendered, or a promissory note or other binding obligation to contribute cash or property or to perform services, which a partner contributes to a limited partnership in his capacity as a partner.

(3) "Event of withdrawal of a general partner" means an event that causes a person to cease to be a general partner as provided in Section 402.

(4) "Foreign limited partnership" means a partnership formed under the laws of any state other than this State and having as partners one or more general partners and one or more limited partners.

(5) "General partner" means a person who has been admitted to a limited partnership as a general partner in accordance with the partnership agreement and named in the certificate of limited partnership as a general partner.

(6) "Limited partner" means a person who has been admitted to a limited partnership as a limited partner in accordance with the partnership agreement.

(7) "Limited partnership" and "domestic limited partnership" mean a partnership formed by two or more persons under the laws of this State and having one or more general partners and one or more limited partners.

(8) "Partner" means a limited or general partner.

(9) "Partnership agreement" means any valid agreement, written or oral, of the partners as to the affairs of a limited partnership and the conduct of its business.

(10) "Partnership interest" means a partner's share of the profits and losses of a limited partnership and the right to receive distributions of partnership assets.

(11) "Person" means a natural person, partnership, limited partnership (domestic or foreign), trust, estate, association, or corporation.

(12) "State" means a state, territory, or possession of the United States, the District of Columbia, or the Commonwealth of Puerto Rico.

Section 102. Name.

The name of each limited partnership as set forth in its certificate of limited partnership:

(1) shall contain without abbreviation the words "limited partnership";

(2) may not contain the name of a limited partner unless (i) it is also the name of a general partner or the corporate name of a corporate general partner, or (ii) the business of the limited partnership had been carried on under that name before the admission of that limited partner;

(3) may not be the same as, or deceptively similar to, the name of any corporation or limited partnership organized under the laws of this State or licensed or registered as a foreign corporation or limited partnership in this State; and

(4) may not contain the following words [here insert prohibited words].

Section 103. Reservation of Name.

(a) The exclusive right to the use of a name may be reserved by:

(1) any person intending to organize a limited partnership under this [Act] and to adopt that name;

(2) any domestic limited partnership or any foreign limited partnership registered in this State which, in either case, intends to adopt that name;

(3) any foreign limited partnership intending to register in this State and adopt that name; and

(4) any person intending to organize a foreign limited partnership and intending to have it register in this State and adopt that name.

(b) The reservation shall be made by filing with the Secretary of State an application, executed by the applicant, to reserve a specified name. If the Secretary of State finds that the name is available for use by a domestic or foreign limited partnership, he [or she] shall reserve the name for the exclusive use of the applicant for a period of 120 days. Once having so reserved a name, the same applicant may not again reserve the same name until more than 60 days after the expiration of the last 120-day period for which that applicant reserved that name. The right to the exclusive use of a reserved name may be transferred to any other person by filing in the office of the Secretary of State a notice of the transfer, executed by the applicant for whom the name was reserved and specifying the name and address of the transferee.

Section 104. Specified Office and Agent.

Each limited partnership shall continuously maintain in this State:

(1) an office, which may but need not be a place of its business in this State, at which shall be kept the records required by Section 105 to be maintained; and

(2) an agent for service of process on the limited partnership, which agent must be an individual resident of this State, a domestic corporation, or a foreign corporation authorized to do business in this State.

Section 105. Records to Be Kept.

(a) Each limited partnership shall keep at the office referred to in Section 104(1) the following:

(1) a current list of the full name and last known business address of each partner, separately identifying the general partners (in alphabetical order) and the limited partners (in alphabetical order);

(2) a copy of the certificate of limited partnership and all certificates of amendment thereto, together with executed copies of any powers of attorney pursuant to which any certificate has been executed;

(3) copies of the limited partnership's federal, state and local income tax returns and reports, if any, for the three most recent years;

(4) copies of any then effective written partnership agreements and of any financial statements of the limited partnership for the three most recent years; and

(5) unless contained in a written partnership agreement, a writing setting out:

(i) the amount of cash and a description and statement of the agreed value of the other property or services contributed by each partner and which each partner has agreed to contribute;

(ii) the times at which or events on the happening of which any additional contributions agreed to be made by each partner are to be made;

(iii) any right of a partner to receive, or of a general partner to make, distributions to a partner which include a return of all or any part of the partner's contribution; and

(iv) any events upon the happening of which the limited partnership is to be dissolved and its affairs wound up.

(b) Records kept under this section are subject to inspection and copying at the reasonable request and at the expense of any partner during ordinary business hours.

Section 106. Nature of Business.

A limited partnership may carry on any business that a partnership without limited partners may carry on except [here designate prohibited activities].

Section 107. Business Transactions of Partners with Partnership.

Except as provided in the partnership agreement, a partner may lend money to and transact other business with the limited partnership and, subject to other applicable law, has the same rights and obligations with respect thereto as a person who is not a partner.

Article 2
FORMATION; CERTIFICATE OF LIMITED PARTNERSHIP

Section 201. Certificate of Limited Partnership.

(a) In order to form a limited partnership, a certificate of limited partnership must be executed and filed in the office of the Secretary of State. The certificate shall set forth:

(1) the name of the limited partnership;

(2) the address of the office and the name and address of the agent for service of process required to be maintained by Section 104;

(3) the name and the business address of each general partner;

(4) the latest date upon which the limited partnership is to dissolve; and

(5) any other matters the general partners determine to include therein.

(b) A limited partnership is formed at the time of the filing of the certificate of limited partnership in the office of the Secretary of State or at any later time specified in the certificate of limited partnership if, in either case, there has been substantial compliance with the requirements of this section.

Section 202. Amendment to Certificate.

(a) A certificate of limited partnership is amended by filing a certificate of amendment thereto in the office of the Secretary of State. The certificate shall set forth:

(1) the name of the limited partnership;

(2) the date of filing the certificate; and

(3) the amendment to the certificate.

(b) Within 30 days after the happening of any of the following events, an amendment to a certificate of limited partnership reflecting the occurrence of the event or events shall be filed:

(1) the admission of a new general partner;

(2) the withdrawal of a general partner; or

(3) the continuation of the business under Section 801 after an event of withdrawal of a general partner.

(c) A general partner who becomes aware that any statement in a certificate of limited partnership was false when made or that any arrangements or other facts described have changed, making the certificate inaccurate in any respect, shall promptly amend the certificate.

(d) A certificate of limited partnership may be amended at any time for any other proper purpose the general partners determine.

(e) No person has any liability because an amendment to a certificate of limited partnership has not been filed to reflect the occurrence of any event referred to in subsection (b) of this section if the amendment is filed within the 30-day period specified in subsection (b).

(f) A restated certificate of limited partnership may be executed and filed in the same manner as a certificate of amendment.

Section 203. Cancellation of Certificate.

A certificate of limited partnership shall be cancelled upon the dissolution and the commencement of winding up of the partnership or at any other time there are no limited partners. A certificate of cancellation shall be filed in the office of the Secretary of State and set forth:

(1) the name of the limited partnership;

(2) the date of filing of its certificate of limited partnership;

(3) the reason for filing the certificate of cancellation;

(4) the effective date (which shall be a date certain) of cancellation if it is not to be effective upon the filing of the certificate; and

(5) any other information the general partners filing the certificate determine.

Section 204. Execution of Certificates.

(a) Each certificate required by this Article to be filed in the office of the Secretary of State shall be executed in the following manner:

(1) an original certificate of limited partnership must be signed by all general partners;

(2) a certificate of amendment must be signed by at least one general partner and by each other general partner designated in the certificate as a new general partner; and

(3) a certificate of cancellation must be signed by all general partners.

(b) Any person may sign a certificate by an attorney-in-fact, but a power of attorney to sign a certificate relating to the admission of a general partner must specifically describe the admission.

(c) The execution of a certificate by a general partner constitutes an affirmation under the penalties of perjury that the facts stated therein are true.

Section 205. Execution by Judicial Act.

If a person required by Section 204 to execute any certificate fails or refuses to do so, any other person who is adversely affected by the failure or refusal may petition the [designate the appropriate court] to direct the execution of the certificate. If the court finds that it is proper for the certificate to be executed and that any person so designated has failed or refused to execute the certificate, it shall order the Secretary of State to record an appropriate certificate.

Section 206. Filing in Office of Secretary of State.

(a) Two signed copies of the certificate of limited partnership and of any certificates of amendment or cancellation (or of any judicial decree of amendment or cancellation) shall be delivered to the Secretary of State. A person who executes a certificate as an agent or fiduciary need not exhibit evidence of his [or her] authority as a prerequisite to filing. Unless the Secretary of State finds that any certificate does not conform to law, upon receipt of all filing fees required by law he [or she] shall:

(1) endorse on each duplicate original the word "Filed" and the day, month, and year of the filing thereof;

(2) file one duplicate original in his [or her] office; and

(3) return the other duplicate original to the person who filed it or his [or her] representative.

(b) Upon the filing of a certificate of amendment (or judicial decree of amendment) in the office of the Secretary of State, the certificate of limited partnership shall be amended as set forth therein, and upon the effective date of a certificate of cancellation (or a judicial decree thereof), the certificate of limited partnership is cancelled.

Section 207. Liability for False Statement in Certificate.

If any certificate of limited partnership or certificate of amendment or cancellation contains a false statement, one who suffers loss by reliance on the statement may recover damages for the loss from:

(1) any person who executes the certificate, or causes another to execute it on his behalf, and knew, and any general partner who knew or should have known, the statement to be false at the time the certificate was executed; and

(2) any general partner who thereafter knows or should have known that any arrangement or other fact described in the certificate has changed, making the statement inaccurate in any respect within a sufficient time before the statement was relied upon reasonably to have enabled that general partner to cancel or amend the certificate, or to file a petition for its cancellation or amendment under Section 205.

Section 208. Scope of Notice.

The fact that a certificate of limited partnership is on file in the office of the Secretary of State is notice that the partnership is a limited partnership and the persons designated therein as general partners are general partners, but it is not notice of any other fact.

Section 209. Delivery of Certificates to Limited Partners.

Upon the return by the Secretary of State pursuant to Section 206 of a certificate marked "Filed," the general partners shall promptly deliver or mail a copy of the certificate of limited partnership and each certificate of amendment or cancellation to each limited partner unless the partnership agreement provides otherwise.

Article 3
LIMITED PARTNERS

Section 301. Admission of Additional Limited Partners.

(a) A person becomes a limited partner on the later of:

(1) the date the original certificate of limited partnership is filed; or

(2) the date stated in the records of the limited partnership as the date that person becomes a limited partner.

(b) After the filing of a limited partnership's original certificate of limited partnership, a person may be admitted as an additional limited partner:

(1) in the case of a person acquiring a partnership interest directly from the limited partnership, upon compliance with the partnership agreement or, if the partnership agreement does not so provide, upon the written consent of all partners; and

(2) in the case of an assignee of a partnership interest of a partner who has the power, as provided in Section 704, to grant the assignee the right to become a limited partner, upon the exercise of that power and compliance with any conditions limiting the grant or exercise of the power.

Section 302. Voting.

Subject to Section 303, the partnership agreement may grant to all or a specified group of the limited partners the right to vote (on a per capita or other basis) upon any matter.

Section 303. Liability to Third Parties.

(a) Except as provided in subsection (d), a limited partner is not liable for the obligations of a limited partnership unless he [or she] is also a general partner or, in addition to the exercise of his [or her] rights and powers as a limited partner, he [or she] participates in the control of the business. However, if the limited partner participates in the control of the business, he [or she] is liable only to persons who transact business with the limited partnership reasonably believing, based upon the limited partner's conduct, that the limited partner is a general partner.

(b) A limited partner does not participate in the control of the business within the meaning of subsection (a) solely by doing one or more of the following:

(1) being a contractor for or an agent or employee of the limited partnership or of a general partner or being an officer, director, or shareholder of a general partner that is a corporation;

(2) consulting with and advising a general partner with respect to the business of the limited partnership;

(3) acting as surety for the limited partnership or guaranteeing or assuming one or more specific obligations of the limited partnership;

(4) taking any action required or permitted by law to bring or pursue a derivative action in the right of the limited partnership;

(5) requesting or attending a meeting of partners;

(6) proposing, approving, or disapproving, by voting or otherwise, one or more of the following matters:

(i) the dissolution and winding up of the limited partnership;

(ii) the sale, exchange, lease, mortgage, pledge, or other transfer of all or substantially all of the assets of the limited partnership;

(iii) the incurrence of indebtedness by the limited partnership other than in the ordinary course of its business;

(iv) a change in the nature of the business;

(v) the admission or removal of a general partner;

(vi) the admission or removal of a limited partner;

(vii) a transaction involving an actual or potential conflict of interest between a general partner and the limited partnership or the limited partners;

(viii) an amendment to the partnership agreement or certificate of limited partnership; or

(ix) matters related to the business of the limited partnership not otherwise enumerated in this subsection (b), which the partnership agreement states in writing may be subject to the approval or disapproval of limited partners;

(7) winding up the limited partnership pursuant to Section 803; or

(8) exercising any right or power permitted to limited partners under this [Act] and not specifically enumerated in this subsection (b).

(c) The enumeration in subsection (b) does not mean that the possession or exercise of any other powers by a limited partner constitutes participation by him [or her] in the business of the limited partnership.

(d) A limited partner who knowingly permits his [or her] name to be used in the name of the limited partnership, except under circumstances permitted by Section 102(2), is liable to creditors who extend credit to the limited partnership without actual knowledge that the limited partner is not a general partner.

Section 304. Person Erroneously Believing Himself [or Herself] Limited Partner.

(a) Except as provided in subsection (b), a person who makes a contribution to a business enterprise and erroneously but in good faith believes that he [or she] has become a limited partner in the enterprise is not a general partner in the enterprise and is not bound by its obligations by reason of making the contribution, receiving distributions from the enterprise, or exercising any rights of a limited partner, if, on ascertaining the mistake, he [or she]:

(1) causes an appropriate certificate of limited partnership or a certificate of amendment to be executed and filed; or

(2) withdraws from future equity participation in the enterprise by executing and filing in the office of the Secretary of State a certificate declaring withdrawal under this section.

(b) A person who makes a contribution of the kind described in subsection (a) is liable as a general partner to any third party who transacts business with the enterprise (i) before the person withdraws and an appropriate certificate is filed to show withdrawal, or (ii) before an appropriate certificate is filed to show that he [or she] is not a general partner, but in either case only if the third party actually believed in good faith that the person was a general partner at the time of the transaction.

Section 305. Information.

Each limited partner has the right to:

(1) inspect and copy any of the partnership records required to be maintained by Section 105; and

(2) obtain from the general partners from time to time upon reasonable demand (i) true and full information regarding the state of the business and financial condition of the limited partnership, (ii) promptly after becoming available, a copy of the limited partnership's federal, state, and local income tax returns for each year, and (iii) other information regarding the affairs of the limited partnership as is just and reasonable.

Article 4
GENERAL PARTNERS

Section 401. Admission of Additional General Partners.

After the filing of a limited partnership's original certificate of limited partnership, additional general partners may be admitted as provided in writing in the partnership agreement or, if the partnership agreement does not provide in writing for the admission of additional general partners, with the written consent of all partners.

Section 402. Events of Withdrawal.

Except as approved by the specific written consent of all partners at the time, a person ceases to be a general partner of a limited partnership upon the happening of any of the following events:

(1) the general partner withdraws from the limited partnership as provided in Section 602;

(2) the general partner ceases to be a member of the limited partnership as provided in Section 702;

(3) the general partner is removed as a general partner in accordance with the partnership agreement;

(4) unless otherwise provided in writing in the partnership agreement, the general partner: (i) makes an assignment for the benefit of creditors; (ii) files a voluntary petition in bankruptcy; (iii) is adjudicated a bankrupt or insolvent; (iv) files a petition or answer seeking for himself [or herself] any reorganization, arrangement, composition, readjustment, liquidation, dissolution, or similar relief under any statute, law, or regulation; (v) files an answer or other pleading admitting or failing to contest the material allegations of a petition filed against him [or her] in any proceeding of this nature; or (vi) seeks, consents to, or acquiesces in the appointment of a trustee, receiver, or liquidator of the general partner or of all or any substantial part of his [or her] properties;

(5) unless otherwise provided in writing in the partnership agreement, [120] days after the commencement of any proceeding against the general partner seeking reorganization,

arrangement, composition, readjustment, liquidation, dissolution, or similar relief under any statute, law, or regulation, the proceeding has not been dismissed, or if within [90] days after the appointment without his [or her] consent or acquiescence of a trustee, receiver, or liquidator of the general partner or of all or any substantial part of his [or her] properties, the appointment is not vacated or stayed or within [90] days after the expiration of any such stay, the appointment is not vacated;

(6) in the case of a general partner who is a natural person,

   (i) his [or her] death; or

   (ii) the entry of an order by a court of competent jurisdiction adjudicating him [or her] incompetent to manage his [or her] person or his [or her] estate;

(7) in the case of a general partner who is acting as a general partner by virtue of being a trustee of a trust, the termination of the trust (but not merely the substitution of a new trustee);

(8) in the case of a general partner that is a separate partnership, the dissolution and commencement of winding up of the separate partnership;

(9) in the case of a general partner that is a corporation, the filing of a certificate of dissolution, or its equivalent, for the corporation or the revocation of its charter; or

(10) in the case of an estate, the distribution by the fiduciary of the estate's entire interest in the partnership.

Section 403. General Powers and Liabilities.

(a) Except as provided in this [Act] or in the partnership agreement, a general partner of a limited partnership has the rights and powers and is subject to the restrictions of a partner in a partnership without limited partners.

(b) Except as provided in this [Act], a general partner of a limited partnership has the liabilities of a partner in a partnership without limited partners to persons other than the partnership and the other partners. Except as provided in this [Act] or in the partnership agreement, a general partner of a limited partnership has the liabilities of a partner in a partnership without limited partners to the partnership and to the other partners.

Section 404. Contributions by General Partner.

A general partner of a limited partnership may make contributions to the partnership and share in the profits and losses of, and in distributions from, the limited partnership as a general partner. A general partner also may make contributions to and share in profits, losses, and distributions as a limited partner. A person who is both a general partner and a limited partner has the rights and powers, and is subject to the restrictions and liabilities, of a general partner and, except as provided in the partnership agreement, also has the powers, and is subject to the restrictions, of a limited partner to the extent of his [or her] participation in the partnership as a limited partner.

Section 405. Voting.

The partnership agreement may grant to all or certain identified general partners the right to vote (on a per capita or any other basis), separately or with all or any class of the limited partners, on any matter.

Article 5
FINANCE

Section 501. Form of Contribution.

The contribution of a partner may be in cash, property, or services rendered, or a promissory note or other obligation to contribute cash or property or to perform services.

Section 502. Liability for Contribution.

(a) A promise by a limited partner to contribute to the limited partnership is not enforceable unless set out in a writing signed by the limited partner.

(b) Except as provided in the partnership agreement, a partner is obligated to the limited partnership to perform any enforceable promise to contribute cash or property or to perform services, even if he [or she] is unable to perform because of death, disability, or any other reason. If a partner does not make the required contribution of property or services, he [or she] is obligated at the option of the limited partnership to contribute cash equal to that portion of the value, as stated in the partnership records required to be kept pursuant to Section 105, of the stated contribution which has not been made.

(c) Unless otherwise provided in the partnership agreement, the obligation of a partner to make a contribution or return money or other property paid or distributed in violation of this [Act] may be compromised only by consent of all partners. Notwithstanding the compromise, a creditor of a limited partnership who extends credit, or, otherwise acts in reliance on that obligation after the partner signs a writing which reflects the obligation and before the amendment or cancellation thereof to reflect the compromise may enforce the original obligation.

Section 503. Sharing of Profits and Losses.

The profits and losses of a limited partnership shall be allocated among the partners, and among classes of partners, in the manner provided in writing in the partnership agreement. If the partnership agreement does not so provide in writing, profits and losses shall be allocated on the basis of the value, as stated in the partnership records required to be kept pursuant to Section 105, of the contributions made by each partner to the extent they have been received by the partnership and have not been returned.

Section 504. Sharing of Distributions.

Distributions of cash or other assets of a limited partnership shall be allocated among the partners and among classes of partners in the manner provided in writing in the partnership agreement. If the partnership agreement does not so provide in writing, distributions shall be made on the basis of the value, as stated in the partnership records required to be kept pursuant to Section 105, of the contributions made by each partner to the extent they have been received by the partnership and have not been returned.

Article 6
DISTRIBUTIONS AND WITHDRAWAL

Section 601. Interim Distributions.

Except as provided in this Article, a partner is entitled to receive distributions from a limited partnership before his [or her] withdrawal from the limited partnership and before the dissolution and winding up thereof to the extent and at the times or upon the happening of the events specified in the partnership agreement.

Section 602. Withdrawal of General Partner.

A general partner may withdraw from a limited partnership at any time by giving written notice to the other partners, but if the withdrawal violates the partnership agreement, the limited partnership may recover from the withdrawing general partner damages for breach of the partnership agreement and offset the damages against the amount otherwise distributable to him [or her].

Section 603. Withdrawal of Limited Partner.

A limited partner may withdraw from a limited partnership at the time or upon the happening of events specified in writing in the partnership agreement. If the agreement does not specify in writing the time or the events upon the happening of which a limited partner may withdraw or a definite time for the dissolution and winding up of the limited partnership, a limited partner may withdraw upon not less than six months' prior written notice to each general partner at his [or her] address on the books of the limited partnership at its office in this State.

Section 604. Distribution Upon Withdrawal.

Except as provided in this Article, upon withdrawal any withdrawing partner is entitled to receive any distribution to which he [or she] is entitled under the partnership agreement and, if not otherwise provided in the agreement, he [or she] is entitled to receive, within a reasonable time after withdrawal, the fair value of his [or her] interest in the limited partnership as of the date of withdrawal based upon his [or her] right to share in distributions from the limited partnership.

Section 605. Distribution in Kind.

Except as provided in writing in the partnership agreement, a partner, regardless of the nature of his [or her] contribu-

tion, has no right to demand and receive any distribution from a limited partnership in any form other than cash. Except as provided in writing in the partnership agreement, a partner may not be compelled to accept a distribution of any asset in kind from a limited partnership to the extent that the percentage of the asset distributed to him [or her] exceeds a percentage of that asset which is equal to the percentage in which he [or she] shares in distributions from the limited partnership.

Section 606. Right to Distribution.

At the time a partner becomes entitled to receive a distribution, he [or she] has the status of, and is entitled to all remedies available to, a creditor of the limited partnership with respect to the distribution.

Section 607. Limitations on Distribution.

A partner may not receive a distribution from a limited partnership to the extent that, after giving effect to the distribution, all liabilities of the limited partnership, other than liabilities to partners on account of their partnership interests, exceed the fair value of the partnership assets.

Section 608. Liability Upon Return of Contribution.

(a) If a partner has received the return of any part of his [or her] contribution without violation of the partnership agreement or this [Act], he [or she] is liable to the limited partnership for a period of one year thereafter for the amount of the returned contribution, but only to the extent necessary to discharge the limited partnership's liabilities to creditors who extended credit to the limited partnership during the period the contribution was held by the partnership.

(b) If a partner has received the return of any part of his [or her] contribution in violation of the partnership agreement or this [Act], he [or she] is liable to the limited partnership for a period of six years thereafter for the amount of the contribution wrongfully returned.

(c) A partner receives a return of his [or her] contribution to the extent that a distribution to him [or her] reduces his [or her] share of the fair value of the net assets of the limited partnership below the value, as set forth in the partnership records required to be kept pursuant to Section 105, of his [or her] contribution which has not been distributed to him [or her].

Article 7
ASSIGNMENT OF PARTNERSHIP INTERESTS

Section 701. Nature of Partnership Interest.

A partnership interest is personal property.

Section 702. Assignment of Partnership Interest.

Except as provided in the partnership agreement, a partnership interest is assignable in whole or in part. An assignment of a partnership interest does not dissolve a limited partnership or entitle the assignee to become or to exercise any rights of a partner. An assignment entitles the assignee to receive, to the extent assigned, only the distribution to which the assignor would be entitled. Except as provided in the partnership agreement, a partner ceases to be a partner upon assignment of all his [or her] partnership interest.

Section 703. Rights of Creditor.

On application to a court of competent jurisdiction by any judgment creditor of a partner, the court may charge the partnership interest of the partner with payment of the unsatisfied amount of the judgment with interest. To the extent so charged, the judgment creditor has only the rights of an assignee of the partnership interest. This [Act] does not deprive any partner of the benefit of any exemption laws applicable to his [or her] partnership interest.

Section 704. Right of Assignee to Become Limited Partner.

(a) An assignee of a partnership interest, including an assignee of a general partner, may become a limited partner if and to the extent that (i) the assignor gives the assignee that right in accordance with authority described in the partnership agreement, or (ii) all other partners consent.

(b) An assignee who has become a limited partner has, to the extent assigned, the rights and powers, and is subject to the restrictions and liabilities, of a limited partner under the partnership agreement and this [Act]. An assignee who becomes a limited partner also is liable for the obligations of his [or her] assignor to make and return contributions as provided in Articles 5 and 6. However, the assignee is not obligated for liabilities unknown to the assignee at the time he [or she] became a limited partner.

(c) If an assignee of a partnership interest becomes a limited partner, the assignor is not released from his [or her] liability to the limited partnership under Sections 207 and 502.

Section 705. Power of Estate of Deceased or Incompetent Partner.

If a partner who is an individual dies or a court of competent jurisdiction adjudges him [or her] to be incompetent to manage his [or her] person or his [or her] property, the partner's executor, administrator, guardian, conservator, or other legal representative may exercise all of the partner's rights for the purpose of settling his [or her] estate or administering his [or her] property, including any power the partner had to give an assignee the right to become a limited partner. If a partner is a corporation, trust, or other entity and is dissolved or terminated, the powers of that partner may be exercised by its legal representative or successor.

Article 8
DISSOLUTION

Section 801. Nonjudicial Dissolution.

A limited partnership is dissolved and its affairs shall be wound up upon the happening of the first to occur of the following:

(1) at the time specified in the certificate of limited partnership;

(2) upon the happening of events specified in writing in the partnership agreement;

(3) written consent of all partners;

(4) an event of withdrawal of a general partner unless at the time there is at least one other general partner and the written provisions of the partnership agreement permit the business of the limited partnership to be carried on by the remaining general partner and that partner does so, but the limited partnership is not dissolved and is not required to be wound up by reason of any event of withdrawal if, within 90 days after the withdrawal, all partners agree in writing to continue the business of the limited partnership and to the appointment of one or more additional general partners if necessary or desired; or

(5) entry of a decree of judicial dissolution under Section 802.

Section 802. Judicial Dissolution.

On application by or for a partner the [designate the appropriate court] court may decree dissolution of a limited partnership whenever it is not reasonably practicable to carry on the business in conformity with the partnership agreement.

Section 803. Winding Up.

Except as provided in the partnership agreement, the general partners who have not wrongfully dissolved a limited partnership or, if none, the limited partners, may wind up the limited partnership's affairs; but the [designate the appropriate court] court may wind up the limited partnership's affairs upon application of any partner, his [or her] legal representative, or assignee.

Section 804. Distribution of Assets.

Upon the winding up of a limited partnership, the assets shall be distributed as follows:

(1) to creditors, including partners who are creditors, to the extent permitted by law, in satisfaction of liabilities of the limited partnership other than liabilities for distributions to partners under Section 601 or 604;

(2) except as provided in the partnership agreement, to partners and former partners in satisfaction of liabilities for distributions under Section 601 or 604; and

(3) except as provided in the partnership agreement, to partners first for the return of their contributions and secondly respecting their partnership interests, in the proportions in which the partners share in distributions.

Article 9
FOREIGN LIMITED PARTNERSHIPS

Section 901. Law Governing.

Subject to the Constitution of this State, (i) the laws of the state under which a foreign limited partnership is organized govern its organization and internal affairs and the liability of its limited partners, and (ii) a foreign limited partnership may not be denied registration by reason of any difference between those laws and the laws of this State.

Section 902. Registration.

Before transacting business in this State, a foreign limited partnership shall register with the Secretary of State. In order to register, a foreign limited partnership shall submit to the Secretary of State, in duplicate, an application for registration as a foreign limited partnership, signed and sworn to by a general partner and setting forth:

(1) the name of the foreign limited partnership and, if different, the name under which it proposes to register and transact business in this State;

(2) the State and date of its formation;

(3) the name and address of any agent for service of process on the foreign limited partnership whom the foreign limited partnership elects to appoint; the agent must be an individual resident of this State, a domestic corporation, or a foreign corporation having a place of business in, and authorized to do business in, this State;

(4) a statement that the Secretary of State is appointed the agent of the foreign limited partnership for service of process if no agent has been appointed under paragraph (3) or, if appointed, the agent's authority has been revoked or if the agent cannot be found or served with the exercise of reasonable diligence;

(5) the address of the office required to be maintained in the state of its organization by the laws of that state or, if not so required, of the principal office of the foreign limited partnership;

(6) the name and business address of each general partner; and

(7) the address of the office at which is kept a list of the names and addresses of the limited partners and their capital contributions, together with an undertaking by the foreign limited partnership to keep those records until the foreign limited partnership's registration in this State is cancelled or withdrawn.

Section 903. Issuance of Registration.

(a) If the Secretary of State finds that an application for registration conforms to law and all requisite fees have been paid, he [or she] shall:

(1) endorse on the application the word "Filed", and the month, day, and year of the filing thereof;

(2) file in his [or her] office a duplicate original of the application; and

(3) issue a certificate of registration to transact business in this State.

(b) The certificate of registration, together with a duplicate original of the application, shall be returned to the person who filed the application or his [or her] representative.

Section 904. Name.

A foreign limited partnership may register with the Secretary of State under any name, whether or not it is the name under which it is registered in its state of organization, that includes without abbreviation the words "limited partnership" and that could be registered by a domestic limited partnership.

Section 905. Changes and Amendments.

If any statement in the application for registration of a foreign limited partnership was false when made or any arrangements or other facts described have changed, making the application inaccurate in any respect, the foreign limited partnership shall promptly file in the office of the Secretary of State a certificate, signed and sworn to by a general partner, correcting such statement.

Section 906. Cancellation of Registration.

A foreign limited partnership may cancel its registration by filing with the Secretary of State a certificate of cancellation signed and sworn to by a general partner. A cancellation does not terminate the authority of the Secretary of State to accept service of process on the foreign limited partnership with respect to [claims for relief] [causes of action] arising out of the transactions of business in this State.

Section 907. Transaction of Business Without Registration.

(a) A foreign limited partnership transacting business in this State may not maintain any action, suit, or proceeding in any court of this State until it has registered in this State.

(b) The failure of a foreign limited partnership to register in this State does not impair the validity of any contract or act of the foreign limited partnership or prevent the foreign limited partnership from defending any action, suit, or proceeding in any court of this State.

(c) A limited partner of a foreign limited partnership is not liable as a general partner of the foreign limited partnership solely by reason of having transacted business in this State without registration.

(d) A foreign limited partnership, by transacting business in this State without registration, appoints the Secretary of State as its agent for service of process with respect to [claims for relief] [causes of action] arising out of the transaction of business in this State.

Section 908. Action by [Appropriate Official].

The [designate the appropriate official] may bring an action to restrain a foreign limited partnership from transacting business in this State in violation of this Article.

Article 10
DERIVATIVE ACTIONS

Section 1001. Right of Action.

A limited partner may bring an action in the right of a limited partnership to recover a judgment in its favor if general partners with authority to do so have refused to bring the action or if an effort to cause those general partners to bring the action is not likely to succeed.

Section 1002. Proper Plaintiff.

In a derivative action, the plaintiff must be a partner at the time of bringing the action and (i) must have been a partner at the time of the transaction of which he [or she] complains or (ii) his [or her] status as a partner must have devolved upon him by operation of law or pursuant to the terms of the partnership agreement from a person who was a partner at the time of the transaction.

Section 1003. Pleading.

In a derivative action, the complaint shall set forth with particularity the effort of the plaintiff to secure initiation of the action by a general partner or the reasons for not making the effort.

Section 1004. Expenses.

If a derivative action is successful, in whole or in part, or if anything is received by the plaintiff as a result of a judgment, compromise, or settlement of an action or claim, the court may award the plaintiff reasonable expenses, including reasonable attorney's fees, and shall direct him [or her] to remit to the limited partnership the remainder of those proceeds received by him [or her].

Article 11
MISCELLANEOUS

Section 1101. Construction and Application.

This [Act] shall be so applied and construed to effectuate its general purpose to make uniform the law with respect to the subject of this [Act] among states enacting it.

Section 1102. Short Title.

This [Act] may be cited as the Uniform Limited Partnership Act.

Section 1103. Severability.

If any provision of this [Act] or its application to any person or circumstance is held invalid, the invalidity does not affect other provisions or applications of the [Act] which can be given effect without the invalid provision or application, and to this end the provisions of this [Act] are severable.

Section 1104. Effective Date, Extended Effective Date, and Repeal.

Except as set forth below, the effective date of this [Act] is _____ and the following acts [list existing limited partnership acts] are hereby repealed:

(1) The existing provisions for execution and filing of certificates of limited partnerships and amendments thereunder and cancellations thereof continue in effect until [specify time required to create central filing system], the extended effective date, and Sections 102, 103, 104, 105, 201, 202, 203, 204 and 206 are not effective until the extended effective date.

(2) Section 402, specifying the conditions under which a general partner ceases to be a member of a limited partnership, is not effective until the extended effective date, and the applicable provisions of existing law continue to govern until the extended effective date.

(3) Sections 501, 502 and 608 apply only to contributions and distributions made after the effective date of this [Act].

(4) Section 704 applies only to assignments made after the effective date of this [Act].

(5) Article 9, dealing with registration of foreign limited partnerships, is not effective until the extended effective date.

(6) Unless otherwise agreed by the partners, the applicable provisions of existing law governing allocation of profits and losses (rather than the provisions of Section 503), distributions to a withdrawing partner (rather than the provisions of Section 604), and distributions of assets upon the winding up of a limited partnership (rather than the provisions of Section 804) govern limited partnerships formed before the effective date of this [Act].

Section 1105. Rules for Cases Not Provided For in This [Act].

In any case not provided for in this [Act] the provisions of the Uniform Partnership Act govern.

Section 1106. Savings Clause.

The repeal of any statutory provision by this [Act] does not impair, or otherwise affect, the organization or the continued existence of a limited partnership existing at the effective date of this [Act], nor does the repeal of any existing statutory provision by this [Act] impair any contract or affect any right accrued before the effective date of this [Act].

The Revised Model Business Corporation Act (Excerpts)

Chapter 2.
INCORPORATION

§ 2.01 Incorporators

One or more persons may act as the incorporator or incorporators of a corporation by delivering articles of incorporation to the secretary of state for filing.

§ 2.02 Articles of Incorporation

(a) The articles of incorporation must set forth:

(1) a corporate name * * * ;

(2) the number of shares the corporation is authorized to issue;

(3) the street address of the corporation's initial registered office and the name of its initial registered agent at that office; and

(4) the name and address of each incorporator.

(b) The articles of incorporation may set forth:

(1) the names and addresses of the individuals who are to serve as the initial directors;

(2) provisions not inconsistent with law regarding:

(i) the purpose or purposes for which the corporation is organized;

(ii) managing the business and regulating the affairs of the corporation;

(iii) defining, limiting, and regulating the powers of the corporation, its board of directors, and shareholders;

(iv) a par value for authorized shares or classes of shares;

(v) the imposition of personal liability on shareholders for the debts of the corporation to a specified extent and upon specified conditions;

(3) any provision that under this Act is required or permitted to be set forth in the bylaws; and

(4) a provision eliminating or limiting the liability of a director to the corporation or its shareholders for money damages for any action taken, or any failure to take any action, as a director, except liability for (A) the amount of a financial benefit received by a director to which he is not entitled; (B) an intentional infliction of harm on the corporation or the shareholders; (C) [unlawful distributions]; or (D) an intentional violation of criminal law.

(c) The articles of incorporation need not set forth any of the corporate powers enumerated in this Act.

§ 2.03 Incorporation

(a) Unless a delayed effective date is specified, the corporate existence begins when the articles of incorporation are filed.

(b) The secretary of state's filing of the articles of incorporation is conclusive proof that the incorporators satisfied all conditions precedent to incorporation except in a proceeding by the state to cancel or revoke the incorporation or involuntarily dissolve the corporation.

§ 2.04 Liability for Preincorporation Transactions

All persons purporting to act as or on behalf of a corporation, knowing there was no incorporation under this Act, are jointly and severally liable for all liabilities created while so acting.

§ 2.05 Organization of Corporation

(a) After incorporation:

(1) if initial directors are named in the articles of incorporation, the initial directors shall hold an organizational meeting, at the call of a majority of the directors,

to complete the organization of the corporation by appointing officers, adopting bylaws, and carrying on any other business brought before the meeting;

(2) if initial directors are not named in the articles, the incorporator or incorporators shall hold an organizational meeting at the call of a majority of the incorporators:

(i) to elect directors and complete the organization of the corporation; or

(ii) to elect a board of directors who shall complete the organization of the corporation.

(b) Action required or permitted by this Act to be taken by incorporators at an organizational meeting may be taken without a meeting if the action taken is evidenced by one or more written consents describing the action taken and signed by each incorporator.

(c) An organizational meeting may be held in or out of this state.

*   *   *   *

Chapter 3.
PURPOSES AND POWERS

§ 3.01 Purposes

(a) Every corporation incorporated under this Act has the purpose of engaging in any lawful business unless a more limited purpose is set forth in the articles of incorporation.

(b) A corporation engaging in a business that is subject to regulation under another statute of this state may incorporate under this Act only if permitted by, and subject to all limitations of, the other statute.

§ 3.02 General Powers

Unless its articles of incorporation provide otherwise, every corporation has perpetual duration and succession in its corporate name and has the same powers as an individual to do all things necessary or convenient to carry out its business and affairs, including without limitation power:

(1) to sue and be sued, complain and defend in its corporate name;

(2) to have a corporate seal, which may be altered at will, and to use it, or a facsimile of it, by impressing or affixing it or in any other manner reproducing it;

(3) to make and amend bylaws, not inconsistent with its articles of incorporation or with the laws of this state, for managing the business and regulating the affairs of the corporation;

(4) to purchase, receive, lease, or otherwise acquire, and own, hold, improve, use, and otherwise deal with, real or personal property, or any legal or equitable interest in property, wherever located;

(5) to sell, convey, mortgage, pledge, lease, exchange, and otherwise dispose of all or any part of its property;

(6) to purchase, receive, subscribe for, or otherwise acquire; own, hold, vote, use, sell, mortgage, lend, pledge, or otherwise dispose of; and deal in and with shares or other interests in, or obligations of, any other entity;

(7) to make contracts and guarantees, incur liabilities, borrow money, issue its notes, bonds, and other obligations (which may be convertible into or include the option to purchase other securities of the corporation), and secure any of its obligations by mortgage or pledge of any of its property, franchises, or income;

(8) to lend money, invest and reinvest its funds, and receive and hold real and personal property as security for repayment;

(9) to be a promoter, partner, member, associate, or manager of any partnership, joint venture, trust, or other entity;

(10) to conduct its business, locate offices, and exercise the powers granted by this Act within or without this state;

(11) to elect directors and appoint officers, employees, and agents of the corporation, define their duties, fix their compensation, and lend them money and credit;

(12) to pay pensions and establish pension plans, pension trusts, profit sharing plans, share bonus plans, share option plans, and benefit or incentive plans for any or all of its current or former directors, officers, employees, and agents;

(13) to make donations for the public welfare or for charitable, scientific, or educational purposes;

(14) to transact any lawful business that will aid governmental policy;

(15) to make payments or donations, or do any other act, not inconsistent with law, that furthers the business and affairs of the corporation.

*   *   *   *

Chapter 5.
OFFICE AND AGENT

§ 5.01 Registered Office and Registered Agent

Each corporation must continuously maintain in this state:

(1) a registered office that may be the same as any of its places of business; and

(2) a registered agent, who may be:

(i) an individual who resides in this state and whose business office is identical with the registered office;

(ii) a domestic corporation or not-for-profit domestic corporation whose business office is identical with the registered office; or

(iii) a foreign corporation or not-for-profit foreign corporation authorized to transact business in this state whose business office is identical with the registered office.

* * * *

§ 5.04 Service on Corporation

(a) A corporation's registered agent is the corporation's agent for service of process, notice, or demand required or permitted by law to be served on the corporation.

(b) If a corporation has no registered agent, or the agent cannot with reasonable diligence be served, the corporation may be served by registered or certified mail, return receipt requested, addressed to the secretary of the corporation at its principal office. Service is perfected under this subsection at the earliest of:

(1) the date the corporation receives the mail;

(2) the date shown on the return receipt, if signed on behalf of the corporation; or

(3) five days after its deposit in the United States Mail, if mailed postpaid and correctly addressed.

(c) This section does not prescribe the only means, or necessarily the required means, of serving a corporation.

Chapter 6.
SHARES AND DISTRIBUTIONS
* * * *

Subchapter B. Issuance of Shares
* * * *

§ 6.21 Issuance of Shares

(a) The powers granted in this section to the board of directors may be reserved to the shareholders by the articles of incorporation.

(b) The board of directors may authorize shares to be issued for consideration consisting of any tangible or intangible property or benefit to the corporation, including cash, promissory notes, services performed, contracts for services to be performed, or other securities of the corporation.

(c) Before the corporation issues shares, the board of directors must determine that the consideration received or to be received for shares to be issued is adequate. That determination by the board of directors is conclusive insofar as the adequacy of consideration for the issuance of shares relates to whether the shares are validly issued, fully paid, and nonassessable.

(d) When the corporation receives the consideration for which the board of directors authorized the issuance of shares, the shares issued therefor are fully paid and nonassessable.

(e) The corporation may place in escrow shares issued for a contract for future services or benefits or a promissory note, or make other arrangements to restrict the transfer of the shares, and may credit distributions in respect of the shares against their purchase price, until the services are performed, the note is paid, or the benefits received. If the services are not performed, the note is not paid, or the benefits are not received, the shares escrowed or restricted and the distributions credited may be cancelled in whole or part.

* * * *

§ 6.27 Restriction on Transfer or Registration of Shares and Other Securities

(a) The articles of incorporation, bylaws, an agreement among shareholders, or an agreement between shareholders and the corporation may impose restrictions on the transfer or registration of transfer of shares of the corporation. A restriction does not affect shares issued before the restriction was adopted unless the holders of the shares are parties to the restriction agreement or voted in favor of the restriction.

(b) A restriction on the transfer or registration of transfer of shares is valid and enforceable against the holder or a transferee of the holder if the restriction is authorized by this section and its existence is noted conspicuously on the front or back of the certificate or is contained in the information statement [sent to the shareholder]. Unless so noted, a restriction is not enforceable against a person without knowledge of the restriction.

(c) A restriction on the transfer or registration of transfer of shares is authorized:

(1) to maintain the corporation's status when it is dependent on the number or identity of its shareholders;

(2) to preserve exemptions under federal or state securities law;

(3) for any other reasonable purpose.

(d) A restriction on the transfer or registration of transfer of shares may:

(1) obligate the shareholder first to offer the corporation or other persons (separately, consecutively, or simultaneously) an opportunity to acquire the restricted shares;

(2) obligate the corporate or other persons (separately, consecutively, or simultaneously) to acquire the restricted shares;

(3) require the corporation, the holders of any class of its shares, or another person to approve the transfer of the restricted shares, if the requirement is not manifestly unreasonable;

(4) prohibit the transfer of the restricted shares to designated persons or classes of persons, if the prohibition is not manifestly unreasonable.

(e) For purposes of this section, "shares" includes a security convertible into or carrying a right to subscribe for or acquire shares.

* * * *

Chapter 7.
SHAREHOLDERS

Subchapter A. Meetings

§ 7.01 Annual Meeting

(a) A corporation shall hold annually at a time stated in or fixed in accordance with the bylaws a meeting of shareholders.

(b) Annual shareholders' meetings may be held in or out of this state at the place stated in or fixed in accordance with the bylaws. If no place is stated in or fixed in accordance with the bylaws, annual meetings shall be held at the corporation's principal office.

(c) The failure to hold an annual meeting at the time stated in or fixed in accordance with a corporation's bylaws does not affect the validity of any corporate action.

* * * *

§ 7.05 Notice of Meeting

(a) A corporation shall notify shareholders of the date, time, and place of each annual and special shareholders' meeting no fewer than 10 nor more than 60 days before the meeting date. Unless this Act or the articles of incorporation require otherwise, the corporation is required to give notice only to shareholders entitled to vote at the meeting.

(b) Unless this Act or the articles of incorporation require otherwise, notice of an annual meeting need not include a description of the purpose or purposes for which the meeting is called.

(c) Notice of a special meeting must include a description of the purpose or purposes for which the meeting is called.

(d) If not otherwise fixed * * *, the record date for determining shareholders entitled to notice of and to vote at an annual or special shareholders' meeting is the day before the first notice is delivered to shareholders.

(e) Unless the bylaws require otherwise, if an annual or special shareholders' meeting is adjourned to a different date, time, or place, notice need not be given of the new date, time, or place if the new date, time, or place is announced at the meeting before adjournment. * * *

* * * *

§ 7.07 Record Date

(a) The bylaws may fix or provide the manner of fixing the record date for one or more voting groups in order to determine the shareholders entitled to notice of a shareholders' meeting, to demand a special meeting, to vote, or to take any other action. If the bylaws do not fix or provide for fixing a record date, the board of directors of the corporation may fix a future date as the record date.

(b) A record date fixed under this section may not be more than 70 days before the meeting or action requiring a determination of shareholders.

(c) A determination of shareholders entitled to notice of or to vote at a shareholders' meeting is effective for any adjournment of the meeting unless the board of directors fixes a new record date, which it must do if the meeting is adjourned to a date more than 120 days after the date fixed for the original meeting.

(d) If a court orders a meeting adjourned to a date more than 120 days after the date fixed for the original meeting, it may provide that the original record date continues in effect or it may fix a new record date.

Subchapter B. Voting

§ 7.20 Shareholders' List for Meeting

(a) After fixing a record date for a meeting, a corporation shall prepare an alphabetical list of the names of all its shareholders who are entitled to notice of a shareholders' meeting. The list must be arranged by voting group (and within each voting group by class or series of shares) and show the address of and number of shares held by each shareholder.

(b) The shareholders' list must be available for inspection by any shareholder, beginning two business days after notice of the meeting is given for which the list was prepared and continuing through the meeting, at the corporation's principal office or at a place identified in the meeting notice in the city where the meeting will be held. A shareholder, his agent, or attorney is entitled on written demand to inspect and, subject to the requirements of section 16.02(c), to copy the list, during regular business hours and at his expense, during the period it is available for inspection.

(c) The corporation shall make the shareholders' list available at the meeting, and any shareholder, his agent, or attorney is entitled to inspect the list at any time during the meeting or any adjournment.

(d) If the corporation refuses to allow a shareholder, his agent, or attorney to inspect the shareholders' list before or at the meeting (or copy the list as permitted by subsection (b)), the [name or describe] court of the county where a corporation's principal office (or, if none in this state, its registered office) is located, on application of the shareholder, may summarily order the inspection or copying at the corporation's expense and may postpone the meeting for which the list was prepared until the inspection or copying is complete.

(e) Refusal or failure to prepare or make available the shareholders' list does not affect the validity of action taken at the meeting.

* * * *

§ 7.22 Proxies

(a) A shareholder may vote his shares in person or by proxy.

(b) A shareholder may appoint a proxy to vote or otherwise act for him by signing an appointment form, either personally or by his attorney-in-fact.

from unjustly receiving a benefit at the expense of another. This is known as a *quasi contract* and provides a basis for Nursing Services to recover the value of the services it provided while Janine was in the hospital. As for the at-home services that were provided to Janine, because Janine was aware that those services were being provided for her, Nursing Services can recover for those services under an implied-in-fact contract. Under this type of contract, the conduct of the parties creates and defines the terms. Janine's acceptance of the services constitutes her agreement to form a contract, and she will probably be required to pay Nursing Services in full.

10–2A.   QUESTION WITH SAMPLE ANSWER

A novation exists when a new, valid contract expressly or impliedly discharges a prior contract by the substitution of a party. Accord and satisfaction exists when the parties agree that the original obligation can be discharged by a substituted performance. In this case, Fred's agreement with Iba to pay off Junior's debt for $1,100 (as compared to the $1,000 owed) is definitely a valid contract. The terms of the contract substitute Fred as the debtor for Junior, and Junior is definitely discharged from further liability. This agreement is a *novation*.

11–2A.   QUESTION WITH SAMPLE ANSWER

The entire answer falls under UCC 2–206(1)(b), because the situation deals with a buyer's order to buy goods for prompt shipment. The law is that such an order or offer invites acceptance by a prompt promise to ship conforming goods. If the promise (acceptance) is sent by a medium reasonable under the circumstances, the acceptance is effective when sent. Therefore, a contract was formed on October 8, and it required Martin to ship 100 model Color-X television sets. Martin's shipment is nonconforming, and Flint is correct in claiming that Martin is in breach. Martin's claim would be valid if Martin had not sent its promise of shipment. The UCC provides that shipment of nonconforming goods constitutes an acceptance *unless* the seller seasonably notifies the buyer that such shipment is sent only as an accommodation. Thus, had a contract not been formed on October 8, the nonconforming shipment on the 28th would not be treated as an acceptance, and no contract would be in existence to breach.

12–2A.   QUESTION WITH SAMPLE ANSWER

To answer this question, you must first decide if there is a legal theory under which Harley may be able to recover. You may recall from your reading the intentional tort of "wrongful interference with a contractual relationship." To recover damages under this theory, Harley would need to show that he and Martha had a valid contract, that Lothar knew of this contractual relationship between Martha and Harley, and that Lothar intentionally convinced Martha to break her contract with Harley. Even though Lothar hoped that his advertisements would persuade Martha to break her contract with Harley, the question states that Martha's decision to change bakers was based solely on the advertising and not on anything else that Lothar did. Lothar's advertisements did not constitute a tort. Note, though, that while Harley cannot collect from Lothar for Martha's actions, he does have a cause of action against Martha for her breach of their contract.

13–3A.   QUESTION WITH SAMPLE ANSWER

If Colt can prove that all due care was exercised in the manufacture of the pistol, Colt cannot be held in an action based on negligence. Under the theory of strict liability in tort, however, Colt can be held liable regardless of the degree of care exercised. The doctrine of strict liability states that a merchant-seller who sells a defective product that is unreasonably dangerous is liable for injuries caused by that product (even if all possible care in preparation and sale is exercised), provided that the product has not been substantially changed after the time of sale. Therefore, if Wayne can prove the pistol is defective, unreasonably dangerous, and caused him injury, Colt as a merchant is strictly liable, because there is no evidence that the pistol has been altered since the date of its manufacture.

14–2A.   QUESTION WITH SAMPLE ANSWER

(a) Ursula will not be held liable for copyright infringement in this case because her photocopying pages for use in scholarly research falls squarely under the "fair use" exception to the Copyright Act.

(b) While Ursula's actions are improper, they could constitute trademark infringement, not copyright infringement. Copyrights are granted for literary and artistic productions; trademarks are distinctive marks created and used by manufacturers to differentiate their goods from those of their competitors. Trademark infringement occurs when a mark is copied to a substantial degree, intentionally or unintentionally.

(c) As with the answer to (a) above, Ursula's actions fall within the "fair use" doctrine of copyright law. Her use of the taped television shows for teaching is the exact type of use the exception is designed to cover.

15–2A.   QUESTION WITH SAMPLE ANSWER

Three basic actions are available to Holiday:

(a) Attachment—a court-ordered seizure of nonexempt property prior to Holiday's reducing the debt to judgment. The grounds for granting the writ of attachment are limited, but in most states (when submitted), the writ is granted on introduction of evidence that a debtor intends to remove the property from the jurisdiction in which a judgment would be rendered. Holiday would have to post a bond and reduce its claim to judgment; then it could sell the attached property to satisfy the debt, returning any surplus to Kanahara.

(b) Writ of execution, on reducing the debt to judgment. The writ is an order issued by the clerk directing the sheriff or other officer of the court to seize (levy) nonexempt property of the debtor located within the court's jurisdiction. The property is then sold, and the proceeds are used to pay for the judgment and cost of sale, with any surplus going to the debtor, (in this case, Kanahara).

(c) Garnishment of the wages owed to Kanahara by the Cross-Bar Packing Corp. Whenever a third person, the garnishee, owes a debt, such as wages, to the debtor, the creditor can proceed to have the court order the employer-garnishee to turn over a percentage of the take-home pay (usually no more than 25 percent) to pay the debt. Garnishment actions are continuous in some states; in others, the action must be taken for each pay period.

Holiday can proceed with any one or a combination of these three actions. Because the property may be removed from the jurisdiction, and perhaps Kanahara himself may leave the jurisdiction (he may quit his job), prompt action is important.

16–2A. QUESTION WITH SAMPLE ANSWER

The court would likely conclude that National Foods was responsible for the acts of harassment by the manager at the franchised restaurant, on the ground that the employees were the agents of National Foods. An agency relationship can be implied from the circumstances and conduct of the parties. The important question is the degree of control that a franchisor has over its franchisees. Whether it exercises that control is beside the point. Here, National Foods retained considerable control over the new hires and the franchisee's policies, as well as the right to terminate the franchise for violations. That its supervisors routinely approved the policies would not undercut National Foods' liability.

17–3A. QUESTION WITH SAMPLE ANSWER

(a) A limited partner's interest is assignable. In fact, assignment allows the assignee to become a substituted limited partner with the consent of the remaining partners. The assignment, however, does not dissolve the limited partnership.

(b) Bankruptcy of the limited partnership itself causes dissolution, but bankruptcy of one of the limited partners does not dissolve the partnership unless it causes the bankruptcy of the firm.

(c) The retirement, death, or insanity of a general partner dissolves the partnership unless the business can be continued by the remaining general partners. Because Dorinda was the only general partner, her death dissolves the limited partnership.

18–2A. QUESTION WITH SAMPLE ANSWER

(a) As a general rule, a promoter is personally liable for all preincorporation contracts made by the promoter. The basic theory behind such liability is that the promoter cannot be an agent for a nonexistent principal (a corporation not yet formed). It is immaterial whether the contracting party knows of the prospective existence of the corporation, and the general rule of promoter liability continues even after the corporation is formed. Three basic exceptions to promoter liability are:

(1) The promoter's contract with a third party can stipulate that the third party will look only to the new corporation, not to the promoter, for performance and liability.

(2) The third party can release the promoter from liability.

(3) After formation, the corporation can assume the contractual obligations and liability by *novation*. (If it is by *adoption*, most courts hold that the promoter is still personally liable.)

Peterson is therefore personally liable on both contracts, because (1) neither Owens nor Babcock has released him from liability, (2) the corporation has not assumed contractual responsibility by novation, and (3) Peterson's contract with Babcock did not limit Babcock to holding only the corporation liable. (Peterson's liability was conditioned only on the corporation's formation, which did occur.)

(b) Incorporation in and of itself does not make the newly formed corporation liable for preincorporation contracts. Until the newly formed corporation assumes Peterson's contracts by novation (releasing Peterson from personal liability) or by adoption (undertaking to perform Peterson's contracts, which makes both the corporation and Peterson liable), Babcock cannot enforce Peterson's contract against the corporation.

19–2A. QUESTION WITH SAMPLE ANSWER

On creation of an agency, the agent owes certain fiduciary duties to the principal. Two such duties are the duty of loyalty and the duty to inform or notify. The duty of loyalty is a fundamental concept of the fiduciary relationship. The agent must act solely for the benefit of the principal, not in the agent's own interest or in the interest of another person. One of the principles invoked by this duty is that an agent employed to sell cannot become a purchaser without the principal's consent. When the agent is a partner, contracting to sell to another partner is equivalent to selling to oneself and is therefore a breach of the agent's duty. In addition, the agent has a duty to disclose to the principal any facts pertinent to the subject matter of the agency. Failure to disclose to Peter the knowledge of the shopping mall and the increased market value of the property also was a breach of Alice's fiduciary duties. When an agent breaches fiduciary duties owed to the principal by becoming a recipient of a contract, the contract is voidable at the election of the principal. Neither Carl nor Alice can hold Peter to the contract, and Alice's breach of fiduciary duties also allows Peter to terminate the agency relationship.

20–2A. QUESTION WITH SAMPLE ANSWER

The Occupational Health and Safety Act (OSHA) requires employers to provide safe working conditions for employees. The act prohibits employers from discharging or discriminating against any employee who refuses to work when the employee believes in good faith that he or she will risk death or great bodily harm by undertaking the employment activity. Denton and Carlo had sufficient reason to believe that the maintenance job required of them by their employer involved great risk, and therefore, under OSHA, their discharge was wrongful. Denton and Carlo can turn to the Occupational Safety and Health Administration, which is part of the Department of Labor, for assistance.

21–2A. QUESTION WITH SAMPLE ANSWER

The Age Discrimination in Employment Act (ADEA) prohibits discrimination in employment on the basis of age against individuals forty years of age or older. For the ADEA to apply, an employer must have twenty or more employees, and interstate commerce must be affected by the employer's business activities. Because Jones worked at a resort (presumably employing more than twenty persons), the court would probably find that its activities affected interstate commerce because it was frequented by out-of-state travelers. Because Jones was not demoted due to any apparent job-performance problems, the fact that he was replaced by a person half his age coupled with Blair's statement about getting rid of all the "senile" men would be enough to shift the burden to the employer to show that it was not discriminating on the basis of age.

22–3A. QUESTION WITH SAMPLE ANSWER

The NLRB has consistently been suspicious of companies that grant added benefits during election campaigns. These benefits will be considered as an unfair labor practice that biases elections, unless the employer can demonstrate that the benefits were unrelated to the unionization and would have been granted anyway.

23–3A. QUESTION WITH SAMPLE ANSWER

Yes. A regulation of the Federal Trade Commission (FTC) under Section 5 of the Federal Trade Commission Act makes it a violation for door-to-door sellers to fail to give consumers three days to cancel any sale. In addition, a number of state statutes require this three-day "cooling off" period to protect consumers from unscrupulous door-to-door sellers. Because the Gonchars sought to rescind the contract within the three-day period, Renowned Books was obligated to agree to cancel the contract. Its failure to allow rescission was in violation of the FTC regulation and of most state statutes.

24–2A. QUESTION WITH SAMPLE ANSWER

Fruitade has violated a number of federal environmental laws if such actions are being taken without a permit. First, because the dumping is in a navigable waterway, the River and Harbor Act of 1886, as amended, has been violated. Second, the Clean Water Act of 1972, as amended, has been violated. This act is designed to make the waters safe for swimming, to protect fish and wildlife, and to eliminate discharge of pollutants into the water. Both the crushed glass and the acid violate this act. Third, the Toxic Substances Control Act of 1976 was passed to regulate chemicals that are known to be toxic and could have an effect on human health and the environment. The acid in the cleaning fluid or compound could come under this act.

25–3A. QUESTION WITH SAMPLE ANSWER

Because all land-use regulations necessarily limit the ways in which property may be used, a regulation by itself will not generally be considered a compensable taking. Compensation will be required only if the regulation itself is found to be overly burdensome and thus subject to the requirement that just compensation be paid. Rezoning the land from industrial use to commercial use—despite the expected reduction in its market value—would probably not be considered a compensable taking because it would not prevent the owner from using the land for any reasonable income-producing or private purpose.

26–3A. QUESTION WITH SAMPLE ANSWER

Super-Tech's unilateral action is a violation of the Sherman Act, Section 2. Super-Tech already controls a substantial portion of the market for computers and thus has a monopoly position in this business field. Super-Tech's action is a misuse of its monopoly power in the marketplace. Any person who shall monopolize or attempt to monopolize any part of trade or commerce may be in violation of the Sherman Act. Therefore, Alcan can file a private action seeking treble damages, costs, and reasonable attorneys' fees, and the Department of Justice can institute criminal and civil proceedings.

27–3A. QUESTION WITH SAMPLE ANSWER

(a) Trujillo's pricing limitations are clearly an attempt at resale price maintenance and vertical price fixing which here are violations of the Sherman Act. The reasons given by the courts for holding these agreements to be illegal are that the limitations (1) tend to provide the same economic rewards to all retailers, regardless of skill, experience, and the like; (2) restrict innovation and deter a retailer from trying out new competitive techniques; and (3) may be so restrictive in the future as to fix a uniform price.

(b) Generally, whenever two or more competitors make any agreement to fix prices, it is considered a *per se* violation of the Sherman Act, Section 1. This is called horizontal price fixing, and generally the court will find any agreement to fix prices among competitors to be illegal. This can result in a criminal conviction. Whether this agreement will be a violation of the Sherman Act with possible criminal conviction will depend on the intent of the parties. Simply "an effect on prices, without more, will not support a criminal conviction under the Sherman Act." If this is truly a patriotic gesture and an aid to assist the unemployed, this intent could be determinative.

(c) Foam Beer's recommended or suggested prices to its distributors is not a violation of the Sherman Act, Section 1. There is no agreement, express or implied, that a distributor *must* resell the beer at those prices to continue to do business with Foam. All facts indicate that the price suggestions are merely a benchmark based on past attempts of distributors to make a reasonable profit. No price restrictions are imposed by Foam.

28–2A. QUESTION WITH SAMPLE ANSWER

No. Under federal securities law, a stock split is exempt from registration requirements. This is because no *sale* of stock is involved. The existing shares are merely being split, and no consideration is received by the corporation for the additional shares created.

GLOSSARY

A

Abandoned property Property with which the owner has voluntarily parted, with no intention of recovering it.

Abandonment In landlord-tenant law, a tenant's departure from leased premises completely, with no intention of returning before the end of the lease term.

Abus de droit A doctrine developed in the French courts. The doctrine modified employment at will and protected workers exercising their rights from wrongful discharge and other employer abuses.

Acceptance In contract law, the offeree's notification to the offeror that the offeree agrees to be bound by the terms of the offeror's proposal. Although historically the terms of acceptance had to be the mirror image of the terms of the offer, the Uniform Commercial Code provides that even modified terms of the offer in a definite expression of acceptance constitute a contract.

Accord and satisfaction An agreement for payment (or other performance) between two parties, one of whom has a right of action against the other. After the payment has been accepted or other performance has been made, the "accord and satisfaction" is complete and the obligation is discharged.

Accredited investors In the context of securities offerings, "sophisticated" investors, such as banks, insurance companies, investment companies, the issuer's executive officers and directors, and persons whose income or net worth exceeds certain limits.

Acquittal A certification or declaration following a trial that the individual accused of a crime is innocent, or free from guilt, and is thus absolved of the charges.

Act of state doctrine A doctrine that provides that the judicial branch of one country will not examine the validity of public acts committed by a recognized foreign government within its own territory.

Actionable Capable of serving as the basis of a lawsuit.

Actual authority Authority of an agent that is express or implied.

Actual malice A condition that exists when a person makes a statement with either knowledge of its falsity or a reckless disregard for the truth. In a defamation suit, a statement made about a public figure normally must be made with actual malice for liability to be incurred.

Actus reus (pronounced *ak*-tus *ray*-uhs) A guilty (prohibited) act. The commission of a prohibited act is one of the two essential elements required for criminal liability, the other element being the intent to commit a crime.

Adequate protection doctrine In bankruptcy law, a doctrine that protects secured creditors from losing their security as a result of an automatic stay on legal proceedings by creditors against the debtor once the debtor petitions for bankruptcy relief. In certain circumstances, the bankruptcy court may provide adequate protection by requiring the debtor or trustee to pay the creditor or provide additional guaranties to protect the creditor against the losses suffered by the creditor as a result of the stay.

Adhesion contract A "standard-form" contract, such as that between a large retailer and a consumer, in which the stronger party dictates the terms.

Adjudicate To render a judicial decision. In the administrative process, the proceeding in which an administrative law judge hears and decides on issues that arise when an administrative agency charges a person or a firm with violating a law or regulation enforced by the agency.

Adjudication The process of adjudicating. *See* Adjudicate

Administrative agency A federal or state government agency established to perform a specific function. Administrative agencies are authorized by legislative acts to make and enforce rules to administer and enforce the acts.

Administrative law The body of law created by administrative agencies (in the form of rules, regulations, orders, and decisions) in order to carry out their duties and responsibilities.

Administrative law judge (ALJ) One who presides over an administrative agency hearing and who has the power to administer oaths, take testimony, rule on questions of evidence, and make determinations of fact.

Administrative process The procedure used by administrative agencies in the administration of law.

Administrator One who is appointed by a court to handle the probate (disposition) of a person's estate if that person dies intestate (without a valid will) or if the executor named in the will cannot serve.

Adverse possession The acquisition of title to real property by occupying it openly, without the consent of the owner, for a period of time specified by a state statute. The occupation must be actual, open, notorious, exclusive, and in opposition to all others, including the owner.

Affidavit A written or printed voluntary statement of facts, confirmed by the oath or affirmation of the party making it and made before a person having the authority to administer the oath or affirmation.

Affirm To validate; to give legal force to. *See also* Ratification

Affirmative action Job-hiring policies that give special consideration to members of protected classes in an effort to overcome present effects of past discrimination.

Affirmative defense A response to a plaintiff's claim that does not deny the plaintiff's facts but attacks the plaintiff's legal right to bring an action. An example is the running of the statute of limitations.

After-acquired evidence A type of evidence submitted in support of an affirmative defense in employment discrimination cases. Evidence that, prior to the employer's discriminatory act, the employee engaged in misconduct sufficient to warrant dismissal had the employer known of it earlier.

After-acquired property Property of the debtor that is acquired after the execution of a security agreement.

Age of majority The age at which an individual is considered legally capable of conducting himself or herself responsibly. A person of this age is entitled to the full rights of citizenship, including the right to vote in elections. In contract law, one who is no longer an infant and can no longer disaffirm a contract.

Agency A relationship between two parties in which one party (the agent) agrees to represent or act for the other (the principal).

Agency by estoppel Arises when a principal negligently allows an agent to exercise powers not granted to the agent, thus justifying others in believing that the agent possesses the requisite agency authority. *See also* Promissory estoppel

Agent A person who agrees to represent or act for another, called the principal.

Agreement   A meeting of two or more minds in regard to the terms of a contract; usually broken down into two events—an offer by one party to form a contract, and an acceptance of the offer by the person to whom the offer is made.

Alien corporation   A designation in the United States for a corporation formed in another country but doing business in the United States.

Allegation   A statement, claim, or assertion.

Allege   To state, recite, assert, or charge.

Alteration   In the context of leaseholds, an improvement or change made that materially affects the condition of the property. Thus, for example, erecting an additional structure probably would (and painting interior walls would not) be considered making an alteration.

Alternative dispute resolution (ADR)   The resolution of disputes in ways other than those involved in the traditional judicial process. Negotiation, mediation, and arbitration are forms of ADR.

Amend   To change and improve through a formal procedure.

American Arbitration Association (AAA)   The major organization offering arbitration services in the United States.

Analogy   In logical reasoning, an assumption that if two things are similar in some respects, they will be similar in other respects also. Often used in legal reasoning to infer the appropriate application of legal principles in a case being decided by referring to previous cases involving different facts but considered to come within the policy underlying the rule.

Annul   To cancel; to make void.

Answer   Procedurally, a defendant's response to the plaintiff's complaint.

Anticipatory repudiation   An assertion or action by a party indicating that he or she will not perform an obligation that the party is contractually obligated to perform at a future time.

Antitrust law   The body of federal and state laws and statutes protecting trade and commerce from unlawful restraints, price discrimination, price fixing, and monopolies. The principal federal antitrust statues are the Sherman Act of 1890, the Clayton Act of 1914, and the Federal Trade Commission Act of 1914.

Apparent authority   Authority that is only apparent, not real. In agency law, a person may be deemed to have had the power to act as an agent for another party if the other party's manifestations to a third party led the third party to believe that an agency existed when, in fact, it did not.

Appeal   Resort to a superior court, such as an appellate court, to review the decision of an inferior court, such as a trial court or an administrative agency.

Appellant   The party who takes an appeal from one court to another.

Appellate court   A court having appellate jurisdiction. Each state court system has at least one level of appellate courts. In the federal court system, the appellate courts are the circuit courts of appeals (intermediate appellate courts) and the United States Supreme Court (the highest appellate court in the federal system).

Appellate jurisdiction   Courts having appellate jurisdiction act as reviewing courts, or appellate courts. Generally, cases can be brought before appellate courts only on appeal from an order or a judgment of a trial court or other lower court.

Appellee   The party against whom an appeal is taken—that is, the party who opposes setting aside or reversing the judgment.

Appraisal right   The right of a dissenting shareholder, if he or she objects to an extraordinary transaction of the corporation (such as a merger or consolidation), to have his or her shares appraised and to be paid the fair value of his or her shares by the corporation.

Appropriation   In tort law, the use by one person of another person's name, likeness, or other identifying characteristic without permission and for the benefit of the user.

Arbitrary and capricious test   The court reviewing an informal administrative agency action applies this test to determine whether or not that action was in clear error. The court gives wide discretion to the expertise of the agency and decides if the agency had sufficient factual information on which to base its action. If no clear error was made, then the agency's action stands.

Arbitration   The settling of a dispute by submitting it to a disinterested third party (other than a court), who renders a decision. The decision may or may not be legally binding.

Arbitration clause   A clause in a contract that provides that, in the event of a dispute, the parties will submit the dispute to arbitration rather than litigate the dispute in court.

Arraignment   A procedure in which an accused person is brought before the court to plead to the criminal charge in the indictment or information. The charge is read to the person, and he or she is asked to enter a plea—such as "guilty" or "not guilty."

Arson   The malicious burning of another's dwelling. Some statutes have expanded this to include any real property regardless of ownership and the destruction of property by other means—for example, by explosion.

Articles of incorporation   The document filed with the appropriate governmental agency, usually the secretary of state, when a business is incorporated; state statutes usually prescribe what kind of information must be contained in the articles of incorporation.

Articles of organization   The document filed with a designated state official by which a limited liability company is formed.

Articles of partnership   A written agreement that sets forth each partner's rights and obligations with respect to the partnership.

Artisan's lien   A possessory lien given to a person who has made improvements and added value to another person's personal property as security for payment for services performed.

Assault   Any word or action intended to make another person fearful of immediate physical harm; a reasonably believable threat.

Assignee   The person to whom contract rights are assigned.

Assignment   The act of transferring to another all or part of one's rights arising under a contract.

Assignor   The person who assigns contract rights.

Assumption of risk   A defense against negligence that can be used when the plaintiff is aware of a danger and voluntarily assumes the risk of injury from that danger.

Attachment   In the context of judicial liens, a court-ordered seizure and taking into custody of property prior to the securing of a judgment for a past-due debt.

Attempted monopolization   Any actions by a firm to eliminate competition and gain monopoly power.

Authority   In agency law, the agent's permission to act on behalf of the principal. An agent's authority may be actual (express or implied) or apparent. *See also* Actual authority; Apparent authority

Authorized means   In contract law, the means of acceptance authorized by the offeror.

Automatic stay   In bankruptcy proceedings, the suspension of virtually all litigation and other action by creditors against the debtor or the debtor's property; the stay is effective the moment the debtor files a petition in bankruptcy.

Award   In the context of litigation, the amount of money awarded to a plaintiff in a civil lawsuit as damages. In the context of arbitration, the arbitrator's decision.

B

Bail   An amount of money set by the court that must be paid by a criminal defendant to the court before the defendant will be released from custody. Bail is set to assure that an individual accused of a crime will appear for further criminal proceedings. If the accused provides bail, whether in cash or in a surety bond, then he or she is released from jail.

Bailee One to whom goods are entrusted by a bailor. Under the Uniform Commercial Code, a party who, by a bill of lading, warehouse receipt, or other document of title, acknowledges possession of goods and contracts.

Bailee's lien A possessory lien, or claim, that a bailee entitled to compensation can place on the bailed property to ensure that he or she will be paid for the services provided. The lien is effective as long as the bailee retains possession of the bailed goods and has not agreed to extend credit to the bailor. Sometimes referred to as an artisan's lien.

Bailment A situation in which the personal property of one person (a bailor) is entrusted to another (a bailee), who is obligated to return the bailed property to the bailor or dispose of it as directed.

Bailor One who entrusts goods to a bailee.

Bait-and-switch advertising Advertising a product at a very attractive price (the "bait") and then informing the consumer, once he or she is in the store, that the advertised product is either not available or is of poor quality; the customer is then urged to purchase ("switched" to) a more expensive item.

Bankruptcy court A federal court of limited jurisdiction that handles only bankruptcy proceedings. Bankruptcy proceedings are governed by federal bankruptcy law.

Bargain A mutual undertaking, contract, or agreement between two parties; to negotiate over the terms of a purchase or contract.

Basis of the bargain In contract law, the affirmation of fact or promise on which the sale of goods is predicated, creating an express warranty.

Battery The unprivileged, intentional touching of another.

Beyond a reasonable doubt The standard used to determine the guilt or innocence of a person criminally charged. To be guilty of a crime, one must be proved guilty "beyond and to the exclusion of every reasonable doubt." A reasonable doubt is one that would cause a prudent person to hesitate before acting in matters important to him or her.

Bilateral contract A type of contract that arises when a promise is given in exchange for a return promise.

Bill of lading A document that serves both as evidence of the receipt of goods for shipment and as documentary evidence of title to the goods.

Bill of Rights The first ten amendments to the U.S. Constitution.

Binding authority Any source of law that a court must follow when deciding a case. Binding authorities include constitutions, statutes, and regulations that govern the issue being decided, as well as court decisions that are controlling precedents within the jurisdiction.

Blue laws State or local laws that prohibit the performance of certain types of commercial activities on Sunday.

Blue sky laws State laws that regulate the offer and sale of securities.

Bona fide Good faith. A bona fide obligation is one made in good faith—that is, sincerely and honestly.

Bona fide occupational qualification (BFOQ) Identifiable characteristics reasonably necessary to the normal operation of a particular business. These characteristics can include gender, national origin, and religion, but not race.

Bond A certificate that evidences a corporate (or government) debt. It is a security that involves no ownership interest in the issuing entity.

Bond indenture A contract between the issuer of a bond and the bondholder.

Bounty payment A reward (payment) given to a person or persons who perform a certain service—such as informing legal authorities of illegal actions.

Boycott A concerted refusal to do business with a particular person or entity in order to obtain concessions or to express displea-

sure with certain acts or practices of that person or business. *See also* Secondary boycott

Breach To violate a law, by an act or an omission, or to break a legal obligation that one owes to another person or to society.

Breach of contract The failure, without legal excuse, of a promisor to perform the obligations of a contract.

Bribery The offering, giving, receiving, or soliciting of anything of value with the aim of influencing an official action or an official's discharge of a legal or public duty or (with respect to commercial bribery) a business decision.

Brief A formal legal document submitted by the attorney for the appellant—or the appellee (in answer to the appellant's brief)—to an appellate court when a case is appealed. The appellant's brief outlines the facts and issues of the case, the judge's rulings or jury's findings that should be reversed or modified, the applicable law, and the arguments on the client's behalf.

Browse-wrap terms Terms and conditions of use that are presented to an Internet user at the time certain products, such as software, are being downloaded but that need not be agreed to (by clicking "I agree," for example) before being able to install or use the product.

Bulk transfer A bulk sale or transfer, not made in the ordinary course of business, of a major part of the materials, supplies, merchandise, or other inventory of an enterprise.

Bureaucracy A large organization that is structured hierarchically to carry out specific functions.

Burglary The unlawful entry into a building with the intent to commit a felony. (Some state statutes expand this to include the intent to commit any crime.)

Business ethics Ethics in a business context; a consensus of what constitutes right or wrong behavior in the world of business and the application of moral principles to situations that arise in a business setting.

Business invitees Those people, such as customers or clients, who are invited onto business premises by the owner of those premises for business purposes.

Business judgment rule A rule that immunizes corporate management from liability for actions that result in corporate losses or damages if the actions are undertaken in good faith and are within both the power of the corporation and the authority of management to make.

Business necessity A defense to allegations of employment discrimination in which the employer demonstrates that an employment practice that discriminates against members of a protected class is related to job performance.

Business plan A document describing a company, its products, and its anticipated future performance. Creating a business plan is normally the first step in obtaining loans or venture-capital funds for a new business enterprise.

Business tort The wrongful interference with the business rights of another.

Buyer in the ordinary course of business A buyer who, in good faith and without knowledge that the sale to him or her is in violation of the ownership rights or security interest of a third party in the goods, purchases goods in the ordinary course of business from a person in the business of selling goods of that kind.

Buyout price The amount payable to a partner on his or her dissociation from a partnership, based on the amount distributable to that partner if the firm were wound up on that date, and offset by any damages for wrongful dissociation.

Buy-sell agreement In the context of partnerships, an express agreement made at the time of partnership formation for one or more of the partners to buy out the other or others should the situation warrant—and thus provide for the smooth dissolution of the partnership.

Bylaws A set of governing rules adopted by a corporation or other association.

Bystander A spectator, witness, or person standing nearby when an event occurred and who did not engage in the business or act leading to the event.

C

C.I.F. or C.&F. Cost, insurance, and freight—or just cost and freight. A pricing term in a contract for the sale of goods requiring, among other things, that the seller place the goods in the possession of a carrier before risk passes to the buyer.

C.O.D. Cash on delivery. In sales transactions, a term meaning that the buyer will pay for the goods on delivery and before inspecting the goods.

Callable bond A bond that may be called in and the principal repaid at specified times or under conditions specified in the bond when it is issued.

Cancellation The act of nullifying, or making void. *See also* Rescission

Capital Accumulated goods, possessions, and assets used for the production of profits and wealth; the equity of owners in a business.

Carrier An individual or organization engaged in transporting passengers or goods for hire. *See also* Common carrier

Case law The rules of law announced in court decisions. Case law includes the aggregate of reported cases that interpret judicial precedents, statutes, regulations, and constitutional provisions.

Case on point A previous case involving factual circumstances and issues that are similar to the case before the court.

Categorical imperative A concept developed by the philosopher Immanuel Kant as an ethical guideline for behavior. In deciding whether an action is right or wrong, or desirable or undesirable, a person should evaluate the action in terms of what would happen if everybody else in the same situation, or category, acted the same way.

Causation in fact An act or omission without ("but for") which an event would not have occurred.

Cause of action A situation or state of facts that would entitle a party to sustain a legal action and give the party a right to seek a judicial remedy.

Cease-and-desist order An administrative or judicial order prohibiting a person or business firm from conducting activities that an agency or court has deemed illegal.

Certificate of incorporation The primary document that evidences corporate existence (referred to as articles of incorporation in some states).

Certificate of limited partnership The basic document filed with a designated state official by which a limited partnership is formed.

Certification mark A mark used by one or more persons, other than the owner, to certify the region, materials, mode of manufacture, quality, or accuracy of the owner's goods or services. When used by members of a cooperative, association, or other organization, such a mark is referred to as a collective mark. Examples of certification marks include the "Good Housekeeping Seal of Approval" and "UL Tested."

Certiorari *See* Writ of *certiorari*

Chain-style business franchise A franchise that operates under a franchisor's trade name and that is identified as a member of a select group of dealers that engage in the franchisor's business. The franchisee is generally required to follow standardized or prescribed methods of operation. Examples of this type of franchise are McDonald's and most other fast-food chains.

Chancellor An adviser to the king at the time of the early king's courts of England. Individuals petitioned the king for relief when they could not obtain an adequate remedy in a court of law, and these petitions were decided by the chancellor.

Charging order In partnership law, an order granted by a court to a judgment creditor that entitles the creditor to attach profits or assets of a partner on dissolution of the partnership.

Charter *See* Corporate charter

Chattel All forms of personal property.

Chattel paper Any writing or writings that show both a debt and the fact that the debt is secured by personal property. In many instances, chattel paper consists of a negotiable instrument coupled with a security agreement.

Checks and balances The national government is composed of three separate branches: the executive, the legislative, and the judicial branches. Each branch of the government exercises a check on the actions of the others.

Citation A reference to a publication in which a legal authority—such as a statute or a court decision—or other source can be found.

Civil law The branch of law dealing with the definition and enforcement of all private or public rights, as opposed to criminal matters.

Civil law system A system of law derived from that of the Roman Empire and based on a code rather than case law; the predominant system of law in the nations of continental Europe and the nations that were once their colonies. In the United States, Louisiana is the only state that has a civil law system.

Claim As a verb, to demand. As a noun, a right to payment.

Click-on agreement An agreement that arises when a buyer, engaging in a transaction on a computer, indicates his or her assent to be bound by the terms of an offer by clicking on a button that says, for example, "I agree"; sometimes referred to as a *click-on license* or a *click-wrap agreement.*

Close corporation A corporation whose shareholders are limited to a small group of persons, often including only family members. The rights of shareholders of a close corporation usually are restricted regarding the transfer of shares to others.

Closed shop A firm that requires union membership by its workers as a condition of employment. The closed shop was made illegal by the Labor-Management Relations Act of 1947.

Closing argument An argument made after the plaintiff and defendant have rested their cases. Closing arguments are made prior to the jury charges.

Collateral promise A secondary promise that is ancillary (subsidiary) to a principal transaction or primary contractual relationship, such as a promise made by one person to pay the debts of another if the latter fails to perform. A collateral promise normally must be in writing to be enforceable.

Collective bargaining The process by which labor and management negotiate the terms and conditions of employment, including working hours and workplace conditions.

Collective mark A mark used by members of a cooperative, association, or other organization to certify the region, materials, mode of manufacture, quality, or accuracy of the specific goods or services. Examples of collective marks include the labor union marks found on tags of certain products and the credits of movies, which indicate the various associations and organizations that participated in the making of the movies.

Comity A deference by which one nation gives effect to the laws and judicial decrees of another nation. This recognition is based primarily on respect.

Comment period A period of time following an administrative agency's publication or a notice of a proposed rule during which private parties may comment in writing on the agency proposal in an effort to influence agency policy. The agency takes any comments received into consideration when drafting the final version of the regulation.

Commerce clause The provision in Article I, Section 8, of the U.S. Constitution that gives Congress the power to regulate interstate commerce.

Commercial impracticability A doctrine under which a seller may be excused from performing a contract when (1) a contingency occurs, (2) the contingency's occurrence makes performance impracticable, and (3) the nonoccurrence of the contingency was a basic assumption on which the contract was made. Despite the fact that UCC 2–615 expressly frees only sellers under this doctrine, courts have not distinguished between buyers and sellers in applying it.

Commingle To mix together. To put funds or goods together into one mass so that the funds or goods are so mixed that they no longer have separate identities. In corporate law, if personal and corporate interests are commingled to the extent that the corporation has no separate identity, a court may "pierce the corporate veil" and expose the shareholders to personal liability.

Common carrier A carrier that holds itself out or undertakes to carry persons or goods of all persons indifferently, or of all who choose to employ it.

Common law That body of law developed from custom or judicial decisions in English and U.S. courts, not attributable to a legislature.

Common stock Shares of ownership in a corporation that give the owner of the stock a proportionate interest in the corporation with regard to control, earnings, and net assets; shares of common stock are lowest in priority with respect to payment of dividends and distribution of the corporation's assets on dissolution.

Community property A form of concurrent ownership of property in which each spouse technically owns an undivided one-half interest in property acquired during the marriage. This form of joint ownership occurs in only nine states and Puerto Rico.

Comparative law The study and comparison of legal systems and laws across nations.

Comparative negligence A theory in tort law under which the liability for injuries resulting from negligent acts is shared by all parties who were negligent (including the injured party), on the basis of each person's proportionate negligence.

Compensatory damages A money award equivalent to the actual value of injuries or damages sustained by the aggrieved party.

Complaint The pleading made by a plaintiff alleging wrongdoing on the part of the defendant; the document that, when filed with a court, initiates a lawsuit.

Complete performance Performance of a contract strictly in accordance with the contract's terms.

Composition agreement See Creditors' composition agreement

Computer crime Any wrongful act that is directed against computers and computer parties, or wrongful use or abuse of computers or software.

Concentrated industry An industry in which a large percentage of market sales is controlled by either a single firm or a small number of firms.

Conciliation A form of alternative dispute resolution in which the parties reach an agreement themselves with the help of a neutral third party, called a conciliator, who facilitates the negotiations.

Concurrent jurisdiction Jurisdiction that exists when two different courts have the power to hear a case. For example, some cases can be heard in either a federal or a state court.

Concurrent ownership Joint ownership.

Concurring opinion A written opinion outlining the views of a judge or justice to make or emphasize a point that was not made or emphasized in the majority opinion.

Condition A qualification, provision, or clause in a contractual agreement, the occurrence of which creates, suspends, or terminates the obligations of the contracting parties.

Confession of judgment The act of a debtor in permitting a judgment to be entered against him or her by a creditor, for an agreed sum, without the institution of legal proceedings.

Confiscation A government's taking of privately owned business or personal property without a proper public purpose or an award of just compensation.

Conforming goods Goods that conform to contract specifications.

Confusion The mixing together of goods belonging to two or more owners so that the separately owned goods cannot be identified.

Conglomerate merger A merger between firms that do not compete with each other because they are in different markets (as opposed to horizontal and vertical mergers).

Consent Voluntary agreement to a proposition or an act of another. A concurrence of wills.

Consequential damages Special damages that compensate for a loss that is not direct or immediate (for example, lost profits). The special damages must have been reasonably foreseeable at the time the breach or injury occurred in order for the plaintiff to collect them.

Consideration Generally, the value given in return for a promise. The consideration, which must be present to make the contract legally binding, must be something of legally sufficient value and bargained for and must result in a detriment to the promisee or a benefit to the promisor.

Consignee One to whom goods are delivered on consignment. See also Consignment

Consignment A transaction in which an owner of goods (the consignor) delivers the goods to another (the consignee) for the consignee to sell. The consignee pays the consignor for the goods when they are sold by the consignee.

Consignor One who consigns goods to another. See also Consignment

Consolidation A contractual and statutory process in which two or more corporations join to become a completely new corporation. The original corporations cease to exist, and the new corporation acquires all their assets and liabilities.

Constitutional law Law that is based on the U.S. Constitution and the constitutions of the various states.

Constructive delivery An act equivalent to the actual, physical delivery of property that cannot be physically delivered because of difficulty or impossibility; for example, the transfer of a key to a safe constructively delivers the contents of the safe.

Constructive discharge A termination of employment brought about by making an employee's working conditions so intolerable that the employee reasonably feels compelled to leave.

Constructive eviction A form of eviction that occurs when a landlord fails to perform adequately any of the undertakings (such as providing heat in the winter) required by the lease, thereby making the tenant's further use and enjoyment of the property exceedingly difficult or impossible.

Consumer credit Credit extended primarily for personal or household use.

Consumer goods Goods that are primarily for personal or household use.

Consumer law The body of statutes, agency rules, and judicial decisions protecting consumers of goods and services from dangerous manufacturing techniques, mislabeling, unfair credit practices, deceptive advertising, and so on. Consumer laws provide remedies and protections that are not ordinarily available to merchants or to businesses.

Contingency fee An attorney's fee that is based on a percentage of the final award received by his or her client as a result of litigation.

Contract An agreement that can be enforced in court; formed by two or more parties, each of whom agrees to perform or to refrain from performing some act now or in the future.

Contract implied in law See Quasi contract

Contract under seal A formal agreement in which the seal is a substitute for consideration. A court will not invalidate a contract under seal for lack of consideration.

Contractual agreement See Contract

Contractual capacity The threshold mental capacity required by the law for a party who enters into a contract to be bound by that contract.

Contribution See Right of contribution

Contributory negligence A theory in tort law under which a complaining party's own negligence contributed to or caused his or her injuries. Contributory negligence is an absolute bar to recovery in a minority of jurisdictions.

Conversion   The wrongful taking, using, or retaining possession of personal property that belongs to another.

Convertible bond   A bond that can be exchanged for a specified number of shares of common stock under certain conditions.

Conveyance   The transfer of a title to land from one person to another by deed; a document (such as a deed) by which an interest in land is transferred from one person to another.

Conviction   The outcome of a criminal trial in which the defendant has been found guilty of the crime with which he or she was charged and on which sentencing, or punishment, is based.

Co-ownership   Joint ownership.

Copyright   The exclusive right of authors to publish, print, or sell an intellectual production for a statutory period of time. A copyright has the same monopolistic nature as a patent or trademark, but it differs in that it applies exclusively to works of art, literature, and other works of authorship, including computer programs.

Corporate charter   The document issued by a state agency or authority (usually the secretary of state) that grants a corporation legal existence and the right to function.

Corporate governance   The system by which corporations are directed and controlled and which governs the relationship of the corporation to its shareholders. The corporate governance structure specifies the distribution of rights and responsibilities among different groups within the corporation and spells out the rules and procedures for making corporate decisions.

Corporation   A legal entity formed in compliance with statutory requirements. The entity is distinct from its shareholders-owners.

Cosign   The act of signing a document (such as a note promising to pay another in return for a loan or other benefit) jointly with another person and thereby assuming liability for performing what was promised in the document.

Cost-benefit analysis   A decision-making technique that involves weighing the costs of a given action against the benefits of the action.

Co-surety   A joint surety. One who assumes liability jointly with another surety for the payment of an obligation.

Counteradvertising   New advertising that is undertaken pursuant to a Federal Trade Commission order for the purpose of correcting earlier false claims that were made about a product.

Counterclaim   A claim made by a defendant in a civil lawsuit that in effect sues the plaintiff.

Counteroffer   An offeree's response to an offer in which the offeree rejects the original offer and at the same time makes a new offer.

Course of dealing   Prior conduct between parties to a contract that establishes a common basis for their understanding.

Course of performance   The conduct that occurs under the terms of a particular agreement; such conduct indicates what the parties to an agreement intended it to mean.

Court of equity   A court that decides controversies and administers justice according to the rules, principles, and precedents of equity.

Court of law   A court in which the only remedies that could be granted were things of value, such as money damages. In the early English king's courts, courts of law were distinct from courts of equity.

Covenant not to compete   A contractual promise to refrain from competing with another party for a certain period of time (not excessive in duration) and within a reasonable geographic area. Although covenants not to compete restrain trade, they are commonly found in partnership agreements, business sale agreements, and employment contracts. If they are ancillary to such agreements, covenants not to compete will normally be enforced by the courts unless the time period or geographic area is deemed unreasonable.

Covenant not to sue   An agreement to substitute a contractual obligation for some other type of legal action based on a valid claim.

Covenant of quiet enjoyment   A promise by a grantor (or landlord) that the grantee (or tenant) will not be evicted or disturbed by the grantor or a person having a lien or superior title.

Covenant running with the land   An executory promise made between a grantor and a grantee to which they and subsequent owners of the land are bound.

Cover   Under the Uniform Commercial Code, a remedy of the buyer or lessee that allows the buyer or lessee, on the seller's or lessor's breach, to purchase the goods from another seller or lessor and substitute them for the goods due under the contract. If the cost of cover exceeds the cost of the contract goods, the breaching seller or lessor will be liable to the buyer or lessee for the difference. In obtaining cover, the buyer or lessee must act in good faith and without unreasonable delay.

Cram-down provision   A provision of the Bankruptcy Code that allows a court to confirm a debtor's Chapter 11 reorganization plan even though only one class of creditors has accepted it. To exercise the court's right under this provision, the court must demonstrate that the plan does not discriminate unfairly against any creditors and is fair and equitable.

Crashworthiness doctrine   A doctrine that imposes liability for defects in the design or construction of motor vehicles that increase the extent of injuries to passengers if an accident occurs. The doctrine holds even when the defects do not actually cause the accident.

Creditor   A person to whom a debt is owed by another person (the debtor).

Creditor beneficiary   A third party beneficiary who has rights in a contract made by the debtor and a third person. The terms of the contract obligate the third person to pay the debt owed to the creditor. The creditor beneficiary can enforce the debt against either party.

Creditors' composition agreement   An agreement formed between a debtor and his or her creditors in which the creditors agree to accept a lesser sum than that owed by the debtor in full satisfaction of the debt.

Crime   A wrong against society proclaimed in a statute and, if committed, punishable by society through fines and/or imprisonment—and, in some cases, death.

Criminal act   *See Actus reus*

Criminal intent   *See Mens rea*

Criminal law   Law that defines and governs actions that constitute crimes. Generally, criminal law has to do with wrongful actions committed against society for which society demands redress.

Cross-border pollution   Pollution across national boundaries; air and water degradation in one nation resulting from pollution-causing activities in a neighboring country.

Cross-examination   The questioning of an opposing witness during a trial.

Cumulative voting   A method of shareholder voting designed to allow minority shareholders to be represented on the board of directors. With cumulative voting, the number of members of the board to be elected is multiplied by the total number of voting shares held. The result equals the number of votes a shareholder has, and this total can be cast for one or more nominees for director.

Cure   Under the Uniform Commercial Code, the right of a party who tenders nonconforming performance to correct his or her performance within the contract period.

Cyber crime   A crime that occurs online, in the virtual community of the Internet, as opposed to the physical world.

Cyber hate speech   Extreme hate speech on the Internet. Racist materials and Holocaust denials disseminated on the Web are examples.

Cyber mark   A trademark in cyberspace.

Cyber tort   A tort committed in cyberspace.

Cyberlaw   An informal term used to refer to all laws governing electronic communications and transactions, particularly those conducted via the Internet.

Cybersquatting The act of registering a domain name that is the same as, or confusingly similar to, the trademark of another and then offering to sell that domain name back to the trademark owner.

Cyberstalker A person who commits the crime of stalking in cyberspace. Generally, stalking consists of harassing a person and putting that person in reasonable fear for his or her safety or the safety of the person's immediate family.

Cyberterrorist A hacker whose purpose is to exploit a target computer for a serious impact, such as the corruption of a program to sabotage a business.

D

Damages Money sought as a remedy for a breach of contract or for a tortious act.

De novo Anew; afresh; a second time. In a hearing de novo, an appellate court hears the case as a court of original jurisdiction—that is, as if the case had not previously been tried and a decision rendered.

Debenture bond A bond for which no specific assets of the corporation are pledged as backing; rather, the bond is backed by the general credit rating of the corporation, plus any assets that can be seized if the corporation allows the debentures to go into default.

Debit card A plastic card issued by a financial institution that allows the user to access his or her accounts online via automated teller machines.

Debtor in possession (DIP) In Chapter 11 bankruptcy proceedings, a debtor who is allowed to continue in possession of the estate in property (the business) and to continue business operations.

Declaratory judgment A court's judgment on a justiciable controversy when the plaintiff is in doubt as to his or her legal rights; a binding adjudication of the rights and status of litigants even though no consequential relief is awarded.

Decree The judgment of a court of equity.

Deed A document by which title to property (usually real property) is passed.

Defalcation The misuse of funds.

Defamation Any published or publicly spoken false statement that causes injury to another's good name, reputation, or character.

Default The failure to observe a promise or discharge an obligation. The term is commonly used to mean the failure to pay a debt when it is due.

Default judgment A judgment entered by a court against a defendant who has failed to appear in court to answer or defend against the plaintiff's claim.

Defendant One against whom a lawsuit is brought; the accused person in a criminal proceeding.

Defense That which a defendant offers and alleges in an action or suit as a reason why the plaintiff should not recover or establish what he or she seeks.

Deficiency judgment A judgment against a debtor for the amount of a debt remaining unpaid after collateral has been repossessed and sold.

Delegatee One to whom contract duties are delegated by another, called the delegator.

Delegation The transfer of a contractual duty to a third party. The party delegating the duty (the delegator) to the third party (the delegatee) is still obliged to perform on the contract should the delegatee fail to perform.

Delegation doctrine A doctrine based on Article I, Section 8, of the U.S. Constitution, which has been construed to allow Congress to delegate some of its power to make and implement laws to administrative agencies. The delegation is considered to be proper as long as Congress sets standards outlining the scope of the agency's authority.

Delegator One who delegates his or her duties under a contract to another, called the delegatee.

Delivery In contract law, the one party's act of placing the subject matter of the contract within the other party's possession or control.

Delivery ex ship Delivery from the carrying ship. A contract term indicating that risk of loss will not pass to the buyer until the goods leave the ship or are otherwise properly unloaded.

Delivery order A written order to deliver goods directed to a warehouser, carrier, or other person who, in the ordinary course of business, issues warehouse receipts or bills of lading [UCC 7–102(1)(d)].

Demurrer See Motion to dismiss

Deposition The testimony of a party to a lawsuit or a witness taken under oath before a trial.

Destination contract A contract for the sale of goods in which the seller is required or authorized to ship the goods by carrier and deliver them at a particular destination. The seller assumes liability for any losses or damage to the goods until they are tendered at the destination specified in the contract.

Digital cash Funds stored on microchips and other computer devices.

Dilution With respect to trademarks, a doctrine under which distinctive or famous trademarks are protected from certain unauthorized uses of the marks regardless of a showing of competition or a likelihood of confusion. Congress created a federal cause of action for dilution in 1995 with the passage of the Federal Trademark Dilution Act.

Direct examination The examination of a witness by the attorney who calls the witness to the stand to testify on behalf of the attorney's client.

Directed verdict See Motion for a directed verdict

Disaffirmance The legal avoidance, or setting aside, of a contractual obligation.

Discharge The termination of an obligation. (1) In contract law, discharge occurs when the parties have fully performed their contractual obligations or when events, conduct of the parties, or operation of the law releases the parties from performance. (2) In bankruptcy proceedings, the extinction of the debtor's dischargeable debts.

Discharge in bankruptcy The release of a debtor from all debts that are provable, except those specifically excepted from discharge by statute.

Disclosed principal A principal whose identity is known to a third party at the time the agent makes a contract with the third party.

Discovery A phase in the litigation process during which the opposing parties may obtain information from each other and from third parties prior to trial.

Disparagement of property An economically injurious falsehood made about another's product or property. A general term for torts that are more specifically referred to as slander of quality or slander of title.

Disparate-impact discrimination A form of employment discrimination that results from certain employer practices or procedures that, although not discriminatory on their face, have a discriminatory effect.

Disparate-treatment discrimination A form of employment discrimination that results when an employer intentionally discriminates against employees who are members of protected classes.

Dissenting opinion A written opinion by a judge or justice who disagrees with the majority opinion.

Dissociation Occurs when a partner ceases to be associated in the carrying on of the partnership business. The severance of the relationship between a partner and a partnership.

Dissolution The formal disbanding of a partnership or a corporation. It can take place by (1) acts of the partners or, in a corporation, of the shareholders and board of directors; (2) the death of a partner; (3) the expiration of a time period stated in a partnership agreement or a certificate of incorporation; or (4) judicial decree.

Distributed network A network that can be used by persons located (distributed) around the country or the globe to share computer files.

Distribution agreement A contract between a seller and a distributor of the seller's products setting out the terms and conditions of the distributorship.

Distributorship A business arrangement that is established when a manufacturer licenses a dealer to sell its product. An example of a distributorship is an automobile dealership.

Diversity of citizenship Under Article III, Section 2, of the Constitution, a basis for federal court jurisdiction over a lawsuit between (1) citizens of different states, (2) a foreign country and citizens of a state or of different states, or (3) citizens of a state and citizens or subjects of a foreign country. The amount in controversy must be more than $75,000 before a federal court can take jurisdiction in such cases.

Divestiture The act of selling one or more of a company's parts, such as a subsidiary or plant; often mandated by the courts in merger or monopolization cases.

Dividend A distribution to corporate shareholders of corporate profits or income, disbursed in proportion to the number of shares held.

Docket The list of cases entered on a court's calendar and thus scheduled to be heard by the court.

Document of title Paper exchanged in the regular course of business that evidences the right to possession of goods (for example, a bill of lading or a warehouse receipt).

Domain name The series of letters and symbols used to identify site operators on the Internet; Internet "addresses."

Domestic corporation In a given state, a corporation that does business in, and is organized under the law of, that state.

Domestic relations court A court that deals with domestic (household) relationships, such as adoption, divorce, support payments, child custody, and the like.

Donee beneficiary A third party beneficiary who has rights under a contract as a direct result of the intention of the contract parties to make a gift to the third party.

Double jeopardy A situation occurring when a person is tried twice for the same criminal offense; prohibited by the Fifth Amendment to the Constitution.

Double taxation A feature (and disadvantage) of the corporate form of business. Because a corporation is a separate legal entity, corporate profits are taxed by state and federal governments. Dividends are again taxable as ordinary income to the shareholders receiving them.

Dram shop act A state statute that imposes liability on the owners of bars and taverns, as well as those who serve alcoholic drinks to the public, for injuries resulting from accidents caused by intoxicated persons when the sellers or servers of alcoholic drinks contributed to the intoxication.

Due process clause The provisions of the Fifth and Fourteenth Amendments to the Constitution that guarantee that no person shall be deprived of life, liberty, or property without due process of law. Similar clauses are found in most state constitutions.

Dumping The selling of goods in a foreign country at a price below the price charged for the same goods in the domestic market.

Durable power of attorney A document that authorizes a person to act on behalf of an incompetent person—write checks, collect insurance proceeds, and otherwise manage the disabled person's affairs, including health care—when he or she becomes incapacitated. Spouses often give each other durable power of attorney and, if they are advanced in age, may give a second such power of attorney to an older child.

Duress Unlawful pressure brought to bear on a person, causing the person to perform an act that he or she would not otherwise perform.

Duty of care The duty of all persons, as established by tort law, to exercise a reasonable amount of care in their dealings with others. Failure to exercise due care, which is normally determined by the "reasonable person standard," constitutes the tort of negligence.

E

E-agent A computer program, electronic, or other automated means used to perform specific tasks without review by an individual.

Early neutral case evaluation A form of alternative dispute resolution in which a neutral third party evaluates the strengths and weakness of the disputing parties' positions; the evaluator's opinion forms the basis for negotiating a settlement.

Easement A nonpossessory right to use another's property in a manner established by either express or implied agreement.

E-commerce Business transacted in cyberspace.

E-contract A contract that is entered into in cyberspace and is evidenced only by electronic impulses (such as those that make up a computer's memory), rather than, for example, a typewritten form.

E-evidence A type of evidence that consists of computer-generated or electronically recorded information, including e-mail, voice mail, spreadsheets, word processing documents, and other data.

Emancipation In regard to minors, the act of being freed from parental control; occurs when a child's parent or legal guardian relinquishes the legal right to exercise control over the child. Normally, a minor who leaves home to support himself or herself is considered emancipated.

Embezzlement The fraudulent appropriation of money or other property by a person to whom the money or property has been entrusted.

Eminent domain The power of a government to take land for public use from private citizens for just compensation.

E-money Prepaid funds recorded on a computer or a card (such as a *smart card*).

Employee A person who works for an employer for a salary or for wages.

Employer An individual or business entity that hires employees, pays them salaries or wages, and exercises control over their work.

Employment at will A common law doctrine under which either party may terminate an employment relationship at any time for any reason, unless a contract specifies otherwise.

Employment discrimination Treating employees or job applicants unequally on the basis of race, color, national origin, religion, gender, age, or disability; prohibited by federal statutes.

Enabling legislation A statute enacted by Congress that authorizes the creation of an administrative agency and specifies the name, composition, purpose, and powers of the agency being created.

Encryption The process by which a message (plaintext) is transformed into something (ciphertext) that the sender and receiver intend third parties not to understand.

Entrapment In criminal law, a defense in which the defendant claims that he or she was induced by a public official—usually an undercover agent or police officer—to commit a crime that he or she would otherwise not have committed.

Entrustment The transfer of goods to a merchant who deals in goods of that kind and who may transfer those goods and all rights to them to a buyer in the ordinary course of business [UCC 2–403(2)].

Environmental impact statement (EIS) A statement required by the National Environmental Policy Act for any major federal action that will significantly affect the quality of the environment. The statement must analyze the action's impact on the environment and explore alternative actions that might be taken.

Environmental law The body of statutory, regulatory, and common law relating to the protection of the environment.

Equal dignity rule In most states, a rule stating that express authority given to an agent must be in writing if the contract to be made on behalf of the principal is required to be in writing.

Equal protection clause The provision in the Fourteenth Amendment to the Constitution that guarantees that no state will "deny to any person within its jurisdiction the equal protection of the laws." This clause mandates that state governments treat similarly situated individuals in a similar manner.

Equitable maxims General propositions or principles of law that have to do with fairness (equity).

Equity of redemption The right of a mortgagor who has breached the mortgage agreement to redeem or purchase the property prior to foreclosure proceedings.

E-signature   As defined by the Uniform Electronic Transactions Act, "an electronic sound, symbol, or process attached to or logically associated with a record and executed or adopted by a person with the intent to sign the record."

Establishment clause   The provision in the First Amendment to the U.S. Constitution that prohibits Congress from creating any law "respecting an establishment of religion."

Estop   To bar, impede, or preclude.

Estoppel   The principle that a party's own acts prevent him or her from claiming a right to the detriment of another who was entitled to and did rely on those acts. *See also* Agency by estoppel; Promissory estoppel

Estray statute   A statute defining finders' rights in property when the true owners are unknown.

Ethical reasoning   A reasoning process in which an individual links his or her moral convictions or ethical standards to the particular situation at hand.

Ethics   Moral principles and values applied to social behavior.

Evidence   Proof offered at trial—in the form of testimony, documents, records, exhibits, objects, and so on—for the purpose of convincing the court or jury of the truth of a contention.

Ex parte contact   Communications with an administrative agency that are not placed in the record.

Ex ship   *See* Delivery ex ship

Exclusionary rule   In criminal procedure, a rule under which any evidence that is obtained in violation of the accused's constitutional rights guaranteed by the Fourth, Fifth, and Sixth Amendments, as well as any evidence derived from illegally obtained evidence, will not be admissible in court.

Exclusive distributorship   A distributorship in which the seller and the distributor of the seller's products agree that the distributor has the exclusive right to distribute the seller's products in a certain geographic area.

Exclusive jurisdiction   Jurisdiction that exists when a case can be heard only in a particular court or type of court, such as a federal court or a state court.

Exclusive-dealing contract   An agreement under which a seller forbids a buyer to purchase products from the seller's competitors.

Exculpatory clause   A clause that releases a contractual party from liability in the event of monetary or physical injury, no matter who is at fault.

Executed contract   A contract that has been completely performed by both parties.

Execution   An action to carry into effect the directions in a court decree or judgment.

Executive agency   An administrative agency within the executive branch of government. At the federal level, executive agencies are those within the cabinet departments.

Executor   A person appointed by a testator to see that his or her will is administered appropriately.

Executory contract   A contract that has not as yet been fully performed.

Export   To sell products to buyers located in other countries.

Express authority   Authority expressly given by one party to another. In agency law, an agent has express authority to act for a principal if both parties agree, orally or in writing, that an agency relationship exists in which the agent had the power (authority) to act in the place of, and on behalf of, the principal.

Express contract   A contract in which the terms of the agreement are fully and explicitly stated in words, oral or written.

Express warranty   A seller's or lessor's oral or written promise, ancillary to an underlying sales or lease agreement, as to the quality, description, or performance of the goods being sold or leased.

Expropriation   The seizure by a government of privately owned business or personal property for a proper public purpose and with just compensation.

F

F.A.S.   Free alongside. A contract term that requires the seller, at his or her own expense and risk, to deliver the goods alongside the ship before risk passes to the buyer.

F.O.B.   Free on board. A contract term that indicates that the selling price of the goods includes transportation costs (and that the seller carries the risk of loss) to the specific F.O.B. place named in the contract. The place can be either the place of initial shipment (for example, the seller's city or place of business) or the place of destination (for example, the buyer's city or place of business).

Family limited liability partnership (FLLP)   A limited liability partnership (LLP) in which the majority of the partners are persons related to each other, essentially as spouses, parents, grandparents, siblings, cousins, nephews, or nieces. A person acting in a fiduciary capacity for persons so related could also be a partner. All of the partners must be natural persons or persons acting in a fiduciary capacity for the benefit of natural persons.

Federal form of government   A system of government in which the states form a union and the sovereign power is divided between a central government and the member states.

Federal question   A question that pertains to the U.S. Constitution, acts of Congress, or treaties. A federal question provides a basis for federal jurisdiction.

Federal Rules of Civil Procedure (FRCP)   The rules controlling procedural matters in civil trials brought before the federal district courts.

Federal system   A system of government in which power is divided by a written constitution between a central government and regional, or subdivisional, governments. Each level must have some domain in which its policies are dominant and some genuine political or constitutional guarantee of its authority.

Fee simple   An absolute form of property ownership entitling the property owner to use, possess, or dispose of the property as he or she chooses during his or her lifetime. On death, the interest in the property descends to the owner's heirs; a fee simple absolute.

Fee simple absolute   An ownership interest in land in which the owner has the greatest possible aggregation of rights, privileges, and power. Ownership in fee simple absolute is limited absolutely to a person and his or her heirs.

Fellow-servant doctrine   A doctrine that bars an employee from suing his or her employer for injuries caused by a fellow employee.

Felony   A crime—such as arson, murder, rape, or robbery—that carries the most severe sanctions, usually ranging from one year in a state or federal prison to the forfeiture of one's life.

Fiduciary   As a noun, a person having a duty created by his or her undertaking to act primarily for another's benefit in matters connected with the undertaking. As an adjective, a relationship founded on trust and confidence.

Fiduciary duty   The duty, imposed on a fiduciary by virtue of his or her position, to act primarily for another's benefit.

Filtering software   A computer program that includes a pattern through which data are passed. When designed to block access to certain Web sites, the pattern blocks the retrieval of a site whose URL or key words are on a list within the program.

Final order   The final decision of an administrative agency on an issue. If no appeal is taken, or if the case is not reviewed or considered anew by the agency commission, the administrative law judge's initial order becomes the final order of the agency.

Firm offer   An offer (by a merchant) that is irrevocable without consideration for a period of time (not longer than three months). A firm offer by a merchant must be in writing and must be signed by the offeror.

Fitness for a particular purpose   *See* Implied warranty of fitness for a particular purpose

Fixture   A thing that was once personal property but that has become attached to real property in such a way that it takes on the characteristics of real property and becomes part of that real property.

Flame   An online message in which one party attacks another in harsh, often personal, terms.

Forbearance   The act of refraining from an action that one has a legal right to undertake.

Force majeure (pronounced mah-*zhure*) **clause**   A provision in a contract stipulating that certain unforeseen events—such as war, political upheavals, acts of God, or other events—will excuse a party from liability for nonperformance of contractual obligations.

Foreclosure   A proceeding in which a mortgagee either takes title to or forces the sale of the mortgagor's property in satisfaction of a debt.

Foreign corporation   In a given state, a corporation that does business in the state without being incorporated therein.

Foreseeable risk   In negligence law, the risk of harm or injury to another that a person of ordinary intelligence and prudence should have reasonably anticipated or foreseen when undertaking an action or refraining from undertaking an action.

Forgery   The fraudulent making or altering of any writing in a way that changes the legal rights and liabilities of another.

Formal contract   A contract that by law requires a specific form, such as being executed under seal, to be valid.

Forum   A jurisdiction, court, or place in which disputes are litigated and legal remedies are sought.

Forum-selection clause   A provision in a contract designating the court, jurisdiction, or tribunal that will decide any disputes arising under the contract.

Franchise   Any arrangement in which the owner of a trademark, trade name, or copyright licenses another to use that trademark, trade name, or copyright, under specified conditions or limitations, in the selling of goods and services.

Franchisee   One receiving a license to use another's (the franchisor's) trademark, trade name, or copyright in the sale of goods and services.

Franchisor   One licensing another (the franchisee) to use his or her trademark, trade name, or copyright in the sale of goods or services.

Fraud   Any misrepresentation, either by misstatement or omission of a material fact, knowingly made with the intention of deceiving another and on which a reasonable person would and does rely to his or her detriment.

Fraud in the execution   In the law of negotiable instruments, a type of fraud that occurs when a person is deceived into signing a negotiable instrument, believing that he or she is signing something else (such as a receipt); also called *fraud in the inception*. Fraud in the execution is a universal defense to payment on a negotiable instrument.

Fraud in the inducement   Ordinary fraud. In the law of negotiable instruments, fraud in the inducement occurs when a person issues a negotiable instrument based on false statements by the other party. The issuing party will be able to avoid payment on that instrument unless the holder is a holder in due course; in other words, fraud in the inducement is a personal defense to payment on a negotiable instrument.

Fraudulent misrepresentation (fraud)   Any misrepresentation, either by misstatement or omission of a material fact, knowingly made with the intention of deceiving another and on which a reasonable person would and does rely to his or her detriment.

Free exercise clause   The provision in the First Amendment to the U.S. Constitution that prohibits Congress from making any law "prohibiting the free exercise" of religion.

Frustration of purpose   A court-created doctrine under which a party to a contract will be relieved of his or her duty to perform when the objective purpose for performance no longer exists (due to reasons beyond that party's control).

Full faith and credit clause   A clause in Article IV, Section 1, of the Constitution that provides that "Full Faith and Credit shall be given in each State to the public Acts, Records, and Judicial Proceedings of every othere States." The clause ensures that rights established under deeds, wills, contracts, and the like in one state will be honored by the other states and that any judicial decision with respect to such property rights will be honored and enforced in all states.

Full warranty   A warranty as to full performance covering generally both labor and materials.

Fungible goods   Goods that are alike by physical nature, by agreement, or by trade usage. Examples of fungible goods are wheat, oil, and wine that are identical in type and quality.

G

Garnishment   A legal process used by a creditor to collect a debt by seizing property of the debtor (such as wages) that is being held by a third party (such as the debtor's employer).

General jurisdiction   Exists when a court's subject-matter jurisdiction is not restricted. A court of general jurisdiction normally can hear any type of case.

General partner   In a limited partnership, a partner who assumes responsibility for the management of the partnership and liability for all partnership debts.

General partnership   *See* Partnership

Genuineness of assent   Knowing and voluntary assent to the terms of a contract. If a contract is formed as a result of a mistake, misrepresentation, undue influence, or duress, genuineness of assent is lacking, and the contract will be voidable.

Good faith   Under the Uniform Commercial Code, good faith means honesty in fact; with regard to merchants, good faith means honesty in fact *and* the observance of reasonable commercial standards of fair dealing in the trade.

Good faith purchaser   A purchaser who buys without notice of any circumstance that would put a person of ordinary prudence on inquiry as to whether the seller has valid title to the goods being sold.

Good Samaritan statute   A state statute that provides that persons who rescue or provide emergency services to others in peril—unless they do so recklessly, thus causing further harm—cannot be sued for negligence.

Grand jury   A group of citizens called to decide, after hearing the state's evidence, whether a reasonable basis (probable cause) exists for believing that a crime has been committed and whether a trial ought to be held.

Grant deed   A deed that simply recites words of consideration and conveyance. Under statute, a grant deed may impliedly warrant that at least the grantor has not conveyed the property's title to someone else.

Grantee   One to whom a grant (of land or property, for example) is made.

Grantor   A person who makes a grant, such as a transferor of property or the creator of a trust.

Group boycott   The refusal to deal with a particular person or firm by a group of competitors; prohibited by the Sherman Act.

Guarantor   A person who agrees to satisfy the debt of another (the debtor) only after the principal debtor defaults; a guarantor's liability is thus secondary.

H

Habitability   *See* Implied warranty of habitability

Hacker   A person who uses one computer to break into another. Professional computer programmers refer to such persons as "crackers."

Hearsay   An oral or written statement made out of court that is later offered in court by a witness (not the person who made the statement) to prove the truth of the matter asserted in the statement. Hearsay is generally inadmissible as evidence.

Hirfindahl-Hirschman Index (HHI) An index of market power used to calculate whether a merger of two businesses will result in sufficient monopoly power to violate antitrust laws.

Historical school A school of legal thought that emphasizes the evolutionary process of law and that looks to the past to discover what the principles of contemporary law should be.

Homestead exemption A law permitting a debtor to retain the family home, either in its entirety or up to a specified dollar amount, free from the claims of unsecured creditors or trustees in bankruptcy.

Horizontal merger A merger between two firms that are competing in the same market.

Horizontal restraint Any agreement that in some way restrains competition between rival firms competing in the same market.

Hot-cargo agreement An agreement in which employers voluntarily agree with unions not to handle, use, or deal in nonunion-produced goods of other employers; a type of secondary boycott explicitly prohibited by the Labor-Management Reporting and Disclosure Act of 1959.

Hung jury A jury whose members are so irreconcilably divided in their opinions that they cannot come to a verdict by the requisite number of jurors. The judge in this situation may order a new trial.

I

Identification In a sale of goods, the express designation of the goods provided for in the contract.

Identity theft The act of stealing another's identifying information—such as a name, date of birth, or Social Security number—and using that information to access the victim's financial resources.

Illusory promise A promise made without consideration, which renders the promise unenforceable.

Immunity A status of being exempt, or free, from certain duties or requirements. In criminal law, the state may grant an accused person immunity from prosecution—or agree to prosecute for a lesser offense—if the accused person agrees to give the state information that would assist the state in prosecuting other individuals for crimes. In tort law, freedom from liability for defamatory speech. *See also* Privilege

Implied authority Authority that is created not by an explicit oral or written agreement but by implication. In agency law, implied authority (of the agent) can be conferred by custom, inferred from the position the agent occupies, or implied by virtue of being reasonably necessary to carry out express authority.

Implied warranty A warranty that the law derives by implication or inference from the nature of the transaction or the relative situation or circumstances of the parties.

Implied warranty of fitness for a particular purpose A warranty that goods sold or leased are fit for a particular purpose. The warranty arises when any seller or lessor knows the particular purpose for which a buyer or lessee will use the goods and knows that the buyer or lessee is relying on the skill and judgment of the seller or lessor to select suitable goods.

Implied warranty of habitability An implied promise by a landlord that rented residential premises are fit for human habitation—that is, in a condition that is safe and suitable for people to live in.

Implied warranty of merchantability A warranty that goods being sold or leased are reasonably fit for the general purpose for which they are sold or leased, are properly packaged and labeled, and are of proper quality. The warranty automatically arises in every sale or lease of goods made by a merchant who deals in goods of the kind sold or leased.

Implied-in-fact contract A contract formed in whole or in part from the conduct of the parties (as opposed to an express contract).

Impossibility of performance A doctrine under which a party to a contract is relieved of his or her duty to perform when performance becomes impossible or totally impracticable (through no fault of either party).

Imposter One who, by use of the mails, telephone, or personal appearance, induces a maker or drawer to issue an instrument in the name of an impersonated payee. Indorsements by imposters are not treated as unauthorized under Article 3 of the Uniform Commercial Code.

In pari delicto At equal fault.

***In personam* jurisdiction** Court jurisdiction over the "person" involved in a legal action; personal jurisdiction.

***In rem* jurisdiction** Court jurisdiction over a defendant's property.

Incidental beneficiary A third party who incidentally benefits from a contract but whose benefit was not the reason the contract was formed; an incidental beneficiary has no rights in a contract and cannot sue to have the contract enforced.

Incidental damages Damages resulting from a breach of contract, including all reasonable expenses incurred because of the breach.

Incontestability clause A provision in an insurance policy that prevents the insurer, after the policy has been in force for a specified length of time (usually two or three years), from disputing the policy's validity based on the policyholder's statements or omissions in the application.

Indemnify To compensate or reimburse another for losses or expenses incurred.

Independent contractor One who works for, and receives payment from, an employer but whose working conditions and methods are not controlled by the employer. An independent contractor is not an employee but may be an agent.

Independent regulatory agency An administrative agency that is not considered part of the government's executive branch and is not subject to the authority of the president. Independent agency officials cannot be removed without cause.

Indictment (pronounced in-*dyte*-ment) A charge by a grand jury that a named person has committed a crime.

Indorsee The person to whom a negotiable instrument is transferred by indorsement.

Indorsement A signature placed on an instrument for the purpose of transferring one's ownership rights in the instrument.

Industry-wide liability Product liability that is imposed on an entire industry when it is unclear which of several sellers within the industry manufactured a particular product. *See also* Market-share liability

Informal contract A contract that does not require a specified form or formality in order to be valid.

Information A formal accusation or complaint (without an indictment) issued in certain types of actions (usually criminal actions involving lesser crimes) by a law officer, such as a magistrate.

Information return A tax return submitted by a partnership that only reports the income earned by the business. The partnership as an entity does not pay taxes on the income received by the partnership. A partner's profit from the partnership (whether distributed or not) is taxed as individual income to the individual partner.

Infringement A violation of another's legally recognized right. The term is commonly used with reference to the invasion by one party of another party's rights in a patent, trademark, or copyright.

Initial order In the context of administrative law, an agency's disposition in a matter other than a rulemaking. An administrative law judge's initial order becomes final unless it is appealed.

Injunction A court decree ordering a person to do or refrain from doing a certain act or activity.

Innkeeper An owner of an inn, hotel, motel, or other lodgings.

Innkeeper's lien A possessory or statutory lien allowing the innkeeper to take the personal property of a guest, brought into the hotel, as security for nonpayment of the guest's bill (debt).

Innocent misrepresentation A false statement of fact or an act made in good faith that deceives and causes harm or injury to another.

Insider A corporate director or officer, or other employee or agent, with access to confidential information and a duty not to disclose that information in violation of insider-trading laws.

Insider trading The purchase or sale of securities on the basis of "inside information" (information that has not been made available to the public) in violation of a duty owed to the company whose stock is being traded.

Insolvent   Under the Uniform Commercial Code, a term describing a person who ceases to pay "his debts in the ordinary course of business or cannot pay his debts as they become due or is insolvent within the meaning of federal bankruptcy law" [UCC 1–201(23)].

Installment contract   Under the Uniform Commercial Code, a contract that requires or authorizes delivery in two or more separate lots to be accepted and paid for separately.

Insurable interest   An interest either in a person's life or well-being or in property that is sufficiently substantial that insuring against injury to (or the death of) the person or against damage to the property does not amount to a mere wagering (betting) contract.

Intangible property   Property that is incapable of being apprehended by the senses (such as by sight or touch); intellectual property is an example of intangible property.

Integrated contract   A written contract that constitutes the final expression of the parties' agreement. If a contract is integrated, evidence extraneous to the contract that contradicts or alters the meaning of the contract in any way is inadmissible.

Intellectual property   Property resulting from intellectual, creative processes. Patents, trademarks, and copyrights are examples of intellectual property.

Intended beneficiary   A third party for whose benefit a contract is formed; an intended beneficiary can sue the promisor if such a contract is breached.

Intentional tort   A wrongful act knowingly committed.

International law   The law that governs relations among nations. International customs and treaties are generally considered to be two of the most important sources of international law.

International organization   In international law, a term that generally refers to an organization composed mainly of nations and usually established by treaty. The United States is a member of more than one hundred multilateral and bilateral organizations, including at least twenty through the United Nations.

Interpretive rule   An administrative agency rule that is simply a statement or opinion issued by the agency explaining how it interprets and intends to apply the statutes it enforces. Such rules are not automatically binding on private individuals or organizations.

Interrogatories   A series of written questions for which written answers are prepared and then signed under oath by a party to a lawsuit, usually with the assistance of the party's attorney.

Investment company   A company that acts on behalf of many smaller shareholder-owners by buying a large portfolio of securities and professionally managing that portfolio.

Invitee   A person who, either expressly or impliedly, is privileged to enter onto another's land. The inviter owes the invitee (for example, a customer in a store) the duty to exercise reasonable care to protect the invitee from harm.

Irrevocable offer   An offer that cannot be revoked or recalled by the offeror without liability. A merchant's firm offer is an example of an irrevocable offer.

Issue   The first transfer, or delivery, of an instrument to a holder.

J

Joint and several liability   In partnership law, a doctrine under which a plaintiff may sue, and collect a judgment from, one or more of the partners separately (severally, or individually) or all of the partners together (jointly). This is true even if one of the partners sued did not participate in, ratify, or know about whatever it was that gave rise to the cause of action.

Joint liability   Shared liability. In partnership law, partners incur joint liability for partnership obligations and debts. For example, if

a third party sues a partner on a partnership debt, the partner has the right to insist that the other partners be sued with him or her.

Joint stock company   A hybrid form of business organization that combines characteristics of a corporation (shareholder-owners, management by directors and officers of the company, and perpetual existence) and a partnership (it is formed by agreement, not statute; property is usually held in the names of the members; and the shareholders have personal liability for business debts). Usually, the joint stock company is regarded as a partnership for tax and other legally related purposes.

Joint tenancy   The joint ownership of property by two or more co-owners in which each co-owner owns an undivided portion of the property. On the death of one of the joint tenants, his or her interest automatically passes to the surviving joint tenants.

Joint venture   A joint undertaking of a specific commercial enterprise by an association of persons. A joint venture is normally not a legal entity and is treated like a partnership for federal income tax purposes.

Judgment   The final order or decision resulting from a legal action.

Judgment n.o.v.   *See* Motion for judgment *n.o.v.*

Judgment rate of interest   A rate of interest fixed by statute that is applied to a monetary judgment from the moment the judgment is awarded by a court until the judgment is paid or terminated.

Judicial lien   A lien on property created by a court order.

Judicial process   The procedures relating to, or connected with, the administration of justice through the judicial system.

Judicial review   The process by which courts decide on the constitutionality of legislative enactments and actions of the executive branch.

Junior lienholder   A person or business who holds a lien that is subordinate to one or more other liens on the same property.

Jurisdiction   The authority of a court to hear and decide a specific action.

Jurisprudence   The science or philosophy of law.

Justiciable   (pronounced jus-*tish*-a-bul) **controversy**   A controversy that is not hypothetical or academic but real and substantial; a requirement that must be satisfied before a court will hear a case.

K

King's court   A medieval English court. The king's courts, or *curiae regis*, were established by the Norman conquerors of England. The body of law that developed in these courts was common to the entire English realm and thus became known as the common law.

L

Laches   The equitable doctrine that bars a party's right to legal action if the party has neglected for an unreasonable length of time to act on his or her rights.

Larceny   The wrongful taking and carrying away of another person's personal property with the intent to permanently deprive the owner of the property. Some states classify larceny as either grand or petit, depending on the property's value.

Last clear chance   A doctrine under which a plaintiff may recover from a defendant for injuries or damages suffered, notwithstanding the plaintiff's own negligence, when the defendant had the opportunity—a last clear chance—to avoid harming the plaintiff through the exercise of reasonable care but failed to do so.

Law   A body of enforceable rules governing relationships among individuals and between individuals and their society.

Lawsuit   The litigation process. *See* Litigation

Leasehold estate   An estate in realty held by a tenant under a lease. In every leasehold estate, the tenant has a qualified right to possess and/or use the land.

Legal positivists   Adherents to the positivist school of legal thought. This school holds that there can be no higher law than a nation's positive law—law created by a particular society at a particular point in time. In contrast to the natural law school, the positivist school maintains that there are no "natural" rights; rights come into existence only when there is a sovereign power (government) to confer and enforce those rights.

Legal rate of interest A rate of interest fixed by statute as either the maximum rate of interest allowed by law or a rate of interest applied when the parties to a contract intend, but do not fix, an interest rate in the contract. In the latter case, the rate is frequently the same as the statutory maximum rate permitted.

Legal realism A school of legal thought that was popular in the 1920s and 1930s and that challenged many existing jurisprudential assumptions, particularly the assumption that subjective elements play no part in judicial reasoning. Legal realists generally advocated a less abstract and more realistic approach to the law, an approach that would take into account customary practices and the circumstances in which transactions take place. The school left a lasting imprint on American jurisprudence.

Legal reasoning The process of reasoning by which a judge harmonizes his or her decision with the judicial decisions of previous cases.

Legislative rule An administrative agency rule that carries the same weight as a congressionally enacted statute.

Levy The obtaining of money by legal process through the seizure and sale of property, usually done after a writ of execution has been issued.

Liability Any actual or potential legal obligation, duty, debt, or responsibility.

Libel Defamation in writing or other form (such as in a videotape) having the quality of permanence.

License A revocable right or privilege of a person to come on another person's land.

Licensee One who receives a license to use, or enter onto, another's property.

Lien (pronounced *leen*) An encumbrance on a property to satisfy a debt or protect a claim for payment of a debt.

Lien creditor One whose claim is secured by a lien on particular property, as distinguished from a general creditor, who has no such security.

Life estate An interest in land that exists only for the duration of the life of some person, usually the holder of the estate.

Limited jurisdiction Exists when a court's subject-matter jurisdiction is limited. Bankruptcy courts and probate courts are examples of courts with limited jurisdiction.

Limited liability Exists when the liability of the owners of a business is limited to the amount of their investments in the firm.

Limited liability company (LLC) A hybrid form of business enterprise that offers the limited liability of the corporation but the tax advantages of a partnership.

Limited liability limited partnership (LLLP) A type of limited partnership. The difference between a limited partnership and an LLLP is that the liability of the general partner in an LLLP is the same as the liability of the limited partner—that is, the liability of all partners is limited to the amount of their investments in the firm.

Limited liability partnership (LLP) A form of partnership that allows professionals to enjoy the tax benefits of a partnership while limiting their personal liability for the malpractice of other partners.

Limited partner In a limited partnership, a partner who contributes capital to the partnership but has no right to participate in the management and operation of the business. The limited partner assumes no liability for partnership debts beyond the capital contributed.

Limited partnership A partnership consisting of one or more general partners (who manage the business and are liable to the full extent of their personal assets for debts of the partnership) and one or more limited partners (who contribute only assets and are liable only to the extent of their contributions).

Limited warranty A written warranty that fails to meet one or more of the minimum standards for a full warranty.

Liquidated damages An amount, stipulated in the contract, that the parties to a contract believe to be a reasonable estimation of the damages that will occur in the event of a breach.

Liquidated debt A debt that is due and certain in amount.

Liquidation (1) In regard to bankruptcy, the sale of all of the nonexempt assets of a debtor and the distribution of the proceeds to the debtor's creditors. Chapter 7 of the Bankruptcy Code provides for liquidation bankruptcy proceedings. (2) In regard to corporations, the process by which corporate assets are converted into cash and distributed among creditors and shareholders according to specific rules of preference.

Litigant A party to a lawsuit.

Litigation The process of resolving a dispute through the court system.

Loan workout *See* Workout

Long arm statute A state statute that permits a state to obtain personal jurisdiction over nonresident defendants. A defendant must have "minimum contacts" with that state for the statute to apply.

M

Magistrate's court A court of limited jurisdiction that is presided over by a public official (magistrate) with certain judicial authority, such as the power to set bail.

Mailbox rule A rule providing that an acceptance of an offer becomes effective on dispatch (on being placed in a mailbox), if mail is, expressly or impliedly, an authorized means of communication of acceptance to the offeror.

Main purpose rule A rule of contract law under which an exception to the Statute of Frauds is made if the main purpose in accepting secondary liability under a contract is to secure a personal benefit. If this situation exists, the contract need not be in writing to be enforceable.

Majority *See* Age of majority

Majority opinion A court's written opinion, outlining the views of the majority of the judges or justices deciding the case.

Maker One who promises to pay a certain sum to the holder of a promissory note or certificate of deposit (CD).

Malpractice Professional misconduct or the failure to exercise the requisite degree of skill as a professional. Negligence—the failure to exercise due care—on the part of a professional, such as a physician or an attorney, is commonly referred to as malpractice.

Manufacturing or processing-plant franchise A franchise that is created when the franchisor transmits to the franchisee the essential ingredients or formula to make a particular product. The franchisee then markets the product either at wholesale or at retail in accordance with the franchisor's standards. Examples of this type of franchise are Coca-Cola and other soft-drink bottling companies.

Mark *See* Trademark

Market concentration A situation that exists when a small number of firms share the market for a particular good or service. For example, if the four largest grocery stores in Chicago accounted for 80 percent of all retail food sales, the market clearly would be concentrated in those four firms.

Market power The power of a firm to control the market price of its product. A monopoly has the greatest degree of market power.

Marketable title Title to real estate that is reasonably free from encumbrances, defects in the chain of title, and other events that affect title, such as adverse possession.

Market-share liability A method of sharing liability among several firms that manufactured or marketed a particular product that may have caused a plaintiff's injury. This form of liability sharing is used when the true source of the product is unidentifiable. Each firm's liability is proportionate to its respective share of the relevant market for the product. Market-share liability applies only if the injuring product is fungible, the true manufacturer is unidentifiable, and the unknown character of the manufacturer is not the plaintiff's fault.

Market-share test   The primary measure of monopoly power. A firm's market share is the percentage of a market that the firm controls.

Marshalling assets   The arrangement or ranking of assets in a certain order toward the payment of debts. In equity, when two creditors have recourse to the same property of the debtor, but one has recourse to other property of the debtor, that creditor must resort first to those assets of the debtor that are not available to the other creditor.

Material alteration   *See* Alteration

Material fact   A fact to which a reasonable person would attach importance in determining his or her course of action. In regard to tender offers, for example, a fact is material if there is a substantial likelihood that a reasonable shareholder would consider it important in deciding how to vote.

Mechanic's lien   A statutory lien on the real property of another, created to ensure payment for work performed and materials furnished in the repair or improvement of real property, such as a building.

Mediation   A method of settling disputes outside of court by using the services of a neutral third party, called a mediator. The mediator acts as a communicating agent between the parties and suggests ways in which the parties can resolve their dispute.

Member   The term used to designate a person who has an ownership interest in a limited liability company.

Mens rea (pronounced *mehns ray*-uh)   Mental state, or intent. A wrongful mental state is as necessary as a wrongful act to establish criminal liability. What constitutes a mental state varies according to the wrongful action. Thus, for murder, the *mens rea* is the intent to take a life; for theft, the *mens rea* must involve both the knowledge that the property belongs to another and the intent to deprive the owner of it.

Merchant   A person who is engaged in the purchase and sale of goods. Under the Uniform Commercial Code, a person who deals in goods of the kind involved in the sales contract; for further definitions, see UCC 2–104.

Merger   A contractual and statutory process in which one corporation (the surviving corporation) acquires all of the assets and liabilities of another corporation (the merged corporation). The shareholders of the merged corporation receive either payment for their shares or shares in the surviving corporation.

Meta tags   Words inserted into a Web site's key-words field to increase the site's appearance in search engine results.

Minimum-contacts requirement   The requirement that before a state court can exercise jurisdiction over a foreign corporation, the foreign corporation must have sufficient contacts with the state. A foreign corporation that has its home office in the state or that has manufacturing plants in the state meets this requirement.

Minimum wage   The lowest wage, either by government regulation or union contract, that an employer may pay an hourly worker.

Mini-trial   A private proceeding in which each party to a dispute argues its position before the other side, and vice versa. A neutral third party may be present and act as an adviser if the parties fail to reach an agreement.

Mirror image rule   A common law rule that requires, for a valid contractual agreement, that the terms of the offeree's acceptance adhere exactly to the terms of the offeror's offer.

Misdemeanor   A lesser crime than a felony, punishable by a fine or imprisonment for up to one year in other than a state or federal penitentiary.

Misrepresentation   A false statement of fact or an action that deceives and causes harm or injury to another. *See also* Fraudulent misrepresentation (fraud); Innocent misrepresentation

Mitigation of damages   A rule requiring a plaintiff to have done whatever was reasonable to minimize the damages caused by the defendant.

Money laundering   Falsely reporting income that has been obtained through criminal activity as income obtained through a legitimate business enterprise—in effect, "laundering" the "dirty money."

Monopolization   The possession of monopoly power in the relevant market and the willful acquisition or maintenance of the power, as distinguished from growth or development as a consequence of a superior product, business acumen, or historic accident.

Monopoly   A term generally used to describe a market in which there is a single seller or a limited number of sellers.

Monopoly power   The ability of a monopoly to dictate what takes place in a given market.

Moral minimum   The minimum degree of ethical behavior expected of a business firm, which is usually defined as compliance with the law.

Mortgage   A written instrument giving a creditor (the mortgagee) an interest in (a lien on) the debtor's (mortgagor's) property as security for a debt.

Mortgage bond   A bond that pledges specific property. If the corporation defaults on the bond, the bondholder can take the property.

Mortgagee   Under a mortgage agreement, the creditor who takes a security interest in the debtor's property.

Mortgagor   Under a mortgage agreement, the debtor who gives the creditor a security interest in the debtor's property in return for a mortgage loan.

Motion   A procedural request or application presented by an attorney to the court on behalf of a client.

Motion for a directed verdict   In a jury trial, a motion for the judge to take the decision out of the hands of the jury and direct a verdict for the moving party on the ground that the other party has not produced sufficient evidence to support his or her claim; referred to as a motion for judgment as a matter of law in the federal courts.

Motion for a new trial   A motion asserting that the trial was so fundamentally flawed (because of error, newly discovered evidence, prejudice, or other reason) that a new trial is necessary to prevent a miscarriage of justice.

Motion for judgment n.o.v.   A motion requesting the court to grant judgment in favor of the party making the motion on the ground that the jury verdict against him or her was unreasonable and erroneous.

Motion for judgment on the pleadings   A motion by either party to a lawsuit at the close of the pleadings requesting the court to decide the issue solely on the pleadings without proceeding to trial. The motion will be granted only if no facts are in dispute.

Motion for summary judgment   A motion requesting the court to enter a judgment without proceeding to trial. The motion can be based on evidence outside the pleadings and will be granted only if no facts are in dispute.

Motion to dismiss   A pleading in which a defendant asserts that the plaintiff's claim fails to state a cause of action (that is, has no basis in law) or that there are other grounds on which a suit should be dismissed.

Multiple product order   An order issued by the Federal Trade Commission to a firm that has engaged in deceptive advertising by which the firm is required to cease and desist from false advertising not only in regard to the product that was the subject of the action but also in regard to all the firm's other products.

Municipal court   A city or community court with criminal jurisdiction over traffic violations and, less frequently, with civil jurisdiction over other minor matters.

Mutual assent   The element of agreement in the formation of a contract. The manifestation of contract parties' mutual assent to the same bargain is required to establish a contract.

Mutual fund   A specific type of investment company that continually buys or sells to investors shares of ownership in a portfolio.

Mutual rescission   An agreement between the parties to cancel their contract, releasing the parties from further obligations under the contract. The object of the agreement is to restore the parties to the positions they would have occupied had no contract ever been formed. *See also* Rescission

N

National law   Law that pertains to a particular nation (as opposed to international law).

Natural law   The belief that government and the legal system should reflect universal moral and ethical principles that are inherent in human nature. The natural law school is the oldest and one of the most significant schools of legal thought.

Necessaries   Necessities required for life, such as food, shelter, clothing, and medical attention; may include whatever is believed to be necessary to maintain a person's standard of living or financial and social status.

Necessity   In criminal law, a defense against liability; under Section 3.02 of the Model Penal Code, this defense is justifiable if "the harm or evil sought to be avoided" by a given action "is greater than that sought to be prevented by the law defining the offense charged."

Negligence   The failure to exercise the standard of care that a reasonable person would exercise in similar circumstances.

Negligence *per se*   An act (or failure to act) in violation of a statutory requirement.

Negligent misrepresentation   Any manifestation through words or conduct that amounts to an untrue statement of fact made in circumstances in which a reasonable and prudent person would not have done (or failed to do) that which led to the misrepresentation. A representation made with an honest belief in its truth may still be negligent due to (1) a lack of reasonable care in ascertaining the facts, (2) the manner of expression, or (3) the absence of the skill or competence required by a particular business or profession.

Negotiation   In regard to dispute settlement, a process in which parties attempt to settle their dispute without going to court, with or without attorneys to represent them.

Nominal damages   A small monetary award (often one dollar) granted to a plaintiff when no actual damage was suffered.

Nonconforming goods   Goods that do not conform to contract specifications.

No-par shares   Corporate shares that have no face value—that is, no specific dollar amount is printed on their face.

Normal trade relations (NTR) status   A status granted through an international treaty by which each member nation must treat other members at least as well as it treats the country that receives its most favorable treatment. This status was formerly known as most-favored-nation status.

Notary public   A public official authorized to attest to the authenticity of signatures.

Notice-and-comment rulemaking   An administrative rulemaking procedure that involves the publication of a notice of a proposed rulemaking in the *Federal Register*, a comment period for interested parties to express their views on the proposed rule, and the publication of the agency's final rule in the *Federal Register*.

Notice of Proposed Rulemaking   A notice published (in the *Federal Register*) by an administrative agency describing a proposed rule. The notice must give the time and place for which agency proceedings on the proposed rule will be held, a description of the nature of the proceedings, the legal authority for the proceedings (which is usually the agency's enabling legislation), and the terms of the proposed rule or the subject matter of the proposed rule.

Novation   The substitution, by agreement, of a new contract for an old one, with the rights under the old one being terminated. Typically, there is a substitution of a new person who is responsible for the contract and the removal of an original party's rights and duties under the contract.

Nuisance   A common law doctrine under which persons may be held liable for using their property in a manner that unreasonably interferes with others' rights to use or enjoy their own property.

O

Objective theory of contracts   A theory under which the intent to form a contract will be judged by outward, objective facts (what the party said when entering into the contract, how the party acted or appeared, and the circumstances surrounding the transaction) as interpreted by a reasonable person, rather than by the party's own secret, subjective intentions.

Obligee   One to whom an obligation is owed.

Obligor   One that owes an obligation to another.

Offer   A promise or commitment to perform or refrain from performing some specified act in the future.

Offeree   A person to whom an offer is made.

Offeror   A person who makes an offer.

Opening statement   A statement made to the jury at the beginning of a trial by a party's attorney, prior to the presentation of evidence. The attorney briefly outlines the evidence that will be offered and the legal theory that will be pursued.

Operating agreement   In a limited liability company, an agreement in which the members set forth the details of how the business will be managed and operated.

Operation of law   A term expressing the manner in which certain rights or liabilities may be imposed on a person by the application of established rules of law to the particular transaction, without regard to the actions or cooperation of the party himself or herself.

Opinion   A statement by the court expressing the reasons for its decision in a case.

Optimum profits   The amount of profits that a business can make and still act ethically, as opposed to maximum profits, defined as the amount of profits a firm can make if it is willing to disregard ethical concerns.

Option contract   A contract under which the offeror cannot revoke his or her offer for a stipulated time period and the offeree can accept or reject the offer during this period without fear that the offer will be made to another person. The offeree must give consideration for the option (the irrevocable offer) to be enforceable.

Order for relief   A court's grant of assistance to a complainant. In bankruptcy proceedings, the order relieves the debtor of the immediate obligation to pay the debts listed in the bankruptcy petition.

Ordinance   A law passed by a local governing unit, such as a municipality or a county.

Original jurisdiction   Courts having original jurisdiction are courts of the first instance, or trial courts—that is, courts in which lawsuits begin, trials take place, and evidence is presented.

Output contract   An agreement in which a seller agrees to sell and a buyer agrees to buy all or up to a stated amount of what the seller produces.

P

Parent-subsidiary merger   A merger of companies in which one company (the parent corporation) owns most of the stock of the other (the subsidiary corporation). A parent-subsidiary merger (short-form merger) can use a simplified procedure when the parent corporation owns at least 90 percent of the outstanding shares of each class of stock of the subsidiary corporation.

Parol evidence   A term that originally meant "oral evidence," but which has come to refer to any negotiations or agreements made prior to a contract or any contemporaneous oral agreements made by the parties.

Parol evidence rule   A substantive rule of contracts under which a court will not receive into evidence the parties' prior negotiations, prior agreements, or contemporaneous oral agreements if that evidence contradicts or varies the terms of the parties' written contract.

Partially disclosed principal A principal whose identity is unknown by a third person, but the third person knows that the agent is or may be acting for a principal at the time the agent and the third person form a contract.

Partner A co-owner of a partnership.

Partnership An agreement by two or more persons to carry on, as co-owners, a business for profit.

Partnership by estoppel A judicially created partnership that may, at the court's discretion, be imposed for purposes of fairness. The court can prevent those who present themselves as partners (but who are not) from escaping liability if a third person relies on an alleged partnership in good faith and is harmed as a result.

Par-value shares Corporate shares that have a specific face value, or formal cash-in value, written on them, such as one dollar.

Past consideration An act done before the contract is made, which ordinarily, by itself, cannot be consideration for a later promise to pay for the act.

Patent A government grant that gives an inventor the exclusive right or privilege to make, use, or sell his or her invention for a limited time period. The word *patent* usually refers to some invention and designates either the instrument by which patent rights are evidenced or the patent itself.

Payee A person to whom an instrument is made payable.

Peer-to-peer (P2P) networking The sharing of resources (such as files, hard drives, and processing styles) among multiple computers without necessarily requiring a central network server.

Penalty A sum inserted into a contract, not as a measure of compensation for its breach but rather as punishment for a default. The agreement as to the amount will not be enforced, and recovery will be limited to actual damages.

Per curiam By the whole court; a court opinion written by the court as a whole instead of being authored by a judge or justice.

Per se A Latin term meaning "in itself" or "by itself."

Per se violation A type of anticompetitive agreement—such as a horizontal price-fixing agreement—that is considered to be so injurious to the public that there is no need to determine whether it actually injures market competition; rather, it is in itself (*per se*) a violation of the Sherman Act.

Perfect tender rule A common law rule under which a seller was required to deliver to the buyer goods that conformed perfectly to the requirements stipulated in the sales contract. A tender of non-conforming goods would automatically constitute a breach of contract. Under the Uniform Commercial Code, the rule has been greatly modified.

Perfection The legal process by which secured parties protect themselves against the claims of third parties who may wish to have their debts satisfied out of the same collateral; usually accomplished by the filing of a financing statement with the appropriate government official.

Performance In contract law, the fulfillment of one's duties arising under a contract with another; the normal way of discharging one's contractual obligations.

Periodic tenancy A lease interest in land for an indefinite period involving payment of rent at fixed intervals, such as week to week, month to month, or year to year.

Personal jurisdiction *See In personam* jurisdiction

Personal property Property that is movable; any property that is not real property.

Petition in bankruptcy The document that is filed with a bankruptcy court to initiate bankruptcy proceedings. The official forms required for a petition in bankruptcy must be completed accurately, sworn to under oath, and signed by the debtor.

Petitioner In equity practice, a party that initiates a lawsuit.

Petty offense In criminal law, the least serious kind of criminal offense, such as a traffic or building-code violation.

Pierce the corporate veil To disregard the corporate entity, which limits the liability of shareholders, and hold the shareholders personally liable for a corporate obligation.

Plaintiff One who initiates a lawsuit.

Plea In criminal law, a defendant's allegation, in response to the charges brought against him or her, of guilt or innocence.

Plea bargaining The process by which a criminal defendant and the prosecutor in a criminal case work out a mutually satisfactory disposition of the case, subject to court approval; usually involves the defendant's pleading guilty to a lesser offense in return for a lighter sentence.

Pleadings Statements made by the plaintiff and the defendant in a lawsuit that detail the facts, charges, and defenses involved in the litigation; the complaint and answer are part of the pleadings.

Police powers Powers possessed by states as part of their inherent sovereignty. These powers may be exercised to protect or promote the public order, health, safety, morals, and general welfare.

Policy In insurance law, a contract between the insurer and the insured in which, for a stipulated consideration, the insurer agrees to compensate the insured for loss on a specific subject by a specified peril.

Positive law The body of conventional, or written, law of a particular society at a particular point in time.

Positivist school A school of legal thought whose adherents believe that there can be no higher law than a nation's positive law—the body of conventional, or written, law of a particular society at a particular time.

Possessory lien A lien that allows one person to retain possession of another's property as security for a debt or obligation owed by the owner of the property to the lienholder. An example of a possessory lien is an artisan's lien.

Potential competition doctrine A doctrine under which a conglomerate merger may be prohibited by law because it would be injurious to potential competition.

Potentially responsible party (PRP) A potentially liable party under the Comprehensive Environmental Response, Compensation and Liability Act (CERCLA). Any person who generated hazardous waste, transported the hazardous waste, owned or operated a waste site at the time of disposal, or currently owns or operates a site may be responsible for some or all of the clean-up costs involved in removing the hazardous chemicals.

Power of attorney A written document, which is usually notarized, authorizing another to act as one's agent; can be special (permitting the agent to do specified acts only) or general (permitting the agent to transact all business for the principal).

Precedent A court decision that furnishes an example or authority for deciding subsequent cases involving identical or similar facts.

Predatory pricing The pricing of a product below cost with the intent to drive competitors out of the market.

Preemption A doctrine under which certain federal laws preempt, or take precedence over, conflicting state or local laws.

Preemptive rights Rights held by shareholders that entitle them to purchase newly issued shares of a corporation's stock, equal in percentage to shares presently held, before the stock is offered to any outside buyers. Preemptive rights enable shareholders to maintain their proportionate ownership and voice in the corporation.

Preference In bankruptcy proceedings, property transfers or payments made by the debtor that favor (give preference to) one creditor over others. The bankruptcy trustee is allowed to recover payments made both voluntarily and involuntarily to one creditor in preference over another.

Preferred creditor In the context of bankruptcy, a creditor who has received a preferential transfer from a debtor.

Preferred stock Classes of stock that have priority over common stock both as to payment of dividends and distribution of assets on the corporation's dissolution.

Prejudgment interest Interest that accrues on the amount of a court judgment from the time of the filing of a lawsuit to the court's issuance of a judgment.

Preliminary hearing An initial hearing used in many felony cases to establish whether or not it is proper to detain the defendant. A magistrate reviews the evidence and decides if there is probable cause to believe that the defendant committed the crime with which he or she has been charged.

Prenuptial agreement An agreement made before marriage that defines each partner's ownership rights in the other partner's property. Prenuptial agreements must be in writing to be enforceable.

Preponderance of the evidence A standard in civil law cases under which the plaintiff must convince the court that, based on the evidence presented by both parties, it is more likely than not that the plaintiff's allegation is true.

Pretrial conference A conference, scheduled before the trial begins, between the judge and the attorneys litigating the suit. The parties may settle the dispute, clarify the issues, schedule discovery, and so on during the conference.

Pretrial motion A written or oral application to a court for a ruling or order, made before trial.

Price discrimination Setting prices in such a way that two competing buyers pay two different prices for an identical product or service.

Price-fixing agreement An agreement between competitors in which the competitors agree to fix the prices of products or services at a certain level; prohibited by the Sherman Act.

Prima facie case A case in which the plaintiff has produced sufficient evidence of his or her conclusion that the case can go to to a jury; a case in which the evidence compels the plaintiff's conclusion if the defendant produces no evidence to disprove it.

Primary liability In negotiable instruments law, absolute responsibility for paying a negotiable instrument. Makers and acceptors are primarily liable.

Principal In agency law, a person who agrees to have another, called the agent, act on his or her behalf.

Principle of rights The principle that human beings have certain fundamental rights (to life, freedom, and the pursuit of happiness, for example). Those who adhere to this "rights theory" believe that a key factor in determining whether a business decision is ethical is how that decision affects the rights of others. These others include the firm's owners, its employees, the consumers of its products or services, its suppliers, the community in which it does business, and society as a whole.

Privatization The replacement of government-provided products and services by private firms.

Privilege In tort law, the ability to act contrary to another person's right without that person's having legal redress for such acts. Privilege may be raised as a defense to defamation.

Privileges and immunities clause Special rights and exceptions provided by law. Article IV, Section 2, of the Constitution requires states not to discriminate against one another's citizens. A resident of one state cannot be treated as an alien when in another state; he or she may not be denied such privileges and immunities as legal protection, access to courts, travel rights, or property rights.

Privity of contract The relationship that exists between the promisor and the promisee of a contract.

Pro rata Proportionately; in proportion.

Probable cause Reasonable grounds to believe the existence of facts warranting certain actions, such as the search or arrest of a person.

Procedural due process The requirement that any government decision to take life, liberty, or property must be made fairly. For example, fair procedures must be used in determining whether a person will be subjected to punishment or have some burden imposed on him or her.

Procedural law Rules that define the manner in which the rights and duties of individuals may be enforced.

Procedural unconscionability Occurs when, due to one contractual party's vastly superior bargaining power, the other party lacks a knowledge or understanding of the contract terms due to inconspicuous print or the lack of an opportunity to read the contract or to ask questions about its meaning. Procedural unconscionability often involves an *adhesion contract*, which is a contract drafted by the dominant party and then presented to the other—the adhering party—on a take-it-or-leave-it basis.

Product liability The legal liability of manufacturers, sellers, and lessors of goods to consumers, users, and bystanders for injuries or damages that are caused by the goods.

Product misuse A defense against product liability that may be raised when the plaintiff used a product in a manner not intended by the manufacturer. If the misuse is reasonably foreseeable, the seller will not escape liability unless measures were taken to guard against the harm that could result from the misuse.

Profit In real property law, the right to enter onto and remove things from the property of another (for example, the right to enter onto a person's land and remove sand and gravel therefrom).

Promise A declaration that something either will or will not happen in the future.

Promisee A person to whom a promise is made.

Promisor A person who makes a promise.

Promissory estoppel A doctrine that applies when a promisor makes a clear and definite promise on which the promisee justifiably relies; such a promise is binding if justice will be better served by the enforcement of the promise. *See also* Estoppel

Promoter A person who takes the preliminary steps in organizing a corporation, including (usually) issuing a prospectus, procuring stock subscriptions, making contract purchases, securing a corporate charter, and the like.

Property Legally protected rights and interests in anything with an ascertainable value that is subject to ownership.

Prospectus A document required by federal or state securities laws that describes the financial operations of the corporation, thus allowing investors to make informed decisions.

Protected class A class of persons with identifiable characteristics who historically have been victimized by discriminatory treatment for certain purposes. Depending on the context, these characteristics include age, color, gender, national origin, race, and religion.

Proximate cause Legal cause; exists when the connection between an act and an injury is strong enough to justify imposing liability.

Proxy In corporation law, a written agreement between a stockholder and another under which the stockholder authorizes the other to vote the stockholder's shares in a certain manner.

Proxy fight A conflict between an individual, group, or firm attempting to take control of a corporation and the corporation's management for the votes of the shareholders.

Public figures Individuals who are thrust into the public limelight. Public figures include government officials and politicians, movie stars, well-known businesspersons, and generally anybody who becomes known to the public because of his or her position or activities.

Public policy A government policy based on widely held societal values and (usually) expressed or implied in laws or regulations.

Public prosecutor An individual, acting as a trial lawyer, who initiates and conducts criminal cases in the government's name and on behalf of the people.

Puffery A salesperson's often-exaggerated claims concerning the quality of property offered for sale. Such claims involve opinions rather than facts and are not considered to be legally binding promises or warranties.

Punitive damages Money damages that may be awarded to a plaintiff to punish the defendant and deter future similar conduct.

Q

Quantum meruit (pronounced *kwahn*-tuhm *mehr*-oo-wuht) Literally, "as much as he deserves"—an expression describing the extent of liability on a contract implied in law (quasi contract). An equitable doctrine based on the concept that one who benefits from another's labor and materials should not be unjustly enriched thereby but should be required to pay a reasonable amount for the benefits received, even absent a contract.

Quasi contract A fictional contract imposed on parties by a court in the interests of fairness and justice; usually, quasi contracts are imposed to avoid the unjust enrichment of one party at the expense of another.

Question of fact In a lawsuit, an issue involving a factual dispute that can only be decided by a judge (or, in a jury trial, a jury).

Question of law In a lawsuit, an issue involving the application or interpretation of a law; therefore, the judge, and not the jury, decides the issue.

Quiet enjoyment *See* Covenant of quiet enjoyment

Quitclaim deed A deed intended to pass any title, interest, or claim that the grantor may have in the property but not warranting that such title is valid. A quitclaim deed offers the least amount of protection against defects in the title.

Quorum The number of members of a decision-making body that must be present before business may be transacted.

Quota An assigned import limit on goods.

R

Ratification The act of accepting and giving legal force to an obligation that previously was not enforceable.

Reaffirmation agreement An agreement between a debtor and a creditor in which the debtor reaffirms, or promises to pay, a debt dischargeable in bankruptcy. To be enforceable, the agreement must be made prior to the discharge of the debt by the bankruptcy court.

Real property Land and everything attached to it, such as foliage and buildings.

Reasonable care The degree of care that a person of ordinary prudence would exercise in the same or similar circumstances.

Reasonable doubt *See* Beyond a reasonable doubt

Reasonable person standard The standard of behavior expected of a hypothetical "reasonable person." The standard against which negligence is measured and that must be observed to avoid liability for negligence.

Rebuttal The refutation of evidence introduced by an adverse party's attorney.

Receiver In a corporate dissolution, a court-appointed person who winds up corporate affairs and liquidates corporate assets.

Recording statutes Statutes that allow deeds, mortgages, and other real property transactions to be recorded so as to provide notice to future purchasers or creditors of an existing claim on the property.

Red herring A preliminary prospectus that can be distributed to potential investors after the registration statement (for a securities offering) has been filed with the Securities and Exchange Commission. The name derives from the red legend printed across the prospectus stating that the registration has been filed but has not become effective.

Redemption A repurchase, or buying back. In secured transactions law, a debtor's repurchase of collateral securing a debt after a creditor has taken title to the collateral due to the debtor's default but before the secured party disposes of the collateral.

Reformation A court-ordered correction of a written contract so that it reflects the true intentions of the parties.

Regulation Z A set of rules promulgated by the Federal Reserve Board to implement the provisions of the Truth-in-Lending Act.

Rejection In contract law, an offeree's express or implied manifestation not to accept an offer. In the law governing contracts for the sale of goods, a buyer's manifest refusal to accept goods on the ground that they do not conform to contract specifications.

Rejoinder The defendant's answer to the plaintiff's rebuttal.

Release A contract in which one party forfeits the right to pursue a legal claim against the other party.

Relevant evidence Evidence tending to make a fact at issue in the case more or less probable than it would be without the evidence. Only relevant evidence is admissible in court.

Remainder A future interest in property held by a person other than the original owner.

Remanded Sent back. If an appellate court disagrees with a lower court's judgment, the case may be remanded to the lower court for further proceedings in which the lower court's decision should be consistent with the appellate court's opinion on the matter.

Remedy The relief given to an innocent party to enforce a right or compensate for the violation of a right.

Remedy at law A remedy available in a court of law. Money damages are awarded as a remedy at law.

Remedy in equity A remedy allowed by courts in situations where remedies at law are not appropriate. Remedies in equity are based on settled rules of fairness, justice, and honesty, and include injunction, specific performance, rescission and restitution, and reformation.

Remitter A person who sends money, or remits payment.

Replevin (pronounced ruh-*pleh*-vin) An action to recover specific goods in the hands of a party who is wrongfully withholding them from the other party.

Reply Procedurally, a plaintiff's response to a defendant's answer.

Reporter A publication in which court cases are published, or reported.

Repudiation The renunciation of a right or duty; the act of a buyer or seller in rejecting a contract either partially or totally. *See also* Anticipatory repudiation

Requirements contract An agreement in which a buyer agrees to purchase and the seller agrees to sell all or up to a stated amount of what the buyer needs or requires.

Res ipsa loquitur (pronounced *rehs ehp*-suh *low*-quuh-duhr) A doctrine under which negligence may be inferred simply because an event occurred, if it is the type of event that would not occur in the absence of negligence. Literally, the term means "the facts speak for themselves."

Resale price maintenance agreement An agreement between a manufacturer and a retailer in which the manufacturer specifies the minimum retail price of its products.

Rescind (pronounced reh-*sihnd*) To cancel. *See also* Rescission

Rescission (pronounced reh-*sih*-zhen) A remedy whereby a contract is canceled and the parties are returned to the positions they occupied before the contract was made; may be effected through the mutual consent of the parties, by their conduct, or by court decree.

Residuary The surplus of a testator's estate remaining after all of the debts and particular legacies have been discharged.

Respondeat superior (pronounced ree-*spahn*-dee-uht soo-*peer*-ee-your) In Latin, "Let the master respond." A doctrine under which a principal or an employer is held liable for the wrongful acts committed by agents or employees while acting within the course and scope of their agency or employment.

Respondent In equity practice, the party who answers a bill or other proceeding.

Restitution An equitable remedy under which a person is restored to his or her original position prior to loss or injury, or placed in the position he or she would have been in had the breach not occurred.

Restraint on trade Any contract or combination that tends to eliminate or reduce competition, effect a monopoly, artificially maintain prices, or otherwise hamper the course of trade and commerce as it would be carried on if left to the control of natural economic forces.

Restrictive covenant   A private restriction on the use of land that is binding on the party that purchases the property originally as well as on subsequent purchasers. If its benefit or obligation passes with the land's ownership, it is said to "run with the land."

Retained earnings   The portion of a corporation's profits that has not been paid out as dividends to shareholders.

Retaliatory eviction   The eviction of a tenant because of the tenant's complaints, participation in a tenant's union, or similar activity with which the landlord does not agree.

Reverse   To reject or overrule a court's judgment. An appellate court, for example, might reverse a lower court's judgment on an issue if it feels that the lower court committed an error during the trial or that the jury was improperly instructed.

Reverse discrimination   Discrimination against majority groups, such as white males, that results from affirmative action programs, in which preferences are given to minority members and women.

Reversible error   An error by a lower court that is sufficiently substantial to justify an appellate court's reversal of the lower court's decision.

Reversionary interest   A future interest in property retained by the original owner.

Revocation   In contract law, the withdrawal of an offer by an offeror. Unless an offer is irrevocable, it can be revoked at any time prior to acceptance without liability.

Right of contribution   The right of a co-surety who pays more than his or her proportionate share on a debtor's default to recover the excess paid from other co-sureties.

Right of first refusal   The right to purchase personal or real property—such as corporate shares or real estate—before the property is offered for sale to others.

Right of redemption   See Equity of redemption; Redemption

Right of reimbursement   The legal right of a person to be restored, repaid, or indemnified for costs, expenses, or losses incurred or expended on behalf of another.

Right of subrogation   The right of a person to stand in the place of (be substituted for) another, giving the substituted party the same legal rights that the original party had.

Right-to-work law   A state law providing that employees are not to be required to join a union as a condition of obtaining or retaining employment.

Robbery   The act of forcefully and unlawfully taking personal property of any value from another; force or intimidation is usually necessary for an act of theft to be considered a robbery.

Rule 10b-5   See SEC Rule 10b-5

Rule of four   A rule of the United States Supreme Court under which the Court will not issue a writ of *certiorari* unless at least four justices approve of the decision to issue the writ.

Rule of reason   A test by which a court balances the positive effects (such as economic efficiency) of an agreement against its potentially anticompetitive effects. In antitrust litigation, many practices are analyzed under the rule of reason.

Rulemaking   The process undertaken by an administrative agency when formally adopting a new regulation or amending an old one. Rulemaking involves notifying the public of a proposed rule or change and receiving and considering the public's comments.

Rules of evidence   Rules governing the admissibility of evidence in trial courts.

S

S corporation   A close business corporation that has met certain requirements as set out by the Internal Revenue Code and thus qualifies for special income tax treatment. Essentially, an S corporation is taxed the same as a partnership, but its owners enjoy the privilege of limited liability.

Sale   The passing of title from the seller to the buyer for a price.

Sale on approval   A type of conditional sale in which the buyer may take the goods on a trial basis. The sale becomes absolute only when the buyer approves of (or is satisfied with) the goods being sold.

Sale or return   A type of conditional sale in which title and possession pass from the seller to the buyer; however, the buyer retains the option to return the goods during a specified period even though the goods conform to the contract.

Sales contract   A contract for the sale of goods under which the ownership of goods is transferred from a seller to a buyer for a price.

Scienter (pronounced *sy-en*-ter)   Knowledge by the misrepresenting party that material facts have been falsely represented or omitted with an intent to deceive.

Search warrant   An order granted by a public authority, such as a judge, that authorizes law enforcement personnel to search particular premises or property.

Seasonably   Within a specified time period, or, if no period is specified, within a reasonable time.

SEC Rule 10b-5   A rule of the Securities and Exchange Commission that makes it unlawful, in connection with the purchase or sale of any security, to make any untrue statement of a material fact or to omit a material fact if such omission causes the statement to be misleading.

Secondary boycott   A union's refusal to work for, purchase from, or handle the products of a secondary employer, with whom the union has no dispute, for the purpose of forcing that employer to stop doing business with the primary employer, with whom the union has a labor dispute.

Securities   Generally, corporate stocks and bonds. A security may also be a note, debenture, stock warrant, or any document given as evidence of an ownership interest in a corporation or as a promise of repayment by a corporation.

Self-defense   The legally recognized privilege to protect one's self or property against injury by another. The privilege of self-defense protects only acts that are reasonably necessary to protect one's self or property.

Seniority system   In regard to employment relationships, a system in which those who have worked longest for the company are first in line for promotions, salary increases, and other benefits; they are also the last to be laid off if the workforce must be reduced.

Service mark   A mark used in the sale or the advertising of services, such as to distinguish the services of one person from the services of others. Titles, character names, and other distinctive features of radio and television programs may be registered as service marks.

Service of process   The delivery of the complaint and summons to a defendant.

Settlor   One creating a trust.

Sexual harassment   In the employment context, the granting of job promotions or other benefits in return for sexual favors or language or conduct that is so sexually offensive that it creates a hostile working environment.

Sham transaction   A false transaction without substance that is undertaken with the intent to defraud a creditor or the government. An example of a sham transaction is the sale of assets to a friend or relative for the purpose of concealing assets from creditors or a bankruptcy court.

Share   A unit of stock. *See also* Stock

Shareholder   One who purchases shares of a corporation's stock, thus acquiring an equity interest in the corporation.

Shareholder's derivative suit   A suit brought by a shareholder to enforce a corporate cause of action against a third person.

Sharia   Civil law principles of some Middle Eastern countries that are based on the Islamic directives that follow the teachings of the prophet Muhammad.

Sheriff's deed   The deed given to the purchaser of property at a sheriff's sale as part of the foreclosure process against the owner of the property.

Shipment contract   A contract for the sale of goods in which the seller is required or authorized to ship the goods by carrier. The buyer assumes liability for any losses or damage to the goods after they are delivered to the carrier.

Short-form merger   A merger between a subsidiary corporation and a parent corporation that owns at least 90 percent of the outstanding shares of each class of stock issued by the subsidiary corporation. Short-form mergers can be accomplished without the approval of the shareholders of either corporation.

Short-swing profits   Profits made by officers, directors, and certain large stockholders resulting from the use of nonpublic (inside) information about their companies; prohibited by Section 12 of the 1934 Securities Exchange Act.

Signature   Under the Uniform Commercial Code, "any symbol executed or adopted by a party with a present intention to authenticate a writing."

Slander   Defamation in oral form.

Slander of quality (trade libel)   The publication of false information about another's product, alleging that it is not what its seller claims.

Slander of title   The publication of a statement that denies or casts doubt on another's legal ownership of any property, causing financial loss to that property's owner.

Small claims courts   Special courts in which parties may litigate small claims (usually, claims involving $5,000 or less). Attorneys are not required in small claims courts, and in many states attorneys are not allowed to represent the parties.

Smart card   Prepaid funds recorded on a microprocessor chip embedded on a card. One type of *e-money*.

Sociological school   A school of legal thought that views the law as a tool for promoting justice in society.

Sole proprietorship   The simplest form of business, in which the owner is the business; the owner reports business income on his or her personal income tax return and is legally responsible for all debts and obligations incurred by the business.

Sovereign immunity   A doctrine that immunizes foreign nations from the jurisdiction of U.S. courts when certain conditions are satisfied.

Spam   Bulk, unsolicited ("junk") e-mail.

Special warranty deed   A deed in which the grantor only covenants to warrant and defend the title against claims and demands of the grantor and all persons claiming by, through, and under the grantor.

Specific performance   An equitable remedy requiring exactly the performance that was specified in a contract; usually granted only when money damages would be an inadequate remedy and the subject matter of the contract is unique (for example, real property).

Spot zoning   Granting a zoning classification to a parcel of land that is different from the classification given to other land in the immediate area.

Standing to sue   The requirement that an individual must have a sufficient stake in a controversy before he or she can bring a lawsuit. The plaintiff must demonstrate that he or she either has been injured or threatened with injury.

Stare decisis (pronounced *ster*-ay dih-*si*-ses)   A common law doctrine under which judges are obligated to follow the precedents established in prior decisions.

Statute of Frauds   A state statute under which certain types of contracts must be in writing to be enforceable.

Statute of limitations   A federal or state statute setting the maximum time period during which a certain action can be brought or certain rights enforced.

Statute of repose   Basically, a statute of limitations that is not dependent on the happening of a cause of action. Statutes of repose generally begin to run at an earlier date and run for a longer period of time than statutes of limitations.

Statutory law   The body of law enacted by legislative bodies (as opposed to constitutional law, administrative law, or case law).

Statutory lien   A lien created by statute.

Statutory period of redemption   A time period (usually set by state statute) during which the property subject to a defaulted mortgage, land contract, or other contract can be redeemed by the debtor after foreclosure or judicial sale.

Stock   An equity (ownership) interest in a corporation, measured in units of shares.

Stock certificate   A certificate issued by a corporation evidencing the ownership of a specified number of shares in the corporation.

Stock option   *See* Stock warrant

Stock warrant   A certificate that grants the owner the option to buy a given number of shares of stock, usually within a set time period.

Stockholder   *See* Shareholder

Strict liability   Liability regardless of fault. In tort law, strict liability may be imposed on defendants in cases involving abnormally dangerous activities, dangerous animals, or defective products.

Strike   An extreme action undertaken by unionized workers when collective bargaining fails; the workers leave their jobs, refuse to work, and (typically) picket the employer's workplace.

Subject-matter jurisdiction   Jurisdiction over the subject matter of a lawsuit.

Subpoena   A document commanding a person to appear at a certain time and place or give testimony concerning a certain matter.

Subrogation   *See* Right of subrogation

Subscriber   An investor who agrees, in a subscription agreement, to purchase capital stock in a corporation.

Substantial evidence test   The test applied by a court reviewing an administrative agency's informal action. The court determines whether the agency acted unreasonably and overturns the agency's findings only if unsupported by a substantial body of evidence.

Substantial performance   Performance that does not vary greatly from the performance promised in a contract; the performance must create substantially the same benefits as those promised in the contract.

Substantive due process   A requirement that focuses on the content, or substance, of legislation. If a law or other governmental action limits a fundamental right, such as the right to travel or to vote, it will be held to violate substantive due process unless it promotes a compelling or overriding state interest.

Substantive law   Law that defines the rights and duties of individuals with respect to each other, as opposed to procedural law, which defines the manner in which these rights and duties may be enforced.

Substantive unconscionability   Results from contracts, or portions of contracts, that are oppressive or overly harsh. Courts generally focus on provisions that deprive one party of the benefits of the agreement or leave that party without remedy for nonperformance by the other. An example of substantive unconscionability is the agreement by a person with a fourth-grade education to purchase a refrigerator for $2,000 under an installment contract.

Suit   *See* Lawsuit; Litigation

Summary judgment   *See* Motion for summary judgment

Summary jury trial (SJT)   A method of settling disputes in which a trial is held, but the jury's verdict is not binding. The verdict acts only as a guide to both sides in reaching an agreement during the mandatory negotiations that immediately follow the summary jury trial.

Summons   A document informing a defendant that a legal action has been commenced against him or her and that the defendant must appear in court on a certain date to answer the plaintiff's complaint. The document is delivered by a sheriff or any other person so authorized.

Superseding cause   An intervening force or event that breaks the connection between a wrongful act and an injury to another; in negligence law, a defense to liability.

Supremacy clause The provision in Article VI of the Constitution that provides that the Constitution, laws, and treaties of the United States are "the supreme Law of the Land." Under this clause, state and local laws that directly conflict with federal law will be rendered invalid.

Surety A person, such as a cosigner on a note, who agrees to be primarily responsible for the debt of another.

Suretyship An express contract in which a third party to a debtor-creditor relationship (the surety) promises to be primarily responsible for the debtor's obligation.

Syllogism A form of deductive reasoning consisting of a major premise, a minor premise, and a conclusion.

Symbolic speech Nonverbal conduct that expresses opinions or thoughts about a subject. Symbolic speech is protected under the First Amendment's guarantee of freedom of speech.

Syndicate An investment group of persons or firms brought together for the purpose of financing a project that they would not or could not undertake independently.

T

Tag In the context of the World Wide Web, a code in an HTML document. *See* Meta tags

Taking The taking of private property by the government for public use. Under the Fifth Amendment to the Constitution, the government may not take private property for public use without "just compensation."

Tangible employment action A significant change in employment status, such as firing or failing to promote an employee; reassigning the employee to a position with significantly different responsibilities; or effecting a significant change in employment benefits.

Tangible property Property that has physical existence and can be distinguished by the senses of touch, sight, and so on. A car is tangible property; a patent right is intangible property.

Tariff A tax on imported goods.

Technology licensing Allowing another to use and profit from intellectual property (patents, copyrights, trademarks, innovative products or processes, and so on) for consideration. In the context of international business transactions, technology licensing is sometimes an attractive alternative to the establishment of foreign production facilities.

Tenancy at sufferance A type of tenancy under which one who, after rightfully being in possession of leased premises, continues (wrongfully) to occupy the property after the lease has been terminated. The tenant has no rights to possess the property and occupies it only because the person entitled to evict the tenant has not done so.

Tenancy at will A type of tenancy under which either party can terminate the tenancy without notice; usually arises when a tenant who has been under a tenancy for years retains possession, with the landlord's consent, after the tenancy for years has terminated.

Tenancy by the entirety The joint ownership of property by a husband and wife. Neither party can transfer his or her interest in the property without the consent of the other.

Tenancy for years A type of tenancy under which property is leased for a specified period of time, such as a month, a year, or a period of years.

Tenancy in common Co-ownership of property in which each party owns an undivided interest that passes to his or her heirs at death.

Tenancy in partnership Co-ownership of partnership property.

Tender An unconditional offer to perform an obligation by a person who is ready, willing, and able to do so.

Tender of delivery Under the Uniform Commercial Code, a seller's or lessor's act of placing conforming goods at the disposal of the buyer or lessee and giving the buyer or lessee whatever notifica-

tion is reasonably necessary to enable the buyer or lessee to take delivery.

Tender offer An offer to purchase made by one company directly to the shareholders of another (target) company; often referred to as a "takeover bid."

Third party beneficiary One for whose benefit a promise is made in a contract but who is not a party to the contract.

Tippee A person who receives inside information.

Tombstone ad An advertisement, historically in a format resembling a tombstone, of a securities offering. The ad informs potential investors of where and how they may obtain a prospectus.

Tort A civil wrong not arising from a breach of contract. A breach of a legal duty that proximately causes harm or injury to another.

Tortfeasor One who commits a tort.

Toxic tort Failure to use or to clean up properly toxic chemicals that cause harm to a person or society.

Trade dress The image and overall appearance of a product—for example, the distinctive decor, menu, layout, and style of service of a particular restaurant. Basically, trade dress is subject to the same protection as trademarks.

Trade fixture The personal property of a commercial tenant that has been installed or affixed to real property for a business purpose. When the lease ends, the tenant can remove the fixture but must repair any damage to the real property caused by the fixture's removal.

Trade libel The publication of false information about another's product, alleging it is not what its seller claims; also referred to as *slander of quality*.

Trade name A term that is used to indicate part or all of a business's name and that is directly related to the business's reputation and goodwill. Trade names are protected under the common law (and under trademark law, if the name is the same as the firm's trademarked property).

Trade secret Information or a process that gives a business an advantage over competitors who do not know the information or process.

Trademark A distinctive mark, motto, device, or implement that a manufacturer stamps, prints, or otherwise affixes to the goods it produces so that they may be identified on the market and their origins made known. Once a trademark is established (under the common law or through registration), the owner is entitled to its exclusive use.

Treasury shares Corporate shares that are authorized by the corporation but that have not been issued.

Treaty An agreement formed between two or more independent nations.

Treble damages Damages consisting of single damages determined by a jury and tripled in amount in certain cases as required by statute.

Trespass to land The entry onto, above, or below the surface of land owned by another without the owner's permission or legal authorization.

Trespass to personal property The unlawful taking or harming of another's personal property; interference with another's right to the exclusive possession of his or her personal property.

Trespasser One who commits the tort of trespass in one of its forms.

Trial court A court in which trials are held and testimony taken.

Trustee One who holds title to property for the use or benefit of another (the beneficiary).

Tying arrangement An agreement between a buyer and a seller in which the buyer of a specific product or service becomes obligated to purchase additional products or services from the seller.

U

U.S. trustee A government official who performs certain administrative tasks that a bankruptcy judge would otherwise have to perform.

Ultra vires (pronounced *uhl*-trah *vye*-reez)   A Latin term meaning "beyond the powers"; in corporate law, acts of a corporation that are beyond its express and implied powers to undertake.

Unanimous opinion   A court opinion in which all of the judges or justices of the court agree to the court's decision.

Unconscionable (pronounced un-*kon*-shun-uh-bul) **contract or clause**   A contract or clause that is void on the basis of public policy because one party, as a result of his or her disproportionate bargaining power, is forced to accept terms that are unfairly burdensome and that unfairly benefit the dominating party. *See also* Procedural unconscionability; Substantive unconscionability

Undisclosed principal   A principal whose identity is unknown by a third person, and the third person has no knowledge that the agent is acting for a principal at the time the agent and the third person form a contract.

Unenforceable contract   A valid contract rendered unenforceable by some statute or law.

Uniform law   A model law created by the National Conference of Commissioners on Uniform State Laws and/or the American Law Institute for the states to consider adopting. If the state adopts the law, it becomes statutory law in that state. Each state has the option of adopting or rejecting all or part of a uniform law.

Unilateral contract   A contract that results when an offer can only be accepted by the offeree's performance.

Union shop   A place of employment in which all workers, once employed, must become union members within a specified period of time as a condition of their continued employment.

Unitary system   A centralized governmental system in which local or subdivisional governments exercise only those powers given to them by the central government.

Unliquidated debt   A debt that is uncertain in amount.

Unreasonably dangerous product   In product liability, a product that is defective to the point of threatening a consumer's health and safety. A product will be considered unreasonably dangerous if it is dangerous beyond the expectation of the ordinary consumer or if a less dangerous alternative was economically feasible for the manufacturer, but the manufacturer failed to produce it.

Usage of trade   Any practice or method of dealing having such regularity of observance in a place, vocation, or trade as to justify an expectation that it will be observed with respect to the transaction in question.

Usurpation   In corporate law, the taking advantage of a corporate opportunity by a corporate officer or director for his or her personal gain and in violation of his or her fiduciary duties.

Usury   Charging an illegal rate of interest.

Utilitarianism   An approach to ethical reasoning in which ethically correct behavior is not related to any absolute ethical or moral values but to an evaluation of the consequences of a given action on those who will be affected by it. In utilitarian reasoning, a "good" decision is one that results in the greatest good for the greatest number of people affected by the decision.

V

Valid contract   A contract that results when elements necessary for contract formation (agreement, consideration, legal purpose, and contractual capacity) are present.

Validation notice   An initial notice to a debtor from a collection agency informing the debtor that he or she has thirty days to challenge the debt and request verification.

Vendee   One who purchases property from another, called the vendor.

Vendor   One who sells property to another, called the vendee.

Venue (pronounced *ven*-yoo)   The geographical district in which an action is tried and from which the jury is selected.

Verdict   A formal decision made by a jury.

Vertical merger   The acquisition by a company at one stage of production of a company at a higher or lower stage of production (such as a company merging with one of its suppliers or retailers).

Vertical restraint   Any restraint on trade created by agreements between firms at different levels in the manufacturing and distribution process.

Vertically integrated firm   A firm that carries out two or more functional phases—for example, manufacture, distribution, retailing—of a product.

Vesting   The creation of an absolute or unconditional right or power.

Vicarious liability   Legal responsibility placed on one person for the acts of another.

Virtual courtroom   A courtroom that is conceptual and not physical. In the context of cyberspace, a virtual courtroom could be a location on the Internet at which judicial proceedings take place.

Virtual property   Property that, in the context of cyberspace, is conceptual, as opposed to physical. Intellectual property that exists on the Internet is virtual property.

Void contract   A contract having no legal force or binding effect.

Voidable contract   A contract that may be legally avoided (canceled, or annulled) at the option of one of the parties.

Voidable preference   In bankruptcy law, a preference that may be avoided, or set aside, by the trustee.

Voir dire (pronounced *vwahr deehr*)   Old French verbs meaning "to speak the truth." In jury trials, the phrase refers to the process in which the attorneys question prospective jurors to determine whether they are biased or have any connection with a party to the action or with a prospective witness.

Voting trust   An agreement (trust contract) under which legal title to shares of corporate stock is transferred to a trustee who is authorized by the shareholders to vote the shares on their behalf.

W

Waiver   An intentional, knowing relinquishment of a legal right.

Warehouse receipt   A document of title issued by a bailee-warehouser to cover the goods stored in the warehouse.

Warehouser   One in the business of operating a warehouse.

Warranty   A promise that certain facts are truly as they are represented to be.

Warranty deed   A deed in which the grantor guarantees to the grantee that the grantor has title to the property conveyed in the deed, that there are no encumbrances on the property other than what the grantor has represented, and that the grantee will enjoy quiet possession of the property; a deed that provides the greatest amount of protection for the grantee.

Warranty disclaimer   A seller's or lessor's negation or qualification of a warranty.

Warranty of fitness   *See* Implied warranty of fitness for a particular purpose

Warranty of merchantability   *See* Implied warranty of merchantability

Warranty of title   An implied warranty made by a seller that the seller has good and valid title to the goods sold and that the transfer of the title is rightful.

Waste   The abuse or destructive use of real property by one who is in rightful possession of the property but who does not have title to it. Waste does not include ordinary depreciation due to age and normal use.

Watered stock   Shares of stock issued by a corporation for which the corporation receives, as payment, less than the stated value of the shares.

Wetlands   Areas of land designated by government agencies (such as the Army Corps of Engineers or the Environmental Protection Agency) as protected areas that support wildlife and that therefore cannot be filled in or dredged by private contractors or parties.

Whistleblowing An employee's disclosure to government, the press, or upper-management authorities that the employer is engaged in unsafe or illegal activities.

White-collar crime Nonviolent crime committed by individuals or corporations to obtain a personal or business advantage.

Will An instrument directing what is to be done with the testator's property on his or her death, made by the testator and revocable during his or her lifetime. No interests in the testator's property pass until the testator dies.

Willful Intentional.

Winding up The second of two stages involved in the termination of a partnership or corporation. Once the firm is dissolved, it continues to exist legally until the process of winding up all business affairs (collecting and distributing the firm's assets) is complete.

Workers' compensation laws State statutes establishing an administrative procedure for compensating workers' injuries that arise out of—or in the course of—their employment, regardless of fault.

Workout An out-of-court agreement between a debtor and his or her creditors in which the parties work out a payment plan or schedule under which the debtor's debts can be discharged.

Writ of attachment A court's order, prior to a trial to collect a debt, directing the sheriff or other officer to seize nonexempt property of the debtor; if the creditor prevails at trial, the seized property can be sold to satisfy the judgment.

Writ of *certiorari* (pronounced sur-shee-uh-*rah*-ree) A writ from a higher court asking the lower court for the record of a case.

Writ of execution A court's order, after a judgment has been entered against the debtor, directing the sheriff to seize (levy) and sell any of the debtor's nonexempt real or personal property. The proceeds of the sale are used to pay off the judgment, accrued interest, and costs of the sale; any surplus is paid to the debtor.

Wrongful discharge An employer's termination of an employee's employment in violation of an employment contract or laws that protect employees.

Z

Zoning The division of a city by legislative regulation into districts and the application in each district of regulations having to do with structural and architectural designs of buildings and prescribing the use to which buildings within designated districts may be put.

TABLE OF CASES

INDEX

A

Acceptance(s)
    of bribe, 150
    contractual, 193, 233
    of delivered goods, 264
        revocation of, 267–269
    online, 274–275
    partial, 264
Accommodation, nonconforming goods
        shipped as, 252
Accord, satisfaction and, 234
Accounting
    agent's demand for, 469
    agent's duty of, 468, 551
    partner's right to, 405
Acid rain, 575
Act(s)
    of commission, 147
    guilty (actus reus), 147
    of omission, 147
    of partners, partnership dissolution by,
        410
Act of state doctrine, 174–175
Actual controversy, 135
Actual malice, 289–290
Actus reus (guilty act), 147
Adjudication, 127, 134–135
Administrative agency(ies), 7
    adjudication by, 127, 134–135
    administrative process and, 129–135,
        188–189
    creation of, 126–127
    investigation by, 132–134
    orders of, 135
    organization and structure of, 127
    powers of
        limitations on, 135–136
        U.S. Constitution and, 127–129
    public accountability and, 136–138
    rulemaking by, 127, 129–131
    selected, listed, 128, 129
    state, 138–140
    types of, 127
Administrative law, 126–143. See also
        Administrative agency(ies);
        Government regulation(s)
    defined, 7, 126
    finding, 15
Administrative law judge (ALJ), 134–135,
        531

Administrative Procedure Act
        (APA)(1946), 129, 130, 134–135, 136
Administrative process, 129–135, 188–189
Admission(s)
    exception to Statute of Frauds and, 254
    request for, 49
Advertisement(s), advertising
    bait-and-switch, 556–557
    contractual offers versus, 201
    counteradvertising and, 558
    deceptive, 94–95
    electronic, 558
    tombstone, 647
Affidavit, 49, 356
Affiliate, 650
Affirmative action, 522–524
AFL-CIO (American Federation of Labor
        and Congress of Industrial
        Organizations), 531, 533
Age
    discrimination on basis of, 507,
        515–516, 553, 560
    of majority, 153, 215
Age Discrimination in Employment Act
        (ADEA)(1967), 507, 515–516, 553
Agency(ies)
    administrative. See Administrative
        agency(ies)
    parallel, conflicts between, 138–140
Agency relationship(s), 460–487. See also
        Agent(s); Principal(s)
    coupled with an interest, 482
    defined, 460
    duties in, 465–469
    employer-employee, 460–461
    employer-independent contractor, 461
    formation of, 464–465
    partnerships and, 400
    rights and remedies in, 469–470
    termination of, 481–483
Agent(s)
    acts of
        authorized, 473–475
        unauthorized, 475–476
    agency termination by, 481–482
    authority of
        agent's renunciation of, 481
        principal's revocation of, 481
        scope of, 470–473
    bankruptcy of, agency termination and,
        483

corporate directors and, 440
corporate officers and executives as, 442
crimes of, 480–481
death or insanity of, agency termination
        and, 482–483
defined, 460
duties of, to principal, 465–468, 551
e-, 476
gratuitous, 466, 468
principal's duties to, 468–469, 551
principal's rights and remedies against,
        469–470
registered, 46, 437
rights and remedies of, against principal,
        469
torts of, 476–480
Agreement(s). See also Contract(s)
    agency formation by, 464
    to agree, 201
    bilateral, 173
    click-on, 275
    collective bargaining, 540
    compromise, 234
    contract discharge by, 233–234
    contractual, 193, 198–208
    creditors' composition, 357
    distribution, 178
    fair trade, 635–637
    hot-cargo, 539–540
    international, 173, 179–180
    lacking consideration, 212–214
    lease. See Lease contract(s)
    multilateral, 173
    mutual, agency termination and, 481
    operating (for LLC), 418–420
    partnership, 402–403
    preliminary, 204–205
    price-fixing, 627–629
    reaffirmation, 376
    resale price maintenance, 635–637
    settlement, 234
    shareholder, 432–434
    shareholder voting, 446
    stock-subscription, 435–436, 450–451
    substituted, 234
    tie-in sales, 611, 638–639
Agricultural associations, exemption of,
        from antitrust laws, 614
AIDS (acquired immune deficiency
        syndrome)
    as disability, 502, 517

INDEX

Helpful Internet Uniform Resource Locators (URLs)

General Legal Resources

http://www.findlaw.com FindLaw, which is a part of West Group, is one of the most comprehensive sources of free legal information. You can access all federal and state cases, codes, and agency regulations, as well as journal articles, newsletters, and links to other useful sites and discussion groups.

http://www.law.cornell.edu The Legal Information Institute (LII) at Cornell Law School also is a great site for legal research and includes federal, state, and international law. You can access materials by topic or by jurisdiction, or you can browse through one of its topical libraries.

http://www.lectlaw.com/bus.html The 'Lectric Law Library has general legal resources.

http://www.lawguru.com/ilawlib The Internet Law Library provides many legal resources relating to American and foreign law.

http://www.law.com/index.shtml This site provides up-to-date legal news articles and information, and has links to other legal news publications, including the *National Law Journal*.

Helpful Government Sites

http://firstgov.gov The U.S. government's official Web site provides links to every branch of the federal government, including federal agencies.

http://www.loc.gov The Library of Congress has links to state and federal government resources, and the THOMAS system allows you to search through several legislative databases.

http://www.sec.gov/edgar.shtml The Web site of the Securities and Exchange Commission offers a searchable electronic database (called EDGAR) of information about public companies.

http://www.gpoaccess.gov/index.html The U.S. Government Printing Office posts official information from each of the three branches of the federal government, including publications such as the *Code of Federal Regulations* and the *Federal Register*.

http://www.uspto.gov The U.S. Patent and Trademark Office has a searchable database of patents and trademarks. This site also provides general information and a way to check the status of pending applications.

http://www.loc.gov/copyright The U.S. Copyright Office provides information on copyrights and a searchable database of copyright records.

http://www.eeoc.gov/index.html The Equal Employment Opportunity Commission (EEOC) posts information on employment discrimination, EEOC regulations, compliance, and enforcement.

http://www.epa.gov The Environmental Protection Agency offers information on environmental laws, regulations, and compliance assistance.

http://www.sbaonline.sba.gov The U.S. Small Business Administration assists in forming, financing, and operating small businesses.

http://www.usdoj.gov The U.S. Department of Justice provides information on many areas of law, including civil rights, employment, crime, and immigration.

http://www.csg.org The Council of State Governments offers state news, information, legislation, and links to state home pages.

http://www.nccusl.org The National Conference of Commissioners on Uniform State Laws posts the text of uniform laws (such as the Uniform Commercial Code) and information on state adoptions and pending state legislation.

Federal and State Courts

http://www.supremecourtus.gov This official site of the United States Supreme Court provides case opinions, orders, and other information about the Court, including its history, procedures, schedule, and transcripts of oral arguments.

http://www.oyez.org/oyez/frontpage This site offers in addition to United States Supreme Court opinions, a multimedia guide to the Court, including a virtual tour of the building and digital audio of selected oral arguments and Court decisions.

http://www.uscourts.gov/index.html The federal judiciary provides access to every federal court (including district courts, appellate courts, and bankruptcy courts).

http://www.ncsconline.org The National Center for State Courts offers links to the Web pages of all state courts.

http://www.abiworld.org The American Bankruptcy Institute is a good resource for bankruptcy court opinions, news, and other information.